ISBN 978-0-332-35373-9
PIBN 10983686

1 MONTH OF
FREE
READING

at
www.ForgottenBooks.com

By purchasing this book you are eligible for one month membership to ForgottenBooks.com, giving you unlimited access to our entire collection of over 1,000,000 titles via our web site and mobile apps.

To claim your free month visit:
www.forgottenbooks.com/free983686

English
Français
Deutsche
Italiano
Español
Português

www.forgottenbooks.com

Mythology Photography **Fiction**
Fishing Christianity **Art** Cooking
Essays Buddhism Freemasonry
Medicine **Biology** Music **Ancient**
Egypt Evolution Carpentry Physics
Dance Geology **Mathematics** Fitness
Shakespeare **Folklore** Yoga Marketing
Confidence Immortality Biographies
Poetry **Psychology** Witchcraft
Electronics Chemistry History **Law**
Accounting **Philosophy** Anthropology
Alchemy Drama Quantum Mechanics
Atheism Sexual Health **Ancient History**
Entrepreneurship Languages Sport
Paleontology Needlework Islam
Metaphysics Investment Archaeology
Parenting Statistics Criminology
Motivational

RAILROAD REPORTS

(Vol. 62 American and English
Railroad Cases, New Series)

A COLLECTION OF ALL

CASES AFFECTING RAILROADS OF EVERY KIND,
DECIDED BY THE COURTS OF
LAST RESORT

IN THE

UNITED STATES.

EDITED BY

THOMAS J. MICHIE.

VOLUME XXXIX.

THE MICHIE COMPANY, PUBLISHERS,
CHARLOTTESVILLE, VA.
1911.

TABLE OF CASES.

RAILROAD REPORTS

SLOPPY *v.* PENNSYLVANIA R. Co.

(Supreme Court of Pennsylvania, July 1, 1910.)

[77 Atl. Rep. 1010.]

Master and Servant—Fellow Servants—"Common Employment."*—Whether an employment is common in the legal sense, so as to render employees fellow servants, is not determined by the character of work done by each, but by the purpose towards which the work is directed, and, if the purpose be a common one and the work of each servant be but complementary to that of the other in accomplishing the general purpose, it is a common employment.

Master and Servant—Fellow Servants.*—The crew of a train switching cars onto a repair track and a railroad car repairer doing his work on such track are fellow servants; the work of each being complementary to that of the other.

Master and Servant—Injuries to Fellow Servant—Liability of Master.†—Where a car repairer, while engaged on a car standing on a repair track, was killed by the negligent shifting of another car upon the track, through failure of the fireman of the shifting crew to give warning, who was decedent's fellow servant, recovery could not be had of the master for the death.

Appeal from Court of Common Pleas, McKean County.

Action by Mrs. David Sloppy against the Pennsylvania Railroad Company. Judgment of nonsuit, and plaintiff appeals. Affirmed.

Argued before FELL, C. J., and BROWN, POTTER, ELKIN, and STEWART, JJ.

R. B. Stone and *Allan Oviatt*, for appellant.
F. D. Gallup, for appellee.

STEWART, J. The accident out of which this action grows occurred on the repair track in the yard of defendant company. The plaintiff's husband was there engaged with an assistant in re-

---

*For the authorities in this series on the subject of the different department limitation of the fellow servant rule, see foot-note of Bennett *v.* Chicago City Ry. Co. (Ill.), 36 R. R. R. 42, 59 Am. & Eng. R. Cas., N. S., 42; last paragraph of foot-note of Meyers *v.* San Pedro, etc., R. Co. (Utah), 35 R. R. R. 21, 58 Am. & Eng. R. Cas., N. S., 21.

†For the authorities in this series on the question whether the master is liable for an injury to his servant caused by the negligence of the latter's fellow servant, see Massy *v.* Milwaukee Elec. Ry. & L. Co. (Wis.), 36 R. R. R. 656, 59 Am. & Eng. R. Cas., N. S., 656; foot-note of Wickham *v.* Detroit United Ry. (Mich.), 35 R. R. R. 321, 58 Am. & Eng. R. Cas., N. S., 321.

Sloppy *v.* Pennsylvania R. Co

pairing a crippled car. At the end of this car nearest the switch opening from the main track was displayed a blue flag, the signal required by the rules of the company to warn against the approach of other cars. Extending back from the cars to the track was a sharp curve for a distance of 200 feet. A yard engine pushing six cars, one of which—the one farthest from the engine—was to be left on this track for repairs, entered from the main track, moving at the rate of four miles an hour. This train of cars collided with the car that was being repaired. Plaintiff's husband was at the time at work under the body of this car. His death resulted from the collision. The negligence charged was not in connection with the construction or maintenance of the track, or in the use of defective cars or imperfect appliances, but that the defendant company, "disregarding its duty, wantonly and negligently, and without permission or consent, or giving any warning of or to the said David Sloppy, ran a train of cars in on said crippled track, and, wantonly, negligently, disregarding its duty, ran and forced the said cars violently against the said car being repaired by the said David Sloppy." At the conclusion of the plaintiff's evidence the court on motion directed a nonsuit, which it subsequently refused to remove. The evidence establishes clearly, as the proximate cause of the accident, the failure on the part of the fireman to communicate to the engineer the order given by the conductor to halt the train. The conductor testified that he saw the blue flag on the crippled car when 200 feet away; that he at once signaled the fireman, whose duty it was to take the signal—the engineer not being in sight because of the curve—to slow down, and then signaled to him to stop immediately; that both signals were disregarded and the collision followed. The witness further testified that at the rate of speed at which the train was moving it could have been brought to a rest within six feet. There was nothing in the evidence which in any way qualified this positive and direct testimony.

The only question then was, Was the plaintiff's husband a fellow servant with those employed in the running of the train? The train was in charge of a conductor, the witness above referred to. It was made up of engine and cars to be distributed through the yard in which plaintiff's husband was employed as a repair man. Conductor, engineer, and fireman were admittedly fellow servants, because engaged in the same common employment, owing obedience to a common authority; but it is contended that those whose duty it was to make repairs were not within this community. There is a clear and manifest distinction between the kinds of work done by these several classes of employees; but that of itself does not disassociate them. Whether a common employment in the legal sense can be affirmed is not determined by the character or kind of work done by each, but by the purpose towards which the work is directed. If the purpose be a common one, and the work of each is but complementary to that of the other in accomplishing the general pur-· pose, then it is a common employment. Here the general purpose on the part of both was to maintain the rolling stock of the company in a state of repair. A track was provided to receive what was known as crippled cars where they were to be repaired by employees engaged to do that particular work. It was the duty of the trainmen to deliver the cars upon this track, and remove them when the repairs had been made. The duties of each class of employees were so related that those employed in the one branch of the service must have known of the required co-operation of those employed in the other to effect the one distinct object in view. They thus became fellow servants in this connection, each individual in the class taking on himself all the ordinary risks of the employment, including the risk of negligent act on the part of others engaged in the same work. To establish this relation in contemplation of law, it is sufficient to show "that they are employed by the same master, engaged in the same common work, and performing duties and services for the same general purpose." Lehigh Val. Coal Co. *v.* Jones, 86 Pa. 432. It is impossible to distinguish this case in its controlling facts from the case of Campbell *v.* Penna. R. R. Co., 2 Atl. 489. "It clearly appears from the testimony," said Sterrett, J., in that case, "that the immediate cause of the unfortunate accident which befell plaintiff was the negligence of the brakeman in recklessly undertaking to drop in on the track where plaintiff was working, a greater number of cars than he was able to control without assistance. The brakeman and plaintiff were engaged in different branches of the same general service, but in the discharge of their respective duties they were brought into such close proximity to each other that the negligence of the former, in carelessly dropping the cars, necessarily endangered the safety of the latter. They were, therefore, in the proper sense of the term fellow servants of the defendant company, and nothing is better settled than that for an injury caused by a fellow servant, without more, there can be no recovery." Fullmer *v.* N. Y. Central & Hudson River R. R. Co., 208 Pa. 598, 57 Atl. 1062, and Peterson *v.* Pennsylvania R. R. Co., 195 Pa. 494, 46 Atl. 112, are directly in line. In all of these cases the difference in the work done by the several classes was just the difference which existed here, and in each case it was held that all were fellow servants because of a common employment owing obedience to common authority.

The assignments of error are overruled, and the judgment is affirmed.

Everingham v. Chicago, B. & Q. R. Co.

(Supreme Court of Iowa, Oct. 21, 1910.)

[127 N. W. Rep. 1009.]

Master and Servant—Assault by Servant—Master's Liability—Evidence.—In an action against a master for an assault committed by his servant, evidence held to show that the assault was not committed in the prosecution of the master's business.

Master and Servant—Assault by Servant—Where Master Not Liable.*—A master is not liable for an assault made by his servant where the servant has stepped aside from the prosecution of the master's business to effect some purpose of his own.

Master and Servant—Assault by Servant—No Ratification by Master.—A master whose servant of his own malice and purpose has committed an assault does not ratify and become liable for such act merely because he thereafter retains the servant in his employ.

Master and Servant—Assault by Servant—Evidence—Servant's Reputation.—In an action for an assault committed by defendant's servant, who stepped aside from the course of his employment to gratify some malice or spite of his own, evidence as to the servant's reputation for quarrelsomeness is immaterial.

Assault and Battery—Evidence—Reputation for Quarrelsomeness —Limits of Question.—A question as to the reputation for quarrelsomeness of a person who has committed an assault is objectionable on account of its generality, where it does not call for testimony as to his reputation in the community in which he lived.

Master and Servant—Master's Liability.—A master does not warrant or insure his servant's good conduct in matters outside the scope of the master's business.

Appeal from District Court, Lee County; Henry Bank, Jr., Judge.

Action to recover damages for an alleged assault made upon plaintiff by one of defendant's employees. Trial to a jury, directed verdict for defendant, and plaintiff appeals. Affirmed.

J. C. Hamilton and *R. N. Johnson,* for appellant.
H. H. Trimble, Palmer Trimble, and *George B. Stewart,* for appellee.

---

*See foot-note of Savannah Elec. Co. *v.* Wheeler (Ga.), 27 R. R. R. 708, 50 Am. & Eng. R. Cas., N. S., 708; foot-note of Charleston, etc., Ry. Co. *v.* Devlin (S. Car.), 35 R. R. R. 341, 58 Am. & Eng. R. Cas., N. S., 341.

For the authorities in this series on the question whether a master's liability for the acts of his servant depends upon whether they were committed within the scope of his employment, see foot-note of Conchin *v.* El Paso, etc., R. Co. (Ariz.), 36 R. R. R. 192, 59 Am. & Eng. R. Cas., N. S., 192.

Everingham *v.* Chicago, B. & Q. R. Co

Deemer, C. J.   Plaintiff is the owner of an elevator in the town of Ft. Madison. A spur track from defendant's railroad leads to this elevator over defendant's own land. Cars for plaintiff's use were to be set out on this spur track, and, when loaded, shipped to the various consignees. He claims that he had very poor switching service, and that he complained thereof to defendant's general agent at Keokuk. William Tordt was defendant's switchman at Ft. Madison, having control of the cars which should be switched for use at plaintiff's elevator. Plaintiff claims that on August 15, 1908, he was delayed in getting cars ordered by him to the elevator, and that, by reason thereof, he had a number of men who were compelled to remain idle; that, while in this situation, Tordt came in with a switching crew upon the spur track to take out some empty cars, and it is shown that plaintiff while standing on the platform of his elevator or in a door leading into said elevator engaged in a wordy controversy with Tordt, who was then standing by some cars which were being moved by an engine attached thereto on this spur track. It seems that plaintiff had notified the Burlington office that he wanted some cars set on this spur track for his use, and that he also informed Tordt of his wishes in the matter. When Tordt got near to plaintiff and while standing on the ground near the cars, he said to plaintiff: "Why in hell don't you leave a list of where you want your cars switched at the office, you God damn farmer, you." In response to this plaintiff said: " 'I would about as soon be a God damn farmer as a damn fool switchman.' Tordt immediately climbed upon the platform, and hit me several times. He was standing a foot or two away at the time he hit me. I think I had my hands in my pockets. No further words passed between us. I can hardly tell where he hit me they came so fast. I was hit once in my right eye, once on the nose, and once on the side of my mouth and probably several other times, could not say exactly where. I did not strike at him. I turned around to protect myself, and Tordt jumped on my back, and continued to hit with one hand." Plaintiff also testified as follows: "Tordt, when he first addressed me, was either reaching to bleed the air out of the car, or else he had hold of the coupling irons. He had hold of the lever with his left hand. It was not the car next the engine. I don't know if he was at the front or rear end of the car. He was switching these cars. I was not anticipating trouble. Tordt was more than a switchman. He was the foreman. He was the man who gave orders. He had charge of the switching and had charge of the bills."

This is plaintiff's case as reproduced from his own testimony, and it is the strongest argument that could be made in support of the proposition that he has no cause of action against the defendant, although liability on the part of Tordt individually is clearly made out. It is fundamental that a master is not liable

Everingham v. Chicago, B. & Q. R. Co

for all assaults made by his servant. It is only for such as
done in the prosecution of the master's business that the ma:
is liable. If the servant steps aside from his master's busir
in order to effect some purposes of his own commits an assa
the master is not liable. This is clearly pointed out in the foll(
ing cases already decided by this court: Alsever v. Railr(
115 Iowa, 338, 88 N. W. 841, 56 L. R. A. 748; Dougherty
Railroad, 137 Iowa, 257, 114 N. W. 902; Kincade v. Railr(
107 Iowa, 682, 78 N. W. 698; Dolan v. Hubinger, 109 Iowa, ‹
80 N. W. 514; Porter v. Railroad, 41 Iowa, 358; Golder
Newbrand, 52 Iowa, 59, 2 N. W. 537, 35 Am. Rep. 257; Ma:
v. Railroad, 59 Iowa, 428, 13 N. W. 415, 44 Am. Rep. 687.
the latter case it is said: "The rule is that an employer is
liable for a willful injury done by an employee, though d
while in the course of his employment, unless the employee's ¡
pose was to serve his employer by the willful act. Where
employee is not acting within the course of his employment,
employer is not liable, even for the employee's negligence,
the mere purpose of the employee to serve his employer has
tendency to bring the act within the course of his employme
One of the best statements of the rule is found in Cooley
Torts (2d Ed.) p. 628, which reads as follows: "So if the ‹
ductor of a train of cars leaves his train to beat a perso
enemy, or from mere wantonness to inflict an injury, the dif
ence between his case and that in which the passenger is remo
from the cars is obvious. The one trespass is the individual t
pass of the conductor, which he has stepped aside from his ‹
ployment to commit. The other is a trespass committed in
course of the employment, in the execution of orders the ma
has given, and apparently has the sanction of the master,
contemplates the furtherance of his interests. * * * The
of the master's responsibility is not the motive of the serv
but whether that which he did was something his employn
contemplated and was something which if he should do it l
fully he might do in the employer's name."

2. It is claimed that defendant ratified the assault by keel
Tordt in its employ, and not discharging him after the ass
was made. That he was so kept is conceded; but surely
cannot be regarded as a ratification of a prior act not done in
fendant's interest, for its benefit or by its authority either
press or implied. No case so holds, and, if any such wer‹
be found, we should not be disposed to follow it. From Kwic:
v. Holmes, 106 Minn. 148, 118 N. W. 668, 19 L. R. A. (N.
255, we extract the following as announcing the true rule a
ratification: "But it is urged that the company became liable
the negligence of Spear because it retained him in its employ a
it had knowledge of this accident. The authorities do not
tain this contention. When there is no original liability for

Everingham *v.* Chicago, B. & Q. R. Co
•
act of a servant, because at the time of the negligence the servant was acting in his own personal business, the master does not become liable merely by reason of the fact that he thereafter retains the servant in his employ. The rule contended for by appellant would seem to render an employer liable for every act of negligence of which he had knowledge which had been committed by the employee prior to the time when he employed him. The fact that an employee is retained after knowledge of a negligent act for which the master is already liable is sometimes important as bearing upon the right to recover exemplary damages, and this is evidently all the Wisconsin court intended to hold in Cobb *v.* Simon, 119 Wis. 597, 97 N. W. 276, 100 Am. St. Rep. 909. This appears with reasonable clearness from the final disposition of the case on a subsequent appeal (124 Wis. 467, 102 N. W. 891), and from the cases cited (Bass *v.* Railway Co., 42 Wis. 654, 24 Am. Rep. 437).

3. Plaintiff offered to prove Tordt's reputation as to being a quarrelsome man, but the offered testimony was rejected. No charge of negligence in employing Tordt or in keeping him in defendant's service was charged in the petition, and no claim of liability on this ground is made. We say this notwithstanding a general allegation in the second count of the petition. These allegations are simply thrown in, and are not relied upon as being the proximate cause of the injury. However, even if such allegations were present, we think there was no error on the part of the trial court in rejecting the offered testimony. Had the assault been upon a passenger, doubtless the testimony would have been admissible, but here, where Tordt clearly stepped aside from his employment to gratify some malice or spite, the testimony as to his reputation for quarrelsomeness was immaterial. Moreover, the trial court was justified in sustaining an objection to the question on account of its generality. In other words, the question did not call for his reputation in the community where he lived. A master holds out his agent as competent and fit to be trusted, and thereby, in effect, warrants his fidelity and good conduct in all matters within the scope of his agency. Story on Bailments, §§ 400, 406. But he does not and should not be held to warrant his servant's conduct in matters outside of the scope of that agency. In other words, he cannot be held to be an insurer in matters not relating to the conduct of the master's business.

There is no error in the record, and the judgment must be, and it is, affirmed.

OREGON R. & NAVIGATION CO. *v.* MCDONALD *et al.*

(Supreme Court of Oregon, Dec. 20, 1910.)

[112 Pac. Rep. 413.]

Railroads—Deed to Right of Way—Condition Subsequent.—A conveyance to a railroad reciting that it was made on the condition that the road would construct its line over the premises within two years created a condition subsequent.

Railroads—Right of Way—Purchase.*—While a railroad may acquire a fee in land by condemnation, yet, where it goes into the market to buy as an ordinary purchaser, it may make its own terms, and may bind itself by conditions subsequent.

Railroads—Conveyance of Right of Way—Forfeiture.†—Grantors of land to a railroad on condition that the line be constructed over the premises within two years were not estopped from claiming a forfeiture by voluntarily permitting the grantee to enter on the land and construct its grade.

Railroads—Right of Way—Forfeiture.†—Where, though, under a grant to a railroad conditioned on the building of the road within a specified time, the grantor was entitled to a forfeiture, it appeared that the road was constructed and in operation, the court would decree the road to be entitled to the land on payment of the damages occasioned by the taking thereof.

Appeal from Circuit Court, Wallowa County; J. W. Knowles, Judge.

Suit by the Oregon Railroad & Navigation Company, a private corporation, against Hector McDonald and another. Decree for defendants, and plaintiff appeals. Decree modified as directed.

This is a suit in equity brought by plaintiff to enjoin defendants from interfering with plaintiff in the construction of its branch line of railway from Elgin to Joseph, where the same crosses defendants' land in Wallowa county. On September 18, 1905, plaintiff purchased of defendants the right of way for the railroad over their land; the amount so purchased comprising in all about 20 acres and the price paid being $600. Defendants, however, declined to sell this land until the following clause was inserted in the deed: "This conveyance is made on the condition that the Oregon Railroad & Navigation Company will construct

---

*For the authorities in this series on the subject of the validity of contracts for the acquisition by a railroad of a right of way, see foot-note of Detroit United Ry. *v.* Smith (Mich.), 21 R. R. R. 347, 44 Am. & Eng. R. Cas., N. S., 347.

†For the authorities in this series on the subject of the forfeiture of a railroad right of way for failure to comply with the terms of the grant, see Treat *v.* Detroit United Ry. (Mich.), 33 R. R. R. 431, 56 Am. & Eng. R. Cas., N. S., 431.

Oregon R. & Navigation Co. *v.* McDonald et al

its line of road over the above described premises within two years from the date hereof." Plaintiff took possession of the land, and had completed its grade along the whole of it by October, 1907, and thereafter ceased work upon the road. Thereupon defendants fenced the land at each end, inclosing it with other fields, and in August, 1908, when work had been resumed on other portions of the road, they posted notices, warning all persons, particularly plaintiff, its agents, and employees, to keep off the premises, and declaring themselves to be the owners and in possession thereof. Plaintiff brought this suit and secured a preliminary injunction under the protection of which it proceeded to complete the construction of its line. On the trial the court rendered a decree for defendants. Plaintiff appeals.

T. H. Crawford (W. W. Cotton and *Arthur C. Spencer,* on the brief), for appellant.
Turner Oliver, for respondents.

McBride, J. (After stating the facts as above). Plaintiff's principal contention, is that the limitation in the right of way deed from defendants is in legal effect a covenant, and not a condition. Forfeitures are not favored in law, and the decisions abound in many subtle distinctions indulged in by the courts to avoid their frequently harsh consequences.

Before discussing the various and frequently unreconcilable decisions on this subject, it may be well to recur to elementary definitions: Littleton defines a condition as follows: "Also, divers words (amongst others) there be, which by virtue of themselves make estates upon conditions; one is the word 'sub conditione.'" And Coke, commenting upon this, says: "This is the most expresse and proper condition in deed, and therefore our author beginneth with it." Coke upon Littleton, § 328. Sheppard says: "Amongst these words there are three words that are most proper, which in and of their own nature and efficacy, without any addition of other words of re-entry in the conclusion of the condition, do make the estate conditional, as 'proviso,' 'ita quod,' and 'sub conditione.' Touch. *122. Tested by these definitions, the language employed in the deed at bar would clearly seem to indicate an intent to create a conditional estate defeasible on the failure of the grantee to perform the condition. It is true that the courts in the cases cited by counsel have held that similar language constitutes a covenant, and not a condition, but in most, if not all, of these cases the words of condition were held to be modified or qualified by other language used in the same connection. Thus in Post *v.* Weil, 115 N. Y. 361, 22 N. E. 145, 5 L. R. A. 422, 12 Am. St. Rep. 809, where the restriction read, "Provided always, and these presents are upon this express condition, that no part of the granted premises shall ever be used or occupied as a tavern," the court held that

Oregon R. & Navigation Co. *v.* McDonald et al

the language used should be construed as a covenant running with the land, placing this construction upon the ground that the original grantor owned adjoining property which might be depreciated in value by the erection of a tavern in the vicinity. But in that case the grantor had an adequate remedy in equity to protect his estate from the erection of the obnoxious building, while in the case at bar defendants would have no such remedy to compel plaintiff to build its road. Hawley *v.* Kafitz, 148 Cal. 393, 83 Pac. 248, 3 L. R. A. (N. S.) 741, 113 Am. St. Rep. 282, was a case where plaintiff executed to defendant a conveyance which contained the following clause: "This deed is given by the parties of the first part, and accepted by the second party, upon the express agreement of the second party to build, or cause to be built, upon the said premises within six (6) months from the date hereof a dwelling house to cost not less than fifteen hundred ($1,500) dollars. Said agreement being considered by the parties hereto as part consideration for this conveyance." This was held by the court as a mere covenant, and not a condition subsequent; the court saying: "There is not only an entire omission on the part of the grantor to use any technical language, such as is ordinarily employed to create an estate on condition subsequent, but there is also an entire absence of any language indicating that, for noncompliance with the stipulation to build, it was the intention of the grantor that the estate granted should be defeated and forfeited. Not only is there no language that would create a condition subsequent, but the language actually employed, 'this deed is upon the express agreement,' implies a personal covenant, and not a condition." The distinction between the case cited and the one at bar is obvious. In Ashuelot Nat. Bank *v.* City of Keene, 74 N. H. 148, 65 Atl. 826, 9 L. R. A. (N. S.) 758, the restriction clause in the deed was as follows: "Provided, however, and this deed is made upon the express condition, that said premises shall be forever held and used for the purpose of erecting and maintaining a public library building thereon, and for utilizing so much thereof as is not used for library purposes for a public park, and for no other purpose whatever; said grantee to take and enjoy the rents and income therefrom until such reasonable time as the same shall be devoted to the purposes aforesaid." There had been some prior negotiations between the parties, which were in writing, and the court, taking into consideration these negotiations and the fact that the city was to have the use of the property and the rents and profits therefrom for a reasonable time, held that the language used was intended to create and define a trust rather than to impose a condition subsequent. The fact that the land was conveyed to the city to be used for a public purpose, and therefore as a public trust, was dwelt upon by the court as a circumstance, indicating that a forfeiture was not intended.

Oregon R. & Navigation Co. v. McDonald et al

It is impossible to discuss within the limits of this opinion all the cases cited by counsel, but, as before observed, it will be found in all that either in the conveyance itself or in some other instrument leading to it there is language qualifying, modifying, or tending to alter the significance of the alleged words of condition. There is no case cited, and it is believed that none can be found, where a bald single condition standing alone as this, has been perverted into a covenant. The case of Blanchard v. Detroit, Lansing & Lake Michigan R. Co., 31 Mich. 43, 18 Am. Rep. 142, is an instructive one. In that case a deed was made in consideration of $500, and the covenant to build a depot "hereafter mentioned." Thereafter it was set forth that the conveyance "is made upon the express condition" that the company shall erect and maintain on the land conveyed a station house "suitable for the convenience of the public," and that one train "each way shall stop at such depot or station each day, and that freight and passengers shall be regularly taken at such depot." The company failed to build such depot and the grantor attempted to compel a specific performance, claiming, as plaintiff does here, that the clause quoted constituted a covenant. The court say: "The question whether there is a limitation or a condition, or whether there is a condition precedent or subsequent, or whether what is to be expounded, is a condition or covenant or something capable of operating both ways, very frequently becomes very perplexing in consequence of the uncertain, ambiguous, or conflicting terms and circumstances involved; and the books contain a great many cases of the kind and not a few of which are marked by refinements and distinctions which the sense of the present day would hardly tolerate. Where, however, the terms are distinctly and plainly terms of condition, where the whole provision precisely satisfies the requirements of the definition, and where the transaction has nothing in its nature to create any incongruity, there is no room for refinement and no ground for refusing to assign to the subject its predetermined legal character. In such a case the law attaches to the act and ascribes to it a definite significance, and the parties cannot be heard to say, where there is no imposition, no fraud, no mistake, that, although they deliberately made a condition, and nothing but a condition, they yet meant that it should be exactly as a covenant." So in the case at bar. We have an instrument in which the clause in controversy is couched in the exact language of a condition subsequent, plain, unambiguous, and unqualified, and we would pervert both law and language to hold that these apt words mean something different from their ordinary import.

The case of Gray v. Blanchard, 8 Pick. (Mass.) 284, is in point. Gray conveyed a parcel of land adjoining his dwelling house by a deed, containing this restriction: "Provided, however, this conveyance is upon the condition, that no windows

Oregon R. & Navigation Co. *v.* McDonald et al

shall be placed in the north wall of the house aforesaid, or any house to be erected on the premises within thirty yea from the date hereof." It will be noticed that the contingen provided against was of trivial character; the only possible e fect of placing a window on the north wall being that such wi dow might overlook the grantor's premises and invade his pr vacy. But the court held the condition good, and declared a fo feiture, saving: "The words are apt to create a condition. Ther is no ambiguity, no room for construction, and they cannot b distorted so as to convey a different sense from that which wa palpably the intent of the parties. The word 'provided' alon may constitute a condition, but here the very term is used which is often implied from the use of other terms. 'This conveyance is upon the condition,' can mean nothing more or less than their natural import; and we cannot help the folly of parties who consent to take estates upon onerous conditions by converting conditions into covenants."

Nor do we see any ground either in law or reason for holding that a railway company cannot bind itself by conditions subsequent. It is true that it may acquire a fee in the land by condemnation, but, when it goes into the market to buy as an ordinary purchaser, it would seem that it ought to be permitted to make its own terms. Mills *v.* Seattle & M. Ry. Co., 10 Wash. 520, 39 Pac. 246, Nicoll *v.* New York & Erie R. Co., 12 N. Y. 121, and Blanchard *v.* Detroit, etc., R. Co., 31 Mich. 43, 18 Am. Rep. 142, are railroad cases, and in each of them a contract containing conditions subsequent is held valid. In the case at bar the plaintiff, having induced defendants to execute the conveyance, which they otherwise declined to execute, by writing in the provision in question, is not in a position to urge that such provision was one of which they had no right to accept.

It is urged that defendants are estopped from urging a forfeiture by reason of the fact that they voluntarily permitted plaintiff to enter upon the land and construct its grade, and the case of Roberts *v.* Northern Pacific R. R. Co., 158 U. S. 1, 15 Sup. Ct. 756, 39 L. Ed. 873, is cited, among others, in support of this contention. It is true that where one stands idly by and permits a railway corporation to enter upon his land and make valuable improvements thereon he will be held to have acquiesced in their act, but this only applies to cases where the entry was not under a specific agreement. Here the entry was made under a contract, which by its terms practically authorized a re-entry by the grantors at the expiration of two years if a road was not constructed within that period. There was no misleading plaintiff to its prejudice. Both parties knew from the beginning the possible consequences of delay. Defendants were unwilling to sell a strip of land across their farm and allow the railroad company to hold it indefinitely, to the detriment of the balance of

Oregon R. & Navigation Co. *v.* McDonald et al

their holdings and to the possible exclusion of some other line of road. They wanted the road built within two years or they wanted their land back. Plaintiff, feeling confident that it could complete the road within that time, took the deed with the condition annexed to it. Owing primarily to the money panic and secondarily to weather conditions, they failed to comply with the conditions which no doubt seemed reasonable enough when the deed was made. Financial stringency has caused many people in this country to forfeit profitable contracts, but the courts cannot compel the beneficiaries of such contracts to be generous and extend the time for performance. We find no reason for holding that defendants have in any way waived this condition. After plaintiff had ceased work, defendants built a fence across that part of the field which had been opened for the purpose of constructing the grade, and, before plaintiff ever attempted to begin work at this point again, they warned the company and its agents that they had taken possession. In this we think that they were within the legal rights and waived nothing.

So far, then, we have found that defendants were entitled to a forfeiture and that the land has reverted, but we now recur to the remedy. The situation is anomalous. Plaintiff has constructed its road and has it in operation, thereby performing an important public function for a large and increasing population. It is reasonable to suppose that it is transporting freight and passengers, and, as is the custom of the country, the United States mail. It is to the interest of the public that it should continue to do so, and that the defendants should not be allowed to acquire a portion of its roadbed to the detriment of public travel. The condemnation of land for railway purposes is usually the function of a court of law, but there are in this case such special circumstances as to authorize this court to end the whole litigation at once and forever. The pleadings show that this land is needed for the purposes of a railway, and the evidence shows that the railway is actually there on the ground. Defendants come into court, submit themselves to the jurisdiction of equity, and ask affirmative relief. Much of the testimony was devoted to showing the value of the land taken, the effect of the taking on the remainder of the tract, and all those things which are usually shown in an action to condemn for a railroad right of way.

Having jurisdiction of this case, we have concluded to assume it for all purposes and to so modify the decree that plaintiff shall take title to the land described in this strip upon the paying to defendants the damage occasioned by such taking, which we assess at $700, and the costs and disbursements of this suit; and that, upon payment of such sum and costs to the clerk of this court, plaintiff be decreed to be the owner in fee for railway purposes of such strip of land.

Southern Ry. Co. et al. *v.* Stewart.

(Court of Appeals of Kentucky, Dec. 14, 1910.)

[132 S. W. Rep. 435.]

Explosives—Negligence.—One whose dwelling near ·a railr
yard was injured by explosion of a car of dynamite in the yard i
not introduce in evidence rules of the railroad company goveri
the conduct of its employees in handling cars of dynamite, or r
of the company which manufactured the dynamite; the care that
ployees of the railroad must exercise in the operation of cars, so
as the general public is concerned, being determinable by princi
of law, and not by such rules.

**Witnesses—Impeachment by Contradictory Statement—Recal
Witness.**—A witness, who, on cross-examination, was asked if
did not, at a certain time and place, make a certain statement ·
certain person, inconsistent with his testimony, having denied
ing so, may, after such person has testified to his having done
be recalled to explain his alleged contradictory statement; it not
ing necessary that his re-examination be when he is on the stan
the first instance.

Appeal and Error—Harmless Error.—Many witnesses, who
served the accident, having testified to an explosion of a car
dynamite having been caused by the shunting of other cars aga
it, error in allowing plaintiff to introduce rules of the railroad c
pany and of a dynamite company as to handling dynamite, an
refusing to allow recall of a witness impeached by a contradic
statement that he so caused the accident, was harmless. .

Appeal from Circuit Court, Whitley County.

Action by Bond Stewart against the Southern Railway C
pany and another. Judgment for plaintiff, and defendants
peal. Affirmed.

*Humphrey & Humphrey, W. A. Henderson, J. W. Alc
William Low,* and *H. H. Tye,* for appellants.
H. C. Faulkner, A. T. Siler, and *J. N. Sharp,* for appellee

Clay, C. On September 21, 1906, a house belonging to
pellee, Bond Stewart, was damaged by an explosion o·
car of dynamite. At the time of the explosion the car was in
railroad yard at Jellico, and this yard was in the joint contro
the appellants, Southern Railway Company and Louisvill
Nashville Railroad Company. Charging that his property
damaged by the negligence of appellants, appellee brought
action to recover damages. The jury returned a verdict in
pellee's favor for $1,660. From the judgment based there
this appeal is prosecuted.

Southern Ry. Co. et al. *v.* Stewart

The car in question contained 450 cases of dynamite and nitroglycerine. It was placed in the yard about 8 o'clock in the evening and remained there until about 7:47 the next morning, when it exploded. By the explosion many persons were killed and a great deal of property destroyed or damaged. No person knew that the car contained explosives except the depot agent and Conductor Yerkes of the train that brought the car in. The car was not guarded, nor was there any warning given to the public that it contained explosives. The proof shows that there was no contents card on the east side of the car. Whether there was such a card on the other side or at the two ends, the evidence is conflicting. Jellico is a town of 3,500 inhabitants. The explosion took place at a point about 150 or 200 yards from the main portion of the town. Many persons lived and performed labor around the place where the car was located. There was evidence to the effect that within about 20 feet of where the car stood there was a common shooting ground where persons shot at marks and turkeys for general amusement, and that this fact was known to appellants, and had been for years. On the trial it was appellee's contention that the explosion was caused by the shunting of other cars against the car loaded with dynamite. Appellants undertook to disprove this theory of appellee by showing that none of the engines which could have shunted the car·were in a position to do so at the time of the accident. They also undertook to show that the explosion was caused by a man by the name of Walter Rodgers shooting into the car with a 22-caliber rifle.

The only two errors relied upon for reversal are: First, the admission of incompetent evidence; second, the exclusion of competent evidence.

On cross-examination, Conductor Yerkes, who was in charge of the train which brought the car of dynamite to Jellico, was asked in regard to certain rules of the Southern Railway Company adopted by it for the purpose of governing the conduct of its employees in handling dynamite cars. These rules were read to the jury, over the objection of appellants. It may be conceded that the admission of this evidence was improper, for this court is committed to the doctrine that the care employees of companies must exercise in the operation of cars, so far as the general public is concerned, is to be determined by the principles of law, and not by the rules adopted by the company for the guidance of its employees. Louisville Railway Co. *v.* Gaugh, 133 Ky. 467, 118 S. W. 276. The court also permitted the rules of the Keystone Powder Manufacturing Company, which manufactured the dynamite in question to be read as evidence. This evidence, while not material one way or the other, should not have been admitted for the same reason.

The witness Stanfill, who was in charge of Southern Railway

Southern Ry. Co. et al. *v.* Stewart

engine No. 686, testified on the trial that it was his duty to take
the engines to the cinder pit for the purpose of cleaning out the
fire boxes, and that on the ocassion in question he had taken engine No. 686 to the cinder pit and was on the engine when the
explosion occurred. On cross-examination he was asked whether
or not, on a trip from Indian Territory to St. Louis, he had not
told Dr. John Siler that he had shoved the cars back and caused
the explosion. He denied making this statement. Dr. Siler was
then introduced by appellee in rebuttal. Siler testified that Stanfill told him that, at the time of the accident, he was a hostler
in charge of the engines in the yard in Jellico, and that he kicked
the car or cars against the one that exploded, and the force of
the explosion knocked him down. Thereafter appellants sought
to introduce Stanfill for the purpose of having the latter tell the
exact conversation with Dr. Siler and explain the circumstances
under which it took place. The court declined to permit this
evidence to go to the jury. The jury was excluded, and the answers of Stanfill to the questions were allowed by agreement to
be made in the nature of an avowal. Stanfill avowed that he
and Dr. Siler sat together on the train from Indian Territory to
St. Louis and had quite a talk; that while they were together—a
period of about four hours—Dr. Siler consumed a quart of
whisky; that in the course of their conversation the question of
the Jellico explosion was brought up, and Dr. Siler asked him
what caused it; that witness stated some people thought the explosion was caused by Walter Rodgers' shooting into the car,
while others thought it was caused by a car or cars being shunted
into the dynamite car; that he told Dr. Siler that, as he was the
hostler in charge of Southern Railway engine No. 686, he was
accused by some people of causing the explosion.

The leading case upon the question of impeaching a witness
by showing that he has made statements contradictory to those
made upon the trial is the Queen's Case, 2 Brod. & Bing. 313,
314. The unanimous opinion of the judges was delivered by
Abbott, C. J., and in the course of his opinion he said: "The
legitimate object of the proposed proof is to discredit the witness. Now, the usual practice of the courts below, and a practice
to which we are not aware of any exception, is this: If it intended to bring the credit of a witness into question by proof of
anything that he may have said or declared, touching the cause,
the witness is first asked, upon cross-examination, whether or
not he has said or declared that which is intended to be proved.
If the witness admits the words or declarations imputed to him,
the proof on the other side becomes unnecessary; and the witness has an opportunity of giving such reason, explanation, or
exculpation of his conduct, if any there may be, as the particular
circumstances of the transaction may happen to furnish; and
thus the whole matter is brought before the court at once, which,

Southern Ry. Co. et al. *v.* Stewart

in our opinion, is the most convenient course. If the witness denies the words or declarations imputed to him, the adverse party has an opportunity afterwards of contending that the matter of the speech or declaration is such that he is not to be bound by the answers of the witness, but may contradict and falsify it; and, if it be found to be such, his proof in contradiction will be received at the proper season. If the witness declines to give any answer to the question proposed to him, by reason of the tendency thereof to criminate himself, and the court is of the opinion that he cannot be compelled to answer, the adverse party has, in this instance, also, his subsequent opportunity of tendering his proof of the matter, which is received, if by law it ought to be received. But the possibility that the witness may decline to answer the question affords no sufficient reason for not giving him the opportunity of answering, and of offering such explanatory or exculpatory matter as I have before alluded to; and it is, in our opinion, of great importance that this opportunity should be thus afforded, not only for the purpose already mentioned, but because, if not given in the first instance, it may be wholly lost; for a witness, who has been examined, and has no reason to suppose that his further attendance is requisite, often departs the court, and may not be found or brought back until the trial be at an end. So that, if evidence of this sort could be adduced on the sudden and by surprise, without any previous intimation to the witness or to the party producing him, great injustice might be done; and, in our opinion, not unfrequently, would be done both to the witness and the party; and this is not only in the case of a witness called by a plaintiff or prosecutor, but equally so in the case of a witness called by a defendant; and one of the great objects of the course of proceeding, established in our courts, is the prevention of surprise, as far as practicable, upon any person who may appear therein."

The purpose of asking the witness, whose testimony is sought to be impeached, as to the time, place, and person involved in the supposed contradiction is twofold: First, to give him an opportunity to correct the statement already made on the witness stand; second, to give him an opportunity, on re-examination, to explain the nature, circumstances, meaning, and design of what he is proved elsewhere to have said. Greenleaf on Evidence (15th Ed.) § 462. But, inasmuch as the impeached witness may not be introduced at all, we are inclined to the opinion that the re-examination should not be limited to the time the witness is on the stand, but that he may be recalled for the purpose of explaining his alleged contradictory statement. This view is sustained by the early case of State *v.* Winkley, 14 N. H. 480, where the court said: "The facts stated in this case render it necessary to inquire how far a witness whose testimony has been impeached by evidence that he has made contradictory

Southern Ry. Co. et al. *v.* Stewart

statements in relation to the same transaction may be permitted, on his re-examination, to give his statement of the conversations in which the contradictions of his present testimony are said to have been made. Holmes, a witness for the state, testified to a certain transaction. The prisoner then introduced three witnesses, Foss, Locke, and Avery, whose testimony tended to prove that Holmes had given accounts of that transaction inconsistent with the truth of his testimony. All these witnesses related conversations between themselves and Holmes. Holmes was then recalled by the Attorney General, and was asked what he said to Foss, Locke, and to Avery, on the several occasions to which their testimony referred. This was objected to, but was permitted by the court to be put; the court ruling that Holmes might state all the conversations he had with these witnesses, at the times to which they referred. To this ruling the prisoner excepts. Holmes was recalled because his testimony had been impeached. Three witnesses had testified that in certain conversations he had made certain statements. Upon these points, therefore, he was entitled to be heard, either by way of express denial that he had made the statements, or by explaining or qualifying them. Their effect upon his credibility might have been destroyed by evidence that they were made in an ironical manner and tone, by showing that they were connected with other remarks in such a way that they ought not to impair his credit, or that he could not have been supposed to be serious in making them." Again: "The inquiry in relation to each of the three witnesses, was limited to the particular conversations to which they alluded, and the only point we intend to decide is that, when the credit of the witness has been impeached by proof that in a certain conversation he had made statements inconsistent with the truth of his testimony, he may on his re-examination state what that conversation was. We are not aware that any direct authorities are to be found on this matter, and we are led to this conclusion by a regard for what, as it seems to us, the interests of truth and justice require. This view of the case, as is appears to us to be a sound one, avoids the objection which exists to proving that the witness has made statements at other times similar to his testimony and thus fortifying his testimony by his declarations made out of court."

The same rule recognized in the case of Hedge *v.* Clapp, 22 Conn. 262, 58 Am. Dec. 424, where the court said: "In the present case, at any rate, we see no cause for the plaintiff's complaint. His witness was still within his reach, and subject to his control, after the impeaching testimony had been heard; and all the cases agree in determining that, in such case, the witness could have been recalled by the plaintiff, for the purpose of explanation."

As the impeached witness may, as it is pointed out in the

Southern Ry. Co. et al. *v.* Stewart

Queen's Case, supra, leave the scene of the trial, and cannot then be introduced, we conclude that it is always proper to permit him, on re-examination, while on the stand, to explain the supposed contradictory statement. On the other hand, as the impeaching witness may not be introduced at all, and there may be, therefore, no necessity for explanation, we conclude that the impeached witness may be recalled and then given an opportunity to explain. In other words, the impeached witness at one stage of the proceedings or another should always be given an opportunity to explain the supposed contradictory statement.

But the question still remains whether the action of the court, in admitting the rules of the Southern Railway Company and of the Keystone Powder Manufacturing Company, and excluding the explanatory statements of the witness Stanfill, was prejudicial to the substantial rights of appellants.

The trial in this case consumed about two weeks. The transcript of testimony consists of 1,852 typewritten pages. Appellee introduced 34 witnesses in chief, to prove what caused the explosion and how it affected and damaged his property, and one witness in rebuttal. Appellants introduced 86 witnesses in chief, to show how the explosion was caused, and 6 witnesses in rebuttal. Eight of appellee's witnesses, who were in a position to see, testified that they saw the loose cars run down the track and strike the car loaded with dynamite, when the explosion occurred. Nine other witnesses for appellee testified that they saw the cars switching and going towards the point where the explosion took place. Four other witnesses for appellee testified that they were close enough to, and did, hear the striking of the cars together, and immediately after heard the explosion. Thus the witness Stanfill was impeached, not merely by evidence of contradictory statements, but by evidence tending to show the falsity of his testimony. When the testimony referred to above is considered in the light of the fact that the car load of dynamite was placed in charge of the car to give the public warning of the habit of passing to and fro, and where there is some evidence tending to show that it was a common shooting ground, and that the car was not properly placarded, and that no person was placed in charge of the car to give the public warning of the fact that it contained dynamite, we conclude that the alleged errors of the trial court respecting the matters above referred to were not prejudicial to the substantial rights of appellant. Indeed, it would be difficult to conduct a trial lasting so long and embracing such a large number of witnesses without making some slight errors in the admission or exclusion of evidence.

Judgment affirmed.

STATE *ex rel.* CORPORATION COMMISSION *et al. v.* SOUTHERN
RY. CO. *et al.*

(Supreme Court of North Carolina, Dec. 7, 1910.)

[69 S. E. Rep. 621.]

Railroads—Location—Extensions—Commission.—The Corporation
Commission has not absolute power to order a railroad company
to put in a side track, but is limited by Revisal 1905, § 1097 (5) which
provides that the revenue from such a side track must, within the
five years next succeeding, be sufficient to pay the expenses of its
construction.

Appeal and Error—Review—Presumption of Validity of Judgment.
—Where the lower court has refused to affirm an order of the Corporation Commission that a railroad shall put in a side track, and
it does not appear that the revenue from such side track will be
sufficient, within the five years, to pay the cost of its construction
as required by Revisal 1905, § 1097 (5), the presumption in favor of
the correctness of the judgment below is a sufficient ground for
affirmance.

**Eminent Domain—Railroad Commission—Necessity of Legislative
Authority.**—The Corporation Commission cannot grant the power
to condemn land for a siding to a railroad which has no such general
power, even if it may require them under Revisal 1905, § 1097 (5),
to put in side tracks, etc.

**Railroads—Right of Way—Right in Highways—Consent by Mu-
nicipal Authorities.**—Without express legislative authority, the streets
of a city cannot be taken for railroad purposes even with consent of
the town authorities.

**Commerce—Railroads—Statutory Provisions for Side Tracks—In-
terference with Interstate Commerce.**—Revisal 1905, § 1097 (5), requiring that a railroad shall, in certain cases, put in side tracks to
private industrial concerns, is not an interference with interstate
commerce although such a road may run through several states, and
may carry freight over this side track to other states.

Eminent Domain—Railroads—Statutory Provisions—Public Use.*
—Revisal 1905, § 1097 (5), requiring switches to be put in to private
industries on the order of the Corporation Commission, is not a requirement for a private purpose, but is for a public use.

Appeal from Superior Court, Rockingham County; Biggs,
Judge.

Mandamus, on the relation of the Corporation Commission
and the F. R. Penn Tobacco Company, against the Southern

---

*For the authorities in this series on the question what does, and
does not, constitute a public use for which private property may be
condemned, see foot-note of Dubuque, etc., R. Co. *v.* Ft. Dodge, etc.,
R. Co. (Iowa), 36 R. R. R. 292, 59 Am. & Eng. R. Cas., N. S., 292.

Vol. 39 R R R—Vol 62 Am & Eng R Cas N S   21

State ex rel. Corp. Com. v. Southern Ry. Co

Railway Company, in which James L. Butler intervenes. From a judgment for defendants, the F. R. Penn Tobacco Company appeals. Affirmed.

Manly & Hendren, for appellant.
R. C. Strudwick and *W. P. Bynum,* for intervener.
Justice & Glidewell, Brooks & Lane, for appellees.

CLARK, C. J. The subject-matter of this action, laying down a side track by the defendant railroad in a street of Reidsville, outside the railroad right of way, to the plant of the Penn Tobacco Company was before us in Butler v. Tobacco Co., 152 N. C. 416, 68 S. E. 12, where the facts are fully set out, together with a part of the locality. In that case, Butler, who is intervener in this case, was the plaintiff seeking to enjoin the defendant railroad and the tobacco company from laying down such track in derogation of the plaintiff's right as a property owner on said street. In that case we held that the commissioners of Reidsville could not authorize the laying down of the side track outside of the right of way without express legislative power, and that the then plaintiff Butler was entitled to an injunction to prevent such action, although his property was not immediately adjacent. This action was then begun by the Penn Company against the railroad company before the Corporation Commission to compel the railroad to lay down said side track to the Penn Company's plant, and off the right of way, the very act which the railroad had been enjoined against doing. The former plaintiff, Butler, now appears as intervener. The Corporation Commission granted the order asked for, and on appeal to the judge of the district, his honor refused to affirm the order. The Penn Company thereupon appealed to this court. Since our former opinion there has been no legislative action authorizing the defendant railroad to use any part of the street outside its right of way, nor authorizing the town of Reidsville to grant such permission. It would seem therefore that the matter is res judicata. The plaintiff contends that it is not, because under Revisal 1905, § 1097 (5), the Corporation Commission has directed the siding to be put in. For more reasons than one we think that this view cannot be sustained. Revisal, § 1097 (5), authorizes the Corporation Commission "to require the construction of side tracks by any railroad company to industries already established: Provided, it is shown that the proportion of such revenue accruing to such side track is sufficient within five years to pay the expenses of its construction." This is a very important provision of the law and was fully sustained by this court in the Industrial Siding Case, 140 N. C. 239, 52 S. E. 941, which has been cited since with approval in Dewey v. R., 142 N. C. 399, 55 S. E. 292, and in other cases, and which again we now reaffirm in every particular. But it has no application here because:

State ex rel. Corp. Com. v. Southern Ry. Co

(1) The power is conferred on the Corporation Commission not absolutely, but with restrictions, one of which is that the revenue from such side track shall be "sufficient within 5 years to pay the expenses of its construction." This does not appear, and as every presumption is in favor of the correctness of the judgment below this would be sufficient of itself to affirm the judgment. Besides it is reasonably apparent that after payment of damages to every citizen of Reidsville who may recover damages for appropriation of this street for railroad purposes the sum will exceed 5 years' additional revenues to be derived from such siding.

(2) The Corporation Commission cannot confer the power of eminent domain. The defendant, the Southern Railroad Company, being a nonresident corporation, does not possess the power of eminent domain, and the Legislature has not conferred it upon that company, save to the extent of authorizing it to lay a double track upon the right of way, which it has leased.

(3) The court has already held in Butler v. Tobacco Co., 152 N. C. 416, 68 S. E. 12, that without express legislative authority the streets of a city cannot be taken for railroad purposes even with the consent of the town authorities. 27 A. & E. (2d Ed.) 170, and cases cited. In Griffin v. R. R., 150 N. C. 312, 64 S. E. 16, the railroad was ordered to lay its tracks along a street by the Corporation Commission to make connection at a union depot but there was express legislative authority and the board of aldermen also granted their permission under authority conferred upon them in the city charter. See, also, Dewey v. R. R., 142 N. C. 392, 55 S. E. 292.

(4) It is by no means clear, though we do not find it now necessary to decide the point, that the Corporation Commission under Revisal, § 1097 (5), can require or authorize any railroad company to condemn a right of way for a side track to an industrial plant. As there is no reference to the exercise of the right of eminent domain in that section, it would seem that the Corporation Commission can require a railroad company to lay down a side track to an industrial plant only upon the railroad's right of way or when the right of way is tendered by the industrial company that petitions for a siding. In Revisal, § 1097 (3), which authorizes the Corporation Commission to require the establishment of union depots, it is expressly provided that "the railroad so ordered to construct union depots shall have power to condemn land for such purpose, as in case of locating and constructing a line of railroad." The absence of such provision in Revisal, § 1097 (5), seems to indicate clearly that industrial sidings can be ordered only when laid upon the railroad's own right of way or when the petitioner has tendered the right of way. In Commissioners v. Bonner (at this term) 68 S. E. 970, where the county commissioners were authorized in cases

State ex rel. Corp. Com. *v.* Southern Ry. Co.

where the public road ran along the bank of a stream to establish "a public landing," it was held that this did not confer the right to condemn land for that purpose; and that where the statute is silent it is to be presumed that the Legislature intended that the property should be obtained by contract; and this is especially so when the statute makes no provision for compensation.

It is proper, however, that we should say that we do not assent to the contention of the defendant railroad that, inasmuch as the side track, if established, would be largely used in interstate commerce, therefore the Corporation Commission could not order its establishment, because the cost of establishing it would be a burden upon interstate commerce. This point was raised and decided against the railroad company in R. R. *v.* Kansas, 216 U. S. 262, 30 Sup. Ct. 330, 54 L. Ed. ——, where that court held: "The fact that a railroad company is chartered by another state, and has projected its lines through several states, does not make all of its business interstate commerce, and render unconstitutional, as an interference with, and burden upon, interstate commerce, reasonable regulations of state railroad commissions applicable to portions of the lines wholly within, and which are valid under, the laws of that state." The establishment of an industrial siding under the authority of the Corporation Commissions, within the provisions of Revisal, § 1097 (5), is no more an interference with interstate commerce than the establishment of a new depot, or of a union depot, under the orders of the Corporation Commission. From such new station and union depot both freight and passenger traffic will originate, part of which will pass beyond the state line.

While it is true that the siding is sought by the industrial plant for the purpose of facilitating its shipments none the less the function which the defendant railroad company is required to exercise in laying and operating the siding is a public use, and a part of its duty as a common carrier. This is expressly held in Hairston *v.* R. R., 208 U. S. 608, 28 Sup. Ct. 335 (52 L. Ed. 637), where the court says: "The uses for which the track was desired are not the less public because the motive which dictated its location over this particular land was to reach a private industry, or because the proprietors of that industry contributed in any way to the cost." We would not be understood as having intimated anything contrary to this in what was said in Butler *v.* Tobacco Co., 152 N. C. 416, 68 S. E. 12.

The judgment below is affirmed.

ALLERTON v. NEW YORK, L. & W. RY. Co.

(Court of Appeals of New York, Nov. 15, 1910.)

[93 N. E. Rep. 270.]

Property—Scope—Rights of Landowner.—An owner of land may impose on it any burden, however injurious or destiuctive, not inconsistent with his general ownership, not violative of public policy, nor injurious to the property rights of others.

Trespass—Legal and Authorized Acts—Negligence.*—A railroad corporation is not liable for a trespass on the land of others which is purely consequential on the doing of a legal and authorized act, unless there is proof of such negligence in the doing of the act as to render the corporation responsible on that theory.

Railroads—Right of Way—Deeds—Construction—Change of Water Course.†—Defendant railroad company, having filed a plan of its right of way involving a change in a water course, obtained from plaintiff's grantor a deed for all lands in the town taken or in any manner affected by the construction and operation of the railway, or in process of construction the lines shown on the map of location, also all water rights and privileges of the grantor in the waters of the C. river, and all rights in any dams therein with the right to change or remove the same, and to use or deepen the channel; the grantors in addition allowing the railroad company to construct its roadbed on the line located as it deems proper, and to change the bed of the river, as proposed, and to wholly, if it sees fit, cut off the branch running to the grantor's mill, releasing the railroad company from all damages which may result by reason thereof. Held, that the deed conveyed the fee of so much of the grantor's land as was actually taken by the railroad company, with such easements in the remaining land as would be affected by the construction of the railroad, and was not a mere conveyance of the land taken, accompanied by a personal covenant of the grantor in the form of a release by him of all further claims for damages, and hence plaintiff, a subsequent grantee of a portion of the remaining land, could not recover damages for injuries thereto, resulting from flood waters turned on it by defendant's change of the channel of the river.

Appeal from Supreme Court, Appellate Division, Fourth Department.

---

*See foot-note of Tucker v. Vicksburg, etc., Ry. Co. (La.), 35 R. R. R. 517, 58 Am. & Eng. R. Cas., N. S., 517; foot-note of Longenecker v. Wichita R. & L. Co. (Kan.), 34 R. R. R. 610, 57 Am. & Eng. R. Cas., N. S., 610; extensive note, 15 R. R. R. 527, 38 Am. & Eng. R. Cas., N. S., 527.

†For the authorities in this series on the subject of the liability of a railroad for causing the overflow of the land of others, see last foot-note of Southern Ry. Co. v. Lewis (Ala.), 35 R. R. R. 778, 58 Am. & Eng. R. Cas., N. S., 778.

Allerton v. New York, L. & W. Ry. Co

Action by D. Dudley Allerton against the New York, Lackawanna & Western Railway Company. From a judgment for
plaintiff unanimously affirmed by the Appellate Division (132
App. Div. 943, 117 N. Y. Supp. 1128), defendant appeals. Reversed and dismissed.

Halsey Sayles, for appellant.
William H. Nichols, for respondent.

WERNER, J. The plaintiff is the owner of about 40 acres of
land, bounded in part by the Conhocton river, in the town of
Bath, Steuben county. He complains that the defendant has
wrongfully and unlawfully changed and diverted the channel of
that river from its former natural course so as to precipitate upon
plaintiff's land large quantities of flood water, debris; and earth;
which have been torn up, washed out, and flooded his surface
soil to his very substantial damage. The defendant has met this
complaint (1) with a general denial, (2) with the defense that
the plaintiff's damage was occasioned by extraordinary and unprecedented floods which occurred from natural causes   over
which the defendant had no control, and (3) with the allegation
that the defendant acquired from the plaintiff's predecessor in
title a grant in the nature of a perpetual easement, under which
the defendant had the right to so change and deflect the course
of the river as to flood the plaintiff's lands if that should be the
necessary result of a careful, skillful, and proper construction
of its railroad and the works incident thereto. That is, in substance, the controversy as outlined in the pleadings and charac-
terized by the evidence.

The trial court took the view that the deed under which the
defendant seeks to justify its alleged trespass was not broad
enough to convey any easement or interest in the 40 acres described in the complaint, and charged the jury, as matter of law,
"that any attempted release of damages, or any actual release of
damages as stated in that deed, would not be a covenant running
with this 40 acres which would be effectual as against a subsequent purchaser." Under this charge, to which an exception
was duly taken, the case was submitted to the jury upon the issue
whether the injury to the plaintiff's land had been occasioned by
any act of the plaintiff, or whether it was due wholly to the so-
called wrongful and unlawful acts of the defendant. The jury
gave a verdict for the plaintiff. From the judgment entered
upon that verdict an appeal was taken to the Appellate Division,
where there was a unanimous affirmance. As we have not been
favored with an opinion setting forth the reason for the affirmance,
we must assume that the Appellate Division assented to the correctness of the trial court's construction of the deed referred
to, and that view of the case presents the question which this
court is asked to decide upon defendant's appeal. It is essential

Allerton *v.* New York, L. & W. Ry. Co

to an understanding of this question that the salient parts of
the deed and the circumstances surrounding its execution should
be briefly stated.

In 1881 the defendant was preparing to build its railroad
through the town of Bath over a route which embraced a portion
of the lands owned by one Hewlett, consisting of a mill and
water power on the southerly side of the Conhocton river. At
this point there was a sweeping curve in the natural channel of
the stream which intersected the proposed line of the railroad
in two different places, and would apparently have necessitated
the building of two bridges unless the stream should be deflected
into a new channel confined wholly to the northerly side of the
railroad. When the railroad was afterward built in 1882, the
channel of the stream was in fact deflected so as to carry it along
the northerly side of the railroad. In 1881 Hewlett was also the
owner of 40 acres of land on the opposite side of the river and
about a quarter of a mile distant from the mill site above referred
to. The defendant, for the purpose of securing such rights as
were deemed necessary to enable it to construct its railroad according to the plan shown in the map filed, took a deed from
Hewlett for a substantial consideration, which conveyed "all
that certain piece or parcel of land situate in the town of Bath,
in the county of Steuben, and state of New York, bounded and
described as follows, to wit: All lands in said town taken or in
any manner used or affected by the construction and operation
of the railway now being constructed by the party of the second
part, the lines of which are shown on a map of the location of
said railway now on file in Steuben county, N. Y., together with
all my rights to enter on any such land for purpose of repairing or
constructing any water rights, also all water rights and privileges
owned, held or enjoyed by the party of the first part or either
of them in or to the waters of the Conhocton river, and all rights
in or to any dams therein, and rights to maintain, change or remove the same, and all rights to use, alter or deepen the channel;
and for value received we hereby permit and consent to and allow
said second party to construct their roadbed on the line as located
in such manner as they deem proper, and change the bed of the
Conhocton river as proposed by second party, and to wholly, if
they see fit, cut off the branch running from White's Channel to
my mill (party of the first part), and first party hereby for
value received release said company from all damages, claim or
claims for damages resulting or which may result by reason of
such construction, changing of stream or cutting off the branch
or removing of dams."

This deed was executed and delivered in August, 1881. In
December of the same year Hewlett conveyed to one Bedell the
40 acres of land situate on the northerly side of the Conhocton
river, being the side opposite from that on which the defendant's

Allerton *v.* New York, L. & W. Ry. Co

railroad was constructed, and in 1888 Bedell conveyed the same land to the plaintiff. The grievance complained of by the latter is that the change made by the defendant in the channel of the stream has caused the current thereof to wash away the high bank on the southerly side of the stream opposite his land, causing ice jams in the river which have turned the waters upon his land, carrying with them large quantities of dèbris and foreign matter, all of which have resulted in cutting away his surface soil and otherwise injuring his lands.

The concrete question, presented by the pleadings and proofs, is whether the plaintiff is entitled to recover of the defendant the damages which he has suffered, and the determination of that question depends, as we have stated, upon the correctness of the construction, by the courts below, of the deed from Hewlett to the defendant. A careful study and analysis of the instrument has convinced us that there is no logical middle ground between the two extremes contended for by the respective parties. It is either a conveyance in fee of so much of Hewlett's land as was actually taken for and occupied by the defendant's railroad, with such easements in such remaining land as should be affected by the construction or operation of the railroad; or it is simply a conveyance of the land actually taken, accompanied by the mere personal covenant of the grantor in the form of a release by him of all further claims for damages. We think the latter view, adopted by the courts below is untenable. Language could hardly be more broad or sweeping than that used by the grantor. He conveyed all his right, title, and interest in "all lands * * * taken or in any manner used or affected by the construction and operation of the railway * * * the lines of which are shown on a map of the location." The map shows that it was a part of the plan to change the course of the river, and the deed expressly gives the grantee the right to "change the bed of the Conhocton river as proposed." This language clearly indicates the purpose of the grantor to convey every right and interest in all his lands that might be actually taken for the roadbed or that might be affected by the use of the road as constructed, and this use includes such changes in the bed of the river as were contemplated by the plan set forth on the map referred to. That is the plain import of the deed which, under fixed and familiar rules, is to be construed most strongly against the grantor. Elphinstone on Interpretation of Deeds, rule 21, p. 94; Devlin on Deeds (2d Ed.) § 848. The context of the deed is quite in harmony with the explicit terms of the railroad law, under which railroad corporations are expressly authorized to acquire easements in lands (Railroad Law [Laws 1890, c. 565] § 7, subd. 4), and brings the case at bar fairly within the principle applied in Van Rensselaer *v.* Albany & W. S. R. R. Co., 62 N. Y. 65, where it was held that an instrument, containing covenants not unlike those in the deed from Hewlett to the defendant, was a grant

Allerton *v.* New York, L. & W. Ry. Co

of the privilege to maintain an embankment which occasioned landslides and deposits of earth upon Van Rensselaer's land. In view of the very comprehensive stipulations in the deed from Hewlett to the defendant, it is a circumstance of minor importance that the parcel of 40 acres now owned by the plaintiff happens to be situate on the opposite side of the river at some distance from the place where the defendant's railroad actually runs over the other lands formerly owned by Hewlett. Geographical location might be of controlling influence if the deed did not by its very terms embrace all of the grantor's land and provide for the very contingency which has resulted in the condition from which the plaintiff's damage has arisen. The right given to the defendant, to change the course of the river in accordance with the plan indicated on the may filed, was one which Hewlett was competent to convey. The owner of land may impose upon it any burden, however injurious or destructive, not inconsistent with his general right of ownership, if such burden is not in violation of public policy, and does not injuriously affect the property rights of others. It was one of the contemplated results of Hewlett's grant to the defendant that new and possibly burdensome conditions were to be created, even if the plan were most properly, carefully, and skillfully executed. That was one of the things for which Hewlett was paid the substantial sum of $4,000, as is shown by the clause in the deed releasing the defendant from, 'all damages, claim or claims for damages, resulting or which may result" to any of the grantor's land in the town of Bath, affected by the changing of the stream. That, we think, is the only reasonable and logical deduction to be drawn from Hewlett's deed to the defendant which is phrased in such comprehensive terms as to clearly convey notice of record to the plaintiff when he subsequently purchased the 40 acres of land described in the complaint.

This view of the case necessitates the reversal of the judgment; and the complaint must also be dismissed, for the plaintiff's action is based wholly upon the theory that the defendant's acts were inherently wrongful and unlawful, and not upon any claim of negligence in the construction cr maintenance of the works which the defendant erected. In that regard the case at bar is like the case of Gordon *v.* Ellenville & K. R. R. Co., 195 N. Y. 137, 88 N. E. 14, where we held that a railroad corporation was not liable for a trespass purely consequential upon the doing of a legal and authorized act unless there were allegations and proof of such negligence in the doing of the act as to render the corporation responsible upon that ground.

The judgment should be reversed, and the complaint dismissed, with costs to the defendant in all the courts.

CULLEN, C. J., and GRAY, HAIGHT, VANN, and CHASE, JJ. concur.

Judgment reversed, etc.

HARRIS *v.* NORFOLK & W. RY. CO.

(Supreme Court of North Carolina, Dec. 7, 1910.)

[69 S. E. Rep. 623.]

Waters and Water Courses—Natural Water Courses—Riparian Rights—Nature and Extent.—Riparian owners are entitled to have a stream which washes their lands, flow in its natural course without material diminution.

Waters and Water Courses—Natural Water Course—Riparian Rights—Extent of Right to Use.—A riparian owner may use water for any purpose to which it can be beneficially applied, provided he does not inflict substantial injury upon those below him.

Waters and Water Courses—Natural Water Courses—Riparian Rights—Injury.—A .lower riparian owner has no right of action because an upper one takes water from the stream, provided there has been no appreciable diminution of the stream.

Water and Water Courses—Natural Water Courses—Mechanical Purposes.—A railroad company crossing a stream may take water therefrom for its locomotives, provided the quantity taken does not materially reduce the volume.

Waters and Water Courses—Natural Water Courses—Proceeding to Protect—Evidence Sufficient to Carry the Case to Jury.—In an action by a lower riparian owner against an upper one for injury by taking water from a stream, conflicting evidence of damage held properly submitted to the jury.

Appeal from Superior Court, Person County; Lyon, Judge.

Action by C. C. Harris against the Norfolk & Western Railway Company. ·From a judgment for defendant, plaintiff appeals. Affirmed.

These issues were submitted: "(1) Is the plaintiff the owner in fee of the land mentioned and described in the complaint; if so, when did he become the owner thereof? Ans. Yes; April 7, 1902. (2) When did the defendant erect its water tank and pumping apparatus, and begin to take and appropriate the water from the stream mentioned, and described in the complaint? Ans. September 27, 1900. (3) When did the plaintiff erect his mill and begin to take and appropriate the water from the stream mentioned and described in the complaint? Ans. January, 1903. (4) Has the defendant unlawfully and wrongfully diverted and used the water from plaintiff's mill pond, as alleged in the complaint? Ans. No. (5) Did the plaintiff commence this action against the defendant within three years next ensuing from and after the time when the defendant erected its water tank and pumping station and first began the use of the water from the stream on which plaintiff's mill and pond are situated? Ans. No. (6) Did plaintiff commence this action

Harris *v.* Norfolk & W. Ry. Co

against the defendant within five years next ensuing from and after the time when the defendant erected its water tank and pumping station and first began the use of the water from the stream on which plaintiff's mill and pond are situated. Ans. No. (7) Is the plaintiff's alleged claim for damages barred by the statutes of limitation? Ans. ———. (8) What amount of permanent damages, if any, is plaintiff entitled to recover of the defendant? Ans. ———. (9) What damage has plaintiff sustained, if any, by reason of the use and diversion of water by defendant for three years next before the bringing of this action?"

Upon the finding of the jury in favor of the defendant upon the fourth issue, the court rendered judgment that the plaintiff take nothing by his writ, and that defendant go without day and recover costs. From this judgment, plaintiff appealed. The facts are stated in the opinion of the court.

J. F. Cothran, R. P. Reade, V. S. Bryant, and *H. A. Foushce,* for appellant.

Guthrie & Guthrie, for appellee.

BROWN, J. The evidence discloses that the plaintiff is the owner of a tract of land known as Burton's old mill situated on Flat river, upon which plaintiff has a water mill. The mill gets its flowage of water from both the North and South forks of Flat river. It is two miles by the river from the mill tract to the defendant's bridge across the South fork. The North fork and South fork come together between the mill and the bridge. Defendant has a water tank at its bridge across South fork from which it supplies its engines with water pumped from the stream. It is claimed by the plaintiff that the taking of the water by the defendant is unlawful and wrongful in that it materially lowers the stream to the injury of plaintiff's mill. This is denied by the defendant which contends that the quantity of water taken is so small that it does not appreciably affect the flowage of the stream. Both parties introduced evidence. The only assignment of error relied upon on argument or presented in plaintiff's brief is to the refusal of the court to give the following instruction asked by plaintiff: "If the jury believe the evidence they will answer fourth issue 'Yes.'" There being no exceptions, except this, the charge of the court is not sent up.

It is well settled that riparian proprietors, in the absence of specific limitation upon their rights, are entitled to have the stream which washes their lands flow as it is wont by nature, without material diminution. The proprietors of lands along streams have no property in the flowing water, which is indivisible and not the subject of riparian ownership. They may use the water for any purpose to which it can be beneficially applied, but in doing so they have no right to inflict material or substantial injury upon those below them. Williamson *v.* Canal Co., 78 N. C. 157; Gould *v.* Waters, pp. 394, 395; Angell on Water Com'rs (7th Ed.) pp. 96, 97. What, then, gives to the lower riparian proprietor the right to complain? Not the mere taking of the water by the upper proprietor, because the water itself is not the subject of ownership as it flows in nature's course. The right of action accrues from the taking it in such unreasonable quantity as to materially, substantially injure the lower proprietor in some legitimate use he is making of the water. As Mr. Farnham expresses it: "Since the right to make use of the stream is common to all who own property upon its shores, there would prima facie seem to be no cause of complaint on the part of one for any use made by another unless he was actually injured by such use." 2 Waters & Water Rights, p. 1584, § 468. It seems to be generally conceded that the seize and character of the stream has much to do with the quantity of water which may be withdrawn from it, and that where there has been no appreciable, perceptible diminution of the volume of the stream by the upper proprietor, the lower has no cause of action. Elliot *v.* Fitchburg R. R. Co., 10 Cush. (Mass.) 191, 57 Am. Dec. 86; Newhall *v.* Ireson, 8 Cush. (Mass.) 595, 54 Am. Dec. 790.

It is generally held that a railroad company, being a riparian proprietor, may take a reasonable amount of water from a stream for the purpose of supplying its locomotives. Mr. Farnham says: "Therefore the water cannot be taken from the stream for use in locomotive engines so as to interfere with the rights of the riparian owner in the stream.' But if the water can be taken for such purpose without interfering with other rights on the stream it may be done." 2 Waters & Water Rights, p. 1583. In England it is held that a railroad company, which crosses a river, may take a reasonable quantity of water for the supply of its engines from the river and "the quantity will not be held unreasonable if it does no injury in wet weather and never shortens the working hours of mills lower down the stream more than a few minutes a day at any time." Sandwich *v.* Great Northern R. R. Co., L. R. 10 Ch. Div. 27. The English courts also held that equity will not restrain the taking of water from a stream by a railroad company for its locomotives when the quantity taken deprives the lower riparian owner of but eleven-twelfths of one horse power. Graham *v.* Northern R. Co., 10 Grant Ch. 259. In this country it seems well settled that a railroad company crossing a stream may take water for its locomotives provided the quality taken does not materially, appreciably, perceptibly, or sensibly (some authorities use one word and some the other) reduce the volume of water flowing down the stream. If it materially lowers the stream, it is liable to a lower proprietor who suffers a substantial injury thereby. 2 Elliott on R. R. § 977, and notes; Elliot *v.* Fitchburg R. R., 10 Cush. (Mass.) 191,

Harris v. Norfolk & W. Ry. Co

57 Am. Dec. 86, a case in which Chief Justice Shaw discusses the subject with his usual thoroughness. Fay v. Salem R. R., 111 Mass. 27; Penn. R. R. v. Miller, 112 Pa. 34. 3 Atl. 780. In this case Mr. Justice Paxson closes a learned discussion of the matter with these words: "As before observed, the railroad company may use this water by virtue of its rights as riparian owner; but such use must be such as not to sensibly diminish the stream to the riparian owner below. The water belongs to both, and if the former wants more than its share it must take it under its right of eminent domain and pay for it." In the case of Garwood v. N. Y. R. R., 83 N. Y. 400, 38 Am. Rep. 452, the right of the defendant as riparian owner to take water for its locomotives is recognized, but the jury having found that the quantity taken was sufficient to "materially reduce or diminish the grinding power of plaintiff's mill," and "to perceptibly reduce the volume of water in the stream," the court held the taking wrongful and unlawful, and that the defendant was liable for the damage sustained. But a diminution of the stream which is not sensible, appreciable, perceptible, is not actionable. Gould on Waters, § 410, and cases cited in notes; Wadsworth v. Tillotson, 15 Conn. 366, 39 Am. Dec. 391; George v. Wabash Western Ry. Co., 40 Mo. App. 433.

Although the charge of the court, there being no exceptions to it, not before us, yet we can perceive from the character of the evidence and examination of witnesses on both sides that the case was properly tried and upon the true theory of liability. It requires only a cusory perusal of the evidence to bring us to the conclusion that the court committed no error in refusing plaintiff's prayer upon the fourth issue. The plaintiff's evidence tends to prove that at times the water taken by defendant from the South fork materially lowers the water in the stream and inflicts substantial damage upon plaintiff by compelling him to shut down his mill. The defendant introduced a number of witnesses who testified that plaintiff's mill was not damaged by the water taken by defendant, and that it does not perceptibly or appreciably decrease the volume of the stream; that water runs over plaintiff's dam when he is grinding, and that the lowest water some witnesses have seen is a foot from the top of the dam. Defendant also proves by a civil engineer that he measured the stream and calculated its volume; that he made surveys and calculations at different times; that the flow of the stream in 24 hours is 293,000,000 gallons, and that the quantity taken out during that time by the railroad company is only 26,000 gallons, or about one-fiftieth part of 1 per cent. of the total flowage. The civil engineer further testifies that: "The pumping of 26,000. gallons of water out of the stream of South fork every 24 hours with the total flowage of the stream would not be appreciable. It would be about 3 two-hundredths (3-200) of one part of 1

Jageriskey *v.* Detroit United Ry

per cent. A person standing on the bank of the river could not see any difference at all. To the eye it would show no difference."

In view of the conflicting character of the evidence his honor properly submitted the question to the jury, and denied the plaintiff's prayer. As the jury found there had been no unlawful and wrongful taking and usage of the water by the defendant, the issues in regard to the statute of limitations and damages were properly left unanswered.

No error.

JAGERISKEY *v.* DETROIT UNITED RY.

(Supreme Court of Michigan, Dec. 7, 1910.)

[128 N. W. Rep. 726.]

Trial—Misconduct of Trial Court—Improper Remarks.—The statement of the court in an action by plaintiff, suing for a personal injury and testifying to her holding peculiar religious views and practicing them as a faith healer, that it was not religion, that it was too fakey, made in response to the objection that the testimony was incompetent because a part of her religious rites, was reversible error, as a comment on her religious beliefs in a manner to mitigate the damages.

Trial—Instructions—Failure to Charge.—Under Comp. Laws, § 10,243, requiring the court to charge the jury only as to the law of the case, failure of the court to instruct as to the law of the case is error, and a court, in a personal injury action, which merely charges that it cannot determine the sum to be allowed, but that is entirely for the jury, without pointing out the elements on which a recovery may be had, does not comply with the statute, especially where there is a proper requested charge on the measure of damages.

Error to Circuit Court, Wayne County; Joseph W. Donovan, Judge.

Action by Anna Jageriskey against the Detroit United Railway. There was a judgment granting insufficient relief, and plaintiff brings error. Reversed.

Argued before BIRD, C. J., and MCALVAY, BROOKE, BLAIR, and STONE, JJ.

William Van Dyke, for appellant.
Corliss, Leete & Joslyn (A. B. Hall, of counsel), for appellee.

BIRD, C. J. This is a personal injury case, in which plaintiff recovered a judgment of $100 in the Wayne circuit court. On account of the inadequacy of the judgment she brings the case to this court for review.

It was the claim of plaintiff that she was a passenger on one of defendant's cars in the city of Detroit and when she was in the act of alighting therefrom, at the intersection of Jefferson and Beauford streets, the car suddenly started and threw her to the ground with such force that it injured her back and side; that she was laid up on account of her injuries for three months, and had not fully recovered at the time of the trial; that she was obliged to have help to care for her during the time, and that her doctor's bill was $187. The negligence relied upon was the sudden starting of the car, without any notice to her, as she was about to step to the ground. Defendant's counsel took part in the trial, but offered no testimony. The errors of which the plaintiff complains relate to the remarks of the court during the progress of the trial, the charge of the court, and the court's refusal to give his requests to charge.

The testimony disclosed that plaintiff was a seamstress, and that she gave "faith healing" treatments, and that she was on her way to see one of her patients when the accident occurred. While upon the witness stand she was cross-examined at a considerable length about her efforts at "faith healing." She testified that she and her brother and a 10-year old girl took a car and went to Delray about three o'clock in the morning, and there behind a billboard dug a hole. The cross examination then proceeded as follows: "Q. What did you do? A. I stood there and prayed while my brother dug the hole. Q. What did you dig a hole for? (Objected to as incompetent and immaterial, inquiring into this woman's rites.) The Court: I do not think that is religion anyway; you may ask about it. Q. What did you dig a hole for? A. For a woman that had been under operation, and she wanted to go home to Cleveland, and she could not get out of bed, and I knew if I would do as I was told to do, I would have her strong enough to get out of bed and go home to Cleveland. Q. Who told you to do this? A. That is the angel? Q. What angel? A. Casimir. (Objected to, and I ask that it be stricken out.) The Court: I think that it has a direct bearing whether she is able to do what she says. Mr. Van Dyke: I want an exception to the court's ruling. Q. It is the Angel Casimir? Mr. Van Dyke: May all this be taken, subject to the objection and the exception? The Court: Certainly. Q. Does Angel Casimir live on this earth, or some other place? A. Lives with God in heaven. Q. And Angel Casimir told you to go down and dig a hole in Delray? A. Yes, sir. Q. What did you have the little child with you for? A. To pray." The cross-examination proceeded further along these lines, when plaintiff's counsel again objected that the testimony was incompetent, irrelevant, and immaterial, "as it is part of her religious rites.

Jageriskey *v.* Detroit United Ry

The Court: I do not think this is religion; you cannot make this
religion with me; it is too fakey. If that is religion, I don't
want to hear anything more about it." It is claimed that these
remarks of the court were prejudicial to the plaintiff's case;
that the result of such remarks was to stamp plaintiff as a religious faker, and destroy her standing before the jury, and lead
them to disbelieve her injuries, and doubt her loss on account of
them.

We argree with counsel that the remarks of the court were
harmful to the plaintiff's case. However absurd the plaintiff's
acts and beliefs might appear to others, she was evidently sincere
in them, and was entitled while in court to have them passed
without question or comment, except so far as was necessary to
show her physical condition and activity. We feel that something more than this was done in plaintiff's examination. Her
acts and beliefs were unduly developed and commented on in
such a manner as to mitigate the damages, to which the testimony
showed she was justly entitled. When one's peculiar views are
made use of for this purpose and it is obvious, as it is here, that
the use had the desired effect, the verdict ought to be set aside.

Plaintiff's counsel requested the court to charge upon the
question of damages, as follows: "I charge you that the amount
of the damages which you must award the plaintiff must be for
such a sum as will make her whole or compensate her for such
injuries as you find she has, or will in the future suffer on account of the accident and negligence of the defendant." The
court refused this, and instead gave the following: "I am unable to determine what sum you are to determine upon. That
is entirely for the jury." This has the merit of brevity, but not
of sufficiency. It was the duty of the trial court to instruct the
jury as to the law applicable to the case. Comp. Laws, § 10,243.
A failure to do so is error. Simons *v.* Haberkorn, 139 Mich.
131, 102 N. W. 659.

Jurors are not supposed to know, without instruction, of the
different elements of damage in a personal injury case, and it
is the duty of the trial court to point out those elements on which
a recovery may be had. This comes clearly within the duty
enjoined upon him by the statute. In this instance the court
not only failed to cover the question of damages in his general
charge, but refused to give the unobjectionable request of counsel on that subject. We think the refusal of the trial court to
give the request was error.

For the errors pointed out, the judgment is reversed, with
costs of both courts, and a new trial ordered.

Simon *et al. v.* Metropolitan St. Ry. Co.

(Supreme Court of Missouri, Division No. 2, Nov. 29, 1910.)

[132 S. W. Rep. 250.]

Street Railroads—Injuries—Negligence—Injuries to a Child.*—
That the motorman sees a child four years of age approaching the
street car track from the sidewalk ahead of the car is in itself sufficient to require him to stop the car to prevent injury.

Street Railroads—Injuries—Action—Sufficiency of Evidence.—In
an action for the death of a four year old child by being struck by
defendant's street car, evidence held to show that the child made
only a momentary stop in the street before going on the track or
merely hesitated from childish indecision.

Street Railroads—Injuries—Negligence—Failure to Stop Car.*—
That a four year old child after leaving the curb merely hesitated for
a brief time in the street from childish indecision before advancing
onto the track did not give the motorman the right to proceed under the idea that the child did not intend to go onto the track.

Street Railroads—Injuries—Negligence.—The distance from the
street car track at which young children are placed in a perilous
position so as to require the motorman of an approaching car to stop
is greater than in the case of adults.

Trial—Instruction—Assumption of Fact.—An instruction in an action against a street railway company for an infant's death that if
the motorman saw the child leave the sidewalk and come into the
street, and stop before going to the track, he could proceed, etc., was
erroneous for assuming that here was evidence that the motorman
saw the child leave the sidewalk and stop; the evidence showing that
he did not do so.

Street Railroads—Injuries to Child—Action—Instructions.—An instruction, in an action against a street car company for death of a
four year old child on the track, that if the motorman after seeing
the child start towards the track, after making its last stop in the
street, used ordinary care to stop the car, he was not negligent, was
erroneous in making the motorman's exercise of ordinary care to
stop after seeing the child start after making its "last stop" in the
street the full measure of his duty, where there was evidence that
he was negligent in not seeing the child until just before striking it,
and in not ringing the bell or observing the efforts of bystanders
to warn him of the child's peril, and was also erroneous for only
requiring the motorman to stop after seeing the child start towards

---

*For the authorities in this series on the subject of the care re-
quired to be exercised by those in charge of street cars to avoid
collisions with children, see last foot-note of Perryman *v.* Chicago
City Ry. Co. (Ill.), 34 R. R. R. 93, 57 Am. & Eng. R. Cas., N. S., 93;
last foot-note of United Rys. & Elec. Co. *v.* Carneal (Md.), 34 R.
R. R. 705, 57 Am. & Eng. R. Cas., N. S., 705.

the track after making "its last stop," the evidence showing that it
first stopped at the edge of the curb, and then momentarily hesitated
in the street before finally toddling towards the tracks.

Street Railroads—Injury Actions—Jury Question—Negligence.—
In an action against a street car company for the death of a four
year old child on the track, the evidence held to make defendant's
negligence a question for the jury.

**Appeal and Error—Findings—Conclusiveness—Weight of Evi-
dence.—**It is not the province of the Supreme Court to pass upon the
weight of the evidence.

Negligence—Imputed Negligence—Care of Parents.—In an action
against a street car company for the death of plaintiff's child upon
the track, evidence held not to show that plaintiff was negligent in
permitting the child to go upon the street.

Appeal from Circuit Court, Jackson County; H. L. McCune,
Judge.

Action by Abraham Simon and another against the Metropolitan Street Railway Company. From an order granting a
new trial, after verdict for defendant, it appeals. Affirmed.

Jno. H. Lucas and *Chas. N. Sadler,* for appellant.
Leon Block and *Daniel O'Byrne,* for respondents.

GANTT, C. J. This is an appeal from an order of the circuit
court of Jackson county granting the plaintiffs a new trial. The
action was for $10,000, brought by the plaintiffs for the death
of their minor daughter. The trial resulted in a verdict for the
defendant, and the court set aside the verdict and granted plaintiffs a new trial on the ground that the court erred in giving instruction "No. 3 A" on behalf of the defendant.

The petition stated that the plaintiffs were husband and wife,
and, respectively, the father and mother of Sarah Simon, who
was at all times a minor and unmarried; that the defendant was
at all times mentioned a corporation operating an electric car
line over and upon the streets of Kansas City, among other streets
an electric car line and electric cars over and upon Third street,
between Walnut and Grant avenue; that on or about July 11,
1905, about 5 o'clock in the afternoon on said Third street, and
about 60 feet west of Grand avenue, Sarah Simon, the minor
child of plaintiffs, while attempting to cross said Third street
from the south side thereof to the north side thereof, the said
Third street running east and west, was run into, her left leg
fractured, and she was terribly injured otherwise by an electric
car which was then and there run, conducted, and managed by
the employees of the defendant, and as a result of said injuries
said Sarah Simon died within ten hours thereafter; that the said
Sarah was thus run into and injured by said car through the
negligence and unskillfulness of the servants and employees of

Simon et al. *v.* Metropolitan St. Ry. Co

the defendant whilst running and managing said electric car, in this: First, the motorman running said car and in charge thereof negligently failed to sound any bell or give any other warning of the approach thereof; second, the said motorman failed to stop the said car within a reasonable time after he saw the dangerous situation of the said Sarah; third, that the said motorman negligently failed to stop the said car with a reasonable time after he might have seen the dangerous situation of the said Sarah; and, fourth, that the agents, servants, and employees of said defendant negligently failed to attach a good and sufficient fender to the front end of said car, which in the exercise of ordinary care they should have done. The answer was a general denial and a plea of contributory negligence on the part of the said Sarah Simon and the plaintiffs directly contributing to the injury of the said Sarah.

The evidence tended to show that on July 11, 1905, the plaintiffs resided on the north side of Third street just east of the alley between Walnut street and Grant avenue of Kansas City. They were the parents of several minor children, and among them the deceased child, Sarah, age four years and three months. The father conducted a clothes pressing shop at said place, and his family lived in the rear of it. Third street runs east and west. Almost directly across the street from the plaintiffs' business place and home Mrs. Barman, with her husband conducted a millinery establishment. In the afternoon of the 11th day of July, 1905, Mrs. Barman, who testified she was a childless woman, went over to the plaintiffs' residence, and, on the parents' consent, took their three minor children across the street to her business place. They played around her establishment inside of the house and store. She had the youngest child on her knee, and did not notice that Sarah had gone outside until she heard shouts and cries in the street about 5 o'clock that afternoon. She went out and found that Sarah, the deceased child, had been struck and run over by an electric car. There was no one on the car except the motorman and the conductor. She testified that the child was never permitted to cross the street unaccompanied.

George Chapman testified that he was walking along Third street, proceeding east along between Walnut and Grand avenue, on the south side of the street, and passed the little girl Sarah about the time she was leaving the curb to cross the street; that at the time the child first started in the sreet the car was at Walnut street curve; that he stopped four or five feet after he passed her, and leaned against the iron post, one of the posts that supports the electric line of the defendant; that he saw the child standing four or five feet from the curb of the street; that the child started again, and, when she did so, the car was about to the vacant lot west of the alley. He saw she was in danger.

Simon et al. *v.* Metropolitan St. Ry. Co

There was no object between the child and the street car. The witness heard no bell and the car's speed was about five or six miles an hour. The child toddled; did not run. She was dragged six or seven feet after she was struck.

A colored policeman took the child from under the car.

Edwin J. Shannahan testified that he had made measurements for the plaintiffs, and that it was 17 feet 4 inches from the south curb to the rail of the alley; that it was 61 feet 7 inches from the alley to Grand avenue, and 29 feet 1 inch east of the east line of the alley to the east line of the door in Barman's place; that the vacant lot alluded to by Chapman in his testimony was over 40 feet west of Mrs. Barman's door, out of which the child came.

Mrs. Bernstein testified that she was coming from Grand avenue into Third street; that, when she was six or seven feet from the corner of Grand avenue, she saw the child coming from the sidewalk into the street, and also saw the car coming. She holloed to the motorman to stop the car, but he paid no attention. He was looking toward the north side of the street (all of the testimony showed that the child came from the south side of the street). Mrs. Bernstein testified that she halloed when the child was leaving the curb of the sidewalk. At that time the car was 50 or 55 feet west of the place where it struck the child. She testified, further, that no bell was rung, and that the child was walking, and did not stop. Mrs. Emma Bernstein testified that she saw the child and then saw the car about 50 feet on the other side of the alley. She raised her hand and halloed to the motorman, but he was looking to the other side. He paid no attention. No bell was rung.

Lee J. Hill testified that he was an ex-motorman; that he had operated similar cars to this one over similar grades; that this grade was 3 or 4 per cent., and in this connection it may be remarked that Mr. Satterlee, defendant's assistant superintendent, corroborated this witness as to the grade of the track. Hill testified that this car under the circumstances, in evidence, could have been stopped within 10 or 15 feet. The motorman himself testified that he stopped the car within from 20 to 25 feet. The father of the deceased child testified that at the time the child was hurt he was at work in his shop on the north side of Third street between Grand avenue and Walnut street, and just east of the alley, which extends south through the block; that there was no window in the west side of his shop, but there were large windows in the front; that he could see about 50 feet up towards Walnut street through the front window; that from time to time he looked across the street and saw his children in Mrs. Barman's store; that he saw the car that injured his child when it was about 50 feet west of the alley; that the motorman was looking toward the west side of the street and upward at the point above witness' shop; that he heard no bell.

Simon et al. *v.* Metropolitan St. Ry. Co

Irvin Schofield, on behalf of the defendant, testified that he was the motorman in charge of the car which killed the child, and that the accident happened at 4:55 p. m. He said: "Well, I was coming from Third and Walnut going down towards Grand. I got probably two-thirds of the way down. There is an alley there. I got somewhere close to the alley, maybe not quite to it, or maybe a little past it, and ahead of me between the curbing and the rail I seen a little child starting towards the track running fast, and I seen that we were going to come together the way we were going, and I holloed, 'Look out!' at the child just as loud as I could, and applied the brakes at the same time. By that time we had pretty near come together. We had come close, and the little child ran right in ahead and back of the fender and fell back, and I had the car pretty near stopped." On cross-examination he testified that he did not see the child on the curb, that she was probably half way between the curbing and the rail when he first saw her, and she was running towards the track. The only thing he did to avert the injury was to apply his brake and holloe to the child. He was moving five or six miles an hour. He was about to the alley when he first saw her. He stopped the car with a hand brake within from 20 to 25 feet.

Peter Cambell, a witness for the defendant, did not hear the bell ring. He was a police officer. He and Sergeant Lynch and Mr. Thompson were standing somewhere near Third street and Grand avenue looking west up Third street and saw some children playing on the sidewalk up the street, saw a little girl start across the street. At the time she started the car was about opposite her. She started due north across the street, and, when near the track, turned notheast and ran between the fender and the bumper of the car, and was knocked down. The car ran three or four feet after she was struck. The front wheel mashed the child's leg. She was not on the track or in front of the car. Witness took the child from under the wheel. The child ran faster than the car when she started towards the track. The motorman made a quick stop. He did not think the motorman knew what had happened. "Q. You do not think then that he saw the child? A. I do not think he did. Q. He did not give any evidence or make any alarm which would indicate as far as you heard? A. No, sir. Of course, the child began to holloe, and I halloed and he stopped. I halloed and told him to back up. Of course, he knew there was something wrong there, and then he backed up."

Jerry Lynch, a sergeant of the police, testified in behalf of the defendant. His evidence is substantially the same as that of Peter Cambell, except that he testified that the motorman holloed, but he did not hear any bell ring, and that at the time the child hesitated in the street the street car was close to the alley.

William Spenamen, for the defendant, testified that he was

Simon et al. *v.* Metropolitan St. Ry. Co

looking out of his window on the north side of the street, did not see the accident, but saw the child start to run across the street and the car came between him and the child and he did not see her any more; that, when the child was stepping off the curb, the front of the car was about at the west line of the alley. When the child was halfway between the curb and the track, the car was about 100 feet west of the little girl. The first motion on the part of the motorman to use his brake was after the car had gotten across the alley.

This was substantially the evidence in the case. At the close of the evidence the defendant requested an instruction in the nature of a demurrer to the evidence, which was refused. The court then instructed the jury, and the jury returned a verdict for the defendant, and thereupon the plaintiffs filed their motion for a new trial, alleging, among other grounds, that the court erred in giving instructions as asked by the defendant. The court sustained the motion for new trial on the ground that it had erred in giving instruction No. 3 A on behalf of the defendant, and from this order the defendant takes its appeal to this court. Said instruction No. 3 A is in these words: "The court instructs the jury that the fact that a person leaves the sidewalk and comes near the track is not enough in itself to impose the duty on the motorman to stop the car.. There must be something noticeable in the conduct of the person coming towards the track to apprise the motorman that such person is about to enter into a position of danger to make it incumbent on the motorman to stop the car. Now, if the jury believe from the evidence that the motorman saw the child leave the sidewalk and come into the street and stop before getting to the track, then the motorman in charge of the car in controversy had the right to proceed with his car, and he was not required to stop the car until there was a movement by the child, which indicated that it was about to run into a position of danger; and, if the motorman after seeing the child start towards the track after making its last stop in the street used ordinary care with the means at his command, to stop said car and prevent a collision with the child, then there was no negligence, and the plaintiff cannot recover in this case, and the jury must return a verdict for the defendant company."

1. The defendant insists that the order of the circuit court granting plaintiffs a new trial should be reversed because the court erred in reaching the conclusion that its instruction No. 3 A, given in behalf of the defendant, was erroneous, and asserts that the said instruction correctly stated the law. The statement in that instruction "that the fact that a person leaves the sidewalk and comes near the track is not enough in itself to impose the duty on the motorman to stop the car, that there must be something noticeable in the conduct of the person coming towards the track to apprise the motorman that such a person is about to

Simon et al. *v.* Metropolitan St. Ry. Co

enter a place of danger to make it incumbent upon the motorman to stop the car" is well enough when "the person is an adult," but it is inapplicable to a child of the tender years that the deceased child of the plaintiffs was in this case. On the contrary, numerous cases in this court assert the doctrine that when a child of tender years, as the plaintiffs' child was in this case, is seen by the engineer or motorman in charge of a train or car approaching the track in its front, then he sees the child in a perilous or dangerous position. In Cytron *v.* Railroad, 205 Mo., loc. cit. 719, 104 S. W. 117, it was said by this court in banc: "The motorman knew his car was bound to occupy with crushing force the very spot the child's steps were directed to. It was obvious to the motorman that the child did not know that fact." Under such circumstances it was said: "Both danger and duty began the instant the child left the sidewalk bound headlong into the peril." Livingston *v.* Railroad, 170 Mo. 452, 71 S. W. 136; Meeker *v.* Railroad, 178 Mo., loc. cit. 176, 77 S. W. 58; Heinzle *v.* Street Ry. Co., 213 Mo., loc. cit. 114, 111 S. W. 536; Cornovski *v.* Transit Co., 207 Mo. 263, 106 S. W. 51. In the last-mentioned case, it was said: "Our every instinct teaches that when a four year old child unattended leaves the curb of a sidewalk, that is a place of safety, and heads across the street devoted to traffic in a great city, with a car track 12 feet away on which a car is approaching, the little one as surely and instantly plunges into danger as that the square of the hypotenuse of a right angled triangle equals the sum of the squares of the other two sides—i. e., speaking broadly—it is axiomatic. Danger to the child and duty on the motorman's part began the instant such a child left the sidewalk bound headlong for the track. Cytron *v.* Railroad, 205 Mo., loc. cit. 720 [104 S. W. 109]; Livingston *v.* Railroad, 170 Mo. 452 [71 S. W. 136]." We are cited, however, by the defendant to the decision of the Kansas City Court of Appeals in Gabriel *v.* Railroad, 130 Mo. App. 656, 109 S. W. 1043, in which that court in speaking of a child of six years of age used this language: "But there was no action upon the part of the child to indicate that she was unaware of her danger in time for the defendant's motorman to have avoided striking her. The mere fact that a person is on the street with the intent purpose of crossing it while a car is approaching is no evidence in itself that he intends to place himself in a position of peril"— citing Reno *v.* Railroad, 180 Mo. 469, 79 S. W. 464. Reno *v.* Railroad was a case in which an adult was the plaintiff who walked across the street car track in broad daylight when there was no obstruction either way, but that case, as is pointed out in Heinzle *v.* Railway, has no application to a case of a minor child of tender age who is incapable of contributory negligence, and that decision did not follow the decisions of this court on this point.

Simon et al. *v.* Metropolitan St. Ry. Co

But counsel say that this statement in the instruction is a mere
abstract statement of the law, and we infer from this that in his
opinion, even though it should be held erroneous with reference
to the facts in evidence in this record, still it would not justify
the circuit court in granting a new trial on account of its error.
The remainder of the instruction must be considered, and it is
in these words: "Now, if the jury believe from the evidence
that the motorman saw the child leave the sidewalk and come
into the street and stop before going to the track, then the motorman in charge of the car in controversy had the right to proceed with his car, and he was not required to stop the car until
there was a movement by the child which indicated that it was
about to run into a position of danger." The plaintiffs chal-
lenge the predicate of this part of the instruction, because they
insist that the fact that the child stopped for an instant, or hesitated in its movement towards the car, did not absolve he motorman from the duty of taking precaution to prevent its injury and
death. Defendant insists, however, that this instruction is based
on the plaintiffs' own evidence in the case, and contends that the
witness Chapman testified that he saw the little girl playing in
the street near the curb and the fact that she was playing or
standing there, and when she started to cross the street whether
she was playing just off the curb, or just on the curb, would not
affect the matter, because, in either event, the motorman was not
bound to stop the car or slacken the speed of it until there was
something to indicate the purpose of the child to cross the street.
We have carefully examined this evidence of Chapman and the
other testimony in the case, and, while some of the witnesses
speak of other children being along there, neither Chapman nor
any other witness states that this child was playing in the street
or on the sidewalk at any time. The witness Chapman states
that he saw the child step off of the curb, and start across the
street, and, when it had gone a few feet, it stopped, and then,
to use the language of the witness, "toddled on towards the
track." The instruction directs the jury that if the motorman
saw the child leave the sidewalk and come into the street, and
stop before going to the track, then the motorman·was under no
obligation to stop his car. When the whole evidence of Chapman and others is taken into account with the necessarily short
time within which the whole transaction occurred, it is perfectly
obvious, we think, that the child made only a momentary stop or
hesitation either from confusion in seeing the wagon cross, or
from childish indecision, but whatever the occasion of the stop,
and even though the motorman might have seen its action from
the time it left the curb, and understood the likelihood that it was
going to continue its journey across the track, under this instruction the motorman was free from any duty towards the
child to prevent its injury at all after it made a subsequent start

Simon et al. *v.* Metropolitan St. Ry. Co

across the track. We think the instruction is too strong in this respect. It was not enough that the child merely stopped or hesitated to give the motorman the right to proceed, but it must have been a stop, as gave him the idea that the child did not intend to go forward. If it looked like a stop and was a mere pause or hesitation, as was testified to by various witnesses, it was his duty to have stopped his car before the child made the further movement which indicated that it was about to run into a position of danger. The size of the child, its extreme infancy, its position in a public street, upon which ponderous cars were constantly running, its having left a place of safety on the sidewalk, and started to cross the street, was enough to warn the motorman that it might capriciously proceed in his journey, and enough to cast upon him the duty of stopping his car until the danger to the child was passed. In Jones *v.* Traction Company, 201 Pa. 344, 50 Atl. 826, the injured child was not upon the track, but was walking upon another track upon which cars ran in an opposite direction, and the Supreme Court said: "She was not at the time, it is true, on the track (that track is the track of the motorman whose car ran over her), but he was bound to know that in her childish caprice she was as likely to cross over in front of his moving car as to go back to the pavement, and his duty the instant he saw her, or if exercising the proper care and watchfulness he ought to have seen her, was to stop or to so absolutely control his car as to avoid the risk before him." Counsel for defendant properly concede that this court and other courts of last resort have placed the danger line for children further away from the track than for adults, and have held that it is the duty of a motorman to stop his car sooner for children than for adults who are presumed to know the danger and to stop before going upon a car track, but insist that even these cases do not require a motorman to stop his car until there is some movement of the child indicating its intention to cross the track or come near enough to the car to put himself in danger of being struck and this is what the instruction declares, and it is on this that the error lies. We think this court announced the true rule as to children of tender age in Cornovski *v.* Transit Co., 207 Mo., loc. cit. 274, 106 S. W. 55, when it said: "Danger to the child and duty on the motorman's part began the instant such a child left the sidewalk, bound headlong for the track." Presence in the street where horses, wagons, and cars were constantly moving in broad daylight of a child $3\frac{1}{2}$ years old, with only a few feet within the curb and the car track with its face to the track, every instinct of a normal man and universal experience teaches him that the child is already in imminent danger, and the law having regard for human life required a motorman in charge of a ponderous car on a public street to stop until the danger to the child is averted. He is

Simon et al. *v.* Metropolitan St. Ry. Co

not to speculate that it may not run upon the track, and cannot indulge the presumption that he may indulge, as to adults, that it may not go into further danger. It has already entered into the danger zone. As said by the Supreme Court of Pennsylvania: "He was bound to know that in her childish caprice she was as likely to cross over in front of his moving car as to go back to the pavement and his duty the instant he saw her, or, if exercising proper care and watchfulness, he ought to have seen her, was to stop or to so absolutely control his car as to avoid the risk before him." The mere temporary stop of the little child caused either by its caprice or hesitation on account of the wagon or car did not absolve the motorman from his duty to stop his car until danger to the child was certainly averted, but this instruction did, and the jury were told that his duty only arose and began when the child again started on its journey to its destruction. Thus instructed the jury might well have found that after that last start the motorman could not have stopped his car in time to have prevented the injury and death of the child and hence they must find for defendant. Moreover, this instruction was erroneous because it assumes there was evidence that the motorman saw the child leave the sidewalk and stop, whereas the motorman himself testified he first saw the child when it was only a few feet away from the track, and another witness, Officer Cambell, testified he did not think the motorman saw the child at all until the collision had occurred, and other witnesses testified the motorman was looking upward in the opposite direction from that from which the child approached the car. The instruction concludes: "If the motorman after seeing the child start towards the track after making its last stop in the street used ordinary care with the means at his command to stop said car and prevent a collision with the child, then there was no negligence, and the plaintiff cannot recover in this case, and the jury must return a verdict for the defendant." In a word, the jury were told that, if the motorman used ordinary care after he saw the child start towards the track after making its last stop, then there was no negligence and no liability. Every other fact was eliminated from their consideration, notwithstanding there was evidence tending to show the motorman was negligent in not seeing the child, and the jury might have believed that, by the exercise of ordinary care, he would have seen her in time to have avoided injury to her, and the instructions wholly ignored the testimony as to his failure to ring the bell and the efforts of bystanders to warn him of the child's peril. Especially harmful was the making the "last step" the point when the duty of the motorman began, inasmuch as there was testimony that the little child stopped first at the edge of the curb, and then other testimony that it made another step and then toddled on towards the track, and under this part of the instruction the jury were given

Simon et al. *v.* Metropolitan St. Ry. Co

to understand that the motorman was required to take no step to stop until after this last step, though the whole evidence shows it was only momentary. Officer Campbell, a witness for the defendant, testified that she might have stopped a second; not over that anyway. In our opinion this instruction was erroneous and harmful, and occasions the verdict against plaintiffs, and the circuit court did not err in so holding and in granting a new trial on that account.

2.   But it is urged that, even though the instruction was erroneous, the circuit court erred in granting a new trial because this court ought to have sustained the demurrer to the evidence and taken the case from the jury. The statement of the facts already set forth we think required the court to submit the question of defendant's negligence to the jury under the first instruction given in behalf of plaintiffs, without the instruction 3 A, given in behalf of defendant.

3.   As to the proposition that the verdict was for the right party, it is sufficient to say that the plaintiffs' evidence entitled them to have the jury pass upon the negligence of defendant under proper instructions, and we have held they did not have that privilege and the learned circuit court so held.   There are instances in which the appellate court has well said that, notwithstanding the circuit court has given an improper or incorrect instruction, the whole record shows that the verdict was right, and the judgment would not be reversed where it was evidently for the right party.   Under the evidence in this case, there was an issue for the jury under proper instructions, and it is not our province to pass upon the weight of the evidence.   It should also be said that instructions Nos. 4 and 8 were improper, in that they submitted to the jury whether the plaintiffs were guilty of contributory negligence in permitting the child to be upon the street.

We think there was no evidence tending to show the plaintiffs were negligent in this regard.   In our opinion the circuit court had the right to grant a new trial, and there was no error in its action in so doing, and the judgment is therefore affirmed.

BURGESS, J., concurs. KENNISH, J., not having been a member of the court when the cause was argued, takes no part in the decision.

HOFF *et ux. v.* LOS ANGELES-PACIFIC CO.

(Supreme Court of California, Nov. 19, 1910.   Rehearing Denied Dec. 19, 1910.)

[112 Pac. Rep. 53.]

Trial—Motion for Nonsuit—Evidence.—A motion for nonsuit admits the truth of the plaintiff's evidence, and every inference of fact that can be legitimately drawn therefrom.

Negligence—Jury Question.—Negligence is a question of fact for the jury, though there be no conflict of evidence, if different conclusions can be therefrom rationally drawn.

Street Railroads—Duty of Person Crossing Track—Care ' Required.*—While one about to cross a street railway track is not held to that high degree of care required in case of a steam railroad running through the country, he must exercise such care as is reasonable under all the circumstances.

Negligence—Contributory Negligence—Jury Questions.†—One in great peril, where immediate action is necessary to avoid it, is not required to exercise that carefulness required of a prudent man under ordinary circumstances, and the reasonableness of his effort to escape injury after discovering the danger is for the jury.

Street Railroads—Collision with Vehicle—Contributory Negligence —Jury Question.—In an action for injuries in a collision between plaintiff's automobile and defendant street railway's car, whether plaintiff was guilty of contributory negligence held, under the evidence, for the jury.

Department 1.   Appeal from Superior Court, Los Angeles County; N. P. Conrey, Judge.

Action by Cory C. Hoff and wife against the Los Angeles-Pacific Company (a corporation).   From a judgment of nonsuit, plaintiffs appeal.   Reversed and remanded for new trial.

Gray, Barker & Bowen and *Allen, Van Dyke & Jutten,* for appellants.
J. W. McKinley and *Gurney E. Newlin,* for respondent.

---

*See foot-note of Talley *v.* Chester Traction Co. (Pa.), 36 R. R. R. 339, 59 Am. & Eng. R. Cas., N. S., 339; second head-note of McCormick *v.* Ottumwa Ry. & L. Co. (Iowa), 36 R. R. R. 350, 59 Am. & Eng. R. Cas., N. S., 350; last foot-note of Sontum *v.* Mahoning, etc., Ry. & L. Co. (Pa.), 35 R. R. R. 574, 58 Am. & Eng. R. Cas., N. S., 574.

†See second foot-note of Steverman *v.* Boston Elev. R. Co. (Mass.), 36 R. R. R. 736, 59 Am. & Eng. R. Cas., N. S., 736; third foot-note of Erie R. Co. *v.* Schomer (C. C. A.), 35 R. R. R. 303, 58 Am. & Eng. R. Cas., N. S., 303; Bruggeman *v.* Illinois Cent. R. Co. (Iowa), 35 R. R. R. 241, 58 Am. & Eng. R. Cas., N. S., 241; South, etc., Ry. Co. *v.* Crutcher (Ky.), 35 R. R. R. 199, 58 Am. & Eng. R. Cas., N. S., 199.

Hoff et ux. v. Los Angeles-Pacific Co

Angellotti, J. This is an appeal from a judgment of non-suit in an action for damages for personal injuries sustained by plaintiff Alta May Hoff, the wife of her coplaintiff, in a collision in the city of Los Angeles between an automobile in which she was riding and which was being operated by her husband, and two electric cars of defendant, coupled together and operated by defendant's servants. The collision occurred at the intersection of Sixteenth street, along which defendant operated a double-track electric street railway, with Western avenue, about 5 o'clock p. m. on August 23, 1908. Mr. Hoff was endeavoring to cross defendant's tracks at such intersection with his automobile, containing himself, his wife, and four other persons, when the machine was struck a little back of its center by defendant's cars, which were proceeding along Sixteenth street from the west, with the result that the machine was violently thrown quite a distance, and Mrs. Hoff severely injured.

The motion for a nonsuit was granted on the ground that the plaintiffs' evidence showed that Mr. Hoff was guilty of contributory negligence. It is conceded by defendant for the purposes of this appeal that such evidence showed negligence on the part of defendant's motorman, in that at the time of the collision defendant's cars were being propelled at a rate of speed in excess of that allowed by an ordinance of the city; such ordinance prohibiting a rate of speed in excess of eight miles per hour over any crossing in the district including the intersection of Sixteenth street and Western avenue, and that no bell was rung and no whistle blown as the cars approached this crossing.

Learned counsel for defendant freely concede the correctness of the rule stated as to the review of the action of trial courts in granting nonsuits in cases of this character in Kramm v. Stocton Electric R. R. Co., 3 Cal. App. 606, 609, 86 Pac. 738, 739, as follows: "The motion for nonsuit admits the truth of plaintiff's evidence, and every inference of fact that can be legitimately drawn therefrom, and upon such motion the evidence should be interpreted most strongly agains the defendant. If there is any evidence tending to sustain plaintiff's action, the nonsuit should be denied, without passing upon the sufficiency of such evidence, and, where there is a conflict in the evidence, some of which tends to sustain the plaintiff's case, a motion for a nonsuit should not be granted. Nor is there any dispute as to the well-settled rule "that negligence is a question of fact for the jury, even when there is no conflict in the evidence, if different conclusions upon the subject can be rationally drawn from the evidence," and that, if but one conclusion can reasonably be reached from the evidence, it is a question of law for the court; but if one sensible and impartial man might decide that the plaintiff had exercised ordinary care, and another equally sensible and impartial man that he had not exercised such care, it must

Hoff et ux. v. Los Angeles-Pacific Co

be left to the jury." Herbert v. Southern Pacific Co., 121 Cal. 227, 229, 53 Pac. 651. "It has often been said by this court that it is very rare that a set of circumstances is presented which enables a court to say, as a matter of law, that negligence has been shown. As a general rule, it is a question of fact for the jury, an interference to be deduced from the circumstances of each particular case and it is only where the deduction to be drawn is inevitably that of negligence that the court is authorized to withdraw the question from the jury. * * * If the conceded facts are such that reasonable minds might differ upon the question as to whether or not one was negligent, the question is one of fact for the jury." Seller v. Market Street Ry. Co., 139 Cal. 268, 271, 72 Pac. 1006. In view of these well-established rules, we are of the opinion that the trial court erred in granting the motion for a nonsuit.

While it is true that one about to cross the track of a street railway is, as said in Kernan v. Market Street Ry. Co., 137 Cal. 326, 70 Pac. 81, "not held to that high degree of care which is required in the case of an ordinary steam railroad running through the country, on which heavy trains of cars are moved at a high rate of speed and cannot be quickly stopped or controlled" (see, also, Clark v. Bennett, 123 Cal. 275, 55 Pac. 908), he must, of course, exercise such care as is reasonable under all the conditions, rights, and circumstances (Scott v. San Bernardino, etc., Co., 152 Cal. 604, 610, 93 Pac. 677), and, if he fails to do so with the result that his own negligence contributes to the accident in which he is injured, he cannot recover, in the absence of the application to the other party of the doctrine of what is called in our decisions the last clear chance doctrine. The care required has been declared to be "that degree of care which people of ordinarily prudent habits—people in general—could be reasonably expected to exercise under the circumstances of a given case" (Driscoll v. Cable Ry. Co., 97 Cal. 553, 567, 32 Pac. 591, 592, [33 Am. St. Rep. 203]), "that degree of care and prudence and good sense which men who possess those qualities in an ordinary or average degree exercise" under similar conditions (Clark v. Bennett, 123 Cal. 278, 55 Pac. 908). While undoubtedly in some cases the facts may be such as to leave no room for doubt in the mind of any reasonable person as to the negligence of a plaintiff, as in Bailey v. Market Street, etc., Co., 110 Cal. 320, 42 Pac. 914, where the plaintiff standing between two tracks waiting for a car stepped backward without looking upon one of the tracks in the face of an approaching car that was within a very few feet of her, the question of negligence is generally one upon which reasonable persons may well differ. We think that the evidence in this case construed most favorably to plaintiffs, as they are entitled to have it construed, presents such a case.

Hoff et ux. v. Los Angeles-Pacific Co

It is not seriously contended that the evidence compels the conclusion that Dr. Hoff's conduct after he first saw the approaching cars was such as to show contributory negligence on his part as matter of law. At that time he was from six to eight feet from the track upon which the cars were approaching, with the front of his machine nearly on the track, and traveling at a rate of speed of five or six miles an hour. As we must on this appeal, we are considering the evidence in the light most favorable to plaintiffs. He then saw the cars approaching at a point apparently about 100 or 125 feet away. He almost immediately increased his speed in an endeavor to get over the track. It is not at all clear that this was not his only chance to escape a collision under the existing circumstances, for the evidence is such as to warrant the conclusion that he could not then have stopped his machine before it reached the railroad track. But it is to be remembered "that a person in great peril, where immediate action is necessary to avoid it, is not required to exercise all of that presence of mind and carefulness which are justly required of a careful and prudent man under ordinary circumstances," and that the reasonableness of his effort to escape injury after discovery of the danger is a question for the jury to be determined by them in view of all the circumstances. Harrington v. Los Angeles Ry. Co., 140 Cal. 514, 521, 74 Pac. 15, 63 L. R. A. 238, 98 Am. St. Rep. 85; Bilton v. Southern Pacific Co., 148 Cal. 443, 450, 83 Pac. 440. It is further to be born in mind that the evidence is of such a nature that it may reasonably be concluded that Mr. Hoff was warranted in assuming that the cars were approaching at such a rate of speed that they would not cross Western avenue at a greater rate than eight miles an hour, the speed allowed by the ordinance (see Scott v. San Bernardino, etc., Co., 152 Cal. 604, 93 Pac. 677), and that, if such had been the fact, it would have been entirely reasonable to assume that the crossing would be made in safety.

Learned counsel for defendant assumes that Mr. Hoff was in a position of peril at the time he discovered the approaching cars, and say that "his negligence consisted in getting into a position of peril through failure to use his sense of sight at the proper point in his approach towards the track." Mr. Hoff testified that he was traveling along Western avenue, between 12 and 15 miles an hour, that he saw the railroad track when he was about half a block away, that he at once looked and listened in both directions as far as he could see, that he heard or saw nothing to indicate the approach of a car, that he began to slow down when about 40 or 50 feet south of the track and decreased his speed until he was going only 5 or or 6 miles an hour, that when about 35 feet from the track he looked to the west 150 feet or so and saw no car, that he then looked to the east to see if a car was approaching from that direction, that he then just

Hoff et ux. v. Los Angeles-Pacific Co

looked at the track in front seeking a smooth place to go over and then to the west again when he saw the car as before stated, apparently some 100 or 125 feet away. The evidence does not compel the conclusion that he should have seen the car when he looked from a point about 35 feet from the tract. We are at a loss to understand how upon this evidence it can be held as a matter of law that Hoff was guilty of negligence. There is nothing to indicate that the situation at this crossing was such that it was negligent to approach it at a rate of speed of 6 miles an hour. Of course, it was incumbent upon Hoff in so approaching the crossing to use ordinary care to detect the approach of cars on either track, and this involved the exercise of the senses of both sight and hearing on his part to the extent that an ordinarily careful person, regardful of the safety of himself and his companions, would exercise those faculties. See Bailey v. Market St., etc., Co., supra; Scott v. San Bernardino, etc., Co., supra. But we cannot agree that the evidence compels the inference that he refrained from the exercise of such faculties when once he had arrived at a point 35 feet from the track. It must be borne in mind that traveling at 6 miles an hour not more than 4 seconds would elapse between the time he looked to the west 35 feet from the track and the time he again looked and saw the car. In the meantime he had looked to the east to see if there was danger from that point, as it was his clear duty to do, and in so doing was necessarily compelled to momentarily withdraw his eyes from the west, and he had also looked to the front to see that his proposed crossing place was all right, the rails being slightly elevated above the ground, and then immediately looked west again, all this in the short space of four seconds. The best we can say for defendant upon the evidence in this record is that the question whether Hoff was negligent in approaching this crossing is one upon which reasonable men might well differ. This being so, it was a question for the jury, and the trial court should not have granted the motion for a nonsuit. We find nothing in the cases cited by learned counsel for defendant that warrants a different conclusion.

In view of our conclusion upon the point discussed, it is unnecessary to consider any other point made for reversal.

The judgment is reversed, and the cause remanded for a new trial.

We concur: Shaw, J., Sloss, J.

UNITED RYS. & ELECTRIC CO. OF BALTIMORE *v.* KOLKEN.

(Court of Appeals of Maryland, Nov. 16, 1910.)

[78 Atl. Rep. 383.]

Street Railroads—Duty of Motorman—Lookout.*—It is the duty of those in charge of a street car to keep a sharp lookout as they approach a street crossing, and to slacken speed sufficiently to have the car under control, so as not to injure those who may be crossing the street.

Street Railroads—Injury to Pedestrians—Contributory Negligence.†—Plaintiff, while crossing a street at a crossing, was struck by a rapidly moving street car. There was evidence that the motorman had a clear view of the crossing as he approached it for a considerable distance, but was not looking ahead and did not ring his bell. Held, that the court properly refused to charge that plaintiff could not recover, since, even though she was negligent in attempting to cross the street in front of the car, she might still recover if the motorman could, by the exercise of due care, have avoided the accident after he saw, or by proper care might have seen, plaintiff as she was about to cross the track.

Street Railroads—Crossing Accident—Contributory Negligence—Elements—Discovered Peril.—The rule of discovered peril applies to a street car crossing accident, notwithstanding plaintiff's contributory negligence, whether such negligence consisted in plaintiff's ven-

---

*For the authorities in this series on the subject of the duty of those in charge of street cars to maintain a lookout in order to avoid collisions with other users of streets, see last foot-note of South, etc., Ry. Co. *v.* Crutcher (Ky.), 35 R. R. R. 199, 58 Am. & Eng. R. Cas., N. S., 199, where all those preceding are collected; first head-note of Engvall *v.* Des Moines City Ry. Co. (Iowa), 35 R. R. R. 266, 58 Am. & Eng. R. Cas., N. S., 266.

For the authorities in this series on the subject of the duty of those in charge of street cars to regulate speed in order to avoid collisions with other users of streets, see last foot-note of Denver City Tramway Co. *v.* Wright (Colo.), 36 R. R. R. 360, 59 Am. & Eng. R. Cas., N. S., 360; last foot-note of Engvall *v.* Des Moines City Ry. Co. (Iowa), 35 R. R. R. 266, 58 Am. & Eng. R. Cas., N. S., 266; Wilson *v.* Seattle, etc., Ry. Co. (Wash.), 35 R. R. R. 80, 58 Am. & Eng. R. Cas., N. S., 80; foot-note of Louisville Ry. Co. *v.* Flannery (Ky.), 34 R. R. R. 310, 57 Am. & Eng. R. Cas., N. S., 310.

†See third foot-note of Bruggeman *v.* Illinois Cent. R. Co. (Iowa), 35 R. R. R. 241, 58 Am. & Eng. R. Cas., N. S., 241; first foot-note of St. Louis, etc., R. Co. *v.* Summers (C. C. A.), 35 R. R. R. 117, 58 Am. & Eng. R. Cas., N. S., 117; last foot-note of Garison *v.* St. Louis, etc., Ry. Co. (Ark.), 34 R. R. R. 543, 57 Am. & Eng. R. Cas., N. S., 543; last paragraph of last foot-note of Farris *v.* Southern R. Co. (N. Car.), 36 R. R. R. 523, 59 Am. & Eng. R. Cas., N. S., 523; foot-note of Denver City Tramway Co. *v.* Wright (Colo.), 36 R. R. R. 360, 59 Am. & Eng. R. Cas., N. S., 360; third head-note of Clark *v.* St. Louis, etc., R. Co. (Okla.), 36 R. R. R. 247, 59 Am. & Eng. R. Cas., N. S., 247.

United Rys. & Electric Co. of Baltimore *v.* Kolken

turing to cross the street without looking to see if a car was coming, or in attempting to cross after seeing a car, as she believed, a safe distance away, and in not looking again.

Appeal from Baltimore Court of Common Pleas; Charles W. Heuisler, Judge.

Action by Rebecca Kolken against the United Railways & Electric Company of Baltimore. Judgment for plaintiff, and defendant appeals. Affirmed.

The following are plaintiff's prayers referred to in the opinion:

"(1) The plaintiff prays the court to instruct the jury that if they believe from the evidence that the plaintiff received the injuries to her person as mentioned in the evidence, by being run into, struck, and knocked down by a car of the defendant in charge of the motorman and conductor in the employ of the defendant, and that said running into, striking, and knocking down was caused by the negligence of the defendant's motorman in the management of the car of which he was the motorman, and that the plaintiff was, at the time of the accident, walking across Charles street at the crossing thereon near Hill street, both being streets of Baltimore city, using due care in so doing, then the plaintiff is entitled to . recover." Granted.

"(2) Even if the jury find that there was want of ordinary care on the part of the plaintiff, yet she is entitled to recover, provided the motorman could have avoided the accident by the exercise of ordinary care after he saw, or by the use of ordinary care might have seen, that the plaintiff was approaching near to the track and in danger of being struck by the car." Granted.

"(3) In estimating damages, the jury are to consider the health and condition of the plaintiff before the injuries complained of, as compared with her present condition in consequence of such injuries, and whether the same are in their nature permanent, and how far they are calculated to disable the plaintiff from engaging in those business pursuits for which, in the absence of such injuries, she would have been qualified; and also the physical and mental suffering to which she had been subjected by reason of said injuries, and the jury are to allow such damages as, in their opinion, will be a fair and just compensation for the injuries suffered." Granted.

The following are the defendant's prayers referred to in the opinion:

"(1) The defendant prays the court to instruct the jury that there is no evidence in this case legally sufficient to entitle the plaintiff to recover, and their verdict must be for the defendant." Refused.

"(2) The court instructs the jury that from the uncontradicted evidence in this case, the plaintiff was guilty of negligence directly contributing to the accident complained of, and therefore their verdict must be for the defendant." Refused.

"(3) The defendant prays the court to instruct the jury that if the plaintiff was injured in consequence of the plaintiff's failure to act on the occasion of the accident as a person of ordinary care and prudence would have acted under the circumstances, and that such failure to use ordinary care and prudence directly contributed to the accident, the verdict must be for the defendant." Granted.

"(5) The defendant prays the court to instruct the jury that if they find from the evidence that the plaintiff could, by the use of reasonable care and diligence, have seen the defendant's car approaching in time to avoid the alleged accident, then there can be no recovery in this case, and the verdict must be for the defendant." Refused.

"(6) The defendant prays the court to instruct the jury that, notwithstanding the jury may believe from the evidence that the defendant was guilty of negligence, yet if they shall further believe from the evidence that the plaintiff was also guilty of negligence, and that the injury was directly caused, partly by the defendant's negligence, and partly by the negligence of the plaintiff, then the verdict must be for the defendant, without regard to · whose negligence was the greater." Refused.

"(7) The defendant prays the court to instruct the jury that if they find that on the occasion mentioned in the evidence the car of the defendant company was running south on Charles street, and that after leaving York street the speed of the car was increased to full speed, and that from that point to the place where the plaintiff was struck the car continued to run at full speed, and if the jury shall further find from the evidence that when the car left York street, the motorman in charge thereof was not looking ahead. but was looking to the east at girls, who were skylarking on the east side of Charles street, if the jury shall so find. and if the jury shall further find that at the time the car left York street, the plaintiff was standing on the pavement at the northwest corner of Charles and Hill streets, and looked in the direction from which the car was coming, and saw, or by the use of reasonable diligence could have seen, the speed at which the car was running, and that the motorman was not looking ahead, but was looking to the east, and if the jury shall find that the plaintiff then left the pavement and started across the street and across the tracks upon which the car was running, and was struck and injured in the manner mentioned in the evidence, then there can be no recovery in this case, and the verdict must be for the defendant." Refused.

"(8) The court instructs the jury that if they shall find from the evidence that at the time the car left York street, the plaintiff was standing on the pavement at the northwest corner of

United Rys. & Electric Co. of Baltimore *v.* Kolken

Charles and Hill streets, and that she looked in the direction in which the car was coming and saw, or by the use of ordinary care could have seen, the car and the speed at which it was coming, if the jury shall so find, and if the jury shall further find that she thereafter started to cross the street, and did not look again for the approaching car before entering upon the track upon which it was approaching, and if the jury shall further find that if she had looked when near to the track and before entering upon the line thereof, the danger of being struck by the oncoming car would have been seen by her, and that she could then have avoided the accident by the use of ordinary care by stopping in a place of safety, if the jury shall so find, then the verdict must be for the defendant." , Refused.

"(9) The court instructs the jury that if they shall find from the evidence that the plaintiff saw, or by the use of ordinary care could have seen, a car approaching before she started to cross the street, and shall further find that she did not look again before attempting to cross the track to see how close the car was upon her, and if the jury shall further find that if she had so looked, while she was still in a position of safety, to the side of the track, and before entering upon the line of travel of the car, she would have seen that the car was close upon her, and that if she entered upon the line of its progress an accident was inevitable, if the jury shall so find, then the verdict must be for the defendant." Refused.

"(10) The court instructs the jury that it was the duty of the plaintiff, before crossing a car track on which she knew that the car was approaching, if the jury shall find that she did know that a car was approaching thereon, to look to see how close the car was upon her before getting in the way thereof, and if the jury shall find that the plaintiff failed to look before getting in the way of the car, and shall further find that if she had so looked, and she could have avoided the accident by the use of ordinary care, then the verdict must be for the defendant." Refused.

"(11) The court instructs the jury that it is the duty of a pedestrian, before crossing a street railway track, to look to see if a car is approaching, and if the jury shall find from the evidence that the plaintiff failed to look before crossing the track, and shall further find that if she had looked, she could, by the use of ordinary and reasonable care, have prevented the accident complained of, if the jury so find, then her negligence directly contributed to the accident, and there can be no recovery in this case, and the verdict must be for the defendant." Refused.

Argued before Boyd, C. J., and Briscoe, Pearce, Schmucker, Burke, Thomas, Pattison, and Urner, JJ.

United Rys. & Electric Co. of Baltimore v. Kolken

J. Pembroke Thom and *Joseph C. France,* for appellant.
Robert F. Leach, Jr., for appellee.

THOMAS, J. This appeal is from a judgment recovered by
the plaintiff in the court below for injuries alleged to have been
caused by the negligence of the employees of the defendant,
the United Railways & Electric Company of Baltimore, and the
only exception in the record is to the ruling of that court granting the plaintiff's prayers and rejecting the first, second, fifth,
sixth, seventh, eighth, ninth, tenth and eleventh prayers of the
defendant. The reporter is requested to set out the prayers in
his report of the case.

The accident which resulted in the injury complained of
occurred between 6 and 7 o'clock in the morning on the 5th of
March, 1909, at the crossing of Charles and Hill streets, in Baltimore city. There are two railway tracks on Charles street,
which runs north and south, one called the west or south bound
track, and the other the east or north bound. One square north
of Hill street is Lee street, and between Hill and Lee streets
there is a narrow street which ends at Charles street, called York
street. The distance between the south side of Lee street and
the north side of Hill street is 366 feet, and it is about 150 feet
from the north side of York street to the crossing from the
northwest corner to the northeast corner of Charles and Hill
streets. At this crossing, the west or south bound track is 12
feet from the curb. The plaintiff, Rebecca Kolken, who lived
on Hill street, east of Charles street, states that on the morning
of the accident she left her home at No. 30 Hill street and went
across Charles street to Berman's grocery store, on the northwest
corner of Charles and Hill streets, to buy her breakfast; that
as she was returning home, carrying a bottle of milk and a small
dish of cream, just as she was about to step from the pavement
to the crossing, she looked up Charles street and saw a car coming south; that the car was then between Lee and York streets,
nearer to Lee street, and was going slow"; that seeing that the
car was a long distance away, and that the motorman had an unobstructed view of the crossing, she strated across the street, and
that as she was crossing the tracks, the car struck her and threw
her on the fender. She further testified that she did not hear a
bell, and on cross-examination stated that after seeing the car,
as she started across the street, she did not look again, because,
when she saw it, the car was a long distance away and the motorman could see her. A number of the plaintiff's witnesses who
saw the accident testified that as the plaintiff started across the
street, they saw the car above or about York street; that there
was nothing on the street to obstruct the motorman's view of
the crossing; that the speed of the car was increased as it passed
York street, and that it was going rapidly or at full speed when
it reached the crossing; that as the car approached the crossing,

United Rys. & Electric Co. of Baltimore v. Kolken

the motorman was looking to the east at some girls on the east side of Charles street, and that he did not ring the bell or check the speed of the car until it reached the crossing and struck the plaintiff. Other evidence in the case shows that the motorman did not succeed in stopping the car until it had nearly reached the opposite side of Hill street; that the plaintiff was carried some distance on the fender, and was finally thrown to the east side of the car, and that one of her arms was so badly crushed that it had to be amputated just below the shoulder.

The motorman in charge of the car at the time of the accident was not present at the trial in the court below, but the conductor testified that "from the time it left Lee street," the car "was going between six and seven miles an hour"; that the motorman was ringing his bell as he approached the crossing, and that "as he drew up to the corner, he reversed the car, putting down brakes." Other witnesses for the defendant also testified that the car was moving at moderate speed, and that they heard the bell before the car got to the crossing.

By its first and second prayers the defendant sought to have the case withdrawn from the jury, first, because there was no evidence legally sufficient to entitle the plaintiff to recover, and, second, because she was guilty of contributory negligence, and by the other rejected prayers the court was asked to instruct the jury that if they found that the plaintiff was guilty of contributory negligence, she was not entitled to recover. All of these prayers, in effect, entirely ignore the evidence adduced by the plaintiff to show that the motorman had a clear view of the crossing, that he was not looking ahead, that he did not ring his bell, and that the car was running at full speed when it reached the crossing and struck the plaintiff. It is the duty of those in charge of a car to keep a sharp lookout as they approach a street crossing, and to slacken the speed of the car sufficiently to enable them to have it under control, so as to avoid injuring those who may be crossing the street, and the evidence adduced by the plaintiff tended to show, not only that the defendant was negligent in the management of its car, but that the motorman saw, or by the exercise of proper care could have seen, the plaintiff in time to have stopped the car before it struck her. Under such circumstances, it would have been error to have taken the case from the jury upon either of the grounds stated in the first and second prayers, or to have instructed the jury that if they found that the plaintiff was negligent, she was not entitled to recover, for even if the plaintiff was guilty of contributory negligence in attempting, under the circumstances, to cross the street in front of the approaching car, she was still entitled to recover, if the motorman could, by the exercise of due care, have avoided the accident, after he saw, or by the exercise of proper care, might have seen the plaintiff as she was about to cross the tracks. This is the rule that has been repeatedly recognized by this court as applicable to cases like the one at bar. Lake Roland Co. *v.* McKewen, 80 Md. 593, 31 Atl. 797; Baltimore Traction Co. *v.* Appel, 80 Md. 603, 31 Atl. 964; Consolidated Ry. Co. *v.* Rifcowitz, 89 Md. 338, 43 Atl. 762; United Railways Co. *v.* Ward (No. 62, January term, 1910) 77 Atl. 593.

In McKewen's Case, the prayer which this court said was "quite as favorable to the defendant as it had any right to expect," instructed the jury that the plaintiff was guilty of contributory negligence, and was not entitled to recover, "unless the jury believe from the evidence that the motorman of the car in question, after he saw, or by the exercise of due care might have seen, that the plaintiff was approaching the track and was apparently about to cross in front of his car, and that the attempt to do so would be dangerous to the plaintiff, might still, by the exercise of reasonable care in the management of said car have avoided the collision, but failed to exercise said care." In the case of Consolidated Ry. Co. *v.* Rifcowitz, supra, the defendant offered a prayer instructing the jury that the plaintiff's evidence was not satisfactory or legally sufficient to entitle her to recover, and the court below granted it after having modified it by adding these words: "Unless the jury shall further find that after the motorman saw, or could reasonably have seen, the peril of the plaintiff, he failed to exercise ordinary care to avoid the accident." In reference to this prayer, the court said: "The modification which the learned judge below made in the first prayer of the defendant before granting it was an entirely proper one, and was requisite to make it conform to the law governing the case. * * * Mere negligence or want of ordinary care will not disentitle a plaintiff to recover if the defendant might, by the exercise of care on his part, have avoided the consequence of the neglect or carelessness of the plaintiff. * * * If the court had not modified the prayer, it would have taken from the jury the question of relative negligence of the parties." In the later case of Consolidated Ry. Co. *v.* Armstrong, 92 Md. 554, 48 Atl. 1047, counsel for the company insisted that the rule we have stated, or rather the modification of the doctrine of contributory negligence, should be limited to cases in which the defendant could have avoided the accident by the exercise of due care, after he actually saw the plaintiff's peril, but this court refused to adopt that view, and said: "It cannot be seriously contended that when the defendant is in a position from which he ought to see, or by the exercise of reasonable care could see, the plaintiff's peril, he may avert his face or close his eyes and not see it, and then escape liability for an injury resulting from such conduct on his part. * * * The law will not permit the loss of life or limb, or even property, to be deliberately or care-

United Rys. & Electric Co. of Baltimore *v.* Kolken

lessly inflicted, when it could by reasonable care and caution be averted, merely because the injured person was negligent." And in Ward's Case we said: "But even if we assume that the appellee did not, before attempting to cross the tracks, look to see if a car was approaching, and that he was to that extent negligent, the court below would not have been justified in directing a verdict for the defendant on the ground of contributory negligence, or because there was no evidence of negligence on the part of the defendant. * * * If the motorman in charge of the car in question saw the appellee, or by the exercise of due care could have seen him, in the act of crossing the tracks in time to have prevented the accident, it was his duty to have stopped the car in time to avoid the collision; and if the accident occurred by reason of his failure to do so, under such circumstances, his negligence, and not the negligence of the appellee, was the proximate cause of the injury."

Learned counsel for the appellant, while recognizing the rule referred to, contend that it does not apply to the case at bar, because here the plaintiff saw the car as she started across the street. But it can make no difference in the application of the principle whether the plaintiff's negligence consisted in venturing across the street without looking to see if a car was coming, or in attempting to cross after seeing the approaching car; the rule relates to the duty of the defendant after the motorman saw, or by the exercise of reasonable care could have seen, her peril. Counsel for the appellant, relying upon cases like the case of McNab *v.* United Railways Co., 94 Md. 728, 51 Atl. 421, further contend that even if the motorman saw the plaintiff crossing the street, he had a right to assume, up to the very moment she stepped on the tracks, that she would not venture to cross until after the car had passed, and that the act of negligence was committed by her. In McNab's Case, the accident happened at a crossing in the open country, where cars are permitted and known to run at much greater speed than is allowed on the streets of a city. and Judge McSherry, quoting from Neubeur's Case, 62 Md. 401, said: "It was not the duty of those in charge of the train to anticipate the conduct of the plaintiff, and because they saw him approach the crossing, to conclude that he would attempt to cross in advance of the train." But, as was distinctly recognized in that case, a very different rule applies to the running of cars on the crowded thoroughfares of a city, where the motorman is required to anticipate the conduct of those crossing the streets to the extent of keeping a sharp lookout, giving proper warning, and reducing the speed of his car, so as to have it under control, for the purpose of avoiding injury to those who may be on the crossing. In the case of Heying *v.* United Railways Co., 100 Md. 281, 59 Atl. 667, cited by counsel for the appellant, Judge Fowler said that there

State *v.* Cleveland

was no evidence "to show that after the motorman saw her in a place of danger, or could have so seen her by the exercise of any, even the greatest degree of, care, he could have stopped the car in time to have avoided the collision."

What we have said in regard to the rejected prayers of the defendant disposes of the exception to the granting of plaintiff's second prayer, and we do not understand the appellant as excepting to the plaintiff's first and third prayers, to which we see no objection, except upon the ground presented in the contention that the case should have been taken from the jury.

Finding no error in the ruling of the court below, the judgment will be affirmed.

Judgment affirmed, with costs.

STATE *v.* CLEVELAND.

(Supreme Court of Ohio, Oct. 25, 1910.)

[93 N. E. Rep. 467.]

Street Railroads—Offenses—Statutes—Construction—Matters Embraced by Inference.—A statute may include by inference a case not originally contemplated when it deals with a genus within which a new species is brought. Thus a statute making it unlawful to willfully throw a stone at a railroad car includes an interurban or traction railway car, although such cars were not known or in use at the time the statute was enacted.

(Syllabus by the Court.)

Exceptions from Court of Common Pleas, Champaign County.

One Cleveland was indicted for throwing a stone at a railroad car. There was a directed verdict of not guilty, and the State files exceptions. Exceptions sustained.

George Waite, Pros. Atty., for the State.
E. E. Cheney and *Frank A. Zimmer*, for defendant.

Per Curiam. The Ohio Electric Railway Company operates interurban or traction railways. In April of the present year the defendant was a passenger in a car that left Urbana for Springfield. He asked to be let off the car at one of the streets in the city of Urbana. He had a controversy with the conductor in charge of the car, and the conductor ejected him at a point outside of that city. This angered the defendant and he picked up a stone about the size of a man's fist and hurled it at the car in the direction of the conductor. The stone struck on the inside of the rear vestibule and just missed striking several passengers and struck a window, breaking it.

State v. Cleveland

The defendant was indicted under section 12,497 Gen. Code, which reads as follows: "Sec. 12,497. Whoever willfully throws a stone or other hard substance or shoots a missile at a railroad car, train, locomotive, cable railway car or street railway car, or at a steam vessel or water craft used for carrying passengers or freight, or both, on any of the waters within or bordering on this state, shall be fined not less than fifty dollars nor more than five hundred dollars and imprisonment in the penitentiary not more than three years or in the county jail not more than six months."

The first count in the indictment charged the defendant with throwing a stone at a railroad car, and the second count charged him with throwing a stone at a street railway car.

The court, on motion, excluded the evidence from the jury and instructed the jury to bring in a verdict of not guilty, and the prosecutor files exceptions in this court.

It is said that the court directed the verdict on the ground that an interurban car does not come within the terms of the statute.

The first act was passed in 1879 (Act January 30, 1879; 76 Ohio Laws, p. 11), and provided: "That whoever willfully throws any stone or other hard substance, or shoots any missile at any railroad car, train or locomotive, shall be fined," etc.

The law was amended in 1884 (Act April 10, 1884; 81 Ohio Laws, p. 125), by adding "steam vessels or water craft," and in 1887 (84 Ohio Laws, p. 81), by adding "or at any cable railway car or street railway car." It is contended that interurban cars were not known at the inception of the statute, and that therefore they could not have been intended to be comprised in its terms, and that under the maxim, "Exclusio unius est exclusio alterius," such cars are clearly excluded from the terms of the statute.

We do not think either contention is sound. The rule is well settled "that a statute may include by inference a case not originally contemplated when it deals with a genus within which a new species is brought by a subsequent statute." The cases illustrating this rule are numerous. People v. Kriesel, 136 Mich. 80, 98 N. W. 850, 4 Am. & Eng. Ann. Cas. 5, note; U. S. v. Nihols, 4 McLean, 23. Fed. Cas. No. 15,880; State v. Becton, 7 Baxt. (Tenn.) 138; Reg. v. Cottle, 16 Q. B. 412; Collier v. Worth, 1 Ex. D. 464; Taylor v. Goodwin, 4 Q. B. D. 228; Parkyns v. Preist, 7 Q. B. D. 313. The rule applies also to new species that come into existence otherwise than by statute. And when the new species is clearly within the mischief intended to be prevented, the rule is not inapplicable because of the rule of strict construction of penal statutes. Endlich on Interpretation of Statutes, §§ 112 and 335.

The rule referred to is not of universal application, but is to be applied only as an aid in arriving at intention, and not to de-

Nappli *v.* Seattle, R. & S. Ry. Co

feat the apparent intention. The statute as originally enacted unquestionably was broad enough to comprise any kind of a railroad car. The amendments were not intended to narrow the statute, but to add other things, and the subsequent enumeration of cable railway cars and street railway cars was not the addition of new things, but was intended to remove any question as to such cars being within the terms of the statute.

Exceptions sustained.

SUMMERS, C. J., and CREW, SPEAR, DAVIS, SHAUCK, and PRICE, JJ., concur.

NAPPLI *v.* SEATTLE, R. & S. RY. CO.

(Supreme Court of Washington, Dec. 12, 1910.)

[112 Pac. Rep. 89.]

Street Railroads—Street Crossing—Use.*—The right of a street car approaching a street crossing and the driver of a team to use the crossing are equal, the driver of the vehicle under ordinary circumstances being justified in proceeding to cross in the face of the approaching car only when he has reasonable ground to believe that he can pass in safety if both he and those in charge of the car act with reasonable regard to the right of each other; the vehicle driver, however, having no right to calculate close chances as to his ability to reach the track before the car, and whether the chances were close under the particular circumstances is ordinarily a question for the jury.

Street Railroads—Crossing Accident—Contributory Negligence *—Plaintiff endeavored to drive over certain street car tracks at a crossing in front of an approaching car, and was struck before he got across. The track approaching the crossing was on a heavy downgrade, and the car which struck him was from 100 feet to a block away when he got on the track, and was approaching at the rate of 60 miles an hour, in violation of a city ordinance limiting the speed to 12 miles. Held, that plaintiff had the right to assume that the car was under control, and when it was that far away that he would be in no danger, and was therefore not negligent as a matter of law.

Street Railroads—Crossing Accident—Rights of Travelers.*—That a street car is approaching a crossing in plain sight does not determine the right of a traveler to cross the street. Such right depends on what a reasonably careful man would do under the circumstances. If the car is so close and coming so fast that it cannot be stopped

---

*See extensive note, 36 R. R. R. 374, 59 Am. & Eng. R. Cas., N. S., 374.

Nappli *v.* Seattle, R. & S. Ry. Co

in time to avoid a collision, and such fact is known or should have been observed, then the traveler attempting to cross would be negligent as a matter of law, but if the car is far enough away to be stopped after the person has passed on the track, or when a reasonably careful man would undertake to cross ahead of it, then it could not be said as a matter of law that he was negligent in attempting to do so.

Department 1. Appeal from Superior Court, King County; John A. Shackleford, Judge.

Action by Frank Nappli against the Seattle, Renton & Southern Railway Company. Judgment for plaintiff, and defendant appeals. Affirmed.

Morris B. Sachs, for appellant.
William C. Keith, for appellee.

MOUNT, J. The defendant prosecutes this appeal from a judgment rendered on the verdict of a jury in an action for personal injuries. The injury occurred to the plaintiff on April 6, 1908, between the hours of 5 and 6 o'clock in the evening. He was driving a team of horses hitched to an express wagon across the tracks of the appellant company, in Seattle, where Dearborn street crosses the Rainier avenue, when one of the defendant's cars ran upon him, killed his team, and severely injured the plaintiff. The complaint alleged that the car was running at an excessive rate of speed. The defense was a general denial, and also that the plaintiff was guilty of contributory negligence. The action was tried to the court and a jury, and verdict was returned for the plaintiff in the sum of $3,500. After motion for new trial was denied, judgment was entered upon the verdict, and defendant has appealed.

Several assignments of error are made, but the only question upon which a reversal is urged is that the court should have directed a verdict for the defendant. It appears that the appellant operates a line of double track electric street railway, on Rainier avenue in the city of Seattle. This avenue runs north and south. On the west of the railway track the street is planked and used for general travel. On the east of the tracks the street is not improved and is not used. Dearborn street crossed Rainier avenue at right angles. From Dearborn street north, Rainier avenue is straight for four blocks to Jackson street, where another electric street car line crosses Rainier avenue, and where cars always come to a full stop. On Rainier avenue there is a steep downgrade—about 9 per cent.—all the way from Jackson street south to Dearborn street. On the evening of April 6, 1908, about 5:30 p. m., when it was daylight, the respondent was driving south on the west side of the railway tracks on Rainier avenue between Jackson and Dearborn streets. When he came

Nappli *v.* Seattle, R. & S. Ry. Co

to Dearborn street, he attempted to cross east over the railway tracks when he was run down by the car. He testified that, before he came to the crossing, he looked back three different times to see if the car was coming and saw nothing; that he looked back the last time when he was within 25 feet of the crossing, and saw no car; that when he drove upon the street car tracks, one wheel of his wagon dropped into a hole between the tracks, and while his horses were pulling on the wagon the car struck him. Some witnesses testified on his behalf that, when respondent drove upon the track, the car was a block away; others, that it was 100 feet away, coming downgrade from Jackson street to Dearborn street and running at 60 miles an hour. It is agreed that the city ordinance prohibited a greater rate of speed than 12 miles per hour for street cars within the business and settled residence district of the city.

The question in the case is whether the court should have said, as a matter of law, that the respondent was guilty of contributory negligence in crossing the street car tracks as he did. If respondent drove his team in front of a car which he knew, or should have known, was coming down upon him and could not be stopped, he is himself negligent and cannot recover. The rule we think is correctly stated in McCarthy *v.* Consolidated Ry. Co., 79 Conn. 73, 63 Atl. 725, and cited by the appellant as follows: "At highway crossings, a street car has no paramount right as against any other vehicle approaching on the cross street. The right attaching to each is equal, and must be exercised with due regard to that attaching to the other, and so as not to interfere with or abridge it unreasonably. It is not necessarily the duty of the driver of an approaching team to wait until the street car has passed, nor is it necessarily his right to push on and cut off its advance. Each party must act reasonably under all the attending circumstances. The driver of an ordinary vehicle can, under ordinary circumstances, be justified in proceeding at a highway crossing, to go over a street railway in the face of an approaching car, when, and only when, he has reasonable ground for believing that he can pass in safety if both he and those in charge of the cars act with reasonable regard to the rights of each other. The duty to slow up or stop, if necessary to prevent a collision, rests equally on each party. In practical effect these doctrines give any railroad car approaching a highway crossing what amounts to a right to precedence. This follows from the rule respecting contributory negligence. No man has the right to calculate close chances as to his ability to reach the track before the car, and throw the risk of injury on the other party. As to whether the chances were close, however, and the railroad company was not the one really in fault, or whether the party injured did not push forward under circumstances of emergency

Nappli *v.* Seattle, R. & S. Ry. Co

which left him no time for calculation, will ordinarily be a question for the jury."

In this case, assuming that the respondent should have seen the car before he drove upon the track because the car was evidently in plain view at that time, it was 100 feet or possibly a block away. Under these circumstances, we think it cannot be said as a matter of law that the respondent should not have attempted to cross over the tracks. He had a right to assume that the car was under control, and, when the car was that far away, that he would be in no danger, and might pass in safety without risk of danger. At any rate the question whether he was negligent in attempting to cross the track when the car was that far away was a question for the jury. Street crossings are to be used, and the mere fact that an approaching car is in sight does not determine the right of a traveler to cross. His right depends upon what a reasonably careful man would do under the circumstances. If the approaching car is so close and coming so fast that it cannot be stopped in time to avoid a collision, and such facts are or should be observed, then a person attempting to cross may be said to be negligent as a matter of law. But where an approaching car is far enough away to be stopped after a person has passed upon the tracks, or when a reasonbly careful man would undertake to cross ahead of it, then it cannot be said as a matter of law that a person attempting to cross is negligent. This rule was substantially applied in Denny *v.* Seattle, Renton & Southern Ry. Co., 111 Pac. 450.

The question of negligence of the respondent was therefore properly referred to the jury, and the judgment must be affirmed.

RUDKIN, C. J., and PARKER, FULLERTON, and GOSE, JJ., concur.

DEHOFF *v.* NORTHERN CENT. RY. CO.

(Supreme Court of Pennsylvania, July 1, 1910.)

[78 Atl. Rep. 104.]

Railroads—Accident at Crossing—Contributory Negligence.—The care imposed on a driver at a railroad crossing is not fulfilled by stopping 100 feet from the track, where, because of obstructions, he cannot see when there is a clear view 30 feet from the track of at least 500 feet.

Appeal from Court of Common Pleas, York County.

Action by John W. Dehoff against the Northern Central Railway Company. Judgment for defendant, and plaintiff appeals. Affirmed.

Argued before FELL, C. J., and BROWN, MESTREZAT, ELKIN, and MOSCHZISKER, JJ.

E. Dean Ziegler, Jacob E. Weaver, and *Edward D. Ziegler,* for appellant.
Richard E. Cochran and *Smyser Williams,* for appellee.

PER CURIAM. A verdict was directed for the defendant under the following state of facts, as to which there was no dispute: The plaintiff was riding in a carriage and stopped, looked and listened when 105 feet from the crossing of the defendant's road. At this place he could not see a train approaching the crossing because of a building on one side of the road on which he was driving and an embankment on the other side. He drove on at a slow trot, looking as he advanced, and his horse was struck by an engine on the nearest main track. Thirty feet from the crossing he had a clear view in the direction from which the engine came of over 500 feet, and 10 feet from it a clear view of 1,000 feet. The duty of care which the law imposes on every driver at a railroad crossing is not fulfilled by stopping where he cannot see. It is his duty to stop where he can see. The plaintiff, having failed to do this, was properly adjudged to have been negligent.

The judgment is affirmed.

WESTERN RY. OF ALABAMA *v.* MOORE.

(Supreme Court of Alabama, Dec. 1, 1910.   Rehearing Denied Dec. 22, 1910.)

[53 So. Rep. 744.]

Railroads—Crossings—Signals.*—It is negligence for the operatives of a train to fail to give the crossing signals required by Code 1907, § 5473.

Railroads—Injuries to Animals—Evidence.—In an action against a railroad for the killing of an animal, evidence held to sustain a finding that there was negligence in failing to give the signals required by Code 1907, § 5473, and that there was a causal connection between the negligence and the injury.

Appeal from City Court of Selma; J. W. Mabry, Judge.

Action by William Moore against the Western Railway of Alabama. From a judgment in favor of plaintiff, defendant appeals. Affirmed.

George P. Harrison, for appellant.
Reese & Reese, for appellee.

SIMPSON, J. This is an action by the appellee for damages for the killing of a mule by the train of the defendant. The evidence shows that there are two public roads, within one-fourth of a mile of each other, and the station between them, and that the mule was killed between said public roads, and near and after passing the station.

Section 5473, Code 1907, requires the engineer or other person in control to "blow the whistle or ring the bell at least one-fourth of a mile before reaching any public road crossing, or any regular station or stopping place on such railroad, and continue to blow the whistle or ring the bell, at short intervals, until it has passed such crossing, or reached such station or stopping place;" and section 5476 places the burden of proof on the defendant to show compliance with the statute, and that there was no negligence. The engineer states that he did not know that there was but one public road there, that he rang the bell from the time he "got to the public road crossing until [he] got to the depot." On his cross-examination he says that he did know there was another crossing, and he was ringing the bell from that crossing; but he does not say that he continued to ring it until the crossing was passed. The plaintiff testified that "the bell did not ring." The witness Walker testified that the mule was struck after the

---

*See first foot-note of Sprague *v.* Northern Pac. Ry. Co. (Mont.), 35 R. R. R. 578, 58 Am. & Eng. R. Cas., N. S., 578; Conway *v.* Louisville & N. R. Co. (Ky.), 34 R. R. R. 513, 57 Am. & Eng. R. Cas., N. S., 313.

Leffonier v. Detroit & M. Ry. Co

train passed the depot, and that no whistle was blown, or bell rung, after the train passed the depot.

A failure to comply with the statute is negligence. Southern Railway Co. v. Crawford, 51 South. 340, 341; Weatherly v. Nashville, Chattanooga & St. Louis Ry., 51 South. 959, 962. It was for the court, sitting as a jury, to determine whether or not there was negligence, and whether or not there was any causal connection between the negligence and the injury. While we could not say, as a matter of law, that there was any causal connection between the negligence and the injury (Central of Georgia Railway Co. v. Simons, 161 Ala. 337, 50 South. 50, 51), neither could we say, as a matter of law, that there was no such causal connection, or that the court, sitting as a jury, erred in its finding.

The judgment of the court is affirmed.

Affirmed.

Dowdell, C. J., and McClellan and Mayfield, JJ., concur.

LEFFONIER v. DETROIT & M. RY. CO.

(Supreme Court of Michigan, Dec. 7, 1910.)

[128 N. W. Rep. 766.]

Railroads—Fire—Evidence—Verdict.—In an action for destruction of plaintiff's property by fire alleged to have been negligently set out by defendant railroad company, evidence held to sustain a verdict finding that the railroad fire was the cause of the burning of plaintiff's property.

Railroads—Fires Set by Employees—Liability.—Where railroad sectionmen set fires in the course of their employment in clearing up defendant's right of way, and such fires escaped and burned adjoining property, the railroad company was liable, even though the setting of the fires was a direct violation of the railroad company's orders.

Error to Circuit Court, Alpena County; Frank Emerick, Judge.

Action by Joseph Leffonier against the Detroit & Mackinac Railway Company. Judgment for plaintiff, and defendant brings error. Affirmed.

Argued before Ostrander, Hooker, Moore, McAlvay, and Brooke, JJ.

Charles R. Henry and *Guy D. V. Henry* (*James McNamara*, of counsel), for appellant.

Joseph H. Cobb and *Fred P. Smith*, for appellee.

Leffonier v. Detroit & M. Ry. Co

BROOKE, J.   Plaintiff brings this action to recover the value of certain property destroyed by fire.   It is his claim that defendant's sectionmen negligently set fire to a pile of old ties and rubbish upon the railroad right of way during the dry season of the summer of 1907, that the fire was negligently permitted to escape from the premises of the defendant, and, after crossing an intervening farm, it came upon the premises of plaintiff, destroying his property.

Testimony was introduced tending (though not clearly) to show that plaintiff's property was destroyed July 27, 1907.   The only testimony introduced by plaintiff having a tendency to prove that the fire which caused plaintiff's loss originated upon defendant's right of way was given by one Mainville, supervisor of the township of Alpena.   He testified that on one occasion he had seen men upon the defendant's right of way, in the vicinity of plaintiff's farm, clearing up and burning old ties and refuse, that he remonstrated with the men, telling them that they were liable to be prosecuted for setting fires at that time of year. When asked to fix the date of this occurrence, he testified: "Well, it must be in the early part of August, for I had to make a report to the state warden, fire warden, and I went down there with that report, for the July report.   I made it the first couple of days in August.   Q.   Were you by Mr. Leffonier's place a few days after that?   A.   Yes; I was.   Q.   State whether or not at that time the buildings on his place were burned?   A.   When I went by they were burned; yes."   On cross-examination, this witness testified: "Q.   How long was it after that you went by the Hamilton house?   A.   I can't tell exactly, a couple of days, about.   Q.   Could you tell how recently the Leffonier house had been burned?   A.   Well, there was some.   There was smoke there yet; it was still burning.   There was smoke in some of the logs there, some in the stumps.   I have been to the Leffonier place.   I was past there before the fire."   This witness also testified to the spreading of the fire.   After verdict for plaintiff, a motion was made for a new trial upon the ground, among others, that inasmuch as by affidavits in support of the motion it clearly appeared that plaintiff's property was destroyed on the night of July 27th, and Mainville fixed the date of his conversation with defendant's sectionmen on August 1st or 2d, it was evident that the fire he testified about could not have caused plaintiff's injury.   The motion was denied by the learned circuit judge, upon the ground that the other testimony given by Mainville made it clear that plaintiff's house was destroyed after his conversation with the sectionmen, and that therefore he was mistaken in fixing the date.   We think this ruling correct.   As pointed out by the trial judge, this discrepancy was urged upon the jury by defendant's counsel at the trial, and was doubtless given due consideration.

Upon the trial, defendant gave evidence tending to show that

Mobile, etc., R. Co. *v.* J. A. Turnipseed

it had given positive orders to its employees to set no fires upon its right of way during the dry season. Assuming the truths of this testimony (and it need not be questioned), it was claimed by defendant in the court below, and it is urged here, that defendant was entitled to have a verdict directed in its favor, for the reason that, even if the fires were set by the sectionmen, they were set without authority, and therefore the defendant would not be liable. This view is not supported by authority in Michigan. If the sectionmen, in direct violation of the orders of defendant, set the fires in the course of their employment in clearing up defendant's right of way, defendant would still be liable. Fitzsimmons *v.* Railway Co., 98 Mich. 257, 57 N. W. 127. See, also, Cosgrove *v.* Ogden, 49 N. Y. 255, 10 Am. Rep. 361; Ellegard *v.* Ackland, 43 Minn. 352, 45 N. W. 715.

Other errors are assigned which require no discussion.

The judgment is affirmed.

MOBILE, JACKSON, & KANSAS CITY RAILROAD COMPANY, Plff. in Err., *v.* J. A. TURNIPSEED, Administrator, etc.

(Submitted November 30, 1910. Decided December 19, 1910.)

[31 Sup. Ct. Rep. 136.]

Constitutional Law—Equal Protection of the Laws—Classification of Railway Employees.—The abrogation of the fellow-servant rule as to railway employees, made by Miss. Code 1892, § 3559, does not offend against the equal protection of the laws clause of the Federal Constitution because construed as applying to the foreman of a section crew charged with keeping the track in repair.

Constitutional Law—Equal Protection of the Laws—Due Process of Law—Statute Creating Presumption of Negligence.—Neither the equal protection of the laws nor due process of law is denied by Miss. Code 1906, § 1985, under which, in actions against railway companies for damage done to persons or property, proof of injury inflicted by the running of the locomotives or cars is made prima facie evidence of negligence.

In error to the Supreme Court of the State of Mississippi to review a judgment which affirmed a judgment of the Circuit Court of Newton County, in that state, in favor of plaintiff in an action to recover damages for a wrongful death. Affirmed.

See same case below, 91 Miss. 273, 124 Am. St. Rep. 679, 46 So. 360.

The facts are stated in the opinion.

Mr. James N. Flowers and *Messrs. May, Flowers, & Whitfield,* for plaintiff in error.

Mr. C. H. Alexander, for defendant in error.

Mobile, etc., R. Co. *v.* J. A. Turnipseed

MR. JUSTICE LURTON delivered the opinion of the court:

This was an action in tort for the wrongful killing of Ray Hicks, a section foreman in the service of the railroad company. There was a judgment for the plaintiff in a circuit court of the state of Mississippi, which was affirmed by the supreme court of the state.

The Federal questions asserted, which are supposed to give this court jurisdiction to review the judgment of the supreme court of the state, arise out of the alleged repugnancy of §§ 3559 and 1985 of the Mississippi Code to that clause of the 14th Amendment of the Constitution which guarantees to every person the equal protection of the laws.

Section 3559 of the Mississippi Code of 1892, being a rescript of § 193 of the Mississippi Constitution of 1890, abrogates, substantially, the common-law fellow-servant rule as to "every employee of a railroad corporation." It is urged that this legislation, applicable only to employees of a railroad company, is arbitrary, and a denial of the equal protection of law, unless it be limited in its effect to employees imperiled by the hazardous business of operating railroad trains or engines, and that the Mississippi supreme court had, in prior cases, so defined and construed this legislation. Ballard *v.* Mississippi Cotton Oil Co., 81 Miss. 532, 62 L. R. A. 407, 95 Am. St. Rep. 476, 34 So. 533; Bradford Constr. Co. *v.* Heflin, 88 Miss. 314, 12 L. R. A. (N. S.) 1040, 42 So. 174, 8 A. & E. Ann. Cas. 1077.

It is now contended that the provision has been construed in the present case as applicable to an employee not subject to any danger or peril peculiar to the operation of railway trains, and that therefore the reason for such special classification fails, and the provision, so construed and applied, is invalid as a denial of the equal protection of the law.

This contention, shortly stated, comes to this: that although a classification of railway employees may be justified from general considerations based upon the hazardous character of the occupation, such classification becomes arbitrary and a denial of the equal protection of the law the moment it is found to embrace employees not exposed to hazards peculiar to railway operation.

But this court has never so constructed the limitation imposed by the 14th Amendment upon the power of the state to legislate with reference to particular employments as to render ineffectual a general classification resting upon obvious principles of public policy, because it may happen that the classification includes persons not subject to a uniform degree of danger. The insistence, therefore, that legislation in respect of railway employees generally is repugnant to the clause of the Constitution guaranteeing the equal protection of the law, merely because it is not limited to those engaged in the actual operation of trains, is without merit.

Mobile, etc., R. Co. *v.* J. A. Turnipseed

The intestate of the defendant in error was not engaged in the actual operation of trains. But he was nevertheless engaged in a service which subjected him to dangers from the operation of trains, and brought him plainly within the general legislative purpose. The case in hand illustrates the fact that such employees, though not directly engaged in the management of trains, are nevertheless within the general line of hazard inherent in the railway business. The deceased was the foreman of a section crew. His business was to keep the track in repair. He stood by the side of the track to let a train pass by; a derailment occurred, and a car fell upon him and crushed out his life.

In the late case of Louisville & N. R. Co. *v.* Melton, 218 U. S. 36, 54 L. ed. 921, 30 Sup. Ct. Rep. 676, an Indiana fellow-servant act was held applicable to a member of a railway construction crew who was injured while engaged in the construction of a coal tipple alongside of the railway track. This whole matter of classification was there considered. Nothing more need be said upon the subject, for the case upon this point is fully covered by the decision referred to.

The next error arises upon the constitutionality of § 1985 of the Mississippi Code of 1906. That section reads as follows:

"Injury to persons or property by railroads prima facie evidence of want of skill, etc.—In all actions against railroad companies for damages done to persons or property, proof of injury inflicted by the running of the locomotive or cars of such company shall be prima facie evidence of the want of reasonable skill and care on the part of the servants of the company in reference to such injury. This section shall also apply to passengers and employees of railroad companies."

The objection made to this statute is that the railroad companies are thereby put into a class to themselves, and deprived of the benefit of the general rule of law which places upon one who sues in tort the burden of not only proving an injury, but also that the injury was the consequence of some negligence in respect of a duty owed to the plaintiff.

It is to be primarily observed that the statute is not made applicable to all actions against such companies. Its operation is plainly limited, first, to injuries sustained by passengers or employees of such companies; second, to injuries arising from the actual operation of railway trains or engines; and third, the effect of evidence showing an injury due to the operation of trains or engines is only "prima facie evidence of the want of reasonable skill and care on the part of the servants of the company in reference to such injury."

The law of evidence is full of presumptions either of fact or law. The former are, of course, disputable, and the strength of any inference of one fact from proof of another depends upon

Mobile, etc., R. Co. v. J. A. Turnipseed

the generality of the experience upon which it is founded. For a discussion of some common-law aspects of the subject, see Cincinnati, N. O. &· T. P. R. Co. v. South Fork Coal Co., 1 L. R. A. (N. S.) 533, 71 C. C. A. 316, 139 Fed. 528 et seq.

Legislation providing that proof of one fact shall constitute prima facie evidence of the main fact in issue is but to enact a rule of evidence, and quite within the general power of government. Statutes, national and state, dealing with such methods of proof in both civil and criminal cases, abound, and the decisions upholding them are numerous. A few of the leading ones are Adams v. New York, 192 U. S. 585, 48 L. ed. 575, 24 Sup. Ct. Rep. 372; People v. Cannon, 139 N. Y. 32, 36 Am. St. Rep. 668, 34 N. E. 759; Horne v. Memphis & O. R. Co., 1 Coldw. 72; Meadowcroft v. People, 163 Ill. 56, 35 L. R. A. 176, 54 Am. St. Rep. 447, 45 N. E. 303; Com. v. Williams, 6 Gray, 1; State v. Thomas, 144 Ala. 77, 2 L. R. A. (N. S.) 1011, 113 Am. St. Rep. 17, 40 So. 271, 6 A. & E. Ann. Cas. 744.

We are not impressed with the argument that the supreme court of Mississippi, in construing the act, has declared that the effect of the statute is to create a presumption of liability, giving to it, thereby, an effect in excess of a mere temporary inference of fact. The statutory effect of the rules is to provide that evidence of an injury arising from the actual operation of trains shall create an inference of negligence, which is the main fact in issue. The only legal effect of this inference is to cast upon the railroad company the duty of producing some evidence to the contrary. When that is done the inference is at an end, and the question of negligence is one for the jury, upon all of the evidence. In default of such evidence, the defendant, in a civil case, must lose, for the prima facie case is enough as matter of law.

The statute does not, therefore, deny the equal protection of the law, or otherwise fail in due process of law, because it creates a presumption of liability, since its operation is only to supply an inference of liability in the absence of other evidence contradicting such inference.

That a legislative presumption of one fact from evidence of another may not constitute a denial of due process of law or a denial of the equal protection of the law, it is only essential that there shall be some rational connection between the fact proved and the ultimate fact presumed, and that the inference of one fact from proof of another shall not be so unreasonable as to be a purely arbitrary mandate. So, also, it must not, under guise of regulating the presentation of evidence, operate to preclude the party from the right to present his defense to the main fact thus presumed.

If a legislative provision not unreasonable in itself, prescribing a rule of evidence, in either criminal or civil cases, does not shut

Taylor *v.* New York & L. B. R. Co

out from the party affected a reasonable opportunity to submit to the jury in his defense all of the facts bearing upon the issue, there is no ground for holding that due process of law has been denied him.

Tested by these principles, the statute as construed and applied by the Mississippi court in this case is unobjectional. It is not an unreasonable inference that a derailment of railway cars is due to some negligence, either in construction or maintenance of the track or trains, or some carelessness in operation.

From the foregoing considerations it must be obvious that the application of the act to injuries resulting from "the running of locomotives and cars" is not an arbitrary classification, but one resting upon considerations of public policy, arising out of the character of the business.

Judgment affirmed.

TAYLOR *v.* NEW YORK & L. B. R. Co.

(Court of Errors and Appeals of New Jersey, Nov. 14, 1910.)

[78 Atl. Rep. 169.]

False Imprisonment—Railway Policeman—Scope of Authority.— The duties of a railway policeman, appointed on the application of a railroad company, and commissioned by the Governor pursuant to the "act concerning carriers" (P. L. 1904, p. 322, § 4), are confined to criminal cases.

False Imprisonment—Railway Policemen—Employment in Matters Aside from Duties—Liability of Railroad.*— If railway policemen, appointed and commissioned under the act (P. L. 1904, p. 322, § 4), are employed in matters aside from their duties under the statute, the employer may be held answerable for what they do the same as in other cases of agency.

Former Decision Distinguished.— Tucker *v.* Erie R. R. Co., 69 N. J. Law, 19, 54 Atl. 557, distinguished.

(Syllabus by the Court.)

Error to Supreme Court.

Action by Joseph Taylor against the New York & Long Branch Railroad Company. Judgment for plaintiff, and defendant brings error. Affirmed.

---

*For the authorities in this series on the question whether railroad companies are liable on account of arrests or prosecutions made or instigated by their employees or agents, see last paragraph of last foot-note of Louisville Ry. Co. *v.* Kupper (Ky.), 32 R. R. R. 513, 55 Am. & Eng. R. Cas. N. S., 513; McKain *v.* Baltimore & O. R. Co. (W. Va.), 32 R. R. R 542, 55 Am. & Eng. R. Cas., N. S., 542; Chicago, etc., Ry. Co. *v.* Nelson (Ark.), 31 R. R. R. 785, 54 Am. & Eng. R. Cas., N. S., 785.

Taylor *v.* New York & L. B. R. Co

John S. Applegate & Son, for plaintiff in error.
Aaron E. Johnston, for defendant in error.

PITNEY, Ch.   This was an action of tort for false imprisonment, wherein the verdict and judgment went in favor of the plaintiff.   The sole ground relied upon for reversal is the refusal by the trial judge of a motion, made at the close of the evidence, that a verdict be directed in favor of the defendant.   The proofs tended to show that in July, 1907, the railroad company obtained a judgment against Taylor before a justice of the peace of the county of Monmouth, sitting in the small cause court, in an action of tort, for $1 damages and $4.11 costs, and that on July 9, 1908, a writ of execution was issued thereon against the goods and chattels of Taylor, the writ commanding the officer, for want of sufficient goods and chattels, to take the body of Taylor and convey him to the county jail.   This writ was placed in the hands of one Wilson, a constable, for execution, and by virtue thereof he took Taylor into custody at the Asbury Park station of the railroad company, being assisted in so doing by one Lankinau. Handcuffs were put upon the prisoner's wrists, but were removed shortly afterwards; and subsequently he was taken by the constable to the office of the superintendent of the railroad company at Long Branch, about seven miles from Asbury Park. There, by order of the superintendent, he was set at liberty.   The plaintiff's contentions were that the judgment upon which the execution was issued had been already satisfied, so that the execution was invalid; that, assuming the execution was valid, the use of the handcuffs amounted to unreasonable and excessive force; that the arrest was warranted only by want of sufficient goods and chattels out of which to make the judgment debt, and that Taylor owned and was in visible possession of personal property more than sufficient for this purpose; and that without authority the constable took Taylor to Long Branch, contrary to the direction of the writ of execution, which required him to be taken to the county jail.   Without spending time upon the other points, we think the taking of Taylor to Long Branch was clearly in excess of the warrant of the writ.   But the railroad company was responsible for this only on the ground that Lankinau participated in it, and that Lankinau was in this behalf an agent of the defendant, acting within the scope of his authority.

It is argued for the plaintiff in error that there was no evidence that Lankinau directed or in any way instigated Wilson to take Taylor to Long Branch.   This contention is clearly untenable; there being testimony from which the jury might reasonably infer that Lankinau fully co-operated with Wilson in the arrest, and assented to, if he did not suggest, the taking of Taylor to Long Branch.   Lankinau's agency for the railroad company in the matter was not so clearly demonstrated, but we think there

Taylor *v.* New York & L. B. R. Co

was sufficient evidence to require the submission of the question to the jury.

It appeared from the evidence that Lankinau was a "state detective"—a "state officer." It did not clearly appear, but seems to have been tacitly conceded, that he was a railway policeman appointed on the application of the railroad company and commissioned by the Governor pursuant to P. L. 1904, p. 322, § 4. Assuming, however, that he had such a commission, and by virtue of the statute possessed the powers of a policeman, and of a constable in criminal cases, there was still abundant evidence that he was employed by the company in the performance of duties aside from those of a railway policeman. The evidence was to the effect that he was regularly employed by the company, with the duty of seeing that order was preserved about its railroad station, included in which was the duty of seeing that the hackmen kept their proper places. The plaintiff for ten years or more had been engaged in driving hacks during the summer seasons at Asbury Park. Repeated suits were brought against him by the railroad company in the justice courts during the summer of 1907. The records of four such actions were introduced in evidence, one of which resulted in the judgment upon which the body execution was issued. Lankinau figured as a witness for the company in each of those cases, and it was Lankinau, who, in the month of July, 1908, made the necessary affidavit to show that Taylor was not a freeholder, in order that the justice might issue a body execution against him. Lankinau was not only present when Taylor was arrested, but, according to one view of the evidence, he may be deemed to have acted as a volunteer in the arrest, in the sense that he was not requested by the constable to lend assistance. And it was Lankinau who produced the handcuffs, which, as the jury might believe, were not needed except for their intimidating effect. From this and other evidence the jury might well infer that a somewhat systematic campaign was being conducted by the railroad company in the effort to secure observance by the hackmen at the Asbury Park station of the company's regulations respecting the mode in which they should ply their trade; that Lankinau was especially charged by the company with the conduct of this campaign; and that the arrest of Taylor was only one step in its prosecution. The duties of a railway policeman under the act of 1904 (P. L. 1904, p. 322, § 4) are confined to criminal cases. In his official capacity he has nothing to do with arrests under civil process.

The case of Tucker *v.* Erie R. R. Co., 69 N. J. Law, 19, 54 Atl. 557, cited by plaintiff in error, was quite different from the present. There the plaintiffs were arrested upon a criminal charge, although without warrant, and all that was done by the railway policemen about the arrest and subsequent prosecution

Taylor *v.* New York & L. B. R. Co

was done in the line of their duty under the Governor's commission.   The decision was that for their misconduct in arresting and prosecuting the plaintiffs the railroad company was not responsible, on the ground that although the policemen were appointed upon the application of the company, they were responsible for the proper discharge of their official duties not to the company, but to the state.   But the opinion of the Chief Justice, who spoke for the Supreme Court, distinctly recognizes that if the prosecution of the plaintiffs had been instigated by the company, or its officers or employees, or if what the railway policemen did had been done by them as agents of the company, and not solely as police officers, the company would have been legally responsible.

In our opinion, if railway policemen, appointed and commissioned under the act of 1904, are employed by the railroad company, or any other corporation or person, in matters aside from their duties under the statute, the principal may be held answerable for what they do, the same as in other cases of agency. Their commissions as railway policemen cannot be made a cloak to shield the company from responsibility for what may be done by such agents under the employment of the company aside from the strict and proper performance of their duties as officers under the act.

There being evidence justifying the inference that in what Landinau did about the plaintiff's arrest he was acting within the scope of his authority as agent for the defendant company, and the evidence justifying the further inference that he participated in the act of the constable in taking the plaintiff to Long Branch, in excess of the warrant of the writ of execution, it was proper to submit to the jury the question of defendant's liability to the plaintiff, and the motion for the direction of a verdict in defendant's favor was properly refused.

The judgment under review should be affirmed.

CHICAGO, M. & ST. P. RY. CO. *v.* DUTCHER.

(Circuit Court of Appeals, Eighth Circuit, October 10, 1910.)

[182 Fed. Rep. 494.]

Master and Servant—Action for Injury to Servant—Evidence.*—
Evidence considered, in an action against a railroad company to
recover for the death of a servant, who was killed while employed
about a coal shed on the main track by some cars, which had been
kicked onto such track from the yards over a cut-off track without
warning, and held to sustain a verdict finding that it was the custom of defendant, on which deceased had a right to rely, to send a
brakeman with the cars in such cases to give deceased warning, and
that the failure to do so was negligence, while the custom relieved
deceased from the charge of contributory negligence in not keeping
a lookout for such cars.

In Error to the Circuit Court of the United States for the
District of Minnesota.

Action by Inez Dutcher, administratrix of the estate of George
W. Dutcher, deceased, against the Chicago, Milwaukee & St.
Paul Railway Company. Judgment for plaintiff, and defendant
brings error. Affirmed.

M. B. Webber and *Edward Lees,* for plaintiff in error.
L. L. Brown, W. D. Abbott, and *S. H. Somsen,* for defendant
in error.

Before SANBORN, HOOK, and ADAMS, Circuit Judges.

HOOK, Circuit Judge. George W. Dutcher was run over and
killed by some freight cars of the Chicago, Milwaukee & St.
Paul Railway Company while he was engaged in its service.
His widow, Inez Dutcher, as administratrix of his estate, sued the
company and obtained judgment. The company prosecuted this
writ of error.

The deceased worked on and about a main railroad track,
which ran alongside a coal shed at which engines were coaled.
His duties were to pick up and care for the coal which fell from
the cars and chutes, and to remove cinders from the track and

---

*For the authorities in this series on the subject of the duty of a
master to warn and instruct his servants, see foot-note of Chesa-
peake & O. Ry. Co. *v.* Nash (Ky.), 36 R. R. R. 511, 59 Am. & Eng.
R. Cas., N. S., 511; foot-note of Ryan *v.* Northern Pac. Ry. Co.
(Wash.), 35 R. R. R. 71, 58 Am. & Eng. R. Cas., N. S., 71.
For the authorities in this series on the subject of the right of a
railroad employee to assume that his master has performed or will
perform its duties to him, see second foot-note of Pittsburg, etc.,
R. Co. *v.* Schawb (Ky.), 36 R. R. R. 644, 59 Am. & Eng. R. Cas., N.
S., 644; Smith *v.* Chicago, etc., R. Co. (Kan.), 36 R. R. R. 640, 59
Am. & Eng. R. Cas., N. S., 640.

Chicago, M. & St. P. Ry. Co. *v.* Dutcher

a cinder pit and wheel them away. The main line was connected with the yards of the company by a track called a "cut-off." In making up trains, cars were at times "kicked" from the yards, over the cut-off, and down on the main line, where deceased was working. On such an occasion the accident occurred. The case of the administratrix depended upon the existence of a uniform custom of the company, upon which deceased had a right to rely, to place a trainman on the end of the moving cars, or to have one running beside them, to notify him of their approach. The existence of such a custom was the controlling question of fact at the trial. It was conceded the precaution was not observed by the company.

Complaint is made by the company that the trial court denied its request for a directed verdict. A careful examination of the record has convinced us that there was substantial evidence supporting the case of the administratrix, and that it may be found in the testimony of witnesses Balow, Brown, and Julius Capon. It is sufficient to say, without reciting it in detail, that some of it was direct and positive. Some confusion in the argument may be dissipated by observing that the custom in question related to the main line, on which the deceased was working, not to the tracks in the yards.

Complaint is also made to the refusal to give the following instruction to the jury:

"You are instructed that if you find as a fact that the view west from the coalhouse on the occasion in question was unobstructed, and the deceased could, if he had looked, have seen the approaching cars, and have avoided being hit by them, then he was guilty of negligence contributing to his injuries, and the plaintiff cannot recover."

The requested instruction was properly refused. It wholly ignores the existence of the custom, and the right of deceased to rely for his protection upon its continued observance.

The judgment is affirmed.

Paquette v. Berlin Mills Co.

(Supreme Court of New Hampshire, Coos, Nov. 1, 1910.)

[78 Atl. Rep. 126.]

Master and Servant—Injury to Servant—Negligence.*—A member of a switching crew represented, when he sought employment, that he had had experience in that line of work, but displayed awkwardness in his employment. While at work he was in a position of safety on a car but voluntarily took another position, and, when the car was within a foot of a stationary car, he attempted to jump on the latter car and was killed. Held, as a matter of law, that the master was not liable for his death for failing to instruct him in his work.

Exceptions from Superior Court, Coos County; Chamberlin, Judge.

Action by Elmire Paquette, administratrix of one Paquette, deceased, against the Berlin Mills Company. There was a directed verdict for defendants, and plaintiff brings exceptions. Overruled.

Henry F. Hollis and *Robert C. Murchie*, for plaintiff.
Drew, Jordan, Shurtleff & Morris and *Rich & Marble*, for defendants.

Bingham, J. This action is brought by the administratrix of the estate of one Paquette, who was killed on July 16, 1908, while in the defendants' employment as a member of a switching crew.

The following facts appear from the evidence: On the morning of the day of the accident, the crew in which Paquette was working was called upon to go to a place on the defendants' road, known as the "Cross Power Siding," take two empty cars —a flat car and a box car—down the track and across a bridge that spans the Androscoggin river, and leave them upon a siding that makes off from the main line at a switch 300 feet below the bridge. The shifting crew, in the performance of its duty, went to the Cross Power Siding, attached the front end of the engine to the flat car. and proceeded to back down the track. Before leaving the Cross Power Siding, Seguin, the head switchman, took his position at the brake staff at the end of the box car nearest the flat car, and Paquette, either of his own motion or at the direction of Ross, the yardmaster, went upon and stood in the middle of the flat car. Streeter, a superintendent at one of the defendants' millyards, got upon the rear footboard of the engine, and Ross upon the front footboard next to the flat car.

---

*See first paragraph of foot-note of preceding case.

Paquette *v.* Berlin Mills Co

With the men in these positions, the engineer backed the engine down the track. When they had proceeded about 210 feet and were distant about 450 feet from the siding below the bridge, Ross pulled the pin from the coupling connecting the engine to the flat car, and the engine, released from the cars, increased its speed and proceeded down the track to a point on the main line below the switch. When the engine reached the switch, Ross stepped off and set it so that the cars, which were coming down and were then about 300 feet away, could go in on the side track. At the time the engine was disconnected from the flat car, Paquette remained standing in the middle of the car, and later, when the engine came across the bridge and approached the siding, he was seen sitting on a timber that extended across the flat car between two posts at a point about two feet from the floor and two feet from the front end of the car. When about ten feet from the switch he passed over the crosspiece and stood with his arm around a timber that crossed the car two or three feet above the one on which he had previously sat, or with his arm around one of the posts to which the cross-timbers were attached. About 300 feet below the switch on the siding was a flat car. As Paquette passed the switch, Ross called out to him to get back into the middle of the car, and Paquette either replied that he would look out for himself, or simply looked around and grinned. When about fifteen feet from the stationary car, he released his hold from the cross-timber or stake and stood about two feet from the front end of the car, until it was within a foot or so of the stationary car, and then jumped to that car, fell between the cars, and was run over and killed. When the cars passed the switch, Seguin was standing at the brake staff on the box car applying the brake. The cars were then moving from six to ten miles an hour. The brake worked all right, but Seguin did not tighten it sufficiently; and the car Paquette was on, its speed having been reduced to two or three miles an hour, bumped into the flat car and, its brake not being set, sent it along a distance of some eighteen feet. When the two flat cars came to rest, they were about three feet apart.

The plaintiff says that she should have been permitted to go to the jury on the question of the defendants' failure to warn and instruct Paquette, and of his exercise of care; that there was evidence from which it could have been found that he was inexperienced and ignorant of the dangers to be encountered in the defendants' service; that they were apprised, or ought to have been apprised, of his inexperience and need of instruction and warnings, at a time sufficiently early to have enabled them to give them to him; that they were negligent in failing to warn and instruct him; that his death was the result of their negligence; and that he was in the exercise of due care.

At the time Paquette met his death, he had been in the de-

Paquette *v.* Berlin Mills Co

fendants' employment as a member of the switching crew about two hours. When he sought this employment, he represented that he had had experience in this line of work on a railroad in Canada and in the yard of the International Paper Company. The plaintiff seeks to avoid the effect of this portion of her evidence by other evidence in which it appeared that Paquette joined the switching crew at about 7 o'clock in the morning; that at 20 minutes after 7 they had ridden on the engine down to the Cascade Mill, where Ross joined them; that while there Ross and Streeter noticed that Paquette took an awkward position in setting brakes and acted a little green in throwing switches, and questioned him further as to his experience in railroading; and that later, at the Cross Power Siding, he displayed awkwardness in stepping upon the footboard of the engine. If from this and other evidence it could have been found that the defendants would not be justified in relying upon Paquette's representation that he was experienced in the line of work he had engaged to perform, and that he should have been instructed as to the proper way in which to couple and uncouple cars, set brakes, and throw switches, and where and how to board or depart from moving cars when called upon to do so in the discharge of his duties, and warned as to the hidden or obscure dangers of the employment, the evidence does not disclose that he met his death while doing or attempting to do any of these things, or while encountering any hidden or obscure danger. On the contrary, the evidence is that after having taken a position of safety upon the car, and with nothing to do but remain there until it reached its destination, he went voluntarily, and for no apparent reason other than to satisfy his curiosity, to the front end of the car, being well aware that it was approaching the stationary car, and when within a foot of that car attempted to jump upon it and was killed. He was 26 years of age, and, so far as appears, a man of average intelligence; at least there is no evidence from which it could be found that he was not, and that the defendants knew or should have known that he was not. And under the circumstances it could not be found that the defendants should have anticipated that Paquette, without being required to perform any act of duty, would leave a place of safety and heedlessly attempt to jump from the car he was on to the stationary car, as they were about to come together.

The plaintiff, however, contends that, after Paquette went to the front of the car, Ross saw him there and could have warned him to return to the middle of the car. But this contention cannot be maintained, as the uncontroverted evidence is that, at the time Ross disconnected the engine from the flat car, Paquette was in the middle of the car; that it was after this, and when the engine had gone ahead down the track, that Ross first saw that he had changed his position to the front of the car; and that, when the car passed Ross at the switch, he warned him to return to the middle of the car. Whether the warning was heard and understood by Paquette can never be known, but that is of little importance in view of the fact that the evidence discloses that every reasonable endeavor was made to warn him after his danger was known.

The verdict was properly directed.

Exception overruled. All concurred.

PETERSON *v*. CHICAGO, R. I. & P. Ry. Co.

(Supreme Court of Iowa, Dec. 15, 1910.)

[128 N. W. Rep. 932.]

Master and Servant—Injury to Servant—"Safe Place to Work."—The place in which a servant is directed to work is safe, when all the safeguards and precautions which ordinary experience, prudence, and foresight will suggest have been taken to prevent injury to the servant while exercising reasonable care; and a place which is safe so long as machinery is not in operation, and the peril involved is in the improper method of performing the work by improperly starting the machinery, is safe within the law.

Master and Servant—Fellow Servants—Who Are.*—One who is for some purposes a foreman, and authorized to direct the work of a servant who is injured, is a fellow servant as to acts not involving the exercise of superior authority.

Master and Servant—Fellow Servants—Who Are.*—The act of the foreman, in charge of the work of elevating coal to the top of a building, from which it may be discharged into the tenders of engines, in starting the hoisting engine while a servant was at work in the pit, rendered dangerous only by starting the engine without proper warning, is an act forming a part of the ordinary operation of the work; and the foreman and the servant are as to such work fellow servants, so that the master is not responsible for the negligence of the foreman in starting the engine without warning the servant.

Appeal from District Court, Cass County; O. D. Wheeler, Judge.

Action to recover damages for personal injuries received while in defendant's employment. At the close of the evidence intro-

---

*For the authorities in this series on the question, when a foreman is, and is not, acting as a fellow servant of a hand working under him, see foot-note of Berglund *v*. Illinois Cent. R. Co. (Minn.), 36 R. R. R. 26, 59 Am. & Eng. R. Cas., N. S., 26.

duced for plaintiff, the court sustained defendant's motion for a directed verdict, and plaintiff appeals. Affirmed.

H. M. Boorman, for appellant.

Carroll Wright, J. L. *Parrish,* and J. B. *Rockafellow,* for appellee.

McCLAIN, J. At the time of receiving the injury complained of, plaintiff was in the employment of the defendant as a laborer, engaged in breaking up coal to be elevated in defendant's coal chute at Atlantic. When the coal was sufficiently broken, it was elevated by buckets to bins in the top of the building, from which it might be discharged into tenders of engines. It was necessary from time to time for the plaintiff in the course of his employment to go into the pit at the bottom of the shaft in which the buckets were hoisted and clean out the loose coal. This work was not dangerous in its nature, unless buckets of coal were being elevated at the same time. In that event there was danger of coal falling from the buckets upon the defendant, working below. The work was in charge of one Dreager, as foreman, and he had personal charge of the motive power, and determined when the buckets should be operated. On one occasion not long prior to the accident in question, plaintiff had complained to Dreager that buckets of coal were being run up while he was working in the pit below, and he was thereby put in danger; and Dreager had assured him that thereafter the machinery would never be started while plaintiff was at work in the pit. The evidence tends to show that in violation of this promise, while plaintiff was at work in the pit and with knowledge of that fact, Dreager started the engine, causing a bucket of coal to be elevated, from which a large piece of coal fell, striking the plaintiff beneath and causing him the injury now complained of. The negligence relied upon was in not affording plaintiff a reasonably safe place in which to work and in negligently starting the hoisting apparatus while plaintiff was in a place of danger, thereby occasioning his injury. It is also contended that plaintiff was improperly ordered into a dangerous place to perform labor, without notice or warning as to the danger and hazard involved.

It is quite evident that there was no breach of duty on the part of the defendant in furnishing plaintiff a safe place to work. The place in which he was working was entirely safe so long as the machinery used in elevating the buckets of coal was not in operation. The peril involved was in the improper method of performing the work, and not in any improper conditions under which the work was to be performed. The place in which an employee is directed to work is "safe," within the meaning of the law, "when all the safeguards and precautions which ordinary experience, prudence, and foresight would suggest have been taken to prevent injury to the employee while he is himself exercising reasonable care in the service which he undertakes to perform." Martin v. Des Moines Edison Light Co., 131 Iowa, 734, 106 N. W. 359. The injury to plaintiff was not due to the character of the place in which he was put to work, but to the fault of Dreager in starting the machinery while plaintiff was in such position that the hoisting of the bucket of coal would imperil his safety; and it is practically conceded in argument that the method of doing the business did not necessarily require nor involve the operation of the machinery while plaintiff was in such situation. There was nothing omitted, so far as it appears from the evidence, in providing a safe place and a safe method. What was omitted, resulting in the injury to plaintiff, was proper caution on the part of Dreager in starting the machinery under his control while the plaintiff was so situated as to be placed in peril.

2. It is contended, however, that Dreager as foreman was vice principal, and his negligence was chargeable to defendant. For some purposes he may have been vice principal, but as to the particular negligent act on his part which caused injury to plaintiff he was his fellow servant. So far as the negligent act causing the injury was concerned, it might as well have been performed by another servant of equal rank with the plaintiff as by Dreager, who was for some purposes a superior. Such act was not, therefore, an act of the defendant in the discharge of its duty of supervision, but the act of a fellow servant in carrying on the work. If the engine had been in charge of another employee of equal rank with plaintiff, there could be no claim that the negligent act was not that of a fellow servant in the ordinary course of his employment. In this state we do not treat the relative rank of two employees as of controlling importance, and do not recognize the so-called "superior servant" rule. One who is for some purposes a superior servant or foreman, and authorized to direct the work of the employee who is injured, is nevertheless a fellow servant as to the acts which do not involve the exercise of such superior authority. Scott v. Chicago & G. W. R. Co., 113 Iowa, 381, 85 N. W. 631; Barnicle v. Connor, 110 Iowa, 238, 81 N. W. 452; Beresford v. American Coal Co., 124 Iowa, 34, 98 N. W. 902, 70 L. R. A. 256; Helgeson v. Higley Co. (Iowa) 126 N. W. 769.

3. The cases principally relied upon for appellant are those involving negligence of the employer, acting through a vice principal, in sending the employee into a place which the vice principal knew or should have known was dangerous, without a reasonable appreciation on the part of the employee that such place was in fact dangerous. McGuire v. Waterloo, etc., Mill Co., 137 Iowa, 447, 113 N. W. 850; Schminkey v. Sinclair & Co., 137 Iowa, 130, 114 N. W. 612. But here the place in which plain-

tiff was put to work was not inherently dangerous, either by reason of its natural condition or the method in which the work was usually carried on. It became dangerous only by reason of the fault of Dreager in starting the machinery without proper warning. It is true that we have held that the duty to give warning in case of the use of dangerous explosives rests upon the master as a part of his duty of supervision. Hendrickson *v.* U. S. Gypsum Co., 133 Iowa, 89, 110 N. W. 322, 9 L. R. A. (N. S.) 555. But that case has been explained and limited in Galloway *v.* Turner Imp. Co. (Iowa) 126 N. W. 1033, so that it is not applicable to the case before us. Indeed, the opinion in the Hendrickson Case itself involves the limitations which make in inapplicable here. The Galloway Case is directly in point, in holding that where two employees are co-operating in carrying on a piece of work, although one of them may be superior to the other in authority, yet if the injury results merely from the failure of such superior to give warning to the inferior of his contemplated act which is a part of the ordinary operation of the work, the negligence in failing to give such a warning is that of a fellow servant, and not that of the master. No appliance can be provided which may not under some circumstances, if used by one employee without warning or precaution, involve injury to a coemployee; and there was in this case no suggestion of any negligence in the method of doing the work which the master had authorized.

There was no error in sustaining the motion for a directed verdict, and the judgment thereon is affirmed.

Simpson v. Southern Ry. Co.

(Supreme Court of North Carolina, Dec. 14, 1910.)

[69 S. E. Rep. 683.]

Master and Servant—Injuries to Servant—Actions—Evidence—Accident.—In an action by an employee against a railroad company for injuries caused by ties falling on his foot, while he and others were piling them on a car, evidence held to show that the injury was the result of an accident.

Negligence—"Accident."—An "accident" is an event resulting from an unknown cause, or an unusual and unexpected event from a known cause; chance; casualty.

Negligence—Actions—Defense—Accident.—When an injury results from an event taking place without one's foresight or expectation or an event which proceeds from an unknown cause, or is an unusual effect of a known cause, and therefore not anticipated, the sufferer is without legal remedy.

Master and Servant—Injury to Servant—Safe Place to Work—Care Required of Master—Ordinary Conditions.—The duty of a master to provide for his employee a reasonably safe place to work does not extend to ordinary conditions which arise during the progress of the work, where the employee can see and understand the dangers and avoid them by the exercise of reasonable care; therefore a railroad company is not liable for injuries received by a servant while piling ties, where the servant and others were doing this work in their own way, and there was nothing to indicate that the work was inherently dangerous, or likely to result in injury to any one, if carefully done.

Master and Servant—Injury to Servant—Safe Place to Work—Obvious Dangers.—Where an employee of a railroad company was injured by ties falling on his foot while he and others were piling them on a car without any particular directions from the employer, the principle that a master is not bound to guard the servant against obvious danger applies.

Appeal from Superior Court, Rutherford County; Webb, Judge.

Action by Jesse Simpson against the Southern Railway Company. From a judgment for plaintiff, defendant appeals. Reversed and remanded.

Solomon Gallert and *W. B. Rodman,* for appellant.

Walker, J. This action was brought to recover damages for an injury to the plaintiff alleged to have been caused by the defendant's negligence. Plaintiff and two other employees had been engaged in loading a flat car, which was attached to a "material

Simpson *v.* Southern Ry. Co

or work train," with ties taken from an abandoned section of the defendant's road. The ties were piled at each end of the car and toward the middle, where a vacant space was left. The train was moved out and onto the main track, where the hands were ordered to level the ties by placing some of them in the middle of the car. The plaintiff and the two other hands who assisted him got upon the car, the plaintiff standing between the two piles of ties, and the others on either side of one of the piles. While they were moving the ties, one or two of them fell from the pile and injured the plaintiff's foot. It does not appear with any degree of certainty what caused the ties to fall, unless it was insufficient support or accidental jostling. If they had been carelessly placed upon the car, the plaintiff was as much responsible for their condition as the other hands, but the evidence does not justify the imputation of negligence to any of them in the manner of doing the work. For all that does appear, it was just one of those accidents which sometimes occur without our being able to ascribe it to any particular cause. It would seem to come within the definition of an accident, which is "an event resulting from an unknown cause, or an unusual and unexpected event from a known cause; chance; casualty." Crutchfield *v.* Railroad, 76 N. C. 322, and, as we said in Martin *v.* Manufacturing Co., 128 N. C. 264, 38 S. E. 876, 83 Am. St. Rep. 671, when an injury results from an event taking place without one's foresight or expectation, or an event which proceeds from an unknown cause, or is an unusual effect of a known cause, and therefore not anticipated, the consequences must be borne by the unfortunate sufferer, who is without legal remedy in such a case. Our reading and study of the evidence, as set forth in the record, does not disclose any act of negligence on the part of the defendant. If there was any negligence at all, it could better be imputed to the plaintiff in taking his position on the car between the two piles of cross-ties, if it was a dangerous one, than to any one else. The hands did the work assigned to them in their own way and without any special instruction as to the manner of doing it, and there is nothing to indicate that it was of such a character as to be inherently dangerous or likely to result in injury to any one, if carefully done. There was nothing in its nature which called for anything more than ordinary skill or even any experience in work of a like kind. The plaintiff required no instruction as to the proper method of doing so simple a piece of work. That degree of care which every man of reasonable prudence exercises in the ordinary affairs of life, would have been a sufficient safeguard against injury. The recent decision of this court (at this term) in Warwick *v.* Oil & Ginning Co., 69 S. E. 129, states the rule of law applicable to the facts of this case. We there held that an employer's duty to provide for his employee a reasonably

Simpson *v.* Southern Ry. Co

safe place to work does not extend to ordinary conditions arising during the progress of the work, where the employee, doing his work in his own way, can see and understand the dangers and avoid them by the exercise of reasonable care. In that case the plaintiff was feeding a conveyor with cotton seed. While standing on the pile of seed, which gradually poured into the conveyor, the seed slipped or gave way, and his foot was caught in the machinery and injured. We held that a judgment of nonsuit should have been awarded, there being nothing in the construction of the machinery or in the nature of the work to show any negligence. See, also, Brookshire *v.* Electric Co., 152 N. C. 669, 68 S. E. 215; House *v.* Railway, 152 N. C. 397, 67 S. E. 981; Keck *v.* Telephone Co., 131 N. C. 277, 42 S. E. 610; Lassiter *v.* Railroad, 150 N. C. 483, 64 S. E. 202; Alexander *v.* Manufacturing Co., 132 N. C. 428, 43 S. E. 1003; Dunn *v.* Railroad, 151 N. C. 313, 66 S. E. 134.

The principle stated in Covington *v.* Furniture Co., 138 N. C. 374, 50 S. E. 761, and quoted from Labbatt on Master and Servant, 333, has some application to the facts of our case: "The general rule of law is that when the danger is obvious, and is of such a nature that it can be appreciated and understood by the servant as well as by the master or by any one else, and when the servant has as good an opportunity as the master or any one else of seeing what the danger is, and is permitted to do his work in his own way, and can avoid the danger by the exercise of reasonable care, the servant cannot recover against the master for the injuries received in consequence of the condition of things which constituted the danger. If the servant is injured, it is from his own want of care. * * * This rule is especially applicable when the danger does not arise from the defective condition of the permanent ways, works, or machinery of the master, but from the manner in which they are used, and when the existence of the danger could not well be anticipated, but must be ascertained by observation at the time." This rule was first stated in Lothrop *v.* Railroad, 150 Mass. 423, 23 N. E. 227, where many cases are cited.

A careful examination of the case leads us to the conclusion that, if the injury to the plaintiff was caused by negligence, it was not that of the defendant, and the motion for a nonsuit should have been granted. The action should therefore be dismissed, and judgment to that effect will be entered in the court below.

Reversed.

Lane v. North Carolina R. Co.

(Supreme Court of North Carolina, Dec. 20, 1910.)

[69 S. E. Rep. 780.]

Master and Servant—Negligence—Instructing as to Work.*—It is not negligence of a railroad company to fail to instruct a car inspector, a grown man, of experience in the work, as to the safe and proper method of shutting the doors of freight cars, they being shut by pushing or pulling them shut, either way being simple, and there being no regular or prescribed way.

Master and Servant—Injury to Servant—Assumption of Risk.—A railroad employee, whose duty is to inspect cars for defects and repair them, assumes the risk of injury from such defects.

Master and Servant—Injury to Servant—Contributory Negligence. —A railroad employee, whose duty was to inspect freight cars in a train at a station, close open doors of freight cars, and discover and repair defects in the cars that might interfere with the safe movement of the train, and who in closing a door was injured by its toppling, which accident could not have occurred had a missing shoe at the bottom of the car door the absence of which he could readily have seen had he looked, been replaced by him before he attempted to close it, was guilty of contributory negligence.

Appeal from Superior Court, Davidson County; W. J. Adams, Judge.   •

Action by John A. Lane against the North Carolina Railroad Company. From a judgment on a verdict for plaintiff, defendant appeals. Reversed, and new trial directed.

The plaintiff, in the fourth allegation of his amended complaint, thus details the manner in which he was injured and for which he sues to recover damages: "That on the 28th day of November, 1907, and for some time prior thereto, the plaintiff was employed by the Southern Railway Company as a servant upon defendant's yards in the town of Spencer for a valuable consideration, and while engaged in such work as a safety appliance man and inspecting a train of freight cars which had been assembled for the purpose of being carried out over defendant's road as aforesaid, and which was then standing upon a side track constructed upon defendant's right of way and being used by its lessee, the Southern Railway Company, plaintiff, in the course of his services as such servant, came to a car in the nighttime with the door open, which it was the duty of the plaintiff to close and fasten before allowing the said train to be carried out, when plaintiff endeavored to pull said door

---

*As to the master's duty to warn and instruct his servants, see extensive note, 35 R. R. R. 640, 58 Am. & Eng. R. Cas., N. S., 640.

Lane *v.* North Carolina R. Co

shut in the usual way—by catching one hand inside of said door and the other ouside and under the bottom of said door—and while endeavoring to pull the said door shut, which was constructed to slide or roll on a track at the top of said door and along the side of said car by means of supports with rollers to carry the weight of the door on said track, and while pulling the door as aforesaid, the back hinge or roller of the door broke loose and allowed the part of the door shutter which plaintiff was pulling to swing in the direction that plaintiff was pulling, and the supports which had been placed at the bottom of the door to secure the bottom of the door in place and keep it from falling or swinging were gone, and thereby allowed the shutter to catch plaintiff's arm between the edge of said door shutter and the facing of the door or post at the side of the door, thereby mash. ing, bruising, and mutilating plaintiff's arm in such a way as to cause him to suffer great bodily pain, and mental anguish, and permanently injuring said arm, permanently injuring his nervous system and his general health."

The particular negligent acts are thus stated: "(1) In that said defendant's lessee carelessly and negligently allowed said car to be placed in a train of cars to be carried and transported by the defendant's lessee over its main line of roadbed without having the necessary supports at the bottom of said door to hold it in place, and without examining the hinge or roller at the top of the door, knowing that it would become in a defective condition by being transported without supports to hold the bottom of the door in its proper place. (2) In that the defendant's lessee failed to supply the necessary supports for the bottom of said door when inspecting and repairing said car when it came upon the yards at Spencer, as it was the custom and was the duty of the defendant's lessee to do. (3) In that defendant's lessee carelessly and negligently operated said car in a defective and dangerous condition and required plaintiff to close said door while said door was in a defective and dangerous condition"— and in addition thereto further charged that defendant had failed to properly instruct plaintiff how to perform his duties and to give him a book of rules. The defendant, denying any and all acts of negligence charged, further alleged: "That if the plaintiff was injured at all, it was caused entirely by his own acts and conduct; that, as safety appliance man, it was his duty, not only to fasten and seal the doors, but to examine the doors and other parts of the car as to their condition, and if any was out of order to repair same, with the aid of others, if required, or to report same, and defendant alleges that if the said door or any of its hinges or rollers were in any way out of order, which is expressly denied, it was the duty of the said plaintiff to place the door in proper condition by repairing it, calling in the help of others if he could not repair it himself, or to make report of

Lane *v.* North Carolina R. Co

the same at once, and the defendant alleges that if said door or any of its hinges or rollers were out of order, which is denied as aforesaid, that the plaintiff's injury was occasioned by his own neglect of duty and carelessly or negligently pulling or forcing the door against his arm, and thereby causing any injury which he may have sustained."

The three issues of negligence, contributory negligence and damages were submitted to the jury, who answered them in favor of plaintiff and assessed his damages at $1,000. Judgment was rendered for plaintiff, from which defendant appealed to this court.

Linn & Linn, for appellant.

E. E. Raper, Geo. W. Garland, and *McRary & McRary,* for appellee.

MANNING, J. But one exception is presented in the record— the refusal of his honor to give, at the request of the defendant, the following special instruction: "Upon all the evidence, if believed, the plaintiff was guilty of contributory negligence as a matter of law, and the jury will answer the second issue 'Yes.'" In determining the correctness of his honor's ruling upon this instruction, we must consider the evidence in that view most favorable to the plaintiff, for if his honor had given the requested instruction, it would have been equivalent to a nonsuit of the plaintiff. It must be kept in mind that the admitted duties of the plaintiff were to inspect the freight cars grouped into a train, to discover defects that might render their transportation unsafe, and to repair such defects when discovered, or to have the defective car taken from the train of cars. The defendant had, as appears from the evidence, wisely adopted a system of double inspection of freight cars coming to its yards at Spencer, one upon their arrival and the second after they had been grouped into a train for an out-bound trip. It was the duty of the plaintiff to make this last inspection. Experience, it seems, had demonstrated to the defendant that in shifting cars on its yards from track to track and making up an outgoing train, some injury might be done to the cars that would interfere with the safe movement of the train, and the second inspection was enforced. The plaintiff, being assigned to this duty, was equipped with the necessary appliances to perform it; boxes containing knuckle pins. chains, hasps, staples, nails, grabirons. hammers, shoes, etc., were placed at convenient points on the yards for the use of the inspector and repairer. The plaintiff was also provided with a lantern. specially made for the use of inspectors in their night work. The plaintiff testified that "when they (the freight cars) came to me. I. would look over the train, inspect it to see if the doors were shut or anything broken during the shifting of the train." Again, in answer to a ques-

Lane *v.* North Carolina R. Co

tion, he said that he was what is called the safety-appliance man. The particular manner in which plaintiff was injured is stated in his complaint and testified to by him.   It further appears in the evidence that the doors to the freight cars are sliding doors and "slide or roll on a track at the top of the door and along the side of the car by means of supports with rollers."   This track at the top primarily supports the weight of the door, which varies from 150 to 250 pounds; but it appears and is alleged by the plaintiff that a secondary support for these doors was provided in the shape of two door guides or "shoes" attached to the side of the cars at the bottom of the doors.   While it appears from the evidence that the primary purpose of these door guides or "shoes" was to prevent the doors from swinging out at the bottom, it also clearly appears from the evidence of plaintiff's witness that their secondary purpose was to support the doors in case anything happened to the primary support, and that these "shoes" were efficient for this secondary purpose.   The presence or absence of these "shoes" was easily detected at a glance because of their size and placing, while the condition of the top slide or track was not so easily discovered by the plaintiff.   The door of this particular car at which plaintiff was injured was partly open, and it was his duty to close it, and to discover and supply any missing appliance or defect in it.   It was charged for negligence against the defendant that it did not specifically instruct the plaintiff as to the safe and proper method of shutting these car doors, but the closing of a door is such a simple act that we are unable to say that a grown man of experience in that work should be specifically instructed as to how to do it. any more than it requires a book of instruction or particular directions to be given as to the manner of using a hammer to drive a nail.   The plaintiff's evidence showed that the doors were shut by pushing or pulling them shut, and there was no regular or prescribed way—either way was simple. One of the shoes at the bottom of the car door was off, and when plaintiff undertook to pull the door shut, the hinge or roller at the opposite top corner broke or came loose, and the door swung diagonally down and caught plaintiff's arm against the jamb of the door or door post.   If the missing "shoe" had been replaced by plaintiff before his attempt to close the door, the injury could not have occurred.   Plaintiff admits that if he had looked, he could readily have seen that the "shoe" was missing. Mr. Thompson. in his Commentary on Negligence, § 4617, states it as an accepted principle: "From the foregoing, it may easily be concluded that an employee assumes the risk of injury from defects in premises, machinery, mechanical contrivances, or appliances which he is employed to repair, or which it is his duty, in the course of his employment, to repair."   This is quoted with approval and applied by this court in the recent case of White *v.*

St. Louis, I. M. & S. Ry. Co. *v*. Jones

Power Co., 151 N. C. 356, 66 S. E. 210. The application of
this principle determines this case, and we think against the
plaintiff. It will further be observed that the injury to the plaintiff was not caused by the intervening act of any other servant
or in any way aided or participated therein by such other servant; it was the plaintiff's own and sole act. This language of
Chief Justice Bleckley in Spinning Co. *v*. Achord, 84 Ga. 14, 10
S. E. 449, 6 L. R. A. 190, states most clearly the controlling
principle (this is also quoted in White *v*. Power Co., supra):
"While it is the duty of a master to furnish his servant safe
machinery for use, he is under no duty to furnish his machinist
safe machinery to be repaired, or to keep it safe whilst repairs
are in progress. Precisely because it is unsafe for use, repairs
are often necessary. The physician might as well insist on
having a well patient to be treated and cured as the machinist
to have sound and safe machinery to be repaired." The important part of plaintiff's duties was to hunt out and discover defects in the car that might interfere with its safe movement,
and to repair such as he ought to discover. In our opinion, his
honor should have given the instruction prayed, and, in failing
to do so, there was error, for which a new trial is directed.
New trial.

ST. LOUIS, I. M. & S. RY. CO. *v*. JONES.

(Supreme Court of Arkansas, Nov. 28, 1910.)

[132 S. W. Rep. 636.]

Principal and Agent—Scope of Agent's Authority—In General.—In
general an agent has implied authority to do all things necessary to
effectuate the main purpose for which he is employed.

**Principal and Agent—Scope of Agent's Authority—Railroad Con-
ductor—Hiring Assistance.***—Except by reason of unusual circumstances which render outside assistance necessary to carry forward
a train, a conductor has no authority to make contracts of employment.

**Railroads—Injuries to Persons on Trains—Authority of Conductor
—Persons Assisting in Handling Freight.***—A conductor having no

---

*For the authorities in this series on the subject of the implied
authority of a railroad's agents or servants to employ others to work
for the railroad, see second paragraph of second foot-note of Welch
v. Boston (Mass.), 35 R. R. R. 35, 58 Am. & Eng. R. Cas., N. S., 35;
foot-note of Hendrickson *v*. Louisville, etc., R. Co. (Ky.), 35 R. R.
R. 774, 58 Am. & Eng. R. Cas., N. S., 774; Louisville & N. R. Co.
v. Vaughn's Transfer Co. (Ky.), 34 R. R. R. 81, 57 Am. & Eng. R.
Cas., N. S., 81.

For the authorities in this series on the question whether persons
on trains or street cars by invitation of railroad employees are trespassers or licensees, see last foot-note of Welch *v*. Boston (Mass.),
35 R. R. R. 35, 58 Am. & Eng. R. Cas., N. S., 35.

St. Louis, I. M. & S. Ry. Co. *v.* Jones

authority to agree to let a person ride in consideration of his assisting with the freight, one who rides under such an agreement is
neither an employee nor a passenger, but a mere volunteer, who
assumes the risk of his position.

**Principal and Agent—Scope of Agent's Authority—Railroad Con-
ductor—Right to Employ Assistant—Custom.**—For custom to modify
the general rule that a conductor has no right to employ an assistant, it must be one that is actually known by the officials who conduct the affairs of the railroad company, or one so general and of
such long standing that it may be fairly inferred that it was known
and assented to by them.

**Railroads—Injuries to Persons on Trains—Proof—Issues—Elec-
tion.**—Where plaintiff, in an action against a railway company for
personal injuries, testifies he was on board a freight train under an
agreement by the conductor to let him ride free in consideration of
his assisting in handling freight he cannot recover as a passenger
riding gratuitously by permission of the conductor, where he was
not injured on the train, but had left it, carrying freight from the
cars, and was injured while attempting to re-enter it and he carried
according to the unauthorized contract with the conductor.

Kirby, J., dissenting.

Appeal from Circuit Court, White County; H. N. Hutton,
Judge.

Action by Lindsay Jones by N. A. Ford, his mother and next
friend, against the St. Louis, Iron Mountain & Southern Railway Company. From a judgment for plaintiff, defendant appeals. Reversed.

Lindsay Jones by N. A. Ford, his mother and next friend,
brought this suit against the St. Louis, Iron Mountain & Southern Railway Company to recover damages for injuries received
by him while attempting to board one of defendant's local freight
trains.

Lindsay Jones testified in his own behalf and stated the circumstances connected with the happening of the accident substantially as follows: He was a white person and was 19 years
old when he was injured. He had been at Bald Knob, a station
on defendant's line of railroad in Arkansas, hunting work. He
ran out of money and failing to obtain employment, he decided to
return home. Higginson was the station on defendant's line of
road nearest his home. He asked the conductor of one of defendant's local freight trains if he would let him ride and work
his way to Higginson. The conductor answered: "I will see
about it directly," and directly came back and said: "Get on;
you can work your way." The first stop was made at Judsonia,
and he helped load and unload some freight. The conductor
was standing around while the freight was unloaded. The next
stop was at Kensett. Jones worked there, helping to load and

St. Louis, I. M. & S. Ry. Co. *v.* Jones

unload the freight. While he was carrying a piece of freight from one of the cars to the freighthouse, the train without notice or warning of any kind was put in motion. Jones after depositing the piece of freight in the freightroom, turned around to get on the departing train. The train was running and Jones reached up to get the handle of the front end of the caboose to get on it. His foot slipped and fell under the wheels of the caboose. It was mashed so badly that it was necessary to amputate it. On the part of the defendant, it was shown that the conductor had no authority to employ any one to assist the train crew in the operation of the train, or in loading or unloading freight. The conductor, on behalf of the defendant, testified that he did not contract with the plaintiff to carry him from Bald Knob to Higginson in consideration of any services performed by him. He did testify to the fact that he saw the plaintiff on the train and that he intended to collect his fare later, but that he overlooked or neglected to take up his fare. On cross-examination, in response to the question: "Isn't it a fact that people are carried free by the conductors on the local freight train up and down the Iron Mountain Road to assist the crew in the loading and unloading of freight at the stations?" he answered, "Colored men only."

The jury returned a verdict for the plaintiff, and from the judgment the defendant has duly prosecuted an appeal to this court.

W. E. Hemingway, E. B. Kinsworthy, and *Jas. H. Stevenson,* for appellant.

S. Brundidge, Jr., and *Harry Neelly,* for appellee.

HART, J. (after stating the facts as above). It is the contention of the plaintiff that he made a contract with the conductor of one of defendant's local freight trains to carry him from Bald Knob to Higginson, in consideration of services to be performed by him in assisting the train crew in loading and unloading freight.

The undisputed evidence shows that the conductor did not have authority to make such contract. Did he have implied authority to make it? The general rule is that the agent has the implied authority to do all things which are reasonably necessary to effectuate the main purpose for which he is employed.

Mr. Elliott says that the authority of the conductor ordinarily extends to the control of the movements of his trains and to the immediate direction of the movements of the employees engaged in operating the train, and does not extend to making contracts on behalf of the railway company. Elliott on Railroads, vol. 1, § 302. Continuing, the author says: "As we have said, the conductor has no general authority to make contracts on behalf of the company, but he may in rare cases of necessity,

St. Louis, I. M. & S. Ry. Co. *v.* Jones

when circumstances demand it, bind the company by such contracts as are clearly necessary to enable him to carry out his prescribed duties. In order that contracts made by him shall be obligatory upon the company they must be made to enable him to perform the duties required of him and must not relate to collateral matters, nor be outside of the line of duty assigned him. Thus, he may, where other provision has not been made, employ mechanics to repair a break of the cars or machinery which must be repaired before the train can proceed to its destination, and may engage men and teams to render the roadway or bridges secure for the passage of his train, when weakened or partially swept away by unforeseen causes; but in such cases the authority to contract does not exist, unless there is necessity for immediate action. It is the necessity which confers the authority, not simply the position of conductor." Elliott on Railroads, vol. 1, par. 302.

In the case of Eaton *v.* Delaware, etc., R. Co., 57 N. Y. 382, 15 Am. Rep. 513, it is said: "There is nothing in the business of a conductor which 'would lead to the conclusion that he had authority to make contracts with persons to act as brakemen. His apparent duties are to carry forward a train after it is organized. The business of organizing it is in its nature wholly distinct. It is, in fact, committed to a train dispatcher." In Cooper *v.* Lake Erie, etc., R. Co., 136 Ind. 366, 36 N. E. 272, the court said: "While the conductor and brakeman were in charge of the train, it does not appear that they had any authority to employ assistance in its management. No emergency is shown for the employment of the appellant. * * * No custom, rule, or regulation of the appellee company is shown by which the appellant might pay his way by working on the train, assisting the brakeman or other employee. * * * At most, the appellant was upon the train by the sufferance of the conductor and brakeman, who were themselves without authority to receive him. Any dangers to which he might become exposed were wholly at his own risk. The company would be liable only for willful injury to him." As bearing upon the question and recognizing this principle, we also cite the following: Church *v.* Railway Co., 50 Minn. 218, 52 N. W. 647, 16 L. R. A. 861; Louisville & N. R. Co. *v.* Ginley, 100 Tenn. 472, 45 S. W. 348; Everhart *v.* Terre Haute & Ind. R. Co., 78 Ind. 292, 41 Am. Rep. 567; Rhodes *v.* Georgia R. & Banking Co., 84 Ga. 320, 10 S. E. 922, 20 Am. St. Rep. 362; Vassor *v.* Atlantic Coast Line R. Co., 142 N. C. 68, 54 S. E. 849, 7 L. R. A. (N. S.) 950.

This principle was recognized and applied by this court in the case of Railroad Co. *v.* Dial, 58 Ark. 318, 24 S. W. 500. The court held (quoting syllabus): "Where a boy 15 years of age, at the request of the conductor of a freight train, undertakes

St. Louis, I. M. & S. Ry. Co. *v.* Jones

to throw off the brake on a car, and is injured by striking his head on an iron bridge, he cannot recover from the railroad company on account of its negligence in failing to warn him of the danger, if the conductor had no express or apparent authority to employ him, and there was no exigency which called for the exercise of implied authority."

It is not claimed that there was any sudden or unexpected emergency which made it necessary for the proper operation or safety of the train for the conductor to employ the plaintiff. There is no evidence that the injury was wanton or willful.

Applying the general principles above announced to the facts of this case as testified to by the plaintiff himself, and upon which he bases his right of recovery, it is apparent that he is neither a passenger nor employee. He bases his right to recover wholly upon the contract made with the conductor. He testified that he was performing the services usually performed by brakemen while making the trip. He could not be engaged in the immediate and direct duties of a servant and at the same time be considered a passenger. He was not an employee because the conductor had no authority, express or implied, to make the contract of employment. He was a mere volunteer and as such assumed the risks of the situation in which he placed himself.

There was an attempt made to prove by the cross-examination of the conductor the existence of a custom whereby persons were permitted to ride upon local freight trains in consideration of services performed by them in loading and unloading freight. The conductor says this applied to colored men only. But in order to make the company liable, there must be proof not only of the custom, but that it was actually known by the officials who conducted the affairs of the railway company, or that it was so general and of such long continuance that it must be fairly inferred that it was known and assented to by them. Railway Co. *v.* Bolling, 59 Ark. 395, 27 S. W. 492. It might be inferred from the evidence of the conductor in this case that he allowed plaintiff to ride without collecting his fare; that he, the conductor, intended later to collect it, but that he overlooked it, or neglected to collect it, owing to his mind being occupied with other duties. But whatever would be the rights of a person riding gratuitously in a coach provided for passengers by permission of the conductor without any evidence of his right to do so, such as a pass, that question has passed out of the case; for plaintiff was not injured while on the train, but according to his own testimony, he had left the train and was injured while attempting to re-enter it and be carried according to the terms of the contract which we have held the conductor had no authority, either express or implied, to make.

It follows that the court should have directed a verdict for the defendant as requested by it, and for the error in not doing so, the judgment must be reversed, and the cause will be dismissed.

KIRBY, J., dissents.

HOUSTON & T. C. RY. CO. v. CALDWELL.

(Supreme Court of Missouri, Dec. 17, 1910.)

[132 S. E. Rep. 1067.]

Garnishment—Jurisdiction—Amount Involved.—Under Rev. St. 1899. §§ 3447, 3448 (Rev. St. 1909, §§ 2427, 2428), a railroad company is not liable to garnishment proceedings on account of wages due its employees, where the debt sued for is less than $200, unless judgment is first rendered against the defendants; and hence a justice of the peace has no jurisdiction to issue garnishment in such a case, where the defendants are nonresidents and served only by publication.

Constitutional Law—Garnishment—Class Legislation.—Rev. St. 1899, §§ 3447, 3448 (Rev. St. 1909, §§ 2447, 2448), provide the garnishment shall not issue in a case where the sum demanded is not over $200, and where the property sought to be reached is wages due defendant from a railroad company, until after judgment is recovered by plaintiff against defendant, and in such case relieve the garnishee or railroad company of the duty to answer. Held, that the statutes were constitutional.

In Banc. Proceedings for prohibition by the Houston & Texas Central Railway Company against T. C. Caldwell. Writ awarded.

Douglass & Watson, for relator.
Piatt, Lea & Wood and *Harvey C. Clark,* for respondent.

PER CURIAM. This is an original proceeding in this court, the purpose of which is to obtain a writ of prohibition, directed to the respondent, a justice of the peace in Jackson county, to prohibit him entertaining jurisdiction in certain attachment suits instituted in his court against certain employees of the relator, the railroad company, wherein the defendants in those suits are nonresidents, and are served only by publication of notice, and wherein it is sought to reach their wages by process of garnishment served on the railroad company in this state.

There is a question raised in the pleadings in reference to the validity of the constable's return of the process of garnishment on the relator; but it will be unnecessary to decide that question, because, even if it should be admitted that the service was other-

Arkansas S. Ry. Co., etc., *v.* Louisiana & A. Ry. Co

wise sufficient, the railroad company is not liable to garnishment on account of the wages of its employees, where the debt sued for (as in each of the cases mentioned in the pleadings) is less than $200, until judgment is rendered against the employee. Sections 3447 and 3448, Rev. St. 1899, now sections 2427 and 2428, Rev. St. 1909. Therefore the justice of the peace exceeded his jurisdiction when he undertook to hold the railroad company under his process of garnishment in the cases mentioned.

It is contended on the part of the justice of the peace that the above-named sections of our statutes are unconstitutional, but this court has very recently considered that subject, and has decided that those were valid and constitutional sections. White *v.* M., K. & T. Ry. Co. (No. 13,889, not yet officially reported) 130 S. W. 325.

On the authority of that case we hold that the respondent has no authority to entertain jurisdiction in the cases mentioned in the pleading, and the writ of prohibition as prayed is therefore awarded.

ARKANSAS SOUTHERN RAILWAY COMPANY and F. L. Shaw, Sheriff and Tax Collector, Plffs. in Err., *v.* LOUISIANA & ARKANSAS RAILWAY COMPANY.

(Argued November 4, 1910. Decided November 38, 1910.)

[31 Sup. Ct. Rep. 56.]

Courts—United States Supreme Court—Error to State Court—Decision of Federal Question—Impairing Contract Obligations.—A decree of a state court adverse to the contention that, if the state Constitution confers on one railway company an exemption from a special tax granted in aid of another railway company, it impairs contract obligations, is reviewable in the Federal Supreme Court, although the state court rested its decision in part upon the ground that the latter railway company had not acquired all of its contract rights before the adoption of the Constitution.

Courts—United States Courts—State Laws—Conclusiveness of State Decisions.—The construction given by a state court to the immunity of railway companies from taxation, granted by the state Constitution, as extending to a special tax in aid of another railway company, is conclusive on the Federal Supreme Court in determining, on writ of error to the state court, whether such constitutional provision impairs contract obligations.

Constitutional Law—Impairing Contract Obligations—Taxation.—The obligation of a valid municipal grant of a special tax of 5 mills in aid of a specified railway company, effective against all the taxable property in the parish, is not unconstitutionally impaired by the

Arkansas S. Ry. Co., etc., v. Louisiana & A. Ry. Co

subsequent adoption of a new state Constitution under which any property in the parish passing into the possession of any railroad thereafter constructed becomes exempt from the tax.

In error to the Supreme Court of Louisiana to review a decree which, reversing a decree of the District Court in and for the Parish of Winn, in that state, enjoined the collection from one railway company of a tax granted in aid of another railway company. Affirmed.

See same case below, 121 La. 997, 46 So. 994.

The facts are stated in the opinion.

Messrs. A. A. Gunby and *Allen Sholars*, for plaintiffs in error.

Messrs. Henry Moore, Jr., H. H. White, Henry Moore, and *Samuel Herrick*, for defendant in error.

Mr. Justice Holmes delivered the opinion of the court:

This is a writ of error to reverse a decision of the supreme court of Louisiana granting an injunction to the plaintiff, the Louisiana & Arkansas Railway Company, the defendant in error, against the collection from it of a special tax in favor of the Arkansas Southern Railway Company, the plaintiff in error. 121 La. 997, 46 So. 994. The agreed facts are these: By art. 230 of the state Constitution of 1898, any railroad thereafter constructed before January 1, 1904, was to be exempt from taxation for ten years from completion, upon certain conditions. The plaintiff built its road through the parish of Winn and gained the right to the exemption. The defendant, plaintiff in error, claims its rights under a vote of the same parish on February 1, 1898, granting a tax of 5 mills to a predecessor to whose rights the defendant has succeeded. This vote was valid, and effective against all taxable property in the parish. James v. Arkansas Southern R. Co., 110 La. 145, 34 So. 337. Act 35, § 6, 1886. Const. 1879, art. 242. By its terms the grant was for ten years from the completion of the road, the police jury adding a condition that the railroad should be completed into Winnfield within three years from the date of the vote. Afterwards the police jury extended the time to May 1, 1901, on or before which date, and before the acquisition of its right of way and ground by the plaintiff, the road was finished. It was accepted by the police jury and taxes have been levied and paid in accordance with the vote, beginning with the year 1901. The defendant was proceeding to levy on the property of the plaintiff in the parish, and says that if the Constitution of 1898 is construed to confer an exemption from this tax upon the plaintiff, it impairs the obligation of contracts, contrary to art. 1, § 10, of the Constitution of the United States.

The plaintiff says that there is no constitutional question before this court because the supreme court of Louisiana put its decision partly upon the ground that the defendant had not acquired all of its contract rights before the adoption of the Constitution of 1898. Of course, this court must satisfy itself up n that point, and therefore has jurisdiction. Sullivan v. Texas, 207 U. S. 416, 423, 52 L. ed. 274, 277, 28 Sup. Ct. Rep. 215. On the other hand, the defendant asks us to review the construction given to the state Constitution as extending the immunity granted by the above-mentioned art. 230 to special taxes like this. Upon that point, equally, of course, we follow the state court. Louisville & N. R. Co. v. Kentucky, 183 U. S. 503, 508, 46 L. ed. 298, 302, 22 Sup. Ct. Rep. 95; Missouri v. Dockery, 191 U. S. 165, 171, 48 L. ed. 133, 134, 63 L. R. A. 571, 24 Sup. Ct. Rep. 53. Leaving these preliminaries behind, we come to the point of the case.

We shall not consider whether the vote is to be regarded as having been simply an offer at the time of its passage, in consideration of acts to be done thereafter, and as having become a contract only when the road was finished, that is to say, after the Constitution of 1898 went into effect. See Wadsworth v. Eau Claire County, 102 U. S. 534, 538, 539, 26 L. ed. 221, 223, 224. We shall assume, without deciding, that it became binding at once, by statutory authority, after the analogy of a covenant (see Wisconsin & M. R. Co. v. Powers, 191 U. S. 379, 386, 48 L. ed. 229, 231, 24 Sup. Ct. Rep. 107), although liable to be defeated by the nonperformance of the condition attached. We assume also that the condition was satisfied and the right to the tax earned, and that when earned it had the same validity and force as if it had been gained before the Constitution was adopted. It appears further from what we have stated that when the right to the tax accrued, the land now in the hands of the plaintiff's road was liable to taxation. But these facts and assumptions are not enough to make out the defendant's case.

No doubt a state might limit its control over the power of a municipal body to tax by authorizing it to make contracts on the faith of its existing powers (Wolff v. New Orleans, 103 U. S. 358, 26 L. ed. 395; Louisiana ex rel. Hurbert v. New Orleans, 215 U. S. 170, 54 L. ed. 144, 30 Sup. Ct. Rep. 40), although, unless it did limit itself with a certain distinctness of implication, a subordinate body would contract subject, not paramount, to the power of the state (Manigault v. Springs, 199 U. S. 473, 480, 50 L. ed. 274, 278, 26 Sup. Ct. Rep. 127; Knoxville Water Co. v. Knoxville, 189 U. S. 434, 438, 47 L. ed. 887, 891, 23 Sup. Ct. Rep. 531). But there is no limitation by the state, and no contract by the parish that implies it. An authority given by the state to promise and levy a tax in future years on the taxable property in the parish does not purport to limit the power of the state to say what property shall be taxable when the time comes,—at least, by general regulations not aimed at aiding an evasion of the promise it has allowed. A vote by a parish to pay 5 mills on all the taxable property within its boundaries refers on its fact to a determination by the sovereign as to what that property shall be. See Arkansas Southern R. Co. *v.* Wilson, 118 La. 395, 401, 42 So. 976. The notion that the statute and the vote, separately or together, precluded the state from erecting a jail that should be free from such claims, is untenable on its face. The same reasoning allows the state to go farther, as it has done. We agree with the Supreme Court that it did not transgress the Constitution of the United States.

Decree affirmed.

———————

CINCINNATI, INDIANAPOLIS, & WESTERN RAILWAY COMPANY, Plff. in Err., *v.* CITY OF CONNERSVILLE.

(Submitted October 25, 1910.   Decided November 28, 1910.)

[31 Sup. Ct. Rep. 93.]

Constitutional Law—Due Process of Law—Imposing Special Burden on Railway Company.—The expense of constructing a railway bridge over a highway, made necessary by the action of the municipality in opening such highway through the railway company's embankment, may be cast upon the railway company without denying the due process of law guaranteed by the Federal Constitution, which requires that compensation be made when private property is taken for public use.

In error to the Supreme Court of the State of Indiana to review a judgment which affirmed a judgment of the Circuit Court of Henry County, in that state, assessing the damages of a railway company in a steet-opening proceeding, without taking into consideration the expense of constructing a bridge over the highway. Affirmed.

See same case below, 170 Ind. 316, 83 N. E. 503.

The facts are stated in the opinion.

Messrs. John B. Elam, James W. Fesler, Harvey J. Elam, and *Reuben Conner,* for plaintiff in error.

Messrs. Richard N. Elliott, Charles F. Jones, Hyatt L. Frost, and *David W. McKee,* for defendant in error.

MR. JUSTICE HARLAN delivered the opinion of the court:

The common council of Connersville, Indiana, adopted a resolution declaring that a railway embankment maintained by the Cincinnati, Indianapolis, & Western Railway Company, the plaintiff in error, across Grand avenue, in that city, obstructed pas-

Cincinnati, etc., Ry. Co. v. City of Connersville

sage between the north and south ends of the avenue; also, that such avenue should, as a matter of public necessity, be opened as a public street through said railroad embankment.

The question of the expediency, advisability, and public utility of opening up the avenue through the embankment was thereupon referred to the city commissioners, and to the council's committee on streets, alleys, and bridges, for action. Upon consideration of the matter at a time of which public notice was duly given, and after an examination of the ground sought to be appropriated, the commissioners reported that the opening of the avenue through the railroad embankment would be of public utility. The report stated that the real estate to be appropriated by the opening of the avenue was so much of the railroad embankment as extended the entire width of the avenue, as then used and opened, immediately north and south of such embankment. The tract sought to be appropriated was 66 feet square and was occupied by the embankment. The commissioners found and reported that no real estate would be damaged by the proposed opening other than that sought to be appropriated, and that the real estate abutting on both sides of the avenue would be benefited by the proposed opening of the street. There was a hearing—after due notice to all parties concerned, including the railroad company—of the question of injuries and benefits to the property to be appropriated, and of the benefits and damages to all real estate resulting from the opening of the avenue. The result of the hearing was a report by the city commissioners in favor of the opening, and the value of the real estate sought to be appropriated was estimated at $150.

The city council adopted the report of the commissioners, and appropriated for the purpose of opening Grand avenue the real estate described in the report as necessary to such opening,— the property here in question being a part of that to be appropriated. The council also directed that a certified copy of so much of the report as assessed benefits and damages be delivered to the treasurer of the city, and copied in full on the records of the council, with the minute of the adoption of the resolution describing the real estate apropriated.

There were various exceptions by the railway company and by the city, followed by a trial before a jury, which found for the railway company and assessed its damages at $800. A motion by the company for a new trial having been overruled, and a judgment entered for the defendant company, in the state court of original jurisdiction, the case was carried to the supreme court of Indiana (which affirmed the judgment), and it is now here for a re-examination as to certain Federal questions raised by the railway company.

It is not disputed at the trial that the improvement of Grand avenue, as ordered by the city of Connersville, made it neces-

Cincinnati, etc., Ry. Co. *v.* City of Connersville

sary to construct a bridge over and across the avenue as reconstructed.

The trial court gave the following, among other, instructions to the jury: "It being the duty of the defendant railroad company to construct and keep in safe and good condition all highway crossings, the defendant in this action would not be entitled to any damages for constructing the necessary crossing nor abutments and bridge for supporting its railroad over and across said street when constructed."

It refused to give this instruction asked by the railway company: "If the appropriation of the defendant's property under the proceedings set forth in this case will necessarily and proximately cause expense to the defendant in constructing a bridge to carry its railroad over the proposed street, in order that its railroad tracks may have support and its railroad may be operated as such, and as an entire line, and such construction of said bridge will be required for no other purpose, then, in determining the defendant's damages, you should consider the expense of constructing such bridge."

The railway company duly excepted to this action of the trial court, but the supreme court of Indiana held that there was no error.

There are twenty assignments of error, accompanied by an extended brief of argument. In addition, a great many authorities are cited by the learned counsel for the railway company. If we should deal with each assignment and argument separately, and enter upon a critical examination of the authorities cited, this opinion would be of undue length. We think the case is within a very narrow compass. This seems to be the view of learned counsel of the plaintiff in error, for, after a general reference to various questions raised at the trial, counsel say that "the case, upon final analysis, reduces itself to the question whether the police power [of the state] can be so applied as to require the railroad company to build the bridge without compensation."

If the railway company was not entitled to compensation on account of the construction of this bridge,—whether regard be had to the 5th or the 14th Amendments of the Constitution, or to the general reserved police power of the state,—then it is clear that the jury were not misdirected as to to what should be considered by them in estimating the damages which, under the law, the railway company was entitled to recover.

The question as to the right of the railway company to be reimbursed for any moneys necessarily expended in constructing the bridge in question is, we think, concluded by former decisions of this court; particularly by Chicago, B. & Q. R. Co. *v.* Illinois, 200 U. S. 562, 582, 584, 591, 50 L. ed. 601, 605, 606, 608, 26 Sup. Ct. Rep. 341, 4 A. & E. Ann. Cas. 1175; New Orleans Gas‑

Cincinnati, etc., Ry. Co. v. City of Connersville

light Co. *v.* Drainage Comrs., 197 U. S. 453, 49 L. ed. 831, 25 Sup. Ct. Rep. 471; New York & N. E. R. Co. *v.* Bristol, 151 U. S. 556, 571, 38 L. ed. 269, 274, 14 Sup. Ct. Rep. 437; Chicago, B. & Q. R. Co. *v.* Chicago, 166 U. S. 226, 254, 41 L. ed. 979, 990, 17 Sup. Ct. Rep. 581; Northern Transp. Co. *v.* Chicago, 99 U. S. 635, 25 L. ed. 336. See also Union Bridge Co. *v.* United States, 204 U. S. 364, 51 L. ed. 523, 27 Sup. Ct. Rep. 367. The railway company accepted its franchise from the state, subject necessarily to the condition that it would conform at its own expense to any regulations, not arbitrary in their character, as to the opening or use of streets, which had for their object the safety of the public, or the promotion of the public convenience, and which might, from time to time, be established by the municipality, when proceeding under legislative authority, within whose limits the company's business was conducted. This court has said that "the power, whether called police, governmental, or legislative, exists in each state, by appropriate enactments not forbidden by its own Constitution or by the Constitution of the United States, to regulate the relative rights and duties of all persons and corporations within its jurisdiction, and therefore to provide for the public convenience and the public good." Lake Shore & M. S. R. Co. *v.* Ohio, 173 U. S. 285, 297, 43 L. ed. 702, 706, 19 Sup. Ct. Rep. 465, 470.

Without further discussion, and without referring to other matters mentioned by counsel, we adjudge, upon the authority of former cases, that there was no error in holding that the city could not be compelled to reimburse the railway company for the cost of the bridge in question.

Judgment affirmed.

HILL *v.* MINNEAPOLIS ST. RY. CO.

(Supreme Court of Minnesota, Dec. 9, 1910.)

[128 N. W. Rep. 831.]

Negligence—Action—Pleading—General Denial.*—In personal injury actions, where the complaint is silent as to the plaintiff's negligence, contributory negligence on the part of the plaintiff is defensive matter, to be specially pleaded, and is not in issue by a general denial; distinguishing St. Anthony Falls Water Power Co. *v.* Eastman, 20 Minn. 277 (Gil. 249), and Hocum *v.* Weitherick, 22 Minn. 152, wherein the rule is settled that the contributory negligence of the plaintiff is put in issue by a general denial, whenever the complaint negatives the plaintiff's negligence.

Carriers—Carriage of Passengers—Care Required.†—The degree of care to be exercised by a common carrier with reference to its passengers is the highest degree of care and foresight consistent with the conduct of its business, or consistent with the practical operation of its road. Fewings *v.* Mendenhall, 88 Minn. 336, 93 N. W. 127, 60 L. R. A. 601, 97 Am. St. Rep. 519; Campbell *v.* Duluth & Northeastern R. Co., 107 Minn. 358, 120 N. W. 375, 22 L. R. A. (N. S) 190. A common carrier is required to take every reasonable precaution for the safety of its passengers. Smith *v.* St. P. City Ry. Co., 32 Minn. 1, 18 N. W. 827, 50 Am. Rep. 550. That degree of care which would be exercised by the ordinary prudent person under the same circumstances is not the test applicable to a motorman of a street car, and it was error to so charge.

(Syllabus by the Court.)

Appeal from District Court, Hennepin County; Andrew Holt, Judge.

Actions by Elizabeth Hill and by Archibald Hill against the Minneapolis Street Railway Company. Judgment for defendant, and plaintiffs appeal. Reversed.

Mead & Robertson, for appellants.

John F. Dahl, W. O. Stout, and *D. R. Frost,* for respondent.

LEWIS, J. Plaintiff claims to have been injured by the negligent act of the motorman in closing the gate too soon while she was in the act of boarding a street car. A verdict was returned for defendant, and the case comes here for the consideration of two propositions: Was the defendant, under the pleadings, en-

---

*See first foot-note of Chicago, etc., R. Co. *v.* Cook (Wyo.), 33 R. R. R. 530, 56 Am. & Eng. R. Cas., N. S., 530.
†First foot-note of Gardner *v.* Metropolitan St. R. Co. (Mo.), 36 R. R. R. 448, 59 Am. & Eng. R. Cas., N. S., 448.

Hill *v.* Minneapolis St. Ry. Co

titled to have submitted to the jury the question of plaintiff's contributory negligence? and the correctness of the charge as to the degree of care required by defendant.

1. The complaint did not negative the negligence of the plaintiff, and the answer was a general denial. The question seems never to have been definitely settled as to whether, under this state of pleadings, evidence of contributory negligence on the part of a plaintiff was receivable. We believe the subject was first considered in the case of St. Anthony Falls Water Power Co. *v.* Eastman, 20 Minn. 277 (Gil. 249). In that case the complaint negatived the negligence of plaintiff, and it was held that a general denial put in issue the plaintiff's contributory negligence. This decision was approved in Hocum *v.* Weitherick, 22 Minn. 152, where the complaint alleged that the injury was caused by the negligence of the defendant and without the fault of the plaintiff; but it was held that the burden was on the defendant to prove the contributory negligence of plaintiff, even where the complaint stated that he was free from fault. It has generally been assumed that these two cases established the rule that general denial raised the issue whether the complaint negatived plaintiff's negligence or not. But such conclusion is not warranted by an examination of the records. If the contributory negligence of plaintiff is defensive matter, and the burden rests on the defendant to prove it, he must necessarily plead it as a defense, unless the plaintiff had tendered the issue by alleging that the plaintiff was without fault. This particular feature of the question was not embraced in the two decisions.

In order to clear up the confusion, it must be definitely understood that the decision in the first case cited merely holds that a general denial puts plaintiff's negligence in issue when the complaint alleges that he is free from negligence, and that the Hocum Case simply holds that under such a state of pleadings the burden is still on the defendant to prove the contributory negligence of plaintiff. Of course, the plaintiff fails to make out a cause of action against the defendant if, in attempting to prove the negligence of defendant, he proves his own negligence. The subject came up in O'Malley *v.* St. Paul, Minneapolis & Manitoba Ry. Co., 43 Minn. 289, 45 N. W. 440. The complaint in that action also negatived contributory negligence on the part of the plaintiff; but the answer alleged certain specific facts which were claimed to constitute negligence on the part of the child which had been injured, and on the part of his parents. The only question decided was that the defendant was restricted in the offer of evidence to the specific facts pleaded. Hoblit *v.* Minneapolis Street Ry. Co., 126 N. W. 407, was decided in accordance with St. Anthony Falls W. P. Co. *v.* Eastman, supra., although that case was not mentioned. In the case of Woodruff *v.* Bearman Fruit Co., 108 Minn. 118, 121 N. W. 426, the complaint was

Hill *v.* Minneapolis St. Ry. Co

silent as to the negligence of the plaintiff, and the answer was a general denial. It was assumed that the question had not been settled; but the case went off on another point. The rule that a general denial puts the plaintiff's contributory negligence in issue, when the complaint negatives such negligence, has become too well settled to be disturbed; but, when the complaint does not negative the plaintiff's negligence, that issue becomes wholly defensive, and must be pleaded and proved.

2. With reference to the degree of care required of the street railway company, the court instructed the jury as follows: "The defendant is required to use the highest degree of care for the safety of the passengers; that is, the highest degree of care, taking into consideration all the circumstances that it is a common carrier and that it is its duty to carry persons, not only safely, but also to carry them expeditiously and to accommodate the public in that way. Taking all the circumstances into consideration, it is, in view of these circumstances, the duty of the defendant to exercise the highest degree of care for the safety of its passengers, and that includes the duty of giving passengers reasonable time and opportunity to board cars safely. * * * In determining whether or not the motorman was negligent, as claimed by the plaintiff, or in determining whether plaintiff herself was negligent, as claimed by defendant, I have but one rule that I can give to you to go by in determining these questions, and that is this: A person is said to be negligent when he does that which the ordinary prudent person placed in the same circumstances would not have done; or when he omits to do that which the ordinary prudent person placed in the same situation would not have omitted to do, then he is negligent." At the close of the charge, counsel for plaintiff took exception in the following language: "I also take exception to the definition of negligence as applied to this case that the court gave, my idea being they are bound to the highest degree of care, and towards the last of the court's charge I think the court charged that the motorman was only bound to use ordinary care." The Court: "I will state to the jury this: I said that the motorman is bound to use the care that the ordinary person would do in the same circumstances; that is, as motorman, where the motorman is required to use the highest degree of care for the safety of the passengers, that is the circumstances under which he serves, and of course the company is responsible for the acts of the motorman." No further exceptions were taken, and the question is: Did the court present to the jury a reasonably clear definition of the degree of care required of the company?

It is the law in this state that, while a carrier of passengers is not an insurer of their safety, it is required to take every reasonable precaution for their safety. Thus, in Smith *v.* St. P. City R. Co., 32 Minn. 1, 18 N. W. 827, 50 Am. Rep. 550, the rule is

Hill *v*. Minneapolis St. Ry. Co

stated ·as follows: "Street railway companies, as carriers of passengers for hire, are bound to exercise the highest degree of care and diligence consistent with the nature of their undertaking, and are responsible for the slightest neglect." In Fewings *v*. Mendenhall, 88 Minn. 336, 93 N. W. 127, 60 L. R. A. 601, 97 Am. St. Rep. 519, it was said: "A carrier of passengers is charged with the highest degree of care and foresight consistent with the orderly conduct of its business; * * * but it is charged with ordinary care and prudence only to guard against the lawless acts of third persons not under its direction or control." In Campbell *v*. Duluth & Northeastern Ry. Co., 107 Minn. 358, 120 N. W. 375, 22 L. R. A. (N. S.) 190, the rule was stated thus: "A railroad as a common carrier is required to exercise the highest degree of care, skill, and foresight for the safety of passengers consistent with the practical operation of its road." The company would not comply with its duty if it employed ordinary persons to perform the difficult and technical work of controlling a street car. Such employees are required to be experienced, and to have acquired skill in the control of the cars and the manipulation of the gates. It was the duty of the motorman to exercise the highest degree of care consistent with the proper operation of the car. The care which would be exercised by the "ordinary prudent person" in acting as motorman would not be the proper test. No doubt the learned trial court had in mind that degree of care which would ordinarily be exercised by one skilled in the business of operating cars. But, unfortunately, the reference to the "ordinary prudent person" was misleading.

Reversed.

Jansen *v.* Minneapolis & St. L. Ry. Co.

(Supreme Court of Minnesota, Dec. 9, 1910.)

[128 N. W. Rep. 826.]

Carriers—Duty to Passengers—Assault by Other Passengers.*—
Under the doctrine of implied police power, a common carrier is
bound to exercise the utmost diligence in maintaining order and in
guarding its passengers against assaults by other passengers which
might reasonably be anticipated or naturally expected to occur.

Assault and Battery—Damages—Mental Suffering—Humiliation.†
—Not only bodily pain, but mental suffering, anxiety, suspense, and
the sense of wrong from insult, connected with bodily injury may
be considered as an element of the injury, for which damages for
compensation may be allowed. .

Carriers—Assault on Passenger—Damages.—Under the facts of
this case, a verdict of $200, as reduced by the trial court, is not ex-
cessive.

(Syllabus by the Court.)

Appeal from Municipal Court of Minneapolis; C. L. Smith,
Judge.

Action by W. B. G. Jansen against the Minneapolis & St.
Louis Railway Company. Verdict for plaintiff. From an
order denying a motion for judgment notwithstanding the verdict or a new trial, defendant appeals. Affirmed.

W. H. Bremner and *Geo. W. Seevers,* for appellant.
Eliza P. Evans, for respondent.

Lewis, J. The complaint alleges that, while respondent was
being carried in appellant's railway passenger train, a drunken
man, whose name was unknown to respondent, assaulted, struck,
and abused him; that respondent appealed to the conductor in
charge of the train for assistance and protection, but he wrongfully and unlawfully declined and refused to interfere or in
any manner assist to protect respondent against the treatment of
the unknown man, which treatment continued for a long time

---

*For the authorities in this series on the subject of the duty of
railroad to protect its passengers against fellow passengers, see
foot-note of Widener *v.* Philadelphia Rapid Transit Co. (Pa.), 34
R. R. R. 6, 57 Am. & Eng. R. Cas., N. S., 6; first foot-note of Norris *v.* Southern Ry. (S. Car.), 33 R. R. R. 208, 56 Am. & Eng. R.
Cas., N. S., 208.
†For the authorities in this series on the subject of the right to
recover for mental suffering, in actions for personal injuries, see
last foot-note of Caldvell *v.* Northern Pac. Ry. Co. (Wash.), 35 R.
R. R. 161, 58 Am. & Eng. R. Cas., N. S., 161; foot-note of St. Louis,
etc., R. Co. *v.* Buckner (Ark.), 33 R. R. R. 780, 57 Am. & Eng. R.
Cas., N. S., 780.

Jansen *v.* Minneapolis & St. L. Ry. Co

after the conductor was appealed to. The jury returned a verdict for $300, and the court filed an order granting a new trial unless respondent should accept the sum of $200 in lieu of the amount returned by the verdict. Respondent accepted the reduction, and appeal was taken from the order denying the motion for judgment notwithstanding the verdict or for a new trial.

Appellant offered no evidence, and that offered in behalf of respondent was to the effect that respondent, who is an elderly Catholic priest, boarded the smoking car of the appellant's train at Excelsior for the purpose of riding to Minneapolis. While he was in the act of closing the door, an intoxicated man, who was one of the passengers, slapped him over the head with his hat and hand. Respondent pushed him to one side, and took the only vacant seat, which was near the middle of the car. The conductor came through immediately after to collect fares, and respondent complained of what had occurred, whereupon the conductor, replied, "What can you do when the party has the whiskey in him?" and then went back to the baggage car, without saying anything to the intoxicated person. After a little while the attack was repeated, and again a third time, and some of the passengers seemed to consider it a joke, and laughed at the performance, until some friends of respondent in another part of the car were attracted and stopped the disorder.

Appellant claims that it owed no duty to respondent under the circumstances, and relies upon the case of Mullan *v.* Wisconsin Central Ry. Co., 46 Minn. 474, 49 N. W. 249. It was there said that railway carriers are bound to exercise the highest degree of care and diligence in the conduct and management of their business to prevent accidents or injuries to passengers on their trains, and that in respect to the danger of injuries from the misconduct of fellow passengers the obligation of the carrier is qualified or limited by the nature of its relation to the passenger; that it must exercise the greatest diligence consistent with its obligations to the public and all the passengers, and neglect no reasonable precaution to protect passengers from insult or injury from its servants or fellow passengers; but as respects passengers there is no such privity between them and the carrier as to make the latter directly liable for their wrongful acts, and it can only interfere under an implied police power to prevent an abuse of their privileges as passengers; that the carrier is bound to exercise the utmost diligence in maintaining order and guarding the passengers against violence, from whatever source arising, which might reasonably be anticipated or naturally be expected to occur, in view of all the circumstances and the number and character of the persons on board. This, no doubt, is a correct statement of the principles of law applicable in such cases; but in that case the trial court was justified in dismissing it, for the reason that the plaintiff provoked the attack which resulted in his being assaulted by a fellow passenger.

Jansen *v.* Minneapolis & St. L. Ry. Co

In the present case, respondent had a right to assume that the people whom he found riding in the smoking car would be orderly and would not interfere with him as a passenger. He was just as much entitled to take a seat and remain unmolested in that car as in any other car on the train. He not only did nothing to aggravate or provoke the assault upon him, but, on the contrary, simply tried to ward off the blows and prevent any serious injury. The man who assaulted him may have had no serious intention of doing him bodily harm. He was intoxicated, and in that condition which, no doubt, caused him to feel that he was doing something smart for the entertainment of his companions. But pulling off a man's hat and striking him on his head, with his hat or hand, even for the purpose of merely creating amusement, is no less an assault than if his intention had been to do him physical harm. If, after his attention had been called to the disturbance, the conductor had taken reasonable precautions to prevent its continuance, then there would be no liability. The evidence is to the effect that he did nothing to stop the disturbance. On the contrary, he left the car with the remark that nothing could be done with the man with whiskey in him, which was equivalent to saying that the passenger would have to put up with such annoyances as drunkenness. He was informed of what had been going on. He knew the condition of the man, knew that he was drunk, and gave that as an excuse for not interfering. So, in leaving the car without doing anything to prevent a renewal of the disturbance, it would be fair to assume that he did not intend to take any steps to interfere, and that he expected respondent to put up with it. We think the case comes within the rules of law laid down in the Mullen Case and in Lucy *v.* Chicago Great Western Ry. Co., 64 Minn. 7, 65 N. W. 744, 31 L. R. A. 551. It was a question of fact for the jury to determine whether or not the company expressed that degree of care for its passengers which was reasonably practicable under the circumstances.

Granting that respondent was not permanently or seriously injured, that alone is not a prerequisite for the recovery of damages for an assault of that character. Wounded feelings, or humiliation, are as much grounds for damages as physical injury. Such treatment may cause acute mental anguish, and the extent of such suffering naturally differs with the disposition and condition of different persons. An elderly man of the clerical profession might feel much more humiliated, and feel the loss of protection under such circumstances more, than one accustomed to mingle with such rough characters. It is the general rule that not only bodily pain, but mental suffering, anxiety, suspense, fright, sense of wrong from insult or injury, connected with bodily injury, may be considered, when the facts will justify it, as an element of the injury for which damages for compen-

Nelson v. Illinois Cent. R. Co

sation should be allowed. Sutherland on Damages, vol. 3, p. 259; Head v. Railway Co., 79 Ga. 358, 7 S. E. 217, 11 Am. St. Rep. 434; Mentzer v. W. U. Tel. Co., 93 Iowa, 752, 62 N. W. 1, 28 L. R. A. 72, 57 Am. St. Rep. 294. It is unnecessary to consider whether mental anguish alone, without some personal injury, can be the basis of damages; but under the evidence there was undoubtedly some physical injury, although not of a serious or lasting character. ●

This is not a case which requires the return of only nominal damages. The injury cannot be said to be so trivial as to justify no compensatory damages, and the amount as fixed by the court, considering respondent's age, his profession, and the manner in which he was treated, cannot be considered as excessive.

Affirmed.

NELSON v. ILLINOIS CENT. R. CO.

(Supreme Court of Mississippi, Dec. 5, 1910.)

[53 So. Rep. 619.]

Carriers—Passengers—Sleeping Cars—Negligence of Sleeping Car Company—Liability of Railroad Company.*—Agents and servants of a sleeping car company on its cars, which are attached to and become part of the system of transportation used by a railroad company, are agents of the railroad company; and if a passenger on such a car is injured by the negligence of servants of the sleeping car company, the railroad company is liable in the same way and to the same extent as if the injury had occurred on its ordinary passenger coaches.

Carriers—Passengers—Sleeping Cars—Loss of Baggage—Liability of Railroad Company.*—A railroad company, which uses cars of a sleeping car company on its trains to carry out its contracts of transportation, is liable for the loss, by negligence of servants of the sleeping car company, of hand baggage of a passenger carried with him on such a car under a contract with the sleeping car company, although that company may also be liable therefor; the same duty to protect the person and baggage of the passenger resting on both companies under their separate contracts, and their negligent failure to perform such duty, resulting in a single indivisible injury, making them joint tort-feasors.

Torts—Joint Tort-Feasors.—Where two or more persons owe a common duty to another, they are jointly and severally liable for injuries caused to such other by a common neglect of such duty.

---

*See last foot-note of Taber v. Seaboard Air Line Ry. (S. Car.), 36 R. R. R. 466, 59 Am. & Eng. R. Cas., N. S., 466; Denver & R. G. R. Co. v. Derry (Colo.), 36 R. R. R. 141, 59 Am. & Eng. R. Cas., N. S., 141.

Nelson v. Illinois Cent. R. Co

Judgment—Conclusiveness—Judgment against Joint Tort-Feasor.
—Judgments conclude only parties and privies, and there is no such
privity between joint tort-feasors as to permit a judgment in favor
of one of them for the injury to be pleaded as a bar to an action
against the other; so that a judgment in favor of a sleeping car company, in an action against it by a passenger for loss of baggage in
the sleeping car, does not bar a subsequent action against the railroad company for the same loss, for which both companies were
jointly and severally liable.

Torts—Joint and Several Liability.—When the negligence of two
or more persons concurs in producing a single indivisible injury,
such persons are jointly and severally liable, although there was no
common duty, common design, or concert of action.

Appeal from Circuit Court, Hinds County; W. A. Henry,
Judge.

Action by H. T. Nelson against the Illinois Central Railroad
Company. From a judgment dismissing the declaration, plaintiff appeals. Reversed and remanded.

Watkins & Watkins, for appellant.
Mayes & Longstreet, for appellee.

MAYES, C. J.   While traveling over the line of railway owned
by the Illinois Central Railroad Company, H. T. Nelson claims
to have lost a suit case and contents, through the negligence of
the company, valued at $227, or thereabouts, and the object of
this suit is to compel reimbursement by the company. The cause
is here on the pleadings, and the case made is about as follows,
viz.: Mr. Nelson alleges in his declaration that he procured
transportation over the Illinois Central Railroad from Memphis,
Tenn., to Durant, Miss. At the same time he purchased his
railroad ticket, and from the same agent, Nelson alleges that he
also purchased a sleeping car ticket entitling him to a berth on a
sleeping car from Memphis to Durant; the sleeping car being
attached to and being a part of the train. Nelson further alleges
in his declaration that he boarded the train at Memphis, bound
for Durant, at about 11:30 p. m., entered the sleeping car, and
was assigned to "lower No. 4 in a car named Saffola." Nelson
further alleges that he had with him a suit case containing
articles of necessary apparel for the contemplated journey, and
of the value, including the suit case, of the sum stated above;
that when he retired he left the suit case and contents by the side
of his berth, and on reaching his destination it was discovered
that the case and contents were gone; and that because of the
negligence, willful conduct, or gross negligence on the part of the
company, etc., the case and its contents were lost. The railroad
company filed the general issue and two special pleas. The first
special plea was to the effect that Nelson instituted a suit on the

Nelson v. Illinois Cent. R. Co

same cause of action in the justice of the peace court in the state of Tennessee; that this court had full and final jurisdiction, and that the suit was instituted there in June, 1909, long prior to the bringing of the suit then on trial; that the suit brought in Tennessee was upon the identical cause of action, was instituted against the Pullman Palace Car Company, and resulted in a judgment against Nelson and in favor of the Pullman Company; that afterwards Nelson appealed the case from the judgment of the justice of the peace to the circuit court of the same county in Tennessee, this appellate court having full jurisdiction of the cause so appealed; and that court again rendered a judgment against Nelson and in favor of the Pullman Company. Wherefore it is claimed by this plea that the cause is res adjudicata and should be dismissed. The second special plea alleges that the suit should not be maintained because, at the time his baggage is claimed to have been lost or destroyed, Nelson was a general passenger, traveling upon an ordinary ticket, and his loss did not occur in an ordinary passenger coach of the railroad company, nor in the baggage car; that the suit case was never placed in the care or custody of any employee of the railroad company, and it did not have any notice of the existence of the baggage; that Nelson went into a sleeping car of the Pullman Company, and paid to it a special consideration for additional accommodation and protection, and placed himself and his hand baggage specially in the custody and care of the employees of the Pullman Company; and that the baggage was then lost while the plaintiff was in the care of the Pullman Company. To these two pleas a demurrer was interposed, the effect of which was to allege that neither of the pleas constituted any defense. The demurrers were overruled, and, Nelson declining to plead further, final judgment was taken, dismissing the declaration, from which judgment an appeal is prosecuted here.

It is our judgment that neither of the pleas offered by the railroad company presented any defense to the suit of Nelson, and the demurrer to both pleas should have been sustained. The agents and servants of the sleeping car company are undoubtedly the agents of the railroad company. The cars of the sleeping car company are attached to and become a part of the system of transportation used by the railroad company in carrying out its contracts of transportation. When a passenger is injured by any neglect on the part of the sleeping car company, and while a passenger on same, the railroad company is liable in the same way and to the same extent as it would be if the injury had occurred on one of its ordinary passenger coaches. As is said in the case of Railroad Co. v. Roy, 102 U. S. 451, 26 L. Ed. 141: "The law will not permit a railroad company, engaged in the business of carrying persons for hire, through any device or arrangement with a sleeping car company, whose cars are used

Nelson *v.* Illinois Cent. R. Co

by and constitute a part of the train of the railroad company, to throw off the duty of providing proper means for the safe conveyance of those whom it has agreed to convey. 2 Kent. Com. (12th Ed.) 600; 2 Pars. Cont. (6th Ed.) 218, 219; Story, Bailments, §§ 601, 601a, 602; Cooley, Torts, 642; Wharton, Negl. (2d Ed.) § 627 et seq.; Chit. Carriers, 256 et seq.; and cases cited by the authors." Because the railroad company adopts the sleeping car as a part of its train, uses it to carry out its contracts of transportation, and invites its passengers to go into and avail of its comforts when traveling upon its line of railway, the sleeping car company and the railroad have no distinction so far as the passenger is concerned when he seeks redress against the railroad company for injury received through the negligence of the sleeping car company. But, because the railroad company may become liable for the negligence of the servants of the sleeping car company, it does not follow that the sleeping car company may not be liable severally and jointly. The passenger not only has a contract of transportation with the railroad company, but he also has a contract with the sleeping car company. By these two contracts each company imposes on itself the same duty of protection to the person and property of the passenger, and each may be sued separately, or both may be sued jointly. Every duty that the sleeping car company owes a passenger is also a duty that the railroad company owes; but the duty of the railroad and sleeping car company may not be the same when the injury results from the negligent operation of the train, as this seems to be a duty peculiarly assumed by the railroad. It is manifest that the same duty rests on the sleeping car company to protect the person and baggage of Nelson as was imposed on the railroad company, and the converse of this proposition is true. Both the sleeping car company and the railroad company had separate contracts with the passenger; each receiving from him an independent consideration. The sleeping car company was both the agent of the railroad company and also engaged in its own enterprise, taking valuable consideration therefor.

While it is not alleged that this injury occurred in this state, it is not amiss to note that, by section 195 of the Constitution of 1890 of the state, sleeping car companies are made common carriers and liable as such. This simply shows that the laws of this state recognize that there may be an independent liability on the part of the sleeping car companies under their contract of carriage, as well as the agents of the railroad company. The negligence complained of was the loss of appellant's baggage. The negligent failure of both companies to perform their duty to appellant resulted in a single and indivisible injury, for which either or both are liable. In such case, as is stated in the case of Walton, Witten & Graham *v.* Miller, 109 Va. 210, 214, 63

Nelson *v* Illinois Cent. R. Co

S. E. 458, 460, 132 Am. St. Rep. 908, 911, these two companies
are joint tort-feasors. As to when persons are joint tort-feasors, it
is stated in that part of opinion to be found in the above-cited case,
citing many authorities, that: " 'In respect to negligent injuries,
there is considerable difference of opinion as to what constitutes
joint liability. No comprehensive general rule can be formulated
which will harmonize all the authorities. The authorities are,
perhaps, not agreed beyond this: That where two or more owe
to another a common duty, and by a common neglect of that
duty such other person is injured, then there is a joint tort, with
joint liability. The weight of authority will, we think, support
the more general proposition that, when the negligence of two
or more persons concurs in producing a single indivisible injury,
then such persons are jointly and severally liable, although there
was no common duty, common design, or concert of action.' 1
Cooley on Torts (3d Ed.) p. 246."

That the sleeping car company is liable for the loss of a passenger's personal baggage, if it fail to exercise proper care to
guard the same, is settled by many authorities. Pullman Company v. Green, 128 Ga. 142, 57 S. E. 233, 119 Am. St. Rep. 368.
That the railroad company is alike liable is equally well settled.
See Nashville & Chattanooga Ry. Co. *v.* Lillie, 112 Tenn. 331, 78
S. W. 1055, 105 Am. St. Rep. 947. If both are liable, it follows
that they are jointly and severally liable, and where the joint
and several liability is conceded the controlling principles of law
become easy of application. In the case of Pullman Company *v.*
Kelly, 86 Miss. 87, 38 South. 317, this court held "that a sleeping car company owes to all passengers whom it receives all the
obligations and duties which a common carrier owes to passengers, except, of course, that a sleeping car company, not controlling
the motive power, and not having the management of the train
of which its car is a part, cannot be held liable to its
passengers for injuries occurring to them by reason
of any defect or failure in the machinery which furnishes the
motive power, or by reason of any want of care, miscarriage, or
default in the management of the train;" but, because it is the
agent of the railroad company, the latter company is also liable
for every neglect that makes the sleeping car company liable. In
Cooley on Torts (2d Ed.) p. 159, it is said that, where an injury
is produced by joint tort-feasors "the party injured may bring
separate suits against the wrongdoers, and proceed to judgment
in each, and that no bar arises as to any of them until satisfaction is received." In the same authority, on page 157, it is said:
"Whatever may have been the reason for proceeding at first
against less than the whole, it is conceded on all sides that a previous suit against one or more is no bar to a new suit against the
others, even though the first suit be pending, or have proceeded
to judgment, when the second is brought." Of course, where

Nelson *v.* Illinois Cent. R. Co

there is but one injury, there can be but one satisfaction for that injury; but there is a satisfaction the injured party may bring as many separate suits for the injury as there are joint wrongdoers, and in the end elect to take the highest assessment of damage made by any judgment. Cooley on Torts (2d Ed.) p. 159; Marriott *v.* Williams, 152 Cal. 705, 93 Pac. 875, 125 Am. St. Rep. 87; French *v.* Boston Coal Co., 195 Mass. 334, 81 N. E. 265, 11 L. R. A. (N. S.) 993, 122 Am. St. Rep. 257; Cleveland, etc., Ry. Co. *v.* Hilligoss, 171 Ind. 417, 86 N. E. 485, 131 Am. St. Rep. 258.

The suit by Nelson against the sleeping car company in the state of Tennessee, resulting in a judgment in favor of the sleeping car company, cannot be used as a bar to this suit against the railroad company. Judgments conclude only parties and privies, and there is no such privy between joint tort-feasors as would allow one to plea in bar to a suit against him a judgment acquitting another of responsibility for the same act. Each is liable independently of the other, and the utmost that any joint tort-feasor can ask is that there be but one satisfaction allowed for the same and indivisible cause of action, and this the law guarantees. That a judgment in favor of one joint wrongdoer is no bar to a separate action against another was settled in this state by the case of Railroad Co. *v.* Clarke, 85 Miss. 697, 38 South. 97. See also 24 Am. & Eng. Enc. Law (2d Ed.) p. 765. In the Clarke Case, supra, this court said: "The right of action which the appellee had was both joint and several, and each defendant was liable for the whole· damage. * * * The appellee could have instituted suit for the entire amount of damage which he had suffered against either of the parties, or against both, as he chose to do. Had the verdict been against both, this would neither have lessened nor increased the liability of appellant for the entire judgment. Nor is the fact that the jury, no matter by what motive actuated, failed to find a verdict against appellant's codefendant in any wise prejudicial to the rights which may exist between appellant and its codefendant, growing out of the subject-matter of this suit." There may be cases in which a judgment in a suit in which an agent or servant is a party may be conclusive for or against the principal; but we are only interested in the pursuit of this question to an extent sufficient to say that, if there are such cases, this is not one of them.

Reversed and remanded.

MAY v. SHREVEPORT TRACTION CO.

(Supreme Court of Louisiana, Nov. 28, 1910.)

[53 So. Rep. 671.]

Carriers—Carriage of Passengers—Assignment of White and Colored Races to Separate Compartment.—The discretion vested in street railway companies and their officers and agents by Act No. 64 of 1902, with regard to the assignment of the white and colored races, respectively, to separate compartments in street cars, is to be exercised by them at their own peril, and they, and not the sufferers, are liable for the consequences of their mistakes or their abuse of such discretion.

Carriers—Carriage of Passengers—Duty to Protect Passengers.*— A carrier of passengers is as much bound to protect them from humiliation and insult as from physical injury.

Carriers—Carriage of Passengers—Insult of Passenger by Conductor—Right of Recovery.—To apply the term "negro" to a white person is humiliating and insulting, and a suggestive question, such as, "Don't you belong over there?" addressed to a white person, by the conductor of a street car, who points to the seats reserved for negroes, is but little less so. In either case, and whether the language used be heard by others or not, an action in damages will lie against the carrier.

(Syllabus by the Court.)

Appeal from First Judicial District Court, Parish of Caddo; A. J. Murff, Judge.

Action by Mrs. Emma May against the Shreveport Traction Company. Judgment for defendant, and plaintiff appeals. Reversed and rendered.

John B. Files and *Hugh C. Fisher,* for appellant.
Wise, Randolph & Rendall, for appellee.

Statement of the Case.

MONROE, J. Plaintiff sues for damages, on the ground, as stated in her petition, that she boarded one of defendant's cars, in which there were a number of passengers. and, having taken her seat in the compartment assigned to white passengers, and paid her fare, she was asked by the conductor, "Don't you belong over there?" pointing to the seats reserved for negro pas-

---

*For the authorities in this series on the subject of the liability of a railroad company on account of insults by employees to passengers. see foot-note of Pierce *v.* St. Louis, etc., R. Co. (Ark.), 36 R. R. R. 480, 59 Am. & Eng. R. Cas., N. S., 480; first foot-note of Caldwell *v.* Northern Pac. Ry. Co. (Wash.), 35 R. R. R. 161, 58 Am. & Eng. R. Cas., N. S., 161.

May *v.* Shreveport Traction Co   •

sengers, and designated by a large sign, marked "Colored;" that petitioner, with great surprise, asked him what he meant, and the conductor repeated, in a loud and rough tone of voice, "You are in the wrong seat; you belong over there," again pointing to the seats set aside for negro passengers. She alleges that the attention of the passengers was attracted; that they stared at her with suspicion and contept; and that she felt much humiliated and embarrassed. She further alleges that she caused the conductor to be arrested; that he was fined; that defendant's manager. and trainmaster, and the same conductor, thereafter, further abused her by declaring, publicly, that she frequently rode in the colored compartment of the car, and have libeled her by causing to be published, in a newspaper, the statement:

"Mrs. May boarded McCoy's car, on Thursday afternoon (Dec. 24, 1908) and took her seat behind the 'colored' sign."

And by publishing in another paper the statement:

"Mrs. May, once before, rode in the negro department."

She alleges that she is of the Caucasian race, and that the matter complained of has injured her in various ways, which she sets out in detail. None of the passengers to whom the plaintiff refers in her petition appeared as witnesses in the case, save a lady, who testified that she was seated near the front of the car, whilst plaintiff was near the rear end, and that, though she heard plaintiff "jawing" a good deal at the conductor, she did not hear what he said. Plaintiff's version of the matter, as given in her testimony, differs from that given in her petition, in that she says that the conductor, having received her fare, said:

" 'You belong over there.' And I was greatly surprised, and I asked him what he said. I am hard of hearing. And he goes on up the car and receives two more fares, and, as he came back. I says: 'Young man, what did you say? What do you mean?' And there was a gentleman sitting over on the seat opposite me, and I looked over at that man, and I says: 'That man is drunk or crazy—must be crazy.' This fustrated me, so I got off the car and went and had him arrested—went to Judge Fullilove's office."

At another time she tells the story as follows:

"When he came around to me and got my fare, he received the fare. and says, 'You belong over there.' I could not hear very good. and I says, 'What did you say?' He did not answer me, but went on and received two more fares. and, when he came back, I approached him again. and I says: 'What do you mean?' He says: 'You are in the wrong seat. You belong over there. You are a negro woman.' Pointing to the negro seats, seats reserved for negroes, he says: 'You are a negro woman.' "

Our conclusion. after considering the statements above given, the allegations of the petition, which were predicated upon information obtained from plaintiff, the testimony of Messrs.

Wise and Freyer (of the law firm by which defendant was represented before Judge Fullilove), the testimony of the judge, himself, as to the "trend" of the conductor's testimony on the occasion of his trial in the city court, and the testimony of the conductor, as given in this case, is that what took place was about as follows: Plaintiff, having taken her seat in that part of the car assigned to white passengers, and having paid her fare, was asked by the conductor, "Don't you belong over there?" He at the same time pointing to the seats, behind the sign "Colored," intended for the use of negroes. Plaintiff being a little deaf, and surprised at the question, as she understood it, said to him, "What did you say? what do you mean?" The conductor, however, moved on towards the front of the car, and collected some other fares, and, on his return, plaintiff repeated her question, and he repeated his, probably in a somewhat louder voice, again pointing to the seats reserved for negroes. Plaintiff had, by that time, become considerably excited, and the conductor was disposed to drop the subject, and did so, so far as he was allowed, but plaintiff continued talking at, or to, him, until, within a few minutes, she got off the car, and, as she states, went to the city court and preferred a charge upon which the conductor was arrested, and at a hearing, some days later, was fined $5. When notified of the charge against him, the conductor went to the police station and surrendered. Whereupon defendant's manager signed a bond for his appearance, and, on that occasion, we think, he told the manager, in the presence of others, that he had seen, or thought he had seen, plaintiff, on a previous occasion, riding in the negro end of the car, but, being asked whether he could prove it, said he could not. It seems probable that the statement, to the effect that she had so ridden, as published in the papers, originated in that way. No attempt was made on the trial of the case to substantiate the statement, save that the conductor testified that he had seen either the plaintiff or some one who looked like her riding in the negro end of the car. We find no reason to doubt that there were passengers in the car who heard the conductor ask the question here complained of, and who understood the significance of his gestures, in pointing to the seats behind the sign; the fact that the lady who testified on behalf of the company did not hear, or see, him, being natural enough, as she was seated at the other end of the car (which was in motion and making considerable noise) with her face in the other direction. Why no other witnesses were produced we are, of course, unable to say, except that it appears that plaintiff is a very poor woman and did not have the facilities for looking up witnesses and inducing them to come into court that are possessed by others differently situated. We do not find that plaintiff has been injured, in the estimation of her friends and acquaintances, by the incident here in question; but there is no

May *v.* Shreveport Traction Co

doubt that she was very much mortified, at the time, and has been very much distressed and disturbed since. The question, then, is: Do the questions and acts of the conductor, all the circumstances considered, furnish her a sufficient cause of action for damages against defendant? That question was first submitted to a jury, who disagreed over it. It was then submitted to the judge of another division of the district court, who arrived at the facts, as we have done, by reading the typewritten testimony, and answered the question in the negative.

Opinion.

The learned judge a quo has summed up the facts in an able written opinion, and there is but little difference between us on that subject. His view, however, was: That, the conductor was required by law to assign white people to one part of the car and colored people to another; that it was necessary for him, in some way, to obtain the information required for the discharge of that function; and that the method adopted was the least objectionable—the conclusion being that the incidental hurt, sustained by plaintiff should be regarded as damnum absque injuria. We are unable to concur in that conclusion. It is true that, where the law imposes a duty upon an individual or an officer, the courts are usually disposed to be lenient with regard to mistakes committed in the honest effort to discharge such duty; but the rule, which obtains wherever justice is recognized and administered, nevertheless, is that he who makes the mistake, and not the victim, shall, so far as practicable, be made to suffer the consequences. It is thus written in our law:

"Every act whatever of man that causes damages to another obliges him by whose fault it happened to repair it." Civ. Code, art. 2315.

The particular statute relied on by defendant as imposing a duty upon it, and as thereby exempting it from liability for injury to others whilst attempting, in good faith, to discharge that duty, is Act No. 64 of 1902, which requires that all street railway companies shall provide separate accommodations on their cars for the white and colored races, and that:

"No person or persons shall be permitted to occupy seats in cars, or compartments, other than the ones assigned to them on account of the race they belong to."

The act imposes a penalty upon the passenger who insists on going into a compartment, to which, by race, he does not belong, and a penalty upon the officer of the railway company who insists upon assigning the passenger to such compartment, and it empowers and requires the officers of "such street cars to assign each passenger to the car or compartment used for the race to which such passenger belongs." The officer, therefore, who insists upon assigning the passenger to the wrong compartment,

May v. Shreveport Traction Co

violates the law, and thereby subjects himself to its penalty, of a fine or imprisonment, as, also, to an action in damages, by the passenger. Upon the other hand, if he does not insist, in a proper case, he subjects himself to the penalty imposed by the act, and it is argued that, in order to protect himself from such penalty, he may, by his inquiries upon the subject, suggest that any white passenger in the car is a negro, or looks like a negro, or consorts with negroes, and intimate that he belongs in the negro compartment. In other words, no matter what may be the humiliation or injury inflicted upon the passenger, the carrier, to which he has intrusted himself, and from which, under his contract and under the law, he is entitled to protection from injury to his person and feelings, is to be saved harmless from the penalties imposed by the act of 1902, and all responsibility as to the manner in which the discretion vested by that act in the carrier is exercised, so long as the carrier acts in good faith, without express malice, is to be shifted from its (the carrier's) shoulders to those of the passenger.

The position is wholly untenable, on general principles, and has been, in effect, specifically repudiated by this court. Thus, under Act No. 111 of 1890, providing for separate accommodations for the white and colored races, on interstate traffic railroads, one Plessy, a passenger, was prosecuted and convicted for a violation of the act in insisting "on going into a coach, to which, by race, he did not belong," and he brought his case up, by habeas corpus, on the question of the constitutionality of the statute. In an exhaustive opinion, in which the statute was maintained, Mr. Justice Fenner, as the organ of this court, among other things, said:

"It (the statute) undoubtedly imposes a severe burden upon railways; but the Supreme Court of the United States has held that they are bound to bear it. It impairs no right of passengers of either race, who are secured that equality of accommodation which satisfies every reasonable claim. * * * The discretion vested in the officer to decide, primarily, the coach to which each passenger, by race, belongs, is only that necessary discretion attending every imposition of a duty, to determine whether the occasion exists which calls for its exercise. It *is a discretion to be exercised at his peril and at the peril of his employer.*" (Italics by the present writer.) Ex parte Plessy, 45 A. 87, 88, 11 South. 948, 951, 18 L. R. A. 639.

A similar view has, since, been expressed by Mr. Justice Russell of the Court of Appeals of Georgia, in the main opinion, in Wolfe v. Georgia Ry. & Electric Co., 2 Ga. App. 499, 58 S. E. 899 (decided in 1907), though, upon that particular point, the two concurring justices disagreed with the organ of the court. Mr. Justice Russell said:

"In no case where a passenger is mistreated can the fact that

May v. Shreveport Traction Co

the servant of the company was carrying out the provisions of the Penal Code, be used as a defense, unless it appears that such servant was acting outside the scope of his employment. The conductor acts at the peril of his employer. The police power, the duty of executing the law requiring the separating of the races, is not placed upon the conductor as an individual, but upon a particular agent of the company, to enable the carrier to better perform its duty of protecting its passengers—of protecting them, not only from assault and physical injuries, but, also, from abuse and insult."

The case thus cited was one in which it appeared that the plaintiff, a white person, was directed by the conductor of a street car, in Atlanta. to occupy a seat among those which were assigned to the colored race, and in which it was held that the fact stated furnished a cause of action for damages against the company operating the car.

We have, then, the law. already quoted, which obliges him through whose fault damage is sustained to repair the damage; the established doctrine that he upon whom is imposed the duty of executing a law discharges that duty at his own peril; and the universally recognized rule (in support of which we need cite no authority) that a carrier of passengers is as much bound to protect them from humiliation and insult as from physical injuries; and, applying law, doctrine, and rule to this case, we find: That plaintiff, a white woman, was a passenger on a car operated by defendant. and that defendant, through its agent, the conductor. in the discharge of the duty, imposed on it by the act of 1902. to assign passengers of the white and colored races, respectively, to different compartments, intimated to the plaintiff that in his opinion she was a negro, and that her proper place in the car was in the compartment assigned to the negro race. We now apply to the case another doctrine, which is also well established, to wit, that, to charge a white person, in this part of the world. with being a negro, is an insult. which must, of necessity, humiliate, and may materially injure. the person to whom the charge is applied. This court has said:

"Under the social habits, customs, and prejudices prevailing in Louisiana, it cannot be disputed that charging a white man with being a negro is calculated to inflict injury and damage. * * * This was treated as an actionable slander by the court organized under the Constitution of 1868. Toye v. McMahon, 21 La. Ann. 308." Sportorno v. Fourichon. 40 La. Ann. 424, 4 South. 71.

In a later case, a daily newspaper published a dispatch in which the plaintiff was referred to as a negro; the mistake having been made by the telegraph operator who converted the word "cultured" into "colored." An apology was published, im-

May v. Shreveport Traction Co

mediately (and it may here be stated that defendant's conductor
and attorney called upon the plaintiff. in the instant case, the day
following the incident out of which this suit has arisen. and that
the conductor tendered an apology), and it was found by this
court that there was no actual malice. Mr. Justice (now Chief
Justice) Breaux, as the organ of the court, however, said:

"The word complained of was provoking to an extreme degree. Inserted as it was, in one of the daily papers, it was enough
to arouse the most profound indignation of the most patient man. * * * But retraction and apology, even when
timely, are not all that is needful to relieve a publishing company from liability; for injury, resulting from oversight or negligence, may give rise to liability in damages. A newspaper
would yet be liable, if an injurious truth found its way into
columns through the merest accident. The law seeks to protect the innocent who has been injured by libelous reports. The
fact that a management can be all that can be expected to guard
against unfortunate accidents is not, in itself, a protection from
damages and a sufficient defense." Upton v. Times Democrat
Publishing Co., 104 La. 143. 28 South. 971.

In the case of Flood v. News & Courier Co., 71 S. C. 112,
50 S. E. 637, the Supreme Court of South Carolina, after a
careful consideration of the subject (referring to the thirteenth,
fourteenth, and fifteenth amendments), said:

"We therefore hold that these three amendments to the federal Constitution have not destroyed the law of this state. which
makes the publication of a white man as a negro anything but
libel."

It is true that, in the instant case, we do not find it sufficiently
proved that the conductor, in direct terms, applied the word "negro" to the plaintiff; but we consider that immaterial. The question, "Don't you belong over there?" when the person asking it
points to seats in a car set apart for negroes and designated by
a sign, is sufficient to wound the feelings of the white person to
whom it is addressed, and, for that wound, the defendant is
bound to render an account. We are of opinion that there were
passengers who heard the question, and, undoubtedly, the cause
of the trouble was known to them all, or to the most of
them, before plaintiff left the car. Defendant's counsel seems
to think that no one would have known of the matter if plaintiff had not been somewhat deaf, and if she had remained silent,
and that defendant is not responsible for either her deafness or
her loquacity. The injury to plaintiff's feelings would have been
inflicted, however, if no one but she had heard the suggestive
question, and the fact that the conductor was compelled to raise
his voice in order to make her hear a question which it was an
insult to her for him to ask, and that she was unable to restrain
her indignation, can hardly excuse the defendant.

Messenger *v*. Valley City Street & Interurban Ry. Co

Being of the opinion that plaintiff was not injured in the estimation of her friends and acquaintances or of the public at large, and that the only malice which can be attributed to the defendant is such as the law imputes from a wrongful act, done without just cause or excuse, the only remaining question is as to the quantum of damages, and that we fix at $250.

It is therefore ordered, adjudged, and decreed that the judgment appealed from be annulled, avoided, and reversed, and that there now be judgment in favor of the plaintiff, Mrs. Emma May, wife of L. G. May, and against the defendant, the Shreveport Traction Company, in the sum of $250, with legal interest thereon from the date at which this judgment shall become final until paid, and all costs.

Messenger *v*. Valley City Street & Interurban Ry. Co.

(Supreme Court of North Dakota, Nov. 19, 1910.)

[128 N. W. Rep. 1023.]

Carriers—Relation of Carrier and Passenger.*—The relation of carrier and passenger may exist while the passenger is entering the car or vehicle, and before he is seated therein. The fact that no ticket has been purchased does not necessarily prevent such relation arising. An implied acceptance may arise without the purchase of a ticket or other acceptance in express terms.

Carriers—Approaches to Cars—Lights.†—It is the duty of a common carrier to provide reasonably safe approaches to its cars, and to provide such approaches with lights at night.

Appeal and Error—Review—Questions for Jury.—The question of defendant's negligence and plaintiff's contributory negligence is, generally, for the jury, and, when passed upon by it, will not ordinarily be disturbed.

(Syllabus by the Court.)·

---

*For the authorities in this series on the question whether a person may be a passenger before he boards a train or street car, see first foot-note of Metcalf *v*. Yazoo & M. V. R. Co. (Miss.), 36 R. R. R. 743, 59 Am. & Eng. R. Cas., N. S., 743; foot-note of Carter *v*. Boston, etc., Ry. Co. (Mass.), 35 R. R. R. 697, 58 Am. & Eng. R. Cas., N. S., 697.

For the authorities in this series on the subject of the existence of the relation of carrier and passenger as affected by failure to purchase·ticket or pay fare, see last paragraph of foot-note of Thompson *v*. Nashville, etc., Ry. (Ala.), 34 R. R. R. 171, 57 Am. & Eng. R. Cas., N. S., 171.

†For the authorities in this series on the subject of the liabilities of railroad companies, as carriers of passengers, for injuries resulting from defects in station or depot premises or approaches thereto, see first foot-note of Bates *v*. Chicago, etc., Ry. Co. (Wis.), 35 R.

Messenger *v.* Valley City Street & Interurban Ry. Co

Appeal from District Court, Barnes County; Burke, Judge.

Action by Sarah Messenger against the Valley City Street & Interurban Railway Company. Judgment for plaintiff, and defendant appeals. Affirmed.

Herman Winterer and *D. S. Ritchie,* for appellant.
Page & Englert, for respondent.

MORGAN, C. J. On the 3d day of December, 1906, the plaintiff was injured while attempting to board a street car belonging to the defendant company. The complaint alleges that the injury was caused by the failure of the defendant to cause the approach to said street car to be properly lighted, and its failure to have guards or rails placed at such approach. The defendant runs a street car line in Valley City, and runs its cars so as to make connections with all passenger trains of the Soo Railway Company at the depot of said railway company. At the depot or station the railway track is used by the street railway company. Except as to this distance, at the station, the street railway company maintains its own tracks. The street railway company carries passengers to and from said depot, and the car remains at the depot until the arrival of the incoming passenger trains, and until the incoming passengers enter the street car. The approach from the depot platform to the car is made on a plank 4 feet long and about 2 feet wide, resting on the depot platform and the steps of the car, about 18 inches from the ground. The space between the depot platform and the car steps is about 30 inches. At about 8 o'clock on the evening of said 3d day of December, plaintiff was a passenger from the South on said railway, and left the train at Valley City, and immediately proceeded towards the street car. She had been a passenger on the street car at prior times, and knew where it stood. She had stepped on the plank with one foot, and was about to take an-

R. R. 173, 58 Am. & Eng. R. Cas., N. S., 173; Missouri Pac. Ry. Co. *v.* Irvin (Kan.), 35 R. R. R. 187, 58 Am. & Eng. R. Cas., N. S., 187; Moriarty *v.* Boston & M. R. R. (Mass.), 34 R. R. R. 227, 57 Am. & Eng. R. Cas., N. S., 227; second foot-note of Illinois Cent. R. Co. *v.* Daniels (Miss.), 34 R. R. R. 196, 57 Am. & Eng. R. Cas., N. S., 196.

For the authorities in this series on the subject of the duty of a street railway to discharge its passengers at safe places, see first foot-note of Farrington *v.* Boston Elev. Ry. Co. (Mass.), 34 R. R. R. 229, 57 Am. & Eng. R. Cas., N. S., 229; first foot-note of Cossitt *v.* St. Louis, etc., Ry. Co. (Mo.), 35 R. R. R. 501, 58 Am. & Eng. R. Cas., N. S., 501.

For the authorities in this series of the subject of the duty of a railroad to light its depots and stopping places, see last paragraph of second foot-note of Bates *v.* Chicago, etc., Ry. Co. (Wis.), 35 R. R. R. 173, 58 Am. & Eng. R. Cas., N. S., 173; Chesapeake, etc., R. Co. *v.* Robinson (Ky.), 35 R. R. R. 205, 58 Am. & Eng. R. Cas., N. S., 205; last foot-note of Williford *v.* Southern Ry. Co. (S. Car.), 35 R. R. R. 693, 58 Am. & Eng. R. Cas., N. S., 693.

Messenger *v.* Valley City Street & Interurban Ry. Co

other step thereon when she fell to the ground and was injured. Whether she slipped, or failed to step on the plank, does not clearly appear. At this time other passengers were entering the car, and some were in the car waiting for it to start. It started in a few minutes thereafter. She was not directed to the cart at that time by any one of the servants or employees of the street car company, and was actually escorted to the car by her son, who carried her baggage. No servants or employees of the company were at the car when she attempted to enter it. The lights had not been turned on in the car, but it was lighted to some extent by a lantern placed on the inside of the car. She brought this action, and bases her right to recover upon the alleged negligence of the company in failing to provide lights at the place where the street car is entered, and for its failure to provide a proper railing or guard where the plank is placed. The defendant, in its answer, alleges that the relation of carrier and passenger did not exist between the plaintiff and the defendant at the time of the injury, and that if she was a passenger at that time, her injury was caused through her own contributory negligence. The jury found a verdict in her favor for the sum of $200. The defendant has appealed from a judgment entered upon that verdict, and relies upon these two assignments for a reversal of the same.

The appellant's contention is that the relation of carrier and passenger is not created as a matter of law until the passenger enters some conveyance by virtue of a contract express or implied, and has been expressly or impliedly received as a passenger by the servants of the carrier. The plaintiff had not purchased a ticket for the trip, and there was no place at the station for the purchase of tickets, and the custom prevails to pay the fare to the conductor while on the car. There is no custom shown that the servants of the street railway company were to give any actual permission or consent before the passengers could rightfully enter the car. The doors of the car were not locked, and the car was lighted as before stated. From these facts it is to be determined whether the plaintiff was a passenger as a matter of law when the injury occurred.

It is beyond question that she stepped upon the plank intending to become a passenger, and that the car started on its trip in a very short time thereafter. When injured she was using one of the appliances provided by the company for entering the car. The contention that the plaintiff was not a passenger for the reason that she had not paid fare or bought a ticket when injured cannot be upheld. The car was at the station to receive passengers, and that fact may be deemed an invitation for passengers to enter, under the circumstances of this case. There is no dispute in the evidence as to the circumstances under which she entered the car, and from such circumstances we think she be-

Messenger v. Valley City Street & Interurban Ry. Co

came a passenger as a matter of law, and defendant owed her the duty to provide safe approaches to the car. The plank had been placed there for the use of those desiring to enter, and, as a matter of law, this should be deemed an invitation for those wishing to enter as passengers to do so. The company having impliedly invited passengers to enter the car without payment of fare impliedly accepts those entering pursuant to such invitation for the purpose and with the intention of being carried as passengers. No formal acceptance is necessary, nor payment of fare previous to entering. The acts of the officers in permitting passengers to use the appliances for entering provided by the company, as in this case, just before the car started, without any warning not to do so, or any objection, should be presumed to be acquiesced in by the company where no rule of the company is violated. The following statement of the rule is well sustained by the authorities: "The relation of carrier and passenger commences when a person with the good-faith intention of taking passage, and with the express or implied consent of the carrier, places himself in a situation to avail himself of the facilities for transportation which the carrier furnishes." 3 Cyc. 536, and cases cited. "The previous purchase of a ticket is not essential to the beginning of the relation of passenger and carrier, where it is not by the rules or known usage of the company made a condition precedent to the acceptance of the passengers. If there is an intent to pay fare, or to do whatever else is required to entitle the person to transportation, he becomes a passenger by implied acceptance, although his fare has not yet been paid or his ticket called for." 3 Cyc. 537, and cases cited.

In Butler v. Glens Falls Street Railway Co., 121 N. Y. 112, 24 N. E. 187, the court said: "It does not seem reasonable to assume, as a matter of law, that a person who, in an orderly way, attempts to enter a street car as passenger is to be regarded a trespasser until a special contract has been made with the conductor based upon the payment of the required fare."

In Phillips v. Southern Ry. Co., 124 N. C. 123, 32 S. E. 388, 45 L. R. A. 163, the court said: "The party coming to a railroad station with the intention of taking its next train, becomes, in contemplation of law, a passenger on its road, provided that his coming is within a reasonable time for the departure of such train. To constitute him such passenger it is not necessary that he should have purchased his ticket."

The question of defendant's negligence is not seriously denied. That question was submitted to the jury. Having found for the plaintiff under proper instructions, there is no legal ground or reason based upon the evidence for disturbing the verdict. The defendant, therefore, must be held to have violated a legal obligation devolving upon it, as a carrier, to provide the approaches to the car with proper light for the safety of those about to enter it. See 6 Cyc. 609, and cases cited.

Abney v. Louisiana & N. W. R. Co

Defendant insists that plaintiff was guilty of such contributory negligence as to bar her right to any recovery. Its claim is based on the alleged fact that the plaintiff entered the car without any invitation, and before the servants of the defendant gave permission to enter the car, and before the time when passengers could properly enter it; that she unnecessarily attempted to walk on the plank in the dark, knowing the danger. It is sufficient to say on this subject that the jury was correctly instructed on the law of contributory negligence, and found in plaintiff's favor. We think that this verdict finally settles the question as to the plaintiff's contributory negligence, under the evidence. There is no warrant for saying, as a matter of law, that there was contributory negligence fatal to a recovery.

There is a dispute as to whether there was a light at or near the plank. Plaintiff testifies that it was dark, and that she could just see the plank. Defendant testifies that it was not dark, and that surrounding lights threw some light on the location. The jury has passed on the question of the contributory negligence of the plaintiff. The verdict is sustained, and no reason appears for disturbing it. That the questions of negligence and contributory negligence are for the jury, ordinarily, has frequently been held by this court, and in the recent cases of Umsted v. Farmers' Elevator Co., 122 N. W. 390; Pendroy v. G. N. Ry. Co., 17 N. D. 433, 117 N. W. 531; Hall v. N. P. Ry. Co., 16 N. D. 60, 111 N. W. 609.

It follows that the order appealed from should be affirmed, and it is so ordered. All concur.

ABNEY v. LOUISIANA & N. W. R. Co.

(Supreme Court of Louisiana, Nov. 14, 1910. Rehearing Denied Dec. 12, 1910.)

[53 So. Rep. 678.]

On Motion to Dismiss.

Corporations—Service of Summons.—Act No. 261 of 1908 provides that a corporation may be cited by leaving the citation at its office, and a corporation cannot avoid the effect of this act by providing in its charter that its secretary shall be the proper person on whom a citation shall be served.

On the Merits.

Carriers—Injury to Passengers—Liability.*—A railroad company assumes the duty to reasonably care for the safety of its passengers

---

*See last paragraph of last foot-note of preceding case.

Abney v· Louisiana & N. W. R. Co

and to furnish safe egress from its station, and where it fails, on a
dark night, to furnish sufficient light on its station platform, and
if an accident happens to a passenger, leaving the station, because of
this insufficient light, the railroad company is responsible for such
injury.

(Syllabus by the Court.)

Appeal from Third Judicial District Court, Parish of Clai-
borne; B. P. Edwards, Judge.

Action by Henrietta O. Abney against the Louisiana & Northwest Railroad Company. Judgment for plaintiff, and defendant
appeals. Affirmed.

John A. Richardson, for appellant.
W. U. Richardson and *J. E. Moore,* for appellee.

BREAUX, C. J. This is an appeal from a judgment of the district court, without a jury, rendered in favor of plaintiff, condemning defendants to pay to plaintiff the sum of $2,500 with
5 per cent. interest per annum from the 12th day of November,
1909, the date of the judgment.

Plaintiff brought suit for $4,000.

She answered the appeal and asked for an increase of the
judgment to the amount she claims.

Plaintiff was returning from Shreveport with her son, an invalid, upon whom an operation had been performed a short time
previous. The son was assisted by a physician and his brother
at the town of Athens, La., to get from the railroad to the buggy
near by. Plaintiff was following behind these persons, when she
fell, as we will hereafter refer to.

The injuries of which she complains are a broken collar bone
—left—loosening it from the shoulder blade. a broken shoulder
blade, a fractured arm, and bruises, and severe shock. As a result of the injuries, she alleged that she was confined to her bed
many weeks, suffered great pain, and still suffers, and that her
arm and shoulder are permanently injured and rendered of little
use.

The cause of the accident is that on a dark night the depot
gallery at Athens, La., was not lighted; that she could not see
her way over the gallery and platform to the steps, down which
it was necessary for her to walk; that the platform extension
was not protected by rails.

In the darkness, she could not see how near the edge of the
platform she was as she approached the steps. She stepped or
fell off the platform and fell to the ground a distance of about
three feet. She fell on the left side on the west of the platform
—the side away from the railroad track.

The defendant filed an exception alleging want of citation and
service.

. Abney v. Louisiana & N. W. R. Co

The exception was overruled.

Defendant filed a general denial, and alleged that if plaintiff received injury it was the result of her negligence.

Plaintiff is about 53 years of age, is the mother of a family, and was a passenger on defendant's passenger train from Gibbsland on the Vicksburg, Shreveport & Pacific Railroad to her home in Athens, La.

The train was late and arrived at Athens between 8 and 9 o'clock at night—a night in December, 1909, the night plaintiff fell from the platform, as above stated.   .

As to whether it was a dark night, the plaintiff testifies that it was dark, so does the physician, Dr. Simpson, who was present and dressed her wounds. He also corroborates plaintiff in the statement that there was no light about the platform or gallery; that there was a light in the office room of the depot; that it did not extend to the platform off which plaintiff fell.

That the light from the office had, if any, the effect to blind the pedestrian who walked from the lines of light into the darkness.

Another witness, the former mayor of Athens, testified that the platform was some 6 or 7 feet wide, and the extension from where it left the main depot gallery to the steps was about 40 feet; that there was no stationary light on or near the platform, casting light thereon. While there were lamps inside the depot at night, there were none throwing light on or near the platform.

Exception to Citation.

Defendant's plea of want of citation was that there was an absolute failure to serve the citation.

Plaintiff named the secretary of the company as the officer designated by the character of the company on whom to make service.

The defendant seeks to hold plaintiff to the letter of this allegation, and, as it was not served on the secretary, that there was no legal service.

The sheriff in his return states, in substance, that he repaired to the office of the defendant company in the town of Homer, La., the domicile of the corporation, and inquired for the secretary of the corporation; intended to make service upon him. He was informed that the secreary was absent from the office, and, as there were no other officers present, he served the papers by handing them to a person (naming him) working in the defendant's office and having the required age.

The law's requirement is that citation with accompanying papers shall be served by the sheriff upon the corporation by leaving the citation and papers at the office of the corporation cited. Act No. 261 of 1908, p. 381.

This provision of the law was complied with by leaving the

Abney *v.* Louisiana & N. W. R. Co

papers at the office of defendant with a person authorized to receive them for the company.

The exception was properly overruled.

On the Merits.

The weight of the evidence sustains the proposition that the
extension of the platform where plaintiff fell was not sufficiently
lighted; that the night was dark; there was light at the depot;
it did not throw light in the direction of the fall of plaintiff.

There was necessity for light, as there were no rails or guards
around the platform and on the sides of the steps. True that
cannot be required. It is not usual to place rails around platforms and steps. None the less, the platform should be constructed so that there is something to warn the pedestrian not
to step too freely on it on a dark night.

The necessity for light at or near this particular place is em-
phasized by the fact that this was a freight and passenger depot,
and, as there were no rails, there should have been sufficient
light.

The defendant charges that the negligence, carelessness, or
want of caution on the part of plaintiff were the proximate cause
of plaintiff's fall.

The testimony shows that plaintiff, following her wounded
son beforementioned, stepped at the end of the platform at or
near the steps; they passed on to the buggy.

She was standing near the edge of the platform—nearer than
she had any idea of—and, while thus standing, she moved a little
and fell.

Whether she moved to get out of the way of some one passing, as is stated in argument, or without any special motive save
to change positions, can make but little difference. If she did
not know of the edge proximity, or could not see because of the
want of light, these facts are complete answers to the charge of
negligence.

This brings us to the second question: Was the night sufficiently dark to require a light?

The weight of the testimony is that it was sufficiently dark to
require a light.

Reputable witnesses—some of them members of the medical
profession—were positive in their statements as witnesses that
the night was dark and that there were no lights.

There was introduced in evidence the fly sheet of an almanac
to prove that on the night in question (that on the 10th day of
December, 1908) the moon rose at 7:25 p. m.

How bright it was, how much of its light reached the little
town of Athens at that time and place, is not stated.

We can only say that it does not always follow that there will
be moonlight on the earth's surface everywhere about an hour
after the moon is up.

Abney *v.* Louisiana & N. W. R. Co

There may have been obstruction to the moon's light at that particular place.

The defendant's contention is that a hill near by in the westerly direction from the depot obstructed the light—whatever light the moon was casting.

There may have been other causes. The almanac fly sheet, under the circumstances, is not controlling, as to whether there was bright moonlight at Athens at the particular time and place to dispense the defendant from the necessity of having light upon its platform on the arrival of a train.

A railroad corporation assumes the responsibility to reasonably care for the safety of its passengers.

One of its duties is to furnish safe egress from trains and platforms at night and to furnish sufficient lights to enable the passengers to guide their steps.

After carefully reading the testimony, we arrive at the conclusion that the want of light was the proximate cause of the injury.

The defendant urges that others passed near the place of the fall, including among them the sick son of the plaintiff and those attending him, and that they met with no accident; that they did not call for light in leaving the train and walking over the platform.

Argument of learned counsel for defendant on this point is persuasive, not, however, to a degree that is conclusive and convincing, for one or more persons may pass a dark place without asking for light, while another following behind or on the side may not be equally as favored.

We have considered this and other points without finding it possible to arrive at the conclusion that the judgment is erroneous.

The district judge with studied care doubtless, heard the witnesses and observed them.

Quantum of Damages.

In this respect also the judge was careful and conservative. The amount allowed conforms with our opinion.

We therefore will not disturb the judgment.

For reasons stated, the judgment appealed from is affirmed.

KONIESZNY *v.* DETROIT & M. RY. CO.

(Supreme Court of Michigan, Dec. 22, 1910.)

[128 N. W. Rep. 1096.]

Evidence—Judicial Notice—Forest Fires—Danger.—The court takes judicial notice of the desperate situation in which the rural population and inhabitants of the new and small villages in the country near Alpena. Mich., were placed by the forest fires of 1908.

Carriers—Injuries to Passengers—Negligence—Burden of Proof.—In an action against a railroad for death of a passenger killed through the destruction of a train alleged to have been negligently run through a forest fire, plaintiff had the burden of proving that defendant's engineer was negligent in attempting to proceed after discovering the fire.

Carriers—Injury to Passenger—Intoxication—Question for Jury.—Where, in an action against a railroad for death of a passenger through the alleged negligence of defendant's engineer in running his train into a forest fire, there was no evidence that the engineer's judgment was in any way affected by liquor, or that it had anything to do with his conduct or ability to intelligently comprehend his dangers, the court properly refused to submit the question of the effect on him and his crew of having drank liquor.

Carriers—Injuries to Passenger—Negligence—Sufficiency of Evidence.—In an action against a railroad for death of a passenger on a train run into a forest fire, evidence held insufficient to show that defendant was negligent.

Error to Circuit Court, Presque Isle County; Frank Emerick, Judge.

Action by John Konieszny, administrator, against the Detroit & Mackinac Railway Company. Judgment for defendant, and plaintiff brings error. Affirmed.

Argued before OSTRANDER, HOOKER, MOORE, McALVAY, and BROOKE, JJ.

I. S. Canfield (Charles F. Hull, of counsel), for appellant.
James McNamara, Charles R. Henry (Griffin Covey, Jr., and *Guy D. V. Henry,* of counsel), for appellee.

HOOKER, J. The plaintiff and his wife were residents of the village of Metz near Alpena, previous to its destruction by the forest fires, which swept and desolated that region in 1908. We may take judicial notice of the desperate situation in which the rural population and the inhabitants of the new and small villages of that section were placed. It is also plainly shown by this record.

It appears beyond and without dispute that on October 15,

Konieszny v. Detroit & M. Ry. Co

1908, the village of Metz was in great danger of destruction, and that in spite of vigorous efforts to prevent, the fire from the wood burned it up, leaving not a shanty standing. This occurred toward night, and a short time after the train of the defendant departed from the village.

The defendant's railway from Detroit to Mackinac passes through Metz. On the day mentioned messages were sent from Metz and other stations to Mr. Luce, the superintendent of this railroad, advising him that the inhabitants of Metz were in imminent danger. The south-bound local freight was at La Rocque, a station five or more miles north of Metz, and its conductor received the following message from Luce: "Take your engine and way car and go to Metz at once to assist people in danger from fire. C. W. Luce." He immediately released his engine and "ran light" to Metz with his crew of engineer, fireman, and two brakemen. On their arrival the engine was coupled to several cars, including a gondola. Some of the railroad property was hastily put into a box car, and some of the citizens loaded on some of their personal property. Many persons climbed into the gondola, and the train was started south to Posen, distant about 10 miles. The conductor was at the rear of the train. At Nowicki's crossing, a mile and a half from Metz, the train encountered fire, the rails warped or spread, and the train was destroyed with about 20 persons, among whom were the engineer, fireman, and the plaintiff's wife and three children. The plaintiff was a saloon keeper at Metz, and at the time was engaged in the attempt to prevent the fire from reaching Metz. This action was brought by him as administrator of his deceased wife to recover damages for her loss to him. Negligence is charged. The jury found a verdict for the defendant and plaintiff has appealed.

The negligence alleged, as set forth in plaintiff's brief, is: "(1) That defendant allowed its engineer and other trainmen to drink intoxicating liquors and thereafter to run and manage the train in question. (R. 7.) (2) That defendant was negligent in employing an engineer and other trainmen, and put them in charge of said train who would and did drink intoxicating liquors to excess or at all. (R. 7.) (3) That defendant was negligent in not giving plaintiff's decedent warning that it was about to run the train on which she was riding between the piles of burning forest products. (R. 7.) (4) That defendant was negligent in not leaving her in a place of safety. (R. 8.) (5) That defendant was negligent in running its said train while plaintiff's decedent was riding thereon, into a place where the track was covered by fiercely burning flames of fire. (R. 10.)"

The brief states that: "The errors assigned cover four grounds: First. (a) That defendant was allowed to show that, shortly before the trial, plaintiff had remarried. (b) That the court did not strike out all testimony relating to plaintiff's sub-

Konieszny *v.* Detroit & M. Ry. Co

sequent marriage. Second. That the court refused to submit
the question of the effect on the engineer, fireman, and brakeman
of having drank intoxicating liquors and afterwards in the running and management of the train. Third. The charge of the
court in submitting the case to the jury in effect that they must
find, before plaintiff could recover, that defendant's engineer was
guilty of having acted recklessly, wantonly, and willfully in running the train between the burning piles of forest products.
Fourth. That the court used the words 'recklessly, wantonly, and
willfully,' in charging the jury, without defining and explaining
their legal meaning and import."

The defendant's counsel were allowed to show by cross-examination of plaintiff that he had married again since the accident.

There is no testimony in the case that tends to prove negligence on the part of any of the crew. The testimony shows that
they had no personal knowledge of the condition of the forest
fires south of Metz, except what could be seen as the train proceeded. It was through a country filled with smoke. The engineer slowed down his train as he approached the place of the
catastrophe, apparently having it under control. We cannot tell
what he saw or why he proceeded. Were his own administrator
a party plaintiff in an action against this defendant, the presumption of the law would be that he was not negligent under
the rule laid down in the case of Underhill *v.* Grand Trunk Ry.,
81 Mich. 43, 45 N. W. 508. There is not only such a presumption here, but the burden is upon the plaintiff to affirmatively
prove that the engineer was negligent in attempting to proceed.
It is common knowledge that engineers sometimes find themselves
in situations with trains when they must decide between two
dangers, and not only that, but must decide instantly. We do
not know, and plaintiff has offered no testimony tending to show,
that the engineer was negligent, or that he did not do the best
thing to be done from the information he had. His own life was
in the balance, and he lost it. Apparently plaintiff's counsel relied principally on the fact that the engineer drank some beer and
whisky while at Metz. There is no proof that the engineer's
judgment was in any way affected by liquor or that it had anything to do with his conduct or ability to fully and intelligently
comprehend his dangers, and decided upon the proper thing to
do. No one testified that he showed signs of intoxication, and
several witnesses testified that all of the crew were sober. In
short there is nothing to justify an inference that the beer or
whisky was in any way the cause of or contributed to this unfortunate outcome of a charitable and heroic effort to save life.

The suggestion that it was negligence to take these people from
a place of safety or not to leave them in a place of safety or to
warn them of the danger ahead, is without force. A verdict
might properly have been directed for defendant.

The judgment is affirmed.

GODFREY v. PULLMAN CO.

(Supreme Court of South Carolina, Dec. 1, 1910.   Rehearing Denied
Dec. 14, 1910.)

[69 S. E. Rep. 666.]

Carriers—Sleeping Car Company—Loss of Personal Effects—Instructions.—Plaintiff having sued a sleeping car company for loss
of personal effects, the court, in denying a nonsuit, stated that he
would leave it to the jury to say whether defendant was negligent
in the particular transaction, and later charged that the action was
based on negligence, that the burden was on plaintiff to prove his
case by a preponderance of the evidence, and that it was the duty of
the company to use reasonable care to guard its passengers from
loss of personal effects from theft, and if, through a want of such
care, plaintiff's personal effects were lost or stolen, and they were
such as would reasonably be supposed to be carried by him, the
company would be liable; otherwise, not. Held, that such instruction was not objectionable as authorizing the jury to infer negligence
from mere proof of loss.

Carriers—Sleeping Car Company—Passenger's Effects—Loss.*—A
sleeping car company is liable for the loss of a passenger's personal
effects suitable for his journey, due to the negligence of the company's servants.

Carriers—Sleeping Car Company—Passenger's Effects—Negligence.—In an action for loss of a passenger's effects from a sleeping car, evidence that while the train was stopping at a station at
night both the conductor and porter were out on the platform at the
same time, leaving both doors unlocked, and no one to keep watch,
required submission of the issue of the negligence of the company's
servants to the jury.

**Carriers—Sleeping Car Company—Passenger's Effects—Loss—Use
of Property.**—Where, in an action against a sleeping car company
for loss of a diamond ring belonging to plaintiff's wife, by alleged
theft from the car in which they were traveling, the wife testified
that she always wore the ring, and had never had it off her hand
but once to have it fixed, and plaintiff stated that before boarding
the train his wife asked him to keep the ring in a pocketbook until
they could get north and have it repaired. Whether the ring was
carried merely to have it repaired or with the ultimate intention of
its being worn by the wife during the remainder of the trip after
it was repaired, and whether it was reasonably necessary for the
wife's pleasure, comfort, and convenience during the journey, was
for the jury.

---

*See foot-notes of Pullman Company v. Green (Ga.), 25 R. R. R.
66, 48 Am. & Eng. R. Cas., N. S., 66.

Godfrey *v.* Pullman Co

Carriers—Baggage—Liability for Loss.†—A suitable amount of jewelry according to the condition and circumstances in life of a passenger may be carried as baggage for use on any part of the journey.

Carriers—Passengers—Amount and Character of Baggage—Disclosure.‡—The amount of money or the character of the baggage carried by a passenger is not to be limited to the requirements of any particular part of the journey, nor of any particular line of connecting carriers, and the passenger is entitled to carry sufficient money and personal effects as baggage, as will reasonably supply his wants during the entire journey.

Carriers—Passengers—Nature or Value of Baggage.—A passenger, in the absence of a request is not bound to volunteer information to the carrier's servants as to the nature and value of his baggage, or the amount of money he has with him, provided it is only such and so much as he is warranted in carrying for the journey contemplated.

Judgment—Loss of Wife's Property—Action by Husband—Estoppel.—Where a wife knowingly permits her husband to sue for the loss of her property, and aids him in so doing, she is estopped to sue for the same again in her own name.

Bailment—Loss of Property—Action by Bailee.—Where a husband was a bailee of a ring belonging to his wife which was claimed to have been stolen from him while on defendant's sleeping car, the husband had such a special property in the ring as entitled him to recover for its loss as against the sleeping car company.

Appeal from Common Pleas Circuit Court of Chesterfield County; Ernest Gary, Judge.

Action by William Godfrey against the Pullman Company. Judgment for plaintiff, and defendant appeals. Affirmed.

W. F. Stevenson, Barron, Moore & Barron, and *Douglas Mc-Kay,* for appellant.

W. P. Pollock, for respondent.

HYDRICK, J. Plaintiff and his wife took passage on one of defendant's sleeping cars at Cheraw, S. C., and plaintiff paid for a berth for himself and wife to Washington, D. C. They were going to New York on a pleasure trip for a week, but did not inform the conductor of defendant's car of their intention to go further than Washington, the point to which they engaged the berth. On retiring for the night, plaintiff put his purse, containing $145 and his wife's diamond ring, worth $150, under his

†For the authorities in this series on the question, what does, and does not, constitute a passenger's baggage, see first foot-note of Chicago, etc., Ry. Co. *v.* Whitten (Ark.), 32 R. R. R. 152, 55 Am. & Eng. R. Cas., N. S., 152; foot-note of Kansas City S. Ry. Co. *v.* Skinner (Ark.), 31 R. R. R. 423, 54 Am. & Eng. R. Cas., N. S., 423.

‡For the authorities in this series on the subject of money as personal baggage, see fourth foot-note of Chesapeake & O. Ry. Co. *v.* Hall (Ky.), 34 R. R. R. 468, 57 Am. & Eng. R. Cas., N. S., 468.

Godfrey *v.* Pullman Co

wife's pillow, which was on the side farthest from the aisle. The next morning the purse and its contents were missing, and have never been found. The allegation is that it was stolen while plaintiff and his wife were asleep. Plaintiff testified that at two places on the route—at Hamlet, N. C., and at Richmond, Va.— he was up, and the conductor and porter of the sleeping car were both out on the platform of the railway station, no one being left in the car to keep watch, and both the front and rear doors of the car were left unlocked. He also testified that the money carried by him was not more than a reasonable amount for the expenses of himself and wife on such a trip. The defendant offered no testimony, and plaintiff recovered judgment for $295.

The first exception was evidently taken under a misapprehension of the ruling of the circuit judge on the defendant's motion for nonsuit and of his charge to the jury. This exception alleges that his honor held and charged the jury that the mere proof of loss under the circumstances, raised the presumption of negligence, and cast the burden on defendant of proving the exercise of due care. The record shows that his honor did not so rule or charge. In concluding his remarks on the motion for nonsuit, he said: "I will leave it to the jury to say whether or not the sleeping car company was guilty of negligence in this particular transaction." He charged the jury in part, as follows: "The action is based upon negligence. The plaintiff says he has suffered an injury on account of the loss of his property through the negligent and careless acts of the sleeping car company. They deny that; they deny that the loss was due to their negligence, and that puts upon the plaintiff the burden of proving his case by the preponderance or greater weight of the testimony. I am going to read to you what I consider the law to be: It is the duty of a sleeping car company to use reasonable care to guard its passengers from personal injury and their property or personal effects from theft, and if, through want of such care, the personal effects of a passenger, such as he would be reasonably supposed to carry with him, are stolen, the company is liable therefor. I do not wish to be understood as charging you that a sleeping car company is liable to a passenger for any and all of his personal effects that might be stolen through the negligence of those in charge of such car, but in the absence of any special notice to the company they are only liable for the loss of such articles or personal effects that he would be reasonably supposed to have or carry with him. Now, the sleeping car company says they were not reasonably to suppose that the plaintiff had as much as $150 in his pocketbook, or reasonably supposed or believed that he had a diamond ring in there; their contention being that it is more money than they were put on notice of his having, and that they were not supposed to know that he had a diamond ring, as that is not one of the usual

Godfrey *v.* Pullman Co

equipments of a passenger while traveling on a sleeping car."
From the foregoing it will be seen that it is not necessary in this
case to decide the question, whether mere loss, under such circumstances, raises a presumption of negligence, which casts upon
the sleeping car company the burden of proving due care—a
question of great importance both to the traveling public and
sleeping car companies, and one to which the courts of other
jurisdictions have given different answers. But all the authorities agree that such companies are liable for loss of a passenger's baggage due to their negligence. The testimony that
both the conductor and the porter were out of the car at the same
time, leaving no one to keep watch while the passengers were
asleep, both doors being unlocked, made it necessary to submit to
the jury the issue whether defendant was guilty of negligence,
and they have answered that question in the affirmative.

The next question presented is whether the court should have
held, as matter of law, that plaintiff could not recover for the
value of the ring, on the ground that it was not being carried for
the purpose of being worn on that trip by plaintiff's wife, but
merely for the purpose of having it repaired, and therefore could
not be considered as baggage. Plaintiff's wife testified that she
always wore the ring, and had never had it off her hand, except
once before, to have it fixed; that on this occasion she gave it
to her husband, because the stone was loose, and would catch
in things, and she was afraid she would lose it. Plaintiff testified
that his wife gave it to him before going to the train, and asked
him to keep it in his pocketbook, until they could get it fixed, and
that they intended to have it fixed while North. This testimony
made an issue for the jury, whether the ring was being carried
merely for the purpose of having it repaired, or with the ultimate
intention of its being worn by plaintiff's wife during the remainder of the trip after it had been repaired, and also whether,
under all the circumstances, it was reasonably necessary to the
pleasure, comfort or convenience of plaintiff's wife during any
part of the journey. The authorities agree that a reasonable
amount of jewelry, according to the condition and circumstances
in life of the passenger, may be carried as baggage for use on any
part of the journey. When it indisputably appears that the
article in question, or the amount of money carried is not reasonably necessary for the journey, its purpose and extent, and the
condition and circumstances in life of the passenger being considered, the court can say, as matter of law, that it cannot be
carried as baggage. But where the evidence is susceptible of
more than one inference, as it is in this case, it raises an issue
of fact which must be submitted to the jury. Defendant contends that it should not have been held liable for more money
than was necessary for the expenses of the plaintiff and his wife
to Washington, because it was not informed that they were going

elsewhere. The amount of money or the character of the baggage carried by a passenger is not to be limited to the requirements of any particular part of the journey, or any particular line of connecting carriers; nor is the passenger, in the absence of a request, bound to volunteer information as to the nature or value of his baggage, or the amount of money he has with him, if it is only such and so much as he is entitled to carry for the journey contemplated.

The next assignment of error is in holding that plaintiff can recover the value of the ring notwithstanding it is his wife's property. The objection is more technical than substantial, inasmuch as the wife, knowing of the suit by her husband and aiding him by her testimony to recover the value of the ring, would be estopped to sue for it again in her own name. But the plaintiff was a bailee of the ring, and the rule is that a bailee has such special property or right in the thing bailed as entitles him to protect it against wrongdoers. As against third persons, he may sue for and recover damages for its injury, loss, or destruction caused by their negligence. Jones *v.* McNeil, 2 Bailey, 466; Harrison *v.* Lloyd, 9 Rich. Law, 161; Thayer *v.* Hutchinson, 13 Vt. 504, 37 Am. Dec. 607; Poole *v.* Symonds, 1 N. H. 289, 8 Am. Dec. 71; note to Hostler's Administrators *v.* Schull, 3 N. C. 179, 1 Am. Dec. 586; 5 Cyc. 222, 223; 3 A. & E. Ency. L. (2d Ed.) 761. See, also, Battle *v.* R. R., 70 S. C. 329, 49 S. E. 849, where the husband was allowed to sue for and recover the value of his wife's baggage.

Judgment affirmed.

.

LAYNE *v.* CHESAPEAKE & O. RY. CO.

(Supreme Court of Appeals of West Virginia, Nov. 22, 1910.)

[69 S. E. Rep. 700.]

Carriers—Carriage of Passengers—Termination of Relation.*—The general rule is, that the relation of carrier and passenger does not terminate until the passenger has alighted from a railway train and left the place where passengers are discharged, or, after reaching his destination, has had reasonable time to get off the car and leave the premises of the carrier.

---

*For the authorities in this series on the question whether a person may be a passenger of the railroad after he alights from the train or street car, see first foot-note of Louisville R. Co. *v.* Mitchell (Ky.), 36 R. R. R. 710, 59 Am. & Eng. R. Cas., N. S., 710; last foot-note of Layne *v.* Chesapeake & O. R. Co. (W. Va.), 36 R. R. R. 537, 59 Am. & Eng. R. Cas., N. S., 537; last head-note of Denver, etc., Co. *v.* Derry (Colo.), 36 R. R. R. 141, 59 Am. & Eng. R. Cas., N. S., 141.

Layne *v.* Chesapeake & O. Ry. Co

Carriers—Carriage of Passengers—Termination of Relation—Reasonable Time for Leaving Carrier's Premises—Question for Jury.—Another general rule is, that where a passenger is necessarily hindered or delayed in leaving the carrier's premises, the question whether he failed to depart within a reasonable time is one of fact for the jury.

Carriers—Carriage of Passengers—Termination of Relation.—If, as in this case, a passenger on a railway train has alighted at his point of destination and is proceeding by the usual way to leave the railway company's premises, but, before actually doing so, is halted by the discharge of a gun and a report that his brother, a fellow passenger, has been shot by a special police officer of the railway company, and in good faith and without the intention of engaging in the difficulty returns to relieve his brother he should be regarded as reasonably and necessarily delayed, and as continuing to be a passenger, entitled as such to the protection of the railway company and its agents, and if assaulted by such police officer or agent of the railway company the railway company is liable to him in damages for injuries sustained.

Carriers—Carriage of Passengers—Termination of Relation—Questions of Fact.*—In such cases the good faith of a passenger, and the purpose of his return to the place of trouble, are questions of fact for jury determination from all the evidence in the case.

Carriers—Carriage of Passengers—Action for Assault on Passengers—Admissibility of Evidence.—The record of the indictment, conviction and sentence of a special police officer of a railway company, for the murder of the plaintiff's brother, is not admissible in evidence on the trial of an action against such railway company for injuries sustained by the assault or shooting of the plaintiff by such police officer, and the admission thereof, over the objection of defendant, is reversible error.

(Syllabus by the Court.)

Error to Circuit Court, Kanawha County.

Action by Henry O. Layne against the Chesapeake & Ohio Railway Company. Judgment for plaintiff, and defendant brings error. Reversed, and new trial awarded.

Simms, Enslow, Fitzpatrick & Baker, for plaintiff in error.
A. M. Belcher and *Charles Curry,* for defendant in error.

MILLER, J. This is an action by Henry O. Layne against the railway company, to recover damages for injuries alleged to have been sustained by him at the hands of one John L. Howery, a special police officer of defendant, in December, 1905. It grows out of the same transaction involved in Layne's administrator against the defendant company, in which Robert Layne, a brother

---

*See foot-note on peceding page.

Layne *v.* Chesapeake & O. Ry. Co

of plaintiff, was shot and mortally wounded. That case, affirming the judgment below, was decided here November 23, 1909, and is reported in 66 W. Va. 607, 67 S. E. 1103.

The verdict and judgment below in favor of the plaintiff in this case was for the sum of $5,000.00, to reverse which this writ of error is being prosecuted.

This case, involving as it does the same facts and circumstances involved in the case of Robert Layne calls for the application of the same legal rules and principles enunciated and applied in that case, unless there be good reasons for modifying or departing from them, and we perceive none, and none have been presented in the briefs and arguments of counsel.

The only material facts differentiating this from the former case, are that in the Robert Layne case he was shot and fatally wounded just after he had alighted from defendant's train, and had had time to go but a few steps. He had not completed his journey, his destination being a station beyond Malden plaintiff's destination. In this case Henry O. Layne had alighted from the train, and, on demand of the train porter, had paid his fare, not previously demanded or called for by the conductor or other train officer, and, leaving his brother Robert in the act of demanding for him a cash receipt, for the cash fare paid, had gone some twelve or fifteen steps in the direction of the place of exit from the railway property, near the eastern end of the station house, but still on the station grounds or premises, when, on hearing the report of a pistol shot, and the announcement of some one in the crowd at the station, that Howery had shot Robert Layne, he laid down his bundles on the station platform, and went back a few steps in the direction of the pistol shot, found Howery in the act of raising up from over the prostrate body of his brother, who on seeing him leveled his gun at Layne and fired, the ball hitting plaintiff in the left side, inflicting a slight flesh wound. Layne succeeded afterwards in wresting the gun from Howery's hand, and started away with it; pursued by Howery and two other train officers, one of whom fired one or two additional shots at Layne, but the latter made a safe retreat across the public road, and through a store on the opposite side from the railway station.

It would be useless to again recite the facts common to both cases, or to go into a new consideration of the legal principles enunciated and applied in the former case, although able briefs have been filed, and elaborate oral arguments were made at the bar on hearing. We will therefore confine ourselves to a consideration and disposition of those points or questions which counsel for the plaintiff in error regard as peculiar to this case, and not having been involved in the former decision.

First, it is contended that plaintiff, at the time he was shot, and shot at, by Howery, and other servants of the railway company, had ceased to be a passenger, that by returning to the scene of trouble between Howery and Robert he ceased to be a passenger, and forfeited all right as passenger to protection by defendant and its agents. The general rule, alluded to in the opinion in the Robert Layne case, "is that the relation of carrier and passenger does not terminate until the passenger has alighted from the train and left the place where the passengers are discharged." Elliott on Railroads, section 1592. It only ceases, as a general rule, after a passenger has arrived at the place of his destination and has had reasonable time to get off the car or vehicle and to leave the premises of the carrier. 2 Shear. & Red. on Neg. (5th Ed.) section 490, pp. 884-885. And it continues, says this writer, for example, "while a passenger by a train is walking along the station platform, without unreasonable delay, though it be his intention to leave the platform at a point where he will become a trespasser." Reasonable time in such cases, means reasonable time under all the circumstances. Chicago Ry. Co. *v.* Wood, 104 Fed. 663, 44 C. C. A. 118. And "what is a reasonable time must often depend upon the circumstances of the particular case." 4 Elliott on R. R., section 1592. "And where the passenger is necessarily hindered or delayed in leaving the carrier's premises, the question whether he failed to depart within a reasonable time is one of fact for the jury." 2 Hutch. on Carriers (3d Ed.) § 1016. The case of C. & O. Ry. Co. *v.* King, 99 Fed. 251, 40 C. C. A. 432, 49 L. R. A. 102, is an illustration of the application of these general principles. The plaintiff was injured while crossing the railroad tracks intervening between the station house and the nearest public highway to the town. The court held, that "if a passenger on a railroad train alights by direction of the company, or by its implied invitation, at a place where, in order to leave the premises of the company, it is necessary to cross intervening tracks, he remains a passenger until he has crossed such tracks, provided he uses the means of egress which the company has provided, or which is customarily used with its knowledge and consent." Houston &c. R. Co. *v.* Batchler, 37 Tex. Civ. App. 116, 83 S. W. 904, is another illustration of the same character. Batchler, the plaintiff, when he had arrived at the end of his journey, stopped on the platform of the station and talked for a short time with a friend before starting to leave the premises of the railway company. As he started to leave he was assaulted by the conductor of the train on which he had been a passenger, and the defense there, as here, was that the plaintiff was not a passenger at the time of the assault. The court, however, ruled that a passenger does not cease, ipso facto, to be such upon the arrival of the train at the point of his destination, but he has a reasonable time thereafter in which to alight from the train and leave the premises of the company. And the court held, in accordance with Hutchinson on Carriers, supra,

Layne *v.* Chesapeake & O. Ry. Co

that "what, under all the circumstances, is a reasonable time, is a question of fact, which must be determined by the jury." Other cases cited by counsel as illustrating the application of the general rule are: Glenn *v.* Lake Erie &c. R. Co., 165 Ind. 659, 75 N. E. 282, 2 L. R. A. (N. S.) 872, 112 Am. St. Rep. 255; Gaynor *v.* Old Colony &c. Ry. Co., 100 Mass. 208, 97 Am. Dec. 96; and Texas & P. Ry. Co. *v.* Dick, 26 Tex. Civ. App. 256, 63 S. W. 895. In the first of these cases, the court held that, "In case of an accident involving a passenger, who on alighting from the train intended and desired to depart from the place at once, but was hindered and delayed, the question as to what is a reasonable time should be determined from the attendant facts and circumstances given in explanation or excuse for such delay." In the Massachusetts case the plaintiff, a passenger on a train was injured after leaving the train and platform upon which he had been discharged, while crossing a side track in an effort to get to an old car for a necessary purpose, and from which he intended to proceed on an adjoining street to his home. The court held that when injured he was still a passenger and entitled to protection as such, not only while in the car, but while upon the premises of the railway company. The case of Texas & P. Ry. Co. *v.* Dick is a closer case to the one we have here, perhaps, than either of the others. The plaintiff had arrived at destination. After passing along on a graveled way, about ten feet wide, between the standing train and the station platform, a distance of sixty or seventy feet, on reaching the station house the station agent and train porter were engaged in loading some trunks, which practically obstructed the walk. The plaintiff put down his baggage and assisted in loading the trunks, and then continued on his way homeward, and after going but a short distance, and while still on the railway premises, a brother-in-law of the agent assaulted and beat him in the presence and hearing of the agent, who did not interfere. The defense there, as here, was that the plaintiff has ceased to be a passenger, and that the defendant owed him no duty as such, but the Supreme Court of Texas held otherwise.

Applying these principles to the case here, had Henry O. Layne ceased to be a passenger when he was shot by Howery? It does not clearly appear whether or not, if he had continued his journey he could have gotten off defendant's premises within the time it took him to return to where Howery and his brother Robert were. But the fact remains, he was still on defendant's premises, and had not loitered on the way. Can it be said, within the meaning of the authorities cited, that he was necessarily or reasonably delayed or hindered in his departure by the gun shot, and the report that Howery had shot his brother? We think that upon the highest principles of humanity, and ties of blood and brotherly affection, that if Henry O. Layne, on hearing these

Layne *v.* Chesapeake & O. Ry. Co

reports, was actuated by good motives and sincere intentions in laying down his bundles, and going back to the relief of his brother, reported to have been shot, he did not thereby lose his relationship of passenger, or his right as such to the protection of the defendant and its agents. If however, he returned, as one of defendant's instructions to the jury, given, assumes, to engage in a quarrel between Howery and Robert Layne, a question of fact for the jury, and not from motives of humanity and brotherly sympathy, as he claims, another fact for the jury, he was not necessarily or justifiably detained, and thereby severed the relationship of carrier and passenger, and lost his rights as such to the protection of the defendant or its servants.

Second:—Our conclusions on the first proposition condemns defendant's seventh instruction to the jury, refused, and as we think, properly refused by the court below. It is the only instruction differing materially from some of those passed upon in the Robert Layne case. As proposed it would have told the jury assuming as true some of the facts peculiarly for jury determination, that under the evidence in the case plaintiff was not a passenger after he left defendant's train without the intention or returning to it, and if afterwards of his own accord, without being stopped by defendant's agents or servants, turned back after he had left the train, not for the purpose of becoming a passenger again, but for purposes of his own, he ceased to be entitled to the protection of defendant as passenger, and defendant was not liable for the assault committed on him after so turning back.

Third, did the court err, as contended by plaintiff in error, in admitting in evidence the record of the indictment, conviction and sentence of Howery for the murder of Robert Layne? We answer, yes. That record had not the slighest bearing on the issues in this case. It did not constitute rebuttal evidence as to any fact introduced in defense. The parties were not the same. Its only purpose and effect could have been to arouse the sympathy or prejudice of the jury, and was wholly improper and irrelevant for any purpose apparent, or pointed out by counsel. In Rodgers *v.* Bailey, 69 S. E. ——, a recent case, not yet officially reported, it is held, in accordance with approved practice, that "admission of irrelevant testimony, likely to enhance damages, is reversible error unless it plainly appears that the verdict is not in excess of the damages proved." "Nothing outside of the ligitimate facts should be introduced to affect the minds of those who are to decide the case." Sesler *v.* Coal Co., 51 W. Va. 318, 41 S. E. 216, point 4 of the syllabus. Even if this were a suit to recover damages for the same assault, which it is not, the record of the criminal proceeding would not be admissible. 3 Cyc. 1098. And, because of the want of mutuality, not even to establish, as res adjudicata, the fact on which the indictment was founded. Honaker v. Howe, 19 Grat. (Va.) 50. 1 Greenleaf on Ev. (16th Ed.) § 537, referring in note to section 537, to sections 180, 189 and 523. The rule, many times repeated, is that where illegal evidence has been admitted, over the objection of a party, it will be cause for setting aside the verdict, unless it clearly appears that the objecting party was not prejudiced thereby. See the cases digested in 1 Ency. Dig. Va. & W. Va. Reports, 592-693. The record in the criminal case was plainly inadmissible. We can not see, as we are urged to do by plaintiff's counsel, that the error was harmless, and that defendant was not prejudiced thereby. For the error in admitting this record the judgment below must be reversed, the verdict set aside, and the defendant awarded a new trial.

This leaves the question of the alleged excessiveness of the verdict, also relied on by defendant. As the judgment and verdict must be set aside and a new trial awarded on another ground, it would be improper for us on this hearing, to express any opinion on that subject.

Judgment reversed, verdict set aside, and new trial awarded, the costs here to be adjudged in favor of the defendant, in the court below, to abide the result of the new trial awarded.

KYLE v. CHICAGO, R. I. & P. RY. Co. (two cases)

(Circuit Court of Appeals, Eighth Circuit, October 19, 1910.)

[182 Fed. Rep. 613.]

Carriers—Performance of Contract for Carriage of Passengers— Train Service of Railroad.*—A railroad company has the legal right to make reasonable rules and regulations for the running of its trains and the carriage of passengers thereon, and it incurs no legal liability because in following such reasonable regulations and train schedules it does not stop its through or limited trains at all stations, especially when it is not shown that it does not afford to the public adequate facilities for travel upon its road.

Carriers—Carriage of Passengers—Train Service.—Plaintiffs purchased tickets from the agent of defendant railroad company for a station on its line, explaining that a relative residing there was ill and not expected to live, and that they desired to take an evening train, which they were told by the agent passed such station early in the morning. They were told by the conductor that the train did

---

*For the authorities in this series on the subject of the validity of a carrier of passenger's rules and regulations, see first foot-note of St. Louis, etc., R. Co. v. Johnson (Okla.), 36 R. R. R. 165, 59 Am. & Eng. R. Cas., N. S., 165; extensive note, 33 R. R. R. 636, 56 Am. & Eng. R. Cas., N. S., 636.

Kyle *v.* Chicago, R. I. & P. Ry. Co

not stop at such station, and that he could not stop, but that they could, by stopping off at an intermediate station, take a local train using the same tickets and reach their destination before 9 o'clock in the morning. They declined to do this, but paid their fare to a station beyond, from which they did not get a train back until the following evening, arriving after their relative had died. Had they followed the conductor's instructions, they would have arrived before their relative died and in the shortest possible time from their starting point. No deceit or misrepresentation was charged. Held, that such facts did not constitute a cause of action against defendant for the recovery of damages.

Damages—Grounds—Mental Suffering.†—It is the settled rule of the federal courts that mental anguish alone, not arising from some physical injury or pecuniary loss caused by the negligent or other wrongful act of another, is not a basis for an action for damages in the absence of a statute authorizing such a recovery.

In Error to the Circuit Court of the United States for the Western District of Arkansas.

Action by E. P. Kyle against the Chicago, Rock Island & Pacific Railway Company, and by G. B. Kyle against the same. Judgments for defendant, and plaintiffs bring error. Affirmed. See, also, 173 Fed. 238.

Oscar L. Miles, for plaintiffs in error.
Thomas S. Buzbee and *George B. Pugh,* for defendant in error.

Before SANBORN and VAN DEVANTER, Circuit Judges, and REED, District Judge.

REED, District Judge. These cases rest upon the same facts, were consolidated and tried together, are presented to this court on the same record, and may be considered and determined as one case.

The facts as disclosed by the evidence are: That on June 26 1908, the plaintiffs, who then resided at Magazine, a village or town in Western Arkansas upon the line of defendant's railroad in that state, received a letter from Wecharty, Okl., that a brother of one of the plaintiffs and uncle of the other, who resided at or near Wecharty, was sick and not expected to live. Upon receipt of this letter, the plaintiffs began preparations to go to their sick relative and went to the agent of the defendant company in Magazine and informed him that they desired to start upon the evening train from Magazine to Wecharty. The agent informed them that Bilby, a station on defendant's road in Oklahoma, was

†See last foot-note of Caldwell *v.* Northern Pac. Ry. Co. (Wash.), 35 R. R. R. 161, 58 Am. & Eng. R. Cas., N. S., 161; foot-note of St. Louis, etc., R. Co. *v.* Buckner(Ark.), 33 R. R. R. 780, 56 Am. & Eng. R. Cas., N. S., 780.

Kyle v. Chicago, R. I. & P. Ry. Co

the same place as Wecharty, and that the train was scheduled to pass there about 2 o'clock in the morning. They purchased tickets from Magazine to Bilby and took passage upon the train which left Magazine about 6:30 in the evening of that day and scheduled to pass Bilby about 2 o'clock the next morning, but not to stop there. At Boonville, the first station seven miles west of Magazine, the crew of the train changed, and shortly after leaving that place plaintiffs presented their tickets to the train auditor or collector when he called for them, and were then informed for the first time, as they say, that the train did not stop at Bilby. They informed the train auditor of their purpose in going to Bilby and their desire to reach there as early as possible, and requested that the train be stopped at Bilby that they might alight from it there, but were informed by the train officials that they had no authority to stop the train; that it was not scheduled to stop at Bilby, and they could not stop there; that the way for them to reach Bilby was to leave the train at Mc-Alester about midnight, or at Calvin a little later, and from either of these places they would get a local train scheduled to leave McAlester about 7 o'clock in the morning, and arrive at Bilby about 8:50 a. m.; that their tickets were good upon this local train from McAlester to Bilby. This was the usual and customary way for passengers on this through train from points east of McAlester destined to Bilby to reach their destination. Bilby is a small station with only a post office, one store, a small cotton gin, and three or four families. The plaintiffs refused to act upon the suggestions or advice of the train officials, but continued on the train to Holdenville, a station six miles beyond Bilby, at an additional expense to each of 12 cents railroad fare, which they voluntarily paid, expecting to get a train back to Bilby early in the morning. For some reason they were unable to do so and did not get a return train until about 6 o'clock in the evening. They stayed in Holdenville all day, returned upon an evening train, and arrived at Bilby about 6:40 p. m. June 27th. The relative died about noon of that day. The train upon which the plaintiffs took passage from Magazine was known as No. 41, was a through train from Memphis west bound to some point in Oklahoma, and after leaving McAlester ran as a fast train, scheduled to stop at only a few stations, and not at small places like Bilby. From McAlester there were two local trains a day west bound which carried passengers, one leaving about 7 o'clock in the morning arriving at Bilby at 8:50 a. m., the other arriving at Bilby about noon or shortly thereafter; and two from the west which stopped at Bilby, one at 1:20, and the other at 5:35, both in the afternoon. The next train west bound from Magazine after No. 41 was due to leave Magazine about 8 o'clock in the morning of June 27th; but passengers leaving Magazine upon this train would not arrive at Bilby until 8:50 a. m. of the

Kyle *v.* Chicago, R. I. & P. Ry. Co

next day as we understand the evidence, or 24 hours later than those leaving the evening before on No. 41. Each of the plaintiffs sued the defendant for alleged mental inguish suffered by him because he was thus prevented from seeing his dying relative before his death, claiming as actual damages $5,000, and $5,000 as exemplary damages because of the alleged willful and wrongful acts of defendant's employees in refusing to stop the train at Bilby. The defendant denied any negligent, willful, or other wrongful acts upon the part of its employees and contends that if plaintiffs had followed the suggestions or advice of its train officers they would have reached Bilby upon its train scheduled to arrive and stop there at 8:50 in the morning of June 27th, nearly three hours before the death of their relative. At the close of all of the evidence the court upon its own motion directed a verdict, and rendered judgment, in favor of the defendant, and the plaintiffs bring error.

Each of the plaintiffs rests his right to recover solely upon the ground that because the defendant sold him a ticket from Magazine to Bilby and allowed him to take passage upon one of its through trains not scheduled to stop at Bilby, that it was its duty to stop the train and let him alight at that place. But it is admitted, and properly so, in the brief filed in behalf of the plaintiffs, that it is, and was, the right of the defendant to make reasonable rules and regulations for the running of its trains and the carriage of passengers thereon, and that it was not required to stop its through or limited trains at all stations upon its line of road if it otherwise provides reasonable facilities for the public to travel to and from such stations. It follows as a corollary that the defendant had the legal right to run its trains under the regulations and upon the schedules so established, and that it incurs no liability in doing so, especially in the absence of allegations and proof that they were unreasonable and did not afford to the public adequate facilities for travel upon its road. There is neither allegation nor proof in this case that the rules and regulations established by the defendant, and the schedules upon which its trains were run from Magazine to Bilby and beyond, were unreasonable and did not afford ample facilities and accommodation to all who might desire to reach and depart from the station at Bilby. The authorities cited in behalf of the plaintiffs are those in which passengers having tickets which entitled them to ride as such upon a given train were wrongfully ejected therefrom by the train men in charge. They are inapplicable here, for these plaintiffs were not ejected from the train, but were permitted to continue thereon to their destination and to the station beyond; each voluntarily paying the additional fare to that station. These actions are not for deceit or misrepresentation on the part of the company in selling the plaintiffs tickets to a station at which the train upon which

Kyle *v.* Chicago, R. I. & P. Ry. Co

they were to take passage did not stop; on the contrary, each petition alleges:

"That plaintiff went to the station at Magazine and explained to the agent his desire and purpose to take the evening westbound train at Magazine so as to reach Bilby at the earliest possible moment."

The plaintiffs each so testified, but do not say that the agent assured them or even told them that the train would stop there; and the proofs show that the next train west from Magazine left the following morning about 8 o'clock, but would not reach Bilby. certainly until afternoon of that day, and, as we understand the evidence, not until 8:50 in the morning of the 28th, or 24 hours later than they would arrive under the schedules then in effect by taking passage upon train No. 41 as they did. Had they been refused passage upon train No. 41, they might well have said that they were prevented by defendant from reaching the bedside of their relative before his death, for they could not possibly then have reached him before he died; but, by taking passage as they did upon train No. 41, they could have reached Bilby upon the regular train from Magazine, scheduled to arrive and stop at Bilby at 8:50 in the morning of June 27th. Each plaintiff sues alone for the mental anguish he claims to have suffered because he was prevented from seeing his dying relative before his final dissolution. If either suffered any such anguish, it was solely because of his refusal to act upon the suggestion or advice of the train officials to leave the train at McAlester or Calvin and take the regular train scheduled to arrive from Magazine and stop at Bilby at 8:50 in the morning of June 27th, and, if they had acted upon such directions, they would not have been deprived of the privilege they now claim was so dear to them. But aside from this there is not a word of evidence that either suffered any mental anguish because he did not see the dying man before his death; nor is there any fact shown upon which it could be found that either suffered any, save alone the fact of the blood relationship existing between him and his relative. Surely the court cannot judicially know that a brother or nephew of a dying man would suffer great mental anguish because he was prevented from seeing him so short a time before his death; or, if he would suffer any, the extent of such suffering. Neither is there a scintille of evidence that the trainmen were actuated by the slightest ill will towards either of the plaintiffs in refusing to disobey their orders and stop the train at a place where they were not authorized to stop it. There is no possible ground, therefore, upon which a verdict or judgment for more than nominal damages could have been sustained against the defendant, admitting, without deciding, that it is liable to the plaintiffs for not stopping the train at Bilby. But the judgment of the Circuit Court need

Mitchell *v.* Augusta & A. Ry. Co

not be, and is not, made to rest upon this ground, for it is settled in this jurisdiction that mental anguish alone, not arising from some physical injury or pecuniary loss caused by the negligent or other wrongful act of another, is not a basis for an action for damages in the absence of a statute authorizing such a recovery. Western Union Tel. Co. *v.* Butler (C. C. A.) 179 Fed. 92. And see Rowan *v.* Western Union Tel. Co. (C. C. A.) 149 Fed. 550. And no such statute is relied upon the plaintiffs for a recovery.

The judgment of the Circuit Court in each case is affirmed.

, MITCHELL *v.* AUGUSTA & A. RY. CO.

(Supreme Court of South Carolina, Dec. 16, 1910.)

[69 S. E. Rep. 664.]

Carriers—Passengers—Commencement of Relation.*—A passenger assumes such relation when, intending to take passage, he enters a place provided for the reception of passengers as a depot, waiting room, or the like, at a time when such place is open for the reception of persons intending to take passage on the train or cars of the company.

Carriers—Passengers—Duty to Take up Persons Desiring Transportation.—A flag station where plaintiff desired to take one of defendant's cars consisted merely of the word "Station" attached to a trolley pole. Cars did not stop there to receive or let off passengers unless signaled. The car plaintiff desired to take did not stop to receive or let off passengers, but to enter a switch to enable another car to pass in the opposite direction. It remained on the switch a sufficient time to enable persons on the car to have alighted, or for those who were at the station when it arrived to have boarded it. When it stopped at the station, plaintiff was about 125 yards away, and though he ran toward it and hallooed to the conductor to wait for him, he refused to do so and plaintiff was left. Held that plaintiff not being at the station when the car arrived was not entitled to the rights of a passenger, and that defendant owed him no duty to detain the car even for a short time to take him aboard.

Carriers—Receiving Passengers—Time.—Where plaintiff was not at a station when a carrier's car arrived, and was left, he was not in a position to raise the question that the carrier did not hold the car a reasonable time to take up passengers.

---

*For the authorities in this series on the question whether a person may be a passenger before he boards a train or street car, see foot-note of Metcalf *v.* Yazoo & M. V. R. Co. (Miss.), 36 R. R. R. 743, 59 Am. & Eng. R. Cas., N. S., 743; foot-note of Carter *v* Boston, etc., Ry. Co. (Mass.), 35 R. R. R. 697, 58 Am. & Eng. R. Cas., N. S., 697.

Mitchell *v.* Augusta & A. Ry. Co

Appeal from Common Pleas Circuit Court of Aiken County; T. S. Sease, Judge.

Action by J. D. Mitchell against the Augusta & Aiken Railway Company. Judgment for plaintiff, and defendant appeals. Reversed.

This is an appeal from an order of the circuit court, affirming the judgment rendered by a magistrate, in favor of the plaintiff for $100. The complaint (omitting the formal allegations thereof) is as follows:

"That on Sunday, May 23, 1909, the plaintiff being in the town of Bath, and being desirous of taking passage to Langley, on one of the cars of the defendant company, started with several friends, who likewise desired to take passage to Langley, to the regular and duly advertised station of the defendant company, commonly known as the last stop in Bath (towards Aiken). That shortly before they reached said station (at about 12:45 p. m.) car No. 108, a regular passenger car of the defendant company. reached said station and ran about 13 yards beyond. That plaintiff and his friends, then being but a short distance away, immediately, by loudly hallooing to the conductor in charge of said car, attracted his attention, and also in words notified him of their desire to board said car, and ran quickly towards the car, at the same time crying to the conductor to wait and to allow them to board the car, but when plaintiff and his friends had actually gotten within a few yards of the car, and close enough to have boarded said car, had said car stopped at the regular station and had said car waited an instant longer, the conductor in charge thereof negligently, willfully, and wantonly failing to stop his car, as is required by law, at said regular and duly advertised station, for a time sufficient to receive passengers, and after stopping said car for an insufficient time to receive prospective passengers. willfully and wantonly made a rude and taunting sign and signal to the plaintiff and his friends, who were endeavoring to board the car, and signaled his car ahead, whereupon it was moved forward. thereby negligently, willfully, and wantonly leaving the plaintiff and his friends at the station, endeavoring to board the car, and begging to be taken on it."

There was a demurrer to the complaint, on the ground that it failed to state facts sufficient to constitute a cause of action, "in that it appears upon the face thereof that the defendant owed no duty to the plaintiff at the time and place alleged in the complaint, and that the car of the defendant arrived at alleged station and passed it before the plaintiff reached the same." The demurrer was overruled.

The plaintiff testified as follows in his own behalf:

"Mr. Aaron Carroll, William Wooten, Oscar Jones, and Oscar Mitchell started with me from my father-in-law's house, to go to

Mitchell *v.* Augusta & A. Ry. Co

Langley with me. I intended and tried to take a car of the defendant company, at the station known as the first stop in Bath, which is a regular station of the defendant company. There is a switch at that station, and there is a board nailed upon a trolley pole bearing the word 'Station.' This is one of their regular stations. All of the stations are flag stations, except the two terminals; cars stop to take on and let off passengers only upon signal at the flag stations. This switch is about 35 yards long. The pole with the word 'Station' on it is near the end of the switch towards Bath. It was at 12:45 that I tried to catch this car. On Sundays the regular scheduled cars of the company for passengers gets to this stop at 12:45. This same car stopped at the regular Bath stop before it got to the stop I am talking about. I saw that. The five of us that I have already mentioned ran to the car. The car was at that station waiting for the other car going the other way to pass. I was left by the car and did not get on it, because the conductor signaled the car ahead, and went off and left us all there. We were all running along trying to catch the car, when the conductor pulled the bell rope and started up the car. When he did this, the car was standing where it had been standing during the whole stop, and I and the other men and boys were about 15 steps away, running and trying to catch the car. We had already gotten upon the company's property and were about 3 or 4 steps from the station pole. *. * * Just before the conductor pulled the bell rope and started off, and when I was about 20 steps off and running to catch the car, I motioned to the conductor to wait for us, and hollered to him to wait that I was obliged to go. I hollered quite loud, plenty loud for a man a 100 yards off to hear, and there was nothing to keep him from hearing. I hollered several times before he rang the bell. Mr. Carroll and several of the others, also, hollered the same thing. I know that the conductor heard us before he rang the bell, because he was right on the back platform looking towards us. He had been looking at us during our entire run, and, instead of stopping, he laughed. Since that occurrence I have been to the place and run at the same rate of speed that I was going that day, and I found that it would have taken me four seconds to have run from where I was when the conductor started up the car to the rear end of the car; in other words, if he had waited four seconds longer I could have gotten on the car, and so could all the balance of us. If the car had been standing at the station board. The rear end of the car was always about 13 yards at all during the stop. It did not originally stop at the station board. The rear end of the car was always about 13 yards beyond the station board. * * *

"Cross-Examination: When the car reached and ran by the station as above stated, I was about 125 yards off running to catch it. We were all running right along together. * * * On

Mitchell v. Augusta & A. Ry. Co

Sundays the cars run every half hour, and the car going towards Augusta passed the car I was after at the switch. The car I was after pulled out first."

On being recalled he stated "that the car in question stopped at the switch, after he and his friends started to running to catch it. He saw it when it stopped, and it stayed at the switch only the length of time that it took to run 200 yards, which was about two minutes." The plaintiff introduced no other testimony. The defendant made a motion for a nonsuit as to the entire cause of action upon the ground that the evidence failed to show any breach of duty on the part of the defendant towards the plaintiff, which motion was refused. The defendant then made a motion for a nonsuit as to the cause of the action for punitive damages, which was also refused. In his order dismissing the defendant's appeal, the circuit judge found the facts substantially as they are stated in the plaintiff's testimony, from which he deduces the conclusion that the defendant should have waited a reasonable time for the plaintiff to board the car, which it failed to do, and was therefore liable in damages.

Boykin Wright, Geo. T. Jackson, and *J. B. Salley,* for appellant.

Hendersons, for respondent.

GARY, A. J. The first question that will be considered is whether there was error in overruling the demurrer on the ground that the car of the defendant arrived at the alleged station and passed it before the plaintiff reached the same. Our construction of the complaint is that it did not intend to allege that the car had passed the station, but simply that it had proceeded thirteen feet beyond the point, where the word "Station" was written. The testimony explanatory of the surroundings shows that the station was designated by a board nailed on a trolley pole, bearing the word "Station."

The next question is raised by the following exception: "In not sustaining defendant's motion for a nonsuit as to the entire cause of action, and in not holding that the judgment was without any evidence to support it, for the reason that there was no evidence of any breach of duty on the part of the defendant, because the car of the defendant arrived at the alleged station and passed in before the plaintiff reached the same." Section 2134 of the Civil Code of 1902 is as follows: "Every railroad company in this state, shall cause its train of cars for passengers, to entirely stop upon each arrival at a station, advertised by such company as a station, for receiving passengers upon said trains, for a time sufficient to receive and let off passengers." The court commenting upon this provision, in Pickett v. Ry., 69 S. C. 445, 48 S. E. 466, uses this language: "It will thus be seen that *the statute* has made provisions for persons desiring to board the

Mitchell *v.* Augusta & A. Ry. Co

train. The railroad company owes no duty to a belated passenger to stop its train in any other manner than that required
by the statute. Creech *v.* Ry., 66 S. C. 528 [45 S. E. 86]. A
contrary doctrine would tend to disarrange the schedules of the
railroad company, and thus enhance the danger to the traveling
public."

In 5 Am. & E. Ency. of Law (2d Ed.) 488, it is stated: "The
relation of carrier and passenger begins when one puts himself
in the care of the carrier, or directly within its control, with the
bona fide intention of becoming a passenger and accepted as
such by the carrier. Seldom, however, is there any formal act
of delivery of the passenger's person into the care of the carrier,
or of acceptance by the carrier of one who presents himself
for transportation; hence the existence of the relation is commonly to be implied from the circumstances attendant. The rule
is that these circumstances must be such as will warrant an implication that one has offered himself to be carried, and that the
offer has been accepted by the carrier."

In Elliott on Railroads, § 1597, it is stated:

"A person may become a passenger before he has entered the
train or vehicle of the carrier. We think it safe to say that a
person becomes a passenger when, intending to take passage, he
enters a place provided for the reception of passengers as a depot, waiting room, or the like, at a time when such a place is
open for the reception of persons intending to take passage on
the trains of the company."

The annotator in Webster *v.* Railway (Mass.) 24 L. R. A. 521,
thus summarizes the result of the decisions: "Considering all
the decisions on the subject, which establish quite clearly that
a person may sometimes be a passenger when attempting to take
a train, although he has not yet got upon the car or even procured
his ticket, there seems to be no other limitation of the rule so satisfactory as that he must, in order to be regarded as a passenger,
present himself in a proper place and in a proper manner, because he cannot be presumed to have an invitation to present
himself in any other way."

It appears from the plaintiff's testimony that the station was
what is known as a "flag station," where the cars do not stop to
receive and let off passengers unless signaled; that the car on
that occasion did not stop to receive or let off passengers, but for
the purpose of entering the switch, so as to enable another car
to pass in an opposite direction; that it remained on the switch
a sufficient time to have enabled persons on the car, to have
alighted, or for those who were at the station when it arrived, to
have boarded it; that when the car stopped at the station, the
plaintiff was about 125 yards away from it.

Under these circumstances the plaintiff was not entitled to the
rights of a passenger, and the defendant did not owe to him the

duty of waiting. even for a short period of time. As the plaintiff was not at the station when the car arrived, he is not in a position to raise the question that the defendant did not wait a reasonable time.   Therefore the conclusion of the circuit judge is not in accord with the case of Pickett v. Ry.. 69 S. C. 445, 48 S. E. 466, and the other cases herein mentioned.

Judgment reversed.

CENTRAL OF GEORGIA RY. CO. v. STORRS.

(Supreme Court of Alabama, Feb. 10. 1910.   Rehearing Denied Dec. 22, 1910.)

[53 So. Rep. 746.]

Carriers—Injury to Passenger—Negligence—Question for Jury.— In an action for injury to a passenger by getting his foot caught between the bumpers of two passenger cars. as he was crossing from one car to another while the train was stopping at a station, and claimed to have been caused by some improper action of the air brake. or because the space was not covered. the carrier's negligence held for the jury.

Carriers—Who Are Passengers—Train Stopping at Station.*— Where a passenger train has stopped at a station. passengers. during the stop, may walk out of the car in which they are seated onto the station platform. or over the car platforms into another car, without losing their right to protection as passengers.

Damages—Personal Injuries—Earnings—Speculative Charges—Instructions.—An injured passenger testified that he was earning $1.500 for six months' work, and was not able to continue work after the injury.   Held that. in the absence of any intimation that his salary was speculative. or that it was continued to him while he was not working. the court did not err in refusing to charge that there could be no recovery for loss of salary between the date of the injury and the bringing of the suit.

Evidence—Opinions—Qualifications of Witness—Construction of Car Platform.—On an issue of a carrier's negligence in failing to cover the space between passenger cars, plaintiff having testified that he had traveled extensively over railroads all over the United States, except on the Pacific Coast, and especially over all the railroads in

---

*For the authorities in this series on the question whether a person may be a passenger of the railroad company after he has alighted from its train or street car at an intermediate station. see first footnote of Gannon v. Chicago, etc., Ry. Co. (Iowa), 31 R. R. R. 27, 54 Am. & Eng. R. Cas.. N. S., 27, where all those preceding it are collected.

Central of Georgia Ry. Co. *v.* Storrs

Alabama, he was property allowed to testify as to how passenger car platforms were arranged on other well-regulated railroads.

Carriers—Injuries to Passengers—Defective Platform.†—On an issue whether the space between passenger cars on a train was negligently left uncovered, evidence as to whether any cars had been constructed within the last five years with platforms like those on the car in question was admissible.

Appeal from City Court of Montgomery; W. H. Thomas, Judge.

Action by Charles P. Storrs against the Central of 'Georgia Railway Company for personal injuries received while a passenger. Judgment for plaintiff, and defendant appeals. Af. firmed.

The facts sufficiently appear in the opinion of the court. The following charges were refused to the defendant: (1) General affirmative charge. (4) "If you believe the evidence in this case, there was no defect in the construction of the coach or coaches in operation by the defendant at the time and place where plaintiff received his injuries." (5) "There is no evidence in this case of any defect in the equipment of the defendant's train at the time and place when and where the plaintiff was injured." (6) "Under the evidence in this case there can be no recovery for any alleged defect in the cars in use on the occasion when and where plaintiff was injured." (7) "It does not appear from the evidence in this case that defendant violated any duty it owed to the plaintiff in so far as the equipment of defendant's train was concerned." (9) "There can be no recovery in this case for any loss of salary to the plaintiff during any of the period intervening between the injury and the bringing of this suit."

Steiner, Crum & Weil, for appellant.
Hill, Hill & Whiting, for appellee.

SIMPSON, J. This action is by the appellee against the appellant, for damages on account of a personal injury received by the plaintiff while a passenger on defendant's train. The complaint alleges that the "defendant then and there so negligently conducted its said business that, by reason thereof and as a proximate consequence thereof, plaintiff received personal injuries," in having his foot bruised and injured. The second count describes the same injuries to his foot, and alleges the same to be the result of "the negligence of the defendant, or some agent, servant, or employee of the defendant's, while acting within the scope or line of his employment."

The plaintiff's testimony as to how the injury was received is

†See extensive note, 18 R. R. R. 321, 41 Am. & Eng. R. Cas., N. S., 321.

that he was a traveling salesman, a passenger on defendant's train, with a ticket from Samson to Dothan; that when the train reached Hartford, an intermediate station, the conductor called out, "All out for Hartford!" and walked out of the train; that when the train had stopped, plaintiff walked out of the rear coach, in which he had his seat, onto the platform, and undertook to cross to the next coach, intending to look out and see if he could discover a customer who lived at Hartford; that, as he started to cross from the platform of the rear coach to that of the one next in front, the bumpers caught his foot; that the train remained stationary for a while, and he heard no signal to move; that he did not know how it was that his foot happened to get between the bumpers; that the bumpers were a little apart, and he presumed, when he was walking, he put his right foot across, and started to put the other, and his toe must have gotten in between the bumpers; that there was no shield over the bumpers; that he had traveled a good deal over well-regulated railroads in this ano other states; that on other well-regulated railroads on which he had traveled the platforms are square, with a piece of steel across, so, when connected up, the cars fit close together; that "the majority of them have a steel shield that plays back and forth over the motion of the cars;" that this train had no such shield; that he had traveled on this particular road a number of times before; that it was not a vestibuled train, and there was no vestibuled train on that line; that his foot was held between the bumpers for "just an instant;" that the train did not move off until after he had gone back into his car; that the space between the bumpers was six or eight inches; that it was broad, open daylight; that his eyesight was fairly good; that he had been accustomed to travel on trains such as this was; that the opening was in plain view; that the bumpers were the ordinary bumpers that hold one car to the other; that his attention had never been called specifically to bumpers arranged as these were, but he must have seen them, as he had traveled on that train before; that he was not clear, but supposed there must have been similar bumpers and platforms on other roads over which he had traveled; that he never examined or paid any particular attention to the bumpers on this train before, but must necessarily have seen them, because he had traveled on the same train, operated the same way; that he could not well have gone from one car to the other without seeing it; that he supposed his foot must have projected a little over the opening, and naturally, his foot coming up, the two went in between the bumpers, and they came together and caught it.

The plaintiff did not attempt to state how or why it was that the car moved so that the ends of the platform came together at that time; but the conductor, while he stated that he did not see how the plaintiff got hurt, said also that the train was equipped with air brakes, and it is a hard matter to have the brakes all

Central of Georgia Ry. Co. *v.* Storrs

over the train working exactly alike, as sometimes the piston travel is longer; that on this occasion it may have been that the brakes were pulling a little harder on one car than on the other, and, if they were, when the brakes were released, one car would naturally roll up to the other car.

The general foreman of the shops of defendant testified that it was his duty to see that the engines and appliances to trains are in proper condition at each terminal; that the train in question was a standard passenger train, with automatic couplers; that it was in proper condition; that he had never seen a shield that crossed over from one car to the other; that the car in question had been in service for 15 years, and overhauled every year; that platforms have been improved since that car was built; that cars with such platforms had not been built within the last 5 years; that this platform was standard in construction, and the opening open to observation, so that any one could see it; that there is always "a buck motion, a surging back," before the engineer has released the brakes; that "that is sometimes done in bringing the train to a stop, when the brakes are not properly handled; that after the train comes to a full stop there is no movement. The engineer stated that the air brakes were working all right, and he managed them in the usual way in making the stop at Hartford (describing how it was done); that, while the air brakes are constructed with the idea that in stopping the train they will work automatically on each car at the same time," yet it is impossible to adjust them so they will all work at the same second; that he first reduced the pressure on the brakes, so as to bring them to the wheels, and gradually increased the same, so as to avoid the jerking; that there was no movement after the train came to a stop; also that, if the brakes are properly constructed, when the train is brought to a stop, it will stay stopped.

Under this evidence the court could not say, as a matter of law, that there was no defect in the condition of the brakes which caused this surging motion of the car; the passenger had a right to go from one car to another when the train was stopped, and while, if the lack of a shield was a defect, yet that was open to the observation of the plaintiff, yet there is nothing to show that he had any information as to the tendency to "buck" or move up, under certain conditions, and it cannot be said that the danger of stepping from one platform to the other was apparent to him. Consequently the court was not in error in refusing to give the general charge in favor of the defendant.

The next insistence of the appellant is that the court erred in refusing to give charge 8, requested in writing by the appellant. There was no error in this refusal. The charge is misleading, tending to make the impression that the plaintiff had no right to pass from one car to another. When the conductor called. "Hartford!" and the train stopped it was a notice to the passengers

Central of Georgia Ry. Co. v. Storrs

that the train would stop there for the usual time, in order that passengers might get on and off, and while this was the primary purpose of the notice, yet during that interval passengers are at liberty to walk out of the car, onto the station platform, or over the car platform into another car, still retaining their rights to protection as passengers. 2 Hutchinson on Carriers (3d Ed.) p. 1165, § 1012, and notes; Southern R. Co. v. Smith, 95 Va. 187, 28 S. E. 173.

From what has been heretofore said, and other reasons, there was no error in the refusal to give charges 4, 5, 6, and 7, requested by the defendant.

There was no error in the refusal to give charge 9, requested by the defendant. The plaintiff stated that he had been employed by M. & G. to travel, that being his fourth season; that he was earning $1,500 for six months' work, and was not able to continue work after the injury. There is no intimation that his salary was speculative, or that it was continued to him while he was not working. If such were the case, the defendant might have brought it out on cross-examination.

The objections to the questions as to how the platforms were arranged on other well-regulated railroads were properly overruled. The plaintiff had testified that he had traveled extensively over railroads, all over the United States (except the Pacific Slope), and specially over all the railroads in Alabama. He was competent to testify on this matter, and, if it had been desirable to have him distinguish between vestibuled trains and others, it could have been done by cross-examination.

There was no error in overruling the objection to the question to the witness Wagner, on cross-examination, as to whether any cars had been constructed, within the last five years, with platforms like those on the cars in question. Great latitude is allowed, on cross-examination, for the purpose of testing the accuracy and knowledge of the witness, and while it is true that the company was not obliged to adopt all improvements which had been made within five years, yet this was a circumstance proper to go to the jury, in considering whether the cars were properly equipped.

There was no error in overruling the motion for a new trial. As before stated, the matter of the condition of the equipment was for the jury to consider, and we cannot say that the preponderance of the evidence was so great against the verdict as to justify this court in reversing the decision of the trial court on that subject.

The judgment of the court is affirmed.

Affirmed.

Dowdell, C. J., and McClellan and Mayfield, JJ., concur.

Burgess ·v. Atchison, T. & S. F. Ry. Co.

(Supreme Court of Kansas, Dec. 10, 1910.)

[112 Pac. Rep. 103.]

Carriers—Ejection of Passenger—Negligence.—Where a passenger without a ticket takes a train for a station at which the train is not scheduled to stop, it is not negligence to eject such passenger, even if he offers to pay cash fare to the station where he wishes to stop.

Railroads—Injury to Person on Track—Negligence.—In such a case, where the person so ejected sits down on the end of a tie, and takes a position so that he is not plainly visible, and while in such position another train comes along, and the engineer, who sees an object upon the track, is uncertain what the object is until the engine gets so close that he is unable to stop it before it strikes such person, the company is not guilty of culpable negligence.

Railroads—Trespasser on Track—Care Required.*—A person who goes upon a railroad track without the leave or knowledge of the company, and without any business with it, is wrongfully there and a trespasser; and while a trespasser, the company owes him no duty, except not recklessly or wantonly to do him an injury.

(Syllabus by the Court.)

Appeal from District Court, Reno County.

Action by W. C. Burgess against the Atchison, Topeka & Santa Fè Railway Company. Judgment for plaintiff. Defendant appeals. Reversed.

W. R. Smith, O. J. Wood, and *A. A. Scott,* for appellant.
F. L. Martin, for appellee.

Graves, J.   This action was commenced in the district court of Reno county by W. C. Burgess to recover damages for a personal injury received by being struck with one of appellant's passing trains. He recovered therefor, and the company appeals.

Burgess was at Ellinwood, and wished to go to Raymond. He boarded a train which did not stop at Raymond. When about two miles from Raymond, the conductor asked him for his ticket. He had none. When he told the conductor that he wanted to stop at Raymond and would pay cash fare, he was informed that he could not stop the train at that place, and he must get off. The train was stopped and he was ejected. This was not negli-

---

*See first and second foot-notes of Chesapeake & O. R. Co. *v.* Lang (Ky.), 36 R. R. R. 630, 59 Am. & Eng. R. Cas., N. S., 630; last paragraph of foot-note of Chesapeake, etc., Ry. Co. *v.* Ball (Ky.), 35 R. R. R. 238, 58 Am. & Eng. R. Cas., N. S., 238; third head-note of Chesapeake, etc., Ry. Co. *v.* Corbin (Va.). 35 R. R. R. 229, 58 Am. & Eng. R. Cas., N. S., 229.

Burgess v. Atchison, T. & S. F. Ry. Co

gence. Burgess was intoxicated. He was left by the side of the track, and he attempted to follow the train afoot on the track.. After walking a short distance, he sat down on the end of the ties, and was soon overcome with a stupor. While in this condition a train passed along and struck his side, whereby he was pushed off on the side of the track and severely injured.

It is claimed that the men in charge of the train which struck the plaintiff were negligent in not discovering him in time to avoid the injury. It was a clear day, about noon. The track was straight; the ground smooth and practically level. It was in the month of January, when rank vegetation does not stand along the track. The plaintiff was sitting on the end of a tie, crouched down, with his head between his knees, and partially lying down. He would not readily be taken for a human being. He was not at a crossing, or where a human being would be expected. After the engineer discovered that the object was really a human being, he attempted to stop the train, but did not succeed in time to avoid the injury. It must be remembered that, when a person is upon a railroad track without leave and has no business with the company, such person is a trespasser, and the company owes him no duty, except not wantonly to injure him. It is not pretended here that the company was recklessly or wantonly negligent in this case. In the absence of such a degree of negligence, the plaintiff has no cause of action, and should not recover a judgment. The rule of law controlling such a case is clearly and forcibly stated by Chief Justice Doster in the case of Railway Co. v. Prewitt, 59 Kan. 734, 54 Pac. 1067. The following cases decide practically to the same effect; Railway Co. v. Hathaway, 121 Ky. 666, 89 S. W. 724, 2 L. R. A. (N. S.) 498; Railway Co. v. Williams, 69 Miss. 631, 12 South. 957; Railway v. McMillan, 100 Tex. 562, 102 S. W. 103. In harmony with these cases we hold that the company was not guilty of such negligence as creates a liability.

The judgment is reversed, with direction to enter judgment for costs in favor of the defendant. All the Justices concurring.

SHIELDS *v.* SOUTHERN PAC. CO. *et al.*

(Supreme Court of Oregon, Dec. 13, 1910.)

[112 Pac. Rep. 4.]

Railroads—Operation—Injuries to Persons on Tracks—Licensees —Duty to Warn.*—A railroad company owes licensees who cross its tracks no duty to warn them of passing trains; the track itself being a sufficient warning.

Appeal and Error—Prejudicial Error—Instructions—Failure to Give.—Where a jury, in an action against a railroad company for an injury received by a licensee on the track, requests an instruction as to whether or not it was negligence for the railroad to permit persons to cross its track without signals of warning, the failure of the court to instruct them that it is not negligence is reversible error.

Appeal from Circuit Court, Multnomah County; Thomas O'Day, Judge.

Action by Richard Shields against the Southern Pacific Company and another. From a judgment for plaintiff, the Southern Pacific Railway Company appeals. Reversed and remanded.

This is an action for damages sustained by plaintiff on account of an injury, occasioned by being struck by a railway engine of the Southern Pacific Company near the depot in the city of Portland. A railway bridge, which crosses the Willamette river near the depot, has an upper deck for the accommodation of public travel, while the lower deck is used exclusively by the railroad companies for the passage of their trains. This bridge is owned by the Oregon Railway & Navigation Company, but is used also by the Southern Pacific Company under some arrangement, the details of which do not appear in the evidence. There is a stairway upon the north side of the bridge and near its westerly end, leading from its upper deck to the ground, just east of the east line of Front street, where the upper deck of the bridge passes over the street, which was built by the Oregon Railway & Navigation Company. By the side of the stairway, and alongside of the railway track crossing the bridge, are two large piers several feet in diameter, which support the upper deck of the bridge. The railroad track crossing the bridge begins to curve a short distance east of the point where it passes the bridge piers. There is evidence tending to show that a person passing down the steps to the ground would be unable to see along the lower deck of the bridge or to see a train crossing the bridge from the east, until it emerged from between the piers or about 70 feet from where a person descending the stairway on his way to Front

---
*See foot-note of preceding case.

Shields *v.* Southern Pac. Co. et al

street usually crossed the railway track leading from the bridge to the Union Depot. The evidence tends to show that a large number of persons used these steps and crossed the track daily, on their way to Front street, without objection by the railway company; and that no signs, forbidding such use of the stairway, were in existence. An ordinance of the city prohibits trains from running faster than 6 miles per hour within the city limits. There is some testimony, on plaintiff's part, tending to show that, at the time of the accident, the train was running at a speed of from 12 to 20 miles per hour; but this is strongly contradicted by the evidence of defendant. Plaintiff walked across the bridge, toward his place of business, went down the stairway, and was proceeding across the track, in order to reach Front street, when he was struck by a locomotive, attached to a passenger train, and was injured.

Plaintiff testified that, owing to there being a number of tracks at the west end of the bridge, it was impossible for him to tell at a glance upon which of them the train was coming in, and was unable, by using his best endeavor, to escape injury; that he stopped, looked, and listened, before starting to cross the track, and did not hear any bell or noise indicating an approaching train; that he stopped just before he reached the first track and waited a few minutes to make sure there was no train coming, and no danger, then started across, and first saw the train as it emerged from the bridge, when it was about 70 or 80 feet distant; that, being confused as to which track it was on, he attempted to escape by taking the shortest way across the track.

The jury were permitted to view the locality where the accident occurred. Before the cause was submitted, plaintiff took a voluntary nonsuit as to the terminal company, leaving the Southern Pacific Company the sole defendant. After the jury had retired for deliberation, they returned into court and propounded the following question: "Is it unlawful or even a presumption of negligence for a railroad company to permit the use of a path or steps leading to its property on which trains are operated, without giving the public warning of danger?" In answer to this question, the court used the following language: "Gentlemen, this question which you have submitted to me is a combination of law and fact. It is one that I cannot answer directly, because if I did that would be trespassing upon your right to pass upon the facts. I will say, however, that probably I can answer the proposition as to the law without trespassing upon your province to pass upon the facts. And I will promise that by saying that if you find that these steps, where they landed, were on private property, of course it goes without saying that a person who owns private property can prevent others from going thereon. What I desire to say, and what the law is, is this: If the public are permitted to use it, and that use has extended for such a time that the company might have reasonably expected to have notice of its use, they would have to use such ordinary property subject to this use of the public. That is, they would have to use such ordinary care as an ordinarily prudent person would use to prevent injury. It would be akin to the use of a street, and it would be their duty to use such reasonable ordinary care in regard thereto as it would be to use ordinary care where they cross a street." The defendant excepted to the giving of this instruction and the failure of the court to answer the question propounded by the jury, and requested the court to instruct as follows: "I will ask your honor to instruct the jury that it will not be the duty of the company—that is, I mean, it would not be affirmatively the duty of the company—to warn the public, and ᵗhat that question should be answered in the negative as a matter of law." This request was refused by the court and an exception allowed. Thereafter the jury returned a verdict for the plaintiff in the sum of $4,850. Defendant appeals.

Wm. D. Fenton and *Ben C. Dey,* for appellant.
H. H. Riddell and *Jay H. Upton,* for respondent.

McBride, J. (after stating the facts as above). The congested condition of the docket of this court precludes us from any extended discussion of the facts upon which counsel for defendant predicates the contention that a nonsuit should have been granted by the court below. We have carefully considered the evidence and do not agree with counsel in their contention that the physical facts so contradicted the testimony of witnesses that the latter should be rejected as a matter of law. Much of this testimony related to the speed of the train, the opportunity that plaintiff had of observing its approach and protecting himself from danger by the exercise of ordinary care. Upon all these matters we think the plaintiff introduced sufficient testimony to make a case for a jury, and that the court properly refused a nonsuit.

We find one material error, however, which compels us to reverse this case, and that was the refusal to answer the question propounded by the jury. This action was predicated upon the alleged negligence of defendant in two particulars: (1) Running at an unusual and unlawful rate of speed; (2) failing to give warning by ringing the bell or blowing the whistle. No question of posting notices or warnings at or about the steps was involved, and as a matter of law none were necessary. The track itself is a sufficient warning of danger. When the jury came in and asked whether it was unlawful or a presumption of negligence for a railroad company to permit the use by the public of a path or steps leading to its track without giving public warning of danger, they should have been told that, so far as the case at bar was concerned, it was not unlawful and did not in itself create a presumption of negligence. The testimony in regard to defendant's negligence in other respects was contradictory, and, considering the nature of the question propounded by the jury, this court cannot say whether the finding of negligence, upon which the verdict was predicated, was within the issues made by the pleadings or upon a failure to post notices upon the stairway warning the public to beware of locomotives. The instruction actually given practically left the minds of the jurors in the same condition that they were in before the question was asked, and did not tend in any way to dissipate any erroneous impression which they may have had, and which some of them evidently did have, that a recovery could be had because of the failure of the company to give public warning of danger.

For the reason above given, the judgment will be reversed, and a new trial ordered.

Morris v. Illinois Cent. R. Co.

(Supreme Court of Louisiana, Nov. 28, 1910.)

[53 So. Rep. 698.]

Carriers—Injuries to Passengers—Alighting from Moving Train.*
—A passenger, who has every reasonable opportunity to ascertain whether a train from which he is about to alight is still in motion, fails to assure himself that the train has stopped sufficiently to permit him to alight without danger, cannot hold the railroad responsible for injuries received while getting off the moving train.

Carriers—Injury to Passenger—Evidence.†—The fact that a flagman fails to notify a passenger who had left the coach and is standing on the step that the train is moving, and that it is dangerous to attempt to alight while the train is in motion, will not charge the company with negligence, because the fact that the passenger is on the step ready to alight does not warn the flagman that he will do so while the train is in motion, and at a time when it is dangerous to do so.

Carriers—Injuries to Passengers—Alighting from Moving Train.†
—Employees of a railroad should use ordinary care to prevent in-

---

*For the authorities in this series on the question whether it is contributory negligence to alight from a moving train or street car at the direction or invitation of an employee of the carrier, see last foot-note of Owens v. Atlantic Coast Line R. Co. (N. Car.), 36 R. R. R. 483, 59 Am. & Eng. R. Cas., N. S., 483; first foot-note of Chesapeake. etc., R. Co. v. Robinson (Ky.), 35 R. R. R. 205, 58 Am. & Eng. R. Cas., N. S., 205; Missouri Pac. Ry. Co. v. Irvin (Kan.), 35 R. R. R. 187. 58 Am. & Eng. R. Cas., N. S., 187.

†For the authorities on the subject of the duty to warn and in-

Morris v. Illinois Cent. R. Co

juries to passenger; but the failure of these employees to control passengers who will jump from a moving train in disregard of their safety is not a failure of the duty of the trainmen.

Carriers—Injury to Passengers—Alighting from Moving Train.‡— The announcement that the next stop was Kentwood was not an invitation to the passenger to alight before it was safe to do so.

Evidence—Admissibility—Declarations of Injured Party.—While, ordinarily, courts will not give much weight to statements detrimental to the rights of the plaintiff made by him while suffering great pain, and at the persistent importunity of the defendant, still due weight will be given to these statements when made after he has had time for reflection, when these statements are corroborated.

Carriers—Injury to Passenger—Evidence.—The plaintiff failed to sustain the burden of proof that rested upon him.

(Syllabus by the Court.)

Appeal from Twenty-Fifth Judicial District Court Parish of Tangipahoa; R. S. Ellis, Judge.

Action by H. G. Morris against the Illinois Central Railroad Company. Judgment for defendant, and plaintiff appeals. Affirmed.

William H. McClendon, for appellant.

Kemp & Spiller (Hunter C. Leake, of counsel), for appellee.

BREAUX, C. J. Dr. H. G. Morris, a physician, sued the defendant company to recover the sum of $9,395.50.

The facts are: Late in the evening of March 18, 1909, he boarded a through train of the defendant company at McComb City to return to his home in Kentwood, La. He had a patient in Kentwood upon whom he desired to call at earliest possible moment.

He requested, and those in charge of defendant's train granted his request, to be permitted to stop at Kentwood, although the train was not scheduled to stop at that place.

Travel on the regular passenger train would not have served his purpose; that is, of coming to Kentwood early enough to timely call on his patient.

The flagman on this through train had never previous to this trip served on a regular passenger train.

The doctor arrived at Kentwood about 9 o'clock p. m. He had paid his fare upon entering the car at McComb City. He took a seat in the car and fell asleep.

---

struct passengers and negligence in allowing them to expose themselves to danger, see last foot-note of Farrington *v.* Boston Elev. Ry. Co. (Mass.), 34 R. R. R. 229, 57 Am. & Eng. R. Cas., N. S., 229; last head-note of Feil *v.* West Jersey S. R. Co. (N J.), 34 R. R. R. 422, 57 Am. & Eng. R. Cas., N. S., 422.

‡See last foot-note of Powers *v.* Connecticut Co. (Conn.), 34 R. R. R. 434, 57 Am. & Eng. R. Cas., N. S., 434.

Morris *v.* Illinois Cent. R. Co

He was awakened by the flagman of the train shortly before reaching his destination and about the time the train was whistling for the station Kentwood.

The plaintiff in his own behalf said that the flagman told him to get off there, meaning Kentwood; that the flagman left him, and where he went he (plaintiff) did not know. He next saw the flagman bending toward him in the coach at the door with a lantern on his arm and looking at him.

Plaintiff arose from his seat and walked toward the flagman. He passed him in the door and was of the impression at the time that the train had stopped at the station at Kentwood, and that he (the trainman) at that particular moment was standing in the rear of the car with the lantern still in his hand; that he walked out, stepped on the ground, fell over, and was badly hurt. Part of his foot was amputated. His arm was also badly bruised and hurt.

R. H. Hayes, the flagman, says: That at Kentwood, after calling out the station, he opened the door. That Dr. Morris came out with him and walked down the steps, and that he walked down with him. He does not remember whether he (the flagman) was on the top step, but says that Dr. Morris was on the step just below him. That just before the train came to a stop Dr. Morris stepped off before he could prevent him, fell on the walk when he stepped off, and rolled down between the curbing and the track. That he (Morris) knew the train was moving.

One of plaintiff's ankles was weak. Years ago he met with an accident. His ankle was injured. He had not since recovered the full strength of that ankle.

The flagman, Hayes, although this was his first trip, swore that he knew the duties of a passenger flagman. He stood an examination on the rules of the company. He had been in its employ a number of years.

Defendant's counsel suggest in argument that, doubtless, plaintiff felt under obligation to the local railroad authorities, particularly to one of their agents through whose kind offices he had obtained the very legitimate favor of taking the fast through train and of stopping at Kentwood to call as early as possible on a patient awaiting the doctor's visit; that he wished to make the stop as speedily as possible, and in doing this was himself hasty and imprudent.

There is evidence to sustain that theory.

The train was still in motion. Plaintiff testified that it was in motion, but that he was not aware of it at the time.

The question arises: Did it not devolve upon him to satisfy himself before alighting that the train was standing ready to permit passengers to alight?

If a passenger, who has every reasonable opportunity to assure himself that the train is at full stop, fails to make inquiry, he

Morris *v*. Illinois Cent. R. Co

cannot hold others liable for damages in case he alights while it is in motion and is hurt.

There were lights at the depot; also near, and other visible objects, although it was in the night, whereby it was possible to satisfy himself that the train was still moving; besides, the motion of the car is of itself a warning that the train is still moving and has not come to a full stop.

Plaintiff's position is that there was negligence on the part of the flagman, who should have warned him of the danger and should have notified him not to attempt to alight.

Unquestionably, that would have been a very proper act on the part of the flagman.

The question is whether the company is liable for the failure of its flagman to thus notify and warn the plaintiff.

That is not the trend of the decision. In a well-considered case, it was decided:

"That there is an implied contract—the passenger assents to the company's rules and regulations for leaving their cars, and, if injury befall him by reason of his disregard of the regulations necessary for conducting the business, the company is not liable even though the negligence of the servants concurred with his own negligence in causing the mischief." Penn. R. R. *v*. Zebe, 33 Pa. 318.

We do not go that far. We do not hold that the servant was negligent. If we were to arrive at that conclusion, we would decide that plaintiff is entitled to damages.

The flagman had seen plaintiff pass him. He was standing behind him on the steps. He, the testimony states, had no reason to infer that plaintiff would seek to alight at that particular time.

It happens (it is within common knowledge) that passengers frequently step down to that step while on their way to alight without attempting to step off before the car has stopped.

We are not led to infer from the testimony that the flagman had invited the passenger to step off.

It is true, as before stated, that at about the time the whistle sounded for Kentwood he announced that the next stop was that place. There is not in this announcement an invitation to alight before the train has stopped.

The following is from the text of Thompson on Negligence:

"Ordinarily, a railway carrier of passengers is under no duty to assist adult passengers who are in apparent good health and possession of their faculties to get on and off its vehicles or to find seats for them; but its duty is limited to giving them a reasonable time and opportunity to do so without assistance, and this is especially true where there are no special sources of danger."

We do not give entire approval to the utterances of the commentation, based, it is said, on numerous decisions, for the em-

ployees should always exercise ordinary care to prevent accident;
but this, in our opinion, does not involve the necessity of seeking
to control the action of those who will jump off without sufficient
regard to their own safety.

Ordinarily, if one, while suffering excruciating pains, is called
upon to answer by an importunate defendant or other person
equally as persistent and rude, and the wounded person makes
statements to the detriment of his rights, courts will not give
them effect.

Plaintiff, a considerable time after the accident, after he had
had days of reflection, said, in substance, that he was not cautious
enough, or that he alone was to blame.

We would not attach importance to the statement if it did not
agree with our view of the case.

Plaintiff swore that the claim agent of the defendant company
promised to pay the expenses of his illness.

Taking the testimony of the plaintiff and of the agent, we do
not find it possible to render a judgment allowing the amount.
As witnesses, the plaintiff and the agent flatly contradict each
other; one affirms, and the other denies.

It follows, under well-settled jurisprudence, that the claim is
not proven.

We are constrained to affirm the judgment.

For reasons stated, the judgment is affirmed.

State *v.* Wignall.

(Supreme Court of Iowa, Dec. 15, 1910.)

[128 N. W. Rep. 935.]

**Commerce—Intoxicating Liquors—Interstate Shipment—Purchase
for Individual Use.**—The Legislature has no power to deprive a citizen or resident of Iowa of his rights to have liquor shipped from
another state for his personal use, nor to receive such liquor and
remove the same from the express or railway office to his own home
or place of business.

Commerce—Interstate Commerce—Transportation of Liquor.—
Where several residents of Iowa ordered liquor from another state
at the same time, and defendant received the liquor from the railroad
station in Iowa and gratuitously transported it inland to the purchasers as their agents, defendant was not engaged in interstate commerce.

State v. Wignall

Commerce—Interstate Commerce—Transportation of Liquor.*— Code 1897, § 2419, provides that, if any common carrier or person shall transport or convey to any person within the state any intoxicating liquors without first having obtained a certificate from the clerk of the court showing that the consignee is a permit holder, such carrier or person, on conviction, shall be fined, etc. Held, that such section is not unconstitutional as interfering with interstate commerce.

Commerce — Intoxicating Liquors—Regulation—Transportation— Legislative Power.—That the Legislature may not prevent a resident from himself getting intoxicating liquor imported from another state from the station and carrying it to his home for his personal use does not prevent the Legislature from prohibiting the transportation of such liquor from the railroad carrier to his home by means of an employee.

Commerce—Intoxicating Liquors—Regulation — Transportation— "Person."—Code 1897, § 2419, provides that if any common carrier or person, or any one as agent or employee thereof, shall transport to any person within the state any intoxicating liquors without first being furnished with a certificate that the consignee is the holder of a permit to sell intoxicating liquors in the county to which the shipment is made, such carrier or person shall on conviction be fined, etc. Held, that the word "person," as used in such section, means a public or private carrier, and did not include one who transported several interstate shipments of liquor from the railroad company's depot to the consignee's place of residence as a mere gratuity.

Appeal from District Court, Mahaska County; W. G. Clements, Judge.

Defendant was convicted of illegally transporting intoxicating liquors, and from the judgment imposed appeals. Reversed.

Burrell & Devitt, for appellant.

H. W. Byers, Atty. Gen., and *Chas. W. Lyo*, Asst. Atty. Gen., for the State.

DEEMER, C. J. Section 2419 of the Code of 1897, so far as material, reads as follows: "If any express or railway company, or any common carrier, or person, or any one as the agent or employee thereof, shall transport or convey to any persons within

---

*For the authorities in this series on the subject of state interference with interstate commerce, see Detroit, etc., R. Co. v. State (Ohio), 36 R. R. R. 625, 59 Am. & Eng. R. Cas., N. S., 625; last paragraph of last foot-note of Davis v. Cleveland, etc., Ry. Co. (U. S.), 36 R. R. R. 92, 59 Am. & Eng. R. Cas., N. S., 92; foot-note of Missouri Pac. Ry. Co. v. Kansas (U. S.), 35 R. R. R. 728, 58 Am. & Eng R. Cas., N. S., 728; foot-note of Yazoo, etc., R. Co. v. Greenwood Grocery Co. (Miss.), 35 R. R. R. 417, 58 Am. & Eng. R. Cas., N. S., 417.

For the authorities in this series on the subject of interstate transportation of intoxicants into prohibition territory, see foot-note of Adams Express Co. v. Commonwealth (Ky.), 21 R. R. R. 304, 44 Am. & Eng. R. Cas., N. S., 304; State v. Intoxicating Liquors (Me.), 24 R. R. R. 273, 47 Am. & Eng. R. Cas., N. S., 273.

State *v.* Wignall

this state any intoxicating liquors, without first having been furnished with a certificate from the clerk of the court issuing the permit, showing that the consignee is a permit holder and authorized to sell liquors in the county to which the shipment is made, such company, common carrier, person, agent or employee thereof, shall upon conviction, be fined in the sum of one hundred dollars for each offense and pay the costs of prosecution, including a reasonable attorney's fee to be taxed by the court. The offense herein created shall be held committed and complete and to have been committed in any county in the state in which the liquors are received for transportation, through which they are transported, or in which they are delivered."

The information filed under this section was in five counts, each reading in substance as follows: "For that the said defendant on the 5th day of January, 1910, in the county of Mahaska and state of Iowa aforesaid, did willfully, unlawfully, and feloniously transport intoxicating liquor, to wit, beer, over the public highway, from Eddyville, Iowa, to White City, Iowa, and did deliver one case of bottled beer to Lewis Lanphere, contrary to law."

The case was tried upon an agreed statement of facts the material parts of which are as follows: "It is conceded that on or about the 27th day of December, 1909, various persons residing at White City, Iowa, by written orders, ordered from the Hamm Brewing Company of Rock Island, Ill., quantities of intoxicating liquor, as shown by the orders hereto attached, consisting of five orders. That in each case a money order was secured at the post office at White City and inclosed with the order. That the orders, with the money orders in payment of the same, were inclosed and sent by mail to the Hamm Brewing Company at Rock Island, Ill. That the parties sending the orders purchased the intoxicating liqours therein referred to for their own personal use in each case, and that none of said liquor was ordered by any of said persons for the purpose of selling the same within the state. That on or about the 30th day of December said orders were received by the Hamm Brewing Company at Rock Island, Ill., and were filled by them, and that the same were shipped from Rock Island, in the state of Illinois, to White City, in the state of Iowa, consigned and properly labeled 'Beer' according to law, addressed to the persons ordering the same, each in a separate package. That duplicate bills of lading which are hereto attached numbered 1, 2, 3, 4, and 5, being exhibits in the case, and by this reference made a part of the agreed statement of facts, were executed by the railroad company and filed and delivered to the agent of the Rock Island Railroad Company at Eddyville, Iowa. That White City is not upon the Rock Island Railroad, but is an inland town, situated about eight miles from Eddyville, the nearest station on said Rock Island Railroad to White City, in Mahaska county, Iowa. That each

State *v.* Wignall

of the persons so ordering said liquor, to wit, E. J. Brugman, Frank Polito, Louie Abrahamson, L. D. Duprey, and Lewis Lanphere, gave the defendant, Thomas Wignall, an order on the Rock Island Railway Company to deliver to said Thomas Wignall the shipments of intoxicating liquor that they had previously ordered from the Hamm Brewing Company at Rock Island, Ill. That each of said persons employed said Wignall to deliver to them at White City the liquor that had been ordered from Rock Island and was carried on the Rock Island Railroad as far as Eddyville to finish the shipment from Rock Island to White City, by hauling the orders of liquor from the railroad depot at Eddyville to their residences in White City. That the said Thomas Wignall was the agent of the consignee who had ordered the liquor hereinbefore named, and was acting as their agent in hauling the liquor from the railroad station at Eddyville to their residences at White City. That the defendant, Thomas Wignall, as agent for the consignees named, presented the orders given by each of them to the agent of the Rock Island Railway at Eddyville, and said agent at Eddyville delivered to said Wignall, upon presentation of said orders, the packages of liquor that had been ordered by the parties before named, and that said Thomas Wignall, acting as agent for said parties, hauled said packages from the depot at Eddyville to the residences and delivered the same at the residences of each of the said parties in White City; said delivery being made on or about January 5th. Order: '12-27-1909. Hamm Brewing Company, Rock Island, Ill.—Gentlemen: Enclosed please find $1.50. Ship me, freight, one case new brew [Signed] E. J. Brugman. Address, White City, Iowa. Agents not allowed to solicit orders. Cash must accompany orders unless parties are known to us.' The other four exhibits, being orders, are similar to the above, except as to the names. Duplicate bill of lading: The bills of lading are in the ordinary form, showing shipment by Hamm Brewing Company; consigned to E. J. Brugman; destination, Eddyville, for White City; one case bottled beer. And stamped upon said bill of lading is the following: 'Goods to be transferred at Eddyville by you to Thomas Wignall, drayman, to complete the transportation and delivery to consignee at White City.' The other four bills of lading are the same as the above, except as to the names of the parties."

Upon this record a judgment of conviction was rendered.

On this appeal it is contended that: (1) The court erred in holding that Code, § 2419, prohibited the defendant from transporting an interstate shipment of liquor that had been ordered by a citizen of Iowa from the state of Illinois for his own personal use from the depot to the residence of the party ordering the liquor, and it holding that the party ordering the liquor could have transported it himself from the depot to his residence, without

State *v.* Wignall

violating Code, § 2419, but that the defendant could not so transport the same liquor from the depot to the residence of the party
ordering the same.   (2) It is claimed that, if the act is not given
this construction, it is unconstitutional and void.

We do not dispute the proposition announced by many courts
that a resident of the state has the right to have liquor shipped
from another state for his own personal use, and that the Legislature has no power to deprive him of the right to receive such
liquor and to remove it from an express or railway office to his
own home or place of business.   But the question here is, not his
right to do so, but the right of another to get the goods from a
carrier, and as the agent of the purchaser, and not of the carrier
or shipper. deliver the same to the buyer.   The agreed statement
of facts does not disclose that defendant is either a public or
private carrier, except that, without any compensation so far as
shown and as a mere gratuity, he acted as the agent of the purchaser in hauling the packages of liquor from the depot at Eddyville to the residences of the consignees of the liquor.   It will
also be observed that there is no showing of any kind that
the purchasers did not have the permits referred to in the
section of the Code heretofore quoted.   We do not think
that defendant was in any manner engaged in interstate
commerce.   Moreover, we are constrained to hold that the
section of the law under consideration is not, when properly construed. unconstitutional, because it interferes in any way with
commerce between the states.   Defendant was in no other sense
than as already pointed out a carrier of the goods.   He simply
undertook, as agent of the consignee, to get the goods at the depot
and to deliver them to the purchasers without any consideration
so far as shown.   Appellant argues that, so long as the purchaser
himself had the right to get the goods from the carrier and take
them to his home for his own personal use. the state has no right
to prevent his employee from doing the same act for him.   But
this is not sound.   No reason has been given for saying that the
Legislature cannot prohibit one from doing for another what that
other may lawfully do for himself.   Certainly there is no constitutional objection to such an act.   No case has been cited
which so holds and we have not been able to find one after a
somewhat diligent search.   High *v.* State, 2 Okl. Cr. 161, 101
Pac. 115, is not in point, for the opinion merely considers the
right of the purchaser of liquors for personal use to transport it
to his own home.   The drayman was discharged in that case for
the reason that he did not know the contents of the barrel he was
conveying.   In the opinion of the court, in deciding the constitutional question, discussed the case solely from the standpoint of
the purchaser of the liquor.   Moreover. the statute there construed read as follows: "Or who shall ship or in any way convey such liquors from one place within this state to another place

State *v.* Wignall

therein except the conveyance of a lawful purchase as herein-after authorized, shall be punished on conviction thereof, by fine not less than fifty dollars and by imprisonment not less than thirty days for each offense." Bunn's Const. Okl. § 499.   It will thus be seen that the decision of the Oklahoma Court is not in point.   No other case touches the question even incidentally.

We still have left the question of defendant's guilt under the statute.   As already suggested, there is no sufficient showing that defendant was even a drayman.   The case against him is no stronger than one where one neighbor, for the convenience of another, undertakes for a mere gratuity to get liquor ordered by the other for his personal use from the depot of a common carrier and conveys and delivers it to the purchaser.   Is such an act in violation of the statute quoted?   We are constrained to hold that it is not.   Criminal statutes are to be strictly con-strued, and in case of doubt these doubts are to be solved in favor of the accused.   Taking the statute by its four corners, looking to all its provisions, and applying the ordinary rules of construction thereto, we think it only applies to railway and ex-press companies, common carriers, or other persons engaged in the carrying business, and not to private individuals acting with-out consideration and for the purpose of conferring a favor even though he be acting as an agent of the buyer of the goods. It is familiar doctrine that the meaning of a word used in a statute, as "person" in the particular case, must be construed in connection with the words with which it is associated.   And all words should be so limited in their application as not to lead to injustice, oppression, or an absurd consequence.   State *v.* Smith, 46 Iowa, 670; State *v.* Smiley, 65 Kan. 240, 69 Pac. 199, 67 L. R. A. 903; State *v.* Botkin, 71 Iowa, 87, 32 N. W. 185, 60 Am. Rep. 780; Oakland *v.* Oakland, 118 Cal. 160, 50 Pac. 277; State *v.* Fry, 186 Mo. 198, 85 S. W. 328.

While in the abstract general terms are to be given their nat-ural and full significance, yet, where they follow specific words of a like nature, they take their meaning from the latter, and are presumed to embrace only persons or things of the kind desig-nated by them.   Brown *v.* Bell, 124 N. W. 901; State *v.* Eno, 131 Iowa, 619, 109 N. W. 119; Burlington *v.* Leebrick, 43 Iowa, 252; McBride *v.* Des Moines Ry. Co., 134 Iowa, 398, 109 N. W. 618; State *v.* Campbell, 76 Iowa, 122, 40 N. W. 100.

Defendant was not, as we have already seen, shown to have been a carrier, either public or private, and we do not think his guilt is shown by the agreed statement of facts.   Moreover, ex-cept by the barest inference, there is no showing that the pur-chasers of the liquor did not have permits, or that the defendant did not have a certificate showing such permits.

Concluding, we may suggest that the statute does not, as the Attorney General contends, make it unlawful for any person or

Vol 39 R R R—Vol 62 Am & Eng R Cas N S   179

State ex rel. Skeen *v.* Ogden Rapid Transit Co

corporation to transport or convey within this state intoxicating liquors to any person within the state without a certificate, etc. If the Legislature had so intended, it would have been a very easy matter to have said so. That it did not so say is the very best reason for deciding that it did not so intend.

The trail court was in error in finding the defendant guilty under the agreed statement of facts, and its judgment must be, and it is reversed.

STATE ex rel. SKEEN *v.* OGDEN RAPID TRANSIT CO.

(Supreme Court of Utah, Nov. 25, 1910.)

[112 Pac. Rep. 120.]

Railroads—Duties to Stop to Receive and Discharge Passengers—Statutes.—The duties imposed on carriers by Comp. Laws 1907, § 449, requiring every railroad to furnish sufficient accommodations for the transportation of persons and property at any station or stopping place established for receiving and discharging passengers and freight, must be discharged by a carrier at depots or stopping places duly established, and it does not require a carrier to stop its cars at any particular place to discharge or receive passengers.

Railroads—Duties to Establish Stations—Power of Courts.—The statutes do not confer on the courts power to determine whether a carrier should or should not establish and maintain a depot or stopping place for the reception and discharge of passengers or freight, or either, at any particular place or places along its line of road.

Mandamus—Performance of Common-Law Duty.—Where the common law imposes on a person a duty and the right of another to require performance thereof is clear and reasonably free from doubt, mandamus lies to compel such person to discharge that duty.

Railroads—Regulation—Depots.—The Legislature may, within limits, direct where a carrier shall maintain depots or stopping places for the convenience of the public, and it may require a carrier to stop its trains or some of them at such depots, or stopping places or it may confer the power to determine whether a carrier shall do so on some board, and, in either case, the courts may coerce a defaulting carrier by mandamus to comply with the legislative edict or with an order of the board.

Railroads—Regulation—Depots.—Under ordinary circumstances, no inherent power is vested in the courts to control a carrier in its determination of the number of depots or stopping places that it will establish or maintain, or in tha selection of the places where it will establish and maintain them along its line of railroad, but the matter is for legislative regulation.

Carriers—Regulation—Discrimination.—The Courts may prevent discrimination by a carrier.

State ex rel. Skeen *v.* Ogden Rapid Transit Co

Mandamus—Regulation—Discrimination.*—Where the duty of a carrier to receive a particular person at a particular place is clear, the courts may by mandamus compel the carrier to discharge the duty.

Courts—Jurisdiction.—A court is an agency of the state by means of which justice is administered, and it may not exceed the powers vested in it for the sole reason that in its judgment it is necessary to exercise the power in the administration of justice.

Railroads—Train Service—Discrimination—Statutes.—Under Comp. Laws 1907, § 455, providing against disctimination from the same place under like conditions, and independent thereof, an interurban railway which stops its cars to receive and discharge passengers at resorts along its line of road and which refuses to do so at another resort is not guilty of discrimination, in the absence of evidence that any person stopped off at the former resorts simply because he could not do so at the latter resort, though the carrier refuses to stop at the latter resort merely out of ill will, and though there is no ground for its refusal to receive and discharge passengers there.

Carriers—Train Service—Discrimination.—The court in determining whether an interurban railway company is guilty of discrimination because it stops its cars to receive and discharge passengers at resorts along its line and refuses to do so at another resort may not consider the fact that it stops its cars at one resort, where such stop is by virtue of a special contract by it for a valuable consideration.

Railroads—Mandamus—Discrimination — Remedy.*—Where a carrier refuses permission to one person to enter or alight from its cars at a place where under similar circumstances it extends the privilege to others, the carrier is guilty of discrimination against the former, and the court may by mandamus prevent it.

Appeal from District Court, Weber County; J. A. Howell, Judge.

Mandamus by the State, on the relation of J. D. Skeen, against the Ogden Rapid Transit Company. From a judgment for plaintiff, defendant appeals. Reversed and remanded.

Richards & Boyd, for appellant.
J. D. Skeen, for respondent.

FRICK, J. On the 27th day of June, 1910, the plaintiff applied to the district court of Weber county, Utah, for a writ of mandate to require the defendant, as a common carrier of passengers, to stop its cars at a certain place named in the application for the purpose of permitting the plaintiff and others to enter upon said cars as passengers and to alight therefrom at the place stated. The district court, after a hearing, issued a peremptory writ in which the prayer of the plaintiff was granted, and the

---

*See foot-note of State *v.* Chicago & N. W. R. Co. (Neb.), 34 R. R. R. 481, 57 Am. & Eng. R. Cas., N. S., 481.

State ex rel. Skeen *v.* Ogden Rapid Transit Co

defendant now presents the record of the proceedings in due form to this court for review on appeal.

A careful reading of the entire record, including all of the evidence adduced at the hearing, discloses substantially the following facts concerning which there is practically no dispute:

The defendant is a corporation organized as a common carrier of passengers, and owns and operates a certain line of street and interurban railway. The line of railway is operated, as aforesaid. for a distance of about seven miles between the Ogden Union Depot and what is known as the "Hermitage" located in Ogden Canyon, in Weber county, Utah. At the mouth of Ogden Canyon is located what is known as the Ogden Canyon Sanitarium, which is a public summer resort. A hotel for the accommodation of patrons, saloon, dance hall, and other places of amusement are maintained there for the pleasure and amusement of the public generally. The sanitarium is located immediately east of the corporate limits of Ogden City, and west of that point defendant's railway is operated as a street railway while east thereof—that is, within the Ogden Canyon proper— the road is operated as an interurban line. Some distance east of the sanitarium, and within Ogden Canyon, there is what is known as the "Peery Resort," where a few people temporarily live during the summer season. About three-quarters of a mile further east, and up the canyon, is what is known as the "Lewis Resort," which is located on lands owned by J. S. and Eva Lewis, and to which we shall further refer hereafter. Farther up the canyon still is what is known as the "Hermitage," which is the eastern terminus of defendant's line of railway. The Hermitage, like the Ogden Canyon Sanitarium, is a public resort with hotel and other conveniences, dancing pavilion, boating pond, and other attractions similar to those at the sanitarium aforesaid. The Ogden river, a considerable stream of water, flows through Ogden Canyon. The canyon is therefore a desirable place for camping, and for many years has been used by many citizens as a temporary place of residence during the summer or heated months of the year. While the canyon proper at many places is too narrow, and the sides thereof too precipitous, to be used for the purposes of either public or private resorts, yet there are numerous places where the canyon widens out somewhat, and at some of such places public resorts have been established, while at other points resorts for summer residence have been maintained as aforesaid. A good road for all kinds of ordinary vehicles has been constructed and is maintained in the canyon.

It appears that prior to 1909 the line of railway terminated at the sanitarium. but that in that year the road was extended into the canyon to the Hermitage as before stated. In extending the line the road passed through the Peery resort before mentioned, and also through said Lewis resort. In consideration of being

State ex rel. Skeen *v.* Ogden Rapid Transit Co

granted a right of way through the lands owned by the Peerys the defendant entered into a contract whereby it agreed to stop its cars at that point when requested to do so by any person who desired to enter on or to alight from its cars there. Pursuant to this agreement the defendant has stopped and continues to stop its cars on request at said point. When the land owned by Lewis was reached, the defendant was refused permission to construct its road thereon, and it was compelled to condemn a right of way through the same, and a strip of land one rod in width and a little over 2,000 feet in length was accordingly condemned through said lands for a right of way. In the center of said tract defendant laid its track, which is standard guage, namely, 4 feet 8½ inches between rails, while the cars are about 8 feet 10 inches wide, projecting somewhat over each rail. While the Lewises own quite a large tract of land in and along each side of the canyon, the amount that is fit for summer residence is merely an oblong strip embracing between four and five acres of ground through which defendant's line of railway is constructed and operated. When the line of railway was constructed in the summer of 1909, the defendant requested, and was given, permission by Mr. Lewis to stop its cars at a certain private road crossing the strip of land used for summer residences as aforesaid. What is called the Lewis resort is purely private—that is, a small parcel of ground is leased to any one who desires to pitch a tent on the strip, or Mr. Lewis, with the land, also furnishes the tent or summer cottage to any one desirous of renting an abode during the summer months. Mr. Lewis testified that about nine-tenths of all the tenants rent the tent or house from him, while the remainder provide their own tents or summerhouses. Either the parcel of land to live on, or the tent or house, is rented for the summer season commencing some time in June and ending some time in September of each year, and each tenant is given the privilege of taking the same place the following summer if he so desires. The business has been conducted as aforesaid at the so-called Lewis resort for quite a number of years, and the number of those who have rented summer residences or places there has increased somewhat each year. This year there were about 100 persons, children and adults, exclusive of the Lewis household, living at the resort.

In June of this year plaintiff rented a summer residence from Lewis, and in that month moved into it with his family. On the 27th day of April, and before the summer season opened in Ogden Canyon, the defendant posted notices in its cars that after that date it would not stop any of its cars at any point in the canyon "between Peery's and the Hermitage." The defendant also prepared a schedule for the running of its cars between said Ogden Union Depot and the Hermitage, and at the time of plaintiff's demand was operating them in accordance with said schedule. According to this schedule, west of the sanitarium, and within the Ogden city limits, the cars are stopped at regular intervals, and at such places signs are placed on the overhead wires which read: "Cars stop here." In this connection the evidence shows that one of the motormen, perhaps some others, upon request, has stopped and permitted some persons to enter the car at points other than where the signs are put up, but it also appears that to do this was contrary to the orders of defendant, and occurred only on rare occasions. It also is made to appear that during the period of time that the road was being constructed in the summer of 1909 in Ogden Canyon the defendant's motorman also frequently permitted persons to either get on or alight from the cars at the Lewis resort, or at the upper end thereof at the point where the defendant at that time maintained a switch, but which has since been removed. There is no evidence, however, that the defendant stopped its cars for the purpose of permitting any person either to enter on or to alight from them at any point in the canyon except at the sanitarium, Peery's, and the Hermitage after the 27th day of April, 1910. On the contrary, the evidence is all to the effect that within the canyon the cars were stopped only at those three points. On the 16th day of June, 1910, plaintiff demanded from the defendant that it stop its cars at the Lewis resort for the purpose of receiving him as a passenger on one of its cars, and on the same day, while he was returning on one of defendant's cars as a passenger from Ogden City to said Lewis resort to his family, plaintiff timely demanded from defendant's conductor in charge of the car that said car be stopped at the Lewis resort for the purpose of permitting plaintiff to alight therefrom. The defendant, through its conductor, refused, and continues to refuse the request of the plaintiff, and refuses to stop its cars or any of them at said Lewis resort, and refuses to receive the plaintiff or any one else at that point as a passenger, and also refuses to stop its cars or any of them to permit the plaintiff or any other passenger to alight therefrom at said point. The evidence also shows that at least a number of those who have rented summer residences at the Lewis resort carry on or conduct some business in the city of Ogden and are desirous of passing daily over its line between said resort and Ogden City, and that many of them, including the plaintiff, are considerably inconvenienced by defendant's refusal to stop its cars at the Lewis resort because they must either stop off at the Peery resort and walk three-quarters of a mile east on the defendant's track to reach their summer home at the Lewis resort or must pass through that place and go to the Hermitage one mile beyond, and then walk down the track for that distance to reach their summer home.

Mr. Lewis also testified that the permission to stop the cars which he gave the defendant in 1909 has never been withdrawn,

State ex rel. Skeen *v.* Ogden Rapid Transit Co

but further says that he never granted, and that the defendant has not obtained, any other facilities to stop its cars on his land except the one-rod strip which was condemned, and that there are no public roads or highways which enter the resort located on his land. He also says that the resort is purely private, and no one can locate on the land without his permission and without paying rent, and that all ingress and egress to and from the same is shut off between the months of October of one year and June of the following year. It is also made to appear that defendant's cars can be stopped with the same facility at the Lewis resort that they can be at any of the other resorts, and that defendant does stop its cars at at least one place where it has no better facilities to stop them than it has at the Lewis resort.

It is also contended, and the court so found, that the reason for refusing to stop the cars at the Lewis resort is "entirely because of ill will and malice growing out of certain condemnation proceedings instituted against John S. Lewis by the said defendant." This finding is, however, assailed by the defendant upon the ground that it is not supported by the evidence. The only evidence to support it is the testimony of the plaintiff, who, in answer to a question propounded to him while a witness in his own behalf as to whether he did not know that the defendant would not stop its cars at the Lewis resort before he went there in June, 1910, testified: "Well, Matt. Browning told me that they were going to get even with Mr. Lewis on that proposition, and I rather supposed it was of a temporary nature." By this the witness meant that the refusal to stop cars at the Lewis resort would be merely temporary. When, and under what circumstances, the statement was made, and what, if any, relation Matt. Browning sustained to the defendant at the time it was made, is not disclosed. The finding in our judgment is not supported by any evidence. But, in view of all the circumstances, the finding is without controlling force, as will more fully appear hereafter.

We have been thus explicit in stating the facts for the reason that the case is one of first impression in this state, and because no claim is made that the defendant either in its charter or by contract has assumed the duty of stopping its cars at the Lewis resort. The plaintiff, however, contends that the duty to stop its cars is imposed upon the defendant either by the common law which is in force in this state, or by section 449, Comp. Laws, 1907, which reads as follows: "Every railroad company shall furnish sufficient accommodations for the transportation of all persons and property as shall, within a reasonable time previous to the departure of any train, offer or be offered for transportation at any station, siding or stopping place established for receiving and discharging passengers and freight, and at any railroad junction; and shall take, transport, and discharge such pas-

State ex rel. Skeen v. Ogden Rapid Transit Co

sengers and property at, from, and to such places, on the due
payment of tolls, freight, or fare therefor; and if the company
or its agents shall refuse to take and transport any passenger
or property, or to deliver the same at the regularly appointed
places, it shall be liable to the party aggrieved for all accruing
damages, including costs of suit." Upon the other hand, the
defendant insists that no such duty is imposed by either the common law or by the provisions of the foregoing section, and further contends that no authority is vested in the courts of this
state to require the defendant to establish a depot or stopping
place, or to stop its cars, at any particular point along its line of
railroad for the purpose of receiving or discharging either
freight or passengers, and that, therefore the district court has
exceeded its powers in issuing the peremptory writ of mandate.

A mere cursory reading of the foregoing section discloses that
it contains nothing from which the court can deduce a legislative command that a common carrier must establish and maintain
depots or stopping places at any particular place or places along
its line of road. The duties imposed by that section are to be discharged by the common carrier at depots or stopping places.
which have been duly established, and what is there said had no
reference to the establishment of depots or stopping places, or
to the stopping of trains or cars, where there are no regularly
established depots or stopping places. The defendant, therefore,
was not required to stop its cars at the Lewis resort by reason
of the provisions of section 449, supra. Nor is there anything
in that section or in any other to which our attention has been
directed or that we can find which confers upon any of the
courts of this state the right or power to determine whether a
common carrier should or should not-establish and maintain a
depot or stopping place for the receipt and discharge of passengers or freight or either at any particular place or places along
its line of railroad. There was therefore neither a contractual
nor a statutory duty imposed on the defendant to stop its cars
at the Lewis resort.

The next inquiry, therefore, is: Does the common law impose the duty upon a common carrier to establish and maintain
depots or stopping places along its line of railroad for the accommodation and convenience of individuals or communities at
points other than such as the carrier in its judgment deems necessary and proper in the conduct of its business? If the common
law imposes such a duty upon the defendant in this case, and
the right of the plaintiff to require the defendant to comply with
it is clear and reasonably free from doubt, then the power of
the district court to coerce the defendant by mandamus to discharge that duty is likewise beyond question. It is now well
settled that the Legislature of any state may within certain limitations determine and direct at what places a common carrier

State ex rel. Skeen v. Ogden Rapid Transit Co

shall establish and maintain depots or stopping places for the convenience of the public, and that it may require the carrier to stop its trains or cars, or some of them, at such depots or stopping places, and that the Legislature, within what are now well-defined limits, may confer the power to determine whether the carrier shall do so or not upon some board or tribunal. In either case the courts have the power to coerce a defaulting carrier by mandamus to comply with the legislative edict, or with the order of such board or tribunal. 33 Cyc. 43, 44. Upon the qustion whether the courts may inquire into and determine the necessity for establishing a depot at a certain place, and, if it be found by the court that the necessity for one exists, in the absence of statutory authority to do so, may order a carrier to establish such a depot or stopping place for the receipt and discharge of freight and passengers, the courts are not unanimous. A careful analysis of the cases will show that, while a number of cases are usually cited in support of the doctrine that the courts possess inherent power to control the carrier in the establishment of depots or stopping places, yet there is in fact but one case that really goes to that extent, namely, the case of State v. Republican Valley Ry. Co., 17 Neb. 647, 24 N. W. 329, 57 Am. Rep. 424. The cases upon the subject are nearly all collated by Mr. Elliott in notes to section 662 in volume 2 of the second edition of his excellent work on Railroads. The decisions in all of the cases, except the one from Nebraska, are in fact based upon particular statutes. There are quite a number of courts, however, who have given the subject careful consideration, and, after doing so, have arrived at the conclusion that under ordinary circumstances no inherent power is vested in the courts of this country to control a common carrier in its determination of the number of depots or stopping places that it will establish and maintain or in the selection of the places where it will establish and maintain them along its line of railroad. Among the well-considered cases in which the question is passed on are the following: Nashville, etc., Ry. Co. v. State, 137 Ala. 439, 34 South. 401; Northern Pac. Ry. Co. v. Washington ex rel. Dustin, 142 U. S. 492, 12 Sup. Ct. 283, 35 L. Ed. 1092; State ex rel. Smart v. Kansas City, etc., Ry. Co., 51 La. Ann. 200, 25 South. 126; People ex rel. Linton v. Brooklyn, etc., Co., 172 N. Y. 90, 64 N. E. 788; People v. N. Y. L. E. & W. Ry., 104 N. Y. 58, 9 N. E. 856, 58 Am. Rep. 484; State ex rel. Atty. Gen. v. Southern, etc., Co., 18 Minn. 40 (Gil. 21); Chicago, etc., Ry. Co. v. People ex rel. Atty. Gen., 152 Ill. 230, 38 N. E. 562, 26 L. R. A. 224; Honolulu Rapid Trans., etc., Co. v. Hawaii Terr., 211 U. S. 282, 29 Sup. Ct. 55, 53 L. Ed. 186; Atchison, Topeka & S. F. Ry. v. Denver, etc., Ry. Co., 110 U. S. 667, 4 Sup. Ct. 185, 28 L. Ed. 291. In Northern Pac. Ry. Co. v. Washington ex rel. Dustin, supra, Mr. Justice Gray, after discussing at some length

State ex rel. Skeen *v.* Ogden Rapid Transit Co

the lack of the power of the courts in this regard, at page 500 says: "To hold that the directors of this corporation, in determining the number, place and size of its stations and other structures, having regard for the public convenience as well as its own pecuniary interests, can be controlled by the courts by writ of mandamus, would be inconsistent with many decisions of high authority in analogous cases." In support of this doctrine both American and English cases are cited. The case of State *v.* Republican Valley Ry. Co., supra, is referred to by Mr. Justice Gray, but it is disapproved. It is true that in the Northern Pac. Ry. Co. Case, supra, there is a dissenting opinion concurred in by two of the justices, but a careful perusal of the dissenting opinion discloses the fact that the dissenting justices merely assumed the power to be vested in the courts without inquiring from what source such a power is derived. In all of the cases which we have cited above the facts and circumstances were much stronger than they are in the case at bar, but, notwithstanding this, the appellate courts all promulgated the doctrine that the power to control a common carrier with respect to proper depots or stopping places for its trains or cars for the convenience of the public is inherent in the legislative, and not the judicial, department.

When the Legislature has declared when and under what conditions and circumstances depots and stopping places shall be established and maintained, the courts may by mandamus compel the carrier to comply with the conditions imposed by the Legislature, but the courts have no inherent power to determine for themselves when, where, and under what conditions and circumstances a common carrier shall establish and maintain a depot or stopping place for the convenience of the public, or to stop its trains or cars at a particular place either to receive or discharge a passenger or passengers. It is true that courts may prevent discrimination, and, where the duty to receive a particular person at a particular place is clear, the courts may, by writ of mandate, compel the carrier to discharge such duty.

From the record it is made to appear that the district court in issuing the writ of mandate in this case was impelled to do so for the following reasons, which we give in his own words: "It seems to me that inasmuch as the court cannot find any other valid reason for the failure of this company to perform its duty to the public at this particular resort, and inasmuch as the uncontradicted testimony in this case shows that it is a matter of spite against Mr. Lewis on account of the proceedings that were had in this court as it has been shown by the statement which Mr. Browning made as testified to by Mr. Skeen, which is uncontradicted by Mr. Browning, this court should let its mandate issue." The court then proceeds to state that under the decisions of the Supreme Court of the United States there is some doubt

State ex rel. Skeen v. Ogden Rapid Transit Co

of the power of the court to compel the defendant to comply
with plaintiff's demands, but notwithstanding such doubt the
court grants the writ for the reason, as appears from his own
statement, that "this court should not consider itself absolutely
helpless to remedy this obvious discrimination on the part of this
carrier; and, if it is helpless, some other court will have to decide
that it is so." Courts no doubt are often tempted to, and do,
interfere where in their judgment justice demands interference,
although there may be some doubt with respect to their power.
It should be remembered, however, that courts are merely the
agencies of the sovereign state by means of which the sovereign administers justice, not according to the notions of the
judges, but in accordance with fixed rules and forms of law. A
court may in its judgment deem the exercise of a certain power
necessary in order to administer full and complete justice in
a particular case, yet unless the power to be exercised is one of
the inherent powers of the court, or is conferred upon it by the
lawmaking power, the court would be guilty of usurpation if it
exercised the power, although to do so might reflect justice in
that particular case. The doctrine that courts may not exceed
the powers vested in them, for the sole reason that in their judgment the exercise of such a power is necessary in the administration of justice is clearly stated and illustrated by Mr. Justice
Straup in the case of Larson v. Salt Lake City, 34 Utah, 318,
97 Pac. 483, 23 L. R. A. (N. S.) 462. In that case the district
court exercised what in our judgment constituted a legislative
power which the Legislature had not authorized the court to
exercise, and for that reason, and for no other, the judgment
of the lower court was reversed by us. In our judgment the same
principle is involved here. The power that the district court exercised in this case is under the great weight of authority clearly
legislative, and not judicial, and, unless and until the Legislature confers the right upon the courts to exercise such a power,
they cannot legally exercise it, although to do so would reflect
justice in a particular case. It is true that the district court
seemed to be impressed with the thought that this was a case of
discrimination, and that the court, as he expressed it, was not
"helpless to remedy this obvious discrimination." By this the
court meant that because the defendant stopped its cars at the
sanitarium, at Peery's, and at the Hermitage, and did not do
so at the Lewis resort, therefore the defendant discriminated
against the Lewis resort and in favor of the other resorts. That
this so-called discrimination was not in favor of the other resorts is too obvious to require argument. The evidence is conclusive that no person stopped off at any of the other resorts
simply because he could not stop off at the Lewis resort. Moreover, the Lewis resort is a place where certain persons stopped
off only because they had a temporary abiding place there, and

State ex rel. Skeen *v.* Ogden Rapid Transit Co

not because they sought after amusement or entertainment, as was the case at the sanitarium and at the Hermitage. The only discrimination, therefore, that could possibly exist would be one against the Lewis resort, which would have to be based on the mere fact that the cars of the defendant refused to stop at that place while they stopped at the other resorts. The so-called Peery resort cannot be taken into consideration, since the cars stopped there by virtue of a special contract and for a consideration received by the defendant. It is manifest, therefore, that the district court in truth and in fact merely directed the defendant how to conduct its business under particular circumstances under the guise of preventing discrimination. If a common carrier by stopping its trains or cars at one village or settlement and by refusing to do so at another village or settlement through which its trains and cars pass and where the cars can be stopped is guilty of legal discrimination against the latter village, then it follows that a common carrier must stop its trains or cars, or some of them, at every village or settlement through which it passes if requested to do so by the inhabitants or some of them, or it will be guilty of discrimination. In the absence of a statute requiring the carrier to do so, it ordinarily at least commits no breach of duty in failing or refusing to stop its cars at one village, although it does so at another similarly situated. Nor was the defendant guilty of discrimination against the plaintiff or others who, like him are staying at the Lewis resort. Our statute (section 455, Comp. Laws, 1907), which is declaratory of the common law, simply provides against discrimination "from the same place, under like conditions, under similar circumstances and for the same period of time." Nor is the fact that there is no good reason why the defendant does not stop its cars at the Lewis resort, or that it refuses to do so because of ill will of one or more of its managing officers, a matter of controlling importance. Where the power to examine into the question whether the carrier should stop its trains or cars at certain places under certain conditions and circumstances is conferred either upon a court or some other body or tribunal, it may easily become material if not a controlling factor in the case that the carrier refuses to stop its trains or cars at a particular place out of mere ill will. Where, however, as in this case, the court is powerless to compel the carrier to stop its cars at a particular place, it is, to say the least, immaterial upon what ground the refusal to stop is based. We have no hesitancy in saying that, if the matter were left to our judgment or discretion, we would be compelled to hold that under the undisputed facts and circumstances of this case defendant's refusal to stop some of its cars, at least mornings and evenings, at the Lewis resort, is wholly inexcusable, if not entirely arbitrary. This, however, is a matter to be regulated by the Legislature, and not by the courts.

State ex rel. Skeen *v.* Ogden Rapid Transit Co

Where the legitimate power of the court ends and it nevertheless acts, the act is usurpation pure and simple, and any attempt to justify the act upon the ground that in the opinion of the court justice demands the act cannot rescue the act from constituting usurpation, nor does it palliate the offense. If the defendant had refused plaintiff permission either to enter upon its cars or to alight therefrom at the Lewis resort, while, under similar circumstances, it extended the privilege to enter and to alight from its cars to others at that place, it would be a clear case of discrimination against the plaintiff. It would likewise constitute a refusal upon the part of the defendant to discharge a plain legal duty it owed to him. Under such circumstances, the court could require the defendant to discharge its duty by a writ of mandate. But, as we have seen, we are not dealing with such a case, but are dealing with a case where the defendant at a particular place treats all alike who live or are at that place, but does not treat them the same as it does others who live or are at some other places which are surrounded by somewhat different conditions and circumstances. To compel the defendant to treat all of the settlements or communities along its line of railroad alike is, as we have shown, a matter for legislative, and not for judicial, regulation.

We do not wish to be understood as holding that conditions and circumstances may not arise under which a court, even in the absence of a statute, would not be authorized to interfere as against the arbitrary acts of a common carrier in failing to provide facilities and conveniences for the public. When and under what conditions the courts might have power to interfere upon equitable or other grounds is not before us, and upon that question we express no opinion. All that we decide at this time is that, under the undisputed facts and circumstances of this case, the district court was not justified in issuing the writ.

The judgment is therefore reversed and the cause remanded to the district court, with directions to dismiss the proceedings. Appellant to recover costs.

STRAUP, C. J., and McCARTY, J., concur.

HANSON v. CHICAGO, R. I. & P. RY. CO.

(Supreme Court of Kansas, Dec. 10, 1910.)

[112 Pac. Rep. 152.]

Carriers—Injury to Passengers—Demurrer to Evidence.*—In an action for damages for the death of a passenger, evidence was adduced to show that it was the custom on the defendant's night trains to turn down the lights and furnish pillows for passengers who would pay for their use; that a passenger who was asleep on such a train when it reached the place of his destination at 1 o'clock in the morning, was awakened immediately after it left the station; that, assisted by the porter, he went forward in an apparently drowsy condition, and stepped off the train, and was killed; that the conductor was nearby, and observed his departure; and that the train was not stopped nor its speed slackened, nor the passenger restrained, although the danger was apparent to the trainmen. It is held that a demurrer to the evidence was properly overruled, and that there was no error in refusing a request for an instruction to find for the defendant.

(Syllabus by the Court.)

Appeal from District Court, Marion County.

Action by Nettie Hanson against the Chicago, Rock Island & Pacific Railway Company. Judgment for plaintiff, and defendant appeals. Affirmed.

M. A. Low, Paul E. Walker, and *J. S. Dean*, for appellant. *W. H. Carpenter* and *D. W. Wheeler*, for appellee.

BENSON, J. This appeal is from a judgment awarding damages for alleged negligence of the appellant in permitting, advising, and directing a drowsy passenger to alight from a rapidly moving train in the nighttime at a place where there was no platform or light, whereby the passenger was killed.

The deceased, who was 36 years of age, took passage at Bison, Okl., about 5 o'clock p. m., holding a ticket to Lost Springs, Kan., where the train arrived at about 1 o'clock a. m. It was the custom on defendant's trains over this route to turn down the lights in passenger coaches about 10 o'clock p. m., and passengers who paid the charge therefor were furnished pillows by the train porter, and this was done on the night of the accident. Tickets were taken up by a train auditor and checks given to the passengers, and it was the custom of the porter on these night

Hanson v. Chicago, R. I. & P. Ry. Co

trains to awaken passengers who were sleeping on approaching their destination, and take up their checks. Announcement of the station was given, and the train made the usual stop at Lost Springs, where one passenger left the train, and two others entered it. After the train left the station, and while moving with rapid and increasing speed, the deceased was observed with the porter having hold of his shoulder, walking toward the platform. He appeared drowsy, and fell on or brushed against another passenger as he went by. The porter removed the check from his hat, and went with him to the platform, where they disappeared down the steps together, and then the porter returned into the car alone. The body was found about 250 yards from the depot. The deceased had been over this route on defendant's trains running on the same schedule on four previous occasions.

In answer to special questions, the jury found that the custom of taking up checks and awakening sleepy passengers on night trains had existed for a long time prior to the injury; that the deceased was acquainted with this custom: that he was sleeping when the train reached Lost Springs; that he was taken out of his seat by the employees of the company and taken to the platform for the purpose of getting him to leave the train while it was in motion if they could get him off before it gained too much speed; that they knew he was in a sleepy, drowsy condition; that the night was dark; that the deceased was unfamiliar with the place; that the train was running rapidly; that there was no conversation between the porter and the deceased with respect to his waiting until the train stopped; and that he did not leave the train voluntarily.

The porter testified that the vestibule was not closed after leaving the station until after the deceased left the car. Before reaching Lost Springs, he had been informed that this passenger was destined for that place. There is some conflict in the testimony concerning the occurrences just before the deceased left the train. The porter testified that, when he announced the station, the deceased was talking with another gentleman in the seat; that, returning into the car after the train started, and when it had proceeded 50 to 100 feet, he saw the deceased coming out toward the vestibule, and understood him to say that the conductor told him to get off; and that the conductor said "Stop," and pulled the bell rope. He also testified: "Q. Why didn't he stop? You knew that train was going at a rapid rate? A. Yes, sir; I presume it was. Q. Didn't you know that it was impossible for a man to get off or on that train when going at a rapid rate? A. I didn't know what he could do. Q. You thought that there was a great possibility that he would be injured? A. No, sir; I never gave it a thought. Q. Although the train was running rapidly? A. I didn't. Q. Notwithstanding

Hanson *v.* Chicago, R. I. & P. Ry. Co

the fact that he got off in the dark there that night, the train running rapidly, you never undertook to stop that train after the man got off, or to pull that cord once? A. I don't remember whether or not I did. Q. You know as a matter of fact you didn't, don't you? A. I don't think the train did stop any more. * * * Well, it didn't stop."

The conductor testified: "I started into a high-backed coach, the first car back of the smoker. * * * This gentleman came down towards me. I asked him if he wanted to get off there. He said, 'Yes,' he did. I said, 'Well, wait a minute, and I'll stop the train.' With that I reached up and pulled the cord, and at that he passed me, and I did not see him any more. This air didn't sound very loud, and, when I got out into the vestibule, the porter was standing there. I said, 'Did he get off?' He said, 'Yes.' That ended it with me. I turned and went back. That was all that I knew about it. Q. Did you see him get off? A. No, sir. Q. Did you have any other conversation with him except that you have already detailed? A. No, sir." On cross-examination he said: "Q. You did not stop that train. The train was going rapidly, was it not? A. It was gaining speed right along. Q. It was going fast when this man was there at the door, was it not? A. Yes, sir. Q. You knew that it was dangerous to get off, didn't you? A. I would not have got off. Q. You know as a trainman that it was dangerous for that man to get off? A. Yes, sir; he passed me in the alleyway. Q. That is where you pulled the cord? A. Yes, sir. * * * Q. When the porter told you a man got off there in the dark, and the train was running rapidly, why didn't you stop the train when the porter told you? A. He told me the man was gone. Q. Both of you knew it was dangerous to get off, and, although the train was running fast and it was dark there, you just went on and paid no further attention to it, that is the way you done it, was it? A. Yes, sir."

A passenger in another coach opening upon the same platform testified that he saw a man who seemed to be sleepy go to the platform, followed by the porter, and heard one of the employees say, "Let him get off if he will;" that the train was going rapidly at the time; and that the trainmen did not pull the bell cord, and made no effort to stop it. Another witness testified that as the train started out of Lost Springs he saw some one shake another man and take him out of the coach just back of the smoker. This was the coach in which the deceased was riding.

The only errors specified are the decision overruling the demurrer to the evidence, and the refusal to instruct the jury to find for the defendant, and the question now to be decided is whether the evidence is sufficient to sustain the verdict. It is contended that it is not the duty of a carrier to awaken sleeping

Hanson *v.* Chicago, R. I. & P. Ry. Co

passengers in a day coach on arrival at his destination, if due announcement of the station is made, and a reasonable opportunity
is given for him.to alight. This is the general rule, although it
is said that exceptional circumstances might impose the duty. 2
Hutch. on Carriers, § 1128. It is also insisted that the custom
shown by the evidence of turning down the lights and furnishing
pillows on night trains that passengers may sleep more comfortably does not impose the duty. The defendant also contends that
the proper announcement of the station having been made, and
sufficient opportunity given by the egress of passengers, the deceased, by remaining in the coach until the train started, became
a trespasser to whom the company owed no duty except to refrain from willfully or wantonly injuring him.

The district court did not instruct the jury that the custom,
if proven, imposed the duty on the trainmen to awaken a sleeping passenger on arrival at his destination, but did instruct, in
substance, that if they found the custom existed as alleged, and
that it was known to the decedent, and ₜhₐₜ he was asleep on
arrival at his destination to the knowledge of the trainmen, and
they failed to awaken him in proper time to leave the train, and
that immediately after leaving the station they discovered that
he had not left the train because of being asleep, he should be
considered as a passenger, and if the trainmen were negligent in
commanding or directing him to leave the train, which negligence
caused his death, then the plaintiff might recover. But if the deceased voluntarily left the train without being ordered or directed
to do so, or if he was advised to wait and told that the train
would be stopped so that he might leave it, and that notwithstanding this advice he left the train without waiting for it to
stop, there could be no recovery.

Cases are cited in support of the proposition that when a passenger fails to leave a train when his destination is reached, after
a reasonable opportunity to do so, the relation of passenger and
carrier is terminated, and he then becomes a trespasser. This is
not true, however, in all cases. If one in such a situation offers
to pay fare to a station beyond, the relation continues unbroken.
Forbes *v.* Railway Co., 135 Iowa, 679, 113 N. W. 477. It would
be a harsh rule that would hold every person a trespasser who
remains upon a train after it reaches the place designated in his
ticket. Whether he is a trespasser must depend on the circumstances of each case, which may present questions for a jury.
It is held that a person who goes aboard the wrong train or one
upon which his ticket does not entitle him to ride is nevertheless
a passenger, and while he may be ejected it must be done with
all proper care. In such a case it was said: "Although he has
no right to a passage, he cannot be expelled from the train as a
trespasser, but must be treated as a passenger who by mistake
has got upon a train on which by his contract he is not entitled

to ride." Lake Shore & Michigan Southern Railroad Company
v. Rosenzweig, 113 Pa. 519, 6 Atl. 545; Arnold v. Pennsylvania
Railroad Co., 115 Pa. 135, 8 Atl. 213, 2 Am. St. Rep. 542.

In a case in Michigan where a sleeping passenger delayed
leaving the train after a full opportunity to do so had been given,
and was afterward injured by the alleged negligent act of the
conductor, it was held that the claim of the company that the
relation of passenger and carrier had ceased, and that the company owed him no duty of protection, could not be sustained as
matter of law, but was properly left to the jury. Bass v. Cleveland, etc., R. Co., 142 Mich. 177, 105 N. W. 151, 2 L. R. A.
(N. S.) 875. In a note following a report of that case in 7 Am.
& Eng. Ann. Cas. 720, it is said that the rule that no obligation
to arouse a sleeping passenger and to see that he gets off at his
destination "had been laid down in case where passengers have
sought to recover damages for being carried beyond their destinations, and is not in conflict with the holding of the reported
case."

It was held in Railway Co. v. Wimmer, 72 Kan. 566, 84 Pac.
378, that: "The duty which a railway company owes to a passenger to exercise the highest degree of care for his safety which
is reasonably practicable does not cease until the passenger has
reached his destination and left the train." (Syl. 3.)

It is probably true that if a passenger should unreasonably delay his departure from a train in such circumstances as to indicate a willful or wanton disregard for the rights of the carrier
or the traveling public, thereby intending to compel a stop for
his benefit, or because of ill will, or to secure further passage
without pay, or like wrongful purpose, he would thereby forfeit
his right to the high degree of care due to a passenger, and
might, if the circumstances warranted the inference, be considered a trespasser, but the question in case of any doubt or
uncertainty of the facts would be for a jury. Here it is not
claimed, and the circumstances do not indicate, that the delay
of the deceased was caused otherwise than by his being asleep,
or bewildered because of sleepiness. In this situation the court
could not arbitrarily declare that he had forfeited the ordinary
rights of a passenger, and did not err in submitting that matter
to the jury.

The case of C. K. & W. Rd. Co. v. Frazer, 55 Kan. 582, 40
Pac. 923, cited by the appellant, is not in conflict with these
views. It appeared there that passage had been taken upon a
construction train on an unfinished road. At the end of the road,
after nearly half an hour had elapsed and all others had left
the caboose, a passenger who without any apparent cause remained upon it was killed in switching; his presence being unknown to the trainmen. It was held that instructions to the
effect that he was entitled at the time of the injury to the ex-

traordinary care due to a passenger were erroneous. The language of the opinion was correct as applied to the facts of that case, but is not an authority for the contention that it should be held as matter of law that Hanson had forfeited his right to such care before he was killed.

The facts concerning the custom to turn down the lights, furnish pillows for the comfort of those desiring to sleep, and to awaken sleeping passengers and take up their checks were circumstances for the jury explanatory of the delay of the passenger and proper to be considered in deciding whether the relation of passenger and carrier had terminated before he stepped from the train.

It is also contended that the evidence shows such contributory negligence as to defeat a recovery. It is said that the night was dark, the train was running rapidly, the place was unfamiliar, and the departure from the train voluntary. The force of this argument is greatly diminished by the finding of the jury that the deceased did not leave the train voluntarily, and this finding we think is supported by the evidence. He was awakened while upon a moving train which had just left the station where he desired to stop. The rate of speed could hardly be determined by him on the instant, especially in his drowsy condition. Those upon whom he had a right to rely did not oppose, but one at least actually assisted him down the steps, according to the testimony. It is true the conductor says he told him to stop and that he pulled the cord, but it is significant that the train did not stop, nor was its speed slackened, and the fact that the conductor pulled the cord is disputed by other testimony. The porter who was in the vestibule with the passenger testified that he, (the porter) did not pull the cord, and according to testimony, which the jury had a right to believe, although contradicted, one of the employees said: "Let him get off if he will." It cannot be said as a matter of law that a man of ordinary prudence in that situation would not have stepped off the train as he essayed to do. Happily for the traveling public the care, patience, and fidelity of trainmen generally are such that passengers are accustomed to, and ordinarily may, safely rely upon their judgment, knowledge, and skill in such matters, and one should not be held guilty of contributory negligence when he does so merely because it is determined by a fatal result that his confidence was misplaced. It appears that, while the danger was obvious to the porter and conductor, it was not necessarily so to this passenger. St. Louis, I. M. & S. R. R. Co. v. Cantrell, 37 Ark. 519, 40 Am. Rep. 105; Jones v. Chicago, Milwaukee & St. Paul Ry. Co., 42 Minn. 183, 43 N. W. 1114; McCaslin v. Railway Co., 93 Mich. 553, 53 N. W. 724; Waller v. Hannibal & St. Joseph R. R. Co., 83 Mo. 608; Haug v. Great Northern Ry. Co., 8 N. D. 23, 77 N. W. 97, 47 L. R. A. 664, 73 Am. St. Rep.

Commonwealth v. Southern Ry. Co

727; S. K. Co. v. Pavey, 48 Kan. 452, 29 Pac. 593. A passenger who, because of drowsiness, or confusion caused by no wrongful act on his part, attempts to jump from a rapidly moving train in the darkness, while apparently aware of the danger, is we believe entitled to the restraining care of those in whose protection he has placed himself, who fully understood the danger, and are in a situation to prevent it. The fact that he slept longer than he ought to have done, if that be a fact, ought not to deprive him of reasonable protection.

The evidence was sufficient to go to the jury, and sustains the verdict. Evidence explanatory of the conduct of the trainmen and to some extent excusing it is not further referred to; the only question here being whether there was competent evidence for the consideration of the jury sufficient to support their findings.

The judgment is affirmed. All the Justices concurring.

COMMONWEALTH v. SOUTHERN RY. CO. IN KENTUCKY.

(Court of Appeals of Kentucky, Dec. 15, 1910.)

[132 S. W. Rep. 408.]

Intoxicating Liquors—Local Option Law—Transportation by Carrier.—Ky. St. § 2569a (Russell's St. §§ 3641-3644), prohibiting a carrier from transporting liquor into a local option district with certain exceptions, and declaring that the act shall only apply to common carriers who usually carry freight or goods for hire, and that every firm, common carrier, etc., who receives pay for conveying liquors shall be deemed a violator of the provisions thereof, etc., does not apply to a railroad carrying liquor into a local option precinct as the personal baggage of a passenger, receiving no consideration therefor except a fare charged for the passenger's personal transportation.

Appeal from Circuit Court, Mercer County.

Prosecution by the Commonwealth against the Southern Railway Company in Kentucky for violating the local option law. A verdict of not guilty having been directed, the Commonwealth appeals. Affirmed.

James Breathitt, Atty. Gen., Tom B. McGregor, Asst. Atty. Gen., and C. E. Rankin, for the Commonwealth.

Alex P. Humphrey, E. P. Humphrey, and E. H. Gaither, for appellee.

CLAY, C. On April 8, 1910, the following warrant was issued against appellee, Southern Railway Company in Kentucky: "It

Commonwealth *v.* Southern Ry. Co

appearing that there are reasonable grounds for believing that Southern Railway Company in Kentucky, a corporation, did on the 4th day of April, 1910, commit the offense of knowingly bringing and carrying, as a common carrier of goods and passengers, spirituous, vinous, and malt liquors into a local option territory committed on April 4th, 1910, by carrying and bringing six boxes or packages and three jugs for Dewitt Bonta, who was neither a licensed physician or druggist, as his personal baggage and belongings, which said packages and jugs contained more than one gallon of whisky, being between ten and twelve gallons of whisky into Harrodsburg, Ky., from Lawrenceburg, Ky., being brought into local option territory, the said corporation being engaged in the general business and occupation of hauling, transporting and carrying goods and passengers for hire, and having brought and carried said packages and jugs with said whisky therein as such common carrier. You are therefore commanded to summon said Southern Railway Company in Kentucky to answer said charge in my court at Harrodsburg, Ky., on the 12th day of April, 1910, at two o'clock p. m. Witness my hand as police judge of Harrodsburg, Ky., this April 8th, 1910. J. Hal Grimes, J. P. C. H." Upon the hearing in the police court, appellee pleaded guilty, and its punishment was fixed at a fine of $50. From the judgment so entered, appellee prosecuted an appeal to the circuit court. There it demurred to the warrant, but the demurrer was overruled. The case then went to trial, and upon the conclusion of the evidence for the commonwealth the trial court peremptorily instructed the jury to find appellee not guilty. The jury returned a verdict in conformity with the instruction so given, and from the judgment based thereon the commonwealth prosecutes this appeal for the purpose of having the law certified.

The evidence for the commonwealth is substantially as follows: Dewitt Bonta testified that he lived in Lawrenceburg, where he was engaged in the saloon business. On April 4, 1910, he came to Harrodsburg as a passenger on one of appellee's trains. He had with him at the time four or five packages of whisky, which contained three or four gallons. The shipping boxes containing the whisky were of the kind ordinarily used for that purpose. The porter who worked at the saloon brought the packages to the depot. When witness arrived there; they were on the platform. When the train for Harrodsburg arrived, the whisky was put on the front end of the colored coach by witness' porter and a negro on the platform. Witness paid nothing for having the whisky conveyed, but purchased and used a ticket to Harrodsburg, which cost him 62 cents. He had no arrangements with the railroad people about bringing the whisky over, did not have the whisky checked, nor did he say anything to the agent about it. The whisky belonged to one Mr. Bottom,

Commonwealth *v.* Southern Ry. Co

and the witness was bringing it to Harrodsburg for delivery on orders.

Jesse Barbour testified that he was in Lawrenceburg on April 4th. When he first saw the packages of whisky two of them were on a truck and two beside a truck. Afterwards another package was placed on the platform. Was present when the packages were put on the car by two colored men whom he did not know. After the packages were put on, the train porter moved them back. The conductor told the porter not to bother with any of that whisky that was coming on. When he reached Harrodsburg, he saw Mr. Bonta put two of the boxes off. None of the whisky was in a grip, valise, or trunk. Witness was in the colored coach where there were six or eight other negroes. Mr. Bonta rode in the smoking car provided for white people.

It will be observed that this proceeding was instituted under section 2569a, Ky. St. (Russell's St. §§ 3641-3644), the provisions of which are as follows:

"It shall be unlawful for any person or persons, individual or corporation, public or private carrier to bring into, transfer to other person or persons, corporations, carrier or agent, deliver or distribute, in any county, district, precinct, town or city, where the sale of intoxicating liquor has been prohibited, or may be prohibited, whether by special act of the General Assembly, or by vote of the people under the local option law, any spirituous, vinous, malt or other intoxicating liquor, regardless of the name by which it may be called, and this act shall apply to all packages of such intoxicating liquors whether broken or unbroken: Provided, individuals may bring into such district, upon their person or as their personal baggage, and for their private use, such liquors in quantity not to exceed one gallon: And provided, the provisions of this act shall not apply to licensed physicians or druggists, to whom any public carrier may deliver such goods, in unbroken packages, in quantity not to exceed five gallons at any one time.

"(2) Each package of such spirituous, vinous, malt or other intoxicating liquor, regardless of the name by which it may be called, whether broken or unbroken packages, brought into and transferred to other person, corporation, carrier or agent, delivered or distributed in such local option territory, shall constitute a separate offense.

"(3) Any person or persons, individual or corporation, public or private carrier violating the provisions of this act shall be deemed guilty of violating the local option law and shall be fined not less than fifty nor more than one hundred dollars for each offense.

"(4) And the place of delivery of such liquors shall be held to be the place of sale: Provided, further, that the provisions of this act shall only apply to common carriers, corporations, firms

Commonwealth *v.* Southern Ry. Co

or individuals who usually carry freight or goods for hire; and every firm, common carrier, corporation or individual who receives pay for conveying vinous, malt or spirituous liquors shall be deemed a violator of the provisions hereof."

The warrant charges, and the evidence shows, that the witness Dewitt Bonta carried the whisky in question as his personal baggage, and for this the company received no pay in addition to the fare which Bonta paid for his ticket. By subsection 4 of the foregoing section of the statute it is provided that the provisions of the act should apply only to common carriers, corporations, firms, or individuals who usually carry freight or goods for hire, and that every firm, common carrier, corporation, or individual who receives pay for conveying vinous, malt, or spirituous liquors shall be deemed a violator of the law.

Was the purchase of the ticket a receiving of pay by appellee for conveying the whisky? We think not. The railway company received no more from the passenger because of the baggage he carried than it would have received if he had no baggage. In our opinion the statute applies only to those cases where the common carrier actually receives pay for conveying spirituous, vinous, or malt liquors. It does not apply where the passenger by virtue of his ticket is entitled to carry personal baggage, and nothing in addition to the purchase price of the ticket is paid for the privilege. It was not the purpose of the act to make of the carrier an inquisitor with full power to examine and inspect the baggage of a passenger so as to determine whether or not he has whisky concealed in the same. This would necessarily follow if the contention of the commonwealth were upheld. In every case, except in a case where the public carrier delivers in local option territory spirituous, vinous, or malt liquors in unbroken packages in quantity not to exceed five gallons at any one time to licensed physicians or druggists, the common carrier is liable to the penalty imposed by the act where it receives pay for conveying the liquor. In receiving pay for carrying goods, it is therefore the duty of the carrier to act in good faith and to exercise ordinary care to see that the goods received and carried into local option territory do not consist of spirituous, vinous, or malt liquors.

From the foregoing, it follows that the trial court properly instructed the jury to find appellee not guilty; and this opinion is certified to the proper tribunal as the law of the case.

Louisiana Ry. & Navigation Co. *v.* Holly.

(Supreme Court of Louisiana, Nov. 28, 1910.   Rehearing Denied Jan. 3, 1911.)

[53 So. Rep. 882.]

Carriers—Interstate Commerce—Rates.—A railroad company being prohibited by the interstate commerce act from charging any less freight on interstate traffic than prescribed by the Interstate Commerce Commission for the route over which the shipment is actually carried, no contract, and no mistake in naming a wrong rate, can affect the right to collect such prescribed rate.

Carriers—Interstate Commerce.—The right of a railroad to recover its part of the interstate commerce rate for an interstate shipment is not affected by its line being wholly in one state.

Carriers—Interstate Commerce—Rates—Remedy.—A railroad cannot estop itself from right to collect the rate for carriage which, by the interstate commerce act, it is required to charge.

Carriers—Interstate Commerce—Rates—Wrong Routing.—That the initial carrier in an interstate commerce shipment disregarded its duty, in the absence of special instructions, to forward the shipment by that reasonable and practical route to which the lowest charge for transportation applies, does not prevent a connecting carrier, over whose line the shipment is routed and carried, from collecting the interstate commerce rate over its line; the shipper's remedy being against the initial carrier for damages.

(Syllabus by Editorial Staff.)

Action by the Louisiana Railway & Navigation Company against K. D. Holly. Judgment for defendant. Plaintiff applied for writ of certiorari. Judgment set aside, and case remanded.

Wise, Randolph & Rendall, for applicant.
W. A. Wilkinson, for respondent.

Provosty, J.   The plaintiff railroad company sues to recover of the defendant $97.57, being amount of undercharge on a car load of corn consigned to defendant at Coushatta, La., from Chase, Ind. T.

The facts are as follows: The defendant, a merchant at Coushatta, desiring to purchase the corn at Chase, Ind. T., for a customer, applied to the agent of the plaintiff railroad at Coushatta to ascertain what the tariff rates were between Chase and Coushatta, and was informed by the said agent that it was 23 cents per 100 pounds. This was the through rate; but the initial carrier at Chase, the St. Louis & San Francisco Railroad, not receiving any special routing instructions, routed the shipment to Shreveport, and from that point it was transmitted to Coushatta. The rate from Chase to Shreveport is 22 cents, and from Shreveport to Coushatta, 32 cents, making a total rate for the route over which the car was carried of 54 cents. These were the rates as fixed by the Interstate Commerce Commission, and as duly printed and posted in the stations of the said two railroads. When the car reached Coushatta, it had an under-charge notation of $47.50. The defendant paid this, but under protest. The defendant delivered the corn to his customer, and received payment therefor, including the $47.50. Two years later the claim was made for the first time by the plaintiff rail-road that an additional amount was due; and, defendant refusing to pay same, the present suit was brought to enforce payment. The customer of defendant has, in the meantime, become in-solvent; and, if defendant is forced to pay the amount, he loses it.

In his answer the defendant recites the foregoing facts, and denies that he ever owed anything beyond the through rate of 23 cents per 100 pounds. He pleads estoppel and the prescription of one year, and claims, in reconvention, the $47.50 of under-charge paid by him to the plaintiff railroad.

The trial court rejected plaintiff's demand, on two grounds: First, that, there being a through rate between the two points, the plaintiff could not claim more than this through rate; second, estoppel.

In the case of Foster-Glassel Company *v.* K. C. S. Ry. Co., 121 La. 1053, 46 South. 1014, there was no through rate; but that circumstance does not affect the principle governing cases of this kind, which is that by the acts of Congress, the paramount law of the land, a railroad is prohibited from charging any less freight on interstate traffic than is prescribed by the Interstate Commerce Commission for the route over which the shipment has actually been carried. In view of that law, any consent that a local agent may give, or any contract that the entire body of officials of the railroad company, from president down, might enter into, would be no bar to the demand for the freight due according to the rates prescribed by the Interstate Commerce Commission. Any such consent, or agreement, would be in vio-lation of said prohibitory law, and, in consequence, null and void.

In the case of Texas & Pacific R. R. Co. *v.* Mugg & Dryden, 202 U. S. 242, 26 Sup. Ct. 628, 50 L. Ed. 1011, the Supreme Court of the United States said:

"A common carrier may exact the legal rate for an interstate shipment, as shown by its printed and published schedule on file with the Interstate Commerce Commission and posted in the stations of such carrier, as required by the interstate commerce act, although a lower rate was quoted by the carrier to the ship-per, who shipped under the lower rate so quoted."

And in Gulf, Colorado & Santa Fè *v.* Hefley, 158 U. S. 98, 15 Sup. Ct. 802, 39 L. Ed. 910, the court said:

Louisiana Ry. & Navigation Co. *v.* Holly

"Shippers are presumed to know of the existence of schedules and the necessity of compliance therewith, and will be held to have contracted with reference to the rates fixed by the schedule, regardless of the terms of the contract. The schedule rate is payable, although the contract fixes a lower rate."

In line with the above, the Interstate Commerce Commission, in passing on the point, on December 18, 1907, announced the following rule:

"A mistake by a carrier in responding to an inquiry by a shipper, either as to the rate or as to the route, will relieve neither the one nor the other from the obligation of fulfilling the law's requirements. In either event the carrier must collect, and the shipper must pay the rate as published for the route over which the shipment actually moved. This gneral rule is founded, not only on the strict letter of the law, but also on sound policy." Poor *v.* Chicago, B. & Q. Ry. Co., 12 Interst. Com. Com'n R. 469.

The fact that the plaintiff company's line lies wholly within the state does not in any manner affect the situation. Augusta S. R. Co. *v.* Wrightsville & T. R. Co. (C. C.) 74 Fed. 522; Cincinnati, N. O. & T. P. R. Co. *v.* Interstate Commerce Com., 162 U. S. 184, 16 Sup. Ct. 700, 40 L. Ed. 935; Louisville & N. R. Co. *v.* Behlmer, 175 U. S. 658, 20 Sup. Ct. 209, 44 L. Ed. 309.

The estoppel cannot avail; for the same prohibitory law which precludes a railroad from agreeing, or consenting, not to claim the freight rate prescribed by the Interstate Commerce Commission, precludes it from estopping itself from so doing. To allow the railroad thus to preclude itself by estoppel would be to allow it to do indirectly what it is forbidden to do directly. Ackerman *v.* Larner, 116 La. 101, 40 South. 581.

Defendant's remedy in the matter is against the initial line, which misrouted the shipment so as to make the greater rate. On this point, see the decision of the Interstate Commerce Commission in Hennepin Paper Co. *v.* N. P. Ry. Co., 12 Interst. Com. Com'n R. 535, the syllabus of which reads as follows:

"It is the duty of a carrier, in the absence of routing instructions to the contrary, to forward shipments, having due regard to the interests of the shipper, ordinarily by that reasonable and practicable route over which the lowest charge for the transportation applies; and damage resulting to a shipper from a disregard of this obligation by the carrier can only be repaired to the extent of the difference betweeen the higher rate applied over the line by which the traffic improperly moved and the lower rate which would have been applied had the freight been properly forwarded.

"To require reparation in such a case is only to require the carrier to make just compensation for injury resulting from failure to perform its duty; but to require or permit any other

Reid et ux. *v.* Southern Ry. Co

carrier than the one responsible for the misrouting to participate in the making of such reparation would be to permit or require departure from established rates, which is expressly forbidden by law."

The judgment of the district court herein is therefore set aside, and the case is remanded, to be proceeded with according to law.

Reid *et ux. v.* Southern Ry. Co.   .

(Supreme Court of North Carolina, Nov. 30, 1910.)

[69 S. E. Rep. 618.]

Commerce—Carriers—Statutory Regulations—Validity—Penalty— Interstate Shipment.*—Revisal 1905, § 2631, imposing a penalty upon railroad companies for refusing to accept freight for shipment, is not unconstitutional when applied to an interstate shipment; not being an interference with or burden upon interstate commerce.

Carriers—Freight—Duty to Receive Freight.†—It is a common-law duty of a common carrier to receive freight whenever tendered.

Commerce—"Interstate Commerce."‡—"Interstate Commerce" does not begin until the freight has been shipped or started for transportation from one state to another.

Carriers—Freight—Right to Receive—Failure to File Rates.—The interstate commerce act (Act Feb. 4, 1887, c. 104, § 6, 24 Stat. 380 [U. S. Comp. St. 1901, p. 3156]) requires every carrier subject to the act to file with the Interstate Commerce Commission, print, and keep open to public instruction, schedules showing all the rates for transportation between different points on its own route, and between points on its own route and that of any other railroad company, when a through route and a joint rate have been established, and also forbids the carrier to engage in the transportation of property be-

---

*For the authorities in this series on the subject of state interference with interstate commerce, see foot-note of Detroit, etc., R. Co. *v.* State (Ohio), 36 R. R. R. 625, 59 Am. & Eng. R. Cas., N. S., 625; last paragraph of last foot-note of Davis *v.* Cleveland, etc., Ry. Co. (U. S.), 36 R. R. R. 92, 59 Am. & Eng. R. Cas., N. S., 92; foot-note of Missouri Pac. Ry. Co. *v.* Kansas (U. S.), 35 R. R. R. 728, 58 Am. & Eng. R. Cas., N. S., 728; Yazoo, etc., R. Co. *v.* Greenwood Grocery Co. (Miss.), 35 R. R. R. 417, 58 Am. & Eng. R. Cas., N. S., 417.

†See first-note of Pittsburg, etc., Ry. Co. *v.* Chicago (Ill.), 35 R. R. R. 380, 58 Am. & Eng. R. Cas., N. S., 380; last foot-note of Reid & Beam *v.* Southern Ry. Co. (N. Car.), 31 R. R. R. 352, 54 Am. & Eng. R. Cas., N. S., 352.

‡See foot-note of Chicago, etc., Ry. Co. *v.* United States (C. C. A.), 34 R. R. R. 495, 57 Am. & Eng. R. Cas., N. S., 495; first foot-note of Hockfield *v.* Southern Ry. Co. (N. Car.), 34 R. R. R. 492, 57 Am. & Eng. R. Cas., N. S., 492.

Reid et ux. *v.* Southern Ry. Co

tween states without filing such rates. Held, that it was only the "business" of a common carrier, which could not be exercised without filing rates, and a railroad company was not prohibited from receiving freight for transportation to another state by the fact that no through route and joint rates had been established between the points of shipment and delivery.

Carriers—Freight—Penalties—Actions—Defenses—Failure to File Rates.—The fact that the railroad company did not establish and post its rates between a point on its own line and a point in another state would not be a defense to an action for the penalty imposed by Revisal 1905, § 2631, for failure to receive freight for shipment, since the railroad company could have discharged its common-law duty to receive the freight by accepting it to be shipped to the end of its own line and there delivered to another carrier for transportation to its interstate destination, making the freight payable at destination, or could have ascertained by telegraph, while the freight was en route, the amount of the freight charges; the shipper not having demanded but merely having offered to prepay the freight.

Evidence—Presumptions—Compliance with Law.—It is presumed that a railroad company is carrying on its business under the authority of law.

Carriers—Freight—Statutory Regulations—Connecting Carriers—Liability of Initial Carrier.—The interstate commerce act (Act Feb. 4, 1887, c. 104, § 20, 24 Stat. 386 [U. S. Comp. St. 1901, p. 3169]), making the initial carrier who issued a bill of lading liable for the default of each successive carrier to the point of destination, merely declares the common law and is constitutional.

Carriers—Freight—Carriage Beyond Line—Duties.—A common carrier of freight is liable in damages for refusing to receive and carry goods, though destined for points beyond its own line.

Carriers—Freight—Receipt—Penalties for Refusal.—Even if Interstate Commerce Act Feb. 4, 1887, c. 104, § 20, 24 Stat. 386 (U. S. Comp. St. 1901, p. 3169), making the initial carrier who issues a bill of lading liable for the default of each successive carrier to the point of destination, were invalid, its invalidity would not relieve a carrier from the penalty imposed by Revisal 1905, § 2631, for failure to receive freight tendered, though the freight was destined for an interstate point, since the goods should have been received under a bill of lading limiting liability to damages suffered on the initial carrier's own line.

Carriers—Freight—Through Shipment.—In absence of statute or act of Congress, the mere designation in the bill of lading of a point in another state as the point of destination does not make the contract one for through transportation, where the other provisions indicate limitation of the initial carrier's liability to damages occurring on its own line.

Brown and Walker, JJ., dissenting.

Reid et ux. *v.* Southern Ry. Co

Appeal from Superior Court, Mecklenburg County; Webb, Judge.

Action by D. L. Reid and wife against the Southern Railway Company. From a judgment for plaintiffs, defendant appeals. Affirmed.

On September 17, 1907, the feme plaintiff tendered to the defendant at its freight depot in Charlotte, N. C., a lot of household goods for shipment to Davis, W. Va., a station on the West Maryland Railroad. She offered to prepay the freight charges, and asked for a bill of lading. The defendant declined to receive said goods for shipment, as requested. Again, on the 18th, 19th, 20th, 21st, and 23d of September, she renewed her requests to the defendant to receive said freight for shipment, as above stated; but the defendant refused to accept same until September 23, 1907, when it informed the plaintiff that the amount necessary to prepay the freight was $34.08. The plaintiff thereupon paid the same, and the defendant then accepted said freight for shipment, and issued a bill of lading therefor. On September 17th, when the plaintiff first tendered the goods and demanded the bill of lading, the defendant's agent informed the plaintiff that there was no established rate for shipment to Davis, W. Va., and that none had been filed or published, and that he had no authority to receive said goods. Said agent on that day wired the proper authority to obtain the freight rate and for permission to receive said shipment. On September 23d he received such information and permission, and thereupon accepted the freight and issued a bill of lading therefor. At the date of said tender, on September 17th, there was a telegraph office at Davis, W. Va. The plaintiff remained at Charlotte from September 17th to September 23d waiting the shipment of said household goods. The above facts were agreed, and it was further agreed that the plaintiff's damage, if she is entitled to recover any, by reason of said delay in Charlotte, was $25. Upon the facts agreed, the judge rendered judgment for $250, being penalty of $50 per day for refusal to accept freight tendered for shipment on each of five different days, and $25 compensatory damages, and the cost of this action. The defendant appealed.

W. B. Rodman, for appellant.
Stewart & McRae, for appellees.

CLARK, C. J. The defendant contends that Revisal 1905, § 2631, is invalid, so far as it undertakes to impose a penalty on a common carrier for refusing to receive a shipment of freight from one state to another, but concedes that this court has heretofore decided this point against it. In Lumber Co. *v.* Railroad, 152 N. C. 72, 67 S. E. 167, 168, it is said: "We have repeatedly passed against this contention. The defendant's brief admits

Reid et ux. v. Southern Ry. Co

this, and cites eight decisions of this court which it asks us to overrule. In one of the latest of these (Reid v. Railroad, 149 N. C. 423 [63 S. E. 112]), the authorities were reviewed, and the court said: "The defendant contends that Revisal 1905, § 2631, giving a penalty for refusing to accept freight for shipment, is unconstitutional when the freight is to be shipped into another state. But refusing to receive for shipment is an act wholly done within this state, is not a part of the act of transportation, and our penalty statute applies.' " The court then cited Bagg v. Railroad, 109 N. C. 279, 14 S. E. 79, 14 L. R. A. 596, 26 Am. St. Rep. 569, and Currie v. Railroad, 135 N. C. 536, 47 S. E. 654, both of which had been cited and reaffirmed by Walker, J., in Walker v. Railroad, 137 N. C. 168, 49 S. E. 84. In Twitty v. Railroad, 141 N. C. 355, 53 S. E. 957, Brown, J., held that, where the agent refused to give the bill of lading because he did not know what the freight rates were, this was a refusal to receive for transportation, and the carrier was responsible for the penalty, even though he put the goods in the warehouse. In Harrill v. Railroad, 144 N. C. 532, 57 S. E. 383, Walker, J., held that a penalty for a failure to deliver freight was valid though the freight was interstate. There the penalty was incurred after transportation had ceased. Here the penalty occurred before the transportation had been begun, and before the freight was received or accepted for transportation. Reid v. Railroad was again before the court (150 N. C. 753, 64 S. E. 874), and was reaffirmed by Hoke, J., citing Morris v. Express Co., 146 N. C. 167, 59 S. E. 667, 15 L. R. A. (N. S.) 983, which held "the state may, in the absence of express action by Congress or by the Interstate Commerce Commission, regulate for the benefit of its citizens local matters indirectly affecting interstate commerce," and cited as sustaining that position Railroad v. Flour Mill, 211 U. S. 612, 29 Sup. Ct. 214, 53 L. Ed. 352, which laid down the same proposition in a case which involved the right of the state court to compel a railroad company to place cars on a siding for the convenience of a flouring mill engaged in making shipments in interstate commerce. The above decisions were followed by Connor, J., in Garrison v. Railroad, 150 N. C. 575, 592, 64 S. E. 578, with a full review of the authorities and no dissent. In fact, the duty to receive freight "whenever tendered" was a common-law duty. Alsop v. Express Co., 104 N. C. 278, 10 S. E. 297, 6 L. R. A. 271, which was cited and approved in Garrison v. Railroad, 150 N. C. 582, 64 S. E. 578. Interstate commerce does not begin "until the articles have been shipped or started for transportation from one state to the other," was said by Bradley, J., in Coe v. Errol, 116 U. S. 517, 6 Sup. Ct. 475, 29 L. Ed. 715, citing In re Daniel Ball, 10 Wall. 565, 19 L. Ed. 999, which has since been cited with approval in Match Co. v. Ontonagon, 188 U. S. 94, 23 Sup. Ct. 266, 47 L. Ed. 394. The statutory enforcement, under penalty, of the common-law duty to accept freight "whenever tendered," is not within the scope or terms of any act of Congress. It is neither an interference with nor a burden upon interstate commerce.

The second point the defendant makes is that it could not receive for shipment freight going from one state to another, until the rates of freight to such points had been filed with the Interstate Commerce Commission, as required by the United States statute. The defendant's brief concedes that this point also has been held against him by this court. The act of Congress (Interstate Commerce Act Feb. 4, 1887, c. 104, § 6, 24 Stat. 380 [U. S. Comp. St. 1901, p. 3156]) provides: "Every common carrier, subject to the provisions of this act, shall file with the commission created by this act, print and keep open to public instruction schedules showing all the rates, fares and charges for transportation between different points on its own route, and between points on its own route and points on the route of any other carrier by railroad, by pipe line or by water, when a through route and joint rate have been established." If no through route and joint rate from Charlotte to Davis, W. Va., had been established, it was not therefore prohibited to the defendant to receive this freight. It cannot be expected that a freight rate to every railroad station in the Union from Charlotte must be established and published before the railroad can receive freight for any point outside this state, at Charlotte. The federal statute does not prohibit the receipt or forwarding of a single shipment, but forbids the carrier to "engage or participate in the transportation of passengers or property," interstate, without filing its rates. It is the business of a common carrier which the defendant is forbidden to exercise without filing its rates. The statute has no application to this case, where the defendant was carrying on such business, presumptively, at least, under the authority of law. Harrill *v.* Railroad, 144 N. C. 540, 57 S. E. 383. If, however, the defendant was in default in not having complied with the federal statute to establish and post its rates, this would not be a defense to its other default in failing to comply with its common-law duty to receive all freight when tendered, under penalty prescribed by a state statute.

Besides, there was nothing which prevented the defendant from accepting the freight to be shipped to the end of its line, there to be delivered to other carriers to be transported to Davis, W. Va. This it actually did when it finally received this freight and gave its bill of lading therefor on September 23d. The bill of lading recites the receipt of the freight in good order, marked as destined for Davis, W. Va., and stipulates: "Which said carrier agrees to carry to its said destination, if on its own road, or otherwise to deliver to another carrier on the route to said destination." There was no reason why the defendant could not have received

Reid et ux. *v.* Southern Ry. Co

this freight on the very first day it was tendered, as it was its duty to do, and have given a bill of lading in the identical words that it gave on September 23d. It could have shipped the goods and made the freight payable at destination, or it could have fore-gone the receipt of freight till it could have ascertained by wire the amount thereof, which could have been done while the goods were proceeding on their way. The plaintiff did not demand prepayment of freight, as the condition precedent to acceptance of the goods. She merely offered to prepay. In Twitty *v.* Railroad, 141 N. C. 355, 53 S. E. 957, Brown, J., says: "The fact that the agent did not know the freight rates is no excuse. It is his duty to know them. At least, he could readily have telegraphed and ascertained, and need not have refused to give a bill of lading on that account." So, here, it is no defense that the defendant had not established its rates. It was its duty to have done so. It could have received and shipped the freight and ascertained the rates while the goods were in transit. It could not plead its default to the United States government as a defense for its default in its duty to the plaintiff. Currie *v.* Railroad, 135 N. C. 537, 47 S. E. 654; Bagg *v.* Railroad, 109 N. C. 279, 14 S. E. 79, 26 Am. St. Rep. 569, 14 L. R. A. 596. In Tel. Co. *v.* James, 162 U. S. 650, 16 Sup. Ct. 934, 40 L. Ed. 1105, a state statute was held valid which required telegraph companies to receive and deliver promptly all telegrams, and it was held that this applied to interstate messages. This has been quoted and approved in Railroad *v.* Flour Mills, 211 U. S. 622, 29 Sup. Ct. 214, 53 L. Ed. 352. It was held in Tel. Co. *v.* James, supra, that a state statute was not void as affecting interstate commerce, unless "it necessarily affected the conduct of the carrier, and regulated him in the performance of his duties outside and beyond the limits of the state enacting the law." But the state statute is valid if it "can be fully carried out and obeyed without in any manner affecting the conduct of the company with regard to the performance of its duties in other states, and would not un-favorably affect or embarrass it in the course of its employment, and hence, until Congress speaks upon the subject, it would seem that such a statute must be valid." In Morris *v.* Express Co., 146 N. C. 167, 59 S. E. 667, 15 L. R. A. (N. S.) 983, this court held valid Revisal 1905, § 2634, imposing a penalty for failure to adjust and pay in 90 days a valid claim for damages to goods shipped from points without the state. In a very recent case Chief Justice Fuller, in Railroad *v.* Mazursky, 216 U. S. 122, 30 Sup. Ct. 378, 54 L. Ed. ——, held exactly the same proposition, approving what had been said by Mr. Justice Peckham in Tel. Co. *v.* James, supra.

And, finally, the defendant objects that by reason of section 20 of the interstate commerce act the initial carrier who issues a bill of lading is liable for the default not only of itself but of

Reid et ux. *v.* Southern Ry. Co

each of the successive carriers to the point of destination, and
therefore the state ought not to compel it to issue a bill of lading.
It seems to question the constitutionality of the act of Congress.
The act of Congress is merely declaratory of what was the common law in this respect and has been held constitutional in Smeltzer *v.* Railroad (C. C.) 158 Fed. 659, and Railroad *v.* Crenshaw,
5 Ga. App. 675, 63 S. E. 865. The defendant, having held itself
out as a common carrier, was liable if it refused to receive and
carry goods for points beyond its own line. Railroad *v.* Wolcott,
141 Ind. 280, 39 N. E. 451, 50 Am. St. Rep. 320; Railroad *v.* Morton, 61 Ind. 577, 28 Am. Rep. 682. But whether such act of Congress is valid or invalid does not arise in this case. If invalid, the
defendant could have received the goods and asserted its liability
only to the extent of damages received on its own line, as it actually did in the bill of lading which it issued when it received these
goods on September 23d. But, if the act is constitutional, the
defendant could not on that account delay or decline to receive
this shipment as long as it was in the business of a common carrier, and carrying goods for other shippers to be transported to
points outside the state. Unless the act of Congress is constitutional, "the mere designation of the destination of the goods in
the contract with the first carrier will not make it a contract for
through transportation, where the other terms indicate a limitation of liability to the end of the contracting carrier's line." 6
Cyc. 481; Phillips *v.* Railroad, 78 N. C. 294. This question, as
already said, does not arise in this case, and, if it did, it would
in no wise affect the duty of the defendant to receive the plaintiff's goods when tendered for shipment. The measure of responsibility for damages, if any should arise, is entirely separate
and apart from the duty to accept and ship the goods.

No error.

Texas & P. Ry. Co. *v.* Railroad Commission of Louisiana.

(Supreme Court of Louisiana, Nov. 14, 1910. On Rehearing, Dec. 12, 1910.)

[53 So. Rep. 660.]

Evidence—Orders of Railroad Commission—Presumption of Legality.—The orders of the State Railroad Commission are presumably proper and legal, and the burden of showing that they are not is upon the person attacking them.

Railroads—Regulation—Regulation of Transportation—Validity.—An order of the State Railroad Commission, requiring a railroad company to put on additional trains, need not go to the extent of violating the provisions of the federal Constitution for the protection of private property, in order to be illegal.

Railroads—Regulation—Validity.—An order of the Railroad Commission, requiring a railroad company to put on two more daily trains, in addition to the two already provided, to connect a branch station with a main line junction station, in order to connect with night trains on the main line, was unreasonable and illegal, where only 3,600 passengers used the night trains at the junction station in a year, resulting in a revenue to the company of $900, when the expense of operating the two additional trains for the year would be $11,349.

(Syllabus by Editorial Staff.)

Appeal from the Twenty-Second Judicial District Court, Parish of East Baton Rouge; H. F. Brunot, Judge.

Suit by the Texas & Pacific Railway Company against the Railroad Commission of Louisiana to set aside an order of the Commission. Judgment sustaining the order, and the Railway Company appeals. Judgment set aside, and order annulled.

Howe, Fenner, Spencer & Cocke, for appellant.

Walter Guion, Atty. Gen., and *R. G. Pleasant (Phanor Breazeale,* of counsel), for appellee.

Provosty, J. The plaintiff railroad company sues to set aside, as unreasonable and unjust, an order of the Railroad Commission requiring it to operate two additional trains daily between Natchitoches and Cypress. Natchitoches is a town on the plaintiff company's branch road going to Shreveport, and Cypress is the station on the main line where the branch road connects with the main line. The distance between the two is 10 and a fraction miles. There are already on the branch two trains daily. They connect with the day trains on the main line. The order in question requires two more trains daily to be put on, to connect with the two night trains on the main line.

Texas & P. Ry. Co. *v.* Railroad Commission of Louisiana

The reason assigned for the order is that passengers who desire to take or who arrive by the night trains must wait several hours at Cypress, and that the accommodations there are worse than poor. The plaintiff contends that the service now being rendered is adequate, and that this additional service is unnecessary, and would occasion a loss of from $10,000 to $15,000 a year to the railway company, without a corresponding benefit to the public, and that the said order is therefore unreasonable and unjust.

The order was made on October 13, 1909, and the case was tried in the lower court in January, 1910.

Plaintiff introduced in evidence exhibits, showing its passenger business to and from Natchitoches for several years back, and showing, also, what would be the probable cost of this additional service.

The first of these exhibits shows what was the passenger business from and to Natchitoches over the plaintiff company's road during the years 1904, 1905, 1906, 1907, and 1908, together with the number of miles traveled by the passengers and the revenue derived from the passenger traffic. The average for this period of five years was, per year, 39,566 passengers, yielding a revenue of $38,701.45; each passenger traveling 39.1 miles, and paying a fare of 98.1 cents.

Another exhibit shows what was the passenger traffic over the plaintiff company's road during the year ending July 31, 1909. It shows that the total number of passengers who left Natchitoches was 16,890; that of this number 10,176 traveled only on the branch road, and did not go on the main line at all, so that only 6,714 traveled on the main line; that of that number only 792 took the night trains—in other words, that the night trains carried an average of 2.17 passengers per day coming from Natchitoches. The exhibit shows, further, that 16,783 passengers traveled to Natchitoches. The exhibit does not show how many of these traveled on the night trains; but, in view of the fact that the total number traveling from Natchitoches, viz., 16,890, was approximately the same as the total number traveling to Natchitoches, the inference is legitimate that approximately the same number traveled to Natchitoches on the night trains as traveled from, to wit, 792, or an average of 2.17 passengers daily.

Another exhibit shows the distance that was traveled by the 16,890 passengers carried by plaintiff from Natchitoches during the year ending July, 1909, and shows that 94 per cent. of these passengers went to points less than 100 miles from Natchitoches; that is to say, were presumably day passengers, since the day trains are ordinarily used for a short distance. This would leave 890 for the night trains, a number approximating the 792 shown by the other exhibit.

If we adopt the higher of these figures, we find that about

Texas & P. Ry. Co. v. Railroad Commission of Louisiana

1,800 passengers traveled to and from Natchitoches more than 100 miles, or presumably on the night trains, during 1909.

Doubling these figures, for the greater safety of computation, we have 3,600 passengers using the night trains, or an average of about 10 a day—5 in and 5 out.

The average fare from Natchitoches to Cypress is 25 cents. The total revenues, then, from the 3,600 passengers would be $900.

The evidence shows that the expense of this additional service would be $11,349.95 a year; that, therefore, the plaintiff company would carry each passenger at a net loss of $2.90, and would furnish the service at a net yearly loss of $10,549.95. The defendant does not admit the correctness of these figures. In the first place, says defendant, they have not been taken directly from the books of the plaintiff company, but from a so-called "financial exhibit;" then there are a great many cash fares from Natchitoches to Cypress, which do not figure on said exhibits; and, moreover, the night travel will largely increase just as soon as the said night service is established, it having been kept down heretofore by the inconvenience of having to wait at Cypress for the night trains in the case of those going, and for the next day train in the case of those arriving.

The financial exhibit in question, from which the exhibits offered by plaintiff were made out, is shown to be a compilation of what appears on the books, and to form part of the plaintiff company's system of bookkeeping, and that the reports which the plaintiff company is required by law to make to the Interstate Commerce Commission and to the Railroad Commissions of the states of Texas and Louisiana are compiled from it. We fail entirely to see why these figures in the exhibits offered in evidence should be any the less reliable from having taken from a compilation from the books, instead of directly from the books themselves, assuming that the compilation has been made in good faith and by competent persons, as is shown to have been the case with the financial exhibit in question.

Doubtless the number of passengers may have been greater than is shown by these exhibits. There may have been cash fares that were not accounted for, and in other ways the books of the company may fail to show the exact number of passengers; but the necessary margin to cover this difference has been more than allowed when the total number of passengers shown by the books has been doubled for the sake of being on the safe side.

Defendant also questions the estimate made by plaintiff of the probable expense of this additional service. We find no reason for not accepting the said estimate as sufficiently correct to serve the purposes of this case.

The Attorney General, who appears herein for the defendant Railroad Commisson, urges that all such orders of the Railroad

Texas & P. Ry. Co. *v.* Railroad Commission of Louisiana

Commission will be presumed to be correct and legal, and that the burden of proof for showing that they are not rests upon the railroad attacking them. That proposition is abundantly supported by authority. But, in our opinion, the plaintiff has fully discharged that burden in this case. We think that, on the facts as found and hereinabove stated, the order in question in this case is unreasonable and unjust, and therefore illegal.

The learned counsel for plaintiff has argued, and in our opinion demonstrated, that for being illegal, and liable to be set aside by the courts, such an order need not go to the extent of violating the provisions of the federal Constitution for the protection of private property. But we do not understand the learned Attorney General as contending that such an order cannot be set aside unless it violates those provisions of the federal Constitution. All that we understand him as contending is that the fact that the extra service can be rendered by the railroad company only at a loss is not the sole criterion, or, indeed, the most important consideration, but that the true criterion and most important consideration is whether or not the public interest requires that the additional service be rendered, provided, always, that the loss to the railroad be not so great as to constitute a greater sacrifice on its part than the public would have the right to expect and demand, or, in other words, such as would reduce the earnings of its road in Louisiana to an amount below a fair return on the capital invested, etc.

A night service upon this branch would, no doubt, be a great convenience to the people of Natchitoches, and especially to the young lady students of the Normal school located in that town; but so would a night service upon every branch line in the state be a great convenience to the people of the towns along the line. We discover no special reason why there should be this night service upon this branch to accommodate so few people.

It is therefore ordered, adjudged, and decreed that the judgment appealed from be set aside, and that there be judgment annulling, cancelling, and setting aside the order of the Railroad Commission of Louisiana, of date September 30, 1910, by which the Texas & Pacific Railroad Company is commanded and required to operate a passenger train between Cypress, La., and Natchitoches, La., on and after October 15, 1909, so as to make close connection at Cypress, allowing a schedule wait of not more than 30 minutes after its train No. 51, due at Cypress at 3:54 a. m., and its train No. 52, due at Cypress at 11:32 o'clock p. m. and that it should also arrange the schedule so as to leave Cypress, returning to Natchitoches, nor more than 30 minutes after the arrival of the said two trains, and that defendant pay all costs.

On Rehearing.

PER CURIAM. Rehearing denied.

BREAUX, C. J. (concurring in the decree). In the application

Daoust & Welch *v.* Chicago, R. I. & P. Ry. Co

for a rehearing, the defendant presses upon our attention whether the doctrine for which he contends refers to the business done by the main road, or whether it can be made to refer to a branch or very small part of plaintiffs' system.

The contention of defendant is that it ought to be the business of the main road or system within the state.

The question is important.

I withhold my opinion upon the subject.

As to the other questions involved, I have found no reason to dissent.

I therefore concur in the decree.

DAOUST & WELCH *v.* CHICAGO, R. I. & P. RY. CO.

(Supreme Court of Iowa, Dec. 17, 1910.)

[128 N. W. Rep. 1106.]

Carriers — Freight — Delay — Excuses — Extraordinary Passenger Transportation.*—Delay in transporting freight cannot be excused by the fact that crews were taken from freight trains to handle an extraordinary amount of passenger traffic of which the carrier had previous warning and could have provided for.

Carriers—Freight—Delay—Excuses.*—Though a carrier, which has provided facilities for handling the traffic which may ordinarily be expected, need not provide in advance for an extraordinary amount of traffic, and may refuse to accept freight, yet, if it accepts freight without notifying the shipper of the congested condition of the traffic, it cannot excuse delay in delivery because of such condition, so that, even if a carrier could take its freight crews for the purpose of handling an extraordinary passenger traffic, it was bound to notify shippers of freight of the crippled condition of its freight traffic by the diversion of freight crews, in order to excuse delay in transportation from such cause.

Trial — Freight — Delay — Action — Instructions—Applicability to Facts.—An instruction, in an action for delay in transporting horses, that if it was the carrier's custom to forward from Fairbury on train No. 94, on which the horses were shipped, the stock destined to South Omaha, which had been unloaded for feed, etc., at Fairbury,

---

*For the authorities in this series on the question, for what delays a common carrier is and is not liable, see Tiller & Smith *v.* Chicago, etc., R. Co. (Iowa), 33 R. R. R. 743, 56 Am. & Eng. R. Cas., N. S., 743; Cormack *v.* New York, etc., R. Co. (N. Y.), 33 R. R. R. 629, 56 Am. & Eng. R. Cas., N. S., 629.

For the authorities in this series on the subject of the burden of showing excuse for delay in transporting freight, see foot-note of Tiller & Smith *v.* Chicago, etc., R. Co. (Iowa), 24 R. R. R. 581, 47 Am. & Eng. R. Cas., N. S., 581.

Daoust & Welch *v.* Chicago, R. I. & P. Ry. Co

and which came in on train No. 94 on the preceding evening, the carrier, in the absence of instructions from the shipper, was not bound to forward the horses on an earlier train, was properly refused, where there had been a previous delay at another station and train No. 94 left Fairbury nearly five hours late, and after the six hours required by the statute for a rest had elapsed.

Carriers—Live Stock—Actions for Delay—Jury Questions—Contributory Negligence.—Where a shipment of horses had been in the cars only about five hours when they reached P., and the shipper's agent could reasonably rely on the train leaving another station ahead at which they were unloaded for food, etc., at 6:30 p. m. instead of 7:02 p. m. on the next day, in which event the horses would have gone to the final destination in less than the statutory 36-hour limit for keeping stock in the car, it was a question for the jury, in an action for damage for delay in shipment, whether the shipper's agent in charge of the horses was negligent in not permitting them to be unloaded at P. for food, water, and rest, when the yardmaster offered to unload them there.

Carriers—Live Stock—Action for Delay—Jury Question—Proximate Cause.—Whether any such negligence of the shipper's agent contributed to delaying the shipment was also a question for the jury.

Live Stock—Action for Delay—Jury Question—Negligence.— Where the train on which horses were shipped had already been delayed more than eight hours in leaving another point when they were unloaded for food, rest, and water, and they could have well been reloaded and forwarded on the same evening on which they were unloaded, instead of at 7:02 p. m. the next day, and the carrier knew that a large number of passenger trains would pass over the road the next day so as to congest traffic, it was a question for the jury whether the horses should have been reloaded, and forwarded sooner than they were in the exercise of due care.

Carriers—Live Stock—Action for Delay—Jury Question.—In an action against a railroad company for damages for delay in forwarding a shipment of horses, whether defendant was negligent in forwarding the horses held a jury question.

Appeal and Error—Findings—Conflicting Evidence—Conclusiveness.—A question of fact on which the evidence directly conflicted was for the jury to determine.

Appeal from District Court, Pottawattamie County; O. D. Wheeler, Judge.

Action for damages caused by the negligent delay in the shipment of four car loads of horses. There was a judgment against defendant, from which it appeals. Affirmed.

Carroll Wright, J. L. Parrish, and *Saunders & Stuart,* for appellant.

Fremont Benjamin and *Verne Benjamin,* for appellee.

LADD, J. The horses were shipped from Goodland, Kan., July 3, 1908, at 5:50 p. m., billed to South Omaha via Lincoln. Upon their arrival at Lincoln July 6th at 12:45 a. m., the yards were inundated with water. Between 8:20 o'clock and 1:30 a. m. of that day, 3.86 inches of water fell, and this was increased to 5.7 inches by 6 o'clock. Between 10 o'clock in the forenoon and 12:30 p. m., 1.16 inches of water fell. Conditions were such that it was impossible to unload the horses or move the train until July 7th at 9 a. m., when it was taken to South Omaha, reaching that place at 2:39 p. m., where the horses were immediately unloaded. It was conceded on the trial that the company was not responsible for the delay after the arrival of the train at Lincoln; this, as the court instructed, being due to an act of God. The controversy is whether there was unreasonable delay in the shipment of these horses from Goodland, Kan., to Lincoln, Neb., a distance of 325 miles in 55 hours, and, if so, whether if transported with reasonable promptness they would have passed through Lincoln in time to have avoided the flood. If they would, then, under rule announced in Green-Wheeler Shoe Co. v. Railway, 130 Iowa, 123, 106 N. W. 498, 5 L. R. A. (N. S.) 882, the plaintiff was entitled to recover. As the time greatly exceeded that scheduled and ordinarily required, counsel concede that the burden was on defendant to explain the delay consistently with the exercise of ordinary diligence in transporting the stock.

1. The horses were shipped from Goodland, Kan., July 3, 1908, at 5:50 p. m. Central time. The train was late in leaving that point and arrived at Phillipsburg, Kan., at 10:35 o'clock, the same evening, 2 hours and 25 minutes behind scheduled time. The crew required rest, and there was no other to go on in its stead. The scheduled time for leaving was 11 o'clock p. m., three hours being allowed for yard work, but a stop was made until 7:12 a. m. the next morning, when the train pulled out for Fairbury, Neb., where it arrived in the afternoon at 4:15. This was 15 minutes ahead of scheduled time, which fixed the time for departure at 6:30 p. m. At the instance of the chief train dispatcher, the horses were unloaded, fed, and watered. The train crew was ordered out at 10:30 o'clock, but the train did not leave until 11:25 p. m. It arrived in South Omaha at 7:28 o'clock the next morning. The horses were not shipped out on this train, though more than the six hours exacted for rest of the animals by the United States statute had elapsed. Nor was the train ordinarily leaving Fairbury at 10:30 a. m. of July 5th run that day, and the horses were not reloaded and moved until 7:02 p. m. of that day. In explanation of these delays, the evidence disclosed that that at Phillipsburg was owing to there being no crew not entitled to rest under the statutes of the United States prohibiting more than 16 hours' continu-

ous employment on trains, and after such service exacting at least 8 hours' rest, to take the train and continue the journey. For this reason, it did not leave that place until 7:12 o'clock the next morning. The company had in its employment a sufficient number of crews to handle the ordinary and usual freight and passenger traffic over its road.   But there was an extraordinary movement of passengers over the line from Council Bluffs, Iowa, via Lincoln, to Denver, Colo., beginning July 2d owing to the National Democratic Convention convening there July 7th, and during the four days commencing the 2d, besides the regular passenger service, defendant operated 21 passenger trains over this line.   Fourteen of the 26 freight crews, under the direction of the train dispatcher at Fairbury, were withdrawn from the freight service and sent to Council Bluffs to take charge of passenger trains as they came in and operate them through to Denver.   It was shown not to have been feasible to have procured crews from other parts of defendant's railroad system or from other systems, for that, in the safe operation of the road, it is essential that the men be familiar with the road, the equipment of trains, the time cards grade, bridges, and the like, and considerable time is necessary to acquire this information.   The naked inquiry with reference to the delay at Phillipsburg, then, is whether defendant was excusable therefore on the ground that the company had diverted the crews ordinarily and necessarily engaged in the transportation of freight to the operation of its passenger trains necessary to move the extraordinary and unusual number of passengers demanding transportation.

We can think of no rule of law which will permit a carrier thus to abandon the carriage of freight which it has received for the purpose of transporting persons. The company had anticipated the exodus to Denver and planned for it during the month previous; but it continued to receive freight without notice to the shipper of its purpose to cripple that service and notwithstanding its knowledge that the withdrawal of more than one-half the freight crews would be likely to occasion unusual delays in the transportation of freight. Though a common carrier, which has equipped itself with sufficient facilities and appliances to enable it to transport the traffic which may be ordinarily expected to seek transportation over its route, is not bound to provide in advance for extraordinary occasions or an unusual influx of business, and may refuse to accept goods owing to the unusual press of business, yet, if it accepts goods or stock without notice to the shipper of the circumstances or his assent, it cannot be heard to say that a delay is due to such a contingency. Hutchinson on Carriers (4th Ed.) § 496. That author lays down the rule that the carrier "must at his peril inform the shipper of the necessary delay, that the shipper may exercise his own discretion as to the propriety of making the shipment; and even

Daoust & Welch *v.* Chicago, R. I. & P. Ry. Co

though the delay may occur from such a cause upon a connecting route over which he has bound himself to carry the goods to destination, which may be known to him at the time of their acceptance, he is liable for any unreasonable delay in the transportation, and such unavoidable difficulty, though wholly unknown and unanticipated, will not excuse him." The principle is well stated in Russell Grain Co. *v.* Railway Co., 144 Mo. App. 488, 89 S. W. 908: "When, at the time the shipper offers freight to the carrier, conditions exist that will prevent the delivery within a reasonable time, which means the time usually consumed under ordinary circumstances, different principles control. The carrier is not expected to perform the impossible, and may refuse to accept freight unless the shipper will agree to suffer delay in delivery made necessary by the extraordinary conditions. But the acceptance of goods for shipment, without such stipulation or without notifying the shipper of the fact that they cannot be promptly delivered, is tantamount to an assurance that they will be delivered within a reasonable time, except for the intervening of excusing causes of subsequent occurrence. The burden then devolved upon the carrier to show that the delay was caused either by some fortuitous happening that excuses delay, or that the shipper was informed, before delivery to the carrier, of the fact that prompt delivery could not be made." Palmer *v.* Ry., 101 Cal. 187, 35 Pac. 630; Texas & N. O. Ry. Co. *v.* Kolp (Tex. Civ. App.) 88 S. W. 417. Even then if it were conceded that defendant might properly divert its employees from the operation of freight trains to the handling of the extraordinary movement of passengers, it was bound, in receiving freight for transportation, to advise the shipper of the situation in order that he might exercise his discretion as to whether he would turn his property over to the carrier or later, and, not having done so, the extraordinary demand on its service in transporting passengers furnished no excuse for delay in carrying plaintiff's horses.

2. Exception is taken to the refusal of the court on request of defendant to instruct the jury that: "If you find from the evidence that it was the custom of the defendant to forward on train No. 94 the stock with South Omaha destination that was unloaded for feed, water, and rest at Fairbury, and that came in on train No. 94 of the preceding evening, the defendant, in the absence of instructions from the plaintiff, would not be required to forward the same on an earlier train." The instruction as requested overlooked the previous delay at Phillipsburg, Kan., and also that No. 94, instead of leaving on scheduled time, 6:30 p. m.—after the horses had been unloaded but 2 hours and 15 minutes—rendering it necessary that they await another train ordinarily, did not leave Fairbury, Neb., until 11:25 p. m. after the six hours exacted by the United States statute for rest had

elapsed. Because of these circumstances, the court rightly refused the instruction.

3. Appellant complains also of the refusal of the court to instruct that if defendant's yardmaster at Phillipsburg offered to
unload the horses at that point for feed, water, and rest, and
those in charge of the shipment refused such offer and insisted
this was unnecessary, and that such refusal rendered unloading
at Fairbury necessary and precluded running the cars without
unloading from Phillipsburg to South Omaha, a verdict should
be returned for defendant. When the horses reached Phillipsburg, Kan., they had been in the cars only about five hours, and
the man in charge knew nothing of the delays likely to occur
on that way. They might well have reckoned on the train leaving Fairbury at 6:30 p. m., in which event, had it moved on according to scheduled time, it would have reached South Omaha
before 3 o'clock the following morning. This would have been
2 hours and 30 minutes within the 36-hour limit for keeping
stock in the car. Manifestly whether those in charge of the
horses were negligent in not unloading at Phillipsburg, and, if
so, whether such negligence contributed to the delay, were issues
for the jury to decide.

4. Defendant also requested and the court refused to instruct
that defendant was under no obligation to take the horses from
the stockyards at Fairbury prior to the time it did. This instruction was rightly refused. But for the delay at Phillipsburg, the
possibility of reloading and moving the horses out the same
evening, and the circumstance that the 10:30 o'clock train the
next morning would not leave, the instruction might have been
given. As the train had been delayed, and the horses might well
have been reloaded and moved out the same evening, and many
passenger trains would be on the road the next day, whether the
horses should have been taken out of Fairbury sooner than they
were was for the jury to decide.

5. The exception to the twenty-sixth instruction is not well
taken, and the criticism of others has been disposed of by what
has been said. The contention that the evidence was not sufficient to carry the issue as to defendant's negligence to the jury
is not borne out by the record. The horses did not reach Lincoln until 55 hours after leaving Goodland, but 19 hours and 31
minutes of which they were being transported. Though a
portion of this time was Sunday, no part of the delay was shown
to have been due to this, and as defendant was operating
trains on that day, including that on which the horses were taken
out of Fairbury, it is not a situation to insist that this ought to
be taken into account. In view of the entire record, it cannot
be said as a matter of law that the company was not negligent
in unreasonably delaying the shipment but for which the flood
at Lincoln would have been avoided.

Louisville & N. R. Co. *v.* J. R. Rash & Co

That the horses were in good condition when loaded on the cars at Goodland is not controverted, but concerning their condition on arrival at South Omaha the evidence was in conflict; that of plaintiff tending to show that they were gaunt, weak, bruised, had lost about 200 pounds each in weight, many of them lame, and that they were unfit for market, while that of defendant indicated that, aside from being gaunt, they were in salable condition. The issue so raised was for the jury to determine, as was also the extent of damages occasioned by the delay.

We have discovered no error in the record, and the judgment is affirmed.

LOUISVILLE & N. R. CO. *v.* J. R. RASH & CO.

(Court of Appeals of Kentucky, Dec. 16, 1910.)

[132 S. W. Rep. 553.]

Carriers—Carriage of Live Stock—Carrier's Duty to Furnish Safe Appliances—Waiver.—When a carrier agrees to furnish a certain car for a particular purpose, which is known to him, and fails, his negligence is not waived by the shipper's acceptance of the car furnished; and where a shipper of horses ordered an Arms palace car, and was given an inferior kind, he did not waive the negligence of the carrier in using the one sent, and the carrier is liable for injuries to the horses because of the inferior car.

Appeal from Circuit Court, Warren County.

Action by J. R. Rash & Co. against the Louisville & Nashville Railroad Company. From a judgment for plaintiffs, defendant appeals. Affirmed.

Chas. H. Moorman, Benjamin D. Warfield, and *Sims & Rodes,* for appellant.
R. C. P. Thomas and *T. W. Thomas,* for appellees.

CARROLL, J. This action was brought by the appellees to recover damages from the appellant company for injuries received by some of the horses in a car load shipped by the appellees over the railroad of appellant from Lexington to Bowling Green. Upon a trial, the appellees recovered judgment for $250, and the railroad company appeals.

It appears that Porter, a member of the firm of Rash & Co., bought in Lexington 18 thoroughbred horses. These horses were placed in the Gentry stockyards, situated on a belt line that connected with the Louisville & Nashville Railroad. On September 24th, Porter ordered from the appellant company, and they agreed to furnish to him, an Arms palace car that would carry 18 horses, and this car was to be sent to the Gentry stock-

Louisville & N. R. Co. *v.* J. R. Rash & Co

yards, where the horses were to be loaded and shipped to Bowling Green. After making this arrangement, Porter gave directions to the persons in charge of the Gentry stockyards, or R. L. Baker, perhaps both, to load the stock in the car when it was sent around, and then left Lexington for his home in Bowling Green. On the following day the railroad company sent to the stockyards, not the Arms palace car contracted for and stipulated in the bill of lading, but a car known as a Burton car, with a capacity for only 16 horses.

The evidence shows very clearly that the car furnished by the railroad company and in which the horses were loaded was not as well constructed or equipped for the shipment of horses as the car contracted for. Nor was it large enough in which to ship comfortably and safely the horses. After the stock was loaded, they were taken by the Cincinnati Southern Railway to the point on the belt line at which the Louisville & Nashville Railroad intersects it, for the purpose of being delivered to the latter railroad. On their way from the stockyards to this point the horses were injured. Just how the injuries happened is not clearly shown, but there is enough from which to infer that they were due to the fact that the car was not suitable for the purpose of shipping the horses put in it.

When the car reached the line of the Louisville & Nashville Railroad, the horses as well as the car were in such a condition that the agent of the Louisville & Nashville Railroad Company removed the horses from the car and put them in another car, in which they were shipped from Lexington to Bowling Green. The car in which the horses were shipped from Lexington to Bowling Green was an Arms palace car, but an old and unsuitable car—very different from the one that was ordered. There is some evidence that the horses received the injuries on the road from Lexington to Bowling Green, and after they were placed in this substituted car, although the weight of the evidence is that the injuries were received in transit from the stockyard to the Louisville & Nashville Railroad Company's line.

It is the contention of appellant that the facts do not show that it did not furnish the kind of car ordered, and further insisted that the car it did furnish was accepted by the agents of appellees, and the horses loaded therein by them. It is also argued that the injury to the horses was not due to any defect in the car, but to their own viciousness, and therefore the jury should have been peremptorily instructed to find for the appellant.

The evidence is very satisfactory that the appellant did not furnish at the stockyards the kind or quality of car that it agreed to furnish, and it is clear that the horses were not shipped from Lexington to Bowling Green in a car of the kind or quality that was ordered, and that the appellant agreed to furnish. So that the appellant committed two breaches of its contract. The evi-

Louisville & N. R. Co. *v.* J. R. Rash & Co

dence also shows that the horses were injured by the defective construction of one or both of these cars, and not by their own viciousness. It follows, from this, that the railroad company is liable to the appellees for the damage they sustained by reason of its breach of contract, unless appellees are estopped from asserting a claim for damages on account of the failure to furnish the car that was ordered.

Upon this point it is insisted for the railroad company that its breach in this particular was waived by the action of the agents of the appellees in accepting and loading the horses into the car that was furnished. Under no circumstances could the doctrine of waiver be applied to the second car, as it is not claimed that appellees had anything to do with the transfer of the horses into this car. But, as to the first car, there is some evidence that the agents of appellees, with notice that it was not the car ordered, loaded the horses in it. The appellant does not present any sufficient excuse for its failure to furnish the car that was ordered and the one it agreed to furnish. This being so, it is well settled that when a shipper orders a car for a particular purpose, and this purpose is known to the carrier and it agrees to furnish the kind of car ordered, that his acceptance of a car other than the one ordered does not generally constitute a waiver of his right to recover damages for injuries caused by the defective condition or insufficiency of the car that he accepts. There might be a case in which the acceptance of a car other than the one ordered would be a waiver, but the facts of this case do not bring it within the exception.

This point was expressly decided by the Supreme Court of the United States in Ogdensburg R. Co. *v.* Pratt, 89 U. S. 123, 22 L. Ed. 827, a case very similar to this one. In that case an action was brought to recover damages for the value of horses killed and injured while being transported by the railroad company. One of the questions presented was: "Did the plaintiffs, by putting their horses into a car which they knew was defective and unsuitable, thereby assume the risk of such defects, and relieve the company from the responsibility of the same?" In discussing this question the court said: "The loss, it is contended, arose from the defective condition of the car in which the horses were placed, whereby it was exposed to danger from fire. It is said that Pratt was aware of the defective condition of the car, that he voluntarily made use of it, and that the risk of loss by its use thus became his and ceased to be that of the company. The judge charged the jury that it was the duty of the carrier to furnish suitable vehicles for transportation; that if he furnished unfit or unsafe vehicles he is not exempted from responsibility by the fact that the shipper knew them to be defective and used them; that nothing less than a direct agreement by the shipper to assume the risk would have that effect. * * * The judge at the trial

Brown *v.* Missouri, K. & T. Ry. Co

in this case might have gone much further than he did, and have charged that, if the jury found the company to have been negligent and careless in furnishing cars, they would not be relieved from responsibility, although there had been an agreement that they should not be liable therefor." To the same effect is Elliott on Railroads, §§ 1470-1480; Hutchinson on Carriers, §§ 508, 509; Forrester *v.* Southern R. Co., 147 N. C. 553, 61 S. E. 524, 18 L. R. A. (N. S.) 509; Atlantic Coast Line R. Co. *v.* Geraty, 166 Fed. 10, 91 C. C. A. 602, 20 L. R. A. (N. S.) 310; Coupland *v.* Housatonic Ry. Co., 61 Conn. 531, 23 Atl. 870, 15 L. R. A. 534; Railroad Co. *v.* Dies, 91 Tenn. 177, 18 S. W. 266, 30 Am. St. Rep. 871.

A few other minor, but harmless, errors are pointed out; but we do not think it worth while to discuss them, as the principal question raised by counsel, which was his right to a peremptory, has been disposed of.

Wherefore the judgment is affirmed.

BROWN *v.* MISSOURI, K. & T. RY. CO.

(Supreme Court of Kansas, Dec. 10, 1910.)

[112 Pac. Rep. 147.]

Reference—Findings by Referee—Amendment.—Findings of fact returned by a referee may be amended by the court, at least in any case where the changes merely reflect the different views of the court as to the effect of testimony accepted by the referee as truthful.

Carriers—Freight Shipments—Bills of Lading—Conclusiveness.*—Where coal is shipped by rail in bulk, the weights stated in the bill of lading are prima facie evidence of the amount received, in favor of the consignee, against the initial carrier or a connecting carrier that collects charges upon the basis of such statement, notwithstanding such weights were reported by the consignor to the carrier, and adopted by it without verification, and notwithstanding the bill of lading contains the words, "Weights subject to correction."

Carriers—Loss of Freight—Action by Consignee—Evidence.—In an action by a consignee to recover for coal lost in transit, the plaintiff's evidence held insufficient to show that such losses occurred before delivery to him.

(Syllabus by the Court.)

----

*See foot-note of Sumrell *v.* Atlantic Coast Line R. Co. (N. Car.), 36 R. R. R. 758, 59 Am. & Eng. R. Cas., N. S., 758; extensive note, 34 R. R. R. 637, 57 Am. & Eng. R. Cas., N. S., 637; first foot-note of Peele & Copeland *v.* Atlantic Coast Line R. Co. (N. Car.), 33 R. R. R. 153, 56 Am. & Eng. R. Cas., N. S., 153.

Brown v. Missouri, K. & T. Ry. Co

Appeal from District Court, Geary County.

Action by George T. Brown against the Missouri, Kansas & Texas Railway Company. Judgment for plaintiff. Defendant appeals. Reversed and remanded.

John Madden and *W. W. Brown*, for appellant.

William W. Pease and *John F. Brown*, for appellee.

Mason, J. George T. Brown sued the Missouri, Kansas & Texas Railway Company on account of coal alleged to have been lost by it in the course of shipments made to him over its line. The court appointed a referee to report on the facts. The referee, among other findings, reported that no competent evidence had been introduced to show either the quantity of coal shipped to the plaintiff or the quantity actually received by him. The court, being of the opinion that there was competent evidence on both points, modified these findings accordingly, found the amount of shortage shown, and gave judgment for the plaintiff. The defendant appeals, and urges two grounds of error: First, that the court had no authority to change the referee's findings of fact; and, second, that the evidence did not support the judgment.

In 34 Cyc. 885, it is said: "While in some jurisdictions the court may disregard the findings of fact of the referee, and make new findings on the evidence reported, or modify or change the facts as found, the general rule is that the court has no such power." This difference in practice exists, but the preponderance of authority in favor of what is stated as the general rule is not so great as might seem from the number of cases cited. Some of them involve a different phase of the subject, some are affected by statute, and one turns upon the fact that the referee was authorized only by the agreement of the parties. In Missouri, as shown by the note to the text quoted, the court may modify the referee's findings of facts, where the reference is or might be compulsory, but not where no referee could have been appointed except by consent. Boatman's Bank v. Trover Bros. Co. (C. C. A.) 181 Fed. 804, is based upon that distinction. See, also, 17 Dec. Dig. p. 1218, tit. "Reference," § 106. Here the reference was by order of the court and not by consent of the parties. In this state the tendency is to a liberal view of the control of the trial court over the referee's findings. Kelley v. Schreiber, 82 Kan. 403, 108 Pac. 816, and cases there cited; Bethell v. Lumber Co., 39 Kan. 230, 236, 17 Pac. 813. In the present case the findings of the referee, which the court changed, were not based upon conflicting oral evidence. There was nothing in the report of the referee to suggest a doubt of the truthfulness of any witness. On the contrary, it fairly appeared that the testimony given was accepted as true. The referee found that the evidence had no tendency to prove certain facts; the

Brown v. Missouri, K. & T. Ry. Co

court thought it sufficient to establish them. The difference of opinion was not whether the statements in evidence were to be believed, but what inferences were to be drawn from them (a question of fact, which the court had as fair an opportunity to decide as the referee) and what they tended to prove (a question of law). In this situation there was no occasion for a new trial. The evidence was before the court, not only without conflict of testimony, but practically with a finding that it was all true. It remained only for the court to make the inferences of fact and conclusions of law, and render judgment.

Some of the coal shipments originated on the defendant's line, and some on that of another company. The referee found that there was no evidence as to the weight of any shipment. The court changed this finding, so that it read in effect that there was no evidence on this point except the weights given by the consignor to the carrier, which were adopted as a basis for freight charges and inserted in the bills of lading. Ordinarily bills of lading are prima facie evidence against the carrier issuing them of the amount of goods received. 4 A. & E. Encycl. of L. 522; 1 Hutchinson on Carriers, § 158. The defendant maintains that here they have not that effect, because of the insertion of the qualifying words, "in apparent good order" and "weights subject to correction." It is doubtful whether the first phrase can apply to material shipped in bulk (6 Cyc. 418, 419), but in any event it does not change the effect of the instrument as prima facie evidence (4 A. & E. Encycl. of L. 522, 523, note 7; 6 Cyc. 422). The expression, "weights subject to correction," has an important function. It avoids the estoppel which would otherwise under some circumstances preclude the carrier from disputing the weight. 6 Cyc. 418. It does not destroy the prima facie effect of the recital as to quantity. It merely leaves the matter open to further inquiry, instead of being absolutely concluded. Its insertion in a bill of lading has been held, where other rights have intervened, not even to prevent the statement of weight from being conclusive, except as to minor errors. Tibbits v. R. I. & P. Ry. Co., 49 Ill. App. 567, 572.

The question whether the recital of a bill of lading as to quantity is competent evidence against a connection carrier is more difficult. In 3 Hutchinson on Carriers, p. 1594, § 1348, it is said: "The receiving carrier will be regarded as the agent of the succeeding connecting carriers for the purpose of accepting the goods for transportation over the connecting lines, and the receipt or bill of lading given by such receiving carrier will be competent evidence in an action against any of the succeeding carriers, into whose possession the goods may have come, to show the delivery for transportation, the condition of the goods at the time of such delivery, and the terms of the shipment." The only case cited in support of this text is South-

Brown v. Missouri, K. & T. Ry. Co

ern Express Co. v. Hess, 53 Ala. 19, where exceptional circumstances were relied upon as making the company receiving the
goods the agent of the connecting carrier.   In the present case
we think that the act of the defendant in collecting freight
charges upon the basis of the weights stated in the bills of lading was an adoption by it of such weights, which thereby became
prima facie evidence against it of the amount of coal shipped.
The connecting carrier is presumed to have received the quantity
of goods shown to have been delivered to the initial carrier.   3
Hutchinson on Carriers, § 1348, second paragraph of note 6;
Cooper & Co. v. Geo. Pacific Railway Co., 92 Ala. 329, 9 South.
159, 25 Am. St. Rep. 59; S. F. & W. Ry. Co. v. George L. Harris, 26 Fla. 148, 7 South. 544, 23 Am. St. Rep. 551.

The remaining question, therefore, is whether the plaintiff
showed that he received a less quantity of coal than the bills
of lading described.   The plaintiff testified that the custom was
for the railroad company to place a car of coal on the side track
and notify him; that he would then notify his teamsters and have
them unload it, hauling the coal to his scales, where it was
weighed.   The company's liability as a carrier, therefore, ceased
upon his assuming control.   6 Cyc. 457.   The referee found that
the plaintiff correctly weighed the coal that was transferred from
the cars to his scales, but that there was no competent evidence
that all the coal in any car was so transferred.   The court
changed this finding concerning the lack of evidence, and held
that, as the plaintiff had shown due care in the handling of the
coal, there was no presumption of any loss after he took charge.
The plaintiff further testified in general terms that he always
exercised supervision over the drivers; that he was careful to
see that they unloaded the coal as he ordered it; that he oversaw them in the performance of their duties; that he had a
general supervision of everything that went on, and a knowledge of the shortage of every car.   But, upon being asked how
he knew that the teamsters brought all of the coal from the
cars to the scales, he answered: "There is a railroad law that
requires us to do certain things, and when they were not done
we find it out instantly."   No explanation was given as to what
he meant by this.   He also said, in answer to the same question, that the teamsters were paid by the ton for hauling, and
would not be apt to throw any of it away.   At another time
he said he was testifying on the record of the system he used,
and that that was the knowledge he had of the transaction.   It
seems clear, therefore, that he did not profess to be speaking
from personal knowledge.   Again, he testified that there was
some little stealing of coal during the unloading at the yards;
that most of the coal cars were covered, and were sealed on
their arrival; that his effort was to unload the cars so far as
practicable on the day they were delivered, so as to lessen his

Slaats v. Chicago, M. & St. P. Ry. Co

loss; that sometimes, when a night intervened before a car was emptied, he had sealed it, but not always. None of the teamsters was produced, nor was any witness who had inspected this part of their work, or who knew that all of the coal, or substantially all of it, was transferred from the cars to the plaintiff's scales. Of course, it was not necessary to have produced witnesses who had watched the operation of unloading throughout; but no one who testified in behalf of the plaintiff seemed to have known anything personally about the coal until it reached his scales. The loss for which recovery was had was distributed among 36 cars, and averaged about a ton to a car. On one car it was over 5 tons, but with this exception it ran approximately from half a ton to 2½ tons. It seems unlikely that the loss could have occurred wholly after the arrival of the cars, but some considerable portion of it may. The plaintiff had the burden of showing how much of it had taken place before delivery to him, and, having failed to produce any evidence from which that can be ascertained, must be held to have failed in his proof.

The judgment is reversed, and the cause remanded, with directions to enter judgment for the defendant. All the Justices concurring.

SLAATS v. CHICAGO, M. & ST. P. RY. CO.

(Supreme Court of Iowa, Dec. 17, 1910.)

[129 N. W. Rep. 63.]

Master and Servant—Fellow Servant—Statute Limiting Doctrine— Railroad—Injuries in Operating—"Use and Operation"—"Railway."* —Code, § 2071, makes every railroad company liable for damages to employees by the mismanagement of the engineers or other employees, when such wrongs are in any manner connected with the use and operation of any railway about which they shall be employed. Plaintiff was a machinist's helper in the machine shop of defendant railroad company where engines were brought for repairs, his duty being to block the wheels of an engine when placed over the draw pit in the shop and to remove such blocks when the engine was to be moved. After one set of wheels had been put on an engine and it was about to be moved by another engine, in order to

---

*See generally, extensive note, 29 R. R. R. 42, 52 Am. & Eng. R. Cas., N. S., 42; Texarkana & Ft. S. R. Co. v. Anderson (Tex.), 33 R. R. R. 351, 56 Am. & Eng. R. Cas., N. S., 351; Hoveland v. Chicago, etc., Ry. Co. (Minn.), 35 R. R. R. 786, 58 Am. & Eng. R. Cas., N. S., 786; O'Neal v. South & W. R. Co. (N. Car.), 36 R. R. R. 586, 59 Am. & Eng. R. Cas., N. S., 586; Wright v. Caney River Ry. Co. (N. Car.), 36 R. R. R. 29, 59 Am. & Eng. R. Cas., N. S., 29.

Slaats *v.* Chicago, M. & St. P. Ry. Co

put on the second pair of drivers, plaintiff attempted to brush a chock from under the wheel of the dead engine, when the other engine started without warning and crushed his hand. The operating department of the railroad had no control over the machine shops, which were used only for repairing disabled equipment which had been withdrawn from service, and not merely for temporary repairs and cleaning, as were the roundhouses. Held, that the statute referred to the physical "use and operation" of the railroad in transportation, and the rails on the shop floor did not constitute a "railway," nor was the movement of the repaired engine by the other engine done in the "use and operation" of the railway, within the meaning of the statute, so that the company was not liable for the negligence of the engineer in starting the live engine.

Weaver, J., dissenting.

Appeal from District Court, Dubuque County; Robert Bonson, Judge.

Action for damages resulted in a verdict being directed for defendant, and judgment entered thereon. The plaintiff appeals. Affirmed.

Hurd, Lenehan & Kiesel, for appellant.
Glenn Brown and *Cook, Hughes & Sutherland,* for appellee.

LADD, J.   A crew, consisting of two machinists and five helpers, was employed by defendant in stripping engines when brought into its machine shops for repair, and in replacing the parts when put in a state of repair. The plaintiff was one of the helpers, and his duty was to block the wheels of the engine when placed over the draw pit in the shop by putting wooden blocks or iron nuts or burrs under the wheel and removing these when the engine was ready to be taken away. This pit was in the shop with movable rails over it, these being connected with others extending to the turntable on the outside and on with the main tracks of the railroad. When the wheels were to be put on an engine, it was "jacked up and rested on supports, the rails of the pit were then removed, and the wheels put in place. Then, for the purpose of putting in the second set of drivers, the track would be replaced and the engine would be removed so that the drivers which had been attached would rest on the permanent track beyond the pit, when the same plan would be followed for putting on the drivers, which has been described. * * * The engine, after the drive wheels were under it, was removed by another engine, but sometimes by pinch bars." On July 13, 1907, a switch engine was employed to remove that on which the wheels had been replaced. The repairs had not been completed, and, for this reason, two of the helpers sat on the frame holding up part of the machinery so it could

Slaats *v.* Chicago, M. & St. P. Ry. Co

move. After helping couple the live with the dead engine, plaintiff stepped back to see if the blocking was out. Noticing a small burr on the rail, he undertook to brush it out with his hand when, without warning, the engine started and his hand was so crushed that he lost three fingers. The evidence was such as to carry the issue of absence of contributory negligence to the jury, and no question is raised but that the jury might have found that the injury was the direct consequence of the employee's negligence in failing to warn plaintiff before moving the engine. As he was a coemployee of plaintiff, however, a finding for defendant was directed by the court, and the sole issue of law is whether the facts bring the case within the provisions of section 2071 of the Code. As plaintiff's employment was such as to expose him to the dangers incident to the moving of the dead engine, and the negligence of the engineer, if any, was in starting the same without warning, it is evident that the determination of the question depends on whether the work being done was in any manner connected with the use and operation of the railroad. The section of the statute referred to, in so far as pertinent to the inquiry, reads: "Every corporation operating a railway shall be liable for all damages sustained by any person, including employees of such corporation, in consequence of the neglect of the agents or by any mismanagement of the engineers or other employees thereof, and in consequence of the willful wrongs, whether of commission or omission of such agents, engineers, or other employees when such wrongs are in any manner connected with the use and operation of any railway on or about which they shall be employed." In a sense, everything such a corporation does is in some manner connected with the use and operation of its railway, for that is the purpose of its existence. Thus the work of those who solicit freight or passengers for transportation or enter into traffic arrangements with other roads, or procure rolling stock or fuel for the engines and the like, is connected with the successful operation of the enterprise, but no one pretends that work in any of these lines is within the purview of this statute. See Malone *v.* Railway, 61 Iowa, 326, 16 N. W. 203, 47 Am. Rep. 813. It has reference, as we think, to the physical use and operation of the railway and the question for determination is whether the accident occurred on or about a railway or in the operation thereof. The record leaves no doubt but that the engines were in the machine shop, as distinguished from a roundhouse. In the latter, engines in service are run for repair and cleaning necessary to their continued use on the road. Roundhouses are constructed along the way for this purpose, and are made use of in connection with the actual use of the road. Their relation thereto is somewhat like the stable to the livery. But the machine shops are the hospitals. The engines, cars, and the like are only taken there when dis-

Slaats v. Chicago, M. & St. P. Ry. Co

abled and withdrawn from use when this is essential to refit them for actual service in the operation of the railway. Manifestly, when so withdrawn and in course of reconstruction or repair, they are in no wise connected with the operation of the railway. As well say the steam shovels, pile drivers, and the like being repaired in the same shop are so connected. Such reconstruction and repair might proceed as well were the shop that of an individual or other corporation and located apart from the railroad. Over the shop in question the operating department of the railroad exercised no control. Tracks were laid on the floor, and on these the engines and cars were stripped, and so, too, the different parts were assembled and put together, and the engines or car moved about thereon during repair or construction. These tracks were connected with those in the yard and then with the railway, but does this make the tracks in the shop a part of the railroad in the sense in which that word is employed in section 2071? If so, then the tracks in a manufacturing plant on which locomotives are constructed by individuals or corporations other than railways constitute railroads, and employees working thereon are within the protection of the above section. The mere laying of tracks on the floor does not make a railway, nor does the movement of an engine or car thereon necessarily constitute the operation of a railway. If so, this might be affected by the use of a pinch bar or a moving crane or any kind of electric device. A company or individual engaged solely in manufacturing or repairing, might make such use of tracks entirely within plant in the convenient performance of its work and without connection with a railroad, as that term is understood. Of course, a company or individual may operate a railway solely for the purpose of carrying property belonging to it or him and such an one has been held to be within the terms of similar cases. Lodwick Lumber Co. v. Taylor, 39 Tex. Civ. App. 302, 87 S. W. 358; Schus v. Powers-Simpson Co., 85 Minn. 447, 89 N. W. 68, 69 L. R. A. 887; Kline v. Minnesota Iron Co., 93 Minn. 63, 100 N. W. 681; Kibbe v. Stevenson Iron Co., 136 Fed. 147, 69 C. C. A. 145; Hines v. Stanley, G. I. Electric Co., 199 Mass. 522, 85 N. E. 851; Cunningham v. Neal, 49 Tex. Civ. App. 613, 109 S. W. 455; Id., 101 Tex. 338, 107 S. W. 539, 15 L. R. A. (N. S.) 479. See Mace v. H. A. Boedker & Co., 127 Iowa, 721, 104 N. W. 475.

But we have discovered no decision to the effect that a railroad is operated save when in use for the transportation of freight of some kind or passengers or both. Such is the use of all railways, and, when not so employed, they are not in use. It is the use the rails are put to and not the form of rails which determines whether they constitute a railway. The mere moving of the dismantled engine which had been withdrawn from service and sent to the hospital for remedy by the live engine was neither

Slaats v. Chicago, M. & St. P. Ry. Co

connected with the use nor the operation of the railways, but was
in the preparation for use in that connection. The work of these
shops may as well have been carried on apart from the defendant
and without interfering with the operation of its road. The
elimination of the fellow servant rule effected by this statute
repeatedly has been justified against the charge of discrimination
on the ground that the hazards of the employment are peculiar
to railroading. Akeson v. Railway, 106 Iowa, 54, 75 N. W. 676.
These hazards are not only from the nature of the work in
movement of vehicles and machinery of great weight and velocity
by steam on tracks, but because of the coemployees being widely
separated and not in a situation directly to influence the actions
of one another. The hazard in performing other work may be
quite as great, but is of a different kind, and, on this ground, the
classification has been upheld and the legislative intent declared.
Other courts may have interpreted similar statutes more broadly,
and possibly in doing so correctly expressed the designs of the
respective Legislatures in enacting them. See Chicago, R. I. &
P. Ry. v. Stahley, 62 Fed. 363, 11 C. C. A. 88; dissenting opinion
in Dunn v. Ry., 130 Iowa, 580, 107 N. W. 616, 6 L. R. A. (N.
S.) 452. But this court, since Deppe v. Railway, 36 Iowa, 52,
has adhered to the proposition that the General Assembly, in
framing the several statutes, did not purpose to afford protection
to railroad employees not extended to others in like situation.
"The purpose of the lawmakers," as said in the Akeson Case, was
"evidently not to make men, because employed by railroad companies, favorites of the law, but to afford protection owing to the
peculiar hazards of their situation." In what way do the hazards
of work in a railroad machine shop differ from those incident to
employment in other shops where heavy machinery is handled?
None whatever. The machine shop is not recognized in title X
of the Code treating of railroads as an essential part thereof.
No one will pretend that chapter 4 thereof authorized the condemnation of land on which to erect such shops and every section
of chapter 5, of which section 2071 is a part, emphasizes the
thought that the word "railway" as employed therein is meant
all those facilities made use of in the movement of trains, cars,
vehicles, and the like on the track constructed for the carriage
of freight and passengers. In many decisions, this court has
declared that by "operation" of a railway is meant the movement
of engines, cars, and machinery on the tracks, and, to be within
the protection of the statute, the wrong must be in such movement or connected therewith. Akeson v. Ry., supra; Strobble v.
Ry., 70 Iowa, 560, 31 N. W. 63, 59 Am. Rep. 456; Smith v.
Ry., 78 Iowa, 583, 43 N. W. 545; Larson v. Ry., 91 Iowa. 81,
58 N. W. 1076; Foley v. Ry., 64 Iowa, 644, 21 N. W. 124; Red-
dington v. Ry., 108 Iowa, 96, 78 N. W. 800; Dunn v. Ry., 130
Iowa, 580, 107 N. W. 616, 6 L. R. A. (N. S.) 452. In the first

case it was said that if "the injury is received by an employee whose work exposes him to the hazard of moving trains, cars, engines, or machinery on the track, and is caused by the negligence of a co-employee in the actual movement thereof, or in any manner directly connected therewith, the statute applies, and recovery may be had. Beyond this, the statute affords no protection."

We are of opinion that the rails on the shop floor did not constitute a railway within the meaning of the statute, nor was the movement of the dismantled engine on the rails therein by the live engine the use and operation of a railway. See Perry v. Ry., 164 Mass. 296, 41 N. E. 289; Potter v. Ry., 46 Iowa, 399; Hathaway v. Ry., 92 Iowa, 337, 60 N. W. 651.

The ruling of the district court is approved, and its judgment is affirmed.

FURLONG v. NEW YORK, N. H. & H. R. Co.

(Supreme Court of Errors of Connecticut, Dec. 16, 1910.)

[78 Atl. Rep. 489.]

Appeal and Error—Joinder of Appeals—Description—Sufficiency.— Where the words in an appeal, describing the court, and the time and place of holding it, to which it was asked that the evidence be reported, were evidently intended to apply also to the appeal and to describe the court and the time and place of holding it, such description was sufficient to permit the joinder of such appeal, with an additional appeal by amendment.

Appeal and Error—Joinder of Appeals—Bond.—Where an amended appeal was properly joined with the original appeal, the giving of a second bond to prosecute the appeal was unnecessary.

Master and Servant—Injury to Servant—Fellow Servants—Negligence.*—Under the fellow servant law, the mere negligence of a railroad employee to carry back a signal flag did not render the railroad liable for injuries thereby caused to a co-laborer.

Master and Servant—Fellow Servants—Competency—Duty of Master.†—The duty of a master to exercise reasonable care to pro-

---

*For the authorities in this series on the question what are, and are not, the nonassignable duties of a master, see last foot-note of Cleveland, etc., Ry. Co. v. Foland (Ind.), 36 R. R. R. 212, 59 Am. & Eng. R. Cas., N. S., 212; first foot-note of Chamberlain v. Southern Ry. Co. (Ala.), 34 R. R. R. 655, 57 Am. & Eng. R. Cas., N. S., 655.

For illustrations in this series showing who are vice-principals or superior servants, see last foot-note of Massy v. Milwaukee, etc., Co. (Wis.), 36 R. R. R. 656, 59 Am. & Eng. R. Cas., N. S., 656.

†For the authorities in this series on the subject of the liability of the master on account of the incompetency of fellow servants, see

Furlong *v.* New York, N. H. & H. R. Co

vide fit and competent colaborers for his employees is not necessarily fully performed by exercising reasonable care in the original selection of his servants, but he must also exercise ordinary care in the retention of fit and competent servants.

Master and Servant—Fellow Servants—Competency—Duty of Master—"Fit and Competent Persons."—As used in the rule requiring a master to select fit and competent persons as colaborers for his employees, the words "fit and competent persons" means something more than skillful and experienced persons; carefulness and faithfulness being also required.

Master and Servant—Injuries to Servant—Fellow Servants—Negligence—Liability.†—A railroad company which, after actual or constructive knowledge of a trainman's habitual violation of a rule requiring him to flag approaching trains, retains him in service, is not exempt under the fellow-servant rule from liability for injuries to another employee resulting from such trainman's negligent failure to perform his duty.

Master and Servant—Fellow Servants—Competency—Negligence—Vice Principal.†—The failure of a railroad employee charged with seeing that other employees are not negligent or incompetent to perform their duty is the negligence of the railroad.

Appeal from Superior Court, New London County; William S. Case, Judge.

Action by Walter Furlong, administrator, against the New York, New Haven & Hartford Railroad Company. There was a judgment for plaintiff. Defendant's motion to set aside the verdict as against the evidence was denied, and defendant appeals. Plaintiff's plea in abatement to the appeal dismissed, and judgment affirmed.

The decedent, Frank A. Furlong, was on the 10th of November, 1908, killed by a collision of the defendant's extra work train No. 1746, upon which he was employed as a brakeman, with the rear end of the defendant's regular way freight train No. 994, at Deep River station on the Valley Branch of the Shore division of the defendant's railroads, which branch consists of a single-track railroad extending from Hartford south to Saybrook.

The plaintiff claimed to have proved these facts regarding the accident: The extra work train No. 1746 consisted of an engine, coach, and caboose, and had been running on the Valley Branch for several weeks. It carried a conductor Paige, an engineer and a fireman, two brakemen, and many laborers. It worked under a general order, which did not fix the time of arrival at or departure from the stations at which it stopped, but required it to

first foot-note of Pittsburgh Rys. Co. *v.* Thomas (C. C. A.), 36 R. R. R. 36, 59 Am. & Eng. R. Cas., N. S., 36.
†See (†) on preceding page.

Furlong *v.* New York, N. H. & H. R. Co

keep clear of regular trains. On the day of the accident, as on prior days, it backed in going southerly approaching the Deep River station with the caboose in front, the coach in the middle, and the locomotive in the rear. The conductor, Paige, sat in the cupola of the caboose, acting as pilot, and signaling the engineer with his hands, when necessary, from the window of the cupola, and having at his hand an air valve by which he could control the air brakes. Furlong, the deceased, was also in the caboose. This method of running the train was known to the defendant. Just north of the Deep River station, which is on the west of the track, the railroad curves sharply to the west and runs through a deep cut obstructing for a time the view of the station and track near it of a person at the front of a train approaching from the north, and also for a time hiding from the view of the engineer of train 1746 any hand signals which could be made from the cupola window of the caboose. There was no signal board at the north end of the cut, nor any north of the station which could be seen from the front of a train approaching from the north, until it reached a point near the south end of the cut.

When train No. 1746 backed through the cut and around the curve, it was coasting, or running upon a downgrade by force of gravity and its own momentum: The engine whistle of train 1746 was blown as it approached the Deep River station, and shortly thereafter, and when it had passed nearly through the cut, its conductor, Paige, observed the station agent and one D'Arche, a trainman and the flagman of the freight train 994, signaling him to stop. He immediately applied the emergency brake, but the caboose of train 1746 collided with that of the freight train 994, which was standing near the Deep River station, with such force that both were demolished and Furlong was killed.

The crew of the freight train 994 consisted of an engineer and fireman, a conductor (Mitchell), and four trainmen, one of whom (D'Arche) had for nearly three months been acting as flagman, and had been in the defendant's employ as brakeman or flagman for a number of years. Coming south on that day the train 994 passed the work train No. 1746 as it stood upon a siding some eight miles north of the Deep River station. The freight train 994 was 40 minutes behind its schedule time when it arrived at Deep River on that day. The engine and some of the freight cars were detached, and run further south for switching. Two of the four trainmen rode away upon the engine, and the other two trainmen, one of whom was D'Arche, whose duty it was to flag approaching trains, went with the conductor, Mitchell, to the freighthouse, where they and the station agent, Kane, proceeded to handle the freight, leaving the rear portion of the freight train standing upon the main track No one went back from train 994 to flag or warn any train approaching from the north until the trainmen of No. 994, while so engaged in handling the freight, heard the whistle of the approaching No. 1746, when D'Arche and the station agent ran out and attempted unsuccessfully to stop it, as above stated.

Rule 99 of the defendant railroad contained this provision, which was well known to Conductor Mitchell and to D'Arche and other conductors and flagman in the defendant's employ: "When a train stops or is delayed under circumstances in which it may be overtaken by a following train, or needs protection, flagman must go back immediately with danger signals a sufficient distance to insure protection. * * *" Rules for government of conductors provided, among other things, that they would be responsible for the "faithful and prompt performance of duties by the trainman;" that they must report all violations of rules and neglect of duties by the train employees to the superintendent; that, in case of gross misconduct, they might relieve the offending employee for the rest of the trip; that they should see "that the train is supplied with a full set of signals and that they are displayed in accordance with the rules." It was the custom of D'Arche, when the train upon which he was acting as flagman stopped at a station, to signal all regular time-table trains and all other trains of the approach of which from back of his train he received actual notice from the bulletin board at the station, or from the station agent or telegraph operator, that an extra train was expected. He received no such notice at the time in question, and no regular time-table train was then due. Conductor Mitchell knew of such custom of D'Arche regarding the flagging of approaching trains, but never censured or reported him for failure to properly flag trains.

The defendant claimed to have proved, among other things, that both Mitchell and D'Arche were competent men in their respective positions; that they were familiar with the printed rules of the railroad, and understood their duties under them; that it had not been the custom of D'Arche to disregard Rule 99. and that any violations of said rule by D'Arche were not known to any official of the railroad or to Conductor Mitchell except upon the day when this collision occurred, and that the defendant had exercised reasonable care to provide fit and competent workmen, and to see that the rules of the company were enforced. The verdict for plaintiff was rendered June 16. 1909, and the defendant on that day filed a motion to set it aside, which was denied June 30th, which is the date of the judgment filed. On July 2d the defendant filed a notice of appeal from the judgment, and on the same day filed a motion for a new trial for verdict against evidence, addressed to this court at its term in Norwich on the 3d Tuesday of October, 1909, and also on July 2d filed an appeal from the denial of its motion to set aside the verdict, as follows: "And now the defendant, within six days after judgment in said cause, appeals from the refusal of the trial court to set aside the verdict, and moves for a new trial of said cause upon the ground that the verdict is against the evidence in the case; and further moves that the court report the evidence to the Supreme Court of Errors next to be holden at Norwich, in the Second judicial district on the third Tuesday of October, 1909, and make such evidence a part of the record and transmit said record to said court for the determination and judgment of that court." A sufficient bond to prosecute was given when said appeal was filed, and the appeal was allowed July 3, 1909.

The finding of facts in this case was filed April 19, 1910, and on April 28th the defendant filed an "Amended Appeal" to this court at its October session in Norwich on the third Tuesday of October, 1910, stating therein that it thereby amended the appeal of July 3d, and took such appeal for the revision of the errors alleged to have occurred during the trial, and of the question whether the court erred in refusing to set aside the verdict, and requested in such appeal that the court report the evidence to this court for the purpose of correcting the finding, and also for considering whether the court erred in refusing to set aside the verdict. This appeal assigns numerous errors alleged to have occurred during the trial, and also assigns as a reason of appeal that the court erred in refusing to set aside the verdict. No bond was given with this appeal. The plaintiff pleaded in abatement, in this court, to the appeal of July 3, 1909, upon the ground that it did not describe the court to which it was taken, and to the appeal of April 28, 1910, upon the ground that no bond to prosecute the appeal was given with it.

The defendant demurred to these pleas in abatement.

Joseph E. Berry, for appellant.
Hadlai A. Hull and *C. Hadlai Hull,* for appellee.

HALL, C. J. (after stating the facts as above). The pleas in abatement to the two appeals to this court, afterwards united in one by amendment, are dismissed. The words in the appeal of July 3, 1909, describing the court, and the time and place of holding it, to which it was asked that the evidence be reported, were evidently intended to apply also to the appeal, and to describe the court and the time and place of holding it, to which the appeal was taken. This description was sufficient to permit the appeal of April 28, 1910, to be joined with that of July 3d by amendment. Stillman v. Thompson, 80 Conn. 192, 194, 67 Atl. 528. The two appeals having been thus properly joined in one, it was unnecessary to give a second bond to prosecute, when the amended appeal of April 28, 1910, was filed. The bond given July 3, 1909, became, by the amendment joining the two appeals, applicable to both. The motion of July 2d for a new trial addressed to this court was irregular.

Turning to the appeal itself, we find that many of the questions raised by the defendant in the trial court, and some of which are repeated in the reasons of appeal, were practically eliminated by the charge of the court respecting them favorable to the defendant, and by the evidence regarding them which we have before us. Indeed, we think the record before us shows that the controlling questions upon this appeal are those arising upon but one or two of the grounds of negligence alleged in the complaint, and from the action and rulings of the trial court regarding them, in its charge to the jury, and its refusal to set aside the verdict as against the evidence.

The alleged grounds of negligence from which most, if not all, of such questions arise, are in substance these: That the flagman of the freight train (D'Arche) had not for many months before the accident gone back to give proper signals to approaching trains when the freight train was so standing upon the main track; that the "defendant company negligently employed and continued to employ said flagman (D'Arche) who on said day and for many months prior thereto had been so negligent as aforesaid in failing to give signals as aforesaid;" that the defendant was negligent in failing to inspect the method of giving the signals required by the rules; and "in allowing and permitting said flagman (D'Arche) to continue to neglect to give proper signals to approaching trains. * *. * *" The court very properly told the jury that it was clear that D'Arche neglected to go back with his flag, and that his failure to do so was one factor in the accident, but that D'Arche was a fellow servant of Furlong, and that, therefore, the plaintiff could not recover for an injury to Furlong caused by D'Arche's negligence only. Concerning the liability of the defendant for its own alleged negligence, as above stated, the court said to the jury that it was charged that "this conduct of D'Arche (in disregarding rule 99) was his habitual conduct * * * consistently practiced by him, recognized by his associates and tolerated and acquiesced in by the company;" that there was conflicting testimony upon that point; that isolated violations of the rule were not enough to establish such an acquiescence by the company as amounted to an abrogation of the rule; but that it must appear that "the violations were persistent enough to be chargeable to the knowledge of a reasonable vigilant master, and that the master's conduct was such as to tolerate or encourage a continuance of them to fasten upon the company responsibility for such a practice." The court further charged the jury upon this point as follows: "If D'Arche's conduct on the day in question was his habitual method, long enough and persistently enough practiced by him to impute knowledge of it and an acquiescence in its continuance by the defendant, then the negligence of the defendant is established, and it is liable if that negligence directly caused the injury. On this feature of the case, therefore, I charge you that any knowledge of the conductor. Mitchell, of the freight train, of prior and persistent and habitual violations of the rules—if such there were—would be chargeable to his superior, the defendant itself."

The two questions raised- by the appeal respecting these instructions given by the trial court are: (1) Were they correct statements of the law? (2) Was the evidence such as justified the court in submitting to the jury the questions of fact involved in these propositions of law, and in refusing to set aside the verdict of the jury in favor of the plaintiff? This is an action against an employer by the representative of a deceased employee. Clearly, under the fellow servant law, the mere negligence of Furlong's colaborer, D'Arche, to carry back the signal flag, did not render the employer liable for the injury thereby caused to Furlong. Whittlesey *v.* N. Y., N. H. & H. R. Co., 77 Conn. 100, 58 Atl. 459, 107 Am. St. Rep. 21. In order to hold the defendant responsible for Furlong's injury, the plaintiff was required to prove that the railroad company had violated some duty which it owed to its employees. One rule, firmly established by law, growing out of the relation of master and servant, or employer and employee, is that the former shall exercise reasonable care to provide "fit and competent" persons as colaborers of his employees. McElligott *v.* Randolph, 61 Conn. 157, 161, 22 Atl. 1094, 1095, 29 Am. St. Rep. 181. The duty of the employer to so endeavor to provide "fit and competent" colaborers for his employees is not necessarily fully performed by exercising reasonable care in the original selection and employment of his servants. The master who continues in his service with his other employees, one who he has learned is unfit or incompetent to engage in such employment with others, may properly be regarded as careless in endeavoring to provide fit and competent persons to work with others, as one who originally employs such a co-workmen with knowledge of his unfitness. Ordinary care in providing fit and competent servants means ordinary care in the retention as well as in the selection of fit and competent servants. 12 Am. & Eng. Encyc. of Law, p. 915; Coppins *v.* N. Y. Cent., etc., R. 122 N. Y. 557, 25 N. E. 915, 19 Am. St. Rep. 523; Gilman *v.* Eastern R. Co., 13 Allen (Mass.) 433, 90 Am. Dec. 210; Brookside Coal Mining Co. *v.* Dolph, 101 Ill. App. 169. Ordinary care in the retention of fit and competent persons to operate a railroad train means some kind of observation of the manner in which such persons perform their duties, if some kind of observation is practicable. The law only requires the employer to act reasonably. It does not compel the directors or high officials of a corporation to themselves perform the work of selecting and hiring its employees. That duty may be performed by any duly authorized suitable person, but in performing it such persons represent the corporation, and is performing the employer's duty. It would seem to be no more difficult for a railroad company to authorize a suitable person to act in its behalf in observing how trainmen performed their work than to authorize one to act for it in the selection and employment of trainmen.

Again, the words "fit and competent persons" mean something more than skillful and experienced persons. Carefulness and faithfulness are often more essential elements of fitness and competency in an employee than experience and skill. The fitness and competency of a fellow servant may depend as much upon his promptness and willingness to perform his duties as upon his understanding of the duties he is expected to perform. In selecting and retaining in its employ trainmen, a railroad company should select and retain only reliable men. Coppins *v.* N. Y. Cent., etc., supra. A railroad company that knowingly employs a reckless or careless trainman to discharge duties, the negligent performance of which may endanger the lives of his fellow workmen, or that continues such person in its service after actual or constructive knowledge of his habitual violation of a rule so important as that requiring him in stated situations to go back with a flag to signal possibly approaching trains, has not only failed to provide fit and competent persons to be colaborers with its other workmen, who may be injured by such negligence, but has failed to perform the duty imposed upon it by law (Nolan *v.* N. Y., N. H. & H. R. Co., 70 Conn., 159, 194, 39 Atl. 115, 43 L. R. A. 305), to use reasonable care to see that its rules for the protection of person and life are enforced. Such company would not, under the fellow-servant rule, be entitled to exemption from liability for an injury to one of its employees caused by such negligent failure of the trainman to perform his duty.

But it is said that the evidence fails to show that the company knew of D'Arche's delinquencies, and that the court erred in charging the jury that the knowledge of Mitchell the conductor was chargeable to the defendant. We are not prepared to say that the jury might not properly have found from the evidence that D'Arche had so long and openly violated rule 99 that the company was chargeable with knowledge of his negligence. But, as we have pointed out, the duty of the employer to provide fit and competent colaborers for his employees is not ended by the act of selecting and hiring them. The employer continues to provide the colaborers so long as they continue to work under his employment. Less watchfulness and oversight may be required of the employer over the conduct of such workmen as have been carefully selected at the time of their original employment, but it still remains at all times a duty which the master owes to his servant to exercise reasonable care to provide as his colaborers persons who can and will perform those duties which they are employed to perform, and the failure to perform which may endanger the lives of their fellow workmen. He who performs the duty of seeing that the employees of a railroad company are not negligent or incompetent is in that respect performing a duty which the master owes the servant, and his failure to properly perform it is the negligence of the master. Rincicotti v. O'Brien, 77 Conn. 617, 60 Atl. 115, 69 L. R. A. 936. The conductor, Mitchell, was required to perform that duty of the master. The rules of the company required him to note and report to the superintendent "all violations of rules and neglect of duty by the train employees," and authorized him in certain cases to suspend the delinquent. Evidently one of the reasons of requiring him to perform this duty was to enable the company to learn who of its employees were competent and reliable persons to be continued in their employ. In the performance of that duty, although in other respects he may have been, Mitchell was not a fellow servant of Furlong, but a representative of the company (Brennan v. Berlin Iron Bridge Co., 74 Conn. 382, 389, 50 Atl. 1030) and as such his knowledge of D'Arche's disregard of the rules was therefore the company's knowledge. O'Neil v. K. & D. M. R. Co., 45 Iowa, 546. Brookside Coal Mining Co. v. Dolph, supra. With such knowledge of an habitual violation of rule 99, the defendant was negligent at least in continuing D'Arche, if not in continuing Mitchell, in its service. There is no error in the charge of the trial court to the jury.

The trial court committed no error in refusing to direct a verdict for the defendant, nor in denying the defendant's motion to set aside the verdict as against the evidence. It is impracticable to recite here the evidence which in our opinion showed that the defendant was not entitled to exemption under the fellow servant law and justified the verdict rendered. Upon a perusal of it. we think the jury were warranted in finding that D'Arche was negligent in not carrying back the flag to signal train 1746; that in that respect he had habitually violated rule 99; that Mitchell, as representing the company with knowledge of such violations of rule 99 negligently failed to perform the duty imposed upon him, and that the defendant was therefore negligent as alleged in the complaint.

Neither the rulings upon the evidence nor other parts of the charge complained of furnish grounds for a new trial, and we deem it unnecessary to discuss them.

There is no error.   The other Judges concurred.

McGahey v. Citizens' Ry. Co.

(Supreme Court of Nebraska, Jan. 9, 1911.)

[129 N. W. Rep. 293.]

(Syllabus by the Court.)

Street Railroads—Collision with Vehicle—Negligence.*—If the driver of a vehicle at a street intersection is reasonably justified in believing that he can pass over a street railway track before an approaching car, if propelled at its usual and ordinary rate of speed, will reach that point, he should not be held as a matter of law guilty of negligence in attempting to cross.

Street Railroads—Collision with Vehicle—Action for Injuries—Submission of Issues.—If there is evidence tending to prove that a heavy, unwieldy vehicle was almost upon, and being propelled across, a street railway track at the intersection of two public streets and that the motorman in control of a street car approaching said intersection, at right angles to the course of the vehicle, either did not act with reasonable diligence to decrease the speed of said car so as to prevent a collision, or after the car had been brought almost to a standstill permitted it to start suddenly and move at a greatly accelerated rate of speed so as to collide with said vehicle, it is not error to submit to the jury the issue of the motorman's negligence in failing to control the car before, as well as after, he was apprised of the driver's perilous position.

Street Railroads—Collision with Vehicle—Action for Injuries—Submission of Issues.—If the pleader charges a cause of action based upon the defendant's negligence in operating a street car, and also alleges that the motorman in charge, after knowing that the plaintiff was in a dangerous position with respect to said car, negligently failed to exercise ordinary care to control it, and evidence is received tending to support those allegations, the case may be submitted to the jury upon both theories.

Negligence—Contributory Negligence—Burden of Proof.—If the defendant pleads that the plaintiff was guilty of contributory negligence, or that the accident resulted solely from his negligence, the burden is upon the defendant to prove those defenses, and does not shift during the trial of the case, but he should receive the benefit of the plaintiff's evidence tending to prove those issues.

Appeal and Error—Negligence—Comparative Negligence—Instructions—Harmless Error.—The defendant, however, is not prejudiced by an instruction that the burden is not upon him to prove contributory negligence if the plaintiff's testimony proves that fact, and instructions to that effect do not involve the doctrine of comparative negligence.

---

*See extensive note, 36 R. R. R. 374, 59 Am. & Eng. R. Cas., N. S. 374.

McGahey v. Citizens' Ry. Co

Negligence—Contributory Negligence—Proximate Cause.†—The plaintiff's negligence will not defeat a recovery unless it was the sole cause of the plaintiff's injury or concurred or co-operated with the defendant's negligence as a proximate cause of the accident.

Trial—Reception of Evidence—Withdrawal of Evidence.—It is not error to withdraw from the jury's consideration facts which by no reasonable construction tend to establish a defense to the action or to mitigate the plaintiff's damages.

Trial—Refusal of Requests—Requests Substantially Embraced in Charge Given.—"When instructions requested are substantially given in the charge prepared by the court on its own motion, it is not error to refuse to repeat them, though expressed in language different from that used by the court." Curry v. State, 5 Neb. 412.

Sufficiency of Evidence.—The evidence examined and commented upon in the opinion and held sufficient to sustain the verdict.

(Additional Syllabus by Editorial Staff.)

Negligence—Action—Construction of Petition.—In an injury action against a street railway company where the petition, after charging many alleged acts of negligence of defendant, alleged that the motorman negligently failed to stop the car after he knew that plaintiff was in a perilous situation, and defendant did not move to compel plaintiff to make the petition more definite, or to separately number and state the causes of action, it was not error to submit the case upon the theory that it involved the law of the last clear chance.

Appeal from District Court, Lancaster County; Cornish, Judge.

Action by Thomas H. McGahey against the Citizens' Railway Company. Judgment for plaintiff, and defendant appeals. Affirmed.

Hainer & Smith and *Clark & Allen,* for appellant.
H. F. Rose and *W. B. Comstock,* for appellee.

ROOT, J. The gist of this action is the defendant's alleged negligence in operating a street car so that the plaintiff was injured and his vehicle damaged while crossing the defendant's railway at the intersection of Seventeenth and N streets in the city of Lincoln. The plaintiff prevailed and the defendant appeals. The testimony is conflicting and parts of it are extravagant, but since the jury found for the plaintiff, it is our duty to consider the transaction in the light most favorable to him.

It appears that N and Seventeenth streets are each paved and 100 feet in width; that a sidewalk and parkway cover 20 feet of the space on each side of the streets, and the defendant maintains a double track railway on N street which runs east and west; that the surface of N street slopes slightly towards the

---

†See second foot-note of Bourrett v. Chicago & N. W. Ry. Co. (Iowa), 34 R. R. 284, 57 Am. & Eng. R. Cas., N. S. 284.

McGahey v. Citizens' Ry. Co

east, and the gutters are seventeenths of a foot lower than the crest of the street. It further appears that there are dwelling houses along the south side of N street westward from Seventeenth street, so situated that the porches are flush with the lot line, and there are seven shade trees between the curb and sidewalk on the south side of N street west of Seventeenth. The accident occurred about 8 o'clock in the forenoon of a still, clear day in September while the plaintiff was driving northward on the east side of Seventeenth street riding upon an air compressor eight feet in height which weighed about 5,200 pounds and was painted a brilliant red. The plaintiff's vehicle had almost cleared the southernmost railway track when one of the defendant's cars moving eastward collided with a rear wheel of the air compressor, and as a result the vehicle was damaged and the plaintiff injured. The testimony discloses that the plaintiff, about the time his team crossed the footpath on the south side of N street, noticed the car in question, and calculated he could drive over the track before the car would cross Seventeenth street; that subsequently, as he urged his horses forward he raised one hand as a warning. The motorman and conductor upon the car both testify to having noticed the signal, but the testimony is in hopeless conflict concerning the space then intervening between the car and the air compressor. The plaintiff says the distance was about 125 feet; the defendant's employees say about 45 feet. The jury would be justified in finding, from all of the evidence, that the motorman did not see the plaintiff until the latter raised his hand. One witness testifies that the car was well under control as it entered the intersection of said streets, but immediately thereafter the speed rapidly increased until the collision occurred, and that directly after the accident the motorman exclaimed that he "thought the old fool was going to get off the track when he started up this second time." If the motorman did not notice so conspicuous an object as the plaintiff's vehicle until the car was almost upon the footpath on the west side of Seventeenth street, the jury might say he was not on the lookout for teams or pedestrians. If the car was 125 feet distant from the plaintiff when the motorman noticed the former's uplifted hand, and thereupon applied all of his power to the brakes upon the car, it must have been running at a terrific rate of speed or else the appliances were defective or ill-suited for controlling its movements. If, as the witness Skinner testifies, the car was well under control at the time it approached said intersection, but its speed was thereafter suddenly accelerated, there was gross disregard for the plaintiff's safety. The court therefore was justified in submitting the cause in a double aspect; that is to say, to permit the jury to find whether the defendant was negligent in failing to exercise reasonable care to control the speed of its car at the time of and shortly preceding the accident, or to find whether the motorman,

McGahey *v.* Citizens' Ry. Co

after discovering the plaintiff's perilous situation brought about possibly by his own negligence, failed to use ordinary care to avert the accident. Omaha St. R. Co. *v.* Mathiesen, 73 Neb. 820, 103 N. W. 666; Zelenka *v.* Union Stock Yards Co., 82 Neb. 511, 118 N. W. 103; Wally *v.* Union P. R. Co., 83 Neb. 658, 120 N. W. 174; Wenninger *v.* Lincoln Traction Co., 84 Neb. 385, 121 N. W. 237; Smith *v.* Connecticut R. & L. Co., 80 Conn. 268, 67 Atl. 888, 17 L. R. A. (N. S.) 707.

The defendant criticises the instructions in so far as they recognize the "last clear chance" doctrine, and insists that no such a cause of action is stated in the petition. It appears, however, that the pleader after charging many alleged acts of negligence on the part of the defendant and its employees, alleges that the motorman negligently failed to stop the car after he knew the plaintiff was in a perilous situation. The defendant did not move to compel the plaintiff to make the petition more definite or to separately number and state the causes of action, and the court was justified in submitting the case upon the theory that it involved the law of the "last clear chance."

The jury were instructed that the burden of proof was upon the plaintiff to prove by a preponderance of the evidence the material allegations in the petition, and the third instruction is as follows: "When the plaintiff has so shown these facts, then the burden of proof is upon the defendant to prove by a preponderance of the evidence the allegations in its answer constituting its defense to plaintiff's action; that is to say, that any injuries received by the plaintiff were the proximate result of his own negligence, or that his own negligence contributed thereto as a proximate cause thereof. If, however, the plaintiff's own testimony shows that he was guilty of negligence at the time of the accident, then the burden would not be upon the defendant to show such fact."

The defendant insists that these instructions submitted the law of comparative negligence to the jury. We do not so understand the charge. We do not approve of the third instruction because the burden of proving contributory negligence does not shift during a trial, but remains with the defendant if he pleads that defense. Rapp *v.* Sarpy County, 71 Neb. 382, 98 N. W. 1042, 102 N. W. 242. The court evidently desired to instruct the jury that contributory negligence might be established by plaintiff's evidence and they should give the defendant the benefit of all the evidence upon that issue irrespective of the source from which it came. The plaintiff's testimony upon direct as well as upon cross examination is such that the jury might have found that he was guilty of contributory negligence, and the defendant was entitled to an instruction giving him the benefit of that testimony. We are of opinion that the instructions did present that principle to the jury, and, in so far as the court relieved the

McGahey v. Citizens' Ry. Co

defendant of the burden of proof, it has no just ground for complaint. The defendant's counsel, however, argue that the jury should not have been told that contributory negligence to constitute a defense must have been a proximate cause of the accident. A fair construction of this instruction is that the plaintiff's negligence would not bar a recovery unless it concurred or co-operated with the negligence of the defendant as the proximate cause of the accident, or was in itself the proximate cause thereof. Thus considered the instruction is in harmony with the law as announced in Vertrees v. Gage County, 81 Neb. 213, 115 N. W. 863. See, also, authorities collated in 29 Cyc. 505.·

Exception is taken to an instruction to the effect that the plaintiff had a right to "drive his team and air compressor across the tracks of defendant and through the street intersection in question in the condition as to equipment of the vehicle and team disclosed by the evidence." The court further instructed the jury that any failure on the plaintiff's part to exercise ordinary care, in the control of said vehicle would constitute contributory negligence. It appears that the air compressor was not equipped with brakes, and that no breeching was attached to the harness upon the horses, and complaint is made that the instruction withdrew from the jury the alleged negligence of the plaintiff in failing to provide those accessories to his vehicle and harness, but the proof is certain that the want of brakes or of breeching in no manner contributed to the accident. The surface of the street was upgrade from the gutter to the track, and the plaintiff's failure to halt before crossing cannot be attributed to the condition of the harness or to the want of brakes upon the air compressor.

The defendant's counsel print in their brief nine instructions requested by them and not given by the court. The court's charge contained the greater part of the principles of law embodied in those instructions, and, so far as we are advised, no error was committed in not giving them verbatim. Curry v. State, 5 Neb. 412.

Upon a consideration of the entire record we find no error prejudicial to the defendant. The judgment of the district court therefore, is affirmed.

ELLIOTT v. NEW YORK, N. H. & H. R. CO.

(Supreme Court of Errors of Connecticut, June 14, 1910.)

[76 Atl. Rep. 298.]

Railroads—Crossing Accident—Contributory Negligence.*—Negligence of one who drove on the track at a crossing and collided with a train would be too remote to constitute contributory negligence if the company's negligence supervened and caused the collision.

Railroads—Crossing Accident—Negligence.†—Negligence in causing a collision at a crossing cannot ordinarily be inferred from speed alone, and under ordinary circumstances only statutory signals are required.

Negligence—Effect of Contributory Negligence.—Contributory negligence does not justify nonperformance of the duty to use due care not to injure another, but only relieves from liability to pay for its consequences.

Railroads—Crossing Accident—Company's Duty to Avoid Collision.*—The duty to avoid a collision with one who negligently drove on the track at a crossing and was killed in a collision arose when by due care the company would have known of his peril, and was not postponed till it had actual knowledge.

Appeal and Error—Assignments of Error—Amendment.—A proposed amendment to assignments of error, filed only 11 days before the opening of the term of the Supreme Court of Errors, was too late to give appellee proper notice of claims on which it was based, and cannot properly be granted.

Trial—Motion to Direct Verdict—Argument before Jury.—Dis-

---

*For the authorities in this series on the question whether a railroad company is liable for running a train against a highway traveler at a crossing where he was guilty of contributory negligence and the trainmen were negligent after discovering his peril, see third foot-note of Bruggeman *v.* Illinois Cent. R. Co. (Iowa), 35 R. R. R. 241, 58 Am. & Eng. R. Cas., N. S., 241; St. Louis, etc., R. Co. *v.* Summers (C. C. A.), 35 R. R. R. 117, 58 Am. & Eng. R. Cas., N. S., 117; last head-note of Garrison *v.* St. Louis, etc., Ry. Co. (Ark.), 34 R. R. R. 543, 57 Am. & Eng. R. Cas., N. S., 543.

For the authorities in this series on the subject of the combined effect of contributory negligence and negligence on the part of defendant after peril of person injured should have been discovered, see third foot-note of Bourrett *v.* Chicago & N. W. Ry. Co. (Iowa), 34 R. R. R. 284, 57 Am. & Eng. R. Cas., N. S., 284.

†For the authorities in this series on the question whether any rate of speed of a train over a country highway crossing may be negligent, see last paragraph of first-note of Louisville, etc., R. Co. *v.* Engleman (Ky.), 35 R. R. R. 106, 58 Am. & Eng. R. Cas., N. S., 106.

For the authorities in this series on the question whether statutory requirements are the sole measure of a railroad company's duties in regard to crossing signals, see sixth foot-note of Weatherly *v.* Nashville, etc., Ry. (Ala.), 35 R. R. R. 759, 58 Am. & Eng. R. Cas., N. S., 759.

Elliott v. New York, N. H. & H. R. Co

missal of the jury during argument of a motion to direct a verdict is within the court's discretion.

Appeal and Error—Harmless Error—Instructions.—Where the jury are allowed to hear the argument of a motion to direct a verdict, they should be carefully instructed that the arguments are solely for the court's information, and an instruction which informs them that they could take them as fair statements of the facts, and thus ignore the evidence and claims as to conclusions to be drawn therefrom in the closing arguments, was reversible error.

Appeal from Superior Court, Litchfield County; George W. Wheeler, Judge.

Action by James H. Elliott, administrator of Charles S. Tetro, deceased, against the New York, New Haven & Hartford Railroad Company. From a judgment for plaintiff, defendant appeals. Error, and a new trial ordered.

Action to recover damages for injuries claimed to have been caused by the defendant's negligence; brought to the superior court for Litchfield county and tried to the jury before G. W. Wheeler, J.; verdict and judgment for the plaintiff and appeal by the defendant, assigning as error the court's refusal to direct a verdict in its favor or to set aside the verdict which was rendered and certain instructions given the jury.

Donald G. Warner and *J. F. Berry*, for appellant.
Caleb A. Morse and *T. J. Wall*, for appellee.

THAYER, J. The plaintiff's intestate was killed while attempting to drive across the defendant's railroad at a grade crossing located near to its East Litchfield station. The court refused to direct a verdict for the defendant or to set aside the plaintiff's verdict as it was requested to do by the defendant, and those refusals constitute two of the assigned errors upon which this appeal is based. The ground of the motions was that the evidence failed to show that the intestate, Tetro, was free from contributory negligence, but that it showed, on the contrary, that he was guilty of such negligence, in that he did not stop in order to properly use his senses before driving upon the crossing as reasonable care required that he should do under the peculiar circumstances of the case.

Upon reading the evidence it is difficult to avoid the conclusion that Tetro failed to use reasonable care in approaching and driving upon the crossing. But the plaintiff alleged in his complaint and claimed upon the trial that, after Tetro was upon the crossing and in peril, the defendant was negligent in failing to properly manage, control, and stop its train after it knew or ought to have known of that peril. The jury were told in substance that, if they should find the fact to be as thus claimed, the defendant would not be liable unless some negligence of Tetro

Elliott *v*. New York, N. H. & H. R. Co

subsequent to the defendant's knowledge of his peril contributed to his injury. A question for the jury was thus presented whether, entirely apart from Tetro's negligence in getting upon the track, the defendant negligently failed in its duty towards him after it knew or ought to have known of his presence there and his peril. If the charge was correct, and if there was evidence in the case which warranted the charge, a verdict could not properly have been directed for the defendant upon the ground claimed. If the defendant's negligence supervened and caused the collision, Tetro's negligence in driving upon the track would be too remote to constitute contributory negligence. Baldwin, American Railroad Law, 425; Smith *v*. Conn. Ry. & L. Co., 80 Conn. 268, 270, 67 Atl. 888, 17 L. R. A. (N. S.) 707. The motion to direct a verdict for the defendant was therefore properly denied. The motion to set aside the verdict and grant a new trial, based upon the same ground, was properly denied for the same reason; but as no appeal was taken from that refusal the question is not properly here. We decide it because it was argued before us and involves no separate discussion.

The defendant complains that the court instructed the jury that they might find the defendant negligent on account of the speed of the train over the crossing provided they found exceptional circumstances, and that they might find the circumstances to be so exceptional as to require more than the statutory signals to be given. An examination of the charge shows that the instructions complained of were in effect the same as those given with respect to the defendant's liability for supervening negligence already referred to, namely, that if the defendant's engineer knew or ought to have known of Tetro's peril, then, if reasonable care required that something more than the statutory signal should be given, the defendant was bound to give it, and that, if a reasonably prudent man would have slowed down, then the defendant's engineer should have done so. These were the exceptional circumstances referred to, and it was left for the jury to find whether they existed or not. The jury were correctly told that negligence cannot ordinarily be inferred from speed alone, and that under ordinary circumstances only the statutory signals are required. So far as appears from the finding, no claim was made that there were any exceptional circumstances in the physical situation at the crossing and nothing in the charge suggested to the jury that they might so find. The exceptional circumstances which were claimed by the plaintiff and referred to by the court as making the ordinary speed dangerous at the crossing and as calling for other than the statutory warning were the presence and peril of Tetro thereat. This part of the charge may therefore be considered in connection with the part already referred to, as its correctness depends upon the same considerations. If that part of the charge was correct, this part was not erroneous.

The correctness of the court's charge upon the question of the defendant's supervening negligence above mentioned is not questioned so far as it states the duty of the defendant after it had actual knowledge of the intestate's peril. In this respect it is in accordance with the established law in this state. Smith *v.* Conn. Ry. & Ltg. Co., supra. So far as it imposes the same duty upon the defendant before it had such knowledge the charge is claimed to be erroneous. The charge was that if the defendant knew or ought to have known of the peril, it was its duty to do all that a reasonably prudent person would have done to avoid the accident. There are in this state no decisions precisely in point which support the charge in fixing upon a defendant who has no knowledge of a peril which a plaintiff has negligently brought upon himself the duty of doing what a reasonably prudent man with knowledge of the peril would do to avert it. The decisions of other states where the precise question has been raised are not in harmony. In Freedman *v.* N. Y., N. H. & H. R. R. Co., 81 Conn. 601, 610, 71 Atl. 901, a case similar to this, a similar charge was given, and we said that it was proper. But in that case the verdict was for the defendant, the charge upon the point now before us was favorable to the plaintiff, and its correctness was not questioned by him on his appeal. The expression of the court that the charge was proper is not necessarily conclusive of the question now raised.

The rule of duty laid down in the charge is the one which is universally applied where the plaintiff's peril has not been caused by his own negligence. In such cases the defendant is chargeable not only with the knowledge which he actually had, but with that which he ought to have had (which means that which with reasonable care on his part he would have had) of the plaintiff's situation. No question as to the correctness of the charge can be raised where there is not the question of contributory negligence. But how does the fact that there may have been contributory regligence affect the question? When the plaintiff brings his action, he is bound to know that he cannot recover if he was guilty of negligence which was the proximate cause of his injury. The trial proceeds. In the evidence it appears that he was injured while upon a railroad crossing, and that the defendant, although it knew of his peril, or would have known it had it exercised due care, negligently ran its train upon him when it had the means and the opportunity to stop the train and avoid the injury. The defendant claims that the facts show that the plaintiff did not use due care, but was negligent in going upon its track, and that this was a proximate cause of his injury. The plaintiff claims that his negligence was before and had ceased at the time when the defendant saw or should have seen his peril.

Elliott *v.* New York, N. H. & H. R. Co

The jury are to decide under the evidence and claims whether the plaintiff was free from negligence which was a proximate cause of the injury. If they find that he was negligent in going upon the track, but that such negligence was not a proximate cause of the injury, and that there was no subsequent negligence on his part essentially contributing to it, he may recover if the jury also find that the defendant's negligence was the proximate cause of it. Had the jury found that the plaintiff's negligence in going upon the track of his subsequent negligence was a proximate cause of his injury, that negligence would have been called contributory negligence. But the fact that the plaintiff's negligence may be "contributory" under certain circumstances, or that there is a doctrine of contributory negligence, has no bearing upon the question of a defendant's legal duty towards him. The question always is: Whose negligence was the proximate cause of the injury? The legal duty of each party is fixed, and the rules of evidence are fixed in all cases. When the evidence is all in, it is weighed, and the fact determined whether either or both of the parties were guilty of negligence which was a proximate cause of the injury. There is no case in which it can be said that the defendant owed the plaintiff a different duty because the latter was guilty of contributory negligence. Contributory negligence, supervening negligence, and the doctrine of "last clear chance," have no bearing upon the question of the duty of the parties toward each other. They have, however, important bearing upon the rights and liabilities of the parties after an injury has been inflicted. It is the duty of a person to use due care not to injure another. Contributory negligence does not justify the nonperformance of this duty; it only relieves from the liability to pay for its consequences. The defendant neglects this duty at his peril.

When the evidence is in, if the questions of contributory negligence, supervening negligence, or last clear chance have been raised, the court is required to explain the duty owed by the parties to each other and their rights and liabilities under such states of fact as to the negligence of the respective parties as the evidence may warrant them in finding. It cannot say to them that the defendant's duty was different if they find contributory negligence on the part of the plaintiff, but it must tell them how such negligence would affect the defendant's liability for damages. The question may be a nice one for the jury to determine in a railway crossing accident whether the negligence of a plaintiff which placed him in a position of peril continued until the injury was received, so as to be a proximate cause of the accident. But it is a question for them nevertheless. We think that the defendant's duty to avoid the collision arose when by the use of due care it would have known of the intestate's peril, and was not postponed until it had actual knowledge, and that there was no error in the charge as given.

Elliott v. New York, N. H. & H. R. Co

It is claimed that, although the charge was correct in the statement of the law, it was improperly given to the jury because there
was no evidence from which the jury could find that the collision
could have been avoided after the defendant knew or ought to
have known of Tetro's peril.   If there was no evidence to support a verdict upon this ground, it should not have been submitted
to the jury.   But the record shows that there was evidence, and
we think sufficient evidence to warrant the submission of the question to the jury.   At what point Tetro as he approached the
crossing could have been seen by the engineer and fireman on
the train, at what point his danger would have been apparent to
them, within what distance the train could be stopped, what
appliances it had for stopping it, whether these were used and
properly used, and within what distance the train in fact stopped,
were all facts concerning which there was evidence and from
which when found inferences could properly be drawn by them
as to the possibility of avoiding the collision by the use of due
care after the engineer was or ought to have been aware of the
danger.   There was no error in submitting it to them.

The defendant's request to charge raised substantially the same
questions which are raised by the exceptions to the charge and to
the refusal to direct a verdict.   In effect they requested that the
jury be told to find for the defendant.   They were properly refused.

An application to correct the finding is attempted to be made
under Gen. St. § 797.   Several paragraphs of the finding are
claimed to have been found without evidence as appears by the
defendant's brief and proposed amendment to its reasons of appeal.   In a case tried to the jury, the finding does not purport
to be a finding of facts by the court from the evidence.   It does
not establish any of these facts.   Practice Book 1908, p. 267,
§ 6.   It is simply a statement of the facts which the parties
claimed had been proved, with their claims thereon, and the rulings and charge of the court sufficient to present the questions
sought to be raised by the appeal.   If the finding erroneously
states that evidence was offered to prove a fact where in truth
no such evidence was offered, it would seem that a correction
might be readily obtained by applying to the trial court for a
correction.   This does not appear to have been done in the
present case.   Counsel would hardly differ as to what the evidence was, and, if they should, a means would be at hand in the
stenographer's notes to ascertain the truth.   There ought to be
no occasion in a jury case to proceed under section 797 to obtain a
correction.   The defendant's claims for correction are not stated
in its assignments of error, but are found in a proposed amendment thereto and in its brief.   The original printed record therefore gives no notice of the corrections which are claimed.   The
amendment filed only 11 days before the opening of the term

Elliott *v.* New York, N. H. & H. R. Co

was too late to give the appellee proper notice of the claims and cannot properly be granted. Union Trust Co. *v.* Stamford Trust Co., 72 Conn. 86, 95, 43 Atl. 555. No change therefore has been made in the finding.

The court refused the defendant's request that the jury be dismissed while the motion to direct a verdict was being argued, and this refusal is made the ground of one of the defendant's assignments of error. We understand that it has been the custom in this state in such cases, and in cases where a motion for a nonsuit is to be argued, to excuse the jury from attendance while such argument proceeds. It is proper in all cases, and desirable in most, to do so. This course affords counsel an opportunity to admit for the purposes of the argument facts which, if the case goes to the jury, he will seriously controvert, but which, if admitted by him in the presence of the jury, might set their minds against and thus work injury to his cause. Time will generally be saved and a fairer trial be had by excusing the jury in such cases. But the ground of the motion or the nature of the case may be such that no harm would result, and time might be saved by allowing the jury to remain in their seats during the argument. It is a matter within the sound discretion of the court.

The court in its charge, after cautioning the jury against drawing any conclusion as to the court's opinion of the merits of the case because of its denial of the motion to direct a verdict, called their attention to the fact that they had been permitted to hear the arguments upon that motion, and then said to them: "Such arguments made at the conclusion of a case to the court are quite apt to be, in their treatment of the facts, fairer in their statement, more direct in application, freer from heat and prejudice, than the arguments addressed to the jury on the merits; and it is of the utmost advantage to the jury to hear such arguments and have the opportunity to secure further light and instruction and longer to sift, weigh, and balance. The arguments addressed to the court in your hearing were designed to inform and instruct you, and I have no doubt that you are better equipped for your duty for having heard them." The jury were thus invited, in arriving at their conclusions as to questions of fact, to consider what had been said in the arguments which had been addressed to the court upon questions of law. They must from the language have been led to believe that they should rely upon these arguments rather than upon those which had been addressed to themselves, for they were told that such arguments are apt to be fairer in their statements of fact and more direct in their application than arguments which are addressed to a jury. Arguments addressed to the court are or should be designed for the information and instruction of the court, and not for the instruction of the jury. They can hardly be of great

Adams v. Arkansas, L. & G. Ry. Co

advantage to a jury in determining the questions of fact. The tendency of the instruction was to mislead the jury into taking any admission made in the course of the argument upon the motion as a fair statement of the fact, and to thus ignore the evidence and the claims made as to the conclusions to be drawn from it in the later argument to the jury. The instruction was wrong, and we think necessarily harmful to the defendant. Since the jury were permitted to remain in their seats during the argument against the defendant's request, it was due to it that they be carefully instructed that the arguments to which they listened were designed for the court's information and not for theirs. The defendant's exception to this part of the charge is sustained.

There is error, and a new trial is ordered. The other Judges concurred.

ADAMS v. ARKANSAS, L. & G. RY. CO.

(Supreme Court of Louisiana, Dec. 12, 1910. Rehearing Denied Jan. 3, 1911.)

[53 So. Rep. 865.]

Railroads—Collisions—Contributory Negligence.*—Where the motorman of a street car, on approaching a steam railroad crossing, failed to stop, look, and listen for an approaching train at the street intersection, from which the train could have been plainly seen, held, that the motorman was guilty of contributory negligence, which bars recovery on his part, although the servants of the railroad company were at the same time negligent in not stopping their train before it reached the crossing, as required by city ordinance.

Railroads—Collision at Crossing—Last Clear Chance.†—In such a case, the trainmen on seeing the car approaching the crossing had

---

*For the authorities in this series on the subject of the combined effect of contributory negligence and negligence on the part of those in charge of the train or car, in an action for injuries inflicted by a train or street car at a crossing, see third paragraph of second foot-note of Wilkinson v. Oregon Short Line R. Co. (Utah), 34 R. R. R. 360, 57 Am. & Eng. R. Cas., N. S., 360.

†For the authorities in this series on the subject of the right of those in charge of trains or street cars to act on the assumption that persons seen on or near tracks will avoid danger from the trains or cars, see fourth foot-note of Denver City Tramway Co. v. Wright (Colo.), 36 R. R. R. 360, 59 Am. & Eng. R. Cas., N. S., 360; fifth head-note of Clark v. St. Louis, etc., R. Co. (Okla.), 36 R. R. R. 247, 59 Am. & Eng. R. Cas., N. S., 247; first foot-note of Southern Ry. Co. v. Bailey (Va.), 35 R. R. R. 557, 58 Am. & Eng. R. Cas., N. S., 557; last head-note of St. Louis, etc., R. Co. v. Summers (C. C. A.), 35 R. R. R. 117, 58 Am. & Eng. R. Cas., N. S., 117.

For the authorities in this series on the subject of the last clear chance doctrine, see first foot-note of Denver City Tramway Co. v.

Adams *v.* Arkansas, L. & G. Ry. Co

the right to presume that the motorman would exercise his senses so as to avoid a collision by stopping his car short of the crossing; and as the trainmen were keeping a proper lookout, and as soon as they discovered the danger, did all that could have been reasonably expected of them to stop the train, there is no room for the application of the doctrine of the last clear chance.

(Syllabus by the Court.)

Appeal from the Sixth Judicial District Court, Parish of Ouachita; J. P. Madison, Judge.

Action by Oscar T. Adams against the Arkansas, Louisiana & Gulf Railway Company. Judgment for defendant, and plaintiff appeals. Affirmed.

Munholland & Dawkins, for appellant.
Stubbs, Russell & Theus, for appellee.

LAND, J. This is an action for damages for personal injuries resulting from a collision between one of defendant's trains and an electric street car, which on the occasion was being operated by the plaintiff as motorman.

Negligence is charged in that the defendant failed to flag the crossing as it was required to do by municipal ordinance, was running its train at an excessive and dangerous rate of speed, and failed to give proper signals and warning of the approach of the train.

Defendant for answer pleaded the general issue and contributory negligence, and especially in that the plaintiff failed to obey and observe the rule of the municipal street railway, requiring all street cars to come to a full stop upon approaching all railroad crossings, and not to proceed on the same until the way was found to be clear.

There were two trials before juries, the first resulting in a mistrial, and the last in a verdict and judgment in favor of the defendant, from which the plaintiff prosecutes this appeal.

On the occasion of the accident, defendant's train was backing toward the crossing in question, and did not stop and flag the same as required by an ordinance of the city of Monroe. The negligence of the defendant in this respect was admitted by its counsel in the argument at the bar, and therefore the only question for determination is whether or not the plaintiff was guilty of contributory negligence.

Wright (Colo.), 36 R. R. R. 360, 59 Am. & Eng. R. Cas., N. S., 360; last paragraph of third foot-note of Farris *v.* Southern R. Co. (N. Car.), 36 R. R. R. 523, 59 Am. & Eng. R. Cas., N. S., 523; third headnote of Clark *v.* St. Louis, etc., R. Co. (Okla.), 36 R. R. R. 247, 59 Am. & Eng. R. Cas., N. S., 247; third foot-note of Bruggeman *v.* Illinois Cent. R. Co. (Iowa), 35 R. R. R. 241, 58 Am. & Eng. R. Cas., N. S., 241.

Adams v. Arkansas, L. & G. Ry. Co

The facts as testified by the plaintiff are stated in his counsels' brief as follows:

"Plaintiff states that he brought his car to a stop about forty feet south of the crossing; that he could then see about one hundred and fifty feet to the east on the defendant's track; that he looked, listened, and sounded his gong, heard no indications of an approaching train, got two bells from the conductor, as required by the rules of the city, and then proceeded ahead on five points; that having already looked in the direction from which the train came, he swung in on the curve, and his face was turned almost west and down the track of the defendant; that owing to the obstructions on the west side of his track he was also bound to keep a watch on that end as well, and when he looked back again the train was within fifty to one hundred feet of him; that he attempted to stop immediately, within about fifteen feet of the crossing, but on account of the grease on the rails, wheels, and brakes he saw that he would be forced on the crossing, and then fed his motor up to seven points in an effort to clear the crossing sufficiently to avoid injury to himself. This he failed to do, and was struck by the oncoming train."

The street railway belongs to the city of Monroe, and is operated under a book of rules and regulations for conductors and motormen. This book warns every employee "that ignorance of these rules will excuse no one," and requires every employee "to always have a copy of them on hand when on duty." As to crossings the book prescribes the following rules:

"Cars must be brought to a full stop before crossing a steam or street railroad crossing. At steam road crossings conductors must go ahead onto the crossing, and if everything is clear signal the motorman ahead. In no case must the crossing be made contrary to the signal of the conductor or railroad fiagman.

"For Motormen

"Run across railroad crossings, through switches and into curves slowly. Under no circumstances are you to cross steam road crossings until your conductor has gone ahead on to the crossing to see if it is clear and given you a signal to come ahead."

These plain rules were disregarded by the plaintiff and the conductor on the occasion in question.

The result is that the plaintiff was negligent in not obeying said rules and regulations, and that the defendant's servants were also negligent in not stopping and flagging the crossing as required by the city ordinance.

Independently of the rules and regulations, the plaintiff was negligent in not stopping his car at the intersection of the two streets where he could have had a plain view of the track of the defendant for several hundred feet on each side of the crossing.

As it was, the plaintiff stopped his car, or slowed down to nearly a stop, at a point where his view of the track was re-

Adams v. Arkansas, L. & G. Ry. Co

stricted to about 150 feet. After making excuses for not stopping at the street intersection, such as the curve of the street
railway track and the slippery condition of the rails, the plaintiff on cross-examination testified as follows:

"Q. Could you not have pulled up to within thirty feet of the
track where you could have. had a view of the track and stopped?
A. I could have. I could have eased up to six feet and stopped,
but if the train had let me. know they were coming I wouldn't
have come on."

Plaintiff admits that he was looking in another direction; did
not see or hear the. train until his car was within 15 feet of the
track. The approach of the train was observed by the sole passenger in the street car, who, after shouting a warning, jumped
off. This passenger testified that the car never stopped at all
when approaching the railroad crossing; that the conductor was
on the front platform with the motorman, and neither seemed to
pay any attention to his warning. The conductor testified that
he was standing in the aisle about the center of the car when
the passenger cried out, and started towards the rear end of
the car. but that the collision took place before he could get out.
The conductor further testified that the car was about 10 feet
from the railroad track when the passenger gave the warning.
The city engineer testified that the motorman could have had an
unobstructed view of the defendant's track at a distance of 28
feet on a right line from its center, or a few feet further by the
curve of the street railway track. This same witness further
testified that it was easier to stop even on a greased curve than
on a straight track. as a curve opposes a constant resistance to
the movement of the trucks. This common-sense testimony disposes of plaintiff's excuse for not stopping his car on the. curve.

Plaintiff having failed to stop his car at the proper place for
observing the railroad track must be held to have been guilty of
contributory negligence. Snider v. R. R. Co., 48 La. Ann. 1, 18
South. 695; Elliott. §§ 1167, 1170.

On the evening in question, the defendant's train stopped at
a railroad crossing about 400 feet from the street railway crossing at which the collision occurred. The train was about 300
feet in length, and, according to the testimony of the engineer,
its speed was about 5 or 6 miles an hour. The engineer was
watching the rear end of the train for signals, and saw the street
car approaching the crossing, and on seeing in a second that the
motorman did not intend to stop, sounded the whistle, and at
the same time the conductor on the rear end of the train applied
the air brakes, and the engineer completed the emergency application, and stopped the train.

The conductor and flagman on the rear of defendant's train
testified that they were keeping a good lookout and sounding
the air whistle all the way; that as soon as the street car came

Adams *v.* Arkansas, L. & G. Ry. Co

into view the whistle was sounded as a warning, and that as soon as it was discovered that the plaintiff intended to try to cross ahead of the train, the conductor shouted and applied the emergency brakes.

The trainmen had the right to presume that the motorman would exercise his senses so as to avoid an accident by stopping his car short of the crossing. Shulte *v.* Railroad Company, 44 La. Ann. 509, 10 South. 811.

There is the usual conflict of evidence as to the speed of the train and of the car, as to the signals given, as to distances, and other particulars, that may be expected in cases of this kind. But we find sufficient evidence in the record of support the finding that the servants of the defendant did all that could be reasonably expected of them to avoid the injury as soon as the danger of the situation became apparent to them. A perusal of the evidence creates the impression on our minds that the plaintiff on the occasion in question acted not only imprudently but recklessly; that the defendant's trainmen had •the right to believe that the plaintiff would stop his car before reaching the crossing; and that they, after the danger became apparent, used all available means to avoid the accident. If the defendant was negligent in the matter of the operation of its train, the negligence of both parties concurred to produce the accident, and therefore there can be no recovery. Bell Alliance Co. *v.* Texas & Pacific Ry. Co., 125 La. 777, 51 South. 846. In the same case the last clear chance doctrine is thus expressed:

"If, after the engineer has seen the danger of the person on or near the track, he can stop his engine and avert the accident, and fails to do so, the person injured can recover, in spite of his own negligence."

If we qualify this enunciation by interpolating "should have seen," the result in this case would be the same, as the trainmen were keeping a vigilant lookout.

The violation of an ordinance by a railroad company does not necessarily carry with it the abrogation of the rules of contributory negligence. Lopes *v.* Sahuque, 114 La. 1004, 38 South. 810; May *v.* T. P. Ry. Co., 123 La. 647, 49 South. 272.

This is a typical jury case, and, on the record before us, we see no good reasons for disturbing the verdict.

Judgment affirmed.

Arkansas & L. Ry. Co. v. Graves.

(Supreme Court of Arkansas, Dec. 5, 1910.)

[132 S. W. Rep. 992.]

Railroads—Injuries to Pedestrians—Negligence.*—Where employees of a railroad company negligently failed to give the statutory signals on approaching a public street crossing, and a person rightfully at another place on the track and in the exercise of ordinary care was injured by reason of the failure, the company was liable.

Railroads—Persons on Track—Liability.†—Where the public, since a railroad was first put into operation, had openly and continuously, used the track as a crossing, and as an appioach to a depot platform, those who used the crossing did so on the implied invitation of the company, and its servants owed them the duty of exercising ordinary care to avoid injury.

Railroads—Persons on Track—Liability.†—One coming to a depot on business with the railroad company, who leaves the premises by a route commonly used by the public under permission from the company, is not a trespasser while so doing, and the servants of the company must exercise care not to injure him while on the track

Railroads—Injuries to Pedestrian Crossing Track—Negligence—Evidence.‡—In an action for injuries to a pedestrian struck by a car

---

*For the authorities in this series on the question whether it is actionable negligence to have failed to give crossing signals where the person was struck by the train at a point beyond the crossing, see last paragraph of foot-note of Norris v. Atlantic C. L. R Co. (N. Car.), 36 R. R. R. 321, 59 Am. & Eng. R. Cas., N. S., 321.

†For the authorities in this series on the question, what does, and does not constitute an implied license to travel on or cross a railroad track, see first paragraph of foot-note of Chesapeake, etc., Ry. Co. v. Ball (Ky.), 35 R. R. R. 238, 58 Am. & Eng. R. Cas., N. S., 238; fourth head-note of Langenfield v. Union Pac. R. Co. (Neb.), 34 R. R. R. 727, 57 Am. & Eng. R. Cas., N. S., 727.

For the authorities in this series on the question, who are, and are not, licensees on railroad tracks or premises, see first foot-note of Atchison v. Jandera(Okla.), 35 R. R. R. 154, 58 Am. & Eng. R. Cas., N. S., 154.

For the authorities in this series on the subject of the duties and liabilities of a railroad company with respect to licensees and trespassers on its tracks, see first foot-note of Riedel v. West Jersey & S. R. Co. (C. C. A.), 36 R. R. R. 312, 59 Am. & Eng. R. Cas., N. S., 312; Louisville & N. R. Co. v. Morgan (Ala.), 36 R. R. R. 318, 59 Am. & Eng. R. Cas., N. S., 318; last foot-note of Pinson v. Southern Ry. (S. Dak.), 35 R. R. R. 700, 58 Am. & Eng. R. Cas., N. S., 700; first foot-note of Southern Ry. Co. v. Stewart (Ala.), 35 R. R. R. 234, 58 Am. & Eng. R. Cas., N. S., 234.

‡For the authorities in this series on the subject of the precautions and care to be used by those engaged in kicking, backing or switching cars at crossings. see foot-note of Vaden v. North Carolina R. Co. (N. Car.), 34 R. R. R. 407, 57 Am. & Eng. R. Cas., N. S., 407.

For the authorities in this series on the duty to maintain lookouts on trains approaching crossings, see last foot-note of Louisville, etc.,

Arkansas & L. Ry. Co. *v.* Graves

backed by an engine at a customary crossing, evidence held to show a negligent failure to keep a lookout while backing the engine and car.

Railroads—Travelers Approaching Track—Care Required.§—One about to cross a railroad track at a customary crossing must look and listen for the approach of trains, and generally it is negligence for a traveler to fail to observe such precautions.

Railroads — Travelers Approaching Track — Care Required. — Whether one about to cross a railroad track at a customary crossing exercised the proper degree of vigilance in looking and listening for the approach of trains, sufficient to amount to ordinary prudence for one's safety, is ordinarily for the jury, though a traveler must be deemed to have discovered whatever could have been plainly seen by looking or could have been heard by listening.

Railroads — Travelers Approaching Track — Care Required — Whether one struck by a car backed by an engine over a crossing was guilty of contributory negligence, held, under the evidence, for the jury.

Railroads — Travelers Approaching Track — Care Required. ‖ — A person about to cross a railroad track may, to some extent, rely on the trainmen giving signals of the approach of trains, and the jury may take that fact into consideration in determining the issue of contributory negligence.

Railroads—Injuries to Pedestrian Crossing Track—Negligence—Proximate Cause.—In an action for injuries to a person crossing a railroad track by being struck by a car backed by an engine, evidence held to justify a finding that the failure of the trainmen to give signals of the approach of the car was the proximate cause of the injury, though the pedestrian knew that the engine was running near him.

Appeal and Error—Questions Reviewable—Instructions—Objections.—Where, on a trial, a party objected to the first part of an in-

R. Co. *v.* Engleman (Ky.), 35 R. R. R. 106, 58 Am. & Eng. R. Cas., N. S., 106; last paragraph of fourth foot-note of Garrison *v.* St. Louis, etc., Ry. Co. (Ark.), 34 R. R. R. 543, 57 Am. & Eng. R. Cas., N. S., 543; fourth foot-note of Bourrett *v.* Chicago & N. W. Ry. Co. (Iowa), 34 R. R. R. 284, 57 Am. & Eng. R. Cas., N. S., 284.

§For the authorities in this series on the question whether the failure of a highway traveler to stop, look, and listen before attempting to cross the tracks of a steam railroad constitutes contributory negligence per se, see foot-note of Schanno *v.* St. Paul City Ry. Co. (Minn.), 35 R. R. R. 94, 58 Am. & Eng. R. Cas., N. S., 94; Bruggeman *v.* Illinois Cent. R. Co. (Iowa), 35 R. R. R. 241, 58 Am. & Eng. R. Cas., N. S., 241.

‖For the authorities in this series on the question whether a person injured through the negligence of another had the right to assume that the latter had performed or would perform the duties owing to the former, see last paragraph of foot-note of Campbell *v.* Chicago G. W. Ry. Co. (Minn.), 35 R. R. R. 98, 58 Am. & Eng. R. Cas., N. S., 98; first foot-note of Norris *v.* Atlantic C. L. R Co. (N. Car.), 36 R. R. R. 321, 59 Am. & Eng. R. Cas., N. S., 321.

Arkansas & L. Ry. Co. v. Graves

struction on a specified ground, but made no general objection to the whole instruction, an objection to the latter part of the instruction could not be made for the first time on appeal.

Railroads—Injuries to Pedestrian Crossing Track—Contributory Negligence.—Where a pedestrian, when attempting to cross a railroad side track at a customary crossing, looked and listened for the approach of trains, and heard an engine and though it was on the main track, he was not negligent in failing to stop to look and listen, since there was no necessity to stop to look and listen, and doing so would not have availed him anything.

Appeal from Circuit Court, Howard County; Jas. S. Steel, Judge.

Action by J. F. Graves against the Arkansas & Louisiana Railway Company. From a judgment for plaintiff, defendant appeals. Affirmed.

W. E. Hemingway, E. B. Kinsworthy, W. V. Tompkins, and *Jas. H. Stevenson,* for appellant.

W. P. Feazel, for appellee.

McCulloch, C. J. Plaintiff, J. F. Graves, instituted this action against defendant railway company to recover compensation for injuries alleged to have been sustained by being knocked down by one of defendant's trains while he was crossing the tracks near the depot at Nashville, Ark. Negligence of the company's servants is alleged in failing to keep a lookout, and in failing to give signals by bell or whistle. Plaintiff was crossing a side track at the southwest corner of the depot platform, and was struck by a freight car against which an engine backed and set in motion while being coupled to the train. There was a space there of 18 feet between the platform and a seedhouse, and the plaintiff adduced evidence tending to show that for many years past people openly and habitually crossed there afoot and with teams without objection from the railway company. There is a street running north and south parallel with the side track, and the evidence tends to show that at the point mentioned the space is used for a crossing from this street to the station platform and to the premises of the company. The space was used, according to some of the evidence, as a means of access to the premises of the company, and this was with the permission or at least without objection from the company. Plaintiff testified that the crossing was open, and was used clear across the right of way, but all the other witnesses testified that the way was closed on the east side, so that there was no access from that side. The testimony is conflicting as to whether or not there was a crossing on the side track at that place, but there was sufficient to warrant a finding as stated above.

According to the undisputed evidence, there was a public

Arkansas & ·L. Ry. Co. *v.* Graves

street crossing over defendant's tracks, both the side track and the main track, about 40 feet south of the place mentioned on the south side of the seedhouse just described. The main track is on the east side of the depot, and the side track is on the west side. On this occasion a mixed passenger train came in from the south, and, after stopping for a while (Nashville being the northern terminus of the railroad), the engine and two cars were uncoupled from the train and pulled up to a switch north of the depot and then backed down the side track for the purpose of coupling to two cars standing near the place where plaintiff was injured. Plaintiff was a mail and express carrier, and had come to the depot to meet the train to see about some express which had come for him, and was leaving the premises to go to another railroad depot near by. In attempting to do so he started across the side track at the place mentioned, and was struck by one of the cars pushed by the backing engine. The corner of the car struck him just as he got across the track. He testified that before going on the side track he "slowed up," looked and listened for an approaching train, but neither saw nor heard one approaching and proceeded to go across. He stated that he heard the noise of the engine running above the depot, but thought that it was still over on the main line. The depot platform was four or five feet high, and plaintiff testified that a lot of boxes of freight piled on and extending over the corner of the platform obstructed his view to some extent up the side track. The evidence tends to establish the fact that no signals were given, and no lookout was kept.

It is insisted that the evidence does not sustain the verdict in plaintiff's favor, in that it fails to establish negligence on the part of defendant's servants, and that it does indisputably establish contributory negligence on the part of plaintiff. The contention, as to the charge of negligence against defendant in failing to give signals, is that the statutory requirement as to giving signals applies only to legally established public road crossings, and that there is no evidence to show that the place where plaintiff received his injuries was such a crossing. The argument entirely ignores the fact that there was a public street crossing about 40 feet south of the place where plaintiff was struck by the train, that the engine and cars were approaching that crossing, and that the trainmen were then under legal obligation to give the signals for that crossing; that is to say, to keep the bell or whistle sounding until the crossing was reached or the train stopped. Therefore, the point which learned counsel argued with so much earnestness, that the statutory requirements do not apply except to legally establish road crossings, is not reached in this case. If the trainmen were guilty of negligence in the particular named, which caused plaintiff's injury, and if plaintiff was not a trespasser and was not guilty of con-

Arkansas & L. Ry. Co. v. Graves

tributory negligence, then defendant is liable for the damages. St. L., I. M. & S. Ry. Co. v. Shaw, 125 S. W. 654; St. L., I. M. & S. Ry. Co. v. Hudson, 86 Ark. 183, 110 S. W. 590.

The evidence tends to show that the place where the plaintiff was injured had for many years—in fact, since the railroad was first put into operation—been openly and notoriously used by the public as a crossing, and that it was used as one of the approaches to the depot platform. Those who used the crossing did so not only by the permission, but upon the implied invitation of the company, and the latter's servants owed them the duty of exercising ordinary care to avoid injury. Moody v. St. L., I. M. & S. Ry. Co., 89 Ark. 103, 115 S. W. 400, 131 Am. St. Rep. 75; M. & N. A. Ry. Co. v. Bratton, 85 Ark. 326, 108 S. W. 518. The plaintiff on this occasion came to the depot on business with the company, and had the right to leave the premises by the route commonly used by the public under permission from the company. He was not a trespasser, and the servants of the company were under duty to exercise care not to injure him while he was crossing the track. There was also evidence of negligence on the part of the trainmen in failing to keep a lookout while backing the engine and cars down the side track. St. L., I. M. & S. Ry. Co. v. Sparks, 81 Ark. 187, 99 S. W. 73.

There was sufficient evidence to justify a submission to the jury of the question whether plaintiff was guilty of contributory negligence. We cannot say, as a matter of law, that under the evidence adduced he was guilty of negligence. He testified that before he attempted to cross the track he "slowed up," looked and listened for the train; that he heard the noise of the engine running above the depot, but thought it was on the main track. His view up the side track was to some extent obstructed by boxes of freight piled on the platform and also by the two freight cars standing on the side track. A railroad track being a place of danger, it is the duty of one about to cross a track to look and listen for the approach of trains, and it is held in law, except under special circumstances which excuse the omission, to be negligence for a traveler to fail to observe those precautions. It is generally a question for the determination of the trial jury whether or not, under a given state of facts, the degree of vigilance in looking and listening was sufficient to amount to ordinary prudence for one's safety. The traveler is, however, deemed to have discovered whatever could have been plainly seen by looking, and whatever could have been heard by listening. St. L., I. M. & S. Ry. Co. v. Johnson, 74 Ark. 372, 86 S. W. 282; St. L., I. M. & S. Ry. Co v. Dillard, 78 Ark. 520, 94 S. W. 617.

The evidence in this case justified a finding by the jury that plaintiff did look and listen with the vigilance of an ordinarily prudent person, and that, without any negligence in this respect on his part, he failed to discover the approach of the train. Plaintiff admitted that he heard the engine running above the depot, but it was for the jury to determine whether or not it was reasonable for him to have been misled in supposing that the engine was on the main track, where he had last seen it. He had a right to rely to some extent on the giving of signals, and the jury could take that into consideration in determining whether or not he was in the exercise of ordinary care in attempting to cross the track. The jury was warranted in finding, too, that the failure to give signals was the proximate cause of the injury, for notwithstanding the plaintiff knew that the engine was running above the depot, the giving of signals would have apprised him of its approach. If a lookout had been kept, plaintiff would have been discovered and warned when he attempted to cross. We conclude that the evidence was sufficient to sustain the verdict.

The court gave the following instruction, the giving of which is now assigned as error: "(7) It was the duty of the plaintiff in attempting to cross the defendant's track to look and listen, to ascertain if the train was approaching, to the end that he might avoid a collision, and to otherwise use ordinary care to prevent his being injured. So in this case, if you find from the evidence that before plaintiff attempted to cross defendant's track he did look and listen for the approach of the train and exercised such ordinary care and diligence as a man of ordinary prudence would do under the circumstances, and if you further believe that by reason of the failure of the defendant to give the proper signal, or by reason of plaintiff's view up the track being obstructed he failed to discover or hear the approach of the train without any fault on his part, and was struck by said train and injured while attempting to cross, you will find for the plaintiff." The serious defect in this instruction is in telling the jury in the latter part thereof that if, "by reason of plaintiff's view up the track being obstructed, he failed to discover or hear the approach of the train," the defendant would be liable. We cannot understand why this language was used, for in considering the other instruction given it is not thought that the court could have meant to say that the failure of plaintiff, on account of the obstructions, to see up the track would render the defendant liable. It is probable that in framing this instruction it was intended to use the conjunctive participle "and" instead of the disjunctive "or," so as to make the instruction state the law to be that if, by reason of negligence of the trainmen in failing to give signals, and by reason of the plaintiff's view being obstructed, he did not, though in the exercise of due care, discover the approach of the train, defendant would be liable. Learned counsel for defendant must have so construed the instruction at the time it was given, for they did not object

Arkansas & L. Ry. Co. *v.* Graves

to that part of it. They objected only to the first half of the instruction, on the ground, specifically stated in their objection, that plaintiff knew that the train was running and the trainmen were not bound to give signals to warn him. The objection to the other half of the instruction cannot be made here for the first time. There was no general objection to the whole instruction.

Error is assigned in the refusal of the court to give the following instructions asked by defendant:

"(3) You are told that the defendant and the public each have the right to use a public crossing; and that it is the duty of a railroad company to sound the whistle or ring the bell before it runs a train over a public crossing; but this duty applies only to persons lawfully using or about to use the public crossings. So, in this case, if you find that the plaintiff was struck by the train at a place not a public crossing, then the defendant owed him no duty to sound the whistle or ring the bell, and if it failed to do so it was not negligence."

"(10) You are also told that the law requiring notice to be given of the approach of trains to public crossings is for the protection of persons using, or about to use, such crossings, and has no application to persons not using nor about to use them. So, in this case, if you believe from the evidence that the plaintiff was attempting to cross the track at a place other than the public crossing, then the failure of the defendant to sound the whistle or ring the bell, if it did so fail, was not negligence."

The weakness of defendant's contention, even if the statutory requirement for the giving of signals be held to apply only to legally established public crossings, is in assuming that because plaintiff was not at such a crossing defendant owed him no duty of protection. We have already shown the fallacy of this contention, for if there was a duty to give signals on approaching a public crossing, and plaintiff, while at another place where he had a right to be, and in the exercise of care, was injured by reason of such omission to give signals, defendant was liable.

Error is also assigned in modifying, by striking out the italicised words, the following instruction requested by defendant: "(4) You are told that a railroad track is a perpetual reminder of danger, and it is negligence for one to go upon a track without looking and listening, *and, if necessary, stopping,* to ascertain if a train is approaching. So in this case, if you find from the evidence that the plaintiff went upon the track without exercising these precautions and was injured, and that he would not have been injured if he had done so, your verdict should be for the defendant."

The question of the necessity for stopping to look or listen for a train has no place in this case. Plaintiff was walking when he attempted to cross the track and was injured. He says that he "slowed up" and looked and listened, and heard the engine,

Chicago, etc., Ry. Co. *v.* Nebraska State Ry. Com

but thought it was on the main track. Under the facts of this case, there could have been no necessity for stopping to look and listen, as plaintiff's senses of sight and hearing could as effectually have been exercised while walking along slowly as if he had stopped. Moreover, if the instruction had been given with the omitted words in it, the latter part would have been misleading in stating that if the plaintiff "went upon the track without exercising these precautions" he could not recover. The words "these precautions" might have been understood to mean to stop for the purpose of looking and listening, and imposed on plaintiff the duty of stopping, even though he would have availed nothing to have done so.

There are other exceptions to the giving and refusal of instructions, but the views we have already expressed as to the law and facts of the case fully dispose of all of the exceptions. We find no error. Judgment affirmed.

CHICAGO, R. I. & P. RY. CO. *v.* NEBRASKA STATE RY. COMMISSION
et al.

(Supreme Court of Nebraska, Jan. 9, 1911.)

[129 N. W. Rep. 439.]

Railroads—Crossings Over Railways—Power of Railway Commission.[*]—The State Railway Commission has no authority to order a railway company to construct a crossing over its railway at a point within the limits of a village where no street has been opened.

(Syllabus by the Court.)

Appeal from District Court, Lancaster County; Cornish, Judge.

Action by the Nebraska State Railway Commission and others against the Chicago, Rock Island Railway Company. Judgment for plaintiffs, and defendant appeals. Reversed, and proceedings dismissed.

E. P. Holmes and *G. L. De Lacy*, for appellant.
W. T. Thompson and *G. G. Martin*, for appellees.

ROOT, J.   In April, 1907, the trustees of the village of Hallam, acting under subdivision 27, 28, § 69, art. 1, c. 14, Comp. St. 1907, condemned a right of way for a village street over the right of way and railway tracks of the Chicago, Rock Island & Pacific

---

[*]For the authorities in this series on the subject of the duty of railroads to construct and maintain crossings, see foot-note of Chicago, etc., R. Co. *v.* St. Clair Circuit Judge (Mich.), 33 R. R. R. 274, 56 Am. & Eng. R. Cas., N. S., 274; foot-note of Piver *v.* Pennsylvania R. Co., (N. J.), 31 R. R. R. 503, 54 Am. & Eng. R. Cas., N. S., 503.

Railway Company. Subsequently a complaint was filed in the office of the Nebraska State Railway Commission to compel the railway company to "open up said public street and place a crossing across its said line of railway over said street, so that said street may be used by the citizens of Hallam and the traveling public in said village." The railway company answered, challenging the jurisdiction of the commission over the subject-matter of the controversy, and contending that all and singular the condemnation proceedings are void, and that the statute under which the village trustees acted is unconstitutional. After a hearing upon the merits, the commission ordered the railway company "to construct and thereafter maintain a suitable crossing, including such culverts, approaches, and plankings as may be necessary over its roadbed and track where Walnut street in the village of Hallam, Nebraska, intersects the same, and in the construction and maintenance of said crossing to do all that is required in providing a safe and suitable highway by reason of the construction of the railroad roadbed and track." Thereupon the railway company commenced an action in the district court of Lancaster county to annul said order. Issues were joined, and upon a hearing there was judgment for the commission. The railway company appeals.

The principal arguments relate to the jurisdiction of the commission over the subject-matter of the complaint. The commission contends that by virtue of the amendment to the Constitution creating the Railway Commission and the enactment of chapter 90, Laws 1907, § 1 et seq. (article 8, c. 72, Comp. St.), it has exclusive original jurisdiction over the contention between the authorities of the village of Hallam and the railway company. State v. Chicago, B. & Q. R. Co., 29 Neb. 412, 45 N. W. 469, is also cited by the Attorney General. At the time the amendment to the Constitution was adopted, and subsequently when the railway commission statute was enacted, the statutes provided that village trustees might, by ordinance, create, open, widen, extend, improve, and vacate streets within the village limits, "and to take private property for public use: * * * Provided, however, that in all cases the city or village shall make the person or persons, whose property shall be taken or injured thereby, adequate compensation therefor, to be determined by the assessment of five disinterested householders, who shall be elected and compensated as may be prescribed by ordinance and who shall in the discharge of their duties act under oath," etc. Subdivisions 27, 28, § 69, art. 1, c. 14, supra.

Acting under this grant of power, the trustees of the village of Hallam by ordinance extended Walnut street by condemning a right of way across the railway company's right of way. and the company's damage was ascertained by five householders of the village elected in conformity to the provision of the ordinance.

Chicago, etc., Ry. Co. v. Nebraska State Ry. Com

If the statute, the ordinance, and the proceedings thereunder are lawful, the village authorities by legal process can compel the railway company to relax its exclusive control over the right of way thus condemned, and to construct a safe and suitable crossing over its railway. The authorities granted the trustees to locate and open streets is administrative in its character, and its exercise, when pursued within the limitations of the law, should not be reviewed by the courts. Otto v. Conroy, 76 Neb. 517, 107 N. W. 752; Stone v. Nebraska City, 84 Neb. 789, 122 N. W. 63. Notice however, must be given the property owner so that he may appear before the appraisers and protect his rights. Wilber v. Reed, 84 Neb. 767, 122 N. W. 53. The Legislature may authorize a municipality to enact an ordinance defining a reasonable procedure for the exercise of its authority. State v. Cosgrave, 85 Neb. 187, 122 N. W. 885, 26 L. R. A. (N. S.) 207; Paulsen v. Portland, 149 U. S. 30, 38, 13 Sup. Ct. 750, 37 L. Ed. 637. This the trustees attempted to do. The amendment to the Constitution provides that: "The powers and duties of such commission shall include the regulation of rates, service and general control of common carriers as the Legislature may provide by law. But in the absence of specific legislation the commission shall exercise the powers and perform the duties enumerated in this provision." The act of 1907, supra, among other things provides: Section 2: "(b) Said commission shall have the power to regulate the rates and services of, and to exercise a general control over all railroads * * * engaged in the transportation of freight or passengers within the state." "(c) Said commission shall investigate any and all cases of alleged neglect or violation of the laws of the state by any railway company, * * * subject to the provisions hereof, doing business in this state, or by the officers, agents or employees thereof, and take such action with reference thereto as may be provided herein, or under the laws of this state providing for the regulation of railway companies. * * *" "(i) The said commission shall have power to examine into and inspect, from time to time, the condition of each railway, or common carrier, its equipment, and the manner of its conduct and management with regard to the public safety and convenience in this state." Section 110, c. 78, Comp. St., provides that any railroad corporation whose railway crosses "any public or private road shall make and keep in good repair good and sufficient crossings on all such roads, including all the grading, bridges, ditches, and culverts that may be necessary, within their right of way."

The commission statute being general in its scope, repeals by implication all earlier statutes in conflict therewith. It is remedial in character, and should be literally construed, but neither by direct language or fair implication does it vest the commission with power to compel a railroad company to permit any part of

Chicago. etc., Ry. Co. v. Nebraska State Ry. Com

its right of way to be used for a village street. The statute was
enacted for practical purposes, and should not be construed so as
to encourage suitors to engage in fruitless contests before the
commission, and thereby divert its energies from the important
legitimate subjects which demand its undivided attention. In the
instant case any order the commission might make will be a vain
thing. If the crossing is constructed, the public will not thereby
secure any relief, because the railway company controls all approaches thereto. We do not question the commission's authority to inspect railway crossings and to compel a railway company to construct them so as to safeguard the lives of passengers
and employees upon its cars, but no such contention exists in the
case at bar. The evidence introduced before the commission
and in the district court is before us, and it clearly appears therefrom that the commission tried the question of whether the public
interest dictated that Walnut street should be opened across the
railway company's right of way. We are convinced that the
Legislature did not intend to withdraw from the village and city
authorities the jurisdiction theretofore granted them over this
subject. East St. Louis R. Co. v. Louisville & N. R. Co., 149 Fed.
159, 79 C. C. A. 107. The precise point now considered was not
presented in State v. Chicago, B. & Q. R. Co., 29 Neb. 412, 45
N. W. 469. That case refers to a statute subsequently held invalid, and the judgment is controlled by the provisions of section
110. c. 78, Comp. St., supra, which by express terms is limited to
country roads, and does not refer to streets in villages or cities.
Neither does Chicago, R. I. & P. R. Co. v. Nebraska State Railway Commission, 85 Neb. 818, 124 N. W. 477, 26 L. R. A. (N.
S.) 444, sustain the attitude assumed by the commission in the
case at bar. In the reported case we approved an order made to
compel the carrier to furnish its patrons a station and accessories
for the receipt and discharge of passengers and freight. In the
instant case, if the proceedings in condemnation are valid, the
village has an adequate remedy by mandamus, one it will be compelled to pursue should the order of the commission be affirmed
and the railroad build the crossing, but refuse to permit travel
over its right of way. If, as the railroad company contends, the
condemnation proceedings are void, either because the statute is
unconstitutional or because its provisions have not been observed,
the commission can enter no order to aid the one it has made
upon the complaint filed in the case at bar. We should not presume that the Legislature intended the commission to devote its
valuable time to such inconclusive proceedings.

The judgment of the district court therefore is reversed, with
directions to enter an order dismissing the proceedings before the
commission.

REESE, C. J., not sitting.

City of Shreveport *v.* Kansas City Southern Ry. Co. *et al.*

(Supreme Court of Louisiana, Nov. 28, 1910.   Rehearing Denied Jan. 3, 1911.)

[53 So. Rep. 923.]

Railroads—Crossing Over Railroad—Ordinances—Reasonableness. —An ordinance of the city of Shreveport, enacted under its charter (Acts 1898. No. 158), giving it full power over its streets and bridges, etc., makes it unlawful to erect any overhead wooden bridges over any railroad, or make any substantial repairs to such bridges heretofore erected, and requires that all such bridges be built of metal, stone, or concrete, or combinations thereof. and imposes a fine for its violation. Held, that the ordinance was reasonable.

Railroads—Crossing Over Railroad—Ordinances—Violation—"Substantial Repair."—The repair of a wooden viaduct, under which railroad tracks ran and over which the street was carried, by changing 40 per cent. of the materials, was a "substantial repair," within the meaning of the ordinance.

(Syllabus by Editorial Staff.)

Appeal from First Judicial District Court, Parish of Caddo; T. F. Bell, Judge.

Suit by the City of Shreveport against the Kansas City Southern Railway Company and others.   From a judgment for defendants. complainant appeals.   Judgment set aside, and temporary injunction reinstated and perpetuated.

L. C. Butler, for appellant.

Wise, Randolph & Rendall and *Alexander & Wilkinson,* for appellees.

Provosty, J.   The city of Shreveport is given by its charter (Act No. 158 of 1898, p. 295) as full and complete authority over its streets and bridges as the Legislature can confer upon a city. In the exercise of this authority, it adopted the following ordinance:

"That it shall be unlawful for any person or for any railroad company to build or erect any overhead wooden bridges over any railroad in the city of Shreveport, or make any substantial repairs to any such wooden bridge heretofore erected; but that all such bridges shall be built of metal, stone, or concrete, or combination of the same. That any person or railroad company violating the provisions of this ordinance shall be subject to arrest, and shall be fined in a sum,"

Murphy street, one of the streets upon which there is the most traffic, is intersected by a deep cut made by the railroads, defendants in this case, and over this cut, along the bottom of which are four railroad tracks, the street is carried by a wooden viaduct constructed by the same railroads. The defendant railroads were about to repair this bridge, which had become rotten and unsafe, when the present suit was brought to enjoin them from doing so, under the above transcribed ordinance.

The defense is that the said bridge is not a menace to the public or to surrounding property, but is substantial, strong, and safe, needing only ordinary repairs, and that the said ordinance is unconstitutional, illegal, null, and void, because unreasonable and ultra vires.

Judgment went in favor of defendants in the lower court. We are not advised upon what grounds. Certainly the repairs necessary to be made were not mere ordinary repairs, but "substantial," within the purview of said ordinance. Forty per cent. of the material had to be changed. And we can see nothing unreasonable in an ordinance requiring street viaducts to be constructed, or reconstructed, of a material less inflammable and less liable to decay than wood.

The judgment appealed from is set aside, and the injunction herein sued out is reinstated and perpetuated, at the cost of defendants.

NORFOLK & W. RY. CO. *v.* OVERTON'S ADM'R.

(Supreme Court of Appeals of Virginia, Jan. 12, 1911.)

[69 S. E. Rep. 1060.]

Railroads—Operation—Accidents at Crossing—Crossing by Custom.*—Where a pathway across a railroad is used by 60 to 100 persons per day with the knowledge of the servants of the railroad, one injured while crossing the railroad on the pathway is a licensee, and not a trespasser.

Railroads—Operation—Accidents at Crossings—Action for Injuries—Instruction.—In an action for a death at a railroad crossing, where the engineer testified that the cab of his engine had reached the tower house beside the track when the deceased appeared beyond the tower house, approaching and close to the track, while plaintiff's witnesses testified that the engine was still some distance away when the deceased came near the track, so as to be seen beyond the tower house, an instruction that it was the duty of the railroad company to use reasonable care to discover deceased, and that if

---

*For the authorities in this series on the question what does, and does not, constitute a license to travel on or across a railroad track, see first foot-note of Chesapeake, etc., Ry. Co. *v.* Ball (Ky.), 35 R. R. R. 238, 58 Am. & Eng. R. Cas., N. S., 238; fourth foot-note of Langenfeld *v.* Union Pac. R. Co. (Neb.), 34 R. R. R. 727, 57 Am. & Eng. R. Cas., N. S., 727.

Norfolk & W. Ry. Co. *v.* Overton's Adm'r

it did not use such care, and by its failure to do so the accident occurred, the finding should be for plaintiff, was properly given, on the
theory that, if plaintiff's testimony were true, the engineer was negligent either in not seeing deceased, or in not giving an alarm or
trying to stop the train before the engine reached the place of the
accident.

**Railroads—Operation—Accidents at Crossings—Action for Injuries
—Instruction.—**In an action for the death at a railroad crossing of
a boy 13 years old, an instruction barring recovery if deceased failed
to look and listen before attempting to cross the railroad track, if
the deceased was sufficiently intelligent to be guilty of contributory
negligence, was properly modified by basing the effect of his failure
to look and listen on the condition that he was capable of knowing
the danger of crossing the railroad track on which trains were frequently passing, and that he failed to use that intelligence which
his age, experience, and capacity indicated.

**Railroads—Operation—Accidents at Crossings—Precautions as to
Persons Seen at or Near Crossing.†—**An engineer has the right to
presume that a pedestrian will stop before reaching the track in
front of a moving train, where there is nothing in his appearance
to indicate that he is not conscious of the danger.

**Railroads—Operation—Accidents at Crossing—Actions for Injuries
—Evidence.—**Evidence that a train was from 50 to 96 feet from a
crossing when deceased first appeared beyond a tower house within
12 feet of the track, approaching it, apparently unconscious of his
danger, having his attention fixed upon a freight train passing on
a further track, and that he was struck and killed on stepping upon
the first track, is insufficient to sustain a finding that the railroad
company was guilty of negligence resulting in his death.

Error to Circuit Court, Norfolk County.

Action by the administrator of Leroy Overton against the Norfolk & Western Railway Company. From a judgment for plaintiff, defendant brings error. Reversed and remanded for new
trial.

Hughes & Little, for plaintiff in error.

O. L. Shackelford and *Daniel Coleman,* for defendant in
error.

---

†For the authorities in this series on the subject of the right of
those in charge of trains or street cars to act on the assumption that
persons seen on or near tracks will avoid danger from the train or car,
see fourth foot-note of Denver City Tramway Co. *v.* Wright (Colo.),
36 R. R. R. 360, 59 Am. & Eng. R. Cas., N. S., 360; third foot-note of
Clark *v.* St. Louis, etc., R. Co. (Okla.), 36 R. R. R. 247, 59 Am. & Eng.
R. Cas., N. S., 247; seventh foot-note of Weatherly *v.* Nashville, etc.,
Ry. (Ala.), 35 R. R. R. 759, 58 Am. & Eng. R. Cas., N. S., 759; first
foot-note of Southern Ry. Co. *v.* Bailey (Va.), 35 R. R. R. 557, 58
Am. & Eng. R. Cas., N. S., 557; last foot-note of St. Louis, etc., R.
Co. *v.* Summers (C. C. A.), 35 R. R. R. 117, 58 Am. & Eng. R. Cas.,
N. S., 117.

Norfolk & W. Ry. Co. v. Overton's Adm'r

CARDWELL, J. This action was brought to recover damages for the death of Leroy Overton, an infant 13 years or more of age, which it is alleged was caused through the negligence of the defendant railway company.

It appears that the place where the fatal accident which is the basis of this suit occurred was a point on the defendant's right of way located in Norfolk county, outside of Norfolk city, in the direction of Suffolk, being the point where the defendant's tracks are crossed by the tracks of the Virginian, formerly known as the Tidewater, Railroad. At this point the defendant's tracks run approximately north and south, and the Virginian Railroad crosses in a direction approximately northeast and southwest. At this crossing the Virginian has one track and the defendant three tracks; the latter being the regular double tracks of the main line at that point for trains inbound and outbound to and from Norfolk city, together with a siding to the east of the main line. The defendant's train which struck and instantly killed plaintiff's intestate was the morning express, commonly known as the "Cannon Ball Express."

The plaintiff's intestate was a white boy, about five feet in height, who had resided in Berkeley ward of Norfolk city, and had employment in a silk mill in the vicinity of the place of the accident. Near the intersection of the two railroads, west of the defendant's tracks and north of the Virginian's single track, there stands a signal tower maintained by the Virginian for the purpose of operating the trains of the two roads over this crossing in safety. On the morning of the accident the "Cannon Ball" train was running on the regular outbound track from Norfolk towards Suffolk—i. e., in a southerly direction—going at the speed of about 25 miles an hour, slower than the usual speed of that train, but the speed provided in the regulations for passing this crossing and the interlocking system adjacent thereto, and struck decedent at a point south of the tower. At the time of the accident a freight train of the defendant was passing the point of the accident on the other or inbound track for Norfolk, to the left of the tower and track on which the "Cannon Ball" train was running, viewed from the direction that the last-named train was approaching, and the freight train had just about half passed the point of the accident, so that its middle was opposite the said point. The engineman on the "Cannon Ball" train, who was at his station on the right of his cab keeping a lookout as he approached the crossing, had signals from the tower which showed that the crossing was open for his train, and that he could proceed without stopping. When his engine was approaching the crossing, but some distance away, the engineman saw three boys approaching the crossing along a path leading to the tracks at right angles,

Norfolk & W. Ry. Co. v. Overton's Adm'r

on the right side of the tower, which path runs along a line of trees, and it was a very common thing for the engineman to see people, men, women, and children, approaching this crossing as the train neared it, so that there was nothing to cause him to suppose that these boys would go upon the track in front of his on-rushing train.   Soon after the engineman saw these boys in the path walking towards the track in front of his train, they disappeared behind the tower, and, when he next saw plaintiff's intestate he appeared from behind the tower, still walking in the direction of the track.   At this time, according to the statement of the engineman when testifying for the defendant in this case, his engine was practically at the tower, but according to plaintiff's witnesses, as we shall see later on, it was some distance away. There was a system of rods, consisting of small steel rods forming a corduroy surface of 6 feet, 5½ inches, connecting with an interlocking switch equipment, which rods ran parallel to the west rail of the defendant's track, upon which its "Cannon Ball" train was running, and the distance from the nearest rail of the defendant's track to the outer edge of the interlocking switch system was 11 feet.   When the engineman, as he claims, saw the decedent appear from behind the tower, he was then to the right of these rods, so that the situation was such as not to cause him to entertain any idea that the decedent would go upon the track in a position of danger until his first suspicions were aroused by seeing that the boy was in the act of stepping upon the rods, and was looking across the tracks and not towards his train, whereupon he, at this moment of suspicion, rapidly blew four sharp alarm whistles, and simultaneously applied the emergency brake, but it was impossible to check the train at that point, because, before the signals had entirely ended, the boy had stepped upon the track in front of the train, and was struck by the pilot and immediately killed.

Before the building of the Virginian Railway, there had been in use for a number of years a neighborhood road extending in a southeasterly and northwesterly direction across the defendant's tracks at the point of this accident, but, when the Virginian Railway was built, its roadbed was elevated above the original level, so that the neighborhood road could no longer be used as formerly and was thereafter used only as a pathway for pedestrians going from one side of defendant's tracks to the other. The number of persons using this pathway during the course of a day was by various witnesses estimated at from 60 to 100, and this use was known to the servants of the defendant, so that in this case the plaintiff's intestate is to be regarded as a licensee, and not as a trespasser upon the right of way of the defendant.

The trial resulted in a verdict and judgment for $2,500 in favor of the plaintiff, which we are asked to review and reverse.

Defendant insists here on its exception taken at the trial to the

Norfolk & W. Ry. Co. *v.* Overton's Adm'r

giving of the seventh and eighth instructions asked by the plaintiff; the exception to the seventh instruction being upon the ground that there was no evidence in the case upon which to base it.

The instruction is as follows: "The court instructs the jury that even though they may believe from the evidence that the plaintiff's intestate, when seen by the defendant's servant, was not then in a position of danger, still if they further believe from the evidence that the said servant of the defendant suspected, or, in the exercise of ordinary foresight, would have suspected from the surrounding circumstances that the plaintiff's intestate was unaware of the approaching train, and was in close proximity to the track upon which said train was running, and would likely get into a dangerous position on or near said tracks, and be injured by said approaching train, then it was the duty of the said defendant to exercise ordinary care to prevent injury to the plaintiff's intestate."

We are of opinion that the evidence was not sufficient to justify the giving of this instruction, as we shall see later in this opinion.

Plaintiff's eighth instruction is as follows: "The court instructs the jury that if they believe from the evidence that the place at which the accident complained of occurred had been in daily use as a cross-way for pedestrians for a long time by a large number of persons, including women and children, in that vicinity, and that its use was well known to the defendant, it was then the duty of the defendant company to us reasonable care to discover Leroy Overton if on or about to cross the railroad track on which the train was proceeding and in danger at that place, and that if the said defendant did not use such care, and that by its failure so to do the accident occurred, then they must find for the plaintiff's intestate, even though they may believe from the evidence that the plaintiff's intestate was guilty of contributory negligence, provided they believed from the evidence that the servants of the said defendant in charge of its engine did not do all they could, consistently with their own safety, to avoid the injury after the said danger to the said Leroy Overton was known or might have been discovered by the said servants of the defendant by the exercise of the ordinary care in keeping a lookout for persons at the place where the accident occurred."

The objection to this instruction is directed at the following language contained therein: "* * * It was then the duty of the defendant company to use reasonable care to discover Leroy Overton if on or about to cross the railroad track on which the train was proceeding and in danger at that place, and that if the said defendant did not use such care, and that by its failure so to do the accident occurred, then they must find for the plaintiff's intestate. * * *"

The two theories intended to be presented by this instruction, and which the evidence tended to sustain, were, first, that the

Norfolk & W. Ry. Co. *v*. Overton's Adm'r

engineer's statement to the effect that the cab of his engine had reached the tower house when the deceased stepped upon the interlocking switch system was inaccurate. Therefore, if this act on deceased's part took place when the engine was some distance north of the tower, as testified to by plaintiff's witnesses, the engineer either did not see it, or, if he saw it, did not take immediate means of warning the decedent of his danger, wherefore the jury might take this statement of the engineer in connection with the statement of plaintiff's witnesses and reach the conclusion that the engineer did not see the boy in the act of crossing the interlocking switch system, nor until he was about to step on the tracks; that if the engineer saw deceased and his danger, as he stepped upon the interlocking switch system, when the engine was 50 feet or more to the north of the tower, he was negligent in not giving the alarm or trying to stop the train before the engine reached the platform, or if, on the other hand, he did not see the deceased until the engine had reached the platform, when according to plaintiff's witnesses the deceased had reached the tracks, then the engineer's negligence consisted in .failing to discover deceased crossing the switch system.

We are of opinion that the plaintiff had the right to submit the two theories set forth in the instruction to the jury, especially as the defendant had presented its theory of the case in the seven instructions it asked, and which were given. See the case of Adamson's Adm'r *v*. Norfolk & Portsmouth Trac. Co. (just decided by this court) 69 S. E. 1055.

The refusal of the circuit court to give defendant's instruction No. 3, and the giving in lieu thereof the court's own instruction marked No. 3A, is assigned as error.

The instruction refused is as follows: "It was the duty of the plaintiff to look and listen before attempting to cross the defendant's tracks at any point or points from which he might, by the exercise of ordinary care, have seen or heard the approaching train. And if you believe from the evidence that he might, by so doing, have ascertained the approach of the train in time to avoid the accident, it must be conclusively presumed that he disregarded the rule of the law and common prudence and did not look and listen, or if he looked and listened that he went negligently into an obvious danger, if you believe from the evidence that the deceased was sufficiently intelligent to be guilty of contributory negligence."

The court's instruction No. 3A is: "If the jury believe from all the evidence that the deceased was a boy capable of knowing the danger of crossing a railroad track upon which trains were frequently passing, then it was his duty to look and listen before attempting to cross the defendant's tracks at any point or points from which he might have seen or heard the approaching trains, and, if he failed to use or exercise that intelligence which his age, experience, and capacity indicated by. failing to look and listen, then you shall find for the defendant."

We think that instruction No. 3, as asked, was defective, in that it confined the test of an infant's capacity for negligence to his intelligence only, while the rule of law that the capacity of an infant between the age of seven and fourteen years for contributory negligence is dependent not only upon his general intelligence, but also upon his experience and maturity, is well settled. Therefore the circuit court rightly changed the instruction so that the capacity of the deceased was to be determined not alone by his intelligence but also by his experience and capacity, and this was not unfavorable, but favorable, to the defendant.

The remaining assignment of error is to the refusal of the trial court to set aside the verdict and award the defendant a new trial, on the ground that the verdict is contrary to the law and the evidence.

The first question presented under this assignment is: Was the evidence sufficient to warrant the jury's finding that the defendant's servants were guilty of negligence, and that their negligence was the proximate and sole cause of the death of plaintiff's intestate?

In considering this question, we may say in the outset, and without reference to the evidence in detail, that it is conclusively shown that the deceased, who was certainly not under 13 years of age and from the shadowy evidence as to his age might have. been as much as 14 years old, was of sufficient intelligence, experience, and capacity to be held guilty of contributory negligence, considered with reference to the particular situation presented in this case. It may also be stated here that it is not seriously claimed that when the engineman of the defendant first saw the deceased and his companions walking along the footway leading to the defendant's tracks, before a view of them became obstructed by the tower and when the approaching train was some 500 feet away, a duty was imposed upon him to take precautions to prevent deceased from going upon the tracks in front of the rapidly approaching train; nor is it claimed that the train by reason of the engineman's seeing the deceased and his companions walking along the pathway towards the tracks and before they reached the tower should have been brought to a stop before its engine reached the tower.

The question, therefore, upon which the case turns, is: What was the negligence of the defendant's servants that alone caused the death of plaintiff's intestate? In other words, when did the engineman have reason to believe that the deceased was going into a dangerous position, or when should he have discovered the intention of the deceased to disregard his own duty to look and listen for the train and to walk upon the tracks in front of the rapidly approaching train; and, if after the engineman saw,

Norfolk & W. Ry. Co. *v.* Overton's Adm'r

or ought to have seen, the deceased's dangerous situation, did he
or did he not use all reasonable means at his command to prevent injury to the deceased?

According to plaintiff's own witnesses, the deceased was paying
no attention to the approach of any other train to the crossing,
but, with his eyes fixed on the moving freight train in front of
him, he walked, at the speed of from three to four miles an hour,
over the interlocking switch system, in the path passing near to the
tower, and upon the track in front of the on-rushing train, which
instantly struck him, and that, when deceased stepped upon the
switch rods, the train was at least 50 feet away, none of the
witnesses putting it at a distance greater than 96 feet, while the
engineer running the train says that, when deceased stepped upon
the switch rods and had taken a second step indicating a purpose to keep on in the direction of the tracks, the engine was
right at the tower house.   All the witnesses agree that deceased
was struck the very moment that he stepped upon the railroad
track, and that his nearest companion was but a few feet behind
him. Accepting as true the statement of plaintiff's witnesses
that, when deceased stepped upon the switch rods and when the
engineman first saw him after he emerged from behind the tower,
the train was not less than 50 nor more than 96 feet away, what
duty did he owe to the deceased which he neglected to perform?
Certainly it was not his duty to stop the train, for all the authorities agree that he had the right to presume that the deceased would
stop before reaching the track in front of the moving train, there
being nothing in his appearance to indicate that he was not conscious of the dangerous situation he was approaching.   A conclusion that, if the alarm whistle of the engine had been sounded,
deceased would have heard it and would not have gone upon the
track, would be purely conjectural, especially in view of the uncontradicted evidence that the moving freight train but a short
distance from deceased was making a great noise, and an unusual rattling by reason of its crossing over the Virginian Railway
track.   Under the presumption that operates in favor of enginemen in such a situation, the engineman was under no duty to do
anything until he discovered deceased's danger, and this was not,
under the facts and circumstances shown, until he had stepped
upon the tracks.   The track itself admonished him of danger,
and the noise of the freight train in front was sufficient to ad-
monish one of his age, intelligence, experience, and capacity to
take care before walking upon the railroad track; yet he neither
looked nor listened for an approaching train.   A finding that the
defendant upon the evidence in the case considered as upon a
demurrer thereto was guilty of negligence, which alone caused
the death of the deceased, could proceed only from conjecture
and speculation as to what the defendant could, might, or ought
to have done to avoid the injury to deceased.

In Humphreys *v.* Valley R. Co., 100 Va. 749, 42 S. E. 882, the contention was made that, if the engineman on the train had sounded the alarm whistle when he discovered Humphreys to be in danger, it would have caused him to get off the track, but it was held that, under the circumstances of the case, even if the expert witnesses had said that the sounding of the whistle would have caused him to get off the track, it would have been nothing more than conjecture. So. Ry. Co. *v.* Bruce, 97 Va. 92, 33 S. E. 548.

In N. & W. Ry. Co. *v.* Cromer, 99 Va. 794, 40 S. E. 58, it was held that the trial court erred in refusing an instruction which told the jury "that the burden of proof is on the plaintiff to prove negligence, and that the proof must amount to more than a probability of a negligent act; that the verdict cannot be founded upon conjecture."

In an action to recover damages for an injury inflicted through the alleged negligence of the defendant, the burden is on the plaintiff to prove the negligence alleged, and the evidence must show more than a mere probability of negligence. It is not sufficient that the evidence is consistent equally with the existence or nonexistence of negligence. There must be affirmative and preponderating proof of the defendant's negligence. N. & W. Ry. Co. *v.* Cromer, supra.

The decisions of this court as to the duties and obligations resting upon those operating a railway train towards persons observed to be near or upon the track in front of an approaching train lay down as a guiding principle of law that an honest discretion is permitted the trainmen in the exercise of that common-sense presumption which the law everywhere allows, that persons in front of a train, in the apparent exercise of their faculties, will keep out of the way, and the only limit and qualification of the presumption is that, when to the observation of the trainmen there first appears some indication calling for a suspicion of peril, then for the first time arises the duty to take such precaution as may be required by ordinary care to warn and avoid injury to a person in such suspected danger.

In the case at bar the engineman, as we have seen, stated that, when the deceased stepped upon the switch rods, his suspicion was aroused, but this was not sufficient to take away from the engineman the right to indulge the presumption that he (deceased) would keep out of the way of the on-rushing train, and the right to that presumption continued until there was reason to believe that the deceased was not going to keep out of the way of the train, and then all was done that it was possible to do to avoid injury to him. "I was looking for him to stop," says the engineman. It is shown that from the farthest side of the switch rods to the nearest rail of the track on which the train was approaching was 11 feet, and, as the path that the deceased was traveling ran diagonally from the switch rods to the track, the deceased had to travel 12 feet to get on the track, while the train, traveling at 25 miles an hour, had, according to plaintiff's evidence, to travel only 50 feet or a little more before reaching the deceased.

In N. & W. Ry. Co. v. Dean, 107 Va. 505, 59 S. E. 389, the injured party was upon the railway track, and there, as here, a recovery of damages was sought on the ground that the engineman had not taken proper precaution to avoid injury to Dean, but the recovery was denied, and the opinion by Keith, P., in discussing the rule governing in such a case, held: "If his presence is observed by careful and experienced men operating the train, and they, in the exercise of their best discretion, do not regard him in danger until on getting nearer to him he appears to be unconscious of his peril, and they then do all in their power to prevent injury to him, though without avail, the company is not liable."

The opinion in that case also uses the following language: "If the emergency brake had been applied at the instant Whitworth (conductor) discovered the presence of Dean upon the track, the accident would have been averted; but, in the honest exercise of his discretion, in the light of his long experience, he did not at that moment consider Dean in a position of peril. He appears to have been an intelligent official; and there is no reason to suppose that his conduct was not controlled by an honest purpose to do his duty, or that he did not give the signal to steady and then to stop to the engineer as soon as the danger of Dean's position became apparent to him." See, also, N. & W. Ry. Co. v. Solenberger, 110 Va. 606, 66 S. E. 726, 857.

It is made clearly to appear in this case that Cousins, the engineman running the engine which struck the deceased, was an intelligent and capable official of long experience in the employ of the defendant company, and in this connection we refer again to the fact that, when he first saw the deceased after the latter emerged from behind the tower, he (deceased) was at least 12 feet out of danger, and there is no evidence even tending to prove that after he got in a perilous situation by stepping upon the track it was possible for the engineman to prevent his being struck by the engine, for plaintiff's witnesses say that he was struck at the instant he got upon the track and before the alarm had ended.

In Humphreys v. Valley R. Co., supra, it is shown that a situation may appear different to those operating the train, and to those in different positions; and in Southern Ry. Co. v. Daves, 108 Va. 378, 61 S. E. 748, in which an infant eight years of age who had been seen by the engineer approaching the track got upon the railway track in front of a backing train and was struck and severely injured, it was held that "a railroad company can-

Norfolk & W. Ry. Co. v. Overton's Adm'r

not be held liable for the failure of its engineer to anticipate that a person, whether an infant or adult, approaching a crossing is going to step upon the track immediately in front of a moving engine, unless there is something to suggest that such person does not intend to remain in a place of safety until the train has passed."

In C. & O. Ry. Co. v. Hall's Adm'x, 109 Va. 296, 63 S. E. 1007, after stating that the doctrine of the last clear chance had no application to the facts of the case, the opinion by Harrison, J., says: "The fireman first saw the deceased when she was about to turn upon the little bridge in the direction of the crossing, but he did not know that she was going to attempt to cross, and he had a right to presume that she was not going to drive on the track in front of a rapidly moving train in plain view. So. Ry. Co. v. Daves, 108 Va. 378, 61 S. E. 748. When he realized that she was going to attempt to cross, there was nothing that he could do to save her. He did not even have time to call to the engineer."

We are of opinion that the verdict of the jury in this case, finding the defendant guilty of negligence resulting in the death of plaintiff's intestate, is without sufficient evidence to support it. Therefore the judgment of the circuit court upon the verdict must be reversed, the verdict set aside, and the cause remanded for a new trial.

Reversed.

WHITTLE, J., absent.

Wilson v. Illinois Cent. R. Co.

(Supreme Court of Iowa, Jan. 12, 1911.)

[129 N. W. Rep. 340.]

Railroads—Accidents at Crossing—Question for Jury.*—In an action for injury at railroad crossing, the testimony of several witnesses that no bell was rung or whistle sounded, is sufficient to take
the case to the jury on the question of negligence of defendant.

Death—Contributory Negligence of Decedent—Presumptions.†—
Where there are no eyewitnesses to death by accident, the law will
presume that the person killed was in the exercise of ordinary care,
but this rule does not obtain where there are eyewitnesses.

Railroads—Crossing Accident—Contributory Negligence.—In an
action for death at railroad crossing, evidence examined, and held
that deceased was guilty of contributory negligence.

Railroads—Crossings—Duty of Public.‡—Where a person traveling
on the highway approaches a railroad track upon which he knows
the view of approaching trains is somewhat obscured, it is his duty
to stop and look and listen for trains, before attempting to cross the
tracks, and unless his attention is suddenly distracted, he is guilty
of contributory negligence in failing to do so.

Railroads—Last Fair Chance.§—Where the deceased was guilty of
contributory negligence in crossing railroad tracks, the only theory
upon which his representatives can recover is that the engineer or
fireman on defendant's train, saw deceased in a place of peril, and
thereafter failed to take the necessary steps to avoid a collision.

Railroads—Accident at Crossing—Last Clear Chance—Evidence.§
—In an action for death at a railroad crossing, evidence held insuffi-

---

*For the authorities in this series on the subject of the value of
negative testimony as to whether train signals were given, see foot-
note of Anspach v. Philadelphia, etc., Ry. Co. (Pa.), 35 R. R. R.
91, 58 Am. & Eng. R. Cas., N. S., 91; last foot-note of Slattery v.
New York, etc., R. Co. (Mass.), 34 R. R. R. 795, 57 Am. & Eng. R.
Cas., N. S., 795; foot-note of Louisville & N. R. Co. v. O'Nan (Ky.),
34 R. R. R. 528, 57 Am. & Eng. R. Cas., N. S., 528.

†See second paragraph of first foot-note of Illinois Cent. R. Co. v.
O'Neill (C. C. A.), 37 R. R. R. 99, 60 Am. & Eng. R. Cas., N. S., 99;
last foot-note of Sontum v. Mahoning, etc., Light Co. (Penn.), 35
R. R. R. 574, 58 Am. & Eng. R. Cas., N. S., 574; third foot-note of
Louisville, etc., R. Co. v. Engleman (Ky.), 35 R. R. R. 106, 58 Am.
& Eng. R. Cas., N. S., 106.

‡See first paragraph of foot-note of New York, etc., R. Co. v.
Maidment (C. C. A.), 32 R. R. R. 681, 55 Am. & Eng. R. Cas., N. S.
681.

§For the authorities in this series on the subject of the last clear
chance doctrine, see second foot-note of Belle Alliance Co. v. Texas,
etc., Ry. Co. (La.), 37 R. R. R. 43, 60 Am. & Eng. R. Cas., N. S., 43;
fifth foot-note of Illinois Cent. R. Co. v. O'Neill (C. C. A.), 37 R. R.
R. 99, 60 Am. & Eng. R. Cas., N. S., 99; last paragraph of last foot-
note of Farris v. Southern R. Co. (N. Car.), 36 R. R. R. 523, 59 Am

Wilson *v*. Illinois Cent. R. Co

cient to show that the engineer was negligent after he saw decedent in a position of peril, or that such negligence, if there was any, was the proximate cause of the accident.

Appeal from District Court, Dubuque County; M. C. Matthews, Judge.

Action at law to recover damages for the death of John Semmens, caused by his being struck by a train at a highway crossing. The trial court directed a verdict for defendant, and plaintiff appeals. Affirmed.

A. M. Cloud and *J. W. Kintzinger*, for appellant.
Kelleher & O'Connor and *T. J. Fitzpatrick*, for appellee.

DEEMER, J. John Semmens was killed in Dubuque county, Iowa, by a train operated by defendant, which collided with deceased at and in a public highway crossing in said county. The negligence charged against defendant is "that there was a high embankment on either side of said defendant's tracks at and easterly of said railway crossing; that said defendant railroad company was negligent in allowing obstruction consisting of tall weeds, trees, and grass to be and remain upon and along the top of said embankment alongside of its tracks so as to prevent persons approaching the same from the north from having a clear and unobstructed view of its tracks and cars approaching thereon from the east. Said railroad company was also negligent in failing to sound any bell or whistle at the regular whistling post for said crossing, or give any other warning of the approach of said train before reaching said crossing; plaintiff further states that said defendant was further negligent in this: That defendant's engineer operating the engine of said train saw the team driven by said deceased approaching said public crossing in time to have averted the accident had he used ordinary care in attempting so to do; that said engineer at the time he first saw said team approach said crossing knew of the dangerous position in which the deceased was placed, and said engineer could, by the exercise of ordinary care, have avoided the injury to said John Semmens, deceased, had he used ordinary care in attempting to do so or to slacken or stop the speed of the train sooner than he did, but said defendant's engineer knowing of the dangerous and perilous position in which deceased was placed failed to stop said train or slacken its speed sufficiently to have averted said injury." These allegations of negligence were denied by de-

& Eng. R. Cas., N. S., 523; first foot-note of Denver City Tramway Co. *v*. Wright (Colo.), 36 R. R. R. 360, 59 Am. & Eng. R. Cas., N. S., 360; first foot-note of Clark *v*. St. Louis, etc., R. Co. (Okla.), 36 R. R. R. 247, 59 Am. & Eng. R. Cas., N. S., 247; third foot-note of Bruggeman *v*. Illinois Cent. R. Co. (Iowa), 35 R. R. R. 241, 58 Am. & Eng. R. Cas., N. S., 241; first foot-note of Bourrett *v*. Chicago, etc., Ry. Co. (Iowa), 34 R. R. R. 284, 58 Am. & Eng. R. Cas., N. S., 284.

Wilson v. Illinois Cent. R. Co

fendant, and it also pleaded contributory negligence on the part of plaintiff's intestate. The motion to direct was evidently sustained upon the theory that plaintiff's intestate was guilty of contributory negligence, and that because thereof there should be no recovery.

1. There was sufficient testimony to take the case to the jury on the question of defendant's negligence. Several witnesses testified that no bell was rung or whistle sounded while the train was approaching the highway crossing.

2. We are also of opinion that the testimony shows contributory negligence on the part of the deceased in approaching the crossing. The railway tracks at the point in question run east and west. The highway over which deceased was driving runs north and south, and crosses the railway tracks at right angles. This crossing is about one mile west of the town of Farley. Four hundred and sixty-five feet north of the crossing is what is known as the Glew house, and the highway from this house to the railway tracks is somewhat higher than the general lay of the land toward the town. There were no embankments on either side of the highway. The land to the east of the highway crossing is practically level and somewhat lower than the traveled part of the highway until it approaches a cut made for the railway tracks. This cut ran easterly from the highway crossing a distance of 450 feet, the deepest point of this cut being 5½ feet to the top of the rail and this deepest part was at the eastern end of the cut. On the north side of the railroad right of way was a snow fence 5 2-10 feet hight extending the entire length of the cut. The cars and engines used by defendant in the train which struck deceased were approximately 14 feet in height. While there was a cornfield north of the cut and in close proximity thereto, this field was something like 540 feet east of the highway, and did not obstruct the view of oncoming trains. There were no other obstructions which would in any way interfere with sight of the train, save a few weeds on the inside of the railway fences, but these weeds offered no particular obstruction in any way interfering with a view of the approaching train. There was one small tree near the right of way which at some points in the highway offered a measure of obstruction to the sight of an approaching train, at least there was testimony to that effect. Plaintiff's intestate was driving south on the highway which we have described past the Glew house, and according to the undisputed testimony he could have seen the approaching train at any point in the highway after leaving the Glew house after the train left Farley, and at all times until it reached the highway crossing. It may be that under the testimony a jury would have been warranted in finding that there was a point 60 feet north of the crossing where one could not well see the approach of a train from the east, and that this condition existed

Wilson *v*. Illinois Cent. R. Co

to a point 150 feet north from the track, being a distance of 90 feet where the train could not be seen or at least the view thereof was obstructed. Ordinarily where one is killed and there are no eyewitnesses of the transaction the law will presume that the person killed was in the exercise of ordinary care and doing nothing to jeopardize his life or limb. But this rule does not obtain where there are eyewitnesses. Here there was an eyewitness and he testifies as follows: "I knew John Semmens in his lifetime. I remember of the Clipper train going east from Farley the afternoon that John Semmens was killed. Prior to the time the Clipper train came west I was going after my cow; she was tied up alongside the railroad. I know where the public highway is that runs east and west near Farley, and am familiar with where the highway turns off north to go up to the Glew home. My cow was tied about 100 feet east from the corner of the fence as the road turns up to go to Glew's. The cow was tied about 80 or 90 feet from the point where the road crosses the tracks coming south. I heard the Clipper train leaving Farley that day. When I heard the Clipper train come I was a little east of where my cow was tied. I kept right on going after the cow. The next I heard was the train whistling at the whistling post. I was right near the cow at that time. I saw John Semmens that day, but not to speak to him, I noticed Semmens, as he left Glew's to go south. He left Glew's about the same time the Clipper train left Farley. Semmens had a box hayrack, and the team was a bay and a gray. After Semmens left Glew's I observed that he was standing in the middle of the wagon with his face to the west and back to the east. The team trotted right along down the road after he started. At the time the train sounded the whistle for the whistling post Semmens was about halfway between the railroad and Glew's. At that time I saw he was in the wagon. He was standing in the middle with his face to the west and back to the east. I saw and observed Semmens after the whistle sounded for the crossing at the whistling post as he came down the road toward the railroad. Q. Just tell the jury what he did, if anything? A. Didn't do anything; kept right on driving. Q. Tell the jury whether or not, from the time you saw him midway between Glew's house and the crossing and after the signal sounded, Semmens turned at any time to look easterly? A. No, sir; he didn't. Q. How did his team continue to go? A. Trotted right along. Q. You may tell the jury whether or not you heard any danger signals being sounded? A. Yes, sir; I did. Q. Did you see where Semmens was at that time? A. Yes, sir; he was right even with the snow fence. Q. At that time, tell the jury what was done, if anything, that you saw toward stopping this team or driving it forward? A. No, sir; he kept right on driving it. Q. How long did you see him? A. I saw him until the train came between me and

Wilson *v.* Illinois Cent. R. Co

him. I did not notice the position the lines were in. During all the time from the time he left the Glew Crossing he was looking west. Q. Then you say that you noticed Mr. Semmens as he was coming down from the Glew road? A. Yes, sir. Q. As he came down the Glew road, you saw him look to the east at one time; you say he looked to the east? A. No, sir. Q. Did you ever see him look to the east? A. No, sir. Q. At the time of the short whistles the team was just inside the snow fence, just about at the snow fence?"

The engineer testified that when he first saw deceased he was approaching the right of way, and "I judged from the motion of the horses' heads that they were moving at that rate of speed; that the driver or party who was with them did not know that the train was approaching. I immediately shut off steam, set the brake and commenced to blow the alarm."

Under this state of facts it is clear that deceased was guilty of contributory negligence. In Schaefert *v.* C., M. & St. P. R. R., 62 Iowa, 624, 17 N. W. 893, we said: "If the plaintiff's son had stopped four or five rods from the track and looked for the train this accident would not have occurred, or if he had not stopped but looked for the train at a place where it could have been seen, the accident would not have occurred. Where a person traveling on the highway and approaching a known crossing of the railway track with knowledge that the view of the approaching train is, to an extent obscured, heedlessly permits the team he is driving to pass over such highway pretty fast or allowed the horses to trot, and makes no effort to look or listen for the approaching train for a distance of eighteen rods from the track, he is guilty of such contributory negligence as will prevent him from recovering if a collision occurs, providing there are no circumstances which are calculated to distract his attention. Under the circumstances above stated and the uncontroverted evidence in this case, we think ordinary care required that the deceased should have stopped and looked or listened at some place between the place where the team was stopped and the track. There was nothing to prevent his doing so and nothing to distract his attention." See, also, Sala *v.* R. R., 85 Iowa, 678, 52 N. W. 664; Bloomfield *v.* R. R., 74 Iowa, 607, 38 N. W. 431; Reeves *v.* R. R., 92 Iowa, 32, 60 N. W. 243; Payne *v.* R. R., 108 Iowa, 188, 78 N. W. 813; Crawford *v.* R. R., 109 Iowa, 433, 80 N. W. 519; McLeod *v.* R. R., 125 Iowa, 270, 101 N. W. 77; Swanger *v.* R. R., 132 Iowa, 32, 109 N. W. 308; Williams *v.* R. R., 139 Iowa, 552, 117 N. W. 956.

In view of the contributory negligence of the deceased there can be no recovery in this case, unless it be on the theory that the engineer or fireman on defendant's train saw plaintiff's intestate in a place of peril, and thereafter failed to take the necessary steps to avoid the collision, and that but for such failure the accident would not have happened.

3. The doctrine of last fair chance as applied to the facts of this case is very well settled by our recent decisions. In Bruggeman v. R. R., 123 N. W. 1007, we said: "In application of that doctrine it is not necessary to find that the negligence of the plaintiff had ceased to operate before the accident occurred, and that, if it had ceased to operate, the defendant with knowledge of plaintiff's danger, due to his own negligence, had failed to take reasonable precautions to avoid the injury to him. It was enough to call for the application of that doctrine that the defendant's employees knew of plaintiff's danger in time to have avoided injury to him by the exercise of reasonable care, even though he was negligent in putting himself in a place of danger, and continued to be negligent in not looking out for his own safety. V. Barry v. R. R. Co., 119 Iowa, 62, 93 N. W. 68, 95 N. W. 229; Doherty v. R. R. Co., 137 Iowa, 358, 114 N. W. 183; Purcell v. R. R. Co., 109 Iowa, 629, 80 N. W. 682, 77 Am. St. Rep. 557; Kelley v. R. R. Co., 118 Iowa, 390, 92 N. W. 45. There is a general agreement in the authorities that where an engineer actually sees a person in a position of danger, and then fails to do what he reasonably can to prevent an accident, the railroad company is held responsible for the resulting injury, irrespective of the question of contributory negligence. If just before the climax only one party had the power to prevent the catastrophe, and he neglected to use it, the legal responsibility is his alone. The trial court evidently had in mind the rule which applies when neither party discovers the other and the negligence is concurrent, or to a case where one has no better opportunity than the other to anticipate the accident, or any better means of preventing it than the other. But there was enough testimony in this case to take the question to the jury as to whether or not the defendant might not have prevented the injury, although the plaintiff was negligent down to the very time of the collision. It is one thing to hold that the continuing negligence of a plaintiff will prevent a recovery for a negligent omission of defendant to discover his peril, and quite another to hold that plaintiff's continuing negligence will prevent a recovery for the negligence of defendant in failing to take proper care to avert the accident after the plaintiff's danger had been discovered and ought to have been appreciated. If each party is negligent in failing to discover the danger, then the doctrine of last fair chance does not apply. But if defendant discovered plaintiff's negligence and his peril in time to have avoided the injury, and did not take the necessary means to do so, then the doctrine does apply in full force; for in such cases the defendant has the last opportunity of avoiding the collision. This thought was not presented to the jury by the instruction given. Indeed that view of the case was distinctly withdrawn. In this there were manifest error."

Again in Welsh v. R. R., 126 N. W. 1118, we said: "While

Wilson v. Illinois Cent. R. Co

it is true that a motorman is not bound to anticipate that a person not already in a position of danger from the approaching car will negligently put himself in such position of danger, yet when the motorman sees that a person on the streets is apparently placing himself in a position of danger without being aware of the approaching car, it is plainly his duty to take cognizance of that fact and avoid injury to him if practicable, and we have recognized the rule that under such circumstances the negligence of the person in danger, which has thus become apparent to the motorman, will not relieve the street car company from liability for the negligence of the motorman in not taking reasonable precautions to avoid an accident. * * * In Kelly v. Chicago, B. & Q. R. R. Co., 118 Iowa, 387, 92 N. W. 45, which is analogous in view of the fact that the engineer in charge of the engine saw the person who was in danger on the track negligently failing to keep any watch for the approaching engine, it was held that notwithstanding the negligence of the person on the track the railway company was liable if the engineer failed to use reasonable care in avoiding injury to him. * * * The motorman was bound to use reasonable care not to injure the plaintiff in the condition in which the plaintiff had placed himself, even though he was guilty of negligence in thus putting himself in a position of danger which he might have avoided by reasonable precautions."

It is not true as appellee contends that as plaintiff's intestate was negligent down to the very time he was struck, there can be no recovery, even though the engineer saw the deceased in a position of peril and did nothing toward stopping his train. The doctrine of last fair chance presupposes negligence on the part of the party injured and proceeds upon the theory that notwithstanding this negligence, if the other party, being cognizant of that negligence and of the peril in which the party had placed himself, failed to take the necessary precautions to avoid injuring him, he is liable on the theory that he had a fair chance to avoid the catastrophe by the use of ordinary care and his failure to exercise it is in such cases the proximate cause of the injury. It is defendant's subsequent negligence, after discovering the peril differing in every essential from the mere continuation of the original negligence for which he is held liable. In order that this rule may be available to an injured party he must show that the party whom he seeks to charge with negligence knew of the perilous position or saw the injured party, and knew or should have known that he was in a position of peril. It is not enough that he should have been on the lookout for him, for in such cases it is the equal duty of each to look out for the other, and mere failure to look for another who is a trespasser or who is just as much bound as the party charged to keep a lookout, does not come within what is known as the last clear chance doc-

Wilson *v.* Illinois Cent. R. Co

trine. In such cases there is nothing more than continuing negligence on the part of each, each having a duty to perform which he neglects. To apply the doctrine of last fair chance to such a case would be. to introduce into our law the rule of comparative negligence, which did not, before the adoption of the employer's liability act of Congress, obtain in this state. It is important to find from the record where. the employees saw the. deceased and what they did after discovering him in a place of peril. The engineer testified as follows regarding this matter:

"We were running about 35 miles an hour when we got in the. vicinity of the Glew Crossing. The engine was working steam. The first thing that attracted my attention after leaving the whistling post was that I noticed on the south side (the wagon road is parallel there with the railroad) a threshing outfit and a vehicle ahead with horse or horses attached to it. The team ahead was getting fractious. I didn't really know whether the. party was trying to hurry the team along or whether they were acting that way themselves, purposely, but this road runs parallel to the Central track there on south side as you go up. This crossing comes, and you can't turn a thing on that. I didn't know but that the man who was driving the team was trying to go ahead, and come across the crossing ahead of me. When I got to a certain point where I knew I was going to get to the crossing first I paid no more attention to them. After I looked away from that team I looked toward the track of the right of way of the company, my eyes turned back to the track. As my eyes came around I noticed horses' heads just approaching the right of way of the company on this crossing. I judged from the motion of the horses' heads that they were moving at that rate of speed that the driver or party who was with them did not know that the train was approaching. I immediately shut off steam, set the brake and commenced to blow the alarm. The alarm was the first thing that was done because that was the first thing I reached for to warn. I reached for that with the right hand. The whistle rope reaches from the whistle lever to the back end of the cab so we can reach it from any point in the cab. We can reach it whether sitting down or standing up. I grabbed that with my right hand, and with my left hand shut off steam and set the brake. From the time I saw the team as it came trotting onto the right of way I made no delay in shutting off the steam and throwing on the emergency. I observed the team as it came up the line of the right of way where I first saw it until it got onto the tracks. They didn't reduce their speed as I could see any. The lines were hanging slack when the team came into view so I could see the lines and they continued hanging. There was no change at all in the speed of the team from the time I saw them come onto the right of way until the

Wilson v. Illinois Cent. R. Co

team went onto the track. I have been an engineer 30 years, and it was impossible for me, by the use of any appliance within the cab or within my power, to stop the train within that distance to avoid this collision. I done everything I could to warn the team and stop the train. The engine ran about 450 or 500 feet by the crossing when the train stopped. * * * I pulled the whistle and shut off the steam at the same time, and then applied the air. At the time the air was put on and the steam shut off I was blowing the whistle. The putting on of the air brake and shutting off the steam and blowing the whistle was all done in the same instant—instantaneously, you might say. At that time I was 200 feet from the crossing. I consider 650 feet a good stop."

The fireman in the engine testified as follows: "At that time the engineer was between two or three hundred feet from the crossing. * * * The engineer sounded the whistle. As we proceeded toward the crossing the bell was rung by myself. As we proceeded toward the crossing, after leaving the whistling post, I noticed something in the roadway on the south or left-hand side of the track. I was on that side of the engine. There was a threshing machine and a team and buggy ahead of the threshing machine. The team and buggy were near to the Glew Crossing, and the team seemed to be excited, and the driver was having to hold on to them pretty tightly. The next thing that attracted my attention as we went toward the crossing was the sounding of the alarm whistle. I noticed that the emergency brake was applied within a second after the danger whistle. The first I saw of the accident was the horses on the left-hand side of the track after they had been struck."

The only thing which plaintiff offers to meet this testimony is some computations based upon the speed of the train, the place where it stopped, the distance traveled after the engineer saw the deceased, the fact that people riding in the train did not notice any application of brakes until after the team was struck, and the supposed distance traveled by the train after the engineer saw it. There was some testimony to the effect that such a train running at 35 miles an hour, as this one was, could be stopped within 300 feet; but the testimony also shows that it would run at least 75 feet after the engineer saw one in peril before he could get his brake to working, sound the alarm and shut off his steam. The most favorable testimony for plaintiff showed that in a distance of 200 feet a train running at 35 miles an hour might be slowed down to 10 or 12. There was also testimony to the effect that the emergency brake was not set until after the team was struck. There is no method of telling mathematically where the train was when the engineer and fireman first saw the team which deceased was driving. The exact place where the team was when first seen by the engineer is a

Wilson v. Illinois Cent. R. Co

mere guess, but it was certainly not more than 50 feet from the track. According to some of the testimony the team was going on a jog trot at the rate of about five miles per hour. If we were to assume these guesses correct, and that the train was go-ing 7 times as fast as the horses, and the horses covered 50 feet after the engineer saw them, then the train must have run 350 feet after the engineer first saw the team. All this, however, is mere guesswork, and should not be allowed to prevail over direct testimony as to the facts. Plaintiff's case is this: The engineer saw the team not more than 300 feet from the crossing, he could have stopped his train, taking into account the shortest length of time needed to sound the alarm, shut off steam, etc., in 375 feet. This would not have avoided the collision, however, for plaintiff who was wholly oblivious of his surroundings and of the warnings given was still traveling toward his death, and his wagon, if not his team, would have been struck by the train. Whether or not he would have been killed had the engine struck the wagon an another place than where it did is of course a matter of merest conjecture. A train going 35 miles an hour covers something like 50 feet per second, and in the short space of six seconds covers 300. Giving the engineer time to sound the alarm, shut off steam, apply the emergency brake, and perhaps reverse his engine, it becomes perfectly clear that he could not, in this case, have stopped his engine in time to have avoided a collision. There is not, therefore, in our opinion sufficient testimony to justify a verdict for plaintiff on the theory that the engineer was negligent after he saw deceased in a position of peril or that such negligence, if any there be, was the proximate cause of the injury. In other words, even if it be conceded that the engineer did not apply the emergency brakes as soon as he might, there is no sufficient showing that had he done so the accident would have been avoided. Verdicts cannot be based upon mere surmise and conjecture. Of course circumstantial evidence is sufficient provided it shows that the fault of the engineer was the proximate cause of the harm. But the circumstances must be such as to exclude any other natural and reasonable hypothesis. The circumstances themselves must be something more than mere guesses. A conclusion is no stronger than the premises upon which it is based, and if these be mere guesses or surmise, the conclusion must also be so regarded. The trial court did not err in directing the verdict, and its judgment must be, and it is, affirmed.

CENTRAL OF GEORGIA RY. CO. v. BLACKMON.

(Supreme Court of Alabama, Nov. 17, 1910.   Rehearing Denied Dec. 22, 1910.)

[53 So. Rep. 805.]

Railroads—Operation of Trains—Duty of Trainmen to Trespassers.*—Trainmen do not owe to a trespasser on the track any duty to keep a lookout, but they owe him the duty of preventing injury if they can do so after discovering his peril, and after becoming aware that he cannot, or will not, extricate himself therefrom.

Railroads—Injuries to Trespasser on Track—Complaint—Sufficiency.—A complaint in an action for the death of a person struck by a train, which shows that decedent was a trespasser, must allege willful or wanton misconduct on the part of the trainmen, or negligence on their part subsequent to a discovery of decedent's peril.

Railroads—Injuries to Trespasser on Track—Complaint—Sufficiency.—A complaint in an action for the death of a person struck by a train, which charges only simple negligence, must show that decedent was not a trespasser.

Railroads—Injuries to Trespasser on Track—Complaint—Sufficiency.—A complaint in an action for the death of a person struck by a train, which alleges that decedent was struck by a train while on a path on the roadbed, and that the trainmen discovered decedent's peril and negligently managed the train and thereby caused the accident, is sufficient as against a demurrer, because it alleges negligence after the discovery of the peril of decedent who was, as shown by the complaint, a trespasser.

Railroads—Injury to Trespassers—Negligence—Contributory Negligence.†—The act of a trespasser on a railroad track in remaining on the track after becoming aware of his danger because of an approaching train is negligence concurrent with or subsequent to the negligence of the trainmen failing to exercise proper care after discovering his peril and defeats an action for his death.

Railroads—Operation of Trains—Care Required.*—Trainmen need not warn an adult trespassing on the track and facing the train, until they discover him and have reason to believe that he is not aware of the approaching train, but they may assume that he can see and hear the train.

Railroads—Operation of Trains—Care Required.*—The duty of

---

*For the authorities in this series on the subject of the care due from trainmen to licensees and trespassers on tracks before their presence is discovered, see first foot-note of Chesapeake & O. R. Co. v. Lang (Ky.), 36 R. R. R. 630, 59 Am. & Eng. R. Cas. N. S. 630; last paragraph of foot-note of Chesapeake & O. Ry. Co. v. Ball (Ky.), 35 R. R. R. 238, 58 Am. & Eng. R. Cas. N. S. 238; last foot-note of Chesapeake, etc., Ry. Co. v. Corbin (Va.), 36 R. R. R. 58 Am. & Eng. R. Cas., N. S., 229.

†For the authorities in this series on the subject of concurrent or

Central of Georgia Ry. Co. v. Blackmon

an adult trespasser on a railroad track, facing an approaching train, to get off the track at any particular time or place, is not of itself sufficient to give notice to the engineer that he cannot or will not get off before the train reaches him, and the mere fact that the track is elevated with sloping embankments from four to five feet on each side with weeds and briers, where the embankment ends, does not show an inability to leave the track, and unless he is unable to leave the track and the engineer is aware of the disability, the company is not liable for his death.

Appeal from Circuit Court, Dale County; M. Sollie, Judge.

Action by James H. Blackmon, administrator, against the Central of Georgia Railway Company, for damages for the death of his intestate. From a judgment for plaintiff, defendant appeals. Reversed and remanded.

Count 1 is as follows: "The plaintiff, as administrator, claims of the defendant the sum of $20,000 as damages, for this: That the defendant, on or about September 9, 1908, was engaged in operating a railroad in said county and running trains thereon for the transportation of passengers and freight. That on or about said date one of defendant's trains, consisting of an engine and cars thereto attached, was being run on its said railroad by its servants and agents in said county near a public road crossing, said public road leading out from Ozark towards Barnes' Crossroads, and crossing defendant's said railroad at a point a little over a mile from the courthouse in the town of Ozark. Plaintiff avers that his intestate was walking along a path that was on a roadbed of defendant, and that he was walking said path at a point about 150 to 250 yards from the said public road crossing; that said intestate was coming towards Ozark, Ala., walking along said pathway, and that, while said intestate was walking along said pathway along said roadbed, the said engine and cars were coming from Ozark, being propelled by steam, and were approaching said intestate, being under the management and in charge of defendant's agents and servants; that plaintiff's intestate was put in peril of his life or great bodily harm by said approaching train; that the agents and servants of defendant in charge of said engine and cars saw said peril of plaintiff's intestate, and saw that plaintiff's intestate could not avoid being injured; that after the discovery of intestate's peril the agents and servants of the defendant in charge of said engine and cars so negligently and carelessly conducted themselves in the management of said engine and cars that said engine was caused by reason

---

ligence, see third foot-note of Farris v. Southern R. Co. (N. Car.), 36 R. R. R. 523, 59 Am. & Eng. R. Cas., N. S., 523; last head-note of Southern Ry. Co. v. Bailey (Va.), 35 R. R. R. 557, 58 Am. & Eng. R. Cas., N. S., 557; St. Louis, etc., Ry. Co. v. Shaw (Ark.), 35 R. R. R. 451, 58 Am. & Eng. R. Cas., N. S., 451.

Central of Georgia Ry. Co. v. Blackmon

of such negligence to run upon intestate, and inflicted upon him injuries from which he died in a very few hours."

The demurrers raise the points indicated in the opinion. The following were the pleas filed by the defendant: "(2) That plaintiff's intestate. was himself guilty of negligence, which proximately contributed to his injuries and death, in this: Plaintiff's said intestate got upon defendant's track and roadbed, and walked along the same for some distance, and at the time he received the injuries from which he died was walking along defendant's said track and roadbed, and was at the time walking in the direction from which the train which struck him was coming; that is, he was facing or meeting said train, and he negligently remained on said track or roadbed in dangerous proximity to said train then and there approaching, and until he was struck and injured, and that said acts on the part of the plaintiff's said intestate were done by him or committed by him with the knowledge on his part of his danger or peril.   (3) That plaintiff's said intestate was himself guilty of negligence, which proximately contributed to his injuries and death, in this: Plaintiff's said intestate negligently went to the defendant's track or roadbed, and negligently remained on said track or roadbed when the train which struck him was in dangerous proximity to him, and remained on said track or roadbed until said train ran against him and struck him, with the knowledge on his part of his peril in so doing.   (4) That plaintiff's intestate negligently went upon defendant's track or roadbed, and walked down the same in the direction from which the train which struck him was coming, until he was struck by said train, and with the knowledge on his part of his peril in so doing."

G. L. Comer, for appellant.
H. L. Martin, for appellee.

ANDERSON, J. The intestate being a trespasser on the defendant's track at the time he was run over or against, and at a point where the defendant owed him no duty to keep a lookout, the defendant's servants owed him only the duty of preventing the injury, if they could do so. after discovering his peril on the track, and after becoming aware that he could not or would not extricate himself therefrom.   Southern R. Co. v. Gullatt. 150 Ala. 318, 43 South. 577; Southern R. Co. v. Bush, 122 Ala. 470, 26 South. 168.   Therefore. the complaint would not be good after showing that the intestate was a trespasser unless it charged willful or wanton misconduct or negligence subsequent to a discovery of peril.   Birmingham R. Co. v. Jones. 153 Ala. 168, 45 South. 177.   We do not understand the authorities to hold that the only duty owing a trespasser is not to willfully or wantonly injure him, but they also permit a recovery for subsequent negligence as well—that is,   for a negligent   failure   to   use

Central of Georgia Ry. Co. v. Blackmon

preventative means to avert injury after a discovery of peril, and after a knowledge that the trespasser cannot extricate himself in time to avoid being injured—notwithstanding the act or omission of the servants in charge of the train did not amount to willful misconduct or wanton negligence. It is true we have authorities, as noticed in section 414, p. 636, vol. 4, Mayfield's Digest, which in effect hold that a complaint which shows that the plaintiff was a trespasser when injured is bad on demurrer if it fails to aver wanton or willful misconduct. But these cases were decided before the doctrine of subsequent negligence had gained much footing in this state, and the negligence there charged was original or initiative negligence as distinguished from subsequent negligence or negligence after a discovery of peril. We think the true rule as testing the sufficiency of a complaint, is that when simple negligence only is charged—that is, initial negligence—it should bring the plaintiff within the protection of the rule and show that he was not a trespasser. Holland v. L. & N. R. R. Co., 51 South. 366; Gadsden R. R. Co. v. Julian, 133 Ala. 373, 32 South. 135. On the other hand, although the injured party was a trespasses when injured, and this fact is set out in the complaint, it would not be subject to demurrer if it charged that the injury was willfully or wantonly inflicted, or that it was due to negligence subsequent to a discovery of peril, and which last fact is charged in the only count in the present complaint that went to the jury—count 1. Count 1 does not charge wanton or willful misconduct, but charges a mere negligent failure to prevent the injury after a discovery of peril. It does charge that defendant's servant's knew of intestate's peril, and knew that he could not extricate himself or avoid being injured, but it does not charge that they then willfully run over or against him, or that they wantonly neglected to discharge the duties required in order to avoid running over or against him. The complaint did not charge wanton or willful misconduct. L. & N. R. R. Co. v. Brown, 121 Ala. 226, 25 South. 609, and cases there cited. But although it showed upon its face that the intestate was a trespasser, it charged negligence subsequent to a discovery of peril, and was not subject to the defendant's demurrers, and the trial court did not err in overruling same. The rule, as laid down by this court, as well as in other jurisdictions, including England, is that while the plaintiff's intestate's negligence in being on the track would defeat a recovery for initial or antecedent negligence, yet he could recover if defendant's servants, in charge of the train, became aware of the intestate's peril in time to avoid running over him by the proper use of preventative means at their command, and negligently failed to resort to such means, to converse his safety, provided the intestate himself was free from negligence after becoming conscious of his danger. Ala. G. S. R. R. Co. v.

McWhorter, 156 Ala. 269, 47 South. 84; Louisville & N. R. Co. v. Young, 153 Ala. 232, 45 South. 238, 16 L. R. A. (N. S.) 301; Central of Ga. R. R. Co. v. Foshee, 125 Ala. 199, 27 South. 1006; L. & N. R. R. Co. v. Brown, 121 Ala. 227, 25 South. 609, and cases there cited. As was also held and properly so, in the case of Louisville & N. R. Co. v. Young, supra, and in the case of St. Louis R. Co. v. Schumacher, 152 U. S. 77, 14 Sup. Ct. 479, 38 L. Ed. 361, the plaintiff cannot recover if his negligence is not only subsequent to, but concurrent with, the subsequent negligence of the defendant. If the special pleas 2, 3, and 4 only set up contributory negligence on the part of plaintiff's intestate, anterior to the subsequent negligence of the defendant's servants as averred in the complaint, such as negligently going on the track, they would not be good, and would be subject to the grounds of the demurrer interposed thereto, but said pleas not only set up the intestate's negligence in going upon and being on the track, but invokes his negligently remaining on the track until he was struck, with a knowledge or consciousness of his danger. If he remained on the track after becoming aware of his danger, this would be negligence concurrent with or subsequent to the negligence charged to the defendant's servants, and would be a complete defense to the complaint, and the trial court erred in sustaining the demurrers to defendant's pleas 2, 3, and 4, as they were certainly not subject to the grounds assigned in the demurrer.

While this case must be reversed because of certain rulings upon the pleadings, we are also of the opinion that the trial court erred in refusing the general charge as requested by the defendant. If the defendant's evidence was true, the enginemen did all they could to avoid injury, as soon as they discovered the intestate, whether he was at the time in peril or not. It may be conceded, however, that there was a conflict in the testimony as to whether or not the engineer did not discover him sooner, as some of the plaintiff's evidence tended to show that the track was straight some distance between the approaching train and the intestate, and that the engineer could have seen him 200 feet, but did not attempt to stop until getting within about 60 feet of the intestate, and at too close a range to do so before striking him. There was also a conflict in the evidence as to whether or not an alarm was given the intestate, by the blowing of the whistle, after discovering him on the track. The trainmen owed him no duty to warn until they discovered he had reason to believe that he was not aware of the approaching train. While the evidence is not very full or definite on the subject, we can only gather from same that the intestate was facing the train, when it collided with him, and the engineer, we think, the right to assume that he could see and hear, and did see and hear the train; one or both, as he was meeting

Central of Georgia Ry. Co. *v.* Blackmon

and they were under no duty to warn him of the approach or to assume that he was not aware of its approach because he did not get off the track as soon as they saw him. It may also be conceded that the engineer saw him before he says he did; but the question that arises, Was the intestate, when discovered by him in peril? If the engineer discovered him walking on the roadbed, meeting the train, his failure to get off at any particular time or place, was not, of itself, sufficient to impress the engineer with the fact that he could not or would not get off before meeting and colliding with the engine. Coming as he was, facing the approaching train, and using the roadbed as a path, the engineer had the right to assume that he saw or heard the train, and would step aside before it reached him. Of course, if he was down on the track, or in such a reclining position, as to indicate, that he could not get off, then the engineer should have resorted to all means to stop the train upon discovering him in such a position. Or if he was at a point on the track where he could not get off, such as being on a high trestle, the engineer should make every reasonable effort to stop the train upon discovering him. Or if the trespasser is a child, of such tender years as to not appreciate danger, although it may see or hear the approaching train, it would doubtless be the duty of the engineer to stop the train or attempt to do so upon discovering said child as he might not have the right to assume that an infant, of tender years, would get off. There might also be cases where the injured party is going from the approaching train, and continued to remain on the track, when the engineer should warn, and, as a last resort, stop his train, upon the idea that the person did not see or hear the train, and was not aware of its approach. But no such facts exist in this case as the engineer had the right to assume that the intestate, an old but not disabled man, who was meeting the train, saw and heard it, one or both, and would get off the track before the engine met him, notwithstanding a delay in doing so. Neither does the proof show that the intestate could not get out of the way at the point where he was injured. True, the plaintiff's proof shows that the track was elevated with sloping embankments from 4 to 5 feet on each side, with weeds and briars where the embankments ended, but this does not show that the intestate could not have gotten off the track or that the engineer did not have the right to assume that he would not do so. Presumptively the engineer had the right to assume that the intestate was aware of the approach of the train, and that he would get out of the way before it struck him, notwithstanding he may have encountered a slight embankment and weeds and briars in doing so; and unless this presumption was overcome, by showing that some disability to get out of the way existed, either due to the condition of the person, track, or other cause, and that the

Stewart v. Omaha & C. B. St. Ry. Co

engineer was aware of such disability, the defendant was entitled to the general charge.

The trial court erred in permitting the plaintiff to introduce in evidence the ordinance of the town of Ozark, as it was immaterial to the issue. In the first place, the collision was not within the corporate limits of the town, secondly, if it had occurred in said t wn, a violation of the ordinance would only show initial or antecedent negligence, and not subsequent negligence as counted on in count 1 of the complaint.

The judgment of the circuit court is reversed and the cause is remanded.

Reversed and remanded.

DOWDELL, C. J., and SAYRE and EVANS, JJ., concur.

STEWART v. OMAHA & C. B. ST. RY. CO.

(Supreme Court of Nebraska. Jan. 9, 1911.)

[129 N. W. Rep. 440.]

Street Railroads—Rights in Street.*—A street railway company and an ordinary traveler have equal rights of travel on the street of a city but each must observe due care to avoid accidents, taking into account the fact that the street car is confined to the track while pedestrians have freedom of movement.

Street Railroads—Operation—Care Required at Street Intersection.†—The employees in charge of the operation of a street car are held to great caution when crossing a street intersection at a point where a car upon the opposite track is or has been, very recently discharging passengers. The motorman should keep a sharp lookout, give ample and timely warning of the approach of the car, and have it under such control that it can be readily stopped if necessary.

Street Railroads—Collision—Actions—Questions for Jury.—Questions as to whether a bell was sounded or as to whether the rate of speed of the car was excessive where the evidence is conflicting, should be submitted to the jury.

(Syllabus by the Court.)

---

*See third foot-note of Donohoe v. Portland Ry. Co. (Ore.), 31 R. R. R. 66, 60 Am. & Eng. R. Cas., N. S., 66; last paragraph of footnote of Carroll v. Boston Elev. Ry. (Mass.), 36 R. R. R. 401, 59 Am. & Eng. R. Cas., N. S., 401; foot-note of Denver City Tramway Co. v. Wright (Colo.), 36 R. R. R. 360, 59 Am. & Eng. R. Cas., N. S., 360; first foot-note of Palmer v. Portland Ry., etc., Co. (Ore.), 38 R. R. R. 68, 59 Am. & Eng. R. Cas., N. S., 68.

†See first foot-note of Engvall v. Des Moines City Ry. Co. (Iowa), 35 R. R. R. 266, 58 Am. & Eng. R. Cas., N. S., 266; second foot-note of South, etc., Ry. Co. v. Crutcher (Ky.), 35 R. R. R. 199, 58 Am. & Eng. R. Cas., N. S., 199.

Stewart *v.* Omaha & C. B. St. Ry. Co

Appeal from District Court, Douglass County; Redick, Judge.

Action by Robert A. Stewart against the Omaha & Council Bluffs Street Railway Company. Judgment for plaintiff, and defendant appeals. Affirmed.

W. J. Connell and *Jno. L. Webster,* for appellant.
H. C. Brome and *Clinton Brome,* for appellee.

LETTON, J.   A statement of the evidence given at a former trial of this case may be found in the opinion in Stewart *v.* Omaha & Council Bluffs St. Ry. Co., 83 Neb. 97, 118 N. W. 1106.   At the second trial, the result was a verdict for the plaintiff, from which defendant has appealed.   At this trial much of the testimony taken at the former trial was read and some other testimony adduced.   The evidence on behalf of the plaintiff as to the distance he was carried and the place where the north-bound car stopped is practically the same as at the former trial. His testimony now is that the car from which he alighted was from 10 to 20 feet away when he looked to the south, while at the former trial he said he thought it was about 10 feet.   As to this he was not positive, however.   A plat is in evidence which shows that, if he had looked to the south from the point where he alighted at a time when the south-bound car was 10 feet away, he would have had an unobstructed view of the other track for a long distance, except so far as his view was cut off by the south-bound car.

The plaintiff's testimony is that in his opinion the car that struck him was moving at the rate of about 20 miles an hour. The motorman and other employees of defendant testify that the north-bound car was moving at the rate of about 8 miles an hour when the plaintiff was struck, and that he was struck when he was about the middle of the intersection.   On the former appeal we held that there was sufficient evidence that the car was being operated at a dangerous rate of speed, and of negligence in failing to give sufficient warning of its approach to require the submission of those questions to a jury, and we further held that the evidence of contributory negligence was not clear enough to justify the court in directing a verdict for the defendant on that account.

The defendant claims that new and additional evidence was produced at the trial destructive of any interference that the plaintiff had used reasonable prudence in stepping in front of the approaching car in the manner he did, and also that the evidence fails to show any negligence on its part.   A large number of cases have been collected through the industry of counsel which hold, in substance, that under facts somewhat similar to those in this case plaintiff will be held as a matter of law to be guilty of such negligence as will preclude a recovery.   What-

Stewart *v.* Omaha & C. B. St. Ry. Co

ever the rule in some states may be with respect to the rights
of pedestrians and street cars upon the streets of a city, the law
in this state is settled that neither the street car nor the pedestrian
has any priority or privileged right over the other, that an electric
street railway company and an ordinary traveler upon the street
are required to observe an equal degree of care to prevent accidents, and that neither has a right of way superior to that of the
other. Omaha St. Ry. Co. *v.* Cameron, 43 Neb. 297, 61 N. W.
606; Mathiesen *v.* Omaha St. Ry. Co., 3 Neb. (unof.) 747, 97
N. W. 243; Omaha St. Ry. Co. *v.* Matheisen, 73 Neb. 820, 103
N. W. 666; Olney *v.* O. & C. B. St. Ry. Co., 78 Neb. 767, 111
N. W. 784. We agree with counsel for defendant that under
ordinary circumstances one who negligently attempts to cross a
street railway track in front of an approaching car cannot recover for injuries caused by a collision therewith, unless those
in charge willfully or wantonly produce the collision, or fail to
exercise ordinary care to prevent the accident after knowledge
of the probable danger. Harris *v.* Lincoln T. Co., 78 Neb. 681,
111 N. W. 580; Wood *v.* Omaha & C. B. St. R. Co., 84 Neb. 282,
120 N. W. 1121, 22 L. R. A. (N. S.) 228. But the crucial question is whether or not the person injured negligently attempted
to cross. We find no evidence in the record which leads us to
change the conclusion we arrived at on the former appeal, that
under the circumstances of this case the question of whether the
plaintiff was negligent or not was a matter for the jury to determine. We think that the employees in charge of a street car
should be held to great caution when crossing a street intersection at a point where a car upon the opposite track is or very
recently has been discharging passengers, that the motorman should
keep a sharp lookout, give ample and timely warning of the approach of the car, and have it under such control that he can
promptly stop it upon the appearance of danger. This seems
to be the more humane and modern doctrine. We see no reason
to adopt one which will in any degree relax the care and caution
of employees engaged in the operation of such dangerous instrumentalities as electrically operated street railways within the
busy streets of a city.

The Supreme Court of Minnesota recently had before it for
consideration the question of the relative degree of care required
of pedestrians and the motorman in charge of a street car approaching a crossing where a street car upon a parallel track is
discharging passengers. The opinion collects the authorities
and reaches the same conclusion as that arrived at by this court.
Bremer *v.* St. Paul C. R. Co., 107 Minn. 326, 120 N. W. 382, 21
L. R. A. (N. S.) 887. Other authorities are collected in the
note to it in 21 L. R. A. (N. S.) 887. This is the rule adopted
in states containing cities of the magnitude of New York, Chicago, Washington, Cincinnati, Cleveland, St. Paul, and Min-

Stewart *v.* Omaha & C. B. St. Ry. Co

neapolis. Pelletreau *v.* Met. St. R. Co., 74 App. Div. 192, 77 N. Y. Supp. 386, affirmed in 174 N. Y. 503, 66 N. E. 1113; Dobert *v.* Troy City R. Co., 91 Hun, 28, 36 N. Y. Supp. 105; Chicago City R. Co. *v.* Robinson, 127 Ill. 9, 18 N. E. 772, 4 L. R. A. (N. S.) 126, 11 Am. St. Rep. 87; Capitol Traction Co. *v.* Lusby, 12 App. D. C. (D. C.) 295; Cincinnati St. Ry. Co. *v.* Snell, 54 Ohio St. 197, 43 N. E. 207, 32 L. R. A. 276. A case which perhaps goes to the limit in holding street car companies liable under such circumstances is Louisville C. R. Co. *v.* Hudgins, 124 Ky. 79, 98 S. W. 275, 30 Ky. Law Rep. 316, 7 L. R. A. (N. S.) 152. We merely cite this case as showing the modern tendency, and not as indicating that this court would take the same view under like circumstances.

2. As to the claim that there is no proof of negligence, no one except the conductor and motorman seems to have heard the gong or bell until just an instant before the plaintiff was struck. Several witnesses were standing upon the street corner and none of them heard it. If the bell had been ringing loudly when the plaintiff was within a few feet of the track, it is probable that he would have noticed it, although the fact that he did not hear it is not conclusive that it was not rung. People often absent-mindedly disregard the most obvious warnings. The testimony being conflicting it was for the jury to consider.

3. The motorman testified that the car was moving at the rate of eight miles an hour. The district court instructed the jury that eight miles an hour might be a negligent rate of speed under some circumstances. This is strongly urged as erroneous, but we see nothing wrong in it. If a street car approaching behind another car at the rate of eight miles an hour without signals of its approach and at a point where persons alighting from another car might reasonably be expected to appear, this might be a negligent rate of speed, while ordinarily eight miles an hour is not a negligent rate. The question as to whether the rate of speed was negligent under the circumstances was properly left to the jury, and we think the evidence sustains the verdict.

4. Defendant complains that the court erred in permitting the plaintiff to give his opinion as to the rate of speed of the car that struck him. He was asked whether he could approximately state the speed, to which he replied affirmatively. He was then asked what his judgment was as to the speed of the car at the time it struck him. Counsel for defendant objected that no proper foundation had been laid for such testimony, and was allowed to conduct a lengthy cross-examination for the purpose of eliciting the facts upon which the witness based his estimate. It is apparent from this cross-examination that his opinion was based upon his observations during the short interval from the time he saw the car until he was struck, from a view of the

Stewart *v.* Omaha & C. B. St. Ry. Co

buildings and surrounding objects with respect to the moving car, and from the force with which it struck him. He testified that he thought the car was moving at the rate of 20 miles an hour, but it might be more and it might be less. This is very indefinite. We are inclined to think that, his opportunities for observation being so limited, his opinion was of little or no value, but, since all of these facts were before the jury, we think defendant suffered no prejudice by allowing them to determine for themselves what weight they would give to his opinion. Counsel himself argues that from his cross-examination it clearly appeared that the plaintiff was utterly unable to judge speed. Probably the jury took this view, and believed the testimony of the defendant on this point.

5. It is also urged that it was error to instruct the jury that the burden of proof was upon the defendant to show the fact of contributory negligence on the part of plaintiff. This, however, is settled law in this state. Rapp *v.* Sarpy County, 71 Neb. 382, 385, 98 N. W. 1042, 102 N. W. 242. We think counsel misapprehends the instruction given. He argues that, if the plaintiff was guilty of negligence directly contributing to his own injuries and this appeared from his own testimony, he could not recover. But the instruction expressly took care that the jury were not misled by saying: "If you find from a preponderance of the testimony offered by both parties that the plaintiff was guilty of negligence in attempting to cross the track in the manner and under all the facts and circumstances in evidence before you, and that his negligence directly contributed in any degree to the cause of his injury, then the plaintiff cannot recover and you should find for the defendant."

The facts in this case with respect to contributory negligence lie very close to the line, but the whole matter was for the jury.

We find no error, and the judgment of the district court is affirmed.

REESE, C. J., not sitting.

PIERSON *et al. v.* NORTHERN PAC. RY. CO.

(Supreme Court of Washington, Jan. 4, 1911.).

[112 Pac. Rep. 509.]

Parties—Capacity to Sue—Filing Name of Firm—Waiver of Objection.—Under Laws 1907, c. 145, providing for the filing of the names of persons doing business under an assumed name, and that no person carrying on business under such a name can sue in the courts of this state without alleging and proving that they have filed a certificate, the objection to the capacity of partners to sue because of failure to file such a certificate is waived where it is not presented by demurrer or answer.

Carriers—Carriage of Live Stock—Limitation of Liability—Effect.*—A contract for the shipment of live stock, stating the value of each of the animals shipped, if freely and fairly entered into, measures the rights and obligations of the parties to the contract.

Carriers—Carriage of Live Stock—Action for Injuries—Evidence.—In an action for injury to live stock, evidence held insufficient to impeach a contract limiting the liability of the carrier for injuries.

Carriers—Carriage of Live Stock—Limitation of Liability—Validity.†—That a contract limiting the liability of a carrier was not read or explained to the shipper of live stock, that he asked no questions, and that the contract was signed hurriedly, does not relieve the shipper from its obligations.

Carriers—Carriage of Live Stock—Limitation of Liability—Consideration.—Where a contract limiting the liability of a carrier of live stock recites, as the consideration, a reduced rate for the shipment, it is presumed that a fair consideration was given, and such a consideration need not be proved.

Carriers—Carriage of Live Stock—Limitation of Liability—Effect of Violation of Statute.—That the injury to live stock shipped was caused by confining the stock in a car for more than 28 hours, in violation of a federal statute, does not relieve the shipper from the limitation of liability in contract of shipment.

Carriers—Carriage of Live Stock—Limitation of Liability—Notice of Claim for Injury.‡—An agreement by a shipper of live stock that,

*See first foot-note of Atlantic C. L. R. Co. *v* Coachman (Fla.), 36 R. R. R. 775, 59 Am. & Eng. R. Cas., N. S., 775: second foot-note of Pittsburg, etc., R. Co. *v.* Mitchell (Ind.), 36 R. R. R. 760, 59 Am. & Eng. R. Cas., N. S., 760; last foot-note of Stringfield *v.* Southern Ry. Co. (N. Car.), 35 R. R. R. 624, 58 Am. & Eng. R. Cas., N S., 624.

†See last foot-note of Bartett *v.* Oregon R., etc., Co. (Wash.), 35 R R. R. 400, 58 Am. & Eng. R. Cas., N. S., 400; second foot-note of McIntosh *v.* Oregon R. & N. Co. (Idaho), 33 R. R. R. 768, 56 Am. & Eng. R. Cas., N. S., 768.

‡See foot-note of Atchison, etc., R. Co. *v.* Coffin (Ariz.), 36 R. R. R. 428, 59 Am. & Eng. R. Cas., N. S., 428; first foot-note of Cleveland, etc., Ry. Co. *v.* Rudy (Ind.), 35 R. R. R. 120, 58 Am. & Eng. R. Cas., N. S., 120.

as a condition precedent to a recovery for loss or injury to any of
the stock, he will give notice in writing of his claim therefor to some
agent of the company before the stock has been removed from the
place of destination or mingled with other stock, is unreasonable and
inapplicable to animals surviving, where the nature and extent of the
injury could not be ascertained with any degree of certainty within
the limited time.

**Carriers—Carriage of Live Stock—Limitation of Liability—Notice
of Claim for Injury.**—Such agreement has no application to animals
which died before their removal from the place of destination.

Department 2.   Appeal from Superior Court, Spokane County;
E. H. Sullivan, Judge.

Action by Victor Pierson and another, doing business under
the name of Pierson Brothers, against the Northern Pacific Railway
Company. From a judgment in favor of plaintiffs, defendant
appeals. Reversed and remanded.

*Edward J. Cannon, Arthur B. Lee, George M. Ferris, Charles
E. Swan,* and *Thomas A. E. Lally,* for appellant.
D. W. Hurn and *C. C. Upton,* for respondents.

RUDKIN, C. J. On the evening of August 6, 1906, the plaintiffs,
Pierson Bros., shipped a car load of horses over the Oregon
Short Line Railroad from Dillon, Mont., to Silver Bow, Mont., a
distance of 60 miles. On the arrival of the train at the latter
point soon after midnight of the same day, the car containing the
horses was transferred from the Oregon Short Line to the road
of the defendant company for shipment to Sandpoint, Idaho.
Before the train left Silver Bow for Sandpoint, the plaintiff
Victor Pierson, who had charge of the horses, entered into the
common form of live stock contract with the defendant company,
which contained the following stipulations and provisions, among
others: "And it is hereby further agreed that the value of the
live stock to be transported under this contract does not exceed
the following mentioned sums, to wit: Each horse, seventy-five
dollars; each mule, seventy-five dollars; each stallion, one hundred
dollars; each jack, one hundred dollars; each ox or steer, fifty
dollars; each bull, fifty dollars; each cow, thirty dollars; each
calf, ten dollars; each pig, ten dollars; each sheep or goat, three
dollars; such valuation being that whereon the rate of compensation
to said carrier for its services and risks connected with said
property is based. * * * The said shipper further agrees
that as a condition precedent to his right to recover any damages
for loss or injury to any of said stock, he will give
notice in writing of his claim therefor to some officer or
station agent of the said company before said stock has
been removed from the place of destination or mingled with other
stock." The car arrived at Sandpoint on the afternoon of

Pierson et al. *v.* Northern Pac. Ry. Co

August 8th, and after their removal from the train 11 head of the horses died, and the remaining 8 head were materially injured through the alleged negligence of the defendant in the course of the shipment. The present action was instituted to recover damages for the loss thus sustained. A more detailed statement of the case will be found in Pierson *v.* Northern Pacific Ry., 52 Wash. 595, 100 Pac. 999. From a judgment in favor of the plaintiffs, the railroad company has appealed.

The first assignment of error is based on the denial of a motion for nonsuit, interposed at the close of the respondents' testimony, on the ground that they failed to allege or prove a compliance with chapter 145 of Laws of 1907, which provides for the filing of the names of persons doing business under an assumed name, and that "no person or persons carrying on, conducting or transacting business as aforesaid, or having an interest therein, shall hereafter be entitled to maintain any suit in any of the courts of this state without alleging and proving that such person or persons have filed a certificate as provided for in section 1 hereof, and failure to file such certificate shall be prima facie evidence of fraud in securing credit."

Waiving the question whether "Pierson Brothers" is an assumed name, and whether the act applies to a copartnership doing business in the state of Idaho, we held, in Rothchild Bros. *v.* Mahoney, 51 Wash. 633, 99 Pac. 1031, that section 7 of the act of March 12, 1907 (Laws 1907, p. 270), which contains a similar provision relating to the commencement and maintenance of suits by corporations, only goes to the capacity to sue, and that the objection is waived unless raised by demurrer or answer. That case is decisive of the question here presented.

The remaining assignments of error are based on the refusal of the court to give effect to the stipulations in the contract of shipment as above set forth. If this contract was freely and fairly entered into, it measures the rights and obligations of the parties under repeated rulings of this and other courts. Hill *v.* Northern Pacific R. Co., 33 Wash. 697, 74 Pac. 1054; Jensen *v.* Spokane Falls & N. R. Co., 51 Wash. 448, 98 Pac. 1124; Windmiller *v.* Northern Pac. R. Co., 52 Wash. 613, 101 Pac. 225; Gomm *v.* Oregon R. & Nav. Co., 52 Wash. 685, 101 Pac. 361, 25 L. R. A. (N. S.) 537; Hart *v.* Pennsylvania R. Co., 112 U. S. 331, 5 Sup. Ct. 151, 28 L. Ed. 717.

The testimony offered by the respondents to impeach the contract is, as a matter of law, utterly insufficient for that purpose. The following given by Victor Pierson, one of the respondents, is the only testimony bearing upon that question: "Q. Who presented that contract to you for signature, if you know? A. Why, supposed to be the agent, or I thought it was the agent. Q. What did he say to you when he came to you with it? A. 'Are you the man that owns this car of horses?' I said, 'Yes,

Pierson et al. v. Northern Pac. Ry. Co

sir,' and then, 'Well,' he says, 'you got to come in here and sign this contract if you want to go. You have only 10 minutes. because they are ready to pull out.' And I went in and signed the contract. Q. Did you say anything to him when he said that to you? A. I said that I had a contract. Q. What did he say? A. 'Well,' he said, 'you got to sign this contract in order to go your horses as well as yourself.' Q. What did you do then or say? A. I just went in and signed the contract, took one of them. Q. Where did you sign the contract? A. I signed the contract in the office. I went into the office and signed the contract, or two of them rather, and I got one of them and walked right out of the depot and went right to the train. We started right out of the yards, but backed in again. Q. What kind of an office was that? That is, how many rooms did you go into? A. It had on room, just one room. Q. How was that room lighted? A. With one lamp. Q. What, if anything, did this contract lay on when you signed it? A. Laid on the desk, or whatever you might term it, as in front or kind of to one side of the partition, and he says just sign up here. It was quite dark in there on account of the lamp was small, and I just signed it, and I was in a hurry to catch the train because the car had already passed. Q. Where was that lamp with reference to where you signed? A. It was right on the desk, the counter. Q. How far from where you signed? A. Just a foot or two. Q. Then you could see to read the contract? A. Not plain; no, sir. Q. What did the agent say to you, if anything, about when your car was going to leave while you were in there with him signing the contract? A. In 10 minutes. Q. Where were you when he told you that? Were you in the office, or was that before you went into the office? A. Just as we went into the office. Q. Did he say anything to you at the time you signed that contract about there being more than one rate of freight? A. No, sir. Q. Did he say anything to you at the time as to what rate of freight you would have to pay under that contract? A. No, sir. Q. Was anything said at any time or place about rates. A. No, sir. Q. Was anything said to you in any way about the value of the horses? A. Nothing. Q. Have you told us all that was said between you and the agent as far as you can tell us at the time you signed that contract? A. As far as I can recollect now. It is so long ago that is all I can recollect. Q. Was there anything said about a pass or your having a pass? A. Yes, sir. Q. Who said it to you, and when? A. This man that had the the contract. Q. What did he say? A. He said, 'This is your pass for yourself and horses.' Q. When did he say that? A. When I was in the office. It was before—after I signed the contract. Q. Well, after signing the contract, what did you do? A. I went right to the caboose and we pulled right out. Q. How long after you got on the caboose before it pulled out?

A. Just a few minutes, not over five minutes. Q. Where did it go then? A. It went out of the yard limits and backed in again. Something wrong with the train, the boys said; that is, the trainmen."

At another point in his testimony the witness testified that he did not read or examine his contract until the horses were dying at Sandpoint two or three days after its execution. The claim of the witness that he already had a contract for the shipment to Sandpoint is not borne out by the testimony. The Oregon Short Line contract only covered the shipment from Dillon to Silver Bow, and the freight was only paid between these points. It is a significant fact that this was also a limited liability contract, differing in degree but not in kind from the contract now under consideration. Under the first contract the animals were shipped as range horses, and the liability in such cases was limited to not exceeding $10 per head. The fact that the contract was not read or explained to the shipper, or that he was asked no questions, or that the contract was signed hurriedly, cannot be permitted to relieve the respondents from its obligations. Written contracts will prove of little avail if parties can avoid the burdens imposed by signing in haste and closing their eyes to their contents. "The shipper cannot evade the limitations imposed by the special contract by showing that he executed it hurriedly or without due care, nor by showing that he was ignorant of the provisions of the contract. If he executes the contract by affixing his signature, or by accepting without objection a receipt containing the limitation, he will be conclusively presumed to have assented to its provisions; no fraud on the part of the carrier appearing." 5 Am. Enc. of Law (2d Ed.) p. 300. "A contract, ex vi termini, implies the assent of two or more minds to the same proposition. It follows, therefore, if one sign a written instrument containing mutual stipulations between himself and another, without any knowledge of its contents, there will not be in fact, in the strict sense of the term, a contract between them, though in a legal sense there may be. Where a party of mature years and sound mind, being able to read and write, without any imposition or artifice to throw him off his guard, deliberately signs a written agreement without informing himself as to the nature of its contents, he will nevertheless be bound, for in such case the law will not permit him to allege, as a matter of defense, his ignorance of that which it was his duty to know, particularly where the means of information are within his immediate reach, and he neglects to avail himself of them. Applying this elementary principle to the case in hand, it was clearly the duty of appellant to have examined the contract in question, and fully advised himself as to its contents, before signing it; and if, by a failure to perform this duty, he has sustained an injury, he must suffer the consequences, unless such failure was occasioned by the fraud or artifice of appellee—and this, we understand, appellant claims was the case." Black *v.* W., St. L. & P. Ry. Co., 111 Ill. 351, 53 Am. Rep. 628. "The shipper was not obliged to sign the contract without reading it. and, if he saw fit to do so, he must take the consequences." Johnstone *v.* Richmond, 39 S. C. 55, 17 S. E. 512. "It would tend to disturb the force of all contracts if one in possession of ordinary capacity and intelligence were allowed to sign a contract and act under it in the enjoyment of all its advantages, and then to repudiate it upon the ground that its terms were not brought to his attention. In the absence of all fraud, misrepresentation, or mistake, it must be presumed that he read the contract. and assented to its provisions." Bethea *v.* Northwestern R. R. Co., 26 S. C. 96, 1 S. E. 376. "There being no special parol contract, and there being nothing in the written contract contrary to public policy, plaintiff cannot now assert that the written contract is not binding because he signed it in haste. without reading." Hengstler *v.* Flint & P. M. Ry. Co., 125 Mich. 530, 84 N. W. 1067. See, also, N. C. & St. L. Ry. *v.* Stone & Haslett. 112 Tenn. 348, 79 S. W. 1031, 105 Am. St. Rep. 955; McMillan *v.* Mich. Southern Ry., 16 Mich. 79, 93 Am. Dec. 208; Arthur et al. *v.* T. & P. Ry., 139 Fed. 127, 71 C. C. A. 391; Cau *v.* T. & P. Ry., 194 U. S. 431, 24 Sup. Ct. 663, 48 L. Ed. 1053. But his rule is elementary. and sound public policy would not permit of the adoption of any other. We are therefore clearly of opinion that the rights of the parties are measured by the limitations contained in this contract.

It is said that no evidence was offered tending to show that the stock was shipped at a reduced rate, but the contract so recites, and there is no evidence to the contrary. "In the absence of any proof to the contrary, it will be presumed that a fair consideration was given for the special contract in the way of reduced rates of transportation or of special privileges, and such a consideration need not be proved." 5 Am. & Eng. Ency. of Law (2d Ed.) p. 300.

Again, it is said that the injury was caused by confining the stock in the car for more than 28 hours, in violation of a federal statute, and that the contract does not relieve the carrier in such cases. We are not aware that any such distinction exists. This was an act of negligence and nothing more. and in the Windmiller Case, supra, we held that the limited liability would prevail even in a case of theft.

As stated above, the contract contained a further stipulation that, as a condition precedent to the right to recover damages for loss or injury to any of the stock, the shipper would give notice in writing of his claim therefor to some officer or station agent of the company. before the stock was removed from the place of destination or mingled with other stock. This clause

Pierson et al. *v.* Northern Pac. Ry. Co

of the contract would perhaps be effectual in some cases; but in a case like the present, where the nature and extent of the injuries to the animals surviving could not be ascertained, with any degree of certainty, within the limited time provided in the contract, the stipulation is unreasonable and inapplicable. Western R. Co. *v.* Harwell, 97 Ala. 341, 11 South. 781; Harned *v.* Missouri Pac. R. Co., 51 Mo. App. 482; Gulf, etc., R. Co. *v.* Stanley. 89 Tex. 42, 33 S. W. 109; Houston, etc., R. Co. *v.* Davis, 11 Tex. Civ. App. 24, 31 S. W. 308; Ormsby *v.* Union Pac. R. Co. (C. C.) 4 Fed. 170. Nor has it any application to the animals which died before their removal from the place of destination. Kansas, etc., R. Co. *v.* Ayers, 63 Ark. 331, 38 S. W. 515.

On the entire record we are therefore of opinion that the recovery should have been limited to $75 per head for the animals that died, with legal interest from the date of the commencement of the action, and to such further sum as the jury might award for injuries to the remaining animals. Inasmuch as the record does not disclose the amount allowed by the jury for this latter claim, we are unable to direct a final judgment at this time. The judgment will therefore be reversed, and the cause remanded for further proceedings not inconsistent with this opinion.

It is so ordered.

DUNBAR, CROW, CHADWICK, and MORRIS, JJ., concur.

CENTRAL OF GEORGIA RY. CO. *v.* CHICAGO VARNISH CO.

(Supreme Court of Alabama, Nov. 24, 1910.)

[53 So. Rep. 832.]

Carriers—Freight—Means of Transportation—Duty of Carrier.—A carrier must provide safe and suitable cars for transporting goods, and cannot avoid liability for not doing so by using another's cars, the latter being its agent; but, if the consignor undertakes to furnish the cars used in transportation, the carrier is not liable for a loss resulting from their defective condition.

Carriers—Freight—Means of Transportation.—Where the freight was shipped in cars leased by the carrier from the consignor under an agreement by which the carrier was to keep the cars in repair at the consignor's cost, the carrier was liable for loss of freight caused by defects therein.

Carriers—Freight—Loss—Liability—What Law Governs.—The liability of the several connecting carriers with respect to loss of freight en route are to be determined by the law as it was when the contract of shipment was made.

Carriers—Freight—Liability of Connecting Carriers.—Before the enactment of Act June 29, 1906, c. 3591, § 7, 34 Stat. 595 (U. S. Comp. St. Supp. 1909, p. 1166), and Code Ala. 1907, § 5546, in effect making the initial carrier responsible for any loss or injury caused by any carrier to which the property is delivered, or over whose line it passes, each of several connecting carriers was responsible only for loss occurring on its own line.

Carriers—Freight—Loss—Actions—Presumptions.[*]—Under the presumption that a fact, continuous in its nature, continues to exist until the contrary is shown, it is presumed, as against a connecting carrier, that the goods were received in the same order as when received by the initial carrier; but such presumption does not affect the liability of the latter, and when loss is shown the burden is upon the initial carriers, or any subsequent carrier shown to have had possession of the goods, to prove that they were not lost while in its possession, if they are sued for such loss.

Trial—Instructions—Construction.—Instructions should be considered in connection with the facts of the particular case.

Trial—Responsiveness of Answer—Who May Object—An objection that answers to questions asked were not strictly responsive can only be taken by the party asking such questions.

Appeal and Error—Motion for New Trial—Necessity.—Where the

[*]See first foot-note of Kansas City So. Ry. Co. *v.* Carl (Ark.), 15 R. R. R. 406, 58 Am. & Eng. R. Cas., N. S., 406; Gibson *v.* Little Rock etc., R. Co. (Ark.), 35 R. R. R. 690, 58 Am. & Eng. R. Cas., N. S., 690; foot-note of Colbath *v.* Bangor & A. R. Co. (Me.), 34 R. R. R. 468, 57 Am. & Eng. R. Cas., N. S., 488.

Central of Georgia Ry. Co. *v.* Chicago Varnish Co

question of excessive damages was not called to the trial court's attention by motion for new trial or otherwise, that question cannot be assigned as error on appeal.

Appeal from Circuit Court, Geneva County; H. A. Pearce, Judge.

Action by the Chicago Varnish Company against the Central of Georgia Railway Company. From a judgment for plaintiff, defendant appeals. Affirmed.

R. D. Crawford, for appellant.
C. D. Carmichael, for appellee.

SAYRE, J.   This suit was for a failure to deliver 448 gallons of turpentine spirits. The complaint is in code form, and is ex contractu. The spirits had been consigned by the Jackson Lumber Company to the plaintiff company in Chicago in 1905. When the tank car in which the shipment was made arrived at its destination, it was found that a part of its original contents (according to plaintiff's contention) had disappeared. Plaintiff insisted that the shortage resulted from a leak in the tank. Pleas 7 and 8 put forward the defense that the spirits had been shipped in a car belonging to and furnished by the consignor and delivered to the defendant for use in the transportation of its turpentine, and that the loss occurred by reason of a defect in the tank at the time of delivery, and without negligence on the part of defendant. To this plaintiff replied, to state the substance of its special replication, that at and prior to the date of the shipment the defendant had a lease of the car from the consignor under an agreement by which the consignor was to furnish defendant with cars for the shipment of consignor's turpentine, defendant paying rent for the use of same, and keeping them in repair at the consignor's cost, and that the car in question had been furnished and used for the shipment of the turpentine under said agreement. Demurrer to this replication was overruled, and that ruling is assigned for error. It is the duty of the carrier to provide safe and suitable vehicles for the carriage of goods. He cannot avoid this responsibility by using the cars of another—this upon the theory that in such case the person furnishing the cars becomes the agent of the carrier. But, where the consignor undertakes to furnish cars, it cannot in reason be that the carrier is responsible for a loss which arises out of the condition of the cars alone; and pleas 7 and 8 stated a case which, in facie, called for the application of this principle. The replication, however, added a material element to the case so stated, by showing that, notwithstanding the shipper furnished the car, the ordinary rule of responsibility obtained between the parties, because the duty in respect to the condition of the car was left by the contract under which it was furnished where the law would have put it if the car had been furnished by defendant. The demurrer was properly ruled.

The shipment was to pass, and the car containing it did pass, over the lines of several connecting carriers. The bill of lading contained the usual stipulation exempting the initial carrier from liability for loss or damage occurring beyond its own terminal. Defendant's engagement, therefore, was to safely carry the goods to its own terminal and there put them in due course of shipment over the line of the proximate connecting carrier. As the law then was—and by the law of that time the rights of the parties here are to be determined—each carrier was responsible only for the loss or injury occurring on its own line. Jones v. C. S. & M. R. R. Co., 89 Ala. 376, 8 South. 61; McNeil v. Atlantic Coast Line, 161 Ala. 319, 49 South. 797. Federal and state statutes, passed since the date of the contract in litigation, have made such stipulations void, and hold the initial carrier responsible for any loss, damage, or injury caused by the receiving carrier or by any common carrier, railroad, or transportation company to which property may be delivered, or over whose lines it may pass. Act June 29, 1906, c. 3591, § 7, 34 Stat. 595 (U. S. Comp. St. Supp. 1909, p. 1166); Code 1907, § 5546. It results that the plaintiff must show the goods to have been in the possession of the carrier sued at the time of the loss or injury. This may, of course, be shown by circumstantial evidence. To effectuate a just conclusion in such cases the law has recourse to the evidential presumption that a fact, continuous in its nature, continues to exist until the contrary appears, and, loss or injury being shown, lays the burden of accounting for it on the bailee whose duty requires him to know. When receipt of the goods by any subsequent carrier is shown, it is presumed, as against such carrier, that the goods were then in the same order as when received by the initial carrier; but this presumption does not concern nor benefit the initial carrier. Loss or injury being shown, the burden is then cast upon the initial carrier, or upon the delivering carrier, or upon any intermediate carrier shown to have been in possession, to prove that the goods were not lost or injured while in its possession, as one or the other may be sued. This we understand to be the rule sanctioned by the decisions of this court. Ga. Pac. Rwy. Co. v. Hughart, 90 Ala. 36, 8 South. 62; Louisville & Nashville R. R. Co. v. Jones, 100 Ala. 263, 14 South. 114; Cooper v. Ga. Pac. Rwy. Co., 92 Ala. 329, 9 South. 159, 25 Am. St. Rep. 59; M. & E. R. R. Co. v. Culver, 75 Ala. 587, 51 Am. Rep. 483. See also Moore on Carriers, p. 490, where cases to this general effect are collated from other jurisdictions. The court's instructions to the jury are to be considered in their application to the facts of the case on trial. The suit was against the initial carrier, whose receipt of the car was not denied. The court properly instructed the jury, in substance, that if the car was loaded, in the beginning with plaintiff's turpentine spirits in the quantity alleged—a question left to the jury—it was for the defendant to account for the entire quantity by showing its delivery to the next succeeding carrier.

We have found no error in those assignments relating to rulings upon the admissibility of evidence, which are noticed in argument. In each case relevant facts only were permitted to go to the jury. If the answers in some instances were not strictly responsive, that was an objection which could be taken only by the party asking the questions.

The amount of damages assessed by the jury may have been somewhat in excess of the amount properly assessable under the evidence. If so, the trial court should have been given an opportunity to make the correction. It does not appear that this fact was called to the attention of the trial court, by motion for new trial or otherwise, or that any ruling was there invoked, or made, which can now be assigned for error. Ritch *v.* Thornton, 65 Ala. 309; Gilliland *v.* Dunn, 136 Ala. 327, 34 South. 25.

The judgment is affirmed.

Affirmed.

Dowdell, C. J., and Anderson and Evans, JJ., concur.

Eli Hurley & Son *v.* Norfolk & W. Ry. Co.

(Supreme Court of Appeals of West Virginia, Dec. 20, 1910.)

[69 S. E. Rep. 904.]

Carriers—Liability—Receipt of Goods—Warehouseman.*—If, after a common carrier has transported goods to the place to which it agreed to carry them, the consignee pays the freight on them, receipts for them, makes a contract for reshipment thereof with another carrier, and leaves them in the warehouse or freightroom of such first carrier, to await reshipment, duty and liability as carrier under the first contract are thereby changed to those of warehouseman.

Trial—Instructions—Issues.—Such a state of facts being admitted on the trial of an action to recover for loss of goods by fire, while so stored, it is error to submit to the jury the question of liability as carrier.

Carriers—Receipt of Goods—Delay in Removal.—It is proper to refuse to instruct the jury, in an action by a consignee against a carrier for loss of goods by fire at the place of delivery, that it was

---

*See foot-note of Knight *v.* Southern R. Co. (S Car.), 35 R. R. R. 393, 58 Am. & Eng. R. Cas., N. S., 393.

Eli Hurley & Son v. Norfolk & W. Ry. Co

the duty of the consignee to remove them without delay for the
law allow's a reasonable time for removal thereof.

Carriers—Contract of Carriage—Termination.*—It is proper, in
such case, to refuse to instruct that payment of the freight alone
terminates the contract of carriage.

(Syllabus by the Court.)

Error from Circuit Court. Mingo County.

Action by Eli Hurley & Son against the Norfolk & Western
Railway Company. Judgment for plaintiff, and defendant brings
error. Reversed and remanded.

Williams, Scott & Lovett, for plaintiff in error.

John S. Marcum, for defendant in error.

Poffenbarger, J. The defendant complains of a judgment
for the sum of $275.37, rendered upon the verdict of a jury in
an appeal from the judgment of a justice of the peace, in a civil
action to recover the value of merchandise, destroyed by fire in
the burning of its station and warehouse at the village of Devon,
on the theory of liability therefor as a carrier of goods, on the
one hand, and negligence as warehouseman, on the other.

The property destroyed consisted of clothing delivered to the
defendant at Cincinnati, Ohio, on the 5th day of October, 1906,
for shipment to Devon, where it arrived on the 9th day of that
month, according to memoranda and the testimony of the agent.
The ultimate destination was Argo, in the state of Kentucky,
but there was no contract of carriage to that point by the defendant. On the 13th day of the month a member of the firm of
Hurley & Son, plaintiffs, came to Devon, paid the freight, got
a receipt for the goods, and then went to the station or office of
the Big Sandy & Cumberland Railroad, a narrow-gauge road,
running from Devon, and made a contract with it for carriage
of the goods from Devon to Argo. This occurred on Saturday.
As the Big Sandy & Cumberland Road ran no freight trains on
that nor the next day, the goods remained in the freight
warehouse of the defendant. On Monday morning, about 3
o'clock, a fire broke out in a neighboring building, standing close
to the station, spread to the latter, and burned it, together with
the goods. These facts are undisputed. Some of the agents or
servants of the defendant company, having been notified of the
fire, went to the station, and removed such of the contents as
they could. They succeeded in getting out the office fixtures,
ticket case, and the express and baggage matter and some of the
freight. The place is small, and, other buildings and their contents being endangered, many of those present were engaged in
efforts to prevent the fire from spreading and save the other

*See (*) on preceding page.

Eli Hurley & Son *v.* Norfolk & W. Ry. Co

·buildings and their contents. One man says he offered his assistance to a servant of the defendant, and that he declined it, saying the railroad company had insurance sufficient to cover everything in the station. To extend or continue liability as carrier, the plaintiffs rely upon the testimony of a member of the firm to the effect that he made an inquiry for the goods on the Wednesday, next preceding the date of the fire, according to his recollection and belief, with a view to paying the freight, and was informed that they had not arrived. He says the agent, in response to the inquiry, examined the books, and then said they had not arrived. The agent denies the recollection of the alleged inquiry.

At the conclusion of the evidence, the defendant asked for several instructions, of which Nos. 1, 2, 6, 7, 8, and 9 were refused, and the benefit of the ruling thereon was saved by an exception. Instruction No. 1 amounted to a motion to direct a verdict for the defendant. The propriety of the ruling of the court on this depends upon certain legal principles in the light of which the evidence must be considered. We think the contract of carriage had been completed before the fire. The defendant was under no duty to give notice of the arrival of the goods. It is incumbent upon the shipper to watch for and remove them within a reasonable time after arrival. His failure to do this changes the character of the possession and responsibility of the defendant from that of carrier to warehouseman. As carrier a railway company is an insurer. As warehouseman it is not, and the measure of its duty is reasonable and prudent care and provision for the safety of the property. Berry *v.* W. Va., etc, Ry. Co., 44 W. Va. 538, 30 S. E. 143, 67 Am. St. Rep. 781; Hutchinson *v.* Express Co., 63 W. Va. 128, 59 S. E. 949, 14 L. R. A. (N. S.) 393. It does not matter that plaintiffs lived some miles from the station, or that the removal of the goods was attended with difficulty or inconvenience. The duty rested upon them, and these difficulties were not matters for which the defendant was in any sense responsible. Berry *v.* Railway Co., cited. All the evidence bearing on the question indicates that the goods arrived some days before the fire. Hurley's alleged call for them on Wednesday is the only circumstance, denying arrival on Tuesday, October 9th. Whether he called in the morning or evening of that day is not stated. They may have arrived on that day, after his inquiry. There was no further inquiry until Saturday. That day their previous arrival was admitted, and they could have been removed. They were left in the station to await reshipment. The defendant maintained a freight-room for that purpose as well as for storage. This was mere storage by agreement, ending liability as carrier, and establishing the relation of warehouseman and patron or depositor. The goods were there, awaiting fulfillment of the contract of carriage

Eli Hurley & Son *v.* Norfolk & W. Ry. Co

made by the plaintiffs with the Big Sandy & Cumberland Railroad Company. That company was to call for the goods. Until it did so, they were to remain in the defendant's freightroom. Plaintiffs had ample time to take them out, but elected to leave them there for safe-keeping. They not only had ample time on Saturday to remove them, but arrival and opportunity to get them at an earlier date are almost conclusively shown. No inquiry was made on Thursday or Friday, conceding one to have been made on Wednesday. Nor will it do to say that the failure of the Big Sandy & Cumberland Railroad Company to run a freight train on Saturday or Sunday before the fire constitutes any excuse. Plaintiffs elected to let the goods remain in the station until it should be able to ship them. These conclusions are fully sustained by the text in Elliott on Railroads, §§ 1412, 1443, founded upon numerous well-considered decisions.

Coming now to the question of negligence as warehouseman, we observe that the fire did not originate on the premises of the defendant, and that there is no evidence tending to show it arose from any negligence on the part of its servants or any act of theirs. Hence the only inquiry in this connection is whether there is sufficient evidence in the conduct of the servants with reference to the safety of the building or the goods after the fire was discovered to sustain the verdict. The substance of it has been stated. Nothing in it indicates that it was possible to prevent the burning of the defendant's building in which the goods were. The neighboring building in which the fire occurred stood close to it. While no effort was made to keep the fire from it, there is nothing to indicate that such an effort would have availed anything. One witness says the fire started between a store room and a saloon, which stood only four feet apart. If so, the store and a boarding house, both frame, stood between it and the station; but another witness says it started in the boarding house, the building next to the station, and only a few feet from it, a witness says only six or eight feet from the platform. In any view of the evidence, these burned buildings, all nearly connected and readily combustible, came right close to the station. Only one of the defendant's servants, the night operator, was at the station when the fire occurred. What he did before the others arrived is not disclosed. At the date of the trial, he was absent and his location unknown. The other two, rooming some distance away, responded to the alarm promptly. Of course, the fire had then made some progress. The station took fire within a half or three quarters of an hour. These two servants, deeming it impossible to save the building, gave their attention and efforts to its contents. Both say this. Others say they made no effort to save the building, but do not say it could have been saved, nor state facts from which the jury could infer it. There was a well nearby and a river close, but nobody says the fire could

Eli Hurley & Son *v.* Norfolk & W. Ry. Co

have been kept out of the building by the use of these means. All admit rapid progress of the fire and shortness of time. How long it had been in progress before the arrival of the two agents does not appear. They thought an effort to save the building, as a measure of protection to its contents, in which alone the plaintiffs had an interest, would be futile, and nobody says it would have availed. Instead of attempting it, they removed such of the contents as they could. Three witnesses, Coleman, Preece, and Charles, say they did not see these men doing much, but all three were fighting fire and saving goods at other buildings. Preece tried to save his store, rendered assistance to others, and then went to the station and found its exterior on fire. Coleman says he had no opportunity to see just what the agents did, but did see them carrying some things out. Charles says he was busy. In passing the station several times he observed closed doors of the freightroom, but admits the express office, which was in the freightroom was open. The closed doors he speaks of were only the outer doors, not the one opening into another room, through which express and baggage matter and freight was carried out. He admits he saw the agents there, does not deny their having taken things out, says only he did not see them do so, and finally admits he saw them carrying a book or two out of the express office. In passing the station he was carrying water to the boarding house. His testimony is not inconsistent with probability of the truth of all the agents say. The two who testified say all three worked diligently and removed office supplies and fixtures, express and baggage matter and freight, and continued their efforts until the fire drove them out. Nobody in a condition to know the contrary asserts it. No assistance from bystanders was asked, but nobody, except Charles, says such assistance was available. The agents say everybody was busy. Charles says the absent agent declined his offered services. Taking this as true, he does not say it would have saved all the freight or the goods of the plaintiffs, if accepted. We may say there is some evidence of negligence in all this; but, to justify refusal of the peremptory instruction, it must be sufficient to sustain a verdict. A request for such an instruction challenges the sufficiency of the evidence, and should be granted, when the state of the evidence is such as to make it the duty of the court to set aside a verdict founded upon it. Stronger evidence is required to sustain a verdict or preclude such an instruction than to justify an instruction, on the evidence, that leaves the case in the hands of the jury. State *v.* Clifford, 59 W. Va. 1, 52 S. E. 981. Our analysis of the evidence convinces us that under this rule the peremptory instruction should have been given, and, of course, this conclusion necessitates reversal. Unable to see that a better case cannot be made, we grant a new trial also.

Eli Hurley & Son *v.* Norfolk & W. Ry. Co

There was no error in refusing defendant's instruction No. 2, reciting salient facts, pertaining to liability as carrier, and leaving the question of liability as warehouseman for negligence to the jury. All of this was substantially covered by its instructions Nos. 3 and 4, which were given. Its instruction No. 6, intended to apprise the jury that the defendant was under no duty to select and save the goods of the plaintiffs in preference to others, was proper, and should have been given. They had no right of preference. In instruction No. 7, saying it was not incumbent upon the defendant to keep a night watchman at the station, was properly refused; its failure to do so not having been proved as a ground of liability. Its instruction No. 8, attempting to impose upon the plaintiff's duty to remove their goods "without delay," was properly refused. The law allowed them a reasonable time for that purpose. There was no error in the refusal of its instruction No. 9, saying payment of freight alone terminates liability as carrier, since it would exclude reasonable time for removal, allowed by law.

As the state of the evidence left no room for the jury function on the question of liability of the defendant as carrier, plaintiffs' instruction No. 1, leaving it to the jury to say whether, under all the circumstances of the case, the relation of shipper and carrier had ceased, should have been refused. The goods had been receipted for and a contract of reshipment made with another road. These facts are undisputed. Hence the question was one of law for the court. There was no error, however, in the giving of plaintiffs' instruction No. 2, submitting to the jury the question of the defendant's negligence as warehouseman; there being evidence tending slightly to prove it. The objection was likely based on the theory of total lack of such evidence.

For the reasons stated, the judgment will be reversed, the verdict set aside, and the case remanded for a new trial.

Southern Ry. Co. v. Moody.

(Supreme Court of Alabama, Dec. 1, 1910.)

[53 So. Rep. 1016.]

Damages—Direct or Remote Consequences—Breach of Contract.
—The damages recoverable for breach of contract are those flowing
directly and naturally from the breach; special damages being recoverable only when contemplated by the parties at the time the
contract was made.

Carriers—Carriage of Goods—Delay—Liability for Conversion.*—
A carrier is not liable as for converting goods unreasonably delayed, in the absence of a demand for delivery and refusal thereof
while the goods are in its possession.

**Damages—Direct or Remote Consequences—Delay in Carriage of
Goods.†**—A carrier is liable for deterioration in goods unreasonably
delayed, but not for special damages not contemplated at the time
of shipment, such as deterioration in eggs because of delay in a
shipment of material to be used in constructing packing boxes.

Appeal from Circuit Court, Jackson County; W. W. Haralson,
Judge.

Action by W. L. Moody against the Southern Railway Company. Judgment for plaintiff, and defendant appeals. Reversed
and remanded.

Lawrence E. Brown, for appellant.
Bilbro & Moody, for appellee.

Simpson, J. This action is by the appellee for damages for
failure, on the part of the appellant, a common carrier, to deliver
certain goods, to wit, certain material for constructing shipping
boxes for eggs. The facts are that the material in question was
delivered to the defendant, at Huntsville, Ala., on June 5, 1906,
for shipment to the plaintiff, at Scottsboro, Ala.; that on the
11th day of June, the goods not having been delivered, the plaintiff brought this suit; that on the 12th day of June the goods
arrived and were tendered to the plaintiff, but he refused to receive the same, as he had already ordered by telephone, and

---

*For the authorities in this series on the question, what does,
and does not, constitute conversion of freight by the carrier, see
Spokane Grain Co. *v.* Great Northern Express Co. (Wash.), 34
R. R. R. 463, 57 Am. & Eng. R. Cas., N. S., 463.

†For the authorities in this series on the subject of the right to
recover special damages against carrier of freight as affected by
carrier's knowledge or lack of knowledge of the urgency of the
shipment, or other special circumstances, see first foot-note of Chicago, etc., Ry. Co. *v.* Miles (Ark.), 35 R. R. R. 134, 58 Am. & Eng.
R. Cas., N. S., 134; Clyde Coal Co. *v.* Pittsburgh, etc., R. Co. (Penn.),
36 R. R. R. 750, 59 Am. & Eng. R. Cas., N. S., 750.

Southern Ry. Co. *v.* Moody

received, other material and shipped his eggs. There was a train each day from Huntsville to Scottsboro, leaving at 10:35 a. m., and reaching Scottsboro at 2:50 p. m. Over the objection of the defendant, the plaintiff, while on the stand as a witness, was allowed to testify that "in June eggs will depreciate 20 per cent." The court, trying the case without a jury, made a special finding of the facts, and rendered a judgment against the defendant for $20.

The decisions of this court are clear to the effect that the damages recoverable for the breach of a contract must be those which flow directly and naturally from the breach, and that any special damages claimed must be shown to have been within the contemplation of the parties at the time of making the contract. Nichols *v.* Rasch, 138 Ala. 372, 35 South. 409; Ala. Chemical Co. *v.* Geiss, 143 Ala. 591, 39 South. 255; Southern Railway Co. *v.* Coleman, 153 Ala. 266, 44 South. 837. Although the delivery of goods be delayed for an unreasonable time, the carrier cannot be charged for the conversion of the goods, unless demand has been made and refused while the goods are in its possession. Its only liability is for damages caused by the deterioration in value of the goods themselves during the time of delay. 2 Hutchinson on Carriers (3d Ed.) p. 717, § 651; 6 Cyc. 442, 444, 449. The Supreme Court of Florida has had occasion to consider a case very similar to the one now under consideration, where a carrier was sued for delay in delivering orange boxes, and damages were claimed on account of the oranges freezing, and on account of the shipper's not being able to pack and ship his oranges for the Christmas market; and that court held that, in order to hold the common carrier liable for such damages, the carrier should have been notified, at the time of shipment, of the peculiar facts and circumstances. Williams *v.* Atlantic Coast Line Railroad Co., 56 Fla. 735, 48 South. 209, 24 L. R. A. (N. S.) 134, 131 Am. St. Rep. 169. It follows that the court erred in permitting proof of the deterioration in the eggs.

There is no claim in the complaint for special damages, and no proof of general damages. The judgment of the court is reversed, and the cause remanded.

Reversed and remanded.

Dowdell, C. J., and McClellan and Mayfield, JJ., concur

Jeffries *v.* Chicago, B. & Q. Ry. Co.

(Supreme Court of Nebraska, Jan. 9, 1911.)

[129 N. W. Rep. 273.]

Appeal and Error—Review—Legal Propositions Not Germane to Evidence.—Legal propositions not germane to the evidence in the case under review will not be considered.

Carriers—Carriage of Goods—Duty to Carry without Unnecessary Delay.*—It is the duty of a railroad company, engaged as a common carrier, receiving freight to be transported, to carry it without unnecessary delay. A delay of 24 hours at a station on the way is an unnecessary delay, unless it is explained and excused by something which the law recognizes as sufficient. Under the evidence in this case, the excuse that the company had annulled a regular freight train scheduled to leave a connecting point an hour after the arrival of a car of horses at such point held not a sufficient excuse.

Carriers—Carriage of Stock—Right of Carrier to Rely upon Caretaker.—When a shipper of live stock is provided by the railroad company with free transportation for a caretaker and the caretaker actually accompanies the stock during the entire time of such shipment, the carrier has a right to rely upon the caretaker to notify its agents in charge of its train whenever he thinks the necessities of the case require the unloading or feeding and watering of such live stock.

Appeal and Error—Presentation of Question—Instructions—Duty to Request.—"Before error can be predicated upon the failure of the court to present a particular feature of a case to the jury, the party complaining should, by an appropriate instruction, request the court to charge upon that feature." German National Bank of Hastings *v.* Leonard, 40 Neb. 676, 59 N. W. 107.

Carriers—Trial — Instructions — Requests — Instructions Already Given.—A judgment will not be reversed because the trial court refused to give an instruction asked, when the substance of such instruction is included in other instructions given.

Carriers—Carriage of Stock—Contracts—Release from Liability for Negligence.†—"A common carrier of live stock cannot, by contract with a shipper, relieve, itself, either in whole or in part, from liability for injury or loss resulting from its own negligence." Chicago, R. I. & P. R. Co. *v.* Witty, 32 Neb. 275, 49 N. W. 183, 29 Am. St. Rep. 436.

---

*For the authorities in this series on the question as to what delays a carrier of freight is liable for, see first foot-note of Tiller *v.* Chicago, etc., R. Co. (Iowa), 33 R. R. R. 743, 56 Am. & Eng. R. Cas., N. S., 743; Cormack *v.* New York, etc., R. Co. (N. Y.), 33 R. R. R. 629, 56 Am. & Eng. R. Cas., N. S., 629.

†See second foot-note of Santa Fe, etc., R. Co. *v.* Grant Bros. Const. Co. (Ariz.), 36 R. R. R. 420, 59 Am. & Eng. R. Cas., N. S., 420; first foot-note of St. Louis, etc., R. Co. *v.* Copeland (Okla.), 32 R. R. R. 236, 55 Am. & Eng. R. Cas., N. S., 236.

Jeffries v. Chicago, B. & Q. Ry. Co

Appeal and Error—Harmless Error—Errors Not Affecting Substantial Right.—It is the duty of this court in reviewing a case on appeal to disregard any error or defect in the proceedings in the court below which does not affect the substantial rights of the adverse party; and, in obedience to that duty, no judgment will be reversed by reason alone of such error or defect.

(Syllabus by the Court.)

Appeal from District Court, Red Willow County; Orr, Judge.

Action by William Jeffries against the Chicago, Burlington & Quincy Railway Company. Judgment for plaintiff, and defendant appeals. Affirmed.

W. S. Morlan, Ritchie & Wolff, James E. Kelby, and *Arthur R. Wells,* for appellant.

P. E. Reeder and *E. B. Perry,* for appellee.

Fawcett, J. The issues are fairly stated in defendant's brief: "The petition in this action stated two causes of action. The first seeks to recover $250 damages to a shipment of horses from Norton, Kan., to Palisade, Neb., March 25, 1906, and the second asks for $1,300 damages to a shipment of six horses and one jack from Orleans, Neb., to Palisade, Neb., March 23, 1907. In the first cause of action the charges of negligence are (a) negligent rough handling; (b) failure to unload for the purpose of water and feed; and (c) negligent delay. In the second cause of action the same grounds of negligence are alleged as in the first, and, in addition, it is claimed that there was a verbal agreement that the said shipment should be transported on fast freight train No. 77 from Oxford to McCook. The answer to each cause of action denied the charges of negligence contained in the petition, and by the way of further answer pleaded written and printed contracts of shipment, under which it was alleged (a) that in consideration of free transportation furnished by the defendant for a caretaker who accompanied each of said shipments, it was agreed that the said animals should be loaded, unloaded, fed and watered by the owner or his agents, and that said animals were to be in the sole charge of such caretaker for the purpose of attention to and care of said animals, and the defendant should not be responsible for such attention and care, and that the plaintiff should load, unload, water and feed said animals, and that a caretaker did, in fact, accompany each shipment; (b) that the defendant should not be liable for injury to said animals in loading or unloading or injuries which said animals might cause to themselves or to each other or which resulted from the nature or propensity of such animals; and (c) that defendant did not agree to deliver said animals at destination at any specified time. The plaintiff recovered $150 on the first cause of action and $770 on the second, a total of $920, with interest."

Jeffries *v.* Chicago, B. & Q. Ry. Co

. The reply denies every allegation of new matter contained in the answer, and alleges that no notice was ever brought to the attention of plaintiff as to any limitation contained in the purported contracts between plaintiff and defendant, that plaintiff had no knowledge of any such limitations and did not in any manner assent thereto, and that such limitations are not effective as between plaintiff and defendant. There was a trial to the court and jury which resulted in a verdict and judgment, as above indicated, from which defendant appeals. Defendant in its brief assigns six grounds for a reversal of the judgment, which we will consider in their numerical order.

1. "Damage Due to Inherent Propensities of the Animals."

It is argued that there is an exception to the rule of the carrier's liability as an insurer which exempts it from responsibility for injuries so caused. The law unquestionably is as contended for by defendant, but the trouble is the facts in this case do not fit the law. There is an entire absence of evidence even tending to show that the injuries complained of were caused by the animals themselves or were the result of the nature or propensities of the animals. This point need not therefore be further considered.

2. "Delays."

Under this assignment, defendant insists that the court erred in stating the issues to the jury, in that it stated plaintiff's cause of action in substantially the terms of the petition, and objects to instructions 4 and 4 "continued," for the reason that negligent delay was given as one of the grounds upon which the jury might find against the defendant. The evidence shows that the horses included in the first cause of action were loaded at Norton, Kan., March 25, 1906, at 2 o'clock a. m.; that they were shipped as a car load lot; that an employee of plaintiff, called a "caretaker," accompanied the shipment. The car left Norton one hour later, and arrived at Republican City at 8 o'clock the same morning. A regular freight train was scheduled to leave Republican City for McCook on defendant's road at 9 a. m., but on this particular morning, upon arrival at Republican City, the caretaker was advised that the regular freight train for that morning had been annulled and an extra "run out at an earlier hour." The result was that the shipment was delayed at Republican City for 12 hours, and did not leave there until 8 o'clock of that evening, which was 11 hours later than it would have left if the regular morning freight train had not been annulled and the extra run out ahead of schedule time. The car reached McCook, a connecting point, at 8 a. m. the next morning, March 26th, about 15 minutes after the freight train had left McCook for Palisade. The result was that the car was delayed at McCook until 10 o'clock the next morning—a delay of 26 hours. From McCook to Palisade, the point of destination, there was no further delay.

Jeffries *v.* Chicago, B. & Q. Ry. Co

It will be seen that if the regular freight train out of Republicant City on the morning of the 25th had not been annulled, or when it was annulled if the extra had been held until its scheduled time, there would have been a delay of only one hour at that point, and the car would have reached McCook in ample time to have connected with the train for Palisade on the morning of March 26th. The evidence shows that, when the horses arrived at Palisade, they were in bad condition; a part of that bad condition being stiffness and swollen joints. In the light of this record, we cannot say that the court erred in submitting that question to the jury. The shipment covered by the second cause of action was a shipment of six horses and a jack. This also was shipped as a car load lot. The car left Orleans at 1 o'clock p. m., March 23, 1907. The petition alleges that defendant agreed to attach the car, when it reached Oxford, the point connecting with its main line, to train No. 77, which was due to leave Oxford that evening. When interrogated as to that, plaintiff testified: "Q. You may state what train, if any, the agent at Orleans told you when he accepted this car load of horses and jack for shipment with the horses would be shipped on from Oxford to McCook? A. I don't remember that he told me the train, but I remember that he told me that I would get out of there in the evening." It is contended by defendant that the contract of shipment was in writing; that the defendant did not agree to transport the shipment in any particular time, and that verbal evidence to vary the terms of the written contract was inadmissible; that the written contract is conclusively deemed to contain the contract of shipment. As a proposition of law, this contention is sound, but we do not think the testimony above quoted should be held to vary the terms of the written contract. It stated the information that was imparted to plaintiff by defendant's agent at the time he accepted the shipment, as to what progress would be made in transporting plaintiff's stock under the written contract. The car reached Oxford at 4 o'clock in the afternoon of March 23d. No. 77 was a fast through freight, and passed through Oxford that evening. The agent at Oxford took the matter up with the chief dispatcher at division headquarters, and asked him if the car could be attached to No. 77. The dispatcher answered that 77 had its full tonnage, and could not take any more cars. Defendant offered no evidence to show what constituted the full tonnage of No. 77, or to in any manner substantiate the statement made by the chief dispatcher, but assumes that his statement was true, and argues that the car "was then put upon the first available west-bound train." This train did not leave Oxford until 7:15 p. m., March 24th, causing a delay of 15 hours at that point. It arrived at McCook at 1:05 on the morning of the 25th, and left there some five or six hours later, arriving at Palisade without further delay. March 23d was Saturday. There was no train between McCook and Pali-

Jeffries *v.* Chicago, B. & Q. Ry. Co

sade on Sunday, so that the car was transported from McCook to Palisade upon the same train Monday morning upon which it would have been taken had defendant conveyed it from Oxford to McCook on No. 77 Saturday evening. Hence defendant argues that plaintiff suffered no injury by reason of the delay occurring at Oxford, instead of at McCook, which would necessarily have occurred had the car gone on No. 77. Counsel for plaintiff argues that plaintiff resided at McCook, and had private and suitable accommodations for caring for the horses and jack and permitting them to rest over Sunday, if they had been delivered there Saturday night in accordance with the assurance given him by the agent of the company at the point of shipment; but this contention we think fails to find support in the evidence. It is also contended by plaintiff that McCook was the regular and ordinary feeding place. This fact is supported by the evidence, but there is no evidence to show that the yards at Oxford, in which the stock was kept by defendant during the 15 hours' delay at that point, were not just as good in every way as any yards that might have been used at McCook. When plaintiff shipped this stock from Orleans Saturday noon, he knew they could not reach Palisade until Monday morning. They did, in fact, reach there at that time, and we are unable to discover from the evidence any reason for supposing that there was any material difference to plaintiff whether the stock was taken from the car and rested and fed at Oxford or McCook. If, therefore, the submission of the question of delay as to the second cause of action were prejudicial, it would call for a reversal of the judgment upon the second cause of action; but we are unable to say it was prejudicial, for reasons hereinafter given.

3. "Unloading."

Defendant urges that the court erred in submitting to the jury the question of negligence on the part of the defendant in failing to unload and properly feed and care for the animals in transit, and that the court submitted this issue to the jury in both causes of action. It is argued that it was the duty of the caretakers, who were furnished transportation and accompanied the shipments for that purpose, to care for the animals in transit, and see that they were properly unloaded, fed, and watered; that, if they desired to unload at any point, it was their duty to request the carrier to set the car at the stock yards for unloading. The testimony upon this point offered by plaintiff was that when the car, covered by the first cause of action, reached Republican City, and again when it reached McCook, it was placed upon a side track at points where the stock could not be unloaded. Witnesses testified that the defendant did not furnish plaintiff facilities for unloading, feeding, and watering; but no witness for plaintiff testified that any request was ever made

Jeffries *v.* Chicago, B. & Q. Ry. Co

of defendant to change the location of the car, or to run it up to a chute where the stock could be unloaded. The evidence is substantially the same as to the second cause of action, the only difference being that as to the stock covered by the first shipment defendant did not, upon its own motion, at any time unload the stock and feed and water it, while it did so at Oxford with the second shipment. We think defendant's contention upon this point is sound, that, when a shipper is provided transportation for a caretaker and the caretaker actually accompanies the stock during the entire time of shipment, it is his duty, if the defendant does not offer to unload and feed and water the stock, to request that facilities for so doing be given. We think the company has a right to rely upon the caretaker to notify its agents in charge of the train whenever he thinks the necessities of the case require the unloading or feeding and watering of the stock. The effect of this will be considered in connection with the next assignment.

4. "Duty of the Court to Instruct the Jury."

Under this head the defendant's brief states: "As already pointed out, the court submitted to the jury the issues of negligent delay and negligent failure to unload when the record contain no evidence to sustain the plaintiff's claims. It was prejudicial error on the part of the trial court to thus submit to the jury issues which there was no evidence in the record to sustain. * * * It was the duty of the court to instruct the jury as to the law without request, announcing the correct legal rules applicable to the facts in issue and setting out the material facts which the plaintiff must prove in order to recover." This raises the question whether or not it was the duty of the defendant to request the court to charge the jury that defendant would not be liable for any failure to furnish facilities for unloading and feeding and watering unless requested so to do by the caretaker, or whether the court was bound to charge upon that point upon its own motion. We are inclined to take the former view and to hold that, by reason of defendant's failure to request instructions upon this point, the error of the court discussed under point 3 was waived.

5. "Negligence of the Plaintiff."

Under this assignment, it is contended that the court erred in refusing to give instructions 7 and 8, requested by defendant. No. 7 reads: "The court instructs the jury, if you find from the evidence the negligence of the plaintiff or of those acting for him contributed to the losses and injuries of which he complains in his first cause of action, then you must find for defendant on the first cause of action." No. 8 reads: "The court instructs the jury if you find from the evidence plaintiff by his negligence, or

Jeffries *v.* Chicago, B. & Q. Ry. Co

those acting for him, contributed to the losses of which he complains, you cannot allow plaintiff anything for such losses or damages." We think these instructions are clearly too limited in their scope. Under a fair interpretation of them, if the negligence of plaintiff or his caretaker, in not requesting defendant to furnish facilities to unload and feed and water, contributed to the stiffness of the animals, no recovery whatever could be had by plaintiff, notwithstanding the fact that the evidence clearly shows that, by reason of the rough handling of the trains, the horses were cut, bruised and otherwise seriously injured. Furthermore we think that instruction No. 4 requested by defendant, and given by the court, sufficiently covered this point. It reads as follows: "The court instructs the jury, if you find from the evidence the defendant was not guilty of negligence in handling either or both of the shipments described in plaintiff's petition, then you will go no further, but you must at once render a verdict in favor of the defendant for such shipment or shipments. If you find in favor of the plaintiff upon the above. proposition, you must next inquire whether or not plaintiff or those acting for him were exercising due and reasonable care at the time of the alleged injuries, if, by the exercise of reasonable care the plaintiff, or those acting for him, could have avoided the losses or damages, then he is not entitled to recover in this action notwithstanding you may believe from the evidence that the employees of defendant in charge of these shipments were guilty of negligence in handling them."

6. "Released Valuation."

This assignment relates to the question as to whether or not the company could limit its liability or damage, by reason of its negligence, to any particular sum, in this case not to exceed $100 upon each animal. That precise question was decided adversely to defendant's contention in Miller *v.* Chicago, B. & Q. R. Co., 85 Neb. 458, 123 N. W. 449. That case being decisive of this point, it will not be considered further. No complaint is made in defendant's brief that the verdict of the jury is excessive, nor is any attempt made to justify the manner in which these shipments were handled by the agents in charge of defendant's trains. There is ample testimony both by plaintiff and by disinterested witnesses that in each instance, when the stock was shipped it was in good condition, and, when it reached its destination, the animals without exception were in bad condition. One had a gash four inches long over one eye. Some of the others had the skin knocked off in places. The joints were badly swollen upon several. Others had lumps upon them. The jack, when it reached its destination and was placed in the barn, was standing on three legs. Several instances are related by the witnesses

Jeffries *v.* Chicago, B. & Q. Ry. Co

showing that, when those in charge of the trains were switching, they struck the cars containing plaintiff's stock so violently as to knock the horses down, in one instance also knocked the caretaker down and put out his lantern; that in the first shipment that occurred twice while the car stood at Republican City; that in the second shipment, after one of these bumps, the caretaker went to the man in charge of another car in the train, and asked for assistance. The party appealed to accompanied him to his car and testified that the 2 by 12 timber, which had been spiked to the car as a partition between the jack and one of the stallions, had been broken; that the rope around the jack's neck, by which he had been tied, was also broken, that the jack was lying upon his side under the stallion; that they got him out and got him up. The evidence as to the rough handling is very strong indeed, and the testimony as to the condition the animals were in when they reached their destination we think sufficient to have supported a larger verdict than was returned by the jury. We also think that the evidence as to the condition of the horses were in, when they reached their destination, shows that those injuries were chiefly the result of the rough handling of the stock by defendant's agents. The evidence upon this point is so convincing that we think this judgment would have to be affirmed upon the ground that no other verdict would have been justified under the evidence; so that, even if the court may have given instructions upon other branches of the case, which would have been better not given, we cannot say that the giving of them was prejudicial error. This appears to be a proper case for the application of section 145 of the Code of Civil Procedure.

Upon the whole record, we are all of the opinion that the judgment of the district court is right, and it is affirmed.

Danville & W. Ry. Co. *v.* Lybrook *et al.*

(Supreme Court of Appeals of Virginia, Jan. 12, 1911.)

[69 S. E. Rep. 1066.]

Railroads—Station Facilities—Evidence—Weight.—Evidence in a proceeding to compel a railway company to remove buildings from its station grounds held to show that the buildings facilitate rather than hinder performance of the company's duties as a carrier.

Corporations—Regulation—Use of Property.—Courts will control public service and other corporations in the use of their property only so far as is necessary to secure proper discharge of the corporation's duty to individuals or to the public.

Railroads—Proper Facilities—Warehouses.* —A warehouse or other structure used for the convenience of the public is a proper auxiliary to railroad business.

Railroads—Station Facilities.—A railroad company, being empowered to maintain buildings on its grounds for the storage and delivery of freight and for the convenience of patrons, can permit others to do so, if the company's duty to shippers is discharged without discrimination.

Railroads—Station Facilities—Rights of Patrons.—A railroad must do what is reasonably necessary to accommodate patrons, but need not refrain from using its property to the best advantage to the public and itself; and one desiring to use railroad property for storage, or other than railroad use, cannot complain because others are permitted to use such property for their private business, if sufficient railroad facilities are afforded.

Railroads—Regulation—Power of State.—Neither the State Corporation Commission nor the courts can relieve against individual inconvenience to shippers, if the carrier affords reasonable facilities for reception and delivery of freight for the general public, and denies no individual right.

Appeal from State Corporation Commission.

Petition by S. M. Lybrook and others against the Danville & Western Railway Company. From an order of the State Corporation Commission, the company appeals. Reversed, and petition dismissed.

Eugene Withers, for appellant.
John W. Carter, for appellees.

---

*For the authorities in this series on the question as to what acts and contracts of railroad are, and are not, ultra vires, see foot-note of Western Maryland R. Co. *v.* Blue Ridge Hotel Co. (Md.), 19 R. R. R. 581, 42 Am. & Eng. R. Cas., N. S., 581, where all those preceding it are collected; foot-note of National Car Ad. Co. *v.* Louisville & N. R. Co. (Va.), 33 R. R. R. 179, 56 Am. & Eng. R. Cas., N. S., 179; last foot-note of Blume *v.* Southern R. Co. (S. Car.), 36 R. R. R. 603, 59 Am. & Eng. R. Cas., N. S., 603.

Danville & W. Ry. Co. *v.* Lybrook et al

CARDWELL, J.   This appeal brings under review an order of
the State Corporation Commission, entered on the 21st day of
April, 1909, upon a petition filed by S. M. Lybrook and seven
others, asking that the Danville & Western Railway Company be
required to remove certain buildings, etc., from its grounds at
Stuart, Patrick county, Va., and to place the depot yards and side
tracks of the defendant company at Stuart in proper condition
for the receipt and handling of freight, etc. The proceedings
were had upon the petition, the answer and exhibits therewith
filed by the defendant company, and the evidence of certain
witnesses examined before the commission at Richmond; whereupon the order was entered, requiring and directing the defendant company to remove or cause to be removed, within 60 days
from the date of the order, certain buildings designated upon a
map filed with the petition as Nos. 2, 3, 4, 5, 6, and 7, and certain
platform scales, designated as Nos. 8, 9, and 10; and from that
order the defendant company takes this appeal.

The petition of appellees alleged that appellant had permitted
the erection of certain buildings on its right of way and depot
grounds at Stuart, "to the exclusion of the public and to the great
inconvenience of the reception and delivery of freight to and
from the patrons of the road; that these commercial houses or
buildings interfered with the loading and unloading of freight
on and from cars; that the patrons of the road were hindered
and obstructed thereby, to their inconvenience and loss of time
and money; that the buildings, or certain of them, so erected and
complained of, contracted the space intended for depot grounds
at Stuart; and that the petitioners themselves were hampered
and interfered with in their receipt and delivery of freight by
reason of these buildings located near the railroad tracks. It
is further alleged that the lands upon which the buildings complained of are located were obtained during the pendency of
certain condemnation proceedings by an agreement between appellant's predecessor and A. M. Lybrook, trustee, and others, on
the 6th day of June, 1885.

Of the buildings complained of, Nos. 2, 3, 4, and 5 are located
upon the right of way of appellant, while the buildings Nos. 6
and 7 and the platform or wagon scales are located upon
what is designated in the petition as the "depot grounds"
of the appellant, and styled on the maps and in the answer
of the appellant and in the evidence as "Area A." Both
the right of way and "Area A" were acquired by the Danville
& New River Narrow Gauge Railroad Company, of which the
appellant is successor in title, during the pendency of certain
condemnation proceedings in the county court of Patrick county,
and it appears that, after the report of certain commissioners
appointed by the court for the purpose of ascertaining the value
of the lands sought to be taken, an agreement was, on the 6th

Danville & W. Ry. Co. *v.* Lybrook et al

day of June, 1885, entered into between A. M. Lybrook, in his own right and as trustee for his wife and her children, whereby the Danville & New River Narrow Gauge Railroad Company acquired from the said Lybrook, in his own right and as such trustee, an 80-foot right of way at Stuart, and "Area A" for depot purposes, which agreement was confirmed by an order of the court entered at the July term, 1885, which order did not adjudicate the right of appellant's predecessor in title to acquire the land by condemnation, and did not vest the title in appellant's predecessor by virtue of the condemnation proceedings, but merely confirmed the agreement by which Lybrook, in his own right and as trustee, agreed to the conveyance of the property by the court to the Danville & New River Narrow Gauge Railroad Company, appellant's predecessor.

With the strip of land, 55 feet wide and 800 feet long, parallel to appellant's right of way at Stuart, acquired by appellant from J. A. White, trustee, et al., by conveyance of date March 27, 1905, we are not especially concerned; nor do we, in the view we take of the case upon the facts proved, attach any importance to the question whether or not appellant's predecessor in title acquired the original right of way of the railroad and the lot for a depot by condemnation or purchase.

The charter of the appellant's predecessor, approved March 29, 1873 (Acts 1872-73, pp. 260-262), and as amended (Acts 1881-82, pp. 256-259), plainly vested in the company thereby chartered the right to acquire, by subscription or otherwise lands, etc., needed for the successful operation of its road, and to lease, sell, etc., any and all lands, etc., acquired by authority of section 4 of said act, as amended. Be that, however, as it may, appellant admits, and rightly, that it has no right to erect, or permit the erection of, upon its right of way at Stuart, any structures that hinder or interfere with it in the reasonable performance of its duties as a common carrier.

It will be observed that this proceeding was not instituted by the former owners of the station grounds and right of way of appellant at Stuart, nor by any one claiming under said former owners, but by eight shippers, who allege that they and the public are inconvenienced, hampered, and interfered with in the reception and delivery of freight.

The applicant owns four contiguous parcels of land at Stuart, acquired for right of way and for depot and other terminal purposes, aggregating 4½ acres, and the space or area occupied by the buildings and scales complained of aggregates 4,727 square feet, or one-fortieth of this total area. These buildings and scales were erected and are being used by patrons of the appellant as a convenience to the public, and were intended to facilitate the delivery of freight shipped to and from Stuart, and are a convenience and not a hindrance to the public in ship-

Danville & W. Ry. Co. v. Lybrook et al

ping from and receiving freight at Stuart, as we shall presently
see. Those occupying or using these buildings and scales are
occupying or using them by sufferance only, and pay no rent
therefor to appellant, and all goods, merchandise, etc., stored or
handled in these buildings, are either shipped to or from Stuart
over appellant's line of railway, and the land of appellant designated as "Area A," or depot grounds, not occupied by any of
said buildings or the scales, is used as a camping ground for
shippers delivering or receiving freight at Stuart, of which no
complaint is made. Of the eight signers of the petition asking
that these buildings and wagon scales be removed, only three of
them testified in these proceedings.

S. M. Lybrook, appellees' leading witness, testifies that "Area
A," on which these structures are located, has been used for
standing—i. e., parking—wagons and as a camping ground for
wagons coming from the country ever since the road was built,
and admits that the building No. 6, used as a wholesale store, is
over a ravine, that its supports on the north and east sides are
in the ravine, and just beyond the edge of it on the west side,
and to the front, there is a platform covering the ravine, to enable the public to cross from the main road to Stuart to the Mt.
Airy road; that the buildings in question in no wise obstruct the
space between No. 6 and the depot; and that the removal of No.
6 would not facilitate the public, except in clearing the ground it
takes up, which ground he had already shown to be practically
a ravine and of no use to the public. He in effect further admits
that the complaint was only made after building No. 6 was put
up; that appellant had never been asked to cover the ravine over
which it stands and thereby afford witness and others more space;
and that the complaint was made, although the g und covered
by the building was not usable as vacant ground for any purpose
by appellant's patrons. As to the scales (Nos. 8, 9, and 10), the
witness admits that they furnish the only facilities at Stuart for
weighing tan bark; that tan bark must be weighed before shipment; that there is no other place at which the scales could be
put; that the weighing is without charge; and that he has used
one or more of these scales without charge. He further sta
that, notwithstanding the buildings complained of on "Area A,"
there is no difficulty of approach for wagons to get their fr
and, in short, the witness says that the only way the b
in question interfere with shippers is to cut off their priv
of using the area they occupy as a camping ground; i. e.,
the shippers are thereby deprived of a place to camp their w
and feed their horses. But he does not state, nor is it
any other witness, that appellant had been requested t
the campers from its right of way or terminals;
witness, or any other witness, show wherein the a
quired to furnish camping ground upon its right of

Danville & W. Ry. Co. *v.* Lybrook et al

minals to accommodate shippers, although it had been doing so ever since the railroad was built. It is not claimed by this witness that the buildings or scales on Nos. 6, 7, 8, 9, or 10 inconveniences him, or any of the petitioners, or any patron of the railroad, other than those who seek to camp on "Area A" for convenience, or are seeking peculiar privileges in the matter of receiving or delivering freight.

T. J. George, another of the petitioners examined as a witness for appellees, when asked whether or not the buildings or scales on Nos. 6, 7, 8, 9, and 10 contract the space and are an inconvenience to the public for the purpose of bringing freight or carrying freight away, answered: "Well, Moir's building is over the branch. It may take a little space on each side; and also the Clark Bros. building is right behind the Moir building." Yet the witness, on cross-examination, admits that the scales on Nos. 8, 9, and 10 are used by the public "for weighing the tan bark and other stuff;" that none of the buildings interfere with him; and, after admitting that he and Moir are competitors in business, his objection is to Moir's occupying any of appellant's land while competing with people, like himself, who own real estate adjoining appellant's property, which real estate is for sale.

The sum and substance of the testimony given by R. C. Shepherd, the other signer of the petition who testified, is that no one complained of the buildings in question, and that his only complaint was that he was not allowed to erect a building on the railroad grounds, and that he objected to none of the structures until No. 6, the last one erected, was placed over the ravine; yet he does not show that No. 6 in any way inconvenienced him or the public.

All of the evidence, particularly that of S. M. Lybrook, shows that the removal of the buildings and scales in question would not change the methods or ways of getting to the tracks of the appellant; that means of ingress and egress to the terminus of appellant at Stuart would not be affected in the least by the removal of the buildings, etc., complained of; and almost with one accord do the witnesses who have been examined pro and con testify that no one has complained of these buildings, except the petitioners.

We cannot in an opinion of reasonable length review the evidence in detail. Enough of it has been referred to to show that this proceeding was not begun in the interest of the general public, but merely to give vent to individual complaint, founded more upon a purpose to obtain individual benefits than to improve the service of the appellant to its patrons at Stuart. The specific complaint of the witness Shepherd is that he could not get similar accommodations that others have, and other witnesses for appellees say that they have encountered inconvenience in the receipt

Danville & W. Ry. Co. *v.* Lybrook et al

and delivery of freight at Stuart, but utterly fail to show how the public would be the better served by appellant if the buildings, etc., complained of were removed. On the other hand, the evidence unmistakably shows that, when the lay of the ground and other conditions existing at Stuart are considered, the. appellant affords reasonable facilities to its patrons in the receiving and delivery of freight at that point.

The two witnesses for appellees, Hatcher and Ayers, and the only witnesses besides the three petitioners mentioned examined for appellees, corroborate the other evidence for both parties that the seven or eight petitioners have alone complained of these buildings; Hatcher and Ayers stating positively that no one in Patrick county is complaining or ever had complained of them.

Viewing the evidence of appellees alone, it appears that the allegations of their petition are not well founded, that the structures complained of facilitate rather than hinder appellant in the performance of its duties as a common carrier, and do not interfere with its patrons or the citizens of Patrick county. Just what the evidence shows, in substance, is fairly stated by the learned chairman of the State Corporation Commission in his dissent from the ruling of the commission, as follows:

"The platform scales referred to (used chiefly for the weighing of tan bark) are a public convenience, and no one is charged for using them. The cooper's shop is only 20x24 feet in size, and promotes the business of the railway company by encouraging the manufacture of barrels for the shipment of the large apple. crop of Patrick county over the Danville & Western Railway.

"The houses into which the fertilizer and heavy machinery have been unloaded and stored have relieved the company from the necessity of building warehouses for these purposes and from enlarging its present freight warehouse. To this extent these houses directly promote the public interest and enable the company better to discharge its public duties. This is especially true of the wholesale grocery warehouse of Moir & Co., which is built over a ravine and incommodes no shipper. This view not only is well sustained by the evidence, but also by public sentiment at Stuart; for 27 merchants and shippers at Stuart say that this building of Moir & Co. is a 'great convenience,' and that the place it occupies 'is over a branch,' and cannot be used 'for standing wagons on or any other purpose' (Exhibit No. 7, with defendant's answer)."

The question is not raised, and therefore we are not called upon to consider in this opinion whether or not, where a public corporation is charged with making a use of its property not authorized by law, a private person can sustain a suit to contest it. See Smith *v.* Cornelius, 41 W. Va. 59, 23 S. E. 599, 30 L. R. A. 747, and other authorities cited in 1 Va. & W. Va. Dig. pp. 1944, 1945.

Danville & W. Ry. Co. v. Lybrook et al

The principle controlling in the class of cases to which this belongs is that courts will only control public service and other corporations in the use of their property, so far as may be necessary to secure the proper discharge of the duties which the corporations owe to individuals or to the public.

In Nye v. Stover et al., 168 Mass. 53, 46 N. E. 402, it is held that "the right given a corporation to hold real estate and buildings carries with it the right to lease them, and it is no objection to the validity of such lease that the business in which the property is to be used is one which the corporation is not authorized to carry on, and that the rental is a share of the net profits."

We have seen that in this case the charter of appellant authorizes it to lease any lands acquired by the corporation by gift, purchase, or otherwise, and that the buildings complained of are occupied and used by sufferance only; that they are buildings used for the storage and delivery of freight shipped to or from Stuart by appellant, or for the conduct of a business which facilitates the handling of such freight, and for the convenience of the patrons of appellant and the public. Take as an example the building used for the storage of staves and the manufacture of barrels, which were sold to the farmers of Patrick county, hauled away, and filled with apples and other articles, and returned to the depot of the appellant for shipment. It is proven in this connection, not only that these staves cannot be allowed to lie out on the ground, because of the injury to them that would follow their exposure to the weather, but that this storage house and the manufacture of the staves into barrels is "a great convenience" to the farmers of the county, and facilitates the business of appellant at Stuart. We are unable to find in the evidence any foundation whatever for a complaint that appellant does not provide reasonable facilities for the reception and delivery of freight at its station at Stuart.

A warehouse or other structure used for the convenience of the public is as much an auxiliary to the business of a railroad as a hotel. State v. New Orleans Warehouse Co., 109 La. 64, 33 South. 81, in which the opinion says; "Why should this right to lease be more restricted where storage is concerned than that of a hotel? One is as useful as the other."

There can be no question that appellant has the right to build structures similar to those complained of here, and therefore, may permit others to do so, so long as if fairly discharges its duty to the shippers at Stuart without discrimination, and when this is the case it has denied its patrons or the public no right.

In Mo. Pac. R. Co. v. Nebraska, 164 U. S. 414, 17 Sup. Ct. 130, 41 L. Ed. 489, citing as authority Grand Trunk R. Co. v. Richardson, 91 U. S. 454, 23 L. Ed. 356, it is said: "A railroad corporation holds its station grounds, tracks, and right of way as its private property, but for the public use for which it was in-

Danville & W. Ry. Co. v. Lybrook et al

corporated, and may, at its discretion, permit them to be occupied by other parties with structures convenient for the receipt and delivery of freight upon its railroad, so long as a free and safe passage is left for the carriage of freight and passengers."

In Hartford Ins. Co. v. Chicago, etc., R. Co., 175 U. S. 91. 20 Sup. Ct. 33, 44 L. Ed. 84, also citing Grand Trunk R. Co. v. Richardson, supra, it is said: "A railroad corporation holds its station grounds, railroad tracks, and right of way for the public use for which it is incorporated, yet as its private property, and to be occupied by itself or by others in the manner which it may consider best fitted to promote, or not to interfere with, the public use. It may, in its discretion, permit them to be occupied by others with structures convenient for the receiving and delivering of freight upon its railroad, so long as a free and safe passage is left for the carriage of freight and passengers."   .

A case in point, where the subject is well considered, is Calcasieu Lumber Co. v. Harris, 77 Tex. 18, 13 S. W. 453. In that case the action was brought by one Harris, alleging that the lumber company had constructed certain buildings on the right of way of the Houston & Texas Central Railroad Company for the purpose of carrying on a private business as a dealer in lumber and building materials, and that such buildings were an obstruction to railway traffic carried on by the patrons of the road, and especially to the complainant, who was also a dealer in lumber and building materials; that the lumber company's buildings obstructed complainant in carrying lumber, when unloaded from the cars, to his yards, situated about 200 feet from the railway track. The prayer of the complainant was that the building in question be removed from the railroad's right of way. The court. after distinguishing an easement from a fee simple in this connection. held that complainant had no cause of action. In the opinion it is said that. so long as the occupation and use of the land owned by and leased from the railway company does not create a nuisance directly affecting the complainant, he had no cause of action; that the use to which the lumber company had appropriated the land creates such a nuisance could not be claimed; that it might be that complaint could conduct his business more conveniently if the railroad company's property was not used as it had been, but, if that be a lawful use, the inconvenience resulting from it does not give a cause of action.

In Mich. Cent. R. Co. v. Bullard, 120 Mich. 416, 79 N. W. 635, approved in Detroit v. Little & Co., 146 Mich. 373. 109 N. W. 671, the lease of a portion of the railway company's right of way was in question. and in dealing with the validity of the lease the opinion of the court says: "The lease in question was made subject to termination on 60 days' notice, and was made to a manufacturing company with a view to furnishing facilities for

Danville & W. Ry. Co. v. Lybrook et al

furnishing freight to the company. Such a lease is not invalid"
—citing Railroad Company v. Richardson, 91 U. S. 454, 23 L.
Ed. 356; Railroad Co. v. Wathen, 17 Ill. App. 582; Gurney v.
Elevator Co., 63 Minn. 70, 65 N. W. 136, 30 L. R. A. 534; Roby
v. Railroad Co., 142 N. Y. 176, 36 N. E. 1053.

The authorities agree that the railroad's property must be devoted to public use to the extent necessary for the public objects intended to be accomplished by the construction and maintenance of the railroad as a highway; but, as said by Mr. Justice Harlan in Donovan v. Penn. Co., 199 U. S. 279, 26 Sup. Ct. 91, 50 L. Ed. 192, where the facts were very similar to those in the case at bar: "It by no means follows * * * that the company may not establish such reasonable rules, in respect of the use of its property, as the public convenience and its interest may suggest, provided only that such rules are consistent with the ends for which the corporation was created, and not inconsistent with public regulations legally established for the conduct of its business. Although its functions are public in their nature, the company holds the legal title to the property which it has undertaken to employ in the discharge of these functions."

Of course, as the opinion in that case holds, a railroad is required, under all circumstances, to do what may be reasonably necessary and suitable for the accommodation of passengers and shippers; but it is under no obligation to refrain from using its property to the best advantage of the public and itself. In this view, one who wishes to use railroad property for storage, or any other use not a railroad use, cannot complain that others are permitted to use the railroad property for their private business, so long as sufficient railroad facilities are afforded by the railroad company.

The bona fides of the complaint made in this case is not questioned; but in our view of the evidence the complainants have been deprived of no essential right they possessed before, nor the traveling public or shippers of freight of that reasonable and equal service to which they are entitled.

The Constitution of this state and the statutes enacted in pursuance of the constitutional provisions confer upon the State Corporation Commission control over common carrier and public service corporations, with well-defined constitutional and statutory limitations upon that power. The commission and the courts cannot undertake to remove individual inconveniences to shippers, such as are complained of here, so long as the carrier or public service corporation affords reasonable facilities for the reception and delivery of freight for the general public, and denies no individual or individuals an essential right. That is this case upon the facts proven.

We are therefore of opinion that the order of the Corporation

St. Louis & S. F. R. Co. *v.* Cavender

Commission appealed from is erroneous, and should be reversed, and this court will enter the order that the commission should have entered, dismissing appellees' petition, with costs to appellant.

Reversed.

HARRISON, J., absent.

ST. LOUIS & S. F. R. CO. *v.* CAVENDER.

(Supreme Court of Alabama, Nov. 24 1910.)

[54 So. Rep. 54.]

Carriers—Carriers of Goods—Commencement of Liability.*—A common carrier is responsible as such only when freight is delivered to and accepted by it for immediate transportation in the usual course of business, so that where a common carrier receives goods, and something remains to be done before they can be transported, as whether they are delivered to the carrier without instructions as to their destination, or to await orders or until charges for transportation are paid, the responsibility of a carrier is not that of an insurer, but that of a warehouseman, who is held only to ordinary care for their safety.

Carriers—Carriers of Live Stock—Duty of Carrier to Receive for Transportation.†—A railroad company holding itself out as a carrier of live stock is under legal obligation to provide proper facilities, such as stock yards, for receiving live stock offered to it for shipment.

Action—Carriers of Live Stock—Actions against Carriers of Live Stock—Nature and Form.—In an action against a carrier for alleged injuries to live stock shipped by the plaintiff, the plaintiff averred that the defendant or its servant or agent received said cattle in its stock yard, preparatory to shipment, where it was the duty of the defendant to use due care to receive and safely transport and deliver said cattle to the consignee, and that the defendant so negligently conducted itself in and about receiving said cattle for shipment, that defendant's stock yard was unsecure and unsafe, and that the unsecurity of the yard resulted in injury to plaintiff. Held to state an action in case for negligence in caring for the cattle while held by the shipper pending definite arrangements for their transportation.

---

*See foot-note of Ashley *v.* Central of Georgia Ry. Co. (Ga.), 36 R. R. R. 419, 59 Am. & Eng. R. Cas., N. S., 419; Kansas City, etc., Ry. Co. *v.* Cox (Okla.), 36 R. R. R. 104, 59 Am. & Eng. R. Cas., N. S., 104; Burrowes *v.* Chicago, etc., R. Co. (Neb.), 35 R. R. R. 373, 58 Am. & Eng. R. Cas., N. S., 373.

†See foot-note of Gilliland & Gaffney *v.* Southern Ry. Co. (S. Car.), 37 R. R. R. 4, 60 Am. & Eng. R. Cas., N. S., 4.

St. Louis & S. F. R. Co. *v*. Cavender

Carriers—Carriers of Live Stock—Actions for Injuries—Pleading. —Complaint.—Where a complaint in an action to recover for injuries sustained to live stock has stated a cause of action for negligence of the carrier in caring for the live stock after it had received them preparatory to transportation, the nature of the pleading is not affected by the fact that the pleader adds an averment of further and cumulative negligence also affecting the safe receipt and keeping of the animals for shipment by alleging that an agent of defendant operating a train negligently blew the whistle of his engine as a proximate consequence of which plaintiff's live stock were greatly scattered and damaged.

Carriers—Carriers of Live Stock—Actions against Carriers of Live Stock—Evidence—Presumptions.‡—Station agents are presumed to have power to make contracts for the transportation of freight and to do whatever is necessary to forward it, and where an agent at a station on a railroad holding itself out as a carrier of live stock receives into the carrier's stock yards cattle delivered there for future shipment he must be taken, prima facie at least, as acting within the scope of his duty.

Railroads—Acts of Servant—Liability of Master—Scope of Employment—Presumption.§—There is a presumption that a servant of a railroad company who is operating an engine on its track is acting within the scope of his employment in negligently blowing the whistle, so as to hold the company for injuries to animals frightened by the noise.

Carriers—Carriers of Live Stock—Actions against Carriers of Live Stock—Pleading.—A complaint in an action against a carrier of live stock for alleged injuries to plaintiff's live stock, which alleges in the alternative that defendant or its servant or agent received the live stock without averring that such servant or agent in receiving the live stock was acting for the defendant within the scope of his employment, is good on demurrer.

Carriers—Carriers of Goods—Liability for Injury to Goods—Nature of Liability as Common Carrier.—Carriers are responsible, by reason of the duties imposed by law upon them as carriers, for the negligence of their servants in and about the carriage of freight, including its receipt for future carriage, and where the servant is acting within his authority, the carrier is responsible, though the wrong or damage be done inadvertently and with the purpose to accomplish its business in an unlawful manner.

Carriers—Carriers of Live Stock—Action on Live Stock—Pleading. —In an action against a carrier, where the complaint stated a good cause of action for damages for the carrier's negligence in caring

‡See second foot-note of St. Louis, etc., Ry. Co. *v*. Citizens' Bank (Ark.), 30 R. R. R. 290, 53 Am. & Eng. R. Cas., N. S., 290; first foot-note of Southern Ry. Co. *v*. Nowlin (Ala.), 30 R. R. R. 261, 53 Am. & Eng. R. Cas., N. S., 261.

§See extensive note, 28 R. R. R. 384, 51 Am. & Eng. R. Cas., N. S., 384.

St. Louis & S. F. R. Co. *v.* Cavender

for live stock while held by it, pending the arrangement for its trans-portation, the addition as a part of one of the good counts of an averment of negligence also affecting the safe receipt and keeping of the live stock for shipment by alleging that a servant of the defend-ant operating a train negligently blew the whistle of his engine, as a proximate consequence of which the live stock was frightened and damaged, without alleging that the engineer was engaged in defend-ant's business when he blew the whistle, is good as against a demur-rer to the entire count, in view of the statute which requires plead-ings to be as brief as is consistent with clearness.

Carriers—Carriers of Live Stock—Actions against Carriers of Live Stock—Negligence of Plaintiff.—In an action for damages to live stock received by a defendant into its stock pens for transportation, whether the plaintiff under the contract of affreightment was to load the cattle upon the cars, and under which the defendant was not to be liable by reason of the stock being wild and unruly, or in consequence of fright, it was shown that on the afternoon of the day on which the cattle were received by defendant it furnished a car for loading, but that the plaintiff failed to load them that day and that, after the plaintiff failed to load, the cattle on that same day broke from the pens and inflicted upon themselves or each other the injuries for which the plaintiff sought recovery. Held that, on these facts, the plaintiff was not as a matter of law negligent.

Carriers—Carriers of Live Stock—Limitation of Liability—Evi-dence.§—A recital in a contract, framed as a limitation of the lia-bility of a carrier of live stock, that the rate is a reduced rate is prima facie evidence of that fact, and the shipper having executed the contract, in the absence of fraud or mistake alleged, is presumed to have known and consented to its terms.

Carriers—Carriers of Live Stock—Limitation—Liability—Construc-tion.‖—Contracts creating special limitation on the liability of the carrier for his own defaults are to be strictly construed against the carrier, and the same rule applies as to a release against accrued damages.

Carriers—Carriers of Live Stock—Limitation of Liability.—A con-tract for the transportation of live stock provided that, in consid-eration of a reduced rate, the shipper released all causes of action for any damages that had accrued to him by any prior written or verbal contract concerning the stock. Held, that an action to re-cover for injuries to stock sustained while in the carrier's stock pens awaiting transportation arrangements, and on the day before the execution of the contract set out, being based on the carrier's neg-ligence in the performance of duties imposed upon it by law, and without regard to the will or contract of the carrier, was not af-fected by the release contained in the subsequent freight contract

‖See extensive note, 28 R. R. 384, 51 Am. & Eng. R. Cas., N. S., 384.
§See (§) on preceding page.

St. Louis & S. F. R. Co. *v.* Cavender

Appeal from Circuit Court, Jefferson County; A. O. Lane, Judge.

Action by S. J. Cavender against the St. Louis & San Francisco Railroad Company. Judgment for plaintiff, and defendant appeals. Affirmed.

Campbell & Johnston, for appellant.
Gaston & Pettus, for appellee.

SAYRE, J. It is well settled that a common carrier becomes responsible as such only when freight is delivered to and accepted by it for immediate transportation in the usual course of business. If the goods are received, but something remains to be done before the goods can be sent on their way, "as where the goods are deposited without instructions as to their place of destination, or to await orders, or until the charges for transportation are paid, if that is required by the carrier," the duty and responsibility of the carrier is not that of an insurer, but that of a warehouseman who must exercise ordinary care for their safety. A. G. S. R. R. Co. *v.* Mt. Vernon Co., 84 Ala. 173, 4 South. 356; L. & N. R. R. *v.* Echols, 97 Ala. 556, 12 South. 304; Hutch. on Carriers (3d Ed.) § 72; Moore on Carriers, 258-9; Barron *v.* Eldredge, 100 Mass. 458, 1 Am. Rep. 126; Dixon *v.* Central Rwy. Co., 110 Ga. 173, 35 S. E. 369. Counts 3, 4, and 5—the rest were taken out of the case by rulings favorable to the appellant—proceeded, not upon defendant's responsibility as a common carrier, nor upon a breach of contract for carriage, but for negligence in and about the performance of duty imposed by law upon defendant as a warehouseman after it had received plaintiff's cattle preparatory to putting them on their way—its duty as a warehouseman. The averment of counts 3 and 4 is that "defendant, or its servant or agent at Guin, Alabama, received said cattle in defendant's said stock yard preparatory to shipment," where "it was the duty if the defendant to use due and reasonable care to receive and safely transport and deliver said cattle to the consignee thereof at Birmingham, Alabama." The averment of the fifth count is that "the defendant, its servants or agents, so negligently conducted themselves in and about receiving said cattle for shipment," etc. Some of the language quoted seems to have been used without clear reference to the distinction between the duties and responsibilities which might devolve upon defendant as carrier or warehouseman, but there is no difficulty in the way of the conclusion that it was intended to state an action in case for negligence in caring for the cattle while held by the defendant pending definite arrangements for their transportation.

A railroad company. holding itself out as a carrier of live stock, is under legal obligation, arising out of its relations with

St. Louis & S. F. R. Co. *v.* Cavender

the public, to provide proper facilities, such as stock yards, for receiving live stock offered to it for shipment. Covington Stock Yards *v.* Keith, 139 U. S. 133, 11 Sup. Ct. 469, 35 L. Ed. 73; Moore on Carriers, 500, 501.   This duty on the part of defendant being alleged, and the occasion for the exercise of care, namely, the receipt of plaintiff's cattle, not for immediate shipment, but preparatory thereto and in anticipation of a contract for shipment to be made, the further averment that defendant's stock yard was insecure and unsafe necessarily implies negligence; and it being shown in the complaint that the insecurity and unsafety of the yard resulted in injury to plaintiff. a cause of action is stated.   And the conclusiveness of this result as matter of law is not affected by the fact that the pleader added an averment of further and cumulative negligence, also affecting the safe receipt and keeping of the animals for shipment. by alleging that an agent of defendant, operating a train, negligently blew the whistle of his engine, as a proximate consequence of which—both which, as we think count 3 must be construed, unless violence be done to the language used—plaintiff's cattle were greatly frightened and caused to break out of the stock yard, and were greatly scattered and damaged.

It is insisted, however, that counts 3 and 4 are defective for that in them it is alleged in the alternative that defendant or its servant or agent received the cattle, while it is not made to appear that defendant's servant or agent in receiving plaintiff's cattle was acting for defendant and within the scope of his employment.   And further fault is found with count 3 because it fails to allege that the engineer was engaged in the transaction of the defendant's business when he negligently blew ˙the whistle.   As to the first proposition, it is possible, of course, that defendant's agent at Guin received plaintiff's cattle into the defendant's stock yard for some purpose of his own, without authority from the defendant, and in disregard of defendant's purposes in the operation of its railroad and the maintenance of its stock yard.   But station agents are presumed to have power to make contracts for the transportation of freight and to do whatever is necessary to send it on its way. Moore on Carriers, 369. And we know enough of the customary operation of railroads, and the maintenance by railroad companies of stations in charge of agents, to be able to say with confidence that when an agent at a station on a railroad, holding itself out as a carrier of live stock, received into his employer's stock pens, constructed for that purpose, cattle delivered there for future shipment—all which is stated in counts 3 and 4 by most fair implication, if not in express words—he must be taken, prima facie at least, as acting within the scope of the duties he is employed to discharge.   So likewise, the presumption must be that an agent of a railroad company who operates an engine upon its track is

St. Louis & S. F. R. Co. v. Cavender

acting within the scope of his employment (Woodward Iron Co. v. Herndon, 114 Ala. 214, 21 South. 430), and that the company is responsible for his act in negligently blowing the whistle although that be done in a way not usual or ordinary. Carriers are responsible by reason of the duties imposed by law upon them as carriers for the negligence of their servants in and about the carriage of freight, including its receipt for future carriage, and if the servant or employee is acting in the execution of his authority, the master is responsible though the wrong be done inadvertently or with the purpose to accomplish the master's business in an unlawful manner. In short, to have required of the pleader that he should avoid every construction which appellant has attributed to the complaint, would have greatly overworked the rule that the pleadings on demurrer are to be construed against the pleader, and would have resulted in a multiplication of words contrary to the spirit and letter of the statute which requires that pleadings must be as brief as is consistent with perspicuity and the presentation of issues in an intelligible form. At least it is safe to say that a demurrer addressed to the entire count should not have been sustained on account of a defect in the allegation in respect to the act of the engineer, the statement of which was a nonessential addition to a cause of action already sufficiently stated.

Our cases are legion in which general averments, analagous to those of the fifth count, have been approved.

There was no error in overruling the demurrers to counts 3, 4, and 5.

In the complaint it is alleged that plaintiff's cattle were received into the stock pens on the 7th day of March, 1908, and the averment is that they were injured on that day. Plea 5 brings into notice a contract of affreightment entered into between the parties on the next succeeding day. By the contract plaintiff agreed to load the stock upon the car. It also contained the following clause: "Third. For the consideration aforesaid, it is further agreed that neither the company nor any connecting carrier shall be responsible for any damage or injury sustained by said live stock, by reason of any defect in the cars used in the transportation thereof, in consequence of the escape of any of said live stock through the doors and openings in said cars, or by reason of the stock being wild, unruly, weak, maiming each other or themselves, or from fright of animals, or from crowding of one upon another, or from heat or suffocation, whether caused by overloading of said cars or otherwise." The plea averred that "said cattle were placed in a pen at Guin, Alabama, to be loaded in one of defendant's cars; and said cattle, in charge of plaintiff, were by him placed in said pen on March 7, 1908. Defendant avers that, on said March 7, 1908, to wit, 4 p. m., it furnished plaintiff a suitable cattle car for said stock, but that plaintiff failed or neglected to load them therein, until, to wit, 9 a. m., on March 8th, and defendant avers that on the afternoon or evening of March 7th, after defendant had furnished the car aforesaid, said cattle became unruly or stampeded and broke out of said pen, thereby inflicting upon themselves or upon each other the injury from which plaintiff sustained damage as alleged." The consideration for this special immunity from liability, moving from defendant to plaintiff, was expressed in the contract as an agreement to carry at a reduced rate. We deem it a sufficient response to the argument made for this plea to say that the facts therein set up do not import negligence on the part of plaintiff as matter of law. Plaintiff's failure to load the cattle upon the car within the hours designated—to deal with one alternative of the plea—may have resulted from a cause entirely apart from any negligence on his part. When amended so as to allege that the act of plaintiff was negligently done, as was the course taken in framing the plea lettered "B," identical in all other respects, demurrer was overruled. There was no error in the court's ruling.

Plea 7, demurrer to which was sustained, seems to have been designed to set up a clause of the contract (heretofore referred to) which was in this language: "Seventh. For the consideration aforesaid the shipper agrees to waive and release and does hereby release the company from any and all liability for or on account of delay in shipping said stock after delivery thereof to its agent, and from any delay in receiving the same after the tender of delivery, and for breach of any alleged contract to furnish cars at any particular time, and the shipper hereby releases and does waive and bar any and all causes of action for any damage whatsoever that has accrued to the shipper by any written or verbal contract prior to the execution hereof concerning said stock or any of them." The plea sets out the contract, and then avers that the alleged injuries sustained by plaintiff accrued before the execution of said written agreement. The recital in the contract that the rate is a reduced rate is prima facie evidence of that fact; and, the shipper having executed the contract, we have no choice but to presume, in the absence of fraud, mistake, imposition, or incapacity alleged, that he knew and consented to its terms. But the circumstances usually attending the execution of contracts creating special limitations upon the liability of the carrier for his own defaults are such that the courts unanimously hold that they are to be strictly construed against the carrier. Such must in reason also be the rule in respect to a release against accrued damages obscurely tucked away in the belly of an elaborate contract for carriage. The contract in question stipulated a release of damages accrued to the shipper by any written or verbal contract prior to the execution thereof. But it was no answer to the complaint which proceeded for dam-

Old Dominion S. S. Co. et al. *v.* C. F. Flanary & Co

ages arising out of negligence in the performance of duties imposed by law and without regard to the. will or contract of the carrier. Damages so arising might also have been released upon sufficient consideration, but it does not appear in the letter of the contract that they were so released.

There is no error in the record, and the judgment will be affirmed.

Affirmed.

Dowdell, C. J., and Anderson and Evans, JJ., concur.

Old Dominion S. S. Co. *et al. v.* C. F. Flanary & Co.

(Supreme Court of Appeals of Virginia, Jan. 26, 1911.)

[69 S. E. Rep. 1107.]

Carriers—Contracts—Limiting Liability of Initial Carrier—Validity. —The Carmack amendment to the interstate commerce act (Act June 29, 1906, c. 3591, 34 Stat. 593 [U. S. Comp. St. Supp. 1909, p. 1167]), making the initial carrier of an interstate shipment liable for loss or injury to the shipment caused by it or any connecting carrier, renders void a stipulation in a contract for an interstate shipment limiting the liability of the initial carrier to loss occurring on its own line.

Carriers—Connecting Carriers—Limitation of Liability.—A stipulation in a bill of lading issued by the initial carrier of an interstate shipment that claims for loss must be made to the agent at point of delivery promptly after the arrival of the goods, and if delayed for more than 30 days after due time for delivery no carrier shall be liable, is a reasonable requirement for the protection of the initial carrier. liable under the Carmack amendment to the interstate commerce act (Act June 29, 1906, c. 3591, 34 Stat. 593 [U. S. Comp. St. Supp. 1909, p. 1167]), for loss or injury caused by it or any connecting carrier, and must be complied with or the carrier is relieved from liability, unless the stipulation is waived.

Carriers—Limitation of Liability—Notice of Loss—Waiver.[*]—The act of a carrier in sending at the request of the consignee tracers for a lost shipment after the time fixed in the bill of lading for service of notice on it of a claim for loss essential to hold the carrier liable does not amount to a waiver of its right to rely on its exemption if the goods are not located; there being nothing to indicate that the carrier did not intend to insist on its contract rights nor anything to show that the consignee was prejudiced.

---

[*]See last foot-note of Atlantic C. L. R. Co. *v.* Bryan (Va.), 33 R. R. R. 655, 56 Am. & Eng. R. Cas., N. S., 655.

Old Dominion S. S. Co. et al. *v.* C. F. Flanary & Co

Carriers—Contracts—Loss of Goods—Notice.†—Where a shipment under a bill of lading stipulating that claims for loss be made to the agent at a point of delivery promptly after the arrival of the goods, and if delayed more than 30 days after due time for delivery the carrier shall not be liable, was made on September 5th, and 15 days was a reasonable time to transport the goods, a notice of a claim for loss not given until October 23d was too late.

Error to Circuit Court, Wise County.

Action by C. F. Flanary & Company against the Old Dominion Steamship Company and others. There was a judgment for plaintiff against the defendant named, and it brings error. Reversed and remanded.

Bulitt & Chalkley and *Loyall, Taylor & White,* for plaintiff in error.

Vicars & Peery, for defendant in error.

KEITH, P. On the 5th of September, 1906, goods were shipped by Dunham & Co. and the Claflin Company, of New York, by the Old Dominion Steamship Company and connecting lines, to C. F. Flanary & Co., at Wise, Va. The goods were never delivered, and in the early part of October tracers were sent out by the transportation companies to discover what had become of them, but they were never found, and in December, 1908, Flanary & Co. brought suit in assumpsit against the Virginia & Kentucky Railway Company, the Norfolk & Western Railway Company, and the Old Dominion Steamship Company to recover the value of the goods.

The bill of particulars shows that the bill shipped by Dunham & Co. on the 5th of September, 1906, amounted to $302.01, and the freight paid upon it was $3.65; the shipment by the Claflin Company on the same day was valued at $125.98, and the freight upon it was $2.63; and it was agreed between the parties that, if the plaintiffs were entitled to recover, they should have a judgment for $434.27.

The court directed the jury by their verdict to answer certain questions, as follows:

"(1) Were the goods sued for in this case delivered by Claflin & Co. and Dunham & Co., respectively, to the Old Dominion Steamship Company, on or about September 5, 1906, for shipment to C. F. Flanary & Co. at Wise, Va.?" To which the jury answered: "Yes."

"(2) Were the goods sued for herein ever received by C. F. Flanary & Co. at Wise, Va.?" Answer: "No."

---

†See first foot-note of Atlantic C. L. R. Co. *v.* Bryan (Va.), 35 R. R. 655, 56 Am. & Eng. R. Cas., N. S., 655; first head-note of Atchison, etc., R. Co. *v.* Coffin (Ariz.), 36 R. R. R. 429, 59 Am. & Eng. R. Cas., N. S., 428; first foot-note of Cleveland, etc., Ry. Co. *v.* Reddy (Ind.), 35 R. R. 120, 58 Am. & Eng. R. Cas., N. S., 120.

Old Dominion S. S. Co. et al. *v.* C. F. Flanary & Co

"(3) If the said goods were delivered to the Old Dominion Steamship Company, as set forth in question No. 1, and if they were never received by C. F. Flanary & Co., then how were the said goods lost; that is, were they lost by any of the defendant companies, and, if by any of the defendant companies, then by which of the defendant companies?" Answer: "They were lost by the Old Dominion Steamship Company and never delivered by it to the Norfolk & Western Railway Company."

"(4) Did any of the defendant companies waive their right to insist upon the provision in the bill of lading, or contract of shipment, reading as follows, namely: 'Claim for loss or damage must be made in writing to the agent at point of delivery promptly after the arrival of the property, and if delayed for more than thirty days after the delivery of the property, or after due time for the delivery thereof, no carrier hereunder shall be liable in any event?' And, if so, which of them?" Answer: "Yes, all of them."

"(5) You will find whether or not C. F. Flanary & Co. or the shippers on behalf of C. F. Flanary & Co. filed in writing claims for damages for the loss of the said goods with any of the said defendant companies; if so, which one, when and where?" Answer: "Yes, J. H. Dunham & Co., on behalf of C. F. Flanary & Co., sent tracers from New York on October 2, 1906, and filed claim in writing with Old Dominion Steamship Company in New York on October 27, 1906, for $302.01, for amount of goods contained in case No. 110, shipped by this company. The H. B. Claflin Company, on behalf of C. F. Flanary & Co., sent tracer from New York on October 2, 1906, and filed claim in writing with Old Dominion Steamship Company in New York on October 23, 1906, for $125.98 for amount of goods contained in case No. 72,798, shipped by this company."

The Old Dominion Steamship Company relied upon the facts that it had delivered all of the freight which it had received in good order at Norfolk, Va., to its connecting carrier, the Norfolk & Western Railway Company, and that it was not responsible to the defendant in error because of the stipulation in its bill of lading that "claims for loss or damage must be made in writing at point of delivery promptly after the arrival of the property, and if delayed for more than thirty days after the delivery of the property, or after due time for the delivery thereof, no carrier hereunder shall be liable in any event."

In reply to the first contention, the defendant in error relies upon what is known as the Carmack amendment to the interstate commerce law (Act June 29, 1906, c. 3591, 34 Stat. 593 [U. S. Comp. St. Supp. 1909, p. 1167]) this day passed upon in the case of Norfolk and Western Railway Company *v.* Dixie Tobacco Company, 69 S. E. 1106, in which, upon the authority of the decision of the Supreme Court of the United States in the case of Atlantic Coast Line Railroad Co. v. Riverside Mills (decided at the October term, 1910) 219 U. S. ——, 31 Sup. Ct. 164, 54 L. Ed. ——, we held that the act in question is constitutional and valid. It is in these words:

" * * * Any common carrier, railroad or transportation company receiving property for transporation from a point in one state to a point in another state, shall issue a receipt or bill of lading therefor, and shall be liable to the lawful holder thereof for any loss, damage or injury to said property caused by it or by any common carrier, railroad or transportation company to which such property may be delivered, or over whose line or lines such property may pass, and no contract, receipt, rule or regulation shall exempt such common carrier, railroad or transportation company from the liability hereby imposed, provided that nothing in this section shall deprive any holder of such receipt or bill of lading of any remedy or right of action which he has under existing law."

The effect of that law, which we consider to be not only constitutional but a wise and salutary regulation, is that the contract by which the Old Dominion Steamship Company undertook to limit its liability to loss occurring on its own line is rendered null and void, and it is made liable for all loss occasioned upon the lines of its connecting carriers. That disposes of the first contention of plaintiff in error.

With reference to the provision in the bill of lading by which the shipper is required to make claim for loss or damage in writing to the agent at the point of delivery promptly after the arrival of the property, and if delayed more than 30 days after the delivery of the property or after due time for the delivery thereof the carrier shall not be liable, Flanary & Co. insist that the benefit of this provision was waived by the plaintiff in error; that its conduct was such as to operate as an estoppel upon it; and that it will not be permitted to rely upon this provision in the bill of lading.

In the case of Liquid Carbonic Co. v. Norfolk & Western Ry. Co., 107 Va. 323, 58 S. E. 569, 13 L. R. A. (N. S.) 753, this subject was fully examined and the conclusion reached that: "A condition in a bill of lading that claims for loss or damage shall be made in writing to the carrier's agent at the point of delivery promptly after the arrival of the property, and if delayed more than 30 days after the delivery of the property, or after due time for the delivery thereof, there shall be no liability upon the carrier, is a reasonable provision and will be upheld. Such a provision contravenes no public policy and excuses no negligence, but is a reasonable regulation for the protection of the carrier from fraudulent imposition in the adjustment and payment of claims for goods alleged to have been lost or damaged."

Old Dominion S. S. Co. et al. *v.* C. F. Flanary & Co

The reasonableness of the rule approved in the case just cited receives additional force from the fact that the liability of the initial carrier under the Carmack amendment to the interstate commerce act having been established, thus rendering it responsible for the delinquencies of a connecting carrier, or for those occurring upon a line other than its own, it should receive prompt notice of the fact that it is to be held liable, in order that it may take steps to indemnify itself by fixing the responsibility where it justly belongs.

The case of Atlantic Coast Line R. Co. *v.* Bryan, 109 Va. 523, 65 S. E. 30, construes a similar provision of a bill of lading, reaffirms the position taken in Liquid Carbonic Company *v.* N. & W. Ry. Co., and holds that such a provision is a reasonable one, and, unless waived, is enforceable by the carrier in bar of any action by the shipper for such loss or damage. Treating of waiver, the court there said: "A waiver, to operate as such, must arise either by contract, or by estoppel. If by contract, it must be supported like any other contract, by a valuable consideration. If estoppel by conduct is relied on, the party sought to be estopped must have caused the other party to occupy a more disadvantageous position than he would have occupied but for that conduct." And that "an attempt by a carrier to find a lost shipment after its exemption from liability has attached and become a vested right by reason of the failure of the shipper to present a claim therefor within the time and at the place stipulated for in the bill of lading does not constitute a waiver of its right to claim such exemption, if the goods should not be located."

In the still more recent case of Virginia-Carolina Chem. Co. *v.* Southern Express Co., 110 Va. 666, 66 S. E. 838, the case of Liquid Carbonic Co. *v.* N. & W. Ry. Co., supra, is referred to and again approved. The subject of waiver was also considered, and the court said: "It is true that, after the time limit had expired and the liability of the defendant had ceased, the agents of the company were diligent in their efforts to lessen the plaintiff's damage, as far as practicable, by collections on the lost notes; and from that source the loss was reduced from $1,980.23, the face amount of the notes, to $776.05. Nevertheless, there is nothing in the record to warrant the assumption that the express company has by words or act admitted liability or waived its right to insist upon the exemption afforded by the 30 days' clause."

In this case the only conduct relied upon to estop the plaintiff in error from asserting its exemption under the provision quoted from the bill of lading is that tracers were sent out to find the lost property. It is nowhere suggested in the record that there was any intimation that the carrier did not intend to insist upon its rights. The request that tracers should be sent out is the only

Old Dominion S. S. Co. et al. *v.* C. F. Flanary & Co

act upon the part of the consignee; the sending out of the tracers the only act upon the part of the carrier. It is not perceived that the defendant in error suffered any loss or damage, or was prejudiced, or was placed in any worse attitude, or was injured in any respect or in any degree whatever by what was done. The shipments were made on the 5th day of September. According to the weight of evidence, the goods should have arrived at their destination at Wise, Va., on or about the 15th. But if 15 days instead of 10 be allowed as a reasonable time to cover their transportation, still the notice would be insufficient, for the notice was filed by the H. B. Claflin Company on behalf of C. F. Flanary & Co. on October 23, 1906, and by Dunham & Co. on behalf of C. F. Flanary & Co. on October 27, 1906.

We are therefore of opinion that the court erred in instructing the jury that: "If they believe from the evidence in this case that the bills of lading covering the shipments of goods and merchandise in the declaration mentioned contained a provision that claims for loss or damage must be made in writing to the agent at the point of delivery promptly after arrival of the property, and if delayed for more than 30 days after the delivery of the property, or after due time for the delivery thereof, no carrier thereunder should be liable in any event; yet if they further believe from the evidence that the defendants had notice of the failure to deliver said goods to plaintiffs, and that plaintiffs or some one of them requested defendants to send tracer after said shipments, and that defendants did endeavor to trace and locate said shipments—then plaintiffs would not be required to give such notice in writing, except within 30 days from the time defendants abandoned all efforts to trace and locate said shipments, and so notified plaintiffs of such abandonment.

"And the jury are further instructed that even though they may believe the said bills of lading contained a provision as aforesaid, yet if they further believe that the defendants, through the acts, representations, and conduct of its employees, or through the acts, representations, and conduct of the agent, or agents, of the Virginia & Kentucky Railway Company, at Wise, Va., with whom such claim in writing should be filed as provided in such provision, or clause, waived the requirement of such provision, and led the plaintiffs to believe that the requirement of such provision would not be insisted upon by defendants, then the plaintiffs are not barred from a recovery by reason of any failure on their part to make such claim or claims in writing to the agent at the point of delivery at Wise, Va."

We are further of opinion that the court should have given instruction No. 1, asked for by plaintiff in error, as follows: "The court instructs the jury that there is no evidence in the case that the defendant, the Old Dominion Steamship Company, ever waived the benefit of the stipulation contained in the bill of lading and quoted in paragraph 4 of the questions submitted. And the jury, in answering the question in the said paragraph 4, should not answer that the said defendant, the Old Dominion Steamship Company, so waived the same."

For these reasons, the judgment of the circuit court must be reversed, and the cause remanded for a new trial in accordance with the views herein expressed.

CARDWELL, J., absent.

McMAHON v. NEW ORLEANS RY. & LIGHT CO.

(Supreme Court of Louisiana, Nov. 14, 1910.   Rehearing Denied Jan. 3, 1911.)

[53 So. Rep. 857.]

Carriers — Street Railroads — Injury to Passenger—Contributory Negligence.*—Where a passenger is permitted to stand on the front platform of a motor car, he has the right to assume that if there is any danger to him, requiring the closing of the gates of the platform, that they will be closed, and the same duty of closing these gates, when it is necessary for the protection of a passenger, rests upon an interurban railroad as upon a strictly city railroad.

Carriers—Street Railroads—Injury to Passenger—Negligence.— The employees of a railroad company must use every care commensurate with the danger to a passenger, and where a motorman of a street car fails to sufficiently slow down his car in rounding a curve, and a passenger, who has been standing on the platform with the motorman, is thrown out by the consequent jolting and is injured, the railroad company is liable.

Carriers—Street Cars—Injury to Passenger—Contributory Negligence.†—The fact that the rules of a railroad company provide that passenger may stand on the platform only when there are no seats in the car will not preclude a passenger from obtaining damages for the negligence of the car crew because there were seats in the car and the passenger was riding on the platform with the sanction of the employees of the railroad company.

Damages—Personal Injuries—Determination.—While there should be some similarity in the awards of damages for like injuries, still

---

*See last foot-note of Struble v. Pennsylvania Co. (Pa.), 35 R. R. R. 217, 58 Am. & Eng. R. Cas., N. S., 217; second foot-note of Denver & R. G. R. Co. v. Derry (Colo.), 36 R. R. R. 141, 59 Am. & Eng. R. Cas., N. S., 141; first foot-note of Cossitt v. St. Louis, etc., Ry. Co. (Mo.), 35 R. R. R. 501, 58 Am. & Eng. R. Cas., N. S., 501.

†For the authorities in this series on the question whether it is contributory negligence for a passenger to ride on the platform of a street car, see foot-note of Birmingham, etc., Co. v. Girod (Ala.), 36 R. R. R. 727, 59 Am. & Eng. R. Cas., N. S., 727.

there is no exact rule for the measurement of damages, and the facts of each case must be the basis on which the amount in each case is predicated.

(Syllabus by the Court.)

Provosty, J., dissenting.

Appeal from Civil District Court, Parish of Orleans; T. C. W. Ellis, Judge.

Action by Daniel P. McMahon against the New Orleans Railway & Light Company. Judgment for plaintiff, and defendant appeals. Affirmed.

Dart, Kernan & Dart, for appellant.

E. M. Stafford and *H. W. Robinson,* for appellee.

BREAUX, C. J. This was an action for damages, brought to recover the sum of $15,000 for personal injuries.

The case was tried by jury.

Nine thousand dollars was the amount allowed to plaintiff by the verdict and judgment.

Defendant prosecutes this appeal.

On the 23d day of July, 1909, plaintiff was thrown from the front platform of one of defendant's cars, a few hundred feet before reaching the West End terminus of defendant's line, near the platform known as the "Jackson Brewing Box."

Plaintiff, at the time of the accident, was a fireman in the employ of the New Orleans Fire Department, in whose service he had been for 18 years. He was earning $65 per month. His age was 44 years. His health was good.

On the day that he was hurt, he boarded the car about 1 p. m. at Basin and Canal streets. He had a holiday, and was going to the lake to fish and enjoy the day's vacation.

He had a hand basket and a package, which he placed on the platform where he stood.

While on the platform, he held to a rod on the front of the car.

Before he was thrown from the platform, he stooped down to take up his basket with his right hand, preparatory to his alighting from the car. It was then that he was thrown from the car.

There is a curve in the road where plaintiff was thrown out of the car.

The speed of the train was moderated a little on entering the curve, but not sufficient to prevent the jolting of the car.

Thomas J. Reed. a witness (an armorer of the Naval Brigade), who was a passenger on the train said that there is always a jolting when the car gets to the curve. because they lean to the right as the West End train goes around the curve. He said that at the time the train was moving at the rate of about 18 miles an hour.

McMahon *v.* New Orleans Ry. & Light Co

The other witness for the plaintiff testified to about the same effect.

The front gates of the car were open.

The motorman, on request of plaintiff, was to stop at the Jackson Brewing Box, where plaintiff was to alight from the car.

There were vacant seats in the car.

The train consisted of two cars—the motor and the trailer.

The contention of plaintiff is that when the train struck the curve there was a violent jolting, owing to the speed of the car, and it was then that he was thrown off.

He suffered severe injury. His foot was badly crushed and amputation was necessary.

He was carried to the Charity Hospital, where he remained four months.

His leg was amputated the first time about eight inches below the knee. The physician explained that it became necessary to perform a second operation and to amputate the leg at about four inches below the knee.

Plaintiff charges that it was negligence on the part of the defendant to leave the front gates of the car open.

Plaintiff testified that after the amputation of his leg he had sought work, and had failed to find it owing to the loss of his leg.

Defendant denies all liability, and charges that the injury suffered was through plaintiff's fault and negligence.

The speed of the car was not sufficiently moderated while passing through the curve is the trend of the testimony for plaintiff.

We are of opinion that there is no question but that while running through a curve those in charge of the car should be watchful and careful in order, so far as possible, to protect the lives of the passengers. The care exercised should be commensurate with the situation.

With reference to the jolting of the car, the defense urged that there were no jolts, and referred to the testimony of passengers inside of the car who did not feel jolt or jars.

We have found that there is conflicting testimony upon the subject.

But, be that as it may, passengers quietly seated in the car may not remember when testifying as witnesses in regard to jolts. Those on the outside were in a better position to see the jolt or to feel it.

Moreover, the fact is that plaintiff was thrown out. This fall is not accounted for on any other theory.

The position of the defendant is that the curve amounted to very little.

The testimony is that years ago a curve was carved out of

each side of the New Basin in order to enable schooners to pass. This curve has a shape of a half moon, is the statement of one of the witnesses. In time, when a track was laid, this track was made to bend to the eastward in order to follow the curve.

Some of the witnesses mention it as a curve of forty-five degrees, and others, that it was a slight curve.

We infer that there was enough of a curve to cause jolt or vibration when the car was running at a full speed or near full speed.

The testimony is that it was running at about 18 miles an hour through this curve.

The motorman and the conductor knew that the plaintiff was standing on the platform. The former knew that he was standing behind him and that he had asked him to stop at the Jackson Brewing Box, and that he had assented.

The conductor collected his fare from plaintiff while on the platform.

Neither the motorman nor the conductor warned the plaintiff of the least danger.

These two employees testified that passengers frequently ride on the platform of this train and that it is not considered at all dangerous to do so.

The rule is that passengers may ordinarily stand on the platform of the car if there are no vacant seats. If there are vacant seats and a passenger is allowed to remain on the platform without warning or notice it is not considered negligent on his part in so doing.

There are decisions in other jurisdictions holding that a passenger may ride on the platform whether there are vacant seats or not.

The case before us for decision is a stronger case for the plaintiff for the reason that he was seen by the employees on the platform, and they gave him some sanction for riding thereon by collecting the fare from him, as before mentioned, and in assenting to let him off at the Jackson Brewing Box, as above stated, while he was standing on the front platform of the motor car, near the motoneer.

The following decisions upon the subject are pertinent: Spurlock v. Shreveport, 118 La. 1, 42 South. 575; Brown v. Capital City R. R., 5 Street Railway Reports, 97.

It is stated in defendant's brief that plaintiff crossed over from the right to the left of the platform; that he was thereby negligent, and it was then that he lost his balance and feel over.

This is a contested issue of fact.

Plaintiff testified that he did not move from the right to the left; that he was on the side of the platform from which he was thrown, picking up his packages preparatory to stepping off the car when the jolt came and threw him out.

McMahon *v.* New Orleans Ry. & Light Co

The open gates at the front platform give rise to another question for decision. Plaintiff was standing on the platform of the front (motor) car, where generally these gates are kept closed while on the way.

The only defense at this point is that defendant's railroad should not be judged as if it were a city railroad.

To this we can only say that this road is at least interurban, if not entirely urban, and a street road. The train was moved by electricity from the city to West End, through grounds that are densely settled, except vacant spots here and there, of which it may be said "rures in urbe," for they all form part of the city of New Orleans.

The gates should have been closed. There was as much necessity for closing them as there is for closing the gates of a city car in front where the motorman guides the car. Interurban and strictly street cars are subject to the same regulation. Cincinnati R. R. Co. *v.* Lohe, Adm'r, etc., 68 Ohio St. 101, 67 N. E. 161, 67 L. R. A. 637.

Defendant's cars are as much city railroads as they are interurban.

One of the employees testified in regard to the open gate:

"Yes, sir; there are gates on the motor car."

That these gates are seldom used, unless the car runs over the Canal Belt. Why should they be seldom used except on the Canal Belt is an inquiry that is not answered by the testimony. There is evidently as much use for shutting these gates on the way to West End as anywhere else. Now, since the passengers were permitted to ride in front on the motorman's platform, it devolved upon the motorman to be careful and see that the gates were closed while the train was running and until the moment when the passengers are about to alight.

Defendant cites several decisions of courts of other jurisdictions, decided in favor of defendant, in which it appeared that plaintiff had knowledge of the situation.

Plaintiff was riding on the platform in view of the motorman and conductor, doubtless, without apprehending that there would be less control than the exigencies of the occasion required or that there would be jolt or vibration.

It is true that when plaintiff boarded the car at Canal he saw the gates open at the front platform. He would not have been heard to object to the open gates at that time. There was no necessity for his assuming that they would not be closed if the motorman saw the necessity of closing them at or near the curve before mentioned.

The duty of closing the gates was with the motorman.

Defendant charges that it was extremely negligent for plaintiff to go near the open gate and stoop down just as the car was about to enter the curve.

little distance before rea
not appear that he was ι
contradicted, that while
of the car; that is, he hε
to pick up his lunch bas

In this one act we haν

We have considered
conclusion that, as rela
affirmed.

Qu

That is the only rema

The defendant's cont
$9,000, a sum in excess
severer, it should be red
support of its contention
nell, 120 La. 1009, 45 S
Summit Lumber Co., 11
E. L. & P. Co., 40 La. A

In these cases, the dan

Defendant cites the ca
146, 24 South. 780. In t
$8,500 to $6,500.

Plaintiff, in this cited
leg.

In none of these case.

Damages are controlleι
case. Although there s
necessity for its being al

For reasons assigned,

Provosty, J., dissents.

CHICAGO, R. I. & P. Ry. Co. *v.* NEWBURN.

(Supreme Court of Oklahoma, July 12, 1910.)

[110 Pac. Rep. 1065.]

Carriers—Carriage of Passengers—Ejection.*—Plaintiff purchased a first-class, round-trip, nontransferable ticket, which contained on its face a requirement that he must sign it in ink, and a proviso that, if presented for passage by other than the original purchaser, the same was void; also, a line for his signature with a line for the signature of the agent as witness. Without being signed said ticket was honored for plaintiff's going passage. On his return he was ejected from the train because said ticket was not signed. There was no evidence showing plaintiff had refused to sign the same. Held, even if essential to the validity of the ticket, plaintiff's signature was waived by the company, and his ejection was wrongful.

Principal and Agent—Acts of Agent—Exemplary Damages.†—Under the decisions controlling in the Indian Territory, exemplary or punitive damages were not allowable against the principal, unless the evidence showed that the principal participated in the wrongful act of the agent expressly or impliedly by his conduct authorizing or approving it either before or after its commission, and, where there is a total absence of such evidence, an instruction authorizing a jury to allow plaintiff such damages is erroneous.

Carriers—Carriage of Passengers—Ejection—Damages.—In an action by a passenger for wrongful ejection from a train, plaintiff's loss of time cannot be considered in assessing his damages, in the absence of evidence as to the value of his time.

(Syllabus by the Court.)

Error from District Court, Le Flore County; D. A. Richardson, Judge.

Action by Geary L. Newburn against the Chicago, Rock Island & Pacific Railway Company. From a judgment in favor of plaintiff, defendant brings error. Reversed and remanded.

C. O. Blake, Thos. R. Beman, and *Stuart & Gordon,* for plaintiff in error.

T. T. Varner, for defendant in error.

---

*For the authorities in this series on the subject of the authority of the carrier's employees to waive the conditions of contracts for the transportation of passengers, see foot-note of Johnson v. Michigan United Rys. Co. (Mich.), 30 R. R. R. 346, 53 Am. & Eng. R. Cas., N. S., 346; last foot-note of Baltimore, etc., R. Co. v. Evans (Ind.), 29 R. R. R. 609, 52 Am. & Eng. R. Cas., N. S., 609.

†For the authorities in this series on the subject of the right to recover punitive or exemplary damages for wrongs to passengers, see first foot-note of Owens v. Atlantic C. L. R. Co. (N. Car.), 36 R. R. R. 483, 59 Am. & Eng. R. Cas., N. S., 483; foot-note of St. Louis, etc., R. Co. v. Garner (Miss.), 35 R. R. R. 185, 58 Am. & Eng. R. Cas., N. S., 185; Amann v. Chicago Consol. Traction Co. (Ill.), 35 R. R. R. 141, 58 Am. & Eng. R. Cas., N. S., 141.

Chicago, R. I. & P. Ry. (

DUNN, C. J. This action was be
Court for the Central District of Ir
Poteau, in January, 1907, by Geary J
error, hereafter called "plaintiff," agaiı
recover the sum of $2,000, for damag
ejection from a train of defendant (
a point between McAlester and Hail
Indian Territory. To the complaint (
consisting of a general and specific
allegations contained therein. The c:
1908, and the jury returned a verdict
prayed for. The evidence showed (
first-class, round trip ticket at Poteau (
& San Francisco Railway Company, (
cago, Rock Island & Pacific Railway
Alester and return, the ticket on its
containing a provision that it was nc
"must be signed in ink by the persoı
presented for passage by other than (
shows any alterations by erasures oı
one date or route is designated, it sł
will refuse to honor, and will take
also, an agreement on the part of the
by all the conditions as stated in the c
fully understood. Immediately follow
with "signature for original purchaser
other line with the word "witness" pı
"agent" beneath. Plaintiff testified t
going to McAlester, and that on his
tween McAlester and Haileyville, the
his ticket; that he showed the same
said the ticket was not good and dei
then left him until he had collected the
out the balance of the train, when he
he must either pay his fare or get off (
a while he was grabbed by his shoulde
door, and after stepping off the car he
hurting his leg. The testimony of pla
took place at the time of his ejection.
and porter all testified that they nevei
train did not stop at the time or place
that he was not ejected. This evide
by the testimony of the train dispatch
records no reports of any such occı
him, although it was the duty of the tr:
As the plaintiff does not testify that (
reason for ejecting him, the record is
but counsel for defendant, though rel

Chicago, R. I. & P. Ry. Co. v. Newburn

proposition that the testimony of plaintiff as to his having been ejected is false, assert that, by reason of the fact that plaintiff had failed to sign the ticket, the same was void, and that, even had he been ejected after having refused to pay fare as stated, the action on the part of the train operative was legal, and that plaintiff had no cause of action; hence the question is raised whether or not plaintiff could be lawfully ejected from the train for the sole reason that the ticket which he held, containing the terms above set forth, had not been signed by him. Plaintiff asserts, and it is not denied, that he was the original purchaser of the ticket, and his possession of it carried with it the presumption of ownership. The manifest purpose requiring it to be signed was to render it non-transferable, and to identify the purchaser, and the mere absence of the signature would not render it void. Walker v. Price, 62 Kan. 327, 62 Pac. 1001, 84 Am. St. Rep. 392; Gregory v. Burlington & Missouri River R. R. Co., 10 Neb. 250, 4 N. W. 1025; Kent v. B. & O. R. R. Co., 45 Ohio St. 284, 12 N. E. 798, 4 Am. St. Rep. 539.

The company sold plaintiff the ticket to enable him to take passage thereon. It could not with reason accept his money and give to him a contract which its agent knew was void. The requirement of the signature was for the benefit of the company. It was beneficial to it that no one but the purchaser should use the ticket, and the time when that fact was intended to be made manifest was at the time of its purchase. This is clear, not only from conditions surrounding and existing in the transaction, but from the fact that the face of the ticket itself shows that the agent was expected to witness the purchaser's signature. It may be said to be a matter of common knowledge that passengers purchasing tickets state to ticket agents their route and destination and rely largely on the agents to supply them with tickets meeting their requirements. And certainly it cannot be said to be a reasonable and just rule which would permit the agent of a company to sell and deliver to a passenger a ticket in such condition that the same will be refused and the passenger ejected on its presentation. If, under the facts in this case, the signing of this ticket was essential to its validity, the time to have required that was when the company took plaintiff's money for transportation, and it was too late to insist upon this right under the contract after plaintiff had boarded the train and was taking passage on the return part thereof. In other words, the company cannot accept and keep plaintiff's money, and then refuse to carry him because of an oversight of this character on the part of one of its agents. In the condition that this record comes to us the plaintiff's evidence must be taken as true. He was the original purchaser, and, under the circumstances, his ejection from the train was wrongful. In a similar case, the Supreme Court of Ohio, in the case of Kent v. B. & O. R. R. Co., supra,

Chicago, R. I. & P. Ry. Co. *v.* Newburn.

said: "According to the company's instructions to agents, and by the uniform custom regulating the sale of such tickets, they were required to be signed before their delivery to the purchasers. The company saw fit, in the case at bar, to dispense with this requirement. It received the plaintiff's money, delivered him the ticket, in his ignorance of any request that he sign it, honored it for several trips without first requiring him to sign its conditions. It thereby waived this requirement, and its conductor was not justified, while it still retained plaintiff's money, in ejecting him from its cars by reason of his failure to sign the ticket, which had already gone into full effect between the parties, and his failure to pay the usual fare in money for a passage which was already paid for."

And the Supreme Court of Nebraska, in the cases of Gregory *v.* Burlington & Missouri River R. R. Co., supra, said: "The general rule is 'that proof of possession of personal property is presumptive proof of ownership.' 1 Greenleaf, Evidence, § 34. This presumption certainly obtains in this case. The plaintiff was in possession of a ticket issued by a lawfully authorized agent of the company. It was regular in form, properly stamped; in fact, a first-class ticket, with certain conditions. The conditions were not signed, but there is no proof that the holder was requested to sign the same. There is no allegation in the answer that the ticket was stolen, nor that the plaintiff was not the original purchaser, nor is there a particle of proof to that effect; yet we are asked to declare the ticket void, because the agent selling the same did not require the purchaser to sign the conditions, as it is claimed the rules of the company require. There is no proof whatever that the plaintiff had any knowledge of such rules. And the fact that he presented the ticket for stamping at Lincoln without such signature is evidence tending to prove such lack of knowledge on his part. It will hardly be contended that the plaintiff can be affected by the neglect of the company's agent. He was the agent of their own selection for the sale of tickets. He was authorized to receive the consideration and issue and stamp the ticket and coupons. Can the company plead his default as a defense? Suppose the rules of the company required each conductor of the train to require the holder of such ticket to sign his name to the same, and a portion or all of them neglected to do so, would the ticket thereby be rendered void, if the company retained the consideration? The statement of the proposition shows its absurdity. But even if the agent has failed in some respects in the performance of his duty, still as between the plaintiff and the company is must bear the loss. And in any event, the defendant cannot retain the consideration and plead the laches of its agent as a defense to the ticket."

Counsel for defendant also complain in their third assignment

Chicago, R. I. & P. Ry. Co. *v.* Newburn

that the court erred in giving an instruction authorizing the jury to impose exemplary damages upon the defendant as punishment for the offense of ejecting plaintiff. There is a diversity of judicial expression upon this subject, but it is not necessary for us in this case to enter into any protracted discussion thereof. The facts in this case arose and it was brought in the Indian Territory, prior to the erection of the state of Oklahoma, and, the decisions of the Supreme Court of the United States being controlling in that jurisdiction, this court is bound by the same. See Moore *v.* A., T. & S. F. Ry. Co. (an opinion delivered by this court at this term, but not yet officially reported) 110 Pac. 1059, which, upon this question, is on all fours with the instant case and the cases therein cited, wherein the rule above noted is laid down and observed, and wherein this court, following the case of Lake Shore, etc., Ry. Co. *v.* Prentice, 147 U. S. 109, 13 Sup. Ct. 261, 37 L. Ed. 97, held substantially that, under the decisions controlling in a territory, exemplary or punitive damages not allowable against a principal unless the evidence showed that the principal participated in the wrongful act of the agent, expressly or impliedly by his conduct authorizing or approving it either before or after its commission. Under the authorities noted therein, the instruction given authorizing the jury to return a verdict for exemplary damages was error.

This conclusion on our part renders it unnecessary to notice the other questions raised in the case, except the error of the court alleged to have been committed in instructing the jury to allow plaintiff such damages as would compensate him for loss of time occasioned by the wrongful ejection. As there was no evidence in the record upon which this instruction could be predicated, and no showing of the value of time lost, this was error. Gulf, Colorado & Santa Fè Ry. Co. *v.* Daniels (Tex. Civ. App.) 29 S. W. 426.

The judgment of the trial court is, accordingly, reversed, and the case remanded, with instructions to set the same aside and allow defendant a new trial.

Turner, Williams, Hayes, and Kane, JJ., concur.

CRAIG *v.* BOSTON ELEVATED RY. CO.

(Supreme Judicial Court of Massachusetts, Suffolk, Jan. 6, 1911.)

[93 N. E. Rep. 575.]

Carriers — Injuries to Passengers — Negligence — Evidence. — A street car passenger was injured while sitting down by the car giving a sudden jerk. The car started, and then stopped, and then started again. No one else in the car was thrown over. Held, as a matter of law, that the motorman was not negligent in the operation of the car.

Carriers — Injuries to Passengers — Negligence — Evidence.—The constant starting and stopping of a car to avoid collisions with carriages crossing ahead of the car, or because of cars ahead of it, does not show negligence of the motorman in the operation of the car.

Exceptions from Superior Court, Suffolk County; Wm. Cushing Wait, Judge.

Actions by Jenetta Craig, and by Abraham Craig, prosecuted after his death by George Craig, his administrator, against the Boston Elevated Railway Company. There were verdicts for defendant in each case, and plaintiff in each case brings exceptions. Overruled.

George S. Littlefield and *Calvin S. Tilden,* for plaintiffs.
John T. Hughes, for defendant.

LORING, J. The plaintiff in the first action (a woman 67 years of age) had been to the theater in company with her own daughter, a Mrs. Goodwin and Mrs. Goodwin's daughter. After the theater they waited for a car at the corner of Washington and Boylston streets. The car stopped. The plaintiff entered first, followed by Mrs. Goodwin, then by Mrs. Goodwin's daughter, and lastly by her own daughter. The plaintiff, her own daughter and Mrs. Goodwin testified at the trial; Mrs. Goodwin's daughter did not. The plaintiff's story was that she went to the forward end of the car because there was but one vacant seat at the rear. To quote her own words: "She was in the act of sitting down when the car gave a sudden jerk and threw her forward. She thought she was facing toward the side of the car at the time. She was just in the act of sitting down. She was thrown forward, first with a sudden jerk, and then jerked back. and fell, she thought on Mrs. Goodwin, * * * who had followed her into the car. When she sat down her left knee began to pain, and, as a result of what happened, she suffered from pain and has a weakness in the leg." The plaintiff further testified that Mrs. Goodwin was not thrown down, but "if she hadn't been holding onto a strap, she would have gone down too," and that no one else in the car was thrown over. Mrs. Goodwin testified

Craig v. Boston Elevated Ry. Co

that there were a number of jerks near together and "violent enough to take you off your feet," but that they did not take her off her feet; that the sudden jerks threw the plaintiff off her feet into a passenger's lap, and "jerked me some, but I recovered myself by taking hold of the strap." The plaintiff's daughter testified that "the car started and then stopped, not a dead stop, and then started again;" that one motion followed the other suddenly, and that the car went "a very, very little distance" on the first start before it stopped again; that she had to support herself "by taking hold of the door frame, or it would throw me in the car;" that she did not see her mother thrown and could not do so, being behind Mrs. Goodwin and her daughter. The testimony showed that all four were safely seated, that no other persons boarded the car at the time, and that those previously in the car were seated.

We are of opinion that the evidence did not go far enough to warrant a finding that the motorman was negligent. and that the case comes within McGann v. Boston Elevated Ry., 199 Mass. 446, 85 N. E. 570, 18 L. R. A. (N. S.) 506, 127 Am. St. Rep. 509. A jerk such as is usual might well throw a passenger "just in the act of sitting down" into the lap of a passenger next to her if the passenger was not prepared for it, and a person might well take hold of a door frame to steady himself in such a case. In Byron v. Lynn & Boston R. R., 177 Mass. 303, 58 N. E. 1015, one of the witnesses testified that the motion of the car there in question "knocked me over, my hand against the sash of the window, I came near falling over the lady I gave my seat to." In spite of that it was held in that case that the evidence did not go far enough to warrant a finding that the motorman was negligent.

Mrs. Goodwin's testimony gave the explanation of the series of jerks. She testified "that it was 11:30 and people were going home from the theater." If the constant stopping and starting was to avoid collision with persons or carriages crossing ahead of the car, or because of cars ahead of it. there was no negligence on the part of the motorman. See in this connection Timms v. Old Colony St. Ry., 183 Mass. 193. 194, 66 N. E. 797, and McGann v. Boston Elev. Ry., 199 Mass. 446, 449. 85 N. E. 570, 18 L. R. A. (N. S.) 506, 127 Am. St. Rep. 509.

Exceptions overruled.

WHITE *v.* LEWISTON, A. & W. ST. RY.

(Supreme Judicial Court of Maine, Dec. 17, 1910.)

[78 Atl. Rep. 473.]

Carriers—Carriage of Passengers—Termination of Relation of Passenger and Carrier—Alighting of Passenger from Car.*—Relation of passenger and carrier was not terminated, upon a passenger alighting from a street car, where the carrier's charter (Priv. & Sp. Laws 1889, c. 528. §§ 3, 15) made it liable for injuries sustained by reason of any obstruction placed by it in the street; and, in view of Rev. St. c. 53, § 26. requiring street railway corporations to keep in repair such portions of the streets as shall be occupied by them, it is liable when a passenger alighted from a street car upon a portion of the street occupied by the company's tracks and fell over a grass covered spur track, sustaining injuries.

Carriers—Injury to Alighting Passenger—Dangerous Condition of Street.†—A carrier having the duty to keep in repair the portions of the streets occupied by its tracks, it was responsible for dangerous conditions of its own making existing there; and, where it stopped its car at such a place, it was liable for injuries received by the passenger from such dangerous condition after alighting from the car.

Carriers—Injury to Alighting Passenger—Negligence.—Where a street car company operates an open car with transverse seats, the implied invitation upon the stopping of the car, or the implied representation as to the safety of the points upon the street opposite the seats, is not restricted to one side or the other, in the absence of warning by the company.

Appeal and Error—Review—Verdict on Conflicting Evidence.—Where the evidence was conflicting, the verdict will not be disturbed where it is not indisputably wrong.

Exceptions from Supreme Judicial Court, Kennebec County.

Action by Mary A. White against the Lewiston, Augusta & Waterville Street Railway. Verdict for plaintiff, and defendant moves for a new trial and files exceptions. Overruled.

*For the authorities in this series on the question whether a person may be a passenger of the railroad after he alights from the train or street car, see first foot-note of Louisville R. Co. *v.* Mitchell (Ky.), 36 R. R. R. 710, 59 Am. & Eng. R. Cas., N. S., 710; last foot-note of Layne *v.* Chesapeake & O. R. Co. (W. Va.), 36 R. R. R. 537, 59 Am. & Eng. R. Cas., N. S., 537; last head-note of Denver & R. G. R. Co. *v.* Derry (Colo.), 36 R. R. R. 141, 59 Am. & Eng. R. Cas., N. S., 141.

†For the authorities in this series on the subject of the duties and liabilities of street railways with respect to keeping the streets occupied by their tracks in a safe condition for other users of streets, see foot-note of Dix *v.* Old Colony St. R. Co. (Mass.), 33 R. R. R. 469, 56 Am. & Eng. R. Cas., N. S., 469; Phinney *v.* Boston Elev. R. Co. (Mass.), 33 R. R. R. 6, 56 Am. & Eng. R. Cas., N. S., 6.

White *v.* Lewiston, A. & W. St. Ry

The case as stated by Mr. Justice BIRD, who prepared the opinion, is as follows:

The defendant, successor to the Lewiston, Winthrop & Augusta Street Railway and of the Augusta, Hallowell & Gardiner Railroad Company, was on the 12th day of August, 1907, a common carrier of passengers by its electric railway from Hallowell to Augusta and intermediate points. On that day at about 3 o'clock in the afternoon, the plaintiff, in good health, and weighing 260 pounds, became at Hallowell a passenger on a northbound open car of defendant of the usual type. She occupied the westerly end of the fourth seat from the rear of the car. Her destination being the third or most northerly gate of the Hallowell Cemetery, she gave a signal to the conductor to stop the car when she had arrived about opposite the most southerly gate of the cemetery. The conductor, being engaged upon the opposite side of the car taking fares, did not see her signal and, after a short interval, plaintiff called to the conductor to stop, the bell was rung, and the car stopped. In the locality where the car stopped the main track was situated upon the westerly side of the wrought portion of the street which upon the easterly side of the track was macadamized and in good condition, while upon the west of the main track was a siding several hundred feet long extending southerly from Day's driveway, near which it united with the main track where its grade was coincident therewith. The driveway extends westerly from the street and northerly of the cemetery, and is about 18 feet wide measuring on the westerly main rail. The grade of the siding gradually lowered as it extended southerly until at a distance of 50 feet or more from the southerly side of the driveway the grade of the siding was nearly 14 inches lower than that of the main track, the surface of the street, gradually sloping from the main track to the siding, forming a shoulder. At a distance of 25 feet southerly of the south side of the driveway, the difference in grade between main and spur tracks is 6 inches and the distance between the westerly main rail and the easterly spur rail 33 inches. The spur track was constructed of T rails supported by sleepers, which between the rails and westerly of the rails projected above the surface of the street, but their ends easterly of the easterly rail were covered with earth except that some of those about 25 feet southerly of the driveway were exposed in the neighborhood of the rail. The running board of the car overhung or extended out from the westerly rail of the main track about 22 inches.

The testimony was sharply contradictory as to the place where the car stopped; that produced by plaintiff tending to show that the front of the car reached the southerly edge of the driveway, that of the defendant that it nearly reached the northerly edge of the driveway where the motorman in charge usually stopped his car. If the latter is correct, the place where the plaintiff

White *v.* Lewiston, A. & W. St. Ry

alighted was between the rails of the spur track; if the former, she alighted between the easterly rail of the spur track and the westerly rail of the main track about 25 feet southerly of the driveway. Here, the spur track being seldom used, grass and weeds had grown upon either side of its easterly rail, more or less, as plaintiff claims, obscuring it from view.

When the car stopped, plaintiff alighted from the westerly side, and placed both feet upon the ground. She states that, after alighting, she took a step to the left to let the car go by her, and her right foot caught on the easterly rail of the siding, causing her to fall and sustain injuries for which she seeks damages.

Argued before Savage, Spear, Cornish, King, and Bird, JJ.

Benedict F. Maher, for plaintiff.
Heath & Andrews, for defendant.

Bird, J. The first exception is to the refusal of certain instructions requested by defendant and to certain instructions given against the objection of defendant. Recital of the instructions refused and given may be avoided by adopting the concise statement of counsel of defendant in his brief: "The gist of our contention was that if the plaintiff had safely alighted in the street, as she admitted, and her fall was due to her stumbling over anything lawfully in the street, the defendant was not liable, on the ground that its duty to the passenger ended with her safe alighting in the street. The gist of the rule given was that it was the duty of the defendant to exercise ordinary care in selecting a reasonably safe stopping place."

The rule asked for has been recognized by this court, at least arguendo, but with a limitation of its application to cases where the railway company has no authority or control over the streets, in Conway *v.* Railroad Co., 87 Me. 283, 286, 32 Atl. 901; s. c., 90 Me. 199, 202-204, 38 Atl. 110. See Call *v.* Street Railway, 69 N. H. 562, 565, 45 Atl. 405; Creamer *v.* West End Railway, 156 Mass. 320, 322, 31 N. E. 391, 16 L. R. A. 490, 32 Am. St. Rep. 456; Joslyn *v.* Milford, etc., Railway Co., 184 Mass. 65, 67, 67 N. E. 866. "In the absence of any authority given the street railway company over the streets, it must be evident that it cannot be held as an insurer of their safety for passengers to alight upon." Conway *v.* Horse R. R. Co., 87 Me. 286, 32 Atl. 902. In Robertson *v.* West Jersey & S. R. Co. (N. J. Sup.) 74 Atl. 300, 301, the court, quoting from Creamer *v.* Railway Co., ubi supra, says: " 'The street is in no sense a passenger station for the safety of which a street railway company is responsible when a passenger steps from the car upon the street. He becomes a traveler upon the highway and terminates his relations and rights as a passenger, and the railway company is not responsible to him as a carrier for the condition of the street or for his

White *v.* Lewiston, A. & W. St. Ry

safe passage from the car to the sidewalk.' While we might qualify the statement of this case to exclude the setting down of a passenger at an obviously improper point in the highway, the rule enunciated as to the termination of the relation is approved."

But in the present case it is provided in the charter of one of the corporations whose franchises the defendant is now exercising that "said corporation shall maintain and keep in repair such portions of the streets and roads occupied by the tracks of its railroad, and shall make all other repairs of said streets and roads which may be rendered necessary by the occupation of the same by said railroad: * * * And said corporation shall be liable for any loss or damage which any person may sustain by reason of any carelessness, neglect or misconduct of its agents or servants, or of any obstruction placed by them in the streets or roads of said cities or towns, and shall save and hold said cities and towns harmless from any suits for such loss or damage.

"The said railroad shall be constructed and maintained in such form and manner, and with such rails and appliances, that so much of the streets and roads as are occupied thereby shall be safe and convenient for travelers; and said corporation shall be liable in an action on the case for any loss or damage which any person may sustain by reason of any failure to comply with this provision." Sections 3, 15, c. 528, Priv. & Sp. Laws 1889.

And so by general statute it is provided (Rev. St. c. 53, § 26): "Such corporations (all street railroad corporations) shall keep and maintain in repair such portions of the streets, roads or ways, as shall be by them occupied and shall make all other repairs thereon, rendered necessary by such occupation."

It is unnecessary to say that, having the duty both by special and general law to maintain in repair the portions of the streets occupied, defendant had the authority and power to make necessary repairs. If grass and weeds obscured and concealed its disused rails, the removal of the same was a matter within its power, and to such extent its siding was within the control of defendant. Milton *v.* Railway Co., 103 Me. 218, 222, 223, 68 Atl. 826, 15 L. R. A. (N. S.) 203, 125 Am. St. Rep. 293.

Having control, if not exclusive, of the point where the passenger is impliedly invited to alight, it is responsible for dangerous conditions of its own making. The condition which the jury may have found to exist at the point at which plaintiff claims to have alighted is not unlike that which existed in Cobb *v.* Standish, 14 Me. 198. The rail lawfully located had become "a pitfall to allure and then to injure." See Bourget *v.* Cambridge, 156 Mass. 391, 393, 31 N. E. 390, 16 L. R. A. 605.

The refusal of the requested instructions without exception or modification in the present case was not error. The instructions given and excepted to were in accordance with the law

White v. Lewiston, A. & W. St. Ry.

as laid down in Conway v. Railroad Co., 90 Me. 199, 204, 38 Atl. 110.

The second and third exceptions, as matter of law, are abandoned, and, so far as the second concerns matter of fact, it is urged and considered upon the motion.

Upon its motion defendant urges that the jury erred in finding that the plaintiff alighted at a place about 25 feet southerly of the driveway. But, assuming the credibility of all the witnesses, the evidence upon this point was conflicting, and we can find no cause to hold that the conclusion of the jury was without warrant.

Again, the defendant contends that the plaintiff was guilty of contributory negligence in not alighting from the east side of the car. But "the plaintiff was sitting at the end of one of the transverse seats, * * * and would be expected to alight, as she did from the side of the car at the point opposite her seat." Conway v. Railroad Co., 90 Me. 199, 203, 38 Atl. 110, 111. We cannot hold that with an open car with transverse seats the implied invitation upon the stopping of the car or the implied representation as to the safety of the points upon the street opposite the seats is restricted to one side or the other in the absence of warning on part of defendant. See McKimble v. B. & M. R. R., 141 Mass. 463, 471, 5 N. E. 804; Richmond City Ry. Co. v. Scott. 86 Va. 902, 908, 11 S. E. 404. Whether the plaintiff was guilty of contributory negligence in selecting the west side from which to alight was a question for the jury, and its finding upon the evidence we find no occasion to disturb.

Contributory negligence is also urged in that the plaintiff was careless in stumbling over the rail, and in not seeing and avoiding it. But upon both these questions the evidence was conflicting. The jury had a view of the locality, and we must hold that it is not apparent that the verdict is indisputably wrong.

Exceptions and motion overruled.

Pelot v. Atlantic Coast Line R. Co.

(Supreme Court of Florida, Division B., Dec. 14, 1910.   Headnotes
Filed Jan. 17, 1911.)

[53 So. Rep. 937.]

**Carriers—Carriage of Passengers—Duties of Carrier—Injury to
Passenger—Acts of Employees.***—Passengers do not contract merely
for ship room and transportation from one place to another; but they
also contract for good treatment, and against personal rudeness, and
every wanton interference with their persons, either by the carrier
or his agents employed in the management of the ship or other conveyance. If the wrongful act is inflicted on the plaintiff while he
is a passenger in actual course of transportation, by a servant of the
carrier acting as such at the time of the act, the law will consider
the carrier as responsible therefor, without inquiring whether the
wrong was committed in the execution of the servant's employment.
Whatever may be the motive which incites the servant to commit
an unlawful or improper act towards the passenger during the existence of the relation of carrier and passenger, the carrier is liable
for the act and its natural and legitimate consequences.

Carriers—Carriage of Passengers—Care Required.†—Passenger
carriers, by their contracts, bind themselves to carry safely those
whom they take into their coaches or cars as far as human foresight will go; that is, for the utmost care and diligence of very cautious persons.

**Carriers—Carriage of Passengers—Injury to Passenger—Action—
Declaration.***—A declaration that distinctly alleges that, while the
plaintiff was a passenger in course of transportation on the defendant's train, the defendant's employee, the porter on said train, who
was in the discharge of the duties of his employment, did negligently,
violently, and suddenly, regardless of plaintiff's rights, shove and
push a swinging door in said passenger coach back and upon plaintiff's foot, without any fault upon plaintiff's part, thereby causing
serious injury to plaintiff's foot, states a legal cause of action, and
is not subject to demurrer.

(Syllabus by the Court.)

Error to Circuit Court, De Soto County; J. B. Wall, Judge.

Action by W. A. Pelot against the Atlantic Coast Line Railroad Company. Judgment for defendant, and plaintiff brings
error. Reversed and remanded, with directions.

---

*For the authorities in this series on the question for what acts
or omissions of servants a carrier of passengers is liable, see extensive note. 6 R. R. R. 170, 29 Am. & Eng. R. Cas., N. S., 170.

†For the authorities in this series on the subject of the degree of
care required of a railroad as a carrier of passengers, see first foot-
note of Gardner v. Metropolitan St. R. Co. (Mo.), 36 R. R. R. 448,
59 Am: & Eng. R. Cas., N. S., 448.

Pelot *v.* Atlantic Coast Line R. Co

Leitner & Leitner, for plaintiff in error.
Sparkman & Carter, for defendant in error.

TAYLOR, J. The plaintiff in error, as plaintiff below, sued the defendant in error, as defendant below, in the circuit court of De Soto county; the declaration in the case being as follows:

"Comes now the plaintiff herein, by his attorneys, Leitner & Leitner, and sues the defendant, Atlantic Coast Line Railroad Company, who has an agent in De Soto county, Florida, and who has been summoned to answer plaintiff in an action of trespass on the case.

"For that, whereas, heretofore, to wit, on or about the 6th day of July, 1909, the said defendant was a common carrier for hire, and operated a line of railroad for the carriage of passengers from the city of Jacksonville, Duval county, Florida, through Bradford county, by the way of Lake Butler, to the city of Gainesville, Florida, Alachua county; that on or about the said date, to wit, July 6, 1909, the said plaintiff was a lawful passenger on the defendant's road from said Jacksonville to Gainesville; that in defendant's coach, in which plaintiff was riding, there were two compartments, to wit, the passenger and smoker, with a partition between, and to allow ingress and egress from the passenger portion of said coach into the said smoker there is a swinging door in said partition; that on said train there were servants of defendant, to wit, a porter, whose duty it was to announce to the passengers on said train the several stations through which defendant's road ran; that plaintiff had been riding on the said train in the smoker, but just after passing Lake Butler he got up from his seat in the smoker and started into the passenger portion of said coach; that when plaintiff was within a few feet of said swinging door, and without any fault on the part of plaintiff, the said porter, coming from the passenger portion of said coach into the smoker, in the discharge of his duty, did negligently, violently, and suddenly, regardless of the rights of plaintiff, shove and push the said swinging door back upon plaintiff's foot, which said stroke did then and there crush and bruse plaintiff's foot, causing it to rise and inflame, from which plaintiff was sick and sore for many weeks, to the damage of plaintiff in the sum of $800; that he was forced and compelled to pay out sums of money in endeavoring to cure the said wound, in the sum of $100; that he was forced to lose time from his business on account of said sickness, to his damage in the sum of $100. Wherefore a cause of action has accrued to demand of defendant the sum of $1,000, and therefore he sues the defendant and claims $1,000."

To this declaration the defendant demurred on the following grounds:

"(1) Because the allegations of the declaration are not sufficient to constitute a cause of action.

Pelot v. Atlantic Coast Line R. Co

"(2) Because the declaration shows on its face that the plaintiff has no cause of action against the defendant.

"(3) Because the declaration shows on its face that the injury complained of was due solely to an accident, and was not due to any ne   en e of the defendant or of any of the servants in its employglig c

"(4) Because the declaration shows on its face that the injury complained of was due to the carelessness of the plaintiff himself.

"(5) And for other good and sufficient reasons apparent upon the face of the declaration."

The first three grounds of this demurrer were sustained by the court, and, the plaintiff declining to amend his declaration, final judgment in favor of the defendant was rendered, and this judgment the plaintiff brings here for review by writ of error, assigning as error the ruling of the court upon such demurrer. The following principles of law are applicable to and will govern this case: "Passengers do not contract merely for ship room and transportation from one place to another; but they also contract for good treatment, and against personal rudeness, and every wanton interference with their persons, either by the carrier or his agents employed in the management of the ship or other conveyance." "If the wrongful act is inflicted on the plaintiff while he is a passenger in actual course of transportation, by a servant of the carrier acting as such at the time of the act, the law will consider the carrier as responsible therefor, without inquiring whether the wrong was committed in the execution of the servant's employment." Buswell on Personal Injuries (2d Ed.) § 38, and citations; Pendleton v. Kinsley, 3 Cliff. 416; Fed. Cas. No. 10,922. Whatever may be the motive which incites the servant to commit an unlawful or improper act toward the passenger during the existence of the relations of carrier and passenger, the carrier is liable for the act and its natural and legitimate consequences. Dwinelle v. New York Cent. & H. R. R. Co., 120 N. Y. 117, 24 N. E. 319, 8 L. R. A. 224, 17 Am. St. Rep. 611. Passenger carriers, by their contracts, bind themselves to carry safely those whom they take into their coaches or cars as far as human foresight will go; that is, for the utmost care and diligence of very cautious persons. Wheaton v. North Beach & M. R. R. Co., 36 Cal. 590; Maverick v. Eight Avenue R. R. Co., 36 N. Y. 378.

Applying these principles to the declaration in this case, we think that it alleges a good cause of action. It distinctly alleges that, while the plaintiff was a passenger in course of transportation on the defendant's train, the defendant's employee, the porter on said train, who was in the discharge of the duties of his employment, did negligently, violently, and suddenly, regardless of the rights of plaintiff, shove and push a swinging door in

Atlantic City R. Co. v. Clegg

said passenger coach back and upon plaintiff's foot, without any fault upon plaintiff's part, thereby causing serious injury to plaintiff's foot.

The court below erred in sustaining the demurrer to the plaintiff's declaration, and in rendering final judgment in favor of the defendant, and because of such error the said judgment is hereby reversed, and the cause remanded, with directions to overrule such demurrer. The costs of this writ of error to be taxed against the defendant in error.

HOCKER and PARKHILL, JJ., concur.

WHITFIELD, C. J., and SHACKLEFORD and COCKRELL, JJ., concur in the opinion.

ATLANTIC CITY R. CO. v. CLEGG.

(Circuit Court of Appeals, Third Circuit, November 28, 1910.)

[183 Fed. Rep. 216.]

Carriers—Injury to Passengers—Management of Trains at Railroad Station.*—Plaintiff's intestate entered the waiting room at a station on defendant's railroad, having the return part of a round-trip ticket, and, after inquiring the time of his train sat down and waited for it. There were two tracks in front of the station building and his train passed on the farther one. A street crossed the

---

*For the authorities in this series on the question whether a person may be a passenger before he boards the train or street car, see first foot-note of Texas Midland R. Co. v. Geraldon (Tex.), 37 R. R. R. 106, 60 Am. & Eng. R. Cas., N. S., 106; Metcalf v. Yazoo & M. V. R. Co. (Miss.), 36 R. R. R. 743, 59 Am. & Eng. R. Cas., N. S., 743.

For the authorities in this series on the subject of the right of a passenger to act on the assumption that the carrier has performed or will perform its duties, see second foot-note of Denver & R. G R. Co. v. Derry (Colo.), 36 R. R. R. 141, 59 Am. & Eng. R. Cas., N. S., 141; first foot-note of Illinois Cent. R. Co. v. Daniels (Miss.), 34 R. R. R. 196, 57 Am. & Eng. R. Cas., N. S., 196; last foot-note of Cossitt v. St. Louis, etc., Ry. Co. (Mo.), 35 R. R. R. 501, 58 Am. & Eng. R. Cas., N. S., 501; Struble v. Pennsylvania Co. (Pa.), 35 R. R. R. 217, 58 Am. & Eng. R. Cas., N. S., 217.

For the authorities in this series on the subject of the duties and liabilities of a railroad company with respect to passengers struck by trains between depots or other stopping places and their respective train or car, see second foot-note of Louisville R. Co. v. Mitchell (Ky.), 36 R. R. R. 710, 59 Am. & Eng. R. Cas., N. S., 710.

For the authorities in this series on the subject on the contributory negligence of passengers struck by trains or street cars while crossing tracks between depots or other stopping places and trains or street cars, see first foot-note of Struble v. Pennsylvania Co. (Pa.), 35 R. R. R. 217, 58 Am. & Eng. R. Cas., N. S., 217; last foot-note of Illinois Cent. R. Co. v. Daniels (Miss.), 34 R. R. R. 196, 57 Am. & Eng. R. Cas., N. S., 196.

Atlantic City R. Co. *v.* Clegg

tracks at the end of the station, paved with concrete, and from it and on the same level a paved platform extended on the outer side of each track, there being no division between the pavement of the street and the platforms. A picket fence also extended from the street between the tracks past the station, which prevented crossing except on the street. An automatic bell was rung by every train from the time it approached until it left the station. The train of plaintiff's intestate stopped with the rear car on the street crossing, and, as he was passing to it from the waiting room along the street, he was struck and killed by a through train on the nearer track going in the opposite direction at high speed. Held, that deceased was a passenger, and did not lose that relation by entering upon the street to reach his train which was at the implied invitation of defendant; that he had the right to act on the assumption that defendant would exercise proper care not to injure passengers while passing from the waiting room to the train by the only way open to them; and that the questions of negligence and contributory negligence were for the jury.

In Error to the Circuit Court of the United States for the District of New Jersey.

Action by Mary S. Clegg, administratrix of Charles A. Clegg, deceased, against the Atlantic City Railroad Company. Judgment for plaintiff, and defendant brings error. Affirmed.

Thompson & Cole, for plaintiff in error.
Frank S. Katzenbach, Jr., for defendant in error.

Before BUFFINGTON and LANNING, Circuit Judges, and CROSS, · District Judge.

BUFFINGTON, Circuit Judge. In the court below Mrs. Mary S. Clegg, administratrix and wife of Charles S. Clegg, brought suit against the Atlantic City Railroad Company for its alleged negligence in causing his death. She recovered a verdict, and on entry of judgment thereon in her favor the railroad sued out this writ.

The accident in which the decedent lost his life occurred at the defendant's station at Magnolia, N. J. The ticket office and waiting room are at the side of a platform which runs along the south-bound track, and there is another open platform along the north-bound track. Eversham avenue, a public street, crosses the two tracks at the south end of the station. A picket fence between the two tracks extends from that avenue northward, and prevents passengers crossing from one platform to the other, except by using the avenue. The two platforms and the street are all made of concrete, are on the same level, and there is no dividing or marked line between platforms and street. North-bound trains often stopped at Magnolia station with a car standing on

Atlantic City R. Co. *v.* Clegg

Eversham avenue, and passengers were accustomed to get off the cars on either side, using the street as a disembarking platform.   There was an automatic bell, rung by an approaching train, and which kept ringing until the train left the station. There was neither watchman or gate at the crossing, and the station agent was the only employee.   He was absent at the time of the accident, having gone to the post office to get the mail bag which it was his duty to put on the train.   The testimony on plaintiff's behalf tended to show that on the day before the accident the decedent came to Magnolia on a train from Camden, and had a return round-trip ticket to that place.   The next morning he went to the station shortly before 9 o'clock, reaching it from the waiting room side.   He went into the waiting room, learned from the ticket agent, who had not yet gone out for the mail, the time of his return train to Camden, and then sat down to wait.   His train came in shortly thereafter, and its last car stopped with its rear platform steps beyond the fence and opposite the Eversham avenue crossing.   Its approach set in motion the automatic bell, and it was ringing when the deceased left the waiting room to take his train and crossed the south-bound track on the avenue.   Just before he reached the train and while crossing the latter track, he was struck and killed by a scheduled express train which passed the station on the south-bound track without stopping.   This train, which was ten minutes behind time and was running at high speed, blew for the crossing, and the deceased, had he looked before he crossed the track, could have seen it.

It will thus be seen the case turns on the relation the decedent and the railroad bore to each other, and its reversal is conditioned on the adoption by this court of the contention made in the brief of the railroad's counsel, viz.: "Entering upon the highway over which the railroad had no possible control destroyed the relation of carrier and passenger, if such existed, at any time prior thereto."   This, in effect, would be to say that the decedent at the time of the accident stood in the relation of a stranger to the railroad, and that it owed no greater duty to him than to a pedestrian crossing its tracks by this public street.   We think, however, there was evidence from which a jury was justified in finding the deceased bore at the time of the accident the relation of a passenger to the railroad, and that it failed to exercise due care for his safety.   In point of fact the deceased had a ticket. He was waiting for the train's approach in a place provided by the railroad, and he could only reach its train by using the public street.   The erection by the railroad of its fence, its use of the street as a train approach or platform, and stopping its train on the street, were acts from which a jury could infer the railroad invited the deceased to use the street as an approach or platform. It must be conceded that the relation of passenger existed when

Atlantic City R. Co. v. Clegg

Mr. Clegg entered the waiting room, inquired for his train, and with a ticket in his possession sat down to await his train. If so, did that relation cease when he crossed an invisible and unmarked property line on the level platform and took the only path the railroad provided for him to get upon its train? To hold that under such circumstances the relation of passenger ended when he crossed the street line would seem unreasonable. As between the railroad and the municipality, the platform and the street were two different things, but, as between the passenger and the railroad, the latter had made them one by using it as the only means of approach to its north-bound trains and by impliedly inviting him to take it. The defendant had no one there to direct the decedent. The ringing signal was a warning given by the north-bound train, and, under the circumstances and the implied invitation to cross, the decedent was justified in assuming the railroad would warn him of danger threatening his crossing. While the case is not on all fours with Warner v. Baltimore, etc., R. Co., 168 U. S. 346, 18 Sup. Ct. 68, 42 L. Ed. 491, yet both are governed by the general principle there stated:

"The situation of the tracks, the location of the station building and the waiting room, the coming of the local train, and its stopping to receive passengers in a position which required the latter to cross a track in order to reach the train involved necessarily a condition of things which under one view of the testimony constituted an implied invitation to the passenger to follow the only course which could have followed in order to take the train; that is, to cross the track to the waiting train. Whilst it is true, as was said in Terry v. Jewett, supra, that such implied invitation would not absolve a passenger from the duty to exercise care and caution in avoiding danger, nevertheless it certainly would justify him in assuming that in holding out the invitation to board the train the corporation had not so arranged its business as to expose him to the hazard of danger to life and limb unless he exercised the very highest degree of care and caution. The railroad, under such circumstances, in giving the invitation, must necessarily be presumed to have taken into view the state of mind and of conduct which would be engendered by the invitation, and the passenger, on the other hand, would have a right to presume that in giving the invitation the railroad itself had arranged for the operation of its trains with proper care. The doctrine finds a very clear expression in a passage in the opinion in the Terry Case [78 N. Y. 334], already referred to, where it was said: 'It may be assumed that a railroad corporation, in the exercise of ordinary care, so regulates the running of its trains that the road is free from interruption or obstruction where passenger trains stop at a station to receive and deliver passengers. Any other system would be dangerous to human life, and impose

Kruse v. St. Louis, I. M. & S. Ry Co

great risks upon those who might have occasion to travel on the railroad.' "

The case having been submitted to the jury in accordance with the foregoing principles, and the evidence such as to warrant a verdict based on negligence of the railroad and an absence of contributory negligence of the decedent, the judgment below is affirmed.

Kruse v. St. Louis, I. M. & S. Ry. Co.

(Supreme Court of Arkansas, Jan. 2, 1911.)

[133 So. Rep. 841.]

Carriers—Who Are Passengers—Conveyances and Places Not Proper for Passengers—Through Freight Train.—One entering a train, such as a through freight train, which he knows or has reason to believe is not intended to carry passengers, and upon which the rules of the company forbid passengers to ride, is not legally a passenger.

Carriers—Passengers—Personal Injuries—Passenger on Freight Train.[*]—A person entering a train, such as a through freight train, which he knows or has reason to believe is not intended to carry passengers, and on which the rules of the company forbid passengers to ride, cannot recover damages for injuries received while on the train, unless they were willfully or wantonly inflicted by the carrier's servants.

Carriers—Who Are Passengers—Payment of Fare.[†]—Where a person enters a train without any intention to pay fare, but under a collusive agreement with the conductor to ride free, in violation of the rules of the company, and does not pay any fare, he does not legally become a passenger for whose safety as a passenger the carrier is liable.

Carriers—Passengers—Personal Injuries—Person Not Paying Fare.[*]—Where a person attempts in bad faith to defraud a carrier

---

[*] For the authorities in this series on the subject of the degree of care due trespassers on trains, see first foot-note of Johnson v. Great Northern Ry. Co. (Wash.), 29 R. R. R. 211, 52 Am. & Eng. R. Cas., N. S., 211; last foot-note of Southern Ry. Co. v. Clark (Ky.), 37 R. R. R. 246, 50 Am. & Eng. R. Cas., N. S., 246.

[†] For the authorities in this series on the question whether persons riding on trains or street cars by invitation of railroad employees are trespassers or licensees, see second foot-note of Johnson v. Great Northern Ry. Co. (Wash.), 29 R. R. R. 211, 52 Am. & Eng. R. Cas., N. S., 211.

For the authorities in this series on the subject of the existence of the relation of carrier and passenger as affected by failure to purchase ticket or pay fare, see foot-note of Thompson v. Nashville, etc., Ry. (Ala.), 34 R. R. R. 171, 57 Am. & Eng. R. Cas., N. S., 171.

Kruse v. St. Louis, I. M. & S. Ry. Co

by riding free or for less than full fare, even with the consent of the conductor of the train, he is a trespasser, and the company is not responsible for injuries not wantonly or willfully inflicted.

Carriers—Passengers—Personal Injuries—Actions—Presumptions —Passenger on Freight Train.—Since the enactment of Kirby's Dig. § 6705, providing that local freight trains shall carry passengers, there is no presumption that a person riding on a freight train is not a passenger.

Trial—Instructions—Error Cured by Other Instruction.—In an action for injuries to a person riding on defendant's through freight which did not carry passengers, the error in an instruction that "the presumption is that a person found upon a freight train is not legally a passenger" is cured by a further instruction that plaintiff entered the train with a bona fide intention of becoming a passenger; that is, that he either procured a ticket to ride on the train, or that he intended in good faith to pay his fare.

Trial—Course and Conduct of Trial—Presence of Judge—Prejudicial Error.—The presiding judge, during a trial, and while the plaintiff's counsel was making his closing argument to the jury, without suspending proceedings, left the courtroom and remained out of hearing of the jury for five or ten minutes, and during his absence a disinterested member of the bar sat upon the bench at the invitation of the judge, and counsel for plaintiff continued his argument, and, while so doing, defendant's counsel objected to his reading of a deposition, whereupon counsel suspended argument until the return of the judge. It appeared from affidavits of bystanders that on objection by defendant's counsel there was a heated controversy, but it did not appear what was said. Held that, unless the party complaining showed some misconduct of his adversary actually committed during the absence of the judge, the mere absence of the judge from the courtroom was not prejudicial error.

Kirby and Hart, JJ., dissenting.

Appeal from Circuit Court, Faulkner County; Eugene Lankford, Judge.

Action by C. H. Kruse against the St. Louis, Iron Mountain & Southern Railway Company. Judgment for defendant, and plaintiff appeals. Affirmed.

J. A. Watkins and *T. G. Malloy,* for appellant.
Lovick P. Miles and *Thos. B. Pryor,* for appellee.

McCulloch, C. J. Plaintiff, C. H. Kruse, instituted this action in the circuit court of Faulkner county to recover damages for personal injuries received while riding on one of appellee's freight trains which he had boarded at Malvern, Ark., en route to Texarkana. His injuries were caused by a collision with another train at Witherspoon, Ark. He alleged that he was a passenger on the train and had paid his fare to Texarkana. The

Kruse *v.* St. Louis, I. M. & S. Ry. Co

answer denied that plaintiff was a passenger, alleged that the train was one on which passengers were not allowed, and that plaintiff was a trespasser on the train and had not paid his fare. The jury returned a verdict in favor of the defendant, and plaintiff appealed.

Plaintiff was a telegraph operator, and had been sojourning in Hot Springs. He came over to Malvern over another railroad and desired to go to Texarkana on one of defendant's trains. He testified that he was waiting in the station at Malvern when the freight train came, and asked the conductor if the train carried passengers, and was told that it did; that he inquired of the conductor what the fare was to Texarkana, and was told that it was $2; that he paid that sum to the conductor, who pointed out the caboose and told him to get on.

The testimony adduced by defendant tended to show that the train was a through freight, on which passengers were not allowed to travel without special permission of the train master or superintendent; that plaintiff knew this when he boarded the train; that plaintiff neither paid nor offered to pay fare, nor intended to pay any; but that, on the contrary, he was permitted by the conductor to ride free in violation of the rules of the company. Plaintiff introduced one witness whose testimony tended to show that the train on which plaintiff rode was a local freight and carried passengers, but the preponderance of the evidence was to the effect that it was a through freight and did not carry passengers.

The law is well settled in this state that when one enters a train such as a through freight, which he knows or has reason to believe is not intended to carry passengers, and on which the rules of the company forbid passengers to ride, he is not a passenger in a legal sense, but is a trespasser, and cannot recover damages for injuries received while on the train unless they have been willfully or wantonly inflicted by servants of the railway company. St. L., I. M. & S. Ry. Co. *v.* Reed, 76 Ark. 106, 88 S. W. 836, 113 Am. St. Rep. 78. Chief Justice Cockrill, speaking for this court in such a case, said: "Where there is a division of the freight and passenger business of a railroad, the common presumption is that a person found on a freight train is not legally a passenger; and, if he claims that he is, it devolves upon him to show a state of case that will rebut the presumption." Hobbs *v.* T. & P. Ry. Co., 49 Ark. 357, 5 S. W. 586. The same learned judge, speaking for the court in another such case, said that, if a person "through his own neglect had embarked on a mere wild train which conductor could not delay without the danger of throwing the passenger and freight travel of the road into confusion, it was his duty to refuse to stop merely for a passenger's accommodation. The fact that he took the appellee's ticket could not alter the rule under such circumstances." St. L., I. M. & S. Ry. Co. *v.* Rosenberry. 45 Ark. 256.

Kruse *v.* St. Louis, I. M. & S. Ry. Co

We deem it to be equally sound in justice to say that when a person enters a train without any intention to pay fare, but under a collusive agreement with the conductor to ride free in violation of the rules of the company, and does not pay any fare, he does not legally become a passenger, and the railway company is not responsible for his safety as a passenger. Quoting the language of Judge Riddick in the Reed Case, supra, if, under those circumstances, he "is carried safely to his destination, he gains that much at the expense of the company. On the other hand, if an accident happens, and he is injured, there is no reason or justice in requiring the company to pay for his injuries, unless they have been wantonly or willfully inflicted." The authorities which sustain the proposition are numerous, and among them are found the following, which include cases where persons ride under collusive agreements with the conductor not to pay fare, or to pay less than full fare, and also where persons ride on a pass or ticket procured from the company by fraud. Fitzmaurice *v.* N. Y., etc., R. R. Co., 192 Mass. 159, 78 N. E. 418, 6 L. R. A. (N. S.) 1146, 116 Am. St. Rep. 236, 7 Am. & Eng. Ann. Cas. 586; note to Vassor *v.* Atl. Coast Line R. Co., 9 Am. & Eng. Ann. Cas. 535; 2 Sherman & Redf. on Neg. § 489; 2 Jaggard on Torts, § 1081; Toledo, etc., R. Co. *v.* Beggs, 85 Ill. 80, 28 Am. Rep. 613; Purple *v.* Railroad Co., 114 Fed. 123, 51 C. C. A. 564, 57 L. R. A. 700; Hayes *v.* Southern Ry. Co., 141 N. C. 195, 53 S. E. 847; Duff *v.* Railway Co., 91 Pa. 458, 36 Am. Rep. 675; Mendenhall *v.* Railway Co., 66 Kan. 438, 71 Pac. 846, 61 L. R. A. 120, 97 Am. St. Rep. 380; Way *v.* C., R. I. & P. Ry. Co., 64 Iowa, 48, 19 N. W. 828, 52 Am. Rep. 431; Condran *v.* Railway Co., 67 Fed. 522, 14 C. C. A. 506, 28 L. R. A. 749; Williams *v.* M. & O. Ry. Co. (Miss.) 19 South. 90.

We have no question presented here of the status of a person who attempts in good faith to ride on a ticket or pass on which he is in fact not entitled to ride but is permitted to ride by the conductor. Many cases hold that, under those circumstances, he is deemed to be a passenger and entitled to protection as such; the test being the question of good faith. But where a person attempts in bad faith to defraud the company by riding free or for less than full fare, even with the consent of the conductor of the train, according to sound reason and authority he is a trespasser, and the company is not responsible for injuries not wantonly or willfully inflicted. The instructions given by the court on this subject conform to the law as here expressed, and were therefore correct.

The court gave the following instruction over the objection of the plaintiff: "The court instructs you that the presumption is that a person found upon a freight train is not legally a passenger, and if he claims that he is it devolves upon him to show a state of case that will rebut the presumption. He must show

Kruse *v.* St. Louis, I. M. & S. Ry. Co

that he entered the train with the bona fide intention of becoming a passenger thereon; that is, that he either procured a ticket of defendant to ride upon said train, or that he intended in good faith to pay his fare." The first part of this instruction is erroneous in saying that "the presumption is that a person upon a freight train is not legally a passenger." The language employed is almost identical with that of Chief-Justice Cockrill in Hobbs *v.* T. & P. Ry. Co., supra; but when that opinion was written we had no statute such as was afterwards enacted requiring railroads to carry passengers on local freight trains. Since there is a statute compelling railroads to carry passengers on local freight trains, when a person is permitted to enter a freight train as a passenger there is no presumption arising that he is not legally a passenger. Ark. Midland Ry. Co. *v.* Griffith, 63 Ark. 491, 39 S. W. 550. We conclude, however, that the last sentence of the instruction rendered the error in the first harmless, for it correctly stated the law as to what the plaintiff was required to prove in order to show that he was a passenger. It devolved on him to prove that much, even if it had been a regular passenger train, where the pleadings raised the issue as to his being a passenger. And while this burden was on him, as correctly stated in the instruction, yet there was no presumption that he was not a passenger, merely because he was on a freight train. It was not a matter of presumption at all as to whether or not he was a passenger, but it was a matter of proof. However, the use of the objectionable term was a matter which should have been called to the attention of the court by a specific objection.

It appears from the bill of exceptions that, while one of plaintiff's counsel was making the closing argument to the jury, the presiding judge, without suspending the proceedings, left the courtroom and went to a closet several hundred feet distant, where he remained out of the hearing of the jury for several minutes—probably 5 or 10 minutes. During the absence of the judge, a member of the bar not interested in this trial sat upon the bench upon the invitation of the judge. The counsel continued his argument, and while so doing defendant's counsel objected to him reading from a deposition of one of defendant's witnesses. Counsel then suspended his argument until the return of the judge, who, on his return, permitted counsel to read from the deposition. It also appears from the affidavits of bystanders that when defendant's counsel interposed the objection to the reading of the deposition there was a heated controversy between counsel, but it is not shown what was said. It is insisted that the conduct of the trial judge absenting himself from the courtroom calls for a reversal of the case. In Stokes *v.* State, 71 Ark. 112, 71 S. W. 248, it was held to be error for the judge in the trial of a murder case to leave the courtroom with-

Kruse *v.* St. Louis, I. M. & S. Ry. Co

out suspending the trial. No objections seem to have been interposed in that case to the departure of the judge. But there is this difference between the facts of that case and this, aside from the difference in the character of the cases: There the counsel for the state was making his argument to the jury, and commented on the failure of the defendant to testify, which constituted actual prejudice; whilst in the present case it was plaintiff's counsel who was arguing the case, and he elected to continue the argument in the absence of the judge. Now, without meaning to weaken the force of the wholesome rule laid down in the Stokes Case, we say that a party to a civil case who voluntarily continues the proceedings after the judge has absented himself from the courtroom cannot complain merely on account of the absence of the judge. He must show that some misconduct of his adversary actually occurred during the absence of the judge which operated to his prejudice. During the absence of the trial judge there is really no legal trial in progress, and neither party is compelled to proceed; but, if one of the parties does so, he cannot complain unless his adversary takes advantage of the absence of the judge to commit some act in the presence of the jury which operates to his prejudice.

We do not discover any prejudicial error in the trial of this case. It was tried upon conflicting testimony, and upon instructions which fairly submitted the questions of fact to the jury, and the verdict settled the issues against the plaintiff.

The judgment is therefore affirmed.

Louisville, H. & St. L. Ry. Co. *v.* Gregory's Adm'r.

(Court of Appeals of Kentucky, Jan. 26, 1911.)

[133 S. W. Rep. 805.]

Carriers—Injury to Passenger—Duty to Vestibule Car Platform.*
—Even if a carrier may be negligent in not having the platform of
a car protected by vestibule doors, it is not so negligent as to a passenger, who stands on the platform, after being directed by the
trainmen to go inside the car where he belongs, while the train is
stopped on a trestle.

Carriers—Injury to Passenger—Cause of Injury—Evidence.—A
carrier may not be held liable for the fall of a passenger from the
platform of a car while standing on a trestle, on the ground of negligence in permitting part of the platform to be in a slippery condition; how he came to fall not being shown, and the contributing
thereto of the slippery condition, not shown to exist in front of the
door, being mere speculation.

Carriers—Injury to Passenger—Air Brakes—Breaking of Hose.—
Ky. St. § 778 (Russell's St. § 5327), providing that no passenger train
shall be run without air brakes, which shall at all times be kept in
good condition, does not make a carrier liable, merely because the
air hose breaks, stopping a train on a trestle, and a passenger goes
out on the car platform and falls off.

Carriers — Injury to Passenger — Intoxication — Evidence.— Evidence, in an action for injury to a passenger who went out on the
platform of a car and fell off, held not to show he was so intoxicated
as to put on the trainmen the duty of exercising any more care to
protect him than they would be required to exercise towards any
other passenger.

Carriers—Duty to Intoxicated Passenger.†—That a passenger is
drinking or under the influence of liquor is not enough to require
the trainmen to give to him any more care than to other passengers;
but it is only when a passenger is so much under the influence of
liquor as to be helpless or irresponsible or incapable of protecting

---

*See first foot-note of Brice *v.* Southern Ry. Co. (S. Car.), 37 R.
R. R. 178, 60 Am. & Eng. R. Cas., N. S., 178; first foot-note of Nor-
vell *v.* Kanawha, etc., Ry. Co. (W. Va.), 37 R. R. R. 148, 60 Am. &
Eng. R. Cas., N. S., 148; Clanton *v.* Southern Ry. Co. (Ala.), 37 R.
R. R. 120, 60 Am. & Eng. R. Cas., N. S., 120.

†For the authorities in this series on the subject of the duties and
liabilities of the carrier with respect to passengers or prospective
passengers in a state of intoxication, see foot-note of Bragg *v.* Norfolk & W. R. Co. (Va.), 36 R. R. R. 438, 59 Am. & Eng. R. Cas., N.
S., 438; Pinson *v.* Southern Ry. (S. Car.), 35 R. R. R. 700, 58 Am. &
Eng. R. Cas., N. S., 700; Central of Georgia Ry. Co. *v.* Carleton
(Ala.), 35 R. R. R. 511, 58 Am. & Eng. R. Cas. N. S., 511; St. Louis,
etc., Ry. Co. *v.* Dallas (Ark.), 35 R. R. R. 167, 58 Am. & Eng R. Cas.,
N. S., 167.

Louisville, H. & St. L. Ry. Co. *v.* Gregory's Adm'r

himself from accident, and his condition is, or in the exercise of ordinary care can be, known by them, that they are under a duty to give him any extra care.

Nunn, J., dissenting.

Appeal from Circuit Court, Breckinridge County.

Action by Emmett Gregory's administrator against the Louisville, Henderson & St. Louis Railway Company. Judgment for plaintiff. Defendant appeals. Reversed.

R. A. Miller and *Claude Mercer,* for appellant.

Jno. P. Haswell, Jr., S. M. Payton, and *Hazelrigg & Hazelrigg,* for appellee.

CARROLL, J.   This action was brought by the appellee to recover damages for the death of Emmett Gregory, alleged to have been caused by the negligence of the appellant company while carrying him as a passenger over its road from Louisville to Cloverport. There is a long trestle that runs nearly to the depot at Cloverport, and the usual announcement to passengers for Cloverport to leave the train is made just before the train gets on this trestle. On the night in question, "Cloverport" was called out by the trainmen at the usual place, and as the passengers for Cloverport, including Gregory, were getting ready to leave the train, it suddenly stopped on the trestle. This unexpected stop was caused by the breaking of the air hose, thereby automatically applying the brakes to the wheels of the train. While the train was standing on the trestle, Gregory, who had gone out on the platform of the car, fell from it to the ground, receiving injuries from which he shortly died. The negligence consists: First, in permitting Gregory, who it is alleged was in a helpless state of intoxication, to go out on the platform when the train stopped on the trestle and remain there unprotected; second, in permitting the platform to be and remain covered with ice; and, third, in permitting the air hose to become so defective as to break. The answer placed in issue all the material averments of the petition, and pleaded contributory negligence. Upon a trial before a jury, a verdict was returned in favor of the appellee for $6,000. A reversal of the judgment on this verdict is asked for error in giving and refusing instructions; and the appellee also complains of the ruling of the trial court in refusing to submit to the jury in appropriate instructions the alleged negligence of the company in permitting ice to accumulate on the platform of its cars and in failing to have and keep its air hose in proper condition.

As a result of the rulings of the court, the only issue of negligence submitted was in respect to the intoxicated condition of Gregory and the duty the trainmen owed to him. We have reached the conclusion, for reasons that will be hereafter stated, that the evidence failed to show that Gregory's condition was such as to impose upon the train crew any greater care in protecting him than they exercised, and so, if this was the only issue in the case which should have been submitted to the jury, the appellant company was entitled to the peremptory instruction requested. But, notwithstanding this, if the company was negligent in permitting the platform of its cars to become covered with ice or in permitting its air hose to become in such a defective condition as to break, thereby suddenly stopping the train, and either of these causes contributed proximately to the death of Gregory, then the case should have been sbmitted to the jury upon these issues, although appellee may have failed to make out a case upon the question of neglect on the part of the company in taking proper care of Gregory. Having this view of the matter, we will first consider the correctness of the rulings of the trial judge in refusing to submit instructions upon the issues mentioned before taking up the principal question in the case.

Gregory was riding in what is known as a "chair car." There was attached to the rear end of this chair car a Pullman sleeper, and the car in front of it was an ordinary passenger car. The rear platform of the chair car was protected by vestibule doors, as this end was coupled to a vestibuled car; but the car in front was not equipped with vestibule doors, and so the vestibule doors on the front end of the chair car in which Gregory was riding were not closed and could not be closed, except partially. The result of this was that the front platform of this car was only protected from the weather in the usual way that platforms of cars without vestibule doors are protected; and it was through the door on this end of the car that passengers for way stations entered and made their exit. After the train left Louisville, from which place it started on its journey, it commenced to rain and freeze, and consequently the rain that fell on the front platform of the car formed a slippery surface on one side of the platform and on the car steps on that side, although it does not appear that the platform in front of the door was covered with ice or in a slippery condition. But the failure to have this end of this car protected by vestibule doors was not under the circumstances negligence, although there might be conditions in which it would be. Elliott on Railroads (2d Ed.) vol. 4, § 1589a. A railroad company may run passenger cars without vestible attachments, and there are no facts in this record from which it can be inferred that it was negligent in failing to have the front end of this car protected by vestibule doors, or that the failure to so protect it contributed proximately to Gregory's death. It is probable that, if this end of the car had been protected by vestibule doors, no rain or ice would have gotten on the platform. But the railroad company did not owe Gregory the duty of having vestibule doors. His place was in the car, and not on the platform, and if he had not remained on the platform no injury would have befallen him. It may also be conceded that under certain conditions and circumstances it would be negligence upon the part of the company to permit the platform or steps of its passenger cars to remain covered with ice, or in a slippery condition, and we can easily imagine a state of case in which the company would be liable for injury received by a passenger on account of the slippery condition of the platform or steps of its passenger cars. But the facts of this case do not justify us in reaching the conclusion that the company was negligent as to Gregory in this respect. How he came to fall is not known. It is possible that the slippery condition of a part of the platform contributed to bring about his fall; but whether it did or not is mere speculation. There is nothing to show that he would not have fallen if the platform had been entirely free from ice.

In respect to the breaking of the air hose, section 778 of the Kentucky Statutes (Russell's St. § 5327) provides that: "No regular or other passenger train shall be run without an air brake, or some equally effective appliance for controlling the speed of trains, which may be applied by the engineer to each car composing the train, and which shall, at all times, be kept in good condition and ready for use at the discretion of the engineer. * * *" But there is no evidence that the breaking of the air hose was due to negligence on the part of the company. The evidence upon this subject is that the air hose was properly inspected and in good condition when the train left Louisville, and that no defects in it were discovered until it suddenly parted as the train was approaching Cloverport. It is true that, if the air hose had not parted, the train would not have stopped on the trestle; and also true that, if it had not stopped on the trestle, Gregory would not have fallen from the train through the trestle. But, manifestly, the admission of these two propositions do not in any manner establish that the company was guilty of negligence as to Gregory on account of the condition of the air hose. Trains often stop at unexpected and dangerous places; but this fact in itself is not sufficient to fix liability upon the company for injury to a passenger who falls or steps from the train at a place. at which it unexpectedly and suddenly stops, in the absence of facts or circumstances showing negligence in other respects. And there is no evidence that the breaking of the air hose proximately brought about or contributed to the death of Gregory. Indeed, the evidence that we will presently recite makes it perfectly plain that. if the question of Gregory's intoxicated condition was left out of the case. there would not be a single fact or circumstance from which it could be inferred that the company was guilty of any act of negligence towards Gregory. Nor would there be the slightest doubt that his death was brought about solely by his own negligence. In making this statement we do not, of course. mean to be understood as implying that there is any evidence

Louisville, H. & St. L. Ry. Co. *v.* Gregory's Adm'r

tending to show that the company was guilty of negligence in failing to exercise the required degree of care in protecting Gregory, because we are satisfied that his condition was not such as to impose upon the company 'the duty of rendering him more care than it did other passengers similarly situated. And we are further of the opinion that the court should have, as requested by the company, peremptorily instructed the jury to find a verdict for it. This request was based on the proposition that the condition of Gregory was not such as to charge the company with notice that he was in a helpless condition or unable to take care of himself, and consequently the trainmen were not negligent in failing to exercise reasonable care to protect him. The evidence upon this subject is as follows:

Miss Davis, a passenger, testified as follows: "Q. Tell the jury in your own way what you know about it and what you saw of it. A. We were coming from Louisville, father and myself, on our way to Owensboro, and the train stopped on the trestle, and when it stopped Mr. Gregory started to get off the train and was on the outside of the door, and the conductor put his hand on his shoulder and told him to step off; that we were not to Cloverport; that we had stopped on the trestle. Mr. Gregory turned back and looked in the door, and in few minutes I heard him fall. * * * Q. Do you know whether Mr. Gregory was intoxicated that night? A. No, sir; I do not. Q. You didn't see him do anything or hear him say anything to cause you to think he was? A. No, sir. Q. Did the brakeman lead him to the door? A. Not that I saw. Q. If he did, you didn't notice it? A. No, sir; he was walking by himself when he passed the seat where I was sitting. * * * Q. You say when Mr. Gregory passed by you he was walking alone? A. Yes, sir. Q. Do you know which one of the trainmen it was that told him they was on the trestle and that wasn't the station. A. No, sir; I do not. Q. You heard of it? A. Yes, sir. Q. Did you hear what Mr. Gregory said in reply to that? A. No, sir. Q. Then the trainman went out on the platform? A. Yes, sir. Q. Did Mr. Gregory go out the door? A. Yes, sir. * * * Q. After Mr. Gregory went out the door, did you see him come to the door? A. Come back to the door? Q. Yes. A. Yes, sir. Q. Did he open it? A. Yes, sir. Q. How long had the train been stopped then, Miss Davis; about how many minutes? A. Well, a short time; probably two or three minutes. Q. Did he close the door when he opened it,—did he close it again? A. Yes, sir. Q. Do you know whether the conductor or brakeman were out on the platform at that time, or whether they had gone to see what was the matter with the train? A. I do not know."

W. E. Davis, the father of Miss Annie Davis, testified: "Q. Did you see Mr. Gregory that night on the train? A. Yes, sir; I seen a man that was said to be Mr. Gregory; I didn't know the

Louisville, H. & St. L. Ry. Co. *v.* Gregory's Adm'r

man. Q. Where was he on that train the first time you saw
him? A. Well, I seen him before we left Louisville, before they
left the depot; that is, before the train pulled out. Q. What was
his condition then? A. Well, when I seen him, I was back in
the smoker, and he came back, and there was only two of us in
there when he came in. And he came in, and he and this other
man got to passing the bottle. Q. Drinking? A. Yes, sir. Q.
Well, what was his condition at that time? Was he already intoxicated? A. Well, he was under the influence to some extent.
Q. What size bottle were they passing? A. I think it was a
pint bottle. Q. Well, then, when did you next see him? A. I
never seen him any more until the train stopped down near
Cloverport. Q. What do you know further about him? A.
Well, when they stopped there he came through the train, and
when he got to the door there was three of them as if though
to get off, and when they got to the door of the front end of the
coach they stopped there, and I think the conductor or brakeman
or some of them said to them: 'We are not at the station yet.
Wait a while. Go back and sit down.' And they stopped, and
the lady and one man went back and sat down, and this man
Gregory he didn't come back in the coach. He stood at the door.
* * * Q. State how they went to the door, how Mr. Gregory
went? A. All I seen of those that were there went just like
any other people would go to get off the train. Q. Which went
first, Mr. Gregory or the young lady Miss Willis? Which was in
the lead? A. Mr. Gregory was in the lead. Q. Did you notice
whether, when that train stopped with a thug, that this lady, Miss
Willis, lunged up against the side of the door? A. I don't think
I could state positively about that, because it seems to me that
the train stopped for a little bit before those passengers started,
but I am not positive about that though."

M. L. Howard, the train conductor, introduced by the appellee,
testified: "Q. Did you know Mr. Gregory? A. Yes, sir. Q.
You are acquainted with him? A. Yes, sir. Q. He was a
passenger on your train, was he? A. He was. Q. Where did
he get on? A. Louisville. Q. What was his condition when he
got on there as to sobriety or intoxication? A. Well, he wasn't
a man that I would consider drunk. Q. Well, was he intoxicated? A. Knowing him as I did, if I hadn't known
him possibly I wouldn't have considered him drinking at all.
but I knew him. and in that way I knew that he was
drinking, or thought he was. * * * Q. Where did you see
Gregory first that evening? A. On the train, do you mean?
Q. That evening. on the train or off the train, where did you
see him? A. Do you mean after leaving Louisville? Q. No,
before. A. In the depot. Q. What state of intoxication was
he in then? A. Well, he walked through the depot there. I
wouldn't consider him a drunken man. As I said, knowing him

as I did, I noticed that he was drinking. Q. What degree of intoxication was he in? A. Well, he could get along with what he had. Q. He could walk, you mean? A. Yes. Q. How long was it from the time you saw him in the depot until you saw him getting on the train? A. I didn't see him get on the train. Q. How long was it before you accepted his ticket as a passenger to Cloverport? A. Possibly an hour; I don't remember how long; it might be an hour and a half. Q. At that time was he drinking? A. I considered him so. Q. Well, did you see him at intervals from that time to Cloverport, when you passed through the train? A. Possibly three or four times; I don't remember just how many. Q. Did you see him drinking on the road? A. I did not. Q. Did you talk to him any or hear him talk as you went down? A. I never talked to him any on the train. * * * Q. And you say that Mr. Gregory was intoxicated the first time you saw him, and he was intoxicated the first time you received him as a passenger? A. I didn't say he was intoxicated. I didn't say he was a man I would call intoxicated. I said, knowing him as I did, I thought he was drinking. * * * Q. When you saw him in the station before he got on the train, tell the jury how long that was before the train started; about how long? A. The first time I seen him? Q. Yes. A. An hour or an hour and a half, or something like that; I don't remember just how long it was. Q. Did he ask you any question then? A. Not the first time I seen him, but something like 30 or 40 minutes before leaving time he did. Q. What did he ask you? A. Asked me if he could get on the train. I told him I didn't know whether he could or not. If he could get around the gateman possibly he could. Q. That was about 30 minutes before train time? A. Something like 30 or 40 minutes. Q. Well, was he able to take care of himself at that time? A. There wasn't any one with him that I know of. Q. I didn't ask you if there was any one with him. Was he able to walk around and take care of himself? A. Yes, sir. Q. You didn't see him get on the train? A. I did not; that was the last time I seen him until I saw him on the train, after he asked me about getting on the train. Q. You didn't regard him as being drunk when you saw him either time? A. He wasn't what I call a drunk man; no, sir. * * * Q. Did you say anything to those passengers at all, make any announcement to them? A. When the train stopped there, I did. Q. What did you say? A. I announced in a very loud voice not to get off; that we were stopped on— standing on—the trestle. Q. That was when you went out on the platform? A. That was when the train first stopped. Q. Did some passengers come to the door or near there? A. Passengers were coming up to the door. Q. You don't know who all were in that crowd? A. I couldn't name any one with the exception of young Berry. Q. You didn't notice whether Mr.

Louisville, H. & St. L. Ry. Co. v. Gregory's Adm'r

Gregory was one of the persons that came up there or not?
A. I did not. Q. The train was standing, as I understand you,
perfectly still? A. When I made this announcement? Q. Yes.
A. Yes, sir."

Miss Willis testified as follows: "Q. What coach were you
sitting in? A. In the chair car. Q. Was that the same coach
in which Mr. Gregory was at the time the train stopped? A.
Yes, sir; at the time the train stopped he was at the door of that
coach, on the platform of the coach. Q. At the time the train
stopped he was on the platform of the coach? A. Yes. sir. Q.
Where were you at this time? A. Standing in the door. Q.
How many passengers were there that night for Cloverport, to
get off at Cloverport? A. There was three; myself, Mr. Gregory, and Mr. Berry. Q. You had gotten up from your seat to
get off, and walked down the aisle towards the front door before the train stopped? A. Yes, sir. Q. Now, why did you
do that? A. They called out Cloverport. Q. Who called it out?
A. I don't remember. It was called out, but I don't remember
who it was. Q. Who reached the platform first, you or Mr.
Gregory? A. He did. Q. Was any one with Mr. Gregory?
A. Yes, sir; the flagman was with him. Q. State whether or
not he had hold of Mr. Gregory as he walked up the aisle. A.
Yes, sir; he did. Q. How did he hold him? A. Why, I don't
remember exactly; I just know that he had hold of his arm coming through the car; I don't remember exactly. Q. Now, did
they go past you before you had arisen from your seat? A.
No, sir; I was almost to the door. Q. Why did you let them
pass you? Why did you stand aside? A. Well, because I did,
just wanted them to pass me. Q. Can you tell what the condition of Mr. Gregory was at this time, when you stood aside and
let them pass, with reference to being intoxicated or not? A.
Well, he seemed to be. I thought at the time that he was, and
that was one reason I stood aside. Q. How did the flagman,
Miller, have hold of his body or his arm? A. Had hold of his
arm. Q. Did or not the flagman go through the door onto the
platform of the car? A. The flagman was with him and went
with him out the door onto the platform. Q. Then where did
the flagman go, if he went anywhere? A. I don't know. I
wasn't paying any attention. Q. I will ask you whether or not
you were able to stand when the train stopped without catching
hold of anything? A. I am never that way. I always catch hold
of something when the train stops. Q. Did you upon this occasion? A. I think I did. Q. What was it you caught hold of
to steady yourself when the train stopped? A. I was right in
the door, and I stood up against the door, the doorway. * * *
Q. After the train stopped, what did you do? A. Well, after
the train stopped, I went back and sat down in the car. I was
standing in the door at the time the train stopped, and Mr.

Louisville, H. & St. L. Ry. Co. *v.* Gregory's Adm'r

Howard said that we had stopped on the trestle, so I went back, and he said we had stopped on the trestle, and he turned around to Mr. Gregory then and told him we had stopped on the trestle. Q. Where was Gregory when he told him that? A. He was standing on the platform. Q. Do you know what became of Mr. Gregory? A. No, sir; I do not. Q. Did you see him any more after you turned around to go back? A. After I turned around and went back and sat down, I saw him again after that. * * * Q. Mr. Sam Berry was the other passenger who was to get off at Cloverport that night, I believe? A. Yes, sir. Q. And he closed the door? A. Yes, sir. Q. And left Gregory on the outside of the door on the platform and you and he on the inside of the coach, is that correct? A. Yes, sir; we were inside, and I suppose Mr. Gregory was out there; I don't know where he went. Q. Did he come back in the car? A. He opened the door and looked in the car. Q. When was that? A. Well, I don't know, just a few seconds before the train started, into the station, he opened the door and looked into the car. Q. Did he step inside? A. No, he just opened the door and stood in the door and looked in the car. Q. What do you know as to his movements after that? A. I don't know, only he closed the door; I don't know what he did. Q. You saw no more after that? A. No, sir. * * * Q. Well, the first thing that the conductor said, if I understand your testimony, was that 'this is the trestle,' and 'we are not down at the station yet,' was that about the substance of it? A. He said 'This is the trestle;' not to step off. Q. Now, he or the brakeman, one or the other, turned and repeated the same thing to Mr. Gregory? A. Mr. Howard said the same thing. Q. Did Mr. Gregory make any reply to that? A. No, he didn't that I remember, but he looked as if he understood what the conductor said, but I don't remember of him saying anything. Q. If I understood you, the brakeman simply had his hand on Mr. Gregory's arm as he passed you in the aisle? A. Yes, sir. Q. He was not shoving him or carrying him or anything like that? A. I don't remember anything about them. I remember he had his hand on his arm and seemed to be leading him."

The foregoing is all the testimony introduced for the appellee upon the subject of Gregory's condition. Sam Berry, introduced for the appellant, testified as follows: "Q. Did you see Mr. Gregory on the train when you first got on at Irvington? A. No, sir. Q. Did you see him at any time? A. I seen him standing on the platform of the car. Q. Was it before or after the train stopped? A. After the train had stopped. Q. What was he doing on the platform? A. Just standing there looking through the door. The door was shut. Q. Do you know whether Mr. Gregory went out of the coach in which you were riding before you went out or afterwards? A. I never saw Mr.

Gregory inside the car; I couldn't say. Q. Did you go out on the platform yourself, Mr. Berry? A. Yes, sir. Q. Did you discover that you were on the trestle and not at the station? A. When Mr. Howard told me, yes, sir, the conductor. Q. What did the conductor say? A. He said: 'Look out; Don't get off! We are on the trestle!' Q. Did he say that in a loud voice or in a low voice? A. Yes, sir; he said it in a loud voice. Q. So that everybody could hear? A. Yes, sir. Q. What did you do then? A. I told him, I said, 'I see we are.' Q. What did you do? A. I stood out there a little bit and went back in and sat down. Q. Did you know Mr. Gregory? A. No, sir. Q. Well, you did see him afterwards on the platform there looking in the door? What was his condition so far as you could see? A. I couldn't tell anything about his condition, sir. Q. Couldn't tell anything about it? A. He was just like any other man. Q. Just standing around there like anybody else would be? A. Yes, sir. Q. As far as you could see, was he able to take care of himself? A. He seemed to be able to take care of himself as I was to take care of myself."

Harry Thompson, the flagman, testified: "Q. Where were you sitting when the train stopped? A. I was sitting about the third seat from the rear end, just outside of the compartment from the smoker into the ladies' car, about the third seat from the door. Q. You were in the main body of the chair car? A. Yes, sir. Q. And about three seats from the rear portion of that part of the car? A. Yes, sir. Q. Did you see Mr. Gregory coming through the car on his way to the front end? A. Yes, sir. Q. Where was he at the time the train came to this sudden stop? A. Well, he was just opposite me, just about one seat ahead of where I was sitting at. Q. The train stopped suddenly did it? A. Yes, sir. Q. What kind of stop did the train make? A. It made a sudden stop, nothing unusual, but a sudden stop. Q. What effect does that have on a man standing in the aisle, or walking along, whether he is drunk or sober? A. Well, a stop like that will make anybody stagger. When it first stops, why he will go ahead for two or three steps; and, when the train does stop, he will come backwards two or three steps. Q. Sometimes it throws people down? A. Yes, sir; sometimes it does. Q. What effect did it have on Mr. Gregory when it stopped that way—you say he was near you, and perhaps just a little in advance of you? A. Well, just about the time that he got even with me, I got up out of my seat. Of course, when the train stopped I fell over against the seat, the seat just ahead of me, and, when he started staggering backwards, I steadied him up with my arm to keep him from falling backwards. Q. Did you walk with him from that point to the front of the car? A. I did. Q. Could he walk all right? A. Yes, sir; as good as I could down there. Q. Did he require or need support from you

Louisville, H. & St. L. Ry. Co. v. Gregory's Adm'r

after that motion of the train was over? A. No, sir; he did not. Q. Was there anything in his manner or condition, as far as you could observe it, to indicate that he was drunk? A. No, sir. Q. State to the jury whether you were under the impression also that the train had stopped for Cloverport as you walked forward. A. Yes, sir; I was at that time. Q. When did you learn otherwise? A. When I got down to the door. Q. How did you learn it? A. From what I could see. Q. You saw you were on the trestle? A. Yes, sir. Q. When you saw you were on the trestle, what did you say or do, or both? A. Oh, well, as quick as I saw we were on the trestle, why I pushed Mr. Gregory back on the inside, and told him, I said: 'You stand here until I come back and tell you we are at Cloverport. We are here on the trestle.' And so he said, 'All·right,' and I goes on back to the rear end to see what the trouble was. Q. You left him standing then inside the door of the coach? A. Yes, sir; I did. Q. Well, you say when the train stopped that Gregory got up about one seat ahead of you? A. Yes, sir. Q. And the jar when you stopped threw him out of balance and you grabbed him? A. Yes, sir. Q. Did you hold on to him until you got to the front? A. Yes, sir; after he started backwards I reached out and caught his arm, like I would any one, and started on down to the front of the car with him. Q. Went all the way? A. Yes, sir; all the way. Q. Did anybody else go out of the coach on to the platform? A. Yes, sir. Q. Who? A. Mr. Gregory and myself. Q. Who else? A. Mr. Miller, the flagman. Q. Who else? A. Also the conductor, Mr. Howard."

The foregoing is the only evidence that throws any light upon the condition of Gregory, and in our opinion his condition was not such as to put upon the trainmen the duty of exercising any more care to protect him than they would be obliged to exercise to protect any other passenger. A fair summary of it is that Gregory was drinking, and to some extent under the influence of liquor when the train left Louisville as well as when it stopped on the trestle; but it does not appear that he was at any time in a helpless condition or unable to stand alone or to walk by himself or to take care of himself. When "Cloverport" was called out by the trainman, he got up for the purpose of getting out, as did the other passengers for Cloverport, and, while he was on his way to the door, the breaking of the air hose caused the train to suddenly stop. Gregory, who was then in the aisle, was thrown off his balance, and the flagman, who was immediately behind him, caught him by the arm and walked with him in this way to the door. When the door was reached, and about the time Gregory stepped out on the platform, both the conductor and the brakeman warned passengers not to get off, telling them that the train had stopped on the trestle, and when this direction was given they went to look

Louisville, H. & St. L. Ry. Co. *v.* Gregory's Adm'r

after the cause of the sudden stopping of the train, leaving Gregory standing on the platform in front of the door. Miss Willis and Mr. Berry then went in the car and closed the door, leaving Gregory standing alone on the platform. A few minutes after this, Gregory opened the door, and looked in the car, then closed the door, and was not seen any more until after he fell from the train. No witness testifies that the platform directly in front of the door where Gregory was standing had any ice on it or was slippery, nor is there any evidence from which it can be fairly inferred that when he was left by the conductor and brakeman on the platform his condition was such as to put a person of ordinary prudence upon notice that he was unable to take care of himself. In fact, his conduct in opening the door and looking in, and then closing it, shows that he knew what he was doing and was able to take care of himself. There was nothing in the conduct, manner, or appearance of Gregory when he got on the train at Louisville that would have justified the company in refusing to accept him as a passenger; nor did he do or say anything on the trip that would indicate that he was unable to care for himself. He was at all times orderly and well behaved. There is no suggestion that he did not hear the warning of the conductor, nor is there any circumstance from which it can be inferred that he did not fully understand and appreciate what the conductor said, as well as the dangerous place at which the train stopped. If, when he started to leave the train and got to the door, he had been so intoxicated as to lead a person of ordinary prudence to believe that he could not get back in the car, the trainmen should have put him back; but that he could have gotten back in the car if he desired is made plain by the uncontradicted evidence that, after the trainmen and others left the platform and door, he opened the door and looked in and then closed it again. Under these circumstances the trainmen had the right to assume, when they gave the warning and left, that Gregory would do as the others did—go back in the car. It is the duty of train employees to look after the safety and comfort of all the passengers, and they are not required to extend to one more protection or care than another, except under special circumstances. And the mere fact that a passenger is drinking or under the influence of liquor is not enough to put upon trainmen the extra duty of giving to him more care than to other passengers. This measure of duty is only demanded when the condition of the passenger is such that he is helpless or incapable of taking care of himself. If a passenger on account of intoxication that does not produce helplessness or incapacity is rendered less capable of protecting himself from accident or injury than he otherwise would be, or his condition induces him to become more indifferent to his safety, he must yet take the consequences of his own recklessness, and the company will not be charged with

Louisville, H. & St. L. Ry. Co. *v.* Gregory's Adm'r

the duty of taking especial care of him. His right to recover is no greater than would be that of a sober person of ordinary prudence. A man may be under the influence of liquor and yet be as competent to protect himself from danger as a thoroughly sober man would be. And it often happens that sober men expose themselves to dangers that a partially intoxicated man would avoid. And so there is good sense and reason in the rule that the sober man and the partially intoxicated man are entitled to the same measure of care—one not more than the other. But when a passenger is so much under the influence of liquor as to be helpless or irresponsible or incapable of protecting himself from accident, and his condition is or could be known by the trainmen in the exercise of reasonable care, the plainest dictates of humanity demand that he should not be permitted to remain or place himself in unnecessary peril if the persons in charge of the train by the exercise of reasonable care can prevent it. But trainmen are not obliged to anticipate that a passenger who is under the influence of liquor will unnecessarily expose himself to danger, nor are they under any duty to exercise more than ordinary care to discover whether passengers are drunk or sober. It is only when their attention is directed either by personal observation or information to the helpless, irresponsible, or incapable condition of a passenger or when by the exercise of ordinary care his condition could be discovered, that they are under a duty to exercise reasonable care to protect him. L. & N. R. Co. *v.* Logan, 88 Ky. 232, 10 S. W. 655, 10 Ky. Law Rep. 798, 3 L. R. A. 80, 21 Am. St. Rep. 332; L. & N. R. Co. *v.* Deason. 96 S. W. 1115, 29 Ky. Law Rep. 1259; Thixton *v.* Illinois Central R. Co., 96 S. W. 548, 29 Ky. Law Rep. 910, 8 L. R. A. (N. S.) 298; Cincinnati, Indianapolis, St. L. & C. R. Co. *v.* Cooper, 120 Ind. 469, 22 N. E. 340, 6 L. R. A. 241, 16 Am. St. Rep. 334; Fisher *v.* West Virginia & Pittsburg R. Co., 39 W. Va. 366, 19 S. E. 578, 23 L. R. A. 758; Fox *v.* Michigan Central R. Co., 138 Mich. 433, 101 N. W. 624, 68 L. R. A. 336, 5 Am. & Eng. Ann. Cas. 72; Black *v.* N. Y., N. H. & H. R. Co., 193 Mass. 448, 79 N. E. 797, 7 L. R. A. (N. S.) 148, 9 Am. & Eng. Ann. Cas. 485; Hutchinson on Carriers, § 994; Elliott on Railroads (2d Ed.) vol. 3, § 1172.

When the standard of care and measure of duty we have announced is applied to the condition of Gregory and the conduct of the trainmen, it is manifest that the liability of the company is to be tested by the same rules it would be if Gregory had been perfectly sober. Looking at the matter from this standpoint, it is clear that the company was not guilty of any negligence in the carriage of Gregory, and that his death was due solely to his own carelessness or negligence in remaining on the platform after he had been requested to go back in the car and warned that the train was standing on the trestle.   Therefore, upon the evidence in the record before us, the court should have directed the jury to return a verdict for the railroad company.

Wherefore the judgment is reversed, with directions for a new trial in conformity with this opinion.

NUNN, J., dissents.

MAYFIELD *v.* ST. LOUIS, I. M. & S. RY. CO.

(Supreme Court of Arkansas, Dec. 12, 1910.)

[133 S. W. Rep. 168.]

Appeal and Error—Harmless Error—Case Right on Merits.—Error, if any, in the giving or refusal of instructions, is not prejudicial, where on the whole case the verdict and judgment are right.

**False Imprisonment—Carriage of Passengers—Protection—Care Required—Wrongful Arrest.*—A railroad company, as a common carrier, is bound to use extraordinary care not only to safely carry its passengers, but to also protect them from assault or injury by its agents in charge of the train and by others, and it is therefore liable for a wrongful arrest of a passenger procured by the servants in charge of the train, or for an illegal arrest made by others which in the exercise of due diligence it could have prevented, though it need not prevent an arrest by an officer duly empowered to make the same.

**False Imprisonment—Wrongful Acts of Servant—Liability of Master.*—Defendant railroad was not liable for the act of its station agent in sending a telegram resulting in the wrongful arrest of plaintiff, a passenger, where such agent had no authority, either express or implied, to cause the arrest, even though he believed plaintiff had stolen defendant's property.

Appeal from Circuit Court Ouachita County; Geo. W. Hays, Judge.

Action by Robert Mayfield against the St. Louis, Iron Mountain & Southern Railway Company.   Judgment for defendant, and plaintiff appeals.   Affirmed.

Warren & Smith and *Stevens & Stevens,* for appellant.

W. E. Hemingway, E. B. Kinsworthy, H. S. Powell, and *Jas. H. Stevenson,* for appellee.

---

*For the authorities in this series on the question whether a railroad company is liable on account of arrests and prosecutions made by or at the instigation of its employees or agents, see foot-note of McKain *v.* Baltimore & O. R. Co. (W. Va.), 32 R. R. R. 542, 55 Am. & Eng. R. Cas., N. S., 542; Chicago, etc., Ry. Co. *v.* Nelson (Ark.), 31 R. R. R. 785, 54 Am. & Eng. R. Cas., N. S., 785.

Mayfield v. St. Louis, I. M. & S. Ry. Co

Frauenthal, J. This was an action instituted by Robert Mayfield, the plaintiff below, to recover damages for his alleged wrongful arrest while a passenger upon one of defendant's trains. The plaintiff was a singing teacher, and for some time prior to May 5, 1908, he had been attending a singing convention in the neighborhood where one J. W. Burton resided and a few miles from the town of Donaldson. On that day he eloped with the young daughter of Mr. Burton and proceeded to Donaldson, where he and the young lady took passage on defendant's train for Camden. Upon the same day, and immediately upon learning of the elopement. Mr. Burton went to Donaldson and requested the station agent of defendant at that place, who was his friend, to assist him in stopping and apprehending plaintiff and his daughter before they should be married. He directed the agent to telegraph to officers at points along the line of the railroad to arrest the plaintiff and his daughter and to send any telegram necessary to apprehend them. The agent sent telegraphic messages to several points along the line of the railroad. and in doing so used the defendant's wires and signed his name thereto, in some instances, as agent. Among the persons to whom he thus sent messages was the station agent of defendant at Chidester. He talked to this agent over the telegraphic wire. telling him that plaintiff and the young lady were on the train that would shortly stop at Chidester and to have them arrested, and also stated that plaintiff had stolen $300 from defendant's safe at Donaldson. He sent to the station agent the following telegram to be delivered to the officer: "To conductor: Please advise where young lady and young man that got on at Donaldson got off at and turn them over to marshal or sheriff and wire me. J. P. Dunlap. Agent. St. L., I. M. & S. Ry. Co."

The station agent at Chidester thereupon sent for the marshal of that town and handed to him the above telegram and also told him that plaintiff had stolen $300 from defendant's safe at Donaldson. When the train arrived at Chidester, the marshal boarded same and handed the above telegram to the conductor, who directed him to hand it to the auditor. This the marshal did, and at the same time asked him if the parties were on the train. After reading the telegram, the auditor told him that "there was nothing in it." but that the parties were on the train, and he would point them out to him, which he did. Neither the conductor or auditor requested or assisted the marshal in arresting the plaintiff; but the auditor simply pointed him out to the marshal upon his demand. The marshal thereupon arrested plaintiff and took him from the train and detained him at the hotel at Chidester until the following morning. when the father of the girl arrived. From him the marshal learned that plaintiff had not stolen any money. but was only eloping with his daughter, and thereupon the marshal released plaintiff. Mr. Burton

Mayfield *v.* St. Louis, I. M. & S. Ry. Co

testified that the agent at Donaldson was acting solely for him and at his direction in sending the various telegraphic messages, and that it was stated that plaintiff had stolen the money in order to make the officers more active in apprehending plaintiff. Under the rules and regulations of defendant which were introduced in evidence, the station agent in the performance of the duties of his employment had no authority to arrest or to direct the arrest of any person or to prosecute or instigate the prosecution of any one. By these rules he was given charge of and made responsible for the defendant's property intrusted to his care.

The evidence introduced upon the trial of the case was practically undisputed, and it established a state of case as above set out. If, under this evidence, the plaintiff was entitled to recover, then the verdict which was returned and the judgment which was recovered against him should be reversed. On the other hand, if he was not entitled to recover under this evidence, then no instruction given or refused by the court of which complaint is made could be prejudicial, even if it was erroneous; for upon the whole case the verdict and judgment would be right. It is not necessary, therefore, to set out or discuss the various exceptions which plaintiff interposed to the ruling of the court upon instructions given and refused by it. The question involved in the case for determination, then, is whether or not, under the undisputed evidence, the defendant was responsible for the arrest of plaintiff and for the violation of his rights. The liability can be based only on one of two grounds: Upon the acts of the auditor and conductor in charge of the train when the arrest was made, or upon the acts and conduct of the station agents in sending and delivering the telegram to the marshal, who made the arrest.

1. A railroad company, as a common carrier of passengers, is bound to use extraordinary care not only to carry its passengers safely, but also to protect them during the carriage from assault or injury from its agents in charge of the train and from others. By its contract the railroad company assumes the obligation to protect the passenger against any negligent or willful misconduct of its servants while performing the carriage; it also assumes the obligation to exercise diligence and care in protecting its passengers while in transit from violence or wrongful misconduct of others on the train. The conductor has control not only over the movements of the train, but over persons on it, and has authority to compel observance of the rules of the company by all persons on the train. He has therefore the power, under ordinary circumstances, to protect them from violence or wrongful injury from others, and the law makes the company liable for an injury to a passenger resulting from a negligent failure to exercise such power. It is therefore liable for any wrongful arrest

Mayfield v. St. Louis, I. M. & S. Ry. Co

of a passenger made or procured by its servants in charge of the train; and it is also liable for an illegal arrest of the passenger made by others which in the exercise of due diligence it could have prevented. 2 Hutchinson on Carriers, §§ 980, 1100; 6 Cyc. 598; Dwinelle v. New York Central R. R. Co., 120 N. Y. 117, 24 N. E. 319, 8 L. R. A. 224, 17 Am. St. Rep. 611; Duggan v. Baltimore & O. R. Co., 159 Pa. 248, 28 Atl. 182, 186, 39 Am. St. Rep. 672; Gillingham v. Ohio River R. Co., 35 W. Va. 588, 14 S. E. 243, 14 L. R. A. 798, 29 Am. St. Rep. 827; Brunswick & W. R. Co. v. Ponder, 117 Ga. 63, 43 S. E. 430, 60 L. R. A. 713, 97 Am. St. Rep. 152.

But no obligation rests upon the railroad company or upon its servants in charge of the train to prevent the arrest of one who happens to be upon its train by an officer duly empowered to make such arrest. The law does not impose the duty on the conductor to resist or interfere with the authority of an officer acting under color of his office. As is said in 2 Hutchinson on Carriers, § 987: "The carrier is not required to resist an officer of the law who has apparent authority to arrest a passenger, nor is he under any duty to inquire into the legality of the arrest, or to see that the officer uses only such force as is necessary to make the arrest. * * * Having a right to presume that the arrest is legal, his obeying the command of the officers is no breach of duty to the passenger." The duty to protect the passenger from violence or assault from others does not demand that the conductor should place himself in opposition to the due administration of the law; and he cannot therefore be said to be guilty of misconduct or of negligence where he simply submits to and complies with the request or demands of those officers whose duty it is to enforce the criminal laws. In the case of Duggan v. Baltimore & O. R. Co., 159 Pa. 248, 28 Atl. 182, 186, 39 Am. St. Rep. 672, it is said: "The conductor is not required to enter into a contest with or put himself in opposition to the officers of the law, and if he merely stood by without taking part in the arrest by known police officers he was not bound to inquire into their authority or assert his own against it." While a railroad company is liable in damages for a wrongful arrest and false imprisonment of a passenger made or caused by its conductor in charge of the train without probable cause, although such arrest was in violation of the authority given him by the company, yet it cannot be held liable for an arrest made by an officer without the procurement or instigation of such conductor. Brunswick & W. R. Co. v. Ponder, supra; Mulligan v. New York, etc., R. Co., 129 N. Y. 506, 29 N. E. 952, 14 L. R. A. 791, 26 Am. St. Rep. 539.

The uncontroverted evidence in the case at bar shows that neither the conductor or auditor in charge of the train procured or instigated the plaintiff's arrest. They did not assist in his arrest, but simply refrained from interfering with a duly authorized

Mayfield v. St. Louis, I. M. & S. Ry. Co

police officer in making the arrest. The officer had the apparent right, upon information received by him that plaintiff had committed a felony, to make the arrest with or without warrant, and the servants in charge of the train were guilty of no act of negligence in submitting to the authority of the police officer; and in failing to resist or oppose that authority they did not fail to perform every duty which under the circumstances the company owed to the plaintiff. The defendant cannot be held liable in damages, therefore, by reason of the acts or conduct of its servants in charge of the train at the time of the arrest.

2. It is urged that the defendant is liable because its station agent at Donaldson procured or instigated the wrongful arrest of plaintiff by causing it to be falsely represented to the officer that he had stolen defendant's property. The question thus presented is whether or not the defendant was responsible for this act of its station agent. The station agent had no authority from defendant either to arrest or to prosecute any person, although such person wrongfully took the property of defendant which had been placed in the custody of such station agent. Nor do we think that he had the apparent authority to make such arrest or prosecute such wrongdoer. It was his duty to care for and protect the property in his charge, but, after such property was stolen, it was not his duty, either expressly granted or impliedly given, to put in motion the criminal laws of the land and cause the arrest or prosecution of the person guilty of the larceny. He had the right to protect the property of defendant placed in his charge and to recover it back; but the arrest of the offender and his prosecution would not protect or recover the property. Such act was not within the real or apparent scope of his employment, nor was it in the line of the business with which he was intrusted, nor was it for the benefit of the defendant. It may be that it is for the benefit of the public that an offender shall be prosecuted; but it cannot be said to be for the benefit of any individual, except in his relation to the public and the state, that such offender should be apprehended and prosecuted. The arrest and prosecution would lead to the punishment of the thief; but it would not tend to recover or protect the property.

In the case of Allen v. London & S. W. R. Co., L. R. 6 Q. B. 65, it is said: "There is no implied authority in a person having the custody of property to take such steps as he thinks fit to punish a person who he supposes has done something to the property which he has not done. The act of punishing the offender is not anything done with reference to the property. It is done merely for the purpose of vindicating justice. And in this respect there is no difference between a railway company, which is a corporation, and a private individual." In the case of Carter v. Howe Mach. Co., 51 Md. 290, 34 Am. Rep. 311, the principle is thus stated: "Where the corporation is sought to be held lia-

Mayfield v. St. Louis, I. M. & S. Ry. Co

ble for the wrongful and malicious act of its agent or servant in putting the criminal law in operation against a party upon a charge of having fraudulently embezzled the money and goods of the company, in order to sustain the right to recover it should be made to appear that the agent was expressly authorized to act as he did by the corporation. The doing of such an act could not in the nature of things be in the exercise of the ordinary duties of the agent or servant intrusted with the custody of the company's moneys or goods; and, before the corporation can be made liable for such an act, it must be shown either that there was express precedent authority for doing the act, or that the act has been ratified and adopted by the corporation." In the case of Edwards v. London & N. W. R. Co., L. R. 5 C. P. 446, the court said: "A servant of a railway company has no implied authority as such to give a person into custody on a charge of felony. It is the duty of any one who sees a person committing a felony to give him into custody, and it cannot be assumed that Holmes was acting in the matter as the company's servant and not in accordance with that general duty. * * *   It is said that Holmes was in charge of the property which he believed was being stolen, and that from that fact it may be inferred that he had authority to act as he did; but the same would apply to a shopman in charge of a shop, or a servant in charge of a house, and yet it has never been suggested that if such a person gave a person in charge for a felony the master would be liable." In Wood on Master and Servant, § 546, the doctrine is thus illustrated: "A clerk to sell goods suspects that goods have been stolen and causes an arrest to be made. The master is not liable for the imprisonment or for the assault, because the arrest was an act which the clerk had no authority to do for the master, either express or implied." In the case of Sweeden v. Atkinson Improvement Co., 125 S. W. 439, 27 L. R. A. (N. S.) 124, we said: "It is well settled that the master is civilly liable for an injury caused by the negligent act of his servant when done within the scope of his employment, 'even though the master did not authorize or know of such acts or may have disapproved of or forbidden them.' But it is also well settled that the master is not liable for an independent negligent or wrongful act of a servant done outside of the scope of his employment." In the case of Little Rock Traction & Electric Co. v. Walker, 65 Ark. 144, 45 S. W. 57, 40 L. R. A. 473, it was held that a street railway company was not liable for the act of its conductor in causing the arrest and prosecution of a passenger in the absence of authority from the company because such acts were not within the scope of the conductor's employment. Wright v. Wilcox, 19 Wend. (N. Y.) 345, 32 Am. Dec. 507; Dwinelle v. N. Y. Cent. R. Co., 120 N. Y. 117, 24 N. E. 319, 8 L. R. A. 224, 17 Am. St. Rep. 611; Mulligan v. New York, etc., R. Co., 129 N. Y. 506, 29 N. E.

Mayfield v. St. Louis, I. M. & S. Ry. Co

952, 14 L. R. A. 791, 26 Am. St. Rep. 539; Goodloe v. Memphis, etc., R. Co., 107 Ala. 223, 18 South. 166, 29 L. R. A. 729, 54 Am. St. Rep. 85.

It will thus be gathered from these authorities that the liability of the defendant herein for the act of its station agents in causing the wrongful arrest of plaintiff depends upon whether such act was performed in the line of their duty and within the scope of the authority conferred upon them by the defendant. The evidence adduced in this case most favorable to plaintiff does not bring it within this principle. The procurement of the arrest of plaintiff was not done in the ordinary course of the business of the company, nor was it for its benefit, except in so far as it might be for the benefit of all the people of the state that a criminal should be arrested, prosecuted, and convicted. If the agent, acting from a sense of public duty, should cause the arrest of an offender, his conduct would in no way be connected with his employer so as to fix upon him a liability.

In the present case, therefore, the station agent had no authority, either express or implied, to cause the arrest of plaintiff, even if he had believed that he had stolen the defendant's property and was endeavoring to act for it. So that, in such event, the act not being within the line of his duty or within the real or apparent scope of his authority, it could not fasten upon defendant a liability for the injury resulting therefrom. But under the undisputed evidence adduced in the case the station agent at Donaldson was solely acting for Burton, the father of the girl, in sending the messages. He was doing a service solely for the benefit of his friend, and not for the defendant. He had stepped aside from the defendant's business and from the line of his employment and was acting solely for his own purposes.

The defendant, therefore, was not liable for the act of the station agent at Donaldson in sending the message to the station agent at Chidester which resulted in procuring plaintiff's wrongful arrest. It follows that, under the undisputed evidence introduced at the trial of the case, the defendant was not liable for the wrongful arrest of plaintiff.

The judgment is affirmed.

39 R R R—26

LOUISVILLE RY. CO. v. HUTTI.

(Court of Appeals of Kentucky, Jan. 11, 1911.)

[133 S. W. Rep. 200.]

Carriers—Street Cars—Transfers—Ejection of Passenger.—A rule of defendant street car company provided that conductor should issue transfer tickets when fares were paid. Plaintiff demanded a transfer without paying his fare, but offered to pay the fare only upon condition that the conductor would simultaneously give him a transfer, and after some altercation the conductor ejected him, using no more force than was reasonably necessary. Held, that plaintiff was not entitled to recover for the ejection.

False Imprisonment—Judgment Conclusive.—In an action for damages for false arrest and imprisonment, the judgment of the police court, fining the plaintiff for disorderly conduct, was conclusive of the existence of reasonable grounds for the arrest.

Appeal from Circuit Court, Jefferson County, Common Pleas Branch, Third Division.

Action by Frank Hutti against the Louisville Railway Co. From a judgment for plaintiff, defendant appeals. Reversed and remanded.

Farleigh, Straus & Fairleigh and *Howard B. Lee,* for appellant.

Edwards, Ogden & Peak, for appellee.

O'REAR, J. Appellee took passage on one of appellant's street cars on Fourth street, in Louisville. He wanted to transfer to another car going down Oak street. When approached for his fare on the Fourth street car, he held out his hand containing the fare, a nickel, and offered to pay it, but demanded as a condition that he be then and there handed a transfer ticket. The rule of the company was that conductors should issue and deliver transfer tickets when fares were paid. The conductor did not refuse to give a transfer ticket. According to some of the witnesses, he said that he would issue all transfers after he had collected all fares. According to other testimony, he said that he would issue the transfer to appellee after he had paid his fare. Appellee insisted that he had failed on previous occasions to get his transfer, as the car would pass Oak street before the conductor would pass through issuing transfer slips after he had finished collecting all fares. The conductor insisted upon payment of the fare. He did not refuse to give the transfer ticket, but insisted on the fare being paid first. Appellee insisted on the transfer ticket being handed him simultaneously with the payment of the fare. The altercation between the conductor and the passenger maintained that form; appellee retaining his fare in his hand, but

Louisville Ry. Co. v. Hutti

offering it upon the condition that the transfer ticket be then and there handed to him. The conductor stopped the car and told appellee to get off. He refused. The conductor then took hold of him and tried to put him off, but failed. A policeman was called by the conductor, who arrested appellee on the conductor's complaint, charged with disorderly conduct. He was fined in the police court. He thereupon instituted this proceeding against appellant for the assault upon him by the conductor, and for false arrest and imprisonment. Upon the disclosure of the foregoing facts the court struck out the cause of action based on the false arrest, as the judgment of the police court was conclusive of the existence of reasonable grounds therefor. The ruling was proper. Upon the other branch of the case the circuit court overruled appellant's motion for a peremptory instruction and submitted the question to the jury, who returned a verdict for appellee for $250 damages.

The ground of complaint on this appeal is the refusal of the trial court to grant appellant's motion for peremptory instruction. The propriety of the ruling depends on the nature of the contract to carry the passenger and the rights of the parties upon its breach. It may be assumed that appellee was entitled to a transfer, under his contract, entitling him to continue his journey upon the Oak Street car, provided the contract was consummated. But before he was entitled either to continue his passage on the Fourth Street car, or to transfer to the Oak Street car, he must first have paid or tendered the necessary fare, which was five cents. He did not pay it. He tendered it, but tendered it conditionally; and from what he then said, and from his conduct · as well, it is inferable that, unless the conductor had complied with his demand to deliver simultaneously the transfer ticket, he would not have paid the fare tendered. In this appellee misconceived his right. It was his duty to pay his fare, or to tender it, without condition. If thereupon the conductor refused to allow him to proceed upon the car, and ejected him, he had his demand for damages. Or if the conductor should have received his fare, and have allowed him to remain on the Fourth Street car, but failed to give him in time a transfer ticket entitling him to continue his journey on the Oak Street car, he was entitled to his damages, which would be the sum which he might have been compelled to pay on the Oak Street car in order to complete his passage. But, though the conductor wrongfully intended not to issue appellee a transfer slip, that did not entitle appellee to ride on the Fourth Street car without paying the fare. The conductor had the right to demand the payment of the fare before either allowing appellee to continue upon the car or issuing him a transfer slip. The contract began only upon the payment or tender of the consideration. The acts could not well be simultaneous—at least, are not required to be. One must precede and

City of Tacoma *v.* Boutelle

that is payment. Possibly a more courteous and patient treatment
and explanation by the conductor might have averted the trouble.
But, whether so or not, the conductor was within his legal rights
in demanding the payment of the fare first, and refusing a conditional tender of it. When appellee refused either to pay or
tender the fare unconditionally, he had not the right to remain
on the car. He had not the right to ride there without paying
the fare. When requested to leave the car after it stopped for
that purpose, he was in the wrong in failing to do so; and it was
lawful for the conductor to eject him, using no more force than
was reasonably necessary for that purpose. It is not complained
that the conductor used excessive force.

Under the facts shown, the court erred in not granting appellant's motion for peremptory instruction.

Reversed and remanded for proceedings consistent herewith.

CITY OF TACOMA *v.* BOUTELLE.

(Supreme Court of Washington, Jan. 4, 1911.)

[112 Pac. Rep. 661.]

**Street Railroads—Regulations as to Service—Ordinances—Reason-
ableness.***—A municipal ordinance regulating the frequency of street
car service, enacted under the general power reserved in the ordinance granting a street railway franchise, is valid, provided it is
reasonable, to be determined by considering whether the regulation
has been carried to the point where it has become confiscatory.

**Street Railroads — Regulating Service—Ordinances — Reasonable-
ness.**—The question of such reasonableness is one of fact, and the
burden of proving unreasonableness is on the party asserting it.

Municipal Corporations—Ordinances—Reasonableness.—The question of such reasonableness is a legislative one for the council of the
city, subject to review by the court.

**Constitutional Law—Impairing Obligation of Contracts—Street
Railway Franchise.**—A street railway franchise which reserves to
the city the right to require the cars to make "sufficient" round trips
each day authorizes the city to adopt an ordinance prescribing the
frequency of cars, as against the objection that it impairs the obligation of a contract evidenced by the franchise.

**Constitutional Law—Impairing Obligation of Contracts—Street
Railway Franchise.**—A street railway franchise reserving to the city
the right to regulate the speed of cars, and stipulating that it may

---

*For the authorities in this series on the subject of the power of
municipalities to regulate the operations of street railways, see third
foot-note of Ashley *v.* Kanawha Valley Traction Co. (W. Va.), 26
R. R. R. 520, 49 Am. & Eng. R. Cas., N. S., 520.

City of Tacoma *v.* Boutelle

require cars to be run two round trips each day, fixes the minimum
street car service, and does not prevent the city from requiring more
frequent service; and an ordinance prescribing a five-minute service
is not invalid, as impairing the obligation of a contract evidenced by
the franchise.

**Constitutional Law—Impairing Obligation of Contracts—Street
Railway Franchise.**—A street railway franchise stipulating that the
city may adopt ordinances necessary for the protection of the interests of the city and to carry out the provisions of the franchise reserves to the city power to regulate the frequency of street car service; and an ordinance prescribing the frequency of service is not invalid, as impairing the obligation of a contract as evidenced by the
franchise.

Municipal Corporations—Police Power.—The police power of a
city includes the power to preserve the peace, security, health, morals, and general welfare of the city.

Street Railroads—Regulating Car Service—Police Power.—The
police power reserved to a city in a street railway franchise stipulating that the city may adopt ordinances necessary for the protection
of the interests of the city vests in the city the power to determine
the frequency of street car service, having in mind the general welfare of the traveling public and the health and safety of the citizens.

Municipal Corporations—Police Power—Right to Surrender.—A
city may not, by granting a street railway franchise, divest itself of
its governmental police power, the exercise of which is necessary
for the public welfare and safety.

Street Railroads—Police Power—Regulation of Street Car Service.
—Under Const. art. 11, § 11, authorizing any city to make local, police, and sanitary regulations, and Rem. & Bal. Code, § 7507, subds.
9, 36, authorizing any city to regulate the operation of street railroads
within its limits, and to provide for the punishment of all practices
dangerous to the public safety, a city empowered by its charter to
regulate the operation of street railroads within its limits may adopt
an ordinance requiring a five-minute street car service between designated hours of each day.

Street Railroads—Ordinances—Validity—Reasonableness.—The superintendent of a street railway company in a city in charge of the
operation of the system may not urge that an ordinance providing
for a five-minute street car service during specified hours of each
day, and imposing a fine not exceeding $100 for a violation, is op-
pressive, when applied to him.

Rudkin, C. J., and Chadwick, J., dissenting.

Department 2. Appeal from Superior Court, Pierce County;
C. M. Easterday, Judge.

F. A. Boutelle was convicted of violating an ordinance of the
City of Tacoma, and he appeals. Affirmed.

B. S. Grosscup and *W. C. Morrow*, for appellant.
T. L. Stiles, F. R. Baker, and *F. M. Carnahan,* for respondent.

Morris, J.. Appellant, the superintendent in charge of the running and operation of the street car system of the city of Tacoma, belonging to the Tacoma Railway & Power Company, was convicted of a violation of Ordinance No. 3883 of said city, and prosecutes this appeal. Said ordinance is as follows:

"An Ordinance Regulating the Operation of Certain Street Cars in the City of Tacoma by the Tacoma Railway & Power Company, and Providing a Penalty for the Violation Thereof.

"Whereas, the street railway service rendered by the Tacoma Railway & Power Company over its line from South Ninth street to Union avenue, South Tacoma, along 'C' street, Jefferson avenue, Pacific avenue, Delin street, 'G' street, South 38th street, 'M' street, South Fifty-Sixth street, Railroad street and South Fifty-Fourth street is inadequate, in that a sufficient number of cars are not operated to accommodate the number of passengers:

"Now, therefore, be it ordained by the city of Tacoma:

"Section 1. That from and after October 5th, 1909, the Tacoma Railway & Power Company, its managers, servants and agents, be required to operate at least one passenger street car each way every ten minutes between South Ninth street and Union avenue (South Tacoma), between the hours of 5:30 o'clock a. m., and 12:30 o'clock a. m., following, and one car each way every five minutes between the hours of 6 o'clock and 8 o'clock a. m., and between the hours of 5 o'clock and 7:30 o'clock p. m., over its line along South 'C' street, Jefferson avenue, Pacific avenue, Delin street, 'G' street, South Thirty-Eighth street, 'M' street, South Fifty-Sixth street, Railroad street and South Fifty-Fourth street.

"Sec. 2. Every person violating the provisions of this ordinance shall, on conviction thereof, be fined in any sum not exceeding one hundred dollars.

"Sec. 3. Each day's failure of said Tacoma Railway & Power Company to comply with the provisions of this ordinance shall constitute a separate offense."

Appellant urges two grounds of error: (1) The ordinance is unconstitutional, and violates the guaranties of both state and federal Constitution, in that it seeks to impair the obligations of a contract, and to deprive the street railway company of its property without due process of law; and (2) the city was without authority to pass the ordinance, it was not authorized under the specific provisions of the city charter conferring power over street railways, nor can it be sustained as a valid exercise of the police power. The street railway line referred to in the ordinance, from South Ninth street to Union avenue, South

Tacoma, is known as the South Tacoma line, and is operated over portions of 10 different streets. The right to operate over these different streets was conferred by three different ordinances, passed at as many different times, and containing different' provisions and conditions affecting the franchise therein granted. The tracks on Jefferson avenue, Pacific avenue, and C street are operated under franchise granted by Ordinance No. 152 as amended by Ordinance No. 238. This ordinance was passed in 1887, and section 5, as amended in 1889, provides as follows: "The city council may regulate the speed for running the cars and may require the cars to be run on or over the lines of said railways sufficient round trips each day, and no cars shall be allowed at any time to stop and remain upon any intersection of streets for a longer period than three minutes, and any violation of the provisions of this section shall subject the owners of said railways to a fine of not less than five or more than twenty-five dollars for every offense upon conviction thereof before any court having jurisdiction." The tracks on Delin and G streets are operated under Ordinance No. 188, passed in 1888, section 6 of which is as follows: "The city council may regulate the speed for running the cars and may require cars to be run two round trips each day on all completed portions of said railway after one mile thereof is completed. No car shall be allowed at any time to stop or remain upon any street intersection. The fare upon said railway over the whole, or any part thereof, shall not exceed five cents for each passenger, including ordinary hand baggage. Any violation of the provisions of this section shall subject the owners of said railway to a fine of not less than five or more than twenty-five dollars for every offense, upon conviction thereof before any court having jurisdiction." The franchise for the remaining streets was granted by Ordinance No. 860, passed in 1893, section 12 of which is as follows: "Nothing in this ordinance shall be so construed as to prevent the city council of the city of Tacoma from passing all ordinances and resolutions necessary for the protection of the interests of the city, and to carry out the spirit and provisions of this franchise or ordinance, or from granting to any other street railway the right to cross the tracks of the line or lines of this railway at the same grade."

Appellant's contention is that Ordinance No. 3883, in providing for a five-minute service over the entire South Tacoma line, is an attempted impairment of the obligation of the contracts between the city and the railway company, as established by the various franchises; that, as to the first group of streets, the city is not authorized by the franchise to determine what shall be "sufficient round trips each day," as provided for in section 5, supra; that such clause does not confer upon the council the right to determine arbitrarily the number of round trips each day that

City of Tacoma *v.* Boutelle

will be sufficient, but that the determination of that matter presents a judicial, rather than a legislative, question; that, as to the second group of streets, the provision of section 6, supra, investing the city council with the power to "require cars to be run two round trips each day," is a manifest expression of intention on the part of the council; that it reserved no authority to require a more frequent service than two round trips a day; that the third group of streets controlled by the provisions of section 12, supra, have no reservation whatever as to any authority in the council to require any specific degree of service, or to determine what should be a sufficient service, there being no expressed intention in section 12 to reserve any such power; that inasmuch as, in the ordinances governing the first two groups of streets, a specific authority had been declared, the omission of such declaration in the ordinance governing the third group was intentional and deliberate. The suggestion first advanced in support of these contentions is that a franchise grant to a public service corporation in the nature of a contract, equally binding upon both the city and the railway company, and that an attempt of the city to abrogate any of the rights conferred by the passage of a subsequent ordinance is an impairment of a contract obligation, and hence void. So far as being a correct statement of the law, the above position may be admitted, but in our opinion it has no place in the determination of the question before us.

A good illustration of the correct application of the above rule of law may be found in Minneapolis & Minn. St. Ry. Co., 215 U. S. 417, 30 Sup. Ct. 118, 54 L. Ed. ——, cited by appellant as supporting his application of the rule. In 1875 the city of Minneapolis gave a franchise to the railway company for 50 years, by the terms of which the company had the right to charge a fare not exceeding five cents on any continuous line not exceeding three miles in length. In 1907 the city council enacted an ordinance requiring the railway company to sell 6 tickets for 25 cents, which ordinance was held to be void as impairing the obligation of a contract. The right to charge a five-cent fare was a specific grant of the franchise, and the city could no more violate such a specific grant than it could abrogate the franchise itself. As was said by Chadwick. J., in Peterson *v.* Tacoma Ry. & Power Co., 111 Pac. 338, in reviewing this same case: "The right to charge the fare provided in the franchise was of the essence of the contract, and it could not be abridged by the city." We have confronting us in the present case no attempt on the part of the city to change or destroy by Ordinance No. 3883 any specific or implied right vested in the railway company under any previous ordinances; but rather an enactment under a general power expressly reserved in each of the original ordinances.

City of Tacoma v. Boutelle

The fact that the provisions of Ordinance No. 3883 are more specific than the expression of the general power reserved in the initiating ordinances does not destroy the specific enactment, but leaves for determination the question whether such specific requirement is reasonable. If so, it will be sustained; if not, it will be held invalid. Elliott on Railroads, 1624. And "the question of reasonableness usually resolves itself into this: Is the regulation carried to a point where it becomes prohibition, destruction, or confiscation?" Freund on Police Power, 61. Reasonableness in this connection is a question of fact, and will be presumed; the burden of proof being upon those asserting unreasonableness of which there was no evidence in this case. In People v. Detroit Citizens' St. Ry. Co., 116 Mich. 132, 74 N. W. 520' an ordinance was passed in 1897 requiring the railway company to maintain a six-minute service on certain streets between prescribed hours under a franchise granted the railway company in 1862. It was provided that cars should be run as often as public convenience required, but not oftener than once in 20 minutes. Another provision of the franchise reserved the right to the city to make such further regulations as may be deemed necessary to protect the safety, welfare, and accommodation of the public. This franchise was amended in 1879, extending its life and providing that cars on all lines subject to the ordinance should be operated as public convenience required. The railway company contended, when it was sought to enforce the six-minute service, as appellant here contends, that the city had no power to pass such an ordinance, and that the franchise constituted an inviolable contract, under which they could only be compelled to run cars every 20 minutes. In passing upon this contention, the court referred to the fact that Detroit, in 1862, was a city of about 50,000 people. Its residents all lived within a comparatively short distance of the business center, and it was probably believed that the time fixed for the running of the cars would fully answer the convenience and demands of the people. It was then held that in view of the increased population of the city, with the consequent demands for a quicker and more convenient street railway service, together with the provisions of the amendment of 1879, the ordinance was valid, and a reasonable determination of the power vested in the common council. A like argument might well be used in referring to the city of Tacoma in 1887 and 1888, the years of the passage of the first two ordinances, one of which provided that the city council might require the cars to be run "sufficient round trips each day," and the other "two round trips each day." Sufficient for what? Manifestly not the convenience of the railway company, but the convenience and demands for reasonable transportation on the part of the residents of the city whose inhabitants at that time looked forward to its becoming a great city before the life of the granted franchise had expired, and, as it increased in population, so would there be an increased demand for an improved street railway service, recognized by the city in reserving to itself, as it did in the first franchise, the right to require "sufficient round trips each day" to accommodate the necessities of its residents and their demands for a proper public service.   Nor is this a question for judicial determination, as contended by appellant, but what would be "sufficient round trips each day" is purely a legislative question to be determined and solved by the common council of the city, subject to a review by the courts upon the question of the authority and reasonableness of its act. So the provision of the second ordinance, requiring cars to run two round trips a day, is not, as contended for by appellant, the expression of an intention to not require more trips.   It is nothing more than an expression of the minimum service regarded by the city as being sufficient for the demands of the then city in the territory covered by the franchise.   As to the third provision found in section 12 of Ordinance 860, appellant contends it to be simply a declaration of a reservation of the police power. If it is such a declaration, then such a reservation, if needful, would be ample to invest the city with full power to pass ordinance No. 3883, as we shall argue more fully hereafter.

Referring again to the rule of "reasonableness," as determinative of the effect of subsequent requirements upon franchise regulation, a good case may be found in Trenton Horse R. Co. v. Trenton. 53 N. J. Law, 132, 20 Atl. 1076, 11 L. R. A. 410.   The charter of the city of Trenton conferred general power to pass ordinances necessary and proper for the good government, order, and protection of persons and property; also power to prescribe the manner in which corporations should exercise any granted privilege in the use of the streets.   Under these grants, the city based its right to pass an ordinance requiring horse railways to have an agent, in addition to the driver on each car.   The ordinance being attacked for lack of power, the court held that neither of the above enumerated powers added anything to the right of the city to exercise the police power, and the only question to be considered was the reasonableness of the ordinance, and, if reasonable, no special delegation of power was required to vindicate it; and added: "In concluding whether the ordinance under consideration is a reasonable precaution in favor of the public safety and order, we must regard it in the light of the following conditions, which surround the question: First. A rule of construction to be applied is that, when an ordinance is passed upon a matter clearly within a general power, the presumption is in favor of its reasonableness. The judicial power to declare it void can only be exerted when from the inherent character of the ordinance, or from evidence taken showing its operation, it is demonstrated to be reasonable."   See, also, Mayor,

City of Tacoma v. Boutelle

etc.. v. Dry Dock E. B. & B. R. Co., 133 N. Y. 104, 30 N. E. 563, 28 Am. St. Rep. 609; Van Hook v. Selma, 70 Ala. 361, 45 Am. Rep. 85; North Jersey St. Ry. Co. v. Jersey City, 75 N. J. Law, 349, 67 Atl. 1072. In the present case there was no attempt to show Ordinance No. 3883 was unreasonable. Nor is there in its inherent character anything which would move the court to hold it unreasonable as a matter of law, and thus declare it void. We therefore hold upon the first point reserved by appellant that the ordinance in question is not an attempt to impair the obligations of a contract, and therefore void.

Much of the second assignment of error is involved in what has already been said. We will, however, discuss it more in detail. All courts concede the impossibility of adopting fixed rules by which to test the validity of laws passed under the police power. It covers a wide range of subjects, but is especially occupied with whatever affects the peace, security, health, morals, and general welfare of a community. While originally it was used as a rule to indicate the protective function of the government, its development of late years has been in the direction of the function of the state that cares for the general walfare. Social Progress and the Police Power, 36 Am. Law Review, 681. As was said by Chadwick, J., in Bowes v. Aberdeen, 109 Pac. 369: "Its exercise in proper cases marks the growth and development of the law rather than, as some assert, a tyrannical assertion of governmental powers denied by our written constitution." In its broadest acceptation it means the general power of the state to preserve and promote the public welfare, even at the expense of private rights. Karasek v. Peier, 22 Wash. 419, 61 Pac. 33, 50 L. R. A. 345. That it, when generally reserved, vests ample power in the common council of a city, having in mind the general welfare of the traveling public, and the health and safety of the citizen, endangered by crowded and heavily loaded cars, to determine by ordinance the frequency with which cars should be run upon the public streets, is to our mind demonstrated both upon principle and by authority. In Detroit v. Detroit Citizens' St. Ry. Co., 184 U. S. 368, 22 Sup. Ct. 410, 46 L. Ed. 592, the court held that a general reservation in a franchise to make such regulations as may from time to time be deemed necessary to protect the interest. safety, welfare. or accommodation of the city and public, while not sufficient to permit the city to pass an ordinance changing the rate of fare, was ample in regard to all matter incident to the operation of the road such as "in the interest of public travel, the frequency with which cars should be run for the public convenience." Such a reservation is not as broad as that contained in Ordinance No. 152, supra; nor is it in effect any broader than the reservations contained in Ordinances Nos. 188 and 860. In Lawton v. Steele, 152 U. S. 133, 14 Sup. Ct. 499, 38 L. Ed. 385, the court says the police

City of Tacoma *v.* Boutelle

power is universally conceded to include everything essential to the public safety, health, and morals, and includes "the regulation of railways and other means of public conveyance." Joyce on Franchises thus states the same rule, in section 387: "A municipality under its right to make reasonable regulations concerning the use of its streets by a street railroad company may limit the speed of its cars, or the length of time of service or of running of cars on certain streets." We believe it to be equally well settled that it was not within the power of the city, in any franchise it may have conferred upon the railway company, to divest itself of its governmental police power, the exercise of which is necessary for the public welfare and the preservation of the public safety. Elliott on Railroads, § 1082; Joyce on Franchises, § 366; Abbott on Municipal Corporations, § 854; Beer Company *v.* Massachusetts, 97 U. S. 25, 33, 24 L. Ed. 989; St. Louis & San F. Ry. Co. *v.* Mathews, 165 U. S. 1, 23, 17 Sup. Ct. 243, 41 L. Ed. 611. "The power is continuing and no grant that can be made legally can destroy it. Therefore the municipal corporation in granting franchises for the use of its streets may not divest itself of the authority of control and regulation. It is true under our constitutional system that neither vested rights can be destroyed, nor the obligation of a contract impaired. But public necessity may legally limit or control these fundamental rights only, however, in the reasonable exercise of the sovereign police power. The police power to regulate comprehends all necessary and convenient regulations designed to protect life and limb or to promote the comfort of the public in the use of the streets and thoroughfares. Not only does such power exist, but the duty to exercise it is imposed as a solemn obligation upon the municipal authorities." McQuillan, Mun. Ord. § 473; Petz et al. *v.* Detroit, 95 Mich. 169, 54 N. W. 644.

Maintaining, then, that the city of Tacoma had reserved to itself ample police power to pass Ordinance No. 3883, the next inquiry naturally is, Has the city the power to use this reserved power? The general police power conferred upon municipal corporations by the Constitution is found in article 11, § 11: "Any county, city, town or township may make and enforce within its limits all such local, police, sanitary and other regulations as are not in conflict with general law." The general powers delegated by the state to cities of the first class are enumerated in section 7507, Rem. & Bal., among them: "(9) To authorize or prohibit the locating and construction of any railroad or street railroad in any street, alley or public place in such city and to prescribe the terms and conditions upon which any such railroad or street railroad shall be located or constructed; to provide for the alteration, change of grade, or removal thereof; to regulate the moving and operation of railroad and street railroad trains, cars, and locomotives within the corporate limits of such

City of Tacoma *v.* Boutelle

city, and to provide by ordinance for the protection of all persons and property against injury in the use of such railroad or street railroads." Under subdivision 36 of the same section is granted the right to provide for the punishment of all practices dangerous to public safety, and to make régulations necessary for the preservation of public health, peace, and good order, and to provide for the punishment of all persons violating any of the ordinances. These provisions of the Constitution and statute would seem to be a sufficient conferring of police power upon the municipality by the state. The charter of Tacoma, passed under these general powers, contains, in section 52, subd. 9, the assertion of its authority "to regulate the moving and operation of railroad and street railroad trains, cars and locomotives within the corporate limits, and to provide for the protection of persons and property against injury in the use of such railroads and street railroads;" while, under subdivision 36, it asserts its power to pass penal ordinances, in the language of subdivision 36, supra. These constitutional, statutory, and charter provisions show a sufficient conferring of power upon the municipality by the state, and the assertion on the part of the municipality to use all such power conferred. The police power being ample, then, to sustain Ordinance No. 3883, and the exercise of this power having been conferred upon the city, and the city having exercised is as conferred, appellant's second objection, that the ordinance is not justified and cannot be vindicated as a valid exercise of the police power, must also fail.

Appellant, in connection with his second assignment of error, makes another assertion which we will notice, contending that the ordinance is void because it is oppressive and arbitrary in declaring, "every person violating the provisions of this ordinance shall be fined;" and in support of this contention cites Town of Oxanna *v.* Allen, 90 Ala. 468, 8 South. 79, Townsend *v.* Circleville, 78 Ohio St. 122, 84 N. E. 792, 16 L. R. A. (N. S.) 914, and Ex parte Young, 209 U. S. 123, 28 Sup. Ct. 441, 52 L. Ed. 714, 13 L. R. A. (N. S.) 932. A review of those cases will, we think, show they are based upon reasoning which cannot obtain here. In the Oxanna Case the superintendent of a street railway company was convicted of a violation of an ordinance providing that it should be unlawful for any street railway company to permit its roadbed or tracks to remain so high above the surface of the street as to discommode and seriously interfere with public travel, and declaring that the president, superintendent, or other officer of such railway company violating the foregoing provision should be fined. Held, that the ordinance was unreasonable and oppressive in so far as it concerned the superintendent, as it made him quasi criminally responsible for the failure of the company to expend money in putting its track in suitable repair; that it was the duty of the company to appropriate money to keep its roadbed

City of Tacoma *v.* Boutelle

in repair. The superintendent had no power to make them, nor could he be expected to use his own money for such purpose. He could not be held responsible for a dereliction of duty on the part of the company. In the case before us, the charge is failure to maintain a schedule provided for in the ordinance. It was charged in the complaint, admitted in the answer, and the court expressly found, that appellant was "in charge of the running and operation of the street car system of the city of Tacoma;" hence, he was clothed with the power denied the superintendent in the Oxanna Case, and the reasoning of the court has no application. In fact, it was not attempted to be shown that appellant had no such power. In the Townsend Case the ordinance required an interurban railway to stop its cars at all cross-streets and street intersections. The conductor of one of the cars was arrested and fined for failing so to stop. Held, no power in the municipality to pass such an ordinance under a power granted "to regulate speed of interurban cars within the corporation," or a second provision providing for the control of the streets. The reasoning of the court is best given in its own language: "The street railway is what its name signifies—a railway on a street—to facilitate its use as a way for persons to pass from one point to another in the city or through the city, but with the advent of electricity as a motive power, the street railway was extended to the suburbs, and, as a result of development in its use, it has been found practicable to operate cars for long distances; so that now we have the interurban railway extending from city to city over the streets and upon or along the highways. * * * If every city and village through which such a railway passes may require its cars to be stopped at every street intersection to take on or to discharge passengers and to serve the purpose of a street railway, then its usefulness as a means of interurban transportation may be very much limited because so much time will be consumed in passing through cities and villages that it will no longer be practicable for many to travel in that way. Councils may reasonably be expected to be actuated by considerations of local convenience rather than those of the public, and, in view of the importance of the subject and its comparatively recent origin, it would seem to be a matter for consideration by the Legislature; and it is in view of these considerations that we reach the conclusion that the power has not been conferred by the general terms of section 28." From the above reasoning, it is apparent that the decision on this branch of the case is based upon the character of the railway—an interurban, as distinguished from a local street railway—and the holding of unreasonableness is due to the impracticability of stopping the cars of such a railway at every street crossing in every city. Such reasoning is of no value here. In the Young Case the state of Minnesota passed an act fixing two cents a mile as the maximum passenger rate in that state. The act further declared that "any railroad company or

Martin *v.* Rhode Island Co

any officer, agent, or representative thereof, who shall violate any provision of this act, shall be guilty of a felony, and upon conviction thereof, shall be punished by a 'fine not exceeding $5,000, or by imprisonment in the state prison for a period not exceeding five years, or both such fine and imprisonment." It was held that imposing such enormous fines and possible imprisonment rendered the statute unconstitutional on its face, irrespective of the insufficiency of the rates, as persons affected by the law were, because of the enormous penalties for disobedience, prevented from so doing and resorting to the courts to test the validity of the statute, and thereby denied the equal protection of the law. The penalty fixed by the ordinance under review is a fine not exceeding $100. It does not seem to us, therefore, that the reasoning of the courts, nor the grounds upon which the decision in each of these three cases is made, renders them authoritative upon the question before us.

We therefore conclude that the judgment of the court below was right upon the law, and the same is affirmed.

CROW and DUNBAR, JJ., concur.

MARTIN *v.* RHODE ISLAND CO.

(Supreme Court of Rhode Island, Jan. 13, 1911.)

[78 Atl. Rep. 548.]

Carriers—Carriage of Passengers—Payment of Fare—Right to Establish Rules.*—A carrier has the incidental power to establish reasonable rules regulating the payment of its charges, and such regulations will be sustained upon the sole ground that they are reasonably necessary to protect the carrier, though the rule manifestly result in additional haidship to the passenger but not interfering with his primary right to transportation.

Carriers—Carriage of Passengers—Rules for Payment of Charges—Reasonableness—Question for Court.—The reasonableness of such a rule is a question for the court.

Carriers—Carriage of Passengers—Rules for Payment of Fare—Reasonableness.—A rule of a street railway company requiring payment of fare by its passengers by means of an automatic fare-registering device held in the hand of the conductor, consisting of a small nickel-plated box having a coin-slot on one side, through which the passenger inserts the nickel, the coin being drawn into the de-

---

*For the authorities in this series on the subject of the validity of a carrier of passenger iules and regulations, see first foot-note of St. Louis, etc., R. Co. *v.* Johnson (Okla.), 36 R. R. R. 165, 59 Am. & Eng. R. Cas., N. S., 165.

vice by its mechanism as soon as the edge of the nickel touches certain levers within the slot, whereupon the fare is registered automatically, under which rule a passenger may either insert a coin
possessed by him or may receive one in change from the conductor
and insert it, is not unreasonable as causing great inconvenience and
annoyance to passengers without benefit to the traveling public, as
being solely for the benefit of the carrier, in keeping a check upon
dishonest conductors, as being a reflection upon the honesty of the
conductors, and as not serving the convenience of the conductors in
keeping account of the fares collected; the rule imposing no greater
burden upon the passengers than a permissible rule requiring the
purchase of tickets and being of aid to the carrier and its conductors
in simplifying the accounting for fares, obviating the necessity of
daily settlements between them, securing accuracy, and tending to
prevent fraud and mistake.

Payment—Legal Tender—Statutory Provision—Violation. — The
refusal of a conductor, under the rule, to accept five one-cent pieces
for fare except in exchange for a five-cent piece to be inserted in
the automatic collector by the passenger is not a violation of U. S.
Comp. St. 1901, § 3587, providing that the minor coins of the United
States shall be a legal tender at their nominal value for any amount
not exceeding 25 cents in one payment, under which five separate
cent pieces are legal tender for a debt of five cents, so as to render
the rule unreasonable; such refusal not amounting to a refusal to accept the five coins in payment of the fare within the meaning of the
statute.

**Carriers—Carriage of Passengers—Rules for Collection of Fares
—Reasonableness.**—The requirement that a passenger pay his fare
into the automatic collector is not a demand for a greater fare than
allowed by the carrier's charter fixing a maximum rate of five cents,
since the establishment of such maximum rate does not preclude the
carrier from making reasonable regulations as to its payment.

Certified from Superior Court, Providence and Bristol
Counties; Willard B. Tanner, Judge.

Action by Joseph Martin against the Rhode Island Company.
Certified from the Superior Court on questions of law. Questions answered.

C. M. Van Slyck and *Frederick A. Jones,* for plaintiff.
Joseph C. Sweeney and *Clifford Whipple,* for defendant.

Edwards & Angell (Frank H. Swan and *Francis B. Keeney,*
of counsel), for Rooke Automatic Register Co.

PARKHURST, J.   This case comes before the court for hearing
upon questions of law of such doubt and importance and so affecting the merits of the case that, in the opinion of the Superior
Court, they should be determined by the Supreme Court before
further proceedings, and are certified in accordance with the pro-

Martin v. Rhode Island Co

visions of chapter 298, § 5, of the General Laws of Rhode Island of 1909.

The action is trespass on the case, brought by Joseph Martin against the Rhode Island Company, for damages resulting from being ejected from the defendant's cars. The declaration is in four counts. The first count sets out in general terms that the plaintiff boarded the defendant's car and tendered the conductor in charge of the car a nickel in payment of his fare; that the conductor declined to accept said nickel, stopped the car, and wrongfully ejected the plaintiff therefrom. The second count covers the same ejectment, but sets out with greater detail that the plaintiff boarded a certain car belonging to the defendant and tendered the conductor in charge of the car a nickel in payment of his fare; that the conductor requested the plaintiff to insert said nickel into an automatic fare-registering device held in the conductor's hand; that the plaintiff declined to accede to the request of the conductor, whereupon the conductor stopped the car and wrongfully ejected the plaintiff therefrom. The third count covers an ejectment on a different day, and sets out in general terms that the plaintiff boarded the defendant's car and tendered the conductor in charge of the car five pennies, in payment of his fare; that the conductor declined to accept said five pennies, stopped the car, and wrongfully ejected the plaintiff therefrom. The fourth count covers the same ejectment as the third, but sets out in detail that the plaintiff boarded a certain car belonging to the defendant and tendered the conductor in charge of the car five pennies, in payment of his fare; that the conductor took said pennies, tendered a nickel to the plaintiff, and requested him to insert said nickel into an automatic fare-registering device held in conductor's hand; that the plaintiff declined to accept said nickel and insert it into the automatic fare-registering device, whereupon the conductor stopped the car, and wrongfully ejected the plaintiff therefrom.

The defendant filed a plea of the general issue to each of the four counts of the declaration, and a special plea to each of the four counts. The special pleas to the first and second counts of declaration are practically identical, and set up, in substance, that when the plaintiff entered the defendant's car he failed to comply with the reasonable regulations of the defendant, known to the plaintiff, governing the manner of the payment of fares, and refused to insert his nickel into the automatic collector held in the hand of the conductor, although requested to do so by the conductor; that said plaintiff was informed by the conductor that in accordance with the regulations of the defendant he would have to insert his nickel into said automatic collector, or he would have to leave the car; that, upon the continued refusal of the plaintiff to insert his nickel into the automatic collector, the car was stopped and the plaintiff ejected, using no more force than

Martin *v.* Rhode Island Co

was necessary. The special pleas to the third and fourth counts of the declaration are practically identical, and set up, in substance, that when the plaintiff entered the defendant's car and tendered to the conductor five pennies in payment of his fare, the conductor received said pennies for the sole purpose of providing the plaintiff with a nickel which the plaintiff might insert into the automatic collector, in accordance with the reasonable regulations of the defendant; that the conductor informed said plaintiff of the purpose for which said pennies were received and tendered him a nickel and requested him to insert it into the automatic collector held in the hand of the conductor, in accordance with the regulations of the defendant; that the plaintiff refused to accept said nickel and insert it into the said automatic collector; that thereupon the conductor informed the plaintiff that he must either receive said nickel and insert it into said automatic collector, in accordance with the defendant's regulations, or leave the car; that, upon the continued refusal of the defendant to accept said nickel and insert it into said automatic collector, the car was stopped and the plaintiff ejected, using no more force than was necessary.

The plaintiff demurred to each of the special pleas upon the following grounds: (1) That said pleas contain no allegations which constitute a defense to this action. (2) That, while said pleas purport to be pleas in confession and avoidance, said pleas confess the commission of the grievances complained of, but do not set forth sufficient matter in justification. (3) That the regulations of said defendant set forth in said pleas are not reasonable. regulations, and therefore not a justification of the defendant's conduct complained of in the plaintiff's declaration.

The question of law certified by the superior court to be determined by the Supreme Court are as follows:

(1) Is a rule of a street railway company requiring the payment of fare by its passengers by means of an automatic fare-registering device held in the hand of the conductor, consisting of a small nickel-plated box having a coin-slot on one side through which the passenger inserts a nickel, a reasonable rule or regulation, justifying the ejectment of a passenger by the conductor in charge of the car should the passenger, having notice of such rule or regulation, fail to observe said rule; no undue force being used?

(2) Is a rule of a street railway company requiring by the payment of fare by its passengers by means of an automatic fare-registering device held in the hand of the conductor, consisting of a small nickel-plated box having a coin-slot on one side through which the passenger inserts a nickel, a reasonable rule or regulation, justifying the ejectment of a passenger by the conductor in charge of the car, no undue force being used, who, having notice of such rule or regulation, tenders

Martin *v*. Rhode Island Co

five pennies in payment of his fare, and who refuses to receive in exchange therefor a nickel, and to insert said nickel into the automatic fare-registering device, the passenger being notified at the time said pennies are tendered that they will be received by the conductor only for the purpose of providing said passenger with a nickel?

We understand the word "nickel," used in the first question, to mean the five-cent piece now and long since in common use in the United States, made partly of nickel and colloquially called a "nickel;" and the word "pennies," used in the second question, to mean the single separate one-cent pieces now in common use. Strictly speaking, we know of no coin now in use in the United States which is properly called a "penny." See 2 U. S. Comp. St. § 3515.

The incidental power of a common carrier to establish reasonable rules regulating the time, place, and mode for payment of its reasonable charges is unquestioned on the plaintiff's brief, and is amply sustained by the authorities. 28 Am. & Eng. Enc. of Law, 166; Reese *v*. Pennsylvania R. R., 131 Pa. 422, 19 Atl. 72, 6 L. R. A. 529, 17 Am. St. Rep. 818 (1890). 1 Elliott, Railroads, vol. 1, § 199: "A railroad company has an implied authority (which is necessarily almost absolute) to make and enforce all reasonable rules and regulations for the control of its trains and the persons thereon, of persons using its stations and grounds, and of those transacting business with it, in order to provide for the safety of its passengers and employees, and to protect itself from imposition and wrong." The power to make such regulations is essential to the maintenance of the undoubted right of the carrier to secure to itself, in return for services rendered, the compensation prescribed by law, and is in aid of a right as absolute in the carrier as is the right of the passenger himself to demand transportation. And the courts have repeatedly held that regulations of this character may, and should be, sustained upon the sole ground that they or similar rules are reasonably necessary to protect the carrier in the collection of his lawful charges, even though the rule manifestly results in additional hardship to the passenger but not interferring with his primary right to transportation. Thus in the leading case of Hibbard *v*. N. Y. & Erie R. R. Co., 15 N. Y. 455, 458 (1857), it was held that a railroad company had a right to compel passengers to exhibit their tickets to the conductor as often as requested, because "this or some similar arrangement is absolutely necessary for the company, unless they are willing to transport passengers free." And see other cases cited infra.

It is also well settled and not disputed by either party that the question of the reasonableness or unreasonableness of such a rule is one to be determined by the court, and is not to be submitted to the jury. See Vedder *v*. Fellows, 20 N. Y. 126; Ill.

Martin v. Rhode Island Co

Central R. R. Co. v. Whittemore, 43 Ill. 420, 92 Am. Dec. 138;
Wolsey v. Lake Shore & M. S. R. R. Co., 33 Ohio St. 227;
Hoffbauer v. D. & N. W. R. Co., 52 Iowa, 342, 3 N. W. 121, 35
Am. Rep. 278; Louisville & Nashville R. R. Co. v. Fleming, 18
Am. & Eng. R. R. Cas. 347; Railway Co. v. Hardy, 55 Ark. 134,
17 S. W. 711; Central of Ga. Ry. Co. v. Motes, 117 Ga. 923, 43
S. E. 990, 62 L. R. A. 507, 97 Am. St. Rep. 223; Burge v. Ga.
Ry. & Electric Co., 33 Ga. 423, 65 S. E. 879, and other cases,
infra; 1 Elliott on Railroads, § 202; 1 Thompson on Trials, §
1057.

The plaintiff, in argument, contends that the rules set up by
the defendant are unreasonable; because they cause great inconvenience and annoyance to passengers and without benefit to
the   traveling public; because they are solely for the benefit
of the defendant, in keeping a check upon dishonest conductors
(admitting, however, that the device is effective for such purpose.); because they are a reflection upon the honesty of every
conductor in the defendant's employ, and do not serve the convenience of the conductor in keeping account of the fares collected; and because the adoption of the fare-registering device in
question is unnecessary even to protect the defendant from dishonest conductors, suggesting that the defendant, like all carriers
of passengers, has a right to demand that passengers procure
tickets before entering the cars, and that a rule requiring the
presentation of a ticket by the passenger would be a proper and
effective check upon the dishonesty of conductors.

We are of the opinion that none of the objections urged by the
plaintiff as against the reasonableness of the rules in question,
are tenable.

The plaintiff cites no authorities even tending to show that the
rules here in question are unreasonable; he cites only the case of
Kennedy v. Birmingham Railway, Light & Power Co., 138 Ala.
225, 230, 35 South. 108, 109, in which one question only was
presented, viz., "the reasonableness of a regulation of the defendant company requiring the plaintiff as a passenger to pay in
cash a greater sum than is charged by it for a ticket between the
same points." The plaintiff had no ticket, and there was no
ticket office where he could buy a ticket conveniently; and so it
was held as to him, that the enforcement of the rule was unreasonable, and that the rule furnished no defense to his ejectment
from the car. The court says: "All the cases agree that carriers
of passengers may require persons to purchase tickets before taking passage on their cars, and to this end may adopt a rule or
regulation establishing a higher rate to be paid to the conductor
than the rate charged for a ticket. But, to justify a discrimination in the rates, the carrier must provide the proper facility and
accommodation for so purchasing the ticket. If the carrier
fails to give the passenger a convenient and accessible place and

Martin *v.* Rhode Island Co

an opportunity to buy his ticket before entering the car, the regulation is unreasonable and void and is no defense to an action brought by the passenger for his ejection by the conductor after he has paid the ticket rate"—citing and discussing a number of cases. And the plaintiff also cites 2 Hutchinson on Carriers, § 1032, where the right of carriers of passengers to make reasonable rules requiring the purchase and exhibition of tickets is discussed and upheld.

It being conceded by the plaintiff, and being in accordance with his own citations of authority, as well as with the numerous other cases herein cited, that it is well settled to be a reasonable rule that a carrier of passengers may require the passenger to purchase a ticket before entering the cars and to present the same to the conductor upon request, provided the carrier furnishes proper facility and accommodation for the passenger to purchase such ticket, we think the portion of the rule here under consideration requiring the passenger to present a nickel (five-cent piece) to the conductor in payment of his fare is quite closely analogous to the ticket requirement, and imposes no greater burden upon the passenger than the rule requiring the purchase of a ticket. In fact, the burden upon the passenger is much less under the nickel (five-cent piece) rule here in question, than under the ticket rule, inasmuch as under the ticket rule, as generally applied, the passenger must purchase his ticket at one or more specified stations of the carrier, and is not allowed to purchase it of the conductor; while, under the nickel rule here in question, every conductor becomes a ticket agent and every car a station, where the equivalent of the ticket may be purchased. So that in our opinion that portion of the rule which requires the passenger to present a nickel to the conductor, and to purchase one of the conductor, if the passenger has none, is a simplification of the ticket rule, in favor of the passenger. and favors the passenger to that extent, and is entirely reasonable.

The only portion of the rule that remains to be discussed then, is the requirement that the passenger's nickel, either the one which he originally had or the one which he has purchased of the conductor, shall be inserted by the passenger in the fare-registering box held in the conductor's hand, instead of in the hand of the conductor himself. The device in use by the defendant corporation is called the "Rooke Automatic Register," one of which was exhibited to the court, and its workings explained, at the argument of this case. It consists of a small nickel-plated box, of convenient size to be held in the hand, of neat appearance, with a coin-slot conveniently placed; and the manner of paying fares required by the defendant's rule involves simply the partial insertion by the passenger of a nickel into the slot. As soon as the edge of the nickel touches certain fingers or levers within the slot, the coin is automatically drawn in by the mechanism,

Martin *v.* Rhode Island Co

and at the same time the fare is registered, and the operation is complete. This involves no more labor or delay or trouble on the part of the passenger than the act of placing the coin in the conductor's hand, and the automatic grasp of the coin by the machine is positive and certain. Whatever of delay or trouble may be involved in the obedience to the rule comes from the necessity of making change in case the passenger is not provided with a nickel and is obliged to obtain one from the conductor; and this, as we have already seen, is so far analogous to the principle of the rule regarding the purchase of tickets that we regard the settled law of the cases heretofore cited as amply supporting the principle contended for by the defendant in this case.

It is quite obvious that the rules in question in this case are far less burdensome to the passenger than many rules regarding the manner of payment of fares, purchase and showing of tickets, taking transfers, making change, and other matters incident to the passenger's right to carriage, which have been held to be reasonable by courts of undoubted authority. See cases cited supra. See, also, Burge *v.* Georgia Ry. & El. Co., 133 Ga. 423, 65 S. E. 879; Knoxville Traction Co. *v.* Wilkerson, 117 Tenn. 482, 99 S. W. 992, 9 L. R. A. (N. S.) 579; Funderburg *v.* Augusta & Aiken Ry. Co., 81 S. E. 141, 61 S. E. 1075, 21 L. R. A. (N. S.) 868; Yorton *v.* M., L. S. & W. Ry. Co., 54 Wis. 234, 11 N. W. 482, 41 Am. Rep. 23; Birmingham Ry. L. & P. Co. *v.* Yielding, 155 Ala. 359, 46 South. 747; Same *v.* McDonough, 153 Ala. 122, 13 L. R. A. (N. S.) 445, 127 Am. St. Rep. 18, 44 South. 960; Montgomery *v.* Buffalo Ry. Co., 165 N. Y. 139, 58 N. E. 770; Nye *v.* Marysville & St. Ry. Co., 97 Cal. 461, 32 Pac. 530; Ketchum *v.* N. Y. City Ry., 118 App. Div. 248, 103 N. Y. Supp. 486; Sickles *v.* Brooklyn Heights Rd. Co., 113 App. Div. 680, 99 N. Y. Supp. 953; Percy *v.* St. Ry. Co., 58 Mo. App. 75; Faber *v.* C. G. W. Ry. Co., 62 Minn. 433, 64 N. W. 918, 36 L. R. A. 789.

None of these rules, sustained above as reasonable, contributed to the convenience of the passenger. All of them required affirmative action or restraint, involving some inconvenience on his part, and they were sustained on the ground that a carrier should be allowed to adopt rules which tend reasonably to insure to it the return allowed by law for services rendered. The difficulties incident to the collection of the moneys due the defendant are apparent to any observer and are admitted by the plaintiff in his brief. Thousands of employees on comparatively small salaries must from the nature of the conditions surrounding the street car business be intrusted with the collection from thousands of passengers during the day's run of sums exceedingly small in amount in each transaction but large in the aggregate. Assuming that 100,000,000 nickels are paid during the course of a year by passengers to the agents of the defendant company, it is clear

Martin *v.* Rhode Island Co

that an automatic registering device of the character here under consideration, which imposes only slight (if any) inconvenience upon the passenger, and which is of such manifest aid both to the company and to its conductors in simplifying the accounting for and return of fares collected, securing accuracy, and tending to prevent fraud and mistake, should be approved rather than condemned. The plaintiff shows, at the most, nothing but that slight degree of annoyance incident to the enforcement of these rules, which will generally be found to exist on the part of a certain few passengers, who are always likely to manifest impatience with the use of new devices, even when they are of obvious utility. But there are, in our opinion, several cases of such close analogy to the case at bar, involving a consideration of devices so nearly like that here in use, as related to the question of the convenience of the passenger, as well as to that of the advantage to the company and its conductors, that they are to be regarded as quite conclusive, upon many of the objections urged by the plaintiff.

In the case of Kitchen *v.* Saginaw Circuit Judge (see Morley *v.* Saginaw Circuit Judge, 117 Mich. 254, 75 N. W. 466, 41 L. R. A. 817), an unreported case in the circuit court for the county of Saginaw, in chancery, one Morris C. L. Kitchen filed an application for leave to bring an action at law against the receivers of the Union Railway Company, setting forth the facts that plaintiff boarded a car of the Union Street Railway Company, took his seat, "and when approached by the conductor tendered to him five cents in payment of his fare; but the conductor refused to receive the same and requested the petitioner to drop the same in a small metal box which he held in his hand. This he (the petitioner) declined to do. Whereupon the conductor advised him that a rule had been made for the government of the road, by the receivers, requiring passengers to put fares in boxes carried by the conductors." Upon a second refusal, petitioner was ejected without undue force. And the circuit court held that the rules prescribed by the receivers "are reasonable, that they do not impose any additional burdens or hardships upon the passengers. * * * and that the petition is therefore denied." This decree was sustained by the Michigan Supreme Court on April 19, 1898, and subsequently approved in the reported case of Morley et al. *v.* Saginaw Circuit Judge, 117 Mich. 264, 254, 75 N. W. 466, 41 L. R. A. 817. It is worthy of note that this box was also an automatic register, and the circuit judge comments on its advantages, both to the company and the conductors, in that "By the new system (cash register box in the hand as compared with the old registering system of ringing up fares by the conductor) there can be no shortage to be made up by the conductors, or losses to be borne by the company. The box properly registers every fare, and all the money and tickets

Martin v. Rhode Island Co

received are in the box, and there is no chance for mistake or fraud and no settlements are required at the end of the day with the conductors."

In Morley v. Saginaw Circuit Judge, 117 Mich. 146, 249, 75 N. W. 466, 41 L. R. A. 817, (1898), the reasonableness of a regulation requiring payment into a cash register, rather than into the conductor's hand, is sustained; and in an able opinion which we think completely answers the objection that the use of a cash register reflects on the honesty of conductors as a class, the court says: "Conductors of street cars deal with a great number of persons, some of whom are entering and leaving the cars frequently. It often happens that change must be made, and there are opportunities for mistakes. It is not unreasonable to assume that, like persons in all callings, some of the employees of street car companies will yield to temptation, when presented. Every one at all familiar with business upon a large scale knows that it is desirable to have it so systematized that mistakes or fraud in its conduct shall not occur. Officials, both of the state and nation, and officers charged with the management of banks, railroads, and other corporations are surrounded by checks and safeguards calculated to do away with the possibilities of frauds or mistakes. The cash register is to be found in most places of business. Upon the elevated roads in the large cities, the passenger pays his fare before he enters upon the platform, over which he must pass to get admission to his train. Every one recognizes the checks and safeguards as proper to be used, and no one has a right to regard them as an imputation upon the honesty of any individual using them. Their use is simply a recognition of what we all know to be a fact, with humanity constituted as it is—that, in the conduct of a large business by many persons, there is a liability to make mistakes, and a possibility of the commission of fraud. The Great Teacher, in that prayer which is the model of all prayers, prayed, 'Lead us not into temptation, but deliver us from evil.' It can readily be seen how the unintelligent or dishonest might object to these checks and safeguards; but it is difficult to understand how the honest and intelligent should object to any practical method which would reduce the probability of mistakes, or the opportunities for the commission of fraud, to the minimum."

In Elder v. International Railway Company, 68 Misc. Rep. 22, 122 N. Y. Supp. 880, Mr. Justice Wheeler on May 3, 1910, held that a rule forbidding conductors to take fare from passengers and requiring the passenger, himself, to deposit his fare in a box at the door on a pay as you enter car was a perfectly valid and reasonable regulation.

In Nye v. Maryville, etc., St. Ry. Co., 97 Cal. 461, 32 Pac. 530 (1893), it was held that a rule requiring a passenger on a street car to deposit his fare in a box on entering the car was "reasona-

Martin v. Rhode Island Co

ble and necessary to prevent fraud upon the company," noncompliance with which would justify ejection.

In Curtis v. Louisville City Ry. Co., 94 Ky. 573, 576, 23 S. W. 363, 364, 21 L. R. A. 649 (1893) the court said: "By the rules of the appellee, a passenger that gets on a street car must deposit his fare in the box within one block. The driver must not receive the fare, etc. * * * These rules are reasonable, and the appellant was aware of them."

In Commonwealth v. McGinn, 29 Leg. Int. (Pa.) 124 (1872), a case at nisi prius, the court charged the jury that a rule requiring payment into a box and not to the driver was a reasonable regulation, and says that the passenger by his contract obligates himself not only to pay the established fare, but to observe the reasonable regulations made by the defendant, among which "the mode and time of payment were of the first importance."

At the argument of this cause the question was raised whether the rules in question were in any wise in conflict with the legal tender statutes of the United States. No such question is raised by the pleadings in the case, nor suggested in the questions certified for our determination. But, as the parties have argued the question upon our own suggestion, we will proceed to consider it.

2 U. S. Comp. St. 1901, § 3587 (1873) provides that "the minor coins of the United States shall be a legal tender, at their nominal value for any amount not exceeding twenty-five cents in any one payment." This statute undoubtedly makes the tender of five separate cent pieces legal tender for a debt of five cents. The question therefore arises whether the refusal to take the five separate cent pieces under the conditions described in the second question certified violates the legal tender statute quoted above, and whether the regulation as applied to the facts therein set forth is unreasonable as a violation of statutory right given the plaintiff by the laws of the United States. This objection is not leveled at that part of the rule requiring a passenger to put money into a box in payment of fare, but to the fact that only one kind of a coin can be so placed by him, namely, a nickel, and that the tender of five separate cent pieces, the exact equivalent under the statute quoted above, is refused except on the condition that the passenger exchange them for a nickel supplied by the conductor.

Upon careful consideration of this question, and in view of our finding above set forth that the rule requiring the presentation of a nickel by the passenger in payment of his fare is so closely analogous to the ticket rule (which has been so frequently upheld) as to be reasonable and valid upon similar grounds; and further in view of the fact that the conductor does not refuse the five separate cents on the ground that their purchasing power is not equivalent to a nickel, and not sufficient for full payment of a fare, but, on the contrary, is willing to and does in fact accept

Martin *v.* Rhode Island Co

them and tenders a nickel in exchange therefor, we are satisfied that there is no such refusal to accept the money in payment of a fare on the part of the conductor as constitutes a violation of the legal tender statute. If the plaintiff offered the five separate cent pieces, and received a ticket, and was required to insert the ticket into the register, no one would contend that the legal tender statute was violated. The transaction, as set forth in the plaintiff's declaration, however, is, in our view of it, essentially the same, with the exception that a nickel is given in exchange for the five separate cent pieces rather than a ticket. We hold therefore that the regulation adopted by the defendant is not a violation of the legal tender statute quoted above and is not because of that statute to be deemed unreasonable.

It was also urged in the oral argument that a passenger has, under the charter of the defendant company, and under the transfer act, a right to demand transportation for five cents and no more, and that the requirement that he pay his fare into a box is in effect demanding a greater amount of fare from him than is permitted by law. The fallacy in this position lies in assuming that the establishment of a maximum amount of fare abrogates the power of the carrier to make reasonable regulations. The establishment by law of a maximum rate of fare has never been construed as requiring transportation by the carrier of every passenger presenting the requisite fare unless he also conforms to the reasonable regulations established by the carrier; otherwise, in the absence of express statutory authority, the carrier would be powerless to eject intoxicated or other unfit persons, or make any of the numerous rules which it is under duty to make for the safety of the passenger and the expediting of its business.

In Reese *v.* Pa. R. R. Co., 131 Pa. 422, 19 Atl. 72, 6 L. R. A. 529, 17 Am. St. Rep. 818, the contention stated above was squarely raised, and the question decided in favor of the carrier's power to make regulations as to mode of payment in spite of a maximum rate limit in the charter. There the defendant adopted a train charge in excess of the ticket charge, and also in excess of the maximum rate per mile allowed by its charter; the excess over ticket fare being refunded on the presentation of a rebate slip at defendant's ticket office at the end of the journey. And it was held that the carrier had a right "to make reasonable regulations, not only as to the amounts of fares, but as to time, place and mode of payment," and that the charter provision was a restriction "of the amount of collection, not of the mode of collection, the protection of the traveler from excessive demands, not interference with the time, place, or mode of payment."

In Percy *v.* St. Ry. Co., 58 Mo. App. 75, it was held that a charter provision requiring that the defendant company give a

Martin *v.* Rhode Island Co

continuous trip on parallel lines for one fare did not forbid a regulation requiring the passenger to ask for a transfer designating the particular place from which he wished to board the second car.

In Crandall *v.* International Ry. Co., 133 App. Div. 857, 117 N. Y. Supp. 1055, it was held that the defendant company might require a passenger not only to obtain a transfer, but to demand it at the time he paid his fare, and to give the destination line when asking for a transfer, although the company was compelled by law to carry a passenger on a continuous trip between any two points on its road by the most direct route for no more than a single fare.

In all of these cases something more was demanded of the passenger than the single act of payment, although in each case the full amount legally demandable had been given. The fixing of the amount of fare, therefore, in no way prevents the adoption of the mode of payment contended for in this case.

The plaintiff has wholly failed to show that the rules in question are in any wise so burdensome or inconvenient to the passenger that they should be deemed to be unreasonable. He admits the necessity of some regulation as to the method of payment and collection of fares to enable the defendant to receive its lawful compensation and to prevent fraud and mistake. The regulation in use tends to secure the end desired.

We are therefore of the opinion that, both upon principle and upon authority, the rules set forth in the two questions submitted to this court for its determination are reasonable, and we answer both of said questions in the affirmative.

●

Houston & T. C. R. Co. *v.* Bush.

(Supreme Court of Texas, Jan. 4, 1911.)

[133 S. W. Rep. 245.]

Carriers—Injury to Passenger—Assault by Employee.*—Carriers are not liable for assaults committed by their servants outside of the servants' scope of employment, unless the assaults could have been anticipated and prevented by due care.

Carriers—Duty of Passengers.†—Carriers are not absolute insurers of the safe carriage of passengers, but are only held to the exercise of a high degree of care.

Carriers—Injury to Passenger—Assault by Employee.*—Where a servant in the employ of a railroad at one of its depots, not acting in his capacity as servant, but for a personal grudge, leaves the depot and goes upon a train, and assaults a passenger, the road is not liable.

Error to Court of Civil Appeals of Fifth Supreme Judicial District.

Action by J. T. Bush against the Houston & Texas Central Railroad Company. From a judgment for plaintiff, affirmed by the Court of Civil Appeals (123 S. W. 201), defendant brings error. Reversed, and judgment rendered.

Baker, Botts, Parker & Garwood and *Head, Dillard, Smith & Head,* for plaintiff in error.
E. J. Smith, for defendant in error.

WILLIAMS, J. This was an action by defendant in error (plaintiff below) for damages for an assault committed on him by one of the servants of plaintiff in error (defendant). The only question is whether or not the defendant is liable for the assault. Adams, the servant who committed it, was employed as porter at defendant's station at Groesbeck, and it was his duty to assist about the baggage and express matter in connection with passenger trains, and to receive and deliver the mail sacks car-

---

*For the authorities in this series on the subject of the liabilities of railroads for assaults on their passengers by their employees, see first foot-note of Layne *v.* Chesapeake & O. R. Co. (W. Va.), 36 R. R. R. 537, 59 Am. & Eng. R. Cas., N. S., 537; foot-note of Teel *v.* Coal & Coke R. Co. (W. Va.), 36 R. R. R. 475, 59 Am. & Eng. R. Cas., N. S., 475; foot-note of Rand *v.* Butte Elec. Ry. Co. (Mont.), 35 R. R. R. 480, 58 Am. & Eng. R. Cas., N. S., 480; Goodwin *v.* Cincinnati Traction Co. (C. C. A.), 35 R. R. R. 477, 58 Am. & Eng. R. Cas., N. S., 477.

†For the authorities in this series on the subject of the degree of care required of a carrier of passengers, see first foot-note of Gardner *v.* Metropolitan St. R. Co. (Mo.), 36 R. R. R. 448, 59 Am. & Eng. R. Cas., N. S., 448.

Houston & T. C. R. Co. *v.* Bush

ried on trains. A train on which plaintiff when assaulted was traveling as a passenger between two other points had made its usual stop at Groesbeck, and that was the only reason for plaintiff's presence at that station. Adams, learning that he was on the train and acting on a personal grudge of five months standing, slipped into the car, purposely avoiding the notice of other servants of the defendant, and made the assault.

There is no contention that in assailing plaintiff he was rendering any service to defendant or acting in the scope of his employment, or that the other servants of the defendant were guilty of any want of care in not anticipating and preventing the assault. The recovery is defended wholly upon the theory that Adams, himself a servant, in making the assault, committed a breach of the obligations of the contract of carriage between the carrier and the passenger. In attaching such a consequence to the act of one who did not have and could not have had anything to do with executing or carrying out that contract the case goes beyond any which has come to our knowledge, except one. Hayne *v.* Union Street Railway Co., 189 Mass. 551, 76 N. E. 219, 3 L. R. A. (N. S.) 605, 109 Am. St. Rep. 655. In that case the conductor on a street car standing on one track in sport threw a dead chicken at the motorman on another car standing opposite on another track, and injured plaintiff, who was a passenger on the latter car. The act of the conductor was held to constitute a breach of the contract of carriage of the company operating both cars; this holding being founded upon the broad proposition laid down in the opinion that the duty to protect passengers from assaults is not confined to those servants of the carrier immediately engaged in carrying out the contract of carriage, but is incumbent on all, at least, who are employed in the general business of transportation, and that an assault by any of these is a breach of the carrier's duty to protect. In every other case than that just referred to that we have found, in which the carrier was held liable for an assault on the passenger by a servant, when not acting in the carrier's business and in the scope of his employment, the servant was employed about the particular premises, or conveyance used in performing the obligations of the carrier to the particular passenger, and charged with rendering some part of the various services the aggregate of which was to constitute the execution of the contract of carriage. In other words, there was delegated to the servant the doing of some part of the work, or the rendering of some part of the attention provided for the safety, comfort, or convenience of passengers using the place or conveyance. In discussing cases of that kind judges have expressed the rule as to the liability of the carrier for the servant's mistreatment of the passenger in various language, some of it, if abstracted from the case before the court and disassociated from its context, comprehensive enough, perhaps, to

Houston & T. C. R. Co. *v*. Bush

impute the liability from the act of any servant in any branch of the service whatever. But we have always supposed that such expressions had reference to such servants as those whose actions were brought in question, to whom was intrusted, in part, the execution of the carrier's undertaking with the passenger, and this is the form in which the doctrine is generally expressed. If there is no such limitation, the courts have put themselves to much unnecessary trouble in trying to state the principle so as to indicate the class of servants whose misconduct is treated as a breach of the carrier's contract. It would always have been very easy to have said that the liability arose from the misconduct of any servant, or of any servant "employed in the general business of transportation," if no limitation was intended. The almost uniform modes of expression indicate to our minds the consensus that there is a limitation suggested by the nature of the carrier's undertaking and the means provided to execute it. His undertaking with each passenger, and he has no contract except with the individual passenger, is to carry him safely and to provide for his comfort and convenience, as far as can be done by the exercise of the care which the law exacts. This obligation as to a safe carriage involves the duty to exercise the requisite care to protect the passenger from assaults from all quarters, and hence the carrier himself cannot commit, nor authorize the commission of, an assault without a breach of his undertaking. Most carriers perform that undertaking by servants to whom they commit the doing of everything essential thereto. Railway companies have stations in which passengers are received and servants are there employed, each charged with the rendition of some service which enters into the discharge of the carrier's duty to those coming to that station for transportation. These servants act for the carrier in dealing with passengers at the station where they are employed, but not elsewhere. The performance of the duty of the carrier to those taking passage at other stations is not delegated to them but to a different corps of employees. How, then, is a servant to break the contract of carriage? Since it includes the obligation to carry safely, the carrier breaks it if he makes the carriage unsafe by assaulting the passenger. The same result follows from like acts of one who stands in the carrier's place charged with the performance of his duty, and thus, and not otherwise, servants in whose care the carrier has left the passenger may commit a breach of the contract. Certainly it will be contended that a stranger to a contract can break it. Can it be said with greater force that a servant or agent who has no part either in the making or the carrying of it out can break it? If not, how is the conduct of an employee to constitute a breach of the obligation assumed by the employer except upon the theory of authority delegated by the latter; and how can the delegation be sufficient unless it charge the employee with the duty which forbids the act? There is such a delegation to all those to whom the carrier has intrusted the execution, in whole or in part, of his contract with the passenger, because either an omission or an act of theirs which is inconsistent with his obligation is a breach thereof. To illustrate, where the relation exists either at a station, or in conveyance, it is under the control of a corps of servants to whose care the passenger is committed by the carrier, and, as the duty of protection assumed by the carrier rests on them individually and collectively, while the passenger is under their care, no one of them can do anything or omit anything inconsistent with that duty without breaking the contract. And the liability of the carrier for such acts or omissions, because it arises from the breach of his contract, is as absolute as is that of any other party to a contract for his breach thereof. Further than this the absolute liability in our opinion does not go. It is assumed in the case referred to that the carrier's contract insures the safe transportation and proper treatment of the passenger against the misconduct of all his servants, but there certainly is no such express undertaking, and whether or not it is to be implied depends on the considerations already discussed. The carrier's implied obligation is that which the law raises from the nature of his business. No statement of it with which we are familiar will include any such absolute liability as that under consideration for the conduct of servants other than those to whom he delegates his duty. Such a liability is not one of those which arises from duties imposed by law for reasons of public policy. The law does not make the carrier an insurer of the safety of the passenger, but only requires that, in order to secure it, he exercises the high degree of care and skill so often defined in the books. It does not make him liable for assaults committed by others than himself or those put by him in his stead, unless they could have been anticipated and prevented by the exercise of the requisite care. He must provide an equipment and a force of employees such as that degree of care exacts in order properly to discharge each of his duties, and will be held liable for the consequences of any deficiencies in those respects, but, when he has done that, there is no principle of which we have knowledge that requires him to hold each servant at the service of every passenger, so that every servant must be regarded as his representative in all his conduct towards the passenger. The only good reason for making the carrier responsible for the misconduct of the servant perpetrated in his own interest and not in that of his employer nor otherwise within the scope of his employment, is that the servant is clothed with the delegated authority and charged with the duty by the carrier to execute his undertaking with the passenger. And it cannot be said, we think, that there is any such delegation to the employees

Houston & T. C. R. Co. *v.* Bush

at a station with reference to passengers embarking at another or traveling on the train.   Of course, we are speaking only of the principle which holds a carrier responsible for wrongs done to passengers by servants acting in their own interest and not in that of the employer.   That principle is not the ordinary rule, respondeat superior, by which the employer is held responsible only for acts or omissions of the employee in the scope of his employment; but the only reason in our opinion for a broader liability arises from the fact that the servant in mistreating the passenger wholly for some private purpose of his own, in the very act, violates the contractual obligation of the employer for the performance of which he has put the employee in his place. That reason does not exist where the employee who committed the assault was never in a position in which it became his duty to his employer to represent him in discharging any duty of the latter towards the passenger.   The proposition that the carrier clothes every employee engaged in the transportation business with the comprehensive duty of protecting every passenger with whom he may in any way come in contact, and thereby makes himself liable for every assault committed by such servant without regard to the inquiry whether or not the passenger has come within the sphere of duty of that servant as indicated by the employment, is regarded as not only not sustained by the authorities, but as being unsound and oppressive both to the employer and the employee.   In the present case it may be assumed that Adams performed every duty and tendered every service which he owed to his employer and to those passengers whose safety it was incumbent on him to look after fully and perfectly, and as to everything else he was as free as any stranger.   And this illustrates that, while his assault was a wrong to the individual assaulted, it was not wrongful because it was the breach of any duty which, through the contract of carriage and his own employment, he owed to the latter as a passenger, but because it was an unlawful infraction of a natural right for which he alone was responsible.

Nearly all the authorities state the doctrine as we have endeavored to explain it.   In some of the discussions it is assumed too broadly, we think, that, because the ordinary rule respondeat superior is not controlling, therefore the law of principal and agent has no application at all.   It must have some application when it is sought to hold one person liable in such cases for the acts of another, and its just application is that which we have indicated.   The general doctrine has often been discussed in this state both by this court and the Court of Civil Appeals, but none of our decisions sustains this judgment.   T. M. Ry. Co. *v.* Dean, 98 Tex. 520, 85 S. W. 1135; G., C. & S. F. Ry. Co. *v.* Luther, 40 Tex. Civ. App. 517, 90 S. W. 44; Railway *v.* Tarking-

Parrot et al. v. Mexican Cent. Ry. Co

ton, 27 Tex. Civ. App. 353, 66 S. W. 137; Railway v. Gaines, 35 Tex. Civ. App. 257, 79 S. W. 1104; Railway v. Howlin, 32 S. W. 918; Railway v. Batcher, 32 Tex. Civ. App. 14, 73 S. W. 981.

As matter of law we hold that the plaintiff in error is not liable for the assault, and will reverse the judgment and render judgment in its favor.

Reversed and rendered.

PARROT et al. v. MEXICAN CENT. RY. Co., Limited.

(Supreme Judicial Court of Massachusetts, Suffolk, Jan. 3, 1911.)

[93 N. E. Rep. 590.]

Corporations—Agents—Buyers.*—The general passenger agent and the passenger traffic manager of a railroad company, with duties to exercise direct charge over the work of soliciting passenger traffic for the road, and making arrangements for that purpose, and to supervise generally the work of the passenger department, have apparent authority to contract for the publication, for a money consideration, of a guidebook to make known and popularize the hunting and fishing regions along the line of the railroad, and a party dealing with them in reliance on their ostensible authority is not affected by secret limitations that they must obtain permission from an executive officer before expending money.

Courts—Decisions—Conclusiveness.—The presiding justice on a subsequent trial is not bound by any intimations or expressions of opinion of the judge at the former trial.

Appeal and Error—Exceptions—Questions Reviewable.—Where the presiding justice in an action for breach of contract refused requests for a directed verdict for defendant, and for a ruling that there was no evidence of any breach of contract, without asking counsel for defendant to point out more particularly the propositions of law on which he relied, any question of law actually involved in the requests and refusal, though not referred to or thought of by the judge or counsel at the trial, is reviewable in the Supreme Judicial Court on exceptions.

Evidence—Presumptions—Laws of Other Countries.—The law of a foreign state or country must be established as a fact, either by direct proof or by a proper presumption.

Evidence—Laws of Foreign Countries—Presumptions.—The court

---

*For the authorities in this series on the subject of the implied authority of a railroad's freight or passenger agents, see second foot-note of St. Louis, etc., Ry. Co. v. Citizens' Bank (Ark.), 36 R. R. R. 290, 53 Am. & Eng. R. Cas., N. S., 290; foot-note of Southern Ry. Co. v. Nowlin (Ala.), 30 R. R. R. 261, 53 Am. & Eng. R. Cas., N. S., 261.

Parrot et al. *v.* Mexican Cent. Ry. Co

will not presume that the people in foreign countries have adopted the statutory provisions in force in the state where the court sits.

Evidence—Laws of Foreign Countries—Presumptions.—The court may presume that all states or foreign countries governed by the common law regard the common law in all its details; but countries governed by a different system of law will not be presumed to be governed by the provisions existing only through precedents established by the courts, and it will only be presumed that they recognized fundamental principles of right and wrong lying at the foundation of human society, and that a direct violation of such principles, to the injury of another, creates a legal liability.

Evidence—Laws of Foreign Countries—Presumptions.—The court, in an action on a simple contract executed in a foreign country, to be governed by its laws, will presume, in the absence of evidence of the law of the foreign country not governed by the common law, that the contract creates a liability in force in the foreign country, and that a party thereto may recover for a breach of the contract by the adverse party.

Contracts—Consideration.—The rule that a promise to pay one for doing that which he is under a prior legal duty to do is not binding for want of consideration does not apply where a party, having entered into a contract with the adverse party to do certain work, refuses to proceed with it, and the adverse party, to secure to himself the actual performance of the work in place of a right to collect damages from the party, promises to pay an additional sum, for in that case there is a new consideration for the promise.

Contracts—Consideration.—Where one was required, by a binding written contract made with an agent of a railway company, to publish a guidebook for the company, a subsequent oral agreement, made in a foreign country with other agents of the company, for the publication of the book, was without consideration, and was not enforceable.

Corporations—Actions—Evidence—Instructions.—Where there was evidence that a contract made by an agent of a railway company for the publication of a guidebook was not binding on the company, because not within the scope of the power of the agent, the court could not rule as a matter of law that a subsequent contract for the publication of the book, made by other agents of the company, was without consideration; but the court must submit the issue of the validity of the first contract, and, on the jury finding the same invalid for want of authority, they must find the second contract binding, because executed by agents having authority to bind the company.

Contracts—Breach of Contracts—Remedy.—Where a railroad company agreed to provide for the expenses incurred by plaintiff in publishing a guidebook to popularize the hunting and fishing regions along the line of the railroad, and the general passenger agent of the company told plaintiff to send the bills for his personal expenses

to him, and plaintiff incurred large expenses, which the company refused to pay, though requested, and denied liability, plaintiff could
refuse to go on with his contract, and sue the company for damages
for breach of contract.

Evidence—Conclusion of Witness.—A question asked an agent of
a corporation as to whether he had authority to spend money for a
specified purpose is properly excluded, as calling for a conclusion of
the agent.

Corporations—Instructions—Misleading Instructions.—A statement
of the court that the answers of the vice president of a railroad company to questions as to the powers of its general passenger agent
and passenger traffic manager were evidence of facts showing the
authority or want of authority of the agents, but not evidence so
far as the answers stated the conclusion of the vice president from
the facts as to the extent of their powers, was not objectionable, as
misleading, as to the effect of the testimony of the vice president.

Appeal and Error—Harmless Error—Exclusion of Evidence.—The
exclusion of a part of an answer of a witness to an interrogatory was
not prejudicial, where there was nothing material in the part excluded that had not been fully stated in the earlier part of the answer.

Exceptions from Superior Court, Suffolk County; Henry A.
King, Judge.

Action by Edward G. Parrot and another against the Mexican
Central Railway Company. There was a verdict for plaintiffs,
and defendant brings exceptions. Overruled.

A. H. Russell and *T. H. Russell,* for plaintiffs.
H. S. Davis, for defendant.

KNOWLTON, C. J.   In this case there was evidence from the
two plaintiffs that an oral agreement for the payment of money
was made with them by one McDonald, the defendant's general
passenger agent in the City of Mexico, which, if it was binding
upon the defendant as a contract, justified and required a finding
for the plaintiffs. McDonald was not called as a witness, nor
was Murdock, the defendant's passenger traffic manager, who was
said by the plaintiffs to have been present when this agreement
was made in Mexico, and to have participated in making it and
to have acted under it.

The defense was a general denial that this agreement was
made, and a denial that either McDonald or Murdock had authority to make it, and contention that such an agreement could
not be proved by oral testimony because the previous negotiations between the parties touching the subject had been reduced
to the form of a contract in writing, and that, if there was any
binding contract, it was this writing which could not be contradicted, varied or enlarged by evidence of an oral agreement.

The writing was in the form of a letter from one Carson, the defendant's Eastern agent in the city of New York, to the plaintiffs. The plaintiffs wrote a letter in reply accepting the terms stated by Carson.

The subsequent oral agreement made in Mexico, relied on by the plaintiffs, was to make a payment in money of a reasonable sum, probably $2,000 to $3,000, towards the expenses of the plaintiffs in publishing a sportsman's guide to the Mexican Central Railway, which was the subject to which the previous writing related.

We assume, in accordance with the defendant's contentions, that the writing did not call for the payment of any money by the defendant to the plaintiffs, that is purported to cover the whole subject to the publication of this guidebook, that it was in such a form as merged all previous negotiations between the parties, and that the testimony of what occurred in these negotiations was not competent to show that the writing was incomplete and that the parties contemplated making some further arrangements in regard to the expenses involved in the project. Some of these matters are not plain, and the justices are not unanimous in their view of them.

The exceptions are to the refusal to give numerous instructions requested, to instructions given so far as they were inconsistent with those requested, and to rulings upon evidence. There was a series of requests as to the authority of McDonald and Murdock to make the oral agreement relied on. According to the testimony, McDonald made the agreement, although Murdock was present some of the time, and took part in the conversation. As the case was submitted to the jury it becomes necessary to consider whether there was evidence that either or both of these persons had authority to make such a contract.

There was evidence from the answers of the defendant's vice president to interrogatories that McDonald was the defendant's general passenger agent. with offices in the City of Mexico, and was held out to the public as such by the use of his name on letterheads and otherwise; that his duties "were to exercise direct charge over the work of soliciting and securing passenger traffic for the road, and to make arrangements for that purpose." It also appeared that the proposed guidebook was intended to "make known and popularize the hunting and fishing regions" along the line of the railroad, and that the defendant, before making this arrangement with the plaintiffs, had planned to publish a similar guidebook entirely at its own expense. It appeared from the answers of the vice president that the defendant, at and about the time of making this arrangement, advertised in various newspapers and magazines. and that contracts for such advertising were made either by Murdock or McDonald. Murdock's duties as passenger traffic manager "were generally to supervise the work of the passenger department." The evidence tended to show that these two men represented the defendant generally at the head of this important department of a great railway corporation, and that their duties could not be properly performed without the frequent expenditure of substantial sums of money. Included in their charge was the advertising department, and the vice president answered that they contracted for the advertising, and had authority to give in return for it a certain amount of free or reduced rate transportation over the defendant's lines. But he said that neither of them had authority to make any contract for any purpose that involved the expenditure of money, without first having obtained special authority from an executive officer of the company. The jury might or might not believe this. If it was true, it was in the nature of a secret limitation of the general authority that these men were held out as possessing. Apparently, they were the general and highest representatives of the corporation that had any direct dealings with the public in reference to the business of the passenger department. They seem to have had all the authority that anybody dealing with the public had to bind the corporation by contracts for the expenditure of money in their department. The business which they had in charge called for the expenditure of money. A secret instruction to them, as general agents in charge of such business, that they should obtain permission from an executive officer before expending any money, was not binding upon persons dealing with them in good faith, in reliance upon their ostensible authority. Fay *v.* Noble, 12 Cush. 1; Merchants' National Bank *v.* Citizens' Gaslight Company, 159 Mass. 505, 34 N. E. 1083, 38 Am. St. Rep. 453; McNeal *v.* Boston Chamber of Commerce, 154 Mass. 277-286, 28 N. E. 245, 13 L. R. A. 559; Cincinnati, etc., Railroad Company *v.* Davis, 126 Ind. 99, 25 N. E. 878, 9 L. R. A. 503. Upon the evidence in this case, the requests for rulings in regard to the authority of McDonald and Murdock were rightly refused.

The thirteenth request, relative to the effect of proceedings at the former trial, was rightly refused. The presiding justice was not bound by any intimations or expressions of opinion of the judge at that trial.

The other requests were for the direction of a verdict for the defendant, and a ruling "that there was no evidence that the defendant committed any breach of any contract with the plaintiffs, and the verdict must therefore be for the defendant." Upon the refusal of such requests, if the judge does not ask the requesting counsel to point out more particularly the propositions of law upon which he relies, it is possible to raise in this court any question of law actually involved in the request and refusal, even though it was never referred to or thought of by the judge or counsel at the trial.

Parrot et al. *v*. Mexican Cent. Ry. Co

The defendant now contends that the oral agreement was made in Mexico, a country which has not inherited the common law of England, that no evidence was introduced of what the law is in Mexico, that there is no presumption in regard to the law of a foreign country unless it is one which is known to be governed by the common law, and that therefore the plaintiffs cannot prevail because the court cannot find a rule of law applicable to the case. If this view was in the mind of counsel at the trial. it does not seem to have been stated ; but we are obliged to consider it.

The question is, By what presumption. if any, will the court be, governed under such circumstances? In Story on Conflict of Laws (8th Ed.) 637, in a long and elaborate note is this language of the learned editor: "Presumption has a proper place, within limits, in regard to foreign laws. Thus it could not be necessary to give evidence that in a foreign country breach of contract, battery, conversion or damage caused by fraud or negligence, would give a right of action." In Whitford *v*. Panama Railroad Company, 23 N. Y. 465-468, Judge Denio says in the opinion: "Hence, if one bring a civil action for false imprisonment. or for an assault and battery committed abroad. he need not in the first instance offer any proof that such acts are unlawful and entitle the injured party to a recompense in damages in the place where they are inflicted, for the courts will not presume the existence of a state of the law in any country, by which compensation is not provided for such injuries." Chief Justice Redfield, speaking for the court in Langdon *v*. Young, 33 Vt. 136, used these words: "But in the absence of all proof. courts assume certain general principles of law as existing in all Christian states. as that contracts are of binding obligation and that personal injuries are actionable." In the note of Dean Bigelow to which we have referred, he discusses many decisions of the courts, and criticises those that hold, in the absence of any evidence of the law of a foreign country, that there is a presumption that such country has the same law as the state or country of the forum; or, to put the proposition a little differently, that in the absence of any evidence of the law of a foreign country, the court will administer the law of the forum, thus putting the burden of proof upon the party who would avoid the application of of the forum to his case. He treats the whole subject as ing upon presumptions of fact which the court will apply ing to common knowledge and experience.

Mr. Wigmore, in his work on Evidence, also says in 25-36 that presumption may. within certain limits, be resorted to. He adds: "If the foreign state is not one whose system is founded in the common law, a presumption (that its law is the same as that of the forum) will probably not be made unless the principle involved is one of the law merchant. common to civilized countries." Here is an implication that universal rules

Parrot et al. *v.* Mexican Cent. Ry. Co

or principle, known to be common to all civilized courts, will be presumed to be recognized by the courts of all nations.

In the application of the law there has been a great diversity in the decisions. Some things seem to be generally settled. The law of a foreign state or country is to be established as a fact, either by direct proof or by a proper presumption. It is not to be presumed that the people in other states or countries have made the same statutory provisions that were made by the people of the state where the court sits. These statutes depend upon the views of the legislators, which may differ in different places. So of the common law, that has grown up through judicial decisions into an elaborate system, going very far beyond the fundamental principles that may be supposed to be recognized everywhere. All states and countries that have grown up under this system, or have inherited it, may be presumed to regard it in all its details. But other countries that live under a different system are not presumed to be governed by these provisions that exist only through precedents established by the courts. There is every reason why they should be presumed to recognize fundamental principles of right and wrong which lie at the foundation of human society, and to hold that a direct violation of these principles, to the injury of another person, creates a legal liability. If one should sue on a contract for goods sold and delivered in France, upon a promise to pay a certain price for them, it would seem unreasonable that a plaintiff should be obliged to bring evidence from that country that a breach of such a contract there creates a liability. So if one should sue for damages suffered from an assault and battery, or from a larceny committed there. There ought to be a presumption from common knowledge that a liability exists everywhere in such cases.

Some courts have gone further, and have held that, in the absence of any proof of the foreign law, the court will administer the law of its own jurisdiction. This is the law in New York, · and in the Supreme Court of the United States. Haynes *v.* McDermott, 82 N. Y. 41, 37 Am. Rep. 538; The Scotland, 105 U. S. 24, 29, 30, 26 L. Ed. 1001.

In this commonwealth a plaintiff was permitted to recover under a contract governed by the law of Scotland, where no evidence was introduced to show what the law of that country was. Chase *v.* Alliance Insurance Company, 9 Allen, 311. In Rau *v.* Von Zedlitz, 132 Mass. 164-170, the court said: "It is conceded that, in the absence of any evidence of the law of Saxony, the question of duress or undue influence is to be determined by the law of this commonwealth." The case was decided upon this view of the law. Upon the question whether a protest of a draft was necessary to charge a party under the law of Turkey, it was said in Aslanian *v.* Dostumian, 174 Mass. 328, 54 N. E. 845, 47 L. R. A. 495, 75 Am. St. Rep. 348, that the court

Parrot et al. *v.* Mexican Cent. Ry. Co

would not presume that the rules of the law merchant, or of
the common law relative to such a matter as the protest of commercial paper, prevailed in Turkey, although this is not the
principal ground of the decision. In Harvey *v.* Merrill, 150
Mass. 1-5, 22 N. E. 49 (5 L. R. A. 200, 15 Am. St. Rep. 159),
the court said: "The rights of the parties are to be determined
by the law of Illinois; but there is no evidence that the common
law of Illinois differs from that of Massachusetts." This is
given as the reason for deciding the case under the law of Massachusetts. Mittenthal *v.* Mascagni, 183 Mass. 19-23, 66 N. E.
425, 60 L. R. A. 812, 97 Am. St. Rep. 404, was an action upon a
contract made in Italy, in which no evidence of the law of Italy
was introduced. The court said: "Assuming this, we must also
assume that the law of Italy is like our own," and the plaintiff
was permitted to recover. Bayer *v.* Lovelace, 204 Mass. 327,
90 N. E. 538, was an action involving the rights of a party summoned as a trustee in an action of contract, in which he set up,
as a ground for his discharge, the judgment of a court in
Colombia, South America. The court said: "We are not informed as to what the law of Colombia is in reference to such
conditions as appear in this case, but there is no reason to think
that it is different from that of this country." The case was
decided against the trustee, according to the law of this country,
but the burden was upon the trustee to prove the effect of the
judgment, and to establish the law of Colombia if he relied upon ·
it for his discharge.

In the present case the law upon which the plaintiffs rely is
that creating a liability upon a simple contract to pay money for
a valuable consideration. We are of opinion that in a suit upon
a simple contract of this kind, there is a broad general presumption of fact that such a contract creates a liability in all civilized
countries, which presumption is sufficient to entitle the plaintiff
to recover, if no evidence is introduced of the law of the
place where the contract is made. In so deciding we do not go
so far as the cases which hold that, in the absence of evidence
of the foreign law, the court will in all cases apply the law of
the forum. We treat this, not as a presumption that the law
of the foreign country is the same as the law of the forum, but
as a presumption that all countries, in their courts of justice, will
give effect to universally recognized fundamental principles of
right and wrong in deciding between contending parties.

The defendant contends that there was no consideration for
the promise to pay money to the plaintiffs, because they were
already bound by the writing to do all that they undertook to
do under the oral agreement. As a general proposition, it is
settled in this commonwealth that a promise to pay one for doing
that which he was under a prior legal duty to do is not binding
for want of a valid consideration. Smith *v.* Bartholomew, 1

Metc. 276, 35 Am. Dec. 365; Com. *v.* Johnson, 3 Cush. 454; Pool *v.* Boston, 5 Cush. 219; Warren *v.* Hodge, 121 Mass. 106. It has often been said that the principle involved is the same that lies at the foundation of the doctrine that a promise to accept or pay a less sum in discharge of a debt for a greater amount is not binding. In connection with the general proposition see also Cabot *v.* Haskins, 3 Pick. 83, 92, 93; Tobey *v.* Wareham Bank, 13 Metc. 440-449; Lester *v.* Palmer, 4 Allen, 145; Harlow *v.* Putnam, 124 Mass. 553.

A limitation of the general proposition has been established in Massachusetts, in cases where a plaintiff, having entered into a contract with the defendant to do certain work refuses to proceed with it, and the defendant, in order to secure to himself the actual performance of the work in place of a right to collect damages from the plaintiff, promises to pay him an additional sum. This limitation is not intended to affect the rule that a contract cannot be binding without a consideration; but it rests upon the doctrine that, under these circumstances, there is a new consideration for the promise. Munroe *v.* Perkins, 9 Pick. 298, 20 Am. Dec. 475; Holmes *v.* Doane, 9 Cush. 135; Peck *v.* Requa, 13 Gray, 407; Rollins *v.* Marsh, 128 Mass. 116; Rogers *v.* Rogers, 139 Mass. 440, 1 N. E. 122; Allen, J., in Abbott *v.* Doane, 163 Mass. 433-435, 40 N. E. 197, 34 L. R. A. 33, 47 Am. St. Rep. 465. In Rollins *v.* Marsh, 128 Mass. 116-120, the court said: "The parties had made a contract in writing with which the plaintiff had become dissatisfied, and which she had informed the defendant that she should not fulfill unless the terms were modified. If she had abandoned her contract, he might have made a new arrangement with some one else for the support of his ward, and enforce whatever remedy he had for the breach, against the plaintiff. Instead of this, he made a new contract with her, which operated as a rescission of the original agreement." In such a case the new promise is given to secure the performance, in place of an action for damages for not performing, as was pointed out by this court in Peck *v.* Requa, 13 Gray, 407, 408.

This limitation in the application of the general rule to such facts is not recognized in England, nor in most of the states in this country. See Abbott *v.* Doane, 163 Mass. 433-435, 40 N. E. 197, 34 L. R. A. 33, 47 Am. St. Rep. 465; Leake on Cont. (4th Eng. Ed) 434-436; Pollock on Cont. (7th Eng. Ed. 184-186; Harriman in Cont. §§ 117-120. See also 8 Harvard Law Review, 27; 12 Harvard Law Review, 515, 521, 531; 13 Harvard Law Review, 319; 17 Harvard Law Review, 71. While it is well established in Massachusetts, the doctrine should not be extended beyond the cases to which it is applicable upon the recognized reasons that have been given for it. A majority of the court are of opinion that it is not applicable to the evidence in this case. and that the defendant is right in its contention that, upon the assumption that the parties were bound by the written contract, there was no consideration for the new promise of the defendant.

But the judge could not give either of these two rulings without assuming. and virtually ruling as matter of law. that the writing was a binding contract. For the defendant, it was signed by Carson, the defendant's Eastern agent. The defendant's answer was a general denial of all the plaintiffs' averments. The defendant's vice president's answers to interrogatories were in evidence, in which he said that, "Outside of contracts involving the transportation of freight or passengers, the general Eastern agent had no authority whatever to enter into any contract of any kind or character in behalf of the company. without securing authority from his superior officers, either in the passenger or freight department." This evidence was uncontradicted. While there was testimony indicating that Carson communicated by letter with some superior officer in Mexico before completing the negotiations with the plaintiffs, there was nothing more than the possibility of an inference in regard to what authority he obtained. While the principal dispute between the parties was in regard to the oral agreement made in Mexico, the authority of Carson to bind the defendant by the writing was a fact to be proved in the case before either party could avail himself of the writing as a contract, and the judge, in his charge, submitted to the jury the question of Carson's authority, as he did also questions as to the authority of McDonald and Murdock. A majority of the court are. of opinion that, in dealing with the requests of the defendant, the judge could not assume or rule as matter of law that Carson had authority to bind the defendant by the writing, and he therefore could not rule that there was a valid contract in writing by which the parties were bound when the agreement was made in Mexico, and that the oral agreement was without consideration because the plaintiffs were to do no more under it than they had previously contracted to do. If the jury failed to find that the writing was authorized by the defendant, they might find that an oral agreement was made in Mexico which adopted and included the provisions that previously had been reduced to writing, and that then for the first time became binding, because made a part of the general agreement between the plaintiffs and the defendant's representatives. Under such a possible finding, this question which the defendant now argues could not arise, and the defendant would be liable.

The defendant contends that the plaintiffs cannot recover because they did not completely perform their contract. The declaration is for damages for a breach of the contract. There was evidence that the defendant agreed to provide for the express

Parrot et al. *v*. Mexican Cent. Ry. Co

incurred by the plaintiffs in the prosecution of the work; that McDonald told the plaintiffs to send the bills for their personal expenses to him; that they incurred large expenses, and that the defendant, though requested, refused to pay any money and denied its liability to pay anything or to make any provision for the payment of the expenses. This justified the plaintiffs in refusing to go on with their contract, and in suing the defendant for damages for its breach of the contract.

The question to Carson, "Did you yourself have authority to spend any money for advertising purposes?" put by the defendant, "expecting the witness to answer that he had no such authority," was rightly excluded. It called for a conclusion of the witness as to the legal effect of his relations with the defendant, and not merely for facts which would show whether he had authority. So far as appears, he was permitted to testify fully as to the facts.

We are also of opinion that the language of the judge in regard to the interrogatories and the rulings upon them, when rightly interpreted, was not erroneous. The first part of his statement was, in substance, that the answers were evidence of the facts tending to show the authority or want of authority of the agents; but not evidence so far as they stated the opinion or the conclusion of the vice president from these facts, as to the extent of their powers or duties. While the meaning of the judge was not very clearly expressed, we are of opinion that the jury were not misled in regard to it.

The defendant did not suffer from the exclusion of the last two sentences of the answer to the fourteenth interrogatory. There was nothing material in these sentences that was not fully stated in the earlier part of the answer.

Exceptions overruled.

WASHINGTON, A. & MT. V. RY. CO. *v.* VAUGHAN.

(Supreme Court of Appeals of Virginia, Jan. 12, 1911.)

[69 S. E. Rep. 1035.]

Carriers—Passengers—Carrier's Duty.—A carrier owes to actual and constructive passengers a higher degree of care than to travelers at highway crossings.

Carriers—Alighting Passengers—Duty.*—An alighting passenger is entitled to reasonable protection against accident in passing from the station premises, but must use proper care to avoid danger; the degree required depending upon the particular circumstances.

Carriers—Alighting Passengers—Contributory Negligence.†—That while crossing double tracks to a station shed in the nighttime an alighting electric railway passenger was struck by a train running in the opposite direction without headlight displayed or giving warning does not show contributory negligence as a matter of law, though he failed to look and listen after alighting from his train.

Carriers—Electric Railways—Injury to Passengers—Evidence.—In an action by an alighting electric railway passenger struck in the nighttime by an unlighted train running in the opposite direction, it was not error to receive testimony on the commonly known fact that trolley poles frequently become detached, and that lights in cars are thereby extinguished.

Evidence—Existence of Thing at Another Time.‡—Prior or subsequent existence of a thing is some indication of its probable existence at a given time; the degree of probability arising from existence at a subsequent time depending upon the likelihood of some circumstance intervening, but the admission of such evidence is largely discretionary with trial courts.

Carriers—Injury to Passenger—Evidence—Existence of Thing at Another Time.‡—In an action by an alighting passenger for injury

---

*For the authorities in this series on the subject of the liabilities of a railroad company with respect to its passengers struck by trains or street cars while crossing tracks between depots of other stopping places, and trains or cars, see second foot-note of Louisville R. Co., *v.* Mitchell (Ky.), 36 R. R. R. 710, 59 Am. & Eng. R. Cas., N. S., 710.

†For the authorities in this series on the subject of the contributory negligence of passengers in crossing tracks between trains or street cars and depots or other stopping places, see first foot-note of Struble *v.* Pennsylvania Co. (Pa.), 35 R. R. R. 217, 58 Am. & Eng. R. Cas., N. S., 217; third foot-note of Illinois Cent. R. Co. *v.* Daniels (Miss.), 34 R. R. R. 196, 57 Am. & Eng. R. Cas., N. S., 196.

‡See. generally first foot-note of Washington, etc., Ry. Co. *v.* Trimyer (Va.), 37 R. R. R. 114, 6 Am. & Eng. R. Cas., N. S., 114; last head-note of Missouri, etc., Ry. Co. *v.* Williams (Tex.), 35 R. R. R. 770, 58 Am. & Eng. R. Cas., N. S., 770; last foot-note of American Ice Co. *v.* Pennsylvania R. Co. (Pa.), 33 R. R. R. 535, 56 Am. & Eng. R. Cas., N. S., 535; last foot-note of Neary *v.* Northern Pac. Ry. Co. (Mont.), 31 R. R. R. 758, 54 Am. & Eng. R. Cas., N. S., 758.

Washington, A. & Mt. V. Ry. Co. *v.* Vaughan

to one struck in the nighttime by an electric car, involving an issue whether the car was lighted, it was not an abuse of discretion to exclude testimony showing that the lights were burning about 15 minutes after the accident.

Negligence—Contributory Negligence—Burden of Proof.§—The rule that the burden is on defendant to show contributory negligence is subject to the qualification that the showing on plaintiff's case is available to defendant.

Negligence—Instructions—Contributory Negligence—Burden of Proof.—An instruction that the burden was on defendant to show contributory negligence unless the "evidence of plaintiff himself" showed it was erroneous as tending to exclude consideration of testimony of plaintiff's witnesses other than himself.

Carriers—Alighting Passengers—Carrier's Duty.*—That the way across railway tracks used by an alighting passenger in going to the station was a public highway did not affect the degree of care owing him by the carrier.

Appeal and Error—Harmless Error—Instructions.—An instruction as to the duty of a railway company to a traveler on a highway, while erroneously given in an action for injury to an alighting passenger, was harmless to the company, since there is a higher duty to passengers than to travelers.

Carriers—Electric Railways—Duty to Passengers.‖—It was not error to instruct that electric railway companies must use the greatest possible care and diligence for their passengers' safety.

Negligence—Instructions—Proximate Cause.¶—An instruction making defendant liable if he was negligent unless plaintiff was guilty of contributory negligence is erroneous as ignoring the necessity that the negligence proximately caused the injury.

Error to Circuit Court, Alexandria County.

Action by Wyatt Vaughn against the Washington, Alexandria & Mt. Vernon Railway Company. Judgment for plaintiff, and defendant brings error. Reversed and remanded for a new trial.

---

§See last paragraph of first foot-note of Illinois Cent. R. Co. *v.* O'Neill (C. C. A.), 37 R. R. R. 99, 60 Am. & Eng. R. Cas., N. S., 99; third head-note of Farris *v.* Southern R. Co. (N. Car.), 36 R. R. R. 523, 59 Am. & Eng. R. Cas., N. S., 523; third foot-note of Bates *v.* Chicago, etc., Ry. Co. (Wis.), 35 R. R. R. 173, 58 Am. & Eng. R. Cas., N. S., 173.

‖See last foot-note of Washington, etc, Ry. Co. *v.* Trimyer (Va.), 37 R. R. R. 114, 60 Am. & Eng. R. Cas., N. S., 114; first foot-note of Garden *v.* Metropolitan St. R. Co. (Mo.), 36 R. R. R. 448, 59 Am. & Eng. R. Cas., N. S., 448.

¶See second foot-note of Southern Ry. Co. *v.* Crawford (Ala.), 37 R. R. R. 82, 60 Am. & Eng. R. Cas.. N. S., 82; second foot-note of Weatherly *v.* Nashville, etc., Ry. (Ala.), 35 R. R. R. 759, 58 Am. & Eng. R. Cas., N. S., 759.

Moore, Barbour & Keith and *Jas. R. & H. B. Caton*, for plaintiff in error.

Lewis H. Machen and *R. C. L. Moncure*, for defendant in error.

BUCHANAN, J. The first assignment of error is to the action of the court in overruling a demurrer to the amended declaration and each count thereof.

This action was brought to recover damages for personal injuries suffered by the plaintiff whilst a passenger on the defendant's line of road—an electric railway, which it operated between Washington city and the city of Alexandria. Each of the three counts in the amended declaration makes averments which show that the plaintiff was a passenger for hire on one of the defendant's cars; that when he reached his destination at Addison, one of the defendant's stations, the train or car upon which he was traveling was stopped, and he stepped on the opposite side of the road from the station shed; that, while crossing double tracks of the defendant going towards that shed in the nighttime, another train of the defendant, running on the other track, in the opposite direction, with no headlight displayed or whistle blown or other warning given, struck him, causing the injuries complained of.

As we understand the petition for the writ of error, the principal objection made to the sufficiency of the declaration is that the facts averred in each count show that the plaintiff was guilty of contributory negligence in going from the point where he left the defendant's car across its tracks towards its station building, in the absence of an averment that he looked and listened for an approaching train, before going upon the tracks upon which he was injured.

A railroad company owes to one occupying the relation of a passenger, actually or constructively, a different and higher degree of care than it does to a traveler about to cross its tracks at a highway. While a passenger has the right to pass from the place where the car stopped for him to alight to the station building or off its premises, and the railway company should furnish him reasonable and adequate protection against accident in the enjoyment of this privilege, the passenger is bound to exercise proper care and caution in avoiding danger. What degree of care and caution he is to exercise in a particular case must be governed by the danger to be encountered and the circumstances attending its exercise. Railway Co. v. Lowell, 151 U. S. 209, 14 Sup. Ct. 281, 38 L. Ed. 131; Warner v. B. & O. R. Co., 168 U. S. 339, 18 Sup. Ct. 68, 42 L. Ed. 491; Terry v. Jewett, 78 N. Y. 338; 6 Cyc. 607-8.

It is said in 2 Shear. & Red. on Neg. § 525, that: "Where a passenger is required to cross the company's intervening tracks

Washington, A. & Mt. V. Ry. Co. *v.* Vaughan

in order to take his train or to leave it, or to change from one train to another, it is not per se negligence not to look and listen for approaching trains before so crossing. The passenger has the right to assume that the company will so regulate its trains that the road will be free from obstructions and danger when passenger trains stop at a depot to receive and deliver passengers; and the rule which requires a person to look and listen before crossing a railroad track has little, if any, application where, by the arrangement of the company, it is necessary for passengers to cross the track in passing to and from the depot and the cars."

The facts averred in the declaration do not show that the plaintiff was guilty of contributory negligence as a matter of law, even if he failed to look and listen for approaching trains before he crossed the track of the defendant company in leaving its premises after alighting from its train.

Without discussing the other grounds of demurrer in detail, it is sufficient to say that each count states a good cause of action, and that the demurrer was properly overruled.

The second error assigned is as to the evidence of witness Rucker, set out in bill of exceptions No. 1. As the question involved in that assignment of error is not likely to arise upon another trial, it is unnecessary to pass upon it.

There was no error in permitting the witness Sorrell to testify that trolley poles frequently become detached from the wire, and, when they do that, there is no light inside the car and no electric headlight. That is a matter of common knowledge, and could not have prejudiced the defendant company.

The third error assigned is based upon a mistake of fact. It appears from bill of exceptions No. 3 that the witness Sorrell was permitted to state such facts as would explain why the defendant company did not obtain the name of the only passenger on the train which caused the plaintiff's injury and did not produce him as a witness.

The fifth assignment of error is based upon the refusal of the court to permit two witnesses to testify under the circumstances disclosed by bill of exceptions No. 4, which is as follows:

"* * * After the plaintiff had introduced evidence tending to show that at the time of the accident the car which collided with the plaintiff and injured him was lit by neither electric nor oil headlight and that the car was absolutely dark, and after the conductor and motorman had testified that at the time of the accident both electric and oil headlights were burning at the time of the accident, that the motorman had turned the current of the electric headlight when they started from Luna Park to Washington, on the night in question, and that the oil lamp had previously been lighted by an attendant of the company at

Washington, A. & Mt. V. Ry. Co. *v.* Vaughan

Twelfth street and Pennsylvania avenue, in the city of Washington, at about 15 or 20 minutes before 8, before said car had left the city of Washington for Luna Park, and that they had not lighted the oil light at all on that night, all of which will more fully and at length appear by reference to defendant's bill of exception No. 5, which is hereby referred to and made a part of this bill of exception, the defendant to further maintain the issue upon its part, and to corroborate the testimony of the motorman and conductor, both of whom had previously testified that at the time of the accident both the electric and oil headlights were burning, introduced two witnesses, George Green and John Dunn, both of whom would have testified that they were employed at a point between Addison Station and Twelfth Street Station in the city of Washington, the destination of the car which injured the plaintiff, and that said car on its way to its destination passed by where they were employed about 15 minutes after the accident, and at that time both the electric and oil headlights were burning.   *   *   *   "

The objection made to the evidence rejected is that it was too remote in time and distance from the place of the accident, and that, if the oil headlight was not burning at that time, "it would have been only natural that it should have been lighted very shortly thereafter, especially in view of the fact, as the witness Sorrell testified, that the oil headlight was the only one used in passing through the city."

Where the existence of a thing at a given time is in issue, its prior or subsequent existence is, according to human experience, some indication of its probable existence at a later or earlier period. The degree of probability that a thing was in existence at a given time from its existence at a subsequent period will depend upon the likelihood of some intervening circumstance having occurred and been the true origin. 1 Wigmore on Ev. § 437.

The general principle that a prior or subsequent existence is evidential a later or earlier one has been repeatedly laid down. But, says Prof. Wigmore: "That no fixed rule can be prescribed as to the time or the conditions within which a prior or subsequent existence is evidential is sufficiently illustrated by the precedents, from which it is impossible (and rightly so) to draw a general rule." Section 437.

The cases show that the principle has been applied to all manner of subjects (see notes to section 437 of Wigmore); but, since it is impossible to lay down any general rule as to the time or the conditions within which a prior or subsequent existence is evidential, the question of the admissibility of such evidence must be left largely to the discretion of the trial courts. Whether the length of time which had elapsed and the distance traveled between the accident and where the witnesses offered saw the

Washington, A. & Mt. V. Ry. Co. v. Vaughan

headlights burning was too great under the circumstances disclosed by the record was for the trial court, in the exercise of a reasonable discretion, and we cannot say that its discretion was not properly exercised.

The next error assigned is to the giving of the plaintiff's instruction No. 1, as amended by the court.

It appears from bill of exceptions No. 6 that, after the court had expressed its purpose to grant the instructions asked for by the plaintiff, "the defendant moved the court to amend instruction No. 1 by inserting the words, 'unless the testimony introduced on behalf of the plaintiff shows him to have been guilty of contributory negligence,' immediately after the words, 'the burden is upon the defendant company to prove such contributory negligence by the preponderance of evidence;' but the court overruled said motion, and, in lieu thereof, added the words, 'unless the jury believe from the evidence of the plaintiff that he was guilty of contributory negligence.'"

The amendment, as asked for by the defendant, was proper and the instruction ought to have been so amended; but, as amended by the court, under the circumstances disclosed by the record, it ought not to have been given. It was clearly susceptible of two constructions, one of which was erroneous, and the jury might very well have believed that in applying that instruction to the facts of the case they could only consider the evidence of the plaintiff himself and not the evidence of all the witnesses introduced by him. It was error to give the instruction as amended. Va. Cent. R. Co. v. Sanger, 15 Grat. 230.

It is insisted that, even if the instruction was erroneous, it could not have prejudiced the defendant, since instructions numbered 4 and 5, given on the defendant's motion, correctly stated the law upon that question, and because the evidence of the other witnesses introduced by the plaintiff did not tend to show that he was guilty of contributory negligence.

Instructions Nos. 4 and 5 were not directed to the question of the burden of proof, as was the plaintiff's instruction No. 1, but to the degree of care due from the plaintiff in crossing the track. Neither can it be said that there is nothing in the evidence of the other witnesses introduced by the plaintiff tending to show that he was guilty of contributory negligence.

The giving of instruction No. 2, offered by the plaintiff, is assigned as error.

This is not an action by a traveler on the highway to recover damages for injuries done him as such while crossing the defendant's tracks, but is an action by a passenger to recover damages for injuries done him in going to the defendant's station house, or leaving its premises, immediately after alighting from its train and while the relation of passenger still existed. The

fact that the passway from where he alighted to the station building was over or along a public highway does not affect the question.   That fact did not change the degree of care which the defendant owed the passenger.   The care which a railway company owes a passenger under such circumstances is, as we have
seen in disposing of the demurrer in this case, a different and a
higher degree of care than that which it owes to a traveler crossing its tracks over a public highway.

The instruction seems to have been based upon the view that
the plaintiff was a traveler on the highway rather than a passenger making his way to the station house, or off its grounds
from the point where he alighted from the train.   No instruction
as to the duty which the defendant owed a traveler on the highway should have been given, because no such question was involved in the case, but, as the degree of care required in the
case of a passenger is different and higher than in the case of a
traveler on a public highway, we do not see how the defendant
could have been prejudiced by the instruction.

The remaining assignment of error which it is necessary to
consider is the giving of instruction numbered 3, offered by the
plaintiff.   That instruction is as follows:

"The court instructs the jury that, when common carriers undertake to convey passengers by the powerful and dangerous
agency of electricity, public policy and safety require that they be
held to the greatest possible care and diligence, and any negligence or default of such railway company, or common carrier,
its agents or employees in such cases will make such company or
carrier liable in proper and adequate damages under the statute,
unless the jury believe from the evidence that the plaintiff was
guilty of contributory negligence."

One of the objections made to the instruction is that "no common carrier is required to use the greatest possible care and
diligence" for the safety of its passengers, as declared by the
instruction.   What is meant by the language used in the instruction is that the carrier of passengers is bound to use the highest
practicable degree of care, and that a failure to use it constitutes
actionable negligence.   Various forms of expression are used to
define such care.   The language of the instruction is almost
identical with that of an instruction approved by this court in
the case of B. & O. R. Co. v. Wightman's Adm'r, 29 Grat. 431.
445, 26 Am. Rep. 384, which declared that. "when carriers
undertake to convey passengers by the powerful but dangerous
agency of steam, public policy and safety require that they should
be held to the greatest possible care and diligence, and any negligence or default in such care will make such carrier liable in
damages under the statute."

An instruction containing identically the same language as

used in Wightman's Case was approved in the case of B. & O. R. Co. v. Noell's Adm'r, 32 Grat. 394, 399.

Sometimes the degree of care required is defined or declared to be "the utmost care and diligence of very cautious persons" (Connell v. C. & O. Ry. Co., 93 Va. 44, 55, 24 S. E. 467, 468, 32 L. R. A. 792, 57 Am. St. Rep. 786; Farish v. Reigle, 11 Grat. 697, 62 Am. Dec. 666); "the utmost care and diligence." (N. & W. Ry. Co. v. Tanner, 100 Va. 379, 382, 41 S. E. 721, 722; Reynolds v. Richmond, etc., Ry. Co., 92 Va. 400, 404-405, 23 S. E. 770, 771); "the utmost care and diligence which human prudence and foresight will suggest" (Palmer v. Delaware, etc., R. Co., 120 N. Y. 170, 24 N. E. 302, 17 Am. St. Rep. 629); "the highest possible degree of care and diligence" (Indianapolis R. Co. v. Horst, 93 U. S. 291, 23 L. Ed. 898).

In discussing the language used in the last-named case, which is substantially the same as that used in the instruction complained of, it was said: "The terms in question did not mean all the care and diligence the human mind can conceive of, nor such as will render the transportation free from any possible peril, nor such as would drive the carrier from business. * * * The language used cannot mislead. It well expresses the vigorous requirement of the law, and ought not to be departed from. The rule is beneficial to both parties. It tends to give protection to the traveler, and warns the carrier against the consequences of delinquency."

The language used in the instruction, defining the degree of care which the law requires of a common carrier to its passengers, is fully sustained, not only by our own decisions, but by the authorities generally, and the trial court did not err in using it.

The instruction is objected to upon another ground, viz., that it makes the defendant responsible in the event of any negligence or default on its part, unless the plaintiff was guilty of contributory negligence, without reference to the question whether or not such negligence was the proximate cause of the injury, or whether the defendant owed the plaintiff any duty. The instruction is erroneous in these respects. Although the defendant may have failed to exercise the high degree of care due its passengers, yet it did not owe that duty to the plaintiff, or if such negligence was not the proximate cause of the plaintiff's injury, it was not liable to him.

For giving instructions numbered 1 and 3, asked for by the plaintiff, in the form in which they were given, the judgment complained of must be reversed, the verdict set aside, and the cause remanded for a new trial to be had not in conflict with the views expressed in this opinion.

Reversed.

CARDWELL, J., absent.

WORK v. BOSTON ELEVATED RY. CO.

(Supreme Judicial Court of Massachusetts, Essex, Jan. 6, 1911.)

[93 N. E. Rep. 693.]

Carriers—Injuries to Passengers—Jerks and Jolts.[*]—Jerks while running, and in stopping and starting to let off and take on passengers, jolts in going over frogs or switch points, and lurches in going around curves, are among the incidents in electric cars which every passenger must expect; and if a passenger is injured by such a jerk, jolt, or lurch, the company is not liable. On the other hand, a car can be started and stopped with a jerk so much more abrupt and so much greater than is usual that the motorman can be found to be guilty of negligence.

Carriers—Injury to Passengers—Burden of Proof.—In order for a passenger to recover for an injury from a jerk, jolt, or lurch, he must show, by evidence of what the motorman did, that he was negligent in the way he stopped or started the car, or by evidence of what took place as a physical fact, or by evidence of what appeared to take place as a physical fact, and it is not enough for witnesses to testify that the jerk was unusual.

Carriers—Injury to Passenger—Evidence.—In an action against a carrier for injury to a passenger from the manner in which the car was started, evidence held to warrant a finding that the motorman was negligent.

Exceptions from Superior Court, Essex County: Marcus Morton, Judge.

Action by Charles T. Work against the Boston Elevated Railway Company. Judgment in favor of defendant, and plaintiff brings exceptions. Exceptions sustained.

W. J. Corcoran and *M. F. Cunningham,* for plaintiff.
Endicott P. Saltonstall, for defendant.

LORING, J. It is settled that jerks while running, jerks in stopping and starting to let off and take on passengers, jolts in going over frogs or switch points, and lurches in going around curves are among the usual incidents of travel in electric cars which every passenger on them must expect to encounter, and that, if a passenger is injured by such a jerk, jolt or lurch the company is not liable. On the other hand an electric car can be started and stopped, for example with a jerk so much and so much greater than is usual that the motorman to be guilty of negligence and the company liable. The difference between the two cases is one of degree. The difference be-

---

[*] See first foot-note of Usury v. Watkins (N. Car.), 36 R R R 136, 59 Am. & Eng. R. Cas., N. S., 136.

Work *v.* Boston Elevated Ry. Co

ing one of degree and one of degree only it is of necessity a difficult matter in practice to draw the line between these two sets
of cases in which opposite results are reached. No general rule
can be laid down. Each case must be dealt with as it arises.

But some points are. settled. It is settled that it is not enough
for a plaintiff in such a case to introduce the testimony of witnesses
who characterize the jerk as an unusual one or as worse than
usual. Foley *v.* Boston & Maine R. R., 193 Mass. 332, 79 N.
E. 765, 7 L. R. A. (N. S.) 1076; Saunderson *v.* Boston Elevated
Ry., 194 Mass. 337, 80 N. E. 515; McGann *v.* Boston Elevated
Ry., 199 Mass. 446, 85 N. E. 570, 18 L. R. A. (N. S.) 506, 127
Am. St. Rep. 509; Olund *v.* Worcester Consolidated St. Ry., 206
Mass. 544, 92 N. E. 720. The plaintiff to make out a case must
go further than merely to characterize the jerk, jolt or lurch and
must show (1) by direct evidence of what the motorman did that
he was negligent in the way that he stopped or started the car (as
in Cutts *v.* Boston Elev. Ry., 202 Mass. 450, 89 N. E. 21), or
(2) by evidence of what took place as a physical fact (as in Lacour *v.* Springfield St. Ry., 200 Mass. 34, 85 N. E. 868; Black *v.*
Boston Elev. Ry.. 206 Mass. 80, 91 N. E. 891), or by evidence
of what appeared to take place as a physical fact (as in Nolan *v.*
Newton & Boston St. Ry., 206 Mass. 384, 92 N. E. 505) show
indirectly that the. motorman was negligent. The earlier cases
are collected in McGann *v.* Boston Elev. Ry., 199 Mass. 446, 85
N. E. 570, 18 L. R. A. (N. S.) 506, 127 Am. St. Rep. 509. The
cases which have been decided since then are Stevens *v.* Boston
Elev. Ry., 199 Mass. 471, 85 N. E. 571; Lacour *v.* Springfield
St. Ry., 200 Mass. 34, 85 N. E. 868; Hunt *v.* Boston Elev. Ry.,
201 Mass. 182, 87 N. E. 489; Cutts *v.* Boston Elev. Ry., 202
Mass. 450, 89 N. E. 21; Tupper *v.* Boston Elev. Ry., 204 Mass.
151, 90 N. E. 422; Black *v.* Boston Elev. Ry., 206 Mass. 80, 91
N. E. 891; Nolan *v.* Newton & Boston St. Ry., 206 Mass. 384,
92 N. E. 505; Olund *v.* Worcester Consolidated St. Ry., 206
Mass. 544, 92 N. E. 720.

The plaintiff's story in the case at bar is that he told the conductor when he boarded the car in question that he wanted to get
off at a real estate office, and that later on, seeing the sign of a
real estate office, he "motioned" to the conductor to stop and
he nodded to the plaintiff in answer. At the time he was seated
at the forward end of the car on the right-hand side. The car
was a 30-foot car with seats on each side running lengthwise of
the car. He then turned and gathered up some tin signs which
lay on the. seat beside him. He took them in his right hand and
proceeded to the rear door to alight. The car was then at a
standstill. The conductor was on the platform and with his right
hand he was helping a woman get off the car; that he had his left
hand on the bell rope apparently ready to ring the bell to start the.
car as soon as the woman had stepped off. The plaintiff was then

8 or 10 feet from the rear door. Seeing that the conductor was looking at the woman and not at him and anticipated that the car would be started before he got to the platform he "grabbed" a strap with his left hand, when "the car started instantly with a tremendous jump, it shot right forward and I lost my hold on the strap and I twisted myself and I landed right down in the corner on the opposite side from where I was standing," 8 or 10 feet away. "I struck on the corner of the seat right up on the left side of my head." The plaintiff further testified that the car was not in motion when he took hold of the strap and (to quote his own words) "I took a pretty good hold on it because when I see him reach for the bell I thought the car would start."

There was evidence of negligence on the part of the conductor in that he rang for the car to go ahead without waiting for the plaintiff to get off after the plaintiff had "motioned" to him to stop and he had nodded in answer. But that negligence was not the cause of the injury which the plaintiff suffered. The plaintiff saw that the car was about to be sent forward by the conductor; he had time while the car was standing still to take hold of a strap to steady himself as the car went forward, and he did so. If the car went forward with no more than the usual jump he has no remedy. His right to recover depends upon the way in which the car was started by the motorman.

There is no direct evidence as to what the motorman did in starting the car. But there is indirect evidence that the motorman was negligent in the way he started the car in the fact that although the plaintiff took hold of the strap to steady himself on the starting of the car while it was standing still, and got a "pretty good hold," he was thrown 8 or 10 feet and struck on the corner of the seat on the side of his head.

In Stevens *v.* Boston Elev. Ry., 199 Mass. 471, 85 N. E. 571. the plaintiff's hold on the handle of the car was broken, and in spite of that fact it was held that the evidence did not warrant a finding of negligence on the part of the motorman in starting the car. The trouble with the plaintiff's case there was that he had got down on to the step to get off, thinking that the stopping place was on the nearer in place of the farther side of Dartmouth street, and that he thought that when the car slowed down before crossing the tracks on Dartmouth street it was slowing down to stop for passengers to alight. The fact that under these circumstances the plaintiff had hold of the handle of the car did not justify the inference that the hold taken was a good enough one to guard against the usual jerk incident to a car starting forward; while in the case at bar the plaintiff's hold on the strap was taken when the car was at rest because the plaintiff was afraid that the car was about to start forward. Under these circumstances the jury were justified in thinking that the hold taken was good enough to guard against the usual jerk incident to a car starting forward and in that it was corroborated by the plaintiff's testimony that his hold was a pretty good one.

There was no evidence that there was any other passenger on the car.

We are of opinion that this evidence warranted a finding that the motorman was negligent in the way he started the car and the entry must be:

Exceptions sustained.

GLENNEN v. BOSTON ELEVATED RY. CO.

(Supreme Judicial Court of Massachusetts, Suffolk, Jan. 6, 1911.)

[93 N. E. Rep. 700.]

Carriers—Passengers—Carrier's Duty to Protect.*—A carrier must exercise the highest degree of care to anticipate and protect passengers from violence from other passengers or other persons; the extent of the care required depending upon the particular circumstances.

Carriers—Passengers—Injuries—Actions—Admission of Evidence. —In determining whether a street car company exercised the requisite degree of care to protect a passenger from injury from a crowd which rushed on the car at a public amusement place, the kind of assembly, and of the people likely to attend it, the time of the day, and the natural impatience and turbulence of a crowd boarding the car at such a place, should all be considered.

Carriers—Passengers—Care Required.†—A common carrier does not insure the safety of its passengers, and need not adopt every conceivable precaution, or exercise the utmost conceivable diligence, to prevent injury to them.

Carriers—Passengers—Injuries—Actions—Admission of Evidence. —In an action against a street car company for personal injuries to a passenger by the jostling and turning of the seats by a crowd which rushed onto the car at a public amusement place, where it stopped on the Sunday on which plaintiff was injured, evidence that at about the same hour on Sundays in the amusement season of preceding years the crowd had customarily rushed upon the cars and

---

*See foot-note of Whitlock v. Northern Pac. Ry. Co. (Wash.), 37 R. R. R. 125, 60 Am. & Eng. R. Cas., N. S., 125; first foot-note of Layne v. Chesapeake & O. R. Co. (W. Va.), 36 R. R. R. 537, 59 Am. & Eng. R. Cas., N. S., 537; extensive notes, 6 R. R. R. 435, 29 Am. & Eng. R. Cas., N. S., 435; 4 R. R. R. 217, 27 Am. & Eng. R. Cas., N. S., 217.

†See second foot-note of Washington, etc, Ry. Co. v. Trimyer (Va.), 37 R. R. R. 114, 60 Am. & Eng. R. Cas., N. S., 114; first foot-note of Gardner v. Metropolitan St. R. Co. (Mo.), 36 R. R. R. 448, 59 Am. & Eng. R. Cas., N. S., 448.

Glennen v. Boston Elevated Ry. Co

jostled passengers, was admissible on the question of the degree of care the company should have exercised to protect passengers in alighting at such place on such occasions.

Carriers—Passengers—Care Required.*—A female passenger with a small child in her arms was entitled to protection from being jostled, etc., by other passengers, commensurate with the impairment of her ability to care for herself resulting from carrying the child.

Carriers—Passengers—Injuries—Actions—Jury Questions—Negligence.—In an action against a street car company for personal injuries by a crowd at an amusement resort, where the car stopped, rushing in and attempting to turn the seats while plaintiff was in the car with a child, catching her arm between the seat backs, etc., whether the company's employees were negligent in not protecting plaintiff held a jury question.

Exceptions from Superior Court, Suffolk County; Robert O. Harris, Judge.

Action by Katherine Glennen against the Boston Elevated Railway Company. Verdict for defendant, and plaintiff excepts. Exceptions sustained.

Francis Juggins and *Amos W. Shepard,* for plaintiff.
L. R. Chamberlin and *R. A. Stewart,* for defendant.

RUGG, J. A common carrier of passengers is required to exercise the utmost care consistent with the nature and extent of its business to carry its passengers to their destination in security and enable them to alight there with safety. This extraordinary vigilance is owed, not only as to its own instrumentalities and employees, but also as to other passengers or strangers, so far as any harmful misconduct on their part may be foreseen and guarded against. The highest degree of prudence and circumspection is exacted of the carrier in anticipating and suppressing violence to passengers from all outside sources. The precautions which the carrier must take in the performance of this duty depend upon the facts of each case. No positive regulation of absolute usage has been or can be defined as a final standard for the discharge of its obligation. The natural turbulence of a multitude of people to be expected at a public celebration may require provision against unusual occurrences. The kind of assembly and the character of people likely to attend it, the place from which they have come and to which they are going, the hour of the day and the normally accompanying impatience of restraint, the probable temper and disposition of a crowd in view of the causes which bring it together are all circumstances to be regarded in determining whether in any instance the carrier has

---

*See (*) on preceding page.

Glennen v. Boston Elevated Ry. Co

performed the highly onerous and stringent obligation imposed on it. Kuhlen v. Boston & Northern St. Ry. Co., 193 Mass. 341, 79 N. E. 815, 7 L. R. A. (N. S.) 729, 118 Am. St. Rep. 516, and cases cited; Beverley v. Boston Elevated Ry., 194 Mass. 450, 80 N. E. 507.

On the other hand, a common carrier does not insure to its passengers immunity from harm. It is engaged in a public service which must be managed in such a manner as to be practical and adapted to the needs of contemporary society, both as to expense, convenience, comfort, and rapidity. Hence it cannot be held responsible for manifestations of lawlessness, heedlessness, impetuosity or force which a high degree of prevision and sagacity could not reasonably be expected to forestall. Injury arising from the sporadic act of an individual or the aggregated impulses of a throng, if outside the limits of conduct reasonably to be apprehended by one under a strong legal duty to be most keenly sensitive to guard against preventable wrongs, affords no ground of liability. The carrier is not bound to adopt all possible precautions nor every conceivable safeguard for the safety of passengers, nor to exercise the utmost diligence which human ingenuity can imagine to avert injury. Simmons v. New Bedford Vineyard & Nantucket Steamboat Co., 97 Mass. 361, 93 Am. Dec. 99; Joy v. Winnisimmet Co., 114 Mass. 63; O'Neil v. Lynn & Boston St. Ry. Co., 180 Mass. 576, 62 N. E. 983; Pitcher v. Old Colony St. Ry., 196 Mass. 69, 81 N. E. 876, 13 L. R. A. (N. S.) 481, 124 Am. St. Rep. 513; Lyons v. Boston Elevated Ry., 204 Mass. 227, 90 N. E. 419; McCumber v. Boston Elevated Ry., 93 N. E. 698. These principles are well settled and have been steadily adhered to. It is not necessary to cite or review the many other cases by which they are illustrated, but only to apply them to the facts before us.

The plaintiff was a passenger upon one of the defendant's open cars, and reach the terminus of the route near a portion of the Charles River reservation, between 5 and 6 o'clock on a Sunday afternoon in May. She was accompanied by her son 2½ years old. It was customary at this terminus, which was on a public street, for the trolley to be reversed, the seats turned over, and for the car to start to return on the same track. At the time of the events to be narrated the conductor was on the rear platform. The motorman was at his post on the front platform, and there was a starter in the employ of the defendant 8 or 10 feet away from the car. A great many people were in the habit of going to this reservation, and a boathouse was near by, where canoes were kept. When the car came to a stop at its terminus the plaintiff's description of what happened was as follows: "I started to get out of the car. * * * There was a crowd of people there. There seemed to be about 100 people or more. There was a great crowd rushed onto the car and

Glennen *v.* Boston Elevated Ry. Co

started turning over the seats. There was a great confusion. I started to get out of the car and I was pushed back * * * into my seat again. * * * I grasped hold of the stanchion, but I was forced back again into my seat. * * * [The child] was in my arms. I was going to step down off the car. I had my arm on the back of the seat * * * waiting for a chance to get out of the car when this seat in back was turned over and pinned my arm between the backs of the two seats. * * * Passengers [were] getting onto the railing and on the outside on the right hand and on the left hand as well. * * * Right around me it seemed that most of [the seats] were turned over." She further testified that no employee of the defendant said or did anything to restrain the crowd or assist her, and that the events she had described happened within a period of two or three minutes. The plaintiff offered to show that on preceding Sundays of 1907 and 1906, at about the same hour, there had been rushing and crowding and jostling by passengers in getting upon the cars at this place, but this line of inquiry was excluded subject to her exception.

Evidence as to what has been the custom of a crowd at a particular place or under special circumstances in boarding the defendant's cars was competent, because a railway company has reasonable cause to know what has been habitually done respecting its cars. It bore upon the care which the defendant ought to have exercised and the protection which it ought to have furnished to its passengers who were entitled to alight even in the face of a large number of people desiring to become passengers. Nichols *v.* Lynn & Boston, 168 Mass. 528, 47 N. E. 427. The evidence as to the conduct of crowds of the year before the accident at the same season of the year, when it may be fairly inferred that conditions as to the reservation, boathouses and use of canoes were substantially the same, had some tendency in the same direction. The plaintiff appears to have gone far enough to bring herself within the operation of this rule. The fact that the superior court excluded the line of inquiry excused her from making so complete an offer of proof as would otherwise have been necessary. It is also to be observed that the plaintiff was a woman incumbered with a small child and entitled to protection commensurate with the impaired capacity to care for herself resulting from this burden. Hamilton *v.* Boston & Northern St. Ry. Co., 193 Mass. 324, 79 N. E. 734. Her own testimony as to the length of time elapsing after the car stopped and before her injury and the facts that she had once risen from her seat and been forced back into it by the violence of the crowd and having risen again was compelled to pause for opportunity to step and that while thus waiting the seat was thrown against her tend to show that the boisterousness was not an instantaneous act without forewarning, but was of appreciable duration and might

Norfolk & W. Ry. Co. v. Stone

be found to have afforded in connection with all the other attendant conditions a premonition such as to call for action on the
part of the conductor or starter. That this occurred upon a
public street rather than in a station under the exclusive control
of the defendant is not decisive in its favor. It is not a question
of policing the public way, but of shielding its passenger while
in the car. Evidence of unruly conduct of crowds at this place
on prior occasions when the circumstances were similar should
have been received and the case submitted to the jury.

Exceptions sustained.

Norfolk & W. Ry. Co. v. Stone.

(Supreme Court of Appeals of Virginia, Jan. 12, 1911.)

[69 S. E. Rep. 927.]

Trial—Instructions—Evidence to Sustain.—In an action against a
carrier for requiring a white passenger to ride in a coach provided
for negroes, it was reversible error to instruct that punitive damages could be allowed if the conductor's act was wanton or oppressive, in the absence of evidence tending to show such facts.

Carriers—Passengers—Mistreatment—Instructions.—Where a white
passenger sued a carrier for compensatory damages, an instruction
that, if the conductor forced her to ride in the car set apart for negroes, she was not limited to actual damages, but that her discomfort
and humiliation could be considered, was improper as being misleading.

Carriers — Passengers — Mistreatment — Damages.* — Compensatory damages to a white passenger for being compelled to ride
in a coach set apart for negroes include compensation for discomfort
and humiliation.

Carriers—Passengers—Mistreatment—Instructions.—In an action
against a carrier for requiring a white passenger to ride in a coach
set apart for negroes, it was improper to modify instructions which
precluded recovery if the conductor honestly believed that the passenger was a negro, by the clause "unless plaintiff made known to
the conductor that she was a white woman."

Error to Circuit Court, Nansemond County.

Action by Rosa Stone against the Norfolk & Western Railway

---

*For the authorities in this series on the subject of the liability
of a railroad company on account of insults by employees to passengers, see foot-notes of Pierce v. St. Louis, etc., R. Co. (Ark.), 36
R. R. R. 480, 59 Am. & Eng. R. Cas., N. S., 480; foot-note of Caldwell
v. Northern Pac. Ry. Co. (Wash.), 35 R. R. R. 161, 58 Am. & Eng.
R. Cas., N. S., 161.

Company. Judgment for plaintiff, and defendant brings error.
Reversed.

Bernard & Townsend, E. E. Holland, and *Theo. W. Reath,* for
plaintiff in error.

S. E. Everett and *R. W. Withers,* for defendant in error.

WHITTLE, J. The defendant in error (the plaintiff below), a
white woman, took passage on an east-bound morning train of
the plaintiff in error (the defendant below) at Myrtle for Suffolk, and by the direction of the conductor entered the coach set
apart for colored passengers. The sole occupants of that coach
were the plaintiff, a negro man (who occupied a seat at the opposite end of the car from the plaintiff), and a negro woman,
Georgia Baker. The plaintiff and Georgia Baker had been acquainted for 15 or 20 years, and the latter remarked to her, in
the presence and hearing of the conductor, who had entered the
car to take up tickets: "Law, Miss Rosa, you are wrong." To
which the plaintiff replied: "I know I'm wrong. I'm not in my
right place. I was raised with white people, and am white, and
I'm going out of here." Whereupon the conductor observed:
"Keep your seat. You've got to stay somewhere, and there's
plenty of room." Suffolk is eight miles from Myrtle, and the
first stop after leaving that station; the time between the two
stations being from 10 to 15 minutes. The conductor had no
recollection whatever of the incident, but frankly admitted that
if he had known the facts he would not have subjected the plaintiff to the hazard of going from one car to another on a rapidly
moving train, unless she had specially requested it; that if he had
done so, and injury had ensued, the company would have had to
respond in damages.

It is not pretended that such request was expressly made by
the plaintiff in the present instance. Independently, therefore,
of any blame that may have attached to the defendant by reason
of the original mistake in directing a white woman to go into
the colored car, it can hardly be doubted, in the circumstances indicated, that the course outlined by the conductor would have
been the most prudent one.

There were two trials of the case, practically upon the same
evidence. At the first trial, the jury returned a verdict for the
plaintiff for $500. This verdict, on motion of the defendant, was
set aside. Several grounds were assigned for this motion, but
the reasons which actuated the court in granting it do not appear.
Without considering other assignments, the fact that the jury
were instructed that, if they believed from the evidence the act
of the conductor was "wanton or oppressive and in utter disregard of the plaintiff's rights," they could award punitive damages,
afforded a quite sufficient reason in itself for setting aside the
verdict.

Norfolk & W. Ry. Co. *v.* Stone

Without considering the question of liability of the defendant to answer in punitive damages for such alleged misconduct of the conductor as is contemplated in the instruction, in the absence of previous authority or subsequent ratification by the defendant, the instruction ought not to have been given because there was no evidence whatever to support it.

At the second trial there was a verdict for the plaintiff for $400, which the court refused to disturb.

The grounds of the motion to set aside the last verdict were the giving of a certain instruction on behalf of the plaintiff, and amending two instructions asked by the defendant, and because the verdict was contrary to the law and the evidence and the damages so excessive as to manifest passion and prejudice on the part of the jury.

The instruction for the plaintiff told the jury that if they believed from the evidence that she was directed by the conductor to the colored car, and when he came in to take up her ticket it was made known to him that she was a white person, and she insisted on going into the white car, and the conductor forced her to ride in the colored car, they must find for the plaintiff. And in assessing her damages they were not limited to compensation for the actual damages sustained by her, but might in addition take into consideration the discomforts, mortification, and humiliation suffered by her, if they believed from the evidence that such had been proved with reasonable certainty.

Upon the plaintiff's theory of the case, on the second trial, the damages to which she was entitled were compensatory damages merely, which, if the jury believed the evidence justified it, would include the constituents of discomfort, mortification, and humiliation. If that is the correct interpretation of the instruction, it correctly states the law. It seems to us, however, that the phraseology employed renders the meaning of the instruction obscure, and was calculated to confuse and mislead the jury. They should have been plainly told that, if they believed from the evidence that the facts recited in the instruction were proved, the plaintiff was entitled to recover compensatory damages, and that discomfort, mortification, and humiliation, if proved with reasonable certainty to have been suffered by the plaintiff, constituted elements of such damages.

The court's amendment of the following instructions offered by the defendant is also assigned as error:

"(2) If the jury believe from the evidence that the plaintiff voluntarily entered the car set apart for colored passengers, that the conductor found her in this car and believed that she was a colored person, and, acting in good faith under such belief, when he saw her rise from her seat as if to leave it or the car, told her to take her seat, they must find for the defendant, although

they may further believe from the evidence that the plaintiff was
and is in fact a white person."

"(3) What race a person belongs to cannot always be determined infallibly from appearances. When a mistake is in-
nocently made, the railroad company is not liable in damages
simply because a white person was taken for a negro or a negro
for a white person, where the aggrieved party does not disclose
her race. It is not a legal injury for a white person to be taken
for a negro under such circumstances. It is not contemplated by
the statute of Virginia applicable to such cases that the carrier
should be an insurer as to the race of its passengers. The court
accordingly instructs the jury that, if they believe from the evidence that the conductor made in this case an honest mistake
as to the race of the plaintiff, they must find for the defendant."

The amendment to each of these instructions reads: "Unless
they further believe from the evidence the plaintiff then and there
made known to the said conductor that she was a white woman."

Two theories of the case are submitted for consideration by
the evidence, namely: On behalf of the plaintiff, that the conductor, although it was made known to him that the plaintiff
was a white woman, required her to ride in the car set apart for
colored persons; and, on behalf of the defendant, that the conductor acted in good faith under the honest belief that the plaintiff was a negro. The purpose of the defendant's instructions
(which were practically rendered meaningless by the amendment) was to submit its theory of the case to the jury. In this,
it was plainly within its rights, and the court should have given
the instructions as prayed for without amendment. Jackson's
Case, 96 Va. 107, 30 S. E. 452; Richmond Traction Co. v. Martin's
Adm'r, 102 Va. 209, 45 S. E. 886.

As the judgment must be reversed for the foregoing errors,
and the case remanded for a new trial, the remaining assignment
of error need not be noticed.

Reversed.

Cardwell, J., absent.

McCumber v. Boston Elevated Ry. Co.

(Supreme Judicial Court of Massachusetts, Suffolk, Jan. 6, 1911.)

[93 N. E. Rep. 698.]

Carriers—Passengers—Assumption of Risk—Overloading Car.*—A street car passenger, who voluntarily entered a crowded car, knowing that she could not get a seat and might have to stand in the vestibule, assumes any risk of injury incident to the crowded condition of the car, including the risk from alighting temporarily to enable other passengers to leave the car, even though she were not negligent in entering it.

Carriers—Passengers—Negligence.†—It is not negligence for a street car company to permit passengers to enter cars which are already crowded.

Carriers—Passengers—Injuries—Negligence.‡—When plaintiff entered defendant's elevated street car, it was so crowded that she could not obtain a seat and was compelled to stand in the vestibule, and when the car stopped to permit passengers to alight the conductor told plaintiff that she was blocking the passageway and must stand aside to permit other passengers to alight, and in the jostling which accompanied the efforts of the other passengers to alight plaintiff was pushed off the car. Held, that the company was required to exercise the highest degree of care for plaintiff's safety which was consistent with a similar duty to the other passengers, and it was not negligent under the circumstances, so as to make it liable for plaintiff's injuries.

Carriers—Passengers—Negligence.—The language used by a street car conductor in telling a passenger that she was blocking the passageway and asking her to move aside being proper in form and substance, evidence that his tone of voice was harsh and loud, so as to agitate and ·confuse her, was not admissible in an action for injuries sustained by being pushed off the car by other passengers in alighting.

Exceptions from Superior Court, Suffolk County; Robert O. Harris, Judge.

Action by Mabel S. McCumber against the Boston Elevated

---

*For the authorities in this series on the question whether it is contributory negligence in a passenger to board a crowded car, see second foot-note of Lobner v. Metropolitan St. Ry. Co. (Kan.), 32 R. R. R. 473, 55 Am. & Eng. R. Cas., N. S., 473.

†For the authorities in this series on the duties and liabilities of carriers of passengers with respect to overloading vehicles, see last foot-note of Norvell v. Kanawha, etc., Ry. Co. (W. Va.), 37 R. R. R. 148, 60 Am. & Eng. R. Cas., N. S.. 148; Chesapeake, etc., Ry. Co. v. Austin (Ky.), 35 R. R. R. 716, 58 Am. & Eng. R. Cas., N. S.. 716.

‡See extensive notes, 4 R. R. R. 217, 27 Am. & Eng. R. Cas., N. S., 217; 6 R. R. R. 435, 29 Am. & Eng. R. Cas., N. S., 435.

Railway Company.   Verdict for defendant, and plaintiff excepts.
Exceptions overruled.

C. E. *Tupper* and A. F. *Tupper*, for plaintiff.
W. G. *Thompson*, G. F. *Kimball*, and F. D. *Putnam*, for defendant.

RUGG, J.   The plaintiff with a dress suit case in hand became
a passenger on one of the defendant's closed cars after dark on
a December day.   When she boarded the car she perceived that
it was crowded, and she was able to get only to the door leading
from the vestibule to the aisle.   Later she gave way for the conductor to go inside to collect fares, and thereafter she stood just
in the door, with one foot in the door and the other in the vestibule.   After one stop, at which other passengers came upon the
car, the plaintiff knew by a bell and the slowing of the car that
persons inside were intending to get out, and she saw them begin
to push their way to the door or move down the car "as they
always do."   The conductor, who was near the plaintiff, but inside the car collecting fares, told her she was blocking the passageway, and that she must make room for the other passengers
to alight.   There was some conflict in the plaintiff's testimony
after this point.   She said she tried to push back into the vestibule, but it was so crowded there was no room for her there, that
people on the step and a gentleman beside her got off and left
a narrow passageway, and while she was turning around and trying to see what she could do the crowd surged against her, and
she felt herself going off.   In answer to the question, "How
did you expect those people, who wanted to get off that car
* * *   at that stop, could get by you, standing, filling up that
door?" she testified, "That was the conundrum."   Other portions of her testimony tend to show that she thought other men
would get off the vestibule, or that the conductor would make
room for her by compelling persons to move up inside the door.
It is impossible to understand how she could have reasonably entertained the latter opinion in view of her own observation as
to the number of people there.

The plaintiff voluntarily and intelligently became a passenger
upon a car so crowded that she could not get a seat, and knew
that perhaps she might be obliged to stand in the vestibule.
This was not negligence on her part, but by doing so she assumed
whatever obligation or risk was incident to that condition.   One
of these might be to alight temporarily in order to enable other
passengers to leave the car.   It is not negligence on the part of
a carrier in the present state of transportation to permit passengers to come upon cars which are already crowded.   Jacobs
v. West End St. Ry., 178 Mass. 116, 59 N. E. 639; Tompkins v.
Boston Elev. R. R., 201 Mass. 114, 87 N. E. 488; 20 L. R. A. (N.
S.) 1063, 131 Am. St. Rep. 392.   It was the duty of the defend-

McCumber v. Boston Elevated Ry. Co

ant to exercise the highest degree of care toward the plaintiff as its passenger, which was consistent with its equal duty to all its other passengers of transporting them and affording them a reasonable opportunity to alight at the end of their journey. It owed the plaintiff no higher or more exclusive duty than it owed each one of its other passengers on the car. There is nothing in the evidence to indicate that the passengers inside the car were turbulent or disorderly in any respect. They were simply trying to move to the door in the ordinary way in order to get off the car. It is plain from the testimony of the plaintiff that the narrow door of the car was completely obstructed by her person, and that other passengers could not pass unless she moved. The conductor, in the performance of what appears to have been his obvious duty to other passengers, told the plaintiff she was blocking the passageway, and that she must make room. In this respect he did not fail in his duty to the plaintiff. The plaintiff does not show any conduct on the part of other passengers which would naturally have caused a careful conductor to apprehend any violence or disorder on their part or any disregard by them of the rights of the plaintiff as a fellow passenger. That there was some pushing in the effort to pass the plaintiff is not significant. It is only when done in a disorderly way that it becomes of consequence. Hence there was no evidence of negligence on the part of the defendant. The case is fully covered in principle by Jacobs v. West End St. Ry., 178 Mass. 116, 59 N. E. 639, and Treat v. Boston & Lowell R. R., 131 Mass. 371. Kuhlen v. Boston & Northern St. Ry., 193 Mass. 341, 79 N. E. 815, 7 L. R. A. (N. S.) 729, 118 Am. St. Rep. 516, and Beverley v. Boston Elevated Ry., 194 Mass. 450, 80 N. E. 507, and distinguishable in that they relate to failure to properly control crowds of people under circumstances such that the carrier ought reasonably, in the exercise of the high degree of care required of it, to have anticipated violence.

Exception was taken to the refusal of the trial court to permit the plaintiff to testify that the tone of voice in which the conductor told her she was blocking the passageway and asked her to move was harsh and loud with the result that she was agitated and flustrated. The language used was proper in form and substance and in the performance of duty. It was unaccompanied by threat of speech or gesture. Perturbation of mind which inevitably depends upon individual peculiarities of experience, sensitiveness and nervousness, and fluctuates in the same person with varying conditions of health and happiness, and which is claimed to arise solely from inflection of voice in the course of necessary speech, is too unstable a foundation upon which to rest a standard of legal liability in a case of this kind. See Beal v. Lowell & Dracut St. Ry., 157 Mass. 444, 32 N. E. 653.

Exceptions overruled.

LOUISVILLE & N. R. Co. *v.* SCOTT.

SAME *v.* CLARK.

(Court of Appeals of Kentucky, Jan. 12, 1911.)

[133 S. W. Rep. 800.]

Carriers—Stopping Trains for Passengers—Duty as to Information.*—Carriers, within reasonable limitations, may designate the stations at which trains will stop for passengers; and a traveler, who, without any agreement or arrangement, or without acting on information furnished by some authorized agent of the company, takes passage on a train, scheduled not to stop at the station to which he desires to go, cannot recover for its not stopping there, as, under such circumstances, he must inform himself as to where the train will stop.

Carriers—Local Ticket Agent—Implied Authority.†—The agent of a carrier, in charge of one of its passenger stations at which tickets are sold, has implied authority to agree with and furnish information to persons desiring to become passengers that a train not scheduled to stop at a certain point will stop there to let him on or off, so that the company will be bound by his representations; the person with whom he makes the agreement, or to whom he gives the information, not being shown to have known that it was not within his power or authority to make the arrangement or to give the information.

Carriers—Ejection of Passengers—Punitive Damages.—A passenger ejected from a train may not recover damages for insults or humiliation put on other passengers at the time.

Carriers—Ejection of Passengers—Punitive Damages.‡—Where a conductor, having in the line of his duty a right to require a pas-

---

*For the authorities in this series on the subject of the duty of passengers to inform themselves in regard to the movements of trains, see last paragraph of third foot-note of Black *v.* Atlantic C. L. R. Co. (S. Car.), 32 R. R. R. 603, 55 Am. & Eng. R. Cas., N. S., 603.

†For the authorities in this series on the subject of the implied authority of a railroad's freight or ticket agents, see second foot-note of St. Louis, etc., Ry. Co. *v.* Citizen's Bank (Ark.), 30 R. R. R. 290, 53 Am. & Eng. R. Cas., N. S., 290; foot-note of Southern Ry. Co. *v.* Nowlin (Ala.), 30 R. R. R. 261, 53 Am. & Eng. R. Cas., N. S., 261; foot-note of Johnson *v.* Michigan United Rys. Co. (Mich), 30 R. R. R. 346, 53 Am. & Eng. R. Cas., N. S., 346.

For the authorities in this series on the subject of the liability of carriers on account of mistakes or negligence of their ticket agents, see first foot-note of Arnold *v.* Atchison, etc., Ry. Co. (Kan.), 34 R. R. R. 217, 57 Am. & Eng. R. Cas., N. S., 217; Mace *v.* Southern Ry. Co., 34 R. R. R. 15, 57 Am. & Eng. R. Cas., N. S., 15.

‡For the authorities in this series on the subject of the right to recover exemplary or punitive damages for wrongs to passengers, see first foot-note of Owens *v.* Atlantic C. L. R. Co. (N. Car.), 36 R. R. R. 483, 59 Am. & Eng. R. Cas., N. S., 483; foot-note of St. Louis, etc., R. Co. *v.* Garner (Miss.), 35 R. R. R. 185, 58 Am. & Eng. R. Cas., N. S., 185.

Louisville & N. R. Co. *v.* Scott

senger to leave the train, tells her to get off, and she says she does not intend to get off and will make him pay for putting her off, and he merely says that is all right, and pushes her down the steps, his conduct is not so rude or offensive as to authorize punitive damages.

Trial—Verdict—Severance of Exemplary and Punitive Damages.— The court, deeming that exemplary as well as compensatory damages are allowable, should instruct the jury to find each class of damages separately, so that in case exemplary damages be not allowable there may be a reversal as to such part only, saving a new trial.

Appeals from Circuit Court, Hart County.

Two actions, one by Mamie Scott, the other by Tiny Clark, both against the Louisville & Nashville Railroad Company. Judgment for plaintiff in each case, and defendant appeals. Reversed.

Watkins & Carden, Sims & Rodes, Benjamin D. Warfield, and *Charles H. Moorman,* for appellant.

McCandless & Larimore, H. W. Curle, and *S. M. Payton,* for appellees.

CARROLL, J.   These two appeals present law and facts growing out of the same transaction, and will be disposed of together.

The appellees, who are colored people, live at Horse Cave, a station on the appellant company's line of road. They, and several others, in September, 1909, desiring to attend a baseball game at Bowling Green, also on appellant's line of road, selected Shelby Beard and others of their friends to make arrangements with the railroad company for transportation. The schedule of the passenger trains between Bowling Green and Horse Cave that made regular stops at Horse Cave would not enable the party to go to Bowling Green, and, after seeing the game, return on the same day, and so Shelby Beard and the others requested the depot and ticket agent of the company at Horse Cave to have the train known as No. 2 that passed through Bowling Green about 10 o'clock each night stop at Horse Cave and let the party off. They knew that Horse Cave was not a regular stopping place for this train, and that is only occasionally stopped there to receive and discharge passengers. According to the testimony of Beard and others, the agent at Horse Cave told them that if they would get up a party of as many as 15 he would have train No. 2 stop and let them off. Acting, as they claim, upon this information, a party of more than 20 was made up, and all of them went to Bowling Green on the morning train, and on that night they got on train No. 2 at Bowling Green for the purpose of returning to Horse Cave. About 11 o'clock at night when this train reached Cave City, a station four miles from Horse Cave, at which it was in the habit of stopping, the conductor required the entire party to leave the train, and they were obliged to and did walk

Louisville & N. R. Co. *v.* Scott

from Cave City to their homes at Horse Cave. To recover damages for their alleged wrongful ejection, the appellees brought these suits, setting out in their petitions substantially the facts before stated, and the further fact that the conductor in requiring them to leave the train at Cave City behaved towards them in a rude, violent, and insulting manner. They also averred that the appellant company, for the purpose of intimidating them, falsely and maliciously had them and other members of the party arrested upon the charge of having committed a breach of the peace on the train and at the station in Cave City, and that upon a trial of this charge they were acquitted. Each of them asked damages in the sum of $5,100. In its answer the company, after traversing the averments of the petition, pleaded: (1) That the agent at Horse Cave had no authority to agree with Shelby Beard or others that he would have train No. 2 stop for the purpose of letting them off at Horse Cave; (2) that they were permitted to get on this train at Bowling Green under an agreement with the conductor that they would all leave the train at Cave City; (3) that it had no connection with, and did not instigate, the arrest or prosecution, if any, of the parties for disturbing the peace at Cave City. Upon a special trial before a jury the damages in favor of appellee Mamie Scott were assessed at $250, and the damages in favor of appellee Tiny Clark at $500.

We are asked to reverse the judgments entered upon these verdicts for error of the court in refusing to direct a verdict in favor of the company, for error in giving instructions, in admitting incompetent evidence, and because the damages allowed are excessive.

But, before taking up the errors assigned, it is proper to state that the agent denied that he agreed he would have train No. 2 stopped, and says that he told Shelby Beard, the leader of the party, to see the agent and telegraph operator at Bowling Green and try to procure one of them to get an order to stop the train, as he had no authority to stop it and could not get an order to have it done. It also appears that Shelby Beard did go to see the agent as well as the operator at Bowling Green; but neither of them made any effort to get an order to have the train stopped. When the train came into Bowling Green, and the party went to get on, the conductor testifies that he asked them where they were going, and they said "Horse Cave," and he replied, "This train doesn't stop at Horse Cave and you cannot get on," and they then said, "Well, we will go to Cave City." And that, with the understanding that the party would leave the train at Cave City, he permitted them to get on. While members of the party testify that they did not tell the conductor they would get off at Cave City, and that they got on the train with the belief and expectation that it would stop and let them off at Horse

Louisville & N. R. Co. v. Scott

Cave. It is also shown that Shelby Beard had one ticket for the entire party, from Horse Cave to Bowling Green, and return, and that the conductor took up this ticket. We may add that the evidence upon this point leaves the impression that the conductor, knowing that his train would stop at Cave City, permitted the party to get on, believing that they would get off at Cave City, and we may also observe that Shelby Beard and the well-behaved members of the party did get off at Cave City without objection or resistance.

Taking up now the question of the authority of the agent at Horse Cave to make the agreement or arrangement relied upon by appellees that they could return to Horse Cave from Bowling Green on train No. 2, we may say at the outset that there was sufficient evidence to authorize a submission of the case on this issue to the jury and to sustain a finding that such an agreement was made. But, admitting this, the question is raised by counsel for the railroad company that the agent did not have authority to make any agreement or arrangement of this character that was binding upon his principal, the company. If he did not, of course no cause of action against the company can be founded upon a breach of it, nor could the company be held responsible for failing to stop this train at Horse Cave in the absence of an agreement with some person authorized to agree that it would stop, because railroad companies have the right to establish reasonable rules and regulations for the operation of their trains, and within reasonable limitations to designate the stations at which they will stop to receive and discharge passengers. And if a traveler, in the absence of an agreement or arrangement or without acting upon information furnished by some authorized agent of the company, takes passage upon a train that is scheduled not to stop at the station to which he desires to go, he cannot maintain an action if it fails to stop at such station, because, unless acting under an agreement or arrangement or upon information furnished by the company, the traveler must inform himself of the arrival and departure of trains and the places at which they will and will not stop. It follows from this that, although appellees boarded this train at Bowling Green with the purpose of getting off at Horse Cave, a station at which it was not scheduled to stop, they could not, unless acting under an arrangement with or upon information furnished by the agent at Horse Cave, recover damages for the failure to carry them to Horse Cave and permit them to leave the train. There is no effort made to hold the company liable upon the ground that the conductor permitted them to board the train knowing that they had a ticket for Horse Cave, which he took up; the cause of action being rested entirely upon the agreement made with the agent at Horse Cave.

Coming now to the sufficiency of the agreement between the

Louisville & N. R. Co. *v.* Scott

agent and his party, or the information furnished by him to bind
the company, we have no doubt that an agent of a railroad company in charge of one of its passenger stations at which tickets
for transportation of passengers are sold has authority on behalf of the company to agree with and furnish information to
persons who desire to become passengers that a train not scheduled to stop at a designated station will stop there for the
purpose of permitting them to get on or off, and that the company will be bound by his representations, unless it is shown that
the person with whom he made the agreement or to whom he
gave the information knew that it was not within the power or
authority of the agent to make the agreement or give the information, or unless the ticket upon its face furnished advice sufficient to put a reasonably careful and prudent person upon notice
that the information furnished or the agreement made by the
agent was incorrect or in excess of his authority. But, as this
phase of the question is not here, we need not express any
opinion as to the rights of a passenger when there is conflict
between the information given or the agreement made, and that
furnished by the ticket. Of course, it is elementary that an
agent has no authority to bind his principal, unless he is acting
within the apparent scope of his authority; but we think that
when a railroad company has established a place on its line of
railroad, or elsewhere, at which tickets may be bought for transportation upon its line of road, it thereby invests the agent in
charge of its business, so far as the public is concerned, with the
implied authority to furnish all reasonable information   relating
to the transportation of passengers, and concerning the movement of passenger trains, and with the power to bind it by any
agreements made by him or information furnished by him, within
the line of his duty. And we are also of the opinion that it is
within the line of his duty to give information and make representations in reference to the rights of passengers holding tickets
that he sells to them. The public has the right to go to such an
agent for information concerning the movement of trains upon
which they desire to take passage, and they have the right to
rely upon the statements made by him concerning such matters.
It would be a curious state of affairs if an agent having the express authority to sell tickets for transportation to and from
different points did not also have the authority to give reasonable
and proper information concerning the trains upon which such
tickets might be used and the places at which trains would stop
to receive and discharge passengers holding tickets sold by him.
And so, when the ticket agent of a railroad company agrees with
or informs a person desiring to become a passenger that the ticket
will be good on certain trains, or that certain trains upon which
it may be used will stop at a designated place to let such person
on or off, the company will be bound by his agreements or repre-

Louisville & N. R. Co. *v.* Scott

sentations or by the information furnished by him in the absence of knowledge upon the part of the purchaser of the ticket that the agent had no authority to make such an agreement or that the information given was incorrect, and when the ticket does not contain agreements or conditions by which the passenger's rights are to be determined. It may be true that the agent must submit the request for a change in schedules, or for authority to stop a train at a place it is not scheduled to stop, to his superiors and obtain their consent; but this is a matter between the railroad company and its agent. If its agent having the implied authority to act for it makes agreements or representations in violation of its rules, or in disobedience of its orders, or fails or neglects to procure the necessary authority to do what he agreed or represented should be done, it is the fault of the agent, and not the passenger, and the company as between the passenger and it must suffer the consequences of its agent's negligence or want of power. P. C. C. & St. L. R. Co. *v.* Reynolds, 55 Ohio St. 370, 45 N. E. 712, 60 Am. St. Rep. 706; Atkinson *v.* Southern R. Co., 114 Ga. 146, 39 S. E. 888, 55 L. R. A. 223; Kansas City, etc., R. Co. *v.* Little, 66 Kan. 378, 71 Pac. 820, 61 L. R. A. 122, 97 Am. St. Rep. 376; Hutchinson *v.* Southern R. Co., 140 N. C. 123, 52 S. E. 263; 6 Am. & Eng. Ann. Cas. 22; Hutchinson on Carriers (3d Ed.) vol. 2, § 1060.

The next question to be considered is: Did the court err in instructing the jury that they might allow punitive or exemplary damages? Whether this instruction was proper or not depends upon the manner in which appellees were rejected from or required to leave the train at Cave City. That the company was liable to them for compensatory damages, if the jury believed the agreement heretofore mentioned was made with the ticket agent, we have already decided. This measure of damages they were entitled to on account of the mere act of ejection, without reference to how it was accomplished. But punitive damages should not have been allowed, unless the conductor used more force than was necessary to require appellees to leave the train, or unless his conduct or manner or language was insulting, or abusive, or violent or threatening, or his behavior manifested a wanton and reckless disregard of the rights of appellees or a disposition to oppose or humiliate them. L. & N. R. Co. *v.* Ballard, 88 Ky. 159, 10 S. W. 429, 10 Ky. Law Rep. 735, 2 L. R. A. 694; Memphis, etc., R. Co. *v.* Nagel, 97 Ky. 9, 29 S. W. 743, 16 Ky. Law Rep. 748; Southern R. Co. *v.* Hawkins, 121 Ky. 415, 89 S. W. 258, 28 Ky. Law Rep. 364; L. & N. R. Co. *v.* Fowler, 123 Ky. 450, 96 S. W. 568, 29 Ky. Law Rep. 905; L. & N. R. Co. *v.* Summers, 133 Ky. 684, 118 S. W. 926; Cincinnati, etc., R. Co. *v.* Strosnider, 121 S. W. 971.

The court in each case instructed the jury that: "If they believe from the evidence that the defendant's agents or servants

Louisville & N. R. Co. *v.* Scott

in charge of said train assaulted plaintiff or brandished or menaced her with a pistol, or willfully abused or threatened her in a violent or insulting manner in the presence of the other passengers, they may find such additional damages by way of smart money as they may deem proper." If the evidence justified the giving of this instruction, it is not objectionable. It appears from the evidence that when the train reached Cave City the conductor told this party that they must get off. In obedience to his request, some of them did get off, others refused, saying that their ticket entitled them to be carried to Horse Cave and they were not going to leave the train at Cave City. The efforts of the conductor to force those who declined to leave the train to get off created considerable confusion and disturbance. And several of them testify that he used very abusive and insulting language, and in addition to this drew a pistol and threatened to shoot some of them. But, assuming that the conductor acted in the manner indicated, we do not think his conduct entitled these appellees to punitive damages unless his manner or conduct towards them was insulting, threatening, or abusive. They are not entitled to recover for insults or humiliation put upon other passengers. Their rights of recovery should be confined to what happened to them. It would be manifestly unjust to award these appellees exemplary damages on account of the misconduct of the conductor towards other passengers, as those other passengers may have suits against the company to recover damages for the injuries to them. Limiting, then, the right of appellees to exemplary damages to their treatment by the conductor, we find that Mamie Scott testified that, when the conductor requested the party to leave the train, she got off in obedience to his orders. She does not say that before or while she was alighting from the train the conductor said or did anything to her that was rude, offensive, insulting, or threatening. But it appears that after she had left the train, and while she was standing on the station platform, the conductor and other members of the party became involved in a controversy of difficulty concerning their removal from the train, and that she then went back on the steps or platform of the train for the purpose of interfering in behalf of one of her friends, and that the conductor then pushed her back against the door of the car. As her right to recover exemplary damages is rested entirely upon the fact that the conductor used more force than was necessary and treated her in a rude and insulting manner in ejecting her from the car, it is manifest from her testimony that she did not bring herself within the averments of her pleading or the rule that entitled passengers to recover damages of this character. What the conductor did or said to her after she had left the train and had ceased to be a passenger, and at a time when she was not entitled to the protection afforded passengers, does not entitle her to recover punitive damages.

Louisville & N. R. Co. *v*. Scott

Tiny Clark testifies, in substance, that, when the train arrived at Cave City, the conductor told them to get off, and that she said she did not intend to get off and would make the conductor pay for putting her off, and that he said that was all right, and pushed her down the steps; that he didn't say anything else to her. Whether the act of the conductor in pushing a passenger out of a car or from the train would entitle the passenger to exemplary damages depends very largely upon the circumstances surrounding the parties at the time and the manner in which the force was used. Under some circumstances it might well be considered rude and offensive to push a passenger, who was being ejected, down the steps or at all. Under other circumstances, the conductor might not be using more force than was reasonably necessary to eject the passenger from the train. If the conductor has the right to eject a passenger, then he has the right in a decent and orderly way to take hold of the person of the passenger for the purpose of requiring such passenger to leave the train, if the passenger refuses otherwise to do so. And so we are of the opinion that under the evidence the conduct of the conductor in ejecting Tiny Clark from the train was not so rude or offensive as to authorize the recovery of more than compensatory damages. The conductor on this occasion was confronted by an unusual situation. Acting in the line of his duty, he had the right to require these people to leave the train, some of them willingly did so, others refused, and at least some of those who refused were disorderly and under the influence of liquor. If, in an effort to require those who were disorderly or under the influence of liquor or who refused to leave the train, the conductor was obliged to take hold of them, the company should not be punished by the allowance of smart money for his acts in so doing. As the appellees, although entitled to compensation, were not entitled to exemplary damages, these cases must be reversed, because we are unable to say how much the jury awarded as compensation and how much as smart money. If the jury had separated their findings of compensatory and exemplary damages, and the sum awarded for compensation was not excessive, we would yet reverse the judgment, but would feel authorized to direct a remitter of the amount awarded as smart money, leaving the remainder of the judgment to stand. And this condition brings sharply to our attention the fact that it would be advisable and proper for trial courts in all cases in which compensatory as well as exemplary damages are deemed by them allowable to instruct the jury to find separately the damages awarded for each. This practice, although it may be regarded as an innovation, is not entirely new and is followed by some of the trial courts. It would save a retrial of many cases, and consequently avoid the delay necessarily incident to the granting of new trials. Nor would it do any injustice to either party. If the plaintiff is en-

Louisville & N. R. Co. v. Scott

titled to compensation, and nothing more, there seems no good reason why the amount in excess of compensation, if due to an erroneous instruction, should not be ordered to be remitted by this court, leaving the judgment in other respects to stand. We have authority for this in C. & O. Ry. Co. v. Judd, 106 Ky. 364, 50 S. W. 539, 20 Ky. Law Rep. 1978. In that case the jury separated their finding of damages, allowing $13,500 as compensation, and $5,000 as smart money. The court, holding that the plaintiff was not entitled to exemplary damages and that the instruction permitting the jury to assess such damages was erroneous, said: "It seems to us that this instruction would probably lead the jury to believe that they might find punitive damages in a case of mere ordinary negligence. We are not inclined to the opinion that under the testimony in this case ordinary negligence could or should be considered gross negligence. And inasmuch as the jury has separated its finding as to compensatory and punitive damages, * * * we are of opinion that the ends of justice will be subserved by reversing so much of the verdict and judgment as allows any punitive damages, but allowing the verdict and judgment to the extent of $13,500 to stand. The judgment appealed from is therefore reversed, and the cause remanded, with directions to the court below to set aside the $5,000 verdict and judgment for punitive damages, and to render judgment only for $13,500."

In reference to the admission of incompetent evidence, it may be said that there was some evidence permitted to go to the jury relating to the arrest of appellees for disturbing the peace in Cave City, although in an instruction the jury were properly told to disregard this evidence, as there was no evidence connecting the company with the arrest. However, upon another trial of the case, no evidence upon this question should be admitted unless it is sufficient to show that the company procured the wrongful arrest.

For the error indicated, the judgment in each case must be reversed, and it is so ordered.

Lovell v. Boston & M. R. Co.

(Supreme Court of New Hampshire, Hillsborough, Dec. 6, 1910.)

[78 Atl. Rep. 621.]

Contracts—Validity—What Law Governs.—The validity of a contract is governed by the law of the place of the contract; and, where that law forbids the making of a contract, it will not be enforced in New Hampshire, and a contract which is valid where made will usually be enforced in New Hampshire.

Contracts—Validity—What Law Governs.—The validity of a contract and the legality of an act to be done under it are distinct, for the making of a contract is an act which depends for its validity on the law of the place; the test of the validity of a contract being to inquire whether the law of the place forbids the parties to make it, and not whether such law forbids them to do the acts it contemplates, nor whether the parties are forbidden to do the acts by the law of the place where they are to be done.

Sunday—Validity of Contracts.—A contract executed on Sunday in Vermont for the transportation by a carrier of an animal to New Hampshire through Massachusetts is invalid because such a contract is prohibited by the law of Vermont, so that the contract, though it would have been valid if made in Massachusetts, is not effective to limit the liability of the carrier for injuries to the animal while transported through Massachusetts.

Sunday—Validity of Contracts.—The fact that a carrier receiving and contracting on Sunday for the transportation of an animal completed the shipment under the contract at a time it could have legally made the contract, and the fact that the shipper accepted the animal on its arrival at destination, did not show that the shipper recognized the contract as valid, and did not prevent him from relying on the invalidity of the contract because made on Sunday.

Exceptions from Superior Court, Hillsborough County; Chamberlin, Judge.

Action by L. T. Lovell against the Boston & Maine Railroad for injuring plaintiff's mare while transporting her from Bellows Falls, Vt., to Nashua by way of Ayer Junction, Mass. There was a verdict granting insufficient relief, and plaintiff brings exceptions. Sustained.

On Sunday, July 26, 1908, the plaintiff delivered the mare to the defendants and signed the contract on which they rely. The mare left Bellows Falls Sunday afternoon, was injured at Ayer Junction some time the same night, was shipped thence Monday morning, and was accepted by the plaintiff on arrival at Nashua. An employee of the plaintiff accompanied the mare in transit. By the contract of shipment, the plaintiff agreed that, in the event of loss or damage, the defendants' liability should be limited to

Lovell v. Boston & M. R. Co

$100, and they contended that he was not entitled to recover more than that sum in this action. The plaintiff claimed that the contract relied upon by the defendants was invalid, and sought to recover the full value of the mare on the ground that the defendants' liability was that imposed by the common law upon a common carrier of freight. At the close of all the evidence, the court ruled that the plaintiff could recover no more than $100, and directed a verdict for him in that sum, and the plaintiff excepted.

Doyle & Lucier, for plaintiff.
Edgar J Rich, Matthew Hale, and *Hamblett & Spring*, for defendants.

Young, J. The defendants concede that if the contract "is void because executed on Sunday, and the plaintiff is in a position to interpose this objection," his exception should be sustained. Their first position is that the contract is valid, notwithstanding the parties were forbidden to make it by the lex loci contractus, because it would have been legal if made in Massachusetts, the place where it was to be performed in part and where the accident happened, or because so much of the carriage as was to be done in that state was legal; in other words, they say that at common law the validity of a contract is to be determined by the law of the place where it is to be performed. If by the common law is intended the common law as it is understood in Massachusetts, where the accident happened, the validity of this contract must be determined by the law of Vermont; for, if this action were pending in that commonwealth, that is the rule which would be applied to determine the validity of the contract. 23 Harv. Law Rev. 98, where the Massachusetts cases on this question are cited. That would seem to be a complete answer to the defendants' first position. Limerick Nat. Bank v. Howard, 71 N. H. 13, 51 Atl. 641, 93 Am. St. Rep. 489.

But, however that may be, if it is assumed that the validity of the contract is to be determined by the view of the common law which obtains in this jurisdiction, the defendants' contention cannot be sustained; for the reasoning of Barter v. Wheeler, 49 N. H. 9, 29, 6 Am. Rep. 434, and the cases which follow it, on which the defendants rely, do not sustain the contention that the validity of a contract is to be determined by the law of the place in which it is to be performed. All these cases hold is that a contract will be interpreted in accordance with the law of the place in which it is to be performed (Limerick Nat. Bank v. Howard, 71 N. H. 13, 51 Atl. 641, 93 Am. St. Rep. 489; Rixford v. Smith, 52 N. H. 355, 362, 13 Am. Rep. 42; Gray v. Jackson, 51 N. H. 9, 12 Am. Rep. 1; Barter v. Wheeler, 49 N. H. 9, 6 Am. Rep. 434), and not that its validity is to be determined in that way (Davis v. Osgood, 69 N. H. 427, 44 Atl. 432; Little v. Riley, 43 N. H. 109,

Lovell v. Boston & M. R. Co

113). In short, the reasoning of these cases presupposes a contract the parties were permitted, or at least not forbidden, to make by the lex loci contractus, and they hold that even such a contract will not be enforced when it would not be legal if made in the place in which it is to be performed. Thayer v. Elliott, 16 N. H. 102. These cases therefore do not sustain the contention that this court will enforce a contract the parties were forbidden to make by the lex loci contractus, when it appears that it would have been legal if made in the place in which it was to be performed. Neither does the rule usually applied in this jurisdiction to determine when a contract made in one place, but to be performed in another, is valid. According to that, the validity of the contract is to be determined by the lex loci contractus. In other words, a contract the lex loci contractus forbids the parties to make will not be enforced in this jurisdiction (Davis v. Osgood, 69 N. H. 427, 44 Atl. 432); but one which is valid where it is made will usually be enforced here (Seely v. Insurance Co., 72 N. H. 49, 55 Atl. 425; Dorntee Casket Co. v. Gunnison, 69 N. H. 297, 45 Atl. 318; Cleveland Machine Works v. Lang, 67 N. H. 348, 31 Atl. 20, 68 Am. St. Rep. 675).

Although all contracts to do an illegal act are invalid, the converse of that proposition is not true. It does not follow from the fact that the carriage of the mare on Sunday was legal in Massachusetts that the contract under which it was done was valid. The legality of an act and the validity of the contract under which it is to be done are as separate and distinct entitles as the act of making the contract and that of doing any of the things it contemplates. The making of a contract is an act and, like all other acts, depends for its validity on the law of the place where it is done; so, when the contract is not made in the place in which it is to be performed, its validity depends on the law of one jurisdiction, and the legality of the act to be done on that of another. A contract may be invalid when the act to be done is legal, both where the contract is made and where it is to be performed (Davis v. Osgood, 69 N. H. 427, 44 Atl. 432), for, not only is a contract to do an illegal act invalid, but one to do a legal act is also invalid if it is made at a time or in a way the lex loci contractus forbids the parties to make it. The test therefore to determine the validity of a contract is to inquire whether the lex loci contractus forbids the parties to make it—not whether it forbids them to do the act or acts it contemplates, nor whether the parties are forbidden to do them by the law of the place where they are to be done. If this test is applied to the facts in this case, the contract is invalid because made at a time when the parties were forbidden to make it by the law of Vermont, the lex loci contractus. This makes it unnecessary to consider the defendants' contention that the common law permits the making of the contract when the act is

Lovell v. Boston & M. R. C

legal in the place in which it is to be done, e\
be illegal if done in the place where the contr
to that contention no opinion is intended to b

The second question to be considered is w\
is in a position to interpose" the objection
invalid because made on Sunday. The answ
depends on whether he has recognized the con:
it could have been legally made by the law of
St. John, 51 Vt. 334, 345. The fact that t\
pleted the shipment of the mare at a time v
been legal to make the contract has no tende:
to prove that the plaintiff recognized it. T\
that he is bound by the acts of the man in (
or that that man was authorized to do anyth
for the mare while in transit. It may well b
tiff had accompanied the mare, his permitt
to continue the shipment on Monday would
the contract; but he did not accompany her.
that the plaintiff accepted the mare on her
sustain a finding that he recognized the co
nothing else he could do; and accepting her 1
stances was at least as consistent with an in:
as with one to recognize the contract. The c
effect, that the defendants would carry the p
Bellows Falls to Nashua for a definite ar
assume the risk of her reaching there in :
them what they were to receive for doing
quently the question whether he has receive
what they did in pursuance of the contract (
the loss he sustained because of the injury to
or less than the difference between the sum h
he would have had to pay, but for the speci:
facts are understood, his loss is much greater
Consequently it is unnecessary to consider '
Vermont permits a person who receives and
of what is done under a contract.to deny its '

Plaintiff's exception sustained. All concurr

VANZANT *v.* SOUTHERN RY. Co. *et al.*

(Supreme Court of Georgia, Dec. 14, 1910.)

[69 S. E. Rep. 721.]

Removal of Causes—Separable Controversy.*—An action, which is brought in a state court by a resident plaintiff against a nonresident railroad corporation and its resident servants jointly, to recover damages in excess of $2,000 for the homicide of the plaintiff's son, involves no separable controversy between the plaintiff and the defendant corporation, entitling the latter to remove the cause on that ground to the Circuit Court of the United States, where the declaration states a prima facie case of joint and concurrent liability against all of the defendants; and this is true, even though a servant of the company participating in the alleged acts of negligence is not a party to the case.

(Syllabus by the Court.)

Error from Superior Court, Fulton County; J. T. Pendleton, Judge.

Action by H. G. Vanzant against the Southern Railway Company and others. From an order granting a removal to the United States court, plaintiff brings error. Reversed.

A. H. Davis, for plaintiff in error.
McDaniel, Alston & Black, for defendants in error.

HOLDEN, J. The plaintiff brought suit against the Southern Railway Company, one of its conductors, and one of its brakemen, for damages caused by the homicide of the son of the plaintiff, making, among others, substantially the following allegations: The deceased was employed by the railway company as a brakeman on one of its freight trains; and while undertaking, in the discharge of his duty, to cross one of the company's tracks, a train other than the one on which he was brakeman, while backing and running at a speed of 10 or 15 miles an hour, struck and killed him. Paragraphs 6, 7, and 8 of the petition are as follows:

"(6) The hour at which this happened was at about 5 minutes after 12 a. m. of July 23d. It was in the nighttime. The train which ran over and killed deceased was being negligently operated by the defendants in the following respects; (a) Said train was running at a greater rate of speed than six miles per hour, although a valid ordinance of the city of Atlanta limits the speed of all trains to six miles per hour; said provision being found in section 1360 of the Code of 1895 of said city, which reads as follows: 'Any engineer or other person in charge of an engine, with or

---

*See foot-note of Southern Ry. Co. *v.* Miller (U. S.), 36 R. R. R. 189, 59 Am. & Eng. R. Cas., N. S., 189.

without cars attached, who shall run the same through any part of the city at a greater rate of speed than six miles an hour, shall, on conviction, be fined not more than five hundred dollars, or imprisoned not longer than thirty days, either or both, in the discretion of the recorder's court.' (b) There were no lights upon the front end of the car, and no brakeman or flagman there to warn any person on the crossing of the approach of the train. (c) There was no flagman or switchman stationed at the crossing or preceding the forward car, to warn persons at the crossing and prevent them from being run over. (d) Defendant employees and defendant company knew the usual mode of operating freight train No. 86, which was then passing Fair street in full view of said defendants, who knew the custom of the brakeman to get waybills for his train at Fair street, and yet neither they nor either of them took any precaution or used any diligence to avoid injuring deceased, but, on the contrary, so recklessly and negligently managed the train on north-bound main line as to run over and kill deceased.

"(7) Plaintiff charges that defendant Hardwick was the brakeman in charge of the forward end of the train which killed deceased, and that it was within his power and duty to control the movements and speed of his train by giving signals to the engineer, and it was further his duty to display a light at the forward end of the foremost car of his train, as provided by the following rule of defendant company: 'When cars are pushed by an engine (except when shifting or making up trains in yards), a white light must be displayed on the front of the leading car by night;' and that it was further his duty to take position on the front of the leading car, as provided by the following rule of defendant company: 'When cars are pushed by an engine (except when shifting and making up trains in yards), a flagman must take a conspicuous position on the front of the leading car and signal the engineman in case of need.' Plaintiff charges that both rules quoted in this paragraph were well known to all of the defendants, as well as to the deceased, and that no one of the defendants complied with either of said rules on the train which killed deceased at the time he was killed. Plaintiff further charges that the engine pushing the cars which ran over deceased was not at that time 'shifting or making up trains in yards' and was not 'shifting and making up trains in yards.'

"(8) Plaintiff shows that defendant Russ was the conductor in charge of the train which killed deceased, and as such had the authority and the duty to control and regulate the movements of said train according to law and with proper diligence, and it was further his duty to see that the train was properly run without negligence for the safety of employees of other trains, who in the course of their duty came properly and with his knowledge within the sphere of action of his own train, and that it was especially his duty to see that his train did not run too fast over a public crossing, and that at such places the rules of the company were observed in regard to displaying lights and having the flagman or brakeman on the front end of the leading car, or else a flagman or switchman preceding the leading car on the ground. Plaintiff charges that said conductor failed to perform these duties, and concurred with the other defendants in running said train negligently and with reckless disregard of the safety of deceased, as aforesaid."

Upon application of the railway company, alleging that it was a nonresident corporation and that the plaintiff was a resident of this state, the court ordered that the case be removed for trial to the next Circuit Court of the United States for the Northern District of Georgia; and to this order the plaintiff filed exceptions.

1. One of the grounds upon which the railroad company sought a removal of the case to the federal court was that a separable controversy was shown between defendant and the plaintiff in the allegation of negligence, wherein it was stated that the train was run at a greater speed than six miles per hour, in violation of an ordinance of the city of Atlanta, within the limits of which the train was being run. Another ground was that a separable controversy existed between defendant company and the plaintiff, by reason of an allegation as follows: "There was no flagman or switchman stationed at the crossing, or preceeding the forward car, to warn persons at the crossing and prevent them from being run over." We do not think a separable controversy was presented by either of the allegations of negligence above referred to. The petition alleged "The train which ran over and killed deceased was being negligently operated by the defendants in the following respects." Then followed the allegations of negligence, including those above referred to. It was further alleged in the petition, with reference to the brakeman, that "it was within his power and duty to control the movements and speed of his train by giving signals to the engineer." The suit having been brought against the brakeman and the conductor, the allegations that the train was being negligently operated "by the defendants" in the manner stated could have no other meaning than that the brakeman and conductor were engaged in the negligent acts referred to. The allegation that it was within the power and duty of the brakeman to control the movements and speed of the train, coupled with the allegation that the defendants (which included the brakeman) were guilty of negligence in operating the train at a speed exceeding six miles per hour in violation of the city ordinance, necessarily meant that such negligent operation of the train involved the negligent conduct of the brakeman. It is not distinctly stated in what way the brakeman was connected with the negligent act, alleged to consist in there being "no flagman or switchman

Vanzant *v.* Southern Ry. Co. et al

stationed at the crossing or preceding the forward car;" but this is one of the allegations of negligence referred to in the averment of the petition that the train which killed the deceased was being negligently run by the defendants "in the following respects."

The petition having generally charged acts of negligence alleged to be the joint acts of the defendants, the court has no right to say that any separate controversy existed between the plaintiff and any one of the defendants. The plaintiff had a right to bring the suit as he saw fit, and the question as to whether any one defendant was properly charged with an act of negligence alleged against him is not for determination upon a motion to remove the case to the federal court. The conductor was never served, and a return of non est inventus was made by the sheriff as to him. No act of negligence of the company through the conductor, with which the brakeman was wholly disconnected, is alleged to have itself caused the death of the deceased. The alleged negligent acts of the conductor formed only a part of the controversy. Every act of negligence alleged to have caused the death of the deceased is averred to have been concurred in by the brakeman. The brakeman is alleged to have concurred in every act of negligence generally and specially alleged against the conductor, and the latter is alleged to have participated in every act of negligence generally and specially alleged against the former. Hence it makes no difference whether or not the conductor be considered a party to the case, and we do not think there is any merit in that ground of the motion seeking a removal of the case wherein it is alleged that the acts of negligence charged against the conductor, he being no party to the case, are acts of negligence charged against the company in which the brakeman did not participate, and form a separate controversy between the plaintiff and the railway company. If the brakeman committed an act of negligence causing the homicide, the mere fact that the conductor had the authority and it was his duty to prevent the commission of such act, and he failed to prevent it, and that this amounted to negligence on his part, would only form a part of the controversy, and would be inseparably interwoven with the negligence alleged against the brakeman. If the failure of the conductor to have the brakeman perform his duty would be a negligent act giving a right of action, it would necessarily involve a failure of duty on the part of the brakeman, another employee of the railway company, and for whose negligence the company and the brakeman would be jointly responsible. If the negligent act of the conductor could not be one giving a cause of action, without necessarily involving a negligent act of the brakeman relating to the same matter which would give a cause of action, such negligent act of the conductor would only form a part of the controversy, and would not constitute a controversy separate and distinct from the one alleged to exist by reason of

Vanzant v. Southern Ry. Co. et al

the negligent acts of the brakeman.   Where joint and concurrent acts of negligence are alleged against a railroad company and several of its servants, for which they are jointly and severally liable, the fact that all of the servants are not parties defendant does not make a separable controversy removable   under the federal statute.   Fox v. Mackay (C. C.) 60 Fed. 4.

Another ground upon which it was sought to have the case re-moved was that the words "defendant employees," used in the sixth paragraph of the petition, included all of the employees of the railway company in charge of the movements of the train. Whether or not a separable controversy would exist, if this was true, need not be considered, for the reason that the words "defendant employees" only included the brakeman and conductor, who were the employees of the railway company, and who were the only named defendants in the suit other than the railway company.   Besides, the acts of negligence "by the defendant employees and defendant company" were acts of negligence referred to in the allegation charging that the train which killed deceased "was being negligently operated by the defendants in the following respects."   The question as to whether or not there is a separable controversy must be determined from the pleadings of the plaintiff.   The fact that a resident defendant might interpose defense which, if sustained, would relieve him of liability and would leave a controversy only between the plaintiff and the nonresident defendant, does not make a case for removal.   In Louisville & Nashville Railroad Co. v. Ide, 114 U. S. 52, 56, 5 Sup. Ct. 735, 737 (29 L. Ed. 63), it was said: "A defendant has no right to say that an action shall be several which a plaintiff elects to make joint.   Smith v. Rines, 2 Sumn. 338 [Fed. Cas. No. 13,100].   A separate defense may defeat a joint recovery, but it cannot deprive a plaintiff of his right to prosecute his own suit to final determination in his own way.   The cause of action is the subject-matter of the controversy, and that is, for all the purposes of the suit, whatever the plaintiff declares it to be in his pleadings."   All of the defendants are jointly charged with every act alleged to have caused the death of the son of the plaintiff, and the court committed error in granting an order removing the case to the federal court.   In this connection, see 2 Foster's Fed. Prac. § 384; Elliott on Railroads, §§ 650, 650a; Ala. Great So. Ry. Co. v. Thompson, 200 U. S. 206, 26 Sup. Ct. 161, 50 L. Ed. 441, 4 Am. & Eng. Ann. Cas. 1147; Note to Wecker v. Nat., etc., Co., 9 Am. & Eng. Ann. Cas. 757; Miller v. Clifford, 133 Fed. 880, 67 C. C. A. 52, 5 L. R. A. (N. S.) 49; Louisville & N. R. Co. v. Vincent, 116 Tenn. 317, 95 S. W. 179, 8 Am. & Eng. Ann. Cas. 66; Fox v. Mackay (C. C.) Fed. 4.

Judgment reversed.   All the Justices concur.

JOHN *v.* NORTHERN PAC. RY.

(Supreme Court of Montana. Oct. 11, 1910. On
ing, Nov. 10, 1910.)

[111 Pac. Rep. 632.]

Carriers — Passengers — Injuries — Instruction
against a railroad company for injuries received
plaintiff was traveling on a free pass, furnished hii
official of another railroad company, which exen
liability for injuries caused by its negligence or
charged, on plaintiff's request, that a common c
onerated by any agreement from liability for the
itself or servants, so that, if defendant was guilty
causing plaintiff's injuries, the jury must find
that plaintiff, by tendering the instruction, tacitlj
theory that plaintiff was riding on a free pass
question in addition to that of damages was wh
guilty of gross negligence.

**Carriers — Passengers — Action for Injuries-
Negligence.**—Rev. Codes, § 5299, requires a cari
out reward to use ordinary care for their safe
requires a carrier for reward to use the utmost
reasonable degree of skill. Held, that a carrier c
of diligence to one carried for a reward than to
a reward, and was only bound to exercise ordinai
of a passenger carried without reward so that
passenger by the happening of an accident or
negligence by the carrier, and not gross negligʏ

Carriers—Passengers—Injuries—Presumption
presumption of the carrier's negligence arises fr
an accident injuring a passenger, which is cau:
over which the carrier has control.

**Carriers—Passengers—Injuries—Action—Burdı
Negligence.**—Since the happening of an accident
being carried without reward is only evidence
care by the carrier, such a passenger must offer
the presumption, in order to show gross neglig

Negligence — Presumptions — Res Ipsa Loqu

---

*See last foot-note of Taber *v.* Seaboard A.
R. R. R. 466, 59 Am. & Eng. R. Cas., N. S., 46
Gardner *v.* Metropolitan St. R. Co. (Mo.), 36 R
& Eng. R. Cas., N. S., 448; foot-note of Blew *v*
Transit Co. (Pa.), 36 R. R. R. 447, 59 Am. &
447; second foot-note of Williford *v.* Southerɴ
R. R. R. 693, 58 Am. & Eng. R. Cas., N. S.,
sacola Elec. Co. *v.* Alexander (Fla.), 35 R. R. R.
R. Cas., N. S., 193; St. Louis, etc., R. Co. *v.*
R. 443, 57 Am. & Eng. R. Cas., N. S., 442.

John v. Northern Pac. Ry. Co

presumption of want of care, raised by the res ipsa loquitur doctrine, is a want of ordinary care.

Carriers—Passengers—Contract—Exemption from Liability for Negligence.†—A common carrier of passengers may contract to exempt itself from liability for the ordinary negligence of itself or its servant.

Carriers—Passengers—Contract of Carriage—Free Passes—Validity.‡—Const. art. 15, § 7, provides that all individuals shall have equal

---

†For the authorities in this series on the subject of the power of a carrier of passengers to exempt itself from liability, see note at end of case.

‡For the authorities in this series on the subject of free passes, see foot-note of St. Louis, etc., Ry. Co. v. Pitcock (Ark.), 25 R. R. R. 79, 48 Am. & Eng. R. Cas., N. S., 79 (validity of stipulation in free pass purporting to exempt carrier from, or limit its liability); Indianapolis, etc., Co. v. Lawson (C. C. A.), 24 R. R. R. 219, 47 Am. & Eng. R. Cas., N. S., 219 (degree of care due passenger carried free); second foot-note of Harris v. Puget Sound Elec. Ry. (Wash.), 34 R. R. R. 43, 57 Am. & Eng. R. Cas., N. S., 43 (whether railroad employees while riding on passes are passengers); Louisville & N. R. Co. v. Mottley (Ky.), 32 R. R. R. 506, 55 Am. & Eng. R. Cas., N. S., 506 (application of Act Cong. June 29, 1906, c. 3591, § 1, 34 Stat. 584, prohibiting any common carrier from giving any interstate free transportation for passengers); Reed v. Chicago, etc., R. Co. (Neb.), 32 R. R. R. 469, 55 Am. & Eng. R. Cas., N. S., 469 (permit to ride on freight trains, issued without consideration, may be revoked at any time when the holder is not a passenger); Louisville & N. R. Co. v. Mottley (U. S.), 31 R. R. R. 38, 54 Am. & Eng. R. Cas., N. S., 38 (suit to compel specific performance of carrier's agreement to issue free passes was not brought within original jurisdiction of Federal Circuit Court, by certain allegations of the bill); State v. Martyn (Neb.), 30 R. R. R. 136, 53 Am. & Eng. R. Cas., N. S., 136 ("Anti Pass Law" of Nebraska, certain contract between railroad and physician employed by it is prohibited by; and such law is a valid exercise of the police power of the state); Indianapolis Trac. & Term. Co. v. Lawson (C. C. A.), 24 R. R. R. 219, 47 Am. & Eng. R. Cas., N. S., 219 (whether one riding free is a passenger); Marshall v. Nashville, etc., Co. (Tenn.), 25 R. R. R. 151, 48 Am. & Eng. R. Cas., N. S., 151 (liability of carrier to one riding on pass); Bradburn v. Whatcom County Ry. & Light Co. (Wash.), 22 R. R. R. 782, 45 Am. & Eng. R. Cas., N. S., 782 (street railway was liable where officer was injured while being carried free in compliance with ordinance, though the ordinance was in conflict with Wash. Const., art. 2, § 39, prohibiting the granting of passes to police officers); Marshall v. Nashville R., etc., Co. (Tenn.), 25 R. R. R. 151, 48 Am. & Eng. R. Cas., N. S., 151 (consideration for pass given to member of police force by street railway); McNeil v. Durham, etc., Co. (N. Car.), 8 R. R. R. 285, 31 Am. & Eng. R. Cas., N. S., 285 (editor riding on pass issued in violation of law could not recover for his injuries, he and the railroad being in pari delicto); People v. Wadhams (N. Y.), 9 R. R. R. 635, 32 Am. & Eng. R. Cas., N. S. 635 (removal from office for violation of constitutional provision prohibiting use of free pass by public officials); McNeil v. Durham, etc., Co. (N. Car.), 8 R. R. R. 285, 31 Am. & Eng. R. Cas., N. S., 285 (whether person riding on an illegal pass is a passenger); Missouri Pac. Ry. Co. v. Henrie (Kan.), 6 Am. & Eng. R. Cas., N. S., 790 (liability of purchaser of railroad on account of life passes issued by predecessor).

John *v.* Northern Pac. Ry. Co

rights to be transported over any railroad in the state, provided that excursion or commutation tickets may be issued and sold at special rates. Rev. Codes, § 4337, makes it unlawful for any common carrier to charge any person for any ticket a greater sum than is charged for a similar ticket of the same class, and section 8524 makes every railroad corporation which fails to observe any of the duties prescribed by law in reference to railroads subject to a fine, etc. Held, that the giving of all free passes, with certain exceptions recognized by law, was prohibited, so that the carriage of a passenger by defendant on a pass issued without compensation to the employee of another railroad company which issued similar free passes for use by defendant's employees was illegal, and hence a provision therein, exempting the carrier from liability for injuries caused by its negligence, was a nullity.

Constitutional Law—Civil Rights—Equality before the Law.—An arbitrary and unreasonable classification by a statute conferring benefits or imposing a penalty contravenes the constitutional principle that all men are equal before the law, and the Legislature in making classifications as for taxation and license purposes must exercise a reasonable discretion.

Statutes—Construction—Remedial Statute.—The court must construe a remedial statute so as to suppress the injury and advance the remedy contemplated by the statute.

Carriers—Construction—Penal Statute.—A statute may be remedial in part and penal in part for purposes of construction, so that the penalty clause of Rev. Codes, § 4337, making it unlawful for any carrier to transfer a person for a less sum than is charged for a similar ticket of the same class, and making any carrier who shall violate the statute guilty of a misdemeanor, and punishable, etc., should be construed according to the fair import of its terms, with a view to effectuating its object as required by section 8096; but the part prohibiting unjust discrimination in charging for transportation should be liberally construed with a view to carrying out the legislative intention.

Carriers—Passenger on Pass—Personal Injuries—Right to Recover.‡—A passenger injured while traveling under a pass furnished him by defendant gratuitously as the officer of another railroad company, but which, including the provision therein exempting defendant from liability for injuries caused by the negligence of itself or servant, was void as issued in contravention of statute, was not in pari delicto with defendant in violating the statute, so as to prohibit recovery for such injuries; the carrier's duty to passengers being imposed by public policy and not founded on the contractual relation between them.

Appeal and Error—Harmless Error—Variance.—Where, in an action against a railroad company for injuries to a passenger, the com-

---

‡See (‡) on preceding page.

John v. Northern Pac. Ry. Co

pany was liable under the evidence as a matter of law, the fact that the court held that plaintiff was not a passenger for hire, contrary to the theory of the complaint, and yet allowed a recovery, was not prejudicial error.

Appeal and Error—Harmless Error—Parties Not Entitled to Succeed.—Where, in an action against a railroad company for injuries to a passenger, plaintiff was, upon the record, entitled to recover damages as a matter of law, any error in an instruction in defining gross negligence was not reversible.

Appeal and Error—Reversal—New Trial Ineffectual.—A judgment will not be reversed because of variance between the pleadings and proof, where it would merely necessitate an amendment to the pleading, resulting in the same verdict.

Damages—Excessive Damages—Personal Injuries.—A railroad passenger was 39 years of age when injured and in perfect health, and received a salary of $1,800 a year. He now suffers intermittently from a pain in the head, his right side is partially paralyzed, and he has no use of his voice; and the medical testimony was that his injuries were probably permanent and would eventually cause his death, while another witness testified that he was now a physical wreck. Held, that a verdict for him for $25,000 was not excessive.

On Motion for Rehearing.

Carriers — Transportation — Free Passes — Right to Issue.‡—Railroad companies may issue free transportation or sell tickets at reduced rates, as the case may require, to its employees and members of their families; to doctors, nurses, and helpers being taken to wrecks; to soldiers and sailors going to or coming from institutions wherein they are kept; to ministers or persons engaged in charitable and religious works; and, by the direct provision of Rev. Codes, § 4369, to members and employees of the railroad commission traveling on official business, but not when they are traveling on private business, section 4394 prohibiting employees of the commission or the board of commissioners from accepting or requesting any pass for themselves or any other person except as herein otherwise provided.

Holloway, J., dissenting.

Appeal from District Court, Silver Bow County; John B. McClernan, Judge.

Action by Terry A. John against the Northern Pacific Railway Company and another. From a judgment against the defendant named, and from an order denying a motion for new trial, it appeals. Affirmed.

Wm. Wallace, Jr., John G. Brown, and *R. F. Gaines,* for appellant.

Roote & Murray and *J. E. Healy,* for respondent.

---

‡See (‡) on page 485.

John v. Northern Pac. Ry. Co

Smith, J.   This is an appeal by the railway company defendant from a judgment pronounced against it on the verdict of a jury in Silver Bow county, for $25,000, and costs, also from an order denying it a new trial.   The defendant Skones was released from liability on motion for a directed verdict.

The complaint charged that on August 11, 1907, at Butte, the railway company received plaintiff on its passenger train, "and undertook and agreed to transfer him from Butte to Miles City for a certain reward," and that it was its duty to carry him "in safety and with due and proper care."   It further charged that, after he had retired into an upper berth of a sleeping car, the same was negligently, carelessly, and unskillfully derailed, while in rapid motion, and partly turned over, whereby he was thrown out of the berth and injured.   The answer, besides a general denial, admits that, while plaintiff was riding in an upper berth in a car of its passenger train, the car was partly tipped over; but denies that he was received, or was riding, as a passenger, or for a reward, and avers that he boarded the train, intending to ride, and that at the time of the derailment was riding, upon a certain annual pass which he had presented as his ticket and rights to carriage, which pass contained the following conditions: "The person accepting this pass agrees that the Northern Pacific Railway Company shall not be liable under any circumstances, whether of negligence of agents or otherwise, for any injury to the person, or for any loss or damage to the property of the passenger using the same."   It is further alleged "that plaintiff was riding and his rights upon said train were under and pursuant to the terms and provisions of said pass contract of carriage and not otherwise."   The reply admits that the plaintiff had and held this pass, but alleges that it was issued to him as agent of another railroad, the St. Louis & San Francisco Railroad Company, of which he was a general agent, and in consideration of the issuance by such other railroad of annual passes from the latter to certain agents of the defendant company; and avers that his rights were those of a passenger for hire, and not affected by the conditions stated in the pass.

There was no conflict in the evidence.   Desiring to go to Miles City, the plaintiff at about 12:40 a. m., August 12, 1907, at Butte station, boarded train No. 6 of the defendant company, having bought an upper berth in a sleeper from the Pullman Company. The subsequent derailment of the sleeper at a point about seven miles east of Butte caused him to fall from his berth, whereby he was severely and permanently injured.   The cause of the derailment could not be ascertained.   There was no direct evidence of any negligence on the part of the defendant or any of its servants.   The plaintiff was riding on the pass mentioned in the answer, the conditions of which had been by him accepted by signing his name thereto, adding the letters "G. A.," which

John v. Northern Pac. Ry. Co

meant "General Agent." The pass was what is known as an "interchange" pass, and was given to the St. Louis & San Fran-cisco Railroad Company by the defendant company, at the request of the former company, and by it sent to the plaintiff to be used in his business of soliciting passengers and freight for that company. No direct consideration passed for its issuance, but the two railroads were in the habit of exchanging passes for their respective employees, without regard to which company asked for the greater number. The inscription on the face read: "Pass Mr. T. A. John, General Agent St. L. & S. F. R. R." Plaintiff testified that, in his general work of soliciting passengers and freight for his road, certain other railroads, including the defendant company, would receive benefits, by virtue of the fact that such passengers and freight would be carried into and out of Montana over such other roads by connection with his road. He said he had frequently routed goods for his customers so that the shipments would go over the Northern Pacific Road, and that he gave most of the passenger business to that company because it furnished the best service. On the part of the defendant, there was testimony to the effect that there was no consideration for the issuance of such passes, no obligation to issue them, and that their exchange was simply a matter of courtesy between the roads.

At the close of all of the testimony, the defendant moved the court to direct a verdict in its favor, for the following reasons: (a) Because there was no proof that defendant undertook to carry plaintiff for a reward; (b) because mere proof of derailment of the train was no evidence of the actionable negligence toward a person in plaintiff's situation; (c) because of variance between the allegation of the complaint to the effect that plaintiff was being carried for hire, and the proof that he was being carried gratuitously under special contract limiting the liability of the defendant; (d) because plaintiff had voluntarily agreed not to hold the defendant liable for injuries received; (e) because there is no allegation in the complaint of other than ordinary negligence, for which, under its contract, defendant was not liable. The court overruled the motion and instructed the jury, over defendant's objection and on motion of plaintiff, that a common carrier cannot be exonerated by any agreement made in anticipation thereof from any liability for the gross negligence of himself or his servants." "Therefore," the court continued, "if you believe that the defendant corporation was guilty of gross negligence, or that its servants were guilty of gross negligence which proximately caused the derailment of the train, * * * then your verdict must be for the plaintiff." This was the court's instruction No. 1. The court, also over defendant's objection, further charged the jury as follows: "(2) You are instructed that 'gross negligence' is the want of slight care and

John v. Northern Pac. Ry. Co

diligence. 'Gross negligence' is an entire failure to exercise care, or the exercise of so slight a degree of care as to justify the belief that there was an indifference to the rights and welfare of others. * * * (4) The court charges you that the pass on which the plaintiff, John, was riding, on the train of the defendant railway company, at the time of its derailment, was a free or gratuitous pass; that, on account thereof, the defendant railway company cannot be held liable in this case for what is called ordinary negligence; but, before the plaintiff can recover in this action, you must find, by a preponderance or greater weight of the evidence, that the derailment in question was caused by the gross negligence of the defendant railway company, or its agents or servants."

1. We think the district court was correct in charging the jury that John was riding on a free or gratuitous pass. The plaintiff, by tendering instruction No. 1, tacitly assented to this and adopted the court's theory that the only question in the case, aside from that of damages, was whether the defendant had been guilty of gross negligence. It is contended by the defendant that, as the pass was an interstate pass, good over the lines of its road in six states, it was subject to the provisions of the act of Congress approved June 29, 1906, known as the "Hepburn act" (Act June 29. 1906, c. 3591, 34 Stat. 584 [U. S. Comp. St. Supp. 1907, p. 892, Supp. 1909, p. 1149]), and was therefore illegal and void if given in exchange for another pass, for the reason that the act prohibits the receipt of anything save money for transportation. Counsel cite an order of the Interstate Commerce Commission, under date September 15, 1909, and the case of United States v. C., I. & L. Ry. Co. (C. C.) 163 Fed. 114, in support of their position. But we do not find it necessary to base our judgment on this consideration. We find no testimony in the record which would warrant the conclusion that any consideration passed for the giving of the pass. or that it was anything more, as defendant's witnesses testified. than a gratuitous courtesy extended by one railroad company to the other.

2. We are of opinion that the court was in error in submitting to the jury the question of fact whether defendant had been guilty of gross negligence. There is nothing in the record to support an affirmative finding of such negligence. As will be hereafter shown, gross negligence is a matter of proof. But plaintiff's counsel contend that there are, under our laws (1) no degrees of negligence, and (2) that any negligence by which a passenger is injured is gross negligence. We cannot assent to either of these propositions. That degrees of negligence are known to our laws is evidenced by an examination of sections 5253, 5295. 5299, 5300, 5306, 5331, 5354. and 5355, Rev. Codes, and recognized in the cases of Prosser v. Montana C. Ry. Co..

John v. Northern Pac. Ry. Co

17 Mont. 372, 43 Pac. 81, 30 L. R. A. 814; Nelson v. Great Northern Ry. Co., 28 Mont. 297, 72 Pac. 642; Robinson v. Helena L. & Ry. Co., 38 Mont. 222, 99 Pac. 837; and Neary v. Northern Pacific Ry. Co., 41 Mont. —, 110 Pac. 226. That this is so is a matter to be deplored, but the conclusion cannot be avoided. Aside from any question of what the common law was on the subject, plaintiff's second contention is disposed of by the provisions of our statute (sections 5299 and 5300, Rev. Codes, supra), which distinctly recognize the fact that a carrier owes a different and higher duty to a person who is carried for reward, from that owing to one who is carried without reward. Those Code provisions read as follows:

"Sec. 5299. A carrier of persons without reward must use ordinary care and diligence for their safe carriage.

"Sec. 5300. A carrier of persons for reward must use the utmost care and diligence for their safe carriage, must provide everything necessary for that purpose, and must exercise to that end a reasonable degree of skill."

It being the law that a carrier of passengers without reward need only use ordinary care and diligence for their safety, and that a carrier for reward must use the utmost care, it seems to follow that if we should hold this defendant guilty of gross negligence on account of the fact alone that an accident happened, without any evidence as to the cause thereof, we should not only destroy the distinction between gross and ordinary negligence, and slight and ordinary care, but we should be indulging in judicial legislation by declaring that a carrier of passengers without reward must use the utmost care and diligence for their safe carriage, contrary to the expressed will of the Legislature. In case of injury to a passenger, a presumption of negligence arises from the mere fact of an accident, when the injury is caused by some thing or agency for which the carrier is responsible. Knuckey v. Butte Electric Ry. Co., 41 Mont. —, 109 Pac. 979. In the latter case the court said: "Proof of the derailment of the train is sufficient"—citing Pierce v. Great Falls & C. Ry. Co., 22 Mont. 445, 56 Pac. 867, and Hoskins v. Northern Pacific Ry. Co., 39 Mont. 394, 102 Pac. 988. The learned trial judge was evidently of opinion that mere proof of derailment was not prima facie evidence of gross negligence, otherwise he would not have submitted the question whether there was any gross negligence. While it may be true, as contended by plaintiff's counsel, that mere proof of derailment or other accident to a train might under certain circumstances furnish an inference of gross negligence, there are no facts in this case to warrant such conclusion.

3. Plaintiff was a passenger. Not a passenger for reward, but a free passenger. Nevertheless the defendant had undertaken to carry him. It sustained toward him the relation of a

John v. Northern Pac. Ry. Co

carrier without reward and by virtue of section 5299, Rev. Codes, supra, it owed to him the duty of using ordinary care for his safe carriage. It would be liable for ordinary negligence. (This, of course, without consideration of the exemption conditions of the pass.) Section 5298, Rev. Codes, provides that a carrier without reward who has begun to perform his undertaking must complete it in like manner as if he had received a reward, unless he restores the person or thing carried to as favorable a position as before he commenced his carriage. Plaintiff, then, was not a trespasser; nor was he a mere licensee. Having begun his journey with the permission of the defendant, his right to carriage could not be arbitrarily and unconditionally revoked. Defendant was under express legal obligation to do one of the two things mentioned in the statute. At the time of the accident it was in the act of doing the first mentioned. Having determined that plaintiff was a passenger, and that the defendant owed him the duty to refrain from any act of ordinary negligence to his injury, it becomes necessary to ascertain whether a finding of ordinary negligence on the part of the defendant will be justified by the mere fact that the train was derailed.

What degree of negligence is it that is disclosed, as the law presumes, by the fact that a passenger train is derailed? Manifestly, ordinary negligence—a lack of ordinary care. It cannot logically be said that the fact of derailment only raises a presumption of slight negligence, any more than it can be said to raise a presumption of gross negligence. Mr. Thompson, in his admirable and exhaustive work on Negligence (volume 1 [2d Ed.] § 18, p. 19), refers to "the. standard called 'ordinary care.'" He also says in the same connection, commenting upon the common-law duty of a common carrier of passengers to exercise a "very high, exact, and unremitting care and attention:" "But even here it has been often pointed out that the care required of the carrier is no more than reasonable care; that is to say, a care proportioned to the great risks attending his business."

The Supreme Court of the United States, in Philadelphia, P. & R. R. Co. v. Derby, 14 How. 486, 14 L. Ed. 502, and again in Steamboat v. King, 16 How. 469, 14 L. Ed. 1019, said: "When carriers undertake to convey persons by the powerful and dangerous agency of steam, public policy and safety require that they should be held to the greatest possible care and diligence. And, whether the consideration for such transportation be pecuniary or otherwise, the personal safety of passengers should not be left to the sport of chance or the negligence of careless agents. Any negligence in such cases may well deserve the epithet of gross." In both of these cases the plaintiff was being carried gratuitously. While we may not, in the light of our statutes, go so far as to hold, in accordance with the above rulings,

John *v.* Northern Pac. Ry. Co

that any negligence by which a free passenger is injured may be called gross, we feel satisfied that the conclusion is not only logical, but in accordance with the accepted notions of the profession that the term "negligence," standing alone, as applied to a carrier of passengers, should, and does, refer to that common degree, or standard, of negligence known as "ordinary." And in so holding we do no violence to our statutes. Sections 5299 and 5300, Rev. Codes, supra. Those Code provisions in practical application deal, not with presumptions, but with proof. While the presumption arising from the fact of derailment of a passenger train is that the carrier of passengers, both paid and gratuitous, has been guilty of ordinary negligence or a want of ordinary care, and such presumption will serve to make a prima facie case of actionable negligence for either class of passengers, yet when, in the absence of circumstances warranting such presumption, it becomes necessary to prove negligence, it is incumbent upon the free passenger to prove ordinary negligence, while the passenger for reward need only prove slight negligence. A plaintiff relying upon gross negligence must offer proof in supplement of the presumption arising from the fact of derailment; while, on the other hand, derailment being shown, a carrier of passengers without reward has the burden of proving the exercise of ordinary care on his part, and a carrier for reward must show that he exercised the utmost care, in order to escape liability.

Again quoting from Thompson, Law of Negligence, vol. 3 (2d Ed.) § 2754: "In every action by a passenger against a carrier to recover damages predicated upon the negligence or misconduct of the latter, the burden of proof, in the first instance, is of course, upon the plaintiff to connect the defendant in some way with the injury for which he claims damages. But when the plaintiff has sustained and discharged this burden of proof by showing that the injury arose in consequence of the failure, in some respect or other, of the carrier's means of transportation, or the conduct of the carrier's servants, then, in conformity with the maxim *res ipsa loquitur*, a presumption arises of negligence on the part of the carrier or his servants, which, unless rebutted by him to the satisfaction of the jury, will authorize a verdict and judgment against him for the resulting damages. Stated somewhat differently, the general rule may be said to be that where an injury happens to the passenger in consequence of the breaking or failure of the vehicle, roadway, or other appliance owned or controlled by the carrier, and used by him in making the transit, or in consequence of the act, omission, or mistake of his servants, the person entitled to sue for the injury makes out a prima facie case for damages against the carrier, by proving the contract of carriage, that the accident happened in consequence of such breaking or failure, or such act, omission, or mis-

John v. Northern Pac. Ry. Co

take of his servants, and that, in consequence of the accident, the plaintiff sustained damage." It will be observed that the author employs the words "passenger" and "negligence" without any qualification. Again: "It is the essential nature of this presumption that it stands in the place of actual proof of negligence, until it is rebutted and overthrown. This presumption would not be a presumption—would not have any evidentiary value for the purpose of influencing the practical result of the trial—unless the court were allowed to explain it to the jury. The nature of the presumption is such that, unless rebutted to the satisfaction of the jury, it decides the case in favor of the plaintiff, upon his making proof of the damages sustained; or, to say the least, it takes the question of the negligence of the carrier to the jury. If there is no countervailing evidence, nothing to explain the accident consistently with due care on the part of the defendant, the plaintiff is plainly, by force of this presumption, entitled to a verdict, and no sound reason is perceived why the judge should not be allowed to so instruct the jury." 3 Thompson on Negligence, § 2770.

This court in the case of Hardesty v. Largey Lumber Co., 34 Mont. 151, 86 Pac. 29, through Mr. Justice Holloway, said: "It may be conceded that, unaided by any presumption, the evidence offered by plaintiff is insufficient to charge the defendant with negligence. But counsel for respondent invoke the doctrine of the maxim 'res ipsa loquitur,' and insist that this case as made by the plaintiff presents an instance wherein the presumption of defendant's negligence arises from the proof of the accident. Of course. the general rule of law is that negligence is not inferable from the mere occurrence of the accident; but to this rule is the well-understood exception that, where the thing which causes the injury is shown to be under the management and control of the defendant, and the accident is such as in the ordinary course of things does not happen if those who have such management and control use proper care, it affords reasonable evidence, in the absence of explanation by the defendant, that the accident arose from the want of ordinary care by the defendant. Under such circumstances, proof of the happening of the event raises a presumption of the defendant's negligence, and casts upon the defendant the burden of showing that ordinary care was exercised."

Section 5244, Rev. Codes, reads as follows: "An employer must in all cases indemnify his employee for losses caused by the former's want of ordinary care." In the Hardesty Case, supra, the court distinctly held that this section is directly applicable to cases arising between master and servant on account of personal injuries sustained by the latter in the course of his employment. and that an instruction embodying it was properly submitted to the jury. This being so, there can be no longer any question in this state that, where the doctrine of the maxim "res

John v. Northern Pac. Ry. Co

ipsa loquitur" may be invoked to raise a presumption of want of care, it is want or ordinary care to which reference is made. A master owes the same duty to his servant that a carrier owes to an unpaid passenger; that is, to exercise ordinary care for his safety. The statutes so declare. Indeed, we find the following statement in the brief of counsel for the appellant: "Derailment never creates a presumption of gross, or of any other than ordinary negligence." The Supreme Court of North Carolina, in Wright v. Southern Railroad Co., 127 N. C. 225, 229, 37 S. E. 221, 222, said: "This presumption [of negligence] extends to the occurrence, regardless of the party injured."

We therefore hold that the happening of the accident complained of by the plaintiff raised a presumption of want of ordinary care on the part of the defendant, and that the district court should have so charged the jury.

4. But it is contended by counsel for the appellant that a common carrier, in this state, may by agreement exonerate himself from liability for the ordinary negligence of himself or his servants. That such is the law is settled by the case of Nelson v. Great Northern Ry. Co., 28 Mont. 297, 321, 72 Pac. 642, 649, where this court, after quoting sections 2876 and 2877 of the Civil Code of 1895 (now sections 5338 and 5339, Rev. Codes), said: "These two sections, construed together, give to the carrier the right by special contract to provide against liability in all cases except when it arises from his gross negligence, fraud, or willful wrong." See, also, Rose v. Northern Pacific Ry. Co., 25 Mont. 70, 88 Pac. 767, 119 Am. St. Rep. 836, and Donlon Bros. v. Southern Pac. Ry., 151 Cal. 763, 91 Pac. 603, 11 L. R. A. (N. S.) 811.

It is further contended that, as to the plaintiff, the defendant was not a common carrier; and, further, that it had been expressly exonerated from liability from its negligence, by the contract on the back of the pass. But it is immaterial whether the defendant was technically a common carrier or not. If it was, and the pass-contract was valid, it was exonerated from liability, for ordinary negligence, by virtue of the terms thereof; and, if it was not, it nevertheless owed to plaintiff the duty of exercising ordinary care for his safe carriage.

5. This brings us to a consideration of an important question: Is the giving of absolutely free passes prohibited by the Constitution or statute of this state? The question is one of first impression, and, so far as we are advised, has never been raised in this jurisdiction. Indeed, it is matter of everyday knowledge that the idea has prevailed, since 1903 at least, that the practice has not been illegal, and that additional legislation was necessary in order to make it so. This is evidenced by the fact that measures designed to prohibit the giving of free transportation have since been often advocated and have been intro-

duced in the legislative assembly, but has nev
laws.

Section 7, art. 15, of the state Constitutio
as follows: "All individuals, associations an
have equal rights to have persons or property
over any railroad, transportation or express
No discrimination in charges or facilities fc
freight or passengers of the same class sha
railroad, or transportation, or express compai
or places within this state; but excursion or
may be issued and sold at special rates, prov
the same to all persons."

Mr. Justice Hunt, in the case of Butte, Ai
Co. v. Montana Union Ry. Co., 16 Mont.
232, 239 (31 L. R. A. 298, 50 Am. St. Rep
upon this constitutional provision, said: "T
considered with section 5 of article 15, dei
Constitution, in its letter, its spirit, and its pc
all railroads as public highways, subject to u
right, amenable to the laws governing comm
forbidding all obnoxious favoritisms betwee
to use such highways. This stable written
the outgrowth of pernicious systems of discr
erence which railroad corporations may have i
out the land where their powers are unrest
tional or other restrictions."

Section 4337, Rev. Codes, is entitled "Discri
Forbidden," and reads, in part, as follows: "
ful for any * * * common carrier * * *
collect or receive from, to sell, barter, transfi
person * * * any ticket * * * of any
titling the purchaser or holder thereof to tr
common carrier issuing such ticket, * * * f
sum or price than is charged, demanded, colle
* * * such common carrier * * * for a si
of the same class. Any * * * common c
* * * shall violate the provisions of this sec
of a misdemeanor and upon conviction there
the sum not exceeding one thousand dollars f

In addition to the foregoing, under the titl
against the Public Health and Safety." we
Rev. Codes, which reads as follows: "Every
tion who owns, carries on or has control of
to observe any of the duties prescribed by
railroads, the penalty for which is not otherwi
this Code, is punishable by a fine not excee
dollars."

Stripped of those portions which are not
this investigation, the constitutional provision

John v. Northern Pac. Ry. Co

"All individuals * * * shall have equal rights to have persons * * * transported on or over any railroad * * * in this state." We understand this to mean that all persons have equal natural rights to be carried on any railroad in the state. "No discrimination in charges * * * for transportation of * * * passengers of the same class shall be made by any railroad between persons * * * within this state." And the Code provision (section 4337, Rev. Codes) reads thus: "It is * * * unlawful * * * for any common carrier * * * to transfer * * * to any person * * * any ticket * * * of any class whatever entitling the * * * holder thereof to transportation * * * for a * * * less sum or price than is charged * * * by such common carrier * * * for a similar ticket * * * of the same class." Or it may perhaps be read thus: "It is * * * unlawful * * * for any common carrier * * * to charge * * * any person (for) any ticket * * * of any class whatever entitling the purchaser * * * to transportation * * * a greater sum or price than is charged by such common carrier * * * for a similar ticket * * * of the same class." The phraseology is not to the commended, but the meaning and the principle involved are clear. This section is a part of the so-called "antiscalpers" law, passed in 1903 (Laws 1893, p. 152, § 7), and its purpose, as we understand it, was not only to benefit the railroad companies by driving the ticket brokers out of business, but to provide against loss, so far as possible, to the purchaser of an unused ticket, by requiring that it should, under certain circumstances, be redeemed by the seller; and so it was enacted that the railroad companies, being relieved of the pest of the ticket "scalpers," should themselves be prohibited from indulging in kindred practices, by pernicious discrimination between persons of the same class. To that end it was enacted that the offense should be a misdemeanor and punishable accordingly.

Recurring to the constitutional provision: It is not permitted to a railroad company to arbitrarily classify the patrons of its road. Even the legislative assembly in making classifications for taxation and license purposes must exercise a reasonable discretion in so doing. Quong Wing v. Kirkendall, 39 Mont. 64, 101 Pac. 250. The idea of arbitrary and unreasonable classification for any purpose, when benefits are to be conferred or penalties imposed, is abhorrent to the principles of all American Constitutions. founded, as they are, upon the consideration that all men are equal before the law.

By the report of the case of State v. Southern Railway Co., 122 N. C. 1052, 30 S. E. 133, 41 L. R. A. 246, it appears that the defendant was indicted for an unlawful discrimination in the transportation of passengers under a statute (Laws 1891, c. 320, § 4) of which the following is a copy: "That if any com-

John v. Northern Pac. Ry. Co

mon carrier subject to the provisions of this act shall directly or indirectly, by any special rate, rebate, draw back or other device, charge, demand, collect or receive from any person or persons a greater or less compensation for any services rendered or to be. rendered in the transportation of passengers subject to the provisions of this act, than it charges, demands or collects or receives from any other person or persons for doing for him or them a like and contemporaneous service in the transportation of a like kind of traffic under substantially similar circumstances and conditions, such common carrier shall be deemed guilty of unjust discrimination, which is hereby prohibited and declared unlawful." The act then goes on to provide for certain exceptions from its general provisions. The particular offense charged against the defendant was that it issued an annual free pass to one Grant, a member of the North Carolina General Assembly, and allowed him to ride thereon between points within the state. The. court said: "The question presented for our decision is: Does the act prohibit and make indictable the giving of free transportation to passengers by common carriers?" This question is then, in an exhaustive opinion, concurred in by all the. justices except Douglas, J., answered in the affirmative as to both propositions involved therein. Douglas. J., concurred in the opinion that the act prohibits the giving of free passes, saying: "Such a construction is in strict accordance with the settled rules of judicial interpretation and with the highest principles of public policy." He, however, held to the view that the case was sui generis, and the defendant not liable to punishment for violation of the act, as long as the giving of free passes was only included therein by implication, and with this view the writer is personally inclined to agree.

We find no difference in principle between the North Carolina act and the provisions of the laws of Montana above quoted. The only difference of any kind is that the Legislature. of North Carolina to an extent classified the general public by providing that free transportation or reduced rates might be given to certain excepted persons and institutions, while our laws provide that there shall be no discrimination between persons of the same class, or in the transfer or sale of tickets of the same class; and as the persons to which this opinion relates. as will hereafter be shown, are. all in the same class, such difference can have no bearing upon the result here. That the North Carolina decision is directly applicable to this case is evidenced by the. fact that conditions here. upon which our laws are designed to operate, are the same as those set forth at length in the opinion of the North Carolina court. There is no greater justification for giving free passes to employees of other railroads than there is for giving like evidences of a right to free carriage to state officials, as such. It is matter of common knowledge in Mon-

John *v.* Northern Pac. Ry. Co

tana that, in accordance with a custom that has obtained for many years, members of the executive, legislative, and judicial branches of the state government, and some county officers, are furnished by the railroad companies with that form of free transportation known as "passes," and in some cases by other transportation companies also. Why should this be so? The practice has popularly come to be known as the "pass evil," and the writer undertakes to say that public sentiment is almost universally opposed to it, and that for the very reason which courts have always felt justified in acting upon, to wit, that it involves an arbitrary, unwarranted, and unjust classification of persons who occupy the same relation toward the transportation companies. It is the constant and natural protest of the givers and receivers of these passes that no consideration is expected in return therefor. A judge who was thought to be influenced in his decisions by the fact that he had a free pass in his pocket would be promptly declared venal and unfit. The law provides ample remuneration, in the way of mileage, for those officers who are obliged to travel on official business. Why should they be furnished with free passes? Honorable members of the legislative assembly would be greatly incensed by the suggestion that the free passes in their pockets influenced their action upon legislation in which the railroads were interested. Why, then, should they ride free of charge? Abundant provision is always made for the payment of their mileage in coming to and going from the capital. Indeed, the recipients of these passes have been often obliged to protest, of late years since the subject has been agitated, that nothing is expected to be given or received in exchange therefor; in other words, that they are purely complimentary. This is no doubt true; it simply emphasizes the fact that such passes are gratuitous. And the whole system of free and unclassified pass giving is made odious by a consideration of the fact that, so long as free passes are so generally given, any judge or public officer who refuses to accept one or who ostentatiously returns it to the giver invites the imputation of hostility towards the railroads. All public officers should be, as Cæsar's wife should have been, above suspicion. What justification can there be for dividing the traveling public into free pass holding and non free pass holding persons?

Our Constitution allows classification, but not unreasonable classification. In the absence of classification by the Legislature, the railroads may themselves make reasonable classifications. But classification into public office holding and non public office holding persons is clearly arbitrary, vicious, unreasonable, and therefore illegal and void; and we believe it will be conducive to a more healthy condition of the body politic to have this made plain without further delay. And if one pays full fare, and his neighbor no fare at all, is the discrimination not more pro-

nounced than would be the case if the latter paid only half fare?
We can find no warrant for holding that this constitutional provision and this statute (section 4337, Rev. Codes) were intended
to apply only to paying passengers, or to passengers using exactly the same kind of ticket.   The evil sought to be counteracted
was fundamental, not merely nominal.   The Constitution seems
to us too plain to require any interpretation.   It distinctly says
that all persons have equal rights to have themselves carried over
railroads, and have no discrimination in charges for being so
carried shall be made between persons of the same class.   That
this provision was intended to be of universal application, except
in the case of excursion or commutation tickets, is evidenced by
the fact that the sale of such tickets is specially permitted.   If
I travel on a free pass, and my neighbor, who is in the same
class with me except that he holds no public office, is obliged to
pay fare, I should not welcome the task of convincing him that
we were enjoying equal rights of carriage or that our relative
situations spoke no discrimination between us.   And the ordinary
layman who has a lawsuit against a railroad company may have
some justification for feeling that he is not on equal terms with
his opponent, if the judge who tries his case or hears his appeal
has accepted a complimentary pass from the latter.   We can see
no difference between an unlimited pass and an unlimited ticket,
or in effect between a pass and a limited ticket, except perhaps
that the holder of the pass enjoys greater privileges than does
the holder of the ticket.   If there were any such difference, the
statute could be nullified by a mere name.   The fact that this
construction has never before been placed upon the Constitution
or statute law, or even the consideration that the lawmakers did
not in terms prohibit that particular form of evil known as the
giving of free "passes," are not of sufficient weight to change
our views of the matter.   It is never too late to put the right
construction upon a law.   That the framers of the Constitution
and the members of the legislative assembly had in view the
general purpose of prohibiting the giving of special privileges
and unjust discrimination between individuals occupying the
same relative situation towards railroad companies is clear;
and, if the giving of free passes is repugnant to this general
purpose, then it is prohibited, although "passes" are not specifically mentioned, either in the Constitution or the statute.   This
same mischief existed at the time of the adoption of the Constitution and the passage of the statute; therefore we may indulge
the inference that, being within the legitimate scope of the general purpose sought to be effected, the intention was to remedy it.
"It is the duty of judges to so construe the act [remedial statute]
as to suppress the mischief and advance the remedy.   This injunction is simply to carry out the intention of the lawmaker,
which is the cardinal aim with reference to all statutes.   The

John v. Northern Pac. Ry. Co

intention in statutes which are for this purpose recognized or enacted pro bono publico is more liberally inferred, and to a greater extent dominates the letter, than is admissible in dealing with those which must be strictly construed. * * * Liberal construction is given to suppress the mischief and advance the remedy. For this purpose it is a settled rule to extend the remedy as far as the words will admit, that everything may be done in virtue of the statute in advancement of the remedy that can be done consistently with any construction." 2 Lewis' Sutherland, Statutory Construction, §§ 583, 605. It is true that there is a penalty attached to the violation of the statute (section 4337, Rev. Codes), and in this regard it should be construed as are other penal statutes (section 8096, Rev. Codes); but that portion which seeks to prohibit in general terms unjust discrimination between individuals should be liberally construed, with a view to carrying out the intention of the lawmaking body. A statute may be remedial in one part or purpose and penal in another. Smith v. Townsend, 148 U. S. 490-497, 13 Sup. Ct. 634, 37 L. Ed. 533.

We conclude, therefore, that the giving of free passes, such as are referred to in this opinion, to the persons we have mentioned as not properly distinguishable by classification from the general public, is prohibited by the Constitution, and also under the penalties mentioned in the statutes above quoted and considered. It therefore follows that the carriage of the plaintiff by the defendant without compensation was an illegal act. The giving of the pass being prohibited by law, it, including the exemption contract on the back thereof, was a nullity.

6. But can this holding avail the plaintiff? Appellant earnestly contends that it cannot, and cites in support of its position the case of Muldoon v. Seattle City Ry. Co., 10 Wash. 311, 38 Pac. 995, 45 Am. St. Rep. 787, wherein the court said: "It is maintained that because the Constitution of the state forbids transportation companies to grant passes to public officers, when that prohibition was violated by respondent, both the pass and the conditions were void and the parties were placed in the position that the railroad company was carrying the appellant as though he were an ordinary free passenger and was subject to its ordinary liabilities in such cases. * * * The appellant received the pass which he knew the corporation had no right to give him, and he availed himself of its privileges, and he ought to be estopped from saying that that which was the very means by which he occupied a place in the respondent's car was unlawfully given him. He was there under the license of a pass, and he cannot be heard to say that his relation to the respondent was any other than that which he voluntarily made it." The cases of Northern Pacific Ry. Co. v. Adams, 192 U. S. 440, 24 Sup. Ct. 408, 48 L. Ed. 513, M., K. & T. Ry. Co. v. Trinity

John v. Northern Pac. Ry. Co

County Lumber Co., 1 Tex. Civ. App. 553, 21 S. W. 290, and Duncan v. Maine Central Ry. Co. (C. C.) 113 Fed. 508, are also cited to the same point. In the Duncan Case the court said: "Rejecting the pass as void, the plaintiff puts himself in the position of one who was on the train of the defendant without its permission, and without any intention of paying the fare which would entitle him to be regarded as a passenger. The consequence, therefore, of the plaintiff putting himself in that position, is to leave him as an unauthorized intruder, and to place him outside of those rules of law which give protection against the mere negligence of the servants of a common carrier."

But, as heretofore pointed out, under our statutes the plaintiff was neither an intruder nor a bare licensee. The defendant, having undertaken to carry him, owed him a certain statutory duty, to wit, to use ordinary care for his safe carriage. We doubt if it can properly be said that the parties were in pari delicto. At any rate, the plaintiff did not stand in the same relation to the railway company as would have been the case had the pass been issued to him personally for his own individual use. The courtesy extended was not to John, but to his employer, the St. Louis & San Francisco Railroad Company. He was on business for his company. The pass ran to him as general agent, and he so signed the agreement on the back thereof. It may be presumed that he was not an entirely free agent, but was required to travel on the pass. Under the circumstances, it must have been expected that he would do so. No penalty attached to receiving the pass or the free transportation, while, on the other hand, the act of the defendant was prohibited by law. It may well be considered that by the joint action of the defendant railway company and the St. Louis & San Francisco Railroad Company John was placed in the situation in which he found himself.

But we are able to place our decision on this branch of the case on other and higher grounds. Asserting again that John was a passenger: He was in the care and custody of the defendant. The law declares that no valid contract existed between them. The pass and its conditions were nullities—in legal effect they had never existed. The duty which a carrier owes to its passengers is founded, not in contractual relation, but in public policy. The preservation of human life and the safety of human limbs are so highly regarded by the law that it has always been its policy to safeguard both when intrusted to the keeping of those who, as was so well said by Mr. Justice Grier, in Philadelphia, etc., Railroad Co. v. Derby, supra, "undertake to convey persons by the powerful but dangerous agency of steam." John was in a situation created, not by himself, but by the law. The legal relation which he bore to the defendant was created by the law. Being a passenger, he had not the power to place himself as an individual in a legal situation which would leave him out-

John v. Northern Pac. Ry. Co

side the pale of those beneficent principles upon which is founded the public policy of the state. We quote from the opinion of the Supreme Court of North Carolina in the case of McNeill v. Durham & C. R. Co. (on rehearing), 135 N. C. 682, 47 S. E. 765, 67 L. R. A. 227: "The pass, issued in pursuance of an illegal contract and for the purpose of carrying out its unlawful purpose, inherits its invalidity. The defendant was free at all times to decline to carry the plaintiff except upon the payment of the usual fare, and to eject him from the train upon refusal to pay. The fact that the pass had expired makes no difference, as, in its character as a contract, it never had any legal existence. Being without legal existence, it was equally devoid of legal effect, and, conferring no rights upon the plaintiff, imposed upon him no obligations which the law will enforce. * * * The pass itself being worthless, the conditions on the back thereof could have no application. * * * It is not the unlawful contract for free transportation which renders a railroad company liable to the penalty, but it is the transportation itself. * * * We must bear in mind that while the statute renders absolutely void any contract for free transportation, so that neither party thereto can acquire any rights thereunder, it imposes the penalty only upon the transportation company. The act of free transportation alone is criminal. The party accepting such transportation is not guilty of a criminal act, whatever moral blame may attach to the reception of unlawful favors. Therefore in contemplation of the law the parties cannot be considered in pari delicto.. * * * It is often said that one becomes a passenger by virtue of a contract. This is not always so. * * * But it may be said that the laws raises an implied contract. Even if we accept that form of expression, it simply means that the law imposes upon a common carrier certain duties and liabilities which adhere to the nature of his calling. We prefer to adopt the more direct expression, and say that those duties and liabilities are imposed by law upon common carriers upon considerations of public policy independent of contract, and arise from the nature of their public employment. * * * One such condition is the inherent liability of the carrier for all injuries proximately resulting from its own negligence or that of its servants. But, as we have already said, in the case at bar there was no legally existing contract, which is equivalent to saying that there was no contract at all." In that case the plaintiff was injured by the negligence of the railroad company while riding on a pass which was void under the statute. On the pass were printed substantially the same conditions of exemption from liability as those we have considered in this case. It was held that plaintiff was a passenger and entitled to recover as such, not being in pari delicto with the company in the violation of the law.

7. As has been seen, the trial resulted, on account of the fact

John v. Northern Pac. Ry. Co

that the court held that plaintiff was not a passenger for hire, in a departure from the original theory of his counsel as evidenced by his complaint; and the court gave to the jury a definition of "gross negligence," which is now claimed by counsel for the appellant to be erroneous. Neither consideration is sufficient to warrant a reversal. It is the policy of the law that immaterial variances between the allegations of a pleading and the proof should be disregarded by the courts, unless the adverse party has been misled thereby to his prejudice. The defendant was, upon the record, liable in damages as a matter of law. No attempt was made to rebut the presumption of negligence arising from the fact of derailment. The court might properly have charged the jury that the only disputed questions of fact were the extent of plaintiff's injuries and the amount of damages sustained. See Consolidated Gold & Sapphire Co. v. Struthers (just decided) 111 Pac. 152. As there arose a presumption of ordinary negligence from the fact of derailment, and plaintiff was entitled to recover, regardless of whether he was a passenger for hire or not, without proof of gross negligence, no prejudice could result to the defendant on account of the errors complained of, conceding them to have been such. And, in any event, a technically proper retrial would simply necessitate an amendment of the pleadings, with the same ultimate result. Under such circumstances, a new trial ought not to be ordered.

8. It is claimed that the damages are excessive. At the time of the injury plaintiff was 39 years of age and in perfect health. His salary was $1,800 per year. He now intermittently suffers from a pain in his head, he sleeps poorly, his right side is partially paralyzed, and he has lost the use of his voice. He testified that at the time of the first manifestation of paralysis he suffered "pain unbearable." One witness said: "He is a physical wreck now." The physicians testified that his injuries were probably permanent and would eventually cause his death. In view of this evidence, we cannot say that the jury, with whom the matter primarily rested, rendered an excessive verdict.

The judgment and order appealed from are affirmed.

Affirmed.

Brantly, C. J., concurs.

On Motion for Rehearing.

Smith, J. The appellant in this case has filed a motion, supplemented by a printed argument, for a rehearing. We are satisfied with the correctness of the conclusions heretofore announced. However, it is stated in the printed argument that the former decision suggests certain questions, which should be answered in order to clear up any uncertainty as to the rights of the appellant and other railroad companies, in the matter of free transportation or reduced rates.

Note

We are unable to answer some of the questions propounded because of the fact that they do not affect the public, but only the railway companies themselves, and we are not sufficiently advised as to the circumstances attendant upon the particular cases instanced. Other questions, however, involve matters of common and everyday knowledge as to the conditions surrounding the persons mentioned; and we have no hesitancy in holding that a railroad company may lawfully issue free transportation, or sell tickets at reduced rates, as the case may warrant, to the following classes of persons: (1) Employees of the issuing road, and the members of their families. (2) Doctors, nurses, and helpers being hurried to wrecks. (3) Soldiers and sailors going to or coming from institutions for their keeping. (4) Ministers of religion and persons engaged in charitable and religious work. Members and employees of the Railroad Commission should be allowed to ride free only when traveling on official business. Section 4369, Rev. Codes, so provides. The state and the railroad companies are alike interested in a speedy physical inspection of the subject-matter of investigation by such officers. When on private business they should pay fare. See section 4394, Rev. Codes. No reason exists why children, and persons who by reason of physical defects, injuries, or deformities, or other misfortune, are unable to compete with mankind in general, should not be placed in classes by themselves and carried free or at reduced rates.

The motion for a rehearing is denied.

BRANTLY, C. J. I concur.

HOLLOWAY, J., having dissented from the original opinion, takes no part in this.

NOTE.

CARRIER OF PASSENGER'S POWER TO EXEMPT ITSELF FROM LIABILITY FOR PERSONAL INJURIES.

Note

Cross-References to Preceding Authorities in This Series on Our Main and Its Kindred Subjects.

Carrier of Passenger's Power to Exempt Itself from, or Limit Its Liability.—See foot-note of Miley *v.* Northern Pac. Ry. Co. (Mont.). 36 R. R. R. 176, 59 Am. & Eng. R. Cas., N. S., 176.

Existence of Relation of Carrier and Passenger as Affected by Failure to Have Ticket or Pay for Transportation.—See last paragraph of foot-note of Thompson *v.* Nashville, etc., Ry. (Ala.). 34 R. R. R. 171, 57 Am. & Eng. R. Cas., N. S., 171.

Express Messengers, Validity of Contracts Purporting to Limit Railroad's Liabilities on Account of Injuries to.—See foot-note of Weir *v.* Rountree (C. C. A.), 35 R. R. R. 144, 58 Am. & Eng R. Cas. N. S., 144.

Necessity of Consideration for Contract Purporting to Limit Liability of Common Carrier of Freight.—See last foot-note of Black *t* Atlantic C. L. R. Co. (S. Car.), 32 R. R. R. 603, 55 Am & Eng. R Cas., N. S., 603.

Power of Carrier of Freight to Limit Amount of Its Liability.—See first foot-note of Atlantic C. L. R. Co. *v.* Coachman (Fla.). 36 R. R. R. 775, 59 Am. & Eng. R. Cas., N. S., 775; second foot-note of Pittsburg, etc., Ry. Co. *v.* Mitchell (Ind.), 36 R. R. R. 760, 59 Am. & Eng. R. Cas., N. S., 760; last foot-note of Stringfield *v.* Southern Ry. Co. (N. Car.), 35 R. R. R. 624, 58 Am. & Eng. R. Cas., N. S., 624.

Power of Carrier to Limit Its Liability for Loss of or Injuries to Passengers' Baggage.—See fourth foot-note of Black *v.* Atlantic C. L. R. Co. (S. Car.), 32 R. R. R. 603, 55 Am. & Eng. R. Cas. N. S. 603; Gomm *v.* Oregon R. & Nav. Co. (Wash.), 32 R. R. R. 495, 55 Am. & Eng. R. Cas., N. S., 495.

Right of Carrier to Exempt Itself from Liability on Account of Baggage of Person Riding on Free Pass.—See foot-note of Hutto *v.*

Note

Southern Ry. Co. (S. Car.), 24 R. R. R. 382, 47 Am. & Eng. R. Cas., N. S., 382.

Whether Carrier's Employees Are Passengers While Riding on Its Trains or Cars, When Off Duty.—See first foot-note of Harris *v.* Puget Sound Elec. Ry. (Wash.), 34 R. R. R. 45, 57 Am. & Eng. R. Cas., N. S., 45.

Whether Carriers of Freight May Limit Their Liability.—See second foot-note of Bartlett *v.* Oregon R., etc., Co. (Wash.), 35 R. R. R. 400, 58 Am. & Eng. R. Cas., N. S., 400.

Whether Carriers of Freight May Limit Their Liability for Negligence.—See second foot-note of Santa Fe, etc., Ry. Co. *v.* Grant Bros. Const. Co. (Ariz.), 36 R. R. R: 420, 59 Am. & Eng. R. Cas., N. S., 420.

Whether Express Messengers Are Passengers.—See fifth paragraph of second foot-note of Birmingham, etc., Co. *v.* Sawyer (Ala.), 29 R. R. R. 779, 52 Am. & Eng. R. Cas., N. S., 779.

Whether Mail Agents and Postal Clerks Are Passengers.—See first foot-note of Southern Ry. Co. *v.* Harrington (Ala.), 36 R. R. R. 148, 59 Am. & Eng. R. Cas., N. S., 148; foot-note of Barker *v.* Chicago, etc., Ry. Co. (Ill.), 35 R. R. R. 470, 58 Am. & Eng. R. Cas., N. S., 470.

I. PASSENGERS FOR HIRE.

A. NEGLIGENCE.

1. Majority Doctrine.

According to the majority doctrine, a common carrier cannot exempt itself, even by a contract provision expressly assented to by the passenger, for liability for injury to a passenger for hire sustained by reason of the carrier's own negligence or that of its servants.

United States.—Hart *v.* Pennsylvania R. Co., 112 U. S. 331, 28 L. Ed. 717; Delaware, etc., R. Co. *v.* Ashley, 14 C. C. A. 368, 67 Fed. Rep. 209; Baltimore, etc., R. Co. *v.* McLaughlin, 19 C. C. A. 551, 73 Fed. 519; Moses *v.* Hamburg-American Packet Co., 88 Fed. Rep. 329; New York Cent. R. Co. *v.* Lockwood, 17 Wall. (U. S.), 357, 21 L. Ed. 627; The Oregon (C. C. A.), 133 Fed. Rep. 609.

Alabama.—Mobile, etc., R. Co. *v.* Hopkins, 41 Ala. 486.

Connecticut.—Griswold *v.* New York, etc., R. Co., 26 Am & Eng. R. Cas. 280, 53 Conn. 371, 55 Am. Rep. 115, 4 Atl. 261.

Delaware.—Flinn *v.* Philadelphia, etc., R. Co., 1 Houst. (Del), 469.

Georgia.—Central of Georgia R. Co. *v.* Lippman, 18 Am. & Eng. R. Cas., N. S., 640, 110 Ga. 665, 678, 36 S. E. 202; Southern Ry. Co. *v.* Watson (Ga.), 18 Am. & Eng. R. Cas., N. S., 209.

Illinois.—Illinois Cent. R. Co. *v.* Beebe, 174 Ill. 13, 50 N. E. 1019; Pennsylvania Co. *v.* Greso, 79 Ill. App. 127.

Indiana.—Louisiana, etc., R. Co. *v.* Keefer, 146 Ind. 21, 44 N. E. 796; Pittsburg, etc., R. Co. *v.* Higgs (Ind.), 24 R. R. R. 201, 47 Am. & Eng. R. Cas., N. S., 201, 76 N. E. 299.

Note

Iowa.—Rose *v.* Des Moines Valley R. Co., 39 Iowa, 246, 9 Am. Ry. Rep. 7, 20 Am. Ry. Rep. 326.

Kentucky.—Louisville, etc., R. Co. *v.* Bell, 100 Ky. 203, 38 S. W. 3·

Massachusetts.—Doyle *v.* Fitchburg R. Co., 166 Mass. 492, 44 N. E. 611, 5 Am. & Eng. R. Cas., N. S., 257.

Mississippi.—Yazoo, etc., Co. *v.* Grant (Miss.), 18 R. R. R. 257, 41 Am. & Eng. R. Cas., N. S., 257, 38 So. 502.

Missouri.—Jones *v.* St. Louis, etc., R. Co., 125 Mo. 666, 28 S. W. 883; Tibby *v.* Missouri Pac. R. Co., 82 Mo. 292.

New Hampshire.—Baker *v.* Boston, etc., R. Co. (N. H.), 23 R. R. R. 592, 46 Am. & Eng. R. Cas., N. S., 592, 65 Atl. 386.

Ohio.—Cleveland, etc., R. Co. *v.* Curran, 19 Ohio St. 1.

Pennsylvania.—Camden, etc., R. Co. *v.* Bausch (Pa.), 7 Atl. 731, 28 Am. & Eng. R. Cas. 172; Crary *v.* Lehigh Valley R. Co., 203 Pa. St. 525, 53 Atl. 363.

South Carolina.—Piedmont Mfg. Co. *v.* Columbia, etc., R. Co., 16 Am. & Eng. R. Cas. 194, 19 S. Car. 353.

Texas.—Missouri Pac. R. Co. *v.* Ivy, 71 Tex. 409, 9 S. W. 346; Ft. Worth, etc., R. Co. *v.* Rogers, 21 Tex. Civ. App. 605, 53 S. W. 366; Gulf, etc., R. Co. *v.* McGown, 65 Tex. 640; Harris *v.* Howe, 74 Tex. 534, 12 S. W. 224; Galveston, etc., R. Co. *v.* Kinnebrew, 7 Tex. Civ. App. 549, 27 S. W. 631.

Utah.—Williams *v.* Oregon Short Line R. Co. (Utah), 12 Am. & Eng. R. Cas., N. S., 61.

Wisconsin.—Alabama *v.* Milwaukee, etc., R. Co., 87 Wis. 485, 58 N. W. 780; Davis *v.* Chicago, etc., R. Co., 93 Wis. 470, 67 N. W. 16, 1132; Feldschneider *v.* Chicago, etc., R. Co., 122 Wis. 423, 99 N. W. 1034, 12 R. R. R. 737, 35 Am. & Eng. R. Cas., N. S., 737.

A common carrier of passengers cannot stipulate for exemption from responsibility for the negligence of itself or its servants. So held in New York Cent. R. Co. *v.* Lockwood, 17 Wall. (U. S.), 357, 21 L. Ed. 627.

In Baltimore, etc., R. Co. *v.* McLaughlin, 19 C. C. A. 551, 73 Fed 519, it is held that a railroad company cannot, by conditions in the contract of carriage, limit its liability for injuries to persons carried on its trains, caused by the negligence of its servants; and an attempt to limit the authority of an agent of such a company to make contracts of carriage, within the ordinary scope of his authority, by requiring such a condition to be inserted in the contracts, is void.

In The Oregon (C. C. A.), 133 Fed. 609, it is held that a provision of a steamship ticket purporting to exempt the carrier from responsibility for its own or its agents' negligence, provided it has used due diligence to make the vessel seaworthy, is void, as against public policy.

The liability of a carrier of passengers is not that of an insurer, but such carrier is bound by law to extraordinary diligence to protect the lives and persons of its passengers. This duty he cannot waive or release, even by an express contract. Being one in which

Note

the public has an interest, public policy forbids such a waiver or release. So held in Central of Georgia R. Co. *v.* Lippman (Ga.), 18 Am. & Eng. R. Cas., N. S., 640, 110 Ga. 665, 36 S. E. 202; Southern Ry. Co. *v.* Watson (Ga.), 18 Am. & Eng. R. Cas., N. S., 209.

The rule that a railroad company may by contract limit its liability for all negligence except gross negligence does not apply to a passenger paying for his transportation. Pennsylvania Co. *v.* Greso, 79 Ill. App. 127.

Where a railroad company is under the duty to carry a passenger, and it undertakes for hire to perform that duty, it cannot by contract legally exempt itself from liability arising out of the negligence of itself or its servants. So held in Pittsburg, etc., R. Co. *v.* Higgs (Ind.), 24 R. R. R. 201, 47 Am. & Eng. R. Cas., N. S., 201, 76 N. E. 299.

In Baker *v.* Boston, etc., R. Co. (N. H.), 23 R. R. R. 592, 46 Am. & Eng. R. Cas., N. S., 592, 65 Atl. 386, it is held that a common carrier cannot by contract relieve itself of the duty to use ordinary care to avoid injuring persons carried on its cars with whom it was apparent its business would bring it in contact.

In Abrams *v.* Milwaukee, etc., R. Co., 87 Wis. 485, 58 N. W. 780, it is held that it is against public policy to allow a common carrier to stipulate for exemption from liability for negligence of its employees resulting in loss or injury to a passenger for hire.

A passenger riding on a free pass given for a valuable consideration is not bound by a condition in the pass purporting to relieve the railroad company from liability for negligence. So held in Griswold *v.* New York, etc., R. Co., 26 Am. & Eng. R. Cas., 280, 53 Conn. 371, 55 Am. Rep. 115, 4 Atl. 261.

In Williams *v.* Oregan Short Line R. Co. (Utah), 12 Am. & Eng. R. Cas., N. S., 61, it is held that where there is a valid consideration for a pass given by a railroad company, conditions printed on such pass, exempting the company from responsibility for the negligence of its servants, do not bind the passenger, and should not be admitted in evidence in an action for damages for injuries caused by negligence.

Carrier's Own Negligence.—In Tibby *v.* Missouri Pac. R. Co., 82 Mo. 292, it is held that a common carrier is not permitted to stipulate against its own negligence; and that especially is this true in regard to its carriage of passengers.

Compared to Carriage of Goods.—In Cleveland, etc., R. Co. *v.* Curran, 19 Ohio St. 1, it is said in the opinion: "It is true, that common carriers are not insurers of the safety of passengers as they are of goods which they undertake to carry; but the principle of law which forbids their being allowed to exempt themselves from liability for the consequences of their negligence in respect of goods, applies with still greater force in the case of passengers."

Liability Limited to Arbitrary Amount.—In Feldschneider *v.* Chicago, etc., R. Co., 12 R. R. R. 737, 35 Am. & Eng. R. Cas., N. S., 737,

Note

99 N. W. 1034, 122 Wis. 423, it is said in the opinion: "A stipulation limiting the liability of a carrier for loss of personal property shipped to an arbitrary sum, not fixed with reference to the agreed or maximum value of the property, is void. Ullman v. C. & N. W. R. Co., 112 Wis. 150, 88 N. W. 41. A fortiori a stipulation limiting the liability for injuries to a passenger for hire to an arbitrary sum must also be void. The question would not seem open to serious discussion."

Making Amount of Fare Measure of Damages—Validity of Stipulation.—A stipulation in a passenger ticket that the amount of fare demanded by a conductor should be the measure of recovery for the violation of the contract of carriage by the carrier, was unreasonable, and would not prevent the passenger from recovering damages for the tort in ejecting him on the ground that his ticket had expired. Galveston, etc., R. Co. v. Kinnebrew, 7 Tex. Civ. App. 549, 27 S. W 631.

Freight Car Attached to Passenger Train at Request of its Owner—Right of Railroad to Repudiate Act of Agents—Liability for Negligence.—In Lackawanna, etc., R. Co. v. Chenewith, 52 Pa. St. 382, it appeared that, at the request of the owner of a freight car, the agents of a railroad company attached his car to a passenger train contrary to the "instructions and rules" of the company, he agreeing "to run all risks" of injuries to his goods or to himself while traveling in such car. It was held that the carrier could not repudiate the act of its agents so as to free itself from responsibility for negligence causing personal injury to the owner of the car.

Collisions between Vessels—Steerage Passenger Killed.—In Moses v. Hamburg-American Packet Co. (D. C.), 88 Fed. Rep. 329, where it appeared that a collision in New York harbor caused the loss of the life of a boy four years old, a steerage passenger, it was held that the steamer, being in fault, was not exempted by the third section of the Harter act, nor by a limitation to $100 for any personal injuries expressed in the ticket, this not being a reasonable provision; nor by exemptions from liability for negligence.

Injury to Minor—Contract with Father.—In Chicago, etc., R. Co. v. Lee (C. C. A.), 14 Am. & Eng. R. Cas., N. S., 264, 92 Fed. Rep. 318, it is held that a stipulation in a contract of carriage that the person who receives free transportation under it agrees to assume all risk of personal injury, except of injuries arising from the gross carelessness of the railroad company, is invalid, where the person injured while being carried under the contract is a minor, and the contract was not his but that of his father.

Chartered Train—Ejection of Passenger—Exemption—Effect of Railroad's Contract.—In Kirkland v. Charleston, etc., R. Co. (S. Car.), 29 R. R. R. 661, 52 Am. & Eng. R. Cas., N. S., 661, 60 S. E. 668, it is held that a railroad company cannot, in chartering one of its trains, to a third person for an excursion, enter into such a contract with such person as will exempt it from liability for negligence

Note

and willful misconduct in the ejectment of a passenger from such train, such third party being in law an agent of the railroad.

2. Minority Doctrine.

But in some jurisdictions it is held that a common carrier may, by contract and for a reasonable consideration, exempt itself from liability for injuries to a passenger for hire caused by negligence for which it would otherwise be responsible.

Louisiana.—Higgins *v.* New Orleans, etc., R. Co., 28 La. Ann. 133.

Maine.—Rogers *v.* Kennebec Steamboat Co., 86 Me. 261, 29 Atl. 1069.

Montana.—John *v.* Northern Pac. R. Co. (Mont.), 111 Pac. 632.

New Jersey.—Kinney *v.* Central R. Co., 32 N. J. L. 407, affirmed , in 34 N. J. L. 513.

New York.—Wilson *v.* New York Cent., etc., R. Co., 21 Am. & Eng. R. Cas. 148, 97 N. Y. 87; Smith *v.* New York Cent. R. Co., 24 N. Y. 222; Blair *v.* Erie R. Co., 66 N. Y. 313; Steers *v.* Liverpool, etc., Steamship Co., 57 N. Y. 1; Bissell *v.* New York Cent. R. Co., 25 N. Y. 442.

South Dakota.—Meuer *v.* Chicago, etc., Ry. Co. (S. Dak.), 2 Am. & Eng. R. Cas., N. S., 493.

In Seybolt *v.* New York, etc., R. Co., 18 Am. & Eng. R. Cas. 162, 95 N. Y. 562, 47 Am. Rep. 75, it is said in the opinion: "It cannot now be disputed that an individual transported over the route of a carrier of passengers may debar himself, by contract founded upon a sufficient consideration, from any claim to damages for injuries to his person or property occasioned by the negligence of such corporation during the course of transportation."

In Bissell *v.* New York Cent. R. Co., 25 N. Y. 442, it is held that a common carrier, in consideration of an abatement in whole or in part of his legal fare, may lawfully contract with a passenger that the latter will assume all risks of damage from the negligence of agents or servants, for which the carrier would otherwise be liable.

In Bissell *v.* New York Cent. R. Co., 25 N. Y. 442, it is held that public policy is satisfied by holding a railroad corporation bound to take the risks when the passenger chooses to pay the fare established by the legislature; and if he voluntarily and for any valuable consideration waives the right to indemnity for personal injuries, the contract is binding upon him.

In John *v.* Northern Pac. R. Co. (Mont.), 111 Pac. 632, it is held that a common carrier of passengers may contract to exempt itself from liability for the ordinary negligence of itself or its servants.

In Gulf, etc., R. Co. *v.* McGown, 65 Tex. 640, it is said in the opinion: "Treating the pass as the evidence of a contract between the parties, and giving to it the most favorable construction for the appellant, the question in the case broadly stated is, can a public carrier of passengers so contract as to relieve itself from liability for an injury to a passenger from the negligence of the carrier or its servants, in the course of their employment. That

Note

there are many cases which hold that a public carrier of passengers
may so limit its liability, cannot be questioned. Such is the rule
asserted in the following English cases. McCawley v. Furness R.
Co., L. R., 8 Q. B. 59, 42 L. J. Q. B. 4, 21 W. R. 140, 27 L. T. 485;
Gallin v. London, etc., R. Co., 23 W. R. 308, 32 L. T. 550, 44 L. J. Q.
B. 89, L. R., 10 Q. B. 212, 215; Neale v. Ry. Co., 10 Q. B. 440."

Rationale of Doctrine.—In Smith v. New York Cent. R. Co., 29
Barb. (N. Y.), 132, it appeared that deceased made a contract with
defendant to transport cattle upon its railroad, and was traveling
with them, under a "drover's pass," which contained a provision that
"the persons riding free to take charge of the stock, do so at their
own risk of personal injury from whatever cause." It was held that
this stipulation did not exempt the carrier from liability for gross
negligence, or from the want of ordinary care; that the carrier was
liable for what would be regarded as fault or misconduct on its
part, and was bound to observe reasonable care and precaution, employ persons of requisite skill, and possess vehicles fit for use and
adapted to the nature of the service required. In this case it is
said in the opinion: "It seems to be well settled, in deference to
the great principle of allowing parties to make their own contracts,
where no rule of public policy or of positive law is violated, that
parties may contract for a less burdensome obligation upon the
carrier of passengers than is imposed by the principle of the common law. (26 Barb. 641., 1 Kern. 490., 14 Barb. 524.)" It does not
seem expressly settled how far the restriction may be carried. It
is generally conceded that it cannot be carried to the extent of relieving the carrier against the consequences of his own fraud or willful
misconduct (cases before cited) and I do not think it ought to be permitted to relieve him against the fraud or misconduct of his servants
or employees. It has been suggested by an eminent judge, that
it might be permitted to cover the latter ground. (Per Gardiner, J.,
in Wells v. St'm Nav. Co., 4 Seld. 381.) But I think the argument
unsound. It would be trifling with human life. Principles of public
policy—a proper regard for the safety of the subject and the citizen
—in my opinion forbid the application of such a rule, or the concession of such a power. Perhaps, also, a party should not be allowed
to bargain for absolving a carrier of passengers from gross negligence; and by that, in this connection, I mean a degree of negligence which amounts to fraud or criminality. And implies a reckless
disregard of human life, and the absence of proper moral sentiments.
"Making these exceptions, I am not prepared to say that parties
may not, if they do it understandingly, stipulate to relieve the carrier to any extent upon which they may deliberately agree, from
the common law obligations of his contract, and from any degree
of negligence of which the passenger, with a full consciousness of
his rights, may consent."

**Cause of Negligence—Public Policy—Compared to Contracts of
Insurance.**—In Trenton Pass. R. Co. v. Guarantors Liability Co., 60

Note

N. J. L. 246, 37 Atl. 609, it is held that a contract to indemnify a common carrier of passengers against losses occurring from injuries to passengers carried by it, is not invalid as against public policy because it covers losses resulting from its negligence or the negligence of its servants. In this case it is said in the opinion: "There is, however, an adjudication precisely in point in which the question thus arose: An incorporated company authorized, among other things, to issue contracts of indemnity of the same character as that before us, became insolvent, its business had not been confined to making such contracts, but had extended to other contracts of indemnity, and the court in distributing the assets had before it creditors whose claims arose from other forms of contracts than those arising upon such contracts of insurance. In behalf of the other creditors the court was urged to declare that the creditors who claimed under such contracts of insurance should not be admitted to partake in the distribution of the assets upon the ground that such contracts of insurance were obnoxious to public policy and unenforceable and void. The opinion of the court was written by Chief Justice McSherry, and contains an admirable discussion of the question, reaching the conclusion that public policy does not avoid these contracts. In respect to the claim that the possession of such indemnity tends to beget negligence he says: 'Nor can we assume as an unvarying rule, of which judicial notice will be taken, that a carrier of passengers, who has secured an indemnity to reimburse himself from losses which his own negligence may produce, will, merely, because and solely in consequence of having such indemnity—which, at best, is but limited and partial—necessarily disregard the duty to exercise the highest degree of care. And unless it be assumed as a postulate that the mere possession of an indemnity will, of itself, necessarily and invariably produce negligence, it does not logically, follow that such policy of indemnity is even incidently or indirectly repugnant to public policy. The indemnity in no way affects the liability of the carrier to the person injured. The utmost that it does, precisely as in the case of a carrier of goods, is to afford him a fund out of which he may be reimbursed, and that, too, perhaps, but partially, for in all these policies the liability of the insured is always limited and confined to a specifically-designated sum. Boston and Albany Merchants Trust and Deposit Co., 34 Atl. 778.' "

Distinction between Carrier's Own Negligence and That of Employee Criticised.—In Gulf, etc., Ry. Co. *v.* McGown, 65 Tex. 640, it is said in the opinion: "In the nature of things, every corporation must act solely through its agents, and that their powers and duties may differ in degree, it seems to us, should make no difference, in so far as duties and liabilities to passengers, whether free or paying full fare, are concerned. The true inquiry, at last, is, did the injury result from the negligence of any agent of the corporation, while acting within the scope of his employment. If a corporation may relieve itself from liability to a passenger for the negligence of one or more classes of agents, why may it not for the negligence of another class? All of a corporation's employees, from the highest official to the humblest laborer, are but agents. Some of them are necessarily clothed with extensive powers, to make contracts which will bind the corporation in reference to many matters, and to control its operations, while others have but simple labors to perform, yet, none of them are the corporation clothed with its full powers or responsible for all its acts."

"We are of the opinion that the distinction sought to be made in the New York and New Jersey cases, to which we have referred, has no solid foundation in reason or public policy, when considered with reference to the right of a corporation pursuing the business of a common or public carrier to limit, by contract, its liability to a passenger for injury resulting from the negligence of any class of its agents."

Shipper Injured—Gross Negligence in Using Unfit and Dangerous Car.—In Smith v. New York Cent. R. Co., 24 N. Y. 222, it appeared that the owner of cattle traveling in charge of them, under a contract stipulating that "the persons riding free to take charge of the stock do so at their own risk of personal injury from whatever cause," and paying no independent consideration for the conveyance of himself, was injured by the gross negligence of an agent of the carrier in using an unfit and dangerous car. The carrier was held liable by a divided court, four of the judges going on the ground that the contract of exemption from liability was void, as against public policy, and the fifth, that the negligence, as it respected the machinery of transportation, was imputable to the carrier itself.

3. Connecting Carriers.

May Limit Liability to Own Line.—A railroad, as a carrier of passengers, may stipulate that it shall be liable only for such injuries as are sustained on its own road and train. Mosher v. St. Louis, etc., R. Co., 127 U. S. 390, 32 L. Ed. 249; Kerrigan v. South Pac. R. Co., 81 Cal. 248, 22 Pac. 677; Spiess v. Erie R. Co. (N. J.), 12 R. R. R. 852, 35 Am. & Eng. R. Cas., N. S., 852, 58 Atl. 116; Baltimore, etc., R. Co. v. Campbell, 3 Am. & Eng. R. Cas. 246, 36 Ohio St. 647, 38 Am. Rep. 617; St. Clair v. Kansas City, etc., R. Co., 77 Miss. 789, 28 So. 957; Alabama, etc., R. Co. v. Holmes, 75 Miss. 371, 23 So. 187; Harris v. Howe, 74 Tex. 534, 12 S. W. 224

Negligence of Person in Charge of Connecting Line—Liability of Railroad Selling Coupon Ticket.—In Kerrigan v. South. Pac. R. Co., 81 Cal. 248, 22 Pac. 677, it is held that if a coupon ticket is sold by a railroad company, containing a coupon over a connecting line, which it issues merely as agent for such line, and the main ticket expressly limits the responsibility of the railway company issuing it to its own line, in the absence of any thing showing that the

Note

railway company undertook differently from what appears from the face of the ticket, it is not liable for the negligence of any person in charge of the connecting line.

Thousand Mile Ticket.—The purchaser of a thousand-mile passenger ticket was bound by an express condition on the ticket that the defendant railroad assumed no responsibility beyond its own lines. So held in Spiess *v.* Erie R. Co. (N. J.), 12 R. R. R. 852, 35 Am. & Eng. R. Cas., N. S., 852, 58 Atl. 116.

Through Tickets.—But in Central R. Co. *v.* Combs, 18 Am. & Eng. R. Cas. 298, 70 Ga. 533, 48 Am. Rep. 582, it is held that a railroad company which sells and issues tickets to passengers over its own lines of road and lines of road of other companies, known as through tickets, is liable for the sure and safe transportation of such passengers to the point of destination, notwithstanding there may be indorsed or printed on the tickets so sold and issued a notice that the company issuing and selling such tickets shall not be liable, except as to its own lines of road.

4. Voluntary Offering to Carry Passengers on Freight Trains.

And it has also been held where a railroad voluntarily offers to carry passengers on freight trains and designates the freight trains upon which it will carry passengers, it can no more limit its liability for injuries to passengers sustained while on such trains, by reason of negligence, than if they were being carried on ordinary passenger trains. Central of Georgia R. Co. *v.* Lippman (Ga.), 18 Am. & Eng. R. Cas., N. S., 640, 110 Ga. 665, 36 S. E. 202; Central of Georgia R. Co. *v.* Almand, 116 Ga. 780, 43 S. E. 67; Illinois Cent. R. Co. *v.* Beebe, 174 Ill. 13, 50 N. E. 1019; Louisville, etc., R. Co. *v.* Bell, 100 Ky. 203, 38 S. W. 3; Richmond *v.* Southern Pac. Co. (Ore.), 2 R. R. R. 49, 25 Am. & Eng. R. Cas., N. S., 49, 67 Pac. 947; Ft. Worth, etc., R. Co. *v.* Rogers, 21 Tex. Civ. App. 605, 53 S. W. 366.

In Louisville, etc., R. Co. *v.* Bell, 100 Ky. 203, 38 S. W. 3, it is held that a railroad cannot by contract relieve itself from liability for injuries sustained by passengers while being carried by them either on freight or passenger trains.

In Illinois Cent. R. Co. *v.* Beebe, 174 Ill. 13, 50 N. E. 1019, it is held that the rule permitting a carrier to exempt itself by a contract from liability except in case of gross negligence, applies only to the carrier of property, and not to the carriage of passengers, whether the passenger is riding on a freight train with the carrier's consent, or on a passenger train.

In Richmond *v.* Southern Pac. Co. (Ore.), 2 R. R. R. 49, 25 Am. & Eng. R. Cas., N. S., 49, 67 Pac. 947, it is held that a railroad company which voluntarily designates freight trains to carry passengers, and permits its agents to sell tickets therefor to passengers generally, is a common carrier of passengers by means of such trains, and its agreement with a passenger whereby he absolves the company from all liability for injuries sustained while riding on such

Note

freight trains in consideration of securing his ticket at a reduced rate is against public policy, and void.

Contract for Exemption from Liability for Negligence.—In Central of Georgia R. Co. *v.* Lippman, 18 Am. & Eng. R. Cas., N. S., 640, 110 Ga. 665, 36 S. E. 202, it is held that an express contract entered into by a carrier and a passenger for transportation on a freight train, the terms of which purport to release the carrier from all liability to the passenger for personal injuries sustained by the passenger while on such train, is, in effect, a contract by which the carrier undertakes to relieve itself from the consequences of the negligence of itself and servants, and cannot be enforced.

In Ft. Worth, etc., R. Co. *v.* Rogers, 21 Tex. Civ. App. 605, 53 S. W. 366, it is held that under Tex. Const., art. 10, § 2, declaring all railroad companies common carriers, and Rev. Stat., art. 319, providing that the duties and liabilities of carriers in Texas shall be the same as at common law, and (art. 320) that railway companies shall not restrict their common-law liability, a railroad company cannot, by a release taken in advance and in consideration of permitting one to be carried as a passenger on a freight train, exempt itself from liability for damages resulting from its own negligence.

Freight Trains—Exemption—Validity of Agreement.—In Central of Georgia R. Co. *v.* Almand, 116 Ga. 780, 43 S. E. 67, it is held that one who purchases from a railroad company a ticket which by its terms is good for passage on way freight trains of the company, and which provides that in consideration of the privilege of traveling on such trains the purchaser agrees that the company shall not be liable for damage to his person or baggage while riding on its freight trains, is not, by reason of the fact that such agreement to relieve the company from liability is invalid and not binding on him, precluded from recovering from the company on account of his wrongful ejection from one of its freight trains.

5. Freight Trains—May Limit Liability.

There are authorities supporting the doctrine that where a railroad company is under no obligation to carry passengers on its freight trains, it may limit its liability for injuries to passengers sustained while riding on such trains, though it cannot exempt itself from liability for such as are caused by negligence, either of itself or that of its servants. Arnold *v.* Illinois Cent. R. Co., 83 Ill. 273; Richmond *v.* Southern Pac. Co. (Ore.), 2 R. R. R. 49, 25 Am. & Eng. R. Cas., N. S., 49, 67 Pac. 947; Central of Georgia R. Co. *v.* Almand, 116 Ga. 780, 43 S. E. 67; Ft. Worth, etc., R. Co. *v.* Rogers, 21 Tex. Civ. App. 605, 53 S. W. 366.

Consideration—Extra Care and Expense.—In Arnold *v.* Illinois Cent. R. Co., 83 Ill. 273, it is held that a railroad company, having passenger trains sufficient to accommodate the public, is under no legal obligation to carry a passenger on its freight trains, and its undertaking to do so, and the extra care and expense required in

Note

such case, is a sufficient consideration for a contract made with a passenger limiting its liability for injuries sustained by a passenger while riding on a freight train.

Assumption of Risk of Boarding Caboose at Stopping Place.— But a railroad company may make suitable and reasonable conditions and regulations for carrying passengers on its freight trains, from which they are excluded except by special permission, and an agreement on the part of the one holding such a permit, by which he assumes the risks incident to boarding the caboose of such trains at any place where it may be stopped for the purpose of conducting the freight business of the company, does not amount to a limitation of the carrier's liability for its own negligence. So held in Chicago, etc., R. Co. *v.* Mann (Neb.), 26 R. R. R. 288, 49 Am. & Eng. R. Cas., N. S., 288, 11 N. W. 379.

6. What Law Governs.

According to one view, contracts exempting a carrier of passengers from liability for negligence are not immoral or illegal, and, therefore, if valid where entered into, should be enforced in other jurisdictions. Illinois Cent. R. Co. *v.* Beebe, 174 Ill. 13, 50 N. E. 1019; Arayo *v.* Currel, 1 La. 528; Dyke *v.* Erie R. Co., 45 N. Y. 113; Mexican Nat. R. Co. *v.* Ware (Tex. Civ. App.), 60 S. W. 343; Pittsburgh, etc., R. Co. *v.* Bishop, 7 Ohio Cir. Dec. 73; Camden, etc, R. Co. *v.* Bausch (Pa.), 28 Am. & Eng. R. Cas. 172, 7 Atl. 731; Meuer *v.* Chicago, etc., Ry. Co. (S. Dak.), 2 Am. & Eng. R. Cas., N. S., 493; Fonseca *v.* Cunard Steamship Co., 153 Mass. 553, 27 N. E. 665; O'Regan *v.* Cunard Steamship Co., 160 Mass. 356, 35 N. E. 1070; Davis *v.* Chicago, etc., R. Co., 93 Wis. 470, 67 N. W. 16, 1132.

Texas Contract—Injured in Mexico.—In Mexican Nat. R. Co. *v.* Jackson (C. C. A.), 118 Fed. 549, it is held that where plaintiff, a resident of Texas, executed a contract with his employer, a sleeping car company, exempting it, and any corporation over whose railroads its cars might be transported, from liability for any injuries to plaintiff, which contract was void under Laws Tex. 1897, Sp. Sess., p. 14, providing that no such contract shall be binding, the fact that plaintiff's injuries, for which suit was brought in the federal court in Texas, occurred in Mexico, was immaterial as affecting the invalidity of such contract, when pleaded as a defense.

Where Portion of Route Is in Other State—Foreign Statute.—In Dyke *v.* Erie R. Co., 45 N. Y. 113, it appeared that plaintiff purchased from defendant, a railroad corporation created by the laws of New York, at a station within such state, a passenger ticket thence to the city of New York, and sustained injuries upon a portion of its road situated in Pennsylvania, through the negligence of defendant's servants. It was held that the amount of damages recoverable for his injuries was not affected by a statute of Pennsylvania limiting the amount of recovery in similar cases.

Foreign Contracts—Both Parties Citizens of United States—Place of Completion of Contract—Public Policy.—But in The Kensington,

36 C. C. A. 533, 94 Fed. 885, it is held that where both carrier
and passenger are citizens of the United States, and the place of
completion of the contract of carriage is within this country, a
stipulation for exemption from liability in the contract, authorized
by the law of a foreign country, by which the contract is by its
terms to be governed, but which is contrary to the public policy
of this country, is not enforceable in its courts.

B. GROSS NEGLIGENCE.

There are authorities holding that while a carrier of passengers
may exempt itself by contract from responsibility for simple negligence, it cannot relieve itself from liability for gross negligence.
Perkins *v.* New York Cent. R. Co., 24 N. Y. 196; Meuer *v.* Chicago,
etc., R. Co. (S. Dak.), 2 Am. & Eng. R. Cas., N. S., 492; Lawson
v. Chicago, etc., R. Co., 64 Wis. 447, 24 N. W. 618

In Pennsylvania R. Co. *v.* McCloskey, 23 Pa. St. 526, it is held
that assuming that a common carrier of passengers may contract
for other exemptions from liability than those allowed by law, still
a contract cannot exempt it from liability for gross negligence.

In Lawson *v.* Chicago, etc., R. Co., 64 Wis. 447. 24 N. W. 618.
it is held that a railroad cannot by stipulation in a special contract
wholly exempt itself from liability for an injury to a shipper accompanying his stock on a train resulting from the carrier's gross
negligence.

Gross Negligence, Fraud, or Willful Wrong.—In Meuer *v.* Chicago,
etc., Ry. Co. (S. Dak.), 2 Am. & Eng. R. Cas., N. S., 492, it is held
that a common carrier of passengers may limit its liability by express contract signed by the parties, except as to gross negligence,
fraud, or willful wrong of such carrier or its servants.

Fraudulent, Willful, or Reckless Misconduct of Employee.—A contract by which a railroad stipulates for exemption from responsibility for personal injuries occasioned to its passengers from the
negligence of its agents or servants is not against public policy,
and may be valid; but a contract cannot relieve the carrier from liability for such injuries if they resulted from the fraudulent, willful,
or reckless misconduct of its agent or employee. So held in Higgins
v. New Orleans, etc., R. Co., 28 La. Ann. 133.

Carrier's Willful Misconduct, or Recklessness.—In Perkins *v.* New
York Cent. R. Co., 24 N. Y. 196, it is held that a railroad corporation cannot, by contract, exempt itself from liability to a passenger
for damages resulting from its own willful misconduct, or recklessness which is equivalent thereto.

II. GRATUITOUS PASSENGERS.
A. NEGLIGENCE.
1. Majority Doctrine.

But according to the weight of authority in the United States,
the liability of a common carrier for negligent injuries to one riding

Note

on a free pass cannot be limited in any respect, whatever the degree
of negligence, or whether that of the carrier itself or that of its
servants.

United States.—Chamberlain v. Pierson, 31 C. C. A. 157, 87 Fed.
420; Farmer's Loan, etc., Co. v. Baltimore, etc., R. Co. (C. C.),
102 Fed. 17.

Alabama.—Mobile, etc., R. Co. v. Hopkins, 41 Ala. 486.

Arkansas.—St. Louis, etc., R. Co. v. Pitcock (Ark.), 25 R. R. R.
79, 48 Am. & Eng. R. Cas., N. S., 79.

Indiana.—Indiana Cent. R. Co. v. Mundy, 21 Ind. 48; Louisville,
etc., R. Co. v. Faylor, 126 Ind. 126, 25 N. E. 869.

Iowa.—Rose v. Des Moines Valley R. Co., 39 Iowa 246, 9 Am. Ry.
Rep. 7, 20 Am. Ry. Rep. 326.

Missouri.—Bryan v. Missouri Pac. R. Co., 32 Mo. App. 228.

North Carolina.—McNeill v. Durham, etc., R. Co., 135 N. Car. 682,
47 S. E. 765.

Texas.—Gulf, etc., R. Co. v. McGown, 65 Tex. 640; Missouri, etc.,
Ry. Co. v. Flood (Tex. Civ. App.), 70 S. W. 331.

Virginia.—Norfolk, etc., Railway v. Tanner, 100 Va. 379, 41 S.
E. 721.

In Chamberlain v. Pierson, 31 C. C. A. 157, 87 Fed. 420, it is
held that one who accepts free carriage on a railroad at his own
risk can nevertheless recover for injuries caused by the negligence
of the railroad, or its employees who are not his fellow servants

In Farmers' Loan, etc., Co. v. Baltimore, etc., R. Co. (C. C.),
102 Fed. 17, it is held that a railroad company cannot relieve itself
by any contract from its duty to exercise the greatest possible care
and diligence for the safety of its passengers, and the fact that the
passenger when injured was traveling on a free pass, by which
he assumed all risk of accident or damage, whether negligence or
otherwise, is no defense to an action to recover for the injury on
the ground that it was caused by the negligence of the company
or its employees.

In Mobile, etc., R. Co. v. Hopkins, 41 Ala. 486, it is held that
public policy forbids that a carrier should contract for exemption
from liability for damages caused by the negligence, willful default,
or tort of himself or his servants; and this rule applies also where
he undertakes to transport passengers gratuitously, or under "free
tickets" containing an express stipulation on the part of the passenger, that, "in consideration thereof, he assumes all risk of accidents, and expressly agrees that the carrier shall not be liable under
any circumstances, whether of the negligence of his agents, or otherwise, for any injury to the person or property."

In St. Louis, etc., R. Co. v. Pitcock (Ark.), 25 R. R. R. 79, 48 Am.
& Eng. R. Cas., N. S., 79, 100 S. W. 725, it is held that under Const.,
art. 17, § 12, making railroads responsible for damages under such
regulations as may be prescribed by the Legislature, and Kirby's
Dig., § 6773, making railroads responsible for damages to persons

caused by the running of trains, a stipulation in a free pass that
the passenger accepting it assumes the risk of accidents is contrary
to public policy, and the passenger injured through the negligence
of the carrier is entitled to recover therefor.

In Louisville, etc., R. Co. *v.* Faylor, 126 Ind. 126, 25 N. E. 869,
it is held that common carriers are subject to the same liability
for injuries resulting from negligence to persons riding on a free
pass as they are to those who pay full fare; and the right of the
carrier to limit the severity of its common-law liability for injuries
sustained by a person while riding on a free pass does not extend
to those which result from its negligence or that of its employees.

In Camden, etc., R. Co. *v.* Bausch (Pa.), 28 Am. & Eng. R. Cas.,
172, 7 Atl. 731, it is held that in Pennsylvania the fact that a person
is riding on a free pass does not relieve the common carrier from
liability for injuries caused by its negligence.

In Gulf, etc., R. Co. *v.* McGown, 65 Tex. 640, it is held that a
common carrier of passengers cannot by contract relieve itself from
responsibility, or ever limit its liability, for injuries to a passenger
caused by the negligence of itself or its employees, or agents, in
the scope of their employment; and this is so with reference as well
to passengers traveling absolutely free of charge as to those paying
full fare.

"Steamboat Man" Carried Gratuitously—Right to Recover for Personal Injuries.—In Steamboat New World *v.* King, 16 How. (U. S.),
469, 14 L. Ed. 1019, it is held that the fact that a passenger was a
"steamboat man," and as such carried, according to custom, gratuitously, did not deprive him of the right of redress against the
carrier for personal injuries enjoyed by other passengers.

2. Minority Doctrine.

On the question whether a stipulation in a free pass purporting
to exempt the carrier from liability for injuries caused by the negligence of the carrier, its agents, or servants, is valid, there is a
wide diversity of opinion. In some of the states the English
doctrine prevails, which is that such an exemption may completely
protect the carrier from liability for negligence.

United States.—Northern Pac. R. Co. *v.* Adams, 192 U. S. 440,
48 L. Ed. 513; Duncan *v.* Maine Cent. R. Co. (C. C.), 113 Fed Rep.
508; Northern Pac. R. Co. *v.* Adams, 192 U. S. 440, 48 L. Ed. 513,
10 R. R. R. 575, 33 Am. & Eng. R. Cas., N. S., 575, 24 Sup. Ct.
Rep. 408; Boering *v.* Chesapeake Beach R. Co., 193 U. S. 442, 48 L.
Ed. 742.

Connecticut.—Griswold *v.* New York, etc., R. Co., 26 Am. & Eng. R.
Cas. 280, 53 Conn. 371, 55 Am. Rep. 115, 4 Atl. 261.

Maine.—Rogers *v.* Kennebec Steamboat Co., 86 Me. 261. 29 Atl.
1069.

Massachusetts.—Doyle *v.* Fitchburg R. Co., 166 Mass. 492, 44 N.
E. 611, 5 Am. & Eng. R. Cas., N. S., 257; Quimby *v.* Boston, etc.,
R. Co., 150 Mass. 365, 23 N. E. 205.

Note

New Jersey.—Trenton Pass. R. Co. *v.* Guarantors Liability Co., 60 N. J. L. 246, 37 Atl. 609.

New York.—Bissell *v.* New York Cent. R. Co., 25 N. Y. 442; Ulrich *v.* New York, etc., R. Co., 108 N. Y. 80, 15 N. E. 60; Wells *v.* New York Cent. R. Co., 24 N. Y. 181.

Washington.—Muldoon *v.* Seattle City R. Co., 10 Wash. 311, 38 Pac. 995.

Wisconsin.—Annas *v.* Milwaukee, etc., R. Co., 67 Wis. 46, 30 N. W. 282.

Canada.—Alexander *v.* Toronto, etc., R. Co., 33 U. C. Q. B. 474.

England.—Gallin *v.* London, etc., R. Co., 23 W. R. 308, 32 L. T. 550, 44 L. J. Q. B. 89, L. R. 10, Q. B. 212; McCawley *v.* Furness R. Co., L. R. 8, Q. B. 57, 42 L. J. Q. B. 4, 21 W. R. 140, 27 L. T. 485.

In Payne *v.* Terre Haute, etc., R. Co. (Ind.), 2 R. R. R. 111, 25 Am. & Eng. R. Cas., N. S., 111, 62 N. E. 472, it is held that one injured through the negligence of a railroad company, while being carried as a passenger on a free pass, which stipulates that the carrier shall not be liable to the holder of the pass for any injuries arising from the carrier's negligence, cannot recover therefor.

A condition in a free pass, given as a pure gratuity, that its user will assume all risk of personal injury is not prohibited by any rule of public policy in Maine, and is effectual to exonerate the carrier from liability for the negligence of its servants. So held in Rogers *v.* Kennebec Steamboat Co., 86 Me. 261, 29 Atl. 1069.

In Quimby *v.* Boston, etc., R. Co., 150 Mass. 365, 23 N. E. 205, it is held that if a person solicits and accepts purely as a gratuity a free pass from a railroad company to ride upon its trains, and agrees to assume all risk of injury therefrom, the agreement is not invalid as against public policy, and he cannot recover for injuries sustained by reason of negligence of the railroad's servants while so riding.

In Kinney *v.* Central R. Co., 34 N. J. L. 513, affirming 32 N. J. Law 407, it is held that a contract in consideration of free passage, that a passenger will assume the risks of injuries to his person from the negligence of the servants of the railroad company, is valid in law; and a passenger who knowingly receives a free ticket with an endorsement of such exemption of liability upon it, will be bound by the terms of such stipulation.

In Muldoon *v.* Seattle City R. Co., 7 Wash. 528, 35 Pac. 422, it is held that a passenger riding upon a free pass which contains conditions limiting the liability of the carrier on account of negligence cannot recover for injuries sustained through the negligence of the carrier's servant.

Public Policy.—In Northern Pac. R. Co. *v.* Adams (U. S.), 10 R. R. R. 575, 33 Am. & Eng. R. Cas., N. S., 575, 24 Sup. Ct. Rep. 408, it is held that a stipulation in a railway pass that the railroad shall not be liable to the user "under any circumstances, whether of negligence of agents or otherwise, for any injury to the person,"

Note

violates no rule of public policy, and relieves the railroad from liability for personal injuries resulting from the ordinary negligence
of its employees to one riding on the pass, who has accepted it with
knowledge of its conditions.

United States—Doctrines Prevailing in Different States.—In Griswold v. New York, etc., R. Co., 26 Am. & Eng. R. Cas. 280, 53 Conn.
371, 55 Am. Rep. 115, 4 Atl. 261, it is said in the opinion: "In the
United States we find much contrariety of opinion. Some state
courts of the highest authority follow the English decisions and
allow railroad companies in consideration of free passage to contract for exemption from all liability for negligence of every degree,
provided the exemption is clearly and explicitly stated. Wells v.
New York Central R. Co., 26 Barb. (N. Y.), 641, and the same
case, 24 N. Y. 181; Perkins v. New York Central R. R. Co., 24 N.
Y. 196; Bissell v. New York Cent. R. R. Co., 25 N. Y. 442; Poucher
v. N. Y. Central R. R. Co., 49 Barb. (N. Y.), 263; Maynir v. Dinsmore, 56 Barb. (N. Y.), 168; Dorr v. New Jersey Steam Nav. Co., 11
N. Y. 485; Kinney v. Central R. Co, 34 N. J. Law 513, affirming
32 N. J. Law 407, and 34 id., 513; Western, etc., R. Co. v. Bishop,
50 Ga. 465." "Other courts, also of high authority, concede the
right to make such exemption in all cases of ordinary negligence,
but refuse to apply the principle to cases of gross negligence.
Illinois Cent. R. Co. v. Read, 37 Ill. 484, 87 Am. Dec. 260: Indiana
Cent. R. Co. v. Mundy, 21 Ind. 48; Jacobus v. St. Paul, etc., R. Co.,
20 Minn. 125. And other state courts of equal authority utterly
deny the power to make a valid contract exempting the carrier from
liability for any degree of negligence. Cleveland, etc., R. Co. v.
Curran, 19 Ohio St. 1; Mobile, etc., R. Co. v. Hopkins, 41 Ala. 486;
Pennsylvania R. R. Co. v. Henderson, 51 Pa. St. 315; Flinn v. Philadelphia, etc., R. Co., 1 Houst. (Del.), 469."

In Muldoon v. Seattle City R. Co., 7 Wash. 528, 35 Pac. 422, it is
said in the opinion: "It is a general rule that carriers of passengers
for hire cannot contract against their liability for damages for injuries to their passengers, and this rule has been frequently held to
be none the less operative when the evidence of the passenger's
right to travel was put in the form of a free pass, if, in fact,
there was a consideration for the issuance of it. Railroad Co. v.
Lockwood, 17 Wall. 357, 21 L. Ed. 627; Railroad Co. v. Stevens, 95
U. S. 655, 24 L. Ed. 535.

"The cases above cited expressly refrain from any expression of
opinion as to what the law would be were the pass purely a gratuity
with a condition against liability. There are dozens of such cases
as Railroad Co. v. Lockwood in the reports, and the language of
many of them is fully strong enough to justify counsel in claiming
that they would cover the case of a gratuitous pass with conditions.
However, nearly all of them are cases where drovers or other
shippers, being under the necessity of accompanying their shipments
of stock or other merchandise to properly care for it while in transit,

Note

were granted transportation without payment of fare eo nomine, but where the federal supreme court found that there was a valuable consideration and therefore a contract of carriage for hire. But of all the cases called to our attention, or discovered by us in a somewhat extended examination of the subject, there are but eight where the naked question of liability under a free pass with conditions was presented. There may be some others, but they are most likely to be found in New York and Illinois, where the right of a carrier to contract against liability has long been recognized in some form or other. "Illinois Central R. Co. *v.* Read (1865), 37 Ill. 484, 87 Am. Dec. 260; held that a passenger traveling on such a pass could not recover, also Kinney *v.* Central R. Co. (1889), 34 N. J. Law 513, affirming 32 N. J. Law 407; Jacobus *v.* St. Paul, etc., R. Co. (1873) 20 Minn. 135, held the opposite, as did Rose *v.* Des Moines Valley R. Co. (1874), 39 Iowa 246, 9 Am. Ry. Rep. 7, 20 Am. Ry. Rep. 326; Griswold *v.* New York, etc., R. Co. (1865), 26 Am. & Eng. R. Cas. 280, 53 Conn. 371, 55 Am. Rep. 115, 4 Atl. 261, and Annas *v.* Milwaukee, etc., R. Co. (1886), 67 Wis. 46, 30 N. W. Rep. 282, held there could be no recovery. Gulf, etc., R. Co. *v.* McGown (1886), 65 Tex. 640, 643, followed Minnesota and Iowa, but Quimby *v.* Boston, etc., R. Co. (1890), 150 Mass. 365, 23 N. E. Rep. 205, decided against recovery. The Iowa case was largely based upon a statute of that state which was construed to prohibit any attempt at limitation by the carrier."

Immaterial Whether Negligence Slight or Gross.—In Wells *v.* New York Cent. R. Co., 24 N. Y. 181, it is held that a contract between a railroad corporation and a gratuitous passenger by which the former is exempted from liability under any circumstances for the negligence of its agents for any injury to the passenger is not against law or public policy and is valid. And it is immaterial whether such negligence of the agent be slight or gross.

Violation of Federal Statute, Effect of.—In Duncan *v.* Maine Cent. R. Co. (C. C.), 113 Fed. Rep. 508, it is held that one riding on a pass, given without consideration, and after assent to conditions that he should assume all risk of accident and that the carrier should not be liable, cannot recover of it for injuries from the negligence of its servants, and it is immaterial that the giving of the pass was a violation of the federal statute in reference to interstate traffic.

Effect of Purchase of Drawing Room Car Ticket.—In Ulrich *v.* New York, etc., R. Co., 108 N. Y. 80, 15 N. E. 60, it appeared that plaintiff while traveling on a regular train of defendant's railroad on a free pass, was injured by reason of a collision caused by defendant's negligence. Upon the pass was an indorsement to the effect that, in consideration of receiving it, the holder assumed all risks of accident and agreed that the company should "not be liable under any circumstances, whether by negligence of their agents or otherwise, for injury to his person or property, and that in the use of the pass he would not consider the company as a common carrier or

Note

liable to him as such." In an action to recover damages for the
injury, it appeared that plaintiff had purchased a ticket entitling
him to a seat in a drawing-room car upon the train, from the
drawing-room car conductor. It was stated in the check given for
the seat that it "with passage ticket or fare" would be taken up by the
train conductor. It was held that this did not make plaintiff a
passenger for hire and did not have the effect to annul or vary,
for the trip, the contract made by the free pass and its indorsement;
that assuming that the purchase of the seat ticket had the same force
and effect as if purchased from the train conductor, it had no effect
upon the status of the purchaser as a passenger; that the purchase
of a right to enjoy particular and exclusive accommodations during
the trip, whether made with defendant or otherwise, did not entitle
him to transportation, and, so long as the pass was used to secure
transportation, did not in any way affect the validity of the exemption from liability expressed therein.

3. Servant's Negligence.

In some jurisdictions, it is held that the carrier may exempt itself
from liability for injuries to a gratuitous passenger caused by the
negligence of its servants who are not its representatives.

Jurisdiction Where Doctrine Prevails.—Thus in Annas v. Milwaukee, etc., R. Co., 67 Wis. 46, 30 N. W. 282, it is said in the opinion:
"By an examination of all the authorities cited by the learned
counsel for the respective parties upon the argument of this case,
as well as others not cited, we find that in England, Canada, New
York, New Jersey, Connecticut, and West Virginia, the courts of
those countries and states have held that a railroad company may,
upon a proper consideration, lawfully contract to relieve itself for
any and all negligence on the part of its servants, employees, and
agents, without any regard to the degree of such negligence; and that such
contract is not against public policy. These courts have therefore held that
where the company agrees to carry a person without compensation, or in
different manner or upon cars in which they do not usually carry
passengers, the company may lawfully contract from exemption from
all liability on account of the carelessness of its agents, servants,
and employees. See the following cases cited by the learned counsel
for the appellant: McCawley v. Furness R. Co., L. R. 8, Q. B. 57, 42
L. J. Q. B. 4, 21 W. R. 140, 27 L. T. 485; Hall v. Northeastern R.
Co., 33 L. T. 306, 23 W. R. 860, 10 Q. B. 437, 44 L. J. Q. B. 164; Duff
v. Great Northern R. Co., L. R. 4 Ir. 178; Alexander v. W. & R. R.
Co., 3 Strob. Law 594; Wells v. New York Cent. R. Co., 26 Barb.
(N. Y.), 641; Wells v. New York Cent. R. Co., 24 N. Y. 181; Per-
kins v. New York Cent. R. Co., 24 N. Y. 196; Smith v. New York
Cent. R. Co., 24 N. Y. 222; Bissell v. New York Cent. R. Co., 25 N.
Y. 442; Magnin v. Dinsmore, 56 N. Y. 168; Kinney v. Central R.
Co., 32 N. J. Law 407, S. C., 34 N. J. Law 513; Griswold v. New York,
etc., R. Co., 26 Am. & Eng. R. Cas. 280, 53 Conn. 371, 55 Am. Rep.
115, 4 Atl. 261; Baltimore R. Co. v. Skeels, 3 W. Va. 556.

Note

"The argument in favor of the rule established in the above cases is perhaps as well stated in the case last cited as in any other. The court says: 'By the rule respondeat superior a corporation is made liable for the negligence of its servants; but when the principal has done the best he could the rule is technical, harsh, and without any basis of inherent justice. As applicable to corporations, it is of great practical convenience and utility. We do not, therefore, advocate its abolition, but we contend that in a case like the present, where there is no actual fault on the part of the principal, it is reasonable in the eye of the law that the party for whose benefit the rule is given should be allowed to waive it in consideration of a free passage. It is not a case where a party stipulates against a liability for imputed negligence in regard to which there is no actual fraud. It is easy to see therefore, that consideration of public policy have no application to such a case' * * * . The foregoing reasoning, as it seems to us, will also furnish a complete answer to the claim that the defendant must be liable on account of the gross negligence of its servants, for it is manifest that the principal is no more culpable in the one case than in the other, and, the rule respondeat superior being waived, the protection is complete."

4. Negligence of Managing Officers.

The view that even in respect to a gratuitous passenger a railroad company cannot, even by express contract, except itself from liability for the negligence of its board of directors, or other managing officers, who represent the corporation itself, is supported by the weight of authority, even by some of the authorities holding the view that the carrier may exempt itself from liability for the negligence of its servants who are not its representatives. Kinney v. Central R. Co., 34 N. J. Law 513, affirming 32 N. J. L. 407; Wells v. New York Cent. R. Co., 26 Barb. (N. Y.), 641; Perkins v. New York Cent. R. Co., 24 N. Y. 196; Smith v. New York Cent. R. Co., 24 N. Y. 222; Camden, etc., R. Co. v. Bausch (Pa.), 28 Am. & Eng. R. Cas. 172, 7 Atl. 731; Muldoon v. Seattle City Ry. Co., 7 Wash. 528, 35 Pac. 422; Annas v. Milwaukee, etc., R. Co., 67 Wis. 46, 30 N. W. 282.

Directors or Managers.—A railroad corporation, in respect to a gratuitous passenger may contract for exemption from liability for any degree of negligence in its servants, other than the board of directors or managers who represent the corporation itself, for all general purposes. So held in Perkins v. New York Cent. R. Co., 24 N. Y. 196.

B. GROSS NEGLIGENCE.

In some jurisdictions, it is held that such a stipulation is not a defense against liability for gross negligence of either the carrier or its servants.

Illinois.—Arnold v. Illinois Cent. R. Co., 83 Ill. 273; Chicago, etc.,

Note

R. Co. *v.* Hawk, 36 Ill. App. 327; Illinois Cent. R. Co. *v.* O'Keefe, 63 Ill. App. 102; Illinois Cent. R. Co. *v.* Read, 37 Ill. 484, 87 Am. Dec. 260; Toledo, etc., R. Co. *v.* Beggs, 85 Ill. 80.

Indiana.—Indiana Cent. R. Co. *v.* Mundy, 21 Ind. 48.

Minnesota.—Jacobus *v.* St. Paul, etc., R. Co., 20 Minn. 125.

Pennsylvania.—Pennsylvania R. Co. *v.* McCloskey, 23 Pa. St. 526.

Wisconsin.—Annas *v.* Milwaukee, etc., R. Co., 67 Wis. 46, 30 N. W. 282.

In Jacobus *v.* St. Paul, etc., R. Co., 20 Minn. 125, it is held that a common carrier of passengers cannot by contract, even with a passenger it carries gratuitously, exempt itself from liability for gross negligence.

In Annas *v.* Milwaukee, etc., R. Co., 67 Wis. 46, 30 N. W. 282, it is held that where a passenger is carried gratuitously the railroad may by contract relieve itself from all liability for injuries caused by the negligence of its employees, except where such negligence is gross or criminal.

Gross Negligence in Running Train.—In Indiana Cent. R. Co *v.* Mundy, 21 Ind. 48, it is held that where a person traveling on a railroad received from the company a free pass, upon which was indorsed the statement that "It is agreed that the person accepting this ticket, assumes all risk of personal injury and loss or damage to property whilst using the same on the trains of the company," such agreement does not cast upon the passenger any risks arising from the gross negligence of the employees of the railroad in running the train.

C. WHO ARE GRATUITOUS PASSENGERS.

Conveyance of Right of Way—Free Transportation for Life.—In Dow *v.* Syracuse, etc., Railway, 81 N. Y. App. Div. 362, 80 N. Y. Supp. 941, it appeared that a street railway, in consideration of the conveyance by plaintiff of a right of way, across a strip of land, agreed to provide her with transportation upon its railroad during her natural life, upon the sole condition that such right should be forfeited if her pass book of tickets should be presented for fare by any person other than herself. In pursuance of such agreement the company delivered to plaintiff a pass book, upon the front cover of which was printed the following clause: "This Pass Book is issued to Adelaide Dow (the plaintiff) and family, who voluntarily releases the company from all claims for damages for personal injuries from whatever cause." It was held that such release was void for want of consideration; that the acceptance of the pass book did not indicate an intention upon plaintiff's part to assent to the clause printed upon its cover; and that the language of such release was not sufficiently explicit to relieve the railroad company from liability for personal injuries sustained by plaintiff while riding upon the cars of defendant in consequence of the latter's negligence.

Note

Agreement to Testify for Railroad—Consideration—Free Transportation for Wife.—In Nickles *v.* Seaboard A. L. Ry. (S. Car.), 20 R. R. R. 755, 43 Am. & Eng. R. Cas., N. S., 755, 54 S. E. 755, 54 S. E. 255, an action for the death of plaintiff's interstate, where the evidence showed that her husband agreed to go to a certain point to testify for a railroad company on condition that it furnish transportation for his wife, if the pass was issued for a consideration, the company is not relieved of liability for negligent killing of the wife by the stipulation on the pass to that effect.

Pass Issued to Employee of Lessee of Railroad's Pleasure Resort. —In Camden, etc., R. Co. *v.* Bausch, 28 Am. & Eng. R. Cas. 172, 7 Pa. 731, it appeared that, plaintiff, a resident of Pennsylvania, was injured while riding on a railroad in New Jersey. It was proved that he was riding on a free pass, which stipulated that the person using it assumed all risk of accident while so doing. Plaintiff proved that the pass was not a mere gratuity but that it was issued to him as part consideration for the leasing to his employer of a pleasure resort owned by the owner of the railroad, and it was not denied that plaintiff's injuries were caused by the negligence of the latter. The court charged that if the pass was accepted by plaintiff upon a good consideration, he was entitled to recover, even by the law of New Jersey, and this was affirmed by a divided court.

Pass Given to Owner of Patented Coupling Device—Mutual Business—Traveling at Request of Railroad.—In Grand Trunk Ry. Co. *v.* Stevens, 95 U. S. 655, 24 L. Ed. 535, it appeared that plaintiff, who was the owner of a patented car-coupling device, for the adoption and use of which by the defendant railroad company he was negotiating, went, at the expense and request of the company, to a point on its road to see one of its officers, about the matter. A free pass was furnished by defendant to carry him in its cars. During the passage, the car in which he was riding was derailed, by reason of the defective condition of the rails, and he was injured. It was held that the pass was given for a consideration; that he was a passenger for hire; and that, therefore, his acceptance of the pass did not estop him from showing that he was not subject to the terms and conditions printed on the back of the pass, exempting the company from liability for any injury he might receive by the negligence of the agents of the company, or otherwise.

Injury to Newsboy—Contracts with News Company and Father— Carrier's Own Negligence.—In Texas & Pac. Ry. Co. *v.* Fenwick, 34 Tex. Civ. App. 222, 78 S. W. 548, it is held that under the constitutional and statutory provisions of Texas declaring railroads to be public highways and all railroad companies common carriers, and prohibiting them from restricting their common-law liability, a railroad cannot escape liability for personal injuries resulting from its own negligence to a newsboy (a minor) serving on its train, by virtue of a provision in a contract made by it with the news company, and also in the contract made by the news company with his father,

Note

purporting to exempt the railroad company from liability for injury sustained while riding on trains in such service.

News Agent—Failure to Stop Train before Reaching Crossing—Violation of Statute—Exemption—Public Policy.—In Starr *v.* Great Northern R. Co. (Minn.), 69 N. W. 632, it appeared that plaintiff while engaged in the business of news agent on defendant's train, was injured by a collision caused by the negligence of defendant in not stopping its train before arriving at a railroad crossing, as required by Minn. Gen. St. 1894, § 2706, which requires railroad companies to cause all their trains to entirely stop not more than sixty rods and not less than ten rods before arrival at the crossing of any other railroad, and provides that every corporation that violates the provisions of the statute is liable to a forfeiture of not more than $100 nor less than $20, and is further liable in the full amount of damages done to person or property in consequence of any neglect to comply with the requirements of the statute. It was held that a contract between defendant and plaintiff purporting to exempt the former from liability for injuries caused by its negligence, is void, as against public policy, as respects negligence consisting of a violation of the statute, and this, too, although defendant may not have borne to plaintiff the relation of common carrier.

Boy Selling Sandwiches on Train—Pass—Consideration.—But in Griswold *v.* New York, etc., R. Co., 26 Am. & Eng. R. Cas. 280, 53 Conn. 371, 55 Am. Rep. 115, 4 Atl. 261, it appeared that a boy of sixteen was employed by the keeper of a restaurant at a station on defendant's railroad to sell sandwiches on trains, and had a free pass for such purpose over the whole road, the pass containing a condition that the company should not be liable for any personal injury caused by the negligence of its agents; that the boy, while going over a part of the road to which he was not called by his business, and for a private purpose, was killed by a collision caused by the gross negligence of defendant's employees. Defendant had no interest in the restaurant and had assumed no obligation to carry the boy over the road, but was incidentally benefited by the accommodation to its passengers, and, to induce the keeper to establish it there, had promised to aid him in every way it could, and gave the boy the pass ·as a means of aiding him. It was held that the pass was to be regarded as given gratuitously and not upon consideration; and that the condition in the pass as to the defendant's exemption from liability for the negligence of its servants was not forbidden by public policy and was binding upon the passenger; and that the boy having capacity to accept the free pass, took it with such condition, and was as much bound by it as an adult.

1. Drover's Pass—View That Exemption Is Valid.

In regard to the validity of exemptions in an ordinary drover's pass, there is also a lack of harmony among the authorities. Some annunciate the doctrine that a person riding on such a pass to ac-

Note

company his stock is not a passenger; that there is no consideration for his carriage, and that, therefore, the carrier may exempt itself from liability on account of injuries sustained by him while accompanying his cattle, even though they are caused by the carrier's own negligence.

Maine.—Rogers *v*. Kennebec Steamboat Co., 86 Me. 261, 29 Atl. 1069.

New Jersey.—Kinney *v*. Central R. Co., 34 N. J. L. 513, affirming 32 N. J. Law 407.

New York.—Bissell *v*. New York Cent. R. Co., 25 N. Y. 442; Boswell *v*. Hudson River R. Co., 18 N. Y. Sup'r Ct. Rep. 699; Poucher *v*. New York Cent. R. Co., 49 N. Y. 263.

South Dakota.—Meuer *v*. Chicago, etc., R. Co. (S. Dak), 2 Am. & Eng. R. Cas., N. S., 492. .

England.—Duff *v*. Great Northern R. Co., L. R. 4 Ir. 178, 3 Ry. & C. T. Cas. XIV; Sallin *v*. London, etc., R. Co., L. R. 10 Q. B. 212.

In Boswell *v*. Hudson River R. Co., 18 N. Y. Sup'r Ct. Rep. (5 Bosw.) 699, it is held that a railroad company may limit its common law liability as carriers of passengers, by express contract with the passenger and upon sufficient consideration, so as not to be liable for injuries not arising from fraud, willfulness, recklessness, or gross negligence, and that this rule applies to one riding on an ordinary "drover's pass."

In Bissell *v*. New York Cent. R. Co., 25 N. Y. 442, it is held that where a cattle dealer paid no independent consideration for the conveyance of himself on the trains of the carrier, but accompanied his cattle, under a contract stating them to be carried at a reduced rate, and providing that "the persons riding free to take charge of the stock do so at their own risk of personal injury from whatever cause," the exemption clause is not void as against public policy, and is binding on the person accompanying the stock under it.

English Doctrine.—In Rogers *v*. Kennebec Steamboat Co., 86 Me. 261, 29 Atl. 1069, it is said in the opinion: "It has been the tendency of the English courts from an early period to recognize the power of carriers to limit their liability with respect to both goods and passengers, and under the construction given to the several acts of Parliament in later years, a common carrier in England has practically unlimited power to provide by contract against liability for negligence. In McCawley *v*. Furness R. Co., L. R. 8 Q. B. 57. 42 L. J. Q. B. 4, 21 W. R. 140, 27 L. T. 485 (1872) the plaintiff was traveling on a "drover's pass," which provided that he should travel at his own risk, and it was held that the defendant was not liable even for gross negligence. Cockburn, C. J., said: 'It was agreed that the plaintiff should be carried at his own risk, which must be taken to exclude all liability on the part of the company for any negligence for which they would have been liable. Qvain, J., said: 'Negligence, even gross, is the very thing which the contract stipulates that the

Note

defendant shall not be liable for.' See also, Gallin *v.* London, etc.,
R. Co., 23 W. R. 308, 32 L. T. 550, 44 L. J. Q. B. 89, L. R. 10 Q. B.
212; Alexander *v.* Toronto R. Co., 33 U. C. Q. B. 474."

Same—Gross or Willful Negligence.—In McCawley *v.* Furness R.
Co., L. R. 8, Q. B. 57, 42 L. J. Q. B. 4, 21 W. R. 140, 27 L. T. 485,
the declaration alleged that plaintiff was a passenger by defendants'
railway, and they so negligently conducted themselves in the management of their railway that an engine and tender came into collision with the train in which plaintiff was traveling, and he was
thereby injured. The plea alleged that defendants received plaintiff
to be carried under a free pass as the drover accompanying cattle,
one of the terms of which was that plaintiff should travel at his own
risk. The replication stated that it was by reason of the gross and
wilful negligence of defendants that the accident happened. It was
held on demurrer that the replication was bad, for that, whatever
gross or wilful negligence might mean, plaintiff, by the terms on the
pass, had agreed that defendants should not be liable for the consequences of any accidents happening in the course of the journey for
which they would otherwise have been liable.

Doctrine Criticised.—In Stinson *v.* New York Cent. R. Co., 32 N.
Y. 333, 337, it is said in the opinion: "But it is insisted that the
contract between the parties, in reference to the use of the car, released the defendant from all liability. Two clauses of the contract
are relied upon as producing this result: 1st * * *. 2d. That
which provides 'that persons riding free, to take charge of the stock,
do so at their own risk of personal injury, from whatever cause.'
The power of the company to make this contract is conceded, under
the late decisions of this court on that subject. (Buell *v.* New York
Cent. R. Co., 25 N. Y. 442; Smith *v.* Same, 24 N. Y. 222.) The fruits
of this rule are already being gathered, in increasing accidents,
through the decreasing care and vigilance on the part of these corporations, and they will continue to be reaped, until a just sense of
public policy shall lead to legislative restriction upon the power to
make this kind of contracts."

Contract for Transportation of Stock and Emigrant Movables.—
In Meuer *v.* Chicago, etc., Ry. Co. (S. Dak.), 2 Am. & Eng. R. Cas.,
N. S., 492, it is held that a special contract for the transportation
of a car-load of live stock and emigrant movables, made between a
railroad company and a shipper, in which it is stipulated that the
shipper shall be entitled to pass upon the same train to care for his
stock, at his "own risk of personal injury, from whatever cause,"
exonerates the railroad company from all liability for any injury to
the shipper while a passenger upon such train, not caused by the
gross negligence, fraud, or wilful wrong of the carrier or its servants.

Injured by Fall of Stick of Wood from Engine Tender.—In
Poucher *v.* New York Cent. R. Co., 49 N. Y. 263, it appeared that
defendant received of plaintiff a car load of sheep, to be transported
under a contract which contained a clause by which plaintiff agreed

Note

to go or send some one with the sheep, "who would take all the risks of personal injury from whatever cause, whether of negligence of defendant, its agents, or otherwise." After the sheep were loaded, plaintiff, who was intending to accompany them, and had a drover's pass, in passing by the engine tender, was injured by a stick of wood negligently thrown thereon. It was held that, under the contract defendant was exempted from liability.

2. Drover's Pass—View That Exemption Is Invalid.

But there are jurisdictions where the directly contrary doctrine prevails, where it is held that one riding on a stock pass is a passenger for hire, in regard to whom the carrier can no more exempt itself from liability than if he were traveling in a passenger coach by virtue of an ordinary passenger ticket.

United States.—Delaware, etc., R. Co. *v.* Ashley, 14 C. C. A. 368, 67 Fed. Rep. 209; New York Cent. R. Co. *v.* Lockwood, 17 Wall. (U. S.), 357, 21 L. Ed. 627.

Arkansas.—Little Rock, etc., R. Co. *v.* Miles, 13 Am. & Eng. R. Cas. 10, 40 Ark. 298, 48 Am. Rep. 10.

Delaware.—Flinn *v.* Philadelphia W. R. R. Co., 1 Houst. (Del.), 469.

Illinois.—Illinois Cent. R. Co. *v.* Anderson, 184 Ill. 294, 56 N. E. 331; Pennsylvania Co. *v.* Greso, 79 Ill. App. 127.

Michigan.—Weaver *v.* Ann Arbor R. Co. (Mich.), 16 R. R. R. 603, 39 Am. & Eng. R. Cas., N. S., 603, 102 N. W. 1037.

Missouri.—Carroll *v.* Missouri Pac. R. Co., 26 Am. & Eng. R. Cas. 268, 88 Mo. 239.

Nebraska.—Missouri Pac. Ry. Co. *v.* Tietken, 49 Neb. 130, 68 N. W. 336.

New Hampshire.—Baker *v.* Boston, etc., R. Co. (N. H.), 23 R R. R. 592, 46 Am. & Eng. R. Cas., N. S., 592, 65 Atl. 386.

Ohio.—Cleveland, etc., R. Co. *v.* Curran, 19 Ohio St. 1; Knowlton *v.* Erie R. Co., 19 Ohio St. 260.

Pennsylvania.—Pennsylvania R. Co. *v.* Henderson, 51 Pa. 315.

Texas.—Missouri Pac. Ry. Co. *v.* Ivy, 71 Tex. 409, 9 S. W. 346; Texas, etc., R. Co. *v.* Avery, 19 Tex. Civ. App. 235, 46 S. W. 897.

Utah.—Saunders *v.* Southern Pac. Co. (Utah), 4 Am. & Eng. R. Cas., N. S., 13.

Vermont.—Sprigg's Adm'r *v.* Rutland R. Co. (Vt.), 17 R. R. R. 628, 40 Am. & Eng R. Cas., N. S., 628, 60 Atl. 143.

Virginia.—Virginia, etc., R. Co. *v.* Sayers, 26 Gratt. (Va.), 328.

West Virginia.—Maslin *v.* Baltimore, etc., R. Co., 14 W. Va. 180.

Wisconsin.—Feldschneider *v.* Chicago, etc., Ry. Co. (Wis.), 12 R. R. R. 737, 35 Am. & Eng. R. Cas., N. S., 737, 99 N. W. 1034, 122 Wis. 423.

Passenger for Hire.—In Lake Shore, etc., Ry. Co. *v.* Teeters (Ind.), 24 R. R. R. 36, 47 Am. & Eng. R. Cas., N. S., 36, 77 N. E. 599, it is held that a person transported on a freight train for the purpose of

Note

caring for certain stock while en route, the carrier being thereby relieved from such care, is a passenger for hire, as to whom the carrier cannot stipulate for exemption from responsibility for negligence of itself or its servants.

In Ohio, etc., R. Co. v. Selby, 47 Ind. 471, 8 Am. Ry. Rep. 177, it appeared that a drover traveling on a freight train for the purpose of taking care of his stock on the train, for which stock he paid freight, received from the railroad company a ticket called a "stock pass," with an indorsement signed by him, as follows: "In consideration of receiving this ticket, I voluntarily assume all risk of accidents, and expressly agree that the company shall not be liable under any circumstances, whether by negligence of their agents, or otherwise, for any injury to my person, or for any loss or injury to my property, and I agree that as for me, in the use of this ticket, I will not consider the company as common carriers, or liable to me as such." It was held in an action for personal injuries to the drover from the negligence of the railroad, that such agreement was invalid and no defense to the answer; the drover, while traveling on the pass, being a passenger for hire.

In Ohio, etc., R. Co. v. Nickless, 71 Ind. 271, it is held that where the complaint alleged that the injuries complained of were received while traveling upon a "shipper's pass" given the plaintiff in consideration of freight paid for the transportation of stock, an answer alleging that such injuries were sustained while riding "upon a free pass," without paying any fare is insufficient on demurrer. In this case it is said in the opinion: "Taking the allegations of the complaint and answer together, it may be gathered that the plaintiff paid nothing as for his own fare, but that a free pass was given in consideration of the freight which he paid on his cattle. Under these circumstances, it is clear that the defendant is liable to the plaintiff for the injury done him, charged in the complaint. Ohio, etc., R. Co. v. Selby, 47 Ind. 471, 8 Am. Ry. Rep. 177."

One riding on a drover's pass is a passenger for hire, and his release of liability for damages on account of negligence of the carrier is invalid. So held in Weaver v. Ann Arbor R. Co. (Mich.), 16 R. R. R. 603, 39 Am. & Eng. R. Cas., N. S., 603, 102 N. W. 1037.

In Pennsylvania R. Co. v. Henderson, 51 Pa. St. 315, it appeared that a drover shipping live stock in the cars of a railroad company received a ticket to "pass the bearer in charge of his stock," on which was endorsed, "The person accepting this free ticket assumes all risks of accidents, and expressly agrees that the company shall not be liable, under any circumstances, whether by the negligence of their agents or otherwise, for any injury to the person, or for any loss or injury to the personal property of the person, using this ticket." It was held that the drover was a paying passenger, and that such endorsement could not relieve the carrier from liability for personal injuries to the drover caused by negligence.

Note

Pass and Shipping Agreement Constitute but Single Contract.—In Cleveland, etc., R. Co. *v.* Curran, 19 Ohio St. 1, it appeared that in making a contract for the shipment of live stock at a specified rate, a railroad company without any additional consideration, delivered to the shipper a "drover's pass" entitling him to go with his stock, and to return on a passenger train. In the written agreement for transporting the stock the holder of the ticket was referred to as "riding free to take charge of the stock." On the pass was an endorsement that it was a "free ticket," and that the holder assumed all risk of accident, and agreed that the company should not be liable under any circumstances, whether of negligence by the company's agents or otherwise, for any injury to his person or property, and that he would not consider the company as common carriers, or liable as such. It was held that the pass and the agreement for transporting the stock constituted together a single contract, and that the holder of the pass, both while going with his stock and returning on the passenger train, was not a gratuitous, but a paying passenger; and that the stipulation in the contract purporting to exempt the company from liability for negligence constituted no defense to an action brought by the shipper for personal injury caused by the negligence of the servants of the carrier in the management of its train, such stipulation being void as against public policy.

Carrier Liable for Any Degree of Negligence.—In Illinois Cent. R. Co. *v.* Anderson, 184 Ill. 294, 56 N. E. 331, it is held that a stock contract, in so far as it purports to limit the carrier's liability for injury to the shipper to acts of gross negligence, is void, since the shipper under such a contract is a passenger, and the carrier is liable for any degree of negligence which causes his injury while accompanying his stock for the purpose of caring for it.

Negligence of Carrier.—In Missouri Pac. Ry. Co. *v.* Tietken, 49 Neb. 130, 68 N. W. 336, it is said in the opinion: "In Chicago, R. I. & P. R. Co. *v.* Witty, 32 Neb. 275, 49 N. W. Rep. 183, it was held that a common carrier of live stock cannot by contract with a shipper relieve itself, either in whole or in part, from liability for loss resulting from its negligence. The liability in that case was with reference to the freight transported, but we can see no reason why the principle is not applicable to an incidental right, that of being transported safely while caring for stock in transit. So far as the shipper is required to assume risks incidental to taking care of his stock he of necessity waives his right to be treated as an ordinary passenger, but this waiver ought never to be extended to negligence on the part of the company to perform its duties proper under the circumstances as a common carrier."

Amount of Liability Limited.—In Feldschneider *v.* Chicago, etc., Ry. Co. (Wis.), 12 R. R. R. 737, 35 Am. & Eng. R. Cas., N. S., 737, 99 N. W. 1034, 122 Wis. 423, it is held that where a contract between a carrier and a shipper provided that the shipper might accompany his stock on the train, but that the carrier should in no

event be liable for any personal injury to him on the carrier's cars
or road in an amount exceeding $500, the clause limiting the car-
rier's liability for personal injuries is void.

**Injuries to Shipper's Employees—Carrier Indemnified—Special
Cars Furnished on Condition.**—In Baker *v.* Boston, etc., R. Co. (N.
H.), 23 R. R. R. 592, 46 Am. & Eng. R. Cas., N. S., 592, 65 Atl. 386, it
is held that a shipper's contract with a carrier by which the carrier
was indemnified against claims for personal injuries to the shipper's
employees by reason of carrying such employees free on cars specially
provided by the shipper is void where the carrier refused to furnish such special cars unless the shipper would furnish men to handle
and care for the shipper's goods, and transportation according to the
shipper's public duty is not afforded the shipper as an alternative, and
no reduction of rates is made.

**Shipment of Poultry—Required by Connecting Carrier to Sign Re-
lease.**—In Delaware, etc., R. Co. *v.* Ashley, 14 C. C. A. 368, 67 Fed.
209, it appeared that plaintiff was employed by a shipper of poultry
in carload lots to travel with the cars of poultry, and care for the
fowls; that the latter shipped by the C. railroad a car of poultry, the
bill of lading stipulating that the same should go to its destination
by the D. railroad from a certain intermediate point; and that the
man in charge should travel free, and the through bill of lading
stated the same condition. Plaintiff accompanied the car, and the
D. railroad received the car with the waybill, and passed plaintiff
free, but required him to sign a release of any claim for damages.
Plaintiff was injured while so traveling on the D. railroad It was
held that the transportation of plaintiff having been part of the
consideration of the contract with the initial railroad company, he
was a passenger for hire, and the D. railroad having been bound,
if it accepted the car of poultry and waybill, to carry plaintiff in accordance with such contract, his release was without consideration
and invalid.

**Injuries from Ordinary Hazards Peculiar to Stock Trains at Sta-
tions—Water Spout Too Near Cars.**—In Fitchburg R. Co. *v.* Nichols,
29 C. C. A. 500, 85 Fed. Rep. 945, it is held that provisions in a contract for the carriage of cattle by rail, that when the person accompanying them shall leave the caboose, and pass over or along the
cars or track, he shall do so at his own sole risk, and that the carrier will not be required to stop or start its trains at or from depots
or platforms, do not extend the exemptions beyond the ordinary
hazards peculiar to the running of stock and freight trains in freight
yards, and, therefore, do not include damages by a waterspout which
is negligently permitted to project too near the moving cars.

Drover Injured in Collision—Negligence—Burden of Proof.—In
Rowdin *v.* Pennsylvania R. Co. (Pa.), 13 R. R. R. 672, 36 Am. & Eng.
R. Cas., N. S., 672, 57 Atl. 1125, it is held that where a drover accompanying live stock on a railroad, whose transportation had been included in the price paid as freight on the stock, is injured by colli-

sion between his car on defendant's track, he sufficiently sustains
the burden of proof to show negligence to relieve him from the effects of the release on the back of the contract of shipment stating
that he assumed all risks of accident or damages to his person.

Application of Statute.—In Chicago, etc., Ry. Co. *v.* Posten, 59
Kan. 449, it is held that an attempt of a railroad company, or its receivers, to limit, without an order of the Board of Railroad Commissioners, its common law liability for injuries to a passenger resulting from the negligence of its employees, is prohibited by section 17,
chapter 69, of Kansas General Statutes of 1897, and, therefore, a provision in a stock-pass, attempting to limit such liability to $1,000, is
invalid.

**Stipulation That Hand Sent with Cattle by Shipper Was Carrier's
Employee.**—In Missouri Pac. Ry. Co. *v.* Ivy, 71 Tex. 409, 9 S. W. 346,
it appeared that a contract with a railroad company for the shipment
of cattle stipulated that the owner should send a hand upon the
train to look after the cattle; that such hand was an employee of
the railroad company; and that as such he assumed the risks of a
railroad employee. The hand thus sent in charge of the stock was
killed in a collision while upon the train in charge of the cattle. It
was held that, as a common carrier cannot limit its liability by express contract, it cannot be done upon false or counterfeited relations; and that such hand while on the train in charge of the cattle was a passenger for hire, and the stipulation purporting to exempt the carrier from liability was invalid.

3. Drover's Employees Are Not Chargeable with Notice, Where.

It has been held that the employees of the shipper are not bound
by an exemption of the carrier's liability provided for by a drover's
pass, unless they were chargeable with notice of its existence and
stipulations before they commenced the trip on the train. Coppack
v. Long Island R. Co., 89 Hun. (N. Y. Sup. Ct.), 186; Porter *v.* New
York, etc., R. Co., 36 N. Y. S. R. 315, 13 N. Y. Supp. 491, 59 Hun. 177,
affirmed in 129 N. Y. 624, mem., 41 N. Y. S. R. 946, 29 N. E 1029.

4. Mail Agents.

A railroad company cannot by contract exempt itself from liability
for negligent injuries to railway mail agents or clerks riding on its
trains in the discharge of their duties. Illinois Cent. R. Co. *v.*
Crudup, 63 Miss. 291; Jones *v.* St. Louis, etc., R. Co., 125 Mo. 666, 28
S. W. 883; Seybolt *v.* New York, etc., R. Co., 18 Am. & Eng. R. Cas.
162, 95 N. Y. 562, 47 Am. Rep. 75.

Lack of Consideration.—In Seybolt *v.* New York, etc., R. Co., 18
Am. & Eng. R. Cas. 162, 95 N. Y. 652, 47 Am. Rep. 75, it appeared that
a mail agent was killed while riding on defendant's train, that upon
the pass issued for his use by defendant was an indorsement by
which the railroad stipulated for an exemption from liability for
damages on account of injuries occurring through its negligence. It

Note

was held that as the authority of the government agents to contract for the transportation of mails is limited by the provisions of the United States Statutes (U. S. R. S. §§ 3997 to 4005), and as to power given them to contract for exemption to a railroad company from liability for such a cause of action, it was not to be assumed that the contract under which defendant carried the mails contained any such provision; that as the contract between the government and defendant contained such a provision it was unauthorized and void; that assuming that decedent received the pass and was chargeable with knowledge of its contents, it did not constitute a contract between him and defendant; that as the absolute duty of carrying the agent in charge of the mail is imposed by said statutes upon the railroad corporation accepting the public for mail transportation, defendant had no right to impose the condition, the agent's acceptance of the pass did not indicate his intention to assent to its provisions, and, even if it might be so construed, and the exemption clause was to be considered as a contract, it was void for want of consideration.

In Illinois Cent. R. Co. *v.* Crudup, 63 Miss. 291, it is held that the acceptance of a "free ticket" by a mail agent running on a railroad, conditioned that he shall take all risk of injury while on such railroad, is not a waiver of his right to damages for an injury occasioned by the negligence of the railroad's servants; for as the company receives compensation from the government for transporting the mail agent such waiver would be without consideration, and such a contract of waiver would be against public policy.

5. Carrier's Employees Injured While Riding on Its Cars.

According to the weight of authority a railroad cannot, by a stipulation in a pass given to one of its own employees for his transportation on its trains or cars, to or from work, or for his own personal ends, exempt itself from liability for injuries caused either by its own negligence or that of its servants. Whitney *v.* New York, etc., R. Co. (C. C. A.), 19 Am. & Eng. R. Cas., N. S., 184; Doyle *v.* Fitchburg R. Co., 166 Mass. 492, 44 N. E. 611, 5 Am. & Eng. R. Cas. N. S., 257; Williams *v.* Oregon Short Line R. Co. (Utah), 12 Am. & Eng. R. Cas., N. S., 61.

Going to and from Work.—A ticket given a railroad to its employees living on the line of its railway, and working in a certain city, cannot be regarded as a gratuity, and an employee traveling on such ticket must be regarded as a passenger; and a contract on the back of such ticket, purporting to exonerate the railroad from liability for its negligence or that of its employees, is invalid. So held in Doyle *v.* Fitchburg R. Co., 166 Mass. 492, 44 N. E. 611, 5 Am. & Eng. R. Cas., N. S., 257.

In Williams *v.* Oregon Short Line R. Co. (Utah), 12 Am. & Eng. R. Cas., N. S., 61, it is held that where a person agrees with a railroad to enter into its employment at a certain place in the future, and in consideration of the mutual interests of both a free pass is given to the place of employment, with conditions on the back purporting to render the railroad not liable for injuries caused by its negligence or that of its agents, and in traveling on such pass to the place of employment the person is injured by the negligence of the carrier's agents, such person must be regarded as a passenger for hire, and not an employee, and the carrier is liable for damages caused the passenger by its negligence, notwithstanding such conditions.

Not Going to or from Work—Conditions Freely Assented to.—In Whitney *v.* New York, etc., R. Co. (C. C. A.), 19 Am. & Eng. R. Cas., N. S., 184, it is held that a railroad employee when traveling over his employer's line for his own convenience, and not in connection with going to or from his work, on a pass which he had received as part of the consideration of his contract of employment, is a passenger; and, in an action for injuries sustained by him through the negligence of the railroad, while so traveling, conditions endorsed on the pass by which the holder expressly assumed all risks arising from the negligence of the agents of the railroad, or otherwise, while using it, will not be enforced, although he freely assented to them.

Ticket Containing More Rides than Necessary in Going to and from Work—Killed While Traveling on Personal Business.—In Doyle *v.* Fitchburg R. Co., 162 Mass. 66, 37 N. E. 770, it appeared that an employee of a railroad company was furnished by it each month with a ticket which contained more rides than were necessary in traveling to and from his work, and on which he was at liberty to ride whether in the service of the company or for his own private interests or pleasure. On the back of the ticket was a contract, one clause of which was as follows: "The person accepting this free ticket thereby and in consideration thereof assumes all risk of accidents, and expressly agrees that the company is not a common carrier in respect to him, and shall not be liable under any circumstances, whether of negligence of agents or otherwise, for injury to the person, or for loss or injury to the property, of the passenger using the ticket." While traveling on the ticket, on his own personal business, when his time was his own, he was killed in a collision caused by the gross negligence of an engineer in the employee of the railroad. It was held that deceased was a passenger at the time of the accident, and not in the employment of the railroad, within the meaning of Mass. Pub. Sts., c. 112, § 212, and that the contract on back of the ticket, did not operate to release the railroad from liability.

6. Express Messengers.

According to the weight of authority, a contract by which a railroad company undertakes to transport the express matter and messengers of an express company, and providing that the railroad company shall not be liable for injuries to the messengers, even where they are caused by its negligence, may be valid.

Note

United States.—Baltimore, etc., R. Co. *v.* Voight, 17 Am. & Eng. R. Cas., N. S., 111, 176 U. S. 498, 44 L. Ed. 560; Kelly *v.* Malott (C. C. A.), 17 R. R. R. 635, 40 Am. & Eng. R. Cas., N. S., 635, 135 Fed. Rep. 74; Long *v.* Lehigh Valley R. Co. (C. C. A.), 12 R. R. R. 508, 35 Am. & Eng. R. Cas., N. S., 508.

Illinois.—Blank *v.* Illinois Cent. R. Co., 182 Ill. 332, 55 N. E. 332.

Indiana.—Louisville, etc., R. Co. *v.* Keefer (Ind.), 5 Am. & Eng. R. Cas., N. S., 26, 146 Ind. 21; Pittsburgh, etc., Ry. Co. *v.* Mahony (Ind.), 8 Am. & Eng. R. Cas., N. S., 441.

Kansas.—Sewell *v.* Atchison, etc., Ry. Co. (Kan.), 30 R. R. R. 86, 53 Am. & Eng. R. Cas., N. S., 86, 96 Pac. 1007.

Massachusetts.—Bates *v.* Old Colony R. Co., 147 Mass 255, 17 N. E. 633.

New York.—Blair *v.* Erie R. Co., 66 N. Y. 313.

Vermont.—Robinson *v.* St. Johnsburg, etc., R. Co. (Vt.), 24 R. R. R. 630, 47 Am. & Eng. R. Cas., N. S., 630, 66 Atl. 814.

Wisconsin.—Peterson *v.* Chicago, etc., R. Co., 9 R. R. R. 286, 32 Am. & Eng. R. Cas., N. S., 286, 96 N. W. 532, 119 Wis. 197.

In Blank *v.* Illinois Cent. R. Co., 182 Ill. 332, 55 N. E. 332, it is held that a contract between a railroad company and an express company, which provides that the former shall not be liable for negligence respecting injuries to the express company's employees, as a condition to granting the right to carry express on trains, is not against public policy.

A contract whereby a railroad company undertook to transport the express matter and messengers of an express company, the latter assuming all risk of accidents happening to its messengers and agreeing to indemnify the railroad company against all claims made by its messengers for injuries received, was valid. So held in Robinson *v.* St. Johnsburg, etc., R. Co. (Vt.), 24 R. R. R. 630, 47 Am. & Eng. R. Cas., N. S., 630, 66 Atl. 814.

A contract by an express messenger, relieving a railroad company from liability for personal injuries sustained by him while riding on its train in the performance of his duties, caused by the ordinary negligence of the railroad's employees, is valid, and not contrary to public policy. So held in Peterson *v.* Chicago, etc., R. Co., 9 R. R. R. 286, 32 Am. & Eng. R. Cas., N. S., 286, 96 N. W. 532, 119 Wis. 197.

Not a Passenger.—In Peterson *v.* Chicago, etc., R. Co., 96 N. W. 532, 9 R. R. R. 286, 32 Am. & Eng. R. Cas., N. S., 286, 119 Wis. 197, it is said in the opinion: "The express messenger is not a person who has applied to a common carrier for transportation, and is entitled to that transportation without condition, upon payment of his fare. But a person who voluntarily goes upon a train, not for transportation, but to transact certain business for the express company which it is allowed to transact, not because the railroad company is a common carrier, but because of a contract between the express company and the railroad company by which the express company

Note

and its messengers were granted rights which the railroad company could not be compelled to grant as a common carrier."

Contract between Express Company and Its Employee—Railroad's Knowledge and Assent.—And it is not essential that the railroad knew of or assented to the contract between the express messenger and the express company before the commencement of an action against the railroad for injuries sustained by the messenger while in the performance of his duties on a train of the railroad company. So held in Peterson *v.* Chicago, etc., R. Co., 9 R. R. R. 286, 32 Am. & Eng. R. Cas., N. S., 286, 96 N. W. 532, 119 Wis. 197.

Cars Used Exclusively by Express Company—Agreement to Assume All Risks.—In Baltimore, etc., Ry. Co. *v.* Voight, 17 Am. & Eng. R. Cas., N. S., 111, 176 U. S. 498, 44 L. Ed. 560, it is held that where a railroad company transports cars used exclusively by an express company, under a contract between the companies exempting the railroad from all liability for injuries sustained by express messengers while being transported on such cars, and an express messenger, in consideration of employment by the express company, assumes the risk of all such injuries, he cannot recover for such an injury sustained by him through the negligence of the railroad, as he cannot evade the agreement exempting the railroad from liability, by invoking that principle of public policy which forbids a common carrier of passengers for hire to contract against responsibility for negligence.

Express Messenger Holding Season Ticket—Permission to Ride in Baggage Car.—In Bates *v.* Old Colony R. Co., 147 Mass. 255, 17 N. E. 633, it is held that if an express messenger holding a season ticket from a railroad company and desiring to ride for the conduct of his business in a baggage car, in contravention of the railroad's rules, agrees to assume all risk of injury therefrom, and to hold the company harmless therefor, such agreement is not invalid as against public policy; and he cannot recover for injuries caused by the negligence of the railroad's servants, to which his presence in the baggage car directly contributed. See also, Hosmer *v.* Old Colony R. Co., 156 Mass. 506, 31 N. E. 652.

Agreement to Indemnify Railroad—Messenger's Implied Assent—Injuries Through Negligence.—But in Robinson *v.* St. Johnsburg, etc., R. Co. (Vt.), 24 R. R. R. 630, 47 Am. & Eng. R. Cas., N. S., 630, 66 Atl. 814, it is held that an express messenger, entering the employ of an express company with knowledge of a contract between the latter and a railroad company whereby the railroad company was to transport the express company's express matter and messengers and to indemnify the railroad company against all claims for injuries received by messengers, must be held to have assented to the contract, but such an assent was not a waiver of the messenger's right to assert the railroad's liability for injuries resulting to him through negligence.

Note

Application of Statute Making Railroad Liable for All Damage from Negligence.—And in Sewell *v.* Atchison, etc., Ry. Co. (Kan.), 30 R. R. R. 86, 53 Am. & Eng. R. Cas., N. S., 86, 96 Pac. 1007, it is held that, at common law, where an express company contracts with the railway company, by means of whose trains it carries on its business, that it assumes all risk of injury to its employees, and undertakes to save the railroad company harmless from any claims with respect thereto, and contracts with one of its employees that neither it nor the railway company shall be liable to him for any injury occurring to him while traveling on any such trains in the course of such employment, such employee cannot, under the common-law rule, maintain an action for injuries received while so traveling, in consequence of the negligence of the agents of the railway company; but that view of the Kansas statutes making a railroad company liable for all damages done to persons or property in consequences of any neglect on its part, and for all damages done to any of its employees, in consequence of any negligence of its agents, or by any mismanagement of its engineers or other employees, that although an express company contracts with the railway company by means of whose trains it carries on its business that it assumes all risk of injury to its employees, and undertakes to save the railway company harmless from any claims with respect thereto, and contracts with one of its employees that neither it nor the railway company shall be liable to him for any injury occurring to him while traveling on any of such trains in the course of such employment, such employee may still maintain an action against the railroad company for injuries received while so traveling, in consequence of the negligence of its agents.

In O'Brien *v.* Chicago & N. W. Ry. Co. (C. C.), 116 Fed. Rep. 502, it appeared that Code Iowa, § 2071, provides that every corporation operating a railroad shall be liable to every person, including employees, for the consequences of the neglect or mismanagement of the company's servants, and that no contract which restricts such liability shall be legal or binding. Section 2074 declares that no contract, receipt, rule or regulation shall exempt any railroad company engaged in transporting persons or property from the liability of a common carrier, and Acts 27th Gen. Assem., c. 49, provides that no contract of insurance, relief, benefit or indemnity in case of injury or death, entered into prior to the injury, shall constitute any bar or defense to any action based on the provisions of Code, § 2071. By a contract made in Iowa, between an express company and a messenger employed by it, the latter, in consideration of his employment, agreed to assume all risk of accidents and injuries resulting from the gross or other negligence of any corporation or person engaged in the operation of any railroad, or any employee thereof, whether resulting in death · or otherwise, and authorized the company to contract with any railroad company on his behalf that no claim should be made against it by him or his

Note

representatives on account of any such injury. By a second contract, made in accordance with such authority, between the express company and a railroad company, the latter agreed to furnish cars for the use of the former over its lines, and the express company agreed to protect the railroad company against liability for injuries to express messengers or agents while being transported over its lines in connection with their duties. It was held that while such contracts would be effectual to protect the railroad company from liability at common law, under such statutory provisions, declaratory of the public policy of the state, they were invalid, and constituted no defense to an action against it for the death of the messenger occurring in the state of Iowa, by reason of the wrecking of the express car in which he was employed, through the negligence and want of ordinary care by defendant railroad or its servants, whether the messenger be regarded as an employee of the railroad or not.

Contract between Express Company and Employee—Case Distinguished.—And in Shannon *v.* Chesapeake, etc., R. Co., 104 Va. 645, 52 S. E. 376, it is said in the opinion: "It will be seen that there is a marked difference between the contract set out in the plea in this case and the tripartite agreement in the Baltimore, etc., R. Co. *v.* Voight, 176 U. S. 498, 44 L. Ed. 560, 20 Sup. Ct. Rep. 385. The only parties to this contract are the express company and its servants; and its purpose is manifest. It stipulates in the first place, to exempt the master from liability for its own negligence to its servants, and, secondly, undertakes to afford similar immunity to defendant (railroad company) for its negligence. It is plain that such contract is violative both of the letter and spirit of the statute (Va. Code 1904, § 1294, c. 25), and illegal. Indeed, independently of statute, the almost unbroken current of authority declares such contracts void. * * * In Voight's case, supra, at page 514, it is said of his relations as an express messenger to the railroad company. 'He was then as a servant, engaged with the servants of the railroad company in the service of transportation on the road. His duties were substantially the same as those of the baggage master in the same car, the latter relating to merchandise carried for passengers, and the former to merchandise carried for the express company. His actual relations to the other servants of the railroad corporation engaged in the transportation were substantially the same as those of the baggage master.' "

Injured in Kentucky—Provision of Virginia Constitution—Application.—And in Davis *v.* Chesapeake, etc., R. Co. (Ky.), 24 R. R. R. 170, 47 Am. & Eng. R. Cas., N. S., 170, 92 S. W. 339, it is held that, under Va. Const., § 196, and Code, Va. 1887, § 1296, prohibiting carriers from contracting away their common-law liability, a Virginia contract, whereby an express messenger at the time of his employment released all claims against the express company or against the carrier for injuries he might receive, whether through

negligence or otherwise, was void, so as not to affect his right
to recover for injuries received in Kentucky.

**Contract between Express Company and Messenger—Railroad
without Knowledge.**—And the mere fact that an express messenger
had entered into a contract with the express company, releasing
the latter from any claim for injuries which might be received
by him in the course of his employment, and authorizing the express company to make a contract in his behalf with any carrier,
in consideration of his free transportation, exempting such carrier
from any liability for injuries which the plaintiff might receive in
transportation, would not entitle a railroad company to the benefit
of it, if it had no notice or knowledge of the contract. So held in
Louisville, etc., R. Co. v. Keefer (Ind.), 5 Am. & Eng. R. Cas., N.
S., 26, 146 Ind. 21.

Agreement to Indemnify Railroad—Construction of Contract.—
And in Kenny v. New York, etc., R. Co., 125 N. Y. 422, 26 N. E. 626,
it appeared that a contract between an express company and defendant railroad company, provided that defendant should be "expressly relieved from and guaranteed against any liability for any
damage done to the agents of" the former, "whether in their employ as messengers or otherwise." Decedent, a messenger in the
employ of the express company, was killed through the negligence
of defendant. It was held that the contract might be construed,
not necessarily as releasing or preventing an action by employees
of the express company against defendant for damages for injuries
received while on the railroad, but as an agreement to indemnify
defendant in the event of such an action; and that plaintiff was entitled to recover.

7. Express Messenger Is Not Chargeable with Notice, Where

But an express messenger is not bound by such a contract between the express company and the railroad company, if he is not
chargeable with notice of its provisions. Long v. Lehigh Valley R.
Co. (C. C. A.), 12 R. R. R. 508, 35 Am. & Eng. R. Cas., N. S., 508,
130 Fed. Rep. 870; Baltimore, etc., R. Co. v. Voight, 176 U. S. 498,
44 L. Ed. 560, 17 Am. & Eng. R. Cas., N. S., 111; Blank v. Illinois
Cent. R. Co., 80 Ill. App. 475; Pittsburgh, etc., R. Co. v Mahony
(Ind.), 8 Am. & Eng. R. Cas., N. S., 441; Sewell v. Atchison, etc.,
R. Co. (Kan.), 30 R. R. R. 86, 53 Am. & Eng. R. Cas., N. S., 86,
96 Pac. 1007; Bates v. Old Colony R. Co., 147 Mass. 255, 17 N. E.
633; Robinson v. St. Johnsburg, etc., R. Co. (Vt.), 24 R. R. R. 630,
47 Am. & Eng. R. Cas., N. S., 630, 66 Atl. 814.

In Chamberlain v. Pierson, 31 C. C. A. 157, 87 Fed. Rep. 420, it is
held that employees of an express company, who had no knowledge
of a contract between such company and a railroad company to the
effect that such employees were to be furnished free transportation
over the railroad at their own risk while in the service of the express company, are not bound thereby.

Note

Contract between Express Company and Railroad—Absence of Knowledge and Assent.—In Brewer *v.* New York, etc., R. Co., 124 N. Y. 59, 26 N. E. 324, an action against defendant railroad to recover for the death of an express messenger, caused by the negligence of defendant, while he was riding in the course of his employment on its train, it appeared that the express company had entered into a contract with a railroad company, to the rights and duties of which defendant had succeeded, by which the railroad company agreed to transport the messengers of the express company and certain specified property free of charge, the latter company assuming all transportation risks and other liabilities arising in respect thereof, and agreeing to indemnify and protect the former therefrom. The responsibility of the railway company in transporting express matter was limited to cases of negligence, it, "in no event, whether of negligence or otherwise," to be responsible for property carried by the railway company free of charge." There was no evidence that decedent had any knowledge or information of the provisions of the contract. It was held that defendant railroad was liable; that decedent was a passenger and could not, without his knowledge or consent, be chargeable with the stipulations in the contract; and that while he entered into the service of the express company he assumed the ordinary hazards incident to that business, there was no presumption of implied understanding that he took upon himself the risks of injury which he might suffer through defendant's negligence.

In Kenney *v.* New York, etc., R. Co., 54 Hun. 143, 7 N. Y. S. 255, it appeared that plaintiff's intestate was a messenger of an express company, and at the time of his death was in charge of goods then being transported by defendant for the express company on the lines of the W. S. R. Co., which lines were then leased to and operated by defendant. Previous to such lease a contract had been made between the W. S. R. Co. and such express company, by which the latter had the right to carry goods on all passenger trains of the former at rates specified in the contract, and "to send one messenger by each train without charge." A clause of the contract read as follows: "Party of the first part is hereby expressly released from, and guaranteed, any liability for any damage done to the agents of the party of the second part, whether in their employ as messengers or otherwise." It was held that, in the absence of an agreement on the part of deceased, or knowledge of such agreement of his employer, which assumed to grant immunity to defendant for injuries done to him, that it was not competent for the express company to waive or compromise the right of deceased to protection against negligent wrong at the hands of the defendant, or to discharge defendant from a cause of action which belonged only to deceased or his personal representatives.

Express Messenger's Knowledge of Contract—Negligence.—The fact that an express messenger on entering the service of an ex-

Note

press company had some knowledge of an arrangement with the railroad company covering his transportation did not charge him with knowledge of anything affecting his right of recovery against the railroad for injuries through negligence. So held in Robinson : St. Johnsburg, etc., R. Co. (Vt.), 24 R. R. R. 630, 47 Am. & Eng R. Cas., N. S., 630, 66 Atl. 814.

Chargeable with Notice of Contract.—An express messenger riding in a railway car in the discharge of the duties of his employment is chargeable with notice of the contract under which he is being transported by the railroad company. So held in Long r. Lehigh Valley R. Co. (C. C. A.), 12 R. R. R. 508, 35 Am. & Eng. R Cas. N. S., 508, 130 Fed. Rep. 870.

8. Sleeping Car Company's Employees.

According to what seems to be the weight of authority, a railroad company in contracting to haul the cars of a sleeping car company in its trains may stipulate for exemption from liability for injuries sustained by the sleeping car company's employees while riding on such cars, even where they are caused by the railroad's negligence. McDermon v. Southern Pac. R. Co. (C. C), 122 Fed Rep. 669; Chicago, etc., Ry. Co. v. Hamler, 215 Ill. 525; Russell r Pittsburgh, etc, Ry. Co. (Ind.), 23 Am. & Eng. R. Cas., N S., 601. 61 N. E. 678; Bissell v. New York Cent. R. Co., 25 N. Y. 442.

In Chicago, etc., Ry. Co. v. Hamler, 215 Ill. 525, it is said in the opinion: "The defendant (railroad company) might undertake to receive and haul the cars of the Pullman Company, but in doing so had a right to impose such terms as it might elect. This has been the opinion of the courts in all cases involving such contracts as the one here in question, which has been enforced in cases of express cars, circus trains and Pullman cars, which the carrier was not bound to receive and haul as a common carrier. (Bates r. Old Colony R. Co., 147 Mass. 255. 17 N. E. 633; Hosmer r. Old Colony R. Co., 156 Mass. 506, 31 N. E. 652; Louisville. etc., R. Co. r Keefer, 146 Ind. 21, 44 N. E. 796; Pittsburg, etc., R. Co. v. Mahoney, 148 Ind. 196, 46 N. E. 917, 47 N. E. 464; Robertson v. Old Colony R Co 156 Mass. 525, 31 N. E. 650; Griswold v. New York, etc.. R. Co.. 25 Am. & Eng. R. Cas. 280, 53 Conn. 371, 55 Am. Rep. 115. 4 Atl 261; Coup v. Wabash, etc., R. Co., 56 Mich. 111, 22 N. W. 215; Express Cases, 117 U. S. 1, 29 L. Ed. 791; Peterson r. Chicago. etc. R. Co., 9 R. R. R. 286, 32 Am. & Eng. R. Cas., N. S., 286. 96 N W. Rep. 532; Donovan v. Pennsylvania Co. (C. C. A.). 130 Fed 215; New York, etc., R. Co. v. Difendaffer (C. C. A.). 125 Fed 893; McDermon v. Southern Pac. R. Co., 122 Fed. 669)."

In Russell v. Pittsburg, etc., R. Co. (Ind.), 23 Am. & Eng. R Cas., N. S., 601, 61 N. E. 678, it is held that as a railroad is under no legal duty to provide or furnish sleeping cars, a contract specifically releasing the company from all liability for negligence toward an employee of the sleeping car company while riding in a sleeping car attached to one of the railroad company's trains is valid.

Note

Indemnity Contract—Validity.—In Chicago, etc., Ry. Co. *v.* Hamler, 215 Ill. 525, it is held that the duties of a railroad company as a common carrier do not require it to haul cars of a sleeping car company, and it has a right, in contracting to haul such cars, to require the sleeping car company to indemnify it against liability for personal injuries received by the sleeping car company's servants.

Negligence of Railroad.—In Russell *v.* Pittsburg, etc., R. Co. (Ind.), 23 Am. & Eng. R. Cas., N. S., 601, 61 N. E. 678, it is held that a contract by a sleeping car employee releasing transportation companies from all claims for "liability of any nature or character whatsoever" includes a release of liability for personal injuries caused by the negligence of the carrier.

Railroad Released from Liability—Validity of Contract between Porter and Sleeping Car Company.—In Chicago, etc., Ry. Co. *v.* Hamler, 215 Ill. 525, it is held that a contract between a sleeping car company and its porter whereby the latter released from liability for negligence any railroad company hauling the sleeping cars, is a good defense to an action by him against the railroad company for any negligence occasioning his injury while discharging his duties as the servant of the sleeping car company, short of willful or intentional negligence.

Pullman Car Porter Not Passenger—Indemnity Contract—Ratification.—In McDermon *v.* Southern Pac. Co. (C. C.), 122 Fed. 669, it is held that a contract made by a Pullman car porter on securing employment, whereby he releases the company from liability for his negligent injury, ratifies contracts made by it with the railroad companies carrying its cars for indemnifying the latter for injuries to Pullman employees, covenants to indemnify the Pullman Company on such account, agrees that the contract may be assigned to a carrying company for purposes of defense and releases carrying companies from such liability, does not contravene public policy, and is valid; the porter not being a passenger of the railroad companies.

Contracts Inures to Benefit of Railroad.—In Russell *v.* Pittsburg, etc., R. Co. (Ind.), 23 Am. & Eng. R. Cas., N. S., 601, 61 N. E. 678, it is held that a contract between a sleeping car company and an employee releasing the sleeping car company and all transportation companies from all liability for personal injuries to the employee sustained while traveling over such lines inures to the benefit of a railroad company transporting the car in which the employee was injured.

Failure to Read Contract.—In New York Cent., etc., R. Co. *v.* Difendaffer (C. C. A.), 125 Fed. 893, it is held that the mere fact that a person entering the employment of the Pullman Company as porter on one of its sleeping cars failed to read the contract which he was required to sign, and which contained a provision

Note

that he assumed all risk of injury from railroad travel while engaged in such employment, does not afford ground for the avoidance
of such stipulation, in the absence of any evidence of fraud or
misrepresentation.

9. Contracts to Haul Show Cars—Injuries to Show Company's Employees.

A railroad, in contracting to haul cars of a circus, menagerie, or
other show company, may stipulate for exemption from liability
for injuries to show company's employees, sustained through the
railroad company's negligence while such cars are being hauled by
the railroad company. Chicago, etc., R. Co. v. Wallace, 14 C. C. A.
257, 66 Fed. 506; Clough v. Grand Trunk, etc., R. Co. (C. C. A.),
26 R. R. R. 660, 49 Am. & Eng. R. Cas., N. S., 660, 155 Fed. 81;
Chicago, etc., Ry. Co. v. Hamler, 215 Ill. 525, 74 N. E. 705; Cleveland,
etc., Ry. Co. v. Henry (Ind.), 29 R. R. R. 266, 52 Am. & Eng. R. Cas., N.
S., 266, 83 N. W. 710; Russell v. Pittsburg, etc., R. Co. (Ind.), 23 Am.
& Eng. R. Cas., N. S., 601, 61 N. E. 678; Robertson v. Old Colony
R. Co., 156 Mass. 525, 31 N. E. 650; Coup v. Wabash, etc., R. Co.,
56 Mich. 111, 22 N. W. 215.

**Contract for Use of Railroad's Motive Power, Tracks and Train-
men—Trainmen as Circus Company's Employees.**—In Clough v.
Grand Trunk, etc., R. Co. (C. C. A.), 26 R. R. R. 660, 49 Am. &
Eng. R. Cas., N. S., 660, 155 Fed. Rep. 81, it appeared that a circus
company, owning its own cars, contracted with a railroad company
for the hire of motive power and the use of tracks, and trainmen,
to be considered as the circus company's servants, for the transportation of the train from one place to another, the contract exempting the railroad company from liability for injuries to any person
or persons using the train from whatsoever cause. It was held that,
the railroad company being under no legal duty to move the circus
company in the manner specified, the contract was not contrary to
public policy.

Same—Reduced Rates—Railroad as Private Carrier.—In Chicago,
etc., R. Co. v. Wallace, 14 C. C. A. 257, 66 Fed. Rep. 506, it appeared that the railroad company made a special contract in writing with the proprietor of a circus, to haul a special train, consisting of cars owned by him, containing the circus property, equipment, and performers, between certain points, on stated days, at
specified charges, which were less than the regular rates of the
company for transportation of passengers and freight. It was provided in the contract that, in consideration of the reduced rate and
of the increased risks to the property of the railroad company in
running such special train, that the railroad should not be liable
for any damage to the persons or property of the circus company
from whatever cause. It was not the regular business or custom
of the railroad company to haul such special trains of private cars,
or to transport persons, animals, and freight on the same trains. It

Note

was held that the railroad company in so hauling the circus train acted as a private, and not as a common carrier; and that, as such, it had the right to make the contract, stipulating against liability for damage, and that such contract was binding upon the parties.

Same—Collision between Sections of Circus Train.—In Clough *v.* Grand Trunk, etc., R. Co. (C. C. A.), 26 R. R. R. 660, 49 Am. & Eng. R. Cas., N. S., 660, 155 Fed. Rep. 81, it is held that where a carrier leases motive power, and the use of its tracks and train operatives to a circus company, under a contract exempting the carrier from liability for all injuries, the relation of passenger and carrier did not exist between the railroad company and an employee of the circus company, traveling solely by virtue of his employment, who was not a party to such transportation contract, so as to entitle such employee to recover against the railroad company for injuries sustained in a collision between two sections of the circus train.

Same—Defective Car.—In Robertson *v.* Old Colony R. Co., 156 Mass. 525, 31 N. E. 650, it appeared that a railroad company agreed to haul certain cars of the proprietors of a circus according to a certain schedule of time, and for a price less than the regular rates for such service, the proprietors agreeing, at their own expense, to load and unload the cars, to save the defendant harmless from all claims for damages to persons and property, however accruing, and to "assume all risk of accident from any cause." An accident occurred by one of the cars running off the track by reason of its trucks not being in proper condition, and an employee of the proprietors who was riding in one of the cars was injured. It was held that he could not recover against the railroad, as it had no control over the condition of the cars and no authority to interfere with them, as the contract was simply to haul the cars as they were, which contract the railroad had a right to make; and it was under no obligation to draw the cars as a common carrier.

Same—Not Common Carrier.—In Coup *v.* Wabash, etc., R. Co., 56 Mich. 111, 22 N. W. 215, it is held that a common carrier's liability does not attach to a railroad which has contracted to move a menagerie in the latter's own cars controlled by its own agents, and though operated by the railroad employees, run upon a time schedule to suit the menagerie, and a stipulation that the railroad shall not be liable for injuries to the menagerie or its employees caused by negligence in thus moving it may be valid.

Same—Show Company's Employee Chargeable with Notice.—In Cleveland, etc., Ry. Co. *v.* Henry (Ind.), 29 R. R. R. 266, 52 Am. & Eng. R. Cas., N. S., 266, 83 N. E. 710, it appeared that a show company contracted with a railroad for the transportation of its show cars from place to place, and agreed to assume all responsibility for damages arising out of the contract and to indemnify the railroad from any claim for personal injuries or damage to property while an employee of the show company was lawfully in one of such cars awaiting transportation to another town; and that the railroad ran a train against the car, whereby such employee was fatally injured. He had made no effort to procure transportation from the railroad, since by his employment he had the right to free transportation in the show cars. It was held that such employee was bound to know that the car would be drawn to its destination under some private arrangement between his employer and the railroad and that whatever right he had to be carried over the railroad arose from such contract; and further that, when he entered the showman's service and accepted the method of transportation provided for his employees, such acceptance was subject to the conditions of the contract limiting the railroad's liability.

Same—Contract to Indemnify Railroad—Application of Statute.— Ind. Acts 1901, p. 516, c. 225, makes void all contracts between employer and employee releasing the employer or a third person from liability for his negligence and all contracts between an employee and a third person releasing the employer "from liability for damage of such employee arising out of the negligence of the employer." A show company contracted with a railroad company for the transportation of its show cars for a stipulated gross sum, and agreeing to assume all responsibility for damages arising out of the contract and "to indemnify and hold said railroad harmless for personal injuries or damage to property." While an employee of the show was in one of the show cars awaiting transportation he was killed by the negligence of the railway company. It was held, in an action against the railroad for the death, that so far as the contract was decedent's contract it was with the railroad, relieving it as a private carrier under a special agreement from liability for accidents from all sources affecting him and was not a contract within the inhibition of the statute. Cleveland, etc., Ry. Co. *v.* Henry (Ind.), 29 R. R. R. 266, 52 Am. & Eng. R. Cas., N. S., 266, 83 N. E. 710.

Negligence.—But in Seaboard, etc., R. Co. *v.* Main, 132 N. Car. 445, 43 S. E. 930, it is held that where a railroad company contracts to transport a circus and is indemnified by the circus company against any loss sustained by injury to the employees of the circus, the carrier is not thereby relieved of liability for negligent injuries to such employees.

III. MISCELLANEOUS.

Free Pass—Scope of Exemption—Death of Passenger.—In Northern Pac. Ry. Co. *v.* Adams (C. C. A.), 3 R. R. R. 734, 26 Am. & Eng. R. Cas., N. S., 734, 116 Fed. Rep. 324, it is held that a contract exempting a railroad company from liability "for any injury to the person, or for any loss or damage to the property," of the passenger using a free ticket, does not extend to the death of the passenger so contracting.

Death of Drover—Statutory Liability to Others—Application of Exemption.—In Clark *v.* Geer, 32 C. C. A. 295, 86 Fed. Rep. 447,

Note

it is held that where a cattle dealer purchases a ticket to ride on a freight train on condition that the company shall not be liable to him in any manner as a passenger, or for any accident, resulting to him, or liable to him for injury to person or property unless caused by the gross negligence of the company, the liability in no case to exceed $1,000, such agreement shows that he was contracting solely with reference to a liability to himself, and not with reference to the statutory liability of the carrier to others in case of his death through the wrongful act of the carrier.

Stock-Pass—Scope of Exemption—Damages Sustained by Widow and Children.—In Chicago, etc., Ry. Co. *v.* Martin, 59 Kan. 437, 53 Pac. 461, it is held that a stipulation in a stock-pass, on which deceased was riding, on terms limiting the liability of the receivers of the railway company for injuries to him resulting from the negligence of their servants, does not limit the recovery of his administratrix for damages sustained by his widow and children through his death, for which a right of recovery is given to her by § 418, chapter 95, of Kansas General Statutes, deceased having had no authority to contract against their rights.

Right to Limit Liability—Statutes.—In Chicago, etc., R. Co. *v.* Hambel (Neb.), 89 N. W. 643, it is held that § 3, art. 1, c. 72, Neb. Comp. Sts., prevents any limitation on the liability of a railroad company for a passenger's safety unless within the exceptions provided for in the section; and that § 5 of the same chapter does not impliedly give the right to a railroad company to limit its liability under § 3 by stipulation; and that the last named section is not unconstitutional.

Particular Form of Ticket—Reduced Fare.—In Miley *v.* Northern Pac. Ry. Co. (Mont.), 36 R. R. R. 176, 59 Am. & Eng. R. Cas., N. S., 176, 108 Pac. 5, it is held that, in the absence of statutory restrictions, a railway company may for a reduced fare sell a particular form of ticket whereby its liability is restricted and its obligations curtailed. See also, Rose *v.* Northern Pac. Ry. Co., 35 Mont. 70, 88 Pac. 767, 119 Am. St. 836.

Excursion Ticket—Assumption of All Risks—Right to Effect of Presumption of Negligence.—In Crary *v.* Lehigh Val. R. Co. (Pa.), 6 R. R. R. 119, 29 Am. & Eng. R. Cas., N. S., 119, 53 Atl. 363, it appeared that a passenger bought from a railroad company an excursion ticket at a reduced rate, with indorsement on it that the person accepting it assumes all risk of accident and damage. It was held that the acceptance of the ticket was waiver of the common-law rule making the carrier liable for the passenger's safety and he must affirmatively prove negligence on the part of the carrier, and cannot avail himself of the presumption of negligence arising in favor of the passenger where he sustains an injury.

Passenger Tickets—Application of Harter Act.—In The Kensington, 36 C. C. A. 533, 94 Fed. 885, it is held that the provisions of § 2 of the Harter act as to the limiting of the carrier's liability by

Note

bills of lading or shipping documents do not apply to passenger tickets. See also, The Rosedale (D. C.), 88 Fed. 324.

Amount of Recovery Limited—Proof of Identity Rejected by Conductor—Good Faith.—In Pierson v. Illinois Cent. R. Co. (Mich.), 24 R. R. R. 591, 47 Am. & Eng. R. Cas., N. S., 591, 112 N. W. 923, it is held that where a passenger, holding a ticket entitling him to transportation on identifying himself as its purchaser, and stipulating that any claim for damages resulting from any bona fide mistake of any conductor in rejecting proof of identity should be limited to the amount which the passenger paid for ticket, was ejected by a conductor who did not act in good faith the passenger was entitled to recover substantial damages.

Assumption of All Risks Pleading.—In Citizens' St. Ry. Co. v. Twiname, 111 Ind. 587, 13 N. E. 55, it is held that in an action against a common carrier for negligence in its transportation of passengers, where an agreement on the part of plaintiff that he will assume all risks is relied upon as a defense, it must be specially pleaded.

Contract between Shipper and His Employee Based on Void Contract between Shipper and Carrier.—A contract between a shipper and its employee indemnifying the shipper against claims for injuries to the employee received while riding on the cars, which is based on a void indemnity contract of the same nature between the shipper and the common carrier, cannot be availed of by the carrier in an action by such employee against the carrier for injuries sustained while riding on the cars. So held in Baker v. Boston, etc., R. Co. (N. H.), 23 R. R. R. 592, 46 Am. & Eng. R. Cas., N. S., 592, 65 Atl. 386.

Validity of Pass Issued to Public Officer—Constitutional Provision—Estoppel.—In Muldoon v. Seattle City R. Co., 10 Wash. 311, 38 Pac. 995, it is held that a public officer traveling upon a free pass issued by transportation company is estopped from setting up, in an action for damages arising from the negligence of the company, that the pass issued to him was void under the constitution, and that the conditions attached to its acceptance and use were, therefore, void.

A. R. Y.

CLOTH v. CHICAGO, R. I. & P. RY. Co.

(Supreme Court of Arkansas, Dec. 19, 1910.)

[132 S. W. Rep. 1005.]

Eminent Domain—Public Use—Determination.*—Whether property taken by power of eminent domain was taken for a public use is a judicial question, which the owner is entitled to have determined by the courts.

Eminent Domain—"Public Use"—Character.†—To constitute a "public use," the public must be concerned in the use, and it must be public in fact.

Eminent Domain—Public Use—Benefit to Third Persons.*—That others would incidentally derive benefit from the condemnation of plaintiff's property for a freight depot did not alter the character of the public use, and it was immaterial, as affecting such use, that a municipality was going to pay part of the compensation.

Eminent Domain—Necessity for Taking.—A railroad company, having the right to condemn property on which to locate a freight depot, had the right to choose plaintiff's property, though the company owned other property which it might have used, or the depot might have been located on the land of others.

Eminent Domain—Appeal—Review of Amount Awarded.—The finding of a jury as to the compensation to be made for property condemned will not be disturbed on appeal, where supported by substantial evidence.

Appeal from Circuit Court, Monroe County; Eugene Lankford, Judge.

Condemnation proceedings by the Chicago, Rock Island & Pacific Railway Company against Caroline Cloth. From a judgment awarding plaintiff certain compensation, she appeals. Affirmed.

Manning & Emerson, for appellant.
C. F. Greenlee, G. Otis Bogle, and *Geo. B. Pugh,* for appellee.

FRAUENTHAL, J. The appellee is a railroad corporation, and for a number of years it has, under due and legal authority, owned and operated a line of railroad in this state and through the town of Brinkley. It instituted proceedings to condemn a

---

*For the authorities in this series on the power to determine the necessity of a proposed condemnation of land for railroad purposes, see foot-note of Chicago, etc., R. Co. v. Mason (S. Dak.), 34 R. R. R. 60, 57 Am. & Eng. R. Cas., N. S., 60.

†For the authorities in this series on the question, what does, and does not, constitute a public use for which private property may be condemned, see foot-note of Dubuque, etc., R. Co. v. Ft. Dodge, etc., R. Co. (Iowa), 36 R. R. R. 292, 59 Am. & Eng. R. Cas., N. S., 292.

· Cloth v. Chicago, R. I. & P. Ry. Co

lot belonging to appellant situated in said town for the purpose of constructing thereon a freight depot. In its petition it alleged that it maintained a station at said town, and that in the due and proper operation of its railroad and the prosecution of its business it was necessary to conduct a freight depot at that place, and it asked the court to ascertain the amount of compensation which it should pay to appellent for said lot. Having deposited the amount designated by the circuit judge as the value of the property, it took possession thereof for said purpose.

In her answer the appellant alleged that the property was of the value of $2,500, and that she was damaged in the additional sum of $1,000 by reason of the appropriation thereof by appellee. She asked for a judgment against appellee for $3,500 for the property and her damages. Also, in her answer, she denied that it was necessary for appellee to construct a freight depot upon her lot, and she asked that the cause be transferred to the chancery court, to determine whether or not appellee had the right to condemn the same. To defeat the right to condemn the property, she alleged that prior to March 8, 1909, appellee owned a lot in the town of Brinkley upon which it had constructed a freight depot, which was destroyed by a cyclone upon that day, and that it still owned this lot, which was suitable for the purpose of a freight depot, and that on this account it was not necessary to take her property for that purpose. It also alleged that appellee had entered into an agreement with citizens of Brinkley, or the municipality itself, by which it was provided that the appellee should change the location of its freight depot from the former site thereof to the lot of appellant, and that said citizens or said town would pay a certain part of the consideration for the taking of her property.

The court refused to transfer the cause to the chancery court, but proceeded to impanel a jury to determine the damages which appellant was entitled to recover by reason of the condemnation of said property. During the progress of the trial appellant offered to prove the allegations of her answer by reason of which she denied the right of appellee to condemn her property. The court refused to permit the introduction of any testimony tending to prove these facts, but only admitted testimony showing the value of her property and the damage thereto. The jury returned a verdict in favor of appellant for $1,000. and from the judgment entered thereon she has appealed to this court.

By virtue of our Constitution the state's right of eminent domain is conceded, and the Legislature, as the representative of the state's sovereignty, or the agency to which the Legislature has granted the power, has the right to take any kind of property for public use. Const. art. 2, §§ 22, 23. But private property can, under the power of eminent domain, be taken only for a public use. It cannot be taken without the owner's consent, and appro-

Cloth *v.* Chicago. R. I. & P. Ry. Co

priated solely to the private use of another person or a corporation; and whether or not the property is taken for a public use is a judicial question, which the owner has the right to have determined by the courts. 2 Lewis on Eminent Domain (3d Ed.) § 599; Railway Co. *v.* Petty, 57 Ark. 359, 21 S. W. 884, 20 L. R. A. 434; Mountain Park Terminal Ry. Co. *v.* Field, 76 Ark. 239, 88 S. W. 897; Gilbert *v.* Shaver, 91 Ark. 231, 120 S. W. 833; 15 Cyc. 632.

In order to constitute a public use, it is necessary that the public shall be concerned in such use thereof, and the purpose for which the property is to be used must be in fact a public one. 15 Cyc. 581; Railway Co. *v.* Petty, 57 Ark. 359, 21 S. W. 884, 20 L. R. A. 434. A railroad corporation is recognized as a public agency, and by the Legislature it is authorized to exercise the power of eminent domain in aid of the purposes for which it is organized. By statutory authority it is empowered to condemn private property for its right of way (Kirby's Dig. § 2947); and the right of way "includes all grounds necessary for side tracks, turnouts, depots, workshops, water stations, and other necessary buildings." Kirby's Dig. § 2958. These uses are for railroad purposes, and they are of a public character; and a railroad company has therefore the right to condemn land for all such purposes. If the use for which the property is desired is in fact a public one, then the right to condemn the property follows. The mere fact that private ends of others will be advanced by such public user will not defeat the right to condemn the property. As is said in the case of Railway Co. *v.* Petty, 57 Ark. 359. 21 S. W. 884, 20 L. R. A. 434: "It is common for the interests of some individuals to be advanced, while that of others is prejudiced, by the location of railway stations and switches, when there is no motive on the part of the railway officials to discriminate between them." But the character of the use is no less public, and that public character is not changed, although private purposes will be incidentally served by the location of the railroad and its stations and buildings. And it is held in the case of Railway Co. *v.* Petty, supra. that "the courts do not assume to interfere with the right of the company to locate its line, stations, or switches," if it does not place an unreasonable restraint on the public to use same, although such location may incidentally subserve the interests of private individuals. And, as is said by the author of the article on "Eminent Domain" in 15 Cyc. 582: "A use is not rendered a private one by the mere fact that a part, or even the whole, of the cost of constructing the improvement, is paid by individuals, although such individuals are the persons most benefited by the improvement."

In her answer the appellant admitted that the railroad company desired to condemn the property involved in this suit for the purpose of locating its freight depot thereon, and therefore

Cloth *v.* Chicago, R. I. & P. Ry. Co

that it sought to condemn it for a public use. This stamped the character of the use to which the property would be put, and the public nature of that use would not be changed by reason of the fact that citizens of the town of Brinkley, or the town itself, agreed to pay a portion of the ascertained compensation for the property. It was, therefore, subject to condemnation, although the town of Brinkley paid a portion of this cost.

But it is urged that no necessity is shown for taking appellant's property, because appellee owned other property in Brinkley, which had been used and was suitable for the location of a freight depot thereon. We do not think that this contention is tenable. It is conceded that the use of the property for freight depot purposes is a public one, and that the employment of it for that purpose is a necessary public use of it. It is only urged that the particular location of the freight depot upon appellant's property is not necessary, because it could be located on other property. If the purpose for which the property is sought to be used is a public one, and such use is necessary in carrying on and in facilitating its business, then the railroad company has the right to determine what particular property it will take for such purpose. The necessity in such event of using the particular property is not affected or lessened by the fact that other property is available for such purpose. If the company has therefore used property for such purpose, the changed condition of the town or of its business may require the change of the location of such use, and of this the company has the right to judge and determine. As is said in the case of Railway Co. *v.* Petty, supra: "Having determined that the side tracks are necessary for the conduct of the company's business, the location must be left to the company's discretion." Upon this phase of this question it is said in 2 Lewis on Eminent Domain (3d Ed.) § 604: "It may be objected that there is no necessity of condemning the particular property, because some other location might be made or other property obtained by agreement. But this objection is unavailing. Except as specially restricted by the Legislature, those invested with the power of eminent domain for a public purpose can make their own location according to their own views of what is best or expedient, and this discretion cannot be controlled by the courts. If the contention were well-founded, the result would be that the plaintiff could not condemn any land; for every other landholder would likewise have the same right to object to his land being condemned." Cane Belt Ry. Co. *v.* Hughes, 31 Tex. Civ. App. 565, 72 S. W. 1020. In the case of Chicago & E. I. R. Co. *v.* People, 222 Ill. 396, 78 N. E. 784, it is held that a railroad company has in the first instance the discretionary power, exercised in good faith, to locate all its passenger and freight depots. It is further held in that case that the power of a railroad company to locate and establish its de-

Cloth v. Chicago, R. I. & P. Ry. Co

pots is not exhausted when it has been once exercised, but such power is a continuing one, which may be exercised in good faith by the company; and the mere fact that it has located a depot at a certain place and used the same for many years does not estop it from changing such location. See, also, Chicago & Northwestern Ry. Co. v. Chicago Mechanics' Institute, 239 Ill. 197, 87 N. E. 933; Kansas & T. Coal Co. v. Northwestern Coal & M. Co., 161 Mo. 288, 61 S. W. 684, 51 L. R. A. 936, 84 Am. St. Rep. 717; St. Louis, H. & K. R. Co. v. Hannibal Union Depot Co., 125 Mo. 93, 28 S. W. 483.

In her answer appellant does not allege, nor is it contended, that the entire lot is not necessary for the purpose of a freight depot. St. L. & S. F. R. Co. v. Tapp, 64 Ark. 357, 42 S. W. 667. It is only alleged that it is not necessary to take her property, because other property is available for this purpose. This allegation was not sufficient, we think, to deprive the appellant of the right to condemn this particular property, which in its discretion the company in good faith determined was necessary in the proper conduct of its business.

The court did not err in refusing to transfer the cause to the equity court, nor did it err in refusing to admit the introduction of the testimony offered by appellant.

It is urged that the amount of damages that was awarded by the jury to appellant was inadequate, and was contrary, not only to the preponderance of the evidence, but to undisputed testimony, which showed the value of the property was larger than the amount of the verdict. A number of witnesses testified relative to the value of the property involved in this case. Some of the witnesses placed its value at $250. The appellant claimed that it was of the value of $2,000; and there was testimony tending to prove that she had been offered from $1,250 to $1,500 therefor. But the great majority of the witnesses testified that the property was of the value of from $500 to $700. The value of the property and the damages which appellant sustained by reason of the condemnation thereof was a question of fact, which it was the province of the jury to determine. If there is substantial evidence to sustain this finding of the jury, then under the repeated rulings of this court such finding should not be disturbed. The jury returned a verdict in favor of appellant for $1,000, and we think there was substantial evidence to sustain that finding. St. L., I. M. & S. R. Co. v. Maxfield Co., 126 S. W. 83, 26 L. R. A. (N. S.) 1111.

The judgment is accordingly affirmed.

Louisiana & A. Ry. Co. *v.* Louisiana Ry. & Nav. Co.

(Supreme Court of Louisiana, Dec. 12, 1910.)

[53 So. Rep. 872.]

Eminent Domain—Expropriation—Extent of Rights Acquired.—
Defendant brought expropriation proceedings for a right of way
across the low lands of what was formerly Silver Lake, and as it
failed to expropriate any of the hill lands, on which the track in
controversy now stands, it acquired no rights to these higher lands.

**Eminent Domain—Expropriation—Reverter upon Termination of
Use.***—The land expropriated by a railroad company for its right of
way reverts back to the owner when it has ceased to be used for the
purpose for which it was expropriated, as the ownership of the soil
continues in the owner from whom the land was taken for the servitude.

**Eminent Domain—Expropriation Proceedings—Necessary Parties
—Owners of Land Sought to Be Taken.—**In order for a railroad to
acquire title to its right of way by expropriation it is necessary that
the owners of the land should be cited and duly made parties to the
expropriation proceedings.

Adverse Possession—Prescription of Ten Years.—Possession and
a title translative of property are necessary as a basis to support the
prescription of 10 years.

Real Actions—Petitory Actions—Defenses.—A defendant in a petitory action cannot demand that the plaintiff should proceed against
the vendors of the defendant for the price paid for it. The right of
the owner is against the one claiming the ownership of the property,
and this right cannot be defeated by any contract entered into by the
defendant and a third party.

(Syllabus by the Court.)

Appeal from First District Court, Parish of Caddo; A. J.
Murff, Judge.

Action by the Louisiana & Arkansas Railway Company against
the Louisiana Railway & Navigation Company. Judgment for
plaintiff, and defendant appeals. Affirmed.

Wise, Randolph & Rendall, for appellant.
Pugh, Thigpen & Herold, for appellee.

Breaux, C. J. The action is petitory.
Plaintiff corporation claims the land by purchase and asks
that the defendant be ousted.

---

*For the authorities in this series on the subject of the title ac-
quired by deed or condemnation proceedings in land conveyed or
condemned for a railroad right of way, see Dilts *v.* Plumville R. Co.
(Pa.), 33 R. R. R. 60, 56 Am. & Eng. R. Cas., N. S., 60.

It traces back its title by mesne conveyance to the government.

Defendant claims ownership by purchase from the Shreveport & Red River Railway Company, and the latter acquired by expropriation against the heirs of W. W. Smith.

If not acquired by expropriation, defendant pleads in the alternative that it went into possession of the land and constructed its track thereon, and that it has occupied the land without objection, and that plaintiff acquiesced in all that was done by the defendant in possession.

The judgment of the district court recognizes plaintiff's title. That court ordered the defendant to remove its track.

Plaintiff pleads res judicata, and to sustain that plea reference is made to the decision in Louisiana & Arkansas Railway Co. v. Louisiana Railway & Navigation Co., 125 La. 756, 51 South. 712.

It is true that there are several questions settled by that decision pertinent in deciding the rights of parties to this suit.

We have given careful attention to the text to that decision.

We will here state that the spur track, which was the subject of controversy in the cited decision, had fallen into innocuous desuetude.

It was never of much use at any time in so far as the public is concerned, for the spur was really not used in the interest of the public. Even as a private enterprise, it was really not in use of late.

It is quite true that in the cited decision, supra, parties in interest as defendants sought to prove that the spur was of some use, but in this they signally failed. The court did not sustain that contention; but, on the contrary, held that it was out of use and subject to expropriation, for which a judgment was rendered.

On the other hand, the defendant's contention is that it acquired its title in an expropriation suit, brought by it against a number of owners, in the year 1898, or by acquiescence of the owners.

Instead of being in favor of defendant, the effect of the decision cited was to put an end to whatever right the defendant had in this right of way.

The court expressly held that, as the spur track was of no further use to defendant, it was property that could be expropriated.

Plaintiff, none the less, chose to go behind these expropriation proceedings on the part of defendant in order to contend that defendant had really acquired no right by virtue of the expropriation suit in 1898 because it had not made all the owners of the land in question parties to the suit. In other words, plaintiff was not content with relying upon the cited decision, but urged that defendant had acquired no right at any time.

In the second place, plaintiff pleads that the petition of defendant for expropriation of the land in 1898, as before stated, was deficient in that the petitioner did not claim the land in controversy.

The defendant here—plaintiff in the proceedings for expropriation—in the petition in question, confined its allegation to a right of way to land situated in Silver Lake.

The lands in this redeemed lake are lower than those of the former shores of the lake. There is a plain line of division between the hill lands and the low lands of the lake. The land now in controversy is not within the area of the former lake lands. It was not possible for defendant, in the expropriation proceedings of 1898, to acquire hill lands in a suit in which it was alleged that the purpose was to expropriate Silver Lake lands.

In alleging that it was the purpose to expropriate lands in this lake, the petition did not include lands on the hill where this spur track is situated.

The fact most fatal to defendant's claim (although one can scarcely be more fatal than the fact just mentioned) is that the owners of the land on which the spur track is built were never cited, never made parties to the expropriation proceedings, and, of course, that being the case, as to them, no title was acquired.

Although the proceedings were virtually null, the plaintiff in the present suit, abundans cautela, avers, in substance, that after a public servitude in the interest of a railway has ceased entirely to be of use it reverts back to the owners of the adjacent lands.

Without this plea, it would be difficult for the defendant, under the null proceedings, to recover the lands on which the spur track lies.

We will here state, none the less, that by the entire abandonment of the use the land passes back to the owner and becomes part of his ownership. Abercrombie v. Simmons, 71 Kan. 538, 81 Pac. 208, 1 L. R. A. (N. S.) 806, 114 Am. St. Rep. 509; Elliott on Railroads, § 40.

Our Code, § 658, provides:

"The soil of public roads belongs to the owners of the land." Bradley v. Pharr, 45 La. Ann. 426, 12 South. 618, 19 L. R. A. 647.

The abandonment above referred to was proven beyond a doubt. That is of itself the end of the case.

Before this court, defendant pleads the prescription of 10 years in support of its asserted title.

That plea cannot be of any avail for it is not shown that defendant was in possession, nor that it has a present title which can serve as a basis of prescription.

Another position of defendant is that the recourse of plaintiff should be against the persons who received the price paid by de-

Louisiana & A. Ry. Co. *v.* Louisiana Ry. & Nav. Co

fendant when it expropriated the land in the year 1898, and that in consequence plaintiff has no right against it.

The pleadings would not sustain such a judgment.

Besides, the owner cannot be made to proceed against those who may have received the price. The plaintiff had a right of its own from which it cannot be deprived by instituting suit against others who were not in the least, either directly or indirectly, authorized to represent the defendant.

For reasons assigned, the judgment is affirmed.

KAYSER *et ux. v.* CHICAGO, B. & Q. R. Co.

(Supreme Court of Nebraska, Jan. 24, 1911.)

[129 N. W. Rep. 554.]

Husband and Wife—Joinder.—The homestead of husband and wife was held in the name of the wife. An action for damages was instituted growing out of the alleged diminution in the value of the property by reason of the contiguous construction of railroad tracks and freightyards. The petition alleged that the real estate was the property of both husband and wife, and they were joined as plaintiffs. No issue as to ownership was specifically raised by the answer. Held, that the plaintiffs were properly joined, and there was no error in overruling an objection to the question as to the ownership or interest of the husband.

Husband and Wife—Parties Plaintiff—Effect of Joinder of Unnecessary Parties.—Had the husband been an unnecessary party plaintiff, that fact would not prevent a recovery, as judgment could have been rendered for either party, if successful, under the provisions of section 429 of the Code of Civil Procedure.

Eminent Domain—Witnesses—Cross-Examination—Injury to Realty—Measure of Damages.—In their efforts to prove the amount of damages sustained by plaintiffs, certain competent witnesses were asked as to the market value of the property immediately before the construction of defendant's tracks and the value after the laying of the tracks and their use for the transfer of freight. This was the proper practice. Chicago, R. I. & P. R. Co. *v.* O'Neill, 58 Neb. 239, 78 N. W. 521. On cross-examination the witnesses were asked as to the elements considered by them in arriving at their valuations, some of which were shown not to be proper to have been taken into consideration. This cross-examination was proper as tending to weaken the force or weight of their testimony, but did not so destroy it as to require the whole thereof, including that which was competent, to be stricken out and withdrawn from the consideration of the jury.

Kayser et ux. v. Chicago, B. & Q. R. Co

Eminent Domain—Measure of Damages—Land Taken for Public Use.—"The jury in fixing the damages sustained by a landowner in consequence of the appropriation or injuiy of his property for a public use may take into account every element of annoyance and disadvantage resulting from the improvement which would influence an intending purchaser's estimate of the market value of such property." Chicago, R. I. & P. R. Co. v. O'Neill, 58 Neb. 239, 78 N. W. 521.

Eminent Domain—Measure of Damages—Land Taken for Public Use.*—Those elements include injury from smoke. noise. soot. cinders, and vibration.

Eminent Domain—Excessive Damages.—The testimony of witnesses as to the extent of the diminution in value of plaintiffs' property by reason of the construction of lines of track and their use by engines and cars was conflicting. The jury was sent out by the court to view the premises. Held, that the verdict, while apparently large, but within the estimates of some of the witnesses, could not be molested.

(Syllabus by the Court.)

Appeal from District Court, Adams County; Dungan. Judge.

Action by George Kayser and wife against the Chicago, Burlington & Quincy Railroad Company. Judgment for plaintiffs, and defendant appeals.

Jas. E. Kelby, Frank E. Bishop, H. F. Rose, and *John C. Stevens,* for appellant.

Tibbetts, Morey & Fuller, for appellees.

REESE, C. J. This is an appeal from the district court of Adams county. The action was instituted for the purpose of recovering damages alleged to have been sustained by reason of the construction of certain railroad tracks on the opposite side of the street in front of plaintiffs' residence in the city of Hastings. The facts briefly stated are that the line and tracks of defendant's railroad had previously been constructed about one block, or from 300 to 350 feet, south of and parallel to First street in said city. Between that street and the tracks was a block of lots with residence improvements thereon; that portion on the north side of the block fronting on First street. Plaintiffs' residence is situated on the north side of said street, fronting to the south thereon. Prior to the commencement of this action, the defendant obtained, by purchase or condemnation, all the lots south of First

---

*See first foot-note of Twenty Second Corp. of Church, etc r Oregon S. L. R. Co. (Utah), 33 R. R. R. 384, 56 Am. & Eng. R Cas. N. S., 384; Wunderlich v. Pennsylvania R. Co. (Pa.), ·33 R. R. R 112, 56 Am. & Eng. R. Cas., N. S., 112; foot-note of Helmer v. Colorado, etc., R. Co. (La.), 32 R. R. R. 5, 55 Am. & Eng. R. Cas. N., 5.

street, removed the dwellings and other buildings, trees, and shrubbery therefrom, excavated the ground from 3 to 7 feet, placed 4 tracks thereon, and constructed its freight depot and platform on and against the curb line on the south side of the street, the platform extending to within the width of an alley (about 20 feet) of a point of and in front of plaintiffs' residence, the tracks extending the whole distance of the block. The action was for the diminution in value of plaintiffs' residence property by reason of the construction of the tracks, the practically constant use thereof by switch engines and freight cars in the transfer of freight, and the "noise, jarring, dust, smoke, soot, cinders, and noxious odors created by such traffic." · With the exception of the allegation of the corporate capacity of defendant, and that it has owned and operated a line of railroad through the city of Hastings for more than 20 years, the answer is a general denial. There was a jury trial which resulted in a verdict and judgment in favor of plaintiffs. Defendant appeals.

The evidence shows the making of the change in defendant's tracks from the main line to the point south of plaintiffs' residence substantially as alleged in the petition, and as above outlined. The plaintiffs are husband and wife. The title to the property is held in the name of the wife, and it is shown to be the homestead of both and their family, consisting of one daughter. The action having been brought in the names of both the husband and wife, it is contended that there is a misjoinder of parties plaintiff; it being insisted that the husband was improperly joined. There was no proof as to by whom the consideration for the purchase of the property was paid, but both plaintiffs testified that the property belonged to both. This evidence was objected to at the time it was offered, and an adverse ruling by the court is now assigned for error. The defendant asked for an instruction directing a verdict in its favor upon that ground which was refused. As this direct issue was not presented by answer, it may be questioned whether or not it was waived. Donahue v. Bragg, 49 Mo. App. 273; Lass v. Eisleben, 50 Mo. 122. However, we are not prepared to say that the husband was not a proper party, even had there been no proof of his ownership. The residence was the homestead of the family—his home—and it was alleged and sufficiently proved that the full enjoyment of that home was interrupted. Should the objection to the evidence that the lots were the joint property of both have been sustained? We think not. The joint ownership was alleged in the petition. The deed showed that the title was held in the name of the wife. It was entirely proper to prove the husband's interest. But, even were this not true, we are unable to see how the joining of the husband could in any event work to the prejudice of defendant. By the provisions of section 429 of the Code of Civil Procedure, a judgment may be given

Kayser et ux. *v.* Chicago, B. & Q. R. Co

for or against one or more of several plaintiffs, and this would
not require a dismissal of the action if it should appear that the
husband was an unnecessary party. The judgment, if in favor
of either plaintiff, could be entered in accordance with the fact.

On the trial of the question of the extent of damages sustained
the testimony offered and received was as to the difference in the
value of the property immediately before and after the construction of defendant's tracks and freight platform on the side of
the street opposite plaintiffs' dwelling. This was the proper
measure of damages (Chicago, R. I. & P. R. Co. *v.* O'Neill, 58
Neb. 239, 78 N. W. 521), and in estimating the amount of damages sustained the jury may take into account every element of
annoyance and disadvantage resulting from the improvement
which would influence an intending purchaser's estimate of the
market value of the property (Chicago, R. I. & P. R. Co. *v.*
O'Neill, supra). And this includes injury from smoke, soot, and
cinders from passing engines where no part of the land is actually
taken (Omaha & N. P. R. Co. *v.* Janecek, 30 Neb. 278, 46 N.
W. 478, 27 Am. St. Rep. 399). also from noise and vibration
caused by the operating of a railroad near the property, though
not along a public highway (Gainesville, H. & W. R. Co. *v.* Hall,
78 Tex. 169, 14 S. W. 259, 9 L. R. A. 298, 22 Am. St. Rep. 42),
and such damages may be recovered if the tracks are on the opposite side of the highway (Lake Erie & W. R. Co. *v.* Scott, 132
Ill. 429, 24 N. E. 78, 8 L. R. A. 330). Upon cross-examination of
the witnesses who had testified to the diminution in value of
plaintiffs' property they were asked as to the elements considered
by them in arriving at their opinions, some of which were not
entitled to consideration in arriving at the conclusion but which
the witnesses testified they considered. Upon the close of their
testimony, defendant's counsel moved to strike out all the testimony of those witnesses, which motion the court overruled. This
ruling is assigned for error. There was no error in the decision.
The cross-examination, while proper, could only have the effect
of weakening the testimony of the witnesses and of which the
jury were the sole judges. A portion, at least, of the testimony
of each witness was competent and material, and the motion to
strike out the whole should not be sustained.

Certain witnesses were asked to state the condition of the
block on the opposite side of the street before the appropriation
of the block by defendant. This was objected to and the objection overruled, to which defendant excepted, and the ruling
is now assigned for error. The answers were that the block
was occupied by residences, trees, shrubbery, etc., which added
to the beauty of the surroundings, and protected plaintiffs' property from the smoke, soot, cinders, and noise caused by the
operation of the trains, engines, and cars on the tracks to the
south, all of which improvements had been removed and the

Kayser et ux. v. Chicago, B. & Q. R. Co

ground appropriated to the use of the tracks within the excavations above referred to, thereby rendering plaintiff's home of less value as residence property. This evidence seems to be of little, if any, importance and might have been well excluded, but the error in receiving it, if such there were, was cured by the giving of instruction numbered 2, given at the request of defendant, which is as follows: "The jury are instructed that, if you find in favor of the plaintiffs in arriving at the amount of your verdict, you must give consideration only to the claims of damage stated in the petition; that is, on account of noise, jarring, dust, smoke, soot, cinders, and noxious odors caused by the operation of the railroad tracks and trains in connection with the freight depot, and you must not allow any damages for any other claims or consideration, even though testimony of witnesses may have been received on other causes and consideration of damage." This eliminated every consideration except those named and left no ground for complaint.

It is contended that the verdict of the jury, which is $1,100, is excessive. Eight witnesses were examined as to values by plaintiffs, and two by defendant. There was considerable discrepancy in their testimony. Of the eight two placed the diminution in value at $1,000, two at from $800 to $1,000, one at $900, one at $600, one at $800, and one at $1,200 to $1,400. Of the two witnesses for defendant, one testified there was no diminution, while the other placed it at from $200 to $300. In addition to the testimony of witnesses, the jury were sent to view the premises and the information there obtained was considered by them. While we are persuaded that the verdict was the full measure of the damage proved, yet we cannot see that the excess, if any there is, calls for the interference of this court.

The judgment of the district court is therefore affirmed.

STATE *ex rel.* CITY OF MILWAUKEE *v.* MILWAUKEE ELECTRIC
RY. & LIGHT CO.'

(Supreme Court of Wisconsin, Jan. 10, 1911.)

[139 N. W. Rep. 623.]

Mandamus—Public Duties—Sprinkling Streets.*—A street railway's duty under an ordinance to sprinkle the part of streets occupied by its tracks is a public one, and enforceable by mandamus

Mandamus—Subjects of Relief—Continuing Duty.—That a duty is a continuing one, does not preclude its enforcement by mandamus.

Mandamus—Jurisdiction—Permanent Relief.—There is no more objection to a court of law granting permanent relief by mandamus than there is to a court of equity granting a mandatory injunction.

Mandamus—Moot Questions.—A proceeding to compel a street railway to sprinkle the part of streets occupied by its tracks from April 1st to November 1st, as required by ordinance, is not defeated as presenting a moot question because pending outside that period and because the duty may be afterwards performed, where the ordinance has been disregarded for five years, and its validity is contested by the railway.

Mandamus—Proper Relators—Municipal Regulations.—A city is the proper relator in a proceeding to compel a street railway to perform its duty under an ordinance to sprinkle the part of streets occupied by its tracks, the ordinance being a health regulation and not merely of private benefit to abutters.

Municipal Corporations—Regulations—Repeal.—A revision of ordinances, including an ordinance requiring street railways to sprinkle streets but not including rules thereunder previously approved by the council, did not repeal the rules, especially where the revision provided that ordinances prescribing regulations against street railways were not repealed.

Appeal and Error—Review—Insufficient Reservation of Ground.—The question whether a revision of ordinances repealed particular rules is not presented for review where appellant did not except to a finding that the rules were not repealed.

Street Railroads—Street Sprinkling Ordinance—Repeal.—Laws 1909, c. 501, authorizing councils of cities of the first class to determine whether streets should be sprinkled during the current year and to charge the cost of sprinkling to abutters; amending existing charters only so far as inconsistent with the act; and providing that the act should expire by limitation December 31, 1910—did not repeal a Milwaukee ordinance requiring street railways to sprinkle the part of streets occupied by their tracks.

---

*See foot-note of State *v.* Chicago & N. W. R. Co. (Neb.), **34** R. R. R. 481, 57 Am. & Eng. R. Cas., N. S., 481.

State *v.* Milwaukee Electric Ry. & Light Co

Municipal Corporations—Ordinances—Repeal.—Implied repeals of ordinances are not favored.

Statutes—Repeal.—An act remains in force unless manifestly inconsistent with or repugnant to a later one, or unless some express notice is taken of the former act plainly indicating an intention to abrogate it.

Statutes—Repeal.—One of two affirmative statutes on the same subject-matter does not repeal the other if both can stand

Statutes—Implied Repeal.—Implication operating to repeal a statute must be necessary, and if it arises out of two acts, the later abrogates the older only so far as they are inconsistent.

Statutes—Repeal—Codification.—Former acts are deemed to be repealed by a revision manifestly intended to cover all existing laws on that subject.

Municipal Corporations—Ordinances—Repeal.—An ordinance requiring street railways to sprinkle the part of streets occupied by them was not repealed by a resolution adopted under Laws 1909, c. 50, authorizing councils to determine whether streets should be sprinkled during the current year and to charge the cost of sprinkling to abutters, where the resolution was adopted as a temporary expedient covering less than three and one-half months.

Street Railroads—Municipal Regulations—Time for Prescribing.—St. 1898, § 1862, subjecting street railroads to such reasonable municipal regulation as shall be prescribed "from time to time," does not require that the rules be adopted when the right to use streets is granted.

Street Railroads—Municipal Regulation—Street Sprinkling.—St. 1898, § 1862, subjecting street railroads to municipal regulation, authorizes adoption of a reasonable ordinance requiring them to sprinkle streets occupied by them.

Street Railroads—Municipal Regulation—Reasonableness—Street Sprinkling.—A municipal regulation requiring a street railroad to sprinkle the part of streets occupied by it so as to prevent dust rising, but not so as to create mud or pools of water, merely requires ordinary care, and is not void as being unreasonable.

Street Railroads—Municipal Regulation—Street Sprinkling—Validity.—An ordinance requiring a street railroad to sprinkle the part of streets occupied by it is not void as discriminating in favor of users of automobiles and other vehicles who are not compelled to bear like expense.

Municipal Corporations—Ordinances—Adoption — Vote — Journal Entries.—Laws requiring the "aye" and "no" vote to be taken on certain questions and entered on the permanent record of the common council of a city are mandatory, being designed to enable constituents to determine how their representatives vote.

Words and Phrases—"Liability"—"Responsibility."—"Liability" in its broadest and most comprehensive use includes any obligation one is bound in law or justice to perform, and is synonymous with "re-

State v. Milwaukee Electric Ry. & Light Co

sponsibility;" in a more restricted and perhaps in its popular sense, it means that which one is under obligation to pay to another.

Municipal Corporations — Ordinances — "Liability." —"Liability," within Milwaukee Charter, c. 4, §§ 2, 4, requiring the vote on ordinances creating "liability" against the city or any fund thereof to be taken by ayes and noes and entered at length on the journal, means more than a naked undertaking involving no expense, covering a claim or obligation presented to the council for audit and allowance against some fund, and hence the section does not apply to an ordinance requiring street railway companies to sprinkle the part of streets occupied by their tracks on the city furnishing the necessary water.

Appeal from Circuit Court, Milwaukee County; W. J. Turner, Judge.

Mandamus proceeding by State of Wisconsin, on the relation of City of Milwaukee, against the Milwaukee Electric Railway & Light Company. Judgment for relator, and respondent appeals. Affirmed.

On July 14, 1902, the common council of the city of Milwaukee passed an ordinance requiring all street railway companies operating lines in the city to sprinkle with water the entire roadbed of the railways operated, between single tracks and double tracks and one foot outside of all tracks, as well as the space between double tracks, such work to be done under the general supervision of the board of public works and under rules and regulations adopted from time to time by said board and approved by the common council. Street railway companies were not required to do any sprinkling between November 1st and the 1st day of April following. The entire expense of such sprinkling was to be borne by the street railway companies, except that the city was to furnish the necessary water free of charge. The ordinance also provided that any violation thereof should be punished by a fine not exceeding $300 and costs. No rules or regulations were adopted by the board of public works until July 10, 1905. Among other things, the rules adopted provided that the sprinkling called for by the ordinance should be done on all days from and including April 1st to November 1st in each year, excepting Sundays and legal holidays and such days as sprinkling was unnecessary by reason of rain or the moist condition of the streets: that sprinkling should be done in such manner and at such intervals as would keep the surface moist and prevent dust from arising between 6 a. m. and 7 p. m. upon each day when the work was required to be done, but not in such a manner as to create mud or pools of water, and that paved streets should be sprinkled lightly to meet the requirements, but graveled or macadamized streets should be thoroughly wetted down. The rules adopted by the board of public works were approved by the common council shortly thereafter. The defendant refused to comply with the ordinance and the rules adopted in pursuance thereof, and the city, on September 21, 1905, commenced a mandamus proceeding to compel the defendant to comply with the terms of the ordinance. From a judgment in relator's favor the defendant or respondent in the court below prosecutes this appeal.

Miller, Mack & Fairchild, for appellant.
Daniel W. Hoan, City Atty., and *John J. Cook,* Asst. City Atty., for respondent.

BARNES, J. (after stating the facts as above). Nine distinct reasons are advanced by the appellant in support of its contention that the judgment appealed from should be reversed; these are: (1) Mandamus is not the proper remedy. (2) The city of Milwaukee is not the proper relator. (3) The rules adopted by the board of public works were not included in the 1906b revision of the charter of the city of Milwaukee and were therefore repealed thereby. (4) Chapter 501, Laws 1909, repealed the street sprinkling ordinance. (5) The street sprinkling ordinance became inoperative because of a resolution adopted by the city council acting under chapter 501, Laws 1909. (6) The city had no power conferred on it to pass an ordinance requiring street railway companies to sprinkle any portion of the public streets. (7) The ordinance is void because its requirements are unreasonable. (8) It is void because it is discriminatory. (9) It was never lawfully passed.

1. It is argued that mandamus will lie only to enforce a clear legal duty, and that no such duty is shown to exist in this case; that the duty imposed is not a public one and therefore performance will not be enforced by mandamus; that mandamus will not lie to enforce the performance of a continuous act, and that it will not lie because the case presents a moot question only. Whether a clear legal duty was imposed on the appellant by the ordinance involved depends on the solution of various legal questions that will hereafter be discussed. We entertain no doubt that the duty attempted to be imposed is of a public nature. The mere fact that the whole or a portion of the expense of sprinkling might be charged to an abutting owner does not determine the nature of the duty. Public streets are built at the expense of abutting property owners where the cost does not exceed the resulting benefits, but the building of streets is none the less a public duty. Sidewalks are built and sewers are constructed in whole or in part at the expense of the abutting owners, regardless of special benefits. This is done by virtue of the police powers lodged in cities and villages, but the duty is as much a public one as if the cost had been defrayed by means of

State *v.* Milwaukee Electric Ry. & Light Co

general taxation. It is somewhat difficult to see wherein any special benefit accrues to the abutting owner by reason of the street in front of his property being sprinkled. In any event the public shares in the benefit. The ordinance was passed to preserve the public health and to promote its comfort, and manifestly such an ordinance operates in the interest of and for the benefit of the public. Neither do we see any good reason for saying that relief should not be afforded by mandamus because the duty to sprinkle is a continuous one. If the legal duty on the part of the appellant is clear, the relator should not be denied an appropriate remedy because the right sought to be enforced is not of a temporary nature. There can be no more objection to a court of law granting permanent relief by mandamus in an appropriate action than there is to a court of equity granting relief in a proper case by a mandatory injunction. The cases of State ex rel. *v.* Associated Press, 159 Mo. 410, 60 S. W. 91, 51 L. R. A. 151, 81 Am. St. Rep. 368, Diamond Match Co. *v.* Powers, 51 Mich. 145, 16 N. W. 314, State ex rel. *v.* Einstein, 46 N. J. Law, 479, and People ex rel. *v.* Dulaney, 96 Ill. 503, cited by the appellant, are for the most part cases where, under the established facts, the right to the continuous or perpetual relief sought was not sufficiently clear to warrant the judgments prayed for. That mandamus will lie to enforce the performance of a continuous legal duty, has been decided at least by inference by this court. State ex rel. *v.* Janesville Street Ry. Co., 87 Wis. 72, 57 N. W. 970, 22 L. R. A. 759, 41 Am. St. Rep. 23. Such is the general current of authority elsewhere. Potwin Place *v.* Topeka Ry. Co., 51 Kan. 609, 33 Pac. 309, 37 Am. St. Rep. 312; State ex rel. *v.* Traction Co., 62 N. J. Law, 592, 43 Atl. 715, 45 L. R. A. 837; Detroit *v.* Fort Wayne, etc., Ry. Co., 95 Mich. 456, 54 N. W. 958, 20 L. R. A. 79, 35 Am. St. Rep. 580; Oklahoma City *v.* Oklahoma Ry. Co., 20 Okl. 1, 93 Pac. 48, 16 L. R. A. (N. S.) 651; State ex rel. *v.* R. R. Co., 48 Fla. 114, 37 South. 652.

The contention that the case presents only a moot question we do not take seriously. It is true that the appellant is not required by the ordinance to do any sprinkling between November 1st and April 1st, and appellant may conclude to comply with its terms beginning April 1st next. This ordinance, if valid, became. operative more than five years ago, and no sprinkling has been done thereunder as yet. Furthermore, the appellant is in court vigorously contesting the right of the city to require it to do any sprinkling thereunder at any time in the future. In view of the situation the city is entitled to have its rights under the ordinance judicially determined.

2. It is argued that the city has no financial interest in the result of the suit, and that the only ones who have are the abutting owners who will be relieved of their burden by the enforcement

State *v.* Milwaukee Electric Ry. & Light Co

of the ordinance, and that the city therefore is not a proper relator. This argument seems to be based on the proposition that street sprinkling is a private matter which inures to the benefit of the abutting owner, and which affects the public in an incidental way only. We have already said that the duty imposed is a public one, and, while the cost may possibly be charged to the lot owner, a point we do not decide, yet the special benefit that accrues to his property may be very slight, if, indeed, any. If we except chapter 501, Laws 1909, which will be discussed later, there is no statute which compels or obligates or in express terms authorizes the city to impose on abutting property owners the burden of sprinkling. The city is authorized by its charter to provide for street sprinkling, and we see no objection to its providing that the expense thereof be met by general taxation. It may be that the city would be restricted to this method of raising the necessary fund to defray the cost of the work. Indeed, under the provisions of the 1909 law the city is directly and pecuniarily interested in requiring street car companies to comply with the ordinance, because it must bear the expense of sprinkling the street crossings, which make up a very considerable fraction of the entire street surface in the city. Besides, the ordinance we are considering purports to be passed in the interest of public health, and the trial court found as a matter of fact that the circulation of dust was injurious to public health and that disease breeding germs were carried therein. There is no difference in principle between the case at bar and Oshkosh *v.* Ry. Co., 74 Wis. 534, 43 N. W. 489, 17 Am. St. Rep. 175, where the court at the suit of the city compelled the railway company to restore a highway used by it to its former state of usefulness. In some respects the present case is stronger, in that it involves the matter of public health. Other cases holding that the city is a proper relator in such a case are: State ex rel. *v.* Traction Co., 62 N. J. Law, 592, 43 Atl. 715, 45 L. R. A. 837; C., B. & Q. Ry. Co. *v.* State ex rel., 47 Neb. 549, 66 N. W. 624, 41 L. R. A. 481, 53 Am. St. Rep. 557; Rutherford *v.* Hudson R. T. Co., 73 N. J. Law, 227, 63 Atl. 84; Pleasantville *v.* Traction Co., 75 N. J. Law, 279, 68 Atl. 60; State ex rel. *v* Railway Co., 42 La. Ann. 11, 7 South. 84; Potwin Place *v.* Topeka R. Co., 51 Kan. 609, 33 Pac. 309, 37 Am. St. Rep. 312; International Water Co. *v.* El Paso (Tex. Civ. App.) 112 S. W. 816.

3. In 1906 an ordinance was passed by the city of Milwaukee to revise, consolidate, and amend the general ordinance of the city. The ordinance requiring the appellant to sprinkle was included in the Revision, but the rules adopted by the board of public works under said ordinance in 1905 were not included therein, and hence it is claimed that such rules were repealed

State v. Milwaukee Electric Ry. & Light Co

by it. The rules adopted by the board of public works having been ratified and approved by the common council, they became to all intents and purposes part and parcel of the ordinance passed by the common council on July 14, 1902, and really make it complete. The Revision does not in express terms purport to repeal the rules adopted and approved as stated, although they do not appear as part of the ordinance therein. But section 3 of chapter 30 of the Revision expressly provides that all ordinances prescribing any rules, regulations, or restrictions upon street railway companies are not repealed. This provision we deem sufficiently broad to save the rules. If they did not become a part of the ordinance, then obviously they were not repealed. The court found that the rules were not repealed by reason of the 1906 codification of the charter provisions, and no exception is taken to such finding, so the question is not really before the court.

4. Chapter 501, Laws 1909, authorized the common council of any city of the first class to provide whether the streets of such city should be sprinkled during the current year, and to charge the cost thereof, with certain exceptions, to the abutting owners in case it decided to sprinkle. The act was made amendatory to existing charters only so far as they were inconsistent with the act, and it was provided that the law should expire by limitation on December 31, 1910. It is argued that this act repeals the ordinance under consideration. The argument is not convincing. In the first place, the act provides that the common council may provide for street sprinkling. Then it recites that it modifies or repeals existing charter provisions only in so far as they are inconsistent therewith. Furthermore, the act has already expired by limitation, and if it should be construed to supersede all existing charter provisions relative to street sprinkling, we would have neither a law nor an ordinance on the subject until one was passed. These considerations are strongly suggestive of a legislative intent to permit existing laws and ordinances on the subject to stand unless they were actually repugnant to the law in question. It is apparent that former laws which confer the power on cities of the first class to proceed in some other way are not inconsistent with the later act. The authority thereby conferred is merely cumulative and supplementary to existing rights. If there was a repeal of the ordinance in question, it must have been by implication, as it was not repealed by any affirmative declaration contained in the 1909 law. Repeals by implication are not favored. The earlier act remains in force unless it is manifestly inconsistent with or repugnant to the later one, or unless some express notice is taken of the former acts in the later one which plainly indicates an intention to abrogate it. State ex rel. v.

State v. Milwaukee Electric Ry. & Light Co

Tomahawk Com. Council, 96 Wis. 73, 71 N. W. 86. Where there are two affirmative statutes on the same subject, one will not repeal the other if both can stand together. Atty. Gen. ex rel. v. Brown, 1 Wis. 513; Atty. Gen. v. Railway Cos., 35 Wis. 425. The implication to be operative must be necessary, and, if it arises out of two acts, the later abrogates the older one only to the extent that it is inconsistent and irreconcilable with it. The two statutes will if possible be construed so as to stand together. Lewis' Sutherland ·Stat. Const. p. 465 (2d Ed.); Maxwell on Int. of Stats. p. 233 (4th Ed.); Black on Int. of Laws, § 53. Other Wisconsin cases illustrating the foregoing rules of statutory construction are Goodrich v. Milwaukee, 24 Wis. 422; Foster v. Hammond, 37 Wis. 185; Vorous v. Ins. Co., 102 Wis. 76, 78 N. W. 162; Bradley v. Cramer, 61 Wis. 572, 21 N. W. 519; First Nat. Bank v. Baker, 68 Wjs. 442, 32 N. W. 523; Peterson v. Baker, 68 Wis. 451, 32 N. W. 527. The exception, if such it may be called, is that where the Legislature legislates on a given subject, and it is manifest that it intended to revise and codify all existing laws and to cover the entire subject, former acts dealing with such subject will be deemed to have been impliedly repealed although there is an absence of an express repealing clause. Gymnastic Ass'n v. Milwaukee, 129 Wis. 429, 109 N. W. 109. No such purpose is apparent in chapter 501, Laws 1909. In fact the intention appears to be quite to the contrary.

5. Acting under the power conferred by chapter 501, Laws 1909, the common council of the city of Milwaukee. on July 6, 1909, passed a resolution authorizing and directing the board of public works to sprinkle certain streets in the city until October 15, 1909, and to charge the expense of such sprinkling to the abutting owners. The resolution further provided that the cost of sprinkling streets at the intersection thereof should be paid out of the street or alley fund. It is argued that this resolution had all the dignity, force, and effect of an ordinance; that it covered all streets upon which appellant maintained a street railroad, as well as the entire width of such streets, and that it operated to repeal the ordinance of July 14, 1902.

Too much is claimed for this resolution. The appellant refused to comply with the 1902 ordinance. This action was brought to compel it to do so and was pending in the courts. Until it was decided, the city must either make some other provision for sprinkling or allow the portion covered by the 1902 ordinance to go unsprinkled. It would not have availed much to sprinkle the balance of the street. To meet the situation the city adopted a temporary expedient covering a period of less than three and one-half months. This was not intended to and in fact did not repeal the original ordinance, which made permanent

State v. Milwaukee Electric Ry. & Light Co

provision for sprinkling that portion of the street occupied by the appellant.

6. The next contention is that there was no authority conferred on the city of Milwaukee to pass the ordinance in question. The city justifies its action on three grounds: (1) A provision in its charter authorizing it to provide for the sprinkling of streets; (2) broad police powers conferred on it empowering it to pass legislation abating nuisances and conserving the public health; (3) section 1862, St. 1898. The statute referred to provides for the organization of corporations to construct, operate, and maintain street railway lines, and authorizes any municipal corporation to grant to such corporation, upon such terms as it deems proper, the right to use the streets and bridges within the limits of the municipality for laying tracks and running cars thereon. The statute then provides: "Every such road shall be constructed upon the most approved plan, and be subject to such reasonable rules and regulations and the payment of such license fees as the proper municipal authorities may by ordinance, from time to time, prescribe."

This statute is as broad and comprehensive as language can well make it. The ordinance in controversy here is unquestionably a regulation. The language quoted precludes the idea that the "regulations" referred to must be passed when the right to use the streets is granted, because they may be passed "from time to time." There is no apparent reason for saying that some particular kind of regulations were intended to be covered and that others were intended to be excluded. The only limitation or restriction which the law fixes is that the "regulations" must be reasonable. It is not seriously contended that it is beyond the power of the lawmaking body to require a street railway company to sprinkle the streets immediately adjacent to its tracks. The reasonableness of this particular regulation is attacked on two grounds, which will be considered later. Being satisfied that section 1862, St. 1898, conferred on the city the power to pass the ordinance, assuming it to be reasonable, it is unnecessary to consider the other acts urged by the city in support of its right to legislate as it did. We apprehend that if the ordinance is not a reasonable regulation it cannot be justified on any ground. Ordinances requiring street railway companies to sprinkle the streets immediately adjacent to their tracks have been held valid by a number of courts. C. & S. Ry. Co. v. Mayor of Savannah, 77 Ga. 731, 4 Am. St. Rep. 106; State v. C. & C. R. Co., 50 La. Ann. 1189, 24 South. 265, 56 L. R. A. 287; Newcomb v. Railway Co., 179 Mass. 449, 61 N. E. 42; Chicago v. Chicago U. T. Co., 199 Ill. 259, 65 N. E. 243, 59 L. R. A. 666. No decisions to the contrary have been cited and we have found none. Only in a case which is clear beyond a reasonable doubt will the courts declare laws void which are adopted under the police power in the interest of the public health. State ex rel. v. Currens, 111 Wis. 431, 87 N. W. 561, 56 L. R. A. 252; Bonnett v. Vallier, 136 Wis. 193, 116 N. W. 885, 17 L. R. A. (N. S.) 486, 128 Am. St. Rep. 1061; State v. Redmon, 134 Wis. 89, 114 N. W. 137, 14 L. R. A. (N. S.) 229, 126 Am. St. Rep. 1003; Benz v. Kremer, 142 Wis. 1, 125 N. W. 99, 26 L. R. A. (N. S.) 842. The validity of a city ordinance is tested by the same rule. E. W. R. & L. Co. v. Hackett, 135 Wis. 464, 481, 115 N. W. 376, 1136, 1139; Stafford v. Railway Co., 110 Wis. 331, 85 N. W. 1036; C. Beck Co. v. Milwaukee, 139 Wis. 340, 120 N. W. 293, 131 Am. St. Rep. 1061. We entertain no doubt that the power existed to pass an ordinance of the general character of the one adopted, provided such power was exercised in a proper mannei. The reasons which support and sustain the imposition of such a burden will be discussed under an assignment of error which raises the alleged discriminatory features of the ordinance.

7. Is the ordinance void because of unreasonableness? It is urged that, assuming the city had power to pass some kind of an ordinance requiring the appellant to sprinkle a portion of the public streets, such power was exercised in an unlawful manner, in that the rules adopted by the board of public works aim at an ideal rather than a practical result, and that such result can only be attained by the expenditure of an extravagant sum of money which it is not reasonable to require the appellant to expend. The obnoxious requirement is found in rule 3, which imposed on the appellant the duty of sprinkling the streets in such a manner as will keep the surface continually moist and prevent the dust from arising at all times each day when the work is done, "but not in such a manner as to create mud or pools of water." It is argued, and reasonably enough, that it may be well nigh impossible to so sprinkle streets that no dust will arise therefrom, and that it is impossible to sprinkle them in the usual and customary way and at the same time keep them entirely free from mud or even pools of water. But the rules must have a reasonable interpretation, and if they are susceptible of one that will make the ordinance valid, it is to be preferred to one which will render it void. It is a matter of common knowledge that streets frequently have depressions in them and that water will run down hill and will collect in these depressions and form little pools, until it seeps into the ground or evaporates. But we think it was not intended that the street railway company should guard against a thing of this kind, but rather to prevent such large quantities of water from being poured onto the streets at any one time as to create continuous pools of water therein. So, too, we all know that dust will accumulate on the street and that when it becomes sufficiently thick it will turn to mud when saturated with water. But here again it is very evident that what the rules were intended to guard against was the excessive use of water at any

State v. Milwaukee Electric Ry. & Light Co

one time or the creation of a permanent condition. This would seem apparent from rule 4, which provides that paved streets shall be sprinkled lightly, but "gravel or macadamized streets shall be thoroughly wetted down." The board of public works did not mean that certain streets should be thoroughly wetted down and at the same time that the laws of nature should be defied in so doing. The rules must be read and construed together and be given a reasonable interpretation; and so interpreted they mean that the appellant must exercise ordinary care and caution in doing the work of sprinkling.

8. It is next claimed that the ordinance is void because it is discriminatory. It is said that some streets are used by steam roads, and that automobiles and teams are constantly using most of them, and that no good reason exists for singling out one user from the many, and compelling it to bear an expense not imposed on other users, and that appellant is therefore being denied the equal protection of the laws.

The question involved is really one of classification. The essentials requisite to constitute legitimate classification have been laid down in a number of cases recently decided, and it is unnecessary to reiterate them. They will be found in Kiley v. Ry. Co., 138 Wis. 215, 119 N. W. 309, 120 N. W. 756; Servonitz v. State, 133 Wis. 231, 113 N. W. 277, 126 Am. St. Rep. 955; State v. Evans, 130 Wis. 381, 110 N. W. 241; and State ex rel. v. Currens, 111 Wis. 431, 87 N. W. 561, 56 L. R. A. 252. In the matter of stirring up dust and setting it in motion street car lines easily fall into a class by themselves. Their cars are large and heavy and run a high rate of speed and with great frequency. The bodies of such cars rest close to the surface of the street. They occupy a very considerable of the best portion of the streets to the exclusion of the general public a large part of the time. They run on tracks which create peculiar conditions for the accumulation of dust and dirt, and they occupy the streets by permission from the common council and not as a matter of absolute right. And finally, they are subjected by statute (section 1862, St. 1898) to reasonable rules and regulations. No other agency stands on the same footing with the street cars in the matter of raising dust. The steam roads occupy a small portion of a few unimportant streets in the outlying districts and cross over some others at grade, but their occupancy of the streets is almost negligible as compared with the street railway system. Of course many different kinds of vehicles occupy the streets, and all stir up more or less dust when the necessary conditions exist, but it does not follow that because all are not called upon to contribute all must escape. This would entirely exclude the idea of classification. The purpose of this law is to provide for the sprinkling of a well-defined portion of the public streets of the city. The appellant has, under the franchise

State *v.* Milwaukee Electric Ry. & Light Co

granted to it, a paramount right to use and occupy this particular part of the street.   In so doing, it is largely responsible for setting in motion the dust that arises therefrom, and falls within a class by itself under the authorities cited.

9. Was the ordinance legally enacted?   The city charter, section 2, c. 4, provided that "on all questions, ordinances, or resolutions for assessing and levying taxes or for the appropriation or disbursement of money, or creating any liabilities or charge against said city or any fund thereof, the vote shall be taken by ayes and noes and every vote by ayes and noes shall be entered at length upon the journal."   Section 4 of chapter 4 of the charter contains a provision substantially like that quoted.   The roll call showed 42 members of the common council present at the meeting at which the ordinance was passed.   An "aye" and "no" vote was taken on the adoption of the ordinance.   Forty-one members voted aye and none voted no.   The clerk preserved the original minutes showing the names of the aldermen who voted on the ordinance and how they voted.   The entry made on the journal, however, was to the effect that 41 votes were cast in favor of the passage of the ordinance and none in opposition, without stating the names of those voting.   Thus it became impossible to tell from the journal what members voted on the passage of the ordinance. Section 5 of chapter 4 of the charter provided that all proposed ordinances should be referred to appropriate committees before their passage, and that if any report was made on any ordinance appropriating money out of or creating any charge against any fund, such report should be countersigned by the city comptroller, and that the report should not be countersigned unless there was a sufficient amount of money in the fund to meet the appropriation.   The ordinance in dispute provided that the city should furnish, free of charge to the street railway companies, the necessary water for sprinkling, and that the water so furnished should be chargeable to and payable out of the general fund of the city. The street railway companies were required to furnish to the board of public works on the 5th of each month a statement of the amount of water used during the preceding month.

The contention of the appellant is that the ordinance created a charge or liability against the city or some fund thereof, and that, the "aye" and "no" vote not having been entered at length upon the journal, it was never legally passed.   Laws requiring the "aye" and "no" vote to be taken on certain questions and entered upon the permanent record of the common council of a city are generally held to be mandatory, and the requirement that the record be kept stands on no different footing from that relating to the manner of voting.   Steckert *v.* E. Saginaw, 22 Mich. 104 ; Pickton *v.* Fargo, 10 N. D. 469, 88 N. W. 90; Cook *v.* Independence, 133 Iowa, 582, 110 N. W. 1029; In re Ryan, 79 Neb. 414, 112 N. W. 599; Rich *v.* Chicago, 59 Ill. 286; City of

State v. Milwaukee Electric Ry. & Light Co

Logansport v. Crockett, 64 Ind. 319, 324; Cutler v. Russellville, 40 Ark. 105; Sullivan v. City of Leadville, 11 Colo. 483, 18 Pac. 736; Dillon on Mun. Corp. § 291. The reason for such enactments is that the people generally, and particularly the constituency of an alderman, are entitled to know how their representatives vote on important questions. In order that they may know, it is quite as important that the record of the vote be preserved as it is that it be taken in such a manner that it can be preserved. While it is possible in the present case to ascertain from the original minutes of the meeting who voted for the passage of this ordinance, it is not possible to do so from the journal, and this is the record which the law requires shall be complete. The only cases we have found which hold that a provision requiring the "aye" and "no" vote to be taken is directory are Striker v. Kelly. 7 Hill (N. Y.) 29, affirmed 2 Denio (N. Y.) 323, and Elemendorf v. New York, 25 Wend. (N. Y.) 693. The reason which impelled the great majority of courts that have passed upon the question to hold such acts mandatory is quite convincing, and such a rule is apt to produce the best results in the administration of municipal affairs, and we adopt it without hesitancy.

It remains to be considered whether the ordinance created a debt or liability against the city or a charge on any fund thereof. Unless it did it was unnecessary that the "aye" and "no" vote be taken or preserved. This presents one of the most serious questions in the case. If it is important that the "aye" and "no" vote shall be taken and preserved in the manner the charter requires, it is just as important that it be taken on all questions falling within the charter provisions. The provisions, it is true, are broad and general, but liberality in construction should not lean in the direction of unduly restricting the application of the statute. That the ordinance does not create a "debt or a charge against any fund" is clear enough, but that it does not create a "liability" is not so clear. If the term is used in its broadest and most comprehensive sense it would include any obligation which a party was bound in law or justice to perform and is synonymous with responsibility. In its more restricted and perhaps in its popular sense, it means that which one is under obligation to pay to another.

The city owns its own waterworks. The object and purpose of the ordinance is not to appropriate money or create any indebtedness, but to require the appellant to sprinkle a portion of the streets which it uses. Incidentally it is provided that no charge shall be made for the water used in sprinkling and which the city must pump into its mains. The city may refuse or decline to permit the appellant to draw water from its hydrants, but if it does the ordinance automatically becomes inoperative. No money is voted out of the city treasury by the ordinance and no expense is contemplated, except it be the fuel consumption in pumping the extra water, and the wear and tear on the pumps in doing the extra work. It is not even certain that these items of expense are real. We are not advised as to whether or not the streets were sprinkled before this ordinance was passed, but the fair presumption is that they were; else there would be little warrant for sprinkling a strip in the center of the streets and neglecting the rest of them. If they were, we must also presume that the city was furnishing water for such sprinkling and was receiving no compensation therefor, unless we assume that the appellant was made a special object of bounty. The resolution of July 6, 1909, provided that the city should furnish water free of charge, which would indicate in some measure what its practice was. We mention these matters as indicating that there is no affimative showing that the expense of the city would be at all increased by the passage of this ordinance. Indeed it may well be that it was relieved of a portion of the cost of sprinkling street crossings at least. We think the word "liability" as used in the ordinance means something other than a mere naked undertaking which may involve no expense to the city at all, and that it was intended to cover some claim or obligation which in the ordinary course of business should be presented to the council for audit and allowance, and which should upon allowance constitute a charge on some fund. Until the amount of expense, if any, incurred under this ordinance, was either ascertained or estimated, there was no charge against any fund, and the expense could be ascertained and provided for after the ordinance was passed as well as at the time of its passage. We conclude that the judgment is right and should be affirmed.

Judgment affirmed.

SOUTHERN RY. CO. *v.* FOSTER'S ADM'R.

(Supreme Court of Appeals of Virginia, Jan. 12, 1911.)

[69 S. E. Rep. 972.]

Trial—Instructions—Applicability to Evidence.—Instructions are to aid the jury to apply the law to the facts, and should be given only on the case which the evidence tends to sustain; so that one declaring the master's duty as to furnishing a safe place to work should not be given, though the declaration alleges negligence in the performance of the duty, in the absence of proof to sustain the allegation.

Master and Servant—Duty of Master—Appliances.*—It is the master's duty to exercise ordinary care to provide, not "safe and suitable" appliances, but "reasonably safe and suitable" appliances, for the use of the servant.

Master and Servant—Assumption of Risk—Manner of Conducting Business.—Notwithstanding Const. 1903, § 162 (Code 1904, p. cclix), and Code 1904, § 1294k, abolish the doctrine of assumption of risk, so far as it applies to knowledge by a servant of a railroad "of the defective or unsafe character or condition of any machinery, ways, appliances or structures," he still assumes all the other ordinary and usual risks incident to the service, including the risks incident to the manner in which he knows, or in the exercise of ordinary care ought to know, the master conducts its business.

Master and Servant—Assumption of Risk—Instruction.†—The instruction given for plaintiff that, "when a person enters the employ of a railroad company as a brakeman, he only assumes the ordinary and usual risks that are incident to such employment," is defective in excluding, at least seemingly, the additional risk, if any, incident to the known manner in which the railroad conducts its business.

Master and Servant—Care Required of Master—Instructions.—Defendant in an action for injury to its brakeman requested an instruction, which, after declaring what constituted ordinary care, stated that, if the jury believed that certain facts were established, they

_____

*For the authorities in this series on the subject of the degree of care required of an employer to furnish safe appliances, see second paragraph of first foot-note of Massy *v.* Milwaukee Elec. Ry. & L. Co. (Wis.), 36 R. R. R. 656, 59 Am. & Eng. R. Cas., N. S., 656; first foot-note of House *v.* Southern R. Co. (N. Car.), 36 R. R. R. 308, 59 Am. & Eng. R. Cas., N. S., 508; first head-note of Delaware, etc., R. Co. *v.* Royce (C. C. A.), 36 R. R. R. 217, 59 Am. & Eng. R. Cas., N. S., 217; second foot-note of Southern Ry. Co. *v.* Lewis (Va.), 35 R. R. R. 743, 58 Am. & Eng. R. Cas., N. S., 743; second head-note of Siegel *v.* Detroit, etc., Ry. Co. (Mich.), 35 R. R. R. 311, 58 Am. & Eng. R. Cas., N. S., 311; first foot-note of Ryland *v.* Atlantic C. L. R. Co. (Fla.), 35 R. R. R. 56, 58 Am. & Eng. R. Cas., N. S., 56.

†For the authorities in this series on the subject of the general principles involved in the doctrine of assumption of risks by serv-

Southern Ry. Co. *v.* Foster's Adm'r

should find for defendant. Between the last of such facts, which was if the car was being handled in the way usual to defendant and other railway companies, and the conclusion that they should find for defendant, the court inserted the words "and with reasonable care under all the circumstances." Held, that the addition, whatever the purpose of making it, made the instruction erroneous, as impos-, ing a higher degree of care than the law requires.

Master and Servant—Care Required of Master.‡—A master is not required to exercise a higher degree of care than that exercised by the average prudent man engaged in like business.

Master and Servant—Ordinary Care of Master—Instructions.—Amending an instruction in an action for injury to defendant's brakeman defining ordinary care as such care as reasonably prudent companies or persons use in the conduct of like business, and stating that defendant was not negligent if it was switching its cars in the usual way adopted by it and other companies engaged in the same business, by adding, and if it "used ordinary care in switching said cars," left the jury without any guide as to what constitutes ordinary care in switching cars.

Appeal from Circuit Court, Pittsylvania County.

Action by C. D. Foster's administrator against the Southern Railway Company. Judgment for plaintiff. Defendant appeals. Reversed and remanded for new trial.

Wm. Leigh, for plaintiff in error.
B. H. Custer and *Geo. T. Rison,* for defendant in error.

BUCHANAN, J. This is an action to recover damages for the death of C. D. Foster, caused, as is alleged, by the negligent act of the Southern Railway Company, in whose service the decedent was employed as an extra brakeman at the time he received the injuries from which he died.

Several grounds of negligence are averred in the original and amended declarations, viz., that the car on which the plaintiff's decedent was riding at the time he was injured was equipped with insufficient brakes; that the brakes on the engine operating the car were insufficient; that the tracks at the station where the

---

ants, see last foot-note of Moyse *v.* Northern Pac. R. Co. (Mont.). 36 R. R. R. 686, 59 Am. & Eng. R. Cas., N. S., 686; second foot-note of Massy *v.* Milwaukee Elec. Ry. & L. Co. (Wis.), 36 R. R. R. 656, 59 Am. & Eng. R. Cas., N. S., 656; Leggett *v.* Atlantic C. L. R. Co. (N. Car.), 36 R. R. R. 636, 59 Am. & Eng. R. Cas., N. S., 636; second foot-note of St. Louis, etc., R. Co. *v.* Corman (Ark.), 35 R. R. R. 48, 58 Am. & Eng. R. Cas., N. S., 48; last foot-note of Vaillancourt *v.* Grand Trunk R. Co. (Vt.), 33 R. R. R. 353, 56 Am. & Eng. R. Cas., N. S., 353.

‡See last foot-note of Southern Ry. Co. *v.* Lewis (Va.), 35 R. R. R. 743, 58 Am. & Eng. R. Cas., N. S., 743; second foot-note of Chamberlain *v.* Southern Ry. Co. (Ala.), 34 R. R. R. 655, 57 Am. & Eng. R. Cas., N. S., 655.

Southern Ry. Co. v. Foster's Adm'r

accident occurred were constructed and maintained at too steep a grade for the handling and switching of cars; that the conductor in charge of the train was negligent in ordering and permitting the car on which the decedent was riding to be cut loose from the engine, and allowed to roll down the grade with defective brakes, and to come in contact with other cars standing on the siding; and that the engineman was negligent in cutting loose the car on which the decedent was riding, and in allowing it to drift or roll down the grade with defective brakes, and come in contact with another or other cars standing on the siding.

There was a verdict and judgment for the plaintiff, to which this writ of error was awarded.

Upon the trial of the cause the plaintiff offered eight instructions, numbered from 1 to 8, inclusive. Instruction No. 1 is objected to on the ground that it told the jury that it was the duty of the defendant to use ordinary care to furnish to the plaintiff's intestate a reasonably safe place in which to work, considering the nature and character of the work, when there was no evidence tending to show that the place in which the accident occurred was not reasonably safe.

While it is the clear duty of the master to exercise ordinary care to furnish his servant a reasonably safe place in which to work, yet if there is no sufficient evidence upon which to base a verdict that he has not done so, as was the fact in this case, an instruction like that complained of ought not to be given. Instructions are given to aid the jury to apply the law to the facts of the case on trial. Although it may be charged in the declaration that the master was guilty of negligence in the performance of his duty in a given particular, yet, if there be no proof to sustain that allegation, the jury have no more right to consider it than if there had been no such charge. The jury should only be instructed upon the case which the evidence tends to sustain. Kincheloe v. Tracewells, 11 Grat. 587; Harvey v. Skipwith. 16 Grat. 393; Bartley v. McKinney, 28 Grat. 750; Scott v. Boyd. 101 Va. 28, 42 S. E. 918; Seaboard, etc., Ry. Co. v. Hickey, 102 Va. 394, 46 S. E. 392; C. & O. Ry. Co. v. Stock & Sons, 104 Va. 97, 51 S. E. 161.

Instruction No. 2 was objected to, and is erroneous, in this: that it imposed a higher degree of care on the master than is imposed by law. It is his duty to exercise ordinary care to provide, not safe and suitable appliances and instrumentalities, but reasonably safe and suitable appliances and instrumentalities for the use of his servant. A. & D. Ry. Co. v. West, 101 Va. 13, 42 S. E. 914; Partlett v. Dunn, 102 Va. 459, 465, 46 S. E. 467, and cases cited.

Instruction No. 3 is as follows: "Actionable negligence is the omission to use that degree of care which the law requires under the circumstances of the particular case. The care re-

Southern Ry. Co. *v.* Foster's Adm'r

quired to prevent the infliction of injury is always proportioned to the probability that an injury will be done under the circumstances which are known to exist."

While the propositions of law announced in the instruction are correct, that stated in the first sentence could not have been of the slightest aid to the jury reaching a correct verdict, and that contained in the last sentence was not applicable to the facts of the case. There was no evidence tending to show that there was any probability that any injury would be done under the circumstances known to exist, or, from past experience, the defendant had any reasonable ground to suppose existed.

Instruction No. 4 will be considered in connection with instruction E, offered by the defendant.

Instruction No. 5 correctly states the law, and we cannot say, as is insisted by the defendant, that it was not applicable to the facts of the case or tended to mislead the jury.

Instruction lettered "E," asked for by the defendant company, and which the court refused to give, was in the following langauge: "The court instructs the jury that an employee assumes the risks incident to the employer's known manner of having its business performed, and if the jury believe from the evidence that the injury to C. D. Foster, complained of in this action, was caused by the manner in which the car on which said C. D. Foster was riding was operated, at the time of the injury, that the manner of operating said car was the usual and ordinary manner in which cars under like circumstances were operated, that C. D. Foster knew, or should have known, of the manner of operating such cars and the danger attending the same, then the said C. D. Foster assumed the risk incident to the operation of said car on which he was injured, and the jury must find for the defendant in this action."

While Const. 1902, § 162 (Code 1904, p. cclix), and section 1294k, Code 1904, do away with the common-law doctrine of the assumption or risk, so far as it applies to knowledge "of the defective or unsafe character or condition of any machinery, ways, appliances or structures," on the part of the servant of a railroad company, they do not change the common-law rule of the assumption of risk as to the manner in which the master conducts his business. When the plaintiff's decedent entered into the service of the defendant company, he assumed all the ordinary and usual risks incident to the service (except those abolished by section 162 of the Constitution and section 1294k of the Code of 1904), including the risks incident to the manner in which he knew, or in the exercise of ordinary care ought to have known, the defendant conducted its business. Moore Lime Co. *v.* Richardson, 95 Va. 326, 28 S. E. 334, 64 Am. St. Rep. 785; Big Stone Gap Iron Co. *v.* Ketron, 102 Va. 23, 45 S. E. 740, 102 Am. St. Rep. 839; Parlett *v.* Dunn, supra, and cases cited.

Southern Ry. Co. *v.* Foster's Adm'r

The plaintiff's counsel does not controvert this in his brief, but insists that the instructions given, especially instructions lettered "D" and "F," fully covered the case.

Instruction No. 4, given upon the motion of the plaintiff, told the jury that, "when a person enters the employ of a railroad company as brakeman, he only assumes the ordinary and usual risks that are incident to such employment."

The defect in that instruction, as applied to the facts of this case, is that it seemed to, if it did not actually, exclude the additional risk, if any, incident to the known manner in which the defendant conducted its business.

None of the other instructions given was upon the question of assumed risk. Instructions D and F, not only were not upon that question, but as amended and given by the court were erroneous.

Instruction D, as given, was as follows: "The court instructs the jury that ordinary care is such care as reasonably prudent men exercise in the conduct of a like business, and if they believe from the evidence that the tracks of the defendant company were not of steeper grade than the tracks of said company, and of other railroad companies, at other places where switching was done, that the brakes on the car on which C. D. Foster was riding were in good order and the kind of brake in ordinary use by said company and other railroad companies, on cars of like character, and that the car was being handled in the way usual to said company and other railway companies *and with reasonable care under all circumstances*, then the jury must find for the defendant in this action.

The italicized words in the instruction were added by the court. As offered by the defendant company, it told the jury what constituted ordinary care, and then instructed them that, if they believed that certain facts which there was evidence tending to prove were established, the defendant company had exercised ordinary care, and they must find for it. It is not clear what was intended by the words added by the court. Whether, as insisted by the defendant company, they were added to tell the jury that, although they believed that such conditions existed and the defendant had acted in such a manner as, under the law, constituted ordinary care, yet in order to relieve itself of liability the jury must believe that those acts which constituted ordinary care were done carefully, thus imposing a higher degree of care than the law requires, or whether they were added because the court was of opinion that all the facts which the evidence tended to prove, and which were necessary to show that the defendant was not liable were not enumerated in the instruction, we cannot say. In either view the amendment was erroneous. If the former, it imposed a higher degree of care upon the defendant than the law did. If the latter, the omitted fact or facts necessary to relieve the defendant of liability should have been added instead of the general

Southern Ry. Co. *v.* Foster's Adm'r

language used by the court. As given, whatever may have been the intention of the court in making the amendment, the instruction was erroneous.

Instruction F, as given, is as follows: "The court instructs the jury that ordinary or reasonable care is such care as other reasonably prudent companies or persons use in the conduct of like business; that it was the duty of the defendant, the railway company, to use reasonable care, as above set out, in conducting its business, but it was not its duty to adopt a mode of conducting its business different from its usual custom, because some one may think such mode a safer way of conducting it. And if the jury believe from the evidence that the railway company was switching its cars at Motleys Station at the time that C. D. Foster was injured in the usual way adopted by it and other companies engaged in like business, *and used ordinary care in switching said cars,* then the said railway company was guilty of no negligence in so switching its cars, and it cannot be held liable therefor in this action."

The words italicized were added by the court. The instruction, as asked for by the defendant, told the jury that ordinary care was such care as reasonably prudent companies or persons use in conducting their business, and that if they believed that the defendant was switching its cars when the plaintiff's decedent was injured, in the usual way adopted by it and other companies engaged in like business, then the defendant was not guilty of negligence in switching its cars in that manner. As offered, the instruction correctly stated the law. No one is held in law to a higher degree of care than the average prudent man engaged in like business. Bertha Zinc Co. *v.* Martin, 93 Va. 791, 22 S. E. 869, 70 L. R. A. 999; N. & P. Traction Co. *v.* Ellington's Adm'r, 108 Va. 245, 250, 61 S. E. 779, 17 L. R. A. (N. S.) 117, and cases cited. The instruction, as amended and given, said in effect to the jury that switching cars in the way in which it is usually done by the defendant and other companies engaged in the same business was not ordinary care, unless the jury further believed that the defendant "used ordinary care in switching said cars," thus leaving the jury without a guide to determine what constitutes ordinary care in switching cars.

As the case will have to be remanded for a new trial, it will serve no good purpose to consider the assignment of error that the verdict is contrary to the evidence.

The judgment complained of must be reversed, the verdict of the jury set aside, and the cause remanded for a new trial to be had not in conflict with the views expressed in this opinion.

Reversed.

Cardwell, J., absent.

KIRBY v. CHICAGO, R. I. & P. RY. Co.

(Supreme Court of Iowa, Feb. 11, 1911.)

[129 N. W. Rep. 963.]

Master and Servant—Locomotive Engineers—Sufficiency of Equipment.—It was proper to refuse to instruct that a railway company was liable for the death of an engineer caused by a boiler exploding, if the lowest gauge-cock on the locomotive was too low, where use of a water glass made gauge-cocks unnecessary.

Master and Servant—Safety of Locomotives—Use by Other Companies.*—General use by reasonably prudent railways of locomotives of particular type can be shown on an issue of negligence in using that kind of a locomotive, but is not conclusive against negligence in a particular respect, and hence, in a suit for death of an engineer caused by a boiler exploding, it was erroneous to direct a finding for the company if locomotives of that class were in general use by other reasonably prudent railways.

Appeal from District Court, Linn County; W. N. Treichler, Judge.

Action to recover damages for the death of plaintiff's intestate while in the employ of the defendant as locomotive engineer, alleged to have resulted from the negligence of the defendant in the use of a defective locomotive. There was a verdict and judgment for defendant. Plaintiff appeals. Reversed.

Dawley & Wheeler, for appellant.
Carroll Wright, J. L. Parrish, and *Grimm & Trewin,* for appellee.

McCLAIN, J. Plaintiff's intestate was killed by an explosion of the locomotive which he was operating on defendant's railroad, and the alleged negligence of the defendant was in continuing to use the engine in question when charged with knowledge that it was defective in construction and repair in such respects as would render it liable to explode.

---

*See first foot-note of preceding case.
See first foot-note of Southern Ry. Co. *v.* Lewis (Va.), 35 R. R. R. 743, 58 Am. & Eng. R. Cas., N. S., 743; foot-note of Bourassa *v.* Grand Trunk Ry. Co. (N. H.), 34 R. R. R. 355, 57 Am. & Eng. R. Cas., N. S., 355; foot-note of Anderson *v.* Louisville & N. R. Co. (Ky.), 34 R. R. R. 220, 57 Am. & Eng. R. Cas., N. S., 220; second head-note of Harris *v.* Puget Sound Elec. Ry. (Wash.), 34 R. R. R. 45, 57 Am. & Eng. R. Cas., N. S., 45; last foot-note of Campbell *v.* Duluth & N. E. R. Co. (Minn.), 32 R. R. R. 490, 55 Am. & Eng. R. Cas., N. S., 490; second head-note of Taylor *v.* Baltimore & O. R. Co. (Va.), 31 R. R. R. 776, 54 Am. & Eng. R. Cas., N. S., 776; foot-note of Lamb *v.* Philadelphia & R. Ry. Co. (U. S.), 27 R. R. R. 180, 50 Am. & Eng. R. Cas., N. S., 180.

1. The locomotive which exploded was of a type described by witnesses as the "1,400 class," and its particular number was 1,422. The characteristics of this class of locomotives seem not to be material to the determination of the questions discussed by counsel except in this respect, that the lowest of the three gauge-cocks by which the engineer tests the height of the water in his boiler should be 4 or 5 inches above the crown sheet of the fire box, while in this locomotive it was only 2½ inches above the crown sheet. The importance of being able to test the height of the water in the boiler above the crown sheet was shown to be that, if the water is so low in the boiler that it does not cover or sufficiently cover the crown sheet, there is danger that the crown sheet will be so affected by the fire in the fire box that the boiler was liable to explode by reason of the resulting weakness at this point. There was evidence tending to show that the crown sheet of this locomotive, when examined after the explosion, had been partially fused and rendered thin in one place, and that the appearances of the metal indicated that the water at the time of the explosion was much lower than the top of the crown sheet. As to this matter, the only assignment of error is as to the refusal of the court on defendant's request, to give the following instruction: "If you find from the evidence that the lowest gauge-cock on engine 1,422 was too low, and that the explosion occurred by reason thereof, and that said William Kirby was not guilty of contributory negligence, then your verdict should be for plaintiff." The evidence shows, however, that in the ordinary operation of a locomotive the engineer depends for information as to the height of water in his boiler on a water glass, and that this locomotive was provided with such water glass located beside the gauge-cocks, and, if the water glass is in operation, the use of the gauge-cocks is wholly unnecessary. Such cocks are useful for determining whether the water glass is working, although that fact may also be determined by the engineer operating the engine by observation of the water in the glass itself. The water glass on this engine was so arranged that the lowest level of the water in the boiler as shown by it would be four inches above the crown sheet.

It therefore appears that, had the lowest gauge-cock been the proper distance above the crown sheet, it would not have given the engineer any information as to the height of the water which he could not have derived from an inspection of the glass; while, as it was in fact situated at a lower level than that of the lowest limit of the water glass, he might have ascertained whether the water had fallen below a level of 2⅛ inches above the crown sheet. It is impossible to see how the fact that the lowest gauge-cock was lower than the lowest limit of the water glass could have been the proximate cause of the explosion. This is apparent for two reasons: First, because the evidence as to

Kirby v. Chicago, R. I. & P. Ry. Co

the condition of the crown sheet after the explosion clearly shows that the water had fallen much below the level of the lowest gauge-cock, so that, if it had been four inches above the crown sheet, it would have given the engineer no information which it would not actually have given him if he had used it with reference to the height of the water; and, second, because there is no evidence whatever that the engineer had any occasion to resort to the gauge-cocks for the purpose of observing the height of the water. If there had been a finding for the plaintiff predicated on the negligence of defendant in having the lowest gauge-cock less than four inches above the crown sheet, it would necessarily have been without support in the evidence, and there was no error, therefore, in refusing the instruction asked.

2. The court gave two instructions relating to the alleged negligence of the defendant in sending out decedent with a locomotive which was defective in construction and repair in such respects as to render it liable to explode. As it is contended that these instructions contained erroneous and conflicting statements of law, they are set out in full:

"(3) You are instructed that, before the plaintiff can recover on this action, you must be satisfied by a fair preponderance of the evidence that decedent was not guilty of contributing to the accident complained of, and also that the accident and injury was the result of the defendant's negligence. You are further instructed that, if you find that the locomotive boiler in question was a design and plan such as are in ordinary and general use by reasonably careful and prudent railways, then your verdict must be for the defendant; but if you find by preponderance of the evidence that the locomotive boiler in question was faulty in design and plan, and that the explosion was due to faulty design, which defects in the boiler construction the defendant in the exercise of ordinary care could have discovered, and you further find the decedent, William J. Kirby, was not himself guilty of contributory negligence, then your verdict should be for plaintiff."

"(5) You are instructed that if you find from the evidence that the locomotive in question was a reasonably safe engine, and it was such as was in general and ordinary use by reasonable and prudent railways, then defendant would not be liable, and you should so find. The defendant was in duty bound to use reasonable care in the selection of the locomotive in question, to see that it was reasonably safe in its design and plans when operated with ordinary care, and if you find by a preponderance of the evidence that the locomotive in question was not properly constructed, and defendant could have, in the exercise of ordinary care, discovered such defects, then, in that event, defendant would be guilty of negligence."

Kirby v. Chicago, R. I. & P. Ry. Co

The objection to these instructions most strongly urged is that the jurors were thereby directed to find the defendant not negligent in the respect complained of if the locomotive boiler was in design and plan such as in ordinary and general use by careful and prudent railways, and it is contended that in several cases decided by this court general usage of other railways has been held no proper test for determining the negligence in a particular case. If the instructions had been to the effect that the jury might find want of negligence from the general use of railways of locomotives of similar design, construction, and condition then the objection urged would have been supported by several decisions of this court. In Hamilton v. Des-Moines Valley R. Co.. 36 Iowa, 31, a requested instruction was held properly refused in which the negligence of the defendant in transporting a car loaded with timbers, which projected beyond the end of the car, was made to depend upon whether the car was loaded as similar cars had been usually and commonly loaded and carried over defendant's road, and the court said that the instruction was properly refused "for the obvious reason that habits of negligence on the part of the defendant or other railroad will not relieve them from the consequence of their negligent acts." In Allen v. Burlington, C. R. & N. R. Co.. 64 Iowa, 94, 19 N. W. 870, where the negligence of the defendant alleged was in allowing a cattle chute to project too near the track, resulting in injury to a brakeman, an instruction was held to have been properly refused which made the negligence of defendant depend upon whether the chute was "constructed at the usual distance from the track at which they are usually located on well regulated railroads generally;" the court saying: "The usual custom or practice of railroad corporations in operating their roads and in constructing their machinery and buildings cannot be the ground of relief from liability for injuries sustained, if the custom or practice disregards the safety of the employees as required by the law. In that case it would simply be nothing more than negligence practiced habitually by the corporations." In Hosic v. Chicago, R. I. & P. R. Co., 75 Iowa, 683, 37 N. W. 963, 9 Am. St. Rep. 518, the question was whether defendant was liable for injury to a brakeman due to failure to provide a platform car on which agricultural implements were loaded with a footboard on which the brakeman might pass over it. and the court said that, if the jury found defendant to be negligent in not providing a footboard, "the fact that such negligence was usual or customary would not relieve defendant from liability for its consequences." In Metzgar v. Chicago, M. & St. P. R. Co., 76 Iowa, 387, 41 N. W. 49. 14 Am. St. Rep. 224, it was said that the liability of the defendant for using an engine which emitted sparks setting out a fire could not be avoided by showing that the engine in question was made like most engines in use, and the court employed this language in stating the proposition: "It was the duty of the defendant to use the best devices available to prevent the escape of fire. * * * This duty would not depend in any manner upon the usage of other roads. A fault is none the less a fault because it is common." Evidence offered tending to show that engines of similar construction were in general use on other roads, for the purpose of showing that defendant was not negligent in the use of the engine in question, was therefore held to have been properly excluded.

It is contended, however, for the appellee, that these cases have been overruled by this court in the case of Austin *v.* Chicago, R. I. & P. Co., 93 Iowa, 236, 61 N. W. 849, where instructions allowing the jury to consider evidence as to the custom in the particular referred to relating to alleged negligence were sustained as against plaintiff's contention that they were in conflict with the announcements of opinion in preceding cases. The view of the court in the case last above cited is well stated, however, in the following quotation: "An act of construction, in such matter, may be said to be, of itself, negligent, when, with the purposes of construction in mind, together with the hazards of its use, a better plan is apparent. If no better plan is apparent, the party is left to inquiry and determination as to what course of conduct will give him legal protection; or, in other words, what course of conduct will amount to diligence. The instructions give the rule that, if in such inquiry and determination they adopt the custom of other well-managed roads in the same particulars, that fact may be considered in finding whether or not they acted as reasonably careful men. It seems to be that, under such conditions, it is the common experience of mankind to be governed more or less by the experience of others. It is a line of inquiry nearest to a demonstration of what is best. In fact, were roads constructed in these particulars without inquiry to know the results of time and experience, that fact alone would be strong, if not conclusive, evidence of negligence. We discover nothing contradictory in the instructions; but, on the contrary, they seem to express pertinently and aptly a wholesome rule of law." It is apparent, therefore, that the adoption of the custom of other well-managed roads in the same particulars is only to be considered in finding whether or not the defendant railroad acted with reasonable care and prudence, and this was the holding in Cooper *v.* Central R. Co. of Iowa, 44 Iowa, 134, cited and quoted from the Austin Case.

In accordance with the views thus expressed, evidence of the general use of locomotives in design and plan such as the one in question by reasonably careful and prudent railways was properly received as bearing on the question of defendant's negligence in using such styles of locomotives; but such evidence, although uncontradicted, would not justify the giving of an instruction to the

Kirby *v.* Chicago, R. I. & P. R*y.* Co

effect that, if locomotives such as that in question were in general use on reasonably careful and prudent railways, then the verdict must be for defendant, for railways which are in general well managed in respect to prudence and care in the selection of machinery may nevertheless in particular instances be negligent, and it cannot be said that the concurrence in such negligence by well-managed railroads changes the character of the act itself. If it be said that, in case they found the use of that style of locomotive was negligent, the jurors would have been justified in finding that the railroads concurring in its use were not reasonably careful and prudent, then it must be said that the instructions left the jury to consider a false issue; that is, the reasonable prudence and care of other roads in using such style engine. At any rate, such form of instruction would be objectionable as making a test of such reasonable care and prudence the care and prudence of such railways in other respects. Assuming, then, that the first of the two instructions above quoted contained an independent and authoritative announcement to the jurors that, if they found the locomotive boiler in question to have been in design and plan such as were in ordinary and general use by reasonably careful and prudent railways, then their verdict must be for the defendant, we reach the conclusion that there was error. There is manifest difference between taking into account the ordinary and general use of careful and prudent railways in determining what a careful and prudent railway should have done in the particular matter, and, on the other hand, accepting such ordinary and general use as conclusive evidence of due care. To give such conclusive weight to the evidence of use is to require the jury to ignore all other evidence as to the defective and dangerous character of the type of engine in question as bearing upon the inquiry whether a reasonably careful and prudent railway would use such style of locomotive.

We find no authority in cases cited by the appellee for a conclusive instruction based on the general usage of other reasonably careful and prudent railways. In Mayer *v.* Detroit, etc., Ry., 142 Mich. 459, 105 N. W. 888, the question was whether the defendant was negligent in failing to provide its street cars with sand boxes which could be automatically used when occasion required, and the court found that on the record there was no evidence that similar cars on other roads were generally equipped with sand boxes, or that such equipment was essential to the safe handling of the cars. In Prybilski *v.* Northwestern Coal R. Co., 98 Wis. 413, 74 N. W. 117, the failure to use a particular form of covering on a coal dock to prevent coal from falling on the employees on the dock from buckets used in hoisting coal overhead was held, in view of the evidence, not to be shown to be negligent; but there is nothing to indicate that evidence of usage

Kirby *v.* Chicago, R. I. & P. Ry. Co

in this respect should be regarded as conclusive. The case of Louisville & R. R. Co. *v.* Allen, 78 Ala. 494, relates also to the question of negligence in fact, rather than to the question of a conclusive instruction, and goes no further than to justify the determination by the jury of the fact of negligence in view of the evidence of general usage on the part of other careful and prudent persons engaged in a like business.

It is contended, however, that in the instruction quoted the court did not make the general usage of reasonably careful and prudent railways conclusive, for it was referred to the jury to say finally from the evidence of such general and ordinary use and from the evidence that the locomotive in question was a reasonably safe engine, whether defendant was negligent. The difficulty is that this argument as to the construction which should be put upon the language used makes the two instructions irreconcilable. In the first of them the jurors were told that, if such locomotives were in general use by other reasonably careful and prudent railways, their verdict should be for the defendant, while the most liberal construction which can be given to the second of the instructions in favor of the defendant is that such fact could be considered only in determining whether the use of such engine by defendant was negligent. In the face of the unequivocal direction in the first instruction, we are unable to say that the jury must have disregarded that direction in favor of the direction contained in the second instruction.

For the error pointed out in the second division of this opinion, the judgment is reversed.

LOUISVILLE & N. R. CO. *v.* MCMILLEN.

(Court of Appeals of Kentucky, Feb. 14, 1911.)

[134 S. W. Rep. 185.]

Master and Servant—Injuries to Servant.*—Where the servant of
a railroad while working under a bridge when a train was passing
over it was injured by being struck by a piece of iron from a freight
car door, the burden was not on the servant to show that the car had
not been inspected, or that a car door on that train was minus the
piece of iron in question.

Master and Servant—Assumption of Risk.†—A servant assumes all
the ordinary risks of his employment.

Master and Servant—Assumption of Risk.‡—A servant does not
assume risks occasioned by the negligence of other servants not
his fellow servants.

Master and Servant—Injuries to Servant.§—Where a servant of a
railroad while working under a bridge when a train was passing on

---

*For the authorities in this series on the subject of plaintiff's bur-
den of proof, in an action against a master for the death of or injury to a servant, see last foot-note of Duvall *v.* Seaboard A. L. Ry.
(N. Car.), 36 R. R. R. 532,.59 Am. & Eng. R. Cas., N. S., 532; second
head-note of Missouri, etc., R. Co. *v.* Foreman (C. C. A.), 36 R. R.
R. 491, 59 Am. & Eng. R. Cas., N. S., 491; third head-note of Pittsburgh Rys. Co. *v.* Thomas (C. C. A.), 36 R. R. R. 36, 59 Am & Eng.
R. Cas., N. S., 36; foot-note of Missouri, etc., Ry. Co. *v.* Jones (Tex.),
35 R. R. R. 346, 58 Am. & Eng. R. Cas., N. S., 346; last head-note
of Siegel *v.* Detroit, etc., Ry. Co. (Mich.), 35 R. R. R. 311, 58 Am.
& Eng. R. Cas., N. S., 311; foot-note of Conrad *v.* Springfield Consol.
Ry. Co. (Ill.), 35 R. R. R. 76, 58 Am. & Eng. R. Cas., N. S., 76.

†For the authorities in this series on the subject of the general
rules and principles involved in the doctrine of assumption of risks
by servants, see second foot-note of Massy *v.* Milwaukee Elev. Ry.
& L. Co. (Wis.), 36 R. R. R. 656, 59 Am. & Eng. R. Cas., N. S., 656;
last foot-note of Smith *v.* Chicago, etc., R. Co. (Kan.), 36 R. R. R.
640, 59 Am. & Eng. R. Cas., N. S., 640; first foot-note of Ross *v.*
Chicago, etc., R. Co. (Ill.), 35 R. R. R. 41, 58 Am. & Eng. R. Cas.,
N. S., 41; last foot-note of Vaillancourt *v.* Grand Trunk R. Co. (Vt.),
33 R. R. R. 353, 56 Am. & Eng. R. Cas., N. S., 353.

‡For the authorities in this series on the question whether a servant assumes the risks from the negligence of his master or that of
another employee of his master, not his fellow servant, see last
foot-note of Moyse *v.* Northern Pac. R. Co. (Mont.), 36 R. R. R.
686, 59 Am. & Eng. R. Cas., N. S., 686; first foot-note of Leggett *v.*
Atlantic C. L. R. Co. (N. Car.), 36 R. R. R. 636, 59 Am. & Eng. R.
Cas., N. S., 636; first foot-note of St. Louis, etc., R. Co. *v.* Corman
(Ark.), 35 R. R. R. 48, 58 Am. & Eng. R. Cas., N. S., 48; first head-
note of St. Louis, etc., R. Co. *v.* Hawkins (Ark.), 35 R. R. R. 46, 58
Am. & Eng. R. Cas., N. S., 46.

§For the authorities in this series on the subject of the care re-
quired of a master in inspecting appliances, see first foot-note of
Erie R. Co. *v.* Schomer (C. C. A.), 35 R. R. R. 303, 58 Am. & Eng.
R. Cas., N. S., 303.

Louisville & N. R. Co. *v.* McMillen

the bridge was struck by a piece of iron from a freight car door, if the train was sent out with a loose piece of iron, or if it was discovered or could have been by the use of ordinary care, it was negligence.

Damages—Personal Injuries.—Where plaintiff was confined to his bed about 10 months, and had pains all the time in his back and one leg, and was compelled to use crutches, a verdict for $2,000 was not excessive.

Appeal from Circuit Court, Bullitt County.

Action by William McMillen against the Louisville & Nashville Railroad Company. From a judgment in favor of plaintiff, defendant appeals. Affirmed.

Charles Carroll, Charles H. Moorman, J. F. Combs, and *Benjamin D. Warfield,* for appellant.
Ben Chapeze, for appellee.

NUNN, J. Appellee was running a pumping station at night for appellant at a point on its road where it crossed Rolling Fork river, the line between the counties of Hardin and Bullitt. He had been so engaged for about 20 months, when on the night of July 21, 1909, he passed from the pumphouse into a coal bin to get some coal to fire the furnace, and while stooping to shovel up the coal something hit him just below the small of the back, and rendered him senseless, in which condition he remained, according to his testimony, from 30 minutes to 2 hours, the exact time not known. When he recovered, he called for a person who was in the pumphouse, who came out and found him sitting upon the floor of the bin with his head leaning forward and a flat piece of iron, about the size of a person's two hands, by his side. Appellee crawled to the pumphouse a few steps away, and remained there about 15 minutes, when he, assisted by Waverly French and Wm. Bryant, who happened to be at the pumphouse, started for home with his wife and children. Appellee used a plank in walking, and the witnesses described to the jury how he used it, but it is not made plain to the court just how he used it, other than he held it with both hands. According to appellee's testimony, he remained at home about two months, and was confined to his bed most of that time by reason of his injuries. He testified that he had pains in the lower part of his back and right leg all the time; that at the end of the two months, when he did get out, he was compelled to use crutches in order to walk, and was using them at the time of the trial in the lower court. He was corroborated in these statements by French, Bryant, and four or five of his neighbors. Two physicians also supported him in his statements, but were contradicted by at least two other physicians who testified for

appellant, and swore that they examined appellee soon after he
received his professed injuries, and found nothing wrong with
him, except his right leg was slightly smaller than the other, and
that this had been caused by nonuse. A freight train passed
upon the bridge at the time appellee was getting the coal, and all
the witnesses swore that the piece of iron found by his side when
he was hurt came off of a freight car door; that it fastened to the
bottom of the door for it to slide on when it was opened or
closed. Appellee said he heard it strike the pumphouse and the
next instant it struck him, and knocked him senseless. The witnesses fix the height of the bridge at from 20 to 30 feet. Appellant also pleaded contributory negligence on the part of
appellee, and proved by two of the managers of·its pumping stations that they had warned appellee not to go into the coal bin
when a train was passing on the bridge. Appellee denied this,
but says he knew it was somewhat dangerous, and that he seldom
went out when a train was going by; that he did not know a
train was passing at the time he arrived at the coal bin; that it
was dark, and he saw no lights; that the train entered upon
the bridge after he went into the coal bin, and that he thought
he would get his coal before he returned to the pumphouse, as
he needed it to fire with.

The lower court gave the jury three instructions. The first,
which fixed the only basis upon which appellant might recover, is
as follows: "The court instructs the jury that if they shall believe from the evidence that the plaintiff was struck and injured
by the piece of iron exhibited in evidence, or a piece of iron
similar thereto, and that said piece of iron was caused to fall
from one of the defendant's trains by negligence upon the part
of its agents and servants in charge of said train, or upon the
part of the agents and servants whose duty it was to inspect said
train, then the law of the case is for the plaintiff, and the jury
should so find." As we understand counsel's brief, they do not
object to the form or substance of the instructions given, but
claim that it was the court's duty to give only a peremptory instruction in behalf of appellant. Their first reason for this contention is that there was no proof showing that this piece of iron
was negligently allowed to fall from the train; and the second
is that the testimony showed that appellee was malingering. The
testimony shows that this piece of iron fell and struck appellee
while a freight train was crossing the bridge, and that it was a
piece of iron which belonged on the door of a freight car. As we
understand the law, it was not required of appellee to show that
the car had not been inspected and made safe to go out on the
road, or that a car door upon that particular train was minus the
piece of iron exhibited to the jury. This burden was upon appellant, and it did prove by its conductor, who was in the caboose,
and its engineer, who was in the engine cab, that they did not see

or hear any iron fall; and it further proved by its two car inspectors in Bowling Green where the train arrived three or four hours after the accident that they inspected the train and found nothing wrong with the cars.

When appellee entered into the employment of appellant, he assumed all the ordinary risks incident to that employment, but he did not assume the risks occasioned by the negligence of other employees who were not his fellow servants. If this train was sent out on the road with a loose piece of iron attached to it, or if it was discovered or could have been by the use of ordinary care after the train was out by those in charge, it was negligence in permitting to be moved in that condition, and it was their duty to make reasonable inspections for the purpose of ascertaining this fact, if it existed, and, if they failed to do so, they were guilty of negligence. The train was shown to have been under the management of appellant, or its servants, and the accident was such as in the ordinary course of things would not have happened if those having the management, use, and care had exercised reasonable diligence. It appears in the case of L. & N. R. R. Co. *v.* Clark, 106 S. W. 1184, 32 Ky. Law Rep. 736, that a lump of coal fell from a tender and struck Clark, a brakeman, upon the head. His evidence showed that fact, and the railroad company claimed that it also devolved upon him to prove the tender was improperly loaded, but this court said it devolved upon the railroad company.

There was no evidence that appellee was guilty of contributory negligence. The question of his malingering was before the jury. If his injuries were as great and as permanent as the testimony tends to establish, the verdict for $2,000 is small.

For these reasons, the judgment of the lower court is affirmed.

CHICAGO, R. I. & P. RY. CO. v. GRUBBS.

(Supreme Court of Arkansas, Feb. 6, 1911.)

[134 S. W. Rep. 636.]

Appeal and Error—Evidence—Review.—The court on appeal, in determining whether there is any evidence warranting the verdict. will consider the testimony in its most favorable aspect to the successful party.

Master and Servant—Injury to Servant—Assumption of Risk.*—A servant assumes the ordinary and usual risks incident to the employment and the risks which he knows or which by the exercise of reasonable care he may know, and, where a master and servant possess equal knowledge of a danger, the servant of sufficient maturity to appreciate the danger assumes the risk.

Master and Servant—Duty to Warn Servant.†—A master need not warn an experienced servant as to obvious dangers, where the master and servant possess equal knowledge of the dangers.

Master and Servant—Injury to Servant—Assumption of Risk.‡—A servant employed to straighten creosoted ties on a car knew that such ties were liable to slip when any weight was applied to them. He climbed on the drawhead of the car and caught hold of a tie with his hand and attempted to pull himself up. The tie slipped, and he lost his hold and fell to the ground and was injured. Held, that he assumed the risk of injury, as a matter of law, though the master negligently failed to provide a safe means of mounting the car to rearrange the ties.

Master and Servant—Injury to Servant—Assumption of Risk.*—A servant, who knows the methods adopted in the work and the place in which the work is to be done, and who continues in the employment, assumes the risks of the dangers resulting therefrom.

Master and Servant—Injury to Servant—Assumption of Risk.—Where the place or work itself was unsafe. a servant voluntarily engaging therein. with knowledge of the danger, assumed the risks.

---

*See second and third foot-notes of preceding case.

†For the authorities in this series on the subject of the duty of the master to warn and instruct his servants, see foot-note of Chesapeake & O. R. Co. v. Nash (Ky.), 36 R. R. R. 511, 59 Am. & Eng. R. Cas., N. S., 511; foot-note of St. Louis, etc., R. Co. v. Wells (Ark.), 35 R. R. R. 638, 58 Am. & Eng. R. Cas., N. S., 638; foot-note of Ryan v. Northern Pac. Ry. Co. (Wash.), 35 R. R. R. 71, 58 Am. & Eng. R. Cas., N. S., 71.

‡For the authorities in this series on the question whether a servant assumes risks arising from his master's negligence, see first foot-note of Leggett v. Atlantic Coast Line R. Co. (N. Car.), 36 R. R. R. 636, 59 Am. & Eng. R. Cas., N. S., 636; first foot-note of St. Louis, etc., R. Co. v. Corman (Ark.), 35 R. R. R. 48, 58 Am. & Eng. R. Cas., N. S., 48; St. Louis, etc., R. Co. v. Hawkins (Ark.), 35 R. R. R. 46, 58 Am. & Eng. R. Cas., N. S., 46.

Chicago, R. I. & P. Ry. Co. *v.* Grubbs

Appeal from Circuit Court, Lonoke County; Eugene Lankford, Judge.

Action by C. W. Grubbs against the Chicago, Rock Island & Pacific Railway Company. From a judgment for plaintiff, defendant appeals. Reversed, and case dismissed.

Thos. S. Bugbee and *John T. Hicks,* for appellant.
J. B. Reed and *Carmichael, Brooks & Powers,* for appellee.

FRAUENTHAL, J. This was an action instituted by C. W. Grubbs, the plaintiff below, to recover damages for a personal injury which he sustained while in defendant's employment and which he alleged was caused by defendant's negligence. The defendant denied the allegations of negligence set out in the complaint and pleaded as a bar to a recovery by plaintiff his alleged contributory negligence and his assumption of the risk of the injury. The jury returned a verdict in favor of the plaintiff, and from the judgment rendered thereon the defendant has appealed to this court.

Upon the trial of the case, the defendant asked for a peremptory instruction in its favor, and now contends that under the uncontroverted testimony in the case the injury which the plaintiff received was due to the risk which was ordinarily incident to the employment in which he was engaged, and which therefore he assumed; and, also, that plaintiff himself was guilty of negligence which contributed to cause the injury. In determining whether or not there was any evidence adduced upon the trial of the case that was legally sufficient to warrant the verdict, this court will consider the testimony in its most favorable aspect to plaintiff and make every legitimate inference in his favor that is deducible therefrom. Viewed in this manner, the case is substantially this: The plaintiff was employed by the defendant as a section hand and had been engaged in that service for about 18 months prior to the time he received the injury complained of. Two cars of creosoted ties had been placed upon the side track at the town of Lonoke. These ties were loaded on flat cars and had become disarranged while being transported. They were placed upon the side track for the purpose of having them rearranged or straightened out, and it was one of the duties of the section hands to do this. The foreman of the section crew directed a number of his hands, amongst whom was plaintiff. to straighten out these ties upon the cars. The ties were loaded upon the cars to a height of about 12 or 14 feet from the ground, and they had become so disarranged that their ends protruded over the cars. The men first attempted to rearrange the ties by the use of a scantling while standing on the ground; but, this method proving unsuccessful, the foreman directed the men to go upon the ties in order to straighten them out. Four of the men got upon the ties safely. The plaintiff went to the end of the flat car, and, climbing upon the drawhead of the car, caught hold of a protruding cross-tie with his hand and attempted to pull himself up. The tie slipped, and the plaintiff, loosening his hold, fell to the ground and was painfully and severely injured. The plaintiff had worked with ties which had been treated with creosote and knew that they were made slick by reason of this treatment; and the section crew to which he belonged had handled a great number of creosoted ties prior to the time of this injury and had straightened the ties on probably one or two cars. The foreman did not direct the section hands, and did not direct the plaintiff, as to the manner in which they should get upon the ties, nor did he warn them of any danger in so doing. He left the manner of mounting the cars to their own discretion and did not see or know of plaintiff's attempt to get on the car until after the injury.

In accepting and continuing in the employment in which he is engaged, a servant assumes the ordinary and usual risks and perils that are incident thereto. He assumes all the obvious risks of the work in which he is engaged, and also the risks which he knows to exist, as well as those which by the exercise of reasonable care he may know to exist. By the contract of service he agrees to bear the risk of all such dangers, and he therefore cannot recover for the injuries resulting therefrom. As is said in the case of Fordyce *v.* Stafford, 57 Ark. 503, 22 S. W. 161: "The employee assumes all risks naturally and reasonably incident to the service in which he engages, where the hazards of the service are obvious and within the apprehension of a person of his experience and understanding." St. Louis, I. M. & S. R. Co. *v.* Touhey, 67 Ark. 209, 54 S. W. 577, 77 Am. St. Rep. 109; Archer-Foster Construction Co. *v.* Vaughn, 79 Ark. 20, 94 S. W. 717; C., O. & G. Ry. Co. *v.* Thompson, 82 Ark. 11, 100 S. W. 83; Graham *v.* Thrall & Shea, 129 S. W. 532; 1 Labatt on Master & Servant, § 259.

In the case at bar the plaintiff knew that the effect of the treatment of creosote upon cross-ties was to make them slick, and therefore liable to slip. The ties had on this account become disarranged upon the cars, and it was for this reason that plaintiff was directed to do the work of straightening them out. Their condition was patent to him, and the manner in which they were disarranged upon the car was also patent. It was obvious, therefore, that these ties were liable to slip whenever any force or weight was applied to them. The risk of injury which might result by reason of the ties slipping or moving was obvious, and, when plaintiff undertook the service of straightening them out, he assumed that risk. The plaintiff knew that these ties had been treated with creosote, and he testified that the effect of such treatment made them sick. He observed that on account of this slick condition these ties had become dislodged and disarranged, and therefore the danger incident to applying force to them, and

598   VOL 39 R R R—VOL 62 AM & ENG R CAS N S

Chicago. R. I. & P. Ry. Co. *v.* Grubbs

thereby causing them to easily move, was obvious and known to the plaintiff. A master is not bound to warn the servant as to dangers which are obvious and patent to him. And, where the master and servant are possessed of equal knowledge of the danger, then it is not incumbent upon the master to warn a servant of sufficient maturity and experience to appreciate the same. In such a case the servant assumes the risk. In the case of L. & A. Ry. Co. *v.* Miles, 82 Ark. 534, 103 S. W. 158, 11 L. R. A. (N. S.) 720, the court, quoting from Labatt on Master & Servant, states the doctrine as follows: "The master is not required to point out the dangers which are readily ascertainable by the servant himself, if he makes an ordinary careful use of such knowledge, experience, and judgment as he possesses. The failure to give instructions, therefore, is not culpable where the servant might by the exercise of ordinary care and attention have known of the danger, or, as the rule is also expressed, where he had all the means necessary for ascertaining the conditions, and there was no danger which could not be discovered."

But it is urged by counsel for plaintiff that, while the servant assumes the ordinary risks incident to the employment, he does not assume the risk of danger caused by the negligence of the master. It is contended that it is incumbent upon the master to furnish the servant with a safe place in which to do the work, and in failing to perform that duty the master is guilty of negligence. It is claimed in this case that it was the duty of the defendant to have provided the plaintiff with a safe means of mounting the car in order to rearrange the ties, and that it failed to furnish same. But, even if the failure to furnish such special appliances or means of mounting the car should be considered an act of negligence on the part of the defendant, still the plaintiff was fully aware of the manner in which the work was being done and the way in which the car was mounted. In the case of Emma Cotton Seed Oil Co. *v.* Hale, 56 Ark. 232, 19 S. W. 600, it is said: "If, having sufficient intelligence and knowledge to enable him to see and appreciate the dangers to which he will be exposed, he knowingly assents to occupy a place set apart for him by the master, and he does so, he thereby assumes the risks incident thereto and dispenses with the obligation of the master to furnish him a better place. It is then no longer a question of whether such place could not with reasonable care and diligence be made safe. Having voluntarily accepted the place occupied by him, he cannot hold the master liable for injuries received by him because the place was not safe. Where the servant knows the methods that are adopted in doing the work and the place furnished in which the work is done, and accepts or continues in the employment under such conditions, he assumes the risks of the dangers which may result therefrom. Railway *v.* Kelton, 55 Ark. 483, 18 S. W. 933, Patterson Coal Co. *v.* Poe, 81 Ark. 343, 99 S. W. 538; Graham *v.* Thrall & Shea, supra.

Chicago, R. I. & P. Ry. Co. *v.* Grubbs

But, in addition to this, in the case at bar the plaintiff was engaged in the work of straightening out the ties, which, on account of their peculiar slick condition, had become disarranged. If the place or the work itself was unsafe, it was a part of the very service which the plaintiff voluntarily engaged in with full knowledge of the unsafety of the place and the dangers of the work. The rule is that under such circumstances the servant assumes the risks of the dangers incident to such duty he has thus engaged to perform. In speaking of the risk which in such a case is assumed by the servant, this court, in the case of Marshall *v.* St. Louis, I. M. & S. R. Co., 78 Ark. 213, 94 S. W. 56, 115 Am. St. Rep. 27, quoted the following with approval from Judge Lurton: "It is not a case where dangerous or defective instrumentalities are supplied by the master to be used in his work and where notice of such danger should be given, but a case where the instrumentalities to be handled and worked with or upon are understood to involve peril and to demand unusual care. In such cases the risk is assumed by the servant as within the terms of his contract and compensated by his wages."

In the case at bar the plaintiff was engaged in rearranging the ties which he knew had become dislodged and displaced on account of their slick condition. He understood the manner in which the work was to be done, and whatever danger was incident to mounting the car and going on and over these ties was obvious to any one with the experience and understanding possessed by plaintiff. The danger of these ties slipping, and the peril arising therefrom, was one of the ordinary incidents of the work in which he was engaged. This risk of injury therefrom was therefore assumed by him. Grayson-McLeod Lumber Co. *v.* Carter, 76 Ark. 69, 88 S. W. 597; C., R. I. & Pac. Ry. Co. *v.* Murray, 85 Ark. 600, 109 S. W. 549, 16 L. R. A. (N. S.) 984; St. Louis, I. M. & S. R. Co. *v.* Goins, 90 Ark. 387, 119 S. W. 277.

Considering the testimony adduced upon the trial of this case most favorably to the cause of the plaintiff, we are of opinion that the injury which he sustained occurred by reason of a risk which under the law he assumed.

The judgment must, accordingly, be reversed, and the case dismissed. It is so ordered.

SMITH *v.* SOUTHERN PACIFIC CO.

(Supreme Court of Oregon, Feb. 7, 1911.)

[113 Pac. Rep. 41.]

**Master and Servant—Injuries to Servant—Railroads—Trackmen—
Looking for Approaching Trains—Degree of Care.**—Where a railroad
trackman is working on the track which is being used for the passage of trains, it cannot be determined as a matter of law how often
he is required to look in order to fulfill the duty of ordinary care;
that being a question for the jury.

Evidence—Negative Testimony—Weight.—Evidence that a witness
was near the point of an accident at the time plaintiff was struck
and injured by an approaching locomotive, and did not hear the
whistle or bell, tends in a measure to show that the whistle·was not
sounded or the bell rung.

**Master and Servant—Injuries to Servant—Railroads—Duty of En-
gineer.***—It is the duty of a railroad engineer to closely observe men
working on the track, and the moment he has reason to believe that
one of them is not going to get out of the way in time to avoid
danger to promptly use the appliances at his command to check or
stop the engine so as to avoid injury.

**Master and Servant—Injuries to Servant—Railroad Track—Care
Required.†**—Where a railroad trackman was engaged in repairing the
track under such circumstances as would justify him in assuming
that ordinary care would be observed to warn him of approaching
danger, he was only required to exercise such care and vigilance in
discovering the peril and avoiding injury as was consistent with the
performance of the work in which he was engaged.

Negligence—Contributory Negligence—Discovered Peril.‡—Where
plaintiff negligently assumed a position of danger in some degree,

---

*For the authorities in this series on the subject of the duties and
liabilities of railroad companies, as employers, with respect to injuries to employees, other than those engaged at the· time of the accident in coupling and uncoupling cars, sustained while they are on
railroad tracks, and caused by the running of trains, locomotives, or
street cars, see first foot-note of Wickham *v.* Louisville & N. R. Co.
(Ky.), 33 R. R. R. 597, 56 Am. & Eng. R. Cas., N. S., 597, where all
those preceding it are collected; second foot-note of Young *v.* St.
Louis, etc., Ry. Co. (Mo.), 36 R. R. R. 197, 59 Am. & Eng. R. Cas.,
N. S., 197.

†For the authorities in this series on the subject of the right of a
railroad employee to assume that his employer has performed, or
will perform, its duties to him, see second foot-note of Pittsburg,
etc., R. Co. *v.* Schaub (Ky.), 36 R. R. R. 644, 59 Am. & Eng. R. Cas.,
N. S., 644; first head-note of Smith *v.* Chicago, etc., Ry. Co. (Kan.),
36 R. R. R. 640, 59 Am. & Eng. R. Cas., N. S., 640.

‡See second foot-note of Hallock *v.* New York, etc., Ry. Co. (N.
Y.), 35 R. R. R. 332, 58 Am. & Eng. R. Cas., N. S., 332; second foot-
note of Chesapeake, etc., Ry. Co. *v.* Gorbin (Va.), 35 R. R. R. 229,
58 Am. & Eng. R. Cas., N. S., 229.

Smith *v.* Southern Pacific Co

which so contributed to his injury as to leave him without right of recovery for defendant's primary negligence, plaintiff could nevertheless recover if the person causing the injury became aware of plaintiff's peril in time to avoid injuring him by the proper use of all the means at his command, and listlessly, inadvertently, or negligently failed to resort to such means, provided plaintiff was himself free from negligence after he became conscious of his danger.

Master and Servant—Injuries to Servant—Contributory Negligence.—Plaintiff, a railroad trackman, working in a snowstorm, was engaged in taking the nuts off an angle plate on a rail near where it connected with and about a foot from the track on which an engine approached in defendant's railroad yards, and struck and injured him. Plaintiff testified that at the time of his injury he was trying to turn off the nut of a bolt that turned, and that it required both his hands on the wrench and one foot to hold the bolt. There was evidence that the train approached without bell or signal at from 20 to 30 miles an hour. Plaintiff also testified that there were other men working between him and the engine, and that he had not been there more than five minutes, during which he looked up and saw no engine coming, that he heard a noise, and just as he raised up he was struck. Held, that plaintiff was not negligent as a matter of law, in that he was not constantly on the lookout for approaching trains.

Appeal from Circuit Court, Douglas County; J. W. Hamilton, Judge.

Action by Lewis N. Smith against the Southern Pacific Company. Judgment for defendant, and plaintiff appeals. Reversed.

This is an action to recover damages for an alleged injury caused by defendant's negligence. Upon the trial the court directed a verdict in favor of defendant, and entered a judgment thereon, from which plaintiff appeals.

Plaintiff, in his complaint, alleged that defendant, by its engineer, carelessly and negligently ran its switch engine against plaintiff, as he was at work on the track, and without fault or negligence on the part of plaintiff; that the engineer saw that the collision was imminent, and could have avoided the same, but carelessly and negligently failed to stop the locomotive, and thereby avoid the collision. In its answer defendant denied the allegations of negligence set forth in the complaint, and affirmatively pleaded the defenses of contributory negligence and assumption of risk. The affirmative matter of the answer was put in issue by plaintiff's reply. At the time of the accident, January 19, 1906, the plaintiff, Lewis N. Smith, had been employed about a month by the defendant company as a section hand, being engaged under the direction of the section foreman in taking the

Smith v. Southern Pacific Co

nuts off an angle plate on the rail near where it connected with, and about a foot from, the track on which the engine came, in the railroad yards, at the crossing of Mosher street in Roseburg, Or. It was snowing at the time very hard. Plaintiff, in substance, testified: "I had just got the wrench, and was taking the nuts off an angle plate on the rail, and there was one bolt that turned, and I got down on one knee and put the other foot up against the bolt to hold it from turning in the angle bar. I was stooping over, facing towards the south, with my wrench on the outside, and I heard a noise of some kind, and just raised up and I was struck, was all the warning I had. The first warning I heard was the time I started to raise up. I did not have time to get up. Q. What length of time transpired between the time you heard that warning and the time that you were struck? A. Just as quick as I could move, because I was afraid all the time I was there that I was going to get hurt. The rest of the men, some six, were north of me, between me and the engine, and I thought if an engine came and they could get out of the way I could. After they got me up and I kind of come too, I said I wanted to see what it was, and, as I turned around, the switch engine was standing at the water tank, 200 feet from where I was struck." He further testified that he was injured, and on cross-examination: "I did not see the engine coming down the track. There was no obstruction to my view unless it was the other men working around there taking out ties. Q. Do you mean to say that those men there would prevent you from seeing this? A. They would unless I straightened up. Yes; clear up. Q. Did you hear the whistle blow at all? A. I heard some noise as I rose up. Q. What was the noise like? A. I can't tell you. I did not have time to distinguish. Q. Did you hear anybody call? A. No, sir. Q. Did you look up the track to see whether the engine was coming or not? A. Well, I had not been to work there but just a little bit. I had just got the wrench. Q. How long had you been in the stooping position? A. Not over five minutes. Q. During that time did you look up the track at all to see if the engine was coming? A. Yes, sir. Q. Did you see the engine? A. No, sir; not from that direction. Q. What time was it that you looked up with reference to the time that you were struck? A. It was not but just a short time before. Q. If you had looked before the engine came down the track, you could have seen it, could you not? A. I suppose I could. Q. How far was the nearest man to you? A. Four or five feet, I suppose. Q. Where were the rest of them? A. They were all at work there on the track north of me. * * * as I remember they were working on the cross-street, taking the ties out of the cross-street. Q. Did you see any flag out of any sort? A. There was no flag on that track. There was a flag out to protect the trains on the track that we were

Smith v. Southern Pacific Co

taking up, not on the other tracks. Q. Not on the track that the engine was on? A. No, sir. Q. If you did not know whether there was a flag out on this other track, why did not you look out and see the engine coming? A. Because the other men were working there, and I thought that if an engine came and they could get out of the way I could. Q. Were you expecting them to call to you? A. No, sir; I was watching the men. Q. You were undertaking to look out for yourself? A. I was undertaking to look out for myself the same as they were. Q. You did not hear the engine except at the moment of the collision? A. No, sir. Q. Were you listening for it? A. I was listening for it. I was on guard all the time."

F. L. Beard, engineer, in detailing the circumstances of the accident, testified, in substance, that he saw the plaintiff on the track some 90 or 100 feet distant, it might have been a little further, before he reached him; that he could have stopped the engine, or closed down so as to have avoided the accident, had he thought it necessary or reasonable to suppose the man would not get out of the way. "As the facts developed later, had I known then at the start I could have stopped." And on cross-examination: "I could see the sectionmen from the time I left opposite the passenger depot. I was on the main track, going south. * * * The bell was rung continuously and had been since we left from where we were at the lower portion of the yard, and, on arrival within 90 or 100 feet or such matter of where the men were working, I sounded a succession of short blasts of the whistle. * * * The speed of the engine was about six miles an hour. * * * I had the engine gradually under control, by that I mean gradually steadying down so as to take the benefit of the doubt in case I had to stop. I noticed the man working as though he was real busy and I began to slow the engine, gradually slowing down from a point 100 or 90 feet away from him, and I sounded the whistle continuously, and, when I reached a point within 30 to 50 feet away, it became apparent to me that he was not going to get out of the way, and I immediately applied the air and emergency. Q. If he had been standing in an erect position, would you not have hit him? A. I do not think it would. I could not see that Smith gave any heed when whistle sounded. I applied service brakes about 100 feet from him. Whistled six to ten times. Sounded whistle about 50 or 60 feet before I applied the emergency. He had his back towards us, looking quartering away from the engine. Q. Did you hear the angle bar strike the engine? I was too busy engaged getting the engine stopped. I made a test with the same engine once, going at a speed of about 7 miles per hour, and it took 62 feet to stop it. At the rate of 10 miles per hour it would take about 80 feet to stop."

H. O. Heidenrich, another section hand, testified: That he

Smith *v.* Southern Pacific Co

was working about 10 or 15 feet from plaintiff at the time of the accident. That he did not see the engine strike him. "Q. Did you see the engine when it was coming at that time? A. I see everybody run and I run too, so I could get out of the way. Q. How fast was the engine going? A. Oh, I don't know, about 20 miles or 30 miles an hour. Q. How close was the engine to you before you saw it? A. Oh, about 10 or 15 feet. Q. Did you hear the whistle blow? A. No, sir. Q. The whistle might have been blown. Were you scared? A. Yes; I was scared." And on cross-examination: "Q. Well, did you see Smith at all? A. No; I see two men take him away. Q. After the accident, you saw two men taking Smith away? Q. Yes, sir. Q. You did not see him before the accident? A. No; I look out for myself. Q. Were there any men south of you? A. Yes; pretty near half jumped that way, and the other half the other way. Q. Now, when did you first see the engine? A. I see everybody run and then I run. I have no time to look around. Q. Your notice was called to the men getting away? A. Yes; I hear some of them. Q. Did you hear anybody yell? A. Yes; they say get out of the way, somebody. I don't know who it was. Q. Did you hear the bell of the engine ringing? A. No; I did not hear that. Q. Or the whistle? A. No, sir. Q. You do not remember about having heard that? A. No, sir. Q. You did not have very much time to see the engine, how fast it was going, did you? A. No. Yes, yes. Q. You think it was going how fast? A. About 20 miles an hour. Q. Where did it stop? A. 60 or 100 feet. Q. Did he put on the brakes? A. Yes. Q. And stopped within 50 or 100 feet from where you were? A. Yes, sir." Redirect examination: "Q. You don't know exactly how far it stopped, do you? A. No. Q. It might have run on a couple of hundred feet as far as you know? A. No; I can't tell exactly."

Defendant's seven witnesses all estimated the speed of the engine, at the time the emergency was applied, at about six miles per hour.

H. Faulkner, witness for defendant, testified that he was about 60 feet away from Smith; that Smith was kneeling down, taking off a pair of angle bars, stooping down with his back to the engine, kind of sideways. He did not know about the bell, but the whistle was sounding; that Smith raised up and the bumper beam of the switch engine caught him on the shoulder and knocked him sidewise, straight out from the engine; that his report shows engine stopped 60 feet beyond where Smith was struck. "When I first saw the engine, 90 feet from where Smith was, it was coming about 6 miles per hour. When it struck him, I do not know the speed. I did not pay any attention. I do not know whether it kept the same gait or not. He did not increase. I do not say he slackened. Bell rings at crossings."

Smith v. Southern Pacific Co

Another witness, C. E. Matthews, fireman, testified that the speed of the engine at the time of the collision, or immediately thereafter, was 2 or 3 miles per hour, and before that 6 miles; that after the brakes were set it would run about 60 feet; that it passed beyond where plaintiff was struck some 35 or 40 feet, or about the length of the engine.

The motion for the directed verdict was based upon the grounds that the plaintiff had not proven a case sufficient to be submitted to the jury, particularly in that no negligence had been shown on the part of defendant, and on the further grounds that it appeared from the testimony that plaintiff had been guilty of contributory negligence, and his injury was a risk assumed by him. The court in passing upon the motion, among other things, stated: "That the allegations upon which this cause is based is that the engineer saw the plaintiff and could have avoided the accident. * * * And one of the acts required of the defendant would be to give warning by proper signals in order that the plaintiff engaged in his work might have the opportunity to get out of the way and protect himself. * * * Now the defendant comes here and brings witnesses who testify, a number of them uncontradicted, as to the signals having been given, the whistling, and others there upon the track getting out of the way, and then evidence also as to the allegation in the complaint that the engineer saw this person at the time that he did, and shows affirmatively by the evidence that all the precaution that could be taken was taken after he saw him, and saw that he was not going to get out of the way."

Albert Abraham, for appellant.
William D. Fenton (Coshow & Rice and *R. A. Leiter,* on the brief), for respondent.

BEAN, J. (after stating the facts as above). It is contended on behalf of plaintiff that the testimony tends to show that his injury was caused by the negligence of defendant and without fault on his part; that the evidence is conflicting in regard to the speed of the engine and the signals; that it is conclusively shown that the engineer was careless and reckless in running the engine against him, when for some distance he had seen, and by the exercise of ordinary care could have stopped the engine and avoided the collision; and that the trial court erred in directing the jury to find a verdict for defendant.

Counsel for defendant contends that it was not guilty of negligence, and that it was the duty of plaintiff to look for the engine; that during the considerable period of time the engine was approaching from the depot he did not look up, and that he was guilty of contributory negligence; that the engineer did all in his power to avoid the injury. As we understand it, the trial court held that the plaintiff was guilty of contributory negligence for the reason that he failed to look. Plaintiff testified that he looked for the engine just as he went to work at the angle plate, and that he was stooping over at work only about five minutes before he was struck. It has been held that the court could not say as a matter of law how often one in a similar position to that of plaintiff should look, and that this is a question for the jury. Shoner v. Pennsylvania Co., 130 Ind. 175, 29 N. E. 775; Austin v. Fitchburg R. R., 172 Mass. 484, 52 N. E. 527; Shultz v. Chicago, M. & St. P., 57 Minn. 271, 59 N. W. 192; St. Louis, I. M. & S. R. Co. v. Jackson, 78 Ark. 100, 93 S. W. 746, 6 L. R. A. (N. S.) 646. "An employee is bound to use ordinary care to avoid the dangers that arise, whether usually incident to the service or not. He is under the same obligation to provide for his own safety from dangers of which he has notice or which he might discover, by the use of ordinary care, that the employer is to provide it for him." 1 White, Personal Inj. on R. R. § 399. In Kunz v. Oregon R. & N. Co., 51 Or. 191, 205, 93 Pac. 141, 146, it was said by Mr. Chief Justice Moore: "If the facts thus supposed were true, and the engineer, seeing the team standing on the track, under the circumstances mentioned, immediately used all available appliances to stop the train, the question as to the measure of such care would nevertheless be for the jury to determine." And in Palmer v. Portland R. L. & P. Co., 108 Pac. 211, 213, it was held, Mr. Justice King speaking for the court: "To test the sufficiency of the proof under a motion for nonsuit, the testimony must be viewed in the light most favorable to plaintiff. * * * It also appears that had the car been under proper control, and not going at an unreasonable speed, it could have been stopped in time to prevent a collision; thus supplementing the plaintiff's proof, tending to establish as a question for the consideration of the jury that defendant's negligence was the primary cause of the accident [citations]. The burden of proving contributory negligence is on the defendant [citation]. And, as held in Eliff v. O. R. & N. Co., 53 Or. 66 [99 Pac. 76], where the proximate cause of the injury is problematical, as certainly appears here, the case should be submitted to the jury." Further, quoting from Mr. Justice Lamar in Grand Trunk Ry. Co. v. Ives, 144 U. S. 408, 12 Sup. Ct. 679, 36 L. Ed. 485: "There is no fixed standard in the law by which a court is enabled to arbitrarily say in every case what conduct shall be considered reasonable and prudent, and what shall constitute ordinary care, under any and all circumstances. The terms 'ordinary care,' 'reasonable prudence,' and such like terms, as applied to the conduct and affairs of men, have a relation significance, and cannot be arbitrarily defined. What may be deemed ordinary care in one case may, under different surroundings and circumstances, be gross negligence. The policy of the law has relegated the determination of such questions to the jury under proper instruc-

Smith *v.* Southern Pacific Co

tions from the court. It is their province to note the special circumstances and surroundings of each particular case, and then say whether the conduct of the parties in that case was such as would be expected of reasonable, prudent men, under a similar state of affairs. It is only where the facts are such that all reasonable men must draw the same conclusion from them that the question of negligence is ever considered as one of law for the court." In the case of Murran *v.* Chicago, M. & St. P., 86 Minn. 470, 90 N. W. 1056, where a sectionman was at work in defendant's yard, cleaning out snow and ice, the foreman and other men being not far distant, snow falling and wind blowing, and where, for convenience in getting the snow and ice out from under a cross-bar which connected the two rails, he had turned his back to the east, and was struck by a single car, which had been thrown over the switch he was cleaning out, and the switchman in charge could easily have stopped the car before it reached plaintiff, but made no effort to do so, the court observed that the plaintiff was at work in an exceedingly perilous place under peculiar and exceptional circumstances. The fact that snow was falling and blowing, and that he was stooped over, engaged in work, with his back toward the approaching car, was all seen and understood by the man in charge of the switching, and a jury could well say that it should have been apparent to the switchman that plaintiff might not discover his peril in time to escape, and as a consequence that he was negligent in not taking active steps to prevent the injury, and that the question of defendant's negligence was for the jury.

If we take the evidence of Heidenrich in regard to the signals and the speed of the engine as correct, if the evidence is conflicting upon the material points, and reasonable men might draw different conclusions from the evidence, taking into consideration all the circumstances of the transaction as disclosed thereby, then they become questions for the jury under proper instructions. Kunz *v.* Oregon R. & N. Co., 51 Or. 191, 205, 93 Pac. 141, 146; Palmer *v.* Portland R. L. & P. Co., 108 Pac. 213. Plaintiff states that he was engaged in his work at the time he was struck, and did not see the engine, nor hear the bell or whistle. The estimate of the speed of the engine at the time, as made by the witness Heidenrich, differs from the testimony of defendant's witnesses. From the circumstances as detailed by the witnesses, as to the manner in which the other men in the crew, at work near the plaintiff, got off the track, and the statement of the engineer that he did not hear the engine strike the angle bar or the wrench, "because he was too busy getting the engine stopped," which was at the very instant that plaintiff was struck, it might be inferred that the engineer did not apply the emergency brake or try to stop the engine until it was close to or practically upon the plaintiff, and that its speed was greater than

Smith *v.* Southern Pacific Co

estimated by some of defendant's witnesses. Heidenrich's testimony that he was near at the time, and did not hear the whistle or bell, coincides with that of plaintiff. This tends in a measure to show that the whistle was not sounded nor the bell rung. 1 Wigmore on Evidence, § 664. From the statement of Mr. H. Faulkner, a section foreman of experience, to the effect that he would not say that the engineer slackened the speed of the engine after the whistle was sounded, and from the estimated distance of 35 or 40 feet that the engine passed plaintiff, it may appear that, if the estimated distance of 60 feet required to stop the engine is assumed to be correct, the engineer did not attempt to stop the locomotive until within 20 or 25 feet of plaintiff.

A railroad company has been held liable where a watchman at a crossing was seen by the engineer of a moving train with a lantern in his hand, if the engineer was carelessly inadvertent as to whether or not he would get out of the way. Betchman *v.* Seaboard Air Line, 75 S. C. 68, 55 S. E. 140. It was the duty of the engineer to closely observe the men on the track, and the moment he had reason to believe plaintiff was not going to get out of the way in time to avoid danger to promptly use the appliances at his command to check or stop the engine, so as to avoid injury to plaintiff. Nelling *v.* Chicago, St. P. & K. C. R. Co., 98 Iowa, 554, 561, 63 N. W. 568, 67 N. W. 404. It would be useless for an engineer to simply observe, if when he plainly sees a track repairer in a place of danger, and as a prudent man has good reason to believe that he is not going to move from the track, he fails to take the proper measures at his command to stop the engine. We think the question of whether the engineer had good reason to believe for a considerable time before he endeavored to stop the engine and avoid the collision that the plaintiff was not going to get out of the way, and was reckless, was, under all the evidence and circumstances, one for the jury. It appears that the engine was being used for switching purposes about the yards, where it was known to the engineer that several men were working; that the necessity for running at a high rate of speed was less than that of a regular train, and the management thereof different from that of an engine and train on its regular run, and the danger of running at a high rate of speed in such a yard, where several men were engaged at work, greater. Therefore, when the engineer saw the plaintiff in a perilous position, and unmindful of the approach of the engine, it was his duty to take active measures, with the means at his command, to avoid the injury. Sullivan *v.* Missouri Pac. R., 97 Mo. 113. 10 S. W. 852. Taking all the evidence, we think it was a question for the jury to determine whether the engineer used ordinary care to avoid the collision, or carelessly and recklessly ran the engine against plaintiff, when he saw for some distance that plaintiff was in danger, and oblivious to the approach of the engine.

Smith *v.* Southern Pacific Co

and whether common prudence demanded of him, as a reasonable man, that he should slacken his.speed so as to have the engine under control and be able to stop it before striking plaintiff. in case he did not see it or move off the track. Doyle *v.* Southern Pac. Co., 108 Pac. 201; Palmer *v.* Portland R. L. & P. Co., 108 Pac. 211.

Defendant asserts that plaintiff was guilty of contributory negligence. "Where the servant is engaged in performing service for the master, under circumstances which justify him in assuming that ordinary care will be observed to warn him of approaching danger, he is required to exercise only such care and vigilance in discovering peril and avoiding injury as is consistent with the performance of the work in which he is engaged. Any other rule would place the servant, while performing work for the master, in the same category as a trespasser upon the premises of the master." St. Louis, I. M. & S. R. Co. *v.* Jackson, 78 Ark. 100, 108, 93 S. W. 746, 748, 6. L. R. A. (N. S.) 646, 656. In Kelly *v.* Union R. & T. Co., 11 Mo. App. 1, the court declares it to be "the settled law of the state, applicable to actions for injuries received by persons while upon railway tracks from passing trains, that, if it appears from the testimony produced by the plaintiff that the person injured, being sui juris, failed to make use of his faculties of sight and hearing, when to do so would have enabled him to avoid the accident, there can be no recovery; and that the principle involved in this rule is equally applicable to the case of a traveler crossing a railway track, or a trespasser, or a bare licensee or person lawfully employed on the track; that a fair statement of the rule is that, when it appears that the person injured did not use his faculties, it is incumbent on him to show a reasonable excuse for failing to do so." Where plaintiff negligently assumed a position of danger in such a degree, and so contributed to his hurt as to leave him without right of recovery for any primary negligence of the other party, he may nevertheless recover, if the person charged with the wrong or injury became aware of his peril in time to avoid, by the proper use of all the means at his command, injuring him, and listlessly, inadvertently, or negligently failed to resort to such means, provided he is himself free from negligence after he became conscious of his danger. Duncan *v.* St. Louis & S. F., 152 Ala. 118, 44 South. 418, 422. See, also, Klutt *v.* Philadelphia & R. R. Co. (C. C.) 145 Fed. 965; Philadelphia & R. R. Co. *v.* Klutt, 148 Fed. 818, 78 C. C. A. 508; 1 White on Per. Inj. on R. R. § 398; 1 Shearman & Redfield on Negligence (5th Ed.) § 99. In the case at bar it may reasonably be believed that the position in which the plaintiff was engaged at work was a perilous one; and if it required both his hands to use the wrench and one foot to hold the bolt to keep it from turning, it would certainly appear that his work would require some care and at-

Dow *v*. Boston Elevated Ry. Co

tention, and it is not proper to assume that plaintiff was negligent in placing himself in a position of danger, or that his fault, while attending to his duty, contributed to his injury. "As a general rule, it is not contributory negligence as a matter of law for a person so employed not to be on a constant lookout for approaching trains." 2 Thompson on Negligence, § 1756. So the question whether the omission to look amounts to contributory negligence is one for the jury. 5 Thompson on Negligence, § 5524. Whether plaintiff exercised ordinary care, or was guilty of contributory negligence in this case, was a question for the jury. Baltimore R. R. Co. *v.* Peterson, 156 Ind. 364, 373, 59 N. E. 1044; Austin *v.* Fitchburg R. Co., 172 Mass. 484, 52 N. E. 527; Comstock *v.* Union Pacific R. R. Co., 56 Kan. 228, 42 Pac. 724; Sullivan *v.* Missouri Pac. R. Co., 97 Mo. 113, 10 S. W. 852; Railroad *v.* Murphy, 50 Ohio St. 135, 144, 33 N. E. 403.

For these reasons, we think it was error for the lower court to direct a verdict for the defendant. The judgment is therefore reversed, and a new trial ordered.

Dow *v.* Boston Elevated Ry. Co.

(Supreme Judicial Court of Massachusetts, Suffolk, Jan. 6, 1911.)

[93 N. E. Rep. 655.]

Master and Servant—Injuries to Servant—Fellow Servant—"Elevated Train."—Surface cars belonging to an elevated railway, which run up an incline to a junction platform, used to discharge passengers from the elevated trains to the surface cars and vice versa, are not elevated trains, within St. 1908, c. 420, which provides that an employee shall, for the negligence of a servant in charge of an "elevated train," have the same rights as if he were not an employee; therefore a conductor of such a surface car, who was injured by the negligence of the motorman of another such car, cannot recover against the company.

Report from Superior Court, Suffolk County; John H. Hardy, Judge.

Action by Timothy J. Dow against the Boston Elevated Railway Company for personal injuries caused by negligence of defendant's motorman while plaintiff was in defendant's employ. On report from superior court. Judgment for defendant.

John S. Richardson, for plaintiff.
Russell A. Sears and *Charles S. French,* for defendant.

Loring, J. The plaintiff was a conductor of a surface car

Dow *v.* Boston Elevated Ry. Co

running from a point in Somerville to the Sullivan Square station of the defendant in Charlestown, where it delivered passengers to and received them from the trains of the defendant running on the tracks of the elevated railway.* This surface car ran upon an incline to a dead end in the station, separate and some 15 feet distant from the track of the defendant's elevated railway. On the day in question the surface car of which the plaintiff was the conductor had reached the end of its run in the Sullivan Square station, and the plainaiff was in the act of pulling out and fastening the fender for the return trip, when he was run into by the negligence of the motorman of another surface car, who ran in for the same purpose on the same track behind the plaintiff's car. The judge ruled that Rev. Laws, c. 106, § 71, as amended by St. 1908, c. 420, applied to such a car, found that the motorman was negligent, that the plaintiff's damages amounted to $500, and reported the case to this court.

Unless this surface car was an "elevated train" within St. 1908, c. 420, the plaintiff's sole remedy is against the motorman whose negligence caused the injury. Fallon *v.* West End St. Ry., 171 Mass. 249, 50 N. E. 536; McGilvery *v.* Boston Elev. Ry., 200 Mass. 551, 86 N. E. 893.

The judge found that the car was not defective. For that reason the question whether the provision of St. 1908, c. 420 (that "an elevated car which is in use by or which is in possession of an elevated railway shall be considered as a part of the ways, works and machinery"), applies to this surface car, does not arise.   •

In our opinion a surface car does not become an "elevated train" by being run up an incline to discharge and receive passengers transferred to it from trains running on the defendant's elevated railway.

Judgment for the defendant.

---

*Note by Reporter.—It appears from the report in Hillman *v.* Boston Elevated Railway, 93 N. E. 653, that the Sullivan Square station was also used for the transfer of passengers from surface lines ending at and starting from that station.

REESE *v.* PENNSYLVANIA R. CO.

(Supreme Court of Pennsylvania, Jan. 3, 1911.)

[78 Atl. Rep. 851.]

Master and Servant—Injuries—Release of Liability.*—Where an application for membership in a railroad employees' relief association stipulates that his acceptance of benefits for injuries shall release all claims against the railroad because of such injuries, a member who accepts benefits cannot, in the absence of fraud, claim additional damages from the master for such injury.

Appeal from Court of Common Pleas, Armstrong County.

Action by Charles Reese against the Pennsylvania Railroad Company. Judgment for defendant, and plaintiff appeals. Affirmed.

Argued before FELL, C. J., and BROWN, MESTREZAT, POTTER. ELKIN, STEWART, and MOSCHZISKER, JJ.

C. E. Harrington and *Harry C. Golden,* for appellant.
Orr Buffington and *O. W. Gilpin,* for appellee.

BROWN, J. Charles Reese, the plaintiff below, was a fireman in the employ of the defendant company. On January 2, 1907, he applied to its relief association for membership. His application was accepted, and his dues were paid up to August 7, 1907, when he sustained the injuries complained of in this action. After being injured he received benefits from August 6, 1907, to April 3, 1908. On April 2, 1908, he was notified by Dr. Sahm, the surgeon for the relief association, to report for examination of his injuries. After having so reported, the doctor gave him what is called a "return to duty card." He returned to duty, and, having worked nearly 6 months, received a furlough for 60 days, but again resumed work as a fireman. and lost one of his legs in March, 1909, while in the employ of the defendant company. The claim in this case, however, is not for the injuries sustained by the appellant in 1909, but for those suffered on August 7, 1907, and his contention is that he is entitled to recover because he was not in a physical condition to return to work when Dr. Sahm gave him his return to duty card. The complaint upon which he seeks to recover is that, if the doctor had examined him as a prudent physician should have done, it would have been discovered that he was not fit to return to duty, and, in view of the alleged fraud practiced upon him by the doctor, he now contends that his agreement when he

*See first foot-note of Barden *v.* Atlantic Coast Line R. Co. (N. Car.), 36 R. R. R. 558, 59 Am. & Eng. R. Cas., N. S., 558.

Reese *v.* Pennsylvania R. Co

became a member of the relief association and what he did under it do not stand in the way of his right to compel his employer to pay him.

What the surgeon for the relief association did on April 2, 1908, is not to be regarded as involved in this controversy. If the appellant were seeking to recover benefits withheld from him by the association as the result of his examination by the surgeon, his complaint of the conduct of that officer might be pertinent, though, under the sixty-fifth regulation of the association, it seems that, it he was dissatisfied with the decision of the surgeon, his right was to appeal to the superintendent of the relief department, and from the latter's decision, if unsatisfactory, to an advisory committee; but on this we need not dwell. The single question before us is whether the appellant, by his own act, has precluded himself from recovering for the injuries for which he sues.

Immediately after he was injured he began to avail himself of the benefits of the relief association, and for a period of eight months continued to do so. In the application for membership in the relief association signed by the appellant there was a stipulation that his acceptance of benefits for injury should operate as a release of all claims for damages against the company arising from such injuries which could be made by or through him, and he accepted membership under a regulation of the association which provided that his acceptance of benefits should operate as a release and satisfaction of all claims against his employer for damages arising from injuries while in its service. Neither when the appellant first accepted the benefits nor at any time during the period that he received them is it pretended that any fraud was practiced upon him to induce him to do so. A very different situation would be presented if it appeared that, by fraud or deception practiced upon him, he was induced to take the benefits, operating as a release from him to the defendant company for any claim he might have had for the injuries that resulted from its negligence; and this is the distinction which seems to be overlooked in pressing his present contention.

With full knowledge of the effect his acceptance of the benefits would have upon any claim that he might have had against his employer for its negligence resulting in the injuries to him, he promptly accepted the benefits and continued to take them for months. His first acceptance of them, in the absence of any fraud or deception inducing him to take them, was an end of his right to recover damages from the defendant. Nothing in his contract of membership in the association barred his right to recover; but what he voluntarily did after he was injured— the effect of which he declared in his application for membership should be a release to the company—is the release upon

Riley *v.* Louisville, H. & St. L. Ry. Co

which, under our own cases and those in other jurisdictions, the defendant has a right to rely for protection from any liability. This case is so squarely ruled by Johnson *v.* Philadelphia & Reading R. R. Co., 163 Pa. 127, 29 Atl. 854, and Ringle *v.* Pennsylvania R. R. Co., 164 Pa. 529, 30 Atl. 492, 44 Am. St. Rep. 628, that nothing more can be said about it, unless it be to call attention to Frank *v.* Newport Mining Co., 148 Mich. 637, 112 N. W. 504, 11 L. R. A. (N. S.) 182, in the notes to which cases from other states are referred to, holding, like our own, that the contract of membership in the relief association entered into by the appellant is not void on the ground of public policy, and that it is not such contract, but the acceptance of benefits, that constitutes the release.

The assignments of error are overruled, and the judgment is affirmed.

————————

RILEY *v.* LOUISVILLE, H. & ST. L. RY. CO.

(Court of Appeals of Kentucky, Feb. 3, 1911.)

[133 S. W. Rep. 971.]

Eminent Domain—Public Use—Use Exclusive of Public.*—Const. § 13, providing that private property shall not be taken for a public use without the consent of the owner, and section 242, relating to compensation, assessment of damages, and procedure, do not authorize the taking of private property for a private use, and a railroad cannot condemn land for a spur track to the premises of a distilling company.

Eminent Domain—Public Use—Test in Determining Use.*—The public character of the business of a corporation, as that of a railroad, is not controlling in determining whether property sought to be taken is to be devoted to a public use; the test being whether on the facts of a particular case the property will be taken for a public use and will be necessary to such use.

Eminent Domain—Public Use—Burden of Proof.—A private corporation seeking to condemn private property has the burden of establishing that the property is needed for a public use.

Eminent Domain—Particular Purpose—Railroads—Spur Track—Statutes.—Ky. St. § 769 (Russell's St. § 5369), providing that any railroad company may build such spurs as may be necessary, and for that purpose shall have all the powers and be subject to the liabilities as in the construction of its main line, is not an attempt to authorize a railroad to take private property for a private purpose.

————————

*For the authorities in this series on the question what does, and does not, constitute a public use for which private property may be condemned, see foot-note of Dubuque, etc., R. Co. *v.* Ft. Dodge, etc., R. Co. (Iowa), 36 R. R. R. 292, 59 Am. & Eng. R. Cas., N. S., 292.

Riley *v.* Louisville, H. & St. L. Ry. Co

Eminent Domain—Particular Use—Railroads—Spur Track—Expense Borne by Party Chiefly Benefited.*—That a private corporation was particularly interested in the construction of a spur track to its premises and intended to furnish the means to construct it does not deprive such track of the public character necessary to authorize the condemnation of private property.

Eminent Domain—Public Use—Extent of Use of Benefit.*—That one or more persons will derive exceptional and special advantages from the construction of a spur track does not show that the track is not for a public use; Const. § 13, permitting the taking of private property only for public use, being satisfied if all the public desiring to use it have the right to do so upon the same terms and conditions as those specially benefited.

Carriers—Preferences and Discrimination—Shipper on Spur Track.—A common carrier cannot discriminate between patrons or give to a shipper to whose premises there is a spur track any preferential rate.

Eminent Domain—Acts Constituting Dedication—Acquiescence in Public Use.*—Where a distilling company, in proceedings by a railroad company to condemn land for a spur track to the distillery, states that the public may use the track on its premises, there is a dedication to the public of such right, and the claim that the appropriation of the land is for a private purpose is negatived.

Eminent Domain—Particular Use—Railroads — Spur Track.*—Where such spur track was about one-half mile long, and, except for a highway crossing, ran entirely through the land of the private owner, and it appeared that it would be extended beyond the premises of the distilling company whenever the business of the company or the public warranted it, and that the railroad company would provide freight facilities at the highway crossing, and that the distilling company would permit persons desiring freight facilities on the branch to enter its premises for that purpose as long as the terminus was on its premises, it cannot be said that the spur track would not serve a public use.

Eminent Domain—Necessity of Appropriation—Spur Track—Extent and Conditions of Use.*—Where such spur track would terminate in the immediate vicinity of two or three large companies, and quite a number of people resided in the neighborhood to whom the track would be a convenience and benefit, and the public could freely use the track, the track was a public benefit.

Contracts—Legality of Object—Contract against Public Policy.†—A contract between a private corporation and a railroad company,

---

†For the authorities in this series on the subject of the validity of contracts to build, maintain, and operate. spur tracks, or sidings, see first foot-note of Whalen *v.* Baltimore & O. R. Co. (Md.), 30 R. R. R. 33, 53 Am. & Eng. R. Cas., N. S., 33.

Riley v. Louisville, H. & St. L. Ry. Co

under which the railroad company was to extend a spur track to
the premises of the private corporation and to retain exclusive operation and control of it, and under which the means for its construction
were to be furnished by the private corporation and to be later reimbursed, is not a contract against public policy.

Appeal from Circuit Court, Daviess County.

Condemnation proceedings by the Louisville, Henderson & St.
Louis Railway Company. From a judgment sustaining petitioner's right to condemn land, Ellen Riley, an owner of property
sought to be taken, appeals. Affirmed.

Clarence M. Finn, for appellant.
R. A. Miller and *J. R. Skillman,* for appellee.

CARROLL, J. In this condemnation proceeding, the only question presented by the record is: Was the land condemned necessary for a public use?

Appellee company is a railway corporation, operating a line·
of railroad from Louisville, Ky., to Evansville, Ind., passing
through the county of Daviess and city of Owensboro therein.
It sought to condemn a strip of ground owned by the appellant,
Mrs. Riley, for the purpose of constructing a spur track from
its main line to a point on the property of the Glenmore Distillery
Company. This company owns about 40 acres of land a short
distance from the corporate limits of the city of Owensboro, and
is one of the largest distilleries in the state. The spur track
proposed to be constructed is about a half mile long, and, except where it crosses the Hardinsburg road, a public highway
that runs immediately along the property line of the distillery
company, ·it runs entirely through the lands of the appellant.
The amount of damages awarded to appellant in the circuit
court is not complained of; but it is insisted that the land cannot be taken because the use to which it is to be put is not a
public one, or, in other words the spur track is not necessary for
a public use. This contention is rested upon the ground that
the appellee company desires to construct and operate the spur
road for the exclusive use and benefit of the Glenmore Distillery
Company. As the present depot of the railway company is some
two miles from the distillery premises and its line of railway a
half mile from it the construction and operation of this spur
track into the distillery company's property would undoubtedly
be of great benefit to it as it would save the heavy cost of
transporting its product, as well as freight received, by wagon
to and from the present depot to the distillery. But, however
beneficial the construction and operation of this spur track might
be to the distillery company, if it was only intended for its use,
and it could not and would not be used by the public, the power

of eminent domain could not be invoked to authorize the taking of the land of the appellant for the purpose of building a railroad across her property to the distillery. The only authority for the taking of private property without the consent of the owner is found in sections 13 and 242 of the Constitution, and these sections do not authorize the taking unless the property is to be applied to a public use and will be necessary for that purpose. Private property cannot be taken for private purposes, and it is plain that, if no one could use this spur road except the distillery company, a private corporation, the taking of appellant's land would be the taking of private property for a private purpose, to wit, the convenience and benefit of the Glenmore Distillery Company. Pittsburg, Wheeling & Kentucky R. Co. *v.* Benwood Iron Works, 31 W. Va. 710, 8 S. E. 453, 2 L. R. A. 680; Pere Marquette R. Co. *v.* Gypsum, 154 Mich. 290, 117 N. W. 733, 22 L. R. A. (N. S.) 181; Kyle *v.* Texas & N. O. R. Co., 3 Wilson, Civ. Cas. Ct. App. (Tex.) § 436, 4 L. R. A. 275. Nor does the fact that the land of the appellant is needed for railroad purposes, and that a railroad will be constructed and operated over it, have the effect of establishing that it will be for a public use. There are what may be called public as well as private railroads, such as railroads built and used by the public generally, and roads built to be used by only one or more persons or business concerns. After the main line of a railroad has been built, it often becomes a matter of importance to the railway company, as well as manufacturing plants or business establishments near the line of the railroad, to have constructed from the main line into their factories or establishments switches or spurs that will cheapen and make more convenient the transportation of freight and property to and from the main line of the railroad and their places of business. And it is in the construction of branches like this that the question of public use most frequently comes up in railroad condemnation proceedings. These branches or spurs may or may not be necessary for a public use. Whether they are or not depends on the facts of each particular case. And it often happens, as is illustrated by this case, that the line that separates a private from a public use may be a very narrow one, for, although it would seem at first impression that there ought to be little difficulty in determining whether or not a railroad was being constructed for a public or private use, there can be no doubt that the use to which it is intended to be put may be exclusively a private one, as where only one person or one factory or establishment could use the road. We may therefore with safety assume that the particular business the corporation is engaged in at the time it seeks to condemn private property is not of controlling importance in determining whether the property sought to be condemned is to be devoted to a public

Riley *v.* Louisville, H. & St. L. Ry. Co

use. The same test in this particular is to be applied in every case in which a private corporation invokes in its behalf the right of eminent domain, and that test is: Will the property taken be for a public use and necessary for such use? If it is, the business in which the corporation is engaged cannot add to or take from its right to condemn. On the other hand, if it is not, then no considerations involving private benefits or advantages will be allowed to confer the right, nor will the character of the corporation strengthen its position. And the burden will be upon the private corporation to establish that the property sought to be taken will be needed for a public use. Henderson *v.* City of Lexington, 132 Ky. 390, 111 S. W. 318, 22 L. R. A. (N. S.) 20.

From the earliest history of the state, its public policy, as expressed in Constitution and statute, is unalterably opposed to the invasion of private rights for private purposes. As said in Robinson *v.* Swope, 12 Bush, 21, in which the court declared unconstitutional a statute authorizing the establishment of a private passway from one track to another: "The right of a citizen to the unmolested use and enjoyment of his land rests upon a sure foundation. He may keep and use it in any lawful manner he chooses, subject only to the right of the public to take it upon compensation previously made for some public use. * * * The provision that private property shall not be taken for public use without just compensation previously made is an implied prohibition of the taking of such property for private use, either with or without compensation." And the principle announced in this case, which has been frequently followed and applied, we have no disposition to depart from in any particular. There can be no such thing in this state as a taking of private property for private purposes. In every case in which the power of eminent domain is invoked, it must appear that the property is desired for a public use and will be reasonably necessary for that use.

Some claim is made that section 769 of the Kentucky Statutes (Russell's St. § 5369), relating to railroads, and providing that: "Any company may build such spurs, switches, tracks or branches as may be necessary to conduct its business or develop business along its line of road, and for that purpose shall have all the power and be subject to the same restrictions and liabilities as are conferred upon it for the construction of its main line * * *"—authorizes condemnation proceedings in behalf of a railroad company when it desires to build tracks or branches that it deems necessary to develop business along its line of road. But this statute was only intended to enable a railroad company to acquire with the consent of the owner or by condemnation proceedings in a proper state of case property upon which it might construct and operate a branch road. It does not mean that a railroad company may take private property for private

Riley v. Louisville, H. & St. L. Ry. Co

purposes, without the consent of the owner, under condemnation proceedings for the purpose of building spurs or branches. If it did, it would be an attempt upon the part of the legislative department of the state to grant authority in violation of the Constitution. When it comes to condemning land for the purpose of establishing branch roads, the same principles apply as do in every case in which it is sought to take private property. Greasy Creek Coal Co. v. Ely Jellico Coal Co., 132 Ky. 692, 116 S. W. 1189.

Having the foregoing view of the principles of law applicable in cases like this, we will now proceed to inquire whether this spur road will serve a public use, and be necessary for such use. Upon this point the argument is made by counsel for the appellant that, as this track runs from the main line of the railway entirely upon the land of the appellant, until it intersects the Hardinsburg road, which it crosses, going immediately into the land of the distillery company, the public cannot use it, as they could not get to it without trespassing upon the land of the appellant, except at the place where it crosses the Hardinsburg road; and it is said that this point is unsuitable for the reception of delivery of freight, and therefore no person can use this spur except the distillery company. It is further said, as evidencing the fact that this road was intended to be built for the exclusive use and benefit of the Glenmore Distillery Company, that it has agreed to furnish the railroad company the money with which to construct it. If it were true that this road could not be used by any person except the Glenmore Distillery Company, it would undoubtedly be constructed and operated for private purposes. But, as we will presently show, it can and will be used by a considerable number of the public besides the distillery company, although it is true the distillery company is deeply concerned in its construction and operation and will receive large benefits therefrom. The fact, however, that the distillery company is vitally interested in the establishment of this branch, and intends to furnish the means to construct it, does not deprive it of the public character necessary to authorize the condemnation proceedings. Henderson v. City of Lexington, 132 Ky. 390, 111 S. W. 318, 22 L. R. A. (N. S.) 20. There is no public improvement, the construction of which does not benefit some persons more than others. In every instance there are certain individuals and business establishments who, on account of their proximity to the road or its stations and the nature of their business, will derive special benefits from the building and operation of railroads that cannot be enjoyed by the public generally. It is therefore plain that the mere fact that one or more persons or establishments on account of the location of their property will derive exceptional advantages from the construction of the road does not furnish any argument in support of the proposition that

Riley *v.* Louisville, H. & St. L. Ry. Co

the road is not for a public use. If it did, no roads would be built. It is also well settled that the improvement need not be used by or necessary to the public generally, or any considerable number thereof. The constitutional requirement will be satisfied if all the public desiring to use it have the right to do so upon the same terms and conditions, although only a few may choose to avail themselves of the opportunity. As was said in Chesapeake Stone Co. *v.* Moreland, 126 Ky. 656, 104 S. W. 762, 31 Ky. Law Rep. 1075, 16 L. R. A. (N. S.) 479, in which it was sought to condemn land to build a tramroad to a rock quarry: "It seems entirely probable that only a few persons aside from the individual at whose instance it was established will have occasion to use this tramway; but this fact does not destroy its public use in the meaning of the Constitution. It is not the number of people who use the property taken under the law of eminent domain that constitutes the use of it a public one; nor does the fact that the benefits will be in a large measure local enter into the question. In short, according to the generally recognized rule, the length of the public way, the places between which it runs, or the number of people who use it, is not the essential inquiry. The controlling and decisive question is: Have the public the right to its use upon the same terms as the person at whose instance the way was established? If they have, it is a public use; if they have not, it is a private one. If the owner can exercise the same kind of dominion over it as he does over other property owned by him, if he can close it up, if he can prohibit all or any part of the public from its use, then it is clear that its establishment would be private and not public; and the right of eminent domain could not be invoked in its creation."
. The fact, however, that only a limited number would use it, is a pertinent inquiry in considering whether or not the improvement is necessary for a public use. And this suggestion brings to mind the utter impracticability of setting down any firm rule that can be applied in all cases when the question of the necessity of the improvement for a public use comes up. Upon this point, each case must be adjudged by its particular facts. Applying to this case the test that it must appear that the public will have the right to use the improvement upon the same terms and conditions as the distillery company, and that they will have free access to it for the purpose of such use, and furthermore that its construction must be necessary for the public use, let us now see how the case stands. At the outset, there can be no doubt that the public will have the right to use this branch road upon the same terms and conditions as the distillery company if it can obtain access to it. The railway company cannot make any discrimination between its patrons in its charges or service. It will be as much under the control of the state as any other part of the railroad, and all the laws in force for the

Riley *v.* Louisville, H. & St. L. Ry. Co

purpose of compelling equal and fair service by the railway company to all shippers will be applicable to this branch. It cannot give any exclusive privilege or preferential rate to the distillery company. In its dealings with the road, the distillery company will occupy precisely the same attitude as any other shipper. L. & N. R. R. Co. *v.* Pittsburg Coal Co., 111 Ky. 960, 64 S. W. 969, 23 Ky. Law Rep. 1318, 55 L. R. A. 601, 98 Am. St. Rep. 447; Bedford & B. G. S. Co. *v.* Oman, 115 Ky. 369, 73 S. W. 1038, 24 Ky. Law Rep. 2274. Now, can the public, desiring to use this branch, do so? Will they have access to it? These questions are satisfactorily answered in the evidence of the president of the railway company and the president of the distillery company. They both say that the branch road may and will be projected through and beyond the premises of the distillery company, whenever the business of the company or the public justifies such an extension, and that persons desiring to receive and ship freight on this branch may enter upon the premises of the distillery company for this purpose, so long as the terminus of the road is on its property. This we construe and hold to be a dedication by the distillery company to the public of the right of ingress and egress over its property to and from the public road adjoining lands to the station or facilities that may be provided on the distillery premises for the reception and delivery of freight. With this right thus guaranteed, there can be no question that the public who desire to use this branch road may do so upon equal terms with the distillery company. In addition to this, it is shown that, at the point where the railroad crosses the Hardinsburg public road, it is the intention of the railway company to provide, and that it can and will provide, facilities for the reception and delivery of freight, and so at this point as well as in the distillery premises persons desiring to use the road can find opportunity to do so.

Coming now to the question as to the need for this branch by any person except the distillery company, which inquiry brings up the question of its necessity for a public use, the facts are these: In the immediate vicinity of the distillery company there are situated two or three large manufacturing plans, with a prospect of others, and in the neighborhood quite a number of people reside. It is clearly shown by the evidence that the construction of this spur track will be a great convenience as well as benefit to the other business establishments in that locality as well as to the public in that section who may desire to receive and ship freight, and that these manufacturing plants and the public will freely use this branch in the conduct of their business. To what extent it will be used is not fully shown, nor indeed could it be. It is, however, sufficient for the purpose of satisfying the requirements of the Constitution to know that it can be and will be used by other of the public than the distillery

Riley *v.* Louisville, H. & St. L. Ry. Co

'company, and by all of the public who desire to use it. This evidence we think shows a sufficient necessity for the construction of this road to justify us in saying that it is necessary for a public use. Warden *v.* Madisonville, H. & E. R. Co., 128 Ky. 563, 108 S. W. 880, 33 Ky. Law Rep. 38.

But it is said that the admitted fact that the distillery company has agreed to furnish to the railway company the money necessary to construct this branch is persuasive, if not controlling, evidence that it is for a private enterprise and not a public use. Although this circumstance is competent as evidence tending to show, if it did so show, that the building of this branch would be a private enterprise, it is not entitled to weighty consideration in determining the nature of the improvement. The railway company was desirous to have this branch built as the distillery company; but it did not have the means with which to construct it, and so it was agreed between the two companies that the distillery company should advance to the railway company the money necessary to build this road, the money so advanced to be repaid by the railway company according to the terms of the agreement between them. But in this agreement it was distinctly stipulated that the railway company should have the exclusive operation and control of the road; the distillery company having no more to do with this than any other shipper. In short, the distillery company merely agreed to advance the money to build the road under a contract by which it is to be reimbursed. There is nothing against public policy in a contract like this. Nor does it carry with it the inference that the road is for private use of the party furnishing the money. It is a matter of no consequence, so far as the legal aspects of the case are concerned, who furnishes the money to build railroads. Zircle *v.* Southern Ry. Co., 102 Va. 17, 45 S. E. 802, 102 Am. St. Rep. 805, and note; Chicago & N. W. R. Co. *v.* Morehouse, 112 Wis. 1, 87 N. W. 849, 56 L. R. A. 240, 88 Am. St. Rep. 918; St. Louis, Iron M. & S. R. Co. *v.* Petty, 57 Ark. 359, 21 S. W. 884, 20 L. R. A. 434; Kansas City, S. & G. R. Co. *v.* La. & W. R. Co., 116 La. 178, 5 L. R. A. (N. S.) 512, 7 Am. & Eng. Ann. Cas. 831, and note.

Tested by all the rules that are to govern in the settlement of cases like this, we are satisfied that the taking of appellant's property is for a public use, and that it will be necessary for such use when appropriated to it.

Wherefore the judgment is affirmed.

CITY OF PARIS *v.* CAIRO, V. & C. RY. CO. *et al.*

(Supreme Court of Illinois, Dec. 21, 1910. Rehearing Denied Feb. 8, 1911.)

[93 N. E. Rep. 729.]

Eminent Domain—Public Necessity—Nature of Question.*—While courts may determine whether the use for which property is proposed to be condemned is public or private in its nature, yet when the use is public, as to extend a city street across a railroad, they cannot inquire into the propriety of exercising the right of eminent domain, and an ordinance passed by the city providing for the extension of such street is decisive of the question.

Judgment—Condemnation Proceedings—Res Judicata.—Where a railroad company, in its suit in the United States court to enjoin a city from extending a street over its tracks, contended that the street had never been so laid out, and that the public had been allowed by mere license to cross the right of way by an overhead bridge, and the decree found such to be the facts, the railroad company, in subsequent proceedings by the city to condemn an extension of the street across the right of way, could not contend that the city was merely attempting to change the grade of the street which already existed as an overhead crossing, and that therefore, having once extended the street by contract across the right of way, the city had exhausted its power and was estopped to extend it in any manner, nor could it contend that the decree in the former case was res judicata, that decree having found that the street never had existed across the right of way, while, in the subsequent case, the city was endeavoring by condemnation to extend the street across the right of way where the former decree had held that it never had been extended.

Evidence—Condemnation Proceedings—Admissibility of Evidence.—In a condemnation suit by a city to acquire a right of way for a street over a railroad track, that witnesses were not familiar with the method of conducting railroads would not render incompetent their testimony whether the location of the street across the right of way would result in damages to the use of the property of the railroad to be occupied by the street.

Eminent Domain—Condemnation Proceedings—Elements of Damage.—In proceedings by a city to condemn a right of way for a street over a railroad track, a question asked witnesses what in their judgment would be the decrease in the value of defendant's property for railroad purposes, which would be caused by the use of the strip in question for street purposes, such use for street purposes being subject to use by defendant of the strip for railroad purposes, eliminat-

---

*See foot-note of Chicago, etc., R. Co. *v.* Mason (S. Dak.), 34 R. R. R. 60, 57 Am. & Eng. R. Cas., N. S., 60.

City of Paris v. Cairo, V. & C. Ry. Co. et al

ing the cost of grading the approaches or of changing the tracks to conform to the grade of the street or planking between the rails, the making of gates or hiring of flagmen, stoppage or slow movement of trains, increased danger of accident, and cutting of trains over crossing, was objectionable as excluding from consideration of the witness as an element of damages those resulting from the change of the railroad tracks to conform to the street grade, but otherwise embraced every element of damage proper to be considered.

Eminent Domain—Condemnation Proceedings—Elements of Damage.—A question asked witnesses as to damages which eliminated from their consideration, the loss to defendant of the use of a portion of the proposed street as a place for standing or storing cars, was erroneous since, if any of the tracks of defendants' railway at the point of the proposed intersection of the street, were used as a place for storage of cars, the opening of the street would necessarily deprive defendants of that use, and the loss of the storage room would be a proper element of damage.

Eminent Domain—Condemnation Proceedings—Issues and Proof.—Defendants having filed a cross-petition for the ascertainment of damages to property not taken, they were entitled to prove any damage sustained to property not taken, and it was error to confine such proof to switch yards of defendants in the immediate vicinity of the land being condemned.

Eminent Domain—Condemnation Proceedings—Compensation—Issues and Proof.—If the extension of the street would necessarily require excavation or removal by defendants of any quantity of earth for the proper operation of their railway, they would be entitled, under their cross-petition for ascertainment of damages to property not taken, to prove such fact as an element of damage.

Eminent Domain—Condemnation—Elements of Compensation—Cost of Observing Police Regulations.†—A railroad company takes a right of way subject to the right of the public to extend streets across it, and. when a street is so extended, the railroad company is not entitled to such damages as result with its compliance with the police regulation of the state. and hence a railroad company, over whose right of way a street is sought to be extended at grade by condemnation, is not entitled to recover compensation for the value of time which would be lost in switching operations in switch yards because of the establishment of the crossing made necessary by the observance of the police regulations of the state.

Appeal from Circuit Court, Edgar County; W. B. Scholfield, Judge.

Action by the City of Paris against the Cairo, Vincennes & Chicago Railway Company and others. From the judgment, defendants appeal. Reversed and remanded.

---

†See foot-note of Chicago, etc., R. Co. v. Village of Fair Oaks (Wis.), 34 R. R. R. 701, 57 Am. & Eng. R. Cas., N. S., 701.

City of Paris *v.* Cairo, V. & C. Ry. Co. et al

George B. Gillespie (L. J. Hackney, Shepherd & Trogdon, and *Gillespie & Fitzgerald,* of counsel), for appellants.
Wilber H. Hickman, Henry S. Tanner, and *Joseph E. Dyas,* for appellee.

Cooke, J. The appellee, the city of Paris, filed a petition in the circuit court of Edgar county to extend, by condemnation, Buena Vista street across a certain railroad right of way owned by the appellant the Cairo, Vincennes & Chicago Railway Company, but used exclusively by the appellant the Cleveland, Cincinnati, Chicago & St. Louis Railway Company as lessee. Appellants filed a motion to dismiss the petition, which, after a hearing thereon before the court, was denied. The appellants then filed a cross-petition for the ascertainment of damages to property not taken. By agreement the hearing was had before the court without a jury, and resulted in a judgment assessing the just compensation to be paid for the land proposed to be taken at $150, and authorizing the city to enter upon, use, occupy, and control the same for the purposes of a street upon payment of that amount. Appellants have prosecuted this appeal from that judgment, and assign various grounds for reversal.

The line of railway owned by appellants was constructed in 1853 to 1854, and extended east and west through what was then the village of Paris. The village had about 500 inhabitants and did not include the proposed crossing. Afterwards the village was organized as a city, the limits were extended so as to embrace the land in question, and Buena Vista street was laid out south of the railroad right of way. Subsequently, during the year 1884, that portion of Buena Vista street north of the right of way was laid out, and by agreement between the city and the railroad company then owning the right of way, the railroad company constructed a bridge over the railroad tracks on a line with Buena Vista street and the city constructed dirt approaches on both sides of the right of way from the street to the bridge, thus furnishing a continuous passageway for travelers upon the street. This bridge, and the approaches thereto, have been used by the public from 1884 to the present time, the railroad companies owning the right of way having kept the bridge in repair. Paris is now a city of about 10.000 inhabitants, and that portion of the city in the vicinity of the proposed crossing is being built up with residences. Appellants' line of railway over which it is sought to extend Buena Vista street is known as the main line, and extends from the city of Indianapolis, in the state of Indiana, to the city of St. Louis, in the state of Missouri. Appellants have another line extending from the city of Danville to the city of Cairo, in this state. It forms a junction with the main line at Paris, and extends south through

City of Paris *v.* Cairo, V. & C. Ry. Co. et al

the city, crossing the main line a considerable distance west of Buena Vista street. A large quantity of freight is transferred at this junction. The first grade crossing east of Buena Vista street is 1,000 feet distant and the first grade crossing west of that street is about 1,700 feet distant. The yards, switches and commercial tracks, as well as the passenger and freight depots and the transfer platform, are located between the bridge above mentioned and the first grade crossing west thereof. Four tracks and a switch point leading to eight tracks in the railroad yards immediately west of Buena Vista street are located under the bridge, and in switching cars to and from and in the railroad yards it is necessary to pass under the bridge. The stock yards are immediately east of the bridge and on the north side of the right of way. The north track is used principally for loading and unloading stock at these yards, and that portion of the track under the bridge is frequently used for storing cars. The railroad at the proposed crossing runs in a cut about eight feet below the natural surface of the land.

On July 20, 1908, the city council of the city of Paris passed an ordinance changing and establishing the grade of Buena Vista street for a distance of 250 feet north and 500 feet south of the appellants' main track, the established grade at the main track being the present grade of that track. A resolution was adopted at the same meeting providing for service of notice upon the appellant the Cleveland, Cincinnati, Chicago & St. Louis Railway Company to conform its right of way to the grade established by the ordinance. The city soon afterwards entered into a contract with a contractor for the removal of the approaches to the bridge and the reduction of the grade of the street in accordance with the ordinance. The Cleveland, Cincinnati, Chicago & St. Louis Railway Company, being a foreign corporation, at once filed a bill in the United States Circuit Court for the Eastern District of Illinois to restrain the city of Paris, the city council, and the contractor from carrying out this contract, and from destroying, removing, or interfering with the abutments and the bridge, and from attempting to change the grade of the street or otherwise interfering with the property of the railway company. The defendants to the bill were duly served with process, but failed to appear in the cause, and a decree pro confesso was entered in accordance with the prayer of the bill. The findings of the decree, so far as necessary to be here shown, were substantially the same as the facts hereinbefore recited, and in addition thereto, that the overhead bridge had been in use for more than 25 years, and that the city had a right of way over said bridge by user or prescription; that the railway company had ever been willing to maintain and renew the bridge with safe, sufficient, and suitable materials for the accommodation of the public; that there was no public necessity requiring the reduction of the bridge and the establishment of a grade crossing; that the city of Paris was not acting from public motives nor for the public welfare, but at the instance and in the interest of one Hardy and contrary to the welfare of the public, and that it was to the interest and for the welfare of the city that said overhead crossing should be maintained as the railway company proposed to maintain it. Thereafter, on December 7, 1908, the city council of the city of Paris passed an ordinance providing that Buena Vista street be opened by condemnation, and that the land involved in this suit, being a strip 51 feet wide and 305 feet long, across the right of way of appellants, be taken for such street purposes, and directing the city attorney to institute the necessary legal proceedings for the condemnation of the same. This proceeding was thereafter, on February 15, 1909, begun by the filing of the petition in the circuit court of Edgar county, and resulted in a judgment assessing $150 as the compensation to be paid appellants for the use of the crossing as a street by the city.

Appellants first urge that the petition should have been dismissed for the reason that there was no necessity for the opening of a street at this place; that the proceeding is a mere attempt to change the grade and not to extend the street across the right of way, as the city already has a right of way over the railway by user, and that the decree of the United States Circuit Court is res judicata as to all the matter presented by the petition.

The appellant companies hold their right of way subject to the right of the public to extend highways, streets, and alleys across the same. Buena Vista street has never been laid across the appellants' right of way. Whether there exists a public necessity for the extension of this street across appellants' right of way is purely a legislative question, and the ordinance passed by the city council of Paris providing for the extension of the street is decisive of that question. Courts have the right to determine whether the use for which property is proposed to be taken is public or private in its nature, but when the use is public, as in this case, courts cannot inquire into the necessity or propriety of exercising the right of eminent domain. Chicago. Rock Island & Pacific Railroad Co. v. Town of Lake, 71 Ill. 333; Illinois Central Railroad Co. v. City of Chicago, 141 Ill. 586, 30 N. E. 1044, 17 L. R. A. 530; Chicago & Alton Railroad Co. v. City of Pontiac, 169 Ill. 155. 48 N. E. 485. In the case last cited, as well as in Chicago & Northwestern Railway Co. v. City of Morrison, 195 Ill. 271, 63 N. E. 96, it was intimated that the courts might interfere in an extreme case of oppression or outrage, but the situation here is not such as would warrant us in taking any cognizance of the question of the necessity or expediency of the extension of Buena Vista street across the right of way of appellants.

City of Paris *v.* Cairo, V. & C. Ry. Co. et al

As to the other grounds urged as to why the petition should be dismissed, the lessee railway company contended in the United States Circuit Court that Buena Vista street had never been extended or laid out across the right of way, and that the public had been allowed by mere license to travel across the right of way by means of the overhead bridge, and the decree of the United States court found such to be the fact. That decree found that Buena Vista street had never been extended, and did not exist, over and across the railway right of way, and that the right of the public to pass over the right of way of the appellants by means of the overhead bridge was a mere license. That having been the contention of the lessee railway company in the United States court as well as the finding and decree of that court, appellants are in no position now either to say here that this is not an attempt on the part of the city of Paris to extend Buena Vista street across its right of way, but a mere attempt to change the grade of that street, or that the decree of the United States court is res judicata as to the matters in issue here. If, as the court decreed in the case in the United States court, Buena Vista street did not exist and never had existed across the railway right of way, appellants cannot now, in attempting to avail themselves of the advantage secured by reason of that decree, contend here that as a matter of fact a street did exist by way of an overhead crossing, and that therefore, having once extended the street by contract across appellants' right of way in that manner, the city has exhausted its power, and is now estopped to extend it in any other manner. Neither can they successfully contend that the decree of the United States court is res judicata as to the matters involved here, as that decree found that Buena Vista street never had existed or been extended across the right of way of appellants, whereas in this proceeding appellee is endeavoring by condemnation proceedings to extend that street across such right of way at the point where the United States court held it never had been extended. The motion to dismiss was properly denied.

Appellants contend that the court erred in the exclusion of testimony offered in their behalf on the hearing, and also in passing upon certain propositions of law submitted. The evidence offered by petitioner was wholly confined to the question whether the location of Buena Vista street across the right of way of appellants would result in damages to the use of the property of appellants to be occupied by Buena Vista street. This proof was made by various citizens of Paris. Propositions of law were submitted by appellants touching the qualifications of the witnesses to testify as to such damages, the theory being that only such witnesses as were shown to have had special and practical knowledge and experience in matters pertaining to the operation of a railroad were qualified to express any opinion as to the damages sustained. The witnesses called on the part of the appellee testified, in answer to preliminary questions, as to their means of knowledge and that they were thoroughly familiar with the use of this property by appellants, and were therefore qualified to give their opinion on the question of damages. The fact that they were not familiar with the methods of conducting railroads does not necessarily render their testimony incompetent. Illinois Central Railroad Co. *v.* City of Chicago, 169 Ill. 329, 48 N. E. 492.

Appellants objected to the question put to each witness for appellee as to the amount of damages sustained by appellants by reason of the taking of the strip of land in question for the purposes of a street. The question so asked of a number of the witnesses for the appellee was substantially as follows: "Eliminating the cost of grading the approaches, or of changing the tracks to conform to the grade of the street, or planking between the rails, the making of gates or hiring of flagmen, stoppage or slow movement of trains, increased danger of accident, cutting of trains over crossings, what, in your judgment, would be the amount of decrease in the value of defendants' property for railroad purposes which would be caused by the use of the strip in question for the purposes of a street, such use for the purposes of a   street being subject to the use by the defendants of said strip for railroad purposes?" This question was objected to upon the ground that it excluded from the consideration of the witness elements of damage which should properly be considered, and for which appellants were entitled to receive compensation for damages to the use of their property as railway property. This objection should have been sustained. If the laying out of this street would make it necessary for appellants to change the tracks of the railway to conform to the grade of the street, that was a proper element of damages, and should not have been eliminated. The remainder of the question was proper and did not eliminate any element of damage which was proper to be considered. Chicago & Northwestern Railway Co. *v.* City of Chicago, 140 Ill. 309, 29 N. E. 1109; Lake Shore & Michigan Southern Railway Co. *v.* City of Chicago, 148 Ill. 509, 37 N. E. 88; Chicago & Northwestern Railway Co. *v.* City of Morrison, supra. The same question was asked the other witnesses for petitioner, except that it also eliminated from the consideration of the witnesses the loss to appellants of the use of a   portion of the proposed street as a place for standing or storing cars as an element of damage. The objection to this question, which was the same as that made to the other question noted, should also have been sustained for the additional reason that if any of the tracks of appellants' railway at the point of the proposed intersection of the street were used as a place for the storage

City of Paris v. Cairo, V. & C. Ry. Co. et al

of cars, the opening of the street would necessarily deprive appellants of that use, and the loss of the storage room was a proper element of damage. Chicago & Northwestern Railway Co. v. City of Chicago, 151 Ill. 348, 37 N. E. 842; Chicago & Northwestern Railway Co. v. City of Morrison, supra.

On the question of consequential damages, or the damages which the appellants would sustain to the property not actually taken for the street, the court expressly confined the proof to the switch yards of appellants in the immediate vicinity of the lands being condemned, and, upon objection, excluded all proof of damages to any of the property of appellants not taken, other than that contained in said switch yards. Under their cross-petition appellants were entitled to prove any damage sustained to property not taken, and we are unable to see upon what theory the court confined this proof to the switch yards alone. If appellants would sustain any damage to their railway aside from the property actually taken and aside from the damage to the switch yards, if any, they were entitled, under the cross-petition, to prove it, and it was error for the court to exclude this testimony. Lake Shore & Michigan Southern Railway Co. v. City of Chicago, 151 Ill. 359, 37 N. E. 880; Chicago, Burlington & Quincy Railroad Co. v. City of Naperville, 166 Ill. 87, 47 N. E. 734. The court, in passing upon the written propositions of law submitted by appellants, held the law to be that the defendants were entitled to recover their just compensation, not merely for the strip of land taken for the purposes of Buena Vista street, but, in addition, such further sum as the evidence might show would justly compensate them for damages to their property not taken. This holding as to the law was inconsistent with the ruling of the court upon the admissibility of the testimony. The law is properly stated in the propositions so held by the court, and proof as to all damages to the property of the railroad not taken, occasioned by the extension of this street, should be admitted, except such as would be occasioned by the enforcement of police regulations, or by delay rendered necessary by the common-law duty of appellants to operate and manage their engines and trains with due care and caution on approaching and passing over said street.

Appellants attempted to prove that the extension of this street as proposed would necessitate the excavation of a considerable amount of earth in the vicinity of the proposed crossing, but outside of the street lines, in order to effect a proper operation of the railway. This testimony was excluded, an objection having been sustained to each question asked along this line. It does not appear from the record where it is claimed this excavation would become necessary or why it would become necessary. If the extension of this street would necessarily require the excavation or the removal by the appellants of any quantity of

City of Paris *v.* Cairo, V. & C. Ry. Co. et al

earth for the proper operation of their railway, they would be entitled, under their cross-petition, to prove that as one element of damage, and appellants should have been permitted to show whether or not they would necessarily be put to this expense.

Appellants complain of the action of the court in disregarding practically all of the testimony offered in their behalf as to the damages to the switch yards occasioned by the extension of this street. The damages to the switch yards testified to by the witnesses for the appellants ranged from $20,000 to $30,000, and were based almost wholly upon the value of the time which would be lost in the switching operation and movements of trains by reason of the establishment of a grade crossing at this point. The lost time testified to was that which would be occasioned by the observance of the police regulations of the state, and was not such an element of damage as appellants were entitled to recover. Appellants are subject to the police power of the state, and are not entitled to recover damages on account of having to stop their trains at any crossing in order to comply with the statute. Every railroad company takes its right of way subject to the right of the public to extend streets across it, and when any street is so extended across the right of way, the railroad company is not entitled to compensation for such damages as result from its compliance with the police regulations of the state. Chicago & Alton Railroad Co. *v.* Joliet, Lockport & Aurora Railway Co., 105 Ill. 388, 44 Am. Rep. 799; Chicago & Northwestern Railway Co. *v.* City of Chicago, supra; Lake Shore & Michigan Southern Railway Co. *v.* City of Chicago, 184 Ill. 509, 37 N. E. 88.

For the error of the court in excluding testimony on the question of damages to the property of appellants not taken, the judgment of the circuit court is reversed and the cause remanded.

Reversed and remanded.

Fowler *et al. v.* Norfolk & W. Ry. Co. *et al.*

(Supreme Court of Appeals of West Virginia, Nov. 29, 1910.)

[69 S. E. Rep. 811.]

Highways—Obstruction—Right of Individual to Sue.*—An action for damages for obstructing a highway cannot be maintained by a citizen, unless he shows injury to himself or his property, peculiar and special in the sense that it is different in nature or kind from that which results to the public generally from the obstruction.

Highways—Obstruction—Right of Individual to Sue.*—A property owner has no right of action against a railway company for destruction of a street crossing in consequence of which his property suffers injury of the same nature or kind as that which results therefrom to all other property owners affected thereby, even though it be greater in degree.

Eminent Domain—Obstruction of Highway—Erection of Overhead Footbridge—Liability for Injury to Abutting Land.—A footbridge or passageway over a railroad, erected by the company owning the railroad at the instance of a city council, by way of partial restoration of a grade crossing which the railroad company has destroyed, is an improvement made by the railroad company, under a duty enjoined upon it by the sixth clause of section 50 of chapter 54 of the Code of 1906; and, for damages occasioned to the property of an abutting landowner by the erection and maintenance of such structure, the railroad company is liable.

Municipal Corporations—Obstruction of Streets—Liability to Abutting Landowners.—Under such circumstances, there is no liability upon the city for injury to abutting land.

Eminent Domain—Obstruction of Highway—Permanent Injury.—In such case, the injury is permanent in its nature, and permanent damages are recoverable.

---

*For the authorities in this series on the question whether abutting owners are entitled to compensation on account of the construction or operation of railroads in streets, see second foot-note of Lund *v.* Idaho & W. N. R. R. (Wash.), 31 R. R. R. 104, 54 Am. & Eng. R. Cas., N. S., 104; foot-note of Hutcheson *v.* International & G. N. R. Co. (Tex.), 33 R. R. R. 105, 56 Am. & Eng. R. Cas., N. S., 105; foot-note of Ft. Collins Development Ry. Co. *v.* France (Colo.), 29 R. R. R. 396, 52 Am. & Eng. R. Cas.. N. S., 396.

For the authorities in this series on the subject of the right of property owners to recover damages on account of the obstruction of egress and ingress caused by the construction or operation of a railroad, see second foot-note of Illinois Cent. R. Co. *v.* Elliott (Ky.), 31 R. R. R. 98, 54 Am. & Eng. R. Cas.. N. S., 98.

For the authorities in this series on the subject of railroads and things pertaining to railroads as nuisances. see foot-note of Tucker *v.* Vicksburg, etc., R. Co. (La.). 35 R. R. R. 517, 58 Am. & Eng. R. Cas.. N. S., 517; foot-note of Longenecker *v.* Wichita R. & Light Co. (Kan.), 34 R. R. R. 610, 57 Am. & Eng. R. Cas., N. S., 610.

Fowler v. Norfolk & W. Ry. Co

Eminent Domain—Obstruction of Highway—Rights of Abutting Property Owners.—In such case, it is immaterial that the owner of abutting land has no title to the fee in the street on which such structure is erected and maintained. The right of action is given by section 9 of article 3 of the Constitution of this state (Code 1906, p. 1), inhibiting the taking or damaging of private property for public use, without just compensation.

Eminent Domain—Public Improvements—Damages.—In an action for damages to property, occasioned by a public improvement, it is error to refuse to instruct the jury to set off, against the damages, the value of peculiar benefits inuring to the property from the construction of the improvement.

Brannon and Williams, JJ., dissenting in part.

(Syllabus by the Court.)

Error from Circuit Court, Mercer County.

Action by William E. Fowler and others against the Norfolk & Western Railway Company and others. From a judgment, both parties bring error. Reversed and remanded.

Sanders & Crockett, for plaintiff Fowler and others.
D. E. French, for defendant City of Bluefield.
A. W. Reynolds, for defendant Norfolk & W. Ry. Co.

POFFENBARGER, J. For injury to the property of William E. Fowler and others, a certain lot in the city of Bluefield, occasioned by the destruction of a public street crossing and the erection of an overhead bridge or passageway for pedestrians, across the tracks of the Norfolk & Western Railway Company, a judgment was rendered against said company for the sum of $5,000. The city of Bluefield, having the supervision and control of said street, was joined as a defendant in the action, upon the theory of liability to the plaintiffs for the injury aforesaid by reason of its having permitted or authorized the destruction of said crossing and the erection of said bridge or passageway, a portion of which extends along the front of the lot aforesaid. The jury found in favor of the plaintiffs against the Norfolk & Western Railway Company. On the issue joined between the plaintiffs and the city, there was a verdict for the latter, under an instruction by the court. The railway company having obtained a writ of error to the judgment, the plaintiffs also sued out one in which they complain of the verdict and judgment in favor of the city.

The Norfolk & Western Railway seems to have been built before the city of Bluefield was laid out. At the time of its construction, it crossed what is said to have been a county road at the point at which the crossing was destroyed and the bridge erected. As to whether there was a county road there, and, if so, whether it had been abandoned or discontinued, there is some controversy, but the evidence is probably sufficient to sustain a finding in favor of the plaintiffs on that question. The City of Bluefield, building and developing on both sides of the railroad, extended its limits beyond this point. South of the railroad there is a street known as Bluefield avenue. About two-thirds of the population of the city is found on that side and the residue on the northern side. Including the one in question, there were three public crossings for the accommodation of travel and transportation between the two sections of the city. The crossing in question is known as Allen street crossing. Said street runs northward from the railroad. As a means of making this crossing available for travel from the northern section to Bluefield avenue, a main thoroughfare in the southern section, the city purchased, from one Karr. a lot adjoining the railway right of way on the south and opened, through it, what is known as Thomas street, or the southern extension of Allen street. The theory of the railway company is that there never was a public crossing at this point, or, if there was, that it had been discontinued long before the opening of Thomas street. They say the city never did acquire any right of way across the railroad, though it did have a public street extending northward from the railway and another extending southward from it. On the other hand, the plaintiffs contend that there was an old public road across which the railway was built at this point and which was never discontinued, so that the city has a public highway over and upon the railway right of way, as well as beyond it in both directions. This crossing is on a sort of hillside, sloping from north to south. About two years before the building of the footbridge, the railway company, needing more tracks,. widened its roadbed and cut back into the hill so as to completely destroy the grade crossing. It left an embankment on the north side about 20 feet high. This was done without any authority or permission from the city, disclosed by the evidence in the record. In response to a protest and remonstrance on the part of citizens, the city authorities concluded to require the railway company to construct an overhead footbridge, by way of partial relief from the public inconvenience. An order was made, requiring the railway company to construct such a bridge. Later, a representative of the railway company appeared before the council with a drawing or plan of the proposed bridge which was approved and accepted. This order was amended by the board of supervisors so as to require the railway company to hold the city harmless from all claims to damages to property owners, occasioned by the construction and maintenance of the bridge. This amendment was concurred in by the council. At a later meeting, the council rescinded the order of concurrence in the amendment, made by the supervisors, and unconditionally accepted the plan proposed by the railway company. An order was also passed by the

Fowler *v.* Norfolk & W. Ry. Co

council, authorizing the street committee to build a wall along the right of way of the railway company on the north side, to prevent the bank from caving in, and to place a substantial railing along the line of the street.

A claim of contractual liability on the part of the railway company is based upon the amendment to the order of the council, made by the board of supervisors and concurred in by the council, notwithstanding the repeal of that order of concurrence; the contention being that concurrence in the amendment put that provision into effect and bound the railway company to indemnify and save harmless the city from all claims for damages. It is also insisted that the city never discontinued this grade crossing nor authorized the destruction thereof. Liability on the part of the railway company is also asserted under the statute giving railway companies the right to cross or occupy public highways, on condition that they do not destroy or impair their efficiency as highways, or, in case they do render them impracticable as highways, that they build new roads for the use of the public in lieu thereof. Finally, it is insisted that if the occupation of this crossing and the destruction thereof was wholly unauthorized and wrongful, the omission to restore the highway to its former condition, or make it available for purposes of travel and transportation, amounts to a nuisance and imposes liability upon the railway company for injuries to adjacent property. Practically the same legal propositions are asserted in respect to the construction and maintenance of the footbridge.

The property of the plaintiffs consists of a lot adjacent to the railway right of way on the south, fronting 90 feet thereon and 90 feet on Thomas street, or the southern extension of Allen street. The footbridge is not built on this lot, but on Thomas street in front of it, and extends from the railway right of way south along the front of the lot for about 50 feet, descending in the form of a stairway to the ground at that point. At its southern end, this lot fronts about 62 feet on Bluefield avenue. The west front of the lot does not extend from the railway to Bluefield avenue. At the distance of 90 feet from the railway line, the boundary line turns east for a distance of 26 feet and then south to Bluefield avenue, and runs parallel to Thomas street. In the corner on the southwest, there is a lot, 26 feet by 93 feet, belonging to J. W. Ruff and others. The plaintiffs claim to have been injured by the destruction of means of access to their lot and also by the maintenance of the footbridge in front thereof.

As to the first element of damages claimed, the loss of the benefit of the street crossing, we are of the opinion that there can be no recovery. A railroad company, occupying a public highway with its tracks, owes the duty of restoration, imposed by the sixth clause of section 50 of chapter 54 of the Code of

Fowler *v.* Norfolk & W. Ry. Co

1906, to the public, and, ordinarily, the discretion of the public tribunals, having the control of highways, is not subject to control by private individuals. County Court *v.* Armstrong, 34 W. Va. 326, 12 S. E. 488; County Court *v.* Boreman, 34 W. Va. 87, 11 S. E. 747; Armstrong *v.* County Court, 54 W. Va. 502, 46 S. E. 131. The railway company has been in possession for many years. The declaration does not deny its rightful occupancy of the crossing. The charge is that, being in the occupancy thereof, which may be presumed to have been rightful, nothing to the contrary being shown, it made alterations in the crossing by which the same was destroyed and rendered impassable. Assuming that this was in violation of law, by reason of failure to comply with the statute, requiring restoration of the crossing to its former condition, or to such state as not necessarily to have impaired its usefulness, the breach or failure was in respect to a duty which the railway company owed to the public. It may have subjected the railway company to criminal liability or civil remedies at the instance of the city. Failure of the city to require a restoration may be taken as an expression of its consent to the alterations. It acted upon the subject of restoration. It demanded a partial restoration, namely, the erection of a footbridge, answering the needs of pedestrians, but wholly unsuited to the requirements of travel or transportation by vehicles. As it saw fit to exercise its sovereign and uncontrollable discretion in reference to this crossing by discontinuing it, there could be no liability upon it. The railway company was already in the occupancy of it and the alterations in the surface of the land, made by it, constituted no invasion of the property rights of the plaintiffs. Nothing in this record discloses any private easement in them, which the railway company was bound to respect. Assuming that there was an old public road at that place, it does not appear that the plaintiffs' property abutted thereon. The general course of that road was parallel with the railroad and this crossing was a curve or turn thereof. It is not shown that the property of the plaintiffs abutted thereon. The northwest corner may have touched it, as it did the crossing, as it was afterwards recognized and maintained by the city and the railway company. That crossing only has been disturbed. The plaintiffs still have Thomas street in front of their property. The only detriment inflicted upon them is that they and the general public can no longer cross the railroad with vehicles. Their property is affected in the same way in which the property of other people in that section of the city has been affected. The inconvenience is just the same in their case as it is in the case of Ruff, whose property adjoins theirs on the same street. They have no street along the railroad right of way and never had. The only injury done their property is the denial of means of crossing the railroad at grade. That same injury has fallen on

Fowler v. Norfolk & W. Ry. Co

all other property owners in that section of the city, as well as upon property in other sections. The advantages of that crossing to them might be somewhat greater than to other people because of their proximity to it, but this is a difference in degree only, not in the nature of the advantage, nor in the detriment ensuing from the denial or loss of that advantage.

The injury resulting to a citizen from the obstruction of a highway, èven though wrongful and unauthorized, creates no right of action in him, unless his injury is peculiar and special in the sense that it differs in kind or character from that which results to the public generally. This court has held in Wees v. Railway Co., 54 W. Va. 421, 46 S. E. 166, and Bridge Co. v. Summers, 13 W. Va. 476, that, to maintain an injunction against such an obstruction, the plaintiff must show injury in that sense. Though it has not been decided in this state, other authorities hold that such peculiar and special injury is necessary to the maintenance of an action for damages. Railway Co. v. Thompson, 34 Fla. 346, 16 South. 282, 26 L. R. A. 410; Railway Co. v. Rasnake, 90 Va. 170, 17 S. E. 879; Dwenger v. Railway Co, 98 Ind. 153; Railway Co. v. Fuller, 63 Tex. 467; Blackwell v. Railway Co., 122 Mass. 1.

The court refused to give two instructions, declaring nonliability for discontinuance of the grade crossing, one of which was applicable to both defendants and the other to the railway company alone. For the reasons stated, this action of the court was erroneous.

As to the construction and maintenance of the footbridge or stairway leading up to it, the liability of the railway company seems to be clear. As we have said, the statute imposed upon it the duty of restoring the crossing to its former condition or to such state as not unnecessarily to have impaired its usefulness and to keep such crossing in repair. Under this statute, the city had the right to compel the railway company to construct the footbridge, and it did so. It had never given any permission to leave the crossing out of repair. The conditions upon which the company had originally constructed its road across the highway had not been altered or changed. Those conditions constituted part of the contract between it and the public authorities, and it could be compelled to comply with them. Town of Mason v. Railroad Co., 51 W. Va. 183, 41 S. E. 418. The occupancy of the crossing by the railroad company made the building of this footbridge necessary in the legal sense of the term, and the duty to build it was imposed upon the railway company by the statute in favor of the public. Legally and substantially, therefore, it is a part of the railway improvement, rather than a city improvement. This view is expressed and enforced in Jordan v. City of Benwood, 42 W. Va. 312, 26 S. E. 266, 36 L. R. A. 519, 57 Am. St. Rep. 859. In that case private property was in⁻

Fowler *v*. Norfolk & W. Ry. Co

jured by the occupancy and alteration of a public street by a
railway company, under a permit from the city, and it was held
that there could be no recovery from the city for injury so inflicted. The holding is expressed in point 7 of the syllabus as
follows: "Where work is done by a railroad company in a street
of a city under authority from the city to occupy the street for
its track, the city is not liable to adjoining lot owners for injury
to their lots from such work, but they must look to the company."
Burkam *v*. Railroad Co., 122 Ind. 344, 23 N. E. 799, fully sustains this position, declaring nonliability on the part of the city
and liability on the part of the railroad company. To the same
effect see Frith *v*. City of Dubuque, 45 Iowa, 406.

As the stairway and footbridge were erected, not upon the
plaintiffs' property, but upon the street in front of the same, in
which the plaintiffs do not own the fee, the street having been
formed out of a lot purchased by the city in fee from other
persons, wherefore the case cannot be brought within the principle of those imposing liability for burdening the plaintiffs' land
with an additional servitude, it is strongly urged that there is
no ground upon which the defendant can be held liable for injury to the plaintiffs' property by reason of the erection and
maintenance of the same. We are of the opinion, however, that
that clause of the Constitution which says private property shall
not be taken or damaged for public use without compensation
affords an amply sufficient basis for liability. The stairway and
bridge were erected for public purposes, and, in the erection
thereof, the property of the plaintiffs has been injured and damaged. The case therefore falls clearly within the terms of this
constitutional provision, and there are numerous precedents
justifying the view of liability, under the circumstances.

The amount of the recovery and the rulings of the court as to
the measure of damages have produced some controversy as
to the character of the damages recoverable; it being contended,
in the brief of the plaintiff in error, that this is not a case for
permanent damages. That portion of the lot, lying adjacent to
the railroad, is vacant and cannot be said to have been seriously
injured thus far. There are no buildings upon it and it has not
been put to any practical use with which the construction and
maintenance of the footbridge have interfered. If, therefore,
the rule of temporary damages is applicable, the recovery could·
not be large, and some of the instructions, embodying the theory
of permanent damages, were erroneous. As the stairway is
intended to stand in lieu of the grade crossing and serve the
public as a highway, the injury is undoubtedly permanent in its
nature, as much so as that which results from the establishment
or alteration of a public highway or the construction and operation of a railway, and the damages would necessarily be of the
same character. That the damages are considered permanent in

Fowler *v.* Norfolk & W. Ry. Co

the similar cases to which reference is here made, there can be no doubt. Stewart *v.* Railroad Co., 38 W. Va. 438, 18 S. E. 604; Blair *v.* City of Charleston, 43 W. Va. 62, 26 S. E. 341, 35 L. R. A. 852, 64 Am. St. Rep. 837; Godby *v.* City of Bluefield, 61 W. Va. 604, 57 S. E. 45.

This conclusion gives a negative answer to the contention that the supposed difference as to the measure of damages, between actions against the city and the railway company, assuming liability on the part of both, makes a case of misjoinder of parties defendant. The measure of damages would be the same in each case, if both were liable.

The court refused to instruct the jury, at the instance of the defendant, that they should set off, against damages to which the plaintiffs were entitled, any peculiar benefits, inuring to the plaintiffs from the construction and public use of the overhead footbridge, but not inuring to other property owners in respect to their property in the locality not similarly situated. It is said this instruction was properly refused for two reasons: First, because the destruction of the grade crossing and erection of the footbridge cannot be regarded as having benefited the property; and, second, because an instruction given for the plaintiffs correctly stated the rule, respecting the measure of damages. Our conclusion, concerning the right of action against the railway company on account of the destruction of the grade crossing, practically disposes of the first reason assigned for the propriety of the ruling. For the purposes in this case, the grade crossing must be regarded as if it had never been. The footbridge is a public improvement, adjacent to the property of the plaintiff. As the grade crossing has ceased to be, the footbridge is to be considered as a separate and independent thing. Its purpose and object is to afford a means of crossing the railroad and connecting two streets. It is built in front of the property of the plaintiffs. Such improvements are generally regarded as conferring peculiar benefits upon the adjacent property. Whether they do is not a matter of law. The facts afford a basis for a finding by the jury. Hence, we cannot say there was no basis in the evidence for this instruction. The facts are such in their general nature as usually call for such an instruction. The instruction given for the plaintiffs which is said to have covered the subject-matter of this one is very general in its terms. It tells the jury the measure of damage is the difference between the fair market value of the plaintiff's property immediately before the commission of the acts complained of and its fair market value immediately afterwards. There is a great volume of law which says peculiar benefits must be deducted from the damages. The eminent domain statute takes cognizance of this element or factor in such cases, allowing only damages in excess of, or beyond, the peculiar benefits which will be derived in respect to

City of Chicago *v.* Pittsburgh, Ft. W. & C. Ry. Co

the residue of the land from the work to be constructed. While there is a presumption of intelligence on the part of the jurors, they are not supposed to be learned in the law. Hence, when legal principles are involved in the determination of questions of fact submitted to them, the parties interested always have the right to call upon the court for a statement of such principles. The jury might know the defendant in a case like this, or the applicant in a condemnation proceeding, is entitled to have the value of peculiar benefits deducted and make their estimate accordingly; but the rule of practice is that the party interested may assume the contrary and obtain from the court an instruction. The refusal to comply with a proper request of this kind is always regarded as an error. While the instruction given for the plaintiffs has been approved in several cases, it has generally been accompanied by other instructions, requiring the deduction of the value of peculiar benefits. The practice of giving such other instructions along with it implies that, by reason of the generality of its terms, it does not sufficiently indicate the elements or factors to be considered by the jury in making up the estimate. See Blair *v.* City of Charleston, 43 W. Va. 62, 26 S. E. 341, 35 L. R. A. 852, 64 Am. St. Rep. 837. We think, therefore, the court should have given defendant's instruction No. 4.

For the error noted, the judgment will be reversed, the verdict set aside, and the case remanded for a new trial.

City of Chicago *v.* Pittsburgh, Ft. W. & C. Ry. Co.

(Supreme Court of Illinois, Dec. 21, 1910.)

[93 N. E. Rep. 307.]

Bridges—Viaduct—"Approach."—Under the common law, and generally under the statutes in this country, a "bridge" includes the abutments and such approaches as will make it accessible and convenient to public travel. Ordinarily an "approach," as the term is used, is considered a part of a viaduct or bridge. The question what is a viaduct proper and what is an approach, where one begins and the other ends, and what is street or highway, as distinguished from an approach to a viaduct or bridge, are more questions of fact than law.

Railroads — Streets — Approach to Viaduct — What Constitutes — Paving—Liability of Railroad Company.—For a block west of a viaduct over the tracks of defendant railroad company the approach was constructed of planking, with a substructure of woodwork and iron, and for another short block west of this the street was filled to its full width, according to the grade established for the approach, and the surface of the fill was paved, manholes provided, curbing

City of Chicago v. Pittsburgh, Ft. W. & C. Ry. Co

set, and sidewalks built; the street, except for the slope or grade of
six or seven feet for such blocks, having all the appearances of a city
street. Held, that that part of the grade so filled and improved did
not constitute a part of the "approach" to the viaduct, and that the
city had no power to require that the same be repaved and improved
at the expense of the railroad company.

Railroads—Street Grade—Change—Rights of Property Owners.*—
Where property owners are damaged by the elevation of the grade
of a street, in order to provide for viaducts over the tracks of a
railroad company, they may recover damages therefor.

Appeal from Municipal Court of Chicago; John H. Hume,
Judge.

Action by the City of Chicago against the Pittsburgh, Fort
Wayne & Chicago Railway Company. Judgment for plaintiff,
and defendant appeals. Reversed.

Loesch, Scofield & Loesch, for appellant.

Edward J. Brundage, Corp. Counsel, and *Charles M. Haft,* for
appellee.

CARTER, J.   This is an appeal from a judgment for $6,377.02
entered against appellant in the municipal court of Chicago May
20, 1910. The judge by whom the case was heard certified that
the rights of the respective parties depended upon the validity of
a municipal ordinance, and the public interests required that the
appeal should be taken directly to this court.

The city of Chicago, October 21, 1907, passed an ordinance
directing appellant to repave Eighteenth street, between the
center line of Canal street and the east line of Mechanic street,
either with granite block or standard pavement, put in new curbing, manholes, and such accessories as are incident to the re-
pavement of streets, and to lay new sidewalks. The ordinance
further provided that if appellant failed to enter upon the performance of the work within seven days the commissioner of
public works should perform the work therein specified and
charge the same to appellant, to be recovered by a suit in a proper
form of action. Appellant refused to do the work required by
the ordinance, which was thereafter performed by the city, and
this suit is brought to recover from appellant a portion of the
cost.

Eighteenth street runs east and west. The appellant's tracks
extend north and south. When said railroad entered the city of
Chicago, it crossed Eighteenth street at grade, and so continued
for years thereafter. The Chicago & Alton Railway Company
parallels the tracks of the appellant company on the east side at

*See foot-note of preceding case.

this point. March 22, 1876, the city council of said city made an appropriation towards the erection of a viaduct over the tracks of appellant and the Chicago & Alton Railway at Eighteenth street. On April 15, 1878, the city council passed an ordinance directing the commissioner of public works to erect a viaduct over said tracks, with stone abutments and iron framework, requesting the appellant to contribute $14,000 towards said construction, and that said viaduct be constructed under the general superintendence of the department of public works and the chief engineer of appellant. The ordinance provided that the city should maintain the approaches and the floor of said viaduct at its own expense and do all ordinary repairs. The viaduct was constructed in accordance with the terms of such ordinance. After this work was completed the grade of Eighteenth street, from the center line of Canal street to the west line of Mechanic street, was established.

Canal street extends north and south across Eighteenth street, and Mechanic street, also extending north and south, is a short block east of Canal. The grade of Eighteenth street, between the center line of Canal street and the west line of Mechanic street, was obtained by depositing earth in the street from building line to building line, to the necessary height. The surface of this fill was paved, manholes were provided, curbing set, and sidewalks built, and the street, except for the slope or grade of six or seven feet between Canal and Mechanic streets, is to all appearances a city street. East of Mechanic street the approach to the viaduct is constructed of planking and a substructure of woodwork or iron. On the south side of Eighteenth street, between Canal and Mechanic streets, stands a large business building, occupying the entire distance between said streets, and abutting on the sidewalk on Eighteenth street. At the northwest corner of Mechanic and Eighteenth streets stands a business house, built to the street line, and abutting on the sidewalk on said streets. Both of these buildings conform to the grade of the street as now established. Appellant does not own any property on Eighteenth street, between Canal and Mechanic streets, and has no interest therein, either directly or indirectly; all such property being owned by private interests for business purposes. No question is raised on this record as to paving the street or keeping up the approach east of Mechanic street.

It is insisted by the city that all of Eighteenth street, from Canal street to the viaduct proper over the railways, including pavement, manholes, catch-basins, curbing, and sidewalks, is a part of the approach to said viaduct, and therefore a part of the viaduct, and for that reason of the city can compel appellant to keep and maintain all of said approach in such condition of repair as the convenience of the public or the safety of lives and property may require; that, notwithstanding the ordinance un-

City of Chicago *v*. Pittsburgh, Ft. W. & C. Ry. Co

der which the viaduct was constructed provided that the city
should maintain and repair these approaches, the city authorities
by said ordinance could not waive the authority of the city, under its police power, to require appellant to maintain and repair
said viaduct, including its approaches. The conclusion that we
have reached in this matter renders it unnecessary for us to consider that question. There can be no doubt that under the provisions of the ordinance granting the appellant the right to construct its railway in the city of Chicago, as well as under the
statutes of the state concerning the control of railways, the public authorities can compel appellant to construct and maintain
proper crossings at streets. alleys, and highways, or, if the safety
and security of the public require, to erect and maintain viaducts,
with proper approaches thereto.

Under the common law, and generally under the statutes in
this country, a bridge includes the abutments and such approaches as will make it accessible and convenient for public
travel. It has been held in some cases that whether a particular
bridge includes approaches depends on the circumstances in
which the word "bridge" is used. State *v*. Illinois Central Railroad Co., 246 Ill. 188, 286, 92 N. E. 814. What is true as to a
bridge and its approaches is equally true of a viaduct and its
approaches. Ordinarily an "approach," as that term is used, is
considered a part of the viaduct. What would be regarded as
approaches would depend largely upon the demands of the
traveling public, and "upon what would be reasonable under
the circumstances and local situation in each case. It is manifest
that they do not, and should not, in all cases, include all that
part of the right of way that is covered by the street or highway
and is not immediately at the crossing." City of Bloomington
v. Illinois Central Railroad Co., 154 Ill. 539, 39 N. E. 478.

What is a viaduct proper, and what is an approach, where one
begins and the other ends, and what is a street or highway, as
distinguished from the approach, are more questions of fact
than of law, and are sometimes not easy to decide. Tolland *v*.
Willington, 26 Conn. 578. The material of which the approach
was constructed might or might not have weight in deciding
whether said approach was a part of the viaduct or of the street.
If the driveway or approach to a viaduct was only of sufficient
width for the use of teams in going over the viaduct, occupying
a comparatively small part of the street or highway, and not of
a character to be used for any other street purposes, the question
whether it was constructed of permanent and lasting material,
or of material that would have to be replaced within a few years,
could have little weight in deciding the matter here under consideration. Such a structure, whether permanent or temporary,
would ordinarily be held to be an approach, and a part of the
viaduct. If a viaduct were to be constructed in a depression

City of Chicago *v.* Pittsbɯrgh, Ft. W. & C. Ry Co

some two or three blocks distant from the higher ground, and the public authorities and owners of adjacent property thought it wise to construct the connection with such viaduct for the entire distance from the viaduct to the ridge, so as to make such connection all on the same level, whether such structure from the viaduct to the ridge would be considered a part of the approach or a part of the street would depend upon the character of the structure and the situation with reference to surrounding property.

No one would contend that if the whole distance, for the full street width, from the viaduct to the ridge, was filled in and made a solid street, and the buildings on either side constructed along such street on that grade, the connection in question would be considered an "approach" to the viaduct, as that term is usually understood. On the other hand, if such structure were built up in the air, and below it was a street bordered by buildings built at the street grade, such a structure might be held to be an approach to the viaduct. If the rise to a viaduct from the ordinary surface of the ground is not more than six or eight feet, it is not generally thought necessary to commence the ascent or approach more than a block away from the viaduct proper. If, however, the public authorities and the property owners along a street for three or four blocks all agree to distribute this grade of six or eight feet over said three or four blocks and have the pavement, curbs, sidewalks, and buildings for that distance conform thereto, it could hardly be argued that the whole of such three or four blocks was a part of the approach, which the railway company constructing the viaduct would be compelled to maintain and keep in repair. As was said by this court in City of Bloomington *v.* Illinois Central Railroad Co., 154 Ill., on page 547, 39 N. E. 481: "What is to be considered as the extent of the approaches to the railroad crossing must be determined by what is reasonable in the particular case."

The railroad must keep and maintain its crossings so that they will continue to meet the needs and requirements of an increasing population in respect to the safety of persons and property. Northern Pacific Railway Co. *v.* Duluth, 208 U. S. 583, 28 Sup. Ct. 341, 52 L. Ed. 630. But this does not necessarily require the railroad to keep and maintain that which is for every practical purpose a street or highway, even though incidentally it is used as a part of the ascent or approach to reach the viaduct. The railroad company, in State *v.* St. Paul, Minneapolis & Manitoba Railway Co., 98 Minn. 380, 108 N. W. 261, 120 Am. St. Rep. 581, was compelled, under the police power of the state, to erect and maintain a viaduct and long approaches over its railroad. But the same court held, in State *v.* Northern Pacific Railway Co., 99 Minn. 280, 109 N. W. 238, 110 N. W. 975, that there were reasonable limitations upon the liability of

City of Chicago v. Pittsburgh, Ft. W. & C. Ry Co

the railway company to maintain and repair the so-called viaduct approach; that where a part of these approaches was filled in permanently the full width of the street, resulting in a mere raising of the street grade, such permanently filled portions of the improvement constituted no part of the viaduct or "approaches;" and that the curbing, paving, and sidewalk upon those portions could not be charged to the railroad company.

This court decided, in People v. Illinois Central Railroad Co., 235 Ill. 374, 85 N. E. 606, 18 L. R. A. (N. S.) 915, where the railroad company had elevated its tracks and constructed a subway at a certain point for a street, that under the provisions of its charter (similar to the provisions of appellant's charter) and the general police power resting in the state, under the principles of law here invoked, the city could not require the railroad to maintain the pavement of the subway or its approaches. The situation of Eighteenth street, between Canal and Mechanic streets, is very similar to that of the approaches to the subway in the case last referred to. The reasoning of this court in that case as to the authority of the city, under its police power, to compel the railroad company to pave the subway and approaches, applies with equal force to the authority of the city in this case to compel appellant, under the police power, to pave Eighteenth street, between Canal and Mechanic streets.

It is insisted by counsel for the city that McFarlane v. City of Chicago, 185 Ill. 242, 57 N. E. 12, and City of Chicago v. Nodeck, 202 Ill. 257, 67 N. E. 39, are controlling in favor of the city on the questions here involved. We cannot so hold. The basis of those decisions was that there was a contract between the railroad company and the city that, in consideration of certain privileges granted to said company, it should construct, maintain, and keep in repair approaches to certain viaducts, and that because of such contract the property owners abutting on the said approaches could not be compelled to pay for the paving of said approaches; that to compel the property owners to pay for the work which the railroad company had agreed to construct would be unjust. This is also the reasoning in City of Chicago v. Newberry Library, 224 Ill. 330, 79 N. E. 666, and the ordinance in each of these three cases, requiring the property owners to pave the portions of the street there in question, was held unreasonable and void. These decisions do not support the contention of the city.

Whether Eighteenth street, between Canal and Mechanic streets, should be repaved and kept in repair by special assessment or by general taxation, is not before us for decision. The argument of counsel for the city that it would be unjust to the abutting property owners to compel them to repave this street, because they have been damaged by the elevation of the street above its former grade, is without force. If the property own-

St. Louis & S. F. R. Co. *v.* State et al

ers have been damaged by such elevàtion, according to the long-settled law of this state that they have a remedy for such damages. Chapman *v.* City of Staunton, 246 Ill. 394, 92 N. E. 905.

On the facts in this record the city of Chicago was without authority to pass or enforce the ordinance in question requiring appellant to repave and keep in repair West Eighteenth street, from Canal to Mechanic streets. The judgment of the municipal court must therefore be reversed.

Judgment reversed.

ST. LOUIS & S. F. R. CO. *v.* STATE *et al.*

(Supreme Court of Oklahoma, Nov. 16, 1910.)

[112 Pac. Rep. 980.]

Railroads—Railroad Commission—Powers—Switches.*—It is beyond the police power of a state to compel a railway company to put in switches at its own expense on the application of the owners of any elevator erected within a specified limit, and section 18 of article 9 of the Constitution does not attempt to confer such power upon the Corporation Commission.

(Syllabus by the Court.)

Appeal from State Corporation Commission.

Proceedings by the St. Louis & San Francisco Railroad Company against the State of Oklahoma and Charles Cottar to review an order of the Corporation Commission. Judgment for defendants, and the railroad company appeals. Reversed.

W. F. Evans, E. T. Miller, and *R. A. Kleinschmidt,* for plaintiff in error.

Geo. A. Henshaw, Asst. Atty. Gen., for defendants in error.

KANE, J. This proceeding was commenced to review an order of the Corporation Commission requiring the plaintiff in error to extend track privileges to the complainant elevator situated on the right of way of the railway company. The Corporation Commission based its order upon the finding that the complainant was discriminated against by the railway company in not being granted the same privileges on the right of way of the company adjoining its switch track as were granted to certain

---

*For the authorities in this series on the subject of the police powers of a state over railroad companies, see first foot-note of People *v.* Erie R. Co. (N. Y.). 36 R. R. R. 587, 59 Am. & Eng. R. Cas., N. S., 587; Downey *v.* Northern Pac. Ry. Co. (N. Dak.), 35 R. R. R. 598, 58 Am. & Eng. R. Cas., N. S., 598.

St. Louis & S. F. R. Co. *v.* State et al

other elevators already located thereon, and the purpose of the order was to put the parties upon an equal footing. The order required the railway company to pay for extending switch facilities to the complainant's elevator, with the exception that the complainant was to pay for the cross-ties and grading.

It is claimed by counsel for the Corporation Commission that the authority to make such an order is conferred upon the commission by section 18, art. 9, of the Constitution, governing unjust or unreasonable discrimination. In C., R. I. & P. Ry. Co. *v.* State et al., 23 Okl. 94, 99 Pac. 901, this court had occasion to examine a question similar to the one presented by the record in the instant case. In that case the complainant sought to require the railway company to build a side track to its place of business, after being refused a location upon its right of way in order to give it equal facilities with others engaged in said business, who were permitted by the railway company to use the right of way. It was held that "the fact that a railroad permitted the location of an elevator, maintained by a private corporation, on the industrial track on the right of way, does not render its refusal to construct, at its own expense, a side track to a competing elevator, located off the right of way, an unlawful discrimination, within Const. art. 9, § 18." The foregoing case was followed in A., T. & S. F. Ry. Co. *v.* State et al., 24 Okl. 616, 104 Pac. 908. Since handing down the opinions in those cases the Supreme Court of the United States, in Mo. Pac. Ry. Co. *v.* State of Nebraska, 217 U. S. 196, 30 Sup. Ct. 461, 54 L. Ed. ——, has passed upon the power of the state of Nebraska to compel a railroad company to put in switches at its own expense on the application of owners of elevators erected within a specified limit under a statute which by its terms required them to do so. In that case it was held: "It is beyond the police power of a state to compel a railroad company to put in switches at its own expense on the application of the owners of any elevator erected within a specified limit. It amounts to a deprivation of property without due process of law; and so held as to the application for such switches made by elevator companies in these cases under the statute of Nebraska requiring such switch connections."

The question involved in the instant case has been passed upon several times by this court, and now that its decision thereon has been followed by the Supreme Court of the United States, we trust that the Corporation Commission will no longer consider it an open one, and will follow the rule laid down in the foregoing cases in cases of that class that may hereafter come before it.

The order of the Corporation Commission is reversed.

Dunn, C. J., and Williams, Hayes, and Turner, JJ., concur.

McCAMMON & LANG LUMBER CO. *et al. v.* TRINITY & B. V.
RY. CO.

(Supreme Court of Texas, Jan. 4, 1911.)

[133 S. W. Rep. 247.]

**Eminent Domain—Compensation—Necessity of Payment before
"Taking."***—The occupation of a street by a railroad is a "taking"
of the property of one owning the fee of the street within the constitutional provision that, when property is taken for public use,
compensation shall be first made or secured by a deposit of money,
and such occupation is not a mere damaging for which compensation
may be made subsequently.

**Eminent Domain—Compensation—Necessity—Effect of Dedica-
tion of Street.**—The dedication of land for a street, the fee being retained by the abutting owners, does not authorize the use of the
street for purposes of commercial railroads without further compensation.

**Eminent Domain—Compensation—Necessity of Payment before
Taking—"Property"—"Taken."**—In the constitutional provision as
to compensation for property taken for public use, the term "property" includes the fee-simple title to the thing owned, whether it be
burdened with an easement or not; and the term "taken" includes
the appropriation of that thing or of some interest or estate in it,
by actual, physical possession, such as exists when a railroad is constructed and operated on it.

**Eminent Domain—Compensation—Necessity of Payment before
"Taking."***—The occupation of a street by a railroad is not a "taking" of property of an abutting owner who does not own the fee in
the street, within the provision of the Constitution that, when property is taken for public use, compensation must be first made.

Error to Court of Civil Appeals of Fifth Supreme Judicial
District.

Action by the McCammon & Lang Lumber Company and
others against the Trinity & Brazos Valley Railway Company.
From a judgment (131 S. W. 85) affirming a judgment dismissing the cause on demurrer, plaintiffs bring error. Reversed
and remanded.

---

*For the authorities in this series on the question whether abut-
ting owners are entitled to compensation on account of the construction and operation of steam railroads in streets, see foot-note
of Hutcheson *v.* International & G. N. R. Co. (Tex.), 33 R. R. R.
105, 56 Am. & Eng. R. Cas., N. S., 105; second foot-note of Lund *v.*
Idaho & W. N. R. R. (Wash.), 31 R. R. R. 104, 54 Am. & Eng. R.
Cas., N. S., 104; foot-note of Ft. Collins, etc., Ry. Co. *v.* France
(Colo.), 29 R. R. R. 396, 52 Am. & Eng. R. Cas., N. S., 396.

McCammon & Lang Lumber Co. *v.* Trinity & B. V. Ry. Co

Richard Mays, for plaintiffs in error.
Andrews, Ball & Streetman and *McClellan & Prince,* for defendant in error.

WILLIAMS, J. This is an action by plaintiffs in error for an injunction to restrain the defendant in error from constructing its track, which is to be that of a commercial railway for the carriage of passengers and freight, along a public street and alley in the city of Corsicana. A general demurrer to the petition was sustained and the cause was dismissed by the district court, whose action was affirmed by the Court of Civil Appeals.

The facts alleged on which the questions of law depend may be stated very briefly. Plaintiffs, as lot owners, are the owners in fee of the land over which the street and alley run and have, abutting thereon, business houses in which they carry on their several businesses for access to and egress from which the street and alley are essential. The allegations are full to the effect that the intended construction would be to appropriate the street and alley to the exclusive use of the defendant for a railroad. The defendant has acquired no other right to occupy the street and alley with its track than legally results from its charter as a railroad company, and the assent thereto of the proper authorities of the city, properly given.

The contention of counsel for the plaintiffs is that the proposed use of the street and alley would be a taking of their property without compensation first paid as required by the Constitution. This is denied by counsel for defendant, who insist that such use of property already dedicated to such purposes would not be a taking of it and would, at most, be only a damaging of plaintiffs' abutting lots for which compensation in advance is not required. The decision, therefore, necessarily depends on the question whether or not the petition shows a threatened "taking." While the Constitution provides that, without consent of the owner, his property should not be "taken, damaged or destroyed" without compensation, it further says that, when it is taken, "compensation shall be first made or secured by a deposit of money." The distinction is thus made by the Constitution itself between taking and damaging, etc., which becomes important when the aid of equity is invoked to prevent action merely threatened. If such action will constitute a taking, the facts that it is without consent and that compensation has not been made render it unlawful, so that the property owner has the right to prevent it by injunction. If it will constitute only a damaging, the attempt is not necessarily unlawful merely because compensation is not made in advance; and, if equity will prevent it at all, it will do so only upon the showing of additional facts. It is unnecessary to discriminate between the street and the alley as the decision will apply to both.

McCammon & Lang Lumber Co. *v*. Trinity & B. V. Ry. Co

It should require only a proper regard for plain physical facts to bring the mind to the conclusion that the location of a railroad, like that of defendant, upon land in which the public have only the easement of a highway and another has the fee, is a taking of that part of the land occupied by the track, at the very least, and hence a taking of property of the owner of the fee. No one disputes that this is the legal effect of such an appropriation of land not burdened with such an easement, for by the construction and use of the railroad the land is actually occupied and, necessarily, to a greater or less extent, the owner is excluded from that complete and exclusive use and control to which his ownership entitles him. Is it otherwise, except in degree, when, instead of only one, there are two interests in the soil to be considered, the public   easement and the fee? Is not the land appropriated and   used in that case in the same way and for the same purposes as in the other? In both instances the railroad company actually occupies and uses the soil itself in the assertion of a right of way in and over it. Is there a taking in one instance and not in the other? To make so fundamental a distinction is to deny to the visible facts necessary consequence. Where, before such occupation of the street, the public, including the owner of the fee, had the use of the highway equally and in common, unimpaired by any appropriation of any part of it to an exclusive use, after such occupation the part actually occupied is to a large extent withdrawn from other uses than those of the railroad company. It is true that such a taking is not entirely from the owner of the fee. The easement of the public is also invaded and taken, at least, to the extent that the highway is actually occupied; but to that extent also the soil belonging to the owner of the fee is taken. The legally authorized consent of the public to such use of the easement makes it lawful, but does not make it any the less a taking, nor justify the taking of that which does not belong to the public—the fee. It is true, also, that the appropriation of part of the land in a street as a way for a railroad does not so completely exclude the public from its use, theoretically at least, as does such an appropriation of land unaffected by any such public use; for the public may   still enjoy the street, as best they can, consistently with the presence of the road. As one of the public, the owner of the fee may participate in such enjoyment of the easement, but his use of the property in his private right is as fully excluded and the land is as completely appropriated to the use of the road as if there were no easement. The fee in the land is not as valuable to him as if it were not burdened with the street, but nevertheless it is property which cannot be taken without compensation first made or secured. If the easement of the street should come to an end, the fee would remain burdened only by the easement of the railroad right of way, and this lays bare

McCammon & Lang Lumber Co. v. Trinity & B. V. Ry. Co

the fact that the private property in the street is diminished to the extent of such right of way. In such situations the entire estate is divided into two interests, the easement of the public and the fee of the private owner, and the construction and use of a railroad over it is as much a taking of the corporeal property as if there were but one interest.

The proposition on which counsel for defendant based the argument that only a damaging and not a taking is threatened would not, if they were sound, tend to establish that conclusion, but rather the one that the taking would be rightful without compensation. Stated shortly, those propositions are that the original dedication of the land was for all the purposes of highways, and that the use of it for a railway is one of such purposes. The conclusion sought to be drawn is, not that such use without compensation is authorized as one to which the owner has consented, but that it is not a taking as distinguished from a damaging. The conclusion has no connection with the premises. If it were true that the dedication authorizes the use of the street for the purposes of commercial railroads, it would follow that such a use would be with the consent of the dedicator, and therefore to be made without compensation, but not that it would not be a taking. That such is not the effect of a dedication in this state is put beyond question by decisions of this court which hold that the construction of tracks of steam commercial railroads in streets constitutes a new servitude or burden not within the purposes of the dedication and calling for compensation. G., C. & S. F. Ry. Co. v. Eddins, 60 Tex. 656; G., C. & S. F. Ry. Co. v. Fuller, 63 Tex. 467.

Whether the compensation is first to be made must, of course, depend upon the answer to the question whether or not there is to be a taking. Whatever may be the full meaning of the words "property" and "taken," in the Constitution, there is no escape from the conclusion that the first includes the fee-simple title to the thing owned, whether it be burdened with an easement or not, and that the latter includes the appropriation of that thing, or of some interest or estate in it, by actual physical possession, such as exists when a railroad is constructed and operated upon it. G., C. & S. F. Ry. Co. v. Lyons, 2 Willson, Civ. Cas. Ct. App. § 139, and authorities cited.

It is urged that the decisions in this state have settled the law to be otherwise, but we think not. There have been conflicting views of the subject in other jurisdictions arising mainly in determining the sense in which the word "property" is used in the Constitution; one view being that it referred to the tangible objects owned as property, and the other that it was used in its correct and legal sense to indicate the several rights of ownership recognized by law with respect to such objects. Differences as to what was essential to a taking necessarily resulted from this

McCammon & Lang Lumber Co. *v.* Trinity & B. V. Ry. Co

fundamental difference as to what was to be regarded as the property. This is fully explained in Lewis on Eminent Domain, c. 3, and the many decisions there referred to. It is alluded to also in G., C. & S. F. Ry. Co. *v.* Fuller, 63 Tex. 469. That which was regarded by a court entertaining the latter view as the taking away of a right of property in the thing which was the subject of ownership, as land or a chattel, for which compensation was exacted by the Constitution, was held by those entertaining the former not to be a taking of the thing or of any part of it, and therefore not to entitle to compensation under a provision exacting it only for takings, however damaging to the owner the act complained of may have been. This history of the subject should be kept in mind when construing our present Constitution.

Several kinds of cases have arisen out of the occupation of streets by railroads: (1) Where the person seeking compensation owned the fee, as in this case; (2) where he did not own the fee, but owned lots abutting on the street with the rights of access and egress, light and air; (3) where he owned neither the fee nor abutting lots, but owned other land so situated with reference to the railroad that he suffered damages peculiar to his situation and was held entitled to compensation under the doctrine of nuisances. G., H. & W. Ry. Co. *v.* Hall, 78 Tex. 169, 14 S. W. 259, 9 L. R. A. 298, 22 Am. St. Rep. 42.

To our minds it seems plain that the first class of cases falls within both views of the meaning of the words "property" and "taken" just noticed. There has been some difference of opinion in other jurisdictions over this proposition; but the overwhelming weight of authority is in favor of the view first stated, and there has been no contrary holding by this court.

In view of this diversity of opinion as to the scope of the original provision in the Constitution, that in the present was so worded as to give compensation for all losses sustained by property owners for the benefit of the public in the construction of public works, whether there was a taking, or only a damaging or destruction of property. Nearly all the actions involving its application that have appeared in this court have been brought to recover compensation, in the form of damages, and the distinction between a taking and a damaging was generally unimportant, as the damages were recoverable whether there had been the one or the other. Dicta in cases merely seeking the recovery of damages could hardly be of controlling effect on the present question, even if they went to the extent claimed for them; but we have not found in those cited even any dicta, besides one noticed below which, properly understood, assert that that is not a taking which is sought to be prevented by the present plaintiff. The cases of that kind are so numerous that we shall not attempt to cite many of them, but shall confine our discussion to those which seem most closely to approach the true question and chiefly to be relied upon.

The case of H. & T. C. Ry. Co. v. Odum, 53 Tex. 343, greatly relied on by the appellee, was an action of the second class above referred to, to recover damages for the location of a railroad in a street, where the fee was not in the plaintiff but in the state. It was controlled by the Constitution of 1869, which gave compensation only for property taken. The court held that "the regulation or enlargement of the use of the street, property of the state, by the Legislature, is not a taking of property within the meaning of the Constitution of 1869, although the lot owner may thereby suffer incidental or consequential inconvenience." It ought not to be necessary to say that this does not apply when the fee is in the person complaining, for then the state is not the owner of the entire estate in the soil, and the Legislature has no power to take or authorize the taking of that part of it which belongs to another.

In G., C. & S. F. Ry. Co. v. Eddins, supra, and in other cases following it too numerous to be cited, the change wrought by the present Constitution has been pointed out, and damages caused by railroads in streets have been allowed whether resulting from takings or not; but none of the cases in this court have decided that there is not a taking of private property by the construction and use of railroads in streets where the fee is privately owned.

In Rische v. Texas Transportation Co., 27 Tex. Civ. App. 33, 66 S. W. 324, such an opinion is expressed; but at the same time it is stated that the pleading did not properly show that the plaintiff owned the fee. The application for writ of error to this court presented an entirely different theory from any involved in this case.

In Settegast v. H. O. L. & M. P. Ry. Co., 38 Tex. Civ. App. 623, 87 S. W. 197, the case was discussed as if it were of the second class above mentioned, in which it was claimed that there had been a taking merely because of the appropriation of a street to railroad purposes, and not because the plaintiff owned the fee in the land actually appropriated. If such a fact existed in that case, there is nothing in the opinion to show that it was relied on or called to the attention of the Court of Civil Appeals.

In Gray v. Dallas Terminal Co., 13 Tex. Civ. App., at page 163, 36 S. W. 352, it is expressly shown that the lots were not invaded; and this is true also of Burton Lumber Co. v. City of Houston et al., 45 Tex. Civ. App. 363, 101 S. W. 825-826, stating the decision in the Settegast Case as we have explained it.

The facts alleged by the plaintiffs in this case, in addition to their claim based on their ownership of the fee, seem to be intended to present the contention that without regard to the fee their right to the use of the street for ingress and egress, light

and air, which is an incident of their ownership of abutting lots,
·is a right of property appurtenant to those lots, and that hence
the threatened inference with that right would constitute a taking of property in the constitutional sense. This contention is in
accord with the authorities holding the second view before mentioned, and with the intimation in Judge Stayton's opinion in
the Fuller Case, supra. It is contrary, we think, to the Odum
Case and to the opinions of the Courts of Civil Appeals in the
four cases above named. If the present Constitution, like former
ones, gave protection only against takings, we should be very
reluctant to agree to a construction that would deny compensation. But no construction we could adopt would deny compensation; the only question being whether or not it must be
made in advance. The words "damaged or destroyed" show the
purpose to secure compensation for losses not within the language
previously used, and evidently were intended to include effects
upon private property of public enterprises which might be held
not to constitute takings. The added words are inserted, not as
a construction, but as an extension of the scope of the language
previously used. It is therefore reasonably certain that the first
view stated above, as to what constitutes the taking of property,
was assumed in the framing of the new provision, and compensation was exacted for injuries which are not regarded as takings
within that view. Since the making of compensation in advance
is required for takings and not for other injuries, the several
words must be held to make an important distinction and not to
have been used out of abundant caution, only, in order to remove
all doubt as to the right to compensation. Hence the word
"taken" ought not to be held to include all cases that are covered
by the others, and we think the Courts of Civil Appeals have
correctly held, in the four cases last above mentioned, that those
kinds of injuries that result to those owning lots abutting on
streets but not owning the fee in the land in the streets from
railroads thereon are not the taking, but the damaging, of property. It is only in reference to that kind of property that the
argument has force that there is no provision for condemnation.
There is provision for the condemnation of land to be actually
occupied by the tracks of railroads and of every estate in it. For
the projectors of a public work to ascertain, and, if necessary,
condemn and pay in advance land actually to be invaded in the
enterprise, is a simple and easy task when compared with the
difficulty and uncertainty that would attend any course intended
to determine in advance all the consequential damages to result
to owners of property not actually touched, and this was probably
the very practical reason for the distinction in the Constitution.
Where the title of the lot owner embraces soil in the street to
be occupied by the railroad, the statute regulating condemnations
applies, and compensation can be made in one proceeding, not

Erie R. Co. *v.* Russell

only for the value of the land actually occupied, but for the consequences to the remainder of the lot.   But this is not true of land not to be occupied and used.

In the Odum Case, supra, there is an intimation that the destruction of a street might be so complete as to constitute a taking of the property in abutting lots.   Whether or not the exercise of the right of access and egress incident to ownership of abutting lots might be so completely prevented by uses made of streets as to constitute a taking of the lots in the sense of the present Constitution we need not now decide, since that which is here threatened is held to be a taking of those parts of the lots extending into the streets so far as the railroad would actually occupy them and that is enough to sustain the application for injunction.

For the same reason it is unnecessary that we discuss the other question whether or not an action for an injunction would lie under proper circumstances to prevent the damaging of property.

For the reason stated, the district court erred in dismissing the cause on demurrer, and the Court of Civil Appeals erred in sustaining that action.

Reversed and remanded.

ERIE R. CO. *v.* RUSSELL.

(Circuit Court of Appeals, Second Circuit, December 2, 1910.)

[183 Fed. Rep. 722.]

Commerce—Safety   Appliance   Act—Construction—Cars   Being "Used."—Under the safety appliance act of March 2, 1893, c. 196, § 2, 27 Stat. 531 (U. S. Comp. St. 1901, p. 3174), which makes it unlawful for any railroad company engaged in interstate commerce to haul or permit to be hauled or used on its lines, any car used in moving interstate traffic, not equipped with couplers coupling automatically by impact, as amended by Act March 2, 1903, c. 976, § 1, 32 Stat. 943 (U. S. Comp. St. Supp. 1909, p. 1143), which provides that the provision of the original and amendatory acts relating to couplers, etc., shall be held to apply to all cars used on any railroad engaged in interstate commerce, a car with a defective coupler, billed for the repair shop, but which was not sent there but was left on a track in ordinary use in a switch yard, to be repaired by the switchmen and then coupled to other cars, was being "used," within the meaning of the statute.

Railroads—Safety Appliance Act—Cars "Used" in Interstate Commerce.*—A car with a defective coupler which, although empty, was

---

*For the authorities in this series on the question whether or not cars were being used in interstate commerce on a particular occasion, see first foot-note of Chicago, etc., R. Co. *v.* United States (C. C. A.), 33 R. R. R. 83, 56 Am. & Eng. R. Cas., N. S., 83; second foot-note of Southern Flour & Grain Co. *v.* Northern Pac. R. Co. (Ga.), 23 R. R. R. 529, 46 Am. & Eng. R. Cas., N. S., 529.

Erie R. Co. v. Russell

brought into a station in an interstate train, left in the switch yards over night, and the next day taken out in another interstate train, was being used in interstate commerce within the meaning of the safety appliance act of March 2, 1893, c. 196, § 2, 27 Stat. 531 (U. S. Comp. St. 1901, p. 3174), not only while being moved in the trains, but also while in the yards.

Master and Servant—Action for Injury to Servant—Questions for Jury—Proximate Cause of Injury.—Plaintiff's intestate, who was a switchman employed by defendant railroad company in its yards, while engaged in repairing a defective coupler on a car standing on a switch track, was caught between such car and others which moved against it, and killed. Held, in an action to recover for his death, that the question whether the defective coupler was a proximate cause of his injury, so as to bring the case within the safety appliance act of March 2, 1893, c. 196, § 8, 27 Stat. 532 (U. S. Comp. St. 1901, p. 3176), was properly submitted to the jury, as was also the question of the contributory negligence of deceased under the evidence.

In Error to the Circuit Court of the United States for the Southern District of New York.

Action at law by Blanche Russell, administratrix of the estate of Harry Russell, deceased, against the Erie Railroad Company. Judgment for plaintiff, and defendant brings error. Affirmed

Writ of error to review a judgment in favor of the plaintiff in an action to recover damages for injuries resulting in the death of the plaintiff's intestate, Harry Russell, while employed by the defendant railroad company. There was evidence in the case sufficient to warrant the jury in finding the following facts which are especially relevant to the questions considered in the opinion:

The defendant railroad company is engaged in interstate commerce and owns a railroad extending from Port Jervis, N. Y., to Newburgh, N. Y., and also running into other states. Port Jervis is two or three miles east of the state line between New York and Pennsylvania. The defendant operates a local freight train between Newburgh and Port Jervis which, when running westerly, carries freight to stations on the road and picks up freight going to all points west, including points in other states. On the easterly trip western freight is carried to local points, and local freight is picked up for eastern points. On the afternoon of June 21, 1907, the car in question in this case was brought into Port Jervis in this train billed to the repair shops there. It had a defective coupler, the knuckle being gone. It was empty, and had been picked up at Greycourt, a station between Port Jervis and Newburgh. This train on said day carried freight going west of Port Jervis and to different states, and one of the cars bore the initials of the Boston & Maine Railroad. There was another

Erie R. Co. *v.* Russell

car in the train which was also in a crippled condition. The train, including the crippled cars, was left standing on a switch in the Port Jervis freight yards. Russell, the plaintiff's intestate, was one of the night switching crew in the yard. On this afternoon this crew had begun work drilling out and switching the cars from the different trains which had come into the yard from east and west. Before supper three cars had been placed on the No. 6 switch in the yard and left standing there. This switch had a slight grade. After supper the switching crew continued work and after some time ran the car in question attached to other cars upon said No. 6 switch. The intention of the switching crew was to repair the defective coupler and after repairing it to couple the train containing this car to the three cars aforesaid which had previously been left upon the switch. In backing up the train this car came in contact with the other three cars but was subsequently pulled away from them some five or six feet. The switching crew then started to look for a knuckle with which to repair the defective coupler. Knuckles were kept in various places in the yard, and the switchmen were accustomed to replace those found missing. Russell, the plaintiff's intestate, was the first to find one, and went in between the cars and attempted to adjust it in the coupling apparatus, but the pin would not fit and one of the other men went to look for another pin. Russell was holding the knuckle in place with his back to said three standing cars when, without any apparent cause, they moved silently down and caught and crushed him, inflicting the injuries from which he died. The car in question was taken the next day on the easterly trip of said local freight train and hauled to Goshen, N. Y.

F. B. Jennings, for plaintiff in error.
George A. Clement, for defendant in error.

Before LACOMBE, WARD, and NOYES, Circuit Judges.

NOYES, Circuit Judge (after stating the facts as above). The first question in the case is whether the acts of the defendant constituted a violation of the federal safety appliance act (Act March 2, 1893, c. 196, 27 Stat. 531 [U. S. Comp. St. 1901, p. 3174], as amended March 2, 1903, c. 976, 32 Stat. 943 (U. S. Comp. St. Supp. 1909, p. 1143), the relevant sections of which are printed in the footnote.*

---

*Act of 1893, § 2: "That * * * it shall be unlawful for any such common carrier to haul or permit to be hauled or used on its lines any car used in moving interstate traffic not equipped with couplers coupling automatically by impact, and which can be uncoupled without the necessity of men going between the ends of the cars."
Amendment of 1903, § 1: " * * * The provisions of * * * [the safety appliance act] * * * shall apply in all cases, whether

Erie R. Co. *v*. Russell

The first phase of this question is whether the car with the defective coupler was, at the time of the accident, in use within the meaning of the amended act. It is pointed out that the car was not being hauled at the time of the accident, but was standing upon a switch track for the insertion of the knuckle in the coupling apparatus, and it is contended that it was not then being used within the contemplation of the statute. We think upon the authority of Johnson *v*. Southern Pacific Co., 196 U. S. 1. 25 Sup. Ct. 158, 49 L. Ed. 363, that this contention is not well founded. The car with the defective coupler was not withdrawn from use. Although billed to the repair shop it was not sent there, nor was it sent to any place used, especially for making repairs. The insertion of the knuckle was a simple matter. The car was stopped only temporarily, and it was intended to couple it to the other cars as soon as repaired. These facts seem clearly to distinguish this case from those cases cited in the defendant's brief where accidents occurred when cars had been sent to repair shops or placed upon dead tracks used for repair purposes.

The second phase of the question of the application of the act is whether the car at the time of the accident was employed in interstate commerce. The car itself does not appear to have been used in any interstate business at the time in question. It was hauled empty from a New York point to Port Jervis in the same state, and the following day in like condition was hauled to another New York point. But the test of the application of the statute is the train rather than the car and we are of the opinion that there was evidence warranting a finding that the train in which this car moved into Port Jervis included other cars loaded with interstate shipments, and that the train in which it moved out of Port Jervis was of a similar character. Upon these facts it is held that the safety appliance act applies. U. S. *v*. International, etc., R. Co., 174 Fed. 638, 98 C. C. A. 302; Chicago, etc., R. Co. *v*. U. S., 165 Fed. 423, 91 C. C. A. 373. 20 L. R. A. (N. S.) 473; U. S. *v*. Wheeling, etc., R. Co. (D. C.) 167 Fed. 198; U. S. *v*. Erie R. R. Co. (D. C.) 166 Fed. 352. The fact that the accident occurred during switching operations, and not during either the regular western or eastern movement of the freight train, does not affect the application of the statute. Johnson *v*. Southern Pacific Co., supra; Wabash R. Co. *v*. U. S. 168 Fed. 1, 93 C. C. A. 393. Certainly if the car came into Port Jervis in the afternoon in an interstate train, and moved out of Port Jervis the next morning in another interstate train, the character of its use was not changed during the switching oper-

---

or not the couplers brought together are of the same kind, mark or type and the provisions and requirements hereof and of said act relating to train brakes, automatic couplers, grabirons, and the height of drawbars shall be held to apply to all trains, locomotives, tenders, cars and similar vehicles used on any railroad engaged in interstate commerce. * * * "

Erie R. Co. *v.* Russell

ations at night. Rosney *v.* Erie R. Co., 135 Fed. 311, 68 C. C. A. 155, is distinguished from the fact that in that case there was no proof of use in interstate commerce.

The second question of importance in₁ the case is whether the trial court properly submitted to the jury the question whether the presence of the defective coupler was a proximate cause of the accident. It is urged with much force that that which caused the injury to the plaintiff's intestate was the unexpected movement of the three cars—an act unrelated to, and independent of, the act of repairing the coupler. Indeed, were the question to be decided free of authority, a majority of the court would have difficulty in holding that the repair of the coupler was a part of a coupling operation, and bore such a relation to the impact of the cars that the necessity for such repairs was an efficient cause of the accident. But still the reason why Russell went to the place where he was injured was the defective coupler, and if he had not gone there the accident would not have occurred. Moreover, it appears that it was intended to couple the car with the defective coupler to the standing cars as soon as the coupler should be repaired. This being true, and in view of the desirability of uniformity in the decisions of the courts of the different circuits in interpreting this act, we feel it our duty to follow the decision of the Circuit Court of Appeals for the Eighth Circuit in Chicago, etc., R. Co. *v.* Voelker, 129 Fed. 522, 65 C. C. A. 226, 70 L. R. A. 264. The facts in that case are very similar to those appearing here. The person injured went upon the track to adjust a defective coupler in a car when, without warning, another car was shoved down upon him, inflicting the injuries complained of. It was held that the defective coupler was a proximate cause of the accident. In Chicago Junction R. Co. *v.* King, 169 Fed. 372, 94 C. C. A. 652, the facts even more closely resembled those appearing here, and a judgment for a person injured by reason of a defective coupler was affirmed, although the question of proximate cause does not appear to have been particularly considered. See, also, the decision of this court in Donegan *v.* Baltimore, etc., R. Co., 165 Fed. 869, 91 C. C. A. 555.

The third question in the case is whether the plaintiff's intestate was, as a matter of law, guilty of contributory negligence. An affirmative answer to this question requires the assumption that the cars which moved down and against Russell moved because he had failed in his duty to break or block them. But this assumption cannot be made. The cars may have been properly blocked and the blocks loosened by the impact with the car in question shortly before the accident. The question of contributory negligence was one for the jury.

The remaining questions raised by the defendant disclose no prejudicial error.

The judgment of the Circuit Court is affirmed.

ATLANTIC COAST LINE R. CO. *v.* DAHLBERG BROKERAGE CO.

(Supreme Court of Alabama, Nov. 22, 1910.   Rehearing Denied Jan. 12, 1911.)

[54 So. Rep. 168.]

Evidence—Parol Evidence Affecting Writings—Admissibility.—In an action against a carrier for failing to deliver freight to plaintiff, who was both consignor and consignee, parol evidence was admissible to show that provision in the bill of lading for delivery to "only" D. meant, according to usage by carriers and shippers, that D. was to be notified of the arrival of the goods, but that they were to be delivered only on plaintiff's order.

Carriers—Bills of Lading—Consignees.—A direction in a bill of lading to "notify" a named person shows that he is not intended as the consignee.

Carriers—Delivery Without Bill of Lading—Carrier's Liability.*—A carrier delivers goods at its peril to one without a bill of lading.

Carriers—Freight—Delivery.—To justify a delivery of freight without the consignor's order, the carrier must prove that the person to whom delivery was made was the true owner entitled to immediate possession.

Pleading—Conformity of Pleading and Proof—Purpose.—Conformity of proof to pleading is required to advise an adversary of what he will be called upon to answer, and to preserve a record as a protection against another proceeding involving the same rights.

Carriers—Delivery of Freight—Variance—Materiality.—In an action against a carrier for failing to deliver freight to plaintiff, who was both consignor and consignee, there was no material variance between allegation that plaintiff drew a draft on a proposed purchaser of the goods with bill of lading attached and proof that the draft was drawn in the name of plaintiff's principal.

Appeal and Error—Objections—Sufficiency.—It being necessary to submit a case to the jury under one count, a request for the affirmative charge on the whole case did not raise for review the question whether plaintiff could recover under another count.

Trial—Misleading Instruction.—In an action against a carrier by the consignor-consignee for wrongful delivery to the buyer, who rejected a draft with bill of lading attached, an instruction that the burden was on plaintiff to show that it reserved title to the goods was properly refused as tending to mislead, where the case presented no theory on which the buyer might have acquired rightful possession without title.

Trial—Instruction—Assumption as to Facts.—In an action against a carrier by the consignor-consignee for wrongful delivery to the

---

*See foot-note of Florence, etc., R. Co. *v.* Jensen (Colo.), 36 R. R. R. 771, 59 Am. & Eng. R. Cas., N. S., 771.

Atlantic Coast Line R. Co. *v.* Dahlberg Brokerage Co

buyer, who rejected a draft with bill of lading attached, an instruction that the burden was on plaintiff to show that it reserved title to the goods was properly refused as assuming a sale of the goods, where plaintiff claimed that there had been no executed agreement for sale.

Carriers—Freight—Delivery.†—A carrier cannot justify delivery of freight to a buyer who had rejected the consignor-consignee's draft with bill of lading attached, on the ground that the buyer had a contract with the consignor's principal for delivery of similar goods.

Trial—Instructions—Conformity to Evidence.—In an action against a carrier by the consignor-consignee of freight for wrongful delivery to a person who had rejected a draft with bill of lading attached, instructions that plaintiff could not recover if such person "bought" the goods on credit were properly refused, where there was no evidence tending to show more than an executory contract for the purchase of goods answering a certain description.

Carriers—Freight—Delivery—Ratification by Consignor.—Where a proposed buyer of goods rejected the consignor-consignee's draft with bill of lading attached, that after the carrier delivered the goods to the buyer the draft was again presented is not conclusive evidence of the consignor's ratification of the delivery.

Appeal from Circuit Court, Montgomery County; W. W. Pearson, Judge.

Action by Dahlberg Brokerage Company against the Atlantic Coast Line Railroad Company for delivering goods to the wrong person. Judgment for plaintiff, and defendant appeals. Affirmed.

The facts and pleadings sufficiently appear from the opinion. The following charges were refused to the defendant: (1) "The burden of proof is upon plaintiff to show that plaintiff reserved the title to the goods and the sale of them to Deans." (2) "The court charges the jury that if plaintiff, after knowing that the draft was rot paid by Deans, had it presented to Deans for payment a second time, then their verdict must be for the defendant." (3) "The court charges the jury that if plaintiff, with knowledge that the defendant had delivered the goods to Deans, had the draft presented to Deans for payment, their verdict must be for the defendant." (4) "If the jury believe from the evidence that Deans bought the goods on a credit, then plaintiff had no right to recover." (5) The general affirmative charge. (6) "The jury must believe, in order to find a verdict for the plaintiff, that Deans consented to the reservation of title to the goods by the plaintiff." (8) "If the jury believe that Deans

†For the authorities in this series on the subject of the duty of the carrier to deliver freight to the person entitled to receive it, see first foot-note of Chicago, etc., Ry. Co. *v.* Pfeifer & Bro. (Ark.), 32 R. R. R. 434, 55 Am. & Eng. R. Cas., N. S., 434.

Atlantic Coast Line R. Co. *v.* Dahlberg Brokerage Co

bought the goods on a credit, and that plaintiff did not reserve title to them, their verdict must be for the defendant."

John R. Tyson, for appellant.
J. Lee Holloway, for appellee.

SAYRE, J.   The complaint was reduced by the voluntary action of the plaintiff, and by rulings of the court not now in question, to counts 6 and 7.   Count 6 declared upon the wrongful delivery of plaintiff's goods by the defendant carrier to one Chas. Deans.   Count 7 declared upon defendant's failure or refusal to deliver to plaintiff.   The bill of lading which evidenced the contract of carriage between the parties provided that the defendant was to make delivery to "only" Chas. Deans.   In the complaint this collocation of letters was averred to have been employed by the parties as meaning "order notify," and the court properly received in evidence the bill of lading, and along with it the testimony of witnesses, familiar with the usage obtaining in the transaction of business between shippers and carriers, by which this sign or technical collocation, not in general use, was shown to have a meaning in accordance with the averment. Mouton *v.* L. & N. R. R. Co., 128 Ala. 537, 29 South. 602.   The direction in a bill of lading to "notify" a named person shows that such person is not intended as a consignee.   Otherwise the direction would mean nothing.   Moore on Carriers, 170.   The meaning of the bill of lading, as explained by the testimony, was that Deans was to be notified of the arrival of the goods at destination, but that they were to be delivered only to plaintiff's order.   Plaintiff was both consignor and consignee.   The sale was to be a sale for cash; at least, that is what the vendor understood it was to be.   In pursuance of this understanding and purpose, plaintiff drew upon Deans, bill of lading attached, for the price.   Deans refusing to pay, the draft and bill of lading were returned to plaintiff.   Nevertheless defendant delivered the goods to Deans.   The carrier delivers at its peril goods to one without a bill of lading.   So far no doubt arises as to plaintiff's right to maintain the action.   But it appeared that in the effort to make a sale and in the shipment of the goods plaintiff was acting as the agent of the Armstrong Packing Company under the following conditions: The Armstrong Company shipped its goods to plaintiff company for distribution in the latter's territory.   Plaintiff shipped the particular goods in question, with a view of delivery to Deans, out of the Armstrong Company's stock in plaintiff's warehouse upon receipt of an order from the Armstrong Company's traveling salesman.   Plaintiff company passed on the credit of proposed buyers, exercising its own judgment in filling orders and accounting to the Armstrong Company, and receiving a commission of 2 per cent. on sales made by it. On these facts the appellant contends that the Armstrong Com-

Atlantic Coast Line R. Co. *v.* Dahlberg Brokerage Co

pany alone could maintain an action for the loss resulting from the delivery of the goods to Deans. A number of cases are cited in which the question was whether the carrier should respond to the consignor or consignee, but they are without influence, for here the plaintiff is both. Certainly the carrier is discharged from liability when it surrenders property, taken for transportation, to the true owner, for that is not a matter of choice. But, to justify a delivery without the order of the consignor, the carrier assumes the burden of proving that the person to whom delivery has been made was the true owner having the right of immediate possession. Moore on Carr. 156. "The rule is that the depositary is bound to redeliver or restore the chattels bailed to the bailor, and that the bailor may recover the goods of his bailee without proving his right of property in them." Riddle *v.* Blair, 148 Ala. 461, 42 South. 560. This rule applies to the common carrier, and the carrier must deliver according to the shipper's order or the terms of the bill of lading, unless the true owner has interposed and asserted his rights. Moore on Carr., supra; Hutch. on Carr., § 750. This disposes of a number of assignments of error in accordance with the rulings of the trial court.

In count 6 "plaintiff avers that it drew a draft on May 21, 1909, through the Montgomery Bank & Trust Company, with said bill of lading thereto attached, and sent the said draft with said bill of lading attached to the People's Bank at Troy, Ala., for collection." Then follows an averment that Deans failed to pay, and that defendant delivered the goods to him notwithstanding he had so failed and had not the bill of lading. The evidence was that the plaintiff drew the draft in the name of the Armstrong Packing Company. It is insisted that this constituted a material and fatal variance. The purpose of the rule requiring correspondence between pleading and proof is that the opposite party may be advised of what he will be called upon to answer and to preserve a record as a protection against another proceeding involving the same rights. Bowie *v.* Foster, Minor, 264. At this time nothing more is insisted upon than substantial conformity. The averment that the bill had been drawn by the Armstrong Company was not material to a statement of plaintiff's cause of action, nor was it descriptive of what was material. The material fact was that defendant had delivered to Deans goods consigned to plaintiff notwithstanding he had no bill of lading. The averment as to which the variance is alleged was the averment of a fact evidential of the material fact otherwise sufficiently averred. The circumstantial particularity was unnecessary. The case was as well stated without it. The reason of the rule did not require that the mere circumstance be proved with liberal exactness, or, indeed, at all. The case would be different, of course, if the suit had been upon the draft as·for a failure to accept or pay.   As for the point here taken, the general charge was well refused to the defendant.

Again, it is insisted that the fact that plaintiff through its agent presented its bill of lading to defendant at Troy, the place to which the goods were consigned, demanding delivery of the goods, and that defendant then and there failed or refused to deliver, as averred in count 7, did not constitute a conversion by the defendant, because it had before that time delivered the goods to Deans.   Without considering the sufficiency of this excuse, the question here made may be properly disposed of on the ground that it could only arise under count 7 of the complaint. It did not affect count 6, which averred a conversion by the delivery to Deans.   It being necessary, on considerations already stated, to submit to the jury the case alleged in count 6, the affirmative charge on the whole case did not raise the question whether plaintiff could recover on count 7.   It was not raised otherwise, and need not now be considered.

Charge 1, refused to the defendant, was so refused without error.   The language of this, and several other of the charges, was misleading to some extent, for that it spoke of the reservation of title by the plaintiff, thereby seeming to imply necessity for the consideration of the case as one in which plaintiff might have parted with the possession to Deans while retaining the title.   No phase of the evidence presented a case in which Deans may have acquired a rightful possession without the title.   But apart from this, and without laying undue stress upon it, the charge assumed a sale of the goods to Deans; whereas, plaintiff's case, finding strong if not undisputed support in the evidence, was that there had been no executed agreement of sale, because, though Deans may have supposed he was buying on credit, the minds of the parties to that transaction were not agreed to that effect, and that its goods had been delivered out of the possession of its agent and bailee without its consent and against its will.

Some charges requested by defendant set up, in different shapes, the proposition that plaintiff could not recover if Deans "bought" the goods on credit.   The giving of these charges would have been justified upon the ground only that if Deans bought the goods, as predicated in the charges, he became the true owner.   Deans' testimony was that he had "bought" the goods on credit.   He leaves it in doubt whether he supposed he was buying the goods from the Armstrong Company directly or from the plaintiff.   He based his conclusion that he had bought upon facts which included no delivery—upon what had passed between him and the traveling salesman, and upon either one or the other of two additional facts, viz., that plaintiff's agreement to the terms of the order to the salesman, as he understood it, was to be implied from the subsequent negotiation and the

Atlantic Coast Line R. Co. *v.* Dahlberg Brokerage Co

shipment of the goods, or that when he received the goods from defendant he supposed they might have come from the Armstrong Company directly and in accordance with his understanding as to terms. Neither party to the suit produced the correspondence which constituted the negotiation between plaintiff and Deans, and they differed diametrically as to its meaning and effect. Conceding the truth of Deans' testimony in its entirety, he had at best acquired, not the title to the specific goods, but an executory contract for the purchase of goods which should answer a certain description. In advance of delivery no title passed. The only delivery shown was a delivery of goods in respect to which plaintiff had rights and responsibilities which could not be changed without its assent. A delivery to Deans of goods held by plaintiff for disposition on its own terms and responsibility, such delivery being unauthorized by plaintiff, was not to be justified on the ground that Deans had a contract with the Armstrong Company for the delivery of goods of similar kind and quality. The testimony, then, as to the terms on which Deans bought the goods, amounted to nothing, and might well have been ignored. Defendant's right to deliver to him depended upon the conditions of the plaintiff's delivery to it— whether it thereby became bailee for plaintiff or for Deans—and that was the sole question in the case. If the word "bought" in these charges be taken as the equivalent of an executed contract of purchase, they were abstract. If taken according to the meaning attached to it by the witness Deans, the charges required the determination of the rights of the parties upon an immaterial issue.

After defendant had delivered the goods to Deans, and after the draft had been returned to plaintiff unpaid, the bill of exceptions shows that it was again "sent to the bank of Troy for collection." Charges were requested by defendant to the effect that, if plaintiff had the draft presented to Deans a second time, plaintiff could not recover. If plaintiff with knowledge of the facts ratified the delivery to Deans, it could not hold defendant company liable. But that is not the statement of the charges. That statement is, in substance, that a second presentation constituted a ratification. Whether it did depended upon the intention. It may have been made for the relief of defendant. At best, this fact was some evidence of ratification, not ratification per se. These charges were properly refused.

What has been said will indicate our opinion on all questions raised.

The judgment will be affirmed.

Affirmed.

Dowdell, C. J., and Anderson and Evans, JJ., concur.

Central of Georgia Ry. Co. v. Sims.

(Supreme Court of Alabama, Nov. 24, 1910.)

[53 So. Rep. 826.]

Commerce—Interstate Commerce—Federal Regulation.—A contract for the transportation of freight from one state to another relates to interstate commerce, and is subject to federal regulation.

Courts—Jurisdiction—Enforcement of Federal Statutes.—A federal statute regulating interstate commerce will be recognized and enforced by state courts.

Courts—Jurisdiction—Enforcement of Federal Statutes.—Interstate Commerce Law (Act Feb. 4, 1887, c. 104, 24 Stat. 386 [U. S. Comp. St. 1901. p. 3169]) § 20, as amended by Act June 29, 1906, c. 3591, § 7, 34 Stat. 593 (U. S. Comp. St. Supp. 1909, p. 1163), making the initial carrier of an interstate shipment liable for loss of or injury thereto, caused by any connecting carrier, will be enforced in a state court.

Constitutional Law—Due Process of Law—Statutes—Construction.—Interstate Commerce Act (Act Feb. 4, 1887, c. 104, 24 Stat. 386 [U. S. Comp. St. 1901, p. 3169]) § 20, as amended by Act June 29, 1906, c. 3591, § 7, 34 Stat. 593 (U. S. Comp. St. Supp. 1909, p. 1163). making the initial carrier of an interstate shipment liable for loss of or injury thereto caused by a connecting carrier, and permitting the initial carrier to recover from the connecting carrier causing the loss or injury the amount it may be required to pay to the owner of the property, as evidenced by any receipt or judgment, makes a judgment against the initial carrier only prima facie evidence against the connecting carrier, and it is not invalid as depriving the connecting carrier of its property without due process of law

Constitutional Law—Party Entitled to Raise Constitutional Questions.—Under the rule that one not within a class affected by a statute may not attack its constitutionality, an initial carrier in an action against it, based on Interstate Commerce Act (Act Feb. 4 1887, c. 104, 24 Stat. 386 [U. S. Comp. St. 1901, p. 3169]) § 20, as amended by Act June 29, 1906, c. 3591, § 7, 34 Stat. 593 (U. S. Comp. St. Supp. 1909, p. 1163), making the initial carrier liable for loss of or injury to interstate shipments caused by any connecting carrier, may not question the validity of the provision permitting it to recover from the connecting carrier for the loss sustained by it.

Carriers—Contracts—Enforcement.—A bill of lading of an interstate shipment. which contains clauses repugnant to the Interstate Commerce Act (Act Feb. 4, 1887, c. 104, 24 Stat. 386 [U. S. Comp. St. 1901, p. 3169]) § 20, as amended by Act June 29, 1906, c. 3591. § 7, 34 Stat. 593 (U. S. Comp. St. Supp. 1909, p. 1163), is not thereby entirely vitiated, but the holder thereof may recover for a failure to safely transport the goods.

Central of Georgia Ry. Co. *v.* Sims

Carriers—Contracts—Exemption from Liability.—A carrier may not by contract limit the liabilities imposed on it by Interstate Commerce Act (Act Feb. 4, 1887, c. 104, 24 Stat. 386 [U. S. Comp. St. 1901, p. 3169]) § 20, as amended by Act June 29, 1906, c. 3591, § 7, 34 Stat. 593 (U. S. Comp. St. Supp. 1909, p. 1163), making the initial carrier of an interstate shipment liable for any loss or injury thereto caused by any connecting carrier, because of the rate charged for the transportation.

Appeal and Error—Harmless Error—Erroneous Rulings on Pleadings.—The error if any, in striking out a bad plea which cannot be amended without departing from the defense therein attempted, instead of disposing of it on demurrer, is not prejudicial.

Appeal from Circuit Court, Russell County; A. A. Evans, Judge.

Action by J. E. Sims against the Central of Georgia Railway Company. From a judgment for plaintiff, defendant appeals. Affirmed.

The pleadings and the issues sufficiently appear in the opinion. The general charge of the court, to which exception is reserved, is as follows: "I charge you, gentlemen of the jury, that if you believe from the evidence in this case that there was an unreasonable delay in the transportation in the said car load of peaches from Seale, Ala., to the city of New York, and that by reason of said unreasonable delay said peaches were damaged, then the defendant in this case would be liable to the plaintiff for whatever damages he sustained by reason of said unreasonable delay in the transportation ,of said peaches, regardless of where, or on what part of the route, or on what line of connecting carriers the damage may have occurred."

G. L. Comer, for appellant.
Glenn & de Graffenried, for appellee.

ANDERSON, J. This was an action for the breach of a contract of shipment, whereby the defendant undertook to transport a number of crates of peaches from Seale, Ala., to New York City, and the breach assigned, in varying forms, was the failure to transport them in such a way as to prevent loss, decrease, or destruction of the value of same, and that the injury or damage to the peaches occurred on defendant's line or the connecting lines over which it undertook to transport them to New York. The special pleas from 2 to 6, inclusive, do not deny that the damage or injury occurred, after the issuance of the bill of lading and before a delivery of the peaches or before they were ready for delivery, but each of them attempts to set up certain clauses of the contract of shipment limiting the defendant's liability. The principal point insisted on being that

Central of Georgia Ry. Co. *v.* Sims

the contract limited the defendant's liability for loss, damage, or destruction on its own line, and that said loss, damage, or destruction occurred after the peaches had been safely delivered to another carrier. These provisions, or some of them, might be effective and binding on the parties, under our decisions as to interstate shipments prior to the enactment of what is known as the Carmack amendment to section 20 of the interstate commerce law of the United States (Act Feb. 4, 1887, c. 104, 24 Stat. 386 [U. S. Comp. St. 1901, p. 3169]), passed June 29, 1906 (Act June 29, 1906, c. 3591, § 7, 34 Stat. 593 [U. S. Comp. St. Supp. 1907, p. 906, Supp. 1909, p. 1163]), and might be now binding as to intrastate shipments, but for section 5546 of the Code of 1907. McNeill *v.* Atlantic Coast Line R. Co., 161 Ala. 319, 49 South. 797; Jones' Case, 89 Ala. 376, 8 South. 61; Landers' Case, 135 Ala. 510, 33 South. 482.

The subject-matter of the present contract, the transportation of goods from one state to another, was an act of interstate commerce, and was subject to federal cognizance and regulation. Southern R. Co. *v.* Harrison, 119 Ala. 539, 24 South. 552, 43 L. R. A. 385, 72 Am. St. Rep. 936. And when federal statutes have been enacted governing and regulating interstate commerce, they will be recognized and enforced by the courts of this and other states. Harrison's Case, supra; M. & O. R. R. Co. *v.* Dismukes, 94 Ala. 131, 10 South. 289, 17 L. R. A. 113; Southern Pac. Co. *v.* Crenshaw, 5 Ga. App. 675, 63 S. E. 865.

So much of the interstate commerce act as amended, and as is necessary to be set out, reads as follows: "That any common carrier, railroad or transportation company receiving property for transportation from a point in one estate to a point in another state shall issue a receipt or bill of lading therefor and shall be liable to the lawful holder thereof for any loss, damage, or injury to such property caused by it or by any common carrier, railroad, or transportation company to which such property may be delivered or over whose line or lines such property may pass, and no contract, receipt, rule, or regulation shall exempt such common carrier, railroad, or transportation company from the liability hereby imposed: provided, that nothing in this section shall deprive any holder of such receipt or bill of lading of any remedy or right of action which he has under the existing law. That the common carrier, railroad, or transportation company issuing such receipt or bill of lading shall be entitled to recover from the common carrier, railroad, or transportation company on whose line the loss, damage, or injury shall have been sustained the amount of such loss, damage, or injury as it may be required to pay to the owners of such property, as may be evidenced by any receipt, judgment, or transcript thereof." While this act is enforceable generally by the interstate Commerce Commission, the above-quoted part has been recognized

Central of Georgia Ry. Co. v. Sims

and enforced by the courts, state and federal. Smeltzer v. St. Louis R. Co. (C. C.) 158 Fed. 649; Riverside Mills v. A. C. L. R. R. Co. (C. C.) 168 Fed. 987; So. Pac. Co. v. Crenshaw, 5 Ga. App. 675, 63 S. E. 865; L. & N. R. R. Co. v. Scott, 133 Ky. 724, 118 S. W. 990; Galveston, H. & S. R. R. Co. v. Piper Co. (Tex. Civ. App.) 115 S. W. 107. So, too, has it been held that this enactment was within the power of Congress and not unconstitutional. Appellant contends that the last part of the above quotation, that is so much thereof as permits the initial carrier to recover from the connecting carrier, upon whose line the loss or damage occurred, the amount of such loss or damage as it was required to pay to the owner, "as may be evidenced by any receipt, judgment, or transcript thereof," is violative of the Constitution because it deprives the carrier, causing the loss or damage, of due process, in that it makes the receipt, judgment or transcript conclusive evidence against him when he was not a party to the cause between the owner and the initial carrier. If they were made conclusive instead of presumptive or prima facie evidence, there might be merit in the contention. Zeigler v. S. & N. R. R. Co., 58 Ala. 594. The act does not say, that the receipt, judgment, or transcript should be conclusive evidence, and if it is reasonably susceptible of being construed as meaning prima facie or presumptive evidence, a construction upholding its constitutionality should be given. Smeltzer v. St. Louis R. R. Co., supra. Moreover, one not within a class affected by the statute cannot attack its constitutionality. Grenada Lumber Co. v. Mississippi, 217 U. S. 433, 30 Sup. Ct. 535, 54 L. Ed. ——. "One who would strike down a statute as unconstitutional must show that it affects him injuriously, and actually deprives him of constitutional right." Southern R. Co. v. King, 217 U. S. 524, 30 Sup. Ct. 594, 54 L. Ed. ——. This defendant would be benefited rather than burdened by this much of the act and could not complain of this constitutional defect, if one existed, but which we do not think is the case.

The case of McNeill v. Atlantic Coast Line R. R. Co., 161 it contained clauses contracting against liability in certain instances, and which were repugnant to the federal statute, this defect did not vitiate the entire contract of shipment so as to preclude the holder from covering for a failure to safely transport the goods. The law does not prohibit the contract to ship, but merely prohibits the carrier from exempting itself from liability by any contract, receipt, rule, or regulation. Each of the special pleas invoked certain clauses of a contract, exempting the defendant from liability and relied upon the contract as an exemption; whether or not the loss occurred upon another line, or whether or not the exemption from liability was due to a failure to make a claim by the consignee within 30 days, or whether or not the contract was based upon the rate of freight

Central of Georgia Ry. Co. v. Sims

charged, each of the pleas referred to and relied upon a contract made at the time of shipment as exempting it from liability, and which was forbidden by law, and void. We do not understand the interstate law as exempting carriers from the influence of the above-quoted part of the statute, because of any particular rate charged, and the plea, which attempts to escape liability, because of the rate charged, did not except the defendant from the influence of so much of the act as renders the contract, exempting from liability, void.

Whether or not the defendant should have resorted to a demurrer rather than by motion to strike (section 5322 of the Code of 1907, and cases noted in citation), we need not decide. For if the court committed the technical error of striking, it was error without injury. The pleas relied upon a contract of exemption, which was void, and in order to become of any benefit to the pleader, there would have to be an abandonment of the contract relied upon, and the amendment would have to be a departure from the original pleas. The rule is, that although a plea may be improperly eliminated, if it could not be amended so as to make it a good plea without departing from the defense therein attempted, the error as to the manner of getting rid of it would be error without injury. Sunflower Co. v. Turner Co., 158 Ala. 191, 48 South. 510, 132 Am. St. Rep. 20; Ryall v. Allen, 143 Ala. 222, 38 South. 851. It is true these two cases deal with the sustaining of inapt or general demurrers, but the same rule should obtain as to striking pleas. In other words, when a plea is bad, and is not capable of being amended, so as to make it a good plea, without departing from the defense therein attempted, it matters not whether it was stricken upon motion or by sustaining a general or inapt demurrer thereto, the trial court will not be reversed for getting rid of same. See, also, Rooks v. State, 83 Ala. 79, 3 South. 720.

The case of McNeill v. Atlantic Coast Line R. R. Co., 161 Ala. 319, 49 South. 797, fully sustains appellant's contention that contracts similar to the one here considered have been enforced in this state, but it should be noted that the contract in said case was made in May, 1905, and the amendment to the federal statute, above discussed, was not enacted until June 29, 1906.

There was no error in the oral charge of the court as excepted to by the appellant.

The judgment of the circuit court is affirmed.

Affirmed.

DOWDELL, C. J., and MAYFIELD and SAYRE, JJ., concur.

ST. LOUIS SOUTHWESTERN RY. CO. *v.* UNITED STATES.

(Circuit Court of Appeals, Fifth Circuit, December 20, 1910. On Rehearing, January 10, 1911.)

[183 Fed. Rep. 770.]

Railroads—Safety Appliance Act—Several Violations.—Where several cars, each without the requisite appliances required by Safety Appliance Act March 2, 1893, c. 196, 27 Stat. 531 (U. S. Comp. St. 1901, p. 3174), are hauled by a carrier in interstate commerce at one and the same time, there are as many distinct violations of the act as there are cars hauled not properly equipped, for every one of which the statutory penalty is recoverable.

Railroads—Safety Appliance Act—Violations—Nature of Proceedings.—Since proceedings against a railroad company to recover penalties for violations of Safety Appliance Act March 2, 1893, c. 196, 27 Stat. 531 (U. S. Comp. St. 1901, p. 3174), are civil in their nature, the government is only required to establish its case by a preponderance of the evidence.

In Error to the District Court of the United States for the Western District of Texas.

Action by the United States against the St. Louis Southwestern Railway Company. Judgment for the United States, and defendant brings error. Affirmed. Petition for rehearing denied.

Before PARDEE and SHELBY, Circuit Judges.

S. P. Ross, .for plaintiff in error.

Chas. A. Boynton and *P. J. Doherty,* for the United States.

PER CURIAM. The judgment of the District Court is affirmed.

On Rehearing.

The hauling by any carrier engaged in interstate commerce of a car not furnished with the safety appliances required by the laws of the United States is a violation of the statute, which entitles the United States to recover a penalty of $100; and as this penalty attaches for each and every such violation, it is recoverable for each and every car not furnished with the requisite safety appliances hauled in violation of the act.

Whether the hauling be of several cars by one act or by several acts is immaterial, so that if several cars, each without the requisite appliances, are hauled by the carrier at one and the same time, there are several distinct violations, for each and every of which the penalty is due and recoverable. See United States *v.* St. Louis & S. W. Ry. (No. 1,895 of this court, recently decided) 183 Fed. ——.

On reason and weight of authority it is considered that actions

Atlantic Coast Line R. Co. v. State

to recover the statutory penalties for violation of the safety appliance law (Act March 2, 1893, c. 196, 27 Stat. 531 [U. S. Comp. St. 1901, p. 3174]) are so far civil in their nature that the strict construction applicable in criminal proceedings is not required, and the United States may recover upon the preponderance of evidence, and the trial judge may in proper cases direct a verdict.

The petition for rehearing herein is denied.

ATLANTIC COAST LINE R. CO. v. STATE.

(Supreme Court of Georgia, Dec. 16, 1910.)

[69 S. E. Rep. 725.]

Statutes—Enactment—Presumption of Legality.—A duly enrolled act, properly authenticated by the regular presiding officers of both houses of the General Assembly, approved by the Governor and deposited with the Secretary of State as an existing law, will be conclusively presumed to have been enacted in accordance with constitutional requirements; and it is not permissible to show, by the legislative journals or other records, that it did not receive on its passage a majority vote of all the members elected to each house, or that there was any irregularity in its enactment.

Railroads—Constitutional Law—Equal Protection of Laws—Regulation—Construction of Statutes—"Railroad Company."*—An act provided "that all railroad companies are hereby required to equip and maintain each and every locomotive used by such company to run on its main line after dark with a good and sufficient headlight which shall consume not less than 300 watts at the arc with a reflector not less than 23 inches in diameter, and to keep the same in good condition." It also provided that "any railroad company violating this act in any respect" should be liable to indictment and a prescribed punishment, and that "this act shall not apply to tram

---

.*For the authorities in this series on the subject of the constitutionality of statutes prescribing penalties to compel railroads to perform their duties, etc., see foot-note of Missouri Pac. Ry. Co v. Nebraska (U. S.), 36 R. R. R. 79, 59 Am. & Eng. R. Cas., N. S., 79; foot-note of Downey v. Northern Pac. Ry. Co. (N. Dak.), 35 R. R. R. 598, 58 Am. & Eng. R. Cas., N. S., 598; Thweat v. Atlantic Coast Line R. Co. (S. Car.), 35 R. R. R. 431, 58 Am. & Eng. R. Cas., N. S., 431; Tracy v. New York, etc., R. Co. (Conn.), 34 R. R R. 105, 57 Am. & Eng. R. Cas., N. S., 105.

For the authorities in this series on the subject of the police powers of a state over railroads, see People v. Erie R. Co. (N. Y.), 36 R. R. R. 587, 59 Am. & Eng. R. Cas., N. S., 587; Downey v. Northern Pac. Ry. Co. (N. Dak.), 35 R. R. R. 598, 59 Am. & Eng. R. Cas., N. S., 598.

Atlantic Coast Line R. Co. v. State

roads, mill roads and roads engaged principally in lumber or logging transportation in connection with mills." Laws 1908, p. 50. Held:

(a) The term "railroad company" employed in the act includes natural persons as well as corporations.

(b) The act is not void, as being violative of the "equal protection" clauses of the state and federal Constitutions because it exempts from its operation tram roads, mill roads, and roads engaged principally in lumber or logging transportation in connection with mills.

(c) Even if receivers of railroads are not within the operation of the act, it would not for this reason be violative of the equal protection clauses referred to in the preceding note.

Constitutional Law—Railroads—Due Process of Law — Police Power—Headlights on Trains.*—The act does not violate the "due process" clauses of the state and federal Constitutions because its enforcement will require a loss of property to the defendant in doing away with the headlights on locomotives now in use, and cause the defendant to incur expense in equipping its locomotives with the headlights required by the act.

(a) The act is not violative of the "due process" clauses of the state and federal Constitutions because it requires an arc electric headlight which shall consume "not less than 300 watts at the arc and with a reflector not less than 23 inches in diameter," on the ground that it deprives the defendant "of its own right to make contracts and manage its own business."

(b) The act was passed in the legitimate exercise of the police power of the state, and is not void on the ground that its requirements are unreasonable.

(c) Nor does the act violate the "due process" clauses of the state and federal Constitutions on the ground that it contains no emergency clause, and absolutely and without exception makes the railroad company guilty of a crime if it operated one of its engines on its main line after dark without the required headlight.

Commerce—Interstate Commerce—Equipment of Trains.†—The act does not violate the "commerce clause" of the federal Constitution on the ground that it would require at the state line a change of headlights on locomotives doing an interstate business, if other states required headlights of a kind different from that prescribed

---

†For the authorities in this series on the subject of state interference with interstate commerce, see foot-note of Detroit, etc., R. Co. v. State (Ohio), 36 R. R. R. 625, 59 Am. & Eng. R. Cas., N. S., 625; last foot-note of Davis v. Cleveland, etc., Ry. Co. (U. S.), 36 R. R. R. 92, 59 Am. & Eng. R. Cas., N. S., 92; foot-note of Missouri Pac. Ry. Co. v. Kansas (U. S.), 35 R. R. R. 728, 58 Am. & Eng. R. Cas., N. S., 728; Yazoo, etc., R. Co. v. Greenwood Grocery Co. (Miss.), 35 R. R. R. 417, 58 Am. & Eng. R. Cas., N. S., 417.

Atlantic Coast Line R. Co. v. State

by the act in question, although such change might involve some loss of time and expense on the part of the railroad company.

(Additional Syllabus by Editorial Staff.)

Words and Phrases—"Company."—The word "company" does not necessarily mean a corporation, but may mean a firm, partnership, or individual.

Statutes—Construction—Penal Laws.—Penal laws should be construed strictly, but not so as to defeat the obvious intent of the Legislature.

Statutes—Construction—Intent of Legislature.—In construing a statute, whether civil or penal in nature, the intent of the Legislature should be sought for, keeping in view the evil and the remedy.

(Syllabus by the Court.)

Certified questions from Court of Appeals.

Action by the State against the Atlantic Coast Line Railroad Company. Judgment for the State, and defendant brought error to the Court of Civil Appeals. On certified questions. Questions answered.

The Court of Appeals certified to this court for its instruction thereon the following questions of law, the determination of which is deemed necessary to a proper decision of the above-stated case:

"(1) Is what purports to be an act of the General Assembly, approved August 17, 1908, and found in the published Acts of 1908, pp. 50, 51, commonly known as the 'headlight law,' a law of this state, as against the specific contention presented in this case that it did not receive on its alleged passage a majority of the votes of all the members elected to the Senate, within the purview of and according to the provisions of article 3, § 7, par. 14, of the Constitution of this state (Civ. Code 1895, § 5777), and that it so affirmatively appears from the journals of the General Assembly, especially the Senate Journal for 1908, pp. 132, 163, 203, 204, 339, 340, 700, and 701?

"(2) Is said act void as being in contravention of article 1, § 1, par. 3, of the Constitution of Georgia (Civ. Code 1895, § 5700), which provides: 'No person shall be deprived of life, liberty or property, except by due process of law'—as against the contention of the defendant [a railway corporation] 'that the said enactment requires defendant to discontinue the use of property already furnishing a sufficient and adequate headlight, forces defendant to abandon the use of material adequate and sufficient for the production of safe and sufficient headlight, compels defendant to purchase expensive machinery for the purpose of generating a specific current of electricity as a means for lighting headlights, and compels defendant to purchase a reflector of a size designated by the statute.' thus not only depriving the defendant of the right to use property already owned, but

Atlantic Coast Line R. Co. v. State

compelling it to purchase property of a given description, and depriving it of its own right to make contracts and manage its own business?

"(3) Is said act void because it violates the provisions of article 1, § 1, par. 2, of the Constitution of Georgia (Civ. Code 1895, § 5699), which provides that 'Protection to person and property is the paramount duty of government, and shall be impartial and complete,' as against the contention that 'the said act does not apply equally to all persons and corporations in the same class or similarly situated; said act makes an unreasonable and arbitrary classification, whereby it excludes from the operation of said act persons owning and operating railroads, and likewise excludes from the operation of said act receivers operating railroads, even though said receivers operate fast trains through cities, towns, and thickly settled districts of the state; nor does said act apply to "tram roads, mill roads, or roads engaged principally in lumber or logging transportation in connection with mills," even though locomotives thereon, for a whole or part of their route, may be operated at a fast schedule, and through thickly populated districts?'

"(4) Is said act void because it violates the provisions of the fourteenth amendment to the Constitution of the United States, which provides that 'No state * * * shall deprive any person of life, liberty, or property without due process of law,' on the alleged ground 'that the said act requires defendant to discontinue the use of property lawfully acquired and lawfully held, although furnishing sufficient and adequate headlight, forces defendant to abandon the use of lamps, reflectors, headlights, and material lawfully held, although adequate and sufficient for the production of safe and sufficient headlight and reasonably adapted to the protection of persons and property, whether on the track or on the locomotive and cars, and compels defendant to purchase expensive machinery for the purpose of generating a specific current of electricity, and to purchase a reflector of a size designated by the statute, thereby depriving defendant of its right to make contracts and to manage its own business'?

"(5) Is said act void because it violates the provisions of the fourteenth amendment to the Constitution of the United States, which declares: 'No state * * * shall deny to any person within its jurisdiction, the equal protection of the laws'—on the alleged ground 'that the said headlight law does not apply equally to all persons and corporations in the same class or similarly situated; said act makes an unreasonable and arbitrary classification, whereby it excludes from the operation of said act persons owning and operating railroads, and likewise excludes from the operation of said act receivers operating railroads, even though said receivers operate fast trains through cities, towns, and thickly settled districts of the state; nor does said act apply to tram

Atlantic Coast Line R. Co. *v.* State

roads, mill roads, or roads engaged principally in lumber or logging transportation in connection with mills,' even though the locomotives used thereon for a whole or part of their route, may be operated at fast speed, and through thickly populated districts?

"(6) Is said act void because repugnant to article 1, § 8, par. 3, of the Constitution of the United States, which provides that 'Congress shall have power to regulate commerce with foreign nations, among the states and with Indian tribes' on the alleged ground 'that the enforcement of said statute and said statute itself interferes with and regulates interstate commerce, hinders and delays the running of locomotives having no such headlight as is required by said statute, although said locomotives are lawfully engaged in hauling cars and trains for interstate commerce, and makes it unlawful for defendant or other companies operating interstate railways to use, in the state of Georgia, locomotives having no headlight of the kind described in said alleged enactment, although said locomotives are lawfully used up to the state line, all with the result of delaying interstate commerce and rendering it impossible for interstate railroad companies crossing the Georgia line to conduct their interstate business with usual customary, and proper dispatch'?

"(7) The plaintiff in error contends that the act in question was never passed by both houses of the General Assembly, according to the method prescribed in the Constitution and set out in the first question above—the specific contention being that it passed the lower House regularly in the form now appearing in the printed Acts; that in the Senate committee to which it was referred reported adversely to the passage of the bill; that the Senate disagreed to the report of the committee and the bill went to second reading; that at the third reading a substitute was offered and adopted; the bill then passed by substitute, 40 senators voting for it in this shape; the bill was transmitted to the House for concurrence in the substitute; the House refused to concur; thereafter the Senate took up the bill for the purpose of receding from the substitute; and the motion to recede prevailed by a vote of 18 to 12. No further action appears. The defendant at the trial in the court below offered to set up by special plea in bar that the substitute passed by the Senate was materially different in its provisions from the bill as passed by the House, and to prove this fact by the exhibition and introduction in evidence of a certified copy of the substitute as filed in the office of the Secretary of State. Was the special plea setting up this fact subject to be stricken on general demurrer thereto, and was the certified copy of the substitute admissible in evidence for the purpose of supplementing, varying, or explaining the entries in the journal of the Senate, and would it, if it had been admitted and had been established that the bill as passed in the Senate

Atlantic Coast Line R. Co. v. State

by substitute was materially different from what it was as originally passed by the lower House, have impeached the validity
of the act, under the circumstances recited above?

"(8) It appears from the record that the defendant was engaged in interstate commerce; that it failed to equip one of its
locomotives engaged in that interstate commerce with a headlight
of the standard required by the act in question. Was the defendant, as to this locomotive, while so engaged in interstate
commerce (it being run partly in this state and partly in South
Carolina), exempt from the provisions of the act, on the ground
that to apply the law to the operation of this locomotive, as so
engaged would be violative of the provision of the Constitution
of the United States quoted above, conferring upon Congress
exclusive power to regulate interstate commerce?

"(9) Where it appears from the proof that the defendant's
locomotives were, prior to the passage of the act, equipped with
oil-burning headlights, or with electric headlights different from
that prescribed by the act in question, is it any defense to a
prosecution under the act that these headlights have in the experience of the defendants and other railroad companies usually
proved reasonably safe and efficient (there being proof, however, that headlights of the prescribed standard are more efficient), and that to substitute electric headlights of the standard
prescribed would entail expense of greater or less amount; the
contention of the defendant being that to enforce the act under
the circumstances would amount to depriving the defendant of
its property without due process of law, in violation of the fourteenth amendment to the Constitution of the United States, and
in violation of article 1, § 1, par. 3, of the Constitution of this
state, because it renders the value of the old headlights less,
or totally destroys it, and entails upon the defendant the expenditure of large sums of money, and deprives the defendant of the
right to regulate its own business and affairs, and causes it to
submit to an arbitrary and unreasonable regulation thereof?"

McDaniel, Alston & Black and *J. R. Lamar*, for plaintiff in
error.

J. C. C. Black, Jr., Sol., and *T. S. Felder*, for the State.

HOLDEN, J. 1. The act referred to in the questions propounded
by the Court of Appeals, known as the "headlight law," was duly
deposited in the office of the Secretary of State as an enrolled
act of the General Assembly, after having been duly signed by
the President of the Senate and the Speaker of the House of
Representatives, and approved by the Governor. The provision
of the Constitution referred to in the first question propounded
is as follows: "No bill shall become a law unless it shall receive a majority of the votes of all the members elected to each
house of the General Assembly, and it shall, in every instance, so

appear on the journal." Civ. Code, § 5777. An act with the status above named cannot be attacked, as being invalid under the constitutional provision above quoted, by showing that the journal of the Senate affirmatively shows that it did not receive on its passage the vote of a majority of all of the members elected to that body. When an enrolled act is signed by the presiding officers of both houses, approved by the Governor, and deposited in the office of the Secretary of State, it will be conclusively presumed that the measure was properly put to a vote in both houses and that it received a constitutional majority; and the court will not upset the act because the journals of the houses happened to show that it did not receive a majority of the votes of either or both branches of the Legislature. 36 Cyc. 971 (G, b). The presiding officer of each branch of the General Assembly, and the Governor, are sworn officers of the state, and it is to be presumed that an enrolled act would not have been signed by these officials, and thereby authenticated as being a valid law, unless the act on its passage had received the number of votes which the Constitution requires in order to enact it. It will be deemed more likely that the subordinate officers of the General Assembly, in the performance of clerical duties, should have made a mistake in recording on the journals the proceedings had by the respective legislative bodies, than that the sworn presiding officers of these bodies should have signed a duly enrolled act as having been lawfully enacted, when it did not in fact receive the number of votes required by the Constitution in order to insure its passage. In the case of De Loach v. Newton, 134 Ga. 739, 68 S. E. 708, it was held: "If an enrolled act of the Legislature was duly signed by the President of the Senate and the Speaker of the House, and approved by the Governor, and deposited in the office of the Secretary of State, it was not competent to attack its validity on the ground that the legislative journals showed that the bill originated in the House, was there passed by a constitutional majority, and transmitted to the Senate, where it was amended and passed by a constitutional majority, and then transmitted to the House, where the Senate amendment was concurred in, but failed to show that this was done by a constitutional majority." See, also, Whitley v. State. 134 Ga. 758, 68 S. E. 716.

If an act is not invalid under the provisions of the Constitution above quoted when the legislative journals fail to show that it received a constitutional majority, it would not be invalid when the journals affirmatively show that it did not receive such majority. If it were permissive to look to the legislative journals to ascertain what occurred with respect to the passage of an act, after it had been duly enrolled, signed, approved, and deposited with the Secretary of State as an existing law, an affirmative showing on the journal that a measure did not receive the

Atlantic Coast Line R. Co. v. State

requisite constitutional majority would be no more fatal to the validity of the act than a failure of the journal to show that it did receive such majority, where the attack is based on a constitutional provision that no bill shall become a law unless it shall receive a majority of all the members elected to each house of the General Assembly, "and it shall, in every instance, so appear on the journal."

The first question propounded by the Court of Appeals must be answered in the affirmative. In answering this question, having ruled that an enrolled act duly signed by the presiding officers of both houses, approved by the Governor, and deposited with the Secretary of State, is conclusively presumed to be valid law, so far as its enactment is concerned, the special plea referred to in the seventh question was subject to be stricken on the general demurrer thereto, and the certified copy of the substitute referred to in the seventh question was not admissible in evidence "for the purpose of supplementing, varying, or explaining the entries in the journal of the Senate." This ruling makes it unnecessary to determine whether or not the journal of the Senate shows that the act in question was, or was not, in fact passed in conformity to the above-quoted provision of the Constitution.

2. The full text of the title and the body of the act referred to in the questions propounded to us is as follows:

"An act to require all railway companies in the state to equip and maintain each and every locomotive used with sufficient electric headlight, to prescribe a punishment for the failure to so equip, and for other purposes.

"Section 1. Be it enacted by the General Assembly of Georgia, and it is hereby enacted by authority of the same, that all railroad companies are hereby required to equip and maintain each and every locomotive used by such company to run on its main line after dark with a good and sufficient headlight which shall consume not less than three hundred watts at the arc, and with a reflector not less than twenty-three inches in diameter, and to keep the same in good condition. The word main line as used herein means all portions of the railway line not used solely as yards, spurs and side tracks.

"Section 2. Be it further enacted, that any railroad company violating this act in any respect shall be liable to indictment as for a misdemeanor in any county in which the locomotive not so equipped and maintained may run, and on conviction shall be punished by fine as prescribed in section 1039 of the Code of 1895.

"Section 3. Be it further enacted, that this act shall go into effect July 1, 1909.

"Section 4. Provided this act shall not apply to tram roads, mill roads and roads engaged principally in lumber or logging transportation in connection with mills.

"Section 5. Be it further enacted, that all laws and parts of laws in conflict with this act be and the same are hereby repealed.

"Approved August 17, 1908." (Acts 1908, pp. 50, 51.)

The act requires "all railroad companies" to equip every locomotive used by "such company to run on its main line" after dark with a light of the kind named, and provides that "any railroad company" violating the act shall be liable to indictment and to be punished by fine as prescribed in Pen. Code, § 1039. Does the term "railroad company" include a natural person, so that the latter would be subject to indictment if such natural person owned and operated a railroad and failed to comply with the provisions of the act? In construing the term "railroad company," we should look to all the provisions of the act, and give proper consideration to the object intended to be accomplished by the act. Section 4 of the act provides: "Provided this act shall not apply to tram roads, mill roads and roads engaged principally in lumber or logging transportation in connection with mills." It should be observed that in making this exception the act does not say that the owner or operator of the roads designated should be excepted, but simply provides that "this act" shall not apply to such "roads," indicating that the purpose of the act was to make the requirement in reference to the use of the named headlights on all other railroads, regardless of whether owned by a corporation or natural persons. The evident purpose was to except certain roads, but not to make any exception in favor of any particular owners of other roads. The object of the act was to require certain headlights on all railroads except those of a named class, and the term "railroad company" was intended to include natural persons as well as corporations. The word "company" does not necessarily mean a corporation. It may mean a firm or partnership. 8 Cyc. 389. If it includes a firm or partnership of two or more individuals, why should it not include one individual? Pen. Code, § 1, par. 4, provides: "The singular or plural number shall each include the other, unless expressly excluded."

Penal laws should be construed strictly, but they should not be so construed as to defeat the obvious intention of the General Assembly. In construing an act, whether of a civil or penal nature, the intention of the General Assembly should be sought for, keeping in view the evil and the remedy. The evil against which protection is sought is the operation of engines without the headlight required by the act. The purpose of the law was to require named headlights on engines on the main line of all railroads except those of a specified character, and it was not the intention to make this requirement of corporations and companies and make no such requirement of an individual owning and operating a railroad. Civ. Code. § 2199, provides that the terms railroad "corporation" and "company" used in the article in which such section appears shall include in their meaning any individual or individuals owning and operating railroads. Much of the law of this state pertaining to the operation of railroads, including the right of condemnation of private property, what is familiarly known as the "blow post" law, and requirements as to the furnishing of heat and light in railroad trains, are embraced in this article. We think the word "company" in the act in question was used in the same sense referred to in Civ. Code, § 2199, as including "individuals." In this connection, see State v. Stone, 118 Mo. 388, 24 S. W. 164, 25 L. R. A. 243, 40 Am. St. Rep. 388; Chicago, etc., Co. v. Garrity, 115 Ill. 155, 3 N. E. 448; Lewis v. Northern Pacific Ry. Co., 36 Mont. 207, 92 Pac. 469; Singer Mfg. Co. v. Wright, 97 Ga. 114, 25 S. E. 249, 35 L. R. A. 497.

(b) The act does not violate the equal protection clauses of the state and federal Constitutions because it provides: "Provided this act shall not apply to tram roads, mill roads and roads engaged principally in lumber or logging transportation in connection with mills." The roads to which the act does not apply do not serve the public generally, but their work is mainly that connected with lumber mills. Their principal business is not the transportation of passengers and freight for the public, but involves work for private enterprises in a small territory. The danger of operating such roads without proper safety appliances is not so great as that attending the operation of ordinary railroads doing a general passenger and freight business for the public. These differences furnish a reasonable basis for requiring a headlight of a certain kind on engines on main lines on ordinary railroads, and not requiring such lights on engines on roads of the kind excepted. The latter form an entirely separate and distinct class of railroads from the former, and the act cannot be said to make an arbitrary classification. N. Y., N. H. & H. R. v. New York, 165 U. S. 628, 17 Sup. Ct. 418, 41 L. Ed. 853; Missouri & N. A. R. Co. v. State (Ark.), 121 S. W. 930; People v. N. Y., N. H. & H. R. Co., 55 Hun, 409, 608, 8 N. Y. Supp. 673; Chicago. I. & L. Ry. Co. v. Railroad Commissioners of Indiana (Ind.), 90 N. E. 1011.

Conceding, without deciding, that receivers of railroads are not within the provisions of the act, we do not think this fact would make the act void as a violation of the equal protection clauses of the state and federal Constitutions. A receiver appointed by a court is one of its officers, and in the absence of any statute imposing a duty on a receiver of a railroad thus appointed, he must handle the property placed in his charge in accordance with the instructions of the court appointing him. His possession and operation of the road are those of the court. Should the court, through its receiver, have possession of a rail-

•   Atlantic Coast Line R. Co. v. State

road whose engines were not equipped with the required headlight, or purchase other engines, the presumption is that the court
—a branch of the government co-ordinate with the General
Assembly—would conform to the policy of the state as declared by the General Assembly, in the exercise of the police
power, and equip the engines with such headlights as it had by
law required of railroad companies.   A railroad is never retained
in possession of and operated by the court longer than is necessary.   The court does not permanently operate railroads; on
the contrary, it only operates them for a short time and from
necessity.   If the act applies to a receiver, and if a receiver were
appointed by the court for a railroad whose engines were not
equipped with the required headlights, how could such a receiver
operate the engines without such lights without subjecting himself to numerous prosecutions and fines, should the court require him to operate the engines in violation of the penal laws
of the state?   If it were a railroad engaged in serving the public,
the latter might suffer to a great extent if the road was not
operated until all the engines were equipped with the required
headlights.   The act provided that it should not go into effect
until a specified date, and thus time was given to railroad companies to equip their engines in accordance with its provisions.
But after the act went into effect, if a receiver were appointed
for a railroad whose engines were not thus equipped, no time is
allowed within which the receiver might comply with the act;
and if the act applies to receivers, they would become subject to
criminal prosecutions the day they were appointed, if they operated engines without the prescribed equipment in disregard of
the act.   The court would dispose of a railroad under receivership as soon as it was proper and practicable to do so.   Those
to whom the receiver delivered it, under a contract of purchase
or otherwise, would be subject to numerous prosecutions under
the act in question, should they not equip the engines as required
by that law, and the public might seriously suffer if the road
should cease operations until its engines could be thus equipped.
It is to be presumed that the court would not allow the road to
be disposed of before its engines were equipped with headlights
as required by the act.   It is not to be presumed that it would
dispose of the road to another when it was in such condition that
the one acquiring it would violate the penal law of the state by
immediately operating it.

Receivers, and courts through receivers, do not construct or
buy railroads; but their ultimate aim is to get rid of the ones of
which they are in possession.   Courts, through receivers, never
operate railroads except from necessity, and when they do so
operate them it is only for a limited time.   If the courts take
possession of a road whose engines are not equipped as required
by the "headlight law," the courts should not require its receiver

Atlantic Coast Line R. Co. v. State

to cease operating the road until the engines should be so equipped, thereby causing inconvenience and suffering to the public. In such cases, the court should yield to the necessity of the situation as it existed when thrust upon it, by immediately operating the road, where possible, to subserve the public convenience and requirements, and impose upon the receiver the duty of equipping the engines as rapidly as possible in accordance with the policy of the law, so as to put the road in a condition where its operation can be continued by those who take charge of it when disposed of by the court without involving a violation of law on their part. We think there was a reasonable basis for a requirement that railroad companies should equip their engines operated on main lines as prescribed in the act, without making such requirements applicable to receivers of railroads.

The answer to the third and fifth questions must be in the negative.

3. All property is held subject to the police power of the state. The determination by the railroad company that the reflector and the light in use by it constituted an adequate light cannot be conclusive on the General Assembly, which has the authority to exercise the police power of the state and in the interest of public safety to declare it inadequate. It is a matter of great importance for the protection of persons and property in the train attached to a locomotive, the persons on the locomotive, persons and property on the track, and persons and property on other trains with which a collision may be had, that there should be an adequate headlight on such locomotive. The General Assembly, in the exercise of the police power of the state, has the right to require adequate headlights on such engines; and if in conformity to the requirements of such law the railroad company is compelled to do away with the headlights already in use by it, and substitute others therefor at its own expense, there is no taking of property without just compensation, in violation of the due process clauses of the state and federal Constitutions. In such a case, there is no taking of property. The due process clauses are not intended to limit the right of the state to properly exercise the police power in the enhancement of the public safety. The fact that the railroad company will, in order to equip its engines with the required headlights, be forced to do away with the reflectors and lights which it has in use is only incidental to a compliance with the police regulation and requirement made in the act, and which is a valid and reasonable requirement. Damages cannot be required by one because he incurs expense in obeying a police regulation enacted for the common welfare and safety of the public. See, in this connection, State v. St. Paul, etc., Ry. Co., 98 Minn. 380, 108 N. W. 261, 120 Am. St. Rep. 581; 1 Thompson on Corp., § 449; C., B. & Q. R. Co. v. Chicago, 166 U. S. 226, 17 Sup. Ct. 581, 41 L. Ed. 979; C., B. & Q. Ry. Co. v.

Atlantic Coast Line R. Co. *v.* State

Drainage Commissioners, 200 U. S. 561, 26 Sup. Ct. 341, 50 L. Ed. 596, and authorities cited in the opinion; Bacon *v.* Boston & M. R. R. (Vt.), 76 Atl. 128 (19).

The act provides that every engine used on a main line after dark shall be equipped "with a good and sufficient headlight, which shall consume not less than 300 watts at the arc and with a reflector not less than 23 inches in diameter." It is not required that the light shall consume more than the specified number of watts at the arc, nor that the reflector shall be exactly a particular size. A light consuming more than 300 watts at the arc and a reflector greater than 23 inches in diameter would be within the provisions of the act. The act requires "a good and sufficient headlight." In the exercise of the police power the General Assembly had the right to prescribe that such light should be an electric light. The fact that the railroad company is prevented from providing a light produced in some way other than by an electric current is no violation of the due process clause, "by depriving it of its own right to make contracts and manage its own business." In McGhee on Due Process of Law, p. 345, it is said: "Although freedom and the liberty to contracts are fundamental rights within the guaranties of the Constitution, they may be limited by the state in the exercise of the police power, in the interest of public safety, health, or morals, or, under certain conditions, in the exercise of the legislative power merely." Also see Freund on Police Power. § 499.

It is to be presumed that the General Assembly satisfied itself that the light power to be used in order to insure the public safety was the one required, and in the exercise of the police power it had the right to require the use of such light. The fact that in obeying the law the railroad company is deprived of the right to use a light other than an electric headlight, or to use an electric light below a specified intensity, or a reflector of less than a designated size, does not violate the due process clause of the state and federal Constitutions. The Legislature has the power to require such a headlight as is best promotive of the public safety, if the requirement is a reasonable one. An act requiring in general terms a light adequate for such purposes would be very indefinite, and would give rise to frequent disputes as to whether or not the law had been observed. A jury in one instance might declare the light in use inadequate, while another jury might declare it adequate, and the user of the light might be uncertain as to whether or not he was complying with the law. In Atchison, Topeka, etc., Railroad *v.* Matthews, 174 U. S. 96, 102, 19 Sup. Ct. 609, 612, 43 L. Ed. 909, the Supreme Court of the United States said: "If, in order to accomplish a given beneficial result—a result which depends on the action of a corporation—the Legislature has the power to prescribe a specific duty and punish a failure to comply therewith by a penalty,

Atlantic Coast Line R. Co. v. State

either double damages or attorney's fees, has it not equal power to prescribe the same penalty for failing to accomplish the same result, leaving to the corporation the selection of the means it deems best therefor? Does the power of the Legislature depend on the method it pursues to accomplish the result? As individuals we may think it better that the Legislature prescribe the specific duties which the corporations must perform; we may think it better that the legislation should be like that of Missouri, prescribing an absolute liability, instead of that of Kansas, making the fact of fire prima facie evidence of negligence; but clearly as a court we may not interpose our personal views as to the wisdom or policy of either form of legislation. It cannot be too often said that forms are matters of legislative consideration; results and power only are to be considered by the courts." In Freund on Police Power, § 34, it is said: "Assuming that several measures are equally efficient to avert danger to health or safety, it would still seem to be within the legislative power to select one method and require its adoption; for it is easier to enforce uniform police regulations than a great variety of measures, the efficiency of each of which would be a question of fact in each particular case."

Requiring a light by virtue of which those on an engine can see a designated distance ahead is practically done by requiring that the light shall be of a certain intensity and behind a reflector of not less than a given size. The act declares that the light which is considered proper for the public safety must be of a kind required. The General Assembly is presumed to have acted after due deliberation and investigation, and after finding that the light proper for the public safety must be of a kind prescribed. The courts cannot say that an electric light, and one of the intensity provided, with a reflector of the size named, is not one necessary for the public safety; nor can we say that the requirement that such a light shall be used on locomotives is an unreasonable requirement, although the act in preventing the use of lights other than an electric light affects the right of the company to contract for any other kind of light. The act is not void for the alleged reason that the government is undertaking to manage the company's business and interfere with its right to contract. In 1 Thompson on Corporations (2d Ed.) § 425, it is said: "The Legislature may exercise its discretion within wide limits in its regulations of corporations under this police power. If the statute appears to be within the apparent scope of such power, it is not for the courts to inquire into its wisdom and policy, or to substitute their discretion or judgment for that of the Legislature. * * * The correct doctrine undoubtedly is that it is for the Legislature to determine the exigency, or the occasion, for the exercise of this power; but it is clearly within the jurisdiction of the courts to determine what

Atlantic Coast Line R. Co. v. State

are the subjects upon which this power is to be exercised, and the reasonableness of that exercise." And in section 486 the same author says: "The position of the courts in passing on the validity of statutes enacted by the Legislature in the exercise of this police power is regarded by them as both delicate and embarrassing. Courts should be, and are, slow to pronounce judgment upon what is purely legislature discretion. It is sufficient to stay the hands of the courts if the exercise of this power by the Legislature is reasonable. And in judging of its reasonableness courts will not look closely into mere matters of judgment, where there may be a reasonable difference of opinion. The courts will assume that this power will always be exercised by the Legislature with the highest discretion; and the rule is that, where the legislative expression is clear and unequivocal, a clear case should be made to authorize an interference by the courts upon the ground of unreasonableness. The courts should and do proceed with the utmost caution, and hold such regulations void only when they clearly pass beyond the limits of the police power and infringe upon rights secured by the federal law. This power rests solely within the legislative discretion, inside constitutional limits. It is for the Legislature to determine when the public safety or welfare requires the exercise of this power, and the courts can interfere only when such exercise conflicts with the Constitution. With the necessity, wisdom, or policy of such legislation they have nothing to do."

The need for the exercise of the police power upon any given subject is a matter in the discretion of the Legislature. The exercise of this power must be reasonable, and the question as to whether or not it is reasonable is one for the courts. We cannot say that the exercise of the power in this instance was unreasonable. In Holden v. Hardy, 169 U. S. 366, 397, 18 Sup. Ct. 383, 390, 42 L. Ed. 780, the following language of the Supreme Court of Utah was approved: "Though reasonable doubts may exist as to the power of the Legislature to pass a law, or as to whether the law is calculated or adapted to promote the health, safety, or comfort of the people, or to secure good order or promote the general welfare, we must resolve them in favor of the right of that department of government." The Legislature has the right to prevent railroad companies from contracting for and using a light not proper to be used for the public safety; and if the light required is one proper for this purpose, the Legislature has the right to require its use, notwithstanding this prevents the use of another kind of light, if the requirement of the act is reasonable—and we cannot say that its requirements are unreasonable.

The act is not void on the ground that it absolutely and without exception makes the company guilty of a crime when it fails to equip its locomotives with the required headlights and operates them on its main line without such headlights. It is contended that the act is void for the reason that in case of accident or other unforeseen cause if the light which the company had provided in conformity with the requirements of the act were injured or destroyed, no provision is made allowing the company to operate its engine without the required headlight to a repair shop, or to the place where another engine could be obtained, without violating the act and becoming liable to punishment thereunder. Every statute must be construed to have a reasonable intendment, and be construed in connection with other statutes. While we will not undertake to detail instances in which the company would be guilty of no offense under the act in question while operating an engine without the required headlight, an act will not be construed so as to require the performance of an impossible act, if any other construction can be legitimately given it. See Southern Ry. Co. *v.* Atlanta Sand & Supply Co., 135 Ga. 36, 68 S. E. 807. The statutes requiring railroad companies to erect blow posts 400 yards on either side of public crossings and to blow the whistle on approaching such crossings, to furnish light and water for passengers, and other statutes imposing duties on railroad companies, and providing a penalty for violation thereof, contain no emergency clauses; and there are many statutes making the commission of specific acts crimes, without providing that there are circumstances under which a technical violation of the letter of the act would constitute no crime; but we are not prepared to hold that such acts are void for this reason. As to whether in any particular instance a person charged with violating a criminal statute has a good defense thereto must depend upon the particular facts in each case.

We do not think that the act is violative of the due process clauses of the state and federal Constitutions, and our answer to the second, fourth, and ninth questions must be in the negative.

4. The commerce clause of the federal Constitution is a limitation on, but is not a destruction of, the police power of the states. The police power has never been surrendered by the states. A railroad company driving an engine engaged in interstate commerce through the territory of this state, with a headlight which endangers the lives and property of the people, cannot claim that under the commerce clause of the federal Constitution it is not subject to reasonable police regulations of this state requiring an adequate headlight for the protection of the lives and property of the people. The act in question does not restrict or prohibit interstate commerce. It is an exercise of the police power, designed to protect persons and property in this state, and does not prohibit or regulate interstate commerce. The statute is not directed against interstate commerce. So far as the act affects interstate commerce, it is in aid thereof. It protects the persons and property on trains brought from another state into this state,

Atlantic Coast Line R. Co. v. State

as it also does persons and property not so brought; and it is the duty of the state to protect the former as well as the latter. One of the highest duties of government is the protection of the lives and property of the people. To the exercise of the police power, all rights of natural persons and corporations are subject.

If an engine doing an interstate business should come into this state from another state, or go out of this state into another state, when such other state had a law requiring a headlight on the engine other than an electric light and a reflector of a size different from that required by the act in question, the mere fact that this would necessitate changes of lights and reflectors, thereby causing expense, loss of time and inconvenience, would not for this reason make the requirement of the act an unlawful interference with interstate commerce. People v. N. Y., N. H. & H. R. Co., 55 Hun, 409, 608, 8 N. Y. Supp. 673; N. Y., N. H. & H. R. Co. v. New York, 165 U. S. 628, 17 Sup. Ct. 418, 41 L. Ed. 853. Many acts requiring trains doing an interstate business to stop at stations and public crossings, and to run at not exceeding a specified rate of speed, have been held not to be violative of the commerce clause. Such acts, however, necessarily to some extent prevent such trains from making the time they would make, but for such stops and slowing up of speed, and also of necessity involve some expense. A violation of the commerce clause would not exist merely because some loss of time, expense, and inconvenience was caused the railroad company in making the necessary changes in its headlight equipment in order to meet the requirements of different states, nor because such changes involved some additional expense. Such expenses and loss of time would impose no substantial burden on interstate commerce. The act is in no sense a regulation of interstate commerce. If every law enacted in the exercise of the police power, with a design to enhance the public safety, be declared void because it to some extent affected interstate commerce, many of the most salutary police regulations of the states must fall. In C. & P. T. Co. v. Manning, 186 U. S. 238, 22 Sup. Ct. 881, 46 L. Ed. 1144, it was declared: "Courts always presume that a Legislature in enacting statutes acts advisedly and with full knowledge of the situation, and they must accept its action as that of a body having full power to act, and only acting when it has acquired sufficient information to justify its action." Every presumption is to be indulged in favor of the constitutionality of an act. There is no legislation by Congress making any requirements with respect to the kind of headlights to be used on engines engaged in interstate business.

The act in question is not violative of the commerce clause of the federal Constitution, and our answer to the sixth and eighth questions is in the negative. All the Justices concur.

ATLANTIC COAST LINE RAILROAD COMPANY, Plff. in Err., v.
RIVERSIDE MILLS.

(Argued October 19, 20, 1910.   Decided January 3, 1911.)

[31 Sup. Ct. Rep. 164.]

Commerce—Federal Power Generally.—No question with reference to the power of Congress to enact a regulation of interstate commerce can arise if the regulating act be one directly applicable to such commerce, not obnoxious to any other provision of the Federal Constitution, and reasonably adapted to the purpose by reason of legitimate relation between such commerce and the rule provided.

Commerce—Federal Power—Regulating Liability of Connecting Carriers.—The imposition upon an interstate carrier voluntarily receiving property for transportation from a point in one state to a point in another state, of liability to the holder of the bill of lading for a loss anywhere en route, with a right of recovery over against the carrier actually causing the loss, which is made by the act of February 4, 1887 (24 Stat. at L. 379, chap. 104, U. S. Comp. Stat 1901, p. 3154), § 20, as amended by the act of June 29, 1906 (34 Stat at L. 584, 595, chap. 3591, U. S. Comp. Stat. Supp. 1909, pp. 1149, 1166), in spite of any agreement or stipulation limiting liability to its own line, is a valid regulation of interstate commerce.

Constitutional Law—Freedom to Contract—Regulating Liability of Connecting Carriers.—The liberty of contract secured by U. S. Const., 5th Amend., was not unconstitutionally denied by the enactment by Congress, in the exercise of its power under the commerce clause, of the Carmack amendment of June 29, 1906, to the act of February 4, 1887, § 20, by which an interstate carrier voluntarily receiving property for transportation from a point in one state to a point in another state is made liable to the holder of the bill of lading for a loss anywhere en route, in spite of any agreement or stipulation to the contrary, with a right of recovery over against the carrier actually causing the loss.

Constitutional Law—Due Process of Law—Regulating Liability of Connecting Carriers.—The property of the initial carrier is not taken in violation of U. S. Const., 5th Amend., to pay the debt of an independent connecting carrier whose negligence may have been the sole cause of a loss, by the Carmack amendment of June 29, 1906, to the act of February 4, 1887, § 20, under which an interstate carrier voluntarily receiving property for transportation from a point in one state to a point in another state is made liable to the holder of the bill of lading for a loss anywhere en route, in spite of any agreement or stipulation to the contrary, with a right of recovery over against the carrier actually causing the loss, since the liability of the receiving carrier which results in such a case is that of a principal, for the negligence of his own agents.

Atlantic C. L. R. Co. *v.* Riverside Mills

Costs—Attorneys' Fees—Under Act to Regulate Commerce.—The attorneys' fee taxable as a part of the costs under the act of February 4, 1887, § 8, where the cause of action is the doing of something made unlawful by some provision of the act, or the omission to do something required by the act, and there is a recovery of damages sustained in consequence of any such violation of the act, may not be taxed to the successful plaintiff in an action by a shipper against an initial carrier for a loss on a connecting line, in which the carrier's liability is dependent upon the Carmack amendment of June 29, 1906, since the cause of action is the loss of property which is in no way traceable to the violation of any provision of the statute.

In Error to the Circuit Court of the United States for the Southern District of Georgia to review a judgment holding an initial carrier in an interstate shipment liable to the shipper for a loss on a connecting line. Affirmed.

See same case below, 168 Fed. 990.

Statement by Mr. Justice Lurton: ·

This was an action to recover the value of goods received by the Atlantic Coast Line Railroad at a point on its line in the state of Georgia for transportation to points in other states. The agreed statement of facts showed that the goods were safely delivered by the Atlantic Coast Line Railroad to connecting carriers, and were lost while in the care of such carriers, and the question is whether the initial carrier is liable for such loss.

The stipulated facts showed that the goods were tendered to the Atlantic Coast Line Railroad, and through bills of lading demanded therefor, which were duly issued, as averred, on the dates named in the petition. That the goods so received were forwarded over the lines of the receiving road and in due course delivered to a connecting carrier engaged in interstate shipment for continuance of the transportation. It was also stipulated "that the Riverside Mill made constant and frequent shipments over the Atlantic Coast Line, and had a blank form of receipt, like the attached, marked 'A,' which the Riverside Mill filled out, showing what goods it had loaded into cars, and the name of the consignee; said receipt containing a stipulation that the shipment is 'per conditions of the company's bill of lading,' and that the Atlantic Coast Line Railroad Company, on said receipts prepared by the Riverside Mill, issued, for each of the sh'pments hereinbefore referred to, bills of lading on forms like that attached, marked exhibit 'B.'"

Upon the reverse side of the bill of lading were certain conditions, one of which was that "no carrier shall be liable for loss or damage not occurring on its portion of the route." The tenth clause thereof was in these words:

Atlantic C. L. R. Co. *v.* Riverside Mills

"This bill of lading is signed for the different carriers who may engage in the transportation, severally, but not jointly, each of which is to be bound by and have the benefits of the provisions thereof, and in accepting this bill of lading the shipper, owner, and consignee of the goods, and the holder of the bill of lading, agree to be bound by all its stipulations, exceptions, and conditions, whether printed or written."

The court below, upon this state of facts, instructed a verdict for the plaintiff, upon which there was a judgment for the amount of the verdict, and, upon motion of the plaintiff, an attorney's fee of $100 was ordered to be taxed as part of the costs in the case. Thereupon error was assigned, and this writ of error sued out by the railroad company.

Messrs. Joseph R. Lamar, Benjamin D. Warfield, Charles H. Moorman, and *Henry Lane Stone,* for plaintiff in error.

Assistant to the Attorney General *Kenyon,* Attorney General *Wickersham, John Maynard Harlan,* and *Lewis W. McCandless,* as amici curiæ.

Messrs. Alexander Akerman, Charles Akerman, and *R. J. Southall,* for defendant in error.

After making the above statement, Mr. JUSTICE LURTON delivered the opinion of the court:

The goods of the defendants in error were lost by a connecting carrier to whom they had been safely delivered. Though received for a point beyond its own line, and for a point on the line of a succeeding carrier, there was no agreement for their safe carriage beyond the line of the plaintiff in error, but, upon the contrary, an express agreement that the initial carrier should not be liable for "a loss or damage not occurring on its own portion of the route." Such a provision is not a contract for exemption from a carrier's liability as such, but a provision making plain that it did not assume the obligation of a carrier beyond its own line, and that each succeeding carrier in the route was but the agent of the shipper for a continuance of the transportation. It is therefore obvious that at the common law an initial carrier under such a state of facts would not be liable for a loss through the fault of a connecting carrier to whom it had, in due course, safely delivered the goods for further transportation. Ogdensburg & L. C. R. Co. *v.* Pratt, 22 Wall. 123, 22 L. ed. 827; Myrick *v.* Michigan C. R. Co., 107 U. S. 102, 27 L. ed. 325, 1 Sup. Ct. Rep. 425; Southern P. R. Co. *v.* Interstate Commerce Commission. 200 U. S. 536, 554, 50 L. ed. 585, 593, 26 Sup. Ct. Rep. 330. Liability is confessedly dependent upon the provision of the act of Congress regulating commerce between the states, known as the Carmack amendment of June 29, 1906 (34 Stat. at L. 584, 595, chap. 3591, U. S. Comp. Stat. Supp. 1909. pp. 1149, 1166). The 20th section of the act of February 4, 1887 (24 Stat. at L.

Atlantic C. L. R. Co. *v.* Riverside Mills

379, chap. 104, U. S. Comp. Stat. 1901, p. 3154), as changed by the Carmack amendment, reads as follows:

"That any common carrier, railroad, or transportation company receiving property for transportation from a point in one state to a point in another state shall issue a receipt or bill of lading therefor, and shall be liable to the lawful holder thereof for any loss, damage, or injury to such property, caused by it or by any common carrier, railroad, or transportation company to which such property may be delivered, or over whose line or lines such property may pass, and no contract, receipt, rule, or regulation shall exempt such common carrier, railroad, or transportation company from the liability hereby imposed. Provided, that nothing in this section shall deprive any holder of such receipt or bill of lading of any remedy or right of action which he has under existing law.

"That the common carrier, railroad, or transportation company issuing such receipt or bill of lading shall be entitled to recover from the common carrier, railroad, or transportation company on whose line the loss, damage, or injury shall have been sustained, the amount of such loss, damage, or injury as it may be required to pay to the owners of such property, as may be evidenced by any receipt, judgment, or transcript thereof."

The power of Congress to enact this legislation has been denied, first, because it is said to deprive the carrier and the shipper of their common-law power to make a just and reasonable contract in respect to goods to be carried to points beyond the line of the interstate carrier; and, second, that in casting liability upon the initial carrier for loss or damage upon the line of a connecting carrier, the former is deprived of its property without due process of law.

The indisputable effect of the Carmack amendment is to hold the initial carrier engaged in interstate commerce and "receiving property for transportation from a point in one state to a point in another state" as having contracted for through carriage to the point of destination, using the lines of connecting carriers as its agents.

Independently of the Carmack amendment the carrier, when tendered property for such transportation, might elect to contract to carry to destination, in which case it necessarily agreed to do so through the agency of other and independent carriers in the line; or, it might elect to carry safely over its own lines only, and then deliver to the next carrier, who would then become the agent of the shipper. In the first case the receiving carrier's liability as carrier extends over the whole route, for, on obvious grounds, the principal is liable for the acts of its agent. In the other case its carrier liability ends at its own terminal, and its further liability is merely that of a forwarder. Having this power to make the one or the other contract, the

Atlantic C. L. R. Co. v. Riverside Mills

only question which has occasioned a conflict in the decided cases was whether it, in the particular case, made the one or the other.

The general doctrine accepted by this court, in the absence of legislation, is, that a carrier, unless there be a special contract, is only bound to carry over its own line, and then deliver to a connecting carrier. That such an initial carrier might contract to carry over the whole route was never doubted. It is equally indisputable that if it does so contract, its common-law carrier liability will extend over the entire route. Ohio & M. R. Co. v. McCarthy, 96 U. S. 258, 266, 24 L. ed. 693, 696; Ogdensburg & L. C. R. Co. v. Pratt, supra; Northern P. R. Co. v. American Trading Co., 195 U. S. 439, 49 L. ed. 269, 25 Sup. Ct. Rep. 84; Muschamp v. Lancaster & P. R. Co., 8 Mees. & W. 421.

The English cases beginning with Muschamp v. Lancaster & P. R. Co., supra, decided in 1841, down to Bristol & E. R. Co. v. Collins, 7 H. L. Cas. 194, have consistently held that the mere receipt of property for transportation to a point beyond the line of the receiving carrier, without any qualifying agreement, justified an inference of an agreement for through transportation, and an assumption of full carrier liability by the primary carrier. The ruling is grounded upon considerations of public policy and public convenience, and classes the receipt of goods so designated for a point beyond the carrier line as a holding out to the public that the carrier has made its own arrangements for the continuance by a connecting carrier of the transportation after the goods leave its own line. There are American cases which take the same view of the question of evidence thus presented. Some of them are Louisville & N. R. Co. v. Campbell, 7 Heisk. 257, Alabama & G. S. R. Co. v. Mt. Vernon Co., 84 Ala. 175, 4 So. 356; Central R. Co. v. Hasselkus, 91 Ga. 384, 44 Am. St. Rep. 37, 17 S. E. 838; Beard v. St. Louis, A. & T. H. R. Co., 79 Iowa, 531, 44 N. W. 803; Kyle v. Laurens R. Co., 10 Rich. L. 382, 70 Am. Dec. 231; Erie R. Co. v. Wilcox, 84 Ill. 240, 25 Am. Rep. 451; East Tennessee & V. R. Co. v. Rogers, 6 Heisk. 143, 19 Am. Rep. 589.

Upon the other hand, many American courts have repudiated the English rule which holds the carrier to a contract for transportation over the whole route, in the absence of a contract clearly otherwise, and have adopted the rule that unless the carrier specifically agrees to carry over the whole route, its responsibility as a carrier ends with its own line; and that, for the continuance of the shipment, its liability is only that of a forwarder. The conflict has therefore been one as to the evidence from which a contract for through carriage to a place beyond the line of the receiving carrier might be inferred.

In this conflicting condition of the decisions as to the circumstances from which an agreement for through transportation of property designated to a point beyond the receiving carrier's line might be inferred, Congress, by the act here involved; has declared, in substance, that the act of receiving property for transportation to a point in another state, and beyond the line of the receiving carrier, shall impose on such receiving carrier the obligation of through transportation, with carrier liability throughout. But this uncertainty of the nature and extent of the liability of a carrier receiving goods destined to a point beyond its own line was not all which might well induce the interposition of the regulating power of Congress. Nothing has perhaps contributed more to the wealth and prosperity of the country than the almost universal practice of transportation companies to co-operate in making through routes and joint rates. Through this method, a situation has been brought about by which, though independently managed, connecting carriers become in effect one system. This practice has its origin in the mutual interests of such companies and in the necessity of an expanding commerce.

In the leading case of Muschamp v. Lancaster & P. R. Co., cited above. Lord Abinger defended the inference of a contract for through carriage from the mere receipt of a package destined to a point beyond the line of the receiving carrier upon the known practice in his day of such carriers. Upon this subject, in speaking of connecting lines of railway, he said: "These railway companies, though separate in themselves, are in the habit, for their own advantage, of making contracts, of which this was one, to convey goods along the whole line, to the ultimate terminus, each of them being agents of the other to carry them forward, and each receiving their share of the profits from the last."

The tenth clause of the conditions annexed to this bill of lading, and shown elsewhere affords a fair illustration of the customary methods of connecting carriers to co-operate for their mutual benefit in carrying on transportation begun by one which must be continued by other lines over which the thing to be transported must go. The receiving carrier makes the rate and the route, and as the agent of every such connecting carrier executes a contract which is to bind each of them, "severally. but not jointly," one of the terms of the agreement being that each carrier shall be liable only for loss or damage occurring on its own line. Through this well known and necessary practice of connecting carriers there has come about, without unity of ownership or physical operation, a singleness of charge and a continuity of transportation greatly to the advantage of the carrier, and beneficial to the great and growing commerce of the country.

Along with this singleness of rate and continuity of carriage there grew up the practice by receiving carriers, illustrated in this case, of refusing to make a specific agreement to transport to points beyond its own line, whereby the connecting carrier, for the purpose of carriage, would become the agent of the primary carrier. The common form of receipt, as the court may judicially know, is one by which the shipper is compelled to make with each carrier in the route over which his package must go a separate agreement limiting the carrier liability of each separate company to its own part of the through route. As a result the shipper could look only to the initial carrier for recompense for loss damage, or delay occurring on its part of the route. If such primary carrier was able to show a delivery to the rails of the next succeeding carrier, although the packages might and usually did continue the journey in the same car in which they had been originally loaded, the shipper must fail in his suit. He might, it is true, then bring his action against the carrier so shown to have next received the shipment. But here, in turn, he might be met by proof of safe delivery to a third separate carrier. In short, as the shipper was not himself in possession of the information as to when and where his property had been lost or damaged, and had no access to the records of the connecting carriers who, in turn, had participated in some part of the transportation, he was compelled in many instances to make such settlement as should be proposed.

This burdensome situation of the shipping public in reference to interstate shipments over routes including separate lines of carriers was the matter which Congress undertook to regulate. Thus, when this Carmack amendment was reported by a conference committee, Judge William Richardson, a congressman from Alabama, speaking for the committee of the matter which it was sought to remedy, among other things, said:

"One of the great complaints of the railroads has been—and, I think, a reasonable, just, and fair complaint—that when a man made a shipment, say, from Washington, for instance, to San Francisco, California, and his shipment was lost in some way, the citizen had to go thousands of miles, probably, to institute his suit. The result was that he had to settle his damages at what he could get. What have we done? We have made the initial carrier, the carrier that takes and receives the shipment, responsible for the loss of the article in the way of damages. We save the shipper from going to California or some distant place to institute his suit. Why? The reasons inducing us to do that were that the initial carrier has a through-route connection with the secondary carrier, on whose route the loss occurred, and a settlement between them will be an easy matter, while the shipper would be at heavy expense in the institution of a suit. If a judgment is obtained against the initial carrier, no doubt exists but that the secondary carrier would pay it at once. Why? Because the arrangement, the concert, the co-operation, the

Atlantic C. L. R. Co. v. Riverside Mills

through route courtesies between them, would be broken up if prompt payment were not made. We have done that in conference." (40 Cong. Rec. Pt. 10, p. 9580.)

It must be conceded that the effect of the act in respect of carriers receiving packages in one state for a point in another, and beyond its own lines, is to deny to such an initial carrier the former right to make a contract limiting liability to its own line. This, it is said, is a denial of the liberty of contract secured by the 5th Amendment to the Constitution. To support this, counsel cited such cases as Allgeyer v. Louisiana, 165 U. S. 589, 41 L. ed. 835, 17 Sup. Ct. Rep. 427; Lochner v. New York, 198 U. S. 45, 49 L. ed. 937, 25 Sup. Ct. Rep. 539, 3 A. & E. Ann. Cas. 1133; and Adair v. United States, 208 U. S. 161, 52 L. ed. 436, 28 Sup. Ct. Rep. 277, 13 A. & E. Ann. Cas. 764.

This power to regulate is the right to prescribe the rules under which such commerce may be conducted. "It is," said Chief Justice Marshall, in Gibbons v. Ogden, 9 Wheat. 1, 196, 6 L. ed. 23, 70, "the power . . . vested in Congress as absolutely as it would be in a single government having in its Constitution the same restrictions on the exercise of the power as are found in the Constitution of the United States." It is a power which extends to the regulation of the appliances and machinery and agencies by which such commerce is conducted. Thus, in Johnson v. Southern P. Co. 196 U. S. 1, 49 L. ed. 363, 25 Sup. Ct. Rep. 158, an act prescribing safety appliances was upheld. And in Interstate Commerce Commission v. Illinois C. R. Co., 215 U. S. 452, 54 L. ed. 280, 30 Sup. Ct. Rep. 155, it was held that the equipment of an interstate railway, including cars used for the transportation of its own fuel, was subject to the regulation of Congress. In Interstate Commerce Commission v. Chicago & A. R. Co., 215 U. S. 479, 54 L. ed. 291, 30 Sup. Ct. Rep. 163, it was held to extend to the distribution of coal cars to the shipper, so as to prevent discrimination. In the Employers' Liability Cases (Howard v. Illinois C. R. Co.) 207 U. S. 463, 52 L. ed. 297, 28 Sup. Ct. Rep. 141, power to pass an act which regulated the relation of master and servant, so as to impose on the carrier, while engaged in interstate commerce, liability for the negligence of a fellow servant, for which at common law there was no liability, and depriving such carrier of the common-law defense of contributory negligence save by way of reduction of damages, was upheld. In Addyston Pipe & Steel Co. v. United States, 175 U. S. 211, 44 L. ed. 136, 20 Sup. Ct. Rep. 96, and Northern Securities Co. v. United States, 193 U. S. 197, 48 L. ed. 679, 24 Sup. Ct. Rep. 436, it was held that this power of regulation extended to and embraced contracts in restrain of trade between the states.

It is obvious, from the many decisions of this court, that there is no such thing as absolute freedom of contract. Contracts

Atlantic C. L. R. Co. *v.* Riverside Mills

which contravene public policy cannot be lawfully made at all; and the power to make contracts may in all cases be regulated as to form, evidence, and validity as to third persons. The power of government extends to the denial of liberty of contract to the extent of forbidding or regulating every contract which is reasonably calculated to injuriously affect the public interests. Undoubtedly the United States is a government of limited and delegated powers, but in respect of those powers which have been expressly delegated, the power to regulate commerce between the state being one of them, the power is absolute, except as limited by other provisions of the Constitution itself.

Having the express power to make rules for the conduct of commerce among the states, the range of congressional discretion as to the regulation best adapted to remedy a practice found inefficient or hurtful is a wide one. If the regulating act be one directly applicable to such commerce, not obnoxious to any other provision of the Constitution, and reasonably adapted to the purpose by reason of legitimate relation between such commerce and the rule provided, the question of power is foreclosed. "The test of power," said Mr. Justice White, speaking for this court in the Employers' Liability Cases, cited above, "is not merely the matter regulated, but whether the regulation is directly one of interstate commerce, or is embraced within the grant [of power] conferred on Congress to use all lawful means necessary and appropriate to the execution of the power to regulate commerce."

That a situation had come about which demanded regulation in the public interest was the judgment of Congress. The requirement that carriers who undertook to engage in interstate transportation, and as a part of that business held themselves out as receiving packages destined to places beyond their own terminal, should be required, as a condition of continuing in that traffic, to obligate themselves to carry to the point of destination, using the lines of connecting carriers as their own agencies, was not beyond the scope of the power of regulation. The rule is adapted to secure the rights of the shipper by securing unity of transportation with unity of responsibility. The regulation is one which also facilitates the remedy of one who sustains a loss, by localizing the responsible carrier. Neither does the regulation impose an unreasonable burden upon the receiving carrier. The methods in vogue, as the court may judicially know, embrace not only the voluntary arrangement of through routes and rates, but the collection of the single charge made by the carrier at one or the other end of the route. This involves frequent and prompt settlement of traffic balances. The routing in a measure depends upon the certainty and promptness of such traffic balance settlements, and such balances have been regarded as debts of a preferred character when there is a receivership. Again, the business association of such carriers affords to each facilities for locating primary responsibility as between themselves which the the shipper cannot have. These well-known conditions afford a reasonable security to the receiving carrier for a reimbursement of a carrier liability which should fall upon one of the connecting carriers as between themselves.

But it is said that any security resulting from a voluntary agreement constituting a through route and rate is destroyed if the receiving carrier is not at liberty to select his own agencies for a continuance of the transportation beyond his own line. This is an objection which has no application to the present case. This action was for loss and damage arising from several distinct shipments to different places beyond the line of the plaintiff in error, who was the initial or receiving carrier. The presumption, from the absence of anything to the contrary in the record, is that the routing was over connecting lines with whom the plaintiff in error has theretofore made its own arrangements and rate. This record presents no question as to the right of the initial carrier to refuse a shipment designated for a point beyond its own line, nor its right to refuse to make a through route or joint rate when such route and rate would involve the continuance of a transportation over independent lines. We therefore refrain from any consideration of the large question thus suggested. The shipments involved in the present case were voluntarily received by an initial carrier who undertook to escape carrier's liability beyond its own line by a provision limiting liability to loss upon its own line. This was forbidden by the Carmack amendment, and any stipulation and condition in the special receipt which contravenes the rule in question is invalid.

Reduced to the final results, the Congress has said that a receiving carrier, in spite of any stipulation to the contrary, shall be deemed, when it receives property in one state, to be transported to a point in another, involving the use of a connecting carrier for some part of the way, to have adopted such other carrier as its agent, and to incur carrier liability throughout the entire route, with the right to reimbursement for a loss not due to his own negligence. The conditions which justified this extension of carrier liability we have already adverted to. The rule of the common law which treated a common carrier as an insurer grew out of a situation which required that kind of security for the protection of the public. To quote the quaint but expressive words of Lord Holt, in Coggs *v.* Bernard, 2 Ld. Raym. 909, when defending and applying the doctrine of absolute liability against loss not due to the act of God or the public enemy, "This rule," said he, "is a politick establishment contrived by the policy of the law for the safety of all persons the necessity of whose affairs oblige them to trust these sorts of persons, that they may be safe in their ways of dealing."

If it is to be assumed that the ultimate power exerted by

Atlantic C. L. R. Co. *v.* Riverside Mills

Congress is that of compelling co-operation by connecting lines of independent carriers for purposes of interstate transportation, the power is still not beyond the regulating power of Congress, since, without merging identity of separate lines or operation, it stops with the requirement of on:ness of charge, continuity of transportation, and primary liability of the receiving carrier to the shipper, with the right of reimbursement from the guilty agency in the route. That there is some chance that this right of recoupment may not be always effective may be conceded without invalidating the regulation. If the power existed and the regulation is adapted to the purpose in view, the public advantage justifies the discretion exercised, and upholds the legislation as within the limit of the grant conferred upon Congress. Touching the range of legislative discretion of the states in respect to occupations or trades which are affected by a public use, this court, in Gundling *v.* Chicago, 177 U. S. 183, 188, 44 L. ed. 725, 728, 20 Sup. Ct. Rep. 633, 635, said:

"Unless the regulations are so utterly unreasonable and extravagant in their nature and purpose that the property and personal rights of the citizen are unnecessarily, and in a manner wholly arbitrary, interfered with or destroyed without due process of law, they do not extend beyond the power of the state to pass, and they form no subject for Federal interference. As stated in Crowley *v.* Christensen, 137 U. S. 86, 34 L. ed. 620, 11 Sup. Ct. Rep. 13: 'The possession and enjoyment of all rights are subject to such reasonable conditions as may be aeemed by the governing authority of the county essential to the safety, health, peace, good order, and morals of the community.' "

But it is said that the act violates the 5th Amendment by taking the property of the initial carrier to pay the debt of an independent connecting carrier whose negligence may have been the sole cause of the loss. But this contention results from a surface reading of the act, and misses the true basis upon which it rests. The liability of the receiving carrier which results in such a case is that of a principal for the negligence of his own agents.

In substance Congress has said to such carriers: "If you receive articles for transportation from a point in one state to a place in another, beyond your own terminal, you must do so under a contract to transport to the place designated. If you are obliged to use the services of independent carriers in the continuance of the transit, you must use them as your own agents, and not as 'the agents of the shipper." It is therefore not the case of making one pay the debt of another. The receiving carrier is, as principal, liable not only for its own negligence, but for that of any agency it may use, although, as between themselves, the company actually causing the loss may be primarily liable.

Atlantic C. L. R. Co. v. Riverside Mills

In Seaboard Air Line R. Co. v. Seegers, 207 U. S. 73, 78, 52 L. ed. 108, 110, 28 Sup. Ct. Rep. 28, 30, legislation by the state of Georgia imposing a penalty on common carriers for failure to adjust damage claims within forty days was held to neither deny due process nor the equal protection of the law. Speaking by Mr. Justice Brewer, the court said of the reasonableness of the requirement and classification, that "the matter to be adjusted is one peculiarly within the knowledge of the carrier. It receives the goods and has them in its custody until the carriage is completed. It knows what it received and what it delivered. It knows what injury was done during the shipment, and how it was done. The consignee may not know what was in fact delivered at the time of the shipment, and the shipper may not know what was delivered to the consignee at the close of the transportation. The carrier can determine the amount of the loss more accurately and promptly and with less delay and expense than anyone else, and for the adjustment of loss or damage to shipments within the state forty days cannot be said to be an unreasonably short length of time."

The conclusion we reach in respect to the validity of the amendment has the support of some well-considered cases. Among them we cite: Smeltzer v. St. Louis & S. F. R. Co. 158 Fed. 649; Pittsburg, C. C. & St. L. R. Co. v. Mitchell (Ind.) 91 N. E. 735; Louisville & N. R. Co. v. Scott, 133 Ky. 724, 118 S. W. 992.

The judgment included an attorneys' fee, taxed as part of the costs. The authority for this is supposed to be found in the 8th section of the act to regulate commerce of February 4, 1887 (24 Stat. at L. pp. 379, 382, chap. 104, U. S. Comp. Stat. 1901, pp. 3154, 3159). The section reads as follows:

"That in case any common carrier subject to the provisions of this act shall do, cause to be done, or permit to be done, any act, matter, or thing in this act prohibited or declared to be unlawful, or shall omit to do any act, matter, or thing in this act required to be done, such common carrier shall be liable to the person or persons injured thereby for the full amount of damages sustained in consequence of any such violation of the provisions of this act, together with a reasonable counsel or attorneys' fee, to be fixed by the court in every case of recovery, which attorneys' fees shall be taxed and collected as part of the costs in the case."

But that section applies to cases where the cause of action is the doing of something made unlawful by some provision of the act, or the omission to do something required by the act, and there is a recovery "of damages sustained in consequence of any such violation of this act," etc. The cause of action in the present case is not for damages resulting from "any violation of the provisions of this act." True, the plaintiff in error attempted

Galveston, H. & S. A. R. Co. v. United States

by contract to stipulate for a limitation of liability to a loss on its own line, and in this action has defensively denied liability for a loss not occurring on its own line. But the cause of action was the loss of the plaintiff's property which had been intrusted to it as a common carrier, and that loss is in no way traceable to the violation of any provision of the act to regulate commerce. Having sustained no damage which was a consequence of the violation of the act, the section has no application to this case.

The judgment was erroneous to this extent, and the provision for an attorneys' fee is stricken out, and the judgment thus modified is affirmed.

GALVESTON, H. & S. A. R. Co. v. UNITED STATES.

(Circuit Court of Appeals, Fifth Circuit, December 20, 1910.)

[183 Fed. Rep. 579.]   •

Railroads—Safety Appliance Statutes—Actions for Violation—Defenses.—The duty of railroads engaged in interstate commerce to comply with the statutes in regard to safety appliances is absolute, and in suits by the United States for penalties thereunder, where the failure to comply with the statutory requirements is clearly proved, no excuses are sufficient to constitute a defense, and it is not error for the court to direct a verdict for the plaintiff.

In Error to the District Court of the United States for the Western District of Texas.

Action by the United States against the Galveston, Harrisburg & San Antonio Railway Company. Judgment for the United States, and defendant brings error. Affirmed.

T. J. Beall, for plaintiff in error.
Chas. A. Boynton and *P. J. Doherty*, for the United States.

Before PARDEE and SHELBY, Circuit Judges.

PER CURIAM. The question is whether, on the evidence admitted in the case without objection, the trial judge erred in directing a verdict for the United States, thus taking away from the jury the right to pass upon the sufficiency of the excuses proved in the case.

That the duty of railroads engaged in interstate commerce to comply with statutes in regard to safety appliances is absolute, and in suits by the United States for penalties thereunder no excuses are sufficient, is held in Atlantic Coast Line R. Co. v. United States, 168 Fed. 175, 94 C. C. A. 35; United States v. Wabash R. Co. (7th Circuit) 182 Fed. 802; United States v.

Commonwealth v. Scott

Denver & Rio Grande R. Co., 163 Fed. 519, 90 C. C. A. 329; United States v. Atchison, Topeka & Santa Fè R. Co., 163 Fed. 517, 90 C. C. A. 327; Chicago, Milwaukee & St. Paul R. Co. v. United States, 165 Fed. 423, 91 C. C. A. 373, 20 L. R. A. (N. S.) 473; United States v. Southern Pacific R. Co., 169 Fed. 407, 94 C. C. A. 629; Chicago, Burlington & Quincy R. Co. v. United States, 170 Fed. 556, 95 C. C. A. 642. And that was evidently the view of the learned trial judge.

On these adjudged cases, and in view of the construction given by Congress in the act of April 14, 1910, the judgment of the District Court is affirmed.

COMMONWEALTH v. SCOTT.

(Court of Appeals of Kentucky, Jan. 24, 1911.)

[133 S. W. Rep. 766.]

Commerce—Interstate Commerce—Intoxicating Liquors—Power of State to Regulate.*—Where intoxicating liquor was shipped from without the state to a resident of a local option district, and a common carrier operating wholly within the state received the liquor outside of the district, paid the charges for carriage to that point, delivered it to the resident of the local option district, and there collected his charges and those advanced, the carriage was an interstate commerce transaction; and the carrier was not guilty under Ky. St. § 2569a (Russell's St. § 3641), making the bringing of liquor for hire into local option territory an offense.

Appeal from Circuit Court, Metcalfe County.

L. B. Scott was acquitted of the crime of bringing spirituous, vinous, and malt liquors for hire into a local option district, and the Commonwealth appeals. Affirmed.

J. W. Kinnaird, Co. Atty., James Breathitt, Atty. Gen., and T. B. Blakey, Asst. Atty. Gen., for the Commonwealth.
M. O. Scott and J. R. Beauchamp, for appellee.

NUNN, J. The grand jury of Metcalfe county returned the following indictment against appellant, to wit:

"The grand jury of Metcalfe county, in the name and by the authority of the commonwealth of Kentucky, accuse L. B. Scott

---

*For the authorities in this series on the question whether a carrier was engaged in interstate commerce on a particular occasion, see first foot-note of Hockfield v. Southern Ry. Co. (N. Car.), 34 R. R. R. 492, 57 Am. & Eng. R. Cas., N. S., 492; Chicago, etc., Ry. Co. v. United States (C. C. A.), 34 R. R. R. 495, 57 Am. & Eng R Cas., N. S., 495.

Commonwealth v. Scott

of the offense of bringing into local option districts spirituous, vinous, and malt liquors for hire, committed as follows, viz.: The said L. B. Scott, on the 27th or 28th day of April, 1910, and within twelve months before the finding of this indictment, in the county and commonwealth aforesaid, did unlawfully for hire bring into Metcalfe county spirituous, vinous, and malt liquors, where the local option law was then and there in full force, contrary to the form of the statutes in such cases made and provided, and against the peace and dignity of the commonwealth of Kentucky."

The case was submitted for trial upon an agreed state of facts, which is as follows:

"It is agreed that the facts in the above-styled action are as follows:

"(1) On the ——— day of ———, 1910, R. E. McCandles, who resides at Edmonton, Ky., was engaged in retailing family groceries and selling spirituous liquors at Edmonton, Ky., and that he by mail ordered to be shipped to him at Edmonton, Ky., via Glasgow, Ky., from New Albany, Ind., whiskey, and that same was shipped to him from New Albany, Ind., to Edmonton, Ky., via Glasgow, Ky., and that when shipped from New Albany, Ind., it was billed or addressed to him at Edmonton, Ky., via Glasgow, Ky.; that same was transported from New Albany, Ind., by Adams Express Company and that the Adams Express Company's line terminated at Glasgow, Ky.

"(2) That the defendant had a long time prior to the day aforesaid, and was at the time, engaged with his own wagons and teams in the business of transportation goods, wares, and merchandise and other chattels for persons who chase to employ and remunerate him therefor from Edmonton, Ky., to Glasgow, Ky., which was the terminus of the Louisville & Nashville Railroad, and also from Glasgow, Ky., to Edmonton, Ky., and the defendant, while so engaged in said business, did transport said whiskey from Glasgow, Ky., to Edmonton, Ky., and there delivered the same to R. E. McCandles, the consignee to whom said whiskey was billed as aforesaid.

"(3) That at the time defendant so transported said whiskey as aforesaid he received and receipted for said whiskey at Glasgow, Ky., and he advanced the money, as was his custom to do for his customers to whom goods were consigned, and paid the freight thereon, and after so transporting same he collected the money so advanced, as well as the money for his charges for transporting the same as aforesaid, and in this way he transported said whiskey for hire to Edmonton, Ky., where he delivered the same to the consignee to whom the same was billed aforesaid, namely, Bud McCandles.

"(4) That the local option law was at that time in full force

Commonwealth *v.* Scott

and effect in Metcalfe county at the place which said liquor was delivered by the defendant as aforesaid to said consignee."

The lower court found Scott not guilty, and the commonwealth appealed.

There can be no question of appellee's guilt under section 2569a, Ky. St. (Russell's St. § 3641), if that section applies to the facts of the case. If the interstate commerce act applies, it takes precedence over section 2569a, and the case must be determined according to it. As shown by the agreed facts, the whiskey was shipped from New Albany, Ind., to McCandles, at Edmonton, Ky.; that the express company carried it to Glasgow, the terminus of its line; that appellee, a common carrier, conveyed it from there to Edmonton, Ky., and delivered it to McCandles, the consignee.

In the case of Rhodes *v.* Iowa, 170 U. S. 412, 18 Sup. Ct. 664, 42 L. Ed. 1088, Rhodes was indicted for carrying a box of whiskey from Burlington, Iowa, to Brighton, Iowa. The package had been billed from Dallas, Ill., to William Horn, Brighton, Iowa. It was carried by the Chicago, Burlington & Quincy Railroad from Dallas to Burlington, and from that point to Brighton by Rhodes. The statute of Iowa, under which Rhodes was prosecuted, is in part as follows: "If any express company, railway company or any agent or person in the employ of any express company, or of any common carrier, or any person in the employ of any common carrier, or if any other person shall transport or convey between points, or from one place to another within this state, for any other person or persons of corporation, any intoxicating liquors, without having first been furnished with a certificate from and under the seal of the county auditor of the county to which said liquor is to be transported or is consigned for transportation, or within which it is to be conveyed from place to place, certifying that the consignee or person to whom said liquor is to be transported, conveyed or delivered, is authorized to sell such intoxicating liquors in such county, such company, corporation or person so offending, and each of them, and any agent of said company, corporation or person so offending, shall, upon conviction thereof, be fined in the sum of one hundred dollars for each offence and pay cost of prosecution," etc. This statute would certainly have reached Rhodes, if it had been applicable to the shipment.

In that case the court said: "The sole question presented for consideration is whether the statute of the state of Iowa can be held to apply to the box in question whilst it was in transit from its point of shipment, Dallas, Ill., to its delivery to the consignee at the point to which it was consigned. That is to say, whether the law of the state of Iowa can be made to apply to a shipment from the state of Illinois, before the arrival and delivery of the merchandise, without causing the Iowa law to be repugnant to

Commonwealth v. Scott

the Constitution of the United States." The court decided in that case that the Iowa statute had no application; that it was an attempt to regulate interstate commerce, which, under the United States Constitution, is a power vested solely in Congress; that the statutes of the state of Iowa did not apply to that shipment until the package which was shipped from Dallas, Ill., had reached Brighton, Iowa, and had been delivered to the consignee, William Horn. The court also decided in that case that, if the statute applied to Rhodes, it would also apply to the man who moved the whiskey from the platform into the freight house in Burlington, as he knew the box contained whiskey. But the court decided that neither he nor Rhodes were subject to the state statute, as the act of Congress applied to the shipment, and that, therefore, all who aided in the shipment and delivery of the whiskey to Horn were amendable under the interstate commerce law, rather than under the state statute.

Since the opinion in the case above mentioned was rendered, that court has again considered the same question in the case of Adams Express Co. v. Kentucky, 206 U. S. 129, 27 Sup. Ct. 606, 51 L. Ed. 987. In that case the grand jury of Laurel county indicted Joe Newland and the Adams Express Company, charging that they were partners engaged in carrying packages, etc.; that they had carried and delivered to Geo. Meece a parcel containing intoxicating liquor, which was to be paid for on delivery at East Bernstadt. It seems that, according to the agreed facts in that case, a Cincinnati whiskey house would obtain the names of citizens of Laurel county, and, without the knowledge of the citizens, ship whiskey to them; that the persons to whom the whiskey was shipped would be notified that there was a package at the express office for them, for which they would call, pay the charges, and receive; and they had been doing this for a long time. Some of the packages remained in the office for a week or more. This court decided that case in favor of the commonwealth. An appeal was taken to the Supreme Court of the United States, which reversed the judgment of this court, and decided, in effect, that the interstate commerce act applied to the shipments, and that it was interstate commerce until the packages were delivered to the persons to whom consigned.

Under these authorities, Scott was not guilty of violating the state law, and the lower court was right in so holding.

For these reasons, the judgment of the lower court is affirmed.

BETUS v. CHICAGO, B. & Q. R. R.

(Supreme Court of Iowa, Feb. 13, 1911.)

[129 N. W. Rep. 962.]

Trial—Order of Proof—Judicial Discretion.—The order of proof being discretionary with the trial court, it was not error to receive evidence of an agent's agreement before proof of his authority.

Corporations — Agents — Implied Authority — Adjustment of Claims.*—A local freight agent has no implied authority to settle claims for injury to a live stock shipment.

Corporations—Ratification of Acts of Agent—Evidence—Weight. —Evidence held to show ratification by a carrier of a settlement agreed upon by its local freight agent for injury to a live stock shipment.

Carriers—Carriage of Live Stock—Limitation of Liability.—Interstate Commerce Act, Feb. 4, 1887, c. 104, 24 Stat. 379 (U. S. Comp. St. 1901, p. 3154), as amended by Act June 29, 1906, c. 3591, 34 Stat. 584 (U. S. Comp. St. Supp. 1909, p. 1149), requiring freight rates to be uniform, does not prevent a shipper from recovering the actual loss to a live stock shipment, though the stock was shipped on the valuation of $100 per head.

Carriers—Freight—Limitation of Liability—Valuation.—Code, §§ 2074, 3136, prohibiting limitation of a carrier's liability, cannot be avoided by a stipulation limiting liability to a fixed valuation in consideration of a lower rate; the shipper being entitled to recover his actual loss, less the difference between freight `charges collected and charges under true valuation.

Carriers—Live Stock—Loss—Right to Recover.—Plaintiff having paid for live stock and shipped it in his own name can recover for injury thereto, though he agreed to pay another a share of the profits, and the damages recoverable were treated by them as profits.

Appeal from District Court, Lee County; W. S. Withrow, Judge.

Action on alleged contract resulted in judgment as prayed. The defendant appeals. Affirmed.

Hazen I. Sawyer and *Palmer Trimble*, for appellant.
A. L. Parsons, for appellee.

LADD, J.   Plaintiff shipped a car load of mules from Grundy Center, billed over the Chicago, Rock Island & Pacific Railway

---

*For the authorities in this series on the subject of the implied authority of a railroad's freight or ticket agents, see second footnote of St. Louis, etc., Ry. Co. v. Citizen's Bank (Ark.), 30 R. R. R. 290, 53 Am. & Eng. R. Cas., N. S., 290; first foot-note of Southern Ry. Co. v. Nowlin (Ala.), 30 R. R. R. 261, 53 Am. & Eng. R. Cas., N. S., 261.

Betus v. Chicago, B. & Q. R. R

to Burlington, and from there over the Chicago, Burlington & Quincy Railroad to East St. Louis, Ill. Between Burlington and Keokuk seven mules were injured, and plaintiff alleged in his petition that, upon discovering their condition, he telegraphed defendant's superintendent, that he turned the shipment over to the company, and that subsequently, by virtue of an agreement with it, he received all but two mules upon the company's promise to pay him $387.50 for these, their legs being supposed to have been broken, and $185 because of injuries to other five. Recovery was sought on this alleged promise. Defendant denied having made any such agreement, alleged that, if made, no more than $100, each, for the two mules might be recovered, and tendered plaintiff $420, said to "cover the damages alleged to have been received by the five mules, as alleged in plaintiff's petition, and the sum of $100 each, for the two head of mules which were alleged to have been a total loss, and interest." Only the difference between the values of the two mules alleged to have been bruised and the amount tendered therefor is in dispute.

1. The evidence tended to show that the mules were injured because of a defective car, and on the morning after plaintiff telegraphed to the superintendent, he and Higgins, the local agent, met at the stockyards and agreed to the appraisement of the damages by three men, who estimated these at amount mentioned. Higgins denied that any agreement concerning the payment of the appraisement was entered into; while plaintiff testified that it was agreed that he should take all but two of the mules, and the defendant would pay the amount of the appraisement. Plaintiff's testimony was corroborated by that of Hull, and sufficiently supported the finding of the trial court. It is said, however, that there was error in receiving the above evidence before Higgins' authority to represent the company was shown, and that such authority was not proven. The order in which the testimony shall be received is discretionary with the trial court, and there was no abuse of such discretion.

Higgins testified that he was without authority to settle damages, and it may be conceded that his employment as local freight agent was not such as to justify an inference in contradiction of his testimony that this was a part of his duties. See McLagan v. Railway, 116 Iowa, 183, 89 N. W. 233. But there was sufficient evidence of ratification to support the court's finding. The superintendent was immediately informed of the retention of the two mules, and, by direction of the assistant general attorney of the company, who was expressly authorized "to look after the legal end of the case," Higgins sold these for $10 each, and the sums were retained by the company. Subsequently defendant's freight claim agent, with authority to adjust such matters, in response to a letter from plaintiff's attorney, wrote, among other things, that, "as we advised Mr. Betts, $185 was the amount of damage agreed upon." Thus it appears that those in authority were aware of the retention of the two mules, and that they were sold at the instance of the attorney having authority to advise as to the proper course to pursue and the money retained by the company, and thereafter the officer authorized to adjust such differences admitted that there was an agreement. We think this evidence sufficient to justify the finding that the company ratified such arrangement as was made.

2. The shipping contract limited defendant's liability on the total loss of any of the mules to not exceed $100 each, and compensation for transportation was determined on the basis of this valuation. There was no proof of any representation of value on the part of plaintiff, save by inference from the contract, stipulating that in case of total loss payment would be made "on the basis of actual cash value at the time and place of shipment, but in no case to exceed $100 for each." Basing its contentions on the act of Congress to regulate commerce, approved February 4, 1887 (Act Feb. 4, 1887, c. 104, 24 Stat. 379 [U. S. Comp. St. 1901, p. 3154]), together with several amendments, the last of which was approved June 29, 1906 (Act June 29, 1906, c. 3591, 34 Stat. 584 [U. S. Comp. St. Supp. 1909, p. 1149]), defendant contested plaintiff's right to recover more than $100 each for the mules. Without quoting from the several sections of the law, it is enough to say that the railroad company is required to make a schedule of rates for transportation and exact the same from all persons alike, and both defendant and the shipper are prohibited from evading this requirement by any devise whatsoever. The rate on the shipment of mules valued above $100 each was 25 per cent. of the tariff on each 100 per cent., or fraction thereof, in excess of the above valuation, and it is argued that, in entering into the shipping contract fixing the value of the mules at not exceeding $100 each, when some of them were worth much more, plaintiff perpetrated a fraud under paragraph 3, section 10, of the above act. For all that appears, the average value may not have been more than $100; each in which event it would not seem deceptive practice to have procured the low rate. Moreover, under the alleged agreement of settlement, the company retained the mules, and they were not a total loss. Even if there were undervaluations, however, it does not follow that the limitation of recovery should be given effect. It may be conceded that many authorities lay down the rule as contended by defendant, that in event of a loss the shipper is estopped from asserting a higher value than that given as a basis upon which to compute freight charges; but this court is committed to the doctrine that the statute prohibiting the limitation of liability of a common carrier (sections 2074, 3136,

Code) cannot be evaded in this way, and that exact justice is administered by awarding the shipper actual value of the animal or article destroyed in being transported, less the difference between the freight charges collected and what would have been charged had the true value been given.   That the act of Congress referred to is not necessarily inconsistent therewith appears from Winn *v.* American Express Company, 128 N. W. 663, and the view therein expressed finds confirmation in a recent decision of the United States Circuit Court of Appeals of the Eighth Circuit.   Latta *v.* Railway, 172 Fed. 850, 97 C. C. A. 198.   There was no error in disregarding the attempt to limit the liability by contract.

3. The point is made that plaintiff cannot maintain this action, for that the shipment was by a partnership consisting of plaintiff and his uncle, C. M. Betts, instead of plaintiff alone.   The evidence warranted no such conclusion.   The plaintiff paid for the mules, shipped them in his name, and was to pay his uncle half of the profits realized.   Subsequently, the amount to be recovered in this case was figured by them as profits; but this did not alter plaintiff's right to recover the damages to the mules, the title being in him, nor relieve him from the obligation of paying one-half the profits realized, regardless of whether measured by this claim.   Having owned the mules, he was entitled to maintain an action for damages thereto, and it is no concern of the defendant in what manner he disposes of the proceeds. See section 3459, Code.

Affirmed.

MARTIN *v.* OREGON R. & NAVIGATION CO.

(Supreme Court of Oregon, Dec. 27, 1910.)

[113 Pac. Rep. 16.]

Commerce—Interstate Commerce—Regulation by State—Police Power.—The states may, under their police power, make reasonable rules regarding the methods of carrying on interstate business, and such rules are inoperative only when conflicting with regulations of Congress on the same subject, and can be supported only when consistent with the general requirement that interstate commerce shall be free and unobstructed, and when not amounting to a regulation of such commerce.

Constitutional Law — Suspension of Laws—"Authority."—Const. art. 1, § 22, provides that the operation of the laws shall never be suspended, except by authority of the legislative assembly. Held, that the word "authority," while meaning power to act, whether original or delegated, is usually used to express a derivative power, and the clause permits the operation of laws to be suspended by an officer or tribunal of the state; and hence Act Feb. 18, 1907 (Laws 1907, p. 77) § 26, requiring railroads to furnish cars on demand by shippers, and authorizing the railroad commission to suspend the operation of the act, is constitutional.

Commerce—Regulation—Railroads—Conflict between State and Federal Statutes.—Since Act Feb. 18, 1907 (Laws 1907, p. 77) § 26, requiring railroads to furnish cars on demand by shippers, covers a field not occupied by the federal act of Feb. 4, 1887, c. 104, 24 Stat. 379 (U. S. Comp. St. 1901, p. 3154), known as the interstate commerce law, as amended by Act June 29, 1906, c. 3591, 34 Stat. 584 (U. S. Comp. St. Supp. 1909, p. 1149), in that it regulates the manner of making the request, the excuses that may be made for a failure to deliver cars, and adds an additional penalty by way of demurrage for failure to comply with its terms, it is not superseded by nor in conflict with the federal statute.

Constitutional Law—Equal Protection of Law—Due Process of Law.*—Act Feb. 18, 1907 (Laws 1907, p. 77) § 26, requiring railroads to furnish cars to shippers on demand, and by section 51 making a railroad liable in treble damages, with attorney's fees, to one injured by a violation of the act, is not void, as denying to railroads the equal protection of the law and depriving them· of property without due process of law.

---

*For the authorities in this series on the subject of the validity of statutes prescribing penalties to compel carriers to perform their duties, etc., see foot-note of Missouri Pac. Ry. Co. *v.* Nebraska (U. S.), 36 R. R. R. 79, 59 Am. & Eng. R. Cas., N. S., 79; first foot-note of Downey *v.* Northern Pac. Ry. Co. (N. Dak.), 35 R. R. R. 598, 58 Am. & Eng. R. Cas., N. S., 598; Thweat *v.* Atlantic Coast Line R. Co. (S. Car.), 35 R. R. R. 431, 58 Am. & Eng. R. Cas., N. S., 431; second head-note of Tracy *v.* New York, etc., R. Co. (Conn.), 34 R. R. R. 105, 57 Am. & Eng. R. Cas., N. S., 105.

Martin v. Oregon R. & Navigation Co

Appeal from Circuit Court, Umatilla County; H. J. Bean, Judge.

Action by F. V. Martin, as surviving partner of the firms of Riggs & Co. and Riggs & Martin, against the Oregon Railroad & Navigation Company. Judgment for plaintiff, and defendant appeals. Affirmed.

This action was begun by F. V. Martin and Ralph Riggs as partners under the firm name of Riggs & Co. and Riggs & Martin. Prior to the trial in the lower courts Riggs died, and his coplaintiff, Martin, as the sole surviving partner, was substituted. The action was to recover damages for defendant's failure to furnish the firm of Riggs & Martin a number of refrigerator cars, demanded by them for shipping apples from Milton station, on defendant's line of road in Umatilla county, to destinations outside the state. The complaint sets forth, in substance: (1) The partnership relation existing between the plaintiffs, who were engaged in buying and selling, packing, and shipping grain and perishable fruits in this state and in the state of Idaho; (2) the corporate existence of defendant, and that its business is that of a common carrier, engaged in the transportation of freight and passengers for hire, having a station with a public switch and side track at Milton in this state; (3) that during 1907 they bought a large amount of apples in the vicinity of Milton, for the purpose of selling and shipping the same from Milton station; that they had the same stored in their packing and ware house, located upon a side track of defendant's railroad at Milton, where cars could be loaded by them and received for shipment by the railroad company; (4) that at several times in October and November of 1907, in compliance with section 26 of the act of the Legislature of this state, approved February 18, 1907 (Laws 1907, pp. 67, 77), they placed written orders with defendant's station agent at Milton for a number of refrigerator cars in which to transport their apples via the Oregon Short Line and Union Pacific Railroads to various eastern and southern points without the state; (5) that they had contracted to sell to one R. O. Applegate of Kansas City, Mo., at prices stated in the complaint, f. o. b. at Milton, all the apples purchased by them at or in the vicinity of that station; that prior to October 21st defendant delivered to plaintiff 12 of such cars, which they caused to be loaded with apples and shipped; that on October 21st, plaintiffs ordered twelve cars, on the 31st, one car, on November 8th, four cars, and at another time in that month four cars; that defendant accepted and received plaintiff's application for cars, which it promised to supply, but failed so to do. Various items of damages are alleged, amounting to $6,316,50, including therein $2 per day for each car in excess of the time allowed defendant to furnish cars by the said act. This item,

Martin *v.* Oregon R. & Navigation Co

amounting to $464, besides $1.000 as attorney's fees, was claimed. Defendant demurred to the complaint.

The main point urged is that it appears in the complaint that the transportation facilities mentioned therein were requested for and were to be used in carrying on interstate commerce; that the action is predicated on section 26 of the railroad commission law, which, it is asserted, is not applicable to such transactions, and if so applied and made to operate, constitutes a regulation of, and an unlawful and unwarranted interference with, interstate commerce, and is violative of clause 3, § 8, art. 1, of the Constitution of the United States. The demurrer was overruled. Defendant answered, putting at issue the material averments of the complaint and setting up two affirmative defenses. By the first, it is averred in substance that defendant's railroad lines extend through the states of Washington, Idaho, and Oregon, its main line connecting with the Oregon Short Line at Huntington, Oregon; that early in the year 1907, it carefully estimated the amount of apples that would probably be offered for shipment upon its lines during that season, and, acting upon such estimate, made adequate provision for the cars necessary for handling all shipments of apples that could reasonably be anticipated; that in the months of October and November, 1907, there was a sudden, unusual, and unanticipated congestion of freight traffic upon its lines, occasioned by a heavy yield of fruit throughout the territory traversed by defendant's lines, and a correspondingly extraordinary and unusual demand for apples in the eastern and middle western states, and that an unusual, unprecedented, and extraordinary quantity of apples was assembled and offered for shipment at various stations along defendant's lines of railroad in said states, and particularly at Milton; that such quantities of apples were collected at such station and offered for shipment at practically one and the same time, and within a period of a few weeks; that large numbers of refrigerator cars were demanded by shippers, including plaintiff, for immediate shipment of such fruit, and as a result an unusual, extraordinary, and unprecedented demand was made upon defendant, far in excess of its available supply, and far in excess of the number and capacity its agents and officers could reasonably have anticipated; and that, although defendant made the utmost effort to supply the necessary cars for transporting the fruit offered for shipment, it was not equal to the task. The second defense avers that the transactions stated in the complaint relate to interstate commerce, and that section 26 of the railroad commission law of this state is void, as in contravention of clause 3, § 8, art. 1, of the Constitution of the United States.

A demurrer to the second defense was sustained, and a reply to the first put the averments thereof at issue. Upon the trial

Martin *v.* Oregon R. & Navigation Co

plaintiff secured a verdict and judgment for $2,758.25 damages and costs, and $500 attorney's fees. Defendant appeals.

W. W. Cotton, Carter & Smythe, and *Arthur C. Spencer,* for appellant.

Charles M. Kahn and *Lowell & Winter,* for respondent.

SLATER, J. (after stating the facts as above). Plaintiff's right to recover in this action is based solely upon section 26 of the railroad commission law of this state, cited in the statement of facts. That section, in so far as is material to the pending action, reads as follows:

"In furnishing cars no discrimination shall be made in favor of any person or place, or any commodity except livestock and perishable property.

"When the owner, manager, or shipper of freight of any kind shall make written application to the railroad to supply cars to be loaded in carload lots with freight of which said railroad is a common carrier, it shall be the duty of such railroad to supply cars so applied for within the time herein prescribed. If the application be for five cars or less. the number of cars applied for shall be furnished to the applicant within five days; if the application be for more than five cars not to exceed ten cars. the number of cars applied for shall be furnished to the applicant within ten days; if the application be for more than ten cars and less than thirty cars. the number of cars applied for shall be furnished to the applicant within fifteen days; if the application be for thirty or more cars, the number of cars applied for shall be furnished to the applicant within twenty days. Said cars shall be suitable for the purpose for which they are ordered, and shall be furnished at a convenient place for loading, at the point where required by the owner, manager or shipper making application therefor.

"Any such application must be made to the railroad upon whose line of railroad the shipment originates. Every such application shall state the number of cars wanted, the time when and place where desired, the kind of freight to be shipped and the final destination thereof. The place where said cars are desired to be loaded for shipment shall be at some station, switch or siding on the line of the railroad to which application is made. The application for cars may be made to any officer or general agent of the railroad required to furnish the same, or to any agent of the railroad at the point nearest the station, switch or siding where said cars are to be furnished. * * *

"When a car or cars are applied for under the provisions of this act. and are not furnished within the time as herein required. the railroad so failing to furnish such car or cars, shall be liable and held to be immediately indebted to the person making application therefor in the sum of two dollars per day

Martin *v.* Oregon R. & Navigation Co

or fraction of a day per car applied for and not furnished within the limit of time and as herein prescribed, until such car or cars are furnished. And to be indebted to the person making such application and not receiving the car or cars therein applied for, within the time and as herein required, in the amount of the actual damages any such applicant may sustain, except as in this section of this act stated. * * *

"No charge for failure of any railroad to furnish a car or cars as herein required shall be made or enforced, or damages therefor claimed, when such failure is caused by public calamity, strikes, washouts, acts of God, the public enemy, mobs, riots, wrecks, fires, or accidents; but the lack of sufficient motive power, cars, equipment, other appliances, terminal facilities, roadbed, facilities for maintenance, repair or transportation, or any thereof, shall not be held to excuse the failure to furnish cars as herein required, or to exonerate any railroad from the payment of the damages and penalties herein prescribed, except during the times when the railroad commission of Oregon shall by order suspend the operation of those portions of this section of this act, requiring the furnishing of cars herein, stated, and then only during the time of such suspension." Laws 1907, pp. 77, 78, 79.

The railroad commission, upon good cause shown and after notice to interested parties and a hearing, is vested with power to suspend for a continuous period not to exceed 30 days the operation of the provisions of this section, in so far as it makes railroads liable for penalties or damages, and such order of suspension may take effect retroactively.

The first and principal contention advanced by defendant's counsel is that the apples, when assembled for shipment at Milton, and tendered by the shippers to defendant for shipment became articles of interstate commerce, and as such were subject to the provisions of the feredal interstate commerce law, and the amendments thereof; that the cars ordered for such freight were instrumentalities with which to accomplish interstate transportation, and as such could be affected by no regulation tending to direct their use or operation, except such regulation emanated from Congress; that if the statute of this state is construed to apply to such transactions, it is an unlawful attempt to regulate interstate commerce; is in contravention of the federal Constitution, and, to that extent, is void.

Without deciding, but conceding for the purpose of this case, that the contemplated transactions heretofore detailed constitute interstate commerce, that alone will not render void the provisions of the act above quoted, if applied to them as we think it should be. Notwithstanding the exclusive nature of the power to regulate interstate commerce vested in the federal government, it has repeatedly been held by the Supreme Court of the United

States that the respective states may, in the exercise of their police power, make reasonable rules with regard to the methods of carrying on interstate business. But such rules are inoperative only when in conflict with regulations upon the same subject enacted by Congress, and can be supported only when consistent with the general requirement that interstate commerce shall be free and unobstructed, and not amounting to a regulation of such commerce. Such is the substance of the language of Mr. Justice Brown in Houston and Tex. Cent. R. Co. *v.* Mayes, 201 U. S. 321, 328, 26 Sup. Ct. 491, 50 L. Ed. 772. That case was like the present one, in that the contemplated shipment originated in Texas and the destination was in Oklahoma, and it involved the validity of a similar statute of the state of Texas, requiring cars to be furnished upon the demand of the shipper. The statute was held void, not because the state could not under its police power prescribe reasonable rules and regulations as to furnishing cars by a railroad company, when the shipment contemplated would constitute interstate commerce, if carried out, but because there was an absolute requirement by that statute that a railroad should furnish a certain number of cars at a specified day, regardless of every other consideration, except strikes and other public calamities. It was held that the act transcended the police power of the state and amounted to a burden upon interstate commerce, but it was admitted that the statute was not far from the line of proper police regulation. The features of the Texas statute, rendering it unreasonable, as pointed out by the court, were that no exception was made in cases of a sudden congestion of traffic, an actual inability to furnish cars by reason of their temporary and unavoidable detention in other states, or in other places in the same state; that there was no allowance for interference of traffic, occasioned by wrecks or other accidents upon the same or other roads, involving a detention thereof, the breaking of bridges, accidental fires, washouts, or other unavoidable consequences of heavy weather. Allowance for all these contingencies is made in our statute, unless it is in the one particular of a sudden congestion of traffic, the absence of which in the Texas statute caused it to be declared arbitrary and burdensome to intestate commerce. The lower court, however, construed the word "accident," used in the statute, to be sufficiently broad to cover the contingency of traffic congestion, and defendant had the benefit of his defense on that ground, and is therefore not in a position as to that to complain. Whether the court was justified in so construing the act is not now before us, but we may say that if the word "accident" is not sufficiently comprehensive in meaning to include "sudden congestion of traffic," then that contingency is provided for in the suspension clause of the statute. This clause, however, has been assailed by defendant because, it asserts, the statute leaves

Martin *v.* Oregon R. & Navigation Co

to the commission to judicially determine when and under what circumstances a suspension of the law and the operation thereof may be justified, and grants the power to suspend the law. It is therefore said to be unconstitutional and void, but there is in the Constitution of this state, as we interpret it, an express warrant for such delegation of power. Section 22 of article 1 provides that "the operation of the laws shall never be suspended, except by the authority of the legislative assembly." "Authority" means power to act, whether original or delegated (Century dictionary), but the term is usually used to express a derivative power. The clause of the Constitution under consideration was intended manifestly as a restrictive or prohibitive clause. If it had been intended to restrict the power to suspend the operation of laws to the enactment of the legislative assembly itself, more direct terms would doubtless have been used, such as, "the operation of the laws shall never be suspended except by the legislative assembly." By the insertion of the words "authority of" we think the intention was to make the restriction less confined, and to permit the operation of laws to be suspended by an officer or tribunal of this state, when so authorized by an act of the legislative assembly. When thus interpreted, the authority conferred upon the railroad commission by the legislative act of 1907 derives its validity from the fundamental law, and cannot be questioned. The law thus construed affords a railroad corporation ample protection under all circumstances and contingencies, and in our opinion is a reasonable exercise by the state of its police power.

In defendant's brief it is pointed out that Congress has legislated upon the same subject, and therefore it is argued that the state statute is superseded. This does not follow, unless the provisions of the two laws so conflict that they cannot stand together. It was said in Sinnot *v.* Davenport, 22 How. 227, 243 (16 L. Ed. 243), that, "In the application of this principal of supremacy of an act of Congress in a case where the state law is but the exercise of a reserved power, the repugnance or conflict should be direct and positive, so that the two acts could not be reconciled or consistently stand together." And in Reid *v.* Colorado, 187 U. S. 137, 148, 23 Sup. Ct. 92, 96 (47 L. Ed. 108), that court again said: "It should never be held that Congress intends to supersede, or by its legislation suspend, the exercise of the police powers of the states, even when it may do so, unless its purpose to effect that result is clearly manifested." The same principle was announced in Houston & Texas Cent. R. Co. *v.* Mayes, supra. By the congressional act of June 29, 1906, c. 3591, 34 Stat. 584 (U. S. Comp. St. Supp. 1909, p. 1149), amendatory of and supplemental to the act of Feb. 4, 1887, c. 104, 24 Stat. 379 (U. S. Comp. St. 1901, p. 3154), known as the interstate commerce law, the term "transportation"

Martin *v.* Oregon R. & Navigation Co

therein was declared to include cars, and it was provided that, "it shall be the duty of every carrier subject to the provisions of this act to provide and furnish such transportation upon reasonable request therefor," etc. By section 8 of the original act, the carrier omitting to do any act or thing required to be done is liable to the person injured thereby for the full amount of damages sustained, together with a reasonable attorney's fees, to be fixed by the court in case of recovery. We see no conflict between that legislation and the provisions of the state law, nor do we see any intent to exclude or supersede the state statute in regulating the furnishing of cars. Indeed, it can hardly be said that the federal act attempts to regulate that matter. It declares the primal duty to furnish cars upon reasonable request therefor, and stops with that. The penalty for a dereliction of that duty is damages suffered and reasonable attorney's fees. So far the two acts, federal and state, are identical, but the state law goes further. It regulates the manner of making the request, the time within which cars shall be furnished, the excuses that may be made for a failure to deliver cars, and adds an additional penalty by way of demurrage for a failure to comply with the terms of the statute. This statute, therefore, covers a field not occupied by the federal statute, and the principles announced in Reid *v.* Colorado, supra, are applicable to the facts of this case.

It is further contended that there is no authority of law to support the allowance to plaintiff of attorney's fees in an action based upon section 26 of the act of 1907. If there is any authorization in the law for attorney's fees, it is only by the terms of section 51 of the same act. This section is a general penal clause, making a railroad liable in treble damages, with attorney's fees, to any person injured by its violation of this act; but by a proviso the damages awarded an aggrieved party, provided for in section 26 of the act, by reason of the cars not being furnished when applied for, shall be in lieu of the treble damages awarded by section 51. The two sections, therefore, by the express terms of the law, are made to co-ordinate, so that the remedy of damages provided by the former section is substituted for those of the same character, but of different degree, named in the latter section. It follows, we think, that the allowance of attorney's fees, not being expressly excluded by the terms of the act, when the action is brought under section 26, plaintiff is entitled to an allowance, if the act is not amenable to defendant's further objections. Is section 51, in so far as it allows attorney's fees, void for the reason that it denies to the railroad company the equal protection of the law, and deprives it of its property without due process of law? Defendant asserts that it is, because it singles out the railroad company from all citizens and other corporations of the state, and requires it to pay attorney's fees to parties

Martin v. Oregon R. & Navigation Co

successfully suing it, while it gives to such company no corresponding right.

Defendant relies upon the case of Gulf, Colorado & S. F. R. Co. v. Ellis, 165 U. S. 150, 158, 17 Sup. Ct. 255, 41 L. Ed. 666. The single question in that case was the constitutionality of a statute of Texas, allowing any attorney's fee not exceeding $10 to a claimant, who demanded of a railroad company damages not exceeding $50, for stock killed or injured by trains, when the claim prior to the action had been presented and not paid within 30 days by the company causing the damage. An exhaustive discussion of the whole question is presented in an opinion by Mr. Justice Brewer. While the majority opinion holds that the particular statute in the respect named is void, still it is not questioned therein that railroad corporations may be for some purposes classified by themselves. This is because "the business in which they are engaged is of a peculiarly dangerous nature, and the Legislature, in the exercise of its police powers, may justly require many things to be done by them in order to secure life and property. Fencing of railroad tracks, use of safety couplers, and a multitude of other things easily suggest themselves. And any classification for the imposition of such special duties—duties arising out of the peculiar business in which they are engaged—is a just classification, and one not within the prohibition of the fourteenth amendment. Thus, it is frequently required that they fence their tracks, and as a penalty for a failure to fence double damages in case of loss are inflicted. Missouri Pac. Ry. Co. v. Humes, 115 U. S. 512 [6 Sup. Ct. 110, 29 L. Ed. 463]. But this and all kindred cases proceed upon the theory of a special duty resting upon railroad corporations by reason of the business in which they are engaged, a duty not resting upon others; a duty which can be enforced by the Legislature in any proper manner; and whether it enforces it by penalties in the way of fines coming to the state, or by double damages to a party injured, is immaterial. It is all done in the exercise of the police power of the state and with a view to enforce just and reasonable regulations."

Now, in that case it was pointed out that there was no special duty resting upon the railroad company to fence its tracks. The Legislature of that state had not deemed it necessary, for the protection of life or property, to require railroads to fence their tracks, and as no duty was imposed, there could be no penalty for nonperformance; hence no valid reason could be found in that case upon which to base the attempted classification. But such it not the situation here. Under this statute a special duty is imposed upon railroads to furnish cars within certain specified times to intending shippers.

In the more recent case of Atchison, Topeka & S. F. R. R. v. Matthews, 174 U. S. 96, 19 Sup. Ct. 609, 43 L. Ed. 909, involving the validity of a similar provision in a statute of Kansas, the court, in an opinion by the same justice, sustained the statute, distinguishing that case from the Ellis Case upon the point above considered. The holding of the court in the Matthews Case has since been cited and followed by that court in a number of cases. Fidelity Mutual Life Ass'n *v.* Mettler, 185 U. S. 308, 22 Sup. Ct. 662, 46 L. Ed. 922; Farmers' M. Ins. Co. *v.* Dobney, 189 U. S. 301, 23 Sup. Ct. 565, 47 L. Ed. 821.

Other errors assigned for a reversal of the judgment have been considered, but we find no substantial error therein.

The judgment is affirmed.

TAUGHER *v.* NORTHERN PAC. RY. CO. *et al.*

(Supreme Court of North Dakota, Nov. 23, 1910. Rehearing Denied Jan. 28, 1911.)

[129 N. W. Rep. 747.]

Witnesses—Credibility—Cross-Examination — Inconsistent Statements.—In an action for damages for conversion of grain by a common carrier, intrusted to it for transportation, one of the defenses relied upon by appellant was that the grain did not belong to the plaintiff consignor, but was the property of one C. In attempting to make proof of such ownership after proper foundation laid and after C. had testified that the grain all belonged to plaintiff, C. was interrogated as to whether he had made statements to the effect that he owned the grain. Held, that such questions were proper as going to the credibility of C. as a witness, when offered for that purpose, and that it was reversible error of the trial court to sustain objections to such questions.

Carriers—Carriage of Grain—Failure to Deliver—Action.—On proof of delivery of property to a common carrier in sound condition and of its failure to redeliver it, a sufficient case is made to sustain a recovery for loss in an action by the shipper on his contract, with certain exceptions which have no application in this case, but other and different proof may be necessary in such case to sustain an action for conversion against the carrier.

Trover and Conversion—"Conversion" Defined.—To constitute conversion, there must be a positive tortious act, a tortious detention of personal property from the owner or its destruction or an exclusion or defiance of the owner's right, or the withholding of possession under a claim of title inconsistent with that of the owner.

Carriers—Carriage of Goods—Failure to Deliver—Action on Contract.—The gist of the action on the contract in such case is the failure to deliver, while the gist of an action in trover is the conver-

Taugher *v.* Northern Pac. Ry. Co. et al

sion; and the mere showing of a breach of contract may not prove conversion.

Carriers—Carriage of Goods—Failure to Deliver—Action.—If a shipper elects to sue for conversion and fails to establish the elements necessary to constitute conversion, his action must fail unless his complaint states facts necessary to sustain a recovery on the contract or some other proper form of recovery, as the burden is on the shipper when he seeks the benefit of the measure of damages for conversion to prove the act of conversion.

Carriers—Conversion—Proof of Demand and Refusal to Deliver Goods.*—While proof of a demand and refusal to deliver the property or thing may establish conversion in connection with other facts, the demand and refusal are only evidence of conversion when the defendant was in such condition that it might have delivered the property if it would, and conversion does not lie against a common carrier for a mere nonfeasance nor for goods stolen from the carrier, nor for negligence causing the loss, nor for bare omission.

Carriers—Carriage of Goods—Attachment—Duty of Carrier to Notify Shipper.†—When goods in transit are taken from the carrier by an officer under a writ of attachment against a third party, it is incumbent on the carrier, in an action for conversion, to give immediate notice to the shipper, and, on failing to give such notice so as to enable the shipper to protect himself, the carrier assumes the burden of establishing the legality of the proceedings on which the attachment was made, and the fact that the writ was regular on its face does not protect the carrier if such writ was in law void.

Justices of the Peace—Attachment—Time for Issuance.—A justice of the peace acquires no jurisdiction to issue a writ of attachment until the summons in the action is issued, as attachment is a provisional or dependent remedy, which has no existence until the commencement of an action.

Carriers—Nondelivery of Goods—Proof of Value.—When delivery by a carrier to an officer, under a valid writ of attachment, constitutes conversion, proof of the value of the property delivered as of the date delivered to the officer is competent proof of value to support a recovery.

Chattel Mortgages—Delivery of Property to Mortgagee for Sale.—In the absence of other existing liens on property, a mortgagor may legally surrender the mortgaged property to the mortgagee and authorize its sale and the application of the proceeds to the mort-

---

*For the authorities in this series on the question what does, and does not, constitute conversion of freight by the carrier, see footnote of Spokane Grain Co. *v.* Great Northern Express Co. (Wash.). 34 R. R. R. 463, 57 Am. & Eng. R. Cas., N. S., 463.

†For the authorities in this series on the subject of the duties and liabilities of the carrier with respect to freight seized while in its possession under legal process, see foot-note of Southern Ry. Co. *v.* Heymann (Ga.), 9 R. R. R. 574, 32 Am. & Eng. R. Cas., N. S., 574; extensive note, 23 R. R. R. 212, 46 Am. & Eng. R. Cas., N. S., 212.

Taugher *v.* Northern Pac. Ry. Co. et al

gage debt, though no default has occurred in the terms of the mortgage.

Evidence—Admissibility.—A justice summons bore date two days after the date of filing with the justice of the complaint, affidavit, and undertaking for attachment and issuance of the writ of attachment. Held that, on the offer of such papers in evidence in an attempt to show that they were simultaneously issued, it was not error to exclude them from evidence.

Evidence—Best and Secondary.—Section 8530, Rev. Codes 1905, requires a justice of the peace to keep a docket and enter therein in continuous order, with the proper date, each act done during the course of litigation, and section 8351 provides that the docket so kept cannot be disputed in a collateral proceeding; that it or a duly certified transcript thereof is competent evidence of the matters to which it relates. Held, that the sections referred to make such docket the best evidence of the facts required to be and which are entered therein by the justice, and that, in the absence of any offer of such docket or a transcript thereof as evidence, no attempt being made to account for its absence, parol evidence is not admissible under the facts disclosed to show that the summons was in fact issued simultaneous with the issuance of a writ of attachment.

(Syllabus by the Court.)

Appeal from District Court Stutsman County; Burke, Judge.

Action by Lillian B. Taugher against the Northern Pacific Railway Company and others. From a judgment for plaintiff and an order denying a new trial, the mentioned defendant appeals. Reversed, and new trial granted appellant.

Ball, Watson, Young & Lawrence, for appellant.

Lee Combs, for respondent.

SPALDING, J. This is an appeal by one of the defendants, the Northern Pacific Railway Company, from a judgment in favor of the plaintiff, Lillian B. Taugher, and from an order overruling and denying said defendant's motion for judgment notwithstanding the verdict or for a new trial. The action was brought against the Northern Pacific Railway Company, a corporation, Peter Kerner, and the firm of Olson, Preszler & Bollinger. The complaint, omitting the formal parts, alleges that on or about the 3d day of January, 1908, plaintiff was the owner and in possession of 550 bushels of flax at the village of Crystal Springs, N. D., of the value of $561, and that on said day and at said place she delivered said flax to the defendant railway company as a common carrier of freight, and caused it to be loaded in one of its cars, No. 4077, to be by it transported for her to Duluth, Minn., upon the customary terms; that on the same day she was entitled to the possession of 374 bushels of other flax at the village of Crystal Springs, and was then and there in possession thereof and then and there delivered the same to the said railway company, together with the flax above mentioned, and loaded it in the same car with the first-mentioned flax; that said company received all such flax, and undertook to transport it to Duluth for plaintiff upon the usual terms, etc., and then and there gave plaintiff a bill of lading therefor; and that the value of the flax last mentioned was $381.48. The complaint then sets forth the plaintiff's right of possession as resting upon a chattel mortgage duly executed, delivered, and filed covering the last-mentioned flax, and that the conditions of such mortgage and the note secured thereby were in default. It alleges the conversion of the said flax between the 3d and 7th days of January, 1908, at or near the village of Medina, N. D., by each and all of the defendants, and a demand thereafter made therefor, and its refusal, and prays judgment for the value of the flax and interest. The defendant and appellant the Northern Pacific Railway Company answered, admitting that on January 3, 1908, there was delivered to it a car load of flax consigned in the name of the plaintiff to the consignee at Duluth, Minn., and alleging that it had no knowledge or information sufficient to form a brief as to the allegations contained in the complaint as to the amount, value, and ownership thereof or of the nature and extent of the plaintiff's interest and rights therein, and denied all other allegations. Defendant Peter Kerner answered, denying every allegation of the complaint not admitted, qualified, or explained, and attempted to justify the taking of 327 bushels and 40 pounds of flax, alleging that it belonged to one Christianson, and was in a Northern Pacific car at Medina, as constable of Stutsman county, on or about the 4th of January, 1908, under an execution (evidently meaning writ of attachment) issued by one Todd, justice of the peace. The defendants Olson, Preszler & Bollinger answered in substantially the same form as defendant Kerner, except that they attempted to justify the taking of 327 bushels and 40 pounds under a writ of attachment delivered to Kerner as constable and the seizure thereof under such writ, and a sale to satisfy a judgment rendered on the 10th of January, 1908. Neither of the answers identifies any of the flax taken as the flax shipped by the plaintiff. A trial was had in district court and two questions were submitted to the jury, namely: "(1) Was there any difference in amount in the grain put into the car at Crystal Springs by Christianson and the amount of grain taken out thereof on the following Monday at Medina?" This was answered in the affirmative. "(2) If so, what was the amount of the difference?" The answer to this question was 503 bushels, gross, and a general verdict was returned in favor of the plaintiff and against all of the defendants, assessing her damages at $835.33, with interest from the

4th of January, 1908, on which verdict judgment was entered. The defendant the Northern Pacific Railway Company appeals separately. The other defendants are not in this court. We seldom have an appeal before us in which the record contains so confusing a mass of objections, motions, and offers. It contains 79 assignments and 137 specifications of error. The objections of plaintiff to questions and the motions to strike out answers in most instances fail to specify adequately the grounds on which they are based. We infer from the briefs that many of those made by respondent were intended to be directed to the admissibility of testimony or evidence of justification under the answer of appellant, but they are invariably inadequate to raise that question. We are at a loss to determine whether the appellant defended the action on the theory that it could justify the delivery of the grain to a third party under its own general denial, or that it might do so under the attempted pleas of justification contained in the answers of the other defendants. We set forth enough of the facts to show the theories of the prosecution and defense and our conclusions on the controlling questions properly before us, but omitting consideration of many which we deem immaterial.

It appears that the plaintiff and one Christianson owned two adjoining quarter sections of land about 1½ miles from Crystal Springs station, in Kidder county. The plaintiff resides during the winter in Minneapolis, Minn., and the remainder of the year on her land near Crystal Springs. The flax first referred to in the complaint was grown on her land, and that last referred to on the land belonging to Christianson. Christianson did the work of cultivating her land and harvesting the crop, and on the 4th day of January, 1908, plaintiff's testimony shows that he completed by her instruction the loading of the flax raised on both places into a car of the defendant railway company at Crystal Springs for which he took a bill of lading in the name of the plaintiff; the flax being consigned by her direction to a firm in Duluth. It was not weighed on shipment. Both plaintiff and Christianson testified that the flax grown on the plaintiff's land belonged to her, and that he was hired to do the work on her place during the season of 1907. She held Christianson's note for $1,000, bearing date May 24, 1907, and due on or before April 1, 1908, secured by chattel mortgage covering the flax raised on his land during the season of 1907. This mortgage bore even date with the note, and contained the usual provisions. Plaintiff and Christianson testified that by agreement between them he turned over to her the flax covered by such mortgage, and it was to be sold with the flax raised on her land and the proceeds of the mortgaged flax retained by her to apply on the indebtedness covered by the mortgage. When the car reached Medina station eight miles from Crystal Springs on Saturday,

Taugher *v.* Northern Pac. Ry. Co. et al

the 4th of January, it was side tracked, and on Monday, the 6th, all the flax then in the car was attached by the defendant Kerner as constable of Stutsman county on the writ of attachment referred to in the pleadings at the suit of the firm of Olson, Preszler & Bollinger instituted in justice court upon a debt due from Christianson to said firm. All the flax then in the car was removed, judgment was obtained against Christianson, and the flax sold on the 10th of February, 1908, and the proceeds paid into justice court. The affidavit and undertaking for attachment and complaint bore date and were filed in such court on the 4th of January, 1908, but the summons bore date January 6, 1908, and the sheriff's return showed that the papers came to his hands on the latter date.

1. It is contended by the appellant that there is no misconduct shown on its part which constitutes an act of conversion such as is necessary to sustain the action of trover. There was much testimony submitted regarding the amount of flax removed from the car at Medina and the amount shipped, but no direct evidence showing what became of the difference of 503 bushels found by the jury, except that Christianson testified that, when the loading was completed at Crystal Springs, he procured locks and closed and locked the car doors. He and others testified that the flax covered the highest grain mark, and reached a point about two feet below the roof of the car. It was shown that, when the car reached Medina and when the attachment was levied, one of the outer doors was partially open, and only about two feet of flax in the car, but men employed on the train, some of whom rode in the caboose, testified that they had seen none upon the track and none leaking from the car, while it was being picked up at Crystal Springs or switched in the yards at Medina and there was no indication of the car being leaky. An inland common carrier is an insurer against loss of property consigned to it for carriage between its receipt at shipping point and arrival at destination, when unaccompanied by the consignor, except through loss occasioned (1) by an inherent defect, vice, or weakness or spontaneous action of the property itself; (2) the act of a public enemy of the United States or of this state; (3) the act of the law; or (4) any irresistible superhuman cause. Section 5690. Rev. Codes 1905; Duncan *v.* G. N. Ry. Co., 17 N. D. 610, 118 N. W. 826, 19 L. R. A. (N. S.) 952. On proof of the delivery of the property to the carrier in sound condition and of the failure to redeliver it, a sufficient case is made to sustain a recovery for loss by the shipper, and the burden is upon the carrier to exonerate itself from liability in case of loss by showing that such loss was occasioned by one or more of the exceptions mentioned. Duncan *v.* Ry. Co., supra. The loss being shown, the burden would fall upon the appellant in a proper action to excuse itself on some of the grounds above mentioned.

Taugher *v.* Northern Pac. Ry. Co. et al

It failed to do so as to the 503 bushels of flax. The plaintiff, having proved the delivery and failure to redeliver, would be entitled to recover in an action on her contract or some other suitable form of action; but does it entitle her to recover in an action for the conversion of the 503 bushels? To constitute conversion, there must be a positive tortious act, a tortious detention of personal property from the owner, or its destruction, or an exclusion or defiance of the owner's right, or the withholding of possession under a claim of title inconsistent with that of the owner. 8 Waits' Actions and Defenses, 1194; Bolling *v.* Kirby, 90 Ala. 215, 7 South. 914, 24 Am. St. Rep. 789; Terry *v.* Bank, 93 Ala. 599, 9 South. 299, 30 Am. St. Rep. 87, and note; 2 Kinkead's Commentaries on Torts, § 582; Tinker *v.* Morrill, 39 Vt. 477, 94 Am. Dec. 345; Magnin *v.* Dinsmore, 70 N. Y. 417, 26 Am. Rep. 608. The gist of an action on the contract is the failure to deliver, but the gist of this action is the conversion. Bigelow *v.* Heintze, 53 N. J. Law, 69, 21 Atl. 109. To maintain the action some wrongful act on the part of the appellant must be shown. The mere showing of a breach of contract does not necessarily prove conversion, though the defendant may be liable on the contract. The rules of evidence and measure of damages are not the same in an action for conversion and in one on the contract for carriage. A common carrier is liable for loss of property in transit in many instances where it is chargeable with no wrongful act, and even where its loss is without fault of the carrier, but the shipper is confined in such cases to the proper remedy. In most cases more than one remedy is applicable and he has his election, while in others an action for conversion does not lie, though one for damages for breach of contract may. If the shipper elects to sue for conversion and is unable or fails to establish the elements necessary to constitute conversion, he must fail in that form of action. The burden is on the shipper, when he elects to seek the benefit of the measure of damages in an action charging conversion, to prove the act of conversion by showing a wrongful disposition or wrongful withholding of the property. Moore on Carriers, 217; Wamsley *v.* Atlas Steamship Co., 168 N. Y. 533, 61 N. E. 896, 85 Am. St. Rep. 699; Tinker *v.* Morrill, supra; Magnin et al. *v.* Dinsmore, supra; Whitney *v.* Slauson, 30 Barb. (N. Y.) 276. In such case the demand and refusal may be prima facie evidence of the conversion, or, when the other facts warrant it, of course, may establish the conversion, but the demand and refusal are only evidence of conversion where the defendant was in such condition that he might have delivered the property if he would. Tinker *v.* Morrill, supra; Whitney *v.* Slauson, supra; Hawkins *v.* Hoffman, 6 Hill (N. Y.) 586, 41 Am. Dec. 767; 24 Am. St. Rep., note page 807. The action for conversion for failure to deliver or return on demand does not lie against a carrier for a

Taugher v. Northern Pac. Ry. Co. et al

mere nonfeasance when the nonfeasance of the defendant was
the cause of the loss of the goods, nor does it lie for goods stolen
from the carrier nor for negligence causing the loss. It must
be for an actual wrong, an injurious conversion, something more
than a bare omission. Goldbowitz v. Met. Express Co. (Sup.)
91 N. Y. Supp. 318; Hawkins v. Hoffman, supra; Abraham v.
Nunn, 42 Ala. 51; Dearbourn v. Bank, 58 Me. 273; Yale v.
Saunders, 16 Vt. 243; Moses v. Norris, 4 N. H. 304; Packard v.
Getman, 4 Wend. (N. Y.) 615, 21 Am. Dec. 166; Bailey v.
Moulthrop, 55 Vt. 13; Bowlin v. Nye, 10 Cush. (Mass.) 416;
Tinker v. Morrill, supra; Magnin v. Dinsmore, supra; Whitney
v. Slauson, supra. It is unnecessary to review these authorities.
The cases of Wamsley v. Atlas Steamship Co. and Tinker v.
Morrill and authorities therein cited and quoted are directly in
point, and we conclude that plaintiff failed to establish the con-
version of the 503 bushels of flax. As we have indicated, she
still has her remedy in a proper action. The complaint in this
case will not justify a recovery upon the contract.

2. Appellant contends that it is not liable in this action for the
flax attached by the officer. In this we think it is mistaken.
As before observed, the appellant did not plead justification, and
in view of the importance of this question and of the fact that
only three members of this court participate in this decision, and
that the objections by respondent to evidence were, in our opinion, inadequate and too indefinite to raise the question, we shall
not pass upon the necessity of pleading justification. If the appellant wrongfully delivered the flax attached to the officer,
it is clear, under the authorities, that this constitutes an act of
conversion, and, as under the pleadings and facts disclosed no
demand was necessary, the date of the conversion was the date
of the delivery, rather than the date of the demand. Wellman
et al. v. English, 38 Cal. 583; Moore v. Murdock, 26 Cal. 515;
Ledley v. Hays, 1 Cal. 160; Boulware v. Craddock, et al., 30
Cal. 190. Appellant urges that the process or writ by which
the flax was attached and taken was regular upon its face, and
that this is as far as the appellant or the court is required to investigate in deciding this question. We have spent much time
in an effort to determine what the law is as applicable to the
facts disclosed, and have concluded that it is unnecessary to pass
upon the regularity of this writ and its justification of the appellant. The authorities, so far as we find them referring to
the subject, are uniform in holding that something more than
the regularity of the writ of attachment on its face may be necessary. The carrier must notify the shipper of the taking of
the property so as to enable him to protect himself by making a
defense or otherwise, and, on the failure of the carrier to give
such notice, it either becomes absolutely liable or assumes the
burden of proving the regularity of all proceedings on which

Taugher v. Northern Pac. Ry. Co. et al

the attachment rested. Without intimating any views as to the first line of authorities, it is sufficient to say that in the case at bar the carrier gave no notice to the shipper of the attachment, and it thereby assumed the burden of establishing the regularity of the proceedings on which the attachment was made. Merz v. C. & N. W. Ry. Co., 86 Minn. 33, 90 N. W. 7; cases cited in note 34 Am. St. Rep. p. 736; Horn v. Corvarubias, 51 Cal. 524; Jewett v. Olsen, 18 Or. 419, 23 Pac. 262, 17 Am. St. Rep. 745. And many authorities hold that a plea of justification is bad unless it avers the giving of such notice. 2 Hutchinson on Carriers, § 743, note 23. None of the answers contained any such averment. That these proceedings were so irregular as to render the writ of attachment void can hardly be questioned. As we have shown, the papers were all filed and the writ of attachment issued on the 4th of January. The summons was not issued until the 6th of January as shown by its date. Section 8358, Rev. Codes 1905, fixes the commencement of an action in justice court at the time of the issuance of the summons, when no voluntary appearance is made, and section 8369 provides that a writ of attachment of personal property of the defendant may be issued by the justice at the time or after the issuance of the summons and before answer, on receiving an affidavit by or on behalf of the plaintiff stating the facts necessary to be stated, as grounds of attachment. It is clear from this provision that the justice acquired no jurisdiction to issue a writ of attachment until the summons is issued, and not having such jurisdiction, the writ issued in the instant case conferred no authority to make the attachment. There must first be an action and there is no action until the summons is issued. Attachment is a provisional or dependent remedy, and has no existence independent of an action. Gans v. Beasley, 4 N. D. 140, 59 N. W. 714; Smith v. Nicholson, 5 N. D. 426, 67 N. W. 296; Hall & Head v. Grogan, 78 Ky. 11. We hold that the appellant failed to bring itself within the rule referred to by failing to show that its default was occasioned by the act of the law, and that, in the absence of other considerations, it would be liable for the flax taken by the constable.

3. It is contended that the proof fails to show the value of the flax at the date of the conversion, if there was a conversion. This contention rests upon the assumption that the conversion occurred on the 11th of February when the demand was made. The proof submitted related to the value of the flax at the date of the delivery to the constable, and this was the date of the conversion.

4. Numerous errors assigned relate to the refusal of the court to allow the defendant to impeach the testimony of the plaintiff's witness Christianson as to statements concerning the ownership of the flax in question. While not pleaded, one theory of the

defense in the trial court was that all the flax belonged to Christianson, and that the shipping of it in the name of the respondent had been arranged between Christianson and her for the purpose of defrauding Christianson's creditors. The witness Christianson was inquired of regarding certain statements as to the ownership of the flax raised on respondent's land during the year 1907, and by the questions it was intimated that an attempt would be made to show that he had told other parties that all the flax on both places raised during 1907 belonged to him.   He denied making such statements, and the court sustained objections to questions asked the witnesses to whom reference was made in the inquiries of Christianson as to his having made them.   These questions were apparently excluded on the theory that they were intended to serve as admissions on the part of Christianson as the agent of respondent, and that she could not be bound by such admissions if made.   We, however, think their exclusion was error prejudicial to appellant.   One of the purposes of the testimony sought to be introduced was to discredit the testimony of Christianson to the effect that a portion of the flax belonged to Miss Taugher.   It is clear that evidence of contradictory statements made by him was admissible for this purpose, and its admission might have influenced the jury in arriving at its verdict, provided there was any evidence to go to the jury as to the ownership of all of the flax by Christianson.   The circumstances and the relations of the parties, as shown, were such as to render impeaching testimony on this subject material, and we cannot say that, had it been received, the jury might not properly have found the ownership in Christianson.

5. It is insisted that proof of default in the terms of the mortgage entitling plaintiff to possession of the flax was necessary. We do not concur in this view.   If the flax belonged to Christianson and if respondent held a valid mortgage on it, in the absence of existing liens held at the time of shipment by any of the interested parties, he could legally surrender the flax to her and authorize her to sell it and apply the proceeds on the mortgage debt, even though no default had occurred in the terms of the mortgage; but even with existing inferior liens they would not have been injured, as its value was less than the debt secured by the mortgage to plaintiff. Lovejoy v. Bank, 5 N. D. 624. 67 N. W. 956.   We are not concerned with what the rights of the parties might have been had the defendant been claiming under a subsisting lien at the time of the shipment.

6. It was not error for the trial court to refuse to admit in evidence the summons, undertaking for attachment, writ of attachment, affidavit for attachment, and complaint.   They did not tend to prove the facts which they were offered to prove. They

tended to show that the ... ...
after the w... ... attachment ... ... and ... ...
sons above stated the ... ...
reject the ... ...
attempt to show that a mistake ... ... the summons, and that ... fact ... was ... ... the writ
of attachment. Such ... ... was ... ... sec. ...
8350. Rev. C... ... the justice is required ... ... a ... ...
in which he shall enter ... ... with ... ...,
each act done during the ... ... section ...
the Legislature has said that ... ... true and
correct in all matters appearing therein as required by law, and
cannot be disputed in a ... ... proceeding and ... ... a
duly certified transcript thereof is ... ... evidence of the
matters to which it relates. Such ... ... and entries thereon of
the dates and facts required to be entered were the best evidence,
and should have been offered before secondary evidence was
admissible. We need not decide whether impeaching evidence
would have been admissible had the docket been offered, and
had it shown the same dates of issuance given on the papers.
No tender was made of such record or a certified transcript
thereof as evidence, and its absence was not excused; hence
secondary evidence was incompetent.

The judgment and the order of the district court denying a
new trial are reversed, and a new trial granted, as to the appeal-
ing defendant the Northern Pacific Railway Company only. All
concur, except ELLSWORTH, J., disqualified, and MORGAN, C. J.,
not participating.

COMMONWEALTH *v.* ILLINOIS CENT. R. CO.

(Court of Appeals of Kentucky, Jan. 11, 1911.)

[133 S. W. Rep. 1158.]

Constitutional Law—Separate Coach Law.*—Ky. St. § 795 (Russell's St. § 5343), providing that a railroad company operating railroad cars in the state shall furnish separate coaches for transportation of white and colored passengers, but that each compartment of a coach divided by a substantial wooden partition with a door therein shall be deemed a separate coach within the act, and that each separate coach and compartment shall bear a notice indicating the race for which it is set apart, is not unconstitutional.

Railroads—Separate Accommodations for White and Colored Races —Duty to Furnish.—A Pullman sleeping car controlled wholly by servants of the Pullman Company, and the fares in which were exclusively received by that company, where it does not appear that the carrier was paid anything by the Pullman Company for handling the sleeper, the only benefit it presumably derived therefor being the inducement for an increased travel, was not operated by the carrier to whom it was delivered for transportation within Ky. St. § 795 (Russell's St. § 5343), and the carrier not being required to furnish sleeping cars under the act, was not liable thereunder for hauling the sleeper which contained no separate compartments for white and colored passengers or for failure to require a colored passenger therein to enter the compartment of the separate day coach set aside for his race where he had provided himself before reaching the state with a ticket entitling him to ride in the sleeper and was a passenger thereof when the sleeper was attached to the carrier's train, and also held a ticket entitling him to be carried through the state upon the carrier's train to which the sleeper was attached.

Railroads—Carriage of Passengers—Separate Accommodations for White and Colored Passengers.—The carrier, having furnished day coaches with the prescribed separate compartments for the white and colored races, and having properly labeled them, even if it were the duty of the conductor of the train to require the colored person to leave the sleeper and take the colored compartment in the day coach, would not be liable under Ky. St. § 795 (Russell's St. § 5343), for his failure to do so; such failure being an offense of the conductor.

Appeal from Circuit Court, McCracken County.

The Illinois Central Railroad was indicted for neglecting to provide separate cars and compartments on cars operated by it for transportation of white and colored passengers. There was

---

*See foot-note of Hart *v.* State (Md.), 16 R. R. R. 622, 39 Am. & Eng. R. Cas., N. S., 622.

a judgment of dismissal, and the Commonwealth appeals. Affirmed.

James Breathitt, Atty. Gen., *Tom B. McGregor*, Asst. Atty. Gen., *John G. Lovett*, Commonwealth's Atty., and *S. E. Clay*, County Atty., for the Commonwealth.

Wheeler & Hughes, Blewitt Lee, and *Trabue, Doolan & Cox*, for appellee.

Settle, J. The grand jury of McCracken county returned against appellee in the circuit court of that county the following indictment: "The grand jurors of the county of McCracken in the name and by the authority of the commonwealth of Kentucky accuse the Illinois Central Railroad Company of the offense of operating and running railroad cars and coaches by steam on a railroad track and line for the transportation of white and colored passengers without having upon each car and coach and compartment thereof in some conspicuous place appropriate words in plain letters indicating the race for which said coach and car and compartment had been and should have been set apart, committed in the manner and form as follows, to wit: The said Illinois Central Railroad Company in the said county of McCracken on the 4th day of May, 1910, and within one year before finding this indictment, did willfully and unlawfully fail, refuse, and neglect to furnish and provide separate cars and coaches and compartments upon the railroad coaches and cars being operated by it by steam on its railroad track and the line for the travel and transportation of white and colored passengers, with each compartment, coach, and car having in some conspicuous place appropriate words in plain letters indicating the race for which it had been and should have been set apart; the said Illinois Central Railroad Company being at the time engaged in operating and running railroad coaches and cars upon a railroad line and track in the state of Kentucky and McCracken county, against the peace and dignity of the commonwealth of Kentucky." Section 795, Ky. St. (Russell's St. § 5343). for the alleged violation of which appellee was indicted, reads as follows: "Any railroad company or corporation, person or persons, running or otherwise operating railroad cars or coaches, by steam or otherwise, on any railroad line or track within this state, and all railroad companies, person or persons doing business in this state, whether upon lines of railroad owned in part or whole, or leased by them; and all railroad companies, person or persons, operating railroad lines that may hereafter be built under existing charters, or charters that may hereafter be granted in this state; and all foreign corporations, companies, person or persons, organized under charters granted or that may be hereafter granted, by any other state. who may now, or may hereafter be, engaged in running or operating any of the railroads of this state, either in part or whole, either in their own name, or that of others, are hereby required to furnish separate coaches or cars for the travel or transportation of the white and colored passengers on their respective lines of railroad. Each compartment of a coach divided by a good and substantial wooden partition, with a door therein, shall be deemed a separate coach within the meaning of this act, and each separate coach and compartment shall bear in some conspicuous place appropriate words in plain letters indicating the race for which it is set apart." Appellee entered a plea of not guilty, and, both parties having waived the right of trial by jury and agreed in writing upon the facts constituting the entire evidence, the court, following the submission of the case, rendered judgment holding appellee not guilty and dismissing the indictment. The commonwealth was refused a new trial, and being dissatisfied with that ruling, as well as the judgment, it has appealed.

According to the agreed statement of facts, appellee's railroad runs from the city of Louisville through the state of Kentucky, by way of Paducah, to Memphis, Tenn., and that on the day and occasion indicated in the indictment appellee ran a train from Louisville to Paducah and points without the state south thereof, which consisted of an engine, tender, baggage car, compartment day car, ordinary day car, and a Pullman or sleeping car; that the compartment car was divided by a substantial wooden partition, on one side of which the seats were exclusively assigned to and occupied by colored passengers, and on the other side by white passengers; that the partition on the side assigned to colored persons contained in a conspicuous place and in plain letters the words, "Exclusively for the use of colored persons," and on the other side in an equally conspicuous place and letters the words, "Exclusively for the use of white persons"; that the ordinary day car also bore in a conspicuous place and letters the words, "Exclusively for the use of white persons"; that the Pullman sleeper was in the rear of the other cars, but did not have therein a sign or contain words indicating to what race it was set apart. It further appears from the agreed statement of facts that the sleeper was delivered to appellee by the Baltimore & Ohio Southwestern Railroad Company at Louisville, to be hauled by it through Kentucky and into Tennessee; that at the time of its delivery to appellee the sleeper contained, among other passengers, one colored man, whose ticket, which had been purchased at a point without Kentucky, entitled him to ride over the Baltimore & Ohio Southwestern Railroad to Louisville, and from that city over appellee's railroad through Kentucky and to Memphis, Tenn.; that the colored passenger in question had also purchased from the Pullman Company, before reaching Kentucky, a sleeper ticket which entitled him to ride in the

sleeper, and to occupy the berth or section designated by the
ticket while being hauled by the Baltimore & Ohio Southwestern
Railroad Company to Louisville, and likewise by the appellee
railroad company from Louisville through Kentucky and Tennessee to Memphis in the latter state, his destination. It also
·appears from the agreed facts that the Pullman car was
manned by a conductor and porter in the employ and under the
control of the Pullman Company, that none of the proceeds
derived from the sale of tickets for berths or space in the
Pullman car belonged to appellee or was received by it, nor did
it derive any revenue from persons purchasing such berths or
space, other than for the sale of transportation on its railroad
train paid by passengers for riding in the day coaches.
     The constitutionality of the statute under consideration has
been repeatedly sustained. Ohio Valley Railway's Receiver v.
Lander, 104 Ky. 431, 47 S. W. 344, 882, 48 S. W. 145, 20 Ky.
Law Rep. 913; Quinn v. L. & N. R. R. Co., 98 Ky. 231, 32 S.
W. 742, 17 Ky. Law Rep. 811; L. & N. R. R. Co. v. Commonwealth, 99 Ky. 663, 37 S. W. 79, 18 Ky. Law Rep. 491; Chesapeake & O. R. Co. v. Commonwealth, 51 S. W. 160, 21 Ky.
Law Rep. 228; C. & O. Ry. Co. v. Commonwealth, 179 U. S.
388, 21 Sup. Ct. 101, 45 L. Ed. 244. A sleeping car owned by
the Pullman Car Company manned and controlled wholly by its
servants and the fares for berths and seats in which were exclusively received and owned by that company was not, because
attached to and hauled with appellee's passenger train, operated
by it within the meaning of the statute, supra. A railroad coach
or car provided with seats and other conveniences is a vehicle
for transporting persons, paying for the privilege. from one
place to another. A sleeping car is a vehicle for repose as well
as transportation. While equipped with seats and greater conveniences than are found in the day coach, the seats are readily
converted into berths or sleeping places for the repose of persons occupying them, but, to entitle such persons to seats or
berths in the sleeper, they must pay the Pullman Company the
fare it charges therefor, and, in addition, pay the railroad company to whose train the sleeper is attached the regular fare it
charges persons for the privilege of riding the same distance
in one of its ordinary or day coaches. It does not appear from
the statement of facts that appellee was paid anything by the
Pullman Company for hauling its sleeper, in view of which
and of the admitted fact that it received no part of the fares
collected by the Pullman Company of persons riding in the
sleeper, we must assume that the only benefit it derived from the
hauling of the sleeper was the increase of travel, which the
greater comfort and security its connection with the train assured, especially to the sick and unprotected who travel alone.
It is patent that the only control appellee had of the sleeper was

Commonwealth v. Illinois Cent. R. Co

such as was necessary to its safe transportation. In other respects the sleeper, together with its occupants, was under the exclusive control of the servants of the Pullman Company in charge of it.

It goes without saying that for any injury to the occupants of the sleeper that might have resulted from the negligence of appellee's servants in charge of the train in operating it appellee would have been liable in a civil action for damages; but that this is true does not make it liable to indictment because of its hauling the sleeping car with its unseparated colored passenger and white passengers within or through the state, because in thus handling the sleeper appellee did not operate it in the meaning of the statute. It is admitted that appellee's train contained a separate coach for white and colored passengers, partitioned and lettered as required by the statute, and, if the colored passenger in the sleeper had become a passenger of the train upon a ticket merely entitling him to ride in an ordinary or day coach, upon his entering the train, it would have been the duty of appellee's conductor to direct and require him to enter the compartment of the separate coach set apart for the use of colored persons. But such was not the way in which the colored person became a passenger. He provided himself before reaching this state with a ticket for the sleeper, and before or after he arrived in this state with a ticket that also entitled him to be carried to Memphis, Tenn., by or upon appellee's train to which the sleeper in which he was a passenger was attached at Louisville. He was therefore a passenger of the sleeper when it was attached to appellee's train, and whether entitled to be classed as an interstate passenger or not (a question we do not decide) appellee's conductor had no such control of the sleeper, its crew, or passengers, as would have authorized him to compel the colored passenger to leave it and enter the compartment of the separate coach set apart for colored persons, nor could he have required the conductor of the sleeper to eject such colored passenger therefrom and assign him to the car designated for persons of his color.

In the case of Louisville & Nashville Railroad Company v. Commonwealth, 99 Ky. 663, 37 S. W. 79, which was a penal prosecution under the statute, supra, against the railroad company for unlawfully and willfully by its agents in charge of its train failing and refusing, as alleged, to furnish a separate coach for white and colored passengers, it appeared from the proof that the train had been chartered by two individuals to run from Greensburg to Campbellsville and return the same day, that they collected the fares and directed at what stations the train should stop, but that the train was operated by the company's crew, including the conductor. Among the passengers on the train were two negroes, Thomas White and his wife.

Commonwealth *v.* Illinois Cent. R. Co

When they boarded the train, they entered the compartment of
the separate coach set apart for persons of their color and which
had theretofore been so used by the railroad company, but, before reaching their destination, they were compelled to give up
the colored compartment to white persons and ride in a mail
and tool car attached to the train. It also appeared from the
proof that the compartment of the separate coach set apart for
colored passengers and from which White and wife were ejected
conformed in its finish and appointments to the requirements of
the statute. Upon the state of facts thus presented, we said:
"Where the company has furnished the kind of cars or coaches
which the law requires, section 799, Ky. St. [Russell's St. §
5347], imposes the duty on the conductor or manager of the
railroad to assign the white and colored passengers to their respective coaches or compartments therein. Section 800 [sec-
tion 5348] provides a penalty to be imposed on the conductor or
manager for his failure to discharge the duty of him. This is not
a proceeding to recover damages of the company for a wrongful
act of its agent or employee. It is a penal prosecution to impose a fine against the company for the alleged violation of a
statute. The company cannot be fined for an act of those whom
it puts in charge of a train because they may have violated a
penal statute. The failure to furnish the coaches for the transportation of white and colored passengers of the kind required
by the statute is an offense of the company. A failure to assign the white and colored passengers to their respective coaches
or compartments is an offense of such conductor or those in
charge of the train. For the offense of the company the conductor cannot be convicted and fined, neither can the company be
convicted and fined for the offense of the conductor or those
in charge of the train, as is the result of this prosecution. The
court should have told the jury to find for the defendant."

No reason is apparent for saying that appellee's conductor
should have required the colored passenger in the sleeper to
leave it and take the compartment in the day coach designated
for his race, but, if such had been his duty, appellee cannot under the statute and in view of the authority, supra, be indicted
or punished because of its nonperformance. The statute does
not require railroad companies to have sleeping cars in their
trains or own them. They are owned and furnished by the Pullman Company. Appellee did, however, have in its train a
separate day coach for white and colored passengers, partitioned
and lettered as the statute requires, and it was not claimed by the
commonwealth that this separate coach did not amply accommodate all white and colored passengers on the train, or that the
compartment thereof set apart for colored passengers was any
less convenient, comfortable, or attractive than the compartment
or other day coaches set apart to the whites. The only com-

plaint is that such a sleeping car or compartment thereof as would afford a separation of white and colored passengers in the manner contemplated by the statute was not provided by appellee. As previously remarked, appellee was under no duty to furnish sleeping cars for its train, and such a construction of the statute, which is a highly penal one, is not warranted by its language or by any rule of construction known to us.

The conclusions already expressed being decisive of the case, we deem it unnecessary to consider other questions discussed in the briefs of counsel.

For the reasons indicated, the judgment is affirmed.

GRAND TRUNK RY. CO. *et al. v.* PARKS.

(Circuit Court of Appeals, Second Circuit, December 12, 1910.)

[183 Fed. Rep. 750.]

Carriers—Liability for Injury to Passenger—Joint Liability—Connecting Carriers—Dangerous Condition of Cars.*—A through passenger train was operated from Chicago to New York, by the Grand Trunk Railway Company to Suspension Bridge and from there eastward by the Lehigh Valley Railroad Company. On reaching Niagara Falls, Ontaria, the train was boarded by car cleaners, employed and paid by the Lehigh Company, who, while the train was passing from there to Suspension Bridge, cleaned the cars. The arrangement between the two companies under which this was done did not appear. Plaintiff, who was a customs inspector riding between such two points in the performance of his duties, without negligence on his part, slipped on a banana peel, which had been negligently left with other sweepings in the aisle of one of the cars by a cleaner, and was injured. Held, that both companies were liable for the injury as joint tort-feasors; the Grand Trunk Company for allowing its cars to become dangerous while passing over its own line, and the Lehigh Company because the negligence which created the dangerous condition was that of its servants, for which it was responsible.

In Error to the Circuit Court of the United States for the Western District of New York.

Action at law by Douglas J. Parks against the Grand Trunk

---

*For the authorities in this series on the subject of the liability of a carrier for wrongs to passengers occurring on a connecting line, etc., see foot-note of Mills *v.* Baltimore, etc., R. Co. (Md.), 33 R. R. R. 666, 56 Am. & Eng. R. Cas., N. S., 666.

For the authorities in this series on the subject of the joint liability of tort-feasors, see second foot-note of Ward *v.* Pullman Car Corp. (Ky.), 31 R. R. R. 548, 54 Am. & Eng. R. Cas., N. S., 548.

Grand Trunk Ry. Co. et al. *v.* Parks

Railway Company and the Lehigh Valley Railroad Company. Judgment for plaintiff, and defendants bring error. Affirmed.

This cause comes here upon appeal from a judgment in favor of defendant in error, who was plaintiff below. The action was brought to recover damages for personal injuries sustained by plaintiff, while engaged in his duties as United States customs inspector on board a train of the Grand Trunk Railway Company between Niagara Falls, Ontario, and Suspension Bridge, N. Y. He slipped upon a banana peel in the aisle of the car, claimed to have been deposited there with other sweepings by a car cleaner, who was engaged in cleaning the car preparatory to the surrender of the train to the Lehigh Valley Railroad Company at Suspension Bridge. It was a through train from Chicago to New York, operated to Suspension Bridge by the Grand Trunk, and from that point on by the Lehigh. The jury found a verdict against both defendants, as joint tort-feasors.

J. W. Ryan, for plaintiff in error Grand Trunk Ry. Co.
L. M. Bass, for plaintiff in error Lehigh Valley R. Co.
A. J. Thibaudeau, for defendant in error.

Beföre LACOMBE, COXE, and NOYES, Circuit Judges.

LACOMBE, Circuit Judge (after stating the facts as above). The plaintiff boarded the train at Niagara Falls, Ontario, and proceeded along the aisles of the several cars from the rear to the front. When he had reached the first car, and was by the doorway with his right foot on the iron threshold of the door, he saw an object ahead of him that looked like newspapers lying on the floor right ahead of him, making a little pile. He stepped with his left foot over this pile, slipped and fell, and then, after being picked up, looked again at the pile, and saw it was made up of papers and dirt, with banana peeling and apple cores.

There was evidence showing that this pile was produced by the car cleaner when sweeping up the car; that it was left in the passageway; that on previous occasions the dirt and debris, when swept up, had been stowed away under the seats, or in some place which was not a thoroughfare for persons moving through the train. There was conflicting evidence as to some of the facts; but it seems too plain for argument that, if the jury accepted the narrative of events relied on by the plaintiff, they were warranted in finding that the accident happened through some one's negligence. Indeed, that proposition seems not to be disputed, for the main reliance of each defendant is that the other defendant was alone responsible for the carelessness of the car cleaner. Both of them contend that the evidence affirmatively established that the plaintiff was guilty of contributory negligence; but there is no force in this contention. Upon the testimony that question was plainly for the jury, who were

Grand Trunk Ry. Co. et al. v. Parks

properly instructed by the court on the branch of the case, and whose finding thereon is conclusive.

. The testimony showed that the car cleaners, one for each car of this train, were selected, employed, and paid by the Lehigh. They came aboard the train while it was still on the Grand Trunk's road for the purpose of having the cars cleaned before the Lehigh took possession of them at Suspension Bridge. This had been the practice for years. The Grand Trunk crew had nothing to do with the cleaning. How this arrangement between the two companies came about, or whether there was some contract between them regulating the matter and fixing the status of the cleaners, did not appear.

Upon this testimony we are satisfied that the Grand Trunk was responsible for the condition in which the cars were maintained while operated on its own road. If it allowed a car to become dangerous by accumulating dirt and banana peelings in its passageway and leaving it there. it was immaterial whether the individual whose carelessness put it in such a condition was one of its regular employees, or was one whom it temporarily borrowed from another road, in whose general employment he was, or was the employee of another road, whom it was accustomed to allow to come on its cars and there conduct operations which, if they were carelessly conducted, would make the car unsafe.

The car cleaner was selected. employed, and paid by the Lehigh, and was its servant. It might have made some arrangement with the Grand Trunk whereby he might have been temporarily turned over exclusively to the service of the latter: but the jury, who were charged on that branch of the case. found against the Lehigh on that proposition. Upon the testimony it is difficult to see how they could reach any other conclusion. The method of car cleaning followed by the two companies apparently was devised to benefit both. By beginning the operation before the train reached Suspension Bridge, the Lehigh secured clean cars the moment the train was turned over to it. without having to wait for that work to be done afterwards. It would seem that for some reason it undertook to do this cleaning itself, since it paid the cleaner's wages, and there is nothing to show that the Grank Trunk was to reimburse it for such expenditure when the work of cleaning was done on the Grand Trunk's road. The cleaner, when engaged in that occupation. was, for all that appears, still the servant of the Lehigh. and for his negligence his master should respond.

We do not find error in the medical testimony which was admitted over objection, and we need not consider any of the exceptions to the charge, in view of the statement, supra, as to the legal obligations of defendants.

The judgment is affirmed.

CHESAPEAKE & O. RY. CO. v. SELSOR.

(Court of Appeals of Kentucky, Feb. 10, 1911.)

[134 S. W. Rep. 143.]

Carriers—Trespassers.*—One who boards a train after the conductor has rightfully refused to carry him because of his intoxication may be ejected, though he has a ticket.

Carriers—Disorderly Persons—Duty to Receive.*—A carrier need not receive as a passenger one who is intoxicated or otherwise in an improper condition.

Carriers—Disorderly Persons—Statutory Provisions—Effect.—Ky. St. § 806 (Russell's St. § 5350), providing for punishment and ejection of disorderly passengers, was enacted for the protection of the carrier, and applies only to persons received on a train, and does not change the common-law rule as to what passengers carriers must receive.

Appeal from circuit court, Lewis County.

Action by M. D. Selsor against the Chesapeake & Ohio Railway Company. Judgment for plaintiff, and defendant appeals. Reversed, and new trial ordered.

Worthington, Cochran & Browning, for appellant.
A. D. Cole and *Jno. E. Littleton,* for appellee.

HOBSON, C. J. M. D. Selsor brought this suit against the Chesapeake & Ohio Railway Company, charging that he .bought a. ticket at Vanceburg, Ky., to go to South Portsmouth, Ky., on April 3, 1910, that he got on board the regular passenger train to go to South Portsmouth, and that the conductor stopped the train and ejected him from it. An answer was filed by the defendant putting in issue the allegations of the petition, and pleading affirmatively facts to warrant his ejection from the train. On a hearing of the case there was a verdict and judgment in his favor for the sum of $200. The railroad company appeals.

The facts in the case are few and simple, and there is little conflict in the evidence. The plaintiff bought his ticket from the ticket agent, and, when the train came, started to get on the train. The conductor saw him, and told him not to get on

*For the authorities in this series on the subject of the duties and liabilities of carriers with respect to passengers or prospective passengers in a state of intoxication, see foot-note of Bragg's Adm'x v. Norfolk & W. R. Co. (Va.), 36 R. R. 438, 59 Am. & Eng. R. Cas., N. S., 438; first foot-note of Pinson v. Southern Ry. (S. Car.), 35 R. R. 700, 58 Am. & Eng. R. Cas., N. S., 700; Central of Ga. Ry. Co. v. Carleton (Ala.), 35 R. R. 511, 58 Am. & Eng. R. Cas., N. S., 511; St. Louis, etc., Ry. Co. v. Dallas (Ark.), 35 R. R. 167, 58 Am. & Eng. R. Cas., N. S., 167.

the train, that he would not carry him. He then went up to the smoker and got on the car, when the brakeman saw him, stopped the train, and put him off. The conductor testified that he told him not to get on the train, that he could not carry him because he was in a very drunken condition, and a young man was leading him. Other witnesses say that he was staggering drunk or helplessly intoxicated, while others say that he was drinking, but not boisterous, and was able to walk. On this evidence the court gave the jury these instructions:

"(1) The jury are instructed that if they shall believe from the evidence that the plaintiff, M. D. Selsor, purchased from the agent of defendant at Vanceburg, Ky., a ticket over the defendant's railroad from said point to Portsmouth on April 3, 1910, and offered to become a passenger on defendant's train on the said day on the ticket so purchased, and the defendant refused to accept him as a passenger, and expelled him from the train after he had entered thereon for the purpose of becoming a passenger, then the law is for the plaintiff, and the jury will find for him such a sum of money as will fairly and reasonably compensate plaintiff for humiliation or mortification, if any, to which he may have been subjected by reason of his being removed from the train, not exceeding. however, the sum of $2,000, the amount claimed in the petition. But, if the jury shall believe from the evidence as indicated in instruction No. 2, they will find for defendant, although they may believe the plaintiff was expelled from defendant's train or refused passage thereon as indicated in this instruction.

"(2) The jury are instructed that it is a public offense for any person while riding on a passenger train in this state to be drunk thereon to the annoyance of other passengers on said train, and it is the right and duty of the conductor in charge of a train upon which such offense is committed either to put the person so offending off the train, or to give notice of such offense to some peace officer at the first stopping place where any such peace officer may be. and it is the duty of such peace officer when so notified by such conductor to arrest such offender, and carry him to the most convenient magistrate of the county in which the arrest is made, and in expelling the offender from the train the conductor ·has the right to use such force as is reasonably necessary therefor, if the conviction be forcibly resisted. And if the jury shall believe from the evidence that the plaintiff, M. D. Selsor, at the time and upon the occasion when he was expelled from the defendant's passenger train on April 3. 1910, mentioned in the evidence. if he was so expelled therefrom, was intoxicated to such an extent as to be an annoyance or offensive to passengers on the train. then the defendant had the right to refuse to accept the plaintiff as a passenger on its train. and to expel him from the train if he got on same in such condition. and if plaintiff was in the condition aforesaid, and was expelled from defendant's train for that reason, the law is for the defendant, and the jury will so find."

It is undisputed in the evidence that the conductor told the plaintiff not to get on the train, that he could not carry him, and that the plaintiff after he was so told by the conductor, in violation of the conductor's instructions, went upon the car. When he so went upon the car, although he had a ticket, he was a trespasser, if the conductor was right in refusing to carry him, and in this event he cannot recover anything for his ejection from the train. The carrier was not obliged to receive the plaintiff as a passenger on its train if he was drunk, although he had bought a ticket. Persons who are not in a proper condition to be received on the train may be refused admittance by the carrier. Section 806, Ky. St. (Russell's St. § 5350), applies to passengers who have been received on the train. It has no application to persons who present themselves to be received. The statute was intended for the protection of the carrier, and not to change the common-law rule as to what persons the carrier is bound to receive. The case of C. & O. R. R. Co. *v.* Crank, 128 Ky. 329, 108 S. W. 276, 16 L. R. A. (N. S.) 197, is not like this case. There the passenger was on the train. He had been accepted as a passenger, and was ejected from the train while on his journey. Section 806, Ky. St., is as follows: "If any person while riding on a passenger or other train, shall, in the hearing or presence of other passengers, and to their annoyance, use or utter obscene or profane language, or behave in a boisterous or riotous manner, or obtain, or attempt to obtain money or property from any passenger by any game or device, he shall be fined for each offense not less than twenty-five nor more than one hundred dollars, or imprisoned in the county jail not less than ten nor more than fifty days, or both so fined and imprisoned; and it shall be the duty of the conductor in charge of any train upon which there is a person who has violated the provisions of this section either to put such person off the train, or to give notice of such violation to some peace officer at the first stopping place where any such officer may be." The statute was applicable in the Crank Case, but it has no application here. The question here is simply: Did the conductor have the right to refuse to receive the plaintiff as a passenger on the train? Louisville, etc., R. R. Co. *v.* McNally, 105 S. W. 124, 31 Ky. Law Rep. 1357, is on all fours with this case. There it was held that the court should instruct the jury that if the plaintiff, when he offered to get on the train was so far intoxicated as to affect his conduct, the conductor had a right to refuse to receive him on the car, and the jury should find for the defendant. In lieu of the instructions given, the court should have instructed the jury as above indicated.

Judgment reversed, and cause remanded for a new trial.

HOUSTON & T. C. RY. CO. *v.* LEE *et al.*

(Supreme Court of Texas, Feb. 1, 1911.)

[133 S. W. Rep. 868.]

Carriers—Passengers—Tickets—Ejection — Identification — Waiver of Stipulations.*—A round trip ticket over connecting lines plainly stipulated that it would not be accepted unless signed in ink by the purchaser and also by the agent of the issuing company, and that no agent or employee on any of the lines had any power to alter, ·modify, or waive any of the conditions of the contract, and that it must be signed in manuscript with ink by the person who was to use it, and not by another for him. A ticket was purchased by a ·husband for his wife, and the issuing agent told the husband that he .might sign the wife's name, which he did. The ticket was accepted for her going passage, but the validating agent refused to validate ·it for the return trip. Held, that the ticket constituted a contract between the wife, her husband, and the carriers, and they having no- .tice by the terms of the ticket that the issuing agent had no author- .ity to modify its terms, the validating agent was within his rights, and no action lay for the company's refusal to accept the ticket for the wife's return passage and in ejecting her from the train.

Carriers—Ejection—Manner.†—Though a carrier's conductor may remove a passenger from a car who is attempting to ride on an in- valid ticket, and who refuses to pay fare except by the ticket, he must do so in a proper manner, and if, instead, he treats her rudely or subjects her to an indignity, she may recover damages against the ·carrier therefor.

Evidence—Witnesses—Conclusion of Witness — Responsiveness.— In an action for ejection of a passenger, plaintiff was asked to state what the carrier's conductor said and did that was ungentlemanly or rude in ejecting plaintiff from the car, to which she answered,

---

*For the authorities in this series on the subject of the validity of a stipulation requiring identification of purchaser of return ticket, see second foot-note of Boling *v.* St. Louis, etc., R. Co. (Mo.), 22 R. R. R. 456, 45 Am. & Eng. R. Cas., N. S., 456.

For the authorities in this series on the right to eject passengers on account of failure to tender valid ticket and refusal or failure to pay fare, see second paragraph of first foot-note of St. Louis, etc., R. Co. *v.* Johnson (Okla.), 36 R. R. R. 165, 59 Am. & Eng. R. Cas., N. S., 165; first head-note of Texas & P. R. Co. *v.* Diefenbach (C. C. A.), 33 R. R. R. 213, 56 Am. & Eng. R. Cas., N. S., 213; last foot-note of Anderson *v.* Louisville & N. R. Co. (Ky.), 34 R. R. R. 220, 57 Am. & Eng. R. Cas., N. S., 220.

†For the authorities in this series on the subject of the liability of railroads on account of insults by employees to passengers, see foot-note of Pierce *v.* St. Louis, etc., R. Co. (Ark.), 36 R. R. R. 480, 59 Am. & Eng. R. Cas., N. S., 480; first foot-note of Caldwell *v.* Northern Pac. Ry. Co. (Wash.), 35 R. R. R. 161, 58 Am. & Eng. R. Cas., N. S., 161.

Houston & T. C. Ry. Co. *v.* Lee et al

"Well, he just gave everybody round to understand the ticket was no good, and just as much as to say I was traveling on a bogus ticket, and every one around where I was said they did not see how they could put anybody off on such a ticket as that." Held, that the answer was objectionable as embracing a conclusion of the witness, and as not responsive.

Error to Court of Civil Appeals of Third Supreme Judicial District.

Action by Lodia Sneed Lee and another against the Houston & Texas Central Railway Company. From a judgment for plaintiffs, affirmed by the Court of Civil Appeals (123 S. W. 154), defendant brings error. Reversed and remanded.

Gregory, Batts & Brooks, J. H. Hart, and *Baker, Botts, Parker & Garwood,* for plaintiff in error.

Warren W. Moore and *Kyrie Thrasher,* for defendants in error.

Brown, C. J. A. T. Lee and his wife, Lodia Sneed Lee, lived at the town of Jennings, in Louisiana, which was on the line of the Morgan's Louisiana & Texas Railroad & Steamship Company, Louisiana Western Railroad Company. Mrs. Lee desired to visit Austin, Tex., and, on the 22d day of December, 1907, her husband, A. T. Lee, went to the ticket office of the railroad company at the above-named place to buy for her a round trip ticket. She was to start on the morning of the 23d of December from that depot. Lee made a purchase of the ticket from H. L. Davis, the agent of the railroad company at that place, and the ticket was prepared, filled out in every way, and signed by the agent, but not signed by Mrs. Lee nor by Lee. The agent wrote on the ticket to identify it "Mrs. Lee." When Lee and his wife went to the depot for her to take passage to Austin, Tex., a different man was in the office, a night agent whose name is not given, and Lee applied for the ticket which was handed to him, and he was told by the agent that he could sign his wife's maiden name to the ticket for her. The price of the ticket was paid by Lee. There is nothing to show whether Lee read the ticket or not, except, as stated by the Court of Civil Appeals, that the time was so short between the delivery of the ticket and the departure of the train that he would not have had time to read so long a document. Mrs. Lee took passage on that railroad to Houston, Tex., and from Houston to Austin on the plaintiff in error's train. When her visit had terminated Mrs. Lee went to the depot of the plaintiff in error and presented her ticket to be stamped by the agent at Austin. When she signed it she wrote the name "Mrs. A. T. Lee." The given name was not the same, nor did it appear to have been in the same handwriting. The agent refused to stamp the ticket be-

Houston & T. C. Ry. Co. *v.* Lee et al

cause of that fact. Mrs. Lee offered to indentify herself, and to prove that she was the party for whom the ticket was intended, and that she had ridden on it from Louisiana to Texas; a lady who accompanied her being present with her. The agent refused, however, to stamp the ticket, and she then went into the car to take passage, after which the agent came in and had a talk with the conductor, and the conductor informed her that she would have to retire. She claims that he treated her very abruptly and unkindly, and mortified her by the manner of his treatment. He required her to leave the train, and she brought this suit for damages.

At the head of the ticket is printed the following words: "Read your ticket carefully." "2nd. It will not be accepted for passage unless this contract is signed in ink by the purchaser, and also by the agent for the issuing company." "3rd. This company is not responsible beyond its own line." There are many other provisions of the ticket which do not bear upon the question before this court, and therefore we will not incumber the record by copying them in this opinion. The tenth provision reads: "No agent or employee of any of the lines named in this ticket has any power to alter, modify or waive in any manner, any of the conditions of this contract." "This contract must be signed in manuscript with ink by the person who is to use this ticket, and not by another for him or her."

The terms of the ticket which was issued by the railroad company to Mrs. Lee constitute a contract between herself, her husband, and the carriers named in the ticket. The terms are definite, and unquestionably come within the terms of many decisions upon that question. 6 Cyc. 574; Howard *v.* Chicago R. R. Co., 61 Miss. 198; Boling *v.* St. Louis & S. F. R. Co., 189 Mo. 219, 88 S. W. 38. In the ticket it was specified that no agent of either of the railroads on whose behalf the ticket was issued had authority to alter or vary the terms of the contract. 6 Cyc. 674. The general rule of law that the terms of a written instrument cannot be varied by parol agreement made at the time the contract is entered into is applicable to this class of contracts, and, in addition, the decisions of the courts, generally, have made specific application of the rule to contracts of this character. In the making of this contract the purchaser was warned that the agent with whom he was then dealing had no authority to make any change in the terms of that instrument. The railroad companies had formulated a ticket applicable to both roads, and had empowered the agent at Jennings to issue that ticket definitely, and specifically denying to him any authority to make changes in it. Not only was the agent thus restricted in his authority, but the purchaser was warned of the fact that the person with whom he or she was dealing at the time had no authority whatever from either road to vary the terms of the contract expressed in the ticket, and such purchaser was equally bound by that contract with the railroad itself. I. & G. N. R. R. Co. *v.* Best, 93 Tex. 344, 55 S. W. 315. In the case just cited the facts, briefly stated, were that a railroad ticket was issued by the Missouri, Kansas & Texas Railway Company at Dallas over its own line and the line of the International & Great Northern Railroad Company to San Antonio and return, which must be continuous after it had been commenced. In the face of the ticket was printed in plain language that no agent of the company had authority to vary the terms of that contract. On the return trip Best was accosted by a conductor on the International & Great Northern Railroad, and asked if he would like to stop over at Austin, and, finally, the conductor indorsed on the ticket words which indicated the right of the passenger to stop at Austin and resume his journey afterwards. Best did stop at Austin, and on the next day when he resumed his journey he was carried by the International & Great Northern Railroad Company to its connection with the Missouri, Kansas & Texas Railway Company, but when he presented his ticket on the last-named company's road, it was rejected because he had broken his return trip by stopping at Austin. Out of this state of facts grew a suit against the two roads, the question being certified to this court, in answer to which Judge Williams said: "We answer that the facts stated show no right of recovery against appellant. The ticket constituted the contract between the two railroad companies and the passenger, and, by its terms, restricted the right of appellee to a continuous trip from San Antonio to Dallas, and notified him that no agent or employee had power to modify such contract. Negligence of the conductor in representing the contract to confer a right on its face it plainly denied cannot be held to be the negligence of appellant, since his act was unauthorized. Appellee could not properly rely on such representation as being within the apparent scope of the conductor's authority, for the reason that the contract itself plainly showed that no such authority existed. It could be properly held, under the authorities, that such act or representation did not bind appellant even to carry appellee over its own road after he had broken his trip by stopping at Austin. Petrie *v.* Railway, 42 N. J. Law 449; Railway *v.* Henry, 84 Tex. 678 [19 S. W. 870, 16 L. R. A. 318]." If the writer were to undertake to add force to the very clear language copied above he would find himself wholly unable to accomplish such purpose; it covers the case now before the court in all of the aspects presented to us.

There is in fact no difference in principle between the Best Case and this case. The only difference is that the statement in this case has reference to a change in the provision for the identification of the party at the terminal station for a return

Houston & T. C. Ry. Co. v. Lee et al

trip which was forbidden by the terms of the contract, while in the Best Case the verbal authority given by the conductor to stop off at Austin was equally forbidden in practically the same terms. If the purchaser of the ticket on the International & Great Northern Railroad Company was required to take notice that by the terms of his contract the conductor had no authority to vary those terms, then it must be true that the purchaser of the ticket in this case was equally charged with notice of the terms of the contract and with notice of the provision that the agent with whom he was dealing was acting beyond the line of his authority when he stated to him that he could sign his wife's name to the ticket, which was most emphatically and positively forbidden in the face of the instrument itself.

Argument cannot add force to the facts of this case and to the rule of law which has been laid down by this court in the Best Case, cited above, which is sustained by the authorities so far as the writer has been able to find. It is the office of the courts to declare the law which is to govern parties in the exercise of their rights under contracts made and entered into by them, and not to vary from the rules already established on account of any supposed public policy and inconvenience of the parties. The question of convenience or inconvenience growing out of the terms of a contract must be considered by the parties who make the contract at the time it is entered into, and cannot be considered in the interpretation of it by the court when its language is not ambiguous.

From what we have said the conclusion follows that the trial court erred in refusing to give this special charge requested by the plaintiff in error: "You are instructed that under the provisions of the ticket involved in this suit no agent or representative of the railroad company issuing it had a right to alter, change, or waive any of the provisions thereof, and you are instructed that in case the agent or agents of the railroad which sold the ticket in controversy at Jennings, La., represented to one or both of the plaintiffs that plaintiff A. T. Lee could sign his wife's name to said ticket, then you are instructed that said agent had no authority to give such instructions to said plaintiff or plaintiffs, and that they were of no effect, and did not authorize the said A. T. Lee to sign his wife's name or his wife's maiden name to the ticket in question, in view of the fact that the ticket provided upon its face that only .the party using same could sign same."

There is evidence in the record to support the claim that the agent at Austin and the conductor dealt harshly and rudely with the plaintiff, which, if true, would give a right of action. Although the conductor had the right to remove Mrs. Lee from the car, he was required to do so in a proper manner, and if he treated her rudely, or subjected her to any indignity, she can

Pittsburg, C., C. & St. L. Ry. Co. *v.* Grom

recover therefor. The plaintiff's counsel propounded to her this question: "Now, if the conductor said or did anything that was ungentlemanly and rough or rude, tell the jury what it was." To which she answered: "Well, he just gave everybody round to understand the ticket was no good, and just as much as to say I was traveling on a bogus ticket, and everyone around where I was said they did not see how they could put anybody off on such a ticket as that."

Defendant's counsel objected to the answer, "because it embraced a conclusion of the witness, and was immaterial and irrelevant, and not responsive to the question, which asked only for what the conductor said and did, and because only what was said and done by the conductor was admissible."

The objection should have been sustained. The answer did not respond to the question, and stated only witness' conclusion as to impressions made upon others. The answer should have been excluded.

The judgments of the district court and of the Court of Civil Appeals are reversed, and the cause is remanded for trial in accordance with this opinion.

PITTSBURG, C., C. & ST. L. RY. CO. *et al. v.* GROM.

(Court of Appeals of Kentucky, Feb. 2, 1911.)

[133 S. W. Rep. 977.]

Pleading—Admission by Failure to Deny.—In a passenger's action for personal injuries, the answer denied that plaintiff was a passenger on defendant's train at the time of the injury, or that defendant had contracted to carry him safely to his final destination, and the amended answer alleged that, when injured, defendant had carried plaintiff safely over its line so far as necessary to enable it to perform its part of the contract of carriage to final destination. Held, that the allegation of the amended answer was merely an affirmative denial, and plaintiff's failure to deny such allegation was not an admission of such fact, so as to authorize a peremptory instruction for defendant.

Appeal and Error—Presumptions—Facts Not Shown.—Where the bill of exceptions does not contain all the evidence, the Supreme Court will assume that there was sufficient evidence to sustain the judgment, so far as the judgment depended upon the evidence.

Continuance—Grounds—Surprise.—In a passenger's action against a railroad company for personal injuries by being struck in the eye while riding in a coach, after plaintiff's evidence was all in and a peremptory instruction for defendant had been refused, a continuance was asked on the ground that defendant was surprised by plain-

Pittsburg, C., C. & St. L. Ry. Co. *v.* Grom

tiff's contention, which he introduced evidence to support, that he was injured by being struck by a chain from a passing freight train, though defendant's counsel had been told generally the day before the trial that such proof would be given. The accident occurred in Pennsylvania, and at the trial the Pennsylvania law on the subject was put in evidence, and counsel knew that under such law proof of injury without proof of facts tending to show a collision or a defect in appliances, etc., would not authorize a recovery. Defendant's counsel also knew that immediately after plaintiff's injury the conductor on his train telegraphed ahead and had all freight trains which had passed inspected to see if anything was attached thereto which could have struck plaintiff, but that nothing was discovered to explain the accident. Held, that a continuance was properly refused to enable defendant to procure evidence to rebut plaintiff's contention.

Carriers—Passengers—Injuries—What Law Governs.*—The lex loci delicti governs in a passenger's action for personal injuries, and not the law of the place where the contract of carriage was made, so that rights given by the law of the place of the injury can only be defeated by defenses permitted by that law.

Evidence—Presumptions.—In the face of evidence introduced to the contrary, there can be no presumption that the law of a foreign state is the same as the law of the forum.

Carriers—Passengers—Injuries—Burden of Proof—Presumptions.†—Under the laws of Pennsylvania, no presumption of negligence by a carrier arises from mere proof of injury to a passenger, negligence being presumed only where a passenger is injured by some act or omission of the carrier or its employees, or by something connected with the appliances of transportation; but the burden of showing negligence still remains upon the passenger where such circumstances are as consistent with due care as with negligence.

Carriers—Passengers—Negligence—Presumptions.†—The evidence in a passenger's action for personal injuries was that while a freight train was passing plaintiff's train he was injured by being struck

---

*See first foot-note of Lake Shore, etc., Ry. Co. *v.* Teeters (Ind.), 24 R. R. R. 36, 47 Am. & Eng. R. Cas., N. S., 36; foot-note of Hoodmacher *v.* Lehigh Valley R. Co. (Pa.), 29 R. R. R. 731, 52 Am. & Eng. R. Cas., N. S., 731.

†For the authorities in this series on the question whether a presumption of negligence arises from proof that a passenger was injured, see first foot-note of Eaton *v.* New York Cent., etc., R. Co. (N. Y.), 37 R. R. R. 252, 60 Am. & Eng. R. Cas., N. S., 252; foot-note of Rhea *v.* Minneapolis St. Ry. Co. (Minn.), 37 R. R. R. 194, 60 Am. & Eng. R. Cas., N. S., 194; foot-note of O'Callaghan *v.* Dellwood Park Co. (Ill.), 37 R. R. R. 182, 60 Am. & Eng. R. Cas., N. S., 182; third foot-note of Gardner *v.* Metropolitan St. R. Co. (Mo.), 36 R. R. R. 448, 59 Am. & Eng. R. Cas., N. S., 448; fifth head-note of Taber *v.* Seaboard Air Line Ry. (S. Car.), 36 R. R. R. 466, 59 Am. & Eng. R. Cas., N. S., 466; second foot-note of Williford *v.* Southern Ry. Co. (S. Car.) 35 R. R. R. 693, 58 Am. & Eng. R. Cas., N. S., 693.

Pittsburg, C., C. & St. L. Ry. Co. *v.* Grom

by something over the eye, and that just prior thereto something rattled against the side of the coach, which sounded like a chain, and that the rattling continued after the injury, and there were marks on the side of the coach indicating that it had been struck by something having an irregular shape, but nothing was found in plaintiff's car by which he might have been struck, and it appeared that if he had been struck by something not attached to something else, such as a stone, it would have remained in the coach. Held, that under the laws of Pennsylvania the evidence raised a presumption of negligence which defendant was required to rebut.

Appeal and Error—Error Favorable to Appellant.—The law of Pennsylvania requires carriers of passengers to exercise the utmost care and prudence to protect the passengers from injury by its negligence, so that an instruction, in a case to which such law was applicable, that the carrier was only required to use the highest degree of care exercised by ordinarily careful and prudent persons engaged in transporting passengers, was, if anything, more favorable to the carrier than to the injured passenger.

Carriers—Passengers—Injuries—Instructions.‡—In a passenger's action for personal injuries by being struck by some hard substance while riding in the coach in Pennsylvania, so that the law of that state governed, the court charged that the carrier was bound to exercise the highest care usually exercised by ordinarily careful and prudent persons engaged in transportation for hire, for plaintiff's protection, and if the trainmen in charge of plaintiff's train or of another train passing it failed to exercise such care whereby a chain or other hard substance was caused to strike plaintiff, injuring him, the jury should find for plaintiff, but unless the jury so believed they should find for defendant, and if they found for plaintiff they should award him such sum, etc. Held, that under the Pennsylvania law the instruction fairly presented the issues raised.

Appeal from Circuit Court, Jefferson County, Common Pleas Branch, Third Division.

·Action by William Grom against the Pittsburg, Cincinnati, Chicago & St. Louis Railway Company and another. From a judgment for plaintiff, defendants appeal. Affirmed.

Charles H. Gibson, for appellants.
Edwards, Ogden & Peak, for appellee.

Clay, C. Appellee, William Grom, brought this action against the appellants, Pittsburg, Cincinnati, Chicago & St. Louis Railway Company and Pennsylvania Railroad Company, to recover

‡For the authorities in this series on the subject of the degree of care required of a carrier of passengers, see Washington, etc.. Ry. Co. *v.* Trimyer (Va.), 37 R. R. R. 114, 60 Am. & Eng. R. Cas., N. S., 114; Gardner *v.* Metropolitan St. R. Co. (Mo.), 36 R. R. R. 448, 59 Am. & Eng. R. Cas., N. S., 448.

damages in the sum of $1,999 for personal injuries, alleged to have been due to the negligence of the railroad companies while he was a passenger on their lines of railroad. The jury awarded him a verdict for the full amount sued for, and the defendants have appealed.

The facts, briefly stated, are as follows: Appellee bought a ticket from Louisville to Atlantic City and return. The accident occurred between Pittsburg and Altoona, in the state of Pennsylvania. At the time of the accident, appellee was sitting in the middle of the sixth seat from the front end of the car. He was struck by some hard and heavy substance over the left eye. The frontal bone was fractured and his eye so seriously injured that the sight thereof is permanently impaired: At the time of the accident a freight train was passing. Just before and after the injury, witnesses heard something rattling against the side of the car. It sounded like a chain. Indentations were found on the side of the car which looked as if they had been made by an irregular object in the form of a chain. One of the witnesses saw a passing shadow of the object that struck appellee, and it looked like a chain. Immediately after the injury several persons searched the car, and nothing was found therein which could have caused the injury. Appellant's testimony was to the effect that on the freight trains ordinarily used there are no chains in a position to be swung out so as to strike or enter a train on an adjacent track, and, even if there were such, they would hang by the side of the car by reason of their own weight, and would not swing out from the car by reason of the velocity of the train. The witnesses, however, had no knowledge of the condition of the particular train in question, and they admit, on cross-examination, that there were numerous chains in and about freight cars.

The following errors are assigned: (1) The failure of the trial court to award the Pittsburg, Cincinnati, Chicago & St. Louis Railway Company a peremptory instruction. (2) The refusal of the court to grant both appellants a continuance on the ground of surprise. (3) The failure of the court properly to instruct the jury under the law of Pennsylvania. These grounds for reversal will be considered in their order.

1. In the original petition the only defendant was the Pittsburg, Cincinnati, Chicago & St. Louis Railway Company. After alleging that that company was a corporation, and that appellee was a resident of Jefferson county, Ky., and had purchased a ticket over its line of railway from Louisville to Atlantic City and return, he charged that by virtue of the ticket so purchased the defendant contracted to carry him in safety over its line of railroad from the city of Louisville to Atlantic City, and that while the train on which he was a passenger, occupying a seat in one of defendant's coaches, was running through the state of Pennsylvania,

Pittsburg, C., C. & St. L. Ry. Co. v. Grom

another train belonging to and operated by the defendant, on one of its tracks near and parallel with the track on which the train on which appellee was a passenger, was running past said train, some hard and heavy substance or object, through the gross carelessness and negligence of defendant, was hurled and thrown with great violence against him, striking him in the head and face, breaking the bones of his face and head, and severely injuring one of his eyes, thereby causing him to suffer great physical pain and anguish, and permanently impairing and destroying the use and sight of his eye. To the petition the Pittsburg, Cincinnati, Chicago & St. Louis Railway Company filed an answer denying the allegations of the petition. Thereupon appellee amended his petition and made the Pennsylvania Railroad Company a party defendant, charging that the two railroad companies were under the same management and control, and operated by the same railway system. The Pennsylvania Railroad Company then filed an answer denying the allegations of the original petition, and later on the two railroad companies filed a joint answer denying the allegations of the amended petition. Thereafter the railroad companies filed an amended answer, wherein they pleaded that their liability was governed and controlled by the laws of the state of Pennsylvania, and set out in general terms the laws of that state. This amended answer also contained an allegation to the effect that when appellee was injured he was in the state of Pennsylvania, and was a passenger on a train of the Pennsylvania Railroad Company; he having been safely carried by its codefendant, the Pittsburg, Cincinnati, Chicago & St. Louis Railway Company, over its railway so far as it was necessary for it to perform its part of the contract. Because of this latter allegation, which was not denied, and because the record contains no proof to the contrary, it is insisted that the court erred in not directing the jury to find for the Pittsburg, Cincinnati, Chicago & St. Louis Railway Company. Inasmuch, however, as that company had already denied that appellee, at the time of the injury, was a passenger on one of its trains, and that it had contracted to carry him safely from Louisville to Atlantic City and return, it is manifest that the allegation in the amended answer, to the effect that he had been carried safely over its line as far as it was necessary for it to perform its part of the contract, was merely an affirmative denial. The failure of appellee to traverse this allegation in his reply was not, therefore, such an admission of the fact as to authorize the court on the face of the pleadings to grant a peremptory instruction. The question, then, is whether or not there was any evidence which justified the submission of the case as to the Pittsburg, Cincinnati, Chicago & St. Louis Railway Company. The record contains no evidence tending to show that the two appellants are not under the same control and

Pittsburg, C., C. & St. L. Ry. Co. *v.* Grom

management, or that the Pittsburg, Cincinnati, Chicago & St. Louis Railway Company did not undertake to carry appellee over its lines in Pennsylvania, or that its lines did not run east of Pittsburg. We find, however, from the record, that the ticket which appellee purchased in Louisville, Ky., was introduced in evidence and exhibited to the jury. We also find that the deposition of one of the witnesses for appellee is not in the record. In the absence of a bill of exceptions containing all the evidence, we must conclude that there was sufficient evidence not only to authorize the submission of the case to the jury, but to sustain the judgment.

2. At the conclusion of the evidence for appellee, appellants' senior counsel filed his affidavit and moved for a continuance on the ground of surprise. In this affidavit counsel stated, in substance, that he had had sole charge of the defense of the action that was being tried; that heretofore he had made a most thorough investigation of the facts of the case and had had submitted to him full reports made by the agents of appellants as to all facts connected with the injury. He had never heard until the day before the trial that any attempt would be made to show that appellee was struck by a chain, when he was then informed in a general way by appellee's counsel that he would show that fact. In all the investigations made and in the reports submitted to him, it had never been suggested that the accident could have happened in that way. He was, therefore, taken completely by surprise, as were the appellants, by the evidence introduced by appellee, and he was not then prepared to rebut such evidence. He had taken the deposition of the train conductor, but did not ask him about a chain, because he had never heard it suggested or thought it possible that a chain could have had anything to do with the accident. If allowed an opportunity to do so, he could and would procure testimony of witnesses—all residing in the state of Pennsylvania—which would prove: (1) That there were no marks on the car on which appellee was injured indicating that it had recently been struck by anything; (2) that all the persons who were in the coach and near appellee were asked by the conductor and brakeman as to the cause of the accident, and none of them could give any explanation of it, and none of them said anything about hearing a chain or seeing a chain, and none of them suggested that a chain had anything to do with the accident; (3) that at the time there were no chains upon or attached to appellants' engine or cars, or forming any part of the equipment thereof, that were long enough to reach into the window of a passenger coach on an adjacent track and strike a passenger, as appellee was struck; (4) that all chains connected with such equipment were, however, short chains, and in the event of their breaking they would drag on the ground, and could not swing out in a horizontal position so as to come

Pittsburg, C., C. & St. L. Ry. Co. *v.* Grom

in contact with a train on an adjacent track; that such a thing is a physical impossibility; (5) that "shortly after the accident to plaintiff the conductor caused telegraphic notice to be given of it, and instructions were immediately given to inspect all west-bound freight trains that had met plaintiff's train to see if any-thing was attached to or projected from them that could have caused the accident, and such investigation was made and nothing found to explain the cause of the accident;" that these facts could be established by the testimony of several witnesses (nam-ing them) and could not be established by any witnesses living in the state of Kentucky. Did not anticipate, nor did the railroad companies anticipate, and no one could reasonably have antici-pated, that appellee would attempt to prove that his injuries were caused in such an unusual or unheard of manner as being struck by a chain. If the railroad companies had known in time that such proof would be offered, they could and would have met it by showing facts to the contrary.

The foregoing affidavit was not filed until appellants' motion for a peremptory instruction, at the conclusion of appellee's evi-dence, had been overruled. Before asking for a continuance on the ground of surprise, therefore, counsel for appellants first took the chance of appellee's failing to make out his case. Though apprised of the fact in a general way, on the day before the trial, that appellee would attempt to show that he was struck by a chain, he did not ask for a continuance of the case when it was called for trial. At the time of the trial the law of Pennsylvania was in proof. Counsel knew that under the law upon mere proof of injury, unaccompanied by any facts tending to show a collision or a defect of cars, track, roadway, machinery, or other negligence, appellee could not recover. The deposition of the conductor showed that there was absolutely nothing the matter with the train on which appellee was a passenger. A search was made to find whether or not the object which struck appellee was in the car, and nothing was found. Knowing the law of Pennsylvania, counsel should have anticipated that appellee would attempt to prove facts tending to show negligence in the operation or mechanical appliances of the passing train, as ap-pellee could not recover by merely showing that he was injured by some object, without showing the source from which it came. Furthermore, counsel admits in his affidavit that, immediately after the accident, the conductor caused telegraphic notice of the fact to be given, and instructions were immediately sent out to inspect all west-bound freight trains that had met the train on which appellee was a passenger, to see if anything was at-tached to or projected from them that could have caused the accident; and such investigation was made and nothing found to explain the cause of the accident. This being true, counsel

Pittsburg, C., C. & St. L. Ry. Co. *v.* Grom

should have taken the depositions of witnesses acquainted with such facts, and should not have gone into the trial in the hope that appellee would fail to make out his case, and, in the event that he did make out his case, appellants would be granted a continuance and a further opportunity to prove facts which they could have established before the trial. We therefore conclude that the court did not err in failing to grant the continuance asked for.

3. But counsel for appellants contend that appellants' liability is governed and controlled by the law of Pennsylvania, and that the trial court failed to instruct the jury in conformity with the law of that state. In actions for personal injuries against carriers of passengers, the law is well settled by the great weight of authority that the lex loci delicti governs, and not the lex loci contractus, and that the rights given by the lex loci delicti can only be defeated by defenses which are given under the lex loci delicti. Hutchinson on Carriers, § 265. This rule has been applied in this state in the case of injuries to employees, but the question has not been determined in a case where the party injured was a passenger. It is insisted by counsel for appellants that the rule should not apply to passengers where the contract to carry is made in the state where the action is brought, and the passenger is injured in another state, for the reason that the contract itself should control. It is a rare thing, however, that the ticket contains any express condition that the carrier is to use proper care to transport the passenger in safety. The duty of the carrier to use proper care in the transportation of the passenger is one imposed by law, and the right of action grows out of the liability which the law imposes, rather than out of the contract of transportation. The ticket is an evidence of the relationship which the passenger sustains to the carrier, and the carrier is liable because of the failure of duty with respect to that relationship, rather than its failure to comply with an implied condition of the contract of carriage. In other words, where the relationship of passenger and carrier exists, whether by reason of the purchase of a ticket or otherwise, the carrier must exercise towards the passenger the care required by law; and for that reason the carrier's negligence must depend upon whether or not it exercised the care required by the law of the place where the injury occurred. That being true, the negligence of appellants in this case must be measured by the law of Pennsylvania. That law has been pleaded and put in proof, and there is, therefore, no presumption that the law of Pennsylvania is the same as that in Kentucky.

The law of Pennsylvania is that where a passenger is injured, either by anything done or omitted by the carrier or its employees, or anything connected with the appliances of transportation, the burden of proof is upon the carrier to show that such

Pittsburg, C., C. & St. L. Ry. Co. *v.* Grom

injury was in no way the result of its negligence; but, to throw this burden upon the carrier, it must first be shown that the injury complained of resulted in the breaking of machinery, collision, derailment of cars, or something improper or unsafe in the conduct of the business or in the appliances of transportation. Following this rule, it was there held that, where a passenger on a railroad train, while sitting at the window of a car, was injured by a missile, the nature and origin of which was unknown, and there was nothing to connect the accident with a defect in any of the appliances of transportation, or any negligence on the part of the company or its employees, there could be no recovery. Pennsylvania Railroad Company *v.* McKinney, 124 Pa. 462, 17 Atl. 14, 2 L. R. A. 820, 10 Am. St. Rep. 601. Briefly stated, then, the Pennsylvania rule is that no presumption of negligence arises from mere proof of injury to a passenger. Negligence will be presumed only from the circumstances of the accident; and, when these circumstances are as consistent with the absence of negligence as with negligence itself, the burden of proof is still upon the party injured. The evidence in this case showed that, at the time of appellee's injury, a freight train was passing the train on which he was a passenger. Just prior to the time he was struck, something rattled against the side of the car that sounded like a chain. One of the passengers saw the shadow of the object which struck appellee. The rattling continued after the injury. There were marks upon the side of the car that indicated it had been struck by something of irregular shape. No object of any kind, which could have struck appellee, was found in the car. If the object that struck him had been a stone, or something of that sort, it would not have struck him and then gone out of the window. It is reasonably certain, therefore, that *the* object which struck appellee was attached to the passing freight train. It was evidence of negligence on the part of appellants to have attached to the train any kind of swinging objects that might enter the window of a car on an adjoining track and strike a passenger. With these facts in evidence, it was incumbent upon appellants to rebut the presumption of negligence.

The court instructed the jury as follows:

"(1) It was the duty of the defendants' agents and servants *in* charge of its engines and cars to exercise for the safety of the plaintiff the highest degree of care usually exercised by ordinarily careful and prudent persons, engaged in the transportation of passengers for hire, and if you believe from the evidence that while the plaintiff was a passenger on a train of the defendants then being operated by the defendants from Pittsburg to Altoona in the state of Pennsylvania, the defendants' agents and servants, in charge of the train on which the plaintiff was a passenger, or in charge of another train of defendants, or whose duty it was to care for and look after said trains or either of them, failed to exercise such care, and by reason thereof a chain or some other hard and heavy substance or object was caused to strike the plaintiff, and he was thereby injured, the law is for the plaintiff, and the jury should so find. But unless the jury believe from the evidence that, while the plaintiff was a passenger on a train of the defendants then being operated by the defendants from Pittsburg to Altoona in the state of Pennsylvania, the defendants' agents and servants in charge of the train on which the plaintiff was a passenger or in charge of another train of defendants, or whose duty it was to care for and look after said trains or either of them, failed to exercise the degree of care specified in the first instruction, and by reason thereof a chain or some other hard and heavy substance or object was caused to strike the plaintiff and he was thereby injured, the law is for the defendants, and the jury should so find.

"(2) If the jury find for the plaintiff, they should award him such a sum in damages as will fairly and reasonably compensate him for the mental and physical pain and suffering endured by him as a direct result of such injury, and for the permanent impairment, if any, of his power to earn money resulting from said injury, if any, not to exceed in all the sum of $1,999, the amount claimed in the petition."

It will be observed that the foregoing instruction imposed upon appellants, in looking after the safety of appellee, only the highest degree of care usually exercised by ordinarily careful and prudent persons engaged in the transportation of passengers for hire. The law of Pennsylvania imposes the utmost degree of prudence and care. Laing *v.* Colder, 8 Pa. 481, 49 Am. Dec. 533. The first portion of the instruction, therefore, is not subject to criticism, for, if anything, it was more favorable to appellants than to appellee. Furthermore, the court did not tell the jury that appellee had been injured, and it was therefore necessary for appellants to introduce evidence to rebut the presumption of negligence, but it permitted a recovery only in the event that appellants failed to exercise the highest degree of care usually exercised by ordinarily careful and prudent persons engaged in the transportation of passengers for hire, and that by reason thereof appellee was struck and injured by a chain or some other hard and heavy substance or object. In other words, the jury had to believe from the evidence that appellants were guilty of negligence in the respect indicated before they could render a verdict for appellee. While the instruction may not have been in the exact form that the Pennsylvania courts would have given, yet we are of the opinion that, under the law of that state, it fairly presented the issues involved.

Judgment affirmed.

Rager *et al. v.* Pennsylvania R. Co.

(Supreme Court of Pennsylvania, Jan. 3, 1911.)

[78 Atl. Rep. 827.]

Carriers — Injury to Passengers — Contributory Negligence.*—
Where a passenger stands on the vestibule of a car while in motion,
and there are vacant seats in the car, and on request of the brakeman he refuses to go inside, and when the doors are opened on approaching a station he falls out and is killed, the railroad company
is not liable.

Appeal from Court of Common Pleas, Cambria County.

Action by Sarah A. Rager and others against the Pennsylvania Railroad Company. Judgment for defendant, and plaintiffs appeal. Affirmed.

The opinion of Reed, P. J., specially presiding, stated the
circumstances of the accident to be as follows:

"The deceased, with a number of others, attended a celebration of some kind at Johnstown, Pa., the evening of October 31,
1907. They resided at South Fork, a short distance from Johnstown, and returned home on the train leaving Johnstown shortly
after 11 o'clock that night. It was a vestibule train, and the
coaches were more or less crowded. The evidence, however,
failed to show the number of cars composing the train, or
whether all were crowded or not. The deceased entered the train
between the first and second coaches, and with several others
remained in the vestibule between these two coaches. He made
no effort to enter either coach, but remained in the vestibule
until the time of the accident which resulted in his death. He,
with the others standing in the vestibule, shortly after the train
left Johnstown, was requested by the brakeman in charge of the
first and second coaches to go inside; but the request was not
complied with. When the train was nearing the South Fork
station the brakeman asked the deceased and others who were
standing on the trapdoor in the vestibule next the second coach
to get off the trap so that he could open the door. They moved
off, and the brakeman opened the floor and outside doors preparatory for the discharge of passengers at the station which the
train was approaching. The doors on the station side were

*For the authorities in this series on the question whether a steam
railroad passenger is guilty of contributory negligence in standing
on the platform of a car, see last foot-note of Central of Ga. Ry.
Co. *v.* Brown (Ala.), 37 R. R. R. 197, 60 Am. & Eng. R. Cas., N.
S., 197; Brice *v.* Southern Ry. Co. (S. Car.), 37 R. R. R. 178, 60
Am. & Eng. R. Cas., N. S., 178; first foot-note of Norvell *v.* Ka-
nawha, etc., Ry. Co. (W. Va.), 37 R. R. R. 148, 60 Am. & Eng. R.
Cas., N. S., 148; first head-note of Clanton *v.* Southern Ry. Co.
(Ala.), 37 R. R. R. 120, 60 Am. & Eng. R. Cas., N. S., 120.

opened both at the rear end of the first coach and at the front end of the second coach, and when opened the train was within about one-half mile of the station. At the rate it was running, it would take about one minute to reach the station. After opening these doors the brakeman was required to pass through the second coach and make similar preparations for the discharge of passengers by opening the doors between the rear end of the second and the front of the third coaches. The accident occurred immediately after the brakeman opened the floor and outside doors at the front end of the second coach. None of the witnesses explained just how it happened."

The court entered a compulsory nonsuit, which it subsequently refused to take off.

Argued before FELL, C. J., and BROWN, MESTREZAT, POTTER, ELKIN, STEWART, and MOSCHZISKER, JJ.

John H. Stephens and *M. B. Stephens,* for appellants.
H. W. Storey, for appellee.

PER CURIAM. A nonsuit was entered on the following state of facts developed by the plaintiff's testimony: Her husband was a passenger on a train composed of vestibule cars, and stood on the front platform of the second car, when there was standing room inside the car and vacant seats in the first car. He was asked by the brakeman in charge of these two cars to go inside, but declined to do so. When the train was half a mile from a station, at which it was to stop, he and others, who were standing on the platform, were asked by the brakeman to step off of the floor door that covered the steps. His request was complied with, and the brakeman raised the floor door and opened the outside door. Immediately thereafter the plaintiff's husband fell from the train and was killed. What caused him to fall did not appear. He rode on the platform, not from necessity, but from choice, when there was room inside the cars, and he disregarded the request of the brakeman to go inside, and he remained on the platform when he knew the doors were open. He fell from some cause unexplained.

Under these circumstances there was no ground upon which the defendant could have been liable for his death. Hopkins *v.* Railroad Co., 225 Pa. 193, 73 Atl. 1104. It provided a place in which he could ride in safety, and it did nothing. except that which was necessary in the operation of its train, to increase the risk that he had voluntarily assumed.

The judgment is affirmed.

HUGHES v. CHICAGO, R. I. & P. RY. Co. et al.

(Supreme Court of Iowa, Feb. 11, 1911.)

[129 N. W. Rep. 956.]

Carriers—Passengers — Injury — Instructions—Contributory Negligence—Intoxication.*—An instruction that a passenger injured while alighting could not recover if he was intoxicated was properly refused, as making any degree of intoxication contributory negligence as a matter of law.

Negligence—Contributory Negligence — Intoxication.†—Intoxication does not bar recovery for personal injury unless the person injured fails to use the ordinary care of a sober man, but intoxication in any degree is a circumstance to be considered in determining a question of contributory negligence.

Carriers—Passengers—Injury—Instructions—Contributory Negligence—Intoxication.*—It was improper to instruct that if just before being injured a passenger became intoxicated, and thereby became careless and negligent contributing to his injury, he could not recover.

Damages—Personal Injuries—Instructions.—On an issue of prospective suffering and diminished earning capacity, plaintiff's life expectancy should have been based on his condition as injured, and hence an instruction basing it on his condition before being injured was erroneous.

Damages—Error Not Cured—Instructions.—The trial court could not by reducing a verdict for plaintiff cure error in an instruction basing his life expectancy on his condition before being injured, instead of on his injured condition; the amount of damages being for the jury's determination.

Appeal from District Court, Jasper County; R. E. Willcockson, Judge.

Action at law to recover damages for personal injuries received by plaintiff while a passenger upon one of defendant's

---

*For the authorities in this series on the subject of the duties and liabilities of carriers with respect to passenger or prospective passengers in a state of intoxication, see foot-note of Bragg's Adm'x v. Norfolk & W. R. Co. (Va.), 36 R. R. R. 438, 59 Am. & Eng R. Cas., N. S., 438; second head-note of Pinson v. Southern Ry. (S. Car.), 35 R. R. R. 700, 58 Am. & Eng. R. Cas., N. S., 700; fifth head-note of Central of Georgia Ry. Co. v. Carleton (Ala.), 35 R. R. R. 511, 58 Am. & Eng. R. Cas., N. S., 511; second head-note of St. Louis, etc., Ry. Co. v. Dallas (Ark.), 35 R. R. R. 167, 58 Am. & Eng. R. Cas., N. S., 167.

†For the authorities in this series on the subject of intoxication as contributory negligence, see last foot-note of St. Louis, etc., Ry. Co. v. Dallas (Ark.), 35 R. R. R. 167, 58 Am. & Eng. R. Cas., N. S., 167; Little Rock, etc., Co. v. Billings (C. C. A.), 34 R. R. R. 788, 57 Am. & Eng. R. Cas., N. S., 788; Coburn v. Moline, etc., Ry. Co. (Ill.). 34 R. R. R. 429, 57 Am. & Eng. R. Cas., N. S., 429.

Hughes v. Chicago, R. I. & P. Ry. Co. et al

trains. Trial to a jury, verdict and judgment for plaintiff, and defendant appeals. Reversed and remanded.

Carroll Wright, J. L. Parrish, and *C. O. McLain,* for appellant.

Matthew Gering and *Tripp & Tripp,* for appellee.

DEEMER, J.   Plaintiff claims that while a passenger on one of defendant's trains from Omaha, Neb., to Colfax, Iowa, and just before the train reached the station at Colfax, supposing that the station had been reached, he was attempting to alight and that while engaged in that act the train started with a jerk, throwing him under the wheels of a coach, resulting in the crushing of the left foot and the final amputation of the limb at a point six or eight inches below the knee.   Defendant denied all allegations of negligence, and, in effect, averred that plaintiff was guilty of contributory negligence.   Upon the issues joined the case was tried to a jury, resulting in a verdict for plaintiff in the sum of $15,000.   This was reduced by the trial court to the sum of $10,000, and for that amount judgment was rendered against the defendant.   This appeal presents but five propositions, and these are so involved as to resolve themselves to but three.

Defendant contended, and introduced testimony to show that at the time plaintiff received his injuries he was intoxicated, and it asked the court to instruct the jury as follows with reference to this matter: "Before you can find for the plaintiff, you must not only find that the defendant was guilty of one or more of the acts of negligence charged in the petition and submitted to you by these instructions, and that such act or acts of negligence was the proximate cause of plaintiff's injury, but you must also find by a preponderance of the evidence that the plaintiff was free from any negligence on his own part which contributed to his injury.   In this connection you are instructed that the fact, if it be a fact, that the plaintiff at the time of the accident was under the influence of intoxicating liquors, would constitute negligence on his part, and, if the same in any degree contributed to his injury, your verdict must be for the defendant."   In lieu thereof the trial court gave the following: "You are instructed that the fact, if it be a fact, that just prior and at the time of the accident the plaintiff was under the influence of intoxicating liquors, and by reason thereof the plaintiff became careless and negligent, and you find such carelessness and negligence contributed to the plaintiff's own injury, and you so find, then the plaintiff cannot recover."

It also gave the following, which should be considered in connection therewith:

"(5) 'Negligence' is the omission to do something which a reasonably prudent man, guided by those considerations which ordinarily regulate the conduct of human affairs, would do, or

Hughes *v.* Chicago, R. I. & P. Ry. Co. et al

doing something which a reasonably prudent man would not do under similar or like circumstances.

"(6) 'Reasonable and ordinary care and diligence' is such care and diligence as an ordinarily prudent man would exercise under similar or like circumstances."

"(11) You are instructed that if you find from the evidence that the plaintiff on April 3, 1907, while a passenger on the cars and train of the defendant company, passed on and along the aisle and through the door of the car and onto the platform of the car on which he was a passenger and hence down from steps of the said car, and while the train was to the plaintiff's knowledge still moving and in motion, or as a reasonably prudent man could have discovered that the train was moving and in motion, he stepped off the car, and was injured substantially as he claims, and you so find, then in that event the plaintiff cannot recover, and your verdict should be for the defendant."

"(13) If you find from the evidence introduced upon the trial of this case, guided by these instructions, that the plaintiff exercised ordinary care, taking into consideration all the facts and circumstances connected with the injury, as shown by the evidence, and you find that he has sustained any injury, then he was not at fault or negligent. If, however, he did not exercise such care the injury of which he complains resulted to him, then he was guilty of contributory negligence."

Defendant contends that the court erred in denying defendant's request, and also committed error in giving instruction No. 15, hitherto quoted.

We shall first consider the instruction refused. This states, in so many words, that if plaintiff, when injured, was under the influence of intoxicating liquors, this in itself would constitute negligence, and that, if this intoxication in any degree contributed to his injury, plaintiff could not recover. It will be noted that the instruction so asked does not refer to the extent of the intoxication, but characterizes any degree as contributory negligence as a matter of law. We think this was too broad, and that the trial court correctly refused to give it. That one is intoxicated when injured does not of itself constitute contributory negligence, but it is a circumstance to be considered in bearing upon the question of his care. Weymire *v.* Wolfe, 52 Iowa, 533, 3 N. W. 541; Cramer *v.* City, 42 Iowa, 315; O'Keefe *v.* Railroad, 32 Iowa, 467; Sylvester *v.* Town, 110 Iowa, 256, 81 N. W. 455. One cannot voluntarily incapacitate himself from the ability to exercise ordinary care, and then recover for an injury to which a want of ordinary care upon his part while so intoxicated proximately contributes. In other words, intoxication is not alone a bar to recovery unless by reason of such intoxication the party injured fails to exercise the ordinary care of a sober man or is unable by reason thereof to take the usual and ordinary precautions to avoid danger. Kingston v. Ft. Wayne Co., 112 Mich. 40, 70 N. W. 315, 74 N. W. 230, 40 L. R. A. 131; Seymer v. Lake, 66 Wis. 651, 29 N. W. 554. Yet intoxication in any degree is a circumstance to be considered in determining the question of contributory negligence. Rhyner v. Menasha, 107 Wis. 201, 83 N. W. 303; Sylvester v. Casey, 110 Iowa, 256, 81 N. W. 455; Wynn v. Allard, 5 Watts & S. (Pa.) 524; Fisher v. Railroad, 42 W. Va. 183, 24 S. E. 570, 33 L. R. A. 69. These propositions are so well fortified by authority that nothing more need be said regarding defendant's request.

Coming now to the instruction given. We find that it is in almost the exact form of the one given in Cramer v. City of Burlington, supra. The court there said in such an instruction: "Again this instruction directs that, in addition to the existence of a state of intoxication, the jury must further find that on account thereof plaintiff became careless or reckless in regard to his safety, and thus caused or contributed to his injury. This was error. An intoxicated person might become neither careless nor reckless, and at the same time might so far lose control of his muscular action as to be unable to avoid injury. If, under such circumstances, he should stumble or stagger over a dangerous precipice, his want of ordinary care may have contributed to the injury, no matter how much he may have wished and endeavored to avoid the danger." To say the least the instruction as given is not happily worded and should not be repeated upon a retrial. In view of other instructions, it may be that this error was without prejudice, and that we should not reverse on this ground alone. The matter is referred to at this time in order that there may be no repetition of the instruction upon a retrial.

2. The trial court gave the jury the following instruction: "(18) It is admitted and conceded by the parties that the tables of life expectancy show that the life expectancy of a man at age of plaintiff on April 3, 1907, was 15 years. Upon this you are instructed that these tables are formed and based upon the lives of individuals who are in the ordinary pursuits of life and in ordinary conditions of health; but the court says to you that these tables are not conclusive, as to the age the plaintiff may continue to live, or the duration of his life, and in considering the expectancy of the life of the plaintiff you should take this concession into consideration together with all the evidence in the case, including the physical condition of the plaintiff at the time and prior to the alleged injury, his general health, his vocation in life, if any, with respect to danger, his habits, whether temperate or intemperate and all other facts and circumstances as entering into the probable duration of life of the plaintiff, as disclosed by the evidence." This was given in order that the jury might have a guide whereby to estimate plaintiff's future and prospective mental and physical suffering and loss of earning capacity. He was asking nothing, even if he could have done

so, for the shortening of his life and the sole inquiry in this connection was, How long will plaintiff, in his present injured condition, live and continue to suffer, and for what length of time will his diminished capacity to make money and acquire a competency exist? As to prospective damages, it is quite clear that plaintiff's condition at the time of trial was a material fact, and the inquiry should have been directed to his expectancy of life in his then injured condition. The instruction given by the trial court referred the jury to plaintiff's condition before he received his injuries and told them to consider his expectancy with reference to a time prior to his injuries and his condition of health at that time. The instruction cannot be sustained. It may possibly be as plaintiff contends that this instruction had no influence upon the verdict; but it is wrong from any point of view, and was presumptively prejudicial. If considered by the jury, as we must assume it was for it was given for that purpose, it must have resulted in increasing the verdict. Plaintiff's counsel insist that as the trial court reduced the verdict this cured the error. But this proposition cannot be indorsed. No one can tell how much the jury allowed as prospective damages for pain and suffering, loss of earning capacity, etc. This matter was peculiarly within the province of the jury. Such damages being unliquidated and incapable of exact measurement, it was impossible for the trial court to know how much was allowed by the jury under the erroneous instruction. This being true, it could not cure the error by reducing the amount of the verdict without trenching upon the province of the jury.

Defendant asked the court to give the following instruction, instead of the one given: "Testimony has been received in evidence which tends to show that the expectancy of life of a man 54 years old, according to the tables of mortality, is 15 years. These tables of mortality, however, do not necessarily apply to the plaintiff, but are based upon the observed expectancy among persons in ordinary pursuits and in ordinary condition of health, and in determining the expectancy of plaintiff you must take into consideration the condition of his health at the present time so far as shown by the evidence or so far as you have been able to observe the same, his prior habits with reference to the use of intoxicating liquors, as well as all other facts and circumstances in evidence and bearing thereon." From the discussion already had upon this proposition it is apparent that this instruction should have been given in lieu of number eighteen.

These conclusions are decisive of this appeal, and render it unnecessary that we consider the other propositions relied upon by appellant. For errors pointed out, the judgment must be reversed and the cause remanded for a new trial.

Reversed and remanded.

Texas & P. Ry. Co. *v.* Williams.

(Circuit Court of Appeals, Fifth Circuit, November 29, 1910.)

[183 Fed..Rep. 576.]

Railroads—Action for Injury by Fire—Questions for Jury.*—In an action against a railroad company to recover for loss by a fire alleged to have been caused by an engine on defendant's road, proof that the appliances of the engine which passed the premises just before the fire were in good condition does not entitle defendant to an instructed verdict.

In error to the Circuit Court of the United States for the Eastern District of Texas.

Action at law by J. S. Williams against the Texas & Pacific Railway Company. Judgment for plaintiff, and defendant brings error. Affirmed.

Cecil H. Smith, for plaintiff in error.
E. S. Conner and *S. B. M. Long,* for defendant in error.

Before Pardee and Shelby, Circuit Judges.

Per Curiam. The assignments of error which question the jurisdiction at law of the court below and the sufficiency of parties in interest are not well taken. See Chicago, St. Louis & New Orleans R. Co. *v.* Pullman Southern Car Co., 139 U. S. 79, 11 Sup. Ct. 490, 35 L. Ed. 97; Southern Bell Telephone & Telegraph Co. *v.* Watts, 66 Fed. 460, 13 C. C. A. 579; Railway *v.* Hall, 64 Tex. 615.

The evidence of George Polk, complained of in the fifth assignment of error, seems to have been, not only relevant, but material. While the undisputed evidence in the case may show that the appliances of defendant's engine that passed plaintiff's premises just before the fire were in good condition, that did not, under the proof, entitle the defendant to an instructed verdict.

As to defendant's negligence, the evidence required a submission to the jury.

The judgment of the Circuit Court is affirmed.

---

*See first foot-note of Cincinnati, etc., Ry. Co. *v.* Sadieville Milling Co. (Ky.), 35 R. R. R. 553, 58 Am. & Eng. R. Cas., N. S., 553.

Owensboro City R. Co. *v.* Wall.

(Court of Appeals of Kentucky, Feb. 7, 1911.)

[133 S. W. Rep. 1145.]

Street Railroads—Negligence—Horses on Highway.*—Where the servants of a street railway company in charge of a car see that its approach frightens a horse on the street, they must use ordinary care not to increase its fright; and if they have reason to believe that the approach of the car frightened the horse, it is negligence to move it nearer.

Appeal from Circuit Court, Daviess County.

Action by W. K. Wall against the Owensboro City Railroad Company. From a judgment for plaintiff, defendant appeals. Affirmed.

E. B. Anderson, Albert W. Funkhouser, and *Arthur F. Funkhouser,* for appellant.

L. P. Tanner, for appellee.

Nunn, J. Appellee, late one afternoon, with his wife and children, was driving over the city of Owensboro, and when coming from the end of Breckenridge street a street car, going the opposite direction, approached him across the tracks of a steam railroad, making a considerable noise, which frightened appellee's horse. The horse turned the buggy around, but was caught by a friend of appellee and stopped, and the motorman stopped the car. Appellee and his friend made an examination, and found that one of the shafts was broken near the cross-bar, and they took a hitch rein and rope and began to tie it up. The motorman told them that he could not wait on them any longer, and they began parleying with him, trying to prevail upon him to wait until appellee got into his buggy before he started the car. When appellee got into his buggy, he started off in the direction the car was going, with the intention of turning out the first street he came to, to a place of safety. As appellee started, the motorman started the car, and, according to appellee's testimony, traveled faster than he was traveling, and overtook him at the street which he intended to turn out, and just as he was turning out, frightened his horse, and caused him to begin to run and kick. Appellee stated that he found that he could not stop the horse, so he turned him into a wire fence; that his knee was injured, and that the horse and buggy were damaged, for which he sued the company, and recovered $397.50. Appellant's

---

*For the authorities in this series on the subject of the duties and liabilities of street railways with respect to frightening teams and saddle horses, see third foot-note of Gould *v.* Merrill Ry., etc., Co. (Wis.), 35 R. R. R. 273, 58 Am. & Eng. R. Cas., N. S., 273.

Owensboro City R. Co. v. Wall

testimony agrees with appellee's, except that it shows that the car was not run upon or near the horse; that appellee had turned into another street, and gone away from the car, when the horse became suddenly freightened and ran away.

The court gave the jury three instructions—one on the question of damages, if they should find for plaintiff, and the other two we copy:

"(1) Gentlemen of the jury, if you believe from the evidence that while plaintiff was passing along Breckenridge street, in or near the city of Owensboro, driving a horse attached to a buggy in which he and his family were riding at the time, and the said horse became frightened at a car belonging to the defendant, Owensboro City Railroad Company, and in charge of one of its servants, and after said agent discovered that said horse was freightened at his car he stopped his car, and negligently, carelessly, and willfully failed to keep it stopped reasonably long enough time for the plaintiff to reach a place of safety, or ran said car close to said horse, and by reason thereof said horse became frightened, ran off, and injured the plaintiff's knee, damaged his buggy, and injured the horse, then you ought to find for the plaintiff, and so state in your verdict."

"(3) If you believe from the evidence that you have heard that the injuries of which the plaintiff complains in his petition and evidence were the result of his own negligence or carelessness, and but for his contributory negligence and carelessness, if any, he would not have been injured or damaged, then you ought to find for the defendant; or, if you believe from the evidence that the horse which the plaintiff was driving was vicious, wild, and unmanageable, and by reason of that alone he received his injuries, than you ought to find for the defendant."

The court should not have given the peremptory instruction asked for by appellant. When it saw that the horse was frightened, it should have used reasonable care, under the circumstances, to not frighten it again, and, if those in charge of the car had reason to believe that it would frighten the horse to move the car near it, they should not have done so, and, if they did, they were guilty of negligence. The instructions submitted this question to the jury, and we are not willing to disturb its finding.

For these reasons, the judgment of the lower court is affirmed.

ACTON v. FARGO & MOORHEAD ST. RY. CO.

(Supreme Court of North Dakota, Sept. 24, 1910. Rehearing Denied
Dec. 30, 1910.)

Appeal and Error—Review—Verdict.—Where, as in this case, the
verdict is supported by substantial evidence, and the trial court has
declined to disturb such verdict when challenged for alleged insufficiency of the evidence, such ruling will not be reversed in this court.

Street Railroads—Extent of Rights in Streets.*—A traveler passing along a city street has a right to use every part of it, regardless
of whether there is a street car track in it or not. In view of the
inability of the cars to leave their tracks, it is the duty of free vehicles not to obstruct unnecessarily, and to turn to one side when
they meet them; but, subject to that, and to the respective powers
of the two, a car and a wagon owe reciprocal duties to use reasonable care on each side to avoid a collision.

Street Railroads—Rights in Streets.†—Street cars have precedence,
necessarily, in the portion of the way designated for their use. This
superior right must be exercised, however, with proper caution and
a due regard for the rights of others; and the fact that it has a prescribed route does not alter the duty of a street railway company to
the public, who have the right to travel upon its track until they are
overtaken by its cars.

**Street Railroads—Collision with Vehicle—Liability of Company—
Discovered Peril.‡**—The court charged the jury as follows: "I
charge you, gentlemen of the jury, as a matter of law, that even if
you find from a preponderance of the evidence that the plaintiff in
this action was guilty of contributory negligence in going upon the

---

*For the authorities in this series on the subject of the mutual
rights and duties of street railways and other users of street, see
foot-note of Carroll v. Boston Elev. Ry. (Mass.), 36 R. R. R. 401,
59 Am. & Eng. R. Cas., N. S., 410; third head-note of Palmer v.
Portland, etc., Co. (Ore.), 36 R. R. R. 68, 59 Am. & Eng. R. Cas.,
N. S., 68.

†For the authorities in this series on the subject of the right of
way as between a street railway car and another vehicle or person,
see second foot-note of Denver City Tramway Co. v. Wright (Colo.),
36 R. R. R. 360, 59 Am. & Eng. R. Cas., N. S., 360; first paragraph
of foot-note of Wilson v. Seattle, etc., Ry. Co. (Wash.), 35 R. R. R.
80, 58 Am. & Eng. R. Cas., N. S., 80.

For the authorities in this series on the subject of the care required of those in charge of street cars in order to avoid collisions
with other users of streets, see second foot-note of Gould v. Merrill
Ry., etc., Co. (Wis.), 35 R. R. R. 273, 58 Am. & Eng. R. Cas. N. S.,
273; third foot-note of Carroll v. Connecticut Co. (Conn.), 34 R. R.
R. 780, 57 Am. & Eng. R. Cas., N. S., 780; Baldie v. Tacoma Ry. &
P. Co. (Wash.), 34 R. R. R. 350, 57 Am. & Eng. R Cas., N. S., 350.

‡For the authorities in this series on the subject of the combined
effect of contributory negligence and negligence on the part of defendant after the latter has discovered the peril of the other, see
first foot-note of St. Louis, etc., R. Co. v. Summers (C. C. A.), 35
R. R. R. 117, 58 Am. & Eng. R. Cas., N. S., 117; third foot-note of

Acton v. Fargo & Moorhead St. Ry. Co

defendant's track, under all the circumstances of the case, that nevertheless, if the defendant or its employees in charge of the car were aware, or should by the exercise of reasonable diligence and care have become aware, of the dangerous position of the plaintiff, in time to have, by the exercise of reasonable diligence and care, avoided the collision with the buggy of the plaintiff, that the prior negligence of the plaintiff would not bar his right to recover in this action." This instruction states the law correctly.

Street Railroads—Collision with Vehicle—Liability of Company—Discovered Peril.‡—The ground upon which a plaintiff may recover, notwithstanding his own negligence, is that the defendant after becoming aware of the danger to which plaintiff was exposed, failed to use a proper degree of care to avoid injuring him.

Street Railroads—Use of Street Occupied by Street Railway—Care Required.*—It is not necessarily negligent to drive a vehicle along a street railway track in the direction in which cars travel upon the track, nor in the direction from which the cars will approach. But when so driving the driver should keep a lookout for cars approaching in the opposite direction, and he should use reasonable diligence, to ascertain the approach of cars from the rear, but he is not, as a matter of law, required to keep a constant watch to the rear to discover approaching cars.

Negligence—Proximate Cause.§—Unless the negligence of the plaintiff proximately contributes to the injury it does not constitute contributory negligence which bars a recovery. The party who last has a clear opportunity of avoiding the accident, notwithstanding the negligence of his opponent, is considered solely responsible for it.

Bruggeman v. Illinois Cent. R. Co. (Iowa), 35 R. R. R. 241, 58 Am. & Eng. R. Cas., N. S., 241; foot-note of Dyerson v. Union Pac. R. Co. (Kan.), 28 R. R. R. 15, 51 Am. & Eng. R. Cas., N. S., 15.

For the authorities in this series on the subject of the combined effect of contributory negligence and negligence on the part of defendant after latter should have discovered the peril of the other party, see last foot-note of Chesapeake, etc., Ry. Co. v. Corbin (Va.), 35 R. R. R. 229, 58 Am. & Eng. R. Cas., N. S., 229; third foot-note of Bourrett v. Chicago & N. W. Ry. Co. (Iowa), 34 R. R. R. 284, 57 Am. & Eng. R. Cas., N. S., 284.

§For the authorities in this series on the question whether contributory negligence must be the proximate cause of the injury in order to prevent recovery, see second foot-note of Bourrett v. Chicago & N. W. Ry. Co. (Iowa), 34 R. R. R. 284, 57 Am. & Eng. R. Cas., N. S., 284.

For the authorities in this series on the subject of the last clear chance doctrine, see first foot-note of Denver City Tramway Co. v. Wright (Colo.), 36 R. R. R. 360, 59 Am. & Eng. R. Cas., N. S., 360; seventh head-note of Farris v. Southern R. Co. (N. Car.), 36 R. R. R. 523, 59 Am. & Eng. R. Cas., N. S., 523; Clark v. St. Louis, etc., R. Co. (Okla.), 36 R. R. R. 247, 59 Am. & Eng. R. Cas., N. S., 247; third foot-note of Bruggeman v. Illinois Cent. R. Co. (Iowa), 5 R. R. R. 241, 58 Am. & R. Cas., N. S., 241.

*See (*) on preceding page.
‡See (‡) on preceding page.

Acton v. Fargo & Moorhead St. Ry. Co

Street Railroads—Use of Streets—Duty to Prevent Collision.†— While it is the duty of vehicles moving along street railway tracks to leave the tracks on the approach of cars so as not to obstruct their passage, still those in charge of cars must use reasonable diligence to prevent collisions, and the company is liable for injury resulting from their failure to do so.

Street Railroads—Use of Streets—Care Required.§—Where a street car is approaching from the rear a vehicle moving along the track, the person operating the car has not the right to proceed without regard to the presence of the vehicle, in anticipation that the vehicle will leave the track in time to give free passage to the car.

Street Railroads—Use of Street—Care Required.‖—In the case of a trolley car approaching another vehicle directly in a line with its progress, and a possible obstacle in the way, a proper regard for the rights of others requires that the car be reduced to such control that it may be brought to a standstill if necessary.

Street Railroads—Use of Street—Care Required.—A street railway company is liable for injuries sustained by a collision between a vehicle and a car, where the employees in charge of the car by the exercise of ordinary care could have avoided the accident, notwithstanding the negligence of the driver in the first instance in placing himself in a situation of peril.

Street Railroads—Use of Street—Failure to Give Warning.—Such timely and reasonable warning of the approach of a street car must be given as will enable others in the exercise of due care to avoid injury from it.

Street Railroads—Collision with Vehicle—Liability of Company—Discovered Peril—Evidence.—If those in charge of a street car discover, or should by the exercise of ordinary care have discovered, plaintiff's peril, while driving a wagon on the track in time to have avoided a collision, and did not do so, plaintiff's negligence in failing to look back for an approaching car would not preclude his recovery. Whether defendant's motorman in charge of a street car which collided with plaintiff's vehicle made proper efforts to avoid the collision if he saw, or by the exercise of ordinary care could have seen, plaintiff's peril, held, under the facts, to be for the jury.

‖For the authorities in this series on the subject of the duty of those in charge of street cars to regulate speed in order to avoid collisions with other users of streets, see last foot-note of Denver City Tramway Co. v. Wright (Colo.), 36 R. R. R. 360, 59 Am. & Eng. R. Cas., N. S., 360; last foot-note of Engvall v. Des Moines City Ry. Co. (Iowa), 35 R. R. R. 266, 58 Am. & Eng. R. Cas., N. S., 266; Wilson v. Seattle, etc., Ry. Co. (Wash.), 35 R. R. R. 80, 58 Am. & Eng. R. Cas., N. S., 80; United Rys. & Elec. Co. v. Carneal (Md.), 34 R. R. R. 705, 57 Am. & Eng. R. Cas., N. S., 705; foot-note of Louisville Ry. Co. v. Flannery (Ky.), 34 R. R. R. 310, 57 Am. & Eng. R. Cas., N. S., 310.

†See (†) on page 767.

Acton *v.* Fargo & Moorhead St. Ry. Co

Street Railroads—Use of Street—Care Required—Presumption.¶—
One driving along the street railway track in daylight has the right
to suppose that if a car is approaching from the rear a proper lookout is maintained, and that ordinary care will be exercised to avoid
injuring him.

Damages—Personal Injuries—Excessiveness.—The jury awarded
plaintiff $2,450 damages without interest. Held not excessive.

Trial—Special Verdict.—An instruction to the jury that the answers to the separate questions must be of such a nature that they
will fully support the general verdict held not error.

Appeal and Error—Harmless Error—Instructions.—The jury having found that the motorman of defendant did not exercise ordinary care and reasonable diligence in stopping his car and preventing the accident after he saw, or might in the exercise of reasonable
diligence have seen, that plaintiff was in a position of danger, for
reasons stated in the opinion the appellant was not prejudiced by
the instructions complained of.

Appeal and Error—Harmless Error—Erroneous Instruction.—A
judgment will not be reversed because of an erroneous instruction
when it affirmatively appears from answers to interrogatories that
such instruction did not influence the jury in reaching its verdict.

Street Railroads—Collision with Vehicles—Actions—Instructions.§
—The court refused to charge the jury that though the motorman
saw the plaintiff driving along and on the track, and (if he was driving thereon) he had a right to assume that the plaintiff would exercise ordinary care to observe the approach of the car and would get
out of danger before the car reached him, and that the motorman is
not required to check his car (if such car is running at an ordinary
rate of speed) until he has reasonable cause to believe that there is
actual danger of a collision, held not error, under the circumstances
of this case.

Special Findings Consistent with General Verdict.—The special
findings made by the jury are sufficient to sustain the general verdict. If the questions not answered, or where the answers are not
proved, were all answered favorably to appellant, the general verdict
would still be consistent with the special findings.

(Syllabus by the Court.)

¶For the authorities in this series on the subject of the duty of
those in charge of street cars to lookout in order to avoid collisions with other users of streets, see second foot-note of South,
etc., Ry. Co. *v.* Crutcher (Ky.), 35 R. R. R. 199, 58 Am. & Eng. R.
Cas., N. S., 199; first foot-note of Engvall *v.* Des Moines City Ry.
Co. (Iowa), 35 R. R. R. 266, 58 Am. & Eng. R. Cas., N. S., 266.

For the authorities in this series on the question whether a person injured through the negligence of another had the right to assume that the latter had performed or would perform the duties
owing to the person injured, see foot-note of Norris *v.* Atlantic C.
L. R. Co. (N. Car.), 36 R. R. R. 321, 59 Am. & Eng. R. Cas., N. S.,
321; Campbell *v.* Chicago G. W. Ry. Co. (Minn.), 35 R. R. R. 98,
58 Am. & Eng. R. Cas., N. S., 98.

§ See (§) on page 768.

Acton *v.* Fargo & Moorhead St. Ry. Co

Appeal from District Court, Cass County, Pollock, Judge.

Action by William Acton against the Fargo & Moorhead Street Railway Company. From a judgment for plaintiff, and an order denying a motion for judgment notwithstanding the verdict or for a new trial, defendant appeals. Affirmed.

Stambaugh & Fowler, for appellant.
Barnett & Richardson, for respondent.

CARMODY, J. This is an action for damages for personal injuries, inflicted upon plaintiff by one of defendant's street cars on October 15, 1907. A trial was had in the district court, and a verdict rendered in favor of the plaintiff. Thereafter the defendant moved for judgment notwithstanding the verdict, or for a new trial, both of which motions were denied, and judgment entered on the verdict. From the order denying such motions, and from the judgment, defendant appeals to this court. The appellant is the owner of a street railway system in the city of Fargo. A portion of its track is laid upon Broadway, which runs north and south. On the day of the accident, the respondent was driving north on the west side of appellant's track, on Broadway. He was driving a double team of work horses attached to a single buggy, without any top. He started to drive north from a point located on the west side of Broadway about midway between First and Second avenues. Before starting north, he looked south but saw no car. He drove north on the west side of the track, at a distance of about 5 or 6 feet from the track, until he reached a point a little north of the center of the block between Third and Fourth avenues, and 60 or 70 feet south of where he was struck. At this point he noticed a team facing him, standing on the west side of the track, attached to a heavy lumber wagon, at a distance of about 6 feet from the west rail of the track. When he saw this team, he looked back over his shoulder for a distance of about 100 feet, and then drove upon the track so that his buggy was astride the west rail. He drove in this position, without looking back for an approaching car, until he reached the point where this team was standing, when he was struck by a car approaching from the rear, and was thrown from his buggy. Just prior to the accident, plaintiff's team was traveling three miles per hour, while appellant's car was traveling about eight miles per hour. The motorman sounded the gong, and responded heard the sound just about the time he was struck by the car. The accident happened at about 11 o'clock in the morning. It is undisputed that there is a clear view of the place of the accident for several hundred feet south. The car in question, under conditions similar to those at bar, could be stopped in between 20 or 25 feet. The car was stopped between 20 and 30 feet north of the point of the accident.

Acton *v*. Fargo & Moorhead St. Ry. Co

In addition to the general verdict, the court submitted 37 questions to the jury. Appellant assigns 18 errors, which are divided into four subdivisions: (1) The evidence fails to show that the defendant was guilty of negligence. (2) The evidence shows that the plaintiff was guilty of such contributory negligence as to prevent his recovery. (3) The damages are so excessive as to appear to have been given under the influence of passion and prejudice. (4) Errors in law occurring at the trial.

We will take up these propositions in the order advanced in the argument of appellant. The jury found a general verdict in favor of the plaintiff, and in addition thereto found that the defendant was guilty of negligence under the law as laid down by the court; that the motorman did not exercise ordinary care and reasonable diligence in stopping his car, and preventing the accident after he saw, or might in the exercise of reasonable diligence have seen, that plaintiff was in a position of danger; that the gong was sounded by the motorman as he approached the point where the accident occurred; that it was not proved as to what distance before the accident he sounded the gong. The jury did not answer the questions as to how far from the point where the accident occurred that the motorman turned the reverse and set the brakes, nor the question how far from the point where the accident occurred did the reversing of the brakes actually begin to take effect. The jury found that the car ran north of the point where the collision occurred from 20 to 30 feet before it came to a stop; that just before the accident the car was running eight miles per hour; and that the plaintiff was driving at the rate of three miles per hour. The first contention of appellant that the evidence fails to show that the defendant was guilty of negligence must be overruled. The jury found in favor of the plaintiff in a general verdict, and found by the special findings that the defendant was guilty of negligence. The defendant having moved for a new trial, or for judgment notwithstanding the verdict on the ground, among others, of the insufficiency of the evidence to justify the verdict, and the trial court having denied such motion, if the verdict is supported by substantial evidence, then it must stand. Taylor *v*. Jones. 3 N. D. 235, 55 N. W. 593; Black *v*. Walker. 7 N. D. 414. 75 N. W. 787; Muri *v*. White, 8 N. D. 58, 76 N. W. 503; Howland *v*. Ink. 8 N. D. 63. 76 N. W. 992; Becker *v*. Duncan. 8 N. D. 600. 80 N. W. 762; Heyrock *v*. McKenzie, 8 N. D. 601. 80 N. W. 762; Magnusson *v*. Linwell, 9 N. D. 157, 82 N. W. 743; Flath *v*. Casselman, 10 N. D. 419. 87 N. W. 988; Drinkall *v*. Movius State Bank, 11 N. D. 10. 88 N. W. 724, 57 L. R. A. 341, 95 Am. St. Rep. 693; Lang *v*. Bailes, 125 N. W. 891.

Under the doctrine laid down by this court in the cases herein cited, an examination of the evidence convinces us that there is substantial evidence to support the verdict, and the learned trial

Acton v. Fargo & Moorhead St. Ry. Co

court did not abuse its discretion in denying the motion for a new trial or for judgment notwithstanding the verdict, on the ground of the insufficiency of the evidence. Appellant argues with much force that, assuming appellant's negligence, plaintiff was guilty of contributory negligence, which, as a matter of law, would prevent his recovery. The jury answered the question, "Was the plaintiff guilty of contributory negligence, as defined by the court in his instructions?" as follows: "To a certain extent." The evidence shows that plaintiff drove north 600 or 700 feet on the west side of the track, and that, seeing a team about 6 feet west of the track, approaching from the north, he looked over his shoulder for a distance of about 100 feet, saw no car, then turned upon the track and drove north, without looking back, for a distance of 60 or 70 feet, to the point where he was struck by the car.

A traveler passing along a city street has a right to use every part of it regardless of whether there is a street car track in it or not. The rights of a street car are, simply, in view of inability of the cars to leave their tracks, it is the duty of free vehicles not to obstruct them, unnecessarily, and to turn to one side when they meet them; but, subject to that, and to the respective powers of the two, a car and a wagon owe reciprocal duties to use reasonable care on each side to avoid a collision. The plaintiff was not a trespasser on the street car tracks in any sense. The right of the street railway in the street is only to use it in common with the public. It has no exclusive right of travel, even upon its track, and is bound to use the same care in preventing a collision, as the driver of a wagon, or any person crossing or entering upon the highway. Street cars have precedence, necessarily, in the portion of the way designated for their use. This superior right must be exercised, however, with proper caution and a due regard for the rights of others; and the fact that it has a prescribed route does not alter the duty of a street railway company to the public, who have the right to travel upon its track until they are overtaken by its cars. In the case at bar, there is no dispute but that the motorman saw, or might have seen, the plaintiff, for some time and for a considerable distance, before he overtook and struck him with the car.

On the question of the contributory negligence of the plaintiff, and the duty of the defendant if plaintiff was guilty of contributory negligence, the court charged the jury as follows: "I charge you, gentlemen of the jury, as a matter of law, that even if you find from a preponderance of the evidence that the plaintiff in this action was guilty of contributory negligence in going upon the defendant's track, under all the circumstances of the case, that nevertheless, if the defendant or its employees in charge of the car were aware, or should by the exercise of rea-

Acton v. Fargo & Moorhead St. Ry. Co

sonable diligence and care have become aware, of the dangerous position of the plaintiff, in time to have, by the exercise of reasonable diligence and care, avoided the collision with the buggy of the plaintiff, that the prior negligence of the plaintiff would not bar his right to recover, in this action." This instruction states the law correctly. If the motorman, after seeing respondent, had any reasonable ground to apprehend, that he was not aware of the approaching train, and was unconscious of the danger that was imminent, a recovery is justified notwithstanding plaintiff's prior negligence. Evans v. Adams Express Co., 122 Ind. 362, 23 N. E. 1039, 7 L. R. A. 678; Evansville, etc., Ry. Co. v. Hiatt, 17 Ind. 102; Krenzer v. Pittsburg, etc., Ry. Co., 151 Ind. 587, 43 N. E. 649, 68 Am. St. Rep. 252; Ry. Co. v. Hamer, 29 Ind. App. 426, 62 N. E. 658. The ground upon which a plaintiff may recover, notwithstanding his own negligence, is that the defendant, after becoming aware of the danger to which the plaintiff was exposed, failed to use a proper degree of care to avoid injuring him. Zimmerman v. R. R. Co., 71 Mo. 476. It is not necessarily negligent to drive a vehicle along a street railway track in the direction in which cars travel upon the track, nor in the direction from which the cars will approach. But when so driving, the driver should keep a lookout for cars approaching in the opposite direction, and he should use reasonable diligence to ascertain the approach of cars from the rear, but he is not, as a matter of law, required to keep a constant watch to the rear to discover approaching cars. Hot Springs St. Ry. Co. v. Hildreth, 72 Ark. 572, 82 S. W. 245.

A driver of a vehicle has a right to assume, and to act upon the assumption, that warning will be given by those in charge of the approaching car behind him, and that the motorman will not knowingly or negligently run him down. The evidence shows conclusively that the car could be stopped in from 20 to 25 feet. The jury found that the plaintiff drove on the track for a distance of 60 to 70 feet, at the rate of 3 miles per hour. The defendant necessarily traveled about 200 feet from the time plaintiff first drove upon the track to the time of the accident. Consequently the motorman had sufficient time to stop the car and avoid the accident. The jury found, further, that the car ran north of the point where the collision occurred before it came to a stop a distance of from 20 to 30 feet. The evidence amply justifies the finding of the jury that the motorman did not exercise ordinary care and reasonable diligence in stopping his car and preventing the accident after he saw, or might in the exercise of reasonable diligence have seen, that plaintiff was in a position of danger. Unless the negligence of the plaintiff proximately contributed to the injury, it does not constitute contributory negligence which bars a recovery. The party who last has a clear opportunity of avoiding the accident, notwithstanding the negligence of his opponent, is considered solely responsible for it. A very full discussion of the doctrine of the last clear chance is found in note to case of Bogan v. Carolina Central Ry. Co., 55 L. R. A. 418.

Thompson on Negligence, vol. 1, § 177 lays down the following rule: "But suppose the traveler had come upon the track without making any use of his faculties to ascertain whether or not a train was approaching, but he had nevertheless arrived upon or near the track so far ahead of the train that those in charge of it, after seeing him thus exposed to danger, might have avoided injuring him; or if the circumstances were such that, by keeping the lookout which is required by law of persons propelling such a dangerous agency over a public highway, they might have seen him in time to have avoided injuring him, by the use of ordinary or reasonable care, by checking the speed of the train or by giving him warning, but negligently failed in these particulars, then the railroad company may be liable to the traveler, or to the person suing for the injury done to him, because its negligence is deemed the proximate cause of the injury, while his is deemed a remote cause of it."

The following is taken from Thompson on Negligence, vol. 2, § 1477: "It is, then, a rule constantly applied by many courts in these cases that, although the traveler may have been guilty of negligence in exposing himself to danger on the tracks of the street railway company, yet if, after discovering him in his exposed position, or if, by the exercise of ordinary diligence and attention to his duties, the driver could have discovered him in that position in time to avoid running upon him and injuring him, by the exercise of the like care in giving him warning, or in checking or stopping the car, the company will be liable."

In 27 Am. & Eng. Ency. of Law, 70, the rule is thus stated: "While it is the duty of vehicles moving along street railway tracks to leave the tracks on the approach of cars, so as not to obstruct their passage, still those in charge of cars must use reasonable diligence to prevent collisions, and the company is liable for injuries resulting from their failure to do so. * * * It has been held that where a street car approaching from the rear runs down a wagon driving along the track, this is of itself sufficient evidence of negligence on the part of the street railway company, in the absence of special circumstances excusing such act to carry the question to the jury. Where a street car is approaching from the rear a vehicle moving along the track, the person operating the car has not the right to proceed without regard to the presence of the vehicle, in anticipation that the vehicle will leave the track in time to give free passage to the car."

"When a motorman discovers a vehicle on the track a short

Acton v. Fargo & Moorhead St. Ry. Co

distance ahead of him, it is his duty to have the power which propels the car under his control, and use it so as to avoid a collision with such vehicle if he can. The fact that the vehicle can be turned in either direction, and that the way is open for it to be turned, does not relieve the motorman of the duty to use ordinary care to avoid a collision. It must be remembered that plaintiff was not a trespasser, but was rightfully upon the street." Flannagan v. St. Ry. Co., 68 Minn. 300, 71 N. W. 379.

In the case of a trolley car overtaking another vehicle directly in a line with its progress, and a possible obstacle in its way, a proper regard for the rights of others requires that the car be reduced to such control that it may be brought to a standstill, if necessary. St. Ry. Co. v. Haight, 59 N. J. Law, 577, 37 Atl. 135; Prendenville v. St. Louis Co., 128 Mo. App. 596, 107 S. W. 453.

The street trolley has no special right of way accorded to it by law, and the duty imposed upon other vehicles is equally imposed upon it. No vehicle can, without reasonable notice of its approach (what is reasonable notice is a question for the jury), violently run into, or force from its way, another, having a legitimate right upon the street, without becoming responsible for any damage which may result. Haight v. Consolidated Traction Co., supra.

One driving upon the side of the street has a right to drive upon a street railway track in order to pass another vehicle standing between the curb and the track. Goodson v. N. Y. City Ry. Co. (Sup.) 94 N. Y. Supp. 10.

Negligence and contributory negligence are questions for the jury, where plaintiff, driving a wagon so loaded with barrels that he could not see behind it without leaning to the side, failing so to look, pulled in towards defendant's street car track to pass a carriage standing by the curb, so that the barrels were struck by an electric car which came from behind, frightening his horses, and causing them to run away and injure him, there being evidence that the wagon, before being struck, traveled 35 feet while within the line of the car, and that the motorman, though seeing the wagon in time to stop, being 30 to 50 feet from it, increased his speed to 6 miles an hour, thinking he had room enough to pass. Blakeslee v. Consolidated St Ry. Co., 112 Mich. 63, 70 N. W. 408.

A driver of a team and wagon, who looked and listened for a car prior to going on a street car track, and who neither saw nor heard a car, was not negligent as a matter of law for not looking for a car within a minute thereafter while driving 470 feet along the track. Bensiek v. St. Louis Transit Co., 125 Mo. App. 121, 102 S. W. 587.

A street railway company is liable for injuries sustained by a collision between a vehicle and a car, where the employees in charge of the car by the exercise of ordinary care could have avoided the accident, notwithstanding the negligence of the driver in the first instance in placing himself in a situation of peril. Bensiek *v.* St. Louis Transit Co., supra.

A driver in a city street has a right to expect that street cars will be managed with reasonable care and a proper regard for the rights of others lawfully using the street, and he may drive along the track in full view of a car approaching from the rear, and the fact that he so proceeds for any distance will not charge him with contributory negligence in case of a collision, if, under all the circumstances, his conduct was consistent with ordinary prudence; the only limitation on his right being that he must not unnecessarily interfere with the passage of the car, which, though entitled to preference, has not an exclusive right to the track. Cohen *v.* Metropolitan St. Ry. Co., 34 Misc. Rep. 186, 68 N. Y. Supp. 830.

The following decisions by various courts of various states cover the case most thoroughly, and are in accord with the principles herein expressed: Vincent *v.* Ry. Co., 180 Mass. 104, 61 N. E. 822 (by Holmes, C. J.) ; Fenner *v.* Wilkes Barre, etc., 202 Pa. 365, 51 Atl. 1034; Consumers' Elec. Co. *v.* Pryor, 44 Fla. 354, 32 South. 797, 806; Manor *v.* Railway Co., 118 Mich. 1, 76 N. W. 139; Schilling *v.* Metropolitan Co., 47 App. Div. 500, 62 N. Y. Supp. 403; Shea *v.* Bay View R. Co., 44 Cal. 414; Mahoney *v.* R. Co., 110 Cal. 471, 42 Pac. 968; Robinson *v.* Louisville R. Co., 112 Fed. 484, 50 C. C. A. 357; Tashjian *v.* Ry. Co., 177 Mass. 75, 58 N. E. 281 ; Tacoma, etc., Co. *v.* Hays, 110 Fed. 496, 49 C. C. A. 115; Hall *v.* R. Co., 13 Utah, 243, 44 Pac. 1046, 57 Am. St. Rep. 726; Saunders *v.* Suburban R. Co., 99 Tenn. 130, 41 S. W. 1031 ; Citizens' R. Co. *v.* Seigrist, 96 Tenn. 119, 33 S. W. 920; Woodland *v.* North Jersey R. Co., 66 N. J. Law, 455, 49 Atl. 479; Shea *v.* St. Paul R. Co., 50 Minn. 395, 52 N. W. 902 ; Laethem *v.* R. Co., 100 Mich. 297, 58 N. W. 996 ; Citizens' R. Co. *v.* Steen, 42 Ark. 321 ; Shaw *v.* R. Co., 21 Utah, 76, 59 Pac. 552; McClellan *v.* R. Co., 105 Mich. 101, 62 N. W. 1025; St. R. R. *v.* Darnell, 32 Ind. App. 687, 68 N. E. 609; Moritz *v.* St. Ry. Co., 102 Mo. App. 657, 77 S. W. 477; Greene *v.* St. R. R., 119 Ky. 862, 84 S. W. 1154; Barry *v.* Street R. R. & Light Co., 119 Iowa. 62, 93 N. W. 68; Traction Co. *v.* Pheanis, 43 Ind. App. 653, 85 N. E. 1040; Street R. R. Co. *v.* Haynes, 112 Tenn. 712, 81 S. W. 374; Benjamin *v.* Holyoke St. Ry. Co., 160 Mass. 3, 35 N. E. 95, 39 Am. St. Rep. 446; Ablard *v.* St. Ry. Co., 139 Mich. 248, 102 N. W. 741 ; Noll *v.* St. Ry. Co., 100 Mo. App. 367, 73 S. W. 907; Funck *v.* Street R. R. Co., 133 Mo. App. 419, 113 S. W. 694; Ball *v.* Camden R. R. Co., 76 N. J. Law, 539, 72 Atl. 76; Mayes *v.* Metropolitan R. R. Co., 121 Mo. App. 614, 97 S. W. 612; St. Ry. Co. *v.* Marschke, 166 Ind. 490, 77 N. E. 945.

In Funck *v.* Metropolitan St. Ry. Co., supra, plaintiff drove

Acton v. Fargo & Moorhead St. Ry. Co

335 feet on defendant's track without looking back for a car although he might have done so. He looked when he first drove onto the track and saw no car. The night was dark except for street lamps. The defendant pleaded contributory negligence on the part of plaintiff. The court says: "If those in charge of a street car discovered, or should by the exercise of ordinary care have discovered, plaintiff's peril while driving the wagon on the track in time to have avoided a collision, and did not do so, plaintiff's negligence in failing to look back for an approaching car would not preclude his recovery;" and further says: "Under the facts, it was the duty of the court to submit to the jury the question whether defendant had performed its duty in the premises in making a proper effort to have avoided the collision after its motorman saw, or could have seen by the exercise of ordinary care, plaintiff's peril."

In Ball v. Camden & T. Ry. Co., supra, the plaintiffs, husband and wife, were in a top buggy with the top up and back curtains down but side curtains up. It was December 2, 1905, a night described by plaintiffs' witnesses as "drizzly and dark." There were two car tracks in the street, and the horse and buggy were being driven in the right-hand track. The plaintiffs became aware of a car coming up behind them, and were in the act of turning out when struck, the buggy being wrecked, and Mrs. Ball more or less injured. The husband and wife both testified that they heard no bell nor any sound of the car. They did not claim to have looked back to see if a car was coming, but both said that its approach was manifested by their seeing the light from the headlight of the car shining under the feet of the horse. Ball immediately pulled his horse to the right, but did not clear the track in time to avoid the car. A motion was made to nonsuit, which was denied. The court says: "We think there was a clear case for the jury on this point. The circumstances, which the jury were entitled to find as facts, that a trolley car driven at high speed on a dark night ran into the rear of a wagon in front of it, and traveling in the same direction, without any warning, and when the car had a headlight bright enough to show by its very reflection on the ground the approach of the car to those in the wagon, and therefore manifestly bright enough to make the wagon plainly visible to an ordinarily watchful motorman, seem to us quite sufficient to justify the jury in concluding that the motorman was not properly attending to his duties, and the court would have been in error to remove such a question from their consideration. The contributory negligence of the plaintiff was also a jury question. It is intimated by plaintiff in error that Ball was guilty of negligence in law by driving on the car track and not keeping a vigilant lookout to his rear; but he was entitled to drive on any

Acton v. Fargo & Moorhead St. Ry. Co

part of the roadway, having due regard for the rights of others, and was not bound to keep a lookout behind him."

In Mayes v. Metropolitan R. R. Co., supra, the court says: "Where plaintiff looked to see if a car was approaching from the rear when she drove into a street, she was not bound to look back while driving close to the car track to guard against a car approaching from the rear, she being entitled to presume that persons in control of such cars and other following vehicles would look out for her safety and avoid running into her."

In St. Ry. Co. v. Marschke, supra, plaintiff was driving at an ordinary trot. There were four street car tracks. She turned toward the track nearest her for the purpose of passing a heavy wagon that was slowly moving in the direction which she was going. Appellee knew that the southeast bound electric cars used the said track, and as she turned in that direction she glanced back up the track, and also listened. She did not hear a gong, nor did she hear a car moving on the viaduct. She continued to drive near the southwest rail of said track until she was opposite the wagon, when the running board of appellant's street car which had approached her from the rear, came into contact with the left hind wheel of her buggy, throwing her out and injuring her. The court held that the question of the contributory negligence of the plaintiff in driving on the track was one for the jury. The court further held that one driving along a street railroad track in daylight has the right to suppose that, if a car is approaching from the rear, a proper lookout is maintained and that ordinary care will be exercised not to injure him.

Appellant claims that the plaintiff's conduct in driving on the track amounted to gross negligence as a matter of law, which should defeat his recovery, and claims further that the jury found as a matter of fact that plaintiff was guilty of contributory negligence. We do not think that this finding helps appellant. Both parties being negligent, the true rule is held to be that the party who last has a clear opportunity of avoiding the accident, notwithstanding the negligence of his opponent, is considered solely responsible for it. It is well settled that a plaintiff may recover damages for an injury caused by the defendant's negligence, notwithstanding the plaintiff's own negligence exposed him to the risk of injury, if such injury was proximately caused by the defendant's omission (after becoming aware of the plaintiff's danger), to use ordinary care for the purpose of avoiding the injury to him. Harrington v. St. Ry., 140 Cal. 514, 74 Pac. 15, 63 L. R. A. 238, 98 Am. St. Rep. 85; Thompson v. St. Ry., 16 Utah, 281, 52 Pac. 92, 40 L. R. A. 172, 67 Am. St. Rep. 621; St. Ry. Co. v. Rifcowitz, 89 Md. 338, 43 Atl. 762; Hart v. St. R. R., 109 Iowa, 631, 80 N. W. 662; Remillard v. Traction Co., 138 Iowa, 565, 115 N. W. 900; Ramsey v. St. R. R., 135 Iowa,

Acton v. Fargo & Moorhead St. Ry. Co

329, 112 N. W. 798; Jett v. St. R. R., 178 Mo. 664, 77 S. W. 738; St. Louis R. R. v. Droddy (Tex. Civ. App.) 114 S. W. 902; Murray v. Transit Co., 108 Mo. App. 501, 83 S. W. 995; Wichita Co. v. Liebhart, 80 Kan. 91, 101 Pac. 457; Ruppel v. United R. R., 10 Cal. App. 319, 101 Pac. 803; St. Louis R. R. v. Thompson, 89 Ark. 496, 117 S. W. 541; 2 Thompson on Negligence, § 1477.

The jury awarded plaintiff $2,450 without interest. The damages so awarded, appellant insists, are so excessive as to appear to have been given under the influence of passion and prejudice. We do not think that the damages are so excessive as to warrant us in setting aside or reducing the verdict on that ground. Plaintiff testified that he suffered more or less pain ever since the accident; that the difficulty was a little above the small of the back and just above the groin on the right side. He tried to do little jobs several times since, but always had to quit. When he attempted to work this pain took him across the back and in the side; previous to the accident he was always well and able to work.

The jury, by the special findings, did not find that plaintiff received any permanent injuries by reason of the accident but did find that he was injured in his kidneys, liver, and head. The court instructed the jury as follows: "May I impress upon you the necessity of the greatest care in making answer to these questions, because, under the law, the answers to the separate questions must be of such a nature that they will fully support the general verdict which you shall find." This, appellant insists, is error, and contends that if the court instructs the jury that the special findings must be consistent with the general verdict, then the value of the special findings amounts to absolutely nothing. The construction complained of immediately precedes the following: "Under our law it is proper to present to juries questions to be answered, as I am doing in this case. The purpose of it is that the court may be fully informed as to the character of the decision which you have made. To aid you in forming your conclusions, in addition to the general instructions, which I will give you, concerning the law, may I suggest to you the following: · You will be permitted to take with you to the jury room the extra copies of the questions which you have been using during the arguments of counsel. By reading those questions in connection with the instructions of the court concerning the law found herein, you will be able to determine which party is entitled to prevail, by making answer to these questions according as you shall find the facts to be. Your answers to these questions should be direct, concise, and couched in as few words as possible. To the end, therefore, that there may be no error, and that your special findings may fully support the general verdict which you render, you had better take one of these extra sets of questions which you have

Acton *v.* Fargo & Moorhead St. Ry. Co

with you, and begin with question No. 1, make your answer thereto, and write it down upon the extra set, then, in their order, question No. 2, and so on throughout the entire series. When you have done this, and thus settled the questions of fact involved in harmony with the instructions concerning the law which I herewith give you, you will then be able to determine which side should prevail."

Section 7034, Rev. Codes 1905, provides that when the special findings of fact are inconsistent with the general verdict, the former controls the latter, and the court must give judgment accordingly. We do not think the court committed any error in the instructions complained of, taken in connection with the balance of the instructions hereinbefore quoted. He merely instructed the jury that the special findings must be consistent with the general verdict, and this the law requires. Section 7034, supra; People *v.* Murray, 52 Mich. 289, 17 N. W. 843; Des Moines & D. Land & Tree Co. *v.* Polk Co. Homestead & Trust Co., 82 Iowa, 663, 45 N. W. 773; Capital City Bank *v.* Wakefield, 83 Iowa, 46, 48 N. W. 1059.

In People *v.* Murray, supra, a number of special questions were put to the jury. The judge said to the jury as to these: "Answer the questions put to you, keeping in mind that the answers to these questions should be consistent with the verdict which you find." This, it is urged, required the jury to conform their special findings to the general verdict. But we think the court merely reminded the jury that the general verdict should be in accord with the facts as they found them; an unnecessary caution, perhaps, but certainly not misleading.

In Des Moines & D. Land Co. *v.* Polk County Homestead & Trust Co., supra, the court submitted two special findings. The jury were instructed to be careful that the answers to these interrogatories supported and were in harmony with the general verdict. The court says: "There was clearly no error in this action of the court. The caution given to the jury was timely, and tended to direct them to a careful consideration of the facts, and the necessity of consistency in their findings and verdict. Special findings are often the cause of much perplexity to jurors, especially, as is sometimes the case, when they are numerous, and requested rather for the purpose of confusing than making clear that about which they are investigating."

In Capital City Bank *v.* Wakefield, supra, the court submitted special interrogatories to the jury with these instructions: "You will decide upon them in the same manner as your general verdict, and answer the same. You will be careful, however, that these answers are in harmony with and support your general verdict." The court says: " The general tenor of previous instructions is that they should decide the case upon the evidence," and then they were specifically told that they must decide upon

Acton *v.* Fargo & Moorhead St. Ry. Co

these special questions in the same manner as the general verdict. Thus far the jury could be in no doubt but that they were to decide the special questions from the evidence. The caution which follows could not lead to a different conclusion. True, it would have been more exactly correct if it had cautioned them to be careful that their general verdict was in harmony with the answers, as the answers control; but we do not think, in view of what preceded, that the jury could have understood that they were to decide upon their answers to the special interrogatories from anything but the evidence.

Appellant in his thirteenth assignment assigns as error the following portion of the charge: "However, the court further instructs you that the plaintiff is bound to exercise that degree of care and caution for his own safety that a person of ordinary prudence would exercise under the same and similar conditions and circumstances, and if you believe that the plaintiff did not exercise such a degree of care and caution, and the accident was occasioned thereby, then the law is for the defendant, and you should so find, unless you further find that the defendant did or could have discovered the peril of the plaintiff in time to have avoided the injury to him, by the exercise of reasonable diligence;" and contends that in effect the court charged the jury: "That in order that the contributory negligence of the plaintiff shall prevent his recovery it must have occasioned (that is, caused) the accident. In other words, must have been the immediate and sole cause of the accident. We do not think that the learned trial court intended to have the jury so understand. What he undoubtedly intended to convey to the jury was that the negligence of the plaintiff must have proximately contributed to the injury. The true rule is that where the injured person's negligence is a mere condition before the accident, and the injury could be prevented by the exercise of reasonable care and prudence on the part of the company after his peril is discovered or should be discovered, his negligence is a remote cause and the company's negligence the proximate cause of the injury, and hence there may be a recovery therefor. 36 Cyc. 1528, and cases cited. The respondent had a right to expect a proper lookout would be kept by those in charge of the cars, and that ordinary care would be exercised by them to avoid injuring him. Greene *v.* Ry. Co., 119 Ky. 862, 84 S. W. 1154; Wenninger *v.* Lincoln Traction Co., 84 Neb. 385, 121 N. W. 237; Randle *v.* Birmingham Ry., Light & Power Co., 158 Ala. 532, 48 South. 114; Pilmer *v.* Boise Traction Co., Ltd., 14 Idaho, 327, 94 Pac. 432, 15 L. R. A. (N. S.) 254, 125 Am. St. Rep. 161; Bensick *v.* St. Louis Transit Co., 125 Mo. App. 121, 102 S. W. 587.

In his fourteenth assignment appellant assigns as error the following portion of the court's charge: "I charge you as a

. Acton *v.* Fargo & Moorhead St. Ry. Co

matter of law that it was the duty of the defendant in this case and its employees, after discovering, if it did so discover, the dangerous position of the plaintiff, if you find from the evidence that his position was dangerous, to use the greatest degree of care to avoid injuring the plaintiff." Appellant particularly objects to the use of the words "greatest degree of care." While a street railway company is required to exercise a very high degree of care in the operation of its road in public streets and highways, it is only required to exercise what under the circumstances is ordinary care and prudence; that is, it is required to exercise such care and vigilance in the management and operation of its cars to avoid injuring persons rightfully upon such streets or highways as a person of ordinary prudence and capacity may be expected to exercise under the same or similar circumstances, but it is not required to exercise the highest degree of care, or guard against unusual and extraordinary dangers. What constitutes ordinary care and prudence within the meaning of the above rule depends upon the known and reasonably to be expected hazards and dangers of the particular case, and varies under different conditions, such as the character of the cars, the agency of propulsion, the locality in which they are operated, whether in the country or in a city, whether over much traveled or unfrequented streets, and the possibility or probability attending their operation as what under some conditions will be ordinary and reasonable care may under other conditions amount even to gross negligence. The plaintiff was not a trespasser, and it was the duty of the defendant to keep a special lookout to avoid a collision with persons or animals lawfully upon the track. The care should be commensurate with the dangers to be reasonably apprehended. The general rule imposes upon street railway companies the duty to exercise exceptional care in operating their cars upon the public streets of a city. 36 Cyc. 1473, and cases cited.

In Bunyan *v.* Citizens' Ry. Co., 127 Mo. 12, 29 S. W. 842, the court says: "It was the duty of the gripman and other employees to keep a vigilant watch for persons on or approaching the track, and, when discovered in danger, to use every possible effort, consistent with the safety of passengers, to avoid striking them. This duty does not depend upon the fact that the person had negligently placed himself in the position of danger. The previous negligence of such person would constitute no defense to an action for an injury resulting from neglect of these duties." Bishop *v.* R. R. Co., 4 N. D. 536, 62 N. W. 605; Johnson *v.* G. N. Ry. Co., 7 N. D. 284, 75 N. W. 250; M., K. & T. Ry. Co. *v.* Reynolds (Tex. Civ. App.) 115 S. W. 341.

In Maxfield *v.* Texas & P. Ry. Co. (Tex. Civ. App.) 117 S. W. 483, the court uses the following language: "It was the absolute duty of the engineer in charge of appellee's train, when he dis-

Acton v. Fargo & Moorhead St. Ry. Co .

covered appellant's peril, to make use of all the means at his command, consistent with the safety of the engine, to stop or check the train and avoid striking appellant."

The eighteenth question submitted to the jury is as follows: "Was the defendant guilty of negligence under the law as laid down by the court?" Answer: "Yes."

The twenty-eighth question submitted to the jury is as follows: "Did the motorman exercise ordinary care and reasonable diligence as those terms are defined by the court, in stopping his car and preventing the accident after he saw, or might in the exercise of reasonable diligence have seen, that plaintiff was in a position of danger?" To which question the jury answered, "No." The court having correctly defined "ordinary care," and the jury having found that the motorman of defendant did not exercise ordinary care and reasonable diligence in stopping his car and preventing the accident after he saw, or might in the exercise of reasonable diligence have seen, that plaintiff was in a position of danger, the appellant was not prejudiced by the instructions complained of. A judgment will not be reversed because of an erroneous instruction when it affirmatively appears from answers to interrogatories that such instruction did not influence the jury in reaching its verdict. 20 Ency. Pleading & Practice, 304; Harriman v. Queen Ins. Co., 49 Wis. 71, 5 N. W. 12; Worley v. Moore, 97 Ind. 15; Cleveland, etc., Ry. Co. v. Newell, 104 Ind. 265, 3 N. E. 836, 54 Am. Rep. 312; Woolery v. Louisville Hampshire Ry. Co., 107 Ind. 384, 8 N. E. 226, 57 Am. Rep. 114; Porter v. Waltz, 108 Ind. 40, 8 N. E. 705; Fisk. Trustee, v. Chicago, Mil. & St. Paul Ry. Co., 83 Iowa, 253, 48 N. W. 1081; Fort Scott Ry. Co. v. Karracker, 46 Kan. 511, 26 Pac. 1027; Atchison, etc., Ry. Co. v. McKee, 37 Kan. 592, 15 Pac. 484; New Omaha Elec. Light Co. v. Dent, 68 Neb. 668, 94 N. W. 819.

In Woolery v. Ry. Co., supra, the court says: "It is now urged that these instructions were erroneous, in that they required the plaintiff to prove more than was necessary in each case, in order to establish the defendant's negligence. However this may be, since it affirmatively appears from the answers to special interrogatories, that the jury found the defendant guilty of negligence, and that their verdict in its favor was the result of finding the decedent guilty of contributory negligence, it is certain that the instructions in reference to this feature of the case were not prejudicial to the plaintiff. A judgment will not be reversed upon an erroneous instruction, when it affirmatively appears from answers to interrogatories that the instruction complained of was not influential in inducing the verdict."

In the case at bar, the jury having found that the motorman of defendant did not exercise ordinary care and reasonable diligence in stopping his car and preventing the accident after he saw, or might in the exercise of reasonable diligence have seen, that plaintiff was in a position of danger, it is plain that the verdict was not arrived at by reason of the court having used the word "occasioned" in the instruction complained of in appellant's thirteenth assignment of error, nor by having instructed the jury that it was the duty of the defendant in this case and its employees after discovering, if it did discover, the dangerous position of the plaintiff, if dangerous, to use the greatest degree of care to avoid injuring the plaintiff, as the jury found that the defendant did not exercise ordinary care. What has heretofore been said in regard to the fourteenth assignment of error disposes of the sixteenth and seventeenth assignments of error.

Appellant contends that the cases in which it has been held that special findings cured erroneous instructions are all those in which the instruction is based upon the existence or absence of a fact, and the special findings has found that such fact exists or does not exist, hence showing clearly and conclusively that the erroneous instruction was not prejudicial. We are unable to concur in the contention of counsel that the rule that erroneous instructions may be cured by the answer to special interrogatories has no application in the case at bar.

The court refused to give the following instruction: "I further charge you that, though the motorman saw the plaintiff driving along, and on the track, and (if he was driving thereon) he had a right to assume that the plaintiff would exercise ordinary care to observe the approach of the car, and would get out of danger before the car would reach him, and that the motorman is not required to check his car (if said car is running at an ordinary rate of speed) until he has reasonable cause to believe that there is actual danger of a collision." The refusal to give this instruction is now assigned as error. This requested instruction does not state the law correctly, as applied to the facts of this case, as the jury found that the plaintiff drove 60 or 70 feet along the railroad track, and that the car was not stopped until it reached a point between 20 and 30 feet north of the accident, when the evidence shows that it could have been stopped in from 20 to 25 feet if the motorman had it under control. The motorman had no right to assume that plaintiff would get off the track before the car reached him. It was his duty to use ordinary care to avoid the accident and have his car under control.

There is no merit in appellant's contention that certain of the special findings are inconsistent with each other and are inconsistent with the general verdict. The special findings made by the jury are sufficient to sustain the general verdict.

If the questions not answered, or where the answers are not proved, were all answered favorably to appellant, the special

Westbrook v. Kansas City, M. & B. R. Co

verdict would not be inconsistent with the general verdict, taking into consideration the answers to the balance of the questions submitted to the jury; and we are unable to see how appellant's rights are prejudicially affected by the answers or lack of answers to these questions.

Finding no prejudicial error in the record, the judgment and order appealed from are affirmed. All concur, except MORGAN, C. J., not participating.

WESTBROOK v. KANSAS CITY, M. & B. R. Co.

(Supreme Court of Alabama, Nov. 24, 1910.   Rehearing Denied Jan. 12, 1911.)

[54 So. Rep. 231.]

Railroads—Invitation Extended for Crossing Cars—Authority to Give.*—A brakeman standing near a crossing obstructed by a freight train has no implied authority to invite a pedestrian to climb over between cars, or to give an assurance of safety to the pedestrian in doing so.

Railroads—Injuries to Travelers—Crossing Train—Contributory Negligence.*—Where plaintiff, on the invitation of a brakeman, started to cross over the cars of a freight train obstructing a crossing and was injured by a movement of the train catching his foot between the bumpers, the brakeman having neither actual nor implied authority to give such invitation, plaintiff was guilty of contributory negligence barring recovery for any simple negligence of the railroad company.

Railroads—Willful Injury.—Where plaintiff was injured while climbing between the cars of a freight train, obstructing a crossing, on the invitation of a brakeman, given without authority, actual or implied, plaintiff could only recover on proof of a willful or intentional injury, by showing that defendant's agents or servants in charge of the train discovered plaintiff's perilous situation in time to prevent his injury by prompt use of available means and failed to do so.

Railroads—Injuries to Pedestrian—Crossing Train—Willfullness.—Where, in an action for injuries to plaintiff by his foot being caught between the bumpers of two cars while climbing between the cars of a train obstructing a crossing, on the unauthorized invitation of the brakeman, there was no evidence that either the con-

---

*For the authorities in this series on the subject of the right of a highway traveler to climb over or go round a train or cars obstructing a crossing, see last paragraph of first foot-note of Lindler v. Southern Ry. Co. (S. Car.), 36 R. R. R. 334, 59 Am. & Eng. R. Cas., N. S., 334; extensive note, 6 R. R. R. 325, 29 Am. & Eng. R. Cas., N. S., 325.

Westbrook *v.* Kansas City, M. & B. R. Co

ductor in charge of the train or the engineer discovered plaintiff before moving the train, and the brakeman was intrusted with no duty to the public or to individuals, so as to render his assurance to plaintiff that he might cross in safety binding on defendant, defendant was not liable as for willful or intentional injury.

Appeal and Error—Conclusion of Evidence—Prejudice.—Where evidence offered by a plaintiff and excluded would not have availed him anything if admitted, the ruling was harmless.

Appeal and Error—Pleadings—Amendment—Refusal to Allow—Prejudice.—Plaintiff was not prejudiced by the court's refusal to allow the addition of a new count to the complaint at the conclusion of the evidence, where the evidence was insufficient to support the case averred in such count, if the court allowed it.

Evidence—Conclusion of Witness.—In an action for injuries to plaintiff while crossing between the cars of a freight train, plaintiff testified that the engine was two or three car lengths from him when he tried to cross, that the track was straight, and that steam was escaping noisily from the engine. He did not know where the conductor was and did not see the engineer. He was then asked whether the brakeman or flagman, who was present and said, "Come across," spoke loud enough for the engineer to hear him. Held, that the question was properly excluded as calling for the witness' conclusion in the absence of preliminary proof showing where the engineer was, or what he was doing, or that the witness knew where he was.

Appeal from Circuit Court, Walker County; James J. Ray, Judge.

Action by Gus Westbrook against the Kansas City, Memphis & Birmingham Railroad Company. Judgment for defendant, and plaintiff appeals. Affirmed.

W. C. Davis and *A. F. Fite,* for appellant.
Bankhead & Bankhead, for appellee.

EVANS, J. The opinion in this cause, following, was prepared by Justice Denson before his retirement as associate justice, and, having been adopted in consultation, it is now announced as the opinion of the court:

At about noon, on the 2d day of October, 1903, a freight train of the defendant's, composed of 18 coal cars and box cars with a locomotive attached, coupled up and ready to move, was standing on defendant's main line across a public crossing at or near defendant's station in the town of Cordova, in Walker county. Five of the coal cars were between the engine and box cars. The bumpers on these cars were $3\frac{1}{2}$ or 4 feet above the track, and the distance from the bumpers to the top of the cars was 4 or $4\frac{1}{2}$ feet, making the height of the coal cars 7 or 8 feet. The direction of the track was east and west, with the engine headed westward. The engineer was in his proper place on the engine—on its north side.

The plaintiff was an employee in the Indian Head Cotton Mills, which were located 175 or 200 yards from defendant's station, and south of the railroad. The signal announcing the noon hour had sounded at the mills, and quite a number of the operatives (plaintiff amongst them), whose homes were located north of defendant's road, were en route to their homes to get lunch. Upon arriving at the point where the train was standing across the public crossing, several of the operatives crossed, by climbing over the bumpers between the coal cars; and while plaintiff was thus in the act of crossing, with his foot on the coupling between the bumpers, there was a backward movement of the train, and plaintiff was severely injured by having his foot caught and mashed.

The plaintiff's case against the defendant railroad company is presented, in some of the counts in the complaint, upon allegations of simple negligence; and these counts seek to justify plaintiff's position on the cars, or his efforts to cross, at the time and place and in the manner stated, upon an invitation extended by the defendant, amounting to an assurance of safety. In other counts of the complaint the injury to plaintiff is alleged to have been willfully, wantonly, and negligently caused.

The evidence in the record, without conflict, shows that, if an invitation was extended or assurance given to plaintiff to cross the train, it was extended or given by a brakeman. But there is a total absence of evidence to show any express authority, on the part of the brakeman, to extend such an invitation or to give the assurance. Therefore, unless it can be properly held that his position as brakeman carried with it the implied authority to extend the invitation or give the assurance, it cannot, upon any just view of the evidence, be said that the plaintiff was entitled to have the case passed upon by the jury—that is to say, the case, as presented by the counts relying upon simple negligence as the gravamen of plaintiff's cause of action—for in going upon the train under the circumstances, if without assurance or invitation by some one in authority, the plaintiff would be guilty of contributory negligence such as would debar him of the right of recovery on the ground of simple negligence. M. & C. A. R. Co. v. Copeland, 61 Ala. 376; Letcher's Case, 69 Ala. 106. 44 Am. Rep. 505; Studer v. Southern Pacific Co., 121 Cal. 400, 53 Pac. 942, 66 Am. St. Rep. 39.

In the absence of a right to recover for simple negligence, plaintiff could only recover upon proof of a wanton, willful, or intentional injury, or upon proof that defendant's agent or servant having the train in charge, discovered plaintiff's perilous situation in time to prevent, by the prompt use of available

Westbrook v. Kansas City, M. & B. R. Co

means, the injuring of plaintiff, and that the agent notwithstanding failed to resort to such means.

We have carefully gone through the entire evidence, but have failed to find any warranting a reasonable inference that either the engineer or the conductor who had the train in charge knew, or had probable cause to believe or know, that the plaintiff was in a position of peril; or was conscious, from the conditions existing, that moving the train would probably result in disaster to a human being.

The evidence shows that the conductor went into the operator's office, as soon as his train stopped, to report his arrival and obtain permission to back his train about a mile, to a water tank, to take on water; and that after getting such permission he came out and signaled to the engineer the result of his efforts.

According to plaintiff's evidence as to the position of the engineer, he was on the right side of the engine, and on the side of the engine or train opposite to that from which the plaintiff mounted the coupling to cross over; and was looking back toward the conductor, who was at the time, as the evidence shows, at the rear end of the train and on the same side of the train that the engineer was on.

When the train moved, plaintiff was on it and between the cars, with his foot on the coupling between the bumpers, and was therefore in the center of the train. In this state of the case, it does seem that it would be nothing short of conjecture or pure speculation to conclude that the engineer, at the time he moved the train, saw the plaintiff.

And on these considerations— ven if it might be decided that the counts in the complaint claiming recovery on the theory of defendant's responsibility for willful, wanton, or intentional acts of its servants are sufficient in form (City Delivery Co. v. Henry, 139 Ala. 161, 34 South. 38))—plaintiff was not entitled, under the evidence to have the case submitted to the jury upon that theory. Nor was he entitled to have it submitted on the doctrine of "last clear chance." L. & N. R. R. Co. v. Brown, 121 Ala. 221, 25 South. 609; Foshee's Case, 125 Ala. 199, 27 South. 1006.

This brings us back to the question of implied authority of the brakeman. We have seen in the evidence that the movement of the train was under the control of the conductor and the engineer. It does not appear that the train's standing over the crossing was a menace to the safety of the public or to that of any individual; neither, indeed, does it appear that the train had been standing an unusual length of time. And there is a total absence of testimony going to show that the brakeman was intrusted with any duty to the public or to individuals at the particular time and place, or with any other duty than ordinarily inheres in the position of brakeman. Therefore, to render bind-

Westbrook v. Kansas City, M. & B. R. Co

ing upon the defendant the assurance given in this instance to the plaintiff by the brakeman, we must assume that he was possessed of and exercising an authority incident to or inhering in the position of brakeman, at the time. Can we, by any known rule of law, indulge such an assumption? In other words, can this court say, as a matter of common knowledge, that the giving of the assurance here claimed to have been extended was within the scope of the duties of a brakeman, the train being stationary at the time?

We have not been furnished by counsel with any case in this jurisdiction decisive of the point at issue, nor has our research discovered such a precedent. The cases cited by appellant, such as A. G. S. R. R. Co. v. Anderson, 109 Ala. 299, 19 South. 516, involving injuries at crossings, attributable to the negligence of a flagman stationed there for the purpose of giving warning and of protecting persons from passing in dangerous proximity to moving trains, are obviously without application.

Counsel for appellee have cited some cases decided in other jurisdictions, which are well reasoned on principle, and which seem to conclude the question. In Skirvin v. L. & N. R. R. Co., 100 S. W. 308, 30 Ky. Law Rep. 1208, it was held that a brakeman had no power to give the assurance of safety to one crossing a train. In the subsequent case of Southern Railway v. Clark, 105 S. W. 384, 32 Ky. Law Rep. 69, 13 L. R. A. (N. S.) 1071, the same court said: "Conceding that the person to whom plaintiff was talking (the brakeman) had said, 'Come right through, you will be safe,' yet the company would not be liable because of the invitation of the brakeman to cross over, for it has been expressly decided in the case of Skirvin v. L. & N. R. R. Co. [100 S. W. 308] 30 Ky. Law Rep. 1208, that a brakeman has not the power by virtue simply of his position to bind his employer, but that the conductor is the representative agent of the company as to the train in his charge." See, also, to the same effect, Renner v. Northern Pacific R. Co. (C. C.) 46 Fed. 344; Andrews v. C. R. & B. Co., 86 Ga. 192, 12 S. E. 213, 10 L. R. A. 58; Sheridan v. B. & O. R. R. Co., 101 Md. 50, 60 Atl. 280; L. & M. S. R. Co. v. Pinchin, 112 Ind. 592, 13 N. E. 677.

Confining ourselves to the facts of the case in hand, upon the authorities above referred to, the court is at the conclusion that the brakeman had no authority, either express or implied, to invite the plaintiff to cross over the train, or to give any assurance that it would be safe for him to do so.

Upon the foregoing considerations it must follow that the defendant, on the evidence, was entitled to have the jury instructed affirmatively in its favor.

If the court had not ruled out the testimony offered by plaintiff, in respect to the invitation, it is manifest that on the foregoing principles it could not have availed plaintiff anything;

Westbrook v. Kansas City, M. & B. R. Co

hence there was no prejudice to the plaintiff by the ruling of the court excluding it.

It is sufficient to say, in justification of the court's refusal to allow plaintiff, at the conclusion of the evidence, to file count D, that the evidence fails to give support to a case as averred in that count, even if the court had allowed it.

One other ground of error must be considered. The plaintiff testified, amongst other things, that "the engine was two or three car lengths from me at the time I tried to cross and was headed west. The track was straight at that point, and I was going north from the south side. Steam was escaping from the engine and making a noise at the time I started to cross." He also testified that he did not know where the conductor was at the time he tried to cross, and did not see the engineer at the time. Plaintiff was then asked by his counsel this question: "I ask you to state whether or not this brakeman or flagman, when he spoke and said, 'Come across,' spoke loud enough for the engineer to hear him."

Obviously the court committed no error in sustaining the defendant's objection to the question. There was no testimony before the court at the time the question was propounded showing where the engineer was or what he was doing, or that witness knew where he was, and therefore it is evident that to have allowed the witness to answer the question would have been to allow him to state a mere conclusion.

In McVay's Case, 100 Ala. 110, 14 South. 862, cited by counsel for plaintiff, the evidence showed the locality of the parties who, as sought to be shown by the state, heard the language, etc., and, the testimony having been admitted, no question arose or could have arisen as to the leading character of the question there propounded. And so, too, the facts in the cases of A. G. S. R. Co. v. Linn. 103 Ala. 135, 15 South. 508, and Birmingham, etc., Co. v. Mullen, 138 Ala. 623, 35 South. 701, differentiate those cases from the one in hand, and render them ineffectual as authorities showing error in the ruling of the court in the instant case.

There is an express waiver of assignments of error presenting for review the judgment of the court overruling the demurrer to plea B. It is further agreed between the parties that the cause shall be here determined as though pleas A and B were not in the record.

No reversible error has been shown, and the judgment of the circuit court will be affirmed.

Affirmed.

Dowdell, C. J., and Anderson and ... JJ., concur.

Blake v. Rhode Island Co.

(Supreme Court of Rhode Island, Jan. 27, 1911.)

[78 Atl. Rep. 834.]

New Trial—Newly Discovered Evidence—Perjury—Sufficiency of Showing.—One is not entitled to a new trial on evidence showing an adverse witness' admission that his testimony was false, he having made no affidavit to that effect, and not being dead, nor convicted of such perjury, since, if a new trial were granted, the showing would be admissible only to contradict or discredit the witness, if he testified again.

Trial—Requested Instructions—Necessity for Giving.—Where the law has been correctly stated in an instruction, the judge need not repeat it in the exact language requested by counsel.

Trial—Instructions—Assumption as to Facts.—In an action for injury to a driver struck by a street car, an instruction that the fact that the running board was down would not affect plaintiff's contributory negligence, if the car was in sight when he looked, since in such a case he would have seen that the board was down and would be bound to manage his team accordingly, was properly refused, as assuming that, if the board was down and plaintiff looked at the car, he must have seen that the board was down.

Street Railroads—Collisions with Vehicles—Instructions—Driver's Duty.—In an action for injury to a driver struck by a street car, an instruction that, if the car was in sight and approaching at a high speed, the plaintiff was bound to stop his horse before reaching the track, was properly refused for failing to specify any distance between plaintiff and the car as he approached the track.

Street Railroads—Collisions with Vehicles—Contributory Negligence.*—One is not negligent in attempting to drive across a street railway track, though a car be rapidly approaching, if a reasonably prudent man would infer that the car was so far away that it could not reach him before he crossed.

Street Railroads—Collisions with Vehicles—Evidence—Sufficiency.—In an action for injury to a driver struck by a street car, evidence held to warrant a finding that the car could have been stopped in time to have avoided the collision.

Exceptions from Superior Court, Providence and Bristol Counties; Darius Baker, Judge.

---

*For the authorities in this series on the subject of the right to cross street railway tracks with knowledge that a car is approaching, see last foot-note of Donohoe v. Portland Ry. Co. (Ore.), 37 R. R. R. 66, 60 Am. & Eng. R. Cas., N. S., 66; Eustis v. Boston Elev. Ry. Co. (Mass.), 37 R. R. R. 60, 60 Am. & Eng. R. Cas., N. S., 60; first foot-note of Rouse v. Michigan United Rys. Co. (Mich.), 35 R. R. R. 289, 58 Am. & Eng. R. Cas., N. S., 289.

Action by Lewis A. E. Blake against the Rhode Island Company. Order granting a new trial conditionally, and both parties bring exceptions. Defendant's exceptions overruled, and plaintiff's exception sustained.

John W. Hogan, for plaintiff.
Joseph C. Sweeney and *Alonzo R. Williams,* for defendant.

JOHNSON, J. This is an action on the case, brought by Lewis A. E. Blake against the Rhode Island Company, to recover damages for personal injuries alleged to have been sustained through the negligence of the defendant company in the operation of one of its street cars. On the 29th day of June, 1906, the plaintiff was driving an ice cart, and had just turned with said cart from Patt street into East avenue, in the city of Pawtucket, when a car of the defendant company, traveling from Providence toward Pawtucket, overtook and collided with said ice cart, and as a result of said collision the ice cart was overturned and the plaintiff was thrown to the ground and injured. The case was tried before a justice of the superior court and a jury on the 18th, 19th, 20th, and 21st days of October, 1909, and resulted in a verdict for the plaintiff for $9,081.50.

Thereafter the defendant duly filed a motion for a new trial upon the grounds: "(1) That said verdict is contrary to the evidence and the weight thereof. (2) That said verdict is contrary to the law. (3) That the amount of damages awarded by said verdict is excessive. (4) That said defendant has discovered new and material evidence in said case, which it had not discovered at the time of the trial thereof, and which it could not with reasonable diligence have discovered at any time previous to the trial of said case, as by affidavits to be filed in court will be fully set forth, said affidavits being made a part of this motion." This motion was heard July 2, 1910, by the justice who presided at the trial, and July 8, 1910, a rescript was filed denying said motion on all grounds except that of excessive damages. With respect to this ground the motion was granted unless the plaintiff should within 10 days remit all of the verdict in excess of $7,000. The plaintiff did not file a remittitur.

Within the time and in accordance with the procedure required by the statute, both parties presented their separate bills of exceptions and transcripts of the testimony, which were severally duly allowed by the justice presiding. The case is now before this court on said two bills of exceptions.

The exceptions pressed by the defendant are the following, as numbered in its bill of exceptions: "(6) To the refusal of said justice, at said trial, to charge defendant's first request to charge, as appears on page 448 of said transcript, exception thereto appearing on page 449 thereof. (17) To the refusal of said justice, at said trial, to charge defendant's fourth request, as

appears on page 449 of said transcript.   (18) To the refusal of
said justice, at said trial, to charge defendant's fifth request, as
appears on page 449 of said transcript.   (19) To the refusal of
said justice, at said trial, to charge defendant's sixth request, as
appears on page 450 of said transcript.   (20) To the refusal of
said justice, at said trial, to charge defendant's seventh request,
as appears on page 450 of said transcript.   (21) To the refusal
of said justice, at said trial, to charge defendant's eighth request,
as appears on page 450 of said transcript, exceptions thereto appearing on page 451 thereof.   (22) To the decision of said court
denying the defendant's motion for a new trial on the ground
that said verdict is contrary to the evidence and the weight
thereof.   (23) To the decision of said court denying the defendant's motion for new trial on the ground that said verdict
is contrary to the law.   (24) To the decision of said court denying the defendant's motion for new trial on the ground that the
amount of damages awarded by said verdict is excessive.   (25)
To the decision of said court denying the defendant's motion for
• a new trial on the ground of newly discovered evidence."

We will first consider the exceptions to the decision of the
superior court denying the motion for a new trial on the grounds
that the verdict was contrary to the evidence, and contrary to
the law, being exceptions numbered 22 and 23.   From an examination of the evidence we are satisfied that the justice presiding at the trial was correct in deciding that "the evidence was
sufficiently conflicting on the three points of defendant's negligence in operating the car at an excessive rate of speed, on the
contributory negligence of the plaintiff, and as to the motorman's
opportunity to stop the car after he saw or should have seen the
ice cart, as to make them matters for the determination of the
jury."

The twenty-fifth   exception is to the decision of the court
denying the defendant's motion for a new trial on the ground of
newly discovered evidence.   In support of the motion on this
ground several affidavits were filed covering three conversations
alleged to have been had with the motorman, Cook, on March
21, Marcn 29, and April 1, 1910.   The affiants state that in said
conversations said Cook admitted that he testified falsely at the
trial of the case and declared that he had lied and perjured himself on the witness stand.   The case seems to come clearly within
the law as laid down by this court in Dexter *v.* Handy, 13 R. I.
474.   In that case the court, Durfee, C. J. (pages 475, 476),
said:

"The ground of the petition is that these witnesses after the
trial was over, severally admitted that their testimony was un-
true.   The affidavits of persons who profess to have heard these
admissions are filed in support of the petition, but no affidavits
are produced from the witnesses themselves, either admitting

Blake *v.* Rhode Island Co

that their testimony was false or stating anything differently from their testimony, while, on the contrary, one of the witnesses, and he the most important, has given an affidavit denying that he ever made the admissions. If another trial were granted, the new evidence would not be admissible in proof of the issue made by the defendant, but only to contradict or discredit the witnesses, if they were again put on the stand by the plaintiff. A new trial is seldom granted for the introduction of newly discovered testimony which goes merely to impeach the witnesses of the prevailing party. We confess that the petition does not commend itself to our minds. If the affidavits introduced by the petitioner are true, the witnesses have confessed themselves perjurers; and yet the petitioner, while he asks us to grant him a new trial on that account, has not, so far as appears, taken any steps to have them prosecuted. It has been decided that a new trial on account of perjury will not be granted until after the perjured witness either has been convicted or is dead; mere evidence of the perjury, or even an indictment for it, being deemed insufficient. Dyche *v.* Patton, 56 N. C. 332; Benfield *v.* Peters, 3 Doug. 24; Seeley *v.* Mayhew, 4 Bing. 561; Wheatley *v.* Edwards, Lofft. 87. Perhaps the rule laid down in these cases may be too strict and exacting for all circumstances, but it is obviously founded in wise policy. Certainly the talk of a witness after trial ought not generally to weigh against the sworn testimony; for there would be no security for verdicts if, without peril to the witnesses, they were liable to be upset by such talk. The best evidence of perjury is the conviction of the perjurer. It is against the petition that the petitioner can find no precedent for it. There is, however, precedent against it. In Commonwealth *v.* Randall, Thacher, Cr. Cas. (Mass.) 500, it was held that expression used by a witness after a trial, contradicting or denying what he said in court, are not ground for setting aside the verdict and for granting a new trial, but are evidence to convict him of perjury. 'In almost every instance,' said the court, 'it would be easy for a losing party to obtain affidavits of that description.' We must therefore refuse a new trial on this ground."

The doctrine of this case has been followed in Roberts *v.* Roberts, 19 R. I. 349, 33 Atl. 872; Jones *v.* N. Y., N. H. & H. R. R. Co., 20 R. I. 214, 37 Atl. 1033; Timony *v.* Casey, 20 R. I. 257, 38 Atl. 370; and State *v.* Lynch, 28 R. I. 463, 68 Atl. 315. In the last-mentioned case, the court, Douglas, C. J. (page 465 of 28 R. I., page 316 of 68 Atl.), said: "On examination of the affidavits submitted we find that they do not divulge any evidence upon the merits of the case but are confined to attempts to discredit the principal witness of the crime. They consist mostly of statements which this witness is said to have made contradictory of her story upon the stand. Such evidence, if well fortified, is not generally admitted to impeach a verdict, as we have frequently decided [citing the cases supra].

The sixteenth exception is to the refusal of the court to charge the defendant's first request, as follows: "It was the plaintiff's duty to look in both directions as he approached East avenue, and to select such a point from which to look as to enable him to determine whether or not a car was coming; and if the jury find that he did not so look, and that his failure so to do contributed to the collision, then he is guilty of contributory negligence and he cannot recover." This request appears to state the law correctly. The court had, however, covered the matter in the general charge. Thus, on page 435 of the transcript, the court said: "So it is the law that a person in the street, in a conveyance or walking, in approaching a track is required to look and listen—to look and see if a car is approaching, and if there is a curve, and the view is obstructed, to listen and see if a car is approaching; and if a person fails to do it, that is negligence in law, because he hasn't done it." And further, on page 436: "Now, if a person is bound to look and listen, of course, he must avail himself of what his looking and listening informs him, and he can't, after looking and seeing a car approaching, say 'I have looked and listened,' and enter on the track with a certainty he can't get across before the car which is approaching reaches that point; that is he must avail himself of what he sees, and he is also charged with knowledge of what he might see." We think the instruction as to the duty "to look and see if a car is approaching, and if there is a curve, and the view is obstructed, to listen and see if a car is approaching." covers the ground quite as fully and completely, from a legal standpoint, as would an instruction that "it was the plaintiff's duty to look in both directions as he approached East avenue, and to select such a point from which to look as to enable him to determine whether or not a car was coming." When the court has correctly instructed the jury as to the law, he is not required to repeat such instructions in the exact language requested by counsel.

The seventeenth exception is to the refusal of defendant's fourth request to charge the jury as follows: "If the jury should find that the running board of the car was down, that fact would have no bearing upon the plaintiff's contributory negligence, if the jury also find that the car must have been in sight of the plaintiff when he says he looked, because in such case he would have seen that the running board was down, and would be obliged to manage his team having such fact in mind." The matter of this request had been fully covered by the charge of the court, except the assumption in the request that, if the running board was down and the plaintiff looked at the car, he

Blake *v.* Rhode Island Co

must have seen that the running board was down. This was an assumption of fact which it would not have been proper for the court to charge.

The eighteenth exception was to the refusal of defendant's fifth request to charge the jury as follows: "If the jury find that the car was in sight of the plaintiff and approaching at a high rate of speed before the plaintiff's team had reached the track, it was the duty of the plaintiff to have stopped his horse; and if the collision was brought about by his failure so to do, there can be no recovery." This request is faulty in failing to specify any distance between the plaintiff and the car as he approached the track; the only limitation as to distance being that the car was in sight. The court had covered the matters involved in the request correctly in the charge (page 436), as follows: "Now, a person may see a car approaching, and it may be at such a distance, even although approaching at a high rate of speed, he may cross the track; and he is not guilty of negligence in doing so because a reasonable, prudent man would infer that the car couldn't reach him at the speed at which he was driving his own conveyance before he got across, and under those circumstances he would not be guilty of negligence in entering upon the track."

The nineteenth exception was to the refusal of defendant's sixth request to charge, as follows: "If the jury find that the plaintiff rounded the corner of East avenue and Patt street with the car running at high speed and but a short distance south of Patt street, in view of the small distance between the curbing on East avenue and the nearest rail, the plaintiff was not in the exercise of due care if the jury also find that in so turning a collision was rendered probable." The court had instructed the jury fully as to the duty of the plaintiff in approaching the track to look and listen, as to the question of the speed of the car and its distance south from Patt street when the plaintiff drove out of said street and the conflicting testimony as to both these matters, as to the distance between the track and the nearest rail on East avenue, and as to the care required of the plaintiff in making the turn from Patt street into East avenue, in view of the testimony as to all these matters. The general instructions upon these matters were sufficiently full and complete, and the court was not bound to repeat such instructions in the form of this request.

The twentieth exception was to the refusal of the defendant's seventh request to charge, as follows: "If the jury find that the motorman was negligent, even grossly so, in the handling of his car, such a finding will not enable the plaintiff to recover, if the jury also find that the conduct of the plaintiff was a contributing cause of the collision, or that the plaintiff could have

Blake *v.* Rhode Island Co

avoided the collision, had he conducted himself as a reasonably prudent person would have done under the circumstances the jury find to have existed just prior to the time of the collision." This request is entirely covered by the charge. Everything contained in it had been charged.

The twenty-first exception was to the refusal of the defendant's eighth request to charge, as follows: "As there is no evidence that the car could have been stopped after it was apparent to the motorman that the plaintiff intended either to get on the track or so near thereto as to make a collision probable, the plaintiff cannot recover upon the ground that, notwithstanding his own negligence, the collision could have been avoided by the motorman." It is true that no witness testified directly that the car could have been stopped after it was apparent to the motorman that the plaintiff intended either to get on the track or so near thereto as to make a collision probable. The motorman testified as follows (page 119): "Q. Did you see the wagon before you got to Patt street? A. Yes, sir. Q. What was the wagon doing when you saw it? A. Coming down Patt street near the corner. Q. Had it got to the corner when you saw it? A. Not quite. Q. Did you see it turn the corner? A. Yes, sir. Q. And when the wagon turned the corner, which direction did it take? A. Went north. Q. In what part of the street? A. The left-hand side of East avenue. Q. When the cart turned the corner, and started north on the left-hand side of East avenue, how far away was your car? A. About 50 feet. Q. What speed were you going? A. About 18 miles an hour. Q. Was the power on or off? A. It was on. Q. When did you put the power off? A. I thought I would clear the ice wagon. Q. When did you shut the power off? A. When I hit the wagon. Q. What made you think you would clear it? A. He just got around the corner, just got straightened out. Q. Why didn't you clear it? A. The running board was down. Q. On which side? A. The left-hand side." He did not testify to the distance his car was from Patt street when he first saw the wagon. He did testify, however, that he saw the wagon coming down Patt street near the corner, that it had not quite got to the corner, and that he saw it turn the corner and go north on the left-hand side of East avenue. There was other testimony as to the distance from Patt street of the car when the ice cart made the turn into East avenue, as to the speed of the car when approaching Patt street, and also as to what the motorman did in regard to stopping the car. The testimony as to all these matters was conflicting. In our opinion, the absence from the testimony of a direct statement by a witness that the motorman could have stopped the car in time to avert the collision was not sufficient to justify the granting of the request in the form in which

Blake *v.* Rhode Island Co

it was presented. Such a statement would have been merely an expression of the opinion of the witness from what he saw. It is the province of the jury to draw inferences from the testimony, rather than of witnesses to draw them from what they see. We think that the jury could properly infer from the testimony that the car could have been stopped in time to avert a collision after it was apparent to the motorman that the plaintiff intended either to get on the track or so near thereto as to make a collision probable.

The defendant's twenty-fourth exception is to the decision of the trial court denying the defendant's motion for a new trial on the ground that the amount of damages awarded by the verdict is excessive. The testimony shows that the plaintiff received a severe and almost fatal injury. He had his ice tongs over his shoulder when thrown to the ground, and one point of the ice tongs penetrated his abdomen, necessitating an operation the evening of the day the injury was received. At the operation it was found that one of the intestines had been pierced, the outer coating of the stomach injured, and a vein completely severed, and that there was a large amount of blood in the abdominal cavity. Two incisions were made in the abdomen by the surgeons, one about 5½ inches in length and the other, at right angles to the first, about 4 inches in length; the second incision being necessary in order to reach the place of hemorrhage and to enable the surgeons to scoop out the blood. At the junction of these two incisions there is, according to the medical testimony, an area, an inch to an inch and a quarter across, where the abdominal wall is thinned and is weakened. The operating surgeon testified that the rectus muscle was cut in the operation, and that such cutting weakened that muscle very much, and that, although it was sewed together and healed pretty fairly well, still the muscle never would be as good as it was before. The plaintiff has to wear a heavy belt five or six inches wide to support the abdominal wall.

The testimony shows a money loss up to the time of the trial of about $2,100, made up of fees for operation and etherization, $1,100; loss of wages from accident to time of trial, $1,000. The plaintiff has not been able to do heavy work, and was not able to do such work at the time of the trial. The medical witnesses testified that he would not be able in the future to do heavy work. According to the medical testimony this injury is permanent. The medical expert called by the defense testified that "it could not be advised that he should do heavy lifting," and in answer to the question, "Would it ever be?" answered, "Not after the reception of this injury." Also, according to the medical testimony, his incapacity to do heavy work will continue, and he will need medical attention in the future. The verdict for

Blake *v.* Rhode Island Co

$9,082.50 does not appear to us, upon the evidence, to be excessive.

The defendant's several exceptions are overruled.

The plaintiff's sole exception is to the decision of the justice presiding that the damages awarded by the jury were excessive, and that, unless within 10 days after the filing of said decision the plaintiff should in writing remit all of said verdict in excess of $7,000, the defendant's motion for a new trial would be granted.

The plaintiff's exception is sustained.

The case is remitted to the superior court, with direction to enter judgment upon the verdict.

INDEX TO NOTES.

CARRIER OF PASSENGERS' POWER TO EXEMPT ITSELF FROM LIABILITY FOR PERSONAL INJURIES.

GRATUITOUS PASSENGERS.

Gross Negligence.

Carrier cannot exempt itself from liability for gross negligence, 525.

Negligence.

Majority doctrine, 518.
Minority doctrine, 520.
Negligence of managing officers, 525.
Servants' negligence, 524.

MISCELLANEOUS.

Illustrations and decisions of questions related to the main subject of the note, 548.

PASSENGERS FOR HIRE.

Gross Negligence.

Carrier cannot exempt itself from liability for gross negligence, 518.

Negligence.

Connecting carriers—may limit liability to own line, 514.
Freight trains—may limit liability, 516.
Majority doctrine, 507.
Minority doctrine, 511.
Voluntary offering to carry passengers on freight trains, 515.
What law governs, 517.

WHO ARE GRATUITOUS PASSENGERS.

Carrier's employees injured while riding on its cars, 536.
Contracts to haul show cars, 546.
Drover's employees are not chargeable with notice, where, 535.
Drover's pass—view that exemption is invalid, 531.
Drover's pass—view that exemption is valid, 528.
Express messenger is not chargeable with notice, where, 542.
Express messengers, 537.
Illustrations, 526.
Mail agents, 535.
Sleeping car company's employees, 544.

39 R R R—51

GENERAL INDEX.

ACCIDENTS ON TRACK.
See CARRIERS OF PASSENGERS; CHILDREN; CROSS-INGS; LICENSEES; MASTER AND SERVANT; TRESPASSERS.

Discovered Peril.
Railroad not liable where engineer is uncertain until too late to stop train in time what the object is when he sees person, ejected from another train, sitting on end of tie. Burgess *v.* Atchison, etc., Ry. Co. (Kan.), 164.

AGENCY.
See CARRIERS; CARRIERS OF PASSENGERS; COMMON CARRIERS; DAMAGES; MASTER AND SERVANT.
Apparent authority of general passenger agent and passenger traffic manager to contract for publication of guidebook to make known and popularize the hunting and fishing regions along the line of the railroad. Parrot *v.* Mexican Cent. Ry. Co. (Mass.), 433.

ANIMALS.
See STOCK, INJURIES TO.

APPEALS.

Review.
Decree of state court adverse to the contention that, if the state constitution confers on one railway company an exemption from a special tax granted to another railroad company, it impairs contract obligations, is reviewable in the federal supreme court, although the state court rested its decision in part upon the ground that the latter railway company had not acquired all of its contract rights before the adoption of the state constitution. Arkansas So. Ry. Co. *v.* Louisiana & Ark. Ry. Co. (U. S.), 100.

ARRESTS AND PROSECUTIONS.
See CARRIERS OF PASSENGERS.

ASSAULTS.
See CARRIERS OF PASSENGERS, MASTER AND SERVANT.

ATTACHMENT.
See COMMON CARRIERS.

BAGGAGE.
See INTOXICATING LIQUORS; SLEEPING CAR COMPANIES.
Information to carrier's servants as to nature and value of his baggage, duty of passenger to volunteer. Godfrey *v.* Pullman Co. (S. Car.), 139.

Sleeping Cars.
Railroad's liability for loss of hand baggage of passenger carried with him on sleeping car belonging to sleeping car company. Nelson *v.* Illinois Cent. R. Co. (Miss.), 114.

BAGGAGE—Continued.

What Is.

Jewelry. Godfrey *v.* Pullman Co. (S. Car.), 139.

Money. Godfrey *v.* Pullman Co. (S. Car.), 139.

Passenger is entitled to carry sufficient money and personal effects as baggage as will reasonably supply his wants during the entire trip, over the line of initial carrier and lines of other railroads. Godfrey *v.* Pullman Co. (S. Car.), 139.

Questions for jury whether ring in question was carried by husband merely to have it repaired or with intention of its being worn by his wife during remaining portion of the trip after it was repaired, and whether it was reasonably necessary for the wife's pleasure and convenience during the journey. Godfrey *v.* Pullman Co. (S. Car.), 139.

Where husband was bailee of ring belonging to his wife, which was claimed to have been stolen from him while on defendant's sleeping car, the husband had such special property in the ring as entitled him to recover for its loss against defendant. Godfrey *v.* Pullman Co. (S. Car.), 139.

Where wife permits her husband to sue for loss of her baggage, and aids him in doing so, she is estopped to sue for the same in her own name. Godfrey *v.* Pullman Co. (S. Car.), 139.

BILLS OF LADING.

See COMMON CARRIERS.

Bill of lading of interstate shipment which contains clause repugnant to the Interstate Commerce Act, as amended by certain statute, is not thereby entirely vitiated, but the holder thereof may recover for a failure to safely transport the goods. Central of Georgia Ry. Co. *v.* Sims (Ala.), 666.

Conclusiveness of bill of lading in regard to weights, where they were reported by consignor to carrier, and adopted by it without verification, and the bill of lading contained the words, "Weights subject to correction." Brown *v.* Missouri, etc., Ry. Co. (Kan.), 224.

Delivery.

Carrier delivers goods at its peril to one without bill of lading. Atlantic C. L. R. Co. *v.* Dahlberg Brokerage Co. (Ala.), 660.

Direction in bill of lading to notify a named person shows that he is not intended as the consignee. Atlantic C. L. R. Co. *v.* Dahlberg Brokerage Co. (Ala.), 660.

Evidence.

Parol evidence was admissible to show that provision in the bill of lading for delivery to "only" D. meant, according to usage by carriers and shippers, that D. was to be notified of the arrival of the goods, but that they were to be delivered only on plaintiff's order. Atlantic C. L. R. Co. *v.* Dahlberg Brokerage Co. (Ala.), 660.

BRIDGES.

See CONSTITUTIONAL LAW; CROSSINGS; RAILROADS IN STREETS.

CARRIERS.

See BILLS OF LADING; COMMON CARRIERS; CONNECTING CARRIERS; CONSTITUTIONAL LAW; INTERSTATE COMMERCE; INTOXICATING LIQUORS; MANDAMUS; RAILROAD COMMISSIONS; RAILROADS; STATIONS AND DEPOTS.

CARRIERS OF LIVE STOCK.

Cars.

Negligence of carrier in failing to furnish proper car is not waived by shipper's acceptance of car furnished. Louisville & N. R. Co. v. J. R. Rash & Co. (Ky.), 221.

Waive negligence of carrier in using car sent by it, and carrier was liable for injuries to plaintiff's horses because of the inferior car, where shipper of horses ordered an Arms Palace car and was given one of an inferior car, he did not. Louisville & N. R. Co. v. J. R. Rash Co. (Ky.), 221.

Contributory Negligence.

Question for jury, in action for delay in shipment, whether shipper's agent in charge of horses was negligent in not permitting them to be unloaded at certain point for food, water, and rest, when yard master offered to unload them there. Daoust & Welch v. Chicago, etc., Ry. Co. (Iowa), 215.

Question whether negligence of shipper's agent contributed in delaying shipment of horses was for jury. Daoust & Welch v. Chicago, etc., Ry. Co. (Iowa), 215.

Where plaintiff failed to load his cattle on the day the carrier furnished a car to receive them, and after plaintiff so failed to load, the cattle on the same day escaped from the pens and inflicted upon themselves or each other the injuries for which plaintiff sought recovery, his negligence did not appear as matter of law. St. Louis, etc., R. Co. v. Cavender (Ala.), 338.

Damages.

Local freight agent has no implied authority to settle claims for injury to live stock shipment. Betus v. Chicago, etc., R. R. (Iowa), 706.

Plaintiff having paid for live stock and shipped it in his own name can recover for injury thereto, though he agreed to pay another a share of the profits, and the damages recoverable were treated by them as profits. Betus v. Chicago, etc., R. R. (Iowa), 706.

Ratification by carrier of settlement agreed upon by its local freight agent for injury to shipment, evidence showed. Betus v. Chicago, etc., R. R. (Iowa), 706.

Degree of Care.

Where its servant is acting within his authority, the carrier is responsible, though the wrong or damage done by him was done inadvertently or with the purpose to accomplish its business in an unlawful manner. St. Louis, etc., R. Co. v. Cavender (Ala.), 38.

Delay.

Question for jury whether carrier was negligent in forwarding plaintiff's horses. Daoust & Welch v. Chicago, etc., Ry. Co. (Iowa), 215.

Question for jury whether plaintiff's horses should have been reloaded and forwarded sooner than they were in exercise of due care. Daoust & Welch v. Chicago, etc., Ry. Co. (Iowa), 215.

Limiting Liability.

Action to recover for injuries to stock sustained while in carrier's stock pens awaiting transportation arrangements was not affected by the release contained in the subsequent freight contract in question. St. Louis, etc., R. Co. v. Cavender (Ala.), 338.

CARRIERS OF LIVE STOCK—Continued.

Insufficiency of evidence to impeach contract fixing value of animals. Pierson *v.* Northern Pac. Ry. Co. (Wash.), 303.

Interstate Commerce Act, Feb. 4, 1887, c. 104, does not prevent shipper from recovering the actual loss to live stock shipment, though the stock was shipped on the valuation of $100 per head. Betus *v.* Chicago, etc., R. R. (Iowa), 706.

Negligence of carrier. Jeffries *v.* Chicago, etc., Ry. Co. (Neb.), 321.

Notice of claim for injury shall be given to carrier before removal or mingling of animals has no application to those which die before their removal from place of destination, agreement providing that. Pierson *v.* Northern Pac. Ry. Co. (Wash.), 303.

Notice to carrier of claim for injury to animals shall be given before their removal or mingling with others, is inapplicable to animals surviving where nature and extent of injuries could not be fully ascertained within limited time, agreement providing for. Pierson *v.* Northern Pac. Ry. Co. (Wash.), 303.

Presumption as to fairness of consideration recited by contract; and effect of. Pierson *v.* Northern Pac. Ry. Co. (Wash.), 303.

Stating value of animals. Pierson *v.* Northern Pac. Ry. Co. (Wash.), 303.

That contract was not read or explained to shipper, that he asked no questions, and that it was signed hurriedly, does not relieve shipper from its obligations. Pierson *v.* Northern Pac. Ry. Co. (Wash.), 303.

That injury to animals was caused by confining them in car for more than 28 hours in violation of federal statute does not relieve shipper from contract limitation of carrier's liability. Pierson *v.* Northern Pac. Ry. Co. (Wash.), 303.

Pleading.

Declaration stated an action in case for negligence of carrier in taking care of plaintiff's cattle while held by shipper pending definite arrangements for their transportation. St. Louis & S. F. R. Co. *v.* Cavender (Ala.), 338.

Presumptions.

Presumption that servant of railroad company who is operating an engine on its track is acting within scope of the employment in negligently blowing the whistle, so as to render the railroad liable for injuries to animals frightened by the noise. St. Louis, etc., R. Co. *v.* Cavender (Ala.), 338.

Presumption that station agents have power to make contracts for transportation of freight and to do whatever is necessary to forward it. St Louis, etc., R. Co. *v.* Cavender (Ala.), 338.

Rely upon shipper's caretaker to notify its agents in charge of train whenever he thinks it necessary to unload stock for feed and right of carrier to. Jeffries *v.* Chicago, etc., Ry. Co. (Neb.), 321.

CARRIERS OF PASSENGERS.

See BAGGAGE; SLEEPING CAR COMPANIES; STATIONS AND DEPOTS; STREET RAILWAYS; TICKETS AND FARES.

Accidents on Track.

Alighting passenger is entitled to reasonable protection against accident while on track in passing from the station premises. Washington, etc., Ry. Co. *v.* Vaughan (Va.), 444.

CARRIERS OF PASSENGERS—Continued.

Carrier's negligence was question for jury where passenger was struck by through train while passing to his train from waiting room along street. Atlantic City R. Co. *v.* Clegg (C. C. A.), 372.

That the way across railway tracks used by alighting passenger in going to station was a public highway did not affect the degree of care in operating its cars owing him by the carrier. Washington, etc., Ry. Co. *v.* Vaughan (Va.), 444.

Appliances.

Ky. St. § 778, providing that no passenger train shall be run without air brakes, which shall at all times be kept in good condition, does not make a carrier liable, merely because the air hose breaks, stopping a train on a trestle, and a passenger goes out on platform and falls off. Louisville, etc., Ry. Co. *v.* Gregory's Adm'r (Ky.), 382.

Arrests.

Liability of carrier for wrongful arrest of passenger procured by trainmen, or for illegal arrest made by others. Mayfield *v.* St. Louis, etc., Ry. Co. (Ark.), 395.

Railroad was not liable for act of its station agent in sending telegram resulting in wrongful arrest of passenger, where such agent had no authority to cause the arrest, even though he believed the passenger had stolen railroad's property. Mayfield *v.* St. Louis, etc., Ry. Co. (Ark.), 395.

Assaults.

By other passengers, degree of care required of carrier to guard its passengers against' assaults. Jansen *v.* Minneapolis, etc., Ry. Co. (Minn.), 111.

Carriers are not liable for assaults committed by their servants outside scope of employment, unless the assaults could have been anticipated and prevented by due care. Houston & T. C. R. Co. *v.* Bush (Tex.), 428.

Record of conviction and sentence of special police officer of railroad company, for murder of plaintiff's brother, in action against the company for injuries sustained by assault or shooting of plaintiff by such officer, admissibility of. Layne *v.* Chesapeake & O. Ry. Co. (W. Va.), 143.

Servant, actuated by personal grudge only, left depot, went upon train, and assaulted passenger, carrier was liable where its. Houston & T. C. R. Co. *v.* Bush (Tex.), 428.

Burden of Proof.

Passenger, injured while alighting from moving train, failed to sustain burden of proof that rested upon him. Morris *v.* Illinois Cent. R. Co. (La.), 169.

Plaintiff had burden of proving that engineer was negligent in attempting to proceed after discovering forest fire, by which train was destroyed. Konieszny *v.* Detroit & M. Ry. Co. (Mich.), 136.

Conductor told plaintiff that she must stand aside to permit other passengers to alight from crowded car, and in the jostling which accompanied efforts of other passengers to alight, plaintiff was pushed off car, carrier was not negligent where. McCumber *v.* Boston Elev. Ry. Co. (Mass.), 463.

Contributory Negligence.

Alighting from moving train. Morris *v.* Illinois Cent. R. Co. (La.), 169.

CARRIERS OF PASSENGERS—Continued.

Assumption of risks by passenger voluntarily entering crowded street car, including risk from alighting temporarily to enable other passengers to leave car. McCumber v. Boston Elev. Ry. Co. (Mass.), 463.

Care required of alighting passenger in crossing tracks in leaving station premises. Washington, etc., Ry. Co. v. Vaughan (Va.), 444.

Electric railway passenger struck at night by unlighted train running in opposite direction without giving warning, where he failed to look and listen after alighting from his train. Washington, etc., Ry. Co. v. Vaughan (Va.), 444.

Even if carrier may be negligent in not having platform of car protected by vestibule doors, it is not so negligent as a passenger, who stands on the platform, after being directed by trainmen to go inside of the car where he belongs, while the train is stopped on trestle. Louisville, etc., Ry. Co. v. Gregory's Adm'r (Ky.), 382.

Intoxication as contributory negligence, erroneous instruction in regard to. Hughes v. Chicago, etc., Ry. Co. (Iowa), 759.

Intoxication of passenger injured while alighting. Hughes v. Chicago, etc., Ry. Co. (Iowa), 759.

Passenger had right to act on assumption that carrier would exercise proper care in operating its trains not to injure passengers while he was passing from waiting room to his train by the only way open to him. Atlantic City R. Co. v. Clegg (C. C. A.), 372.

Passenger standing in vestibule of moving car, and refusing to go inside upon brakeman's request, killed by fall when doors are opened on approaching station. Rager v. Pennslyvania R. Co. (Pa.), 757.

Passenger's duty to inform himself as to whether the train is scheduled to stop at his destination. Louisville & N. R. Co. v. Scott (Ky.), 466.

Question for jury where passenger was struck by another train while passing to his train from waiting room along street. Atlantic City R. Co. v. Clegg (C. C. A.), 372.

Riding on platform of street car in violation of rules, but with sanction of employees. McMahon v. New Orleans, etc., Co. (La.), 351.

Right of passenger permitted to stand on front platform of motor car to assume that the gates are closed. McMahon v. New Orleans, etc., Co. (La.), 351.

Damages.

Compensatory damages to white passenger for being compelled to ride in car set apart for negroes include compensation for discomfort and humiliation. Norfolk & W. Ry. Co. v. Stone (Va.), 459.

In action for ejection of passenger, his loss of time could not be considered in assessing damages, in absence of evidence as to value of his time. Chicago, etc., Ry. Co. v. Newburn (Okl.), 357.

Passenger ejected from train may not recover damages for insults and humiliation put on other passengers at the time. Louisville & N. R. Co. v. Scott (Ky.), 466.

Punitive damages were not recoverable for conduct of conductor, when ejecting passenger, in pushing her down the car steps. Louisville & N. R. Co. v. Scott (Ky.), 466.

$200 was not excessive verdict against carrier for injuries sustained by passenger from an assault upon him by another passenger. Jansen v. Minneapolis, etc., Ry. Co. (Minn.), 111.

CARRIERS OF PASSENGERS—Continued.

Degree of Care.

Carrier must exercise highest degree of care for passenger's safety which is consistent with similar duty to other passengers. McCumber v. Boston Elev. Ry. Co. (Mass.), 463.

Carrier owes actual and constructive passengers higher degree of care than it owes to travelers at highway crossings. Washington, etc., Ry. Co. v. Vaughan (Va.), 444.

Carrier owes higher degree of diligence to one carried for a reward than to one carried gratuitously. John v. Northern Pac. Ry. Co. (Mont.), 484.

Carriers are not insurers of safe carriage of passengers, but are only held to exercise of high degree of care. Houston & T. C. R. Co. v. Bush (Tex.), 428.

Common carrier does not insure safety of its passengers. Glennen v. Boston Elev. Ry. Co. (Mass.), 455.

Common carrier is required to take every reasonable precaution for the safety of its passengers. Hill v. Minneapolis St. Ry. Co. (Minn.), 107.

Employees of railroad must use every care commensurate with the danger to a passenger. McMahon v. New Orleans, etc., Co. (La.), 351.

Highest degree of care and foresight, consistent with the conduct of its business, or consistent with, practical operation of its road, is required of a railroad as a common carrier of passengers. Hill v. Minneapolis St. Ry. Co. (Minn.), 107.

It was not error to instruct that electric railway companies must use the greatest possible care and diligence for their passenger's safety. Washington, etc., Ry. Co. v. Vaughan (Va.), 444.

Ordinary care only due person carried free of charge. John v. Northern Pac. Ry. Co. (Mont.), 484.

Passenger carriers bind themselves to carry safely those whom they take into their cars as far as human foresight will go; that is with the utmost care and diligence of very cautious persons. Pelot v. Atlantic C. L. R. Co. (Fla.), 369.

That degree of care which would be exercised by the ordinary prudent person under same circumstances is not the test applicable to motorman of street car. Hill v. Minneapolis St. Ry. Co. (Minn.), 107.

Delay.

Delay caused by adherence to train service regulation and failure of passenger to follow conductor's instructions in regard to taking certain train at intermediate station, and resulting in failure to arrive before death of relative, right to recover for. Kyle v. Chicago, etc., Ry. Co. (C. C. A.), 149.

Discharging Passengers.

Invitation to alight before it was safe to do so, mere announcement of next stop was not an. Morris v. Illinois Cent. R. Co. (La.), 169.

Street car passenger's right to alight on either side of open car with transverse seats, in absence of warning in regard to dangerous condition of street on one side. White v. Lewiston, etc., Ry. Co. (Me.), 364.

Ejection.

If conductor treats passenger rudely or subjects her to any indignity when ejecting her, she may recover against the carrier for such improper manner of ejection. Houston, etc., Ry. Co. v. Lee (Tex.), 742.

CARRIERS OF PASSENGERS—Continued.

One who boards train after conductor has rightfully refused to carry him may be ejected, though he has a ticket. Chesapeake & O. Ry. Co. *v.* Selsor (Ky.), 739.

Passenger without ticket taking train for station at which it is not scheduled to stop, where he offers to pay cash fare to such station, right to eject. Burgess *v.* Atchison, etc., Ry. Co. (Kan.), 164.

Plaintiff demanded a transfer without paying his fare, only upon condition that conductor would simultaneously give him a transfer, there could be no recovery for his ejection in proper manner, where. Louisville Ry. Co. *v.* Hutti (Ky.), 402.

Evidence.

Circumstances to be considered in determining whether street railway exercised requisite degree of care to protect passenger from injury from crowd which rushed to the car from public amusement place. Glennen *v.* Boston Elev. Ry. Co. (Mass.), 455.

Evidence that at about same hour on Sundays in amusement season of preceding years the crowd had customarily rushed upon the cars and jostled passengers, was admissible on question of degree of care the carrier should have exercised to protect passengers from being jostled when alighting at such place on such occasions. Glennen *v.* Boston Elev. Ry. Co. (Mass.), 455.

Injured passenger was properly allowed to testify as to how passenger car platforms were arranged on other well-regulated railroads. Central of Georgia Ry. Co. *v.* Storrs (Ala.), 159.

On issue whether space between passenger cars on train in question was negligently left uncovered, evidence as to whether any cars had been constructed within last five years with platforms like those on cars in question was admissible. Central of Georgia Ry. Co. *v.* Storrs (Ala.), 159.

That conductor's tone of voice was harsh and loud when telling passenger that she was blocking passageway from car, etc., admissibility of evidence. McCumber *v.* Boston Elev. Ry. Co. (Mass.), 463.

Where alighting passenger was struck by an unlighted train of electric cars, it was not error to receive testimony that trolley poles frequently became detached and that lights in cars are thereby extinguished. Washington, etc., Ry. Co. *v.* Vaughan (Va.), 444.

Freight Trains.

Person on train upon which he knows passengers are not carried, cannot recover for injuries sustained while thereon, unless they were willfully or wantonly inflicted by carrier's servants. Kruse *v.* St. Louis, etc., Ry. Co. (Ark.), 376.

In action for death of passenger on train run into forest fire, the evidence was sufficient to show that carrier was negligent. Konieszny *v.* Detroit & M. Ry. Co. (Mich.), 136.

Insults.

Carrier is as much bound to protect its passengers from humiliation and insult as from physical injury. May *v.* Shreveport Traction Co. (La.), 120.

Liability of carrier where conductor intimates that white passenger belongs in the portion of street car reserved for negroes. May *v.* Shreveport Traction Co. (La.), 120.

CARRIERS OF PASSENGERS—Continued.

Intoxicated Passengers.

Duty of trainmen to give intoxicated passenger special care, when is it the. Louisville, etc., Ry. Co. *v.* Gregory's Adm'r (Ky.), 382.

Evidence did not show that passenger was so intoxicated as to put on trainmen the duty of exercising any special care to protect him. Louisville, etc., Ry. Co. *v.* Gregory's Adm'r (Ky.), 382.

Jars and Jolts.

Constant starting and stopping of street car to avoid collisions with carriages crossing ahead of car, or because of cars ahead of it, does not show negligence of motorman in operating car. Craig *v.* Boston Elev. Ry. Co. (Mass.), 362.

Duty to slow down street car when it is rounding a curve, to passenger standing on platform with motorman. McMahon *v.* New Orleans, etc., Co. (La.), 351.

Evidence warranted finding that motorman was negligent in starting car. Work *v.* Boston Elev. Ry. Co. (Mass.), 452.

Jerks, jolts, or lurches of street cars which render the carrier liable for injuries to passengers, what do, and do not, constitute. Work *v.* Boston Elev. Ry. Co. (Mass.), 452.

Motorman was not negligent, as matter of law, in operating car, where street car passenger was injured while sitting down by the car giving sudden jerk, no one else in the car being thrown over. Craig *v.* Boston Elev. Ry. Co. (Mass.), 362.

What passenger must prove in order to recover for injury from a jerk, jolt, or lurch of street car. Work *v.* Boston Elev. Ry. Co. (Mass.), 452.

Joint Liability.

Where passenger was injured by slipping on banana peel left in aisle of car with other sweepings by car cleaner, both of defendant railroad companies were liable for such injury as joint tort-feasors, one for allowing its cars to become dangerous while passing over its own line, and the other because the negligence which created the dangerous condition was that of its servants. Grand Trunk Ry. Co. *v.* Parks (C. C. A.), 736.

Liability for Acts of Servants.

General statement of rule in regard to carrier's liability to passengers on account of acts or omissions of servants, whether within scope of employment or not. Pelot *v.* Atlantic C. L. R. Co. (Fla.), 369.

Sufficiency of declaration which alleged that porter on train pushed swinging door of car against passenger's foot. Pelot *v.* Atlantic C. L. R. Co. (Fla.), 369.

Lights.

Duty of carrier to provide reasonably safe approaches to its cars, and to provide such approaches with lights at night. Messenger *v.* Valley City Street & Interurban Ry. Co. (N. Dak.), 127.

Limiting Liability.

Common carrier of passengers may contract to exempt itself from liability for the ordinary negligence of itself or its servants. John *v.* Northern Pac. Ry. Co. (Mont.), 484.

Provision in illegal free pass purporting to exempt carrier from liability for injuries caused by its negligence was a nullity. John *v.* Northern Pac. Ry. Co. (Mont.), 484.

CARRIERS OF PASSENGERS—Continued.

Negligence was question for jury where passenger was injured by getting his foot caught between bumpers, as he was crossing from one car to another while train was stopping at station. Central of Georgia Ry. Co. v. Storrs (Ala.), 159.

Overcrowding Cars.

Not negligence for street car company to permit passengers to enter cars which are already crowded. McCumber v. Boston Elev. Ry. Co. (Mass.), 463.

Passes.

Right of passenger to recover for injuries sustained while riding on illegal free pass. John v. Northern Pac. Ry. Co. (Mont.), 484.

Platforms of Cars.

Carrier's liability for fall of passenger from platform of car while it was standing on trestle, on ground of negligence in permitting part of the platform to be in a slippery condition, insufficiency of evidence to establish. Louisville, etc., Ry. Co. v. Gregory's Adm'r (Ky.), 382.

Presumption of Negligence.

Gross negligence by carrier, passenger carried free must offer proof to supplement the presumption of negligence arising from the fact of his injury, in order to show. John v. Northern Pac. Ry. Co. (Mont.), 484.

Injury to passenger carried free by the happening of an accident only shows ordinary negligence on part of the carrier, and not gross negligence. John v. Northern Pac. Ry. Co. (Mont.), 484.

Laws of Pennsylvania, whether presumption of negligence arises against carrier where passenger is injured under. Pittsburg, etc., Ry. Co. v. Grom (Ky.), 747.

Presumption of carrier's negligence arises from mere happening of an accident injuring a passenger, which is caused by some agency over which the carrier had control. John v. Northern Pac. Ry. Co. (Mont.), 484.

Raised by the res ipsa loquitur doctrine, is a want of ordinary care. John v. Northern Pac. Ry. Co. (Mont.), 484.

Under the laws of Pennsylvania, the evidence raised presumption of negligence which carrier was required to rebut, where passenger was struck by something while freight train was passing his train. Pittsburg, etc., Ry. Co. v. Grom (Ky.), 747.

Protection of Passengers.

Carrier must exercise highest degree of care to anticipate and protect passengers from violence from other passengers or other persons. Glennen v. Boston Elev. Ry. Co. (Mass.), 455.

Common carrier need not adopt every conceivable precaution, or exercise the utmost conceivable diligence to prevent injury to its passengers. Glennen v. Boston Elev. Ry. Co. (Mass.), 455.

Failure of railroad employees to control passengers who are about to jump from a moving train in disregard of their own safety is not a failure of the duty of the trainmen. Morris v. Illinois Cent. R. Co. (La.), 169.

Female passenger with small child in her arms was entitled to protection from being jostled, etc., by other passengers, commensurate with the impairment of her ability to care for herself resulting from carrying the child. Glennen v. Boston Elev. Ry. Co. (Mass.), 455.

CARRIERS OF PASSENGERS—Continued.

Question for jury whether railway's employees were negligent in not protecting female passenger with child in her arms from being jostled by crowd of passengers who boarded the car at public amusement resort. Glennen *v.* Boston Elev. Ry. Co. (Mass.), 455.

Receiving Passengers.

Ky. St., § 806, providing for punishment and ejection of disorderly passengers, does not change common-law rule as to what passengers carrier must receive. Chesapeake & O. Ry. Co. *v.* Selsor (Ky.), 739.

Where plaintiff was not at station when a carrier's car arrived, and he was left, he was not in a position to raise the question that the carrier did not hold the car a reasonable time to take up passengers. Mitchell *v.* Augusta & A. Ry. Co. (S. Car.), 154.

Rules and Regulations.

Railroad's right to make reasonable rules and regulations for running of trains and carrying of passengers thereon. Kyle *v.* Chicago, etc., Ry. Co. (C. C. A.), 149.

Railroad's right to omit to stop its through or limited trains at all stations. Kyle *v.* Chicago, etc., Ry. Co. (C. C. A.), 149.

Same duty of closing gates of platforms of cars, when it is necessary for the protection of a passenger, rests upon an interurban railroad as upon a strictly city railroad. McMahon *v.* New Orleans, etc., Co. (La.), 351.

Separation of Colored Passengers.

Constitutionality of Ky. St., § 795. Commonwealth *v.* Illinois Cent. R. Co. (Ky.), 730.

Even if it were the duty of the railroad's conductor to require the colored person in question to leave the Pullman sleeper and take the colored compartment in the day coach, the railroad would not be liable, under Ky. St., § 795 for his failure to do so. Commonwealth *v.* Illinois Cent. R. Co. (Ky.), 730.

It was improper to modify instructions which precluded recovery if the conductor honestly believed that the passenger was a negro, by the clause "unless plaintiff made known to the conductor that she was a white woman." Norfolk & W. Ry. Co. *v.* Stone (Va.), 459.

Liability of street railway for consequences of mistakes or abuse of the discretion vested in them and their officers and agents by La. Act No. 64, of 1902. May *v.* Shreveport Traction Co. (La.), 120.

Pullman sleeping car was not operated by the railroad company to whom it was delivered for transportation, within Ky. St., § 795, so as to render it liable under the statute. Commonwealth *v.* Illinois Cent. R. Co. (Ky.), 730.

Sleeping Cars.

Judgment in favor sleeping car company, in action against it by a passenger for loss of baggage in sleeping car, does not bar subsequent action against the railroad company for the same loss, for which both companies were jointly and severally liable. Nelson *v.* Illinois Cent. R. Co. (Miss.), 114.

Railroad's liability where passenger on sleeping car is injured by the negligence of servants of the sleeping car company. Nelson *v.* Illinois Cent. R. Co. (Miss.), 114.

Same duty to protect person and baggage of passenger rests on both railroad and sleeping car company under their separate

CARRIERS OF PASSENGERS—Continued.

contracts, and their negligent failure to perform such duty, resulting in a single indivisible injury, makes them joint tortfeasors, when does the. Nelson *v.* Illinois Cent. R. Co. (Miss.), 114.

Stopping Places.

Street railway, having the duty to keep in repair the portions of the street occupied by its tracks, was responsible for dangerous condition of its own making there, and where it stopped its car, was liable for injuries received by passenger from such condition after alighting from car. White *v.* Lewiston, etc., Ry. (Me.), 364.

Warn and Instruct.

Demurrer to plaintiff's evidence was properly overruled, it appearing therefrom that passenger, after being awakened immediately after the train had left the station of his destination, at night and while he was in an apparently drowsy condition, was assisted towards the platform by the porter and was suffered to step off the moving train in presence of conductor, was killed, and train was not stopped nor its speed slackened. Hanson *v.* Chicago, etc., Ry. Co. (Kan.), 191.

Duty of flagman to notify passenger who had left car and was standing on its step that the train was moving and that it was dangerous to attempt to alight while the train was in motion, whether it was the. Morris *v.* Illinois Cent. R. Co. (La.), 169.

Employees of railroad should use ordinary care to prevent injuries to passengers. Morris *v.* Illinois Cent. R. Co. (La.), 169.

Ticket agent's implied authority to agree with and furnish information to person desiring to become a passenger that a train not scheduled to stop at a certain point will stop there to let him on or off, so that the carrier will be bound by his representations. Louisville & N. R. Co. *v.* Scott (Ky.), 466.

What Law Governs.

Lex loci delicti govern in passenger's action for personal injuries, and not law of the place where contract of carriage was made. Pittsburg Ry. Co. *v.* Grom (Ky.), 747.

Where alighting passenger was struck by an electric car, claimed to have been unlighted, it was no abuse of discretion to exclude testimony showing that its lights were burning about 15 minutes after the accident. Washington, etc., Ry. Co. *v.* Vaughan (Va.), 444.

Who Are Passengers.

After alighting from street car, passenger was injured by reason of falling over grass-covered spur track in street, carrier was liable, under certain statutes, where. White *v.* Lewiston, etc., Ry. Co. (Me.), 364.

Alighting from car at intermediate station. Central of Georgia Ry. Co. *v.* Storrs (Ala.), 159.

Carrier need not receive as passenger one who is intoxicated or otherwise in an improper condition. Chesapeake & O. Ry. Co. *v.* Selsor (Ky.), 739.

Decease, while in waiting room before arrival of his train, was a passenger, and he did not lose that relation by entering upon the street to reach his train. Atlantic City R. Co. *v.* Clegg (C. C. A.), 372.

Good faith of passenger in delaying his departure from carrier's premises, and the purpose of his return to place of trouble on them, were questions for jury. Layne *v.* Chesapeake & O. Ry. Co. (W. Va.), 143.

CARRIERS OF PASSENGERS—Continued.

Implied acceptance of one as passenger may arise without purchase of ticket or other acceptance in express terms. Messenger *v.* Valley City Street & Interurban Ry. Co. (N. Dak.), 127.

One entering a train, such as a through freight train, which he is chargeable with notice is not intended to carry passengers, and upon which the rules of the railroad forbid passengers to ride, is not a passenger. Kruse *v.* St. Louis, etc., Ry. Co. (Ark.), 376.

Passenger is such until he has had reasonable time to alight from car and leave carrier's premises. Layne *v.* Chesapeake & O. Ry. Co. (W. Va.), 143.

Person on train by virtue of collusive agreement with conductor, who does not pay any fare. Kruse *v.* St. Louis, etc., Ry. Co. (Ark.), 376.

Plaintiff not being at the station when the car arrived, was not entitled to the rights of a passenger, and defendant owed him no duty to detain the car even for a short time to take him aboard. Mitchell *v.* Augusta & A. Ry. Co. (S. Car.), 154.

Question for jury, where passenger was necessarily delayed, whether he failed to leave carrier's premises within reasonable time. Layne *v.* Chesapeake & O. Ry. Co. (W. Va.), 143.

Reasonable and necessary delay of passenger in leaving carrier's premises, ~hat constituted a. Layne *v.* Chesapeake & O. Ry. Co. (W. Va.), 143.

Relation of carrier and passenger may exist while the passenger is entering the car or other vehicle, and before he is seated therein, and the fact that no ticket has been purchased does not necessarily prevent such relation arising. Messenger *v.* Valley City Street & Interurban Ry. Co. (N. Dak.), 127.

Since enactment of Kirby's Dig., § 6705, providing that local freight trains shall carry passengers, there is no presumption that person riding on freight train is not a passenger. Kruse *v.* St. Louis, etc., Ry. Co. (Ark.), 376.

When person enters place provided for reception of passengers, such as a depot, waiting room, or the like, at a time when such place is open for reception of persons intending to take passage on train or cars of the company. Mitchell *v.* Augusta & A. Ry. Co. (S. Car.), 154.

Where person attempts to defraud carrier by riding free or for less than full fare, even with consent of conductor of the train, he is a trespasser, and the company is not responsible for his injuries not wantonly or willfully inflicted. Krause *v.* St. Louis, etc., Ry. Co. (Ark.), 376.

CHILDREN.

Contributory Negligence.

Evidence did not show that parents were negligent in permitting four year old child to go upon street on which was defendant's street car track. Simon *v.* Metropolitan St. Ry. Co. (Mo.), 36.

Discovered Peril.

Distance from street car track at which young children are placed in a perilous position, so as to require motorman of approaching car to stop, is greater than in the case of adults. Simon *v.* Metropolitan St. Ry. Co. (Mo.), 36.

Evidence showed that the child made only a momentary stop in street before going upon defendant's street car track or merely hesitated from childish indecision. Simon *v.* Metropolitan St. Ry. Co. (Mo.), 36.

That four year old child after leaving the curb merely hesitated for a brief time in the street from childish indecision before

CHILDREN—Continued.

advancing onto the track did not give defendant's motorman the right to proceed under the idea that the child did not intend to go on the track. Simon *v.* Metropolitan St. Ry. Co. (Mo.), 36.

That motorman sees child four years of age approaching the street car track from sidewalk ahead of the car is in itself sufficient to require him to stop car to prevent injury. Simon *v.* Metropolitan St. Ry. Co. (Mo.), 36.

COMMON CARRIERS.

Attachment.

When goods in transit are taken from carrier by officer under writ of attachment against third person, the carrier assumes the burden of establishing the legality of the proceedings in which the attachment was made, and the mere fact that the writ was regular on its face does not protect the carrier if such writ was in law void. Taugher *v.* Northern Pac. Ry. Co. (N. Dak.), 719.

Burden of Proof.

Sufficiency of proof to sustain recovery for loss in action by shipper on his contract. Taugher *v.* Northern Pac. Ry. Co. (N. Dak.), 719.

Cars.

Carrier must provide safe and suitable cars, and cannot avoid liability for not doing so by using another's cars. Central of Georgia Ry. Co. *v.* Chicago Varnish Co. (Ala.), 310.

If shipper undertakes to furnish the cars, carrier is not liable for loss resulting from their defective condition. Central of Georgia Ry. Co. *v.* Chicago Varnish Co. (Ala.), 310.

Where freight was shipped in cars leased by carrier from consignor under agreement by which carrier was to keep the cars in repair at consignor's cost, carrier was liable for loss of freight caused by defects therein. Central of Georgia Ry. Co. *v.* Chicago Varnish Co. (Ala.), 310.

Commencement of Liability.

Common carrier is responsible as such only when freight is delivered to and accepted by it for immediate transportation, in usual course of business. St. Louis, etc., R. Co. *v.* Cavender (Ala.), 338.

Liability of carrier where it receives goods, and something remains to be done before they can be transported, as where they are delivered to carrier without instructions as to their destination. St. Louis, etc., R. Co. *v.* Cavender (Ala.), 338.

Conversion.

Carrier not liable as for converting goods unreasonably delayed, in absence of demand for delivery and refusal thereof while the goods are in its possession. Southern Ry. Co. *v.* Moody (Ala.), 319.

Conversion does not lie against common carrier for mere nonfeasance, nor for goods stolen from carrier, nor for negligence causing the loss, nor for bare omission. Taugher *v.* Northern Pac. Ry. Co. (N. Dak.), 719.

Duty of carrier to notify shipper when goods in transit are taken from it by an officer under writ of attachment against third person. Taugher *v.* Northern Pac. Ry. Co. (N. Dak.), 719.

Proof necessary to sustain action for conversion against carrier. Taugher *v.* Northern Pac. Ry. Co. (N. Dak.), 719.

COMMON CARRIERS—Continued.

Damages.

Carrier not liable for special damages not contemplated at time of shipment, such as deterioration of eggs because of delay in shipment of material to be used in constructing packing boxes. Southern Ry. Co. *v.* Moody (Ala.), 319.

Degree of Care.

Carriers are responsible for the negligence of their servants in and about the carriage of freight, including its receipt for future carriage. St. Louis, etc., R. Co. *v.* Cavender (Ala.), 338.

Delay.

Duty to carry freight without unnecessary delay. Jeffries *v.* Chicago, etc., Ry. Co. (Neb.), 321.

Excuse that carrier had annulled a regular freight train scheduled to leave connecting point an hour after arrival of car of plaintiff's horses was insufficient for delay in question. Jeffries *v.* Chicago, etc., Ry. Co. (Neb.), 321.

Excuses as affected by conduct of carrier in accepting freight without notifying shipper of congested condition of traffic. Daoust & Welch *v.* Chicago, etc., Ry. Co. (Iowa), 215.

In transporting freight cannot be excused by fact that crews were taken from freight trains to handle an extraordinary amount of passenger traffic of which carrier had warning and could have provided for. Daoust & Welch *v.* Chicago, etc., Ry. Co. (Iowa), 215.

24 hours delay of freight at way station is unnecessary delay, whether. Jeffries *v.* Chicago, etc., Ry. Co. (Neb.), 321.

Delivery by Carrier.

Carrier cannot justify delivery of freight to buyer who had rejected consignor-consignee's draft with bill of lading attached, on the ground that the buyer had a contract with consignor's principal for delivery of similar goods. Atlantic C. L. R. Co. *v.* Dahlberg Brokerage Co. (Ala.), 660.

In action by consignee to recover for coal lost in transit, evidence was insufficient to show that such losses occurred before delivery to him. Brown *v.* Missouri, etc., Ry. Co. (Kan.), 224.

To justify delivery of freight without consignor's order, the carrier must prove that the person to whom delivery was made was the true owner and entitled to immediate possession. Atlantic C. L. R. Co. *v.* Dahlberg Brokerage Co. (Ala.), 660.

Where proposed buyer rejected consignor-consignee's draft with bill of lading attached, that after the carrier delivered the goods to the buyer the draft was again presented is not conclusive evidence of consignor's ratification of the delivery. Atlantic C. L. R. Co. *v.* Dahlberg Brokerage Co. (Ala.), 660.

Discrimination.

Common carrier cannot discriminate between patrons or give to shipper to whose premises there is a spur track any preferential rate. Riley *v.* Louisville, etc., Ry. Co. (Ky.), 614.

Courts may prevent discrimination by carrier. State *v.* Ogden Rapid Transit Co. (Utah), 179.

Duty to Receive and Carry.

Carrier is liable in damages for refusing to receive and carry freight though it was destined for points beyond its own line. Reid *v.* Southern Ry. Co. (N. Car.), 204.

39 R R R—52

COMMON CARRIERS—Continued.

Common-law duty of carrier to receive freight whenever tendered. Reid *v.* Southern Ry. Co. (N. Car.), 204.

Limiting Liability.

Contract to be strictly construed against carrier. St. Louis, etc., R. Co. *v.* Cavender (Ala.), 338.

Iowa Code, §§ 2074, 3136, cannot be avoided by a stipulation limiting liability to a fixed valuation of the freight in consideration of a lower rate. Betus *v.* Chicago, etc., R. R. (Iowa), 706.

Recital in contract, framed as limitation of liability of carrier, that the rate is a reduced rate is prima facie evidence of that fact. St. Louis, etc., R. Co. *v.* Cavender (Ala.), 338.

Shipper having executed the contract, in absence of fraud or mistake alleged, is presumed to have known and consented to its terms. St. Louis, etc., R. Co. *v.* Cavender (Ala.), 338.

Sunday for carriage of animal completed the shipment under the contract at a time it could have legally made the contract, and fact that shipper accepted the animal on its arrival did not prevent shipper from relying on invalidity of the contract because made on Sunday, the fact that a carrier receiving and contracting on. Lovell *v.* Boston & M. R. Co. (N. H.), 475.

Waiver of right to rely on its exemption, act of carrier in sending at request of consignee tracers for lost shipment after time fixed in bill of lading for service of notice on it for claim for loss did not constitute. Old Dominion S. S. Co. *v.* C. F. Flanary & Co. (Va.), 345.

Where the shipment was made on Sept. 5, and 15 days was a reasonable time to transport the goods, a notice of a claim against the carrier for their loss not given until Oct. 23, was too late, under the contract in question. Old Dominion S. S. Co. *v.* C. F. Flanary & Co. (Va.), 345.

Removal of Goods.

Consignee is entitled to reasonable time to remove freight. Eli Hurley & Son *v.* Norfolk & W. Ry. Co. (W. Va.), 313.

Termination of Liability.

Was proper to refuse to instruct that payment of freight alone, after arrival of freight at destination, terminates contract of carriage. Eli Hurley & Son *v.* Norfolk & W. Ry. Co. (W. Va.), 313.

Warehouseman.

Duty and liability of defendant as carrier under the first contract of shipment were changed to those of warehouseman. Eli Hurley & Son *v.* Norfolk & W. Ry. Co. (W. Va.), 313.

CONNECTING CARRIERS.

See INTERSTATE COMMERCE.

Burden of Proof.

Presumption, as against a connecting carrier, that goods were received by it in same order as when received by initial carrier, effect of. Central of Georgia Ry Co. *v.* Chicago Varnish Co. (Ala.), 310.

Duty to Receive and Carry.

Even if the provision of the Interstate Commerce Act making initial carrier liable for default of each successive carrier to the point of destination were invalid, its invalidity would not relieve

CONNECTING CARRIERS—Continued.

a carrier from the penalty imposed by N. Car. Revisal 1905, §
2631, for refusal to receive freight tendered, though the freight
was destined for an interstate point, since the goods should
have been received under a bill of lading limiting liability to
injuries suffered on initial carrier's own line. Reid v. Southern
R. Co. (N. Car.), 204.

Liability of several connecting carriers with respect to loss of
freight en route is to be determined by the law as it was when the
contract of shipment was made. Central of Georgia Ry. Co. v.
Chicago Varnish Co. (Ala.), 310.

Limiting Liability.

Carrier may not by contract limit the liabilities imposed on it
by Interstate Commerce Act, as amended by certain statute
making initial carrier of interstate shipment liable for loss or
injury thereto caused by any connecting carrier, because of
the rate charged for the transportation. Central of Georgia
Ry. Co. v. Sims (Ala.), 666.

In absence of statute or act of Congress, the mere designation
in the bill of lading of a point in another state as the point of
destination does not make the contract one for through transportation, where the other provisions indicate limitation of the
initial carrier's liability to injuries occurring on its own line.
Reid v. Southern Ry. Co. (N. Car.), 204.

Reasonableness of stipulation in bill of lading issued by initial
carrier of interstate shipment that claims for loss must be made
to agent at point of delivery within certain time, under Carmack amendment to interstate commerce act. Old Dominion
S. S. Co. v. C. F. Flanary & Co. (Va.), 345.

Right of initial carrier to limit its liability to own line as affected by Carmack amendment to interstate commerce act.
Old Dominion S. S. Co. v. C. F. Flanary & Co. (Va.), 345.

Under common-law, each of several connecting carriers was responsible only for loss occurring on its own line. Central of
Georgia Ry. Co. v. Chicago Varnish Co. (Ala.), 310.

CONSTITUTIONAL LAW.

See EMPLOYERS' LIABILITY ACTS; GARNISHMENT;
INTERSTATE COMMERCE; INTOXICATING LIQUORS;
NEGLIGENCE; RAILROAD COMMISSIONS; SPURS
AND SIDETRACKS; STREET RAILWAYS.

Constitutionality of Georgia Laws 1908, p. 50, requiring railroads
to equip every locomotive with certain kind of headlight, as affected by due process clauses of state and federal Constitutions.
Atlantic C. L. R. Co. v. State (Ga.), 672.

Equal Protection of Laws.

Statute in question, requiring railroad companies to equip every
locomotive with a certain kind of headlight, is not void because it exempts from its operation tram roads, mill roads, and
roads engaged principally in lumber or logging transportation
in connection with mills; nor if receivers of railroads are not
within its operation. Atlantic C. L. R. Co. v. State (Ga.), 672.

Obligation of valid municipal grant of special tax in aid of a specified railroad company, effective against all taxable property in
the parish, is not impaired by subsequent adoption of new state
constitution under which any property in the parish passing into
possession of any railroad thereafter constructed becomes exempt from taxation. Arkansas So. Ry. Co. v. Louisiana & Ark.
Ry. Co. (U. S.), 100.

CONSTITUTIONAL LAW—Continued.

Ore. Act, Feb. 18, 1907, requiring railroads to furnish cars on demand of shippers and authorizing the railroad commission to suspend the operation of the act, and making railroads liable in treble damages, with attorney's fees, for its violation is constitutional. Martin *v.* Oregon R. & Nav. Co. (Ore.), 710.

Right to impose upon railroad company expenses of constructing railway bridge over highway, made necessary by action of the city in opening such highway through the railway company's embankment. Cincinnati & W. Ry. Co. *v.* Connersville (C. S.), 103.

CONTRIBUTORY NEGLIGENCE.

See CARRIERS; CHILDREN; CROSSINGS; DEATH BY WRONGFUL ACT; MASTER AND SERVANT; NEGLIGENCE; STREET RAILWAYS.

Burden of Proof.

Instruction·in question was erroneous as tending to exclude consideration of testimony of plaintiff's witnesses, showing contributory negligence, other than himself. Washington, etc., Ry. Co. *v.* Vaughan (Va.), 444.

Plaintiff's negligence as appearing from his case is available to defendant. Washington, etc., Ry. Co. *v.* Vaughan (Va.), 444.

Upon defendant to prove contributory negligence, and does not shift during trial; but he should receive benefit of plaintiff's evidence tending to prove such defense, when is the burden. McGahey *v.* Citizen's Ry. Co. (Neb.), 242.

Defeat recovery, when will and when will not contributory negligence. McCahey *v.* Citizen's Ry. Co. (Neb.), 242.

Emergencies.

Degree of care required of one in great peril. Hoff *v.* Los Angeles-Pacific Co. (Cal.), 47.

Reasonableness of effort of one in great peril to escape injury after discovering the danger is question for jury. Hoff *v.* Los Angeles-Pacific Co. (Cal.), 47.

Intoxication. Hughes *v.* Chicago, etc., Ry. Co. (Iowa), 759.

Is generally question for jury. Messenger *v.* Valley City Street & Interurban Ry. Co. (N. Dak.), 127.

Last Clear Chance. ₁

Ground upon which plaintiff may recover, notwithstanding his own negligence, is that defendant after becoming aware of former's danger failed to use proper care to avoid injuring him. Acton *v.* Fargo, etc., Ry. Co. (N. Dak.), 767.

Only relieves from liability to pay for consequences of nonperformance of duty. Elliott *v.* New York, etc., R. Co. (Conn.), 247.

Pleading.

In personal injury actions, where the complaint is silent as to plaintiff's negligence, such negligence must be specially pleaded by defendant. Hill *v.* Minneapolis St. Ry. Co. (Minn.), 107.

Proximate Cause.

Contributory negligence will not prevent recovery unless it was proximate cause of the injury. Acton *v.* Fargo, etc., Ry. Co. (N. Dak.), 767.

CROSSINGS.

See LICENSEES; RAILROAD COMMISSIONS; RAILROADS IN STREETS; STOCK, INJURIES TO; STREET RAILWAYS.

Construction and Maintenance.

Reasonableness of ordinance requiring that all bridges over railroads be built of metal, stone, or concrete, or combinations thereof, etc. City of Shreveport v. Kansas City So. Ry. Co. (La.), 270.

Repair of wooden viaduct, under which railroad tracks ran and over which street was carried, by changing 40 per cent. of the materials, was a "substantial repair," within meaning of ordinance in question. City of Shreveport v. Kansas City So. Ry. Co. (La.), 270.

Contributory Negligence.

Deceased was guilty of. Wilson v. Illinois Cent. R. Co. (Iowa), 282.

In action for injuries in a collision between plaintiff's automobile and defendant street railway's car, whether plaintiff was guilty of contributory negligence was for jury. Hoff v. Los Angeles-Pacific Co. (Cal.), 47.

Negligence of one who drove on track at crossing and collided with train would be too remote to constitute contributory negligence, if railroad's negligence supervened and caused the collision. Elliott v. New York, etc., R. Co. (Conn.), 247.

Negligent pedestrian might still recover if motorman could, by exercise of due care, have avoided the accident after he saw, or by proper care might have seen, her as she was about to cross the track. United Rys., etc., Co. v. Kolken (Md.), 52.

Pedestrian, on invitation of brakeman, attempting to cross over cars of freight train obstructing crossing, and injured of their movement catching his foot between bumpers. Westbrook v. Kansas City M. & B. R. Co. (Ala.), 786.

Plaintiff had right to assume that street car was under control, and that he would be in no danger in attempting to drive across track. and was, therefore, not negligent as matter of law. Nappli v. Seattle, etc., Ry. Co. (Wash.), 62.

Question for jury whether one struck by car backed by engine over crossing was guilty of contributory negligence. Arkansas & L. Ry. Co. v. Graves (Ark.), 259.

Right of person about to cross track to rely on trainmen to give signals. Arkansas & L. Ry. Co. v. Graves (Ark.), 259.

Right to attempt to drive across street car track·in front of car which driver sees to be approaching, test of. Nappli v. Seattle, etc., Ry. Co. (Wash.), 62.

Right to attempt to drive over track in front of approaching street car. McGahey v. Citizen's Ry. Co. (Neb.), 242.

Street railway, degree of care required of one about to cross a. Hoff v. Los Angeles-Pacific Co. (Cal.), 47.

Discovered Peril.

Duty to avoid collision with one who negligently drove on track at crossing and was killed in a collision arose when by due care railroad would have known of his peril. Elliott v. New York, etc., R. Co. (Conn.), 247.

Engineer's right to presume that pedestrian will stop before reaching track in front of moving train. Norfolk & W. Ry. Co. v. Overton's Adm'r (Va.), 271.

Rule of discovered peril applies to street car crossing accident

CROSSINGS—Continued.

whether plaintiff's negligence consisted in her venturing to
cross street without looking for cars, or in attempting to cross
after seeing a car, as she believed, a safe distance away, and in
not looking again. United Rys., etc., Co. *v.* Kolken (Md.). 52
Trainmen on seeing street car approaching the crossing had
right to presume that motorman would exercise his senses so
as to avoid collision by stopping his car short of the street
intersection. Adams *v.* Arkansas, etc., Ry. Co. (La.). 254.

Last Clear Chance.

As those in charge of steam railroad train were keeping proper
lookout, and as soon as they discovered danger of collision
with the street car, did all they could have been reasonably expected to do to stop train, last clear chance doctrine did not
apply. Adams *v.* Arkansas, etc., Ry. Co. (La.). 254.
Evidence was insufficient to show that engineer was negligent
after he saw decedent in a position of peril, or that such negligence was proximate cause of the accident. Wilson *v.* Illinois Cent. R. Co. (Iowa), 282.
Where deceased was guilty of contributory negligence in attempting to cross tracks, the only theory upon which there
can be recovery for his death is that engineer or fireman saw
him in place peril, and thereafter failed to take necessary steps
to avoid a collision. Wilson *v.* Illinois Cent. Ry. Co. (Iowa),
282.

Lookouts.

Motorman's duty to keep lookout. United Rys., etc., Co. *v.*
Kolken (Md.), 52.

Obstructing Cars.

Brakeman has no implied authority to invite pedestrian to climb
over or between cars, or to give an assurance of safety to the
pedestrian in doing so. Westbrook *v.* Kansas City, M. & R.
R. Co. (Ala.), 786.
Liability of railroad where pedestrian was injured by movement
of cars while he was attempting, at invitation of brakeman,
who had no authority to give it, to cross over cars of freight
train obstructing crossing. Westbrook *v.* Kansas City M. &
B. R. Co. (Ala.), 786.

Proximate Cause.

Failure to give train signals was proximate cause of injury,
though pedestrian knew that the engine was running near him.
Arkansas & L. Ry. Co. *v.* Graves (Ark.), 259.

Right of Way.

Right of way as between street car and other vehicle. Nappli *v.*
Seattle, etc., Ry. Co. (Wash.), 62.

Signals.

Evidence that witness was near point of accident at time plaintiff was struck by locomotive, and did not hear the whistle or
bell, effect of. Smith *v.* Southern Pac. Co. (Ore.), 600.
Liability of railroad where there was failure to give statutory
signals for street crossing and person was struck by the train
at another point. Arkansas & L. Ry. Co. *v.* Graves (Ark.), 259.
Negligence to fail to give statutory signals. Western Ry. *v.*
Moore (Ala.), 67.
Testimony of several witnesses that no bell was rung or whistle
sounded is sufficient to take case to jury on question of negligence. Wilson *v.* Illinois Cent. R. Co. (Iowa), 282.

CROSSINGS—Continued.

Under ordinary circumstances only statutory signals are required. Elliott *v.* New York, etc., R. Co. (Conn.), 247.

Speed.

Motorman's duty to have car under control when approaching street crossings. United Rys., etc., Co. *v.* Kolken (Md.), 52.

Negligence in causing collision at crossing cannot ordinarily be inferred from speed alone. Elliott *v.* New York, etc., R. Co. (Conn.), 247.

Stop, Look, and Listen.

Highway traveler must be deemed to have discovered approach of train if it could have been plainly seen by looking or could have been heard by listening. Arkansas & L. Ry. Co. *v.* Graves (Ark.), 259.

Motorman was guilty of contributory negligence barring recovery, although servants of steam railroad were at same time negligent in not stopping their train before it reached the crossing, as required by ordinance, as he could have seen the train in time had he stopped, looked, and listened at street intersection. Adams *v.* Arkansas, etc., Ry. Co. (La.), 254.

One about to cross railroad track at customary crossing must look and listen for approach of trains. Arkansas & L. Ry. Co. *v.* Graves (Ark.), 259.

Precautions to be taken by highway traveler before crossing railroad tracks where view of approaching trains is obstructed. Wilson *v.* Illinois Cent. R. Co. (Iowa), 282.

Question for jury whether one about to cross at customary crossing exercised due care in looking and listening for trains. Arkansas & L. Ry. Co. *v.* Graves (Ark.), 259.

The care imposed upon a driver at a railroad crossing is not fulfilled by stopping 100 feet from the track, where, because of obstructions, he cannot see, when there is a clear view 30 feet from the track of at least 500 feet. Dehoff *v.* Northern Cent. Ry. Co. (Pa.), 366.

Where pedestrian, when attempting to cross side track at customary crossing, looked and listened for approach of trains, and heard an engine and thought it was on main track, he was not negligent in failing to stop, look, and listen. Arkansas & L. Ry. Co. *v.* Graves (Ark.), 259.

DAMAGES.

See CARRIERS; EMINENT DOMAIN; PERSONAL INJURIES; RAILROADS IN STREETS.

Measure.

Facts of each case must be the basis on which the amount in each case is predicated. McMahon *v.* New Orleans, etc., Co. (La.), 351.

Punitive Damages.

Duty to instruct jury to find each class of damages separately. Louisville & N. R. Co. *v.* Scott (Ky.), 466.

Exemplary or punitive damages are, and are not, allowable against principal for act of agent, when. Chicago, etc., Ry. Co. *v.* Newburn (Okl.), 357.

Remote Damages.

Damages recoverable for breach of contract are those flowing directly and naturally from the breach. Southern Ry. Co. *v.* Moody (Ala.), 319.

DEATH BY WRONGFUL ACT.
Contributory Negligence.
Presumption that person killed exercised ordinary care. Wilson
v. Illinois Cent. R. Co. (Iowa), 282.

DISCRIMINATION.
See CARRIERS, STATIONS AND DEPOTS.

EMINENT DOMAIN.
See RAILROADS IN STREETS; RIGHT OF WAY; SPURS
AND SIDE TRACKS.

Benefits.
Duty to instruct jury to set off, against the damages, the value
of peculiar benefits inuring to property from construction of
public improvement by which it is also injured. Fowler v.
Norfolk & W. Ry. Co. (W. Va.), 632.

Compensation.
In constitutional provision as to compensation for property taken
for public use, the term "taken" includes the appropriation of
the property or of some interest in it, by actual, physical possession, such as exists when a railroad is constructed and operated on it. McCammon & Lang Lumber Co. v. Trinity &
B. V. Ry. Co. (Tex.), 648.
Occupation of street by railroad is a "taking" of the property
of one owning the fee of the street. McCammon & Lang Lumber Co. v. Trinity & B. V. Ry. Co. (Tex.), 648.

Damages.
Cost of observing police regulation, whether railroad company in
proceeding by city to condemn right of way for street over its
track, could recover the. City of Paris v. Cario, V. & C. Ry. Co.
(Ill.), 623.
Elements of damages recoverable in proceedings by city to con-
demn right of way for street over railroad track. City of Paris
v. Cairo V. & C. Ry. Co. (Ill.), 623.
Elements of damages sustained by landowner in consequence of
the appropriation or injury of his property for a public use.
Kayser v. Chicago, B. & S. R. Co. (Neb.), 559.
Injury to landowner from smoke, noise, soot, cinders, and vibra-
tion, resulting from the operation of a railroad. Kayser v.
Chicago, B. & Q. R. Co. (Neb.), 559.
Review of amount awarded by jury. Cloth v. Chicago, etc., Ry.
Co. (Ark.), 551.

Evidence.
Testimony of nonexperts as to whether the location of the street
across railroad right of way would result in damages to the
use of the property of the railroad to be occupied by the street,
admissibility of. City of Paris v. Cario, V. & C. Ry. Co. (Ill.),
623.
Extent of rights acquired by expropriation proceedings in question. Louisiana & A. Ry. Co. v. Louisiana Ry. & Nav. Co.
(La.), 536.

Necessity for Taking.
Courts cannot inquire into the propriety of exercising the right
of eminent domain for the purpose of extending city street
across railroad. City of Paris v. Cairo, V. & C. Ry. Co. (Ill.),
623.

EMINENT DOMAIN—Continued.

Railroad had right to choose plaintiff's property on which to locate freight depot, though it owned other property which it might have used, or the depot might have been located on land of others. Cloth v. Chicago, etc., Ry. Co. (Ark.), 551.

Parties.

In order for railroad to acquire title to its right of way by expropriation it is necessary that owners of the land should be cited and duly made parties to the proceedings. Louisiana & A. Ry. Co. v. Louisiana Ry. & Nav. Co. (La.), 556.

Public Use.

Acquiescence in public use of spur track extended to premises of private corporation, effect of. Riley v. Louisville, etc., Ry. Co. (Ky.), 614.

Burden of proving that the property is needed for public use. Riley v. Louisville, etc., Ry. Co. (Ky.), 614.

Extent and conditions of public use of spur track built to premises of private corporation, effect of. Riley v. Louisville, etc., Ry. Co. (Ky.), 614.

Incidental benefit to third persons by condemnation of land for freight depot. Cloth v. Chicago, etc., Ry. Co. (Ark.), 551.

It could not be said that the proposed spur track would not serve a public use. Riley v. Louisville, etc., Ry. Co. (Ky.), 614.

Judicial question, whether property taken by power of eminent domain was taken for a public use is a. Cloth v. Chicago, etc., Ry. Co. (Ark.), 551.

N. Car. Revisal 1905, § 1097, requiring switches to be put into private industries on the order of the Corporation Commission, is not a requirement for a private purpose, but is for a public use. State v. Southern Ry. Co. (N. Car.), 20.

Spur track to premises of distilling company. Riley v. Louisville, etc., Ry. Co. (Ky.), 614.

Test in determining whether use is public. Riley v. Louisville, etc., Ry. Co. (Ky.), 614.

That one or more persons will derive special advantages from construction of spur track, effect of fact. Riley v. Louisville, etc., Ry. Co. (Ky.), 614.

That private corporation was particularly interested in construction of spur track to its premises and intended to furnish the means to construct it, effect of fact. Riley v. Louisville, etc., Ry. Co. (Ky.), 614.

To constitute a public use, the public must be concerned in the use, and it must be public in fact. Cloth v. Chicago, etc., Ry. Co. (Ark.), 551.

Reverter upon termination of use of land for railroad right of way. Louisiana & A. Ry. Co. v. Louisiana Ry. & Nav. Co. (La.), 556.

EMPLOYERS' LIABILITY ACTS.

Application.

Car with defective coupler, billed for the repair shop, but which was not sent there but was left on a track in ordinary use in a switch yard, to be repaired by the switchmen, and then coupled to other cars, was being "used," within the meaning of U. S. Comp. St. 1901, p. 3174. Erie R. Co. v. Russell (C. C. A.), 655.

Statute in question referred to physical "use and operation" of railroad in transportation; and the rails on the railroad's machine shop floor did not constitute "a railway," nor was the movement of the repaired engine by the other engine done in

EMPLOYERS' LIABILITY ACTS—Continued.

the "use and operation" of the railway, within meaning of such statute, so that the railroad was not liable for negligence of engineer in starting the live engine. Slaats *v.* Chicago, etc., Ry. Co. (Iowa), 228.

Surface cars in question belonging to elevated railway were not elevated trains, within Mass. St. 1908, c. 420, providing that an employee shall, for the negligence of a servant in charge of an "elevated train," have the same right as if he were not an employee. Dow *v.* Boston Elev. Ry. Co. (Mass.), 610.

"Used" in interstate commerce, within meaning of U. S. Comp. St. 1901, p. 3174, car in question with a defective coupler was being. Erie R. Co. *v.* Russell (C. C. A.), 655.

Burden of Proof.

In proceedings against railroad company to recover penalties for violation of Safety Appliance Act March 2, 1893, the government is only required to establish its case by preponderance of the evidence. St. Louis S. W. R. Co. *v.* United States (C. C. A.), 671.

Constitutional Law.

Abrogation of fellow servant rule as to railway employees, made by Miss. Code 1892, § 3559, does not offend against the equal protection of the laws clause of the federal constitution because construed as applying to the foreman of a section crew charged with keeping the track in repair. Mobile, etc., R. Co. *v.* Turnipseed (U. S.), 70.

Duty of railroads to comply with federal statutes requiring the use of the safety appliances in question is absolute. Galveston, etc., R. Co. *v.* United States (C. C. A.), 701.

Proximate Cause.

In an action to recover for death of switchman, question whether defective coupler was proximate cause of his injury, so as to bring the case within U. S. Comp. St. 1901, 3176, was properly submitted to jury. Erie R. Co. *v.* Russell (C. C. A.), 655.

Where several cars, each without the requisite appliances required by Safety Appliance Act March 2, 1893, c. 196, are hauled by carrier in interstate commerce at one and the same time, there are as many distinct violations of the act as there are cars hauled and not properly equipped, for every one of which the statutory penalty is recoverable. St. Louis S. W. Ry. Co. *v.* United States (C. C. A.), 671.

EVIDENCE.

See BILLS OF LADING; CARRIERS; CARRIERS OF PASSENGERS; EMINENT DOMAIN; PERSONAL INJURIES.

FALSE IMPRISONMENT.

See MASTER AND SERVANT.

FELLOW SERVANTS.

See EMPLOYERS' LIABILITY ACTS; MASTER AND SERVANT.

Different Department Limitation.

Common employment, test of what constitutes. Sloppy *v.* Pennsylvania R. Co. (Pa.), 1.

Fellow Servant Rule.

Master is not liable for injury to servant caused by negligence of his fellow servant. Sloppy *v.* Pennsylvania R. Co. (Pa.), 1.

FELLOW SERVANTS—Continued.

Mere neglect of railroad employee to carry back signal flag did not render railroad liable for injuries thereby caused to a co-laborer. Furlong *v.* New York, etc., R. Co. (Conn.), 233.

Railroad which, after actual or constructive knowledge of a trainmen's habitual violation of rule requiring him to flag approaching trains, retains him in service, is not exempt under fellow-servant rule from liability for injuries to another employee resulting from such trainmen's negligent failure to perform such duty. Furlong *v.* New York, etc., R. Co. (Conn.), 233.

Who Are.

Crew of train switching cars onto repair track and car repairer doing his work on such track. Sloppy *v.* Pennsylvania R. Co. (Pa.), 1.

Foreman, in charge of work of elevating coal to top of building from which it may be discharged into tenders of engines, when engaged in starting the hoisting engine while a servant is at work in the pit, rendered dangerous only by starting the engine without warning, is a fellow servant of such servant. Peterson *v.* Chicago, etc., Ry. Co. (Iowa), 83.

Foreman when doing acts not involving exercise of superior authority. Peterson *v.* Chicago, etc., R. Co. (Iowa), 83.

Master is not liable where its car repairer, while engaged on a car standing on repair track, was killed by negligent shifting of another car upon such track, through failure of the fireman of the shifting crew to give warning. Sloppy *v.* Pennsylvania R. Co. (Pa.), 1.

FIRES SET BY LOCOMOTIVES.

Railroad was liable for the destruction of plaintiff's property resulting from fires started by sectionmen in cleaning up railroad's right of way, even though the setting of such fires was in violation of its orders. Leffonier *v.* Detroit & M. Ry. Co. (Mich.), 68.

Origin of Fire.

Proof that the appliances of the locomotive which passed plaintiff's premises just before the fire inflicting the injuries sued for were in good condition did not entitle defendant to an instructed verdict. Texas & P. Ry. Co. *v.* Williams (C. C. A.), 764.

Verdict finding that the fire in question on defendant's railroad right of way was cause of the burning of plaintiff's property was warranted by the evidence. Leffonier *v.* Detroit & M. Ry. Co. (Mich.), 68.

FREE PASSES.

See CARRIERS OF PASSENGERS.

FRIGHTENING TEAMS.

See CARRIERS OF LIVE STOCK.

Where those in charge of street car see that its approach frightens horse on street, they must use ordinary care not to increase its fright, and if they have reason to believe that the approach of the car frightened the horse, it is negligence to move it nearer. Owensboro, City R. Co. *v.* Wall (Ky.), 765.

GARNISHMENT.

Constitutionality of certain statute of Missouri providing that garnishment shall not issue in a case where the sum demanded is not over $200, where the property sought to be reached is

GARNISHMENT—Continued.
wages due defendant from a railroad company, until after judgment is recovered by plaintiff against defendant, and in such case relieves the garnishee railroad of duty to answer. Houston, etc., Ry. Co. v. Caldwell (Mo.), 90.
Under Mo. Rev. St. 1899, §§ 3447, 3448, a railroad is not liable to garnishment proceedings on account of wages due its employees where the debt sued for is less than $200, unless judgment is first rendered against defendants, and hence a justice of the peace has no jurisdiction to issue garnishment in such a case, where defendants are nonresidents and served only by publication. Houston, etc., Ry. Co. v. Caldwell (Mo.), 90.

HUSBAND AND WIFE.
See BAGGAGE.

INTERSTATE COMMERCE.
See BILLS OF LADING; CONNECTING CARRIERS; INTOXICATING LIQUORS.
Attorneys' fees taxable as part of the costs under act of Congress of February 4, 1887, § 8, in action by shipper against initial carrier for loss on connecting line, in which the carrier's liability is dependent upon the Carmack amendment of June 29, 1906, to whom are the. Atlantic C. L. R. Co. v. Riverside Mills (U. S.), 689.

Connecting Carriers.
Validity of imposition, made by act of Congress in question, upon interstate carrier accepting property for transportation from point in one state to point in another state and liability to holder of bill of lading for loss any where en route, with right of recovery over against carrier actually causing the loss. Atlantic C. L. R. Co. v. Riverside Mills (U. S.), 689.
Contract for transportation of freight from one state to another relates to interstate commerce, and is subject to federal regulation. Central of Georgia Ry. Co. v. Sims (Ala.). 666.
Federal statute regulating interstate commerce will be recognized and enforced by state courts. Central of Georgia Ry. Co. v. Sims (Ala.), 666.
General rule as to power of Congress to regulate. Atlantic C. L. R. Co. v. Riverside Mills (U. S.), 689.
Initial carrier, in action based on Interstate Commerce Act, as amended by Act June 29, 1906, c. 3591, § 7, may not question the validity of the provision permitting it to recover from the connecting carrier for the loss sustained by it. Central of Georgia Ry. Co. v. Sims (Ala.), 666.
Interstate Commerce Act, as amended by Act June 29. 1906, makes judgment against initial carrier only prima facie evidence against connecting carrier, and is not invalid as depriving the connecting carrier of its property without due process of law. Central of Georgia Ry. Co. v. Sims (Ala.), 666.
Interstate Commerce Law, making initial carrier of interstate shipment liable for loss of or injury thereto caused by any connecting carrier, will be enforced in state court. Central of Georgia Ry. Co. (Ala.), 666.

Rates.
Fact that the railroad company did not establish and post its rates between a point on its own line and a point in another state would not be a defense to an action for the penalty imposed by N. Car. Revisal 1905, § 2631, for failure to receive

INTERSTATE COMMERCE—Continued.

freight for shipment, why was the. Reid *v.* Southern Ry. Co. (N. Car.), 204.

Railroad being prohibited from charging any less freight on interstate traffic than prescribed by Interstate Commerce Commission for the route over which the shipment is actually made, no contract, and no mistake in naming a wrong rate can affect the right to collect such prescribed rate. Louisiana Ry. & Nav. Co. *v.* Holly (La.), 201.

Railroad cannot estop itself from right to collect rate for carriage which, by interstate commerce act, it is required to charge. Louisiana Ry. & Nav. Co. *v.* Holly (La.), 201.

Railroad's right to recover its part of interstate commerce rate for an interstate shipment is not affected by its line being wholly within one state. Louisiana Ry. & Nav. Co. *v.* Holly (La.), 201.

Under the interstate commerce act, it was only the "business" of a common carrier which could not be exercised without filing freight rates, and a railroad company was not prohibited from receiving freight for transportation to another state by the fact that no through route and joint rates had been established between the points of shipment and delivery. Reid *v.* Southern Ry. Co. (N. Car.), 204.

Wrong routing by initial carrier does not prevent connecting carrier, over whose line the shipment is routed and carried, from collecting the interstate commerce rate over its line. Louisiana Ry. & Nav. Co. *v.* Holly (La.), 201.

State Regulation.

Constitutionality of Iowa Code 1897, § 2419, providing that if any common carrier or person shall transport any intoxicating liquor without first having obtained a certificate from the clerk of the court showing that the consignee is a permit holder, such carrier or person, on conviction, shall be fined, etc. State *v.* Wignall (Iowa), 173.

N. Car. Revisal 1905, § 2631, imposing penalty upon railroad companies for refusing to accept freight for shipment, is not unconstitutional when applied to an interstate shipment, not being an interference with or burden upon interstate commerce. Reid *v.* Southern Ry. Co. (N. Car.), 204.

N. Car. Revisal 1905, § 1095, requiring that a railroad shall, in certain cases, put in side tracks to private industrial concerns, is not an interference with interstate commerce, although such road may run through several states, and may carry freight over their side track to other states. State *v.* Southern Ry. Co. (N. Car.), 20.

Ore. Act. February 18, 1907, requiring railroads to furnish cars on demand of shippers, is not superseded by nor in conflict with the federal statutes in question. Martin *v.* Oregon R. & Nav. Co. (Ore.), 710.

State's right to make reasonable rules regarding the methods of carrying on interstate business. Martin *v.* Oregon B. & Nav. Co. (Ore.), 710.

Validity of Georgia Laws 1908, p. 50, requiring railroads to equip every locomotive with a certain kind of headlight. Atlantic C. L. R. Co. *v.* State (Ga.), 672.

What Constitutes.

"Interstate commerce" does not begin until the freight has been shipped or started for transportation from one state to another. Reid *v.* Southern Ry. Co. (N. Car.), 204.

INTOXICATING LIQUORS.
See INTERSTATE COMMERCE.

Ky. St., § 2569a does not apply to a railroad carrying liquor into a local option precinct as personal baggage of passenger, receiving no consideration therefor except a fare charge for the passenger's personal transportation. Commonwealth *v.* Southern Ry. Co. (Ky.), 197.

Legislature has no power to deprive a citizen of Iowa of his right to have liquor shipped from another state for his personal use, or to receive such liquor and remove the same from the express or railway office to his own home or place of business. State *v.* Wignall (Iowa), 173.

Legislature's power to prohibit the transportation of liquor imported from another state from the railroad carrier to the home of a resident of the state. State *v.* Wignall (Iowa), 173.

The carriage in question was an interstate commerce transaction; and the carrier was not guilty under Ky. St., § 2569a, making the bringing of liquor into local option territory an offense. Commonwealth *v.* Scott (Ky.), 702.

The word "person," as used in Iowa Code 1897, § 2419, means a public or private carrier, and does not include one who transported several interstate shipments of liquor from the railroad company's depot to the consignee's place of residence as a mere gratuity. State *v.* Wignall (Iowa), 173.

Where several residents of Iowa ordered liquor from another state at the same time, and defendant received the liquor from the railroad station in Iowa and gratuitously transported it inland to the purchasers as their agent, defendant was not engaged in interstate commerce. State *v.* Wignall (Iowa), 173.

INTOXICATION.
See CARRIERS OF PASSENGERS; CONTRIBUTORY NEGLIGENCE.

LEASES AND RUNNING POWERS.
See CARRIERS OF PASSENGERS.

LICENSEES.
See CROSSINGS; TRESPASSERS.

Degree of Care.
Ordinary care due from trainmen to persons using track as crossing, and as approach to depot, on implied invitation of railroad. Arkansas & L. Ry. Co. *v.* Graves (Ark.), 259.

Lookouts.
Evidence showed negligent failure to keep lookout while backing engine and car over track at point used as approach to depot on implied invitation of railroad. Arkansas & L. Ry. Co. *v.* Graves (Ark.), 259.

Signals.
Railroad owes licensees who cross its tracks no duty to warn them of passing trains. Shields *v.* Southern Pac. Co. (Ore.), 166.

Who Are.
One coming to depot on business with railroad, who leaves the premises by route commonly used by public under implied permission of company, is not trespasser while so doing. Arkansas & L. Ry. Co. *v.* Graves (Ark.), 259.

One injured by train, while crossing railroad on pathway used by 60 to 100 persons per day with knowledge of railroad's em-

LICENSEES—Continued. ·
ployees is a licensee. Norfolk & W. Ry. Co. *v.* Overton's Adm'r (Va.), 271.
Where public had openly and continuously used track ever since its construction as a crossing, and as approach to depot platform, it did so at implied invitation of railroad. Arkansas & L. Ry. Co. *v.* Graves (Ark.), 259.

MANDAMUS.
See STREET RAILWAYS.
Courts compel carrier to receive particular passenger at particular place, when may. State *v.* Ogden Rapid Transit Co. (Utah), 179.
Courts may coerce carrier by mandamus to comply with legislative edict or with order of railroad commission to maintain depots or stopping places at certain points and require carrier to stop its trains or some of them at such points. State *v.* Ogden Rapid Transit Co. (Utah), 179.
Where carrier refuses permission to one passenger to enter or alight from its cars at a place where under similar circumstances it extends the privilege to others, the carrier is guilty of discrimination against former, and the courts may by mandamus prevent it. State *v.* Ogden Rapid Transit Co. (Utah), 179.

MASTER AND SERVANT.
See CARRIER OF PASSENGERS; DAMAGES; EMPLOYERS' LIABILITY ACTS; FELLOW SERVANTS.

Accidents on Track.
Care due men working on track from engineer of locomotive approaching them. Smith *v.* Southern Pac. Co. (Ore.), 600.

Appliances.
General use by reasonably prudent railways of locomotives of the type of the one whose explosion caused the death of defendant's engineer, effect of evidence of. Kirby *v.* Chicago, etc., Ry. Co. (Iowa), 584.
If the train was sent out with a loose piece of iron on the door of a car, or if the defect was, or could have been, discovered, by the use of ordinary care, it was negligence towards the employee struck by such piece of iron while under a bridge. Louisville & N. R. Co. *v.* McMillen (Ky.), 591.
In action for death of engineer caused by boiler explosion, it was error to direct a finding for the railroad company if locomotives of that class were in general use by other reasonably prudent railways. Kirby *v.* Chicago, etc., Ry. Co. (Iowa), 584.
It is master's duty to exercise ordinary care to provide reasonably safe and suitable appliances for use of servant. Southern Ry. Co. *v.* Foster's Adm'r (Va.), 578.

Assaults.
Evidence of reputation for quarrelsomeness of defendant's servant by whom assault was committed. Everingham *v.* Chicago, etc., R. Co. (Iowa), 4.
Evidence showed that assault in question was not committed in prosecution of master's business. Everingham *v.* Chicago, etc., R. Co. (Iowa), 4.
Master does not ratify and become liable for assault committed by his servant merely because he thereafter retains the servant in his employ. Everingham *v.* Chicago, etc., R. Co. (Iowa), 4.
Master is not liable for an assault made by his servant where

832

MASTER AND SERVANT—Continued.

he has stepped aside from prosecution of master's business to effect some purpose of his own. Everingham *v.* Chicago, etc., R. Co. (Iowa), 4.

Assumption of Risk.

Experienced servant employed to straighten creosoted ties loaded on a car assumed the risk of injury from their slipping, as a matter of law; though his employer negligently failed to furnish a safe means of mounting the car to arrange the ties. Chicago, etc., Ry. Co. *v.* Grubbs (Ark.), 595.

Knowledge of servant that work place is unsafe. Chicago, etc., Ry. Co. *v.* Grubbs (Ark.), 595.

Negligence or other servants not his fellow servants. Louisville & N. R. Co. *v.* McMillen (Ky.), 591.

Notwithstanding Va. Const. 1903, § 162, and Va. Code 1904, § 1294k, a servant still assumes all other ordinary and usual risks incident to the service, including the risks incident to the manner in which he knows, or in the exercise of ordinary care ought to know, the master conducts its business. Southern Ry. Co. *v.* Foster's Adm'r (Va.), 578.

Risks from defects assumed by car inspectors. Lane *v.* North Carolina R. Co. (N. Car.), 90.

Servant assumes all the ordinary risks of his employment. Louisville & N. R. Co. *v.* McMillen (Ky.), 591.

Servant assumes the ordinary and usual risks incident to his employment, which he knows, or by the exercise of reasonable care he may know. Chicago, etc., Ry. Co. *v.* Grubbs (Ark.), 595.

Servant who knows the methods adopted in the work, and the place in which the work is to be done, and who continues in the employment, assumes the risks of the dangers resulting therefrom. Chicago, etc., Ry. Co. *v.* Grubbs (Ark.), 595.

Where master and servant possess equal knowledge of a danger, if the servant is of sufficient maturity to appreciate the danger, he assumes the risk. Chicago, etc., Ry. Co. *v.* Grubbs (Ark.), 595.

Burden of Proof.

Burden was not on servant to show that the car had not been inspected, or that a car door on the train in question was minus the piece of iron which fell off and struck him while at work under a bridge. Louisville & N. R. Co. *v.* McMillen (Ky.), 591.

Contributory Negligence.

Car inspector injured by reason of absence of shoe at bottom door of car he was inspecting. Lane *v.* North Carolina R. Co. (N. Car.), 90.

Right of deceased employee to rely on observance of custom to send the brakeman with cars to be kicked onto main track from the yards over a cut-off track to give deceased warning. Chicago, etc., Ry. Co. *v.* Dutcher (C. C. A.), 78.

Trackman engaged in repairing track was only required to exercise such care and vigilance in discovering peril from locomotive by which he was struck as was consistent with performance of the work in which he was engaged. Smith *v.* Southern Pac. Co. (Ore.), 600.

Trackman's duty to look out for trains when working on track. Smith *v.* Southern Pac. Co. (Ore.), 600.

MASTER AND SERVANT—Continued.

Degree of Care.

Instruction in question left jury without any guide as to what constitutes ordinary care in switching cars. Southern Ry. Co. v. Foster's Adm'r (Va.), 578.

Instruction was erroneous as imposing higher degree of care than the law requires of the master. Southern Ry. Co. v. Foster, Adm'r (Va.), 578.

Master is not required to exercise higher degree of care than that exercised by the average prudent man engaged in like business. Southern Ry. Co. v. Foster's Adm'r (Va.), 578.

Employment of Servant.

"Fit and competent" co-laborers, compliance with rule requiring master to select. Furlong v. New York, etc., R. Co. (Conn.), 233.

Master's duty to exercise ordinary care to retain only fit and competent fellow servants. Furlong v. New York, etc., R. Co. (Conn.), 233.

False Imprisonment.

If railway policemen, appointed and commissioned under N. J. P. L. 1904, p. 322, § 4, are employed by a railroad company in matters aside from their duties under the statute, the company may be held answerable for what they do the same as in other cases of agency. Taylor v. New York & L. B. R. Co. (N. J.), 74.

In action against railroad for injuries caused by ties falling on its servant's foot, while he and others were piling them on car, the evidence showed the injury was result of accident. Simpson v. Southern Ry. Co. (N. Car.), 87.

Master's Liability to Third Parties.

Master does not warrant or insure his servant's good conduct in matters outside the scope of the master's business. Everingham v. Chicago, etc., R. Co. (Iowa), 4.

Nonassignable Duties.

Failure of railroad employee charged with duty to see that other employees are not negligent or incompetent to perform their duties is negligence of the railroad. Furlong v. New York, etc., R. Co. (Conn.), 233.

Relief Department.

Stipulation in application for membership in railroad employees' relief association that applicant's acceptance of benefits for injuries shall release all claims against the railroad because of such injuries, validity of. Reese v. Pennsylvania R. Co. (Pa.), 612.

Scope of Employment.

Conductor's authority to make contracts of employment. St. Louis, etc., Ry. Co. v. Jones (Ark.), 94.

Custom modify general rule that conductor has no authority to employ an assistant, when will. St. Louis, etc., Ry. Co. v. Jones (Ark.), 94.

Duties of railway policeman, appointed on the application of a railroad company and commissioned by the Governor, pursuant to the "act concerning carriers," are confined to criminal cases. Taylor v. New York & L. R. R. Co. (N. J.), 74.

MASTER AND SERVANT—Continued.
Warn and Instruct.
As matter of law, the defendant master was not liable for the death of decedent, member of switching crew, for failing to instruct him in his work. Paquette *v.* Berlin Mills Co. (N. H.), 80.

Duty of railroad to instruct car inspector as to safe and proper method of shutting doors of freight cars. Lane *v.* North Carolina R. Co. (N. Car.), 90.

Master need not warn an experienced servant as to obvious dangers, where the master and servant possess equal knowledge of the dangers. Chicago, etc., Ry. Co. *v.* Grubbs (Ark.), 595.

Negligence in failing to observe custom to send brakeman with the cars to be kicked onto main track to give deceased employee warning. Chicago, etc., Ry. Co. *v.* Ducther (C. C. A.), 78.

Who Are Employees.
Conductor having no authority to agree to let person ride in consideration of his assisting with the freight, one who rides under such an agreement is a mere volunteer, who assumes risks of his position. St. Louis, etc., Ry. Co. *v.* Jones (Ark.), 94.

Work Place.
Duty of railroad to provide for its employee reasonably safe place to work does not extend to ordinary conditions which arise during progress of the work, where the employee can avoid the dangers arising therefrom by exercise of reasonable care. Simpson *v.* Southern Ry. Co. (N. Car.), 87.

Railroad not liable where its employee was injured by ties falling on his foot while he and others were piling them on car without any particular directions from the railroad. Simpson *v.* Southern Ry. Co. (N. Car.), 87.

"Safe place to work," what constitutes. Peterson *v.* Chicago, etc., Ry. Co. (Iowa), 83.

Work place which is safe so long as machinery is not in operation, and the peril involved is in the improper method of performing the work by improperly starting the machinery, is safe within the law. Peterson *v.* Chicago, etc., Ry. Co. (Iowa), 83.

MUNICIPAL CORPORATIONS.
See STREET RAILWAYS.

NEGLIGENCE.
See ACCIDENTS ON TRACK; CARRIERS; CHILDREN; CONTRIBUTORY NEGLIGENCE; CROSSINGS; FELLOW SERVANTS; FIRES SET BY LOCOMOTIVES; LICENSEES; MASTER AND SERVANT; SLEEPING CAR COMPANIES; STOCK, INJURIES TO; STREET RAILWAYS; TRESPASSERS.

Accident, sufferer is without legal remedy when his injury is result of. Simpson *v.* Southern Ry. Co. (N. Car.), 87.

Constitutional Law.
Constitutionality of Miss. Code 1906, § 1985, under which, in actions against railroads for damage done to persons or property, proof of injury inflicted by the running of the locomotives or cars is made prima facie evidence of negligence. Mobile, etc., R. Co. *v.* Turnipseed (U. S.), 70.

NEGLIGENCE—Continued.

Definitions.

Accident is an event resulting from unknown cause, or an unusual and unexpected event from a known cause; chance; casualty. Simpson *v.* Southern Ry. Co. (N. Car.), 87.

Is generally question for jury. Messenger *v.* Valley City Street & Interurban Ry. Co. (N. Dak.), 127.

Joint Tort-Feasors.

When the negligence of two or more persons concurs in producing a single indivisible injury, such persons are jointly and severally liable, although there was no common duty, common design, or concert of action. Nelson *v.* Illinois Cent. R. Co. (Miss.), 114.

Where two or more persons owe a common duty to another, they are jointly and severally liable for injuries caused to such other by a common neglect of such duty. Nelson *v.* Illinois Cent. R. Co. (Miss.), 114.

Last Clear Chance.

Party who has last c[ear chance of avoiding the accident, notwithstanding negligence of the other, is solely responsible for it. Acton *v.* Fargo, etc., Ry. Co. (N. Dak.), 767.

Proximate Cause.

Instruction was erroneous as ignoring necessity that defendant's negligence proximately caused the injury sued for. Washington, etc., Ry. Co. *v.* Vaughn (Va.), 444.

Question for jury, though there be no conflict of evidence, when is negligence a. Hoff *v.* Los Angeles-Pacific Co. (Cal.), 47.

Rules.

The care that railroad employees must exercise in the operation of cars, so far as the general public is concerned, is determined by principles of law, and not rules of the railroad company. Southern Ry. Co. *v.* Stewart (Ky.), 14.

NUISANCES.

See TRESPASS.

ORDINANCES.

See CROSSINGS; STREET RAILWAYS.

PARENT AND CHILD.

See CHILDREN.

PASSES.

See CARRIERS OF PASSENGERS.

PENAL STATUTES.

See CONSTITUTIONAL LAW; EMPLOYERS' LIABILITY ACTS; STREET RAILWAYS.

PERSONAL INJURIES.

Damages.

Bodily pain, mental suffering, anxiety, suspense, and the sense of wrong from insult, connected with bodily injury, may be considered as elements of the injury, for which damage for compensation may be allowed. Jansen *v.* Minneapolis, etc., Ry. Co. (Minn.), 111.

On issue of prospective suffering and diminished earning ca-

PERSONAL INJURIES—Continued.

pacity, plaintiff's life expectancy should have been based on his condition as injured. Hughes *v.* Chicago, etc., Ry. Co. (Iowa), 759.

Trial court could not by reducing verdict for plaintiff cure error in instruction basing his life expectancy on his condition before being injured instead of on his injured condition. Hughes *v.* Chicago, etc., Ry. Co. (Iowa), 750.

$2,000 was not excessive verdict. Louisville & N. R. Co. *v.* Mc-Millen (Ky.), 591.

$25,000 was not excessive verdict for the injuries in question. John *v.* Northern Pac. Ry. Co. (Mont.), 484.

Evidence.

Statements detrimental to right of plaintiff made by him while suffering great pain, and at the persistent importunity of defendant, weight to be given to. Morris *v.* Illinois Cent. R. Co. (La.), 169.

Mental Suffering.

Mental anguish alone, right of recovery for. Kyle *v.* Chicago, etc., Ry. Co. (C. C. A.), 149.

POLICE POWER.

See STREET RAILWAYS.

POLICEMEN.

See MASTER AND SERVANT.

PROCESS.

La. Act No. 261, of 1908 provides that a corporation may be cited by leaving the citation at its office, and a corporation cannot avoid the effect of such act by providing in its charter that its secretary shall be the proper person on whom a citation shall be served. Abney *v.* Louisiana & N. W. R. Co. (La.), 131.

RAILROAD COMMISSIONS.

See SPURS AND SIDE TRACKS.

Order of State Railroad Commission, requiring railroad to put on additional trains, need not go to the extent of violating the provisions of federal Constitution for the protection of private property, in order to be illegal. Texas & P. Ry. Co. *v.* Railroad Commission (La.), 211.

Powers.

State Railway Commission has no authority to order railroad company to construct crossing over railroad at point within limits of village where no street has been opened. Chicago, etc., Ry. Co. *v.* Nebraska State Ry. Commission (Neb.), 266.

Presumption that orders of State Railroad Commission are proper and legal. Texas & P. Ry. Co. *v.* Railroad Commission (La.), 211.

Validity of order in question of Railroad Commission, requiring railroad to put on additional trains. Texas & P. Ry. Co. *v.* Railroad Commission (La.), 211.

RAILROADS.

See AGENCY; CONSTITUTIONAL LAW; EMINENT DOMAIN; GARNISHMENT; RIGHT OF WAY; STATIONS AND DEPOTS; STREET RAILWAYS; TRESPASS.

Presumption that railroad is carrying on its business under authority of law. Reid *v.* Southern Ry. Co. (N. Car.), 204.

RAILROADS—Continued.

Term "railroad company" employed in statute in question includes natural persons as well as corporations. Atlantic C. R. Co. v. State (Ga.), 672.

Use of Property.

Courts will control public service corporations in use of their property only so far as is necessary to secure proper discharge of corporations' duties to individuals or the public. Danville & W. Ry. Co. v. Lybrook (Va.), 329.

RAILROADS IN STREETS.

See CROSSINGS; EMINENT DOMAIN; STREET RAILWAYS.

Abutters.

Dedication of land for street, the fee being retained by abutting owners, does not authorize the use of the street for purposes of commercial railroads without further compensation. McCammon & Lang Lumber Co. v. Trinity & B. V. Ry. Co. (Tex.), 648.

Immaterial that owner of abutting land injured by erection of. overhead bridge by railroad had no title to the fee in the street on which the structure was erected, the right of action being given by section 9 of article 3 of the constitution of West Virginia, prohibiting the taking or damaging of private property for public use, without just compensation. Fowler v. Norfolk & W. Ry. Co. (W. Va.), 632.

Occupation of street by railroad is not a "taking" of property of abutting owner who does not own the fee in the street. McCammon & Lang Lumber Co. v. Trinity & B. V. Ry. Co. (Tex.), 648.

Property owner has no right of action against railroad for destruction of street crossing unless his property sustained some special and peculiar injury thereby. Fowler v. Norfolk & W. Ry. Co. (W. Va.), 632.

Property owners damaged by elevation of grade of street, in order to provide for viaducts over railroad tracks, may recover damages therefor. City of Chicago v. Pittsburgh, etc., Ry. Co. (Ill.), 640.

Railroad's liability for injury to abutting property from erection of overhead bridge at instance of city council, under statute in question. Fowler v. Norfolk & W. Ry. Co. (W. Va.), 632.

Special and peculiar injury to abutting property by destruction of street crossing by railroad, what does, and does not, constitute. Fowler v. Norfolk & W. Ry. Co. (W. Va.), 632.

Damages.

Permanent damages were recoverable by abutting owner against railroad for injury from erection of overhead bridge. Fowler v. Norfolk & W. Ry. Co. (W. Va.), 632.

Improvements.

Part of grade of the street filled and improved at the time in question did not constitute part of the approach to the viaduct over the defendant railroad's tracks, and city had no power to require the same to be repaved and improved at railroad's expense. City of Chicago v. Pittsburgh, etc., Ry. Co. (Ill.), 640.

REMOVAL OF CAUSE.

Separable Controversy.

Action, brought in state court against nonresident railroad cor-

REMOVAL OF CAUSE—Continued.

poration and its resident servants jointly, to recover damages in excess of $2,000 for homicide of plaintiff's son, involves no separable controversy between plaintiff and defendant corporation, entitling latter to remove cause to circuit court of United States, when does an. Vanzant *v.* Southern Ry. Co. (Ga.), 479.

RIGHT OF WAY.

See EMINENT DOMAIN; WATER AND WATERCOURSES.

Conveyance to railroad reciting that it was made on the condition that its line should be constructed over grantor's premises within two years created a condition subsequent. Oregon R. & N. Co. *v.* McDonald (Ore.), 8.

Forfeiture.

Court decree the railroad to be entitled to the forfeited land on payment of damages occasioned by the taking thereof, when will the. Oregon R. & N. Co. *v.* McDonald (Ore.), 8.

Estopped from claiming forfeiture by voluntarily permitting grantee to enter on the land and construct its grade, railroad was not. Oregon R. & N. Co. *v.* McDonald (Ore.), 8.

Railroad, where it goes into the market as an ordinary purchaser to buy land, may make its own terms, and may bind itself by conditions subsequent. Oregon R. & N. Co. *v.* McDonald (Ore.), 8.

Streets of city cannot be used for railroad purposes without express legislative authority even with consent of the city authorities. State *v.* Southern Ry. Co. (N. Car.), 20.

RULES.

See NEGLIGENCE.

SERVICE OF SUMMONS.

See PROCESS.

SLEEPING CAR COMPANIES.

See BAGGAGE; CARRIERS OF PASSENGERS.

In action for loss of passenger's effects from sleeping car, evidence that while train was stopping at station at night both conductor and porter were out on platform at same time, leaving both doors unlocked, and no one to keep watch, required submission of issue of negligence to jury. Godfrey *v.* Pullman Co. (S. Car.), 139.

Sleeping car company is liable for loss of passenger's personal effects suitable for his journey, due to negligence of its servants. Godfrey *v.* Pullman Co. (S. Car.), 139.

SPURS AND SIDE TRACKS.

See EMINENT DOMAIN; INTERSTATE COMMERCE.

Contract between private corporation and railroad company for extension of spur track to premises of former was not against public policy. Riley *v.* Louisville, etc., Ry. Co. (Ky.), 614.

Corporation Commission cannot grant the power to condemn land for a siding to a railroad which has not such general power, even if it may require railroads under N. Car. Revisal 1905, § 1097, to put in side tracks, etc. State *v.* Southern Ry. Co. (N. Car.), 20.

Ky. St. § 769, permitting railroads to build spur tracks when necessary, is not an attempt to authorize a railroad to condemn pri-

SPURS AND SIDE TRACKS—Continued.

vate property for a private purpose. Riley *v.* Louisville, etc., Ry. Co. (Ky.), 614.

Power of Corporation Commission to order railroad to put in side track, under N. Car. Revisal 1905, § 1097, State *v.* Southern Ry. Co. (N. Car.), 20.

State has no power to compel railroad company to put in switches at its own expense on the application of the owners of any elevator erected within a specified limit, and section 18 of art. 9 of Constitution of Oklahoma does not attempt to confer such power upon the Corporation Commission. St. Louis, etc., R. Co. *v.* State (Okl.), 646.

STATIONS AND DEPOTS.

See CARRIERS OF PASSENGERS; EMINENT DOMAIN; LICENSEES; MANDAMUS.

Lights.

Liability of carrier where its passenger is injured after alighting from train by reason of its failure to furnish sufficient light on its station platform. Abney *v.* Louisiana & N. W. R. Co. (La.), 131.

Location.

Legislature may, within limits, direct where carrier shall maintain depots or stopping places, and require carrier to stop its trains or some of them at such depots, or stopping places. State *v.* Ogden Rapid Transit Co. (Utah), 179.

Statutes in question do not confer on courts power to determine whether a carrier should or should not establish and maintain depot or stopping place for reception and discharge of passengers or freight, or either, at any particular place or places along its line of road. State *v.* Ogden Rapid Transit Co. (Utah), 179.

Station Facilities.

Evidence in proceedings to compel railroad company to remove buildings from its station grounds showed that they facilitated rather than hindered performance of company's duties as carrier. Danville & W. Ry. Co. *v.* Lybrook (Va.), 329.

Implied power of railroad to permit others to maintain buildings on its grounds for storage and delivery of freight and for convenience of patrons. Danville & W. Ry. Co. *v.* Lybrook (Va.), 329.

Neither State Corporation Commission nor the courts can relieve against individual inconvenience to shippers, if the carrier affords reasonable facilities for reception and delivery of freight for the general public, and denies no individual right. Danville & W. Ry. Co. *v.* Lybrook (Va.), 329.

One desiring to use railroad property for storage, or other than a railroad use, cannot complain because others are permitted to use such property for their private business, if sufficient railroad facilities are afforded. Danville & W. Ry. Co. *v.* Lybrook (Va.), 329.

Warehouse or other structure used for convenience of public is proper auxiliary to railroad business. Danville & W. Ry. Co. *v.* Lybrook (Va.), 329.

Stopping Places.

Court in determining whether interurban railway is guilty of discrimination because it stops its cars to receive and discharge passengers at resorts along its line and refused to do

STATIONS AND DEPOTS—Continued.

so at another resort may not consider the fact that it stops its cars at one resort, where such stop is by virtue of special contract executed by it for valuable consideration. State *v.* Ogden Rapid Transit Co. (Utah), 179.

Duties imposed on carriers by Utah Comp. Laws 1907, § 449, must be discharged by carrier at duly established stopping places, and the statute does not require carrier to stop its cars at any particular place to discharge or receive passengers. State *v.* Ogden Rapid Transit Co. (Utah), 179.

Judicial power to control carrier in its determination of number of depots or stopping places that it will establish or maintain, or in selection of places where it will establish them. State *v.* Ogden Rapid Transit Co. (Utah), 179.

Under certain statute, interurban railway which stops its cars to receive and discharge passengers at resorts and refused to do so at another resort is not guilty of discrimination, in absence of evidence that any person stopped off because he could not do so at latter resort. State *v.* Ogden Rapid Transit Co. (Utah), 179.

STOCK, INJURIES TO.

Signals.

Evidence sustained finding that there was negligence in failing to give the signals required by Ala. Code 1907, § 5473; and that there was causal connection between such negligence and the killing of plaintiff's mule by defendant's train. Western Ry. *v.* Moore (Ala.), 67.

STREET RAILWAYS.

See CARRIERS OF PASSENGERS; CHILDREN; CROSS-INGS; FRIGHTENING TEAMS; TICKETS AND FARES.

Car Service.

Burden of proving unreasonableness or ordinance regulating frequency of car service is on party asserting it. City of Tacoma *v.* Boutelle (Wash.), 404.

Franchise in question fixed minimum car service, but did not prevent city for requiring more frequent service; and an ordinance prescribing a five-minute service was not invalid as impairing obligation of contract evidenced by the franchise. City of Tacoma *v.* Boutelle (Wash.), 404.

Franchise in question impliedly reserved to city power to regulate frequency of car service. City of Tacoma *v.* Boutelle (Wash.), 404.

Franchise of street railway impliedly authorized city to adopt ordinance prescribing frequency of car service, as against objection that it impaired obligation of contract evidenced by the franchise. City of Tacoma *v.* Boutelle (Wash.), 404.

Police power of city to regulate frequency of car service. City of Tacoma *v.* Boutelle (Wash.), 404.

Police power of city, under certain general constitutional and statutory provisions, to require a five-minute street car service between designated hours each day. City of Tacoma *v.* Boutelle (Wash.), 404.

Reasonableness of ordinance regulating frequency of car service is a legislative one for city counsel, subject to review by courts. City of Tacoma *v.* Boutelle (Wash.), 404.

Reasonableness of ordinance regulating frequency of car service is question of fact. City of Tacoma *v.* Boutelle (Wash.), 404.

STREET RAILWAYS—Continued.

Superintendent of street railway company in charge of operation of system may not urge that ordinance providing for five-minute car service during specified hours of each day and imposing fine not exceeding $100 for a violation, is oppressive, when applied to him. City of Tacoma v. Boutelle (Wash.), 404.

Validity of ordinance regulating frequency of car service. City of Tacoma v. Boutelle (Wash.), 404.

Collisions.

Duty to reduce trolley car approaching vehicle on track from rear to such control that it may be brought to standstill if necessary. Acton v. Fargo, etc., Ry. Co. (N. Dak.), 767.

Evidence warranted finding that car could have been stopped in time to have avoided the collision with ice cart. Blake v. Rhode Island Co. (R. I.), 792.

Reasonable diligence must be used by those in charge of cars to avoid collisions with persons using the tracks as driveways. Acton v. Fargo, etc., R. Co. (N. Dak.), 767.

Contributory Negligence.

Duty of one driving wagon along street car track to keep constant lookout for approaching cars. Acton v. Fargo, etc., Ry. Co. (N. Dak.), 767.

One is not negligent in attempting to drive across street railway track, though he sees car rapidly approaching, if a reasonably prudent man would infer that the car was so far away that it could not reach him before he crossed. Blake v. Rhode Island Co. (R. I.), 792.

Right of one driving along street car track in daylight to assume that if car is approaching from rear, a proper lookout is maintained, and that ordinary care will be exercised to avoid injuring him. Acton v. Fargo, etc., Ry. Co. (N. Dak.), 767.

Right to drive wagon along street car track in direction in which cars travel or in opposite direction. Acton v. Fargo, etc., Ry. Co. (N. Dak.), 767.

Contributory negligence of driver of wagon and failure to exercise ordinary care in operating car, which would have prevented the collision, company was liable where there were both. Acton v. Fargo, etc., Ry. Co. (N. Dak.), 767.

Degree of Care.

Care required in operating car when crossing street intersection where car upon opposite track is, or has been, discharging passengers. Stewart v. Omaha, etc., R. Co. (Neb.), 298.

Discovered Peril.

Question for jury whether motorman failed to use ordinary care to avoid running car into wagon after discovering there was danger of a collision. Acton v. Fargo, etc., Ry. Co. (N. Dak.). 767.

Franchises.

City may not by granting street railway franchise divest itself of its police power. City of Tacoma v. Boutelle (Wash.), 404.

Last Clear Chance.

Contributory negligence in driving wagon on track and negligence of those in charge of street car after they should have, by exercise of reasonable care, discovered the danger in time to avoid the collision with the wagon, company was liable if there were both. Acton v. Fargo, etc., Ry. Co. (N. Dak.), 767.

STREET RAILWAYS—Continued.

If those in charge of street car should, by exercise of ordinary care, have discovered plaintiff's peril while driving wagon along track in time to have avoided collision, and did not do so, plaintiff's negligence in failing to look back for an approaching car, would not prevent his recovery. Acton *v.* Fargo, etc., Ry. Co. (N. Dak.), 767.

Mutual Rights.

Equal right to travel on streets of street cars and other users, effect of. Stewart *v.* Omaha, etc., Ry. Co. (Neb.), 298.

Reciprocal duties of car and wagon to use reasonable care to avoid collision. Acton *v.* Fargo, etc., Ry. Co. (N. Dak.), 767.

Railroads.

Statute making it unlawful to throw stones at railroad car includes an interurban traction railway car, although such cars were not known or in use at time such statute was enacted. State *v.* Cleveland (Ohio), 60.

Right of traveler passing along city street to use every part of it, regardless of whether there is street car track in it or not. Acton *v.* Fargo, etc., Ry. Co. (N. Dak.), 767.

Right of way.

Duty of tree vehicles not to obstruct street car tracks unnecessarily. Acton *v.* Fargo, etc., Ry. Co. (N. Dak.), 767.

Duty of those in charge of street car to exercise its right of precedence with the due regard to rights of other users of street. Acton *v.* Fargo, etc., Ry. Co. (N. Dak.), 767.

Motorman of car approaching from rear wagon moving along track has no right to proceed without regard to presence of the wagon. Acton *v.* Fargo, etc., Ry. Co. (N. Dak.), 767.

Signals.

Duty of those in charge of street car to one using track as driveway. Acton *v.* Fargo, etc., Ry. Co. (N. Dak.), 767.

Sprinkling Streets.

City is the proper relator in proceeding to compel street railway to perform its duty under ordinance to sprinkle the parts of streets occupied by its tracks. State *v.* Milwaukee Elec. Ry. & L. Co. (Wis.), 564.

Ordinance requiring street railway to sprinkle the parts of streets occupied by its tracks is not void as discriminating in favor of users of automobiles and other vehicles who are not compelled to bear like expense. State *v.* Milwaukee Elec. Ry. & L. Co. (Wis.), 564.

Reasonableness of ordinance requiring street railway to sprinkle the parts of streets occupied by its tracks. State *v.* Milwaukee Elec. Ry. & L. Co. (Wis.), 564.

Street railway's duty under ordinance to sprinkle the part of streets occupied by its tracks is enforceable by mandamus. State *v.* Milwaukee Elec. Ry. & L. Co. (Wis.), 564.

Wis. St. 1898, § 1862, subjecting street railways to municipal regulations, authorizes adoption of a reasonable ordinance requiring them to sprinkle portions of streets occupied by their tracks. State *v.* Milwaukee Elec. Ry. & L. Co. (Wis.), 564.

STREETS AND HIGHWAYS.

See EMINENT DOMAIN; RAILROADS IN STREETS; RIGHT OF WAY.

SUNDAY.
See COMMON CARRIERS.

TAXATION.
See APPEALS; CONSTITUTIONAL LAW.

TICKETS AND FARES.
See CARRIERS OF PASSENGERS.

Identification of Passenger.
Ticket in question constituted contract between the wife, her husband, and the carriers, and such persons having notice by the terms of the ticket that the issuing agent had no authority to allow the husband to sign the wife's name to the ticket, the validating agent properly refused to accept it for the wife's return passage, and no action lay for such refusal and her ejection from the train. Houston, etc., Ry. Co. *v.* Lee (Tex.), 742.

Passes.
Right of passenger to recover for injuries sustained while riding on illegal free pass. John *v.* Northern Pac. Ry. Co. (Mont.), 484.
To whom, under certain statute, railroad may issue free transportation or sell tickets at reduced rate. John *v.* Northern Pac. Ry. Co. (Mont.), 484.
Under statutory provision in question, the carriage of a passenger by defendant on a pass issued without compensation to the employee of another railroad company which issued similar free passes for use by defendant's employees was illegal. John *v.* Northern Pac. Ry. Co. (Mont.), 484.

Rules and Regulations.
Incidental power of carrier to establish rules regulating payment of fares. Martin *v.* Rhode Island Co. (R. I.), 415.
Reasonableness of carrier's rule regulating payment of fares is question for court. Martin *v.* Rhode Island Co. (R. I.), 415.
Reasonableness of carrier's rule requiring payment of fare by its passengers by means of an automatic fare registering device held in hand of conductor. Martin *v.* Rhode Island Co. (R. I.), 415.
Refusal of conductor, under certain rule of carrier, to accept five one-cent pieces for fare except in exchange for a five-cent piece to be inserted in automatic fare collector by passenger, was not a violation of legal tender statute. (U S. Comp. St. 1901, § 3587.) Martin *v.* Rhode Island Co. (R. I.), 415.
Requirement that passenger pay his fare into automatic collector is not a demand for a greater fare than allowed by charter fixing maximum rate of five cents. Martin *v.* Rhode Island Co. (R. I.), 415.

Waiver.
Condition requiring plaintiff's signature to round-trip ticket was waived by the ticket being honored for his going passage; and and his ejection was wrongful. Chicago, etc., Ry. Co. *v.* Newburn (Okl.), 357.

TORTS.
See NEGLIGENCE.

TRESPASS.
Railroad is liable for a trespass on land of others which is purely consequential on the doing of a legal and authorized act, whether. Allerton *v.* New York, etc., Ry. Co. (N. Y.), 24.

TRESPASSERS.

See CARRIERS OF PASSENGERS; LICENSEES.

Contributory Negligence.

Act of trespasser in remaining on track after becoming aware of his danger from train is negligence concurrent with or subsequent to the negligence of the trainmen in failing to exercise proper care after discovering his peril; and defeats action for his death. Central of Georgia Ry. Co. *v.* Blackmon (Ala.), 292.

Degree of Care.

Railroad owes trespasser on track no duty, except not to recklessly or wantonly do him injury. Burgess *v.* Atchison, etc., Ry. Co. (Kan.), 164.

Discovered Peril.

Right of trainmen to presume that adult trespasser, seen by them on track facing train, is able to and will get off in time. Central of Georgia Ry. Co. *v.* Blackmon (Ala.), 292.

Trainmen owe trespasser on track the duty of preventing injury to him if they can do so after discovering his peril, and after becoming aware he cannot, or will not extricate himself therefrom. Central of Georgia Ry. Co. *v.* Blackmon (Ala.), 292.

Lookouts.

Trainmen do not owe trespasser on track any duty to keep lookout. Central of Georgia Ry. Co. *v.* Blackmon (Ala.), 292.

Pleading.

Complaint was sufficient as against demurrer, because it alleged negligence after discovery of peril of decedent from the train, who was, as shown by complaint, a trespasser. Central of Georgia Ry. Co. *v.* Blackmon (Ala.), 292.

Complaint which charges only simple negligence on part of trainmen in running train against person must show that he was not a trespasser. Central of Georgia Ry. Co. *v.* Blackmon (Ala.), 292.

Complaint, which shows that decedent was a trespasser on defendant's track when struck by train, must allege willful or wanton misconduct on part of trainmen or negligence on their part after discovery of his peril. Central of Georgia Ry. Co. *v.* Blackmon (Ala.), 292.

Signals.

Trainmen need not warn adult trespasser on track and facing train, until they discover that he is not aware that train is approaching, but may assume that he can see and hear it. Central of Georgia Ry. Co. *v.* Blackmon (Ala.), 292.

TRIAL.

Remarks of Court.

Improper statement of court, in action by person suing for a personal injury and testifying to her holding peculiar religious views and practicing them as a faith healer, that it was not a religion, that it was too fakey, was reversible error. Jageriskey *v.* Detroit United Ry. (Mich.), 33.

ULTRA VIRES.

See STATIONS AND DEPOTS.

VOLUNTEERS.

See MASTER AND SERVANT.

WAREHOUSEMAN.
See COMMON CARRIERS.

WAREHOUSES.
See STATIONS AND DEPOTS.

WATER AND WATER COURSES.

Railroad crossing stream may taking water therefrom for its locomotives, provided the quantity taken does not materially reduce
the volume. Harris *v.* Norfolk & W. Ry. Co. (N. Car.), 29.

Subsequent grantee of portion of the land remaining after defendant railroads' taking of part of it for right of way could not recover damage, on account of the scope of the conveyance in
question, for injuries thereto by defendant's change of the channel of the river in question. Allerton *v.* New York, etc., Ry.
Co. (N. Y.), 24.

Lightning Source UK Ltd.
Milton Keynes UK
UKHW020622051218
333473UK00010B/285/P